Collins

ESSENTIAL
ATLAS
OF THE WORLD

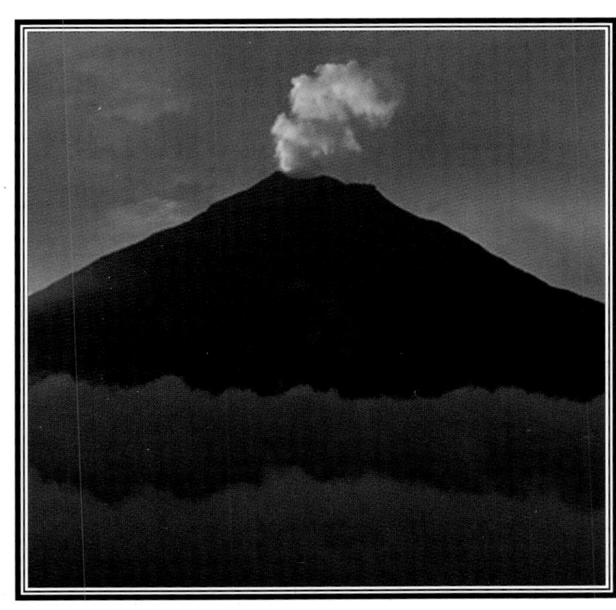

ESSENTIAL ATLAS OF THE WORLD

Collins Essential Atlas of the World

Published 2003 by Borders Press in association with HarperCollins

Borders Press is a division of Borders Group, Inc. 100 Phoenix Drive, Ann Arbor. Michigan, 48108. All rights reserved.

Borders Press is a trademark of Borders Properties, Inc.

First published 1998
Reprinted 1998, 1999 (twice)
Reprinted with changes 2000
Reprinted 2001, 2002 (twice)
Reprinted 2003

Copyright ©HarperCollins*Publishers* Ltd 1998
Maps © Bartholomew Ltd 1998
Collins® is a registered trademark of HarperCollins*Publishers*

The contents of this edition of the Collins Essential Atlas of the World are believed correct at the time of printing. Nevertheless, the publisher can accept no responsibility for errors or omissions, changes in the detail given or for any expense or loss thereby caused.

Printed in Singapore

ISBN 0-681-50234-7

Cover/title page photo : Wayne Lawler; Ecoscene/Corbis

QH11483 Imp 008

Everything **clicks** at www.collins.co.uk

CONTENTS

THE WORLD

EUROPE

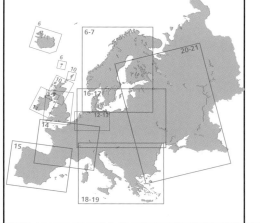

ASIA

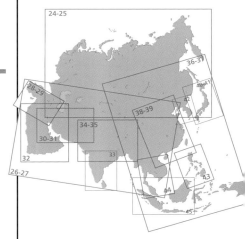

OCEANIA

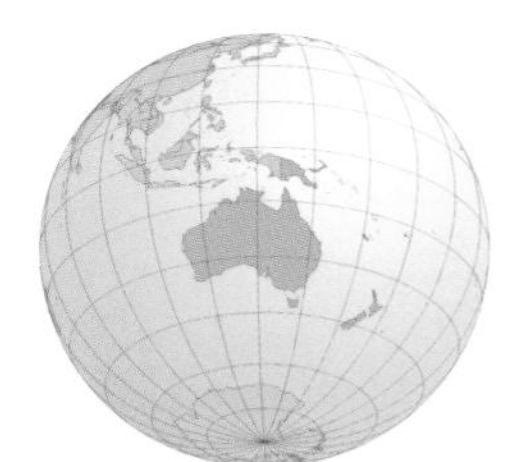

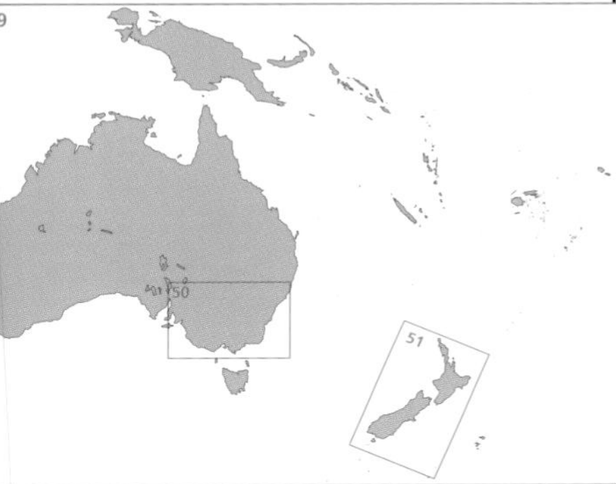

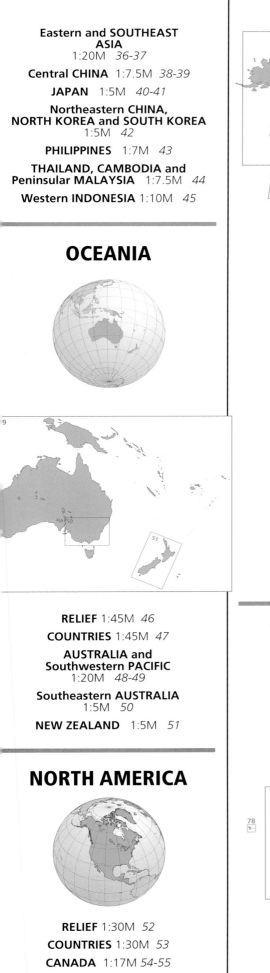

NORTH AMERICA

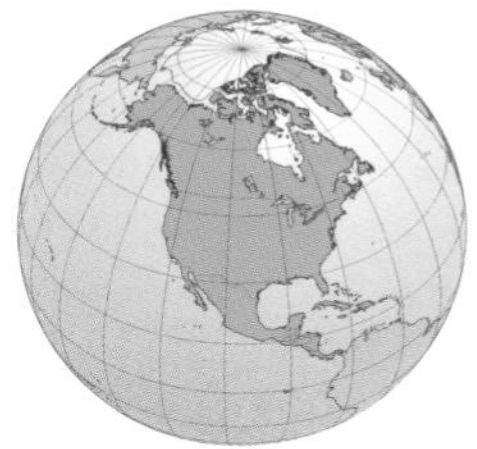

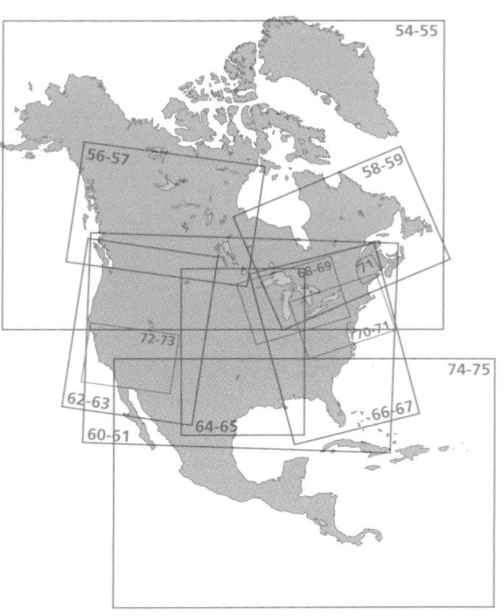

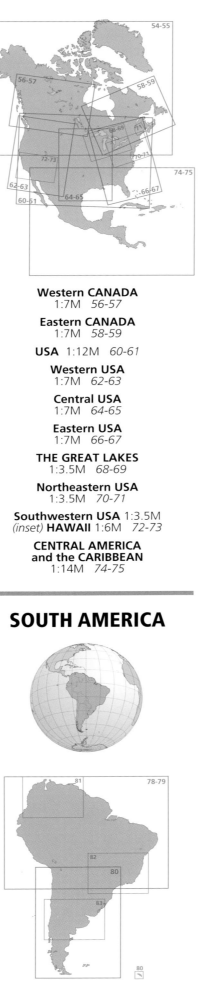

SOUTH AMERICA

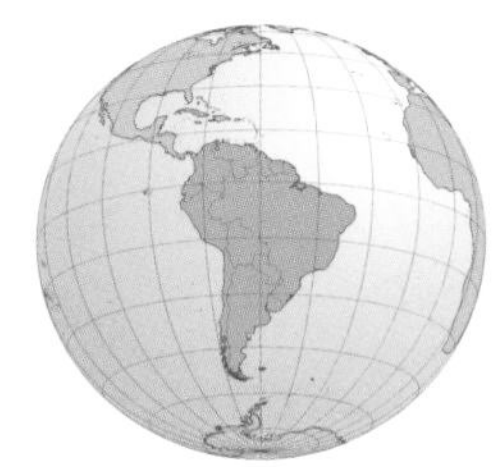

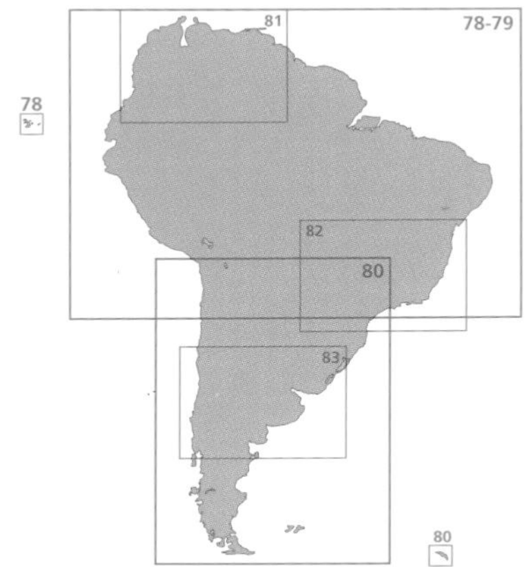

AFRICA

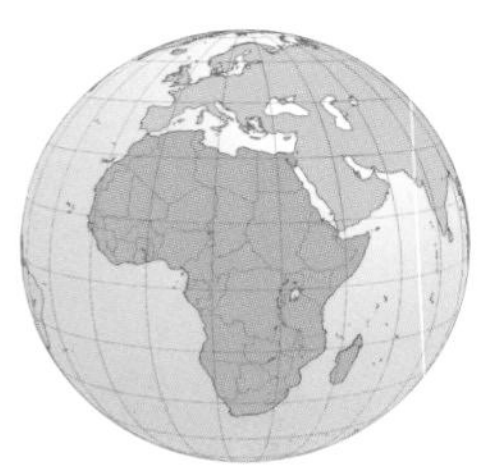

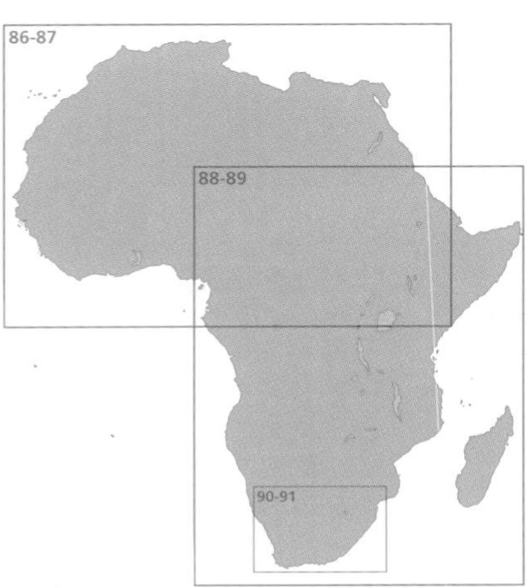

POLAR and OCEANS

COUNTRY	AREA		POPULATION			CITY	LANGUAGES	RELIGIONS	CURRENC
			TOTAL	DENSITY PER		CAPITAL			
	sq ml	sq km		sq ml	sq km				
ALBANIA	11 100	28 748	3 414 000	308	119	Tirana	Albanian	Muslim, Orthodox, Roman Catholic	Lek
ANDORRA	180	465	65 000	362	140	Andorra la Vella	Catalan, Spanish, French	Roman Catholic	Fr franc, S
AUSTRIA	32 377	83 855	8 031 000	248	96	Vienna	German, Serbo-Croat	Roman Catholic, Protestant	Schilling
AZORES	868	2 247	237 800	274	106	Ponta Delgada	Turkish Portuese	Roman Catholic, Protestant	Port. escu
BELARUS	80 155	207 600	10 355 000	129	50	Minsk	Belorussian, Russian, Ukrainian	Orthodox, Roman Catholic	Rouble
BELGIUM	11 784	30 520	10 080 000	855	330	Brussels	Dutch (Flemish), French, German	Roman Catholic, Protestant	Franc
BOSNIA-HERZEGOVINA	19 741	51 130	4 459 000	226	87	Sarajevo	Serbo-Croat	Muslim, Orthodox, Roman Catholic, Protestant	Dinar
BULGARIA	42 855	110 994	8 443 000	197	76	Sofia	Bulgarian, Turkish	Orthodox, Muslim	Lev
CHANNEL ISLANDS	75	195	149 000	1987	764	St Helier, St Peter Port	English, French	Protestant, Roman Catholic	Pound
CROATIA	21 829	56 538	4 777 000	219	84	Zagreb	Serbo-Croat	Roman Catholic, Orthodox, Muslim	Kuna
CZECH REPUBLIC	30 450	78 864	10 336 000	339	131	Prague	Czech, Moravian, Slovak	Roman Catholic, Protestant	Koruna
DENMARK	16 631	43 075	5 205 000	313	121	Copenhagen	Danish	Protestant, Roman Catholic	Krone
ESTONIA	17 452	45 200	1 499 000	86	33	Tallinn	Estonian, Russian	Protestant, Orthodox	Kroon
FAROE ISLANDS	540	1 399	47 000	87	34	Tórshavn	Danish, Faeroese	Protestant	Danish kro
FINLAND	130 559	338 145	5 088 000	39	15	Helsinki	Finnish, Swedish	Protestant, Orthodox	Markka
FRANCE	210 026	543 965	58 375 000	278	107	Paris	French, French dialects, Arabic, German (Alsatian)	Roman Catholic, Protestant, Muslim	Franc
GERMANY	138 174	357 868	81 912 000	593	229	Berlin	German	Protestant, Roman Catholic,	Mark
GIBRALTAR	3	7	28 000	11157	4308	Gibraltar	English, Spanish	Roman Catholic, Protestant,	Pound
GREECE	50 949	131 957	10 426 000	205	79	Athens	Greek	Greek Orthodox	Drachma
HUNGARY	35 919	93 030	10 261 000	286	110	Budapest	Hungarian	Roman Catholic, Protestant	Forint
ICELAND	39 699	102 820	266 000	7	3	Reykjavik	Icelandic	Protestant, Roman Catholic	Króna
ISLE OF MAN	221	572	73 000	331	128	Douglas	English	Protestant, Roman Catholic	Pound
ITALY	116 311	301 245	57 193 000	492	190	Rome	Italian, Italian dialects	Roman Catholic	Lira
LATVIA	24 595	63 700	2 548 000	104	40	Rīga	Latvian, Russian	Protestant, Roman Catholic, Orthodox	Lat
LIECHTENSTEIN	62	160	31 000	502	194	Vaduz	German	Roman Catholic, Protestant	Swiss fran
LITHUANIA	25 174	65 200	3 721 000	148	57	Vilnius	Lithuanian, Russian, Polish	Roman Catholic, Protestant, Orthodox	Litas
LUXEMBOURG	998	2 586	404 000	405	156	Luxembourg	Letzeburgish, Portuguese	Roman Catholic, Protestant	Franc
MACEDONIA, Former Yugoslavian Republic of	9 928	25 713	2 142 000	216	83	Skopje	Macedonian	Orthodox, Muslim, Roman Catholic	Denar
MADEIRA	307	794	253 000	825	319	Funchal	Portuguese	Roman Catholic, Protestant	Port. escu
MALTA	122	316	373 000	3057	1180	Valletta	Maltese, English	Roman Catholic	Lira
MOLDOVA	13 012	33 700	4 350 000	334	129	Chişinău	Romanian, Russian, Ukrainian	Moldovan, Orthodox,	Leu
MONACO	1	2	32 821	32821	16410	Monaco	French, Monegasque, Italian	Roman Catholic	French fra
NETHERLANDS	16 033	41 526	15 517 000	968	374	Amsterdam	Dutch, Frisian	Roman Catholic, Protestant	Guilder
NORWAY	125 050	323 878	4 325 000	35	13	Oslo	Norwegian	Protestant, Roman Catholic	Krone
POLAND	120 728	312 683	38 544 000	319	123	Warsaw	Polish, German	Roman Catholic, Orthodox	Zæoty
PORTUGAL	34 340	88 940	9 902 000	288	111	Lisbon	Portuguese	Roman Catholic, Protestant	Escudo
REPUBLIC OF IRELAND	27 136	70 282	3 571 000	132	51	Dublin	English, Irish	Roman Catholic, Protestant	Punt
ROMANIA	91 699	237 500	22 731 000	248	96	Bucharest	Romanian	Orthodox	Leu
RUSSIAN FEDERATION	6 592 849	17 075 400	147 739 000	22	9	Moscow	Russian, Tatar, Ukrainian, local languages	Orthodox, Muslim, other Christian, Jewish	Rouble
RUSSIAN FEDERATION (in Europe)	1 527 343	3 955 800	105 984 000	69	27				
SAN MARINO	24	61	25 000	1061	410	San Marino	Italian	Roman Catholic	Ital. lira
SLOVAKIA	18 933	49 035	5 347 000	282	109	Bratislava	Slovak, Hungarian, Czech	Roman Catholic, Protestant	Koruna
SLOVENIA	7 819	20 251	1 989 000	254	98	Ljubljana	Slovene, Serbo-Croat	Roman Catholic, Protestant	Tólar
SPAIN	194 897	504 782	39 143 000	201	78	Madrid	Spanish, Catalan, Galician, Basque	Roman Catholic	Peseta
SWEDEN	173 732	449 964	8 781 000	51	20	Stockholm	Swedish	Protestant, Roman Catholic	Krona
SWITZERLAND	15 943	41 293	6 995 000	439	169	Bern	German, French, Italian, Romansch	Roman Catholic, Protestant	Franc
UNITED KINGDOM	94 241	244 082	58 144 000	617	238	London	English, South Indian languages, Welsh, Gaelic	Protestant, Roman Catholic, Muslim	Pound
UKRAINE	233 090	603 700	51 910 000	223	86	Kiev	Ukrainian, Russian, regional languages	Orthodox, Roman Catholic	Karbovane
VATICAN CITY		0.44	1000		2273		Italian	Roman Catholic	Ital. lira
YUGOSLAVIA	39 449	102 173	10 516 000	267	103	Belgrade	Serbo-Croat, Albanian, Hungarian	Serbian and Montenegrin Orthodox, Muslim	Dinar

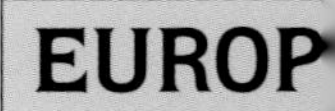

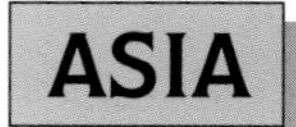

| COUNTRY | AREA | | POPULATION | | | CITY | LANGUAGES | RELIGIONS | CURRENCY |
	sq ml	sq km	TOTAL	DENSITY PER sq ml	sq km	CAPITAL			
FGHANISTAN	251 825	652 225	18 879 000	75	29	Kābul	Dari, Pushtu, Uzbek	Sunni & Shi'a Muslim	Afghani
RMENIA	11 506	29 800	3 548 000	308	119	Yerevan	Armenian, Azeri, Russian	Orthodox, Roman Catholic, Muslim	Dram
ZERBAIJAN	33 436	86 600	7 472 000	223	86	Baku	Azeri, Armenian, Russian,	Shi'a & Sunni Muslim,	Manat
AHRAIN	267	691	599 000	2244	867	Al Manāma	Arabic, English	Shi'a & Sunni Muslim, Christian	Dinar
ANGLADESH	55 598	143 998	120 073 000	2160	834	Dhaka	Bengali	Muslim, Hindu	Taka
HUTAN	18 000	46 620	1 614 000	90	35	Thimphu	Dzongkha, Nepali, Assamese	Buddhist, Hindu, Muslim	Ngultrum
RUNEI	2 226	5 765	280 000	126	49	Bandar Seri Begawan	Malay, English, Chinese	Muslim, Buddhist, Christian	Dollar (ringgit)
AMBODIA	69 884	181 000	9 568 000	137	53	Phnum Penh	Khmer	Buddhist, Muslim	Riel
HINA	3 691 899	9 560 900	1 232 083 000	334	129	Beijing	Chinese, regional languages	Confucian, Taoist, Buddhist	Yuan
YPRUS	3 572	9 251	726 000	203	78	Nicosia	Greek, Turkish, English	Greek Orthodox, Muslim	Pound
AST TIMOR	5 743	14 874	857 000	149	58	Dili	Portuguese, Tetun, English	Roman Catholic	Rupiah
EORGIA	26 911	69 700	5 450 000	203	78	T'bilisi	Georgian, Russian, Armenian	Orthodox, Muslim	Lari
IDIA	1 269 219	3 287 263	944 580 000	744	287	New Delhi	Hindi, English, regional languages	Hindu, Muslim, Sikh, Christian	Rupee
DONESIA	741 102	1 919 445	196 813 000	266	103	Jakarta	Indonesian, local languages	Muslim, Protestant, Roman Catholic	Rupiah
AN	636 296	1 648 000	61 128 000	96	37	Tehrān	Farsi, Azeri, Kurdish	Shi'a & Sunni Muslim	Rial
AQ	169 235	438 317	19 925 000	118	45	Baghdād	Arabic, Kurdish	Shi'a & Sunni Muslim	Dinar
RAEL	8 019	20 770	5 399 000	673	260	Jerusalem	Hebrew, Arabic	Jewish, Muslim, Christian	Shekel
PAN	145 841	377 727	125 761 000	862	333	Tōkyō	Japanese	Shintoist, Buddhist	Yen
RDAN	34 443	89 206	5 198 000	151	58	'Ammān	Arabic	Sunni & Shi'a Muslim	Dinar
AZAKSTAN	1 049 155	2 717 300	17 027 000	16	6	Astana	Kazakh, Russian	Muslim, Orthodox, Protestant	Tanga
UWAIT	6 880	17 818	1 620 000	235	91	Kuwait	Arabic	Sunni & Shi'a Muslim, Christian	Dinar
YRGYZSTAN	76 641	198 500	4 473 000	58	23	Bishkek	Kirghiz, Russian, Uzbek	Muslim, Orthodox	Som
AOS	91 429	236 800	4 742 000	52	20	Vientiane	Lao, local languages	Buddhist, traditional beliefs	Kip
EBANON	4 036	10 452	2 915 000	722	279	Beirut	Arabic, French, Armenian	Shi'a & Sunni Muslim, Protestant, Roman Catholic	Pound
ALAYSIA	128 559	332 965	20 097 000	156	60	Kuala Lumpur	Malay, English, Chinese,	Muslim, Buddhist, Roman Catholic, Christian, trad. beliefs	Ringgit
ALDIVES	115	298	263 015	2287	883	Male	Divehi (Maldivian)	Muslim	Rufiyaa
ONGOLIA	604 250	1 565 000	2 363 000	4	2	Ulaanbaatar	Khalka (Mongolian), Kazakh	Buddhist, Muslim, traditional beliefs	Tugrik
YANMAR	261 228	676 577	43 922 000	168	65	Yangon	Burmese, Shan, Karen	Buddhist, Muslim, Protestant,	Kyat
EPAL	56 827	147 181	21 360 000	376	145	Kathmandu	Nepali, Maithili, Bhojpuri	Hindu, Buddhist	Rupee
ORTH KOREA	46 540	120 538	23 483 000	505	195	P'yŏngyang	Korean	Trad. beliefs, Chondoist	Won
MAN	105 000	271 950	2 096 000	20	8	Muscat	Arabic, Baluchi	Muslim	Rial
KISTAN	310 403	803 940	134 146 000	432	167	Islamabad	Urdu, Punjabi, Sindhi, Pushtu	Muslim, Christian, Hindu	Rupee
ALAU	192	497	17 000	89	34	Koror	Palauan, English	Roman Catholic, Protestant	US dollar
HILIPPINES	115 831	300 000	71 899 000	621	240	Manila	Filipino, Cebuano, local languages	Roman Catholic, Aglipayan, Muslim	Peso
ATAR	4 416	11 437	593 000	134	52	Doha	Arabic, Indian lang.	Muslim, Christian	Riyal
USSIAN FEDERATION	6 592 849	17 075 400	147 739 000	22	9	Moscow	Russian, Tatar, Ukrainian, local languages	Orthodox, other Christian, Muslim, Jewish	Rouble
USSIAN FEDERATION (in Asia)	5 065 506	13 119 600	41 755 000	8	3				
AUDI ARABIA	849 425	2 200 000	17 451 000	21	8	Riyadh	Arabic	Sunni & Shi'a Muslim	Riyal
NGAPORE	247	639	3 044 000	12324	4764	Singapore	Chinese, English, Malay, Tamil	Buddhist, Taoist, Muslim, Christian	Dollar
OUTH KOREA	38 330	99 274	45 547 000	1188	450	Seoul	Korean	Buddhist, Protestant, Roman Catholic	Won
RI LANKA	25 332	65 610	17 865 000	705	272	Colombo	Sinhalese, Tamil, English	Buddhist, Hindu, Muslim	Rupee
YRIA	71 498	185 180	13 844 000	194	75	Damascus	Arabic, Kurdish	Muslim, Christian	Pound
AIWAN	13 969	36 179	21 212 000	1518	586	T'ai-pei	Chinese, local languages	Buddhist, Taoist, Confucian	Dollar
AJIKISTAN	55 251	143 100	5 933 000	107	41	Dushanbe	Tajik, Uzbek, Russian	Muslim	Rouble
HAILAND	198 115	513 115	60 003 000	303	117	Bangkok	Thai, Lao, Chinese	Buddhist, Muslim	Baht
URKEY	300 948	779 452	62 697 000	208	80	Ankara	Turkish, Kurdish	Sunni & Shi'a Muslim	Lira
URKMENISTAN	188 456	488 100	4 010 000	21	8	Ashgabat	Turkmen, Russian	Muslim	Manat
NITED ARAB EMIRATES	30 000	77 700	1 861 000	62	24	Abu Dhabi	Arabic	Sunni & Shi'a Muslim, Christian	Dirham
ZBEKISTAN	172 742	447 400	22 633 000	131	51	Tashkent	Uzbek, Russian, Tajik, Kazakh	Muslim, Orthodox	Som
ETNAM	127 246	329 565	75 181 000	591	228	Ha Nôi	Vietnamese	Buddhist, Roman Catholic	Dong
EMEN	203 850	527 968	12 672 000	62	24	Şan'ā	Arabic	Sunni & Shi'a Muslim	Dinar, rial

NATIONS OF THE WORLD

COUNTRY	AREA		POPULATION			CITY	LANGUAGES	RELIGIONS	CURRENCY
			TOTAL	DENSITY PER		CAPITAL			
	sq ml	sq km		sq ml	sq km				
AMERICAN SAMOA	76	197	55 000	723	279	Pago Pago	Samoan, English	Protestant, Roman Catholic	US dollar
AUSTRALIA	2 966 153	7 682 300	17 838 000	6	2	Canberra	English, Aboriginal languages	Protestant, Roman Catholic, Aboriginal beliefs	Dollar
FIJI	7 077	18 330	784 000	111	43	Suva	English, Fijian, Hindi	Christian, Hindu, Muslim	Dollar
FRENCH POLYNESIA	1 261	3 265	215 000	171	66	Papeete	French, Polynesian languages	Protestant, Roman Catholic,	Pacific franc
GUAM	209	541	146 000	699	270	Agana	Chamorro, English	Roman Catholic	US dollar
KIRIBATI	277	717	77 000	278	107	Bairiki	I-Kiribati (Gilbertese), English	Roman Catholic, Protestant	Austr. doll
MARSHALL ISLANDS	70	181	54 000	773	298	Dalap-Uliga-Darrit	Marshallese, English	Protestant, Roman Catholic	US dollar
FED. STATES OF MICRONESIA	271	701	104 000	384	148	Palikir	English, Trukese, Pohnpeian, local languages	Protestant, Roman Catholic	US dollar
NAURU	8	21	11 000	1357	524	Yaren	Nauruan, Gilbertese, English	Protestant, Roman Catholic	Austr. doll
NEW CALEDONIA	7 358	19 058	184 000	25	10	Nouméa	French, local languages	Roman Catholic, Protestant	Pacific franc
NEW ZEALAND	104 454	270 534	3 493 000	33	13	Wellington	English, Maori	Protestant, Roman Catholic	Dollar
NORTH. MARIANA IS.	184	477	47 000	255	99	Saipan	English, Chamorro, Tagalog	Roman Catholic, Protestant	US dollar
PAPUA NEW GUINEA	178 704	462 840	3 997 000	22	9	Port Moresby	English, Tok Pisin	Protestant, Roman Catholic	Kina
SAMOA	1 093	2 831	164 000	150	58	Apia	Samoan, English	Protestant, Roman Catholic	Tala
SOLOMON ISLANDS	10 954	28 370	366 000	33	13	Honiara	English, Pidgin	Protestant, Roman Catholic	Dollar
TONGA	289	748	98 000	339	131	Nuku'alofa	Tongan, English	Protestant, Roman Catholic, Mormon	Pa'anga
TUVALU	10	25	10 000	1000	400	Fongafale	Tuvaluan, English	Protestant	Dollar
VANUATU	4 707	12 190	165 000	35	14	Port Vila	English, Bislama, French	Protestant, Roman Catholic	Vatu
WALLIS AND FUTUNA	106	274	14 000	132	51	Mata-Utu	French, Polynesian	Roman Catholic	Pacific franc

ECONOMIC GROUPS

EUROPEAN UNION (EU)

Originally the European Economic Community founded by the Treaty of Rome in 1957, signed by Belgium, France, West Germany, Italy, Luxembourg and the Netherlands. Denmark, the Republic of Ireland and the United Kingdom joined in 1973; Greece in 1981 and Spain and Portugal in 1986. The objectives, under the Treaty of Rome, are to lay the foundations of an ever closer union among the peoples of Europe, and to ensure economic and social progress.
Headquarters : Brussels, Belgium

EUROPEAN ECONOMIC AREA (EEA)

On 1 January 1994 the EU nations and the EFTA nations formed the European Economic Area, the World's largest multi-lateral trading area.

ASSOCIATION OF SOUTH EAST ASIAN NATIONS (ASEAN)

Established in 1967, the objectives of ASEAN are to promote economic, political and social co-operation. The founder members were Indonesia, Malaysia, the Philippines, Singapore and Thailand; Brunei joined in 1984 and Vietnam in 1995. Cambodia, Laos and Myanmar have applied for membership.
Headquarters : Jakarta, Indonesia

ASIA PACIFIC ECONOMIC CO-OPERATION FORUM (APEC)

Formed in 1989 to promote trade and economic co-operation, with the long term aim of the creation of a Pacific free trade area. The original members were Australia, Brunei, Canada, Indonesia, Japan, Malaysia, New Zealand, the Philippines, Singapore, South Korea, Thailand and U.S.A.. China, Hong Kong and Taiwan joined in 1991, Mexico and Papua New Guinea in 1993, and Chile in 1994.
Headquarters : Singapore

CARIBBEAN COMMUNITY (CARICOM)

CARICOM was established in 1973. The original members were Barbados, Guyana, Jamaica and Trinidad and Tobago; in May 1974, Belize, Dominica, Grenada, Montserrat, St Lucia, and St Vincent joined followed by Antigua and St Kitts-Nevis in August 1974, the Bahamas in 1984 and Surinam in 1995. The objectives of CARICOM are to foster co-operation, co-ordinate foreign policy, and to formulate and carry out common policies on health, education and culture, communications and industrial relations.
Headquarters : Georgetown, Guyana

MERCADO COMMUN DEL SUR (Southern Common Market MERCOSUR)

Established by a treaty signed in Paraguay in 1991 by Argentina, Brazil, Paraguay and Uruguay, Mercosur's objective is to establish a regional common market.
Headquarters : Mercosur's headquarters rotate between member states' capitals.

NORTH AMERICAN FREE TRADE AREA (NAFTA)

NAFTA grew out of a 1988 free trade agreement between U.S.A. and Canada, which was extended to include Mexico in 1992. The accord came into force in January 1994.

ORGANISATION FOR ECONOMIC CO-OPERATION AND DEVELOPMENT (OECD)

Established in 1961, the OECD's objective is to promote economic and social welfare throughout the OECD area. It does this by assisting member governments in the formulation and co-ordination of policies to meet this objective; it also aims to stimulate and harmonise members' efforts in favour of developing countries.
Headquarters : Paris, France

ORGANIZATION OF PETROLEUM EXPORTING COUNTRIES (OPEC)

Established in 1960 to co-ordinate the price and supply policies of oil-producing states, and to provide member countries with economic and technical aid. Member countries are Algeria, Ecuador, Gabon, Indonesia, Iran, Iraq, Kuwait, Libya, Nigeria, Qatar, Saudi Arabia, U.A.E., and Venezuela.
Headquarters : Vienna, Austria

SOUTHERN AFRICAN DEVELOPMENT COMMUNITY (SADC)

The founder members of SADC were Angola, Botswana, Lesotho, Malawi, Mozambique, Swaziland, Tanzania, Zambia and Zimbabwe. Namibia joined in 1990, South Africa in 1994 and Mauritius in 1995. The objectives are deeper economic co-operation and integration and the promotion of political and social values, human rights and the alleviation of poverty.
Headquarters : Gaborone, Botswana

COUNTRY	AREA sq ml	AREA sq km	POPULATION TOTAL	DENSITY PER sq ml	DENSITY PER sq km	CITY CAPITAL	LANGUAGES	RELIGIONS	CURRENCY
NGUILLA	60	155	8 000	134	52	The Valley	English	Protestant, Roman Catholic	E. Carib. dollar
NTIGUA & BARBUDA	171	442	65 000	381	147	St John's	English, Creole	Protestant, Roman Catholic	E. Carib. dollar
AHAMAS	5 382	13 939	272 000	51	20	Nassau	English, Creole, French Creole	Protestant, Roman Catholic	Dollar
ARBADOS	166	430	264 000	1590	614	Bridgetown	English, Creole (Bajan)	Protestant, Roman Catholic	Dollar
ELIZE	8 867	22 965	211 000	24	9	Belmopan	English, Creole, Spanish, Mayan	Roman Catholic, Protestant	Dollar
ERMUDA	21	54	64 000	3048	1185	Hamilton	English	Protestant, Roman Catholic	Dollar
NADA	3 849 674	9 970 610	29 251 000	8	3	Ottawa	English, French, Amerindian languages, Inuktitut (Eskimo)	Roman Catholic, Protestant	Dollar
YMAN ISLANDS	100	259	31 000	310	120	George Town	English	Protestant, Roman Catholic	Dollar
STA RICA	19 730	51 100	3 071 000	156	60	San José	Spanish	Roman Catholic, Protestant	Colón
BA	42 803	110 860	10 960 000	256	99	Havana	Spanish	Roman Catholic, Protestant	Peso
MINICA	290	750	71 000	245	95	Roseau	English, French Creole	Roman Catholic, Protestant	E. Carib. dollar,
MINICAN REPUBLIC	18 704	48 442	7 769 000	415	160	Santo Domingo	Spanish, French Creole	Roman Catholic, Protestant	Peso
SALVADOR	8 124	21 041	5 641 000	694	268	San Salvador	Spanish	Roman Catholic, Protestant	Colón
REENLAND	840 004	2 175 600	55 000			Nuuk	Greenlandic, Danish	Protestant	Danish krone
RENADA	146	378	92 000	630	243	St George's	English, Creole	Roman Catholic, Protestant	E. Carib. dollar
JADELOUPE	687	1 780	421 000	613	237	Basse Terre	French, French Creole	Roman Catholic	French franc
JATEMALA	42 043	108 890	10 322 000	246	95	Guatemalà	Spanish, Mayan languages	Roman Catholic, Protestant	Quetzal
AITI	10 714	27 750	7 041 000	657	254	Port-au-Prince	French, French Creole	Roman Catholic, Protestant	Gourde
ONDURAS	43 277	112 088	5 770 000	133	51	Tegucigalpa	Spanish, Amerindian languages	Roman Catholic, Protestant	Lempira
MAICA	4 244	10 991	2 429 000	572	221	Kingston	English, Creole	Protestant, Roman Catholic	Dollar
ARTINIQUE	417	1 079	375 000	900	348	Fort-de-France	French, French Creole	Roman Catholic	French franc
EXICO	761 604	1 972 545	96 578 000	127	49	México	Spanish, Amerindian languages	Roman Catholic	Peso
ONTSERRAT	39	100	11 000	285	110	Plymouth	English	Protestant, Roman Catholic	E. Carib. dollar
CARAGUA	50 193	130 000	4 401 000	88	34	Managua	Spanish, Amerindian languages	Roman Catholic, Protestant	Córdoba
NAMA	29 762	77 082	2 583 000	87	34	Panamá	Spanish, English Creole, Amerindian languages	Roman Catholic	Balboa
ERTO RICO	3 515	9 104	3 736 000	1063	410	San Juan	Spanish, English	Roman Catholic, Protestant	US dollar
KITTS & NEVIS	101	261	41 000	407	157	Basseterre	English, Creole	Protestant, Roman Catholic	E. Carib. dollar
LUCIA	238	616	141 000	593	229	Castries	English, French Creole	Roman Catholic, Protestant	E. Carib. dollar
VINCENT & E GRENADINES	150	389	111 000	739	285	Kingstown	English, Creole	Protestant, Roman Catholic	E. Carib. dollar
RKS & CAICOS ISLANDS	166	430	14 000	84	33	Cockburn Town	English	Protestant	US dollar
A	3 787 425	9 809 386	266 557 000	70	27	Washington	English, Spanish, Amerindian languages	Protestant, Roman Catholic	Dollar
RGIN ISLANDS (UK)	59	153	18 000	305	118	Road Town	English	Protestant, Roman Catholic	US dollar
RGIN ISLANDS (USA)	136	352	104 000	765	295	Charlotte Amalie	English, Spanish	Protestant, Roman Catholic	US dollar

INTERNATIONAL ORGANIZATIONS

ARAB LEAGUE

Founded in 1945 in Cairo, by Egypt, Syria, Iraq, Lebanon, Jordan, Saudi Arabia and Yemen. The membership has been extended to include 14 other countries in the region.
Headquarters : Cairo, Egypt

THE COMMONWEALTH

The status and relationship of members of the Commonwealth, which grew out of the British Empire was defined in 1926 and enshrined in the 1931 Statute of Westminster. There are 53 members of the Commonwealth.

COMMONWEALTH OF INDEPENDENT STATES (CIS)

Established by the Minsk agreement and the Alma-Ata Declaration in 1991 following the collapse of the U.S.S.R..
Headquarters : Minsk, Belarus

ORGANIZATION OF AMERICAN STATES (OAS)

e OAS claims to be the oldest regional ganization in the world, tracing its origins ck to 1826. The charter of the present OAS me into force in 1951. There are 34 member tes spread throughout North and South nerica.
adquarters : Washington, U.S.A.

THE UNITED NATIONS

The United Nations is the largest international group of countries. Formed in 1945 to promote world peace and co-operation between nations. The 185 members regularly meet in a General Assembly to settle disputes and agree on common policies to world problems. The work of the United Nations is carried out through its various agencies which include:

Headquarters : New York, U.S.A.

Agency:	Responsibility:
UNESCO	Science, education and culture.
UNICEF	Children's welfare.
UNDRO	Disaster relief.
UNHCR	Aid to refugees.
WHO	Health.
FAO	Food & agriculture.
UNEP	Environment.
UNDP	Development programme.

ORGANIZATION OF AFRICAN UNITY (OAU)

The OAU grew out of the Union of Africa states which was founded in 1961. All continental African countries are members together with Cape Verde, the Comoros, Sao Tome and Principe, and Seychelles.
Headquarters : Addis Ababa, Ethiopia

© Collins

NATIONS OF THE WORLD

COUNTRY	AREA		POPULATION			CITY	LANGUAGES	RELIGIONS	CURRENCY
			TOTAL	DENSITY PER		CAPITAL			
	sq ml	sq km		sq ml	sq km				
ARGENTINA	1 068 302	2 766 889	34 180 000	32	12	Buenos Aires	Spanish, Amerindian languages	Roman Catholic	Peso
ARUBA	75	193	69 000	926	358	Oranjestad	Dutch, Papiamento,	Roman Catholic, Protestant	Florin
BOLIVIA	424 164	1 098 581	7 237 000	17	7	La Paz	Spanish, Quechua, Aymara	Roman Catholic	Boliviano
BRAZIL	3 286 488	8 511 965	157 872 000	48	19	Brasília	Portuguese, Italian, Amerindian languages	Roman Catholic	Real
CHILE	292 258	756 945	13 994 000	48	18	Santiago	Spanish, Amerindian languages	Roman Catholic	Peso
COLOMBIA	440 831	1 141 748	34 520 000	78	30	Bogotá	Spanish, Amerindian languages	Roman Catholic	Peso
ECUADOR	105 037	272 045	11 221 000	107	41	Quito	Spanish, Amerindian languages	Roman Catholic	Sucre
FALKLAND ISLANDS	4 699	12 170	2 000			Stanley	English	Protestant, Roman Catholic	Pound
FRENCH GUIANA	34 749	90 000	141 000	4	2	Cayenne	French, French Creole	Roman Catholic, Protestant	French fran
GUYANA	83 000	214 969	825 000	10	4	Georgetown	English, Creole, Hindi, Amerindian languages	Protestant, Hindu, Roman Catholic, Sunni Muslim	Dollar
NETH. ANTILLES	283	732	158 206	560	216	Willemstad	Dutch, Papiamento	Roman Catholic, Protestant	Guilder
PARAGUAY	157 048	406 752	4 700 000	30	12	Asunción	Spanish, Guaraní	Roman Catholic	Guaraní
PERU	496 225	1 285 216	23 088 000	47	18	Lima	Spanish, Quechua	Roman Catholic	Sol
SURINAME	63 251	163 820	418 000	7	3	Paramaribo	Dutch, Surinamese	Hindu, Roman Catholic, Protestant, Muslim	Guilder
TRINIDAD AND TOBAGO	1 981	5 130	1 250 000	631	244	Port Of Spain	English, Creole, Hindi	Roman Catholic, Hindu, Protestant	Dollar
URUGUAY	68 037	176 215	3 167 000	47	18	Montevideo	Spanish	Roman Catholic, Protestant	Peso
VENEZUELA	352 144	912 050	21 177 000	60	23	Caracas	Spanish, Amerindian languages	Roman Catholic	Bolívar

COUNTRY	AREA		POPULATION			CITY	LANGUAGES	RELIGIONS	CURRENC
			TOTAL	DENSITY PER		CAPITAL			
	sq ml	sq km		sq ml	sq km				
ALGERIA	919 595	2 381 741	27 561 000	30	12	Algiers	Arabic, French, Berber	Muslim	Dinar
ANGOLA	481 354	1 246 700	10 674 000	22	9	Luanda	Portuguese	Roman Catholic, Protestant, traditional beliefs	Kwanza
BENIN	43 483	112 620	5 387 000	124	48	Porto Novo	French, local languages	Trad. beliefs, Roman Catholic	CFA franc
BOTSWANA	224 468	581 370	1 443 000	6	2	Gaborone	English, Setswana	Traditional beliefs, Protestant, Roman Catholic	Pula
BURKINA	105 869	274 200	9 889 000	93	36	Ouagadougou	French, local languages	Traditional beliefs, Muslim, Roman Catholic	CFA franc
BURUNDI	10 747	27 835	6 134 000	571	220	Bujumbura	Kirundi, French	Roman Catholic, Protestant	Franc
CAMEROON	183 569	475 442	12 871 000	70	27	Yaoundé	French, English	Trad. beliefs, Roman Catholic, Muslim, Protestant	CFA franc
CAPE VERDE	1 557	4 033	381 000	245	94	Praia	Portuguese	Roman Catholic	Escudo
CENTRAL AFRICAN REPUBLIC	240 324	622 436	3 235 000	13	5	Bangui	French, Sango	Protestant, Roman Catholic, traditional beliefs	CFA franc
CHAD	495 755	1 284 000	6 214 000	13	5	Ndjamena	Arabic, French	Muslim, traditional beliefs, Roman Catholic	CFA franc
COMOROS	719	1 862	630 000	876	338	Moroni	Comorian, French, Arabic	Muslim	Franc
CONGO	132 047	342 000	2 516 000	19	7	Brazzaville	French, local languages	Roman Catholic, Protestant	CFA franc
CONGO, DEM. REP. OF	905 568	2 345 410	42 552 000	47	18	Kinshasa	French, local languages	Roman Catholic, Protestant	Zaïre
CÔTE D'IVOIRE	124 504	322 463	13 695 000	110	42	Yamoussoukro	French, local languages	Traditional beliefs, Muslim, Roman Catholic	CFA franc
DJIBOUTI	8 958	23 200	566 000	63	24	Djibouti	French, Arabic	Muslim	Franc
EGYPT	386 199	1 000 250	60 603 000	157	61	Cairo	Arabic, French	Muslim, Coptic Christian	Pound
EQUATORIAL GUINEA	10 831	28 051	389 000	36	14	Malabo	Spanish	Roman Catholic	CFA franc
ERITREA	45 328	117 400	3 437 000	76	29	Asmara	Tigrinya, Arabic, Tigre, English	Muslim, Coptic Christian	Ethiopian b
ETHIOPIA	437 794	1 133 880	58 506 000	134	52	Addis Ababa	Amharic, local languages	Ethiopian Orthodox, Muslim, traditional beliefs	Birr
GABON	103 347	267 667	1 283 000	12	5	Libreville	French, local languages	Roman Catholic, Protestant	CFA franc
GAMBIA	4 361	11 295	1 081 000	248	96	Banjul	English	Muslim	Dalasi
GHANA	92 100	238 537	16 944 000	184	71	Accra	English, local languages	Protestant, Roman Catholic, Muslim, traditional beliefs	Cedi
GUINEA	94 926	245 857	6 501 000	68	26	Conakry	French, local languages	Muslim	Franc
GUINEA-BISSAU	13 948	36 125	1 050 000	75	29	Bissau	Portuguese, local languages	Traditional beliefs, Muslim	Peso
KENYA	224 961	582 646	29 292 000	130	50	Nairobi	Swahili, English	Roman Catholic, Protestant, traditional beliefs	Shilling
LESOTHO	11 720	30 355	1 996 000	170	66	Maseru	Sesotho, English	Roman Catholic, Protestant	Loti
LIBERIA	43 000	111 369	2 700 000	63	24	Monrovia	English, local languages	Muslim, Christian	Dollar
LIBYA	679 362	1 759 540	4 899 000	7	3	Tripoli	Arabic, Berber	Muslim	Dinar
MADAGASCAR	226 658	587 041	14 303 000	63	24	Antananarivo	Malagasy, French	Traditional beliefs, Roman Catholic, Protestant	Franc

| UNTRY | AREA | | POPULATION | | | CITY | LANGUAGES | RELIGIONS | CURRENCY |
	sq ml	sq km	TOTAL	DENSITY PER sq ml	sq km	CAPITAL			
ALAWI	45 747	118 484	9 461 000	207	80	Lilongwe	English, Chichewa	Protestant, Roman Catholic, traditional beliefs, Muslim	Kwacha
ALI	478 821	1 240 140	10 462 000	22	8	Bamako	French, local languages	Muslim, traditional beliefs	CFA franc
AURITANIA	397 955	1 030 700	2 211 000	6	2	Nouakchott	Arabic, local languages	Muslim	Ouguiya
AURITIUS	788	2 040	1 134 000	1439	556	Port Louis	English	Hindu, Roman Catholic, Muslim	Rupee
OROCCO	172 414	446 550	26 590 000	154	60	Rabat	Arabic	Muslim	Dirham
OZAMBIQUE	308 642	799 380	16 614 000	54	21	Maputo	Portuguese, local languages	Traditional beliefs,Roman Catholic, Muslim	Metical
MIBIA	318 261	824 292	1 500 000	5	2	Windhoek	English, Afrikaans, German, Ovambo	Protestant, Roman Catholic	Dollar
GER	489 191	1 267 000	8 846 000	18	7	Niamey	French, local languages	Muslim, traditional beliefs	CFA franc
GERIA	356 669	923 768	115 020 000	322	126	Abuja	English, Hausa, Yoruba, Ibo, Fulani	Muslim, Protestant, Roman Catholic, traditional beliefs	Naira
UNION	985	2 551	644 000	654	252	St-Denis	French	Roman Catholic	French franc
VANDA	10 169	26 338	7 750 000	762	294	Kigali	Kinyarwanda, French	Roman Catholic, traditional beliefs	Franc
O TOMÉ AND PRÍNCIPE	372	964	125 000	336	130	São Tomé	Portuguese	Roman Catholic, Protestant	Dobra
NEGAL	75 954	196 720	8 102 000	107	41	Dakar	French, local languages	Muslim	CFA franc
YCHELLES	176	455	74 000	421	163	Victoria	Seychellois, English	Roman Catholic, Protestant	Rupee
RRA LEONE	27 699	71 740	4 402 000	159	61	Freetown	English, local languages	Traditional beliefs, Muslim	Leone
MALIA	246 201	637 657	9 077 000	37	14	Mogadishu	Somali, Arabic	Muslim	Shilling
UTH AFRICA	470 689	1 219 080	40 436 000	86	33	Pretoria/Cape Town	Afrikaans, English, local languages	Protestant, Roman Catholic	Rand
DAN	967 500	2 505 813	28 947 000	30	12	Khartoum	Arabic, local languages	Muslim, traditional beliefs	Dinar
VAZILAND	6 704	17 364	879 000	131	51	Mbabane	Swazi, English	Protestant, Roman Catholic, traditional beliefs	Emalangeni
NZANIA	364 900	945 087	28 846 000	79	31	Dodoma	Swahili, English, local languages	Christian, Muslim, traditional beliefs	Shilling
GO	21 925	56 785	3 928 000	179	69	Lomé	French, local languages	Traditional beliefs, Roman Catholic, Muslim	CFA franc
NISIA	63 379	164 150	8 814 000	139	54	Tunis	Arabic	Muslim	Dinar
ANDA	93 065	241 038	20 621 000	222	86	Kampala	English, Swahili	Roman Catholic, Protestant	Shilling
MBIA	290 586	752 614	9 196 000	32	12	Lusaka	English, local languages	Christian, traditional beliefs	Kwacha
MBABWE	150 873	390 759	11 150 000	74	29	Harare	English, Shona, Ndebele	Protestant, Roman Catholic, traditional beliefs	Dollar

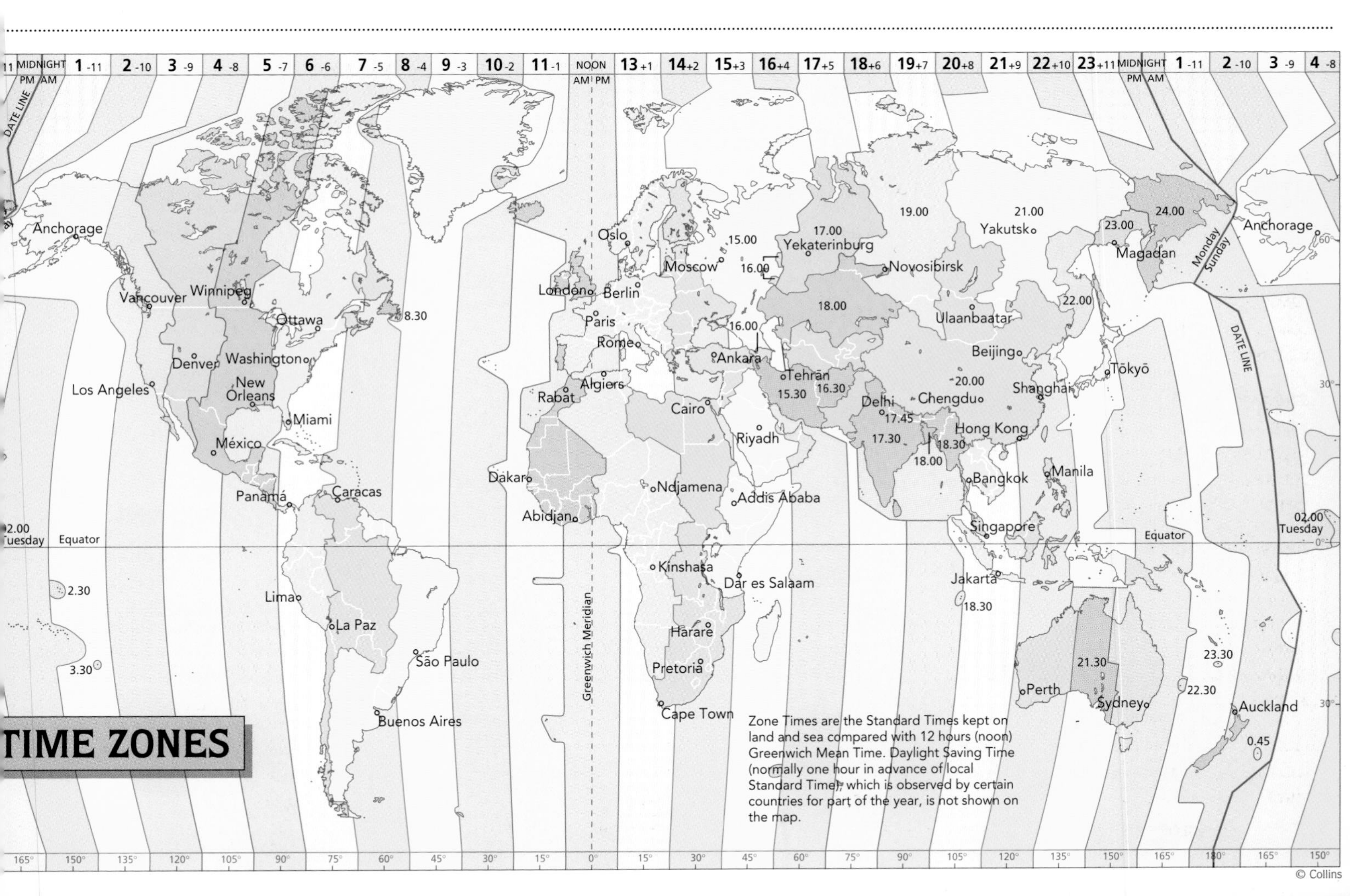

TIME ZONES

Zone Times are the Standard Times kept on land and sea compared with 12 hours (noon) Greenwich Mean Time. Daylight Saving Time (normally one hour in advance of local Standard Time), which is observed by certain countries for part of the year, is not shown on the map.

© Collins

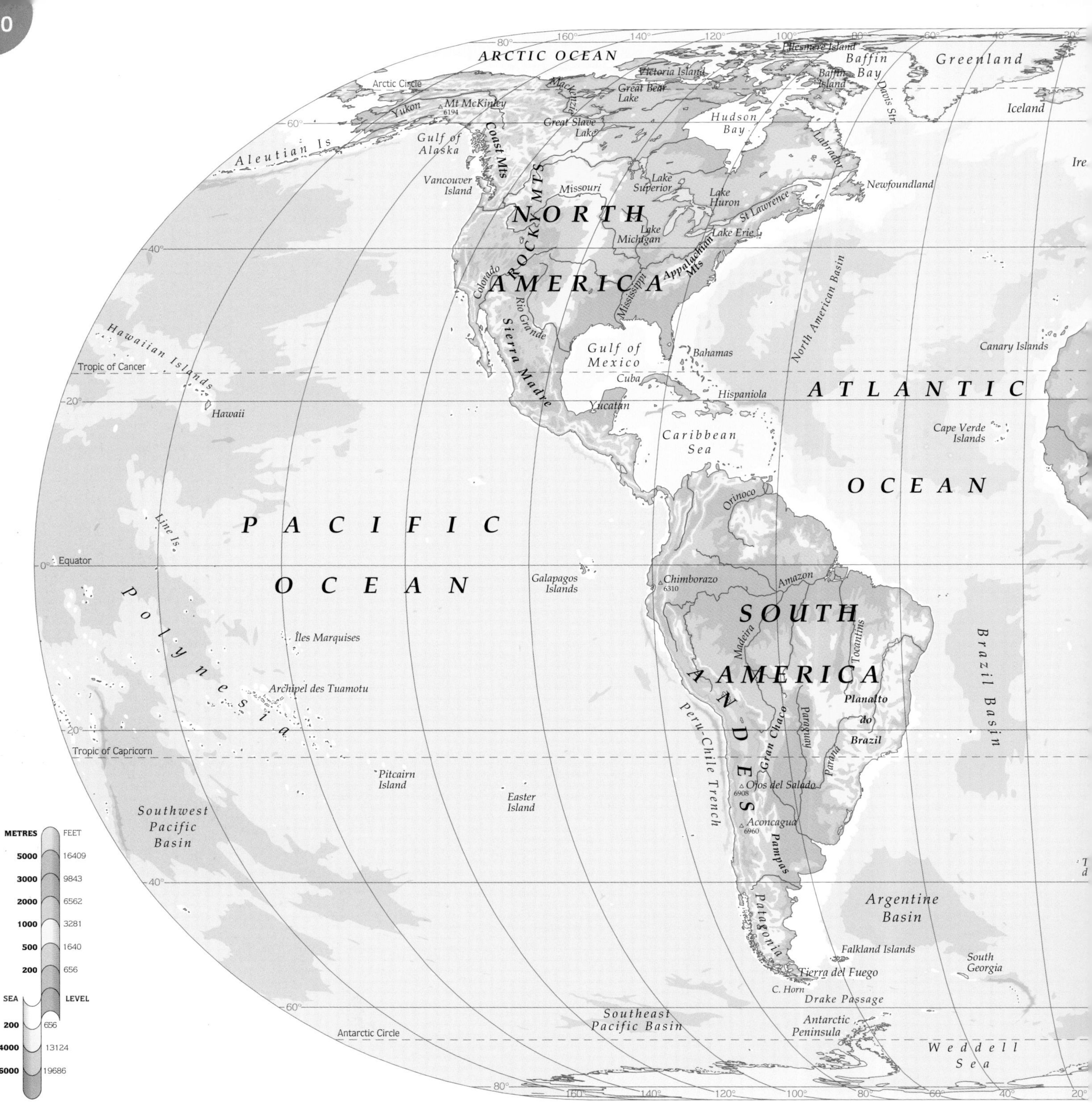

PHYSICAL FEATURES

WORLD EXTREMES

Highest Mountain
8 848 m   MT EVEREST (Asia)   29 028 ft

Largest Inland Water Area
371 000 sq km   CASPIAN SEA (Asia)   143 205 sq mls

Largest Island
2 175 600 sq km   GREENLAND (N. America)   839 780 sq mls

Longest River
6 695 km   NILE (Africa)   4 160 mls

Largest Drainage Basin
7 050 000 sq km   AMAZON (S. America)   2 721 000 sq mls

Deepest Water
11 022 m   MARIANAS TRENCH   36 161 ft
(Pacific Ocean)

CONTINENTS and OCEANS

sq km		sq miles
45 036 492	ASIA	17 388 590
30 343 578	AFRICA	11 715 655
25 680 331	NORTH AMERICA	9 529 076
17 815 420	SOUTH AMERICA	6 878 534
13 340 000	ANTARCTICA	5 150 574
9 908 599	EUROPE	3 825 710
8 504 241	OCEANIA	3 283 487
165 384 000	PACIFIC OCEAN	63 838 000
82 217 000	ATLANTIC OCEAN	31 736 000
73 481 000	INDIAN OCEAN	28 364 000
14 056 000	ARCTIC OCEAN	5 426 000

MOUNTAINS

metres		fe
8 848	MT EVEREST (Nepal/China)	29
8 611	K2 (India/China)	28
8 598	KANGCHENJUNGA (Nepal/India)	28
6 960	ACONCAGUA (Argentina)	22
6 908	OJOS DEL SALADO (Arg./Chile)	22
6 310	CHIMBORAZO (Ecuador)	20
6 194	MT MCKINLEY (USA)	20
5 895	KILIMANJARO (Tanzania)	19
5 642	ELBRUS (Russian Federation)	18
5 199	KIRINYAGA (Kenya)	17
5 030	PUNCAK JAYA (Indonesia)	16
4 808	MONT BLANC (France/Italy)	15

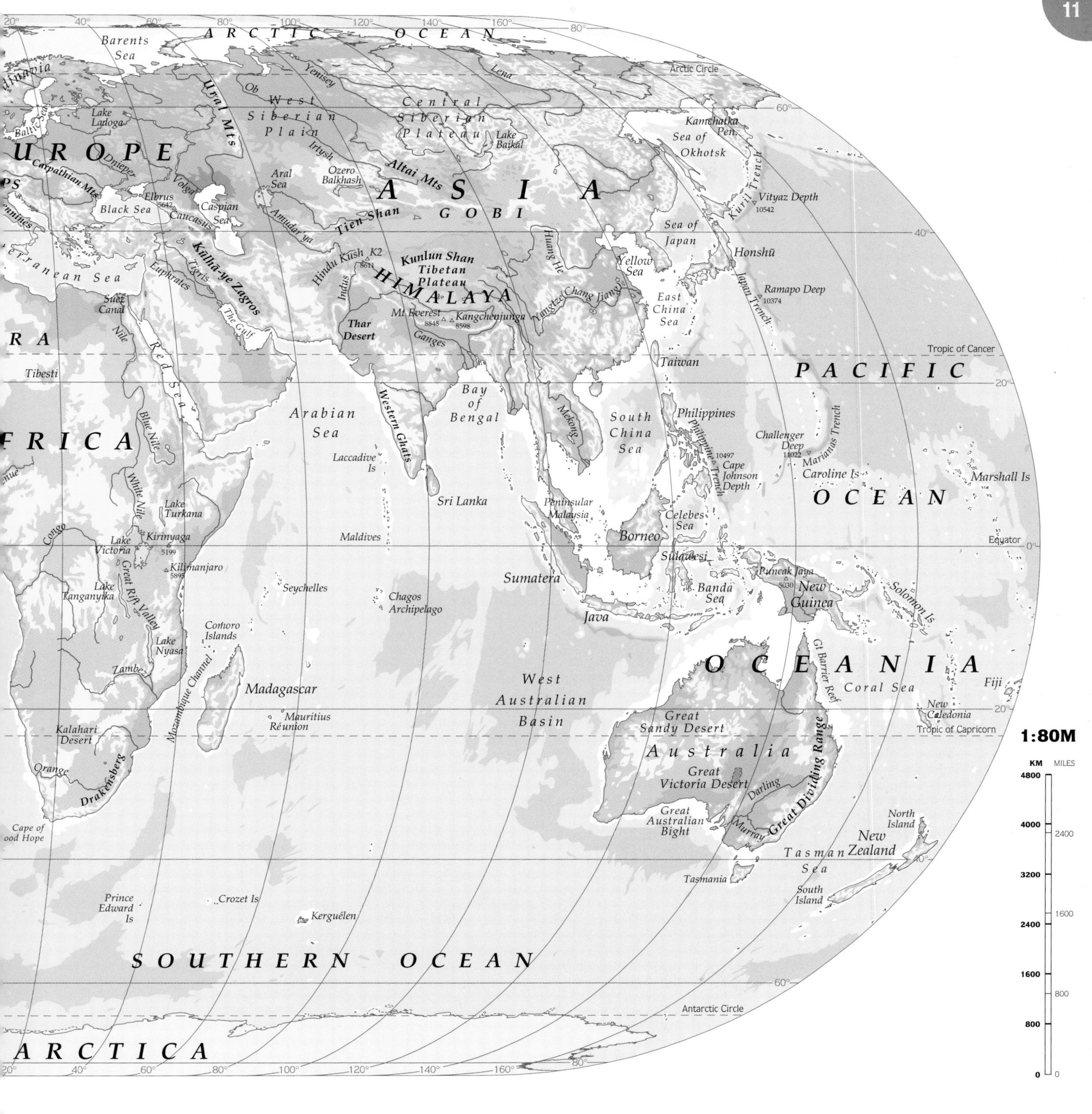

1:80M

KM MILES
4800
4000 — 2400
3200
2400 — 1600
1600 — 800
800
0 — 0

ISLANDS			LAKES			RIVERS		
.m		sq miles	sq km		sq miles	kilometres		miles
600	GREENLAND (N. America)	839 780	371 000	CASPIAN SEA (Asia)	143 205	6 695	NILE (Africa)	4 160
510	NEW GUINEA (Asia/Oceania)	312 085	83 270	LAKE SUPERIOR (N. America)	32 140	6 516	AMAZON (S. America)	4 048
050	BORNEO (Asia)	292 220	68 800	LAKE VICTORIA (Africa)	26 560	6 380	YANGTZE (Chang Jiang) (Asia)	3 964
180	MADAGASCAR (Africa)	229 355	60 700	LAKE HURON (N. America)	23 430	6 020	MISSISSIPPI-MISSOURI (N. America)	3 740
100	SUMATERA (Asia)	202 300	58 020	LAKE MICHIGAN (N. America)	22 395	5 570	OB-IRTYSH (Asia)	3 461
070	BAFFIN ISLAND (N. America)	183 760	33 640	ARAL SEA (Asia)	12 985	5 464	HUANG HE (Asia)	3 395
455	HONSHŪ (Asia)	88 955	32 900	LAKE TANGANYIKA (Africa)	12 700	4 667	CONGO (Africa)	2 900
870	GREAT BRITAIN (Europe)	88 730	31 790	GREAT BEAR LAKE (N. America)	12 270	4 425	MEKONG (Asia)	2 749
690	ELLESMERE ISLAND (N. America)	82 100	30 500	LAKE BAIKAL (Asia)	11 775	4 416	AMUR (Asia)	2 744
200	VICTORIA ISLAND (N. America)	81 190	28 440	GREAT SLAVE LAKE (N. America)	10 980	4 400	LENA (Asia)	2 734
040	SULAWESI (Asia)	72 970	25 680	LAKE ERIE (N. America)	9 915	4 250	MACKENZIE (N. America)	2 640
460	SOUTH ISLAND (Oceania)	58 080	22 490	LAKE NYASA (Africa)	8 680	4 090	YENISEY (Asia)	2 541

ICE CAP

Areas of permanent ice cap around the north and south poles. The intense cold, dry weather and the ice cover render these regions almost lifeless. In Antarctica, tiny patches of land free of ice have a cover of mosses and lichens which provide shelter for some insects and mites.

TUNDRA and MOUNTAIN

Sub-arctic areas or mountain tops which are usually frozen. Tundra vegetation is characterized by mosses, lichens, rushes, grasses and flowering herbs; animals include the arctic fox and reindeer. Mountain vegetation is also characterized by mosses and lichens, and by low growing birch and willow.

TAIGA (NORTHERN FOREST)

Found only in the high latitudes of the northern hemisphere where winters are long and very cold, and summers are short. The characteristic vegetation is coniferous trees, including spruce and fir; animals include beavers, squirrels and deer.

MIXED and DECIDUOUS FOR

Typical of both temperate mid-la and eastern subtropical regions. vegetation is a mixture of broad and coniferous trees, including c beech and maple. Humankind ha a major impact on these regions in many areas little natural vege remains.

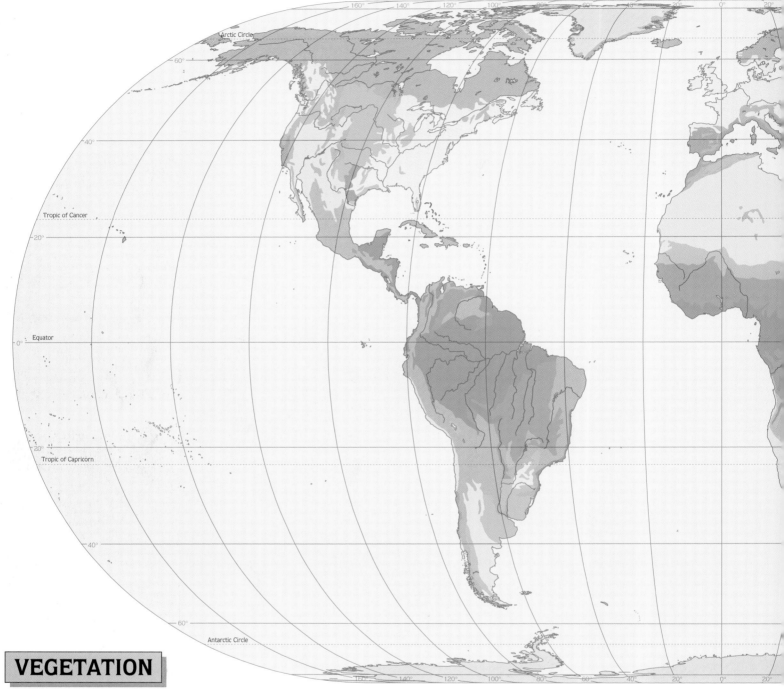

VEGETATION

ICE CAP

TUNDRA and MOUNTAIN

TAIGA (NORTHERN FOREST)

MIXED and DECIDUOUS FOREST

MEDITERRANEAN SCRUB

ng, hot, dry summers and short, warm, et winters characterize these areas. A riety of herbaceous plants grow beneath rub thickets with pine, oak and gorse.

GRASSLAND

Areas of long grasslands (prairies) and short grasslands (steppe) in both the northern and southern hemispheres. These grasslands have hot summers, cold winters and moderate rainfall.

SAVANNA

Tropical grasslands with a short rainy season; areas of grassland are interspersed with thorn bushes and deciduous trees such as acacia and eucalyptus.

DESERT

Little vegetation grows in the very hot, dry climate of desert areas. The few shrubs, grasses and cacti have adapted by storing water when it is available.

RAINFOREST

Dense evergreen forests found in areas of high rainfall and continuous high temperatures. Up to three tree layers grow above a variable shrub layer: high trees, the tree canopy and the open canopy.

DRY TROPICAL FOREST and SCRUB

Low to medium size semi-deciduous trees and thorny scrub with thick bark and long roots characterize the forest areas; in the scrub areas the trees are replaced by shrubs, bushes and succulents.

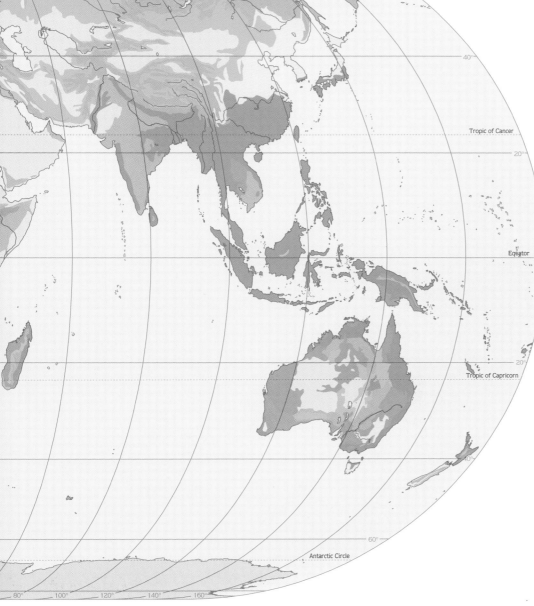

DRY TROPICAL FOREST and SCRUB

DESERT

MEDITERRANEAN SCRUB

GRASSLAND

SAVANNA

RAINFOREST

CLIMATE TYPES

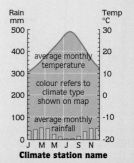

	Ice cap
	Tundra: warmest month below 10°C
	Subarctic: rainy with severe cold winters and less than 4 months over 10°C

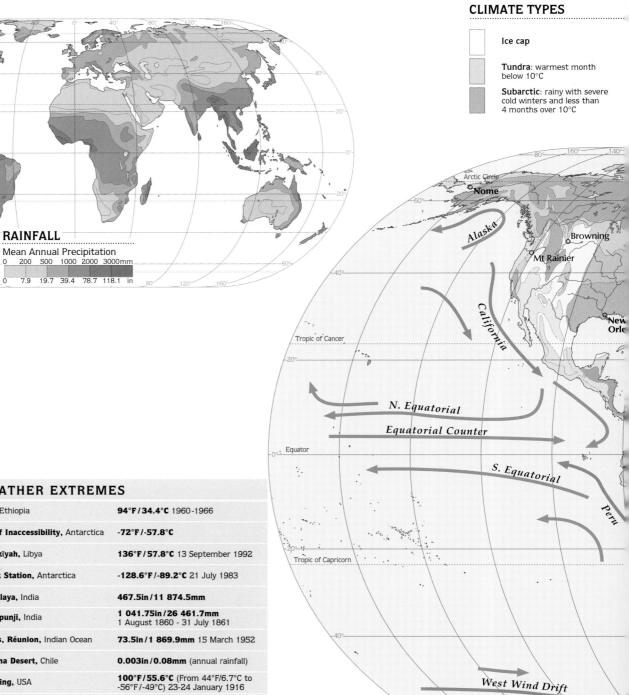

RAINFALL

Mean Annual Precipitation

0 200 500 1000 2000 3000mm
0 7.9 19.7 39.4 78.7 118.1 in

CLIMATE

WEATHER EXTREMES

Hottest annual average	**Dalol**, Ethiopia	**94°F/34.4°C** 1960-1966
Coldest annual average	**Pole of Inaccessibility**, Antarctica	**-72°F/-57.8°C**
Hottest location	**Al 'Azīzīyah**, Libya	**136°F/57.8°C** 13 September 1992
Coldest location	**Vostok Station**, Antarctica	**-128.6°F/-89.2°C** 21 July 1983
Highest annual average rainfall	**Meghalaya**, India	**467.5in/11 874.5mm**
Greatest measured annual rainfall	**Cherrapunji**, India	**1 041.75in/26 461.7mm** 1 August 1860 - 31 July 1861
Greatest 24hr rainfall	**Chilaos, Réunion**, Indian Ocean	**73.5in/1 869.9mm** 15 March 1952
Driest location	**Atacama Desert**, Chile	**0.003in/0.08mm** (annual rainfall)
Greatest 24hr temperature change	**Browning**, USA	**100°F/55.6°C** (From 44°F/6.7°C to -56°F/-49°C) 23-24 January 1916
Greatest annual snowfall	**Mt Rainier**, USA	**1 224.5in/31 102mm** 19 February 1971 - 8 February 1972
Largest hailstone	**Gopalganj**, Bangladesh	**2.25lbs/1.02kg** 14 April 1986
Highest measured wind gust	**Mt Washington**, USA	**231mph/372kph** 12 April 1934

TROPICAL STORMS

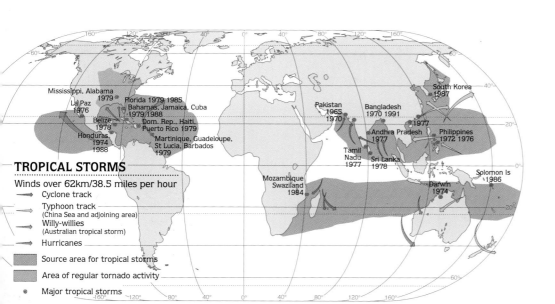

Winds over 62km/38.5 miles per hour

→ Cyclone track
→ Typhoon track (China Sea and adjoining area)
→ Willy-willies (Australian tropical storm)
→ Hurricanes

Source area for tropical storms
Area of regular tornado activity
• Major tropical storms

CLIMATE GRAPHS

The graphs show the average monthly temperature and the average monthly rainfall; the colour relates to the Climate Type shown on the map and key above.

The climate stations are shown on the map in bold type; the names in light type on the map show the locations of the Weather Extremes on the chart on the left.

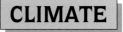

Continental cool summer: rainy
with warmest month below 22°C

Continental warm summer: with
warmest month above 20°C

Temperate: rainy with mild winters
and coolest month above 0°C

Humid subtropical: coolest month
above 0°C and warmest month
above 22°C

Mediterranean: rainy with mild wet
winters and dry summers

Steppe: semi-arid, dry

Desert

Savanna: rainy tropical climate

Rain forest: rainy tropical climate,
constantly wet throughout the year

Warm
Currents

Cold
Currents

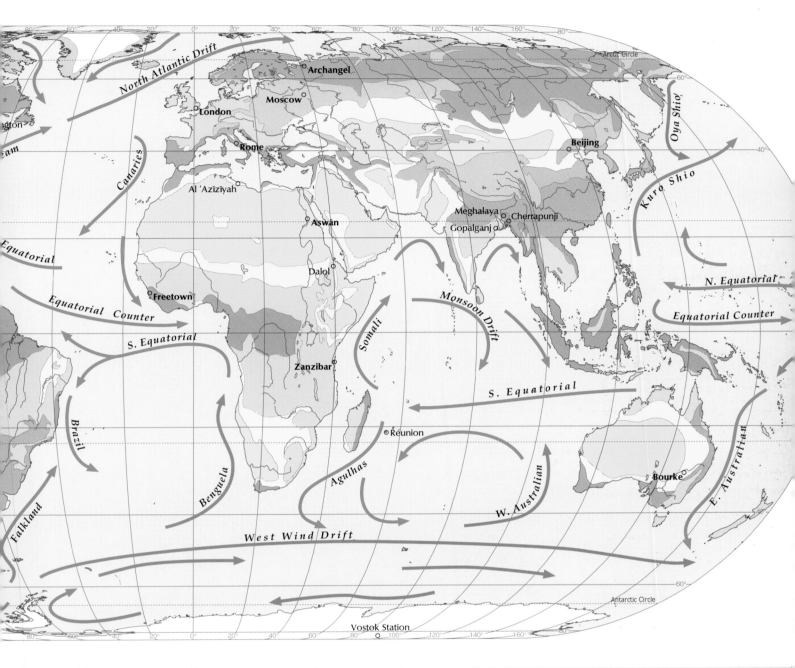

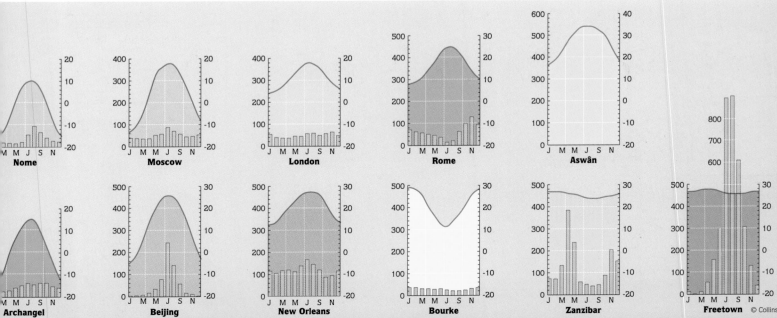

Nome

Moscow

London

Rome

Aswân

Archangel

Beijing

New Orleans

Bourke

Zanzibar

Freetown © Collins

WORLD POPULATION RANKINGS

Rank	Mid 1996 population		Population density 1996 (persons per square kilometre)	
1	CHINA	1 232 083 000	MACAU	25882.4
2	INDIA	944 580 000	MONACO	16410.3
3	U.S.A.	266 557 000	SINGAPORE	4763.7
4	INDONESIA	196 813 000	GIBRALTAR	4307.7
5	BRAZIL	157 872 000	VATICAN CITY	2272.7
6	RUSSIAN FEDERATION	147 739 000	BERMUDA	1185.2
7	PAKISTAN	134 146 000	MALTA	1180.4
8	JAPAN	125 761 000	MALDIVES	882.6
9	BANGLADESH	120 073 000	BAHRAIN	866.9
10	NIGERIA	115 020 000	BANGLADESH	833.9
11	MEXICO	96 578 000	CHANNEL ISLANDS	764.1
12	GERMANY	81 912 000	BARBADOS	607.0
13	VIETNAM	75 181 000	TAIWAN	586.3
14	PHILIPPINES	71 899 000	MAURITIUS	555.9
15	TURKEY	62 697 000	NAURU	523.8
16	IRAN	61 128 000	SOUTH KOREA	458.8
17	EGYPT	60 603 000	PUERTO RICO	410.4
18	THAILAND	60 003 000	SAN MARINO	409.8
19	ETHIOPIA	58 506 000	TUVALU	400.0
20	FRANCE	58 375 000	NETHERLANDS	373.7

POPULATION PATTERNS

THE WORLD'S POPULATION in mid-1996 totalled 5.8 billion, over half of which live in six countries: China, India, USA, Indonesia, Brazil and the Russian Federation. 80% of the world's population live in developing countries - 95% of people added to the world total are born in the developing world.

The total is still rising, but there are signs that worldwide growth is slowly coming under control. Growth rates and fertility rates are declining, although there are great regional variations which still cause concern. The average annual growth rate in the developed world is 0.4% per annum, whilst in the less developed world it is 1.8%, reaching as high as 2.8% in Africa. Developed regions also have lower fertility rates - an average of 1.7 children per woman, below the 'replacement level' target of 2. In the developing world the rate is 3.4 and can reach 5.6 in the poorest countries.

Until growth is brought under tighter control, the developing world in particular will continue to face enormous problems of supporting a rising population.

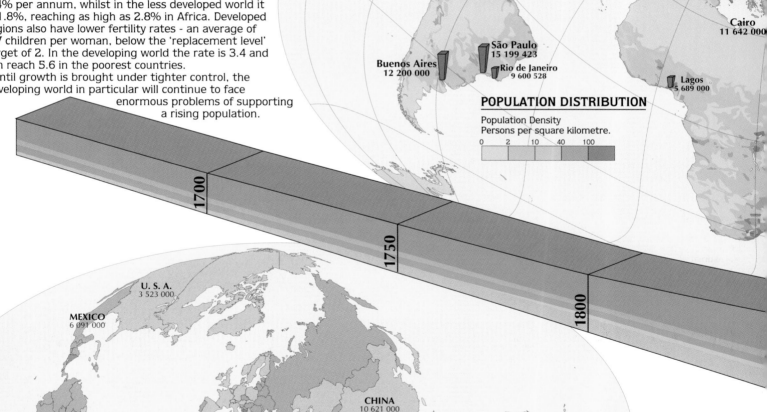

Urban population as a percentage of the total population

North America — 2025 (projected), 1995, 1975
South America — 2025 (projected), 1995, 1975
Europe — 2025 (projected), 1995, 1975
Oceania — 2025 (projected), 1995, 1975
Asia — 2025 (projected), 1995, 1975
Africa — 2025 (projected), 1995, 1975

San Francisco 5 240 000
Los Angeles 11 420 000
Chicago 7 498 000
New York 16 972 000
México 20 200 000
Bogotá 5 025 989
Lima 6 483 901
São Paulo 15 199 423
Rio de Janeiro 9 600 528
Buenos Aires 12 200 000
St Peter 5 004
London 9 227 687
Paris 9 318 821
İstanbul 6 407 215
Cairo 11 642 000
Lagos 5 689 000

POPULATION DISTRIBUTION

Population Density
Persons per square kilometre.

| 0 | 2 | 10 | 40 | 100 |

U. S. A. 3 523 000
MEXICO 6 091 000
BRAZIL 2 050 000
NIGERIA 3 299 000
ETHIOPIA 1 829 000
CONGO (ZAIRE) 2 911 000
CHINA 10 621 000
PAKISTAN 4 338 000
INDIA 8 836 000
INDONESIA 2 249 000

1700

1750

1800

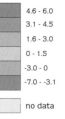

Population change

Average annual population ch 1990-1995 (%)

	4.6 - 6.0
	3.1 - 4.5
	1.6 - 3.0
	0 - 1.5
	-3.0 - 0
	-7.0 - -3.1
	no data

Countries named are those with the 10 greatest populat increases between 1995 and

NIZATION

he dominant themes of world population is that of urbanization - the
nt of people from the countryside to towns and cities. In 1995 43%
orld's population lived in urban areas and the number of urban
is expected to double between 1990 and 2025 to over 5 billion.
gree of urbanization varies between regions. The populations of
North America and South America are over 70% urban compared
0-35% in Africa and Asia. It is the developing regions, however,
experiencing the fastest growth of urban populations. Urban
ates reach over 7% per year in some of the poorest countries of
d, including Burkina and Mozambique.
e effect of urbanization is that fertility rates tend to decrease
ntry's population becomes more urbanized. Decreasing fertility
e a crucial factor in controlling population growth. It seems
t increased urbanization, with all its problems, may
ly help the overall situation

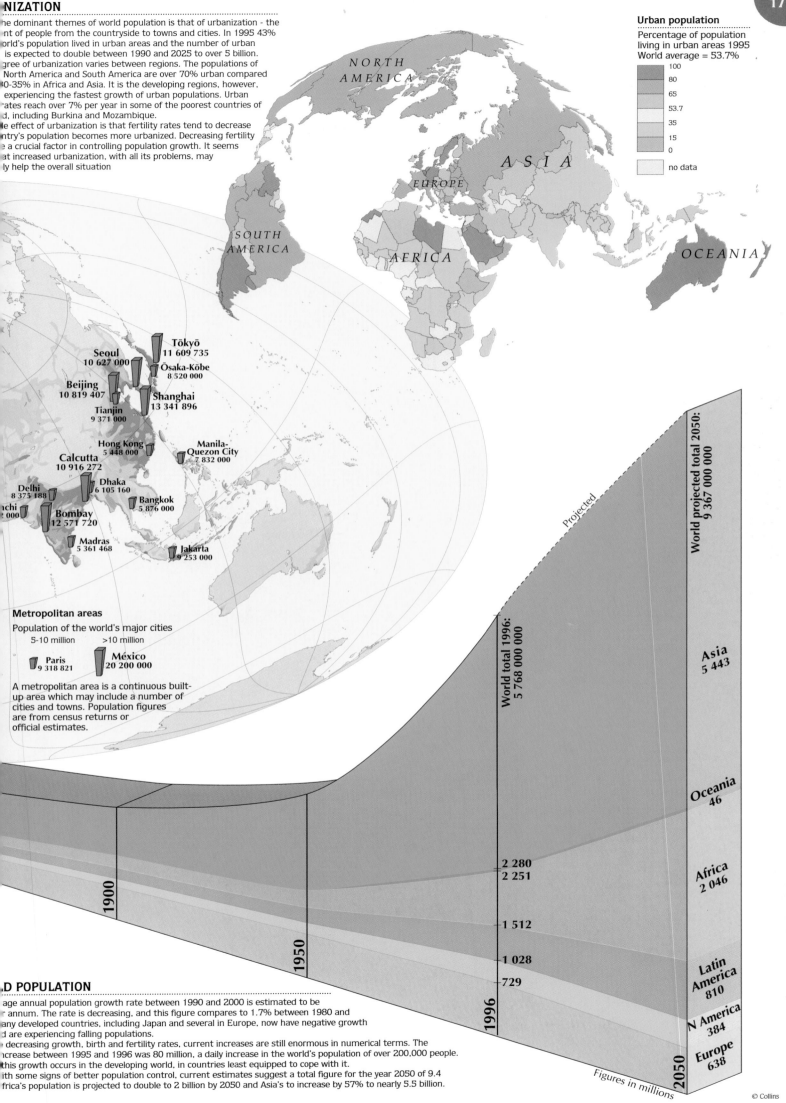

Urban population

Percentage of population
living in urban areas 1995
World average = 53.7%

	100
	80
	65
	53.7
	35
	15
	0
	no data

NORTH
AMERICA

SOUTH
AMERICA

EUROPE

ASIA

AFRICA

OCEANIA

Tōkyō
11 609 735

Seoul
10 627 000

Ōsaka-Kōbe
8 520 000

Beijing
10 819 407

Shanghai
13 341 896

Tianjin
9 371 000

Hong Kong
5 448 000

Manila-
Quezon City
7 832 000

Calcutta
10 916 272

Dhaka
6 105 160

Bangkok
5 876 000

Delhi
8 375 188

Bombay
12 571 720

chi
000

Madras
5 361 468

Jakarta
9 253 000

Metropolitan areas

Population of the world's major cities

5-10 million   >10 million

Paris
9 318 821

México
20 200 000

A metropolitan area is a continuous built-
up area which may include a number of
cities and towns. Population figures
are from census returns or
official estimates.

D POPULATION

age annual population growth rate between 1990 and 2000 is estimated to be
r annum. The rate is decreasing, and this figure compares to 1.7% between 1980 and
any developed countries, including Japan and several in Europe, now have negative growth
d are experiencing falling populations.
decreasing growth, birth and fertility rates, current increases are still enormous in numerical terms. The
crease between 1995 and 1996 was 80 million, a daily increase in the world's population of over 200,000 people.
this growth occurs in the developing world, in countries least equipped to cope with it.
ith some signs of better population control, current estimates suggest a total figure for the year 2050 of 9.4
frica's population is projected to double to 2 billion by 2050 and Asia's to increase by 57% to nearly 5.5 billion.

World projected total 2050:
9 367 000 000

Projected

Asia
5 443

Oceania
46

World total 1996:
5 768 000 000

Africa
2 046

Latin
America
810

N America
384

Europe
638

1900

1950

1996

2050

2 280
2 251

1 512

1 028

729

Figures in millions

© Collins

Health Indicators
(Selected Countries)

	Life Expectancy 1995	Country	Infant Mortality Rate 1995
BEST	80	Japan	4
	79	Sweden	4
	79	Iceland	5
	78	Switzerland	6
	78	Canada	6
	78	Netherlands	6
	78	Italy	7
	78	Australia	7
	78	Spain	8
	77	U.K.	6
WORST	48	Somalia	125
	47	Mali	117
	47	Mozambique	158
	46	Gambia	80
	46	Guinea	128
	45	Guinea-Bissau	134
	45	Malawi	138
	45	Afghanistan	165
	44	Uganda	111
	40	Sierra Leone	164

Infant mortality
Deaths before first birthday per 1000 live births 1995

- 0-9
- 10-49
- 50-99
- 100-149
- >149
- no data

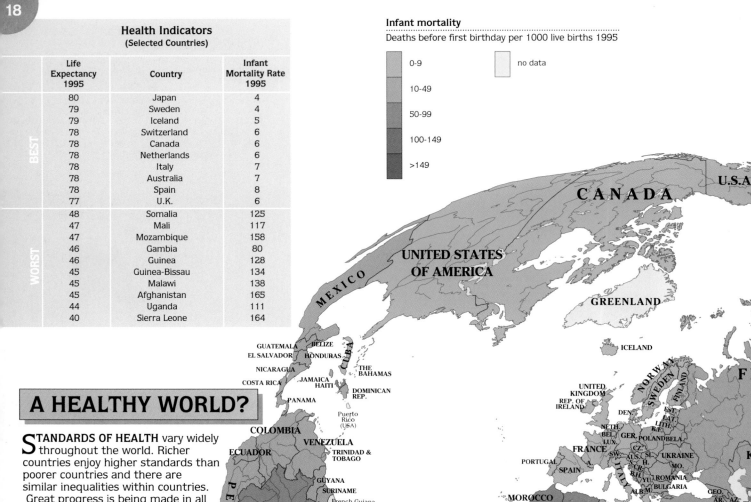

A HEALTHY WORLD?

STANDARDS OF HEALTH vary widely throughout the world. Richer countries enjoy higher standards than poorer countries and there are similar inequalities within countries. Great progress is being made in all aspects of health and there have been significant improvements in the two main indicators of health levels over the last few decades. The world average life expectancy increased from 48 to 65 years between 1955 and 1995; and infant mortality rates have fallen - deaths among children under five declined from 19 million in 1960 to 11 million in 1996. Longer life and a greater chance of survival do not necessarily mean a healthy life. There is still a need to ensure a freedom from additional years of ill-health and poverty - quality of life is as important as quantity.

Life expectancy
Number of years a new b can expect to survive

- <50
- 50-59
- 60-69
- 70-79
- >79
- no data

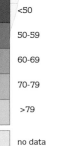

...USES OF DEATH

...dominant causes of death in the developing world are ...tious and parasitic diseases, in particular lower respiratory ...tion, tuberculosis, diarrhoeal diseases and malaria. By ...rast, people in the richer, developed countries suffer more ...circulatory diseases and cancers - illnesses generally ...ring later in life and often associated with life-style. ...s pattern is gradually changing. As living standards and life ...ctancy increase throughout the world there is a ...sponding increase in the risks from diseases prevalent in

the developed world. This provides the developing world with the 'double burden' of coping with existing high rates of infectious diseases and increasing rates of chronic illness.

Patterns in causes of death again reflect relative wealth. Infectious and parasitic diseases are the easiest to prevent and eradicate but, despite great successes in the eradication of smallpox and the imminent demise of polio, the resources are so often lacking in the areas suffering most.

...eveloped countries

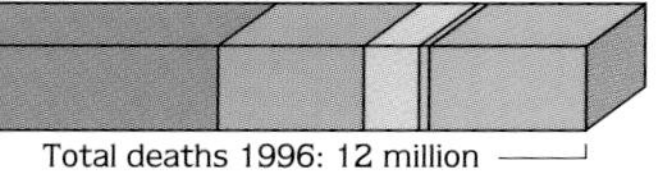

Total deaths 1996: 12 million

...eveloping countries

Total deaths 1996: 40 million

Worldwide causes of death 1996

- Infectious and parasitic diseases
- Circulatory system diseases
- Cancers
- Respiratory system diseases
- Perinatal and neonatal causes
- Maternal causes
- Other and unknown causes

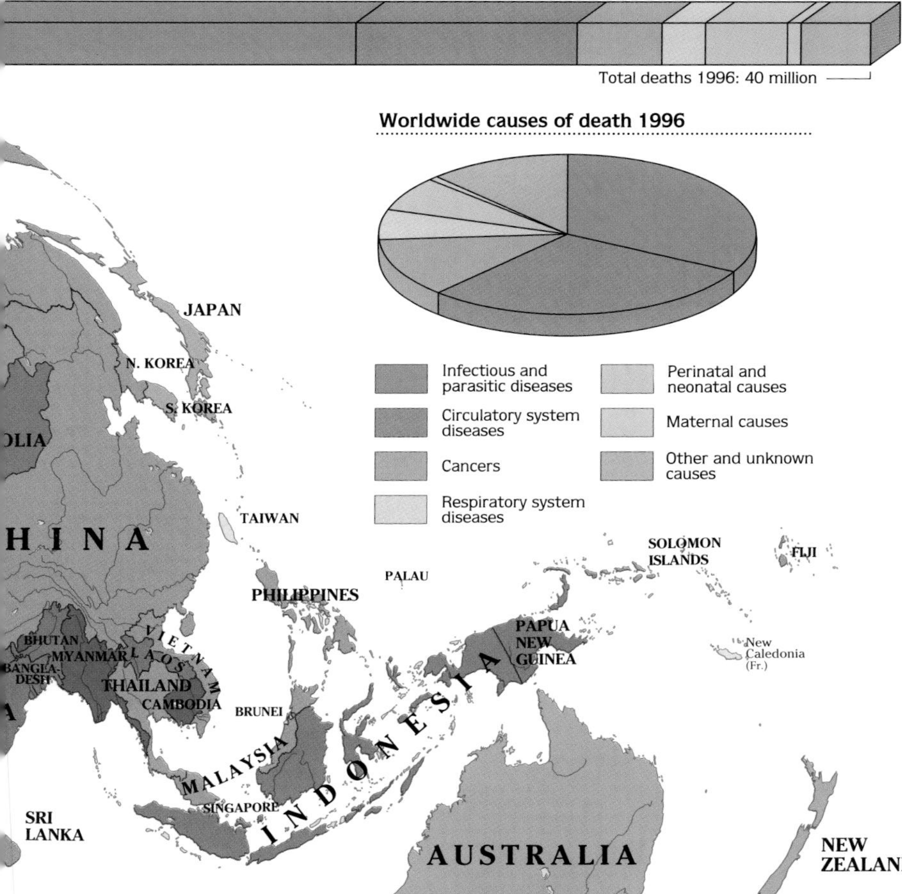

HEALTH PROVISION

Easy access to appropriate health services are taken for granted in the developed world where 100% access for the population can often be assumed. In developing countries, however, such access is often far more limited, as the graph below shows. Social and economic conditions in a country can greatly influence the chances of a healthy life.

The provision of conditions for good health, including trained personnel, medical facilities and equipment as well as those of safe water, food and sanitation, obviously costs money. Some countries are in a much better position to meet these costs than others. This is reflected in the overall differences in standards of health between the developed and developing world. The richer countries not only enjoy better health, but also spend proportionately more of their Gross National Product on health provision. The poorer countries of the world are spending a smaller proportion of much less money on vital facilities.

Health Services
Percentage of population with access to health services
(Selected countries 1990-1995)

Health Spending
Total national expenditure on health
Percentage of Gross National Product
(Selected countries 1989-1993)

...ccess to safe water
...ercentage of population with reasonable ...ccess to sufficient safe water 1995

- 0-20
- 21-40
- 41-75
- 76-90
- 91-100
- no data

© Collins

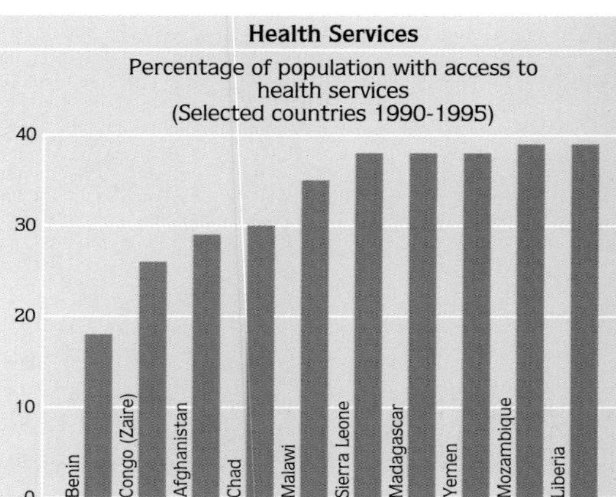

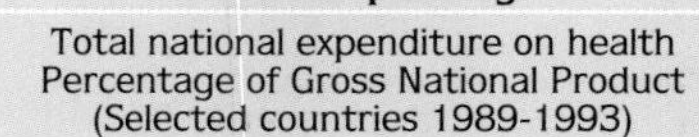

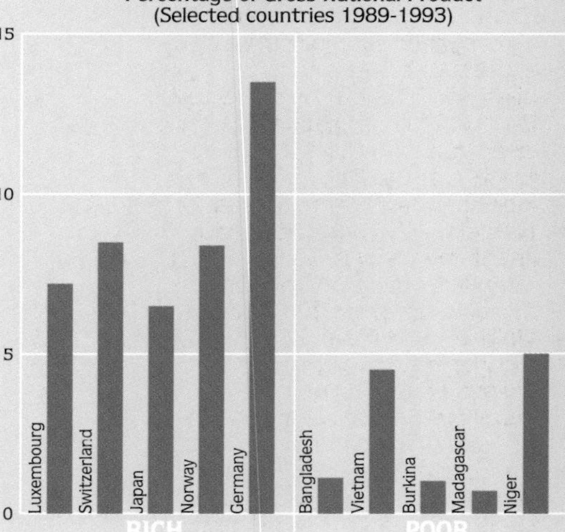

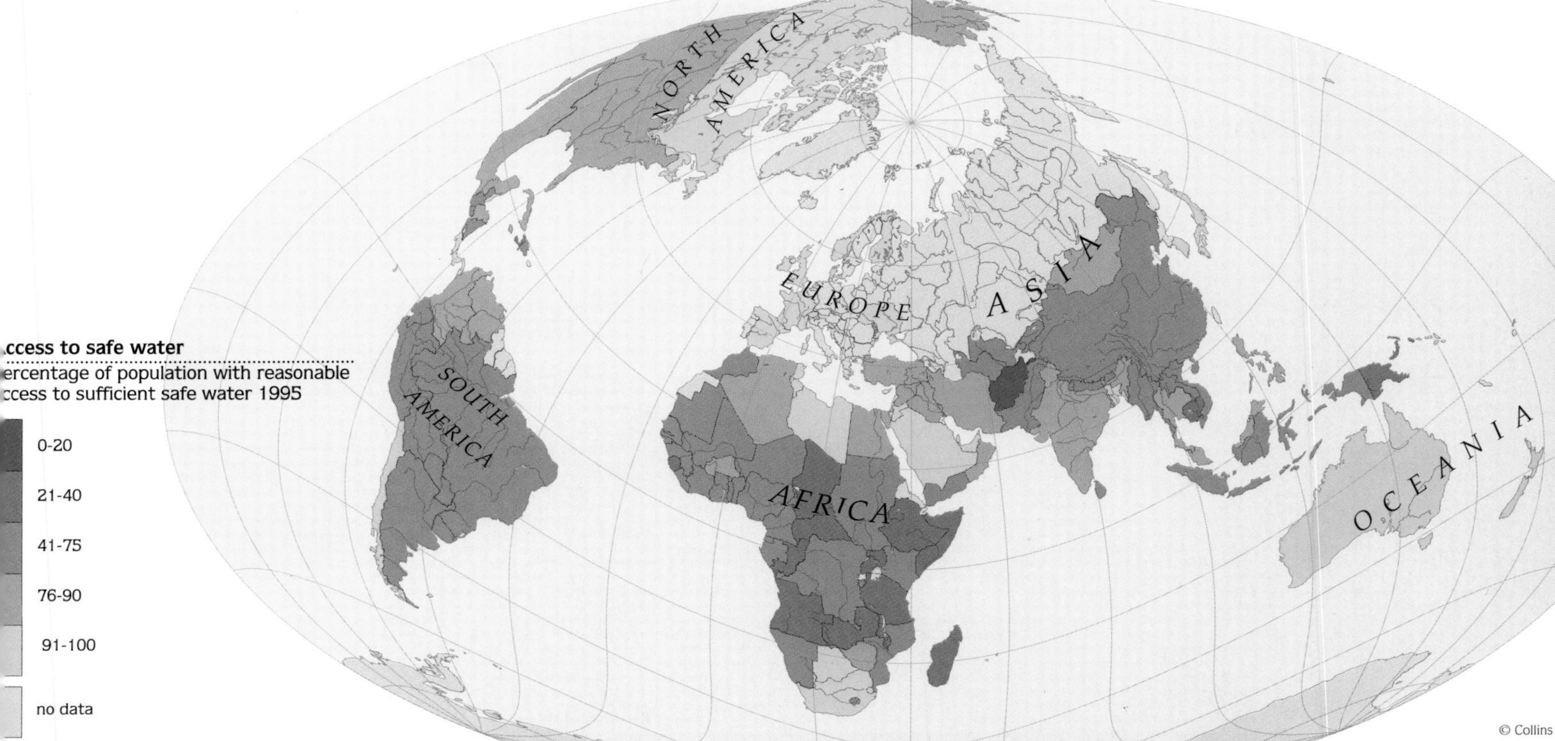

MEASURING THE WORLD'S WEALTH

A commonly used measure of wealth is Gross National Product (GNP). This is the total value of goods and services produced by a country in any one year, including income from investments abroad. If the total GNP figure is divided by the country's population, the average wealth per person is provided as GNP per capita.

GNP per capita statistics provide only an average figure and give no indication of the relative distribution of wealth within the country. They show neither the great inequalities which can exist, nor the relative numbers of people living in poverty. Also, GNP is usually based on valuations in US$ and not in local currencies. Purchasing Power Parity (PPP), measured in International Dollars, is another means of measuring individual wealth which uses local exchange rates and takes account of cost of living differences between countries (see table below).

No method provides a perfect picture of the world's complex ecomomy, but whichever method is used clear patterns of wealth and poverty - the rich and poor of the world - emerge.

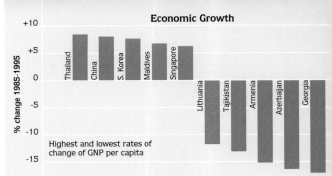

Economic Growth

% change 1985-1995

Highest and lowest rates of change of GNP per capita

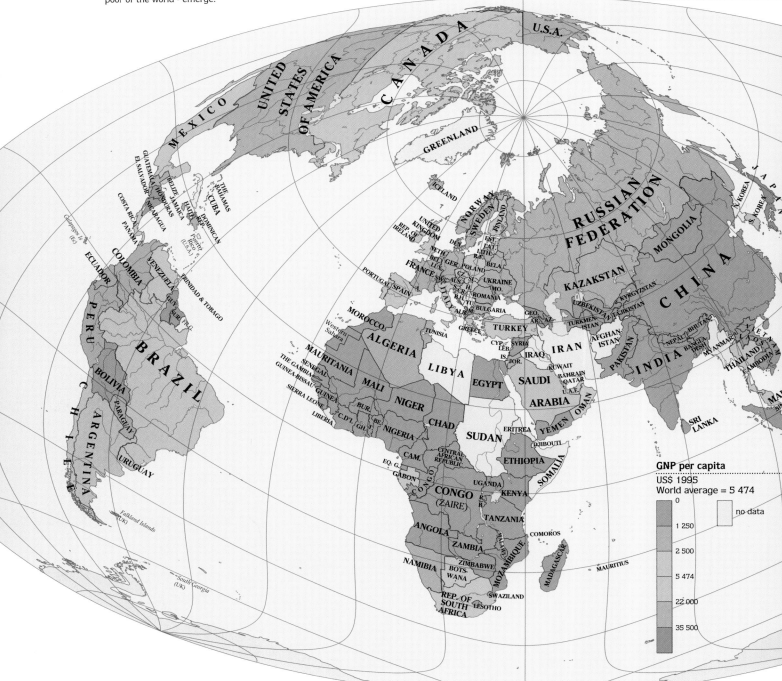

GNP per capita
US$ 1995
World average = 5 474

0	no data
1 250	
2 500	
5 474	
22 000	
35 500	

Rank	GROSS NATIONAL PRODUCT (GNP) (US$ Millions 1995)	GNP PER CAPITA (US$ 1995)	PURCHASING POWER PARITY(PPP) ($ International 1995)	EXTERNAL DEBT (% of GNP 1995) Low- and middle-income economies
1	U.S.A. (7 100 007)	LUXEMBOURG (41 210)	LUXEMBOURG (37 930)	NICARAGUA (520)
2	JAPAN (4 963 587)	SWITZERLAND (40 630)	U.S.A. (26 980)	MOZAMBIQUE (333)
3	GERMANY (2 252 343)	JAPAN (39 640)	SWITZERLAND (25 860)	CONGO (325)
4	FRANCE (1 451 051)	NORWAY (31 250)	KUWAIT (23 790)	ANGOLA (260)
5	UNITED KINGDOM (1 094 734)	DENMARK (29 890)	SINGAPORE (22 770)	GUINEA-BISSAU (235)
6	ITALY (1 088 085)	GERMANY (27 510)	JAPAN (22 110)	CÔTE D'IVOIRE (185)
7	CHINA (744 890)	U.S.A. (26 980)	NORWAY (21 940)	MAURITANIA (166)
8	BRAZIL (579 787)	AUSTRIA (26 890)	BELGIUM (21 660)	TANZANIA (148)
9	CANADA (573 695)	SINGAPORE (26 730)	AUSTRIA (21 660)	ZAMBIA (139)
10	SPAIN (532 347)	FRANCE (24 990)	DENMARK (21 230)	VIETNAM (138)
10	COMOROS (237)	YEMEN (260)	NIGER (750)	KYRGYZSTAN (15)
9	DOMINICA (218)	GUINEA-BISSAU (250)	CHAD (700)	ARMENIA (14)
8	MICRONESIA (215)	HAITI (250)	MADAGASCAR (640)	BOTSWANA (13)
7	ST KITTS & NEVIS (212)	MALI (250)	TANZANIA (640)	UKRAINE (10)
6	VANUATU (202)	BANGLADESH (240)	BURUNDI (630)	LITHUANIA (9)
5	WESTERN SAMOA (184)	UGANDA (240)	SIERRA LEONE (580)	AZERBAIJAN (8)
4	TONGA (170)	VIETNAM (240)	MALI (550)	LATVIA (7)
3	EQUATORIAL GUINEA (152)	BURKINA (230)	RWANDA (540)	UZBEKISTAN (7)
2	KIRIBATI (73)	MADAGASCAR (230)	CONGO (ZAIRE) (490)	BELARUS (6)
1	SÃO TOMÉ & PRÍNCIPE (45)	NIGER (220)	ETHIOPIA (450)	ESTONIA (6)

HIGHEST / LOWEST

FOREIGN DEBT

al problem facing many of the world's poorest countries is
foreign debt. To assist them in development
mmes in the past, many countries borrowed huge
ts from such agencies as the World Bank. Changes in the
economy have created conditions in which it is virtually
ible for these countries to repay their loans.
otal amount of debt need not be a problem if the
y can make its payments (or 'service' the debt),
income from its own exports. Problems arise
the debt service ratio (total debt service as a
tage of exports of goods and services) is
country with a debt service ratio of 50%
to spend half of its income on debt
nts - money which could otherwise
t on developing the country's
ny as a whole.

Debt Service Ratios
Low- and middle-
income economies

10% 25% 50%

other countries / no data

THE WORLD'S WEALTH

Regional distribution of wealth

Total world GNP 1995: US$ 27 110 768 million

Europe 32.6%   Asia 30.4%   N. America 29.7%

S. America 4.3%
Africa 1.5%
Oceania 1.5%

OVERSEAS AID

as Aid is the provision of funds or
s at non-commercial rates for
mental purposes. The flow is from
untries to poor countries, with the
donors generally being those
s with the highest GNP. Aid can
e Official Development Assistance
provided by governments, or
ary Aid from private donations
through non-governmental
ations (NGOs) such as Oxfam.
portant group of donor countries is
velopment Assistance Committee
f the Organization for Economic
ration and Development (OECD). The
commends that its members should
0.7% of their GNP in aid. Most fall
ort of this figure.
ot always the poorest countries
eceive the aid on offer. Political
rations are often a factor, with
countries choosing carefully which
es they support.

Aid donors
Major donors from the OECD
Development Assistance Committee
1994-1995

U.S.A. - Donor
6 042 - Amount (US$M)
(0.1%) - % of donor's GNP

Aid recipients
Major recipients of Official
Development Assistance from the
OECD DAC and other sources 1995

Egypt - Recipient
2 022 - Amount (US$M)
(4.4%) - % of recipient's GNP

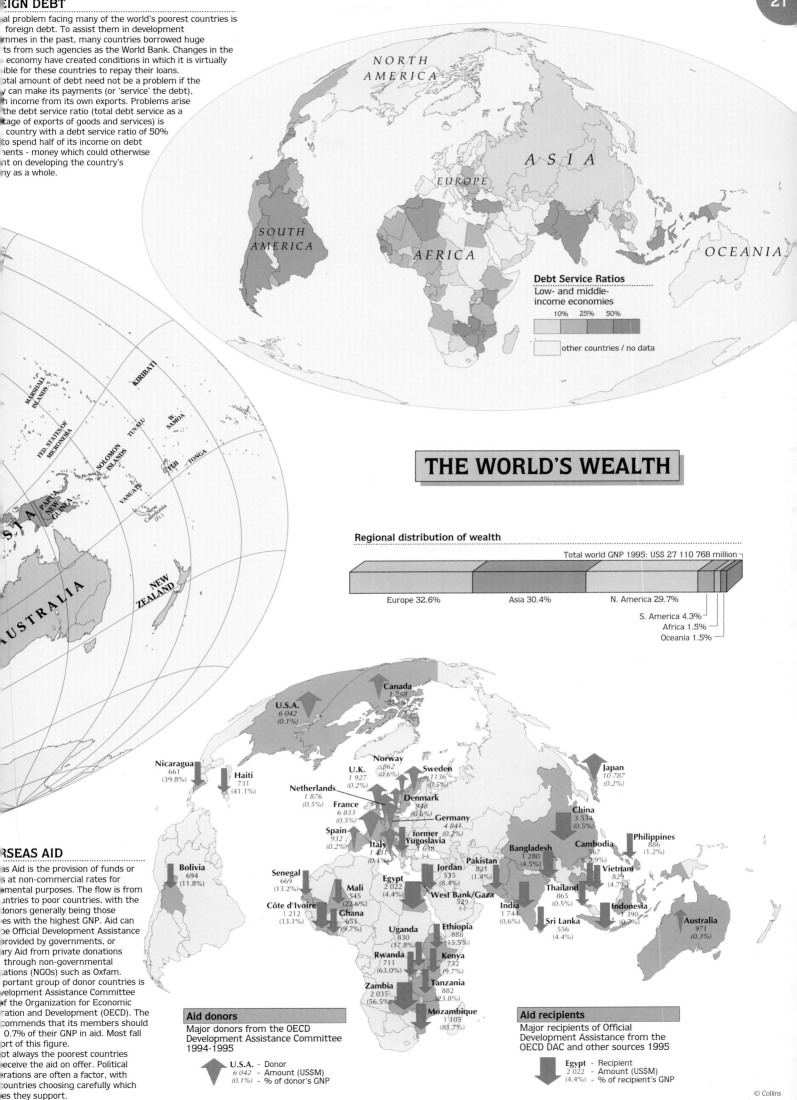

© Collins

INTERNATIONAL TRAVEL

All parts of the world are experiencing steady growth in air travel and tourism. Worldwide, airline traffic for passengers and freight grew by 7% in 1995 and the rise is expected to continue at a similar rate into the next century. Rates of growth vary between regions, with the dominant region being East Asia and the Pacific which is expected to sustain a growth rate in passenger traffic of approximately 12%.

New international airports have recently been completed in Denver, USA and Macau; and Hong Kong's new Chek Lap Kok airport is due to open in 1998 - further indicators of the strength of the aviation business.

Healthy economic conditions, particularly in the developed world, have encouraged recent increases in international tourism. Both tourist arrivals and receipts increased significantly in 1995 with the fastest-growing region again being that of East Asia and the Pacific.

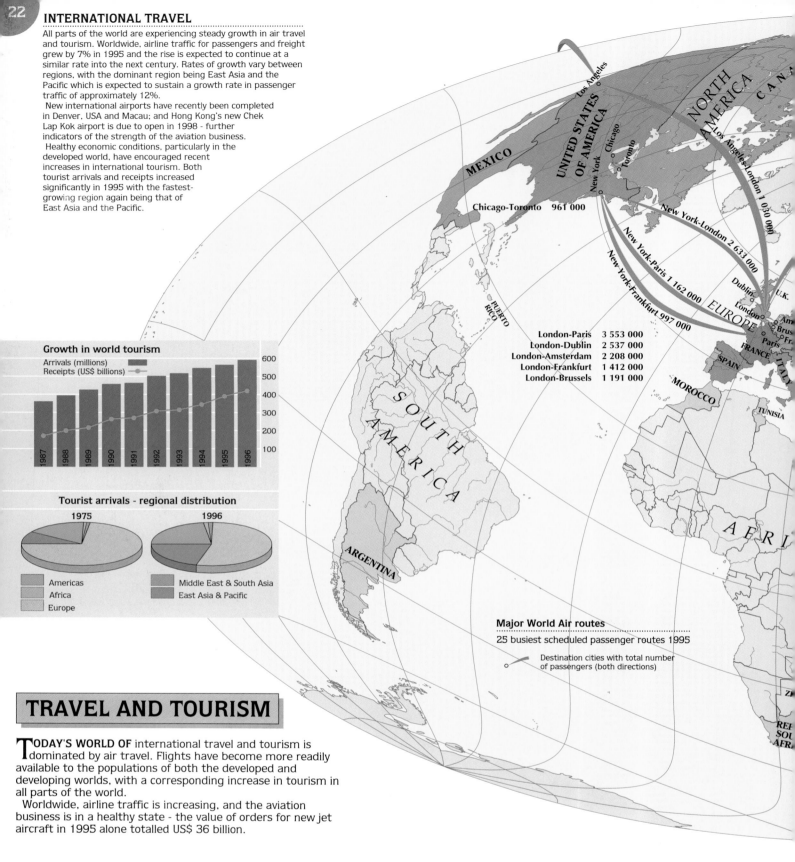

Chicago-Toronto   961 000

New York-London 2 633 000
New York-Paris 1 162 000
New York-Frankfurt 997 000
Los Angeles-London 1 030 000

London-Paris   3 553 000
London-Dublin   2 537 000
London-Amsterdam   2 208 000
London-Frankfurt   1 412 000
London-Brussels   1 191 000

Growth in world tourism

Arrivals (millions)
Receipts (US$ billions)

1987 1988 1989 1990 1991 1992 1993 1994 1995 1996

Tourist arrivals - regional distribution

1975   1996

Americas
Africa
Europe
Middle East & South Asia
East Asia & Pacific

Major World Air routes

25 busiest scheduled passenger routes 1995

○──── Destination cities with total number
         of passengers (both directions)

TRAVEL AND TOURISM

TODAY'S WORLD OF international travel and tourism is dominated by air travel. Flights have become more readily available to the populations of both the developed and developing worlds, with a corresponding increase in tourism in all parts of the world.

Worldwide, airline traffic is increasing, and the aviation business is in a healthy state - the value of orders for new jet aircraft in 1995 alone totalled US$ 36 billion.

SEEING THE WORLD - GLOBAL TOURISM

In 1996 worldwide tourist arrivals and receipts from tourism increased by 4.5% and 7.6% respectively. Growth is expected to continue, largely because of increasing numbers of short-duration overseas visits by travellers from the developed world. Foreign travel from within the developing regions is also increasing steadily.

Europe is the dominant region in terms of arrivals and receipts, but its relative share is decreasing. Its market share has fallen by over 10% since 1975, compared with a corresponding rise of 11.3% in the East Asia and Pacific region. This shift reflects an overall increase in long-haul flights, from Europe in particular, to tourist destinations such as China (including Hong Kong), Malaysia and Thailand.

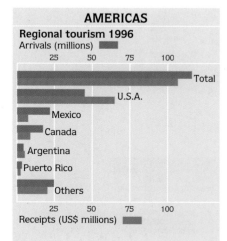

AMERICAS

Regional tourism 1996

Arrivals (millions)
25   50   75   100

Total
U.S.A.
Mexico
Canada
Argentina
Puerto Rico
Others

25   50   75   100
Receipts (US$ millions)

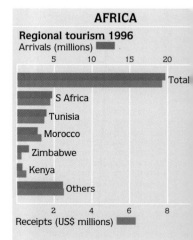

AFRICA

Regional tourism 1996

Arrivals (millions)
5   10   15   20

Total
S Africa
Tunisia
Morocco
Zimbabwe
Kenya
Others

2   4   6   8
Receipts (US$ millions)

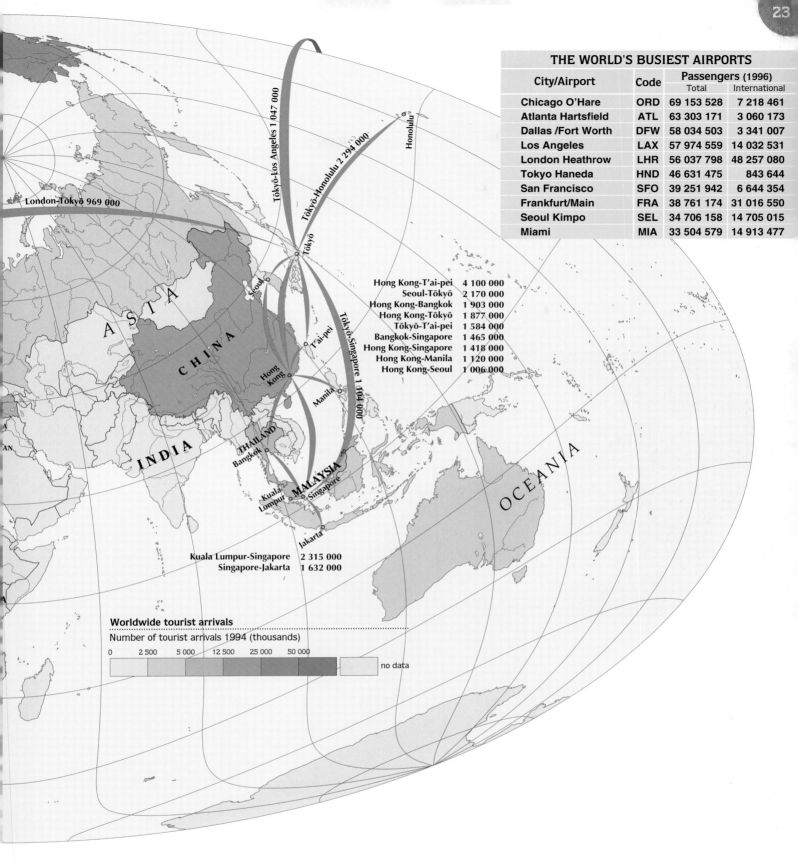

London–Tōkyō 969 000

Tōkyō–Los Angeles 1 047 000

Tōkyō–Honolulu 2 294 000

Tōkyō–Singapore 1 102 000

Honolulu

Tōkyō

Seoul

T'ai-pei

Hong Kong

Manila

Bangkok

THAILAND

Kuala Lumpur

MALAYSIA

Singapore

Jakarta

ASIA

CHINA

INDIA

OCEANIA

Hong Kong–T'ai-pei 4 100 000
Seoul–Tōkyō 2 170 000
Hong Kong–Bangkok 1 903 000
Hong Kong–Tōkyō 1 877 000
Tōkyō–T'ai-pei 1 584 000
Bangkok–Singapore 1 465 000
Hong Kong–Singapore 1 418 000
Hong Kong–Manila 1 120 000
Hong Kong–Seoul 1 006 000

Kuala Lumpur–Singapore 2 315 000
Singapore–Jakarta 1 632 000

THE WORLD'S BUSIEST AIRPORTS

City/Airport	Code	Passengers (1996)	
		Total	International
Chicago O'Hare	ORD	69 153 528	7 218 461
Atlanta Hartsfield	ATL	63 303 171	3 060 173
Dallas /Fort Worth	DFW	58 034 503	3 341 007
Los Angeles	LAX	57 974 559	14 032 531
London Heathrow	LHR	56 037 798	48 257 080
Tokyo Haneda	HND	46 631 475	843 644
San Francisco	SFO	39 251 942	6 644 354
Frankfurt/Main	FRA	38 761 174	31 016 550
Seoul Kimpo	SEL	34 706 158	14 705 015
Miami	MIA	33 504 579	14 913 477

Worldwide tourist arrivals
Number of tourist arrivals 1994 (thousands)

0   2 500   5 000   12 500   25 000   50 000

no data

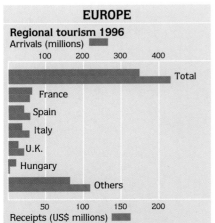

EUROPE
Regional tourism 1996
Arrivals (millions)
100   200   300   400
Total
France
Spain
Italy
U.K.
Hungary
Others
50   100   150   200
Receipts (US$ millions)

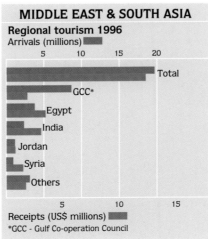

MIDDLE EAST & SOUTH ASIA
Regional tourism 1996
Arrivals (millions)
5   10   15   20
Total
GCC*
Egypt
India
Jordan
Syria
Others
5   10   15
Receipts (US$ millions)
*GCC – Gulf Co-operation Council

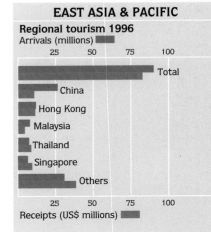

EAST ASIA & PACIFIC
Regional tourism 1996
Arrivals (millions)
25   50   75   100
Total
China
Hong Kong
Malaysia
Thailand
Singapore
Others
25   50   75   100
Receipts (US$ millions)

© Collins

Fibre-optic cable

COMMUNICATIONS TECHNOLOGY

Satellite transmission basics

Satellites are used by earth stations to receive and amplify information which is in the form of high-powered, high-frequency signals, and retransmit it back to stations in another part of the world.

Fibre-optic cables have been developed to overcome the limited capacity of the copper wires traditionally used for communication. Information is encoded into beams of laser light and sent down fine fibres of coated glass which can carry signals over large distances with little loss of quality.

Improving cost:capacity ratios have meant that fibre-optic cables are overtaking satellites in the transmission of point-to-point communications (e.g. telephone calls) but satellites remain the prime carrier of point-to-multi point signals (e.g. television broadcasts).

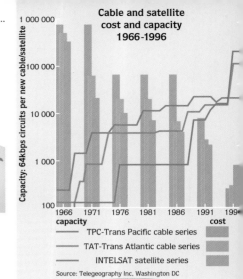

Cable and satellite cost and capacity 1966-1996

Capacity: 64kbps circuits per new cable/satellite

1 000 000 / 100 000 / 10 000 / 1 000 / 100

1966 | 1971 | 1976 | 1981 | 1986 | 1991 | 199

capacity — cost

— TPC-Trans Pacific cable series
— TAT-Trans Atlantic cable series
— INTELSAT satellite series

Source: Telegeography Inc, Washington DC

GLOBAL TELECOMMUNICATIONS

DEVELOPMENTS IN TECHNOLOGY have improved the speed and extent of voice, image and text communication to a level previously unimaginable, now making possible almost instant connection between people throughout the world by means of telephone, television, facsimile, and personal computer.

MAJOR FIBRE-OPTIC SUBMARINE NETWORKS
AND COMMUNICATIONS SATELLITE POSITIONS

Cable capacity in gigabits per second

— 1-5 gb   1gb per second=80 000 calls (approximately)
— 10-20 gb   Pecked lines show cables under construction
— 40-80 gb

Satellite ownership
(shows major international communications satellites transmitting to fixed terminals 1997)

◆ IS 512   INTELSAT
◆ PAS-5   PANAMSAT
◆ ORION1   ORION

TELEPHONE DENSITY 1995

Wireline telephones per 1 000 people

5 or less
6-25
26-100
101-500
>500
No data

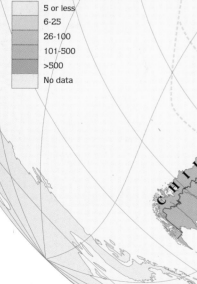

WORLD COMMUNICATIONS EQUIPMENT

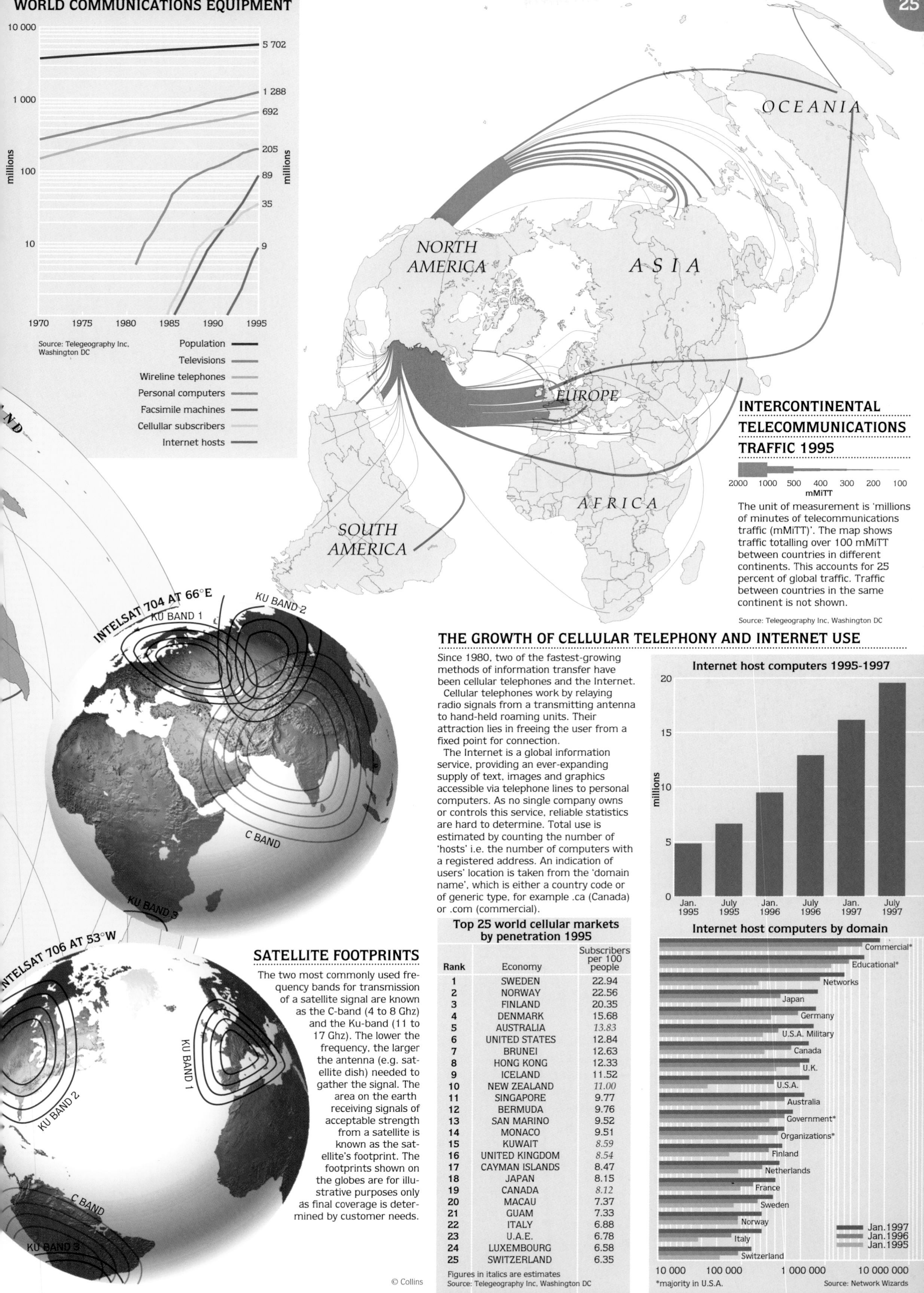

(graph y-axis: millions; markers 10 000, 1 000, 100, 10; right-side values 5 702, 1 288, 692, 205, 89, 35, 9; x-axis years 1970, 1975, 1980, 1985, 1990, 1995)

Source: Telegeography Inc, Washington DC

- Population
- Televisions
- Wireline telephones
- Personal computers
- Facsimile machines
- Cellular subscribers
- Internet hosts

(Map labels) OCEANIA · NORTH AMERICA · ASIA · EUROPE · AFRICA · SOUTH AMERICA

INTERCONTINENTAL TELECOMMUNICATIONS TRAFFIC 1995

2000 1000 500 400 300 200 100
mMiTT

The unit of measurement is 'millions of minutes of telecommunications traffic (mMiTT)'. The map shows traffic totalling over 100 mMiTT between countries in different continents. This accounts for 25 percent of global traffic. Traffic between countries in the same continent is not shown.

Source: Telegeography Inc. Washington DC

THE GROWTH OF CELLULAR TELEPHONY AND INTERNET USE

Since 1980, two of the fastest-growing methods of information transfer have been cellular telephones and the Internet.

Cellular telephones work by relaying radio signals from a transmitting antenna to hand-held roaming units. Their attraction lies in freeing the user from a fixed point for connection.

The Internet is a global information service, providing an ever-expanding supply of text, images and graphics accessible via telephone lines to personal computers. As no single company owns or controls this service, reliable statistics are hard to determine. Total use is estimated by counting the number of 'hosts' i.e. the number of computers with a registered address. An indication of users' location is taken from the 'domain name', which is either a country code or of generic type, for example .ca (Canada) or .com (commercial).

Internet host computers 1995-1997

(bar chart y-axis: millions 0, 5, 10, 15, 20; x-axis: Jan. 1995, July 1995, Jan. 1996, July 1996, Jan. 1997, July 1997)

SATELLITE FOOTPRINTS

The two most commonly used frequency bands for transmission of a satellite signal are known as the C-band (4 to 8 Ghz) and the Ku-band (11 to 17 Ghz). The lower the frequency, the larger the antenna (e.g. satellite dish) needed to gather the signal. The area on the earth receiving signals of acceptable strength from a satellite is known as the satellite's footprint. The footprints shown on the globes are for illustrative purposes only as final coverage is determined by customer needs.

(Globe labels) INTELSAT 704 AT 66°E · KU BAND 1 · KU BAND 2 · C BAND · KU BAND 3 · INTELSAT 706 AT 53°W · KU BAND 1 · KU BAND 2 · C BAND · KU BAND 3

© Collins

Top 25 world cellular markets by penetration 1995

Rank	Economy	Subscribers per 100 people
1	SWEDEN	22.94
2	NORWAY	22.56
3	FINLAND	20.35
4	DENMARK	15.68
5	AUSTRALIA	*13.83*
6	UNITED STATES	12.84
7	BRUNEI	12.63
8	HONG KONG	12.33
9	ICELAND	11.52
10	NEW ZEALAND	*11.00*
11	SINGAPORE	9.77
12	BERMUDA	9.76
13	SAN MARINO	9.52
14	MONACO	9.51
15	KUWAIT	*8.59*
16	UNITED KINGDOM	*8.54*
17	CAYMAN ISLANDS	8.47
18	JAPAN	8.15
19	CANADA	*8.12*
20	MACAU	7.37
21	GUAM	7.33
22	ITALY	6.88
23	U.A.E.	6.78
24	LUXEMBOURG	6.58
25	SWITZERLAND	6.35

Figures in italics are estimates
Source: Telegeography Inc. Washington DC

Internet host computers by domain

(horizontal bar chart; categories top to bottom: Commercial*, Educational*, Networks, Japan, Germany, U.S.A. Military, Canada, U.K., U.S.A., Australia, Government*, Organizations*, Finland, Netherlands, France, Sweden, Norway, Italy, Switzerland)

(x-axis: 10 000, 100 000, 1 000 000, 10 000 000)

Jan.1997
Jan.1996
Jan.1995

*majority in U.S.A.

Source: Network Wizards

OUTBREAK OF THE FIRST WORLD WAR 1914

In 1912 the desire for independence and territory motivated the people in the Balkan peninsula to go to war, first with their Ottoman rulers, and then amongst themselves. These actions had repercussions for the other European powers who saw their security threatened by the instability of the frontier area between three great empires. By this time, Europe had divided itself into two alliance blocs, the Central Powers (Germany, Austria-Hungary, Italy) and the Entente Powers (France, Russia, Britain) whose opposing interests prevented them resolving the Balkan dispute.

The crisis in the Balkans intensified the growing rivalry between the old dynastic empires of Russia and Austria-Hungary, into which their respective allies were inextricably drawn. The turning point came in June 1914 when Austria blamed Serbia for the assassination of the heir to their throne, Franz Ferdinand, and Russia pledged to defend their Balkan ally in the event of war. These actions triggered the wider system of alliances, whose members had considerably reinforced their armies, and so by August the major states of Europe found themselves at war.

mobilizations, with date

ultimata issued, with date

declarations of war, with date

Entente Powers at outbreak of war

joined Entente Powers during war, with date

Central Powers at outbreak of war

joined Central Powers during war, with date

frontiers 1914

North Sea · SWEDEN · DENMARK · Copenhagen · Riga · RUSSIAN EMPIRE
UNITED KINGDOM · 29 July · 4 Aug: to Germany · 4 Aug: against Germany · 12 Aug: against Austria-Hungary
London · NETHERLANDS · GERMAN EMPIRE · Berlin · Warsaw
BELGIUM · Brussels · 31 July: to Russia · 31 July · 1 Aug.
LUX. · Paris · 1 Aug: against Russia · 3 Aug: against Belgium and France
FRANCE · 1 Aug. · Vienna · 23 July: to Serbia
SWITZ. · AUSTRO-HUNGARIAN EMPIRE · 25 July
4 Aug: against Germany · 13 Aug: against Austria-Hungary
28 July: against Serbia · 5 Aug: against Russia
9 Mar. 1916 · PORTUGAL · Lisbon · Madrid · ANDORRA · SPAIN
ROMANIA · 28 Aug. 1916 · Bucharest
ITALY · 25 May 1915 · Rome · Corsica · MONTENEGRO · 25 July · Belgrade · SERBIA
5 Aug: against Austria-Hungary · 11 Aug: against Germany · ALBANIA
Sardinia · Balearic Is · BULGARIA · 5 Oct. 1915 · Sofia · Constantinople (Istanbul)
Gibraltar · British · Mediterranean Sea · GREECE · 29 June 1917 · Sicily · Athens · OTTOMAN EMPIRE · 30 Oct. 1 · Dodecanese Italian

CENTURY OF CHANGE I 1900–1934

COLLAPSE OF CENTRAL POWERS 1918

By September 1918, facing an advancing Allied army in the west, mutinies in the army and navy, and public calls for economic and political change, the Central Powers disunited in the hope of securing a separate peace and better treatment. In the Austro-Hungarian Empire the diverse ethnic groups called for independence, leading to the states of Czechoslovakia and Yugoslavia. Following armistice agreements in November, Austria and Hungary declared themselves republics. Germany followed suit, so that, coupled with revolution in the Russian Empire, by the end of the year three major European empires had disintegrated.

FINLAND · independent 6 Dec. 1917 · Helsingfors (Helsinki) · Petrograd (St Petersburg) · ESTONIA
U.S.S.R. · Riga · LATVIA · Moscow · LITHUANIA · Vilna · Minsk
U.K. · NETHERLANDS · Berlin · Warsaw · POLAND
BELGIUM · Brussels · Cologne · GERMAN EMPIRE · Lemberg
Frankfurt · LUX. · Prague · BOHEMIA · UKRAINE
Paris · FRANCE · Munich · LIECH. · Cracow (Kraków) · occupied by Romania, 11 Nov.
SWITZ. · AUSTRO-HUNGARIAN · Vienna · Budapest · BUKOVINA · BESSARABIA
Trieste · Laibach · Gyulafehérvár · annexed by Romania, April · Odessa
EMPIRE · Zagreb · CROATIA-SLAVONIA · ROMANIA · Black Sea
MONACO · SAN MARINO · BOSNIA-HERZEGOVINA · Belgrade · Bucharest
DALMATIA · Sarajevo · SERBIA · BULGARIA · Sofia · Constantinople (Istanbul)
Rome · MONTENEGRO · Skopje · Tirana · ALBANIA · Salonica · OTTOMAN EMPIRE
ITALY · GREECE · Mudros

USSR, determined by Treaty of Brest-Litovsk, March

controlled by Entente Powers, 30 Sept.

limit of Central Powers' control, 30 Sept.

lost by Central Powers before armistices

evacuated by Central Powers under armistices of 3–11 Nov.

ceded to former nationalities of Austro-Hungarian empire by 6 Dec.

Austria, declared independent 12 Nov.

Hungary, declared independent 16 Nov.

controlled by Czechoslovakia 31 Dec.

★ declaration of independence

▲ overthrow of monarchy

THE POLITICAL WORLD 1900

At the start of the 20th century the political world was dominated by empires, and more than half the land was controlled by European powers. Over the next one hundred years these empires disappeared, being replaced by the nation state.

MEXICO · BRITISH HONDURAS · UNITED STATES OF AMERICA · DOMINION OF CANADA · NEWFOUNDLAND · GREENLAND · ICELAND · SWEDEN · NORWAY
CUBA (occupied by U.S.A.) · Jamaica (U.K.) · The Bahamas (U.K.) · UNITED KINGDOM · NETHERLANDS · DENMARK
PANAMA · COLOMBIA · VENEZUELA · BRITISH GUIANA · DUTCH GUIANA · FRENCH GUIANA · Trinidad (U.K.) · Barbados (U.K.) · Virgin Is (U.K.) · PORTUGAL · SPAIN · FRANCE · AUSTRO-HUNGARIAN EMPIRE · ITALY · GREECE
ECUADOR · PERU · BOLIVIA · BRAZIL · ACRE · Cape Verde Is (Port.) · RIO DE ORO · MOROCCO · ALGERIA · TUNISIA · TRIPOLITANIA · EGYPT · Ottoman dominion under con...
PARAGUAY · URUGUAY · 1899 Franco-British agreement · assigned to France under 1899 Franco-British agreement - not yet effectively occupied
CHILE · ARGENTINA · PORTUGUESE GUINEA · GAMBIA · SIERRA LEONE · LIBERIA · IVORY COAST · GOLD COAST · TOGOLAND · DAHOMEY · RIO MUNI · CAMEROONS · NIGERIA · FRENCH CONGO · LADO · ANGLO-EGYPTIAN SUDAN
CONGO FREE STATE · ANGOLA · Walvis Bay (U.K.) · GERMAN SOUTH WEST AFRICA · BECHUANALAND · N.W. RHOD. · SOUTH RHODESIA · CAPE COLONY · ORANG...
ANTARCTICA

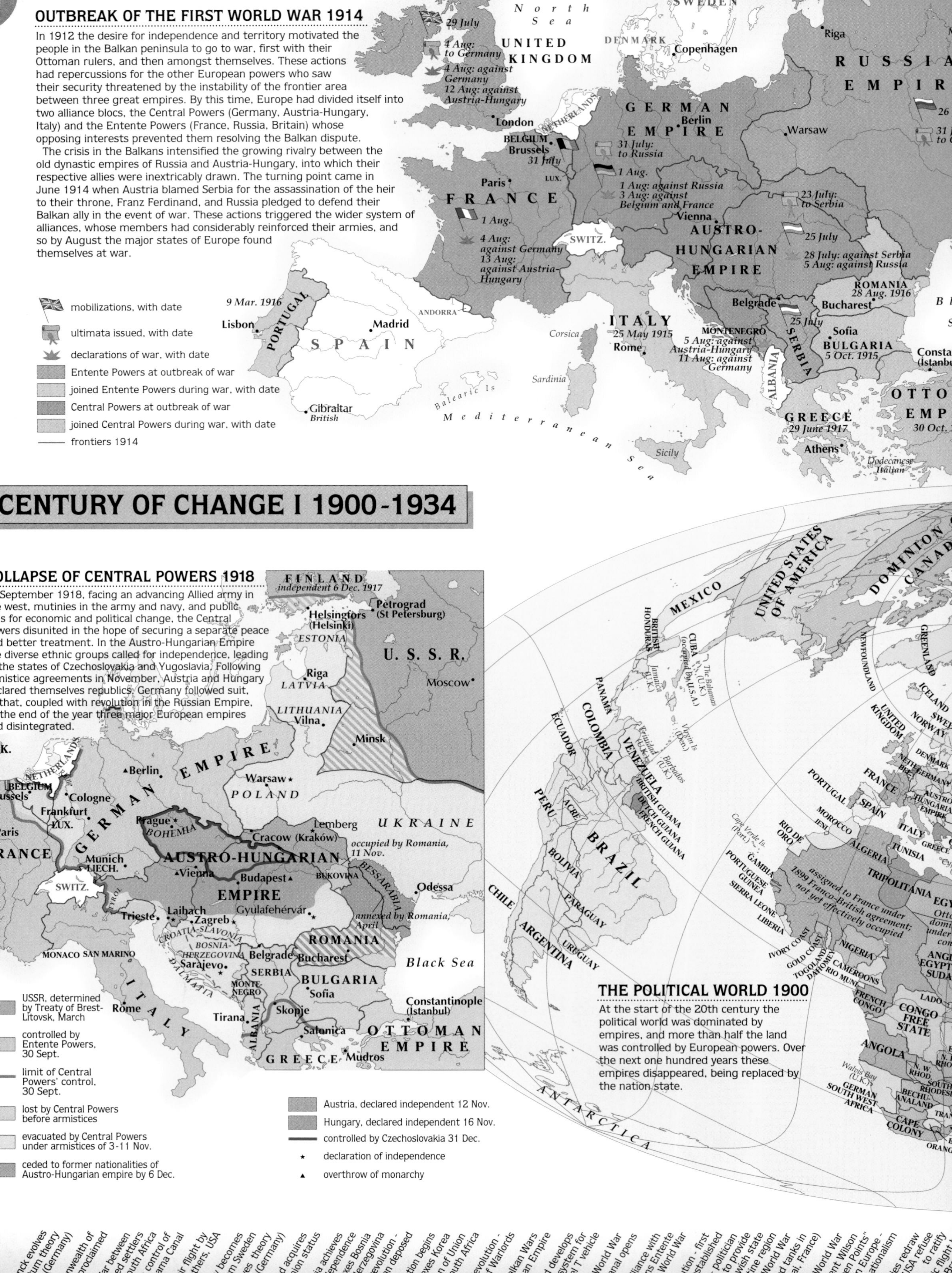

Timeline (bottom):
1900 • Planck evolves quantum theory (Germany)
1901 • Commonwealth of Australia proclaimed
1902 • End of Boer War between British and established settlers for control of South Africa • USA gain control of Panama Canal
1903 • First air flight by Wright brothers, USA
1905 • Norway becomes independent from Sweden • Einstein evolves theory of relativity (Germany)
1907 • New Zealand achieves dominion status
1908 • Bulgaria achieves independence • Austria annexes Bosnia and Herzegovina • Young Turk revolution - Ottoman sultan deposed
1910 • Mexican revolution begins • Japan annexes Korea • Formation of Union of South Africa
1911 • Chinese Revolution - rise to power of Warlords
1912 • Start of Balkan Wars against Ottoman Empire
1913 • Henry Ford develops conveyor belt system for production of Model T vehicle
1914 • Start of First World War • Panama Canal opens
1915 • Italy breaks alliance with Austria and joins Entente Powers in First World War
1917 • Russian Revolution - first socialist state established • Balfour Declaration - politician committing Britain to provide an independent Jewish state in the Palestine region • USA enters First World War • First use of massed tanks in warfare (Cambrai, France)
1918 • End of First World War • USA President Wilson announces his "Fourteen Points" favoured nationalism in Europe
1919 • Paris treaties redraw map of Europe • USA refuse to ratify
1920 • First transatlantic flight by Alcock and Br...

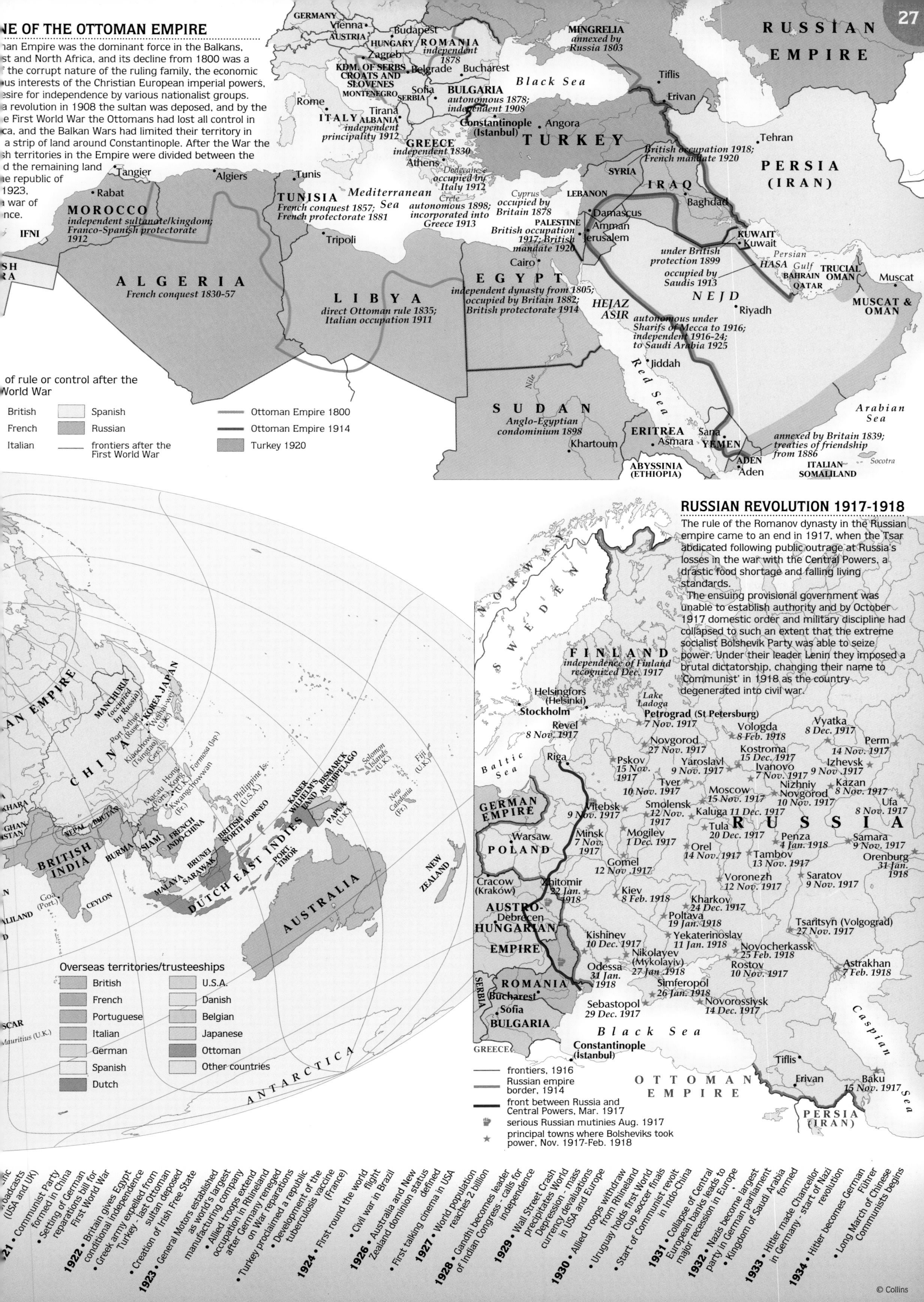

NE OF THE OTTOMAN EMPIRE

...han Empire was the dominant force in the Balkans,
...st and North Africa, and its decline from 1800 was a
... the corrupt nature of the ruling family, the economic
...us interests of the Christian European imperial powers,
...esire for independence by various nationalist groups.
... a revolution in 1908 the sultan was deposed, and by the
...e First World War the Ottomans had lost all control in
...ca, and the Balkan Wars had limited their territory in
... a strip of land around Constantinople. After the War the
...sh territories in the Empire were divided between the
...d the remaining land
...e republic of
...1923,
... a war of
...nce.

of rule or control after the
...World War

- British
- French
- Italian

- Spanish
- Russian

Ottoman Empire 1800
Ottoman Empire 1914
Turkey 1920

frontiers after the
First World War

GERMANY · Vienna · Budapest · AUSTRIA · HUNGARY · ROMANIA *independent 1878* · Zagreb · Belgrade · Bucharest · KDM. OF SERBS CROATS AND SLOVENES · MONTENEGRO · SERBIA · Sofia · BULGARIA *autonomous 1878; independent 1908* · Rome · Tirana · ITALY · ALBANIA *independent principality 1912* · GREECE *independent 1830* · Athens · Constantinople (Istanbul) · Angora · TURKEY · *Dodecanese occupied by Italy 1912* · *Crete autonomous 1898; incorporated into Greece 1913* · Tangier · Rabat · MOROCCO *independent sultanate/kingdom; Franco-Spanish protectorate 1912* · IFNI · Algiers · Tunis · TUNISIA *French conquest 1857; French protectorate 1881* · Mediterranean Sea · *Cyprus occupied by Britain 1878* · LEBANON · SYRIA · *British occupation 1918; French mandate 1920* · IRAQ · Damascus · Amman · PALESTINE *British occupation 1917; British mandate 1920* · Jerusalem · ALGERIA *French conquest 1830-57* · Tripoli · LIBYA *direct Ottoman rule 1835; Italian occupation 1911* · EGYPT *independent dynasty from 1805; occupied by Britain 1882; British protectorate 1914* · Cairo · HEJAZ ASIR · *autonomous under Sharifs of Mecca to 1916; independent 1916-24; to Saudi Arabia 1925* · NEJD · Riyadh · *under British protection 1899; occupied by Saudis 1913* · HASA · KUWAIT · Kuwait · BAHRAIN · QATAR · TRUCIAL OMAN · Muscat · MUSCAT & OMAN · Persian Gulf · RUSSIAN EMPIRE · Tiflis · Erivan · Tehran · PERSIA (IRAN) · Baghdad · Black Sea · MINGRELIA *annexed by Russia 1803* · SUDAN *Anglo-Egyptian condominium 1898* · Khartoum · Nile · Red Sea · Jiddah · ERITREA · Asmara · Sana · YEMEN · *annexed by Britain 1839; treaties of friendship from 1886* · ADEN · Aden · ABYSSINIA (ETHIOPIA) · ITALIAN SOMALILAND · Socotra · Arabian Sea

---

RUSSIAN REVOLUTION 1917-1918

The rule of the Romanov dynasty in the Russian empire came to an end in 1917, when the Tsar abdicated following public outrage at Russia's losses in the war with the Central Powers, a drastic food shortage and falling living standards.

The ensuing provisional government was unable to establish authority and by October 1917 domestic order and military discipline had collapsed to such an extent that the extreme socialist Bolshevik Party was able to seize power. Under their leader Lenin they imposed a brutal dictatorship, changing their name to 'Communist' in 1918 as the country degenerated into civil war.

Overseas territories/trusteeships
- British
- French
- Portuguese
- Italian
- German
- Spanish
- Dutch
- U.S.A.
- Danish
- Belgian
- Japanese
- Ottoman
- Other countries

frontiers, 1916
Russian empire border, 1914
front between Russia and Central Powers, Mar. 1917
serious Russian mutinies Aug. 1917
principal towns where Bolsheviks took power, Nov. 1917-Feb. 1918

NORWAY · SWEDEN · FINLAND *independence of Finland recognized Dec. 1917* · Helsingfors (Helsinki) · Lake Ladoga · Stockholm · Revel *8 Nov. 1917* · Riga · Baltic Sea · Petrograd (St Petersburg) *7 Nov. 1917* · Novgorod *27 Nov. 1917* · Pskov *15 Nov. 1917* · Vyatka *8 Dec. 1917* · Vologda *8 Feb. 1918* · Perm *14 Nov. 1917* · Yaroslavl *9 Nov. 1917* · Kostroma *15 Dec. 1917* · Ivanovo *7 Nov. 1917* · Izhevsk *9 Nov 1917* · Tver *10 Nov. 1917* · Moscow *15 Nov. 1917* · Nizhniy Novgorod *10 Nov. 1917* · Kazan *8 Nov. 1917* · GERMAN EMPIRE · Vitebsk *9 Nov. 1917* · Smolensk *12 Nov. 1917* · Kaluga *11 Dec. 1917* · Ufa *8 Nov. 1917* · Warsaw *7 Nov. 1917* · POLAND · Minsk *7 Nov. 1917* · Mogilev *1 Dec. 1917* · Tula *20 Dec. 1917* · RUSSIA · Gomel *12 Nov .1917* · Orel *14 Nov. 1917* · Tambov *13 Nov. 1917* · Penza *4 Jan. 1918* · Samara *9 Nov. 1917* · Cracow (Kraków) · Zhitomir *22 Jan. 1918* · Kiev *8 Feb. 1918* · Voronezh *12 Nov. 1917* · Saratov *9 Nov. 1917* · Orenburg *31 Jan. 1918* · AUSTRO-HUNGARIAN EMPIRE · Debrecen · Poltava *19 Jan. 1918* · Kharkov *24 Dec. 1917* · Tsaritsyn (Volgograd) *27 Nov. 1917* · Kishinev *10 Dec. 1917* · Yekaterinoslav *11 Jan. 1918* · Nikolayev (Mykolayiv) *27 Jan. 1918* · Novocherkassk *25 Feb. 1918* · SERBIA · Odessa *31 Jan. 1918* · Rostov *10 Nov. 1917* · Astrakhan *7 Feb. 1918* · ROMANIA · Bucharest · Simferopol *26 Jan. 1918* · Sofia · BULGARIA · Sebastopol *29 Dec. 1917* · Novorossiysk *14 Dec. 1917* · Black Sea · GREECE · Constantinople (Istanbul) · OTTOMAN EMPIRE · Tiflis · Erivan · Baku *15 Nov. 1917* · PERSIA (IRAN) · Caspian Sea

...AN EMPIRE · MANCHURIA (occupied by Russia) · Port Arthur (Russ.) · Weihai-wei (U.K.) · KOREA · JAPAN · CHINA · Kiaochow (Tsingtau) (Ger.) · Macau (Port.) · Hong Kong (U.K.) · Formosa (Jap.) · Kwangchowan (Fr.) · Kwangsi · Philippine Is. (U.S.A.) · Solomon Islands (U.K.) · Fiji (U.K.) · KAISER WILHELM'S LAND · BISMARCK ARCHIPELAGO · New Caledonia (Fr.) · PAPUA (U.K.) · NEPAL · BHUTAN · AFGHANISTAN · BRITISH INDIA · BURMA · SIAM · FRENCH INDOCHINA · MALAYA · BRUNEI · SARAWAK · BRITISH NORTH BORNEO · DUTCH EAST INDIES · PORT. TIMOR · AUSTRALIA · NEW ZEALAND · ...BHARA · ...GHAN... · ...ISTAN · Goa (Port.) · CEYLON · ...LILAND · Mauritius (U.K.) · ...SCAR · Madagascar (U.K.) · ANTARCTICA

Timeline (bottom):
...broadcasts (USA and UK) · ...Communist Party formed in China · Setting up of German reparations bill for First World War
1922 · Britain gives Egypt conditional independence · Greek army expelled from Turkey - last Ottoman sultan deposed · Creation of Irish Free State
1923 · General Motors established as world's largest manufacturing company · Allied troops extend occupation in Rhineland after Germany reneged on War reparations · Turkey proclaimed a republic · Development of vaccine for tuberculosis (France)
1924 · First round the world flight
1926 · Civil war in Brazil · Australia and New Zealand dominion status defined
1927 · First talking cinema in USA
1928 · World population reaches 2 billion · Gandhi becomes leader of Indian Congress - calls for independence
1929 · Wall Street Crash precipitates World Depression - mass currency devaluations in USA and Europe
1930 · Allied troops withdraw from Rhineland · Uruguay holds first World Cup soccer finals · Start of Communist revolt in Indo-China
1931 · Collapse of Central European banks leads to major recession in Europe
1932 · Nazis become largest party in German parliament · Kingdom of Saudi Arabia formed
1933 · Hitler made Chancellor in Germany - start of Nazi revolution
1934 · Hitler becomes German Führer · Long March of Chinese Communists begins

© Collins

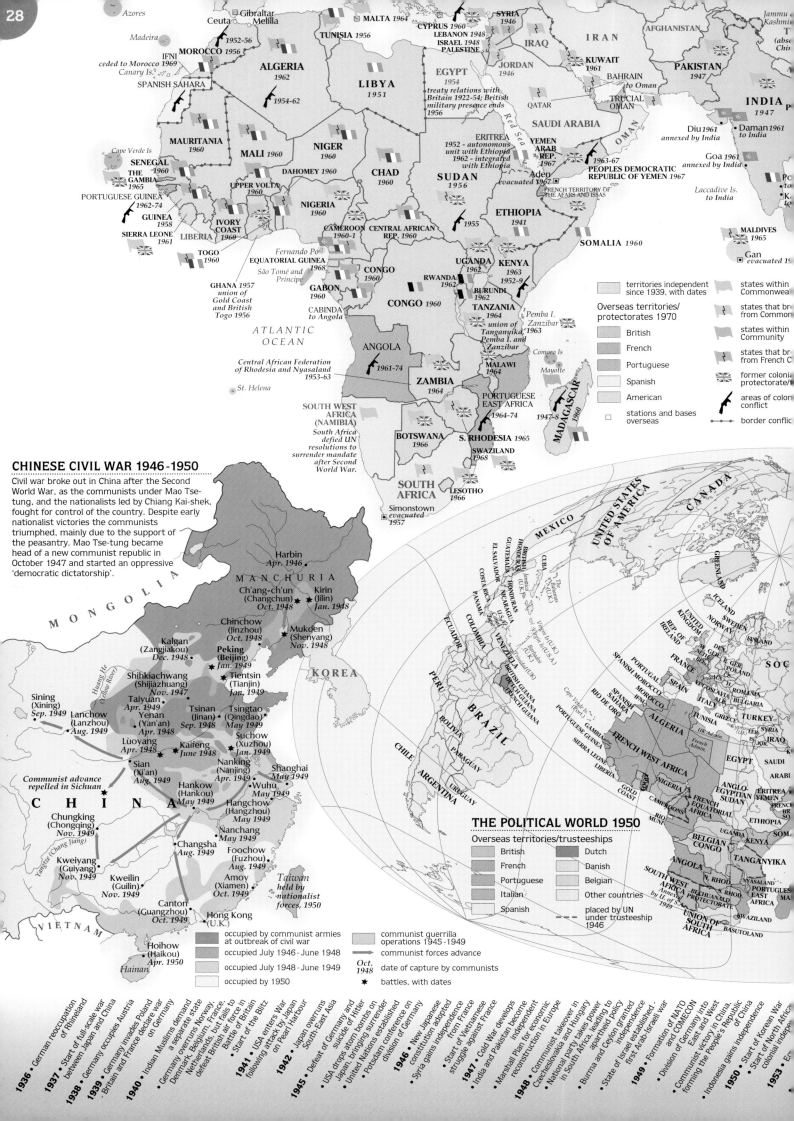

Map labels (Africa, Middle East, Asia — decolonization map)

Azores
Madeira
Gibraltar
Ceuta
Melilla
MALTA 1964
CYPRUS 1960
SYRIA 1946
LEBANON 1948
ISRAEL 1948
PALESTINE
IRAQ
IRAN
AFGHANISTAN
Jammu & Kashmir (absent China)
TUNISIA 1956
1952-56
MOROCCO 1956
IFNI ceded to Morocco 1969
Canary Is.
SPANISH SAHARA
ALGERIA 1962
1954-62
LIBYA 1951
EGYPT 1954 treaty relations with Britain 1922-54; British military presence ends 1956
JORDAN 1946
KUWAIT 1961
BAHRAIN to Oman
QATAR
TRUCIAL OMAN
PAKISTAN 1947
INDIA 1947
MAURITANIA 1960
MALI 1960
NIGER 1960
CHAD 1960
SUDAN 1956
SAUDI ARABIA
ERITREA 1952 - autonomous unit with Ethiopia 1962 - integrated with Ethiopia
YEMEN ARAB REP. 1967
1963-67 PEOPLES DEMOCRATIC REPUBLIC OF YEMEN 1967
Aden evacuated 1967
OMAN
Diu 1961 annexed by India
Daman 1961 to India
Goa 1961 annexed by India
Laccadive Is. to India
MALDIVES 1965
Gan evacuated 19
Cape Verde Is
SENEGAL 1960
THE GAMBIA 1965
PORTUGUESE GUINEA 1962-74
GUINEA 1958
SIERRA LEONE 1961
LIBERIA
IVORY COAST 1960
UPPER VOLTA 1960
DAHOMEY 1960
NIGERIA 1960
CAMEROON 1960-1
CENTRAL AFRICAN REP. 1960
ETHIOPIA 1941
1955
TOGO 1960
GHANA 1957 union of Gold Coast and British Togo 1956
Fernando Po
EQUATORIAL GUINEA 1968
São Tomé and Príncipe
GABON 1960
CONGO 1960
CONGO 1960
UGANDA 1962
KENYA 1963 1952-9
RWANDA 1962
BURUNDI 1962
SOMALIA 1960
CABINDA to Angola
TANZANIA 1964 union of Tanganyika 1963 Pemba I. and Zanzibar
Pemba I. Zanzibar
ATLANTIC OCEAN
ANGOLA 1961-74
Central African Federation of Rhodesia and Nyasaland 1953-63
St. Helena
ZAMBIA 1964
MALAWI 1964
PORTUGUESE EAST AFRICA 1964-74
1947-8
Comoro Is
Mayotte
MADAGASCAR 1960
SOUTH WEST AFRICA (NAMIBIA) South Africa defied UN resolutions to surrender mandate after Second World War.
BOTSWANA 1966
S. RHODESIA 1965
SWAZILAND 1968
SOUTH AFRICA
LESOTHO 1966
Simonstown evacuated 1957

Legend (top right)

territories independent since 1939, with dates	states within Commonwealth
	states that br from Common
Overseas territories/ protectorates 1970	states within Community
British	states that br from French C
French	former coloni protectorate/t
Portuguese	areas of coloni conflict
Spanish	border conflic
American	
stations and bases overseas	

CHINESE CIVIL WAR 1946-1950

Civil war broke out in China after the Second World War, as the communists under Mao Tse-tung, and the nationalists led by Chiang Kai-shek, fought for control of the country. Despite early nationalist victories the communists triumphed, mainly due to the support of the peasantry. Mao Tse-tung became head of a new communist republic in October 1947 and started an oppressive 'democratic dictatorship'.

MONGOLIA
MANCHURIA
Harbin Apr. 1946
Ch'ang-ch'un (Changchun) Oct. 1948
Kirin (Jilin) Jan. 1948
Chinchow (Jinzhou) Oct. 1948
Mukden (Shenyang) Nov. 1948
Kalgan (Zangjiakou) Dec. 1948
Peking (Beijing) Jan. 1949
Tientsin (Tianjin) Jan. 1949
KOREA
Shihkiachwang (Shijiazhuang) Nov. 1947
Taiyuan Apr. 1949
Tsinan (Jinan) Sep. 1948
Tsingtao (Qingdao) May 1949
Sining (Xining) Sep. 1949
Lanchow (Lanzhou) Aug. 1949
Yenan (Yan'an) Apr. 1949
Lùoyang Apr. 1948
Kaifeng June 1948
Suchow (Xuzhou) Jan. 1949
Huang He (Yellow River)
Sian (Xi'an) Aug. 1949
Nanking (Nanjing) Apr. 1949
Shanghai May 1949
Communist advance repelled in Sichuan
CHINA
Hankow (Hankou) May 1949
Wuhu May 1949
Hangchow (Hangzhou) May 1949
Chungking (Chongqing) Nov. 1949
Nanchang May 1949
Foochow (Fuzhou) Aug. 1949
Taiwan held by nationalist forces, 1950
Yangtze (Chang Jiang)
Kweiyang (Guiyang) Nov. 1949
Changsha Aug. 1949
Kweilin (Guilin) Nov. 1949
Amoy (Xiamen) Oct. 1949
Canton (Guangzhou) Oct. 1949
Hong Kong (U.K.)
VIETNAM
Hoihow (Haikou) Apr. 1950
Hainan

Chinese Civil War legend

occupied by communist armies at outbreak of civil war	communist guerrilla operations 1945-1949	
occupied July 1946 - June 1948	communist forces advance	
occupied July 1948 - June 1949	Oct. 1948 date of capture by communists	
occupied by 1950	★ battles, with dates	

THE POLITICAL WORLD 1950

MEXICO
UNITED STATES OF AMERICA
CANADA
GREENLAND
ICELAND
SWEDEN
NORWAY
FINLAND
REP. OF IRELAND
UNITED KINGDOM
FRANCE
W. GER. E. GER. POLAND
NETH. BEL.
YUGOSLAVIA
ITALY
PORTUGAL
SPAIN
ROMANIA
BULGARIA
GREECE
TURKEY
SYRIA
IRAQ
JOR.
EGYPT
SAUDI ARABIA
SOC
GUATEMALA
BRITISH HONDURAS
HONDURAS
EL SALVADOR
NICARAGUA
COSTA RICA
PANAMA
CUBA
Jamaica (U.K.)
The Bahamas (U.K.)
Virgin Is. (U.K.)
Virgin Is. (U.S.A.)
Barbados (U.K.)
COLOMBIA
VENEZUELA
ECUADOR
BRITISH GUIANA
DUTCH GUIANA
FRENCH GUIANA
PERU
BRAZIL
BOLIVIA
PARAGUAY
CHILE
ARGENTINA
URUGUAY
Cape Verde Is.
SPANISH MOROCCO
SPANISH SAHARA
RIO DE ORO
PORTUGUESE GUINEA
GAMBIA
SIERRA LEONE
LIBERIA
GOLD COAST
FRENCH WEST AFRICA
ALGERIA
TUNISIA
Cyprus (UK Admin.)
French Admin.
NIGERIA
CAMEROONS
RIO MUNI
FRENCH EQUATORIAL AFRICA
ANGLO-EGYPTIAN SUDAN
ERITREA Annexed by U.S.A. 1949
FRENCH SOMALI
ETHIOPIA
BELGIAN CONGO
UGANDA
KENYA
SOM.
TANGANYIKA
SOUTH WEST AFRICA
BECHUANA-LAND PROTECTORATE
N. RHOD.
S. RHOD. Annexed by U. of S.A.
NYASALAND
PORTUGUESE EAST AFRICA
MA
SWAZILAND
UNION OF SOUTH AFRICA
BASUTOLAND

Political World 1950 legend

Overseas territories/trusteeships

British	Dutch
French	Danish
Portuguese	Belgian
Italian	Other countries
Spanish	placed by UN under trusteeship 1946

Timeline (bottom)

1936 • German reoccupation of Rhineland
1937 • Start of full-scale war between Japan and China
1938 • Germany occupies Austria
1939 • Germany invades Poland - Britain and France declare war on Germany
1940 • Indian Muslims demand a separate state • Germany overruns Norway, Denmark, Belgium, France, Netherlands, but fails to defeat British air force in Battle of Britain • Start of the Blitz
1941 • USA enters War following attack on Pearl Harbour
1942 • Japan overruns South-East Asia
1945 • Defeat of Germany and suicide of Hitler • USA drops atom bombs on Japan, bringing surrender • United Nations established • Potsdam Conference on division of Germany
1946 • New Japanese constitution adopted • Syria gains independence from France • Start of Vietnamese struggle against France
1947 • Cold War develops • India and Pakistan become independent • Marshall Plan for economic reconstruction in Europe
1948 • Communist takeover in Czechoslovakia and Hungary • National party takes power in South Africa, leading to apartheid policy • Burma and Ceylon granted independence • State of Israel established - first Arab-Israeli war
1949 • Formation of NATO and COMECON • Division of Germany into East and West • Communist victory in China, forming the People's Republic of China
1950 • Indonesia gains independence • Start of Korean War
1953 • Start of North Afri colonial war

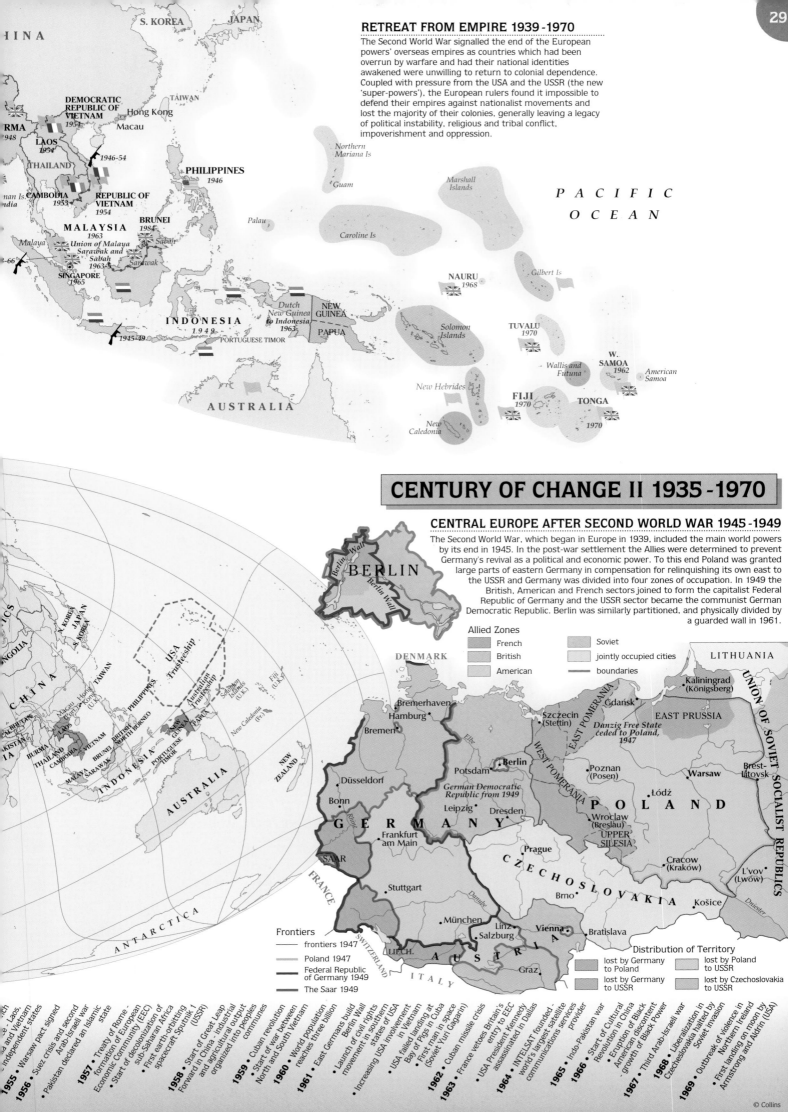

RETREAT FROM EMPIRE 1939-1970

The Second World War signalled the end of the European powers' overseas empires as countries which had been overrun by warfare and had their national identities awakened were unwilling to return to colonial dependence. Coupled with pressure from the USA and the USSR (the new 'super-powers'), the European rulers found it impossible to defend their empires against nationalist movements and lost the majority of their colonies, generally leaving a legacy of political instability, religious and tribal conflict, impoverishment and oppression.

CENTURY OF CHANGE II 1935-1970

CENTRAL EUROPE AFTER SECOND WORLD WAR 1945-1949

The Second World War, which began in Europe in 1939, included the main world powers by its end in 1945. In the post-war settlement the Allies were determined to prevent Germany's revival as a political and economic power. To this end Poland was granted large parts of eastern Germany in compensation for relinquishing its own east to the USSR and Germany was divided into four zones of occupation. In 1949 the British, American and French sectors joined to form the capitalist Federal Republic of Germany and the USSR sector became the communist German Democratic Republic. Berlin was similarly partitioned, and physically divided by a guarded wall in 1961.

Allied Zones
- French
- British
- American
- Soviet
- jointly occupied cities
- boundaries

Frontiers
- frontiers 1947
- Poland 1947
- Federal Republic of Germany 1949
- The Saar 1949

Distribution of Territory
- lost by Germany to Poland
- lost by Germany to USSR
- lost by Poland to USSR
- lost by Czechoslovakia to USSR

© Collins

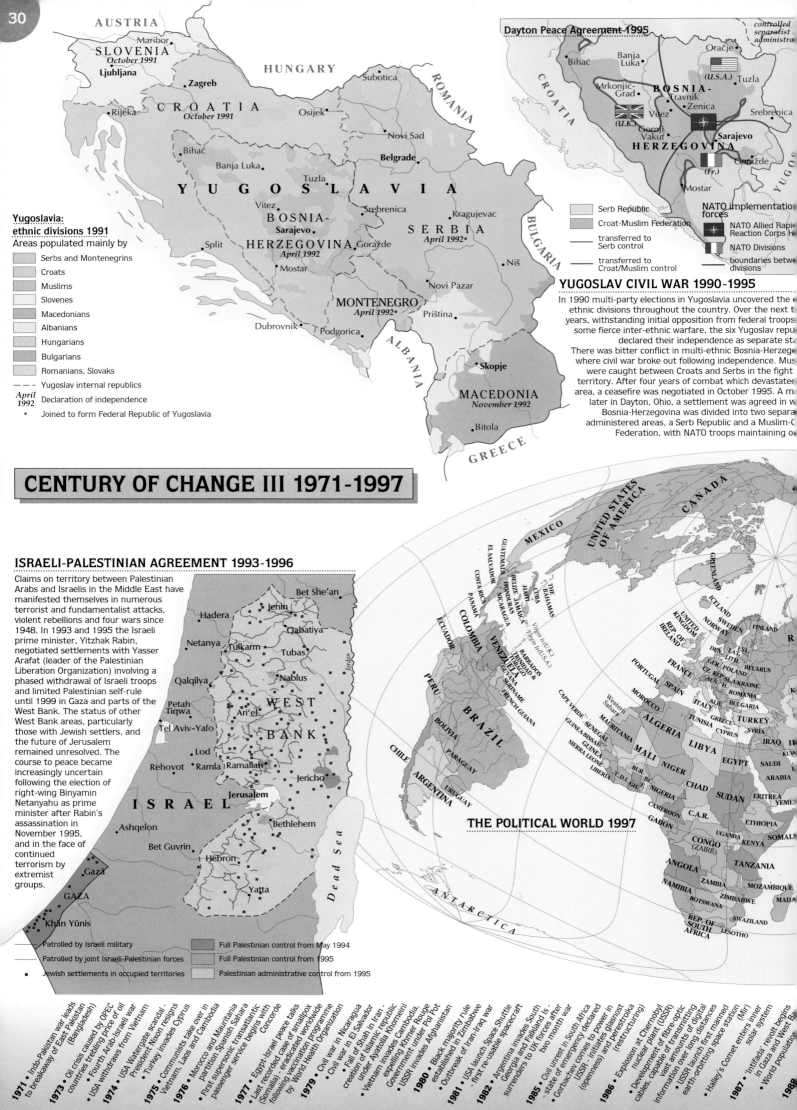

Dayton Peace Agreement 1995

controlled separatist administra

BOSNIA-HERZEGOVINA

Serb Republic

Croat-Muslim Federation

transferred to Serb control

transferred to Croat/Muslim control

NATO implementation forces

NATO Allied Rapid Reaction Corps H

NATO Divisions

boundaries between divisions

YUGOSLAV CIVIL WAR 1990-1995

In 1990 multi-party elections in Yugoslavia uncovered the ethnic divisions throughout the country. Over the next years, withstanding initial opposition from federal troops some fierce inter-ethnic warfare, the six Yugoslav repu declared their independence as separate sta There was bitter conflict in multi-ethnic Bosnia-Herzeg where civil war broke out following independence. Mus were caught between Croats and Serbs in the fight territory. After four years of combat which devastate area, a ceasefire was negotiated in October 1995. A m later in Dayton, Ohio, a settlement was agreed in w Bosnia-Herzegovina was divided into two separa administered areas, a Serb Republic and a Muslim-C Federation, with NATO troops maintaining o

Yugoslavia: ethnic divisions 1991
Areas populated mainly by

- Serbs and Montenegrins
- Croats
- Muslims
- Slovenes
- Macedonians
- Albanians
- Hungarians
- Bulgarians
- Romanians, Slovaks

– – – Yugoslav internal republics

April 1992 Declaration of independence

* Joined to form Federal Republic of Yugoslavia

CENTURY OF CHANGE III 1971-1997

ISRAELI-PALESTINIAN AGREEMENT 1993-1996

Claims on territory between Palestinian Arabs and Israelis in the Middle East have manifested themselves in numerous terrorist and fundamentalist attacks, violent rebellions and four wars since 1948. In 1993 and 1995 the Israeli prime minister, Yitzhak Rabin, negotiated settlements with Yasser Arafat (leader of the Palestinian Liberation Organization) involving a phased withdrawal of Israeli troops and limited Palestinian self-rule until 1999 in Gaza and parts of the West Bank. The status of other West Bank areas, particularly those with Jewish settlers, and the future of Jerusalem remained unresolved. The course to peace became increasingly uncertain following the election of right-wing Binyamin Netanyahu as prime minister after Rabin's assassination in November 1995, and in the face of continued terrorism by extremist groups.

Patrolled by Israeli military
Patrolled by joint Israeli-Palestinian forces
■ Jewish settlements in occupied territories
Full Palestinian control from May 1994
Full Palestinian control from 1995
Palestinian administrative control from 1995

THE POLITICAL WORLD 1997

OLLAPSE OF COMMUNISM IN EUROPE 1985-1991

1991 communist governments had been wiped out in Eastern Europe
ecause of the pressures caused by economic and political reforms introduced
rough modernization. Growing popular unrest contributed to their collapse
nd led to multi-party elections, which brought to power parties committed
democratic reform and economic liberalization.

ERMANY
9: political refugees reach the West via Hungary
v. 1989: protests against leadership
1989: Berlin Wall breached
0: free elections
0: currency union with West German
0: reunified with West Germany

IA
9: economic war between federal
ernment and Slovenia
): free elections
1: federal army tries to regain control
1: federal army withdraws
1: independence declared

1990: free elections
Serbian areas declare
pendence
Slovenian fighting spreads
rbs try to extend territory
oatia and Bosnia
independence declared

GOSLAVIA
7: mass strikes; growing Serb
militancy against minorities
y 1990: provincial autonomies abolished
0-1: increasing tension between federal
government and Slovenia and Croatia

ESTONIA, LATVIA and LITHUANIA
1989: mass anti-communist demonstrations
Mar.-June 1990: independence declared in Lithuania;
economic embargo imposed by USSR
Mar. 1991: referendums in Estonia and Latvia
endorse independence
Aug. 1991: independence declared in Estonia and Latvia
Sep. 1991: independent states recognized by USSR

POLAND
June 1989: partially free elections
Sep. 1989: Solidarity-led
government takes office
Jan. 1990: Communist Party
dissolved
Oct. 1991: free elections

BELARUS
June 1989: Popular Front
founded
Aug. 1991: independence
declared

RUSSIAN FEDERATION
Mar. 1985: Mikhail Gorbachev becomes
leader of Communist Party;
initiates perestroika (restructuring)
and glasnost (openness)
Aug. 1991: hard-line communist coup
against Gorbachev fails
Nov. 1991: Communist Party declared
illegal
Dec. 1991: USSR dissolved

CZECHOSLOVAKIA
Nov. 1989: mass demonstrations end
communist rule
Apr. 1990: new constitution adopted
June 1990: free elections

UKRAINE
1989: opposition mass-movements emerge
Aug. 1991: independence declared
Dec. 1991: referendum endorses independence

HUNGARY
from 1987 communist regime
relaxes control
Sep. 1989: allows East Germans
to travel to the West
Oct. 1990: communist rule ends
Mar.-Apr. 1990: free elections

MOLDOVA
June 1989: Popular Front wins 75%
of votes in election
Aug. 1991: independence declared

ROMANIA
Dec. 1989: mass demonstrations lead to
armed uprisings and overthrow
of Ceaucescu regime
June 1991: free elections
Nov. 1991: new constitution adopted

GEORGIA
Nov. 1988: mass demonstrations
Mar. 1991: referendum endorses
independence
Apr. 1991: independence declared

BULGARIA
Nov. 1989: President Zhivkov
removed from office
June 1990: free elections
July 1991: fresh elections following
adoption of new constitution

ARMENIA
Sep. 1989: economic embargo imposed
by Azerbaijan
Sep. 1991: referendum endorses
independence; independence declared

ALBANIA
Jan.-May 1990: democratic reforms
initiated by leadership
Mar. 1991: free elections

AZERBAIJAN
Jan. 1990: state of emergency declared;
Soviet troops intervene
Oct. 1991: independence declared

Legend
— USSR to 1991
— Soviet-dominated Eastern Europe to 1989
— Yugoslavia to 1991
Communist states outside USSR to 1990/1991
united with West Germany, 1990
independent states, 1991
de-facto independent states, late 1991, on former territory of the Soviet Union, internationally unrecognized
— frontiers, late 1991

THE GULF WAR 1990-1991

Legend
• Iraqi missile plant
• Iraqi chemical weapons plant
• Iraqi biological weapons plant
• Iraqi nuclear installations
states supporting Iraq
members of UN Coalition
— maximum range of Iraqi Scud missiles

In August 1990 Iraqi troops invaded oil-rich Kuwait. Despite pressure from the United Nations (UN), the Iraqi
leader, Saddam Hussein, refused to withdraw his forces, increasingly justifying his actions in anti-Israeli terms.
On 16th January 1991 a coalition of UN forces launched a series of air strikes, followed a month later by a
ground offensive. Iraq responded with anti-aircraft fire, ground-to-air missiles and launched Scud missiles into
Israel and Saudi Arabia. However by the end of February, following heavy casualties and billions of pounds worth
of damage to Iraqi targets, Saddam Hussein was forced to agree to a ceasefire and an unconditional withdrawal.

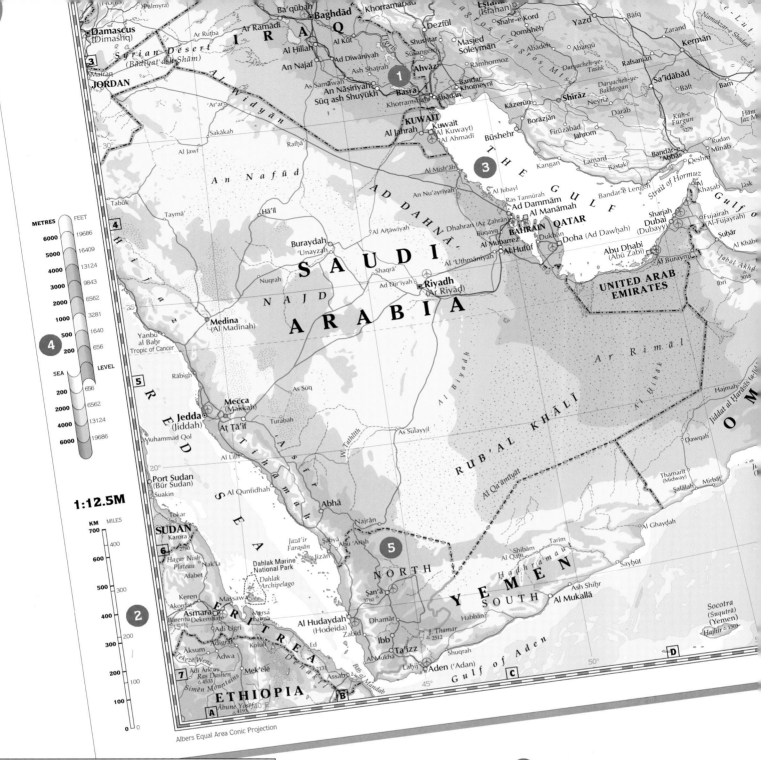

Albers Equal Area Conic Projection

1:12.5M

HOW TO USE THE ATLAS

THIS SECTION HELPS the reader to interpret the reference maps in the Atlas of the World. It explains the main features shown on the mapping and the policies adopted in deciding what to show and how to show it.

The databases used to create the maps provide the freedom to select the best map coverage for each part of the world. Maps are arranged on a continental basis, with each continent being introduced by maps of the political situation and the main physical features. Maps of Antarctica and the world's oceans complete the extensive worldwide coverage.

1 SYMBOLS & GENERALIZATION

Maps show information by using signs, or symbols, which are designed to reflect the features on the earth that they represent. Symbols can be in the form of points - such as those used to show towns and airports; lines - used to represent roads and rivers; or areas - lakes, marsh. Variation in size, shape and colour of these types of symbol allow a great range of information to be shown. The symbols used in

this atlas are explained in the panel to the right.

Not all information can be shown, and much has to be generalized to be clearly shown on the maps. This generalization takes the form of selection - the inclusion of some features and the omission of others of less importance; and simplification - where lines are smoothed, areas combined, or symbols displaced slightly to add clarity. This is done in such a way that the overall character of the area mapped is retained. The degree of generalization varies, and is determined largely by the scale at which the map is drawn.

2 SCALE

Scale is the relationship between the size of an area shown on the map and the actual size of the area on the ground. It determines the amount of detail shown on a map - larger scales show more, smaller scales show less - and can be used to measure the distance between two points, though the projection of the map must also be taken into account when measuring distances.

Scale is shown in two ways. The representative fraction (1:12.5M on the extract above) tells us that a distance of 1 mm on the map actually measures 12,500,000 mm (or 12.5 kilometres) on the ground. The linear scale, or scale bar, converts this into easily measurable units.

3 GEOGRAPHICAL NAMES

The spelling of place names on maps is a complex problem f the cartographer. There is no single standard way of spelling names or of converting them from one alphabet, or symbol set, to another. Changes in official languages also have to be taken into account when creating maps and databases, and policies need to be established for the spelling of names on

individual atlases and maps. Such policies must take account of the local official position, international conventions or

SYMBOLS

Relief

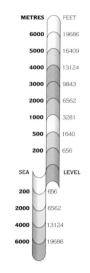

METRES		FEET
6000		19686
5000		16409
4000		13124
3000		9843
2000		6562
1000		3281
500		1640
200		656
SEA		LEVEL
200		656
2000		6562
4000		13124
6000		19686

Additional bathymetric contour layers are shown at scales greater than 1:2m. These are labelled on an individual basis.

213
△ Summit
height in metres

Boundaries

━ ━ ━   International

╫ ╫ ╫   International disputed

● ● ● ● ●   Ceasefire line

▬▬▬   Main administrative (U.K.)

━━━   Main administrative

▬ ▬ ▬   Main administrative through water

Communications

═══   Motorway

┅┅┅   Motorway tunnel

Motorways are classified separately at scales greater than 1:5 million. At smaller scales motorways are classified with main roads.

━━━   Main road

┅ ┅ ┅   Main road under construction

┅┅┅┅┅   Main road tunnel

───   Other road

╴ ╴ ╴   Other road under construction

┅┅┅┅   Other road tunnel

╴ ╴ ╴ ╴   Track

━━━   Main railway

╴ ╴ ╴ ╴   Main railway under construction

┅┅┅┅   Main railway tunnel

───   Other railway

╴ ╴ ╴ ╴   Other railway under construction

┅┅┅┅   Other railway tunnel

✈   Main airport

✦   Other airport

Physical Features

◯   Freshwater lake

◯   Seasonal freshwater lake

◯   Saltwater lake *or* Lagoon

◯   Seasonal saltwater lake

◯   Dry salt lake *or* Salt pan

▢   Marsh

───   River

─┼─   Waterfall

─┼─   Dam *or* Barrage

╴ ╴ ╴   Seasonal river *or* Wadi

┉┉┉   Canal

┈┈┈   Flood dyke

───   Reef

▲   Volcano

▢   Lava field

▢   Sandy desert

▢   Rocky desert

˅   Oasis

┉┉┉┉   Escarpment

≍
923   Mountain pass *height in metres*

◯   Ice cap or Glacier

Other Features

╴╴╴╴╴   National park

┈┈┈┈   Reserve

∿∿∿∿   Ancient wall

∴   Historic or Tourist site

Styles of Lettering

Country name	**FRANCE**	Island	*Gran Canaria*
	BARBADOS	Lake	*LAKE ERIE*
Main administrative name	HESSEN	Mountain	*ANDES*
Area name	*ARTOIS*	River	*Zambezi*

Settlements

POPULATION	NATIONAL CAPITAL	ADMINISTRATIVE CAPITAL	CITY OR TOWN
Over 5 million	▣ **Beijing**	◉ **Tianjin**	◉ **New York**
1 to 5 million	▣ **Seoul**	◉ **Lagos**	◉ **Barranquilla**
500000 to 1 million	▣ **Bangui**	◎ **Douala**	◎ **Memphis**
100000 to 500000	▢ Wellington	○ Mansa	○ Mara
50000 to 100000	▢ Port of Spain	◦ Lubango	○ Arecibo
10000 to 50000	▫ Malabo	◦ Chinhoyi	◦ El Tigre
Less than 10000	▫ Roseau	◦ Áti	◦ Soledad

▢ Urban area

---

traditions, and the purpose of the atlas or map. The policy in this atlas is to use local name forms which are officially recognized by the governments of the countries concerned. However, English conventional name forms are used for the most well-known places. In these cases, the local form is included in brackets on the map and also appears as a cross-reference in the index. Examples of this policy on the above names extract include:

ENGLISH FORM	LOCAL FORM
Kuwait	**Al Kuwayt**
Riyadh	**Ar Riyāḍ**
Doha	**Ad Dawḥah**

Other examples in the atlas include:

Moscow	**Moskva**
Vienna	**Wien**
Crete	**Kriti**
Serbia	**Srbija**

All country names and those for international features appear in their English forms. Other alternative names, such as well-known historical names or those in other languages, may also be included in brackets and as index cross-references.

4 REPRESENTATION OF RELIEF

One important element of mapping the earth is the depiction of relief - the 'shape' of the land. This presents a problem to the cartographer who has to show the earth's three-dimensional surface on the two-dimensional page. The maps in this atlas use two main methods of relief representation.

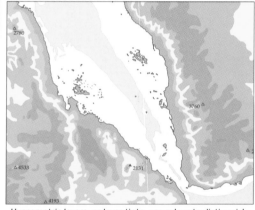

Hypsometric layers, or layer tints, use colour to distinguish areas which lie in specific altitude or relief bands. The colours give an immediate impression of the height and shape of the land and are indicated on the altitude bar in the margin of each map. The height of the land at selected points is shown by summit symbols or spot heights which indicate the height at that point in metres above sea level. On the maps of the oceans, small dots show the depth of the ocean below sea level in metres.

A third method of relief depiction is used on the maps of the oceans and Antarctica - hill or relief shading simulates the effect of a light shining across the landscape, providing an impression of the shape of the land.

5 BOUNDARIES

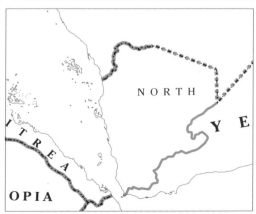

The status of nations and their boundaries are shown in this atlas as they are in reality at the time of going to press, as far as can be ascertained. Where international boundaries are the subject of dispute, the aim is to take a strictly neutral viewpoint, based on advice from expert consultants.

Every attempt is made to show where territorial disputes exist and their depiction varies accordingly, as illustrated on the above extract. Generally, prominence is given to the 'de facto' situation - that existing on the ground.

© Collins

2

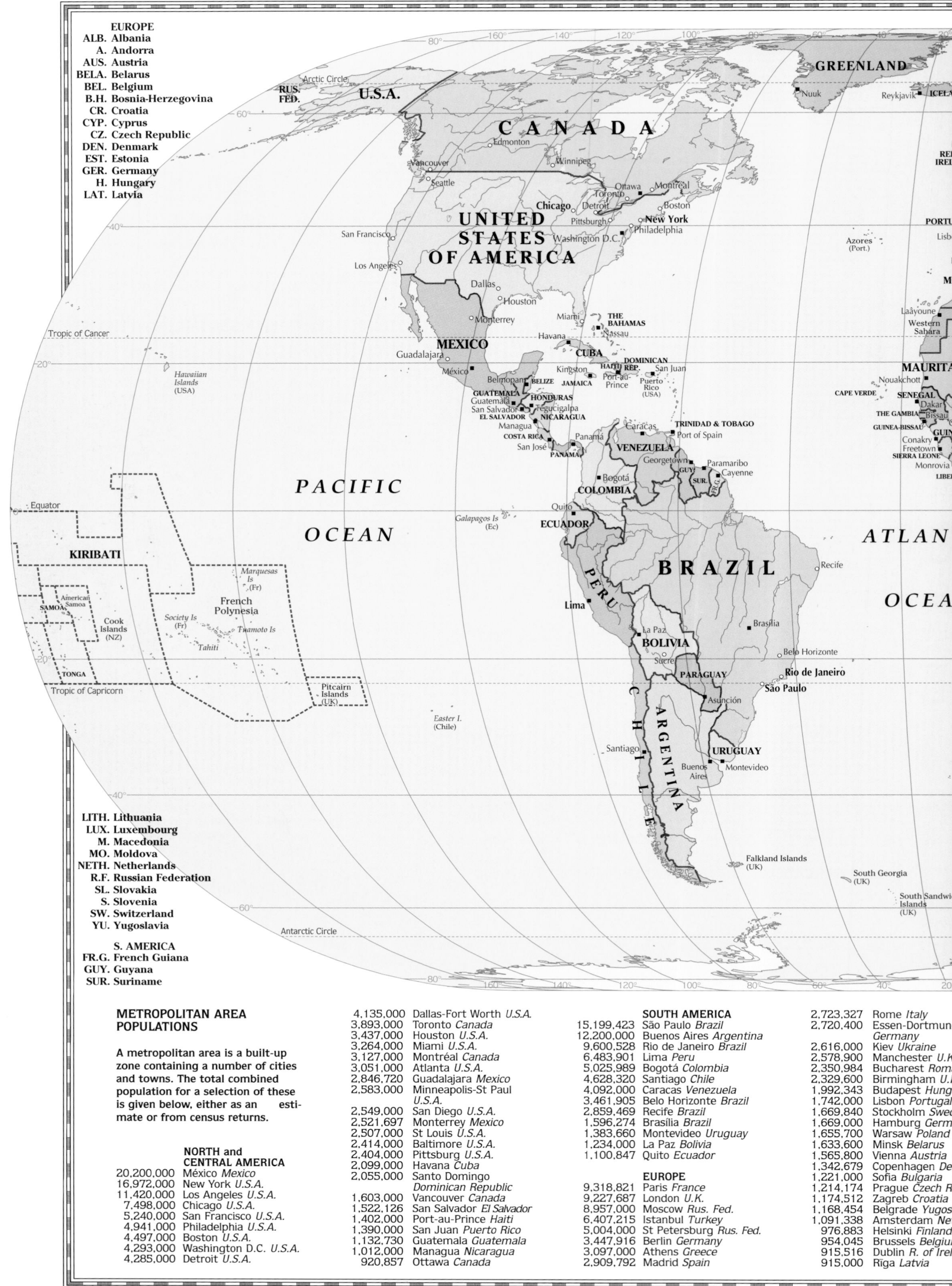

METROPOLITAN AREA POPULATIONS

A metropolitan area is a built-up zone containing a number of cities and towns. The total combined population for a selection of these is given below, either as an estimate or from census returns.

NORTH and CENTRAL AMERICA

20,200,000	México *Mexico*
16,972,000	New York *U.S.A.*
11,420,000	Los Angeles *U.S.A.*
7,498,000	Chicago *U.S.A.*
5,240,000	San Francisco *U.S.A.*
4,941,000	Philadelphia *U.S.A.*
4,497,000	Boston *U.S.A.*
4,293,000	Washington D.C. *U.S.A.*
4,285,000	Detroit *U.S.A.*
4,135,000	Dallas-Fort Worth *U.S.A.*
3,893,000	Toronto *Canada*
3,437,000	Houston *U.S.A.*
3,264,000	Miami *U.S.A.*
3,127,000	Montréal *Canada*
3,051,000	Atlanta *U.S.A.*
2,846,720	Guadalajara *Mexico*
2,583,000	Minneapolis-St Paul *U.S.A.*
2,549,000	San Diego *U.S.A.*
2,521,697	Monterrey *Mexico*
2,507,000	St Louis *U.S.A.*
2,414,000	Baltimore *U.S.A.*
2,404,000	Pittsburg *U.S.A.*
2,099,000	Havana *Cuba*
2,055,000	Santo Domingo *Dominican Republic*
1,603,000	Vancouver *Canada*
1,522,126	San Salvador *El Salvador*
1,402,000	Port-au-Prince *Haiti*
1,390,000	San Juan *Puerto Rico*
1,132,730	Guatemala *Guatemala*
1,012,000	Managua *Nicaragua*
920,857	Ottawa *Canada*

SOUTH AMERICA

15,199,423	São Paulo *Brazil*
12,200,000	Buenos Aires *Argentina*
9,600,528	Rio de Janeiro *Brazil*
6,483,901	Lima *Peru*
5,025,989	Bogotá *Colombia*
4,628,320	Santiago *Chile*
4,092,000	Caracas *Venezuela*
3,461,905	Belo Horizonte *Brazil*
2,859,469	Recife *Brazil*
1,596,274	Brasília *Brazil*
1,383,660	Montevideo *Uruguay*
1,234,000	La Paz *Bolivia*
1,100,847	Quito *Ecuador*

EUROPE

9,318,821	Paris *France*
9,227,687	London *U.K.*
8,957,000	Moscow *Rus. Fed.*
6,407,215	Istanbul *Turkey*
5,004,000	St Petersburg *Rus. Fed.*
3,447,916	Berlin *Germany*
3,097,000	Athens *Greece*
2,909,792	Madrid *Spain*
2,723,327	Rome *Italy*
2,720,400	Essen-Dortmun *Germany*
2,616,000	Kiev *Ukraine*
2,578,900	Manchester *U.K.*
2,350,984	Bucharest *Rom.*
2,329,600	Birmingham *U.*
1,992,343	Budapest *Hung*
1,742,000	Lisbon *Portugal*
1,669,840	Stockholm *Swe*
1,669,000	Hamburg *Germ*
1,655,700	Warsaw *Poland*
1,633,400	Minsk *Belarus*
1,565,800	Vienna *Austria*
1,342,679	Copenhagen *De*
1,221,000	Sofia *Bulgaria*
1,214,174	Prague *Czech R*
1,174,512	Zagreb *Croatia*
1,168,454	Belgrade *Yugos*
1,091,338	Amsterdam *Ne*
976,883	Helsinki *Finland*
954,045	Brussels *Belgiu*
915,516	Dublin *R. of Irel*
915,000	Riga *Latvia*

Eckert IV Projection

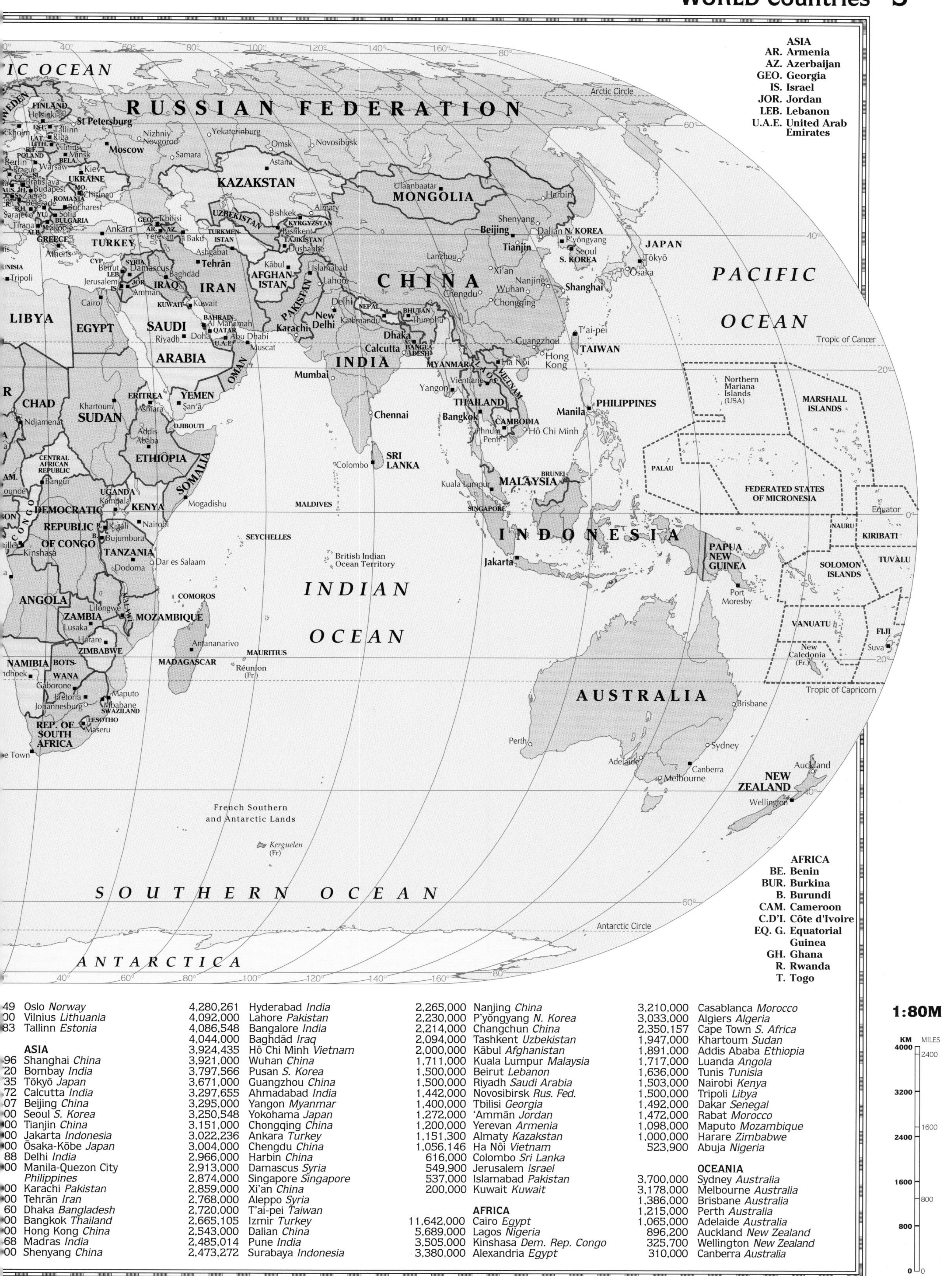

ASIA
AR. Armenia
AZ. Azerbaijan
GEO. Georgia
IS. Israel
JOR. Jordan
LEB. Lebanon
U.A.E. United Arab Emirates

AFRICA
BE. Benin
BUR. Burkina
B. Burundi
CAM. Cameroon
C.D'I. Côte d'Ivoire
EQ. G. Equatorial Guinea
GH. Ghana
R. Rwanda
T. Togo

1:80M

KM   MILES
4000 — 2400
3200 — 1600
2400 —
1600 — 800
800 —
0 — 0

49 Oslo *Norway*	4,280,261 Hyderabad *India*	2,265,000 Nanjing *China*	3,210,000 Casablanca *Morocco*
00 Vilnius *Lithuania*	4,092,000 Lahore *Pakistan*	2,230,000 P'yŏngyang *N. Korea*	3,033,000 Algiers *Algeria*
83 Tallinn *Estonia*	4,086,548 Bangalore *India*	2,214,000 Changchun *China*	2,350,157 Cape Town *S. Africa*
	4,044,000 Baghdad *Iraq*	2,094,000 Tashkent *Uzbekistan*	1,947,000 Khartoum *Sudan*
ASIA	3,924,435 Hồ Chi Minh *Vietnam*	2,000,000 Kābul *Afghanistan*	1,891,000 Addis Ababa *Ethiopia*
96 Shanghai *China*	3,921,000 Wuhan *China*	1,711,000 Kuala Lumpur *Malaysia*	1,717,000 Luanda *Angola*
'20 Bombay *India*	3,797,566 Pusan *S. Korea*	1,500,000 Beirut *Lebanon*	1,636,000 Tunis *Tunisia*
'35 Tōkyō *Japan*	3,671,000 Guangzhou *China*	1,500,000 Riyadh *Saudi Arabia*	1,503,000 Nairobi *Kenya*
'72 Calcutta *India*	3,297,655 Ahmadabad *India*	1,442,000 Novosibirsk *Rus. Fed.*	1,500,000 Tripoli *Libya*
'07 Beijing *China*	3,295,000 Yangon *Myanmar*	1,400,000 Tbilisi *Georgia*	1,492,000 Dakar *Senegal*
'00 Seoul *S. Korea*	3,250,548 Yokohama *Japan*	1,272,000 'Ammān *Jordan*	1,472,000 Rabat *Morocco*
'00 Tianjin *China*	3,151,000 Chongqing *China*	1,200,000 Yerevan *Armenia*	1,098,000 Maputo *Mozambique*
'00 Ōsaka-Kōbe *Japan*	3,022,236 Ankara *Turkey*	1,151,300 Almaty *Kazakstan*	1,000,000 Harare *Zimbabwe*
88 Delhi *India*	3,004,000 Chengdu *China*	1,056,146 Ha Nội *Vietnam*	523,900 Abuja *Nigeria*
'00 Manila-Quezon City	2,966,000 Harbin *China*	616,000 Colombo *Sri Lanka*	
Philippines	2,913,000 Damascus *Syria*	549,900 Jerusalem *Israel*	**OCEANIA**
'00 Karachi *Pakistan*	2,874,000 Singapore *Singapore*	537,000 Islamabad *Pakistan*	3,700,000 Sydney *Australia*
'00 Tehrān *Iran*	2,859,000 Xi'an *China*	200,000 Kuwait *Kuwait*	3,178,000 Melbourne *Australia*
'60 Dhaka *Bangladesh*	2,768,000 Aleppo *Syria*		1,386,000 Brisbane *Australia*
'00 Bangkok *Thailand*	2,720,000 T'ai-pei *Taiwan*	**AFRICA**	1,215,000 Perth *Australia*
'00 Hong Kong *China*	2,665,105 Izmir *Turkey*	11,642,000 Cairo *Egypt*	1,065,000 Adelaide *Australia*
'68 Madras *India*	2,543,000 Dalian *China*	5,689,000 Lagos *Nigeria*	896,200 Auckland *New Zealand*
'00 Shenyang *China*	2,485,014 Pune *India*	3,505,000 Kinshasa *Dem. Rep. Congo*	325,700 Wellington *New Zealand*
	2,473,272 Surabaya *Indonesia*	3,380,000 Alexandria *Egypt*	310,000 Canberra *Australia*

L 2   3   4   5
70°
A S I A

Caspian Sea

U r a l   M o u n t a i n s

Usa

Pechora
Pechora
Mezen
Vychegda
Kama
Kamskoye Vodokhranilishche
Kuybyshevskoye Vodokhranilishche
Volga
Volga
Volga
Volga
Don
Don
Tsimlyanskoye Vodokhranilishche
Elbrus 5642
C A U C A S U S

Barents Sea

Kola Peninsula
White Sea
Lake Onega
Lake Ladoga
Lake Peipus
Rybinskoye Vodokhranilishche
Central Russian Uplands
Valdayskaya Vozvyshennost
Dnieper
Dnieper

Sea of Azov
Crimea
B l a c k   S e a

Ostrov Kolguyev
Chëshskaya Guba
Severnaya Dvina

Oz. Imandra
Inarijärvi
Nordkapp
Lappland
Kemi
Gulf of Finland
Gulf of Riga
Bug
Dniester
Dniester
Danube
Sea of Marmara

Carpathian Mts
Transylvanian Alps
Balkan Mts
Mures
Tisza
Morava
Rôdopi Planina
Pindos
Aegean Sea
Dodecanese

METRES   FEET
5000   16409
3000   9843
2000   6562
1000   3281
500   1640
200   656
SEA   LEVEL
200   656
3000   9843
5000   16409
6000   19686

1:20M

KM   MILES
1200
1000
800
600
400
200
0

Vesterålen
Lofoten
Vestfjorden
Indals
Lule
Ume
Åland
Gulf of Bothnia
Vänern
Vättern
Gotland
Öland
Baltic Sea
Bornholm
Oder
Wisła
Warta
Wisła
Sudety
Elbe
Balaton
Sava
Adriatic Sea
Apennines
Vesuvius 1281
Ionian Sea
Mt Etna 3323
Sicily

S C A N D I N A V I A

Kattegat
Skagerrak
Zealand
Fyn
Weser
Böhmer Wald
Inn
Lac Léman
Mont Blanc 4808
Matterhorn 4478
Alpi Dolomitiche
Po
Lac Constance
A L P S
Tyrrhenian Sea
Corsica
Sardinia
Ligurian Sea

N O R W E G I A N   S E A

Shetland
Faroe Islands
Orkney
Outer Hebrides
Ben Nevis 1344
Penninnes
Great Britain
Snowdon 1085
British Isles
Irish Sea
Thames
English Channel
Channel Islands
Galway Bay
Shannon
Ireland

N O R T H   S E A

Rhine
Maas
Ardennes
Vosges
Jura
Meuse
Marne
Seine
Loire
Allier
Vienne
Saône
Rhine
Moselle
Rhône
Massif Central
Golfe du Lion

A T L A N T I C   O C E A N

Arctic Circle
Snæfell 1833
Vatnajökull
Iceland
Fontur
Faxaflói
Vestmannaeyjar

B a y   o f   B i s c a y

Gulf of Gascony
Pyrenees
Aneto 3404
Ebro
Cabo Fisterra
Cabo de São Vicente
Cantabrian Mts
Douro
Tagus
Sierra Morena
Guadalquivir
Sierra Nevada
Duero

Balearic Is
Menorca
Mallorca
Ibiza

M E D I T E R R A N E A N   S E A

A F R I C A

Albers Equal Area Conic Projection

© Collins

1:20M

KM   MILES
1200
        600
1000
        500
800
        400
600
        300
400
        200
200
        100
0   0

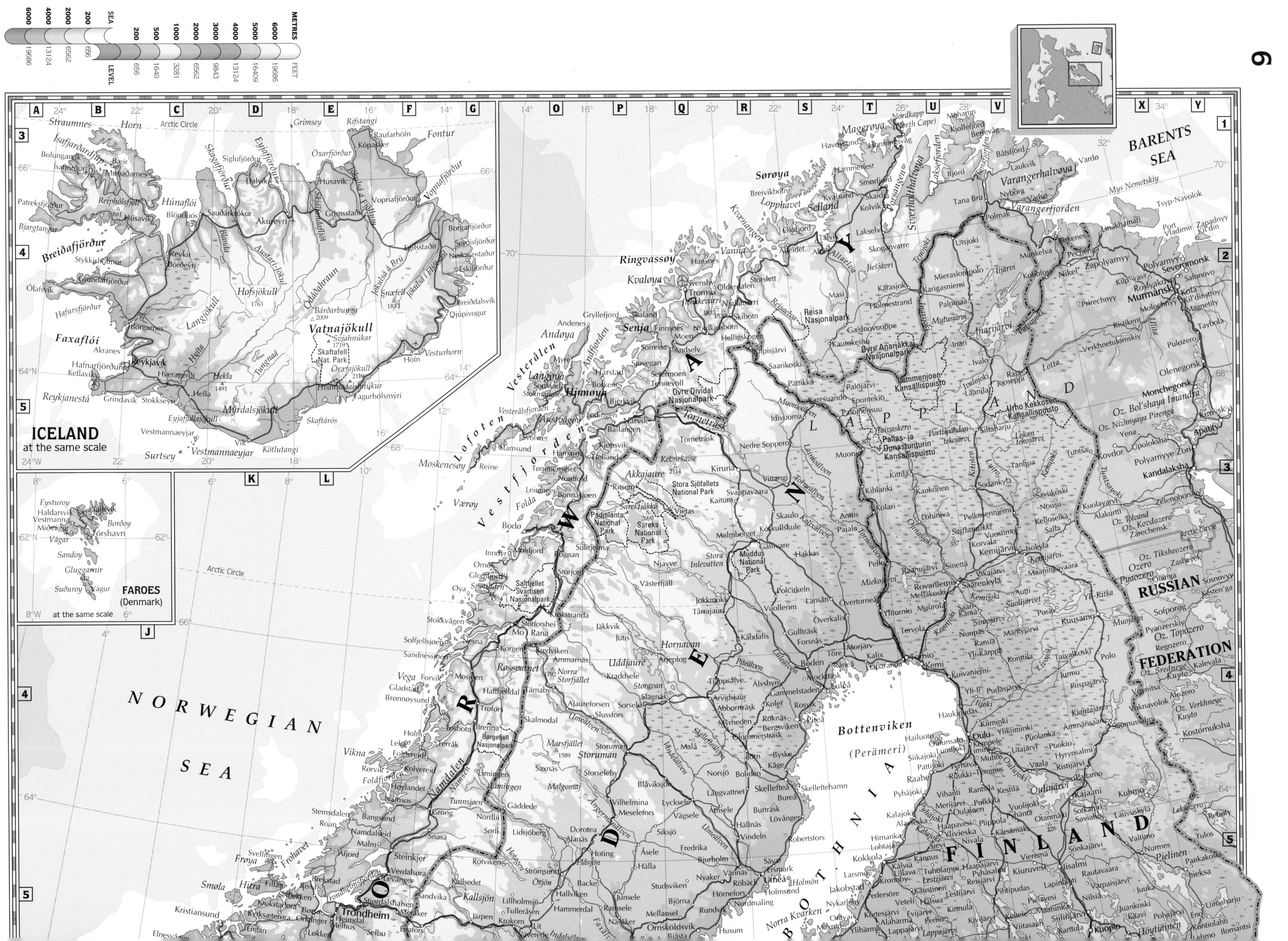

6

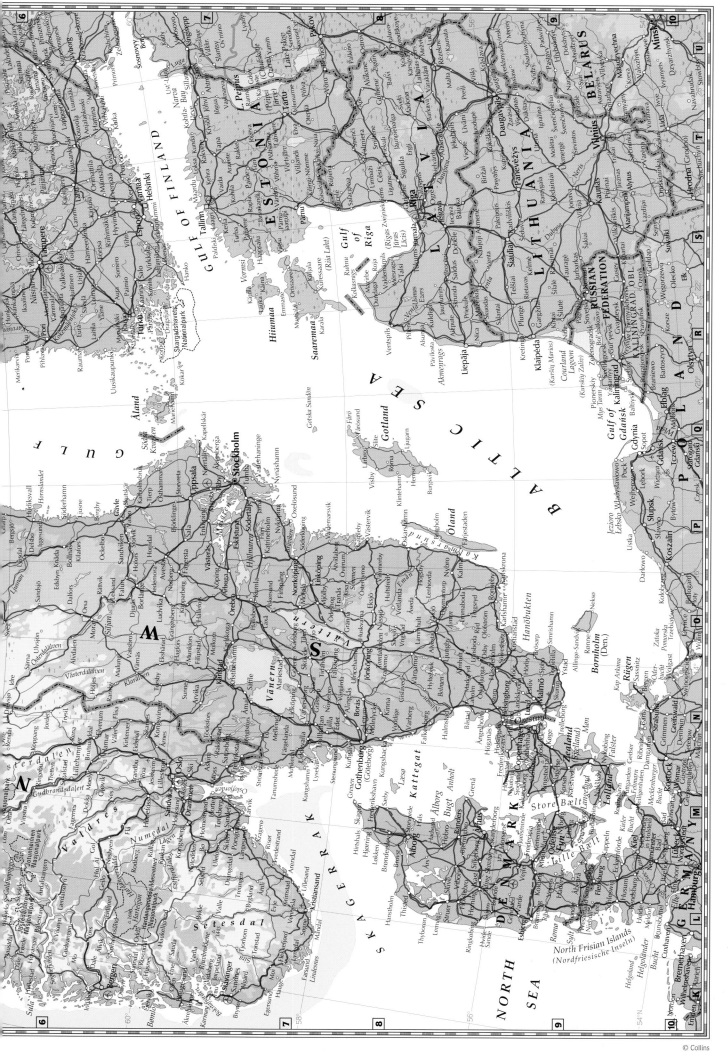

1:5M

KM   MILES

© Collins

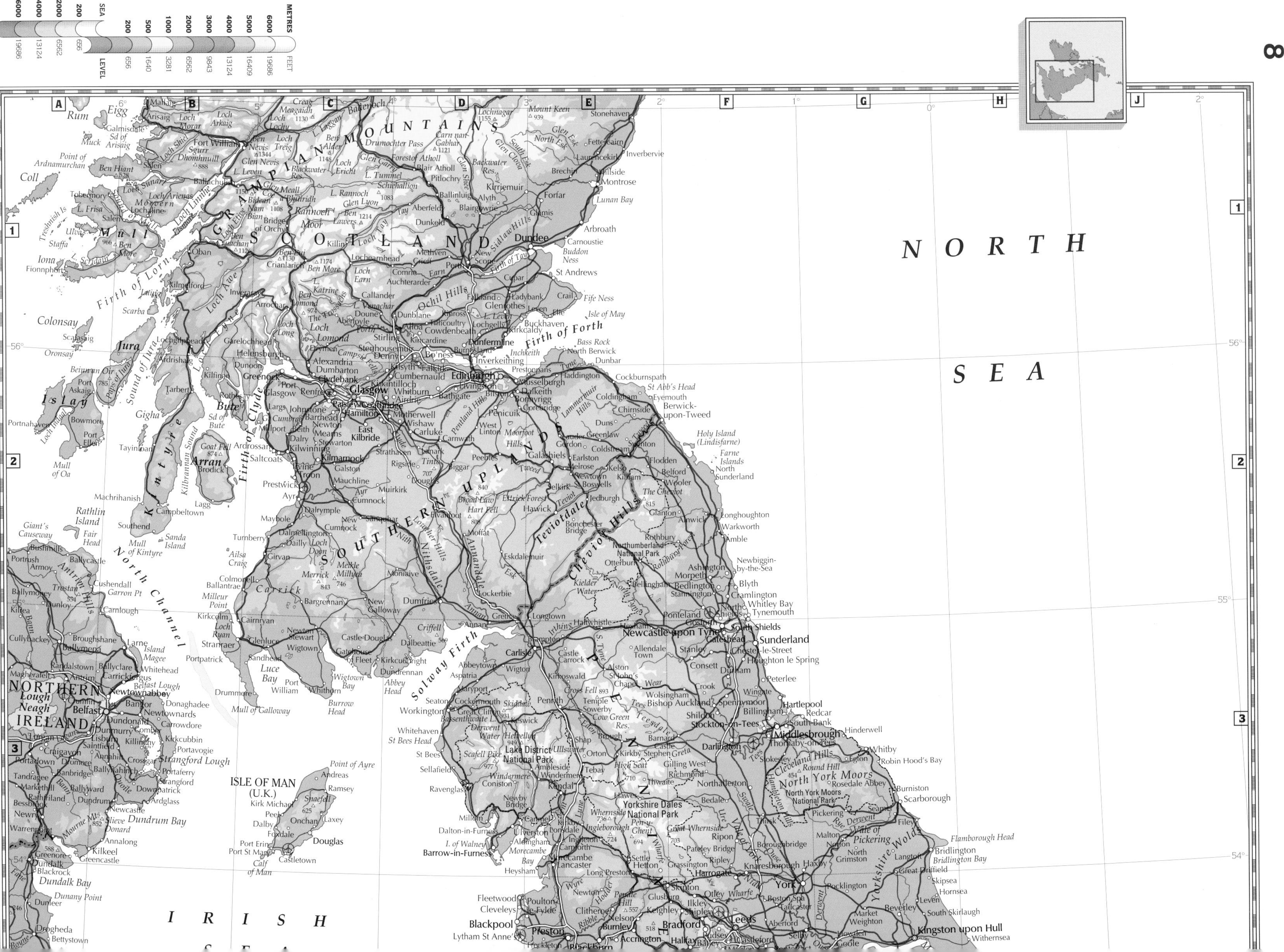

NORTH

SEA

Conic Equidistant Projection

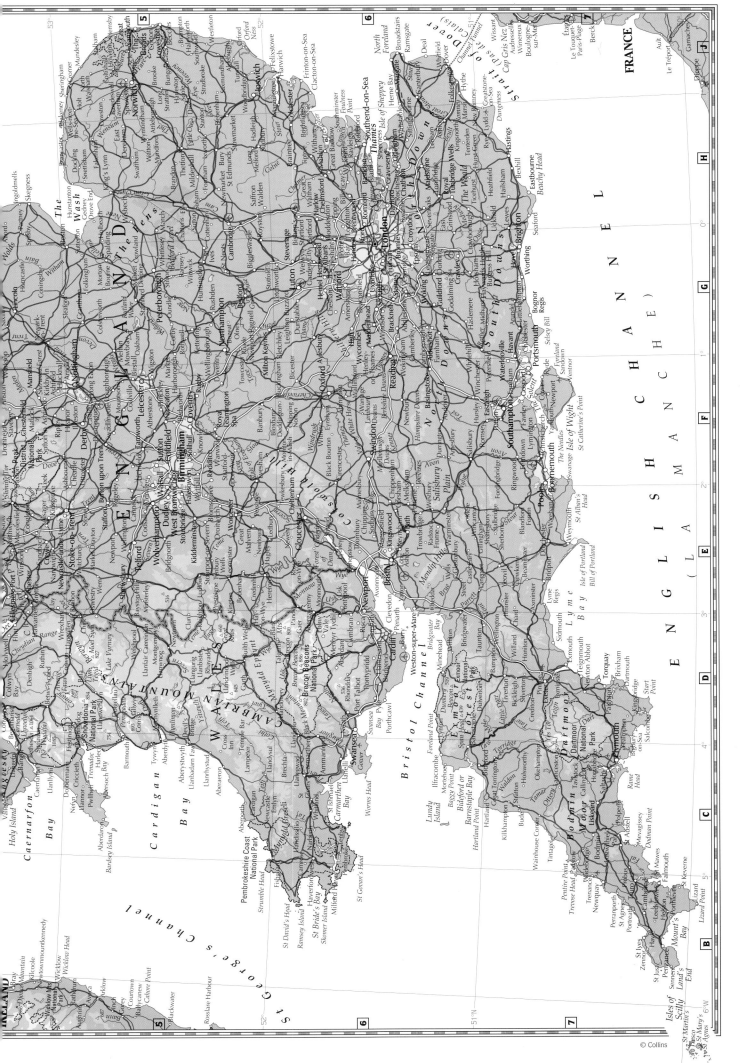

1:2M

KM MILES

© Collins

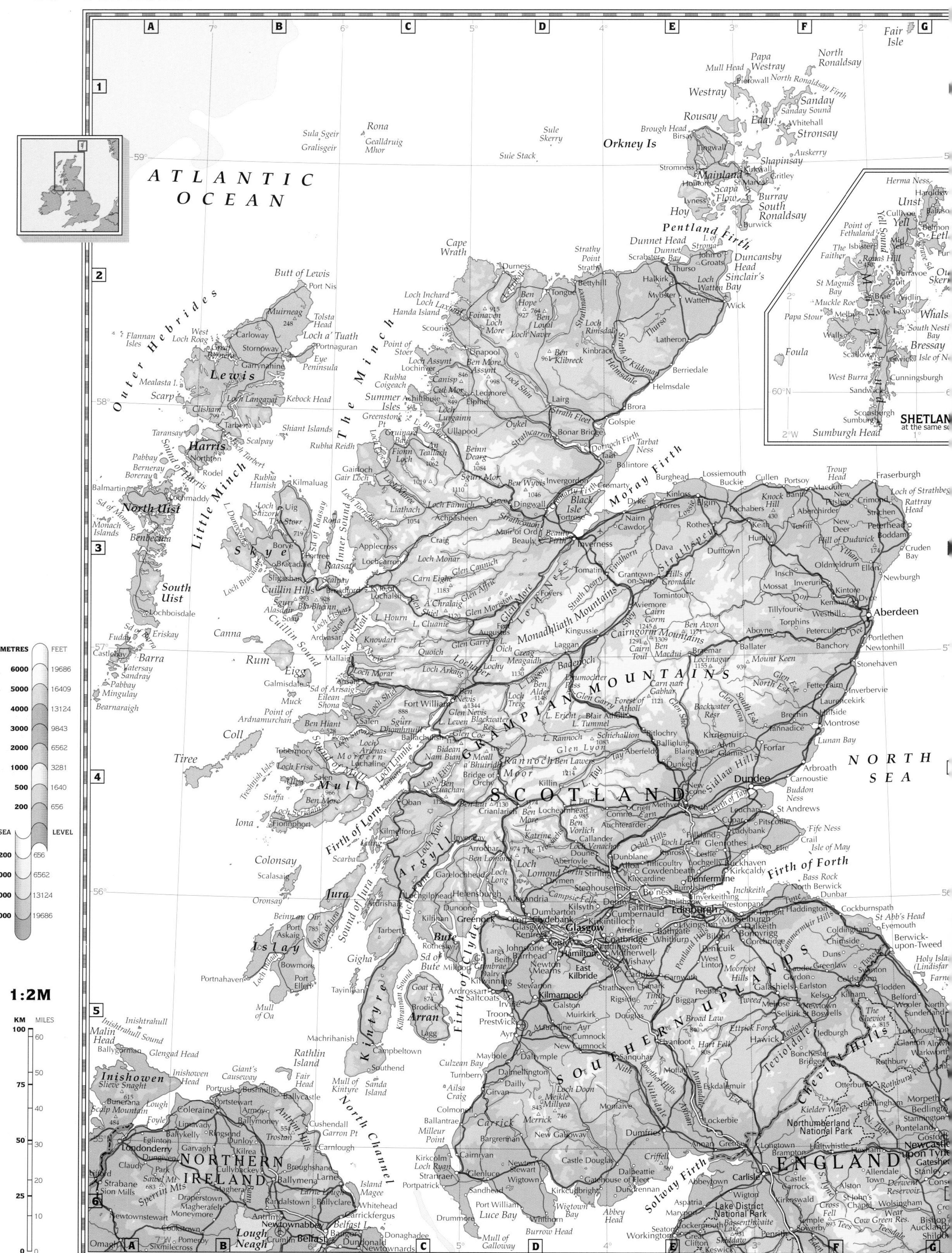

Conic Equidistant Projection

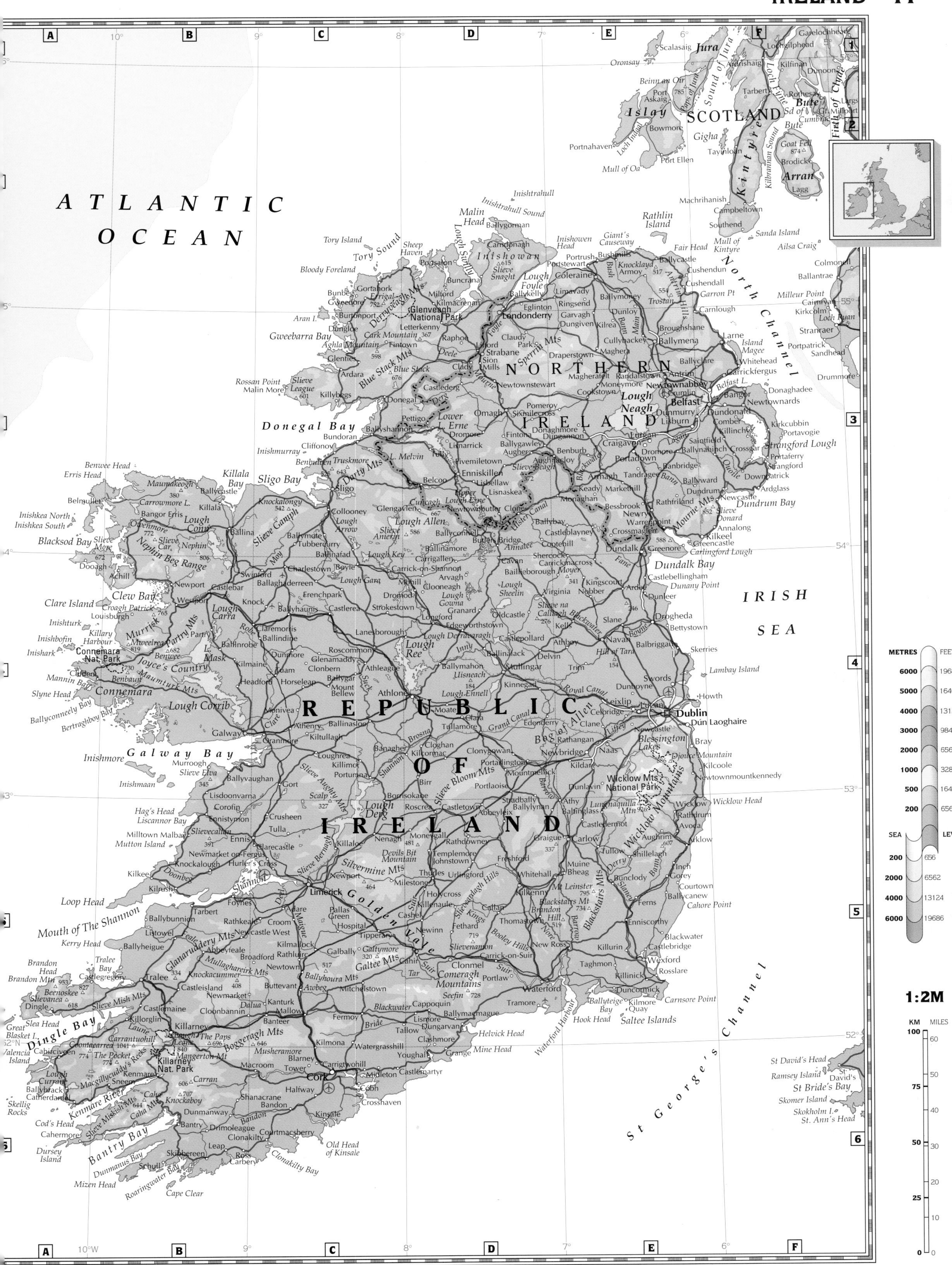
ATLANTIC
OCEAN
IRISH
SEA
NORTHERN
IRELAND
REPUBLIC
OF
IRELAND
SCOTLAND
North Channel
St George's Channel
Jura
Islay
Kintyre
Arran
Bute
Gigha
Mull of Oa
Mull of Kintyre
Rathlin Island
Malin Head
Inishtrahull
Inishtrahull Sound
Tory Island
Tory Sound
Bloody Foreland
Sheep Haven
Inishowen
Lough Foyle
Lough Swilly
Giant's Causeway
Fair Head
Portrush
Portstewart
Coleraine
Ballycastle
Ballymoney
Ballymena
Larne
Carrickfergus
Newtownabbey
Belfast
Belfast L.
Bangor
Newtownards
Donaghadee
Lisburn
Lough Neagh
Antrim
Randalstown
Magherafelt
Cookstown
Dungannon
Omagh
Strabane
Londonderry
Limavady
Dungiven
Sperrin Mts
Armagh
Portadown
Craigavon
Lurgan
Banbridge
Newry
Downpatrick
Strangford Lough
Dundrum Bay
Mourne Mts
Slieve Donard
Kilkeel
Carlingford Lough
Newcastle
Enniskillen
Lower L. Erne
Upper Lough Erne
Letterkenny
Donegal
Donegal Bay
Glenveagh National Park
Derryveagh Mts
Blue Stack Mts
Gweebarra Bay
Aran I.
Killybegs
Bundoran
Ballyshannon
Sligo
Sligo Bay
Killala Bay
Ballina
Lough Conn
Nephin Beg Range
Blacksod Bay
Achill
Clare Island
Clew Bay
Westport
Castlebar
Lough Mask
Lough Corrib
Connemara
Connemara Nat. Park
Maumturk Mts
Joyce's Country
Galway
Galway Bay
Inishmore
Inishmaan
Lough Allen
Carrick-on-Shannon
Roscommon
Athlone
Lough Ree
Longford
Mullingar
Cavan
Monaghan
Dundalk
Dundalk Bay
Drogheda
Navan
Hill of Tara
Skerries
Lambay Island
Swords
Dublin
Dun Laoghaire
Howth
Bray
Wicklow Mts National Park
Wicklow Mountains
Lugnaquilla Mtn
Wicklow
Wicklow Head
Arklow
Gorey
Enniscorthy
Wexford
Rosslare
Carnsore Point
Saltee Islands
Hook Head
Waterford
Tramore
Kilkenny
Carlow
Naas
Kildare
Newbridge
Portlaoise
Tullamore
Birr
Slieve Bloom Mts
Nenagh
Lough Derg
Ennis
Shannon
Limerick
Golden Vale
Galtee Mts
Tipperary
Cashel
Clonmel
Comeragh Mountains
Knockmealdown
Dungarvan
Youghal
Cork
Cobh
Kinsale
Old Head of Kinsale
Clonakilty Bay
Bandon
Macroom
Mallow
Fermoy
Lismore
Killarney
Killarney Nat. Park
Macgillycuddy's Reeks
Carrantuohill
Dingle Bay
Dingle
Tralee
Tralee Bay
Brandon Head
Kerry Head
Listowel
Loop Head
Mouth of The Shannon
Kilkee
Valencia Island
Skellig Rocks
Kenmare River
Bantry Bay
Bantry
Skibbereen
Mizen Head
Cape Clear
Dursey Island
St David's Head
St Bride's Bay
1:2M
METRES
FEET
SEA
LEVEL
KM
MILES

N O R T H

S E A

East Frisian Islands
(Ostfriesische Inseln)

NETHERLANDS

Amsterdam

Rotterdam

The Hague
(Den Haag) ('s-Gravenhage)

Hoek van Holland
(Hook of Holland)

EUROPOORT

BELGIUM

Brussels
Bruxelles

Antwerp

Maastricht

Aachen

Liège

LUXEMBOURG

Luxembourg

ARDENNES

F R A N C E

Paris

Reims

Amiens

METRES	FEET
6000	19686
5000	16409
4000	13124
3000	9843
2000	6562
1000	3281
500	1640
200	656
SEA	LEVEL
200	656
6562
13124
19686

Conic Equidistant Projection

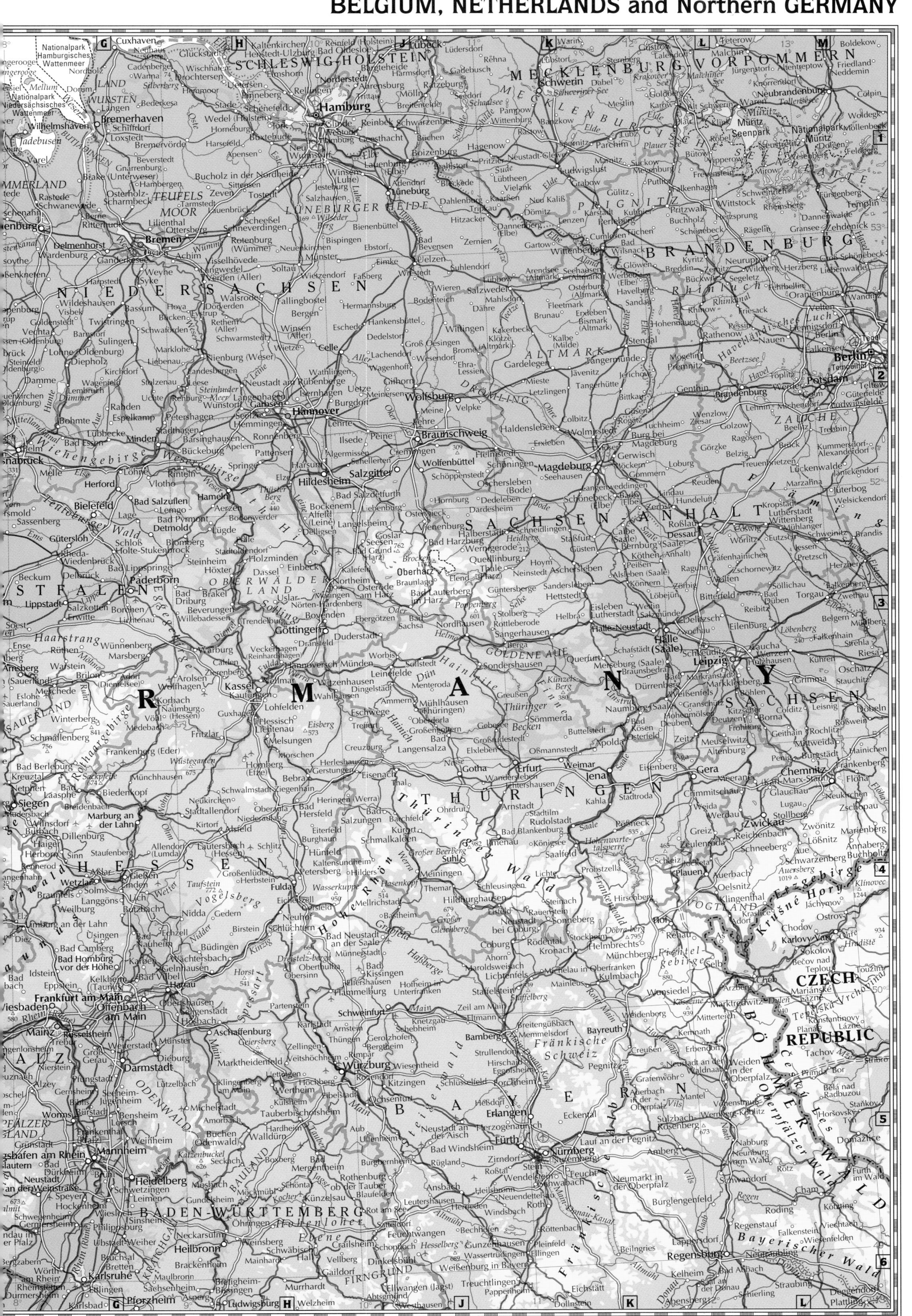
SCHLESWIG-HOLSTEIN
MECKLENBURG-VORPOMMERN
NIEDERSACHSEN
BRANDENBURG
SACHSEN-ANHALT
SACHSEN
THÜRINGEN
HESSEN
BAYERN
BADEN-WÜRTTEMBERG
CZECH REPUBLIC
Hamburg
Bremen
Hannover
Berlin
Magdeburg
Leipzig
Frankfurt am Main
Nürnberg
Würzburg
Regensburg
Erfurt
Kassel
Braunschweig
Mannheim
Heidelberg
Karlsruhe
1:2M
KM
MILES
100
75
50
25
0
60
50
40
30
20
10
0

1:5M

Conic Equidistant Projection

METRES
FEET
6000
19686
5000
16409
4000
13124
3000
9843
2000
6562
1000
3281
500
1640
200
656
SEA
LEVEL
200
656
2000
6562
4000
13124
6000
19686
KM
MILES
BAY OF BISCAY
(MAR CANTÁBRICO)
MEDITERRANEAN SEA
LIGURIAN SEA
English Channel
(La Manche)
Gulf of Gascony
(Golfo de Gascuña)
Strait of Dover (Pas de Calais)
FRANCE
GERMANY
SWITZERLAND
ITALY
SPAIN
BELGIUM
LUXEMBOURG
LIECHTENSTEIN
AUSTRIA
ANDORRA
MONACO
ENGLAND
CHANNEL ISLANDS
(ÎLES NORMANDES)
(U.K)
CORSICA
(CORSE)
(France)
Paris
Lyon
Marseille
Bordeaux
Toulouse
Nantes
Rennes
Brest
Lille
Strasbourg
Dijon
Orléans
Tours
Limoges
Clermont-Ferrand
Grenoble
Montpellier
Toulon
Le Havre
Rouen
Reims
Metz
Nancy
Bern
Zürich
Genève
Turin (Torino)
Milan (Milano)
Genoa (Genova)
Bilbao
Pamplona
Perpignan

BAY OF BISCAY
Gulf of Gascony (Golfo de Gascuña)
ATLANTIC OCEAN
FRANCE
PYRENEES
ANDORRA
SPAIN
PORTUGAL
MEDITERRANEAN SEA
Golfe du Lion
Costa Brava
Golf de Sant Jordi
Golfo de Valencia
Costa Blanca
Costa del Sol
Costa de la Luz
GOLFO DE CÁDIZ
Strait of Gibraltar
MENORCA (MINORCA)
MALLORCA (MAJORCA)
IBIZA (EIVISSA)
Formentera
Balearic Islands (Islas Baleares)
ALGERIA
Madrid
Lisbon (Lisboa)
Barcelona
Valencia
Zaragoza
Bilbao
Seville (Sevilla)
Málaga
Granada
Córdoba (Cordova)
Oporto (Porto)
Toulouse
Marseille
Algiers (Alger)
Oran
1:5M
KM
MILES
METRES
FEET
SEA
LEVEL

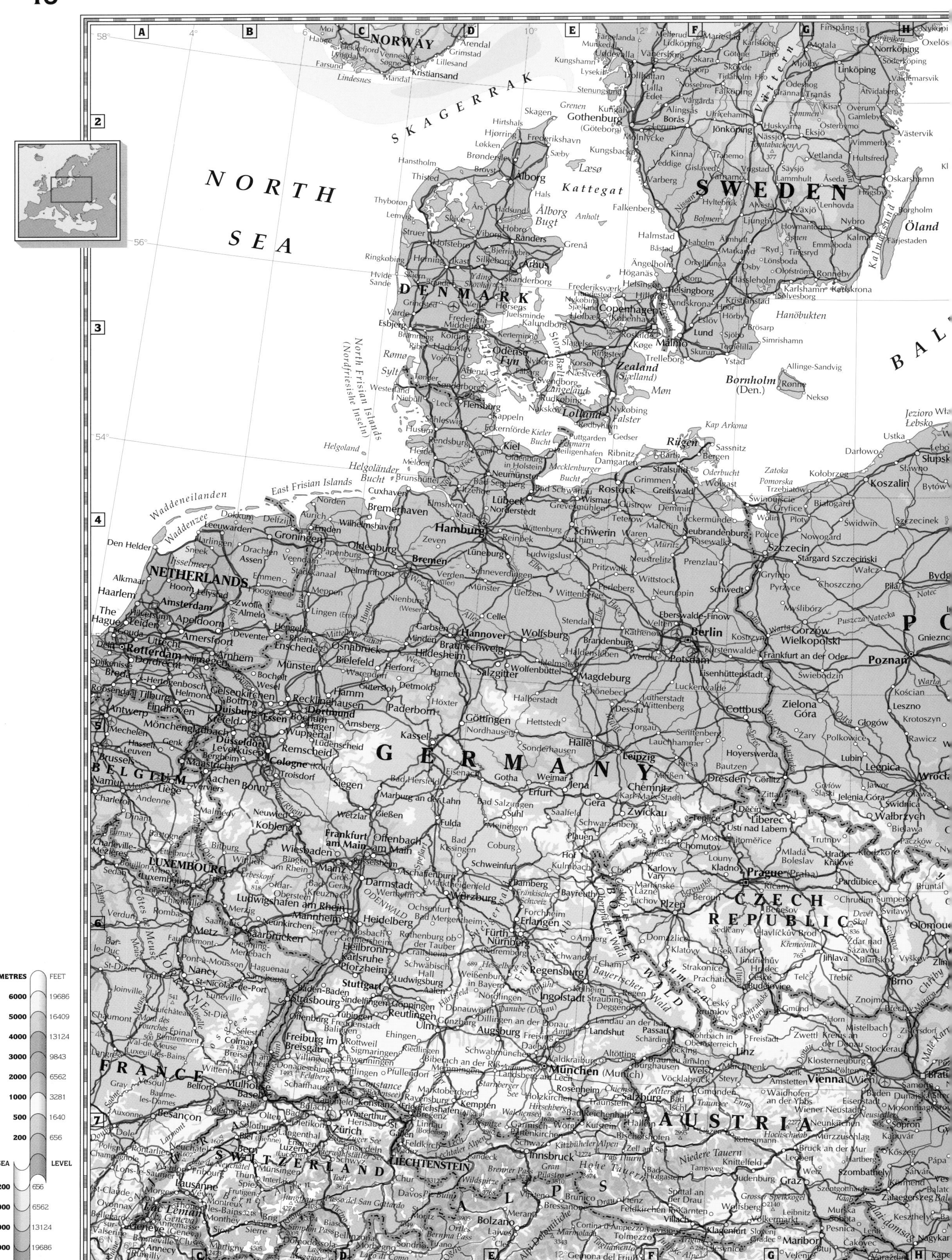

Conic Equidistant Projection

KM MILES

200

300

150

250

200

100

150

100

50

50

0

© Collins

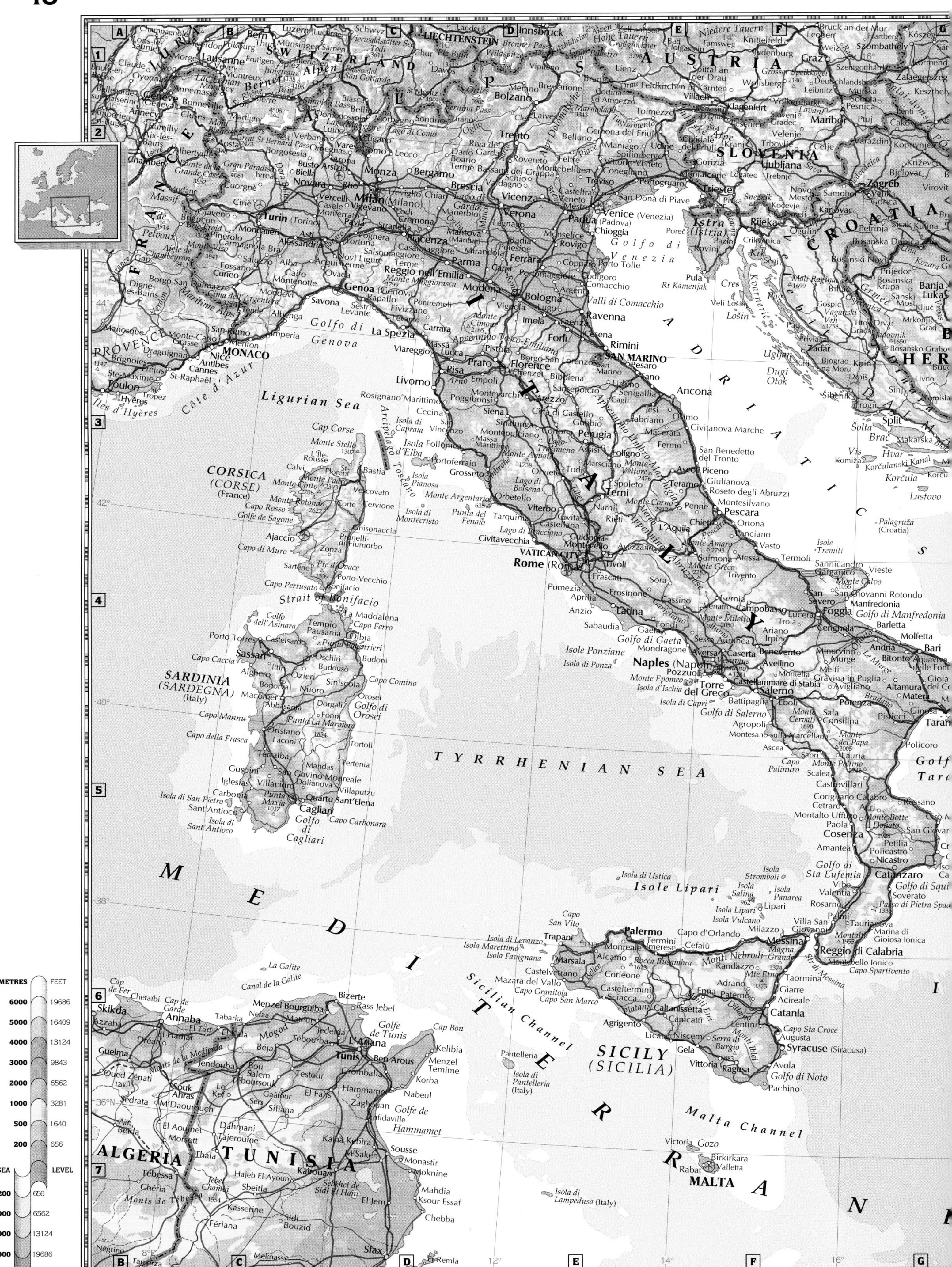

Conic Equidistant Projection

BLACK SEA

AEGEAN SEA

IONIAN SEA

ROMANIA

BULGARIA

YUGOSLAVIA

GREECE

TURKEY

MACEDONIA (F.Y.R.O.M.)

ALBANIA

MOLDOVA

UKRAINE

1:5M

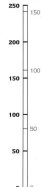

© Collins

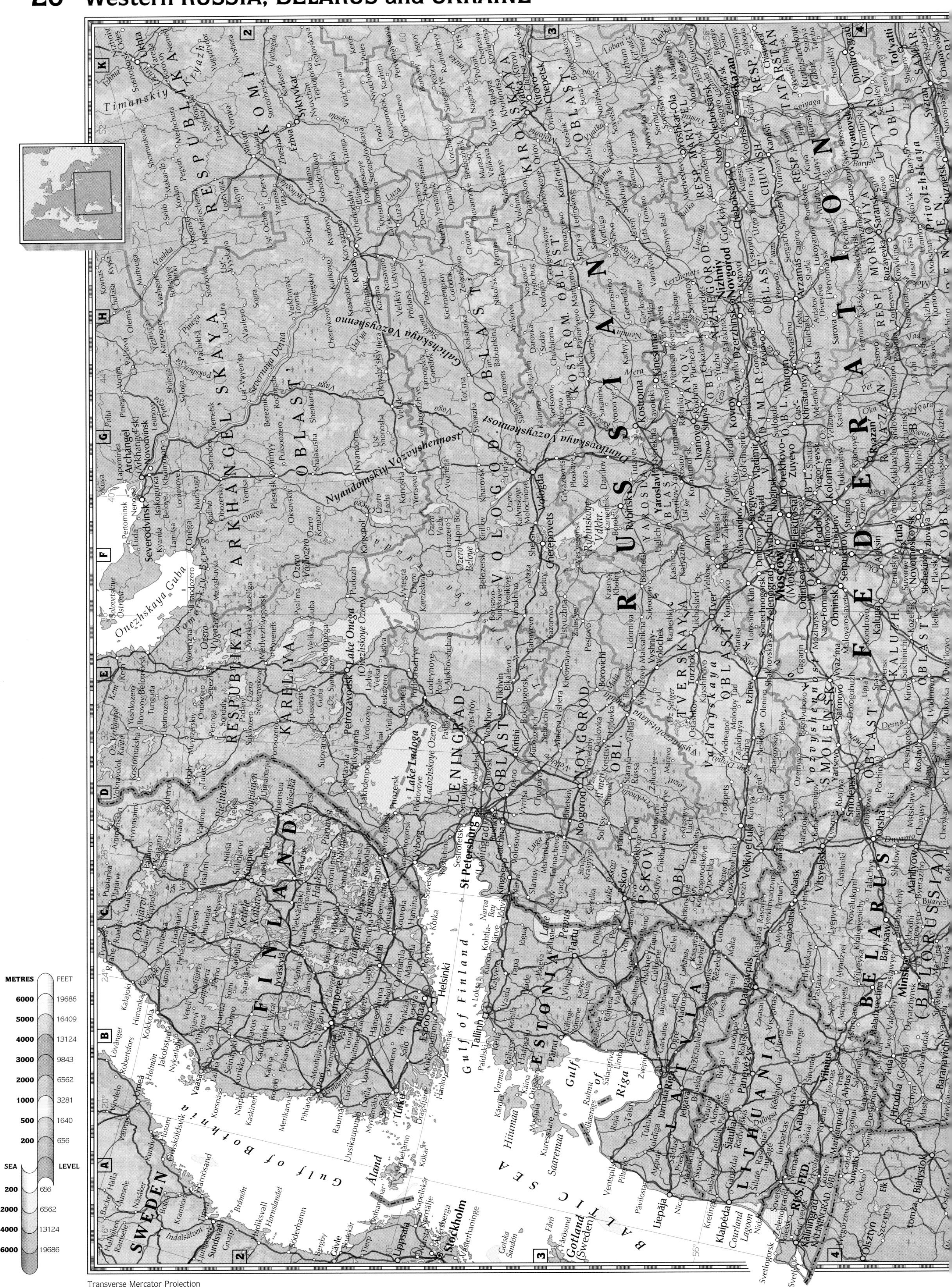

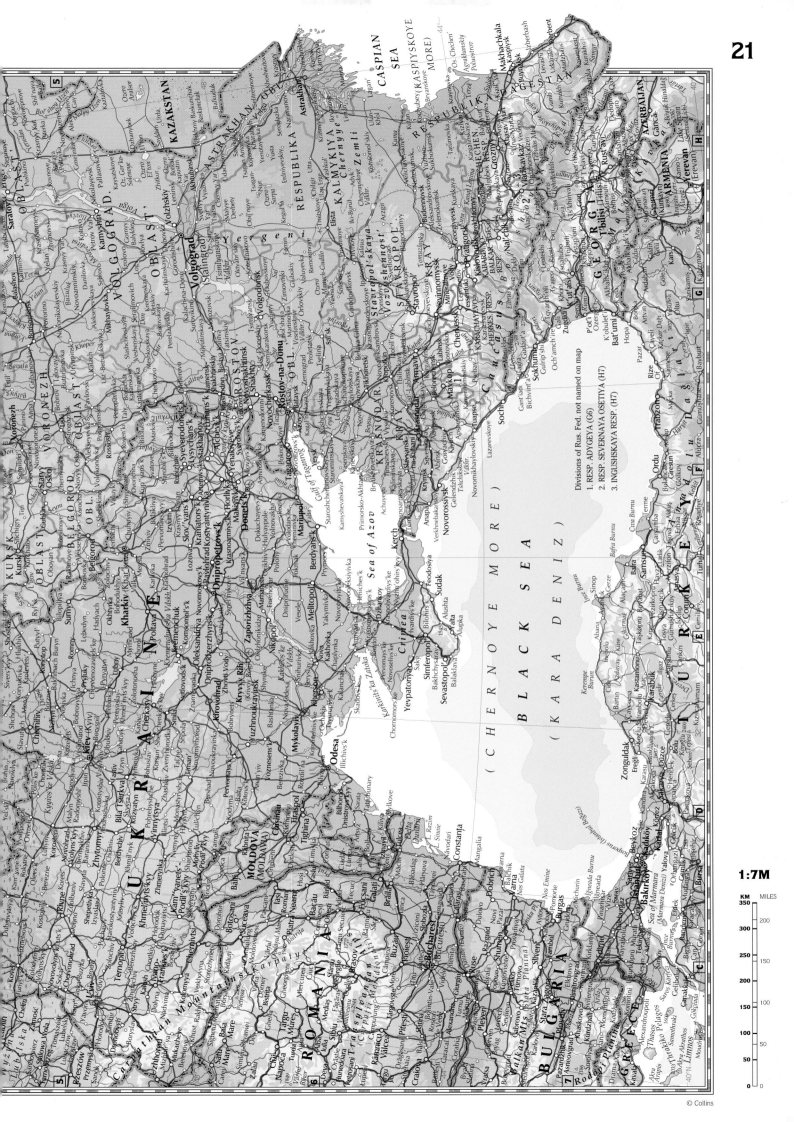

1:7M

Divisions of Rus. Fed. not named on map
1. RESP. ADYGEYA (G6)
2. RESP. SEVERNAYA OSETIYA (H7)
3. INGUSHSKAYA RESP. (H7)

KM   MILES
350
300   200
250
200   150
150   100
100
50
0

METRES | FEET
5000 | 16409
3000 | 9843
2000 | 6562
1000 | 3281
500 | 1640
200 | 656

SEA | LEVEL

200 | 656
3000 | 9843
5000 | 16409
6000 | 19686

1:48M

KM | MILES
2500 | 1500
2000
1500 | 1000
1000
500 | 500
0 | 0

Lambert Azimuthal Equal Area Projection

EUROPE

Bering
Sea

Laptev
Sea

Barents
Sea

ARCTIC OCEAN

Sea
of
Okhotsk

R U S S I A N   F E D E R A T I O N

JAPAN
PACIFIC
OCEAN

Tropic of Cancer

Northern Mariana
Islands

Guam

Koror PALAU

OCEANIA

New
Guinea

EAST
TIMOR

Banda
Sea

Java
Sea

Java

Sumatera

I N D O N E S I A

Borneo

Celebes
Sea

Sulu
Sea

Padang

Palembang

Jakarta

Surabaya

Medan

Bandar Seri
Begawan

BRUNEI

M A L A Y S I A

SINGAPORE

Kuala Lumpur

Davao

PHILIPPINES
Quezon City

Manila

T'ai-pei
TAIWAN
Kao-hsiung

Luzon Strait

Hong
Kong
Macao

South
China
Sea

Hô Chi Minh

V I E T N A M
Ha Nôi

L A O S
Vientiane

CAMBODIA
Phnom Penh

Gulf of
Thailand

THAILAND
Bangkok

MYANMAR
Yangon

Mandalay

Andaman
Sea

BAY OF
BENGAL

SRI LANKA
Colombo

Male
MALDIVES

Chennai

Madurai

Bangalore

Dhārwād

Hyderabad

Mumbai

Pune

Nagpur

Bhopal

I N D I A

Ahmadābād

Karachi

Hyderabad

P A K I S T A N

New Delhi
Delhi

Jaipur
Kanpur
Lucknow

Varanasi
Guwahati
Kathmandu
NEPAL
BHUTAN
Thimphu

BANGLADESH
Dhaka
Calcutta
Chittagong

Mt Everest
8848

TIBET

Ganges

Sutlej

Ludhiana
Lahore
Faisalabad
Islamabad
Kābul

AFGHANISTAN

Mashhad

TURKMENISTAN
Ashgabat

Mary

Tehrān

I R A N

Esfahān

Shīrāz

Kermānshāh

Ahvāz

Baghdād
Basra

IRAQ

Kuwait
KUWAIT

The Gulf

BAHRAIN
Al Manāmah

QATAR
Doha

U.A.E.
Abu Dhabi

O M A N

Muscat

Gulf of Oman

A R A B I A N
S E A

Gulf of Aden

YEMEN

Şan'ā'

Red Sea

Mecca
Medina
Jedda

S A U D I
A R A B I A

Riyadh

JORDAN
Ammān
ISRAEL
Jerusalem
LEBANON
Beirut
Damascus
SYRIA

CYPRUS
Nicosia

Antalya
Konya
Izmir
Ankara

T U R K E Y

Adana

Mosul

Tabrīz

Tigris
Euphrates

AZER.
Baku
ARMENIA
Yerevan
GEORGIA
Tbilisi

Black Sea

Mediterranean Sea

AFRICA

Tropic of Cancer

Equator

Caspian Sea

Volgograd
Astrakhan
okrasnodar

Saratov

Samara

Ufa

Orenburg

St Petersburg
Moscow

Nizhniy
Novgorod
Kazan'

Perm'
Yekaterinburg
Chelyabinsk

Lake
Ladoga

Lake
Onega

Aral
Sea

U Z B E K I S T A N

TAJIKISTAN
Dushanbe

KYRGYZSTAN
Bishkek

Tashkent

Almaty

Astana

Karaganda

Ozero
Balkhash

K A Z A K S T A N

Omsk

Novosibirsk

Barnaul

Tomsk

Novokuznetsk

Krasnoyarsk

Irkutsk

Lake Baikal

SINKIANG

Ürümqi

M O N G O L I A

Ulaanbaatar

INNER
MONGOLIA

C H I N A

Xining

Lanzhou

Chengdu

Chongqing

Guiyang

Kunming

Nanning

Guangzhou

Hengyang

Changsha

Wuhan

Nanchang

Xi'an

Taiyuan

Zhengzhou

Xuzhou

Nanjing

Shanghai

Zibo
Qingdao
Yellow
Sea

Jinan

Huang He

Beijing

Shenyang
Dalian

NORTH
KOREA
Pyongyang

SOUTH
KOREA
Seoul

Changchun

Jilin

Qiqihar

Harbin

Vladivostok

Khabarovsk

Komsomol'sk-na-Amure

Blagoveshchensk

Sapporo

JAPAN
Sendai
Tokyo
Yokohama
Kyoto
Osaka
Kobe
Hiroshima

Sea of
Japan

East
China
Sea

Yangtze

Mekong

Salween

Brahmaputra

Irrawaddy

Lena

Tunguska

Nizhnyaya Tunguska

Yenisey

Ob'

Lena

© Collins

1:48M

KM   MILES
2500   1500

2000
1500   1000

1000
500

500
0   0

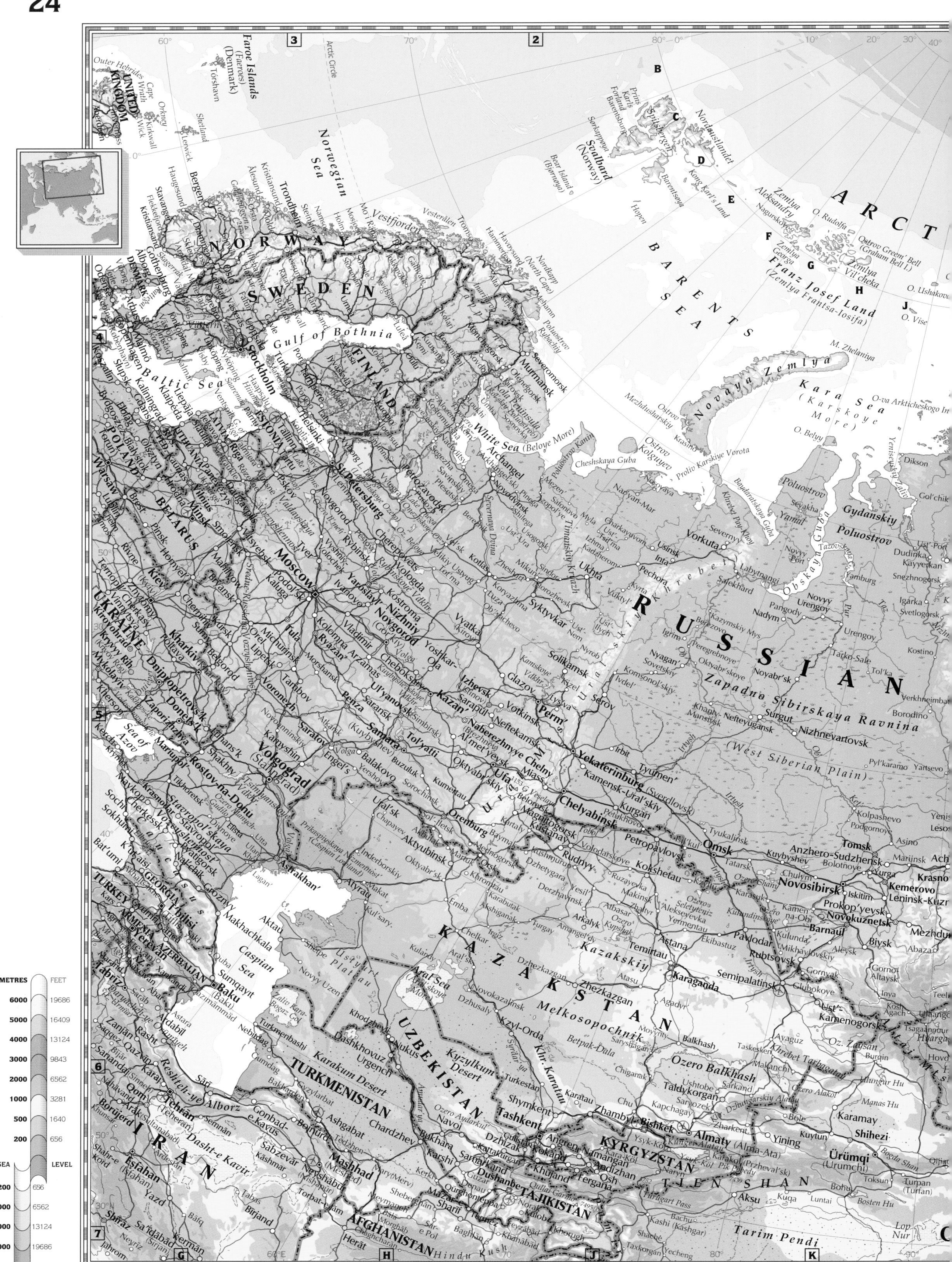

1:21M

KM MILES

1000 600 800 450 600 300 400 150 200 0 0

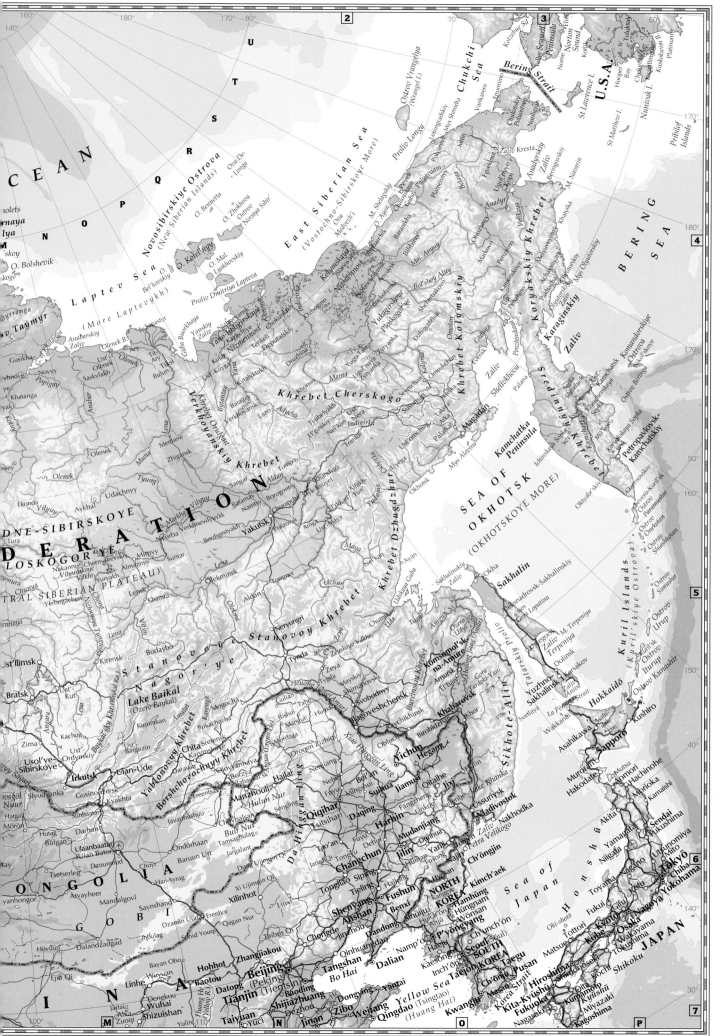

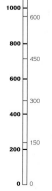

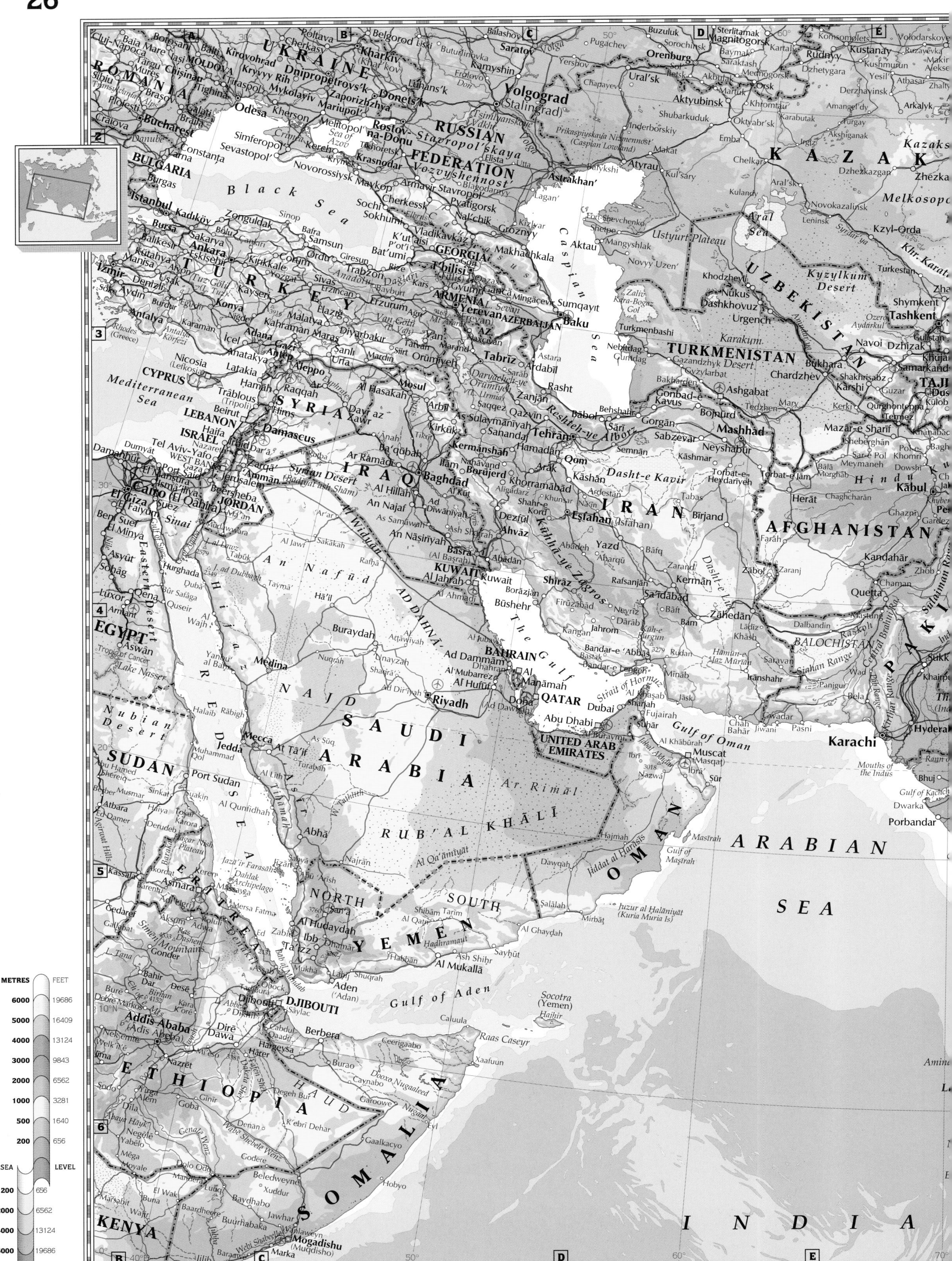

26

Albers Equal Area Conic Projection

METRES		FEET
6000		19686
5000		16409
4000		13124
3000		9843
2000		6562
1000		3281
500		1640
200		656
SEA		LEVEL
200		656
2000		6562
4000		13124
6000		19686

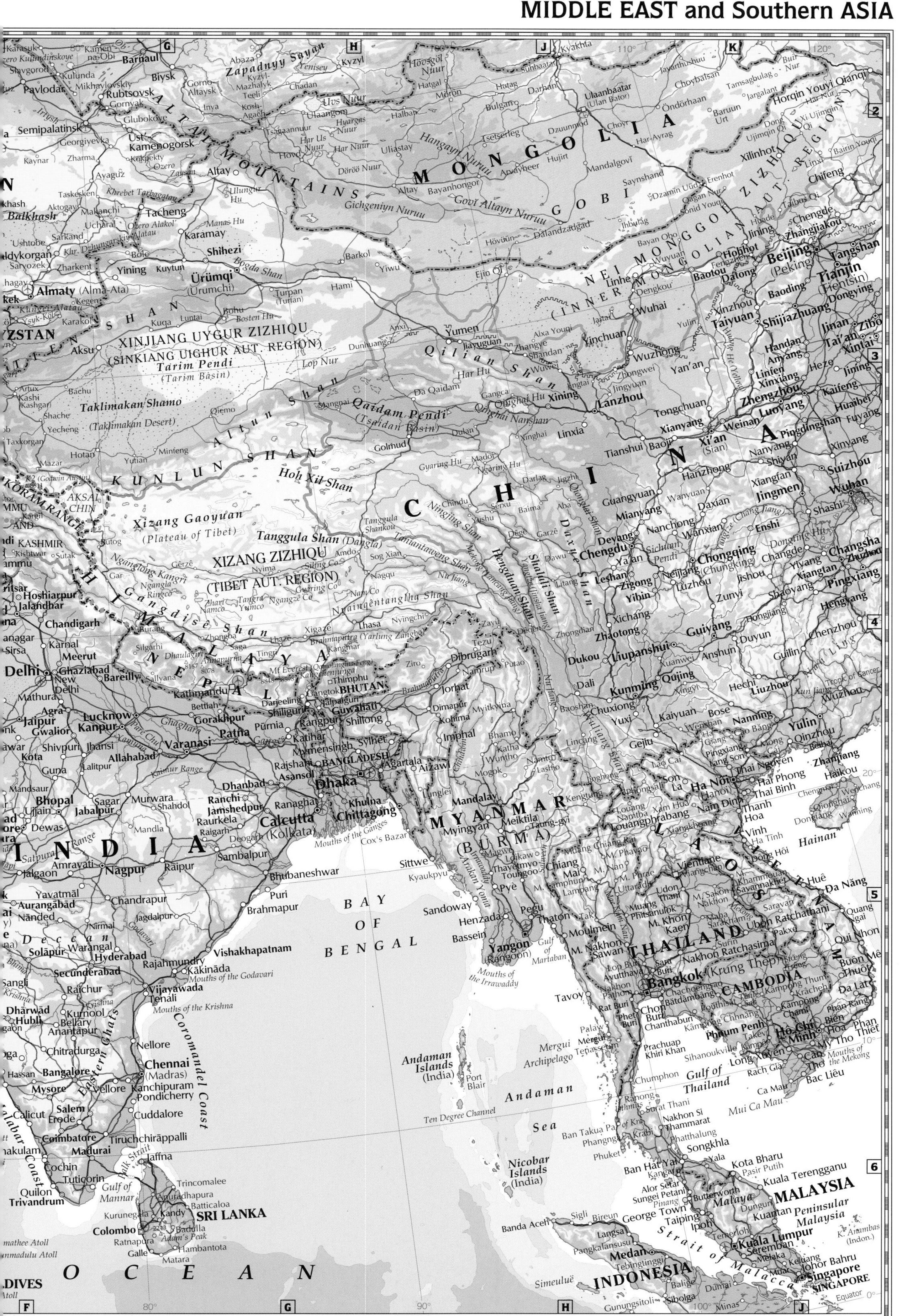

1:20M

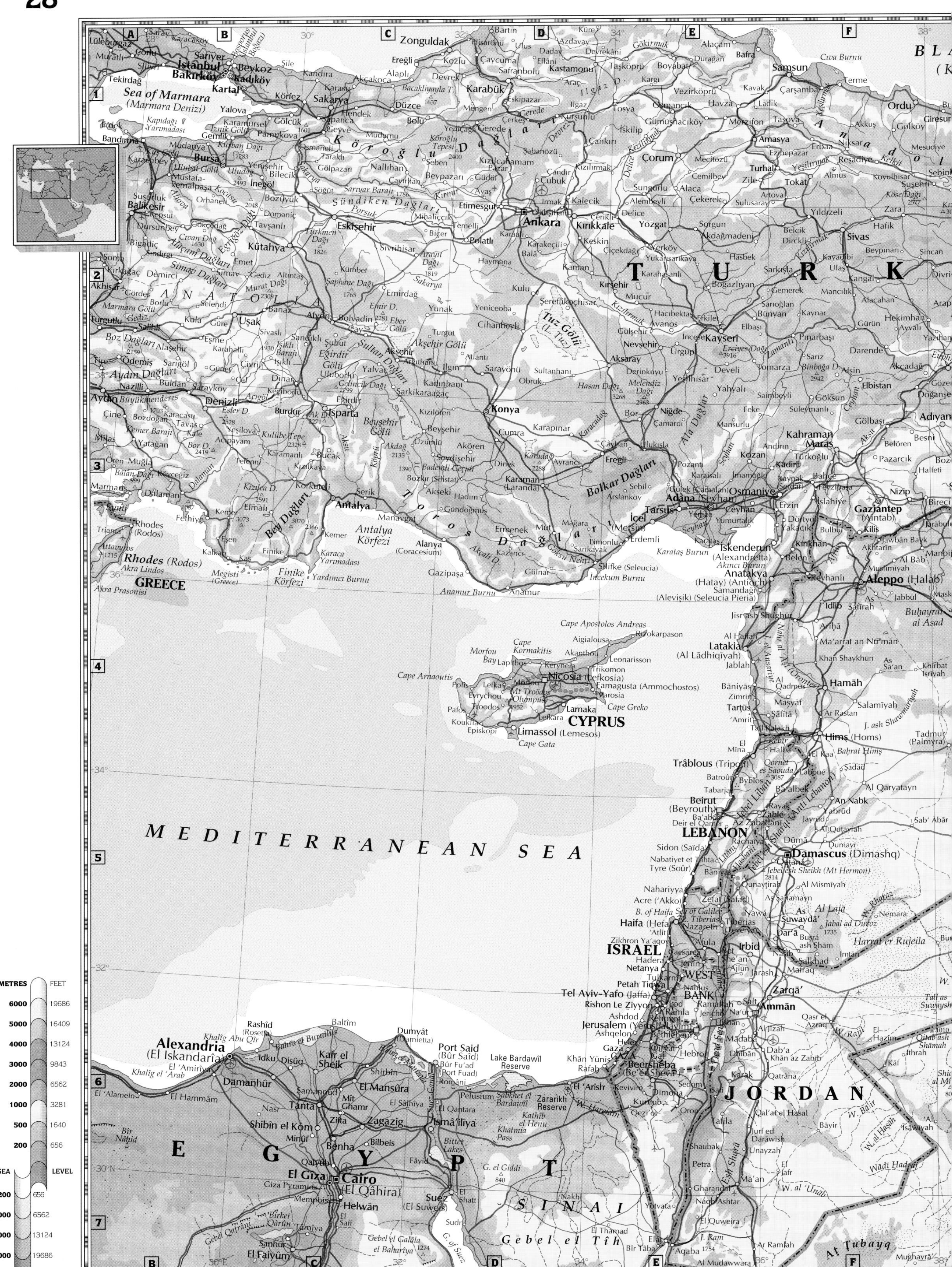

Conic Equidistant Projection

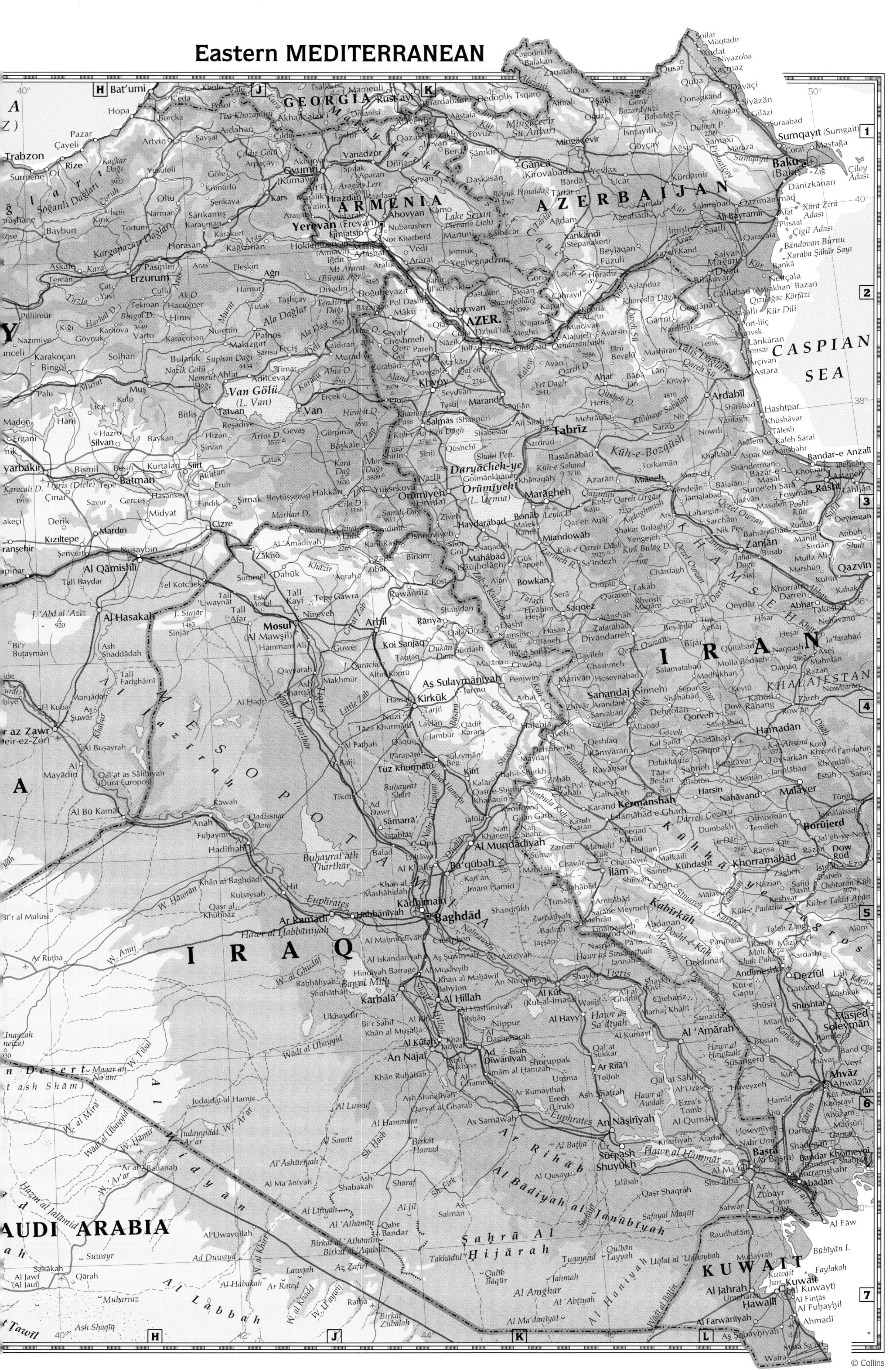
GEORGIA
ARMENIA
AZERBAIJAN
AZER.
IRAN
IRAQ
KUWAIT
SAUDI ARABIA
MESOPOTAMIA
CASPIAN SEA
KHAMSEH
KHALAJESTAN
Tbilisi
Yerevan (Erevan)
Baku (Bakı)
Tabrīz
Baghdād
Mosul (Al Mawşil)
Kirkūk
Arbīl
As Sulaymānīyah
Basra (Al Başrah)
Kuwait (Al Kuwayt)
Van Gölü (L. Van)
Daryācheh-ye Orūmīyeh (L. Urmia)
Orūmīyeh (Urmia)
Erzurum
Kars
Gyumri
Gäncä (Kirovabad)
Sumqayıt (Sumgait)
Ardabīl
Rasht
Qazvīn
Zanjān
Hamadān
Kermānshāh
Sanandaj (Sinneh)
Malāyer
Borūjerd
Khorramābād
Dezfūl
Ahvāz (Ahwāz)
Ābādān
Khorramshahr
Al Hillah
Karbalā'
An Najaf
Al Kūt (Kut-al-Imara)
An Nāşirīyah
Al 'Amārah
Ar Ramādī
Al Qāmishlī
Al Hasakah
Euphrates
Tigris
Kūh-e Bozqūsh
Zagros
Ar Rihāb
Al Bādiyah al Janūbīyah
Şahrā Al Hijārah
Al Labbah
Al Widyān
Al Jazīrah
1:5M
KM
MILES
© Collins

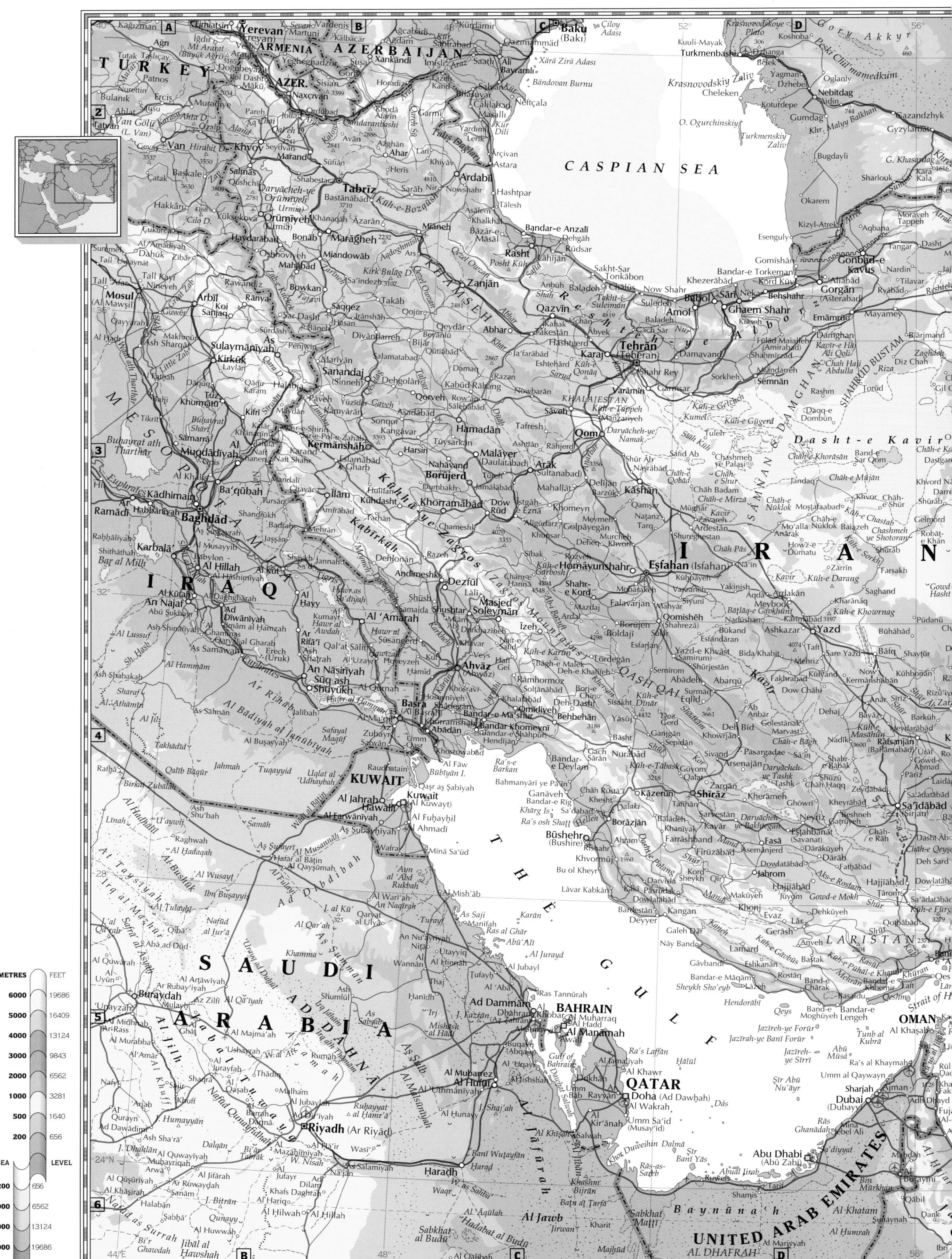

Conic Equidistant Projection

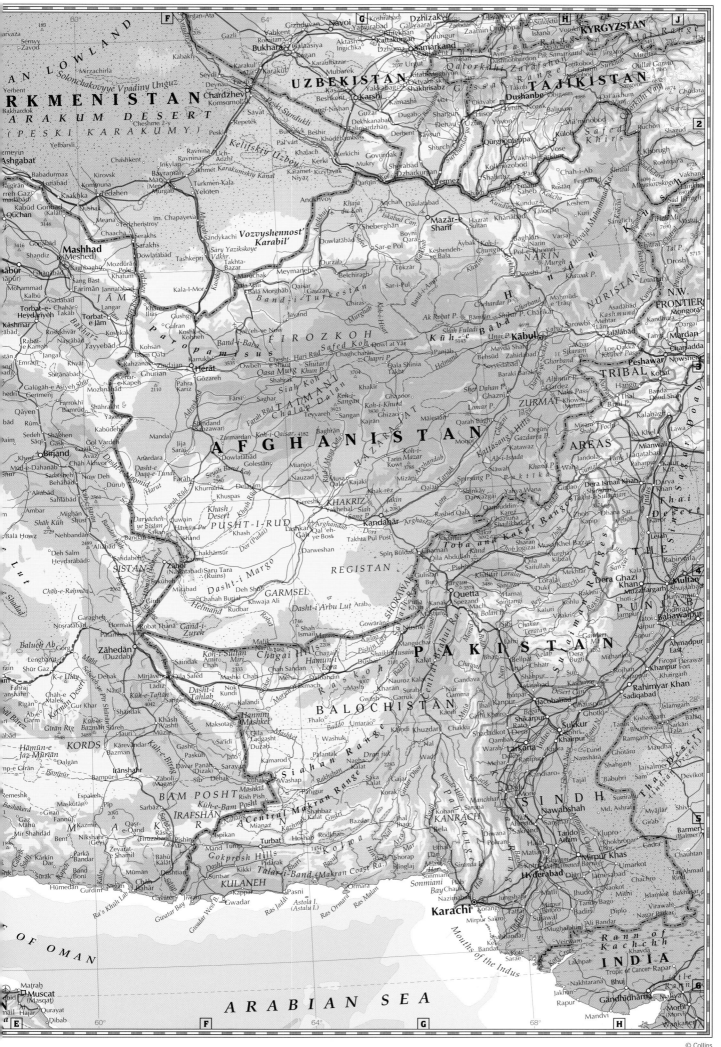

1:7M

KM MILES
350
300 — 200
250 — 150
200
150 — 100
100
50 — 50
0 — 0

© Collins

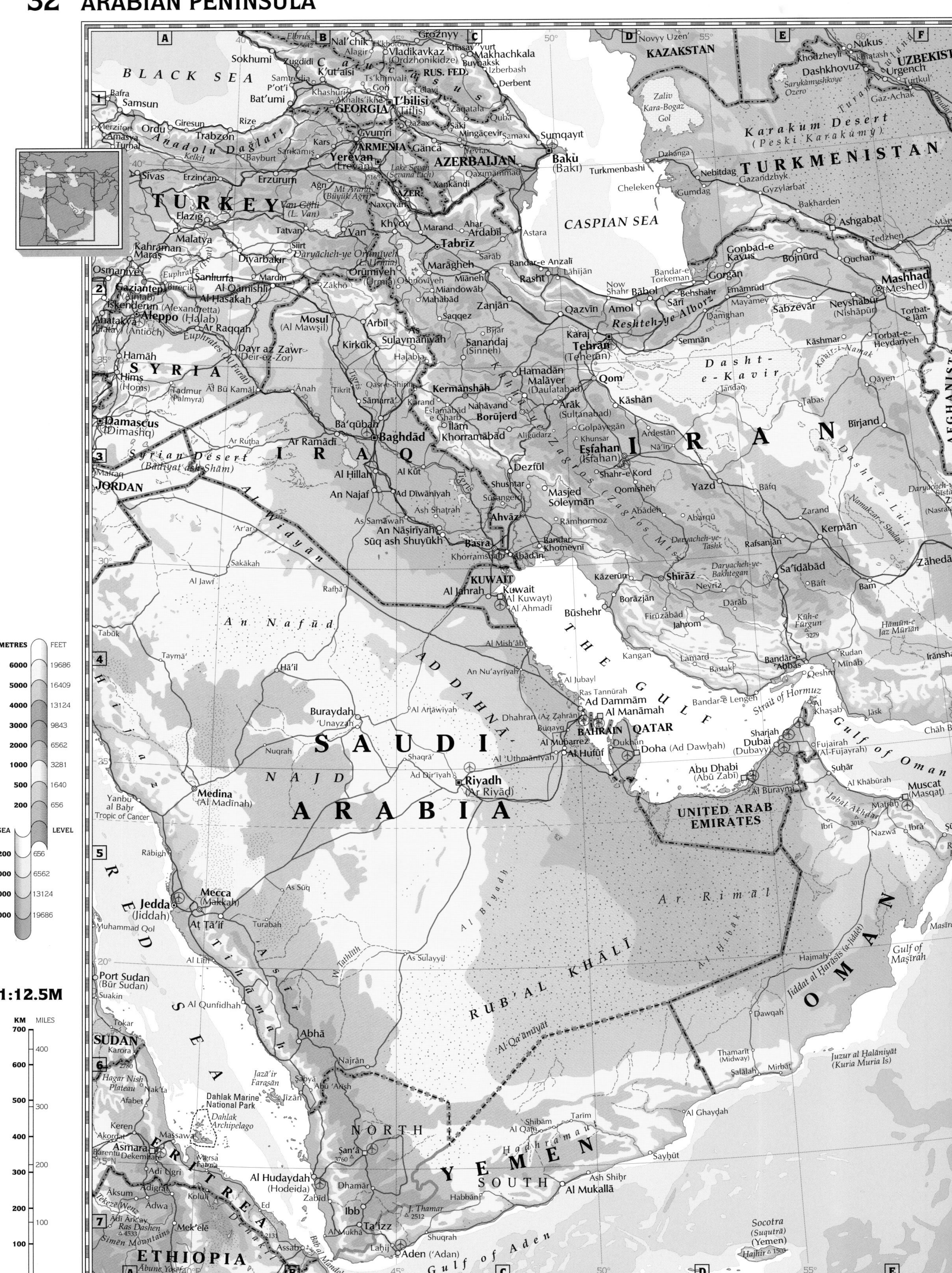

METRES / FEET

6000	19686
5000	16409
4000	13124
3000	9843
2000	6562
1000	3281
500	1640
200	656
SEA	LEVEL
200	656
2000	6562
4000	13124
6000	19686

1:12.5M

KM / MILES

700	
	400
600	
	300
500	
400	200
300	
200	100
100	
0	0

Albers Equal Area Conic Projection

MADHYA PRADESH
MAHARASHTRA
INDIA
ANDHRA PRADESH
KARNATAKA
KERALA
TAMIL NADU
ORISSA
GUJARAT
BIHAR
GOA
SRI LANKA
Ceylon
LAKSHADWEEP
MALDIVES
BAY OF BENGAL
Gulf of Mannar
Palk Strait
Palk Bay
Adam's Bridge
Malabar Coast
Laccadive Islands
Eastern Ghats
Western Ghats
Satpura Range
Vindhya Range
Mahadeo Hills
Ajanta Range
Balaghat Range
Mouths of the Godavari
Mouths of the Krishna
Indore
Vadodara (Baroda)
Surat
Nasik
Aurangābād
Pune (Poona)
Solāpur
Kolhapur
Belgaum
Hubli
Dhārwād
Nagpur
Raipur
Jabalpur
Chandrapur
Nizamabad
Warangal
Secunderabad
Hyderabad
Gulbarga
Bijapur
Kurnool
Guntur
Vijayawada
Rajahmundry
Kākināda (Cocanada)
Vishakhapatnam (Vizagapatam)
Vizianagaram
Nellore
Tirupati
Chennai (Madras)
Pondicherry (Puduchcheri)
Bangalore
Mysore
Mangalore
Calicut (Kozhikode)
Coimbatore
Salem
Tiruchchirāppalli
Thanjavur (Tanjore)
Madurai
Cochin (Kochi)
Alleppey (Alappuzha)
Quilon (Kollam)
Trivandrum (Thiruvananthapuram)
Nagercoil
Kanniyakumari
Cape Comorin (Kanniya Kumari)
Tuticorin
Jaffna
Trincomalee
Anuradhapura
Kandy
Batticaloa
Colombo
Dehiwala-Mount Lavinia
Moratuwa
Galle
Matara (Matturai)
Dondra Head
Minicoy
Thiladhunmathee Atoll
Miladhunmadulu Atoll
Faadhippolhu Atoll
North Maalhosmadulu Atoll
76°E
80°
84°
16°
12°
8°
Indian states not named on map
1. DAMAN & DIU (A1)
2. DADRA & NAGAR HAVELI (A1)
METRES FEET
6000 19686
5000 16409
4000 13124
3000 9843
2000 6562
1000 3281
500 1640
200 656
SEA LEVEL
200 656
2000 6562
4000 13124
6000 19686
1:7M
KM MILES
350 300 250 200 150 100 50 0
200 150 100 50 0
idistant Projection

© Collins

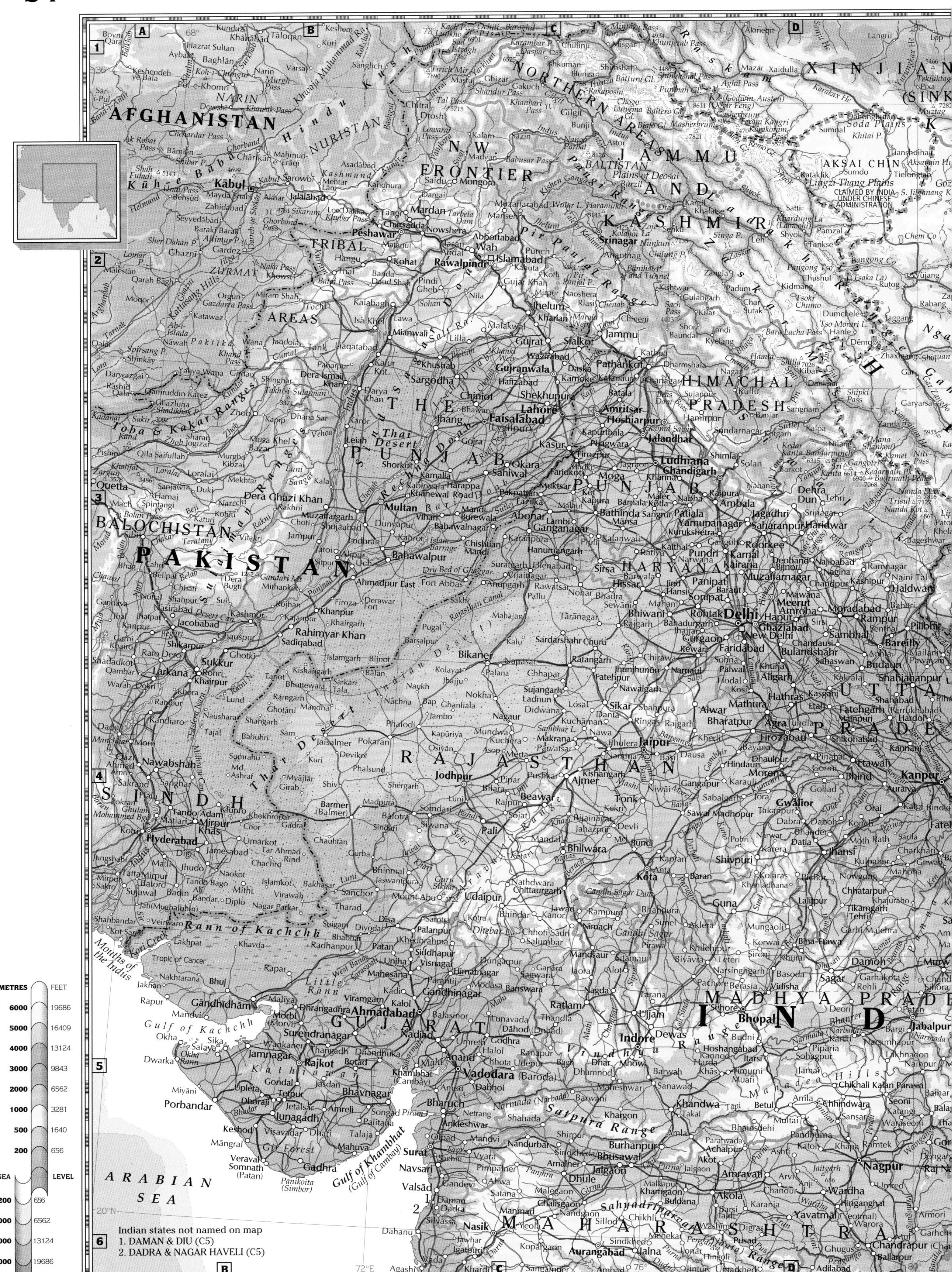

Indian states not named on map
1. DAMAN & DIU (C5)
2. DADRA & NAGAR HAVELI (C5)

Conic Equidistant Projection

CHINA
XIZANG ZIZHIQU
(TIBET AUT. REGION)
XIZANG GAOYUAN
(PLATEAU OF TIBET)
QINGHAI
Hoh Xil Shan
Tanggula (Dangla) Shan
Taniantaweng Shan
NYAINQÊNTANGLHA SHAN
HIMALAYA
NEPAL
Kathmandu
Mt Everest
BHUTAN
SIKKIM
ARUNACHAL PRADESH
ASSAM
MEGHALAYA
NAGALAND
MANIPUR
MIZORAM
TRIPURA
BANGLADESH
Dhaka (Dacca)
Chittagong
BIHAR
Patna
WEST BENGAL
Calcutta (Kolkata)
ORISSA
Bhubaneshwar
Lhasa
Brahmaputra (Yarlung Zangbo)
MYANMAR (BURMA)
Mouths of the Ganges
BAY OF BENGAL
Tropic of Cancer
1:7M
KM
MILES

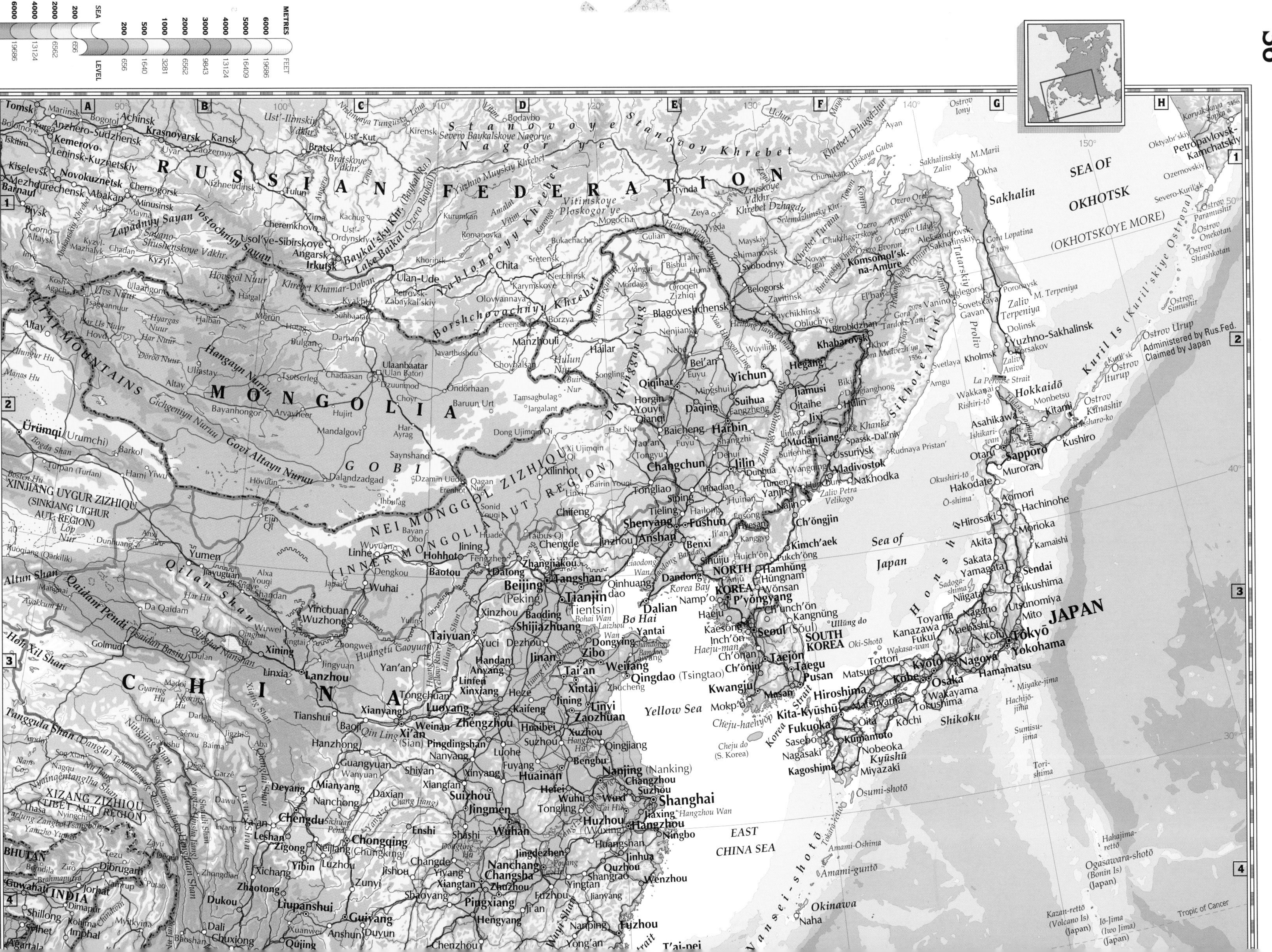

Conic Equidistant Projection

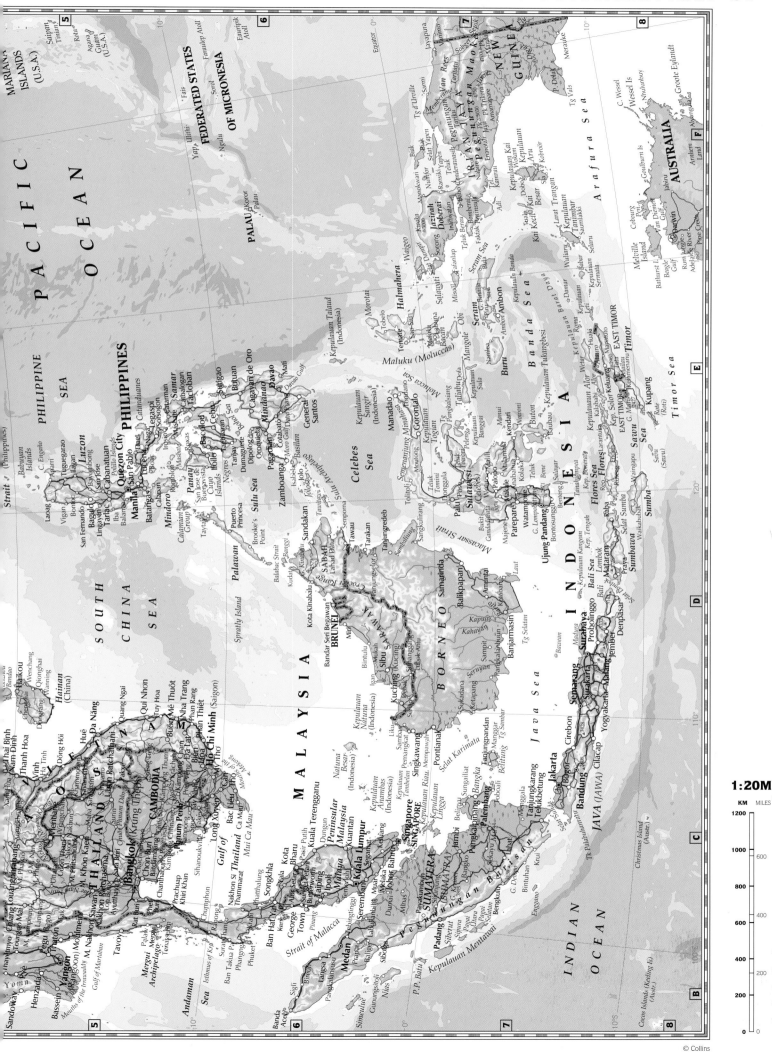

PACIFIC

OCEAN

MARIANA ISLANDS (U.S.A.)
Saipan
Tinian
Rota
Guam (U.S.A.)
Agana

FEDERATED STATES

OF MICRONESIA

Fais
Ulithi
Sorol
Ngulu
Yap
Faraulep Atoll
Eauripik Atoll

PALAU
Koror
Palau

PHILIPPINE

SEA

PHILIPPINES

Luzon
Laoag
Vigan
Bontoc
Baguio
San Fernando
Lingayen
Dagupan
Tarlac
Cabanatuan
Quezon City
Manila
San Pablo
Batangas
Cabanatuan
C. Engaño
Aparri
Tuguegarao
Ilagan
Babuyan Islands
Batan Islands
Strait (Philippines)

Mindoro
Calamian Group
Calapan
Lubang Islands
Polillo Islands
Catanduanes
Naga
Legaspi
Sorsogon
Masbate
Samar
Catbalogan
Tacloban
Romblon
Roxas
Iloilo
Bacolod
Cebu
Panay
San Jose de Buenavista
Cuyo Islands
Negros
Tagbilaran
Dumaguete
Dipolog
Ozamiz
Oroquieta
Pagadian
Cotabato
Zamboanga
Basilan
Jolo
Sulu Archipelago
Tawitawi

Surigao
Butuan
Cagayan de Oro
Davao
General Santos
Mati
Mindanao
Iligan

SOUTH

CHINA

SEA

Spratly Island

Palawan
Puerto Princesa
Brooke's Point
Balabac Strait
Banggi
Kudat

Kepulauan Talaud (Indonesia)
Morotai
Tobelo
Ternate
Halmahera
Tidore
Bacan
Obi
Mangole
Sula
Kepulauan Sula
Buru

Maluku (Moluccas)

Celebes Sea

SABAH
Kota Kinabalu
Crocker Range
Sandakan
Lahad Datu
Tawau
Tarakan
Tanjungselor

BRUNEI
Bandar Seri Begawan
Miri
Bintulu
Mukah
Sibu
Kuching
SARAWAK

BORNEO

Samarinda
Balikpapan
Banjarmasin
Sukadana
Ketapang
Pontianak
Singkawang
Sambas

MALAYSIA

Natuna Besar (Indonesia)
Kepulauan Natuna (Indonesia)
Kepulauan Anambas (Indonesia)
Kepulauan Riau (Indonesia)
Kepulauan Lingga

Singapore
SINGAPORE
Kuala Lumpur
Peninsular Malaysia
Kuantan
Kuala Terengganu
Kota Bharu
Ipoh
George Town
Pinang
Taiping
Butterworth
Melaka
Seremban
Johor Bahru

SUMATERA

Medan
Langsa
Sigli
Banda Aceh

Jambi
Palembang
Pangkalpinang
Bangka
Belitung
Tanjungpandan
Telukbetung
Tanjungkarang
Bengkulu
Padang
Pekanbaru
Dumai

Pematangsiantar
Sibolga

INDONESIA

Manado
Gorontalo
Sulawesi (Celebes)
Palu
Poso
Kendari
Kolaka
Majene
Parepare
Watampone
Ujung Pandang
Selat

Makassar Strait

Java Sea

Semarang
Surabaya
Surakarta
Yogyakarta
Malang
Probolinggo
Jember
Madura
Bandung
Cirebon
Jakarta

JAVA (JAWA)
Cilacap

INDIAN

OCEAN

Christmas Island (Austr.)

Cocos Islands (Keeling Is) (Austr.)

IRIAN JAYA

NEW GUINEA
Jayapura
Merauke
Sarmi
Biak
Manokwari
Sorong
Fakfak
Kaimana

Arafura Sea

Banda Sea

Seram
Ambon
Buru

Kepulauan Aru
Kepulauan Kai
Kepulauan Tanimbar
Dobo

EAST TIMOR
Timor
Kupang
Dili
Kupang
Rote (Roti)

Flores Sea
Flores
Sumbawa
Sumba
Lombok
Bali
Denpasar
Mataram
Bali Sea

Savu Sea

Timor Sea

AUSTRALIA
Darwin
C. Wessel
Wessel Is
Groote Eylandt
Arnhem Land
Melville Island
Bathurst I.
Coburg Pen.
Van Diemen Gulf
Beagle Gulf
Pine Creek

1:20M

KM   MILES
1200
        600
1000
800   400
600
400   200
200
0   0

© Collins

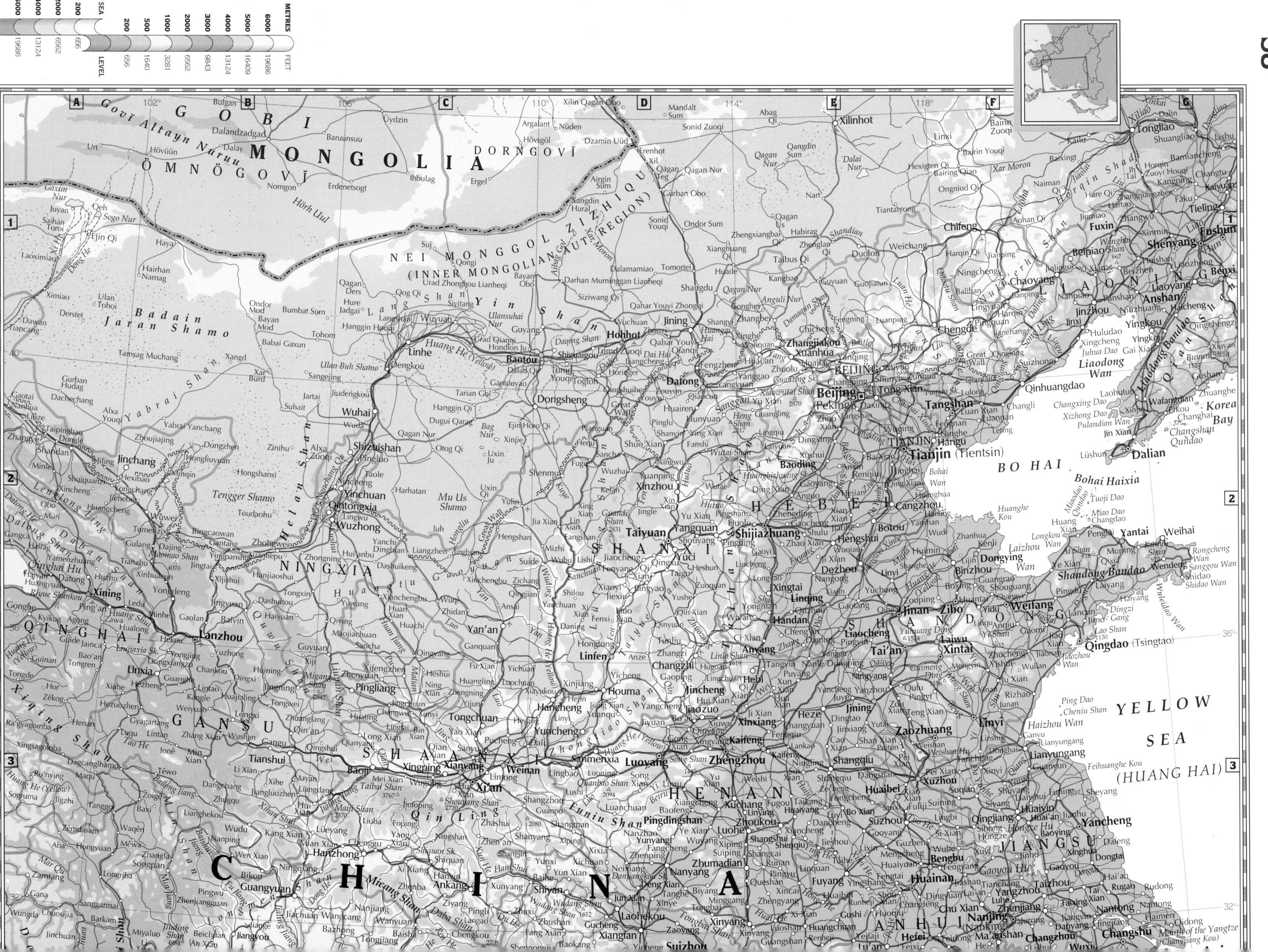

Conic Equidistant Projection

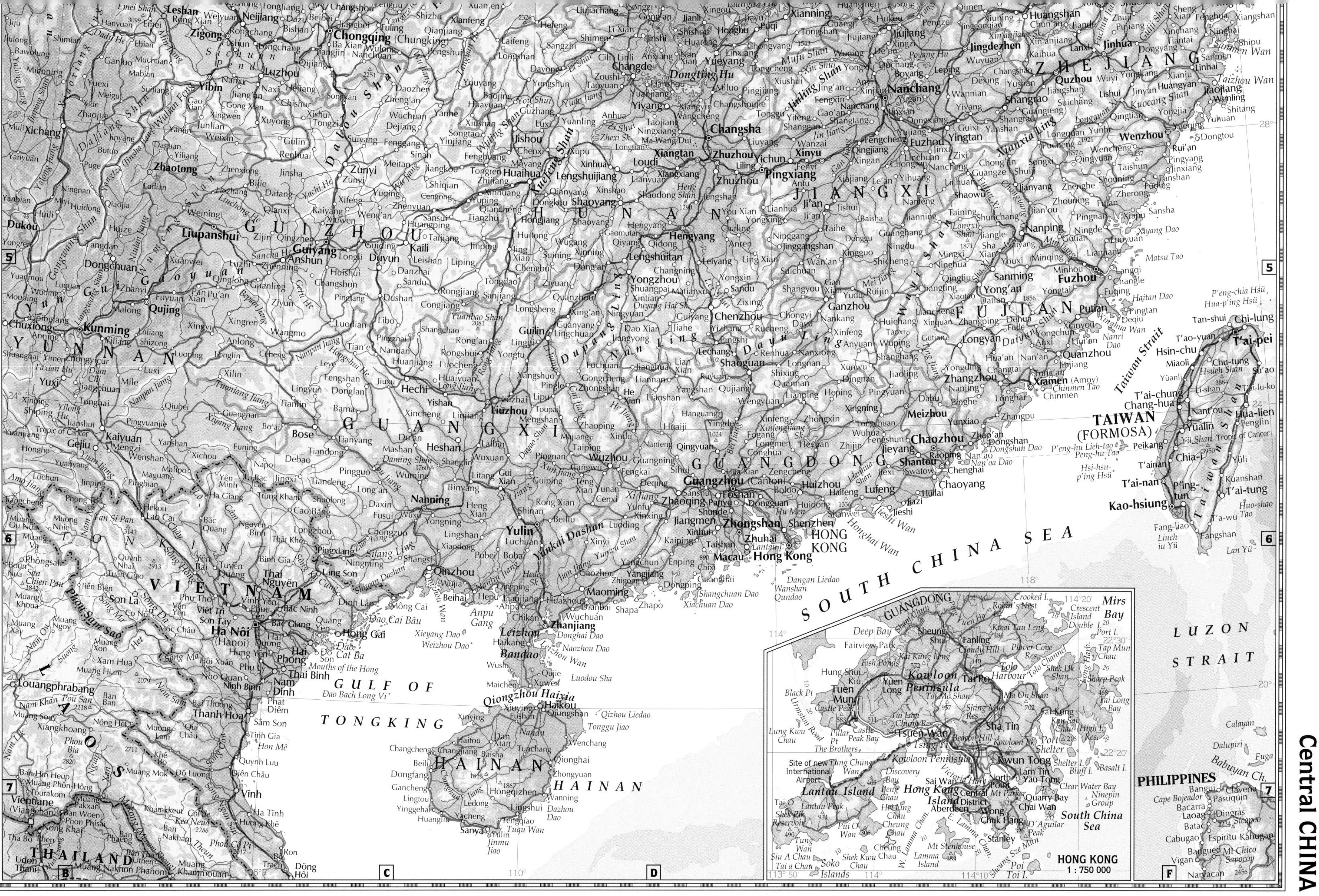

1:7.5M

KM MILES
300
450
375 225
300
150
225
150 75
75
0 0

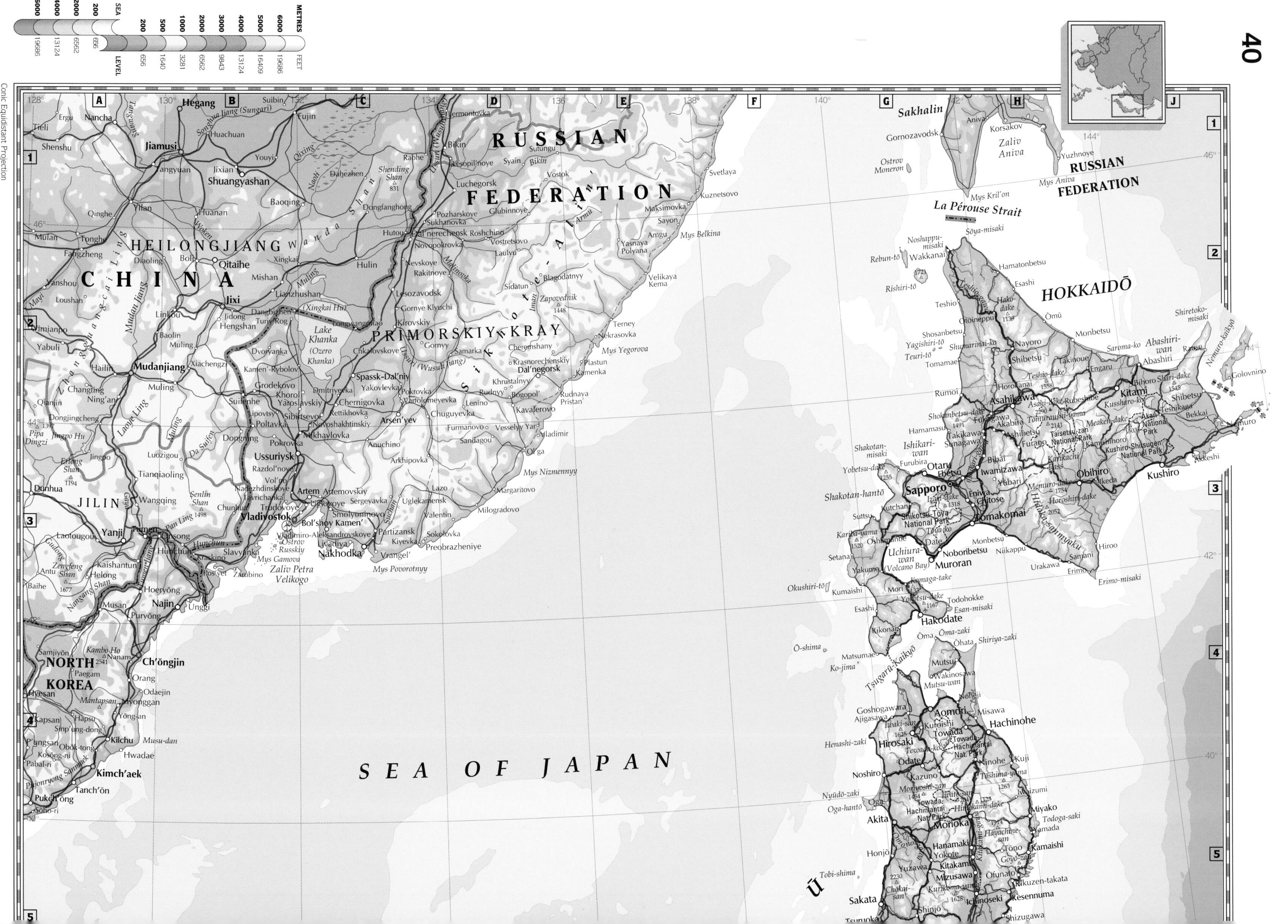

Conic Equidistant Projection

METRES
FEET
6000
19686
5000
16409
4000
13124
3000
9843
2000
6562
1000
3281
500
1640
200
656
SEA
LEVEL
200
656
2000
6562
4000
13124
6000
19686
RUSSIAN FEDERATION
HOKKAIDŌ
Sakhalin
La Pérouse Strait
SEA OF JAPAN
CHINA
HEILONGJIANG
JILIN
NORTH KOREA
PRIMORSKIY KRAY
Sapporo
Asahikawa
Kushiro
Obihiro
Hakodate
Muroran
Otaru
Kitami
Aomori
Hachinohe
Akita
Morioka
Hirosaki
Vladivostok
Nakhodka
Ussuriysk
Lake Khanka
Jixi
Jiamusi
Hegang
Shuangyashan
Qitaihe
Mudanjiang
Yanji
Ch'ŏngjin
Kimch'aek
Dal'negorsk
Artem
Spassk-Dal'niy
Arsen'yev
Lesozavodsk
Luchegorsk
Bikin
Korsakov
Zaliv Aniva
Wakkanai
Rishiri-tō
Rebun-tō
Okushiri-tō
Shakotan-hantō
Tsugaru-kaikyō
Abashiri
Nemuro-kaikyō
Hidaka-sanmyaku
Uchiura-wan (Volcano Bay)

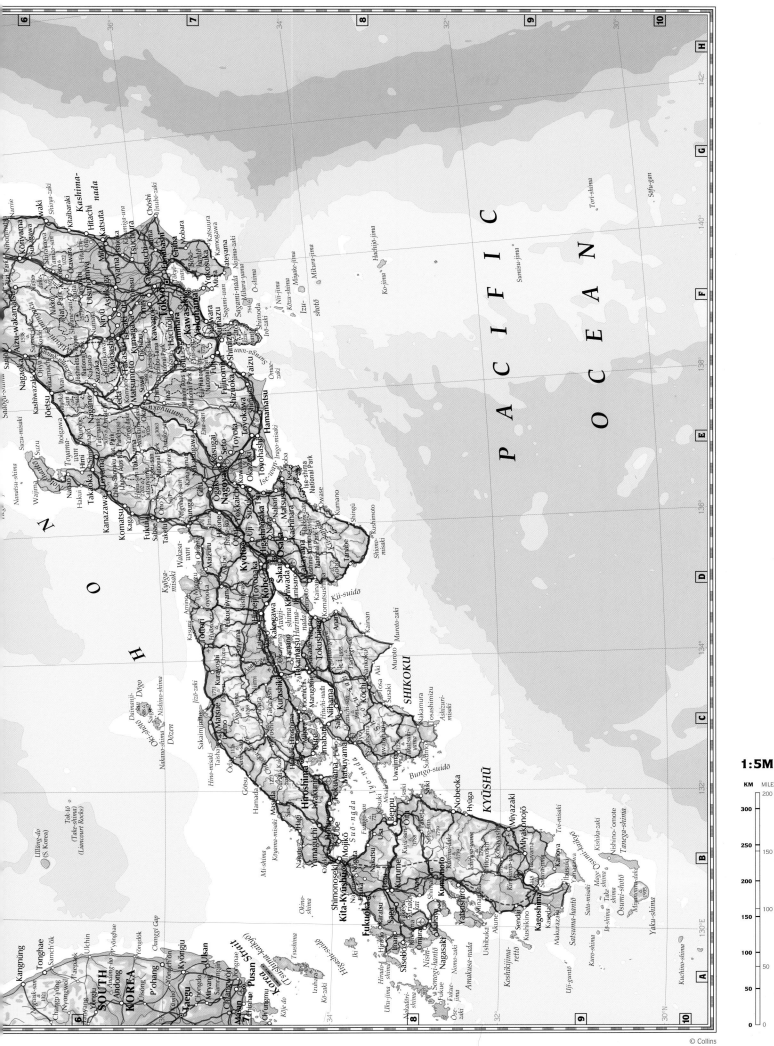

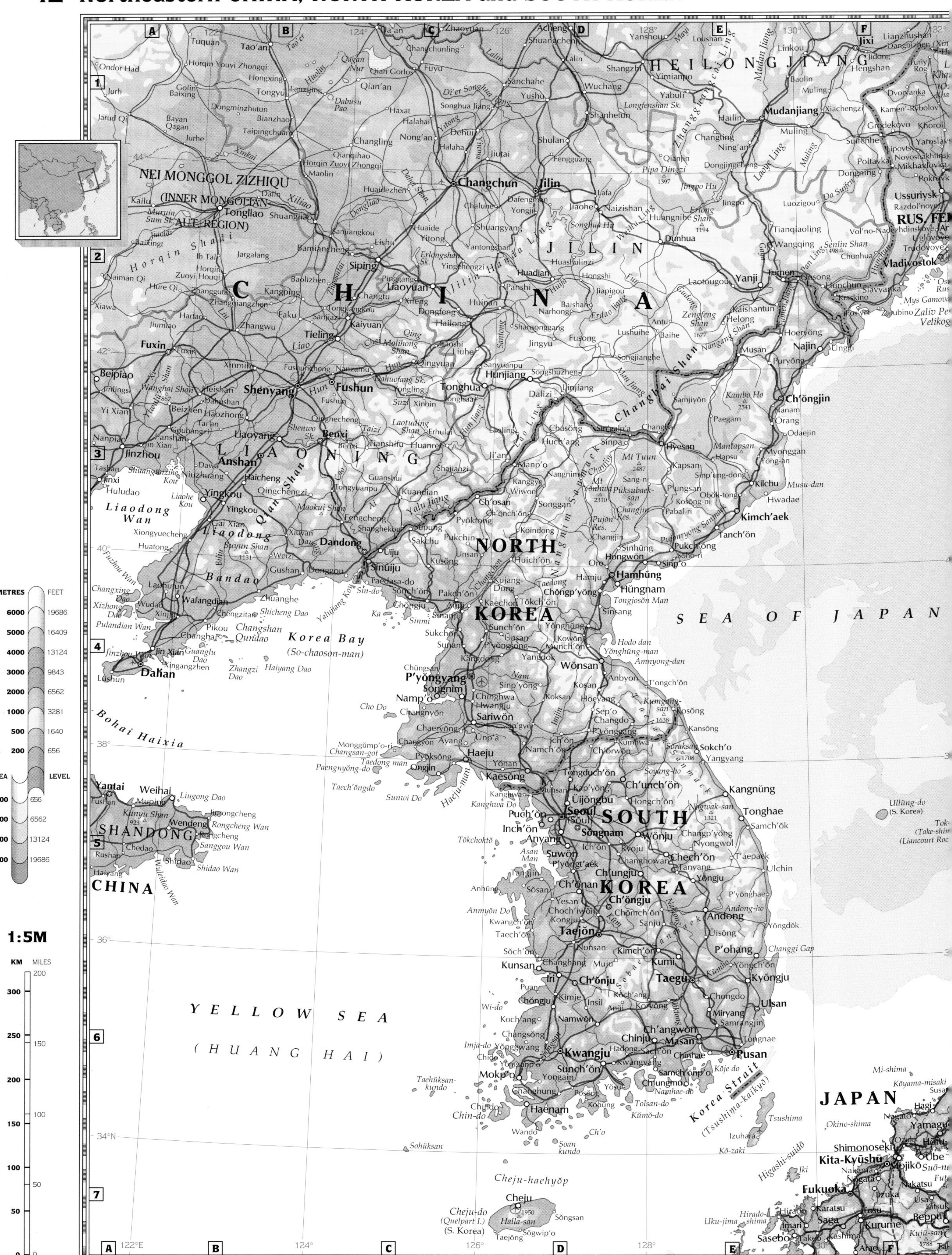

Conic Equidistant Projection

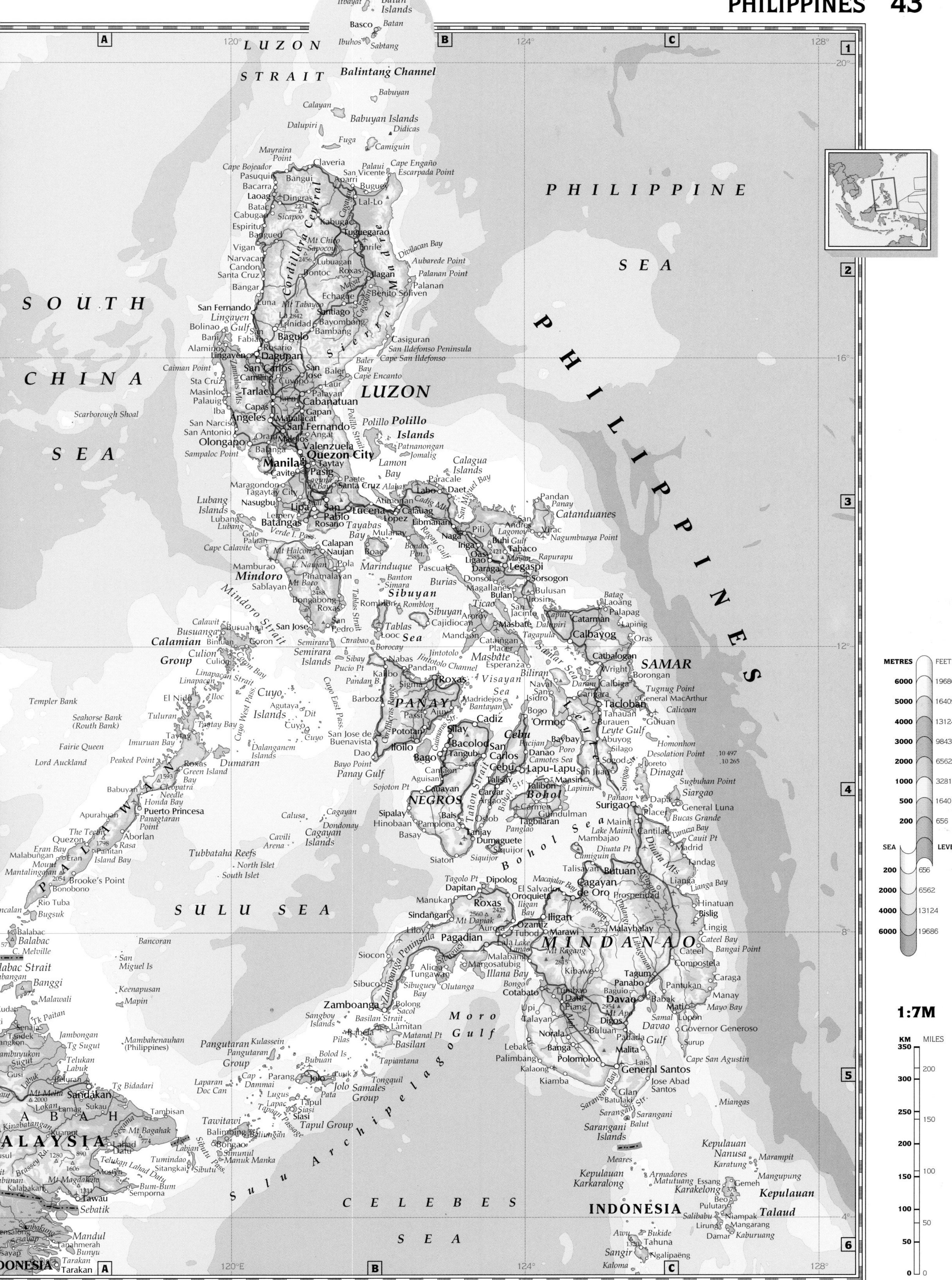

LUZON STRAIT

Balintang Channel

Mabudis North I.
Itbayat Batan Islands
Basco Batan
Ibuhos Sabtang

Babuyan

Calayan
Dalupiri Babuyan Islands Didicas
Fuga Camiguin

PHILIPPINE SEA

Claveria Cape Engaño
Pasuquin San Vicente Escarpada Point
Cape Bojeador Aparri
Bacarra Bangui Buguey Lal-lo
Laoag Dingras
Batac Sicapoo ▲224
Espiritu Mt Chico
Vigan Sapocoy ▲2456 Lubuagan
Narvacan Bontoc Ilagan
Candon Bangued Echague Divilacan Bay
Santa Cruz Luna Mt Tabaco Aubarede Point
Bangar Trinidad ▲2842 Santiago Palanan Point
San Fernando Bayombong Palanan
Lingayen Bambang San Ildefonso Peninsula
Bolinao Gulf Baguio Bayombong Casiguran Cape San Ildefonso
Bani Fabian Rosario Dagupan
Alaminos San Carlos San Jose Baler Bay
Caiman Point Camiling Cuyo Laur Cape Encanto
Sta Cruz Tarlac Jaen Palayan
Masinloc Capas LUZON
Palauig Iba Gapan Cabanatuan
San Carlos Angeles Mabalacat Polillo Strait
San Antonio San Fernando Polillo
Olongapo Angat Polillo Islands
Sampaloc Point Balanga Valenzuela Patnanongan
Manila Quezon City Jomalig
Cavite Pasig Lamon Calagua
Maragondon Santa Cruz Bay Islands
Tagaytay City Paete Paracale Pandan
Nasugbu Lipa Calauag Daet Panay
Lubang San Atimonan Labo Catanduanes
Islands Pablo Lopez Libmanan
Lubang Lemery Lucena Andres
Lubang Batangas Rosario Tayabas Naga Pili Virac
Golo Verde I. Pass. Bay Mulanay Iriga Lagonoy Nagumbuaya Point
Cape Calavite Calapan Boac Ragay Gulf Buhi Gulf
Mt Halcon Naujan Pola Pascual Oas Tabaco
Mamburao ▲2585 Marinduque Bondoc Mayon▲2421 Rapurapu
Mindoro L. Naujan Pen. Ligao Daraga Legaspi
Sablayan Mt Baco Simara Burias Donsol Sorsogon
Pinamalayan Banton Magallanes
Bongabong Tablas Sibuyan Bulan Bulusan
Roxas Romblon Ticao San Jacinto Irosin
San Jose Tablas Masbate Batag
Calawit Busuanga Looc Sea Dalupiri Laoang Palapag
Busuanga Coron Cataingan Catarman Lapinig
Calamian Culion Semirara Cajidiocan Tagapula Calbayog Oras
Group Islands Sibay Nabas Jintotolo Channel Placer
Linapacan Pucio Pt Pandan Masbate SAMAR Wright Borongan
Linapacan Strait Kalibo Sigma Visayan Naval Catbalogan
Cuyon Bay Semirara Cirabao Borocay Sea San Tugnug Point
Templer Bank Cuyo West Pass. Islands Roxas Barbaza Madridejos Isidro General MacArthur
Seahorse Bank Agutaya Dit Sigma Bantayan Daram Caibiran Calicoan
(Routh Bank) El Nido Iloc Cuyo East Pass. Passi PANAY Bogo Carigara Buruen Guiuan
Fairie Queen Tuluran Cuyo Islands Ajuy Cadiz Cebu Ormoc Leyte Gulf
Lord Auckland Taytay Cuyo San Jose de Silay Poro Homonhon
Peaked Point Imuruan Bay Dalanganem Buenavista Pototan Talibon Baybay Camotes Sea Desolation Point .10 497
Roxas Islands Iloilo Bacolod San Poro .10 265
Babuyan Green Island Bayo Point Dao Bago Carlos Lapu-Lapu Abuyog Doreto Dinagat
Cleopatra Panay Gulf Canlaon▲ Danao Maasin Sugbuhan Point
Needle Sojoton Pt ▲2465 Talisay Sogod Siargao
Apurahuan Puerto Princesa NEGROS Cauayan Cardar Bohol Dapa General Luna
The Teeth Panagtaran Aguisan Sipalay Talibon Bucas Grande
Calusa Point Bais Argao Carmen Surigao Placer
Cagayan Dondonay Hinoban Pamplona Guindulman Siargao
Cavili Cagayan Basay Tanjay Panglao Tagbilaran Mambajao
Puerto Princesa Arena Islands Dumaguete Bohol Sea Lake Mainit Cantilan
Siaton Siquijor Talisay Diuata Pt Madrid
Brooke's Point ▲1798 Siquijor Camiguin Lianga Bay
Mount Rasa Tagolo Pt El Salvador Butuan Lianga
Mantalingajan▲2054 Island Bay Dipolog Cagayan de Oro Prosperidad Lianga
Bonobono SULU SEA Dapitan Oroquieta Hinatuan
Rio Tuba Sindangan Iligan Bislig
Bugsuk Liloy Mt Dapiak Ozamiz Aurora MINDANAO Cateel Bay
Balabac Bancoran Siocon ▲2560 Tubod Marawi Cateel Bangai Point
C. Melville San ▲2425 Iligan Malaybalay Compostela
57 Miguel Is Aliona Zamboanga Pagadian Malabang Kibawe Caraga
Banggi Keenapusan Peninsula Panabo Mt Ragang Tagum Pantukan
Malawali Mapin Sibuco Margosatubig Kibawe Baguio Manay
Labac Strait Tandek Tungawan Illana Bay Cotabato Davao Babak
Banggi Jambongan Zamboanga Bongo ▲2954 Samal Mayo Bay
Tg Sugut Mambahenauhan Sibuguey Olutanga Upi Piang Mt Apo Davao Lupon
Sandakan (Philippines) Bay Cotabato Digos Gulf Governor Generoso
Telukan Pangutaran Sacol Moro Kalaong Talayan Malita Surup
Labuk Kulassein Basilan Strait Gulf Norala Buluan Malita Cape San Agustin
Mt Melta▲2000 Pangutaran Bolong Isabela Lamitan Lebak Banga Polomoloc
Gusi Group Parang Basilan Matanal Pt Palimbang General Santos
Beluran Bum-Bum Pilas Tapiantana Kiamba Lais Jose Abad
Mt Madalena Jolo Samales Glan Santos
Tandel Kinabatangan Zamboanga Tapul Group Sarangani Bay Miangas
ABAH Lokan▲1280 Jolo Lapac Tongquil Batulaki Sarangani
MALAYSIA Tambisan Tawitawi Lugus Siasi Sarangani Sarangani
Mt Bagahak Balimbing Siasi Pata Islands Balut
Brassey Ra.▲774 Semporna Tapul Group Kepulauan Marampit
Kuamut Mt Magdalena▲ Tumindao Nanusa Mangupung
Lahad Datu Bongao Laparan Meares Nanusa Karatung
Kalabakan Lahad Datu Bay Doc Can Kepulauan Armadores Essang Gemeh
Telukan Bum-Bum Sitangkai Sibutu Karkaralong Matutuang ▲375
Tawau Simunul Manuk Manka Beo Mangasang
Sebatik Sibutu Pass. Damar Karakelong Pulutan Kepulauan
DONESIA Mandul INDONESIA Awu Bukide Salibabu Talaud
Tarakan Tanahmerah Sangir Niampak Mangarang
Bunyu CELEBES SEA Kaloma Ngalipaëng Tahuna

SOUTH CHINA SEA

Scarborough Shoal

Sibutu Passage

Sulu Archipelago

1:7M

<table>
<tr><th>METRES</th><th>FEET</th></tr>
<tr><td>6000</td><td>19686</td></tr>
<tr><td>5000</td><td>16409</td></tr>
<tr><td>4000</td><td>13124</td></tr>
<tr><td>3000</td><td>9843</td></tr>
<tr><td>2000</td><td>6562</td></tr>
<tr><td>1000</td><td>3281</td></tr>
<tr><td>500</td><td>1640</td></tr>
<tr><td>200</td><td>656</td></tr>
<tr><td>SEA</td><td>LEVEL</td></tr>
<tr><td>200</td><td>656</td></tr>
<tr><td>2000</td><td>6562</td></tr>
<tr><td>4000</td><td>13124</td></tr>
<tr><td>6000</td><td>19686</td></tr>
</table>

<table>
<tr><th>KM</th><th>MILES</th></tr>
<tr><td>350</td><td></td></tr>
<tr><td>300</td><td>200</td></tr>
<tr><td>250</td><td>150</td></tr>
<tr><td>200</td><td>100</td></tr>
<tr><td>150</td><td></td></tr>
<tr><td>100</td><td>50</td></tr>
<tr><td>50</td><td></td></tr>
<tr><td>0</td><td>0</td></tr>
</table>

Projection

© Collins

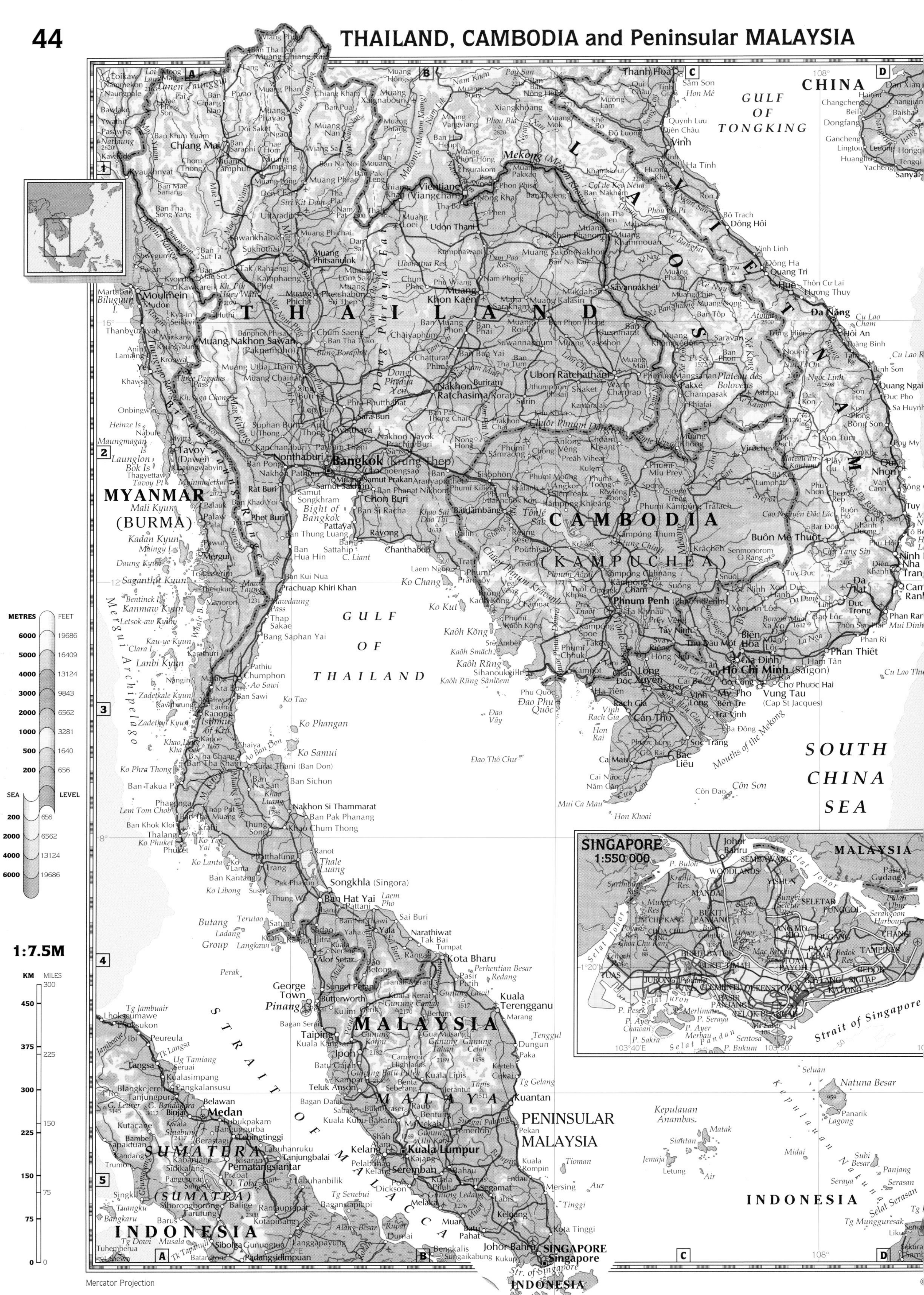
THAILAND
CAMBODIA
(KAMPUCHEA)
MALAYSIA
PENINSULAR MALAYSIA
MYANMAR (BURMA)
LAOS
VIETNAM
CHINA
INDONESIA
SUMATERA (SUMATRA)
GULF OF TONGKING
GULF OF THAILAND
SOUTH CHINA SEA
STRAIT OF MALACCA
Mergui Archipelago
Bangkok (Krung Thep)
Vientiane (Viangchan)
Phnum Penh
Hô Chi Minh (Saigon)
Kuala Lumpur
Singapore
Medan
Chiang Mai
Mekong
SINGAPORE 1:550 000
Strait of Singapore
METRES
FEET
6000
19686
5000
16409
4000
13124
3000
9843
2000
6562
1000
3281
500
1640
200
656
SEA
LEVEL
1:7.5M
KM
MILES
Mercator Projection

SOUTH CHINA SEA
MALAYSIA
THAILAND
Andaman Sea
Celebes Sea
SABAH
BRUNEI
SARAWAK
BORNEO
KALIMANTAN
PENINSULAR MALAYSIA
STRAIT OF MALACCA
SINGAPORE
SUMATERA
(SUMATRA)
PEGUNUNGAN BARISAN
Kepulauan Mentawai
JAVA SEA
INDONESIA
MACASSAR STRAIT
BALI SEA
Selat Karimata
INDIAN OCEAN
Java (Jawa)
Madura
Bali
Lombok
Sumbawa
Sulawesi (Celebes)
Bangka
Belitung
Nias
Siberut
Kepulauan Natuna (Indonesia)
Kepulauan Anambas (Indonesia)
Kepulauan Riau (Indonesia)
Kepulauan Lingga
Kuala Lumpur
Singapore
Jakarta
Bandung
Semarang
Surabaya
Yogyakarta
Malang
Palembang
Medan
Padang
Pekanbaru
Jambi
Bengkulu
Pontianak
Kuching
Banjarmasin
Balikpapan
Samarinda
Ujung Pandang
Bandar Seri Begawan
Kota Kinabalu
Sandakan
Banda Aceh
George Town
Kuantan
Equator
95°E
100°
105°
110°
115°
METRES
FEET
6000
19686
5000
16409
4000
13124
3000
9843
2000
6562
1000
3281
500
1640
200
656
SEA
LEVEL
1:10M
KM
MILES

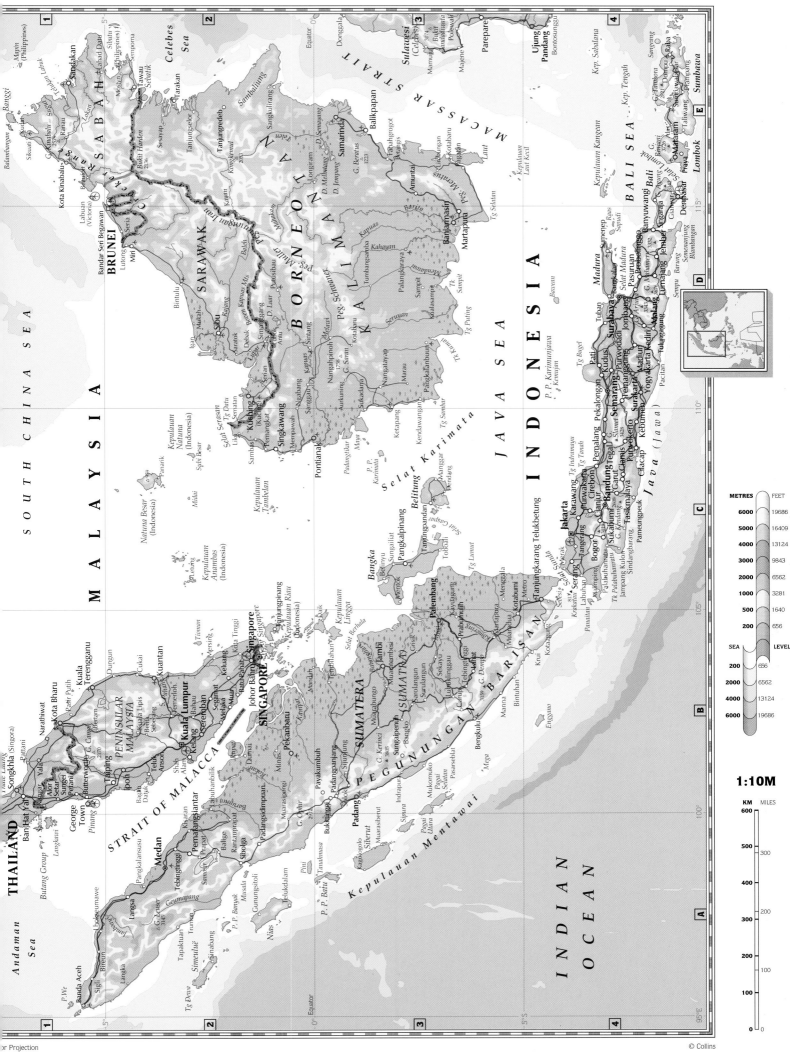

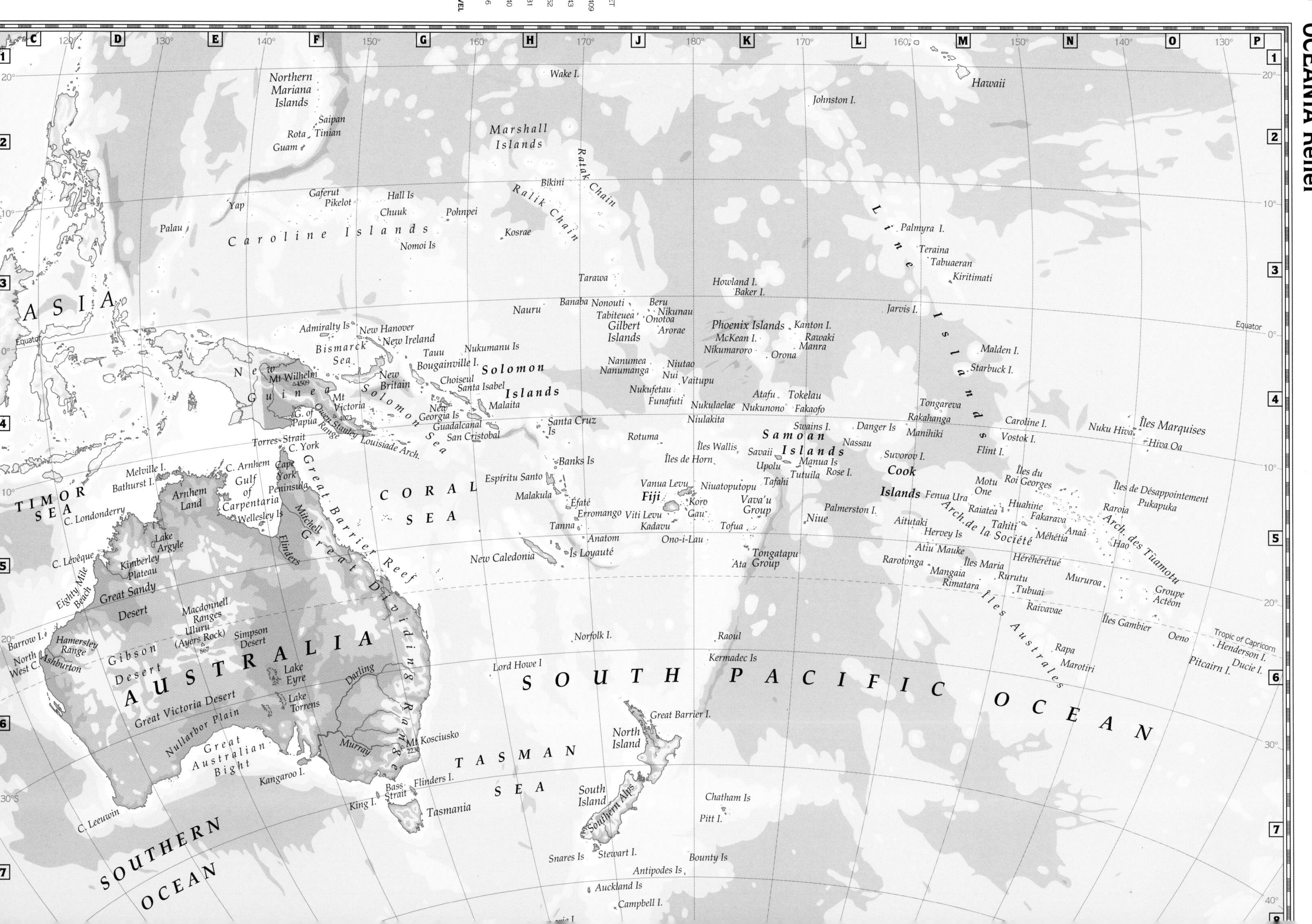

METRES	FEET
5000	16409
3000	9843
2000	6562
1000	3281
500	1640
200	656

SEA	LEVEL
200	656
3000	9843
5000	16409
6000	19686

1:45M

KM	MILES
2500	1500
2000
	1000
1500
	500
1000
500
0	0

Lambert Azimuthal Equal Area Projection

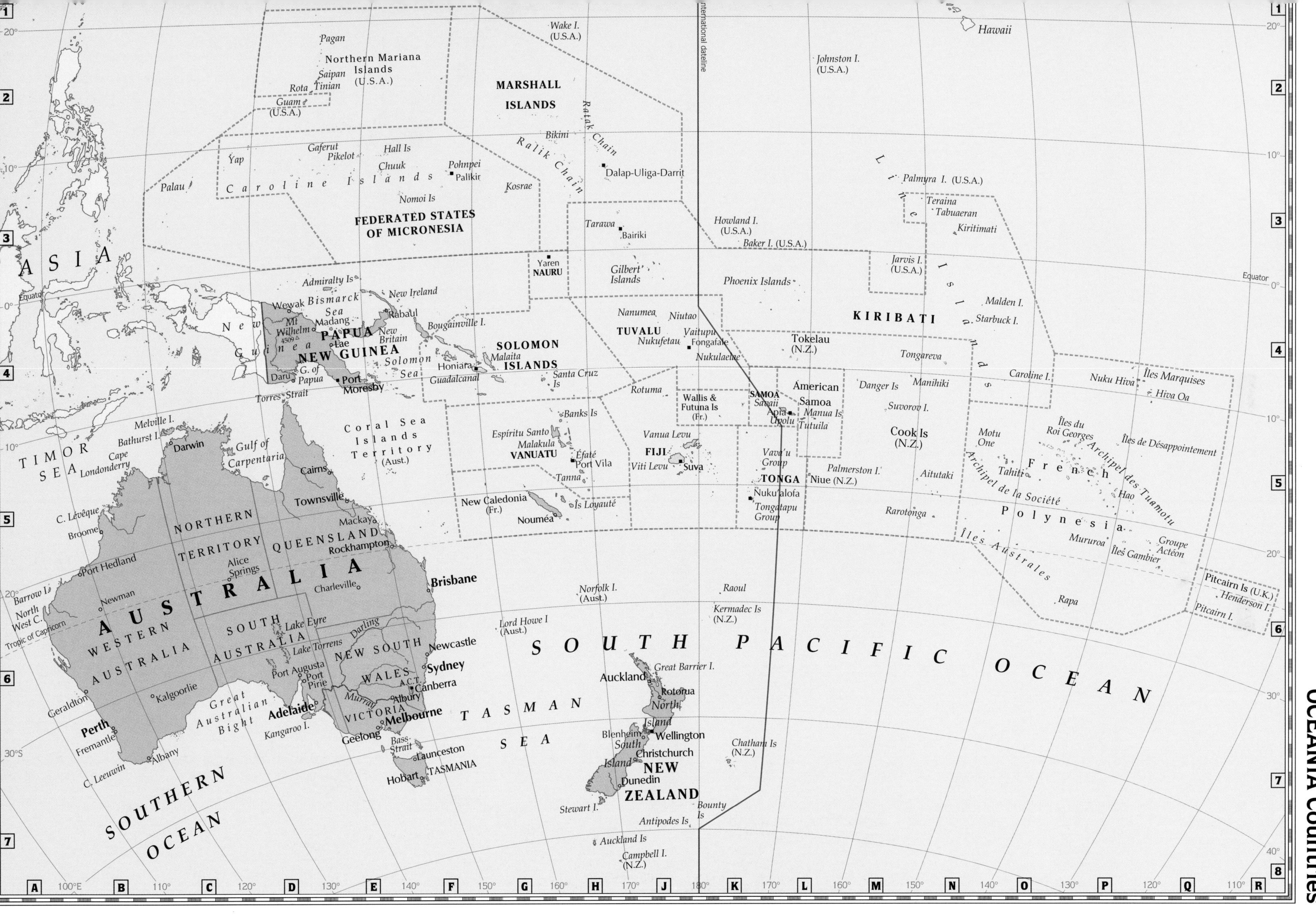

1:45M

t Azimuthal Equal Area Projection

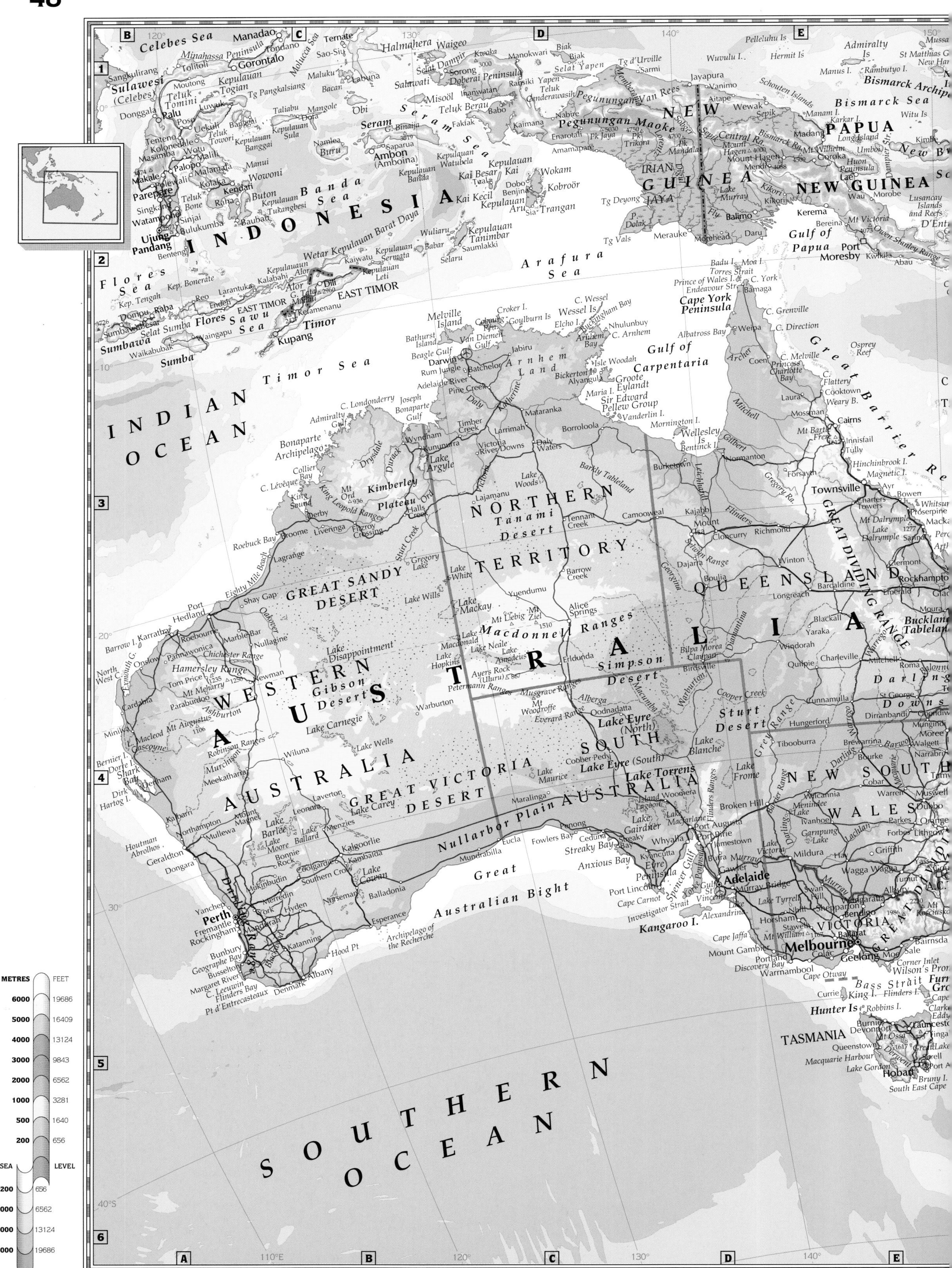

48

Celebes Sea
Manadao
Ternate
Halmahera Waigeo
Pelleluhu Is
Admiralty Is
St Matthias Is
Tolitoli
Tondano
Moluccan Sea
Sao-Siu
Kwoka
Manokwari
Biak
Wuvulu I.
Hermit Is
Manus I.
Rambutyo I.
New Han
Minahassa Peninsula
Gorontalo
Maluku
Labuna
Selat Dampir
Sorong
Doberai Peninsula
Selat Yapen
Tg d'Urville
Sarmi
Jayapura
Vanimo
Schouten Islands
Aitape
Karkar I.
Witu Is
Bismarck Archi
Sulawesi (Celebes)
Kepulauan Togian
Tg Pangkalsiang
Bacan
Salawati
Misoöl
Ihanwatan
Rabsiki
Yapen
Teluk Cenderawasih
Pegunungan Van Rees
Wewak
Sepik
Manam I.
Bismarck Sea
Moutong
Teluk Tomini
Taliabu
Mangole
Dofa
Babo
Kaimana
Pegunungan Maoke
Central Ra
Madang
Long Island
Umboi I.
PAPUA
Donggala
Palu
Poso
Luwuk
Kepulauan Sula
Namlea
Seram Sea
Fakfak
5030
Pk Jaya 4750
Mount Hagen
Mt Wilhelm 4508
Huon Peninsula
Lae
Morobe
Lusancay Islands and Reefs
NEW
Tenteno
Uekuli
Seram
Amamapare
Pk 4700
Mendi
4088
Wau
New B
Masamba
Watu
Malili
Buru
Kepulauan Watubela
Kai Besar
Wokam
IRIAN
Kikori
D'Ent
Makale
Palopo
Ambon (Amboina)
Kai Kecil
Kobroör
JAYA
Kerema
Bereina
Mt Victoria 4073
Queen Stanley Range
Polewali
Malamala
Kolaka
Kendari
Kepulauan Banda
Dobo
Benjina
Lake Murray
Port
Parepare
Singkang
Bone
Raha
Buton
Banda Sea
Saparua
Aru
Sia-Trangan
P. Dolak
Fly
Balimo
Morehead
Daru
Gulf of Papua
Moresby
Kwikila
Abau
Watampone
Sinjai
Bulukumba
Baubau
Kepulauan Tukangbesi
Wuliaru
Kepulauan Barat Daya
Merauke
Tg Vals
I N D O N E S I A
Wetar
Kepulauan Tanimbar
Saumlakki
A r a f u r a   S e a
Badu I.
Moa I.
Torres Strait
Prince of Wales I.
C. York
Endeavour Str.
C. Wessel
Wessel Is
Nhulunbuy
Buckingham Bay
C. Grenville
Osprey Reef
D'Ent

Flores Sea
Kep. Bonerate
Larantuka
Kaiwatu
Serutja
Selaru
Bamaga
Elcho I.
C. Arnhem
Albatross Bay
Weipa
C. Direction
Kep. Tengah
Dompu
Raba
Reo
Endeh
Alor
Kalabahi
Kupang
EAST TIMOR
Croker I.
Coburg Pen.
Goulburn Is
Arnhem Bay
Isle Woodah
Gulf of Carpentaria
Archer
Coen
C. Melville
Laura
Cooktown
Weary B.
Great Barrier Re
Sumbawa
Selat Sumba
Flores
Waingapu
S a w u   S e a
Timor
Melville Island
Van Diemen Gulf
Bathurst Island
Arnhem Land
Maria I.
Sir Edward Pellew Group
Mornington I.
Wellesley Is
Bentinck I.
Gilbert
C. Melville
C. Flattery
Mossman
Cairns
Innisfail
Tully
Sumbawabesar
Waikabubak
Sumba
Kupang
Darwin
Rum Jungle
Batchelor
Pine Creek
Katherine
Groote Eylandt
Alyangula
Vanderlin I.
Borroloola
Normanton
Burketown
Gregory Ra.
Forsayth
Hinchinbrook I.
Magnetic I.
Townsville
Ayr
Bowen
Whitsu
Proserpine
I N D I A N
Timor Sea
C. Londonderry
Joseph Bonaparte Gulf
Adelaide River
Daly River
Timber Creek
Larrimah
Victoria River Downs
Daly Waters
Barkly Tableland
Camooweal
Mount Isa
Kajabbi
Cloncurry
Richmond
Charters Towers
Mt Dalrymple
Lake Dalrymple 1277
Macka
O C E A N
Admiralty Gulf
Bonaparte Archipelago
Drysdale
Wyndham
Kununurra
Lake Argyle
Lajamanu
NORTHERN
Tennant Creek
Barrow Creek
Leichhardt
Flinders
Dajarra
Georgina
Winton
Clermont
Rockhampt
C. Lévêque
King Sound
Derby
Plateau
Halls Creek
Mt Ord 936
Sturt Creek
Gregory Lake
Tanami Desert
TERRITORY
Barrow Creek
QUEENSLAND
Boulia
Diamantina
Longreach
Barcaldine
Emerald
Bucklan Tablelan
Bonaparte Gulf
Kimberley
King Leopold Ranges
Liveringa
Fitzroy Crossing
Lake White
Yuendumu
Mt Liebig
Mt Ziel 1510
Macdonnell Ranges
Alice Springs
Bilpa Morea Claypan
Windorah
Yaraka
Quilpie
Charleville
Roma
Darling
Roebuck Bay
Broome
Lagrange
Eighty Mile Beach
Shay Gap
GREAT SANDY DESERT
Lake Disappointment
Lake Mackay
Lake Macdonald
Lake Neale
Lake Amadeus
Ayers Rock (Uluru) 867
Simpson
Desert
Birdsville
Cooper Creek
Hungerford
Cunnamulla
Mitchell
Dirranbandi
Morei
Gonil
Port Hedland
Roebourne
Marble Bar
Nullagine
Newman
Lake Hopkins
Petermann Ranges
Musgrave Ranges
Mt Woodroffe
Everard Range
Alberga
Macumba
Warburton
Sturt Desert
Grey Range
Tibooburra
Bourke
Brewarrina
Wa
Barrow I.
Karratha
Pannawonica
Onslow
Chichester Range
Hamersley Range
Mt Meharry
Paraburdoo
Ashburton
WESTERN
Gibson
U Deserts
Warburton
AUSTRALIA
SOUTH
Oodnadatta
Coober Pedy
Lake Eyre (North)
Lake Eyre (South)
Lake Blanche
Broken Hill
NEW
Wilcannia
Menindee
Cobar
Nyngan
Dubbo
SOUTH
North West C.
Exmouth G.
Tom Price 1235 1250
Robinson Ranges
Lake Carnegie
AUSTRALIA
Lake Wells
Lake Eyre (South)
Lake Torrens
Island Lagoon
Woomera
Lake Frome
Flinders Ranges
Darling
Lake Cargelligo
Parkes
Forbes
Orange
Lithgow
WALES
Minilya
Cardabia
Bernier I.
Dorre I.
Shark Bay
Denham
Carnarvon
Gascoyne
Mt Augustus 1106
Murchison
Meekatharra
Wiluna
Lake Carey
Lake Maurice
Lake Gairdner
Lake Macfarlane
Port Augusta
Lake Victoria
Mildura
Wagga Wagga
Griffith
Allbury
Dirk Hartog I.
Geraldton
Northampton
Mount Magnet
Leonora
Laverton
Maralinga
Penong
Ceduna
Streaky Bay
Whyalla
Port Pirie
Kimba
Cleve
Lake Tyrell
Shepparton
Bendigo
Mt Kosciusko 2230
Houtman Abrolhos
Dongara
Mullewa
Lake Barlee
Menzies
GREAT VICTORIA DESERT
Lake Carey
Eucla
Fowlers Bay
Streaky Bay
Anxious Bay
Kyancutta
Spencer Gulf
Port Lincoln
Adelaide
Murray Bridge
Swan Hill
Horsham
Stawell
Ballarat
Bairnsda
Sale
Kalgoorlie
Coolgardie
Southern Cross
Lake Cowan
Balladonia
Nullarbor Plain
Mundrabilla
Great
Cape Carnot
Yorke Peninsula
Kangaroo I.
Cape Jaffa
Mt William 1167
Mount Gambier
Portland
Melbourne
Geelong
Colac
Perth
Fremantle
Rockingham
Yanchep
York
Mandurah
Hyden
Narrogin
Esperance
Australian Bight
Investigator Strait
Alexandrina
Cape Otway
Warrnambool
Discovery Bay
Corner Inlet
Wilson's Prom.
Furn Gro
Bunbury
Busselton
Geographe Bay
Margaret River
Katanning
Archipelago of the Recherche
Hood Pt
Bass Strait
King I.
Flinders I.
Currie
Hunter Is
Robbins I.
Cape
Clarke
Eddy
C. Leeuwin
Flinders Bay
Pt d'Entrecasteaux
Denmark
Albany
Burnie
Devonport
Launceston
TASMANIA
Queenstown
Macquarie Harbour
Lake Gordon
Hobart
Bruny I.
South East Cape

A U S T R A L I A

S O U T H E R N   O C E A N

Lambert Azimuthal Equal Area Projection

METRES		FEET
6000		19686
5000		16409
4000		13124
3000		9843
2000		6562
1000		3281
500		1640
200		656
SEA		LEVEL
200		656
2000		6562
4000		13124
6000		19686

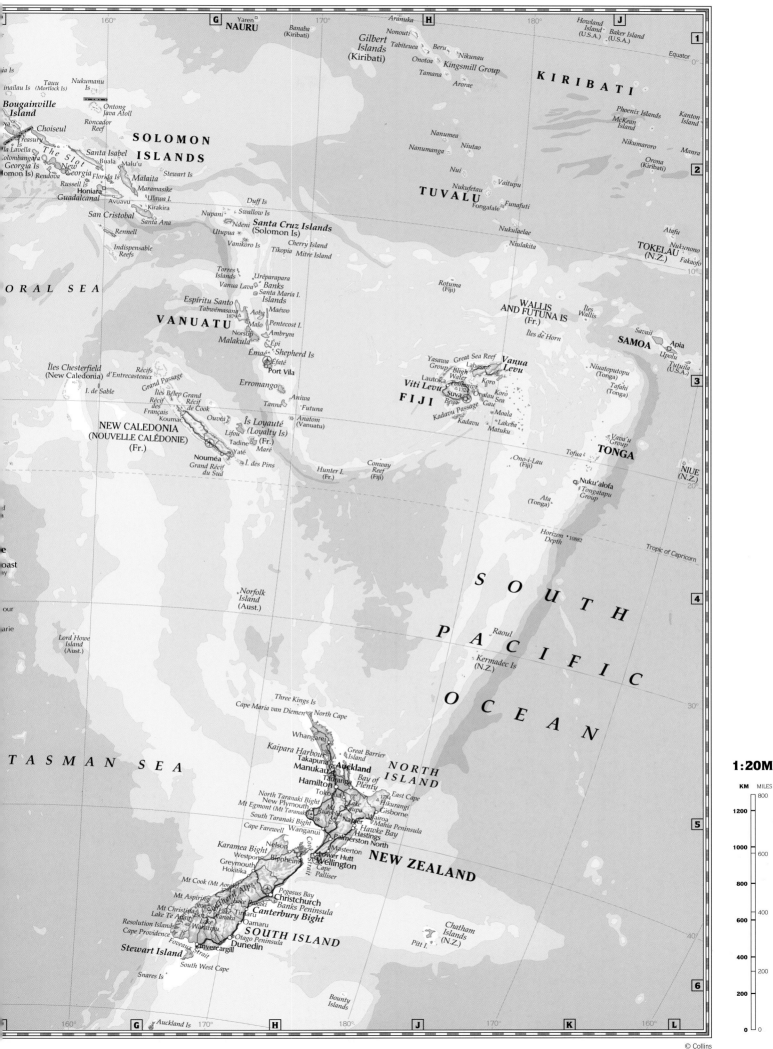

1:20M

KM   MILES
800
1200
600
1000
800
400
600
400
200
200
0   0

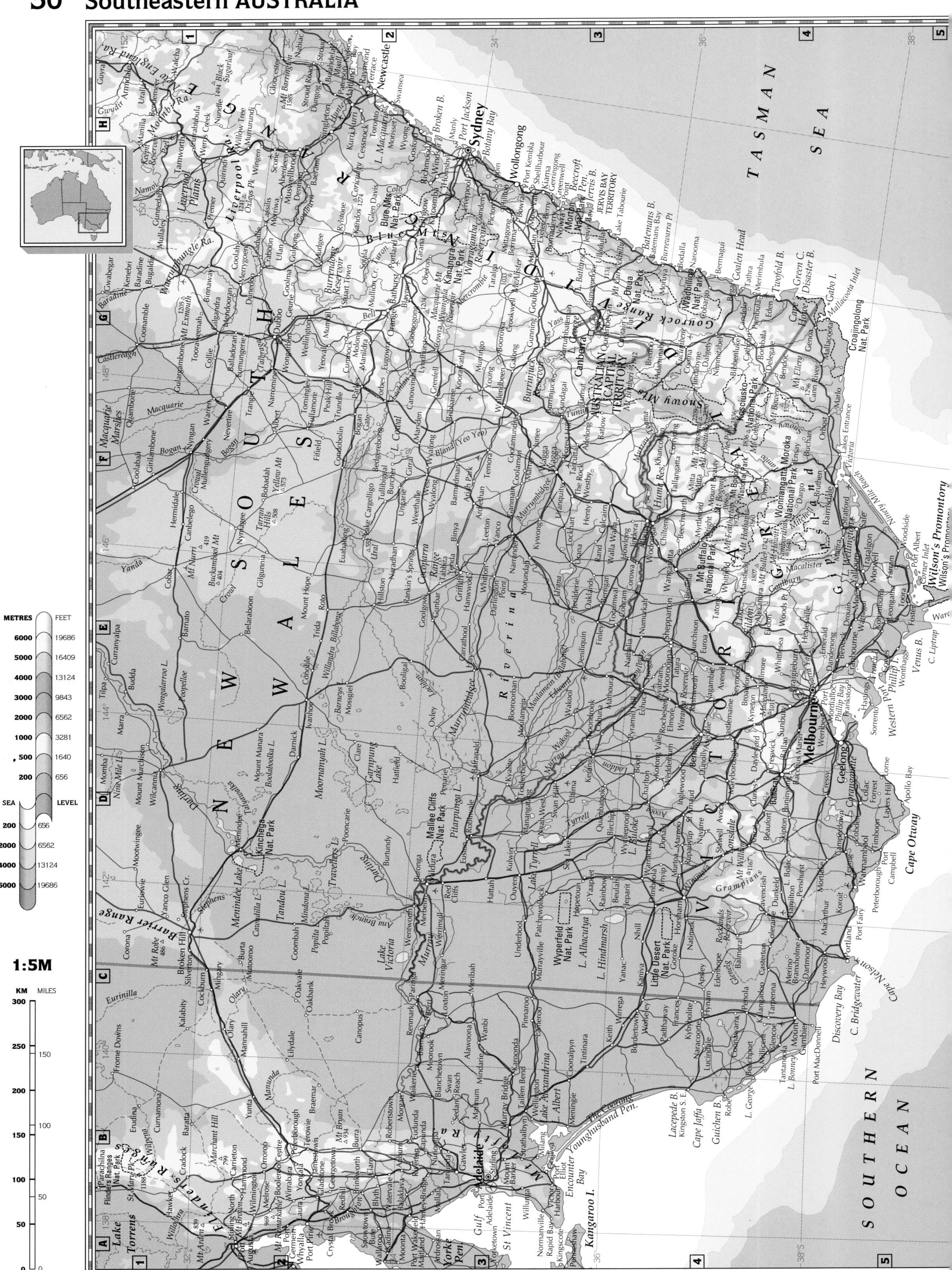

1:5M

Lambert Azimuthal Equal Area Projection

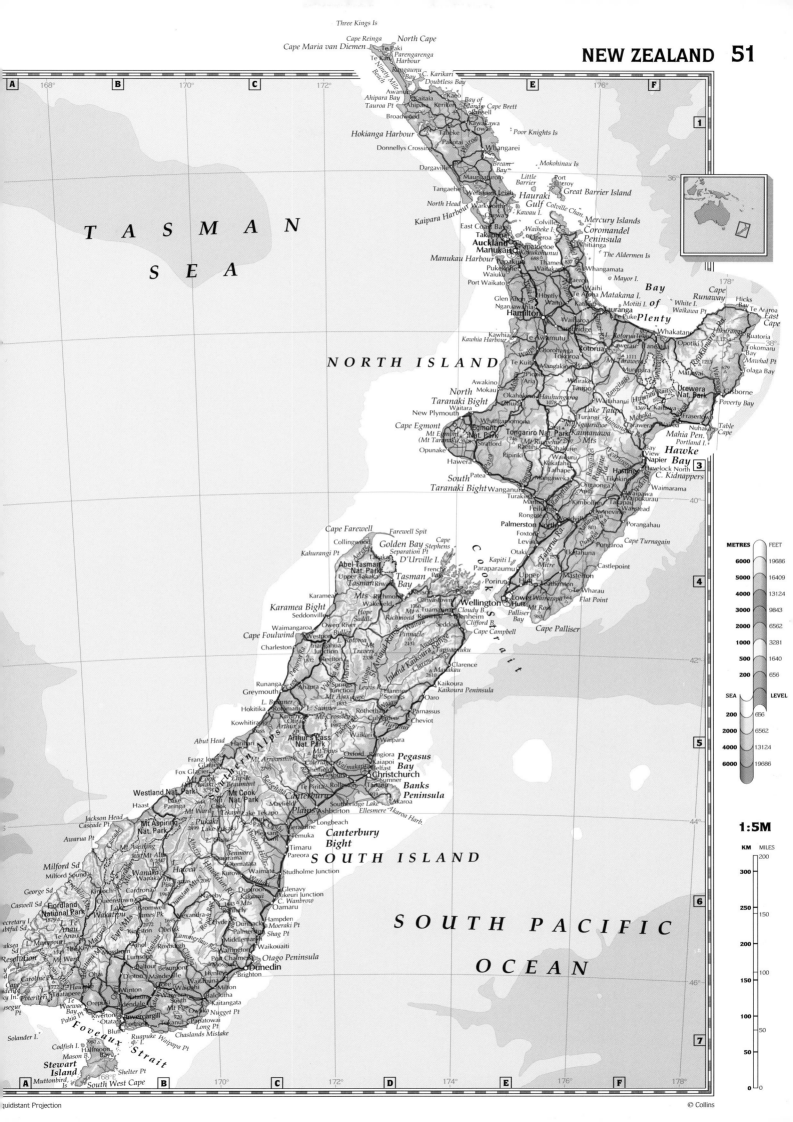

TASMAN SEA

NORTH ISLAND

SOUTH ISLAND

SOUTH PACIFIC OCEAN

Three Kings Is
Cape Reinga   North Cape
Cape Maria van Diemen
Te Paki
Parengarenga Harbour
Rangaunu Bay
Doubtless Bay
C. Karikari
Awanui
Ahipara Bay   Kaeo   Bay of Islands   Cape Brett
Tauroa Pt   Ahipara   Kaitaia   Kerikeri   Russell
Broadwood   Kawakawa Towai   Poor Knights Is
Hokianga Harbour   Taheke   Pakotai
Donnellys Crossing   Whangarei
Dargaville   Bream Bay   Mokohinau Is
Maungaturoto   Little Barrier   Port Fitzroy
Tangaehe   Wellsford Leigh   Great Barrier Island
North Head   Warkworth   Colville Chan.
Kaipara Harbour   Orewa   Kawau I.   Mercury Islands
East Coast Bays   Colville   Coromandel Peninsula
Takapuna   Waiheke I.   Whitianga
Auckland   Oneroa   The Aldermen Is
Manukau   Papatoetoe   Mayor I.
Manukau Harbour   Papakura   Waitakaruru   Bay of Plenty
Pukekohe   Thames   Cape Runaway
Waiuku   Waihi   Te Araroa
Port Waikato   Waihi   Matakana I.   White I.   Hicks Bay
Glen Afton   Huntly   Katikati   Motiti I.   Waikawa Pt   East Cape
Ngaruawahia   Tauranga   Whakatane   Hikurangi   Ruatoria
Hamilton   Te Puke   Opotiki   Tokomaru Bay
Waiharoa   Rotorua   Tarawera   Mawhai Pt   Tolaga Bay
Cambridge   Kawerau   Matawai
Te Awamutu   Tokoroa   Mt Tarawera   Urewera Nat. Park   Gisborne
Kawhia   Otorohanga   Murupara   Poverty Bay
Kawhia Harbour   Mangakino   Mt Tarawera   Frasertown
Te Kuiti   Wairakei   Waikaremoana   Wairoa
North Taranaki Bight   Piopio   Taupo   Mohaka   Mahia Pen.
Awakino   Aria   Lake Taupo   Nuhaka   Portland I.   Table Cape
Mokau   Okahukura   Haumunaroa   Turangi   Bay View
Waitara   Ohura   Mt Ngauruhoe   Napier   Hawke Bay
New Plymouth   Whangamomona   Tongariro Nat. Park   Kaimanawa Mts   Hastings   Havelock North
Cape Egmont   Egmont Nat. Park   Raetihi   Mt Ruapehu   Ohakune   Taihape   C. Kidnappers
Mt Egmont   Stratford   Waiouru   Waimarama
(Mt Taranaki)   Ongaonga   Waipawa
Opunake   Ohakune   Apiti   Waipukurau
Hawera   Ripiriki   Kakatahi   Porangahau
South Taranaki Bight   Patea   Mangaweka   Feilding   Dannevirke   Cape Turnagain
Wanganui   Turakina   Woodville
Marton   Palmerston North   Pongaroa
Rongotea   Foxton   Levin   Pahiatua
Otaki   Eketahuna   Castlepoint
Cape Farewell   Waikanae   Mitre
Farewell Spit   Kapiti I.   Upper   Masterton
Collingwood   Cape Stephens   Paraparaumu   Hutt   Carterton
Golden Bay   Separation Pt   Porirua   Lower Hutt   Flat Point
Kahurangi Pt   Takaka   D'Urville I.   Wellington   Te Wharau
Abel Tasman   French Pass   Cloudy B.   Palliser Bay   Cape Palliser
Nat. Park   Upper Takaka   Tasman Bay   Blenheim   Clifford B.
Tasman   Riwaka   Nelson   Renwick   Seddon   Cape Campbell
Mts Richmond   Canvastown
Karamea   Wakefield   Richmond   Tuamarina   Inland Kaikoura Range
Karamea Bight   Hope   Mt   Kaikoura Peninsula
Seddonville   Saddle   Tapuaenuku   Kaikoura
Cape Foulwind   Owen River   Pinnacle   Clarence   Oaro
Waimangaroa   Buller   Clarence Range   Parnassus
Charleston   Westport   Mt Travers   Hanmer Springs   Cheviot
Inangahua Junction   Lewis P.   Rotherham
Reefton   Springs Junction   Culverden   Pegasus Bay
Runanga   Mt Ajax   Waiau   Waikari
Greymouth   Ahaura   Waipara
Hokitika   L. Brunner   Mt Crossley   Culverden
Kowhitirangi   Otira   Oxford   Rangiora   Christchurch
Abut Head   Harihari   Arthur's Pass   Kaiapoi   Sumner
Franz Josef Glacier   Nat. Park   Sheffield   Belfast   Banks Peninsula
Fox Glacier   Mt Arrowsmith   Rolleston   Akaroa
Mt Cook   Aylesbury   Akaroa Harb.
Westland Nat. Park   Mt Cook Nat. Park   Mayfield   Ellesmere
Haast   Lake Paringa   Mt Ward   Ashburton   Southbridge Lake
Jackson Head   Mt Aspiring   Mt Cook   Lake Tekapo   Geraldine
Cascade Pt   Nat. Park   Lake Pukaki   Temuka
Awarua Pt   Benmore   Canterbury Bight
Milford Sd   Mt Aspiring   Lake Ohau   Timaru
Milford Sound   Wanaka   Otematata   Pareora
George Sd   Lake Wanaka   Kurow   Studholme Junction
Cardrona   Longbeach
Caswell Sd   Glenavy   Waimate
Fiordland   Queenstown   Duntroon   Pukeuri Junction
National Park   Lake Wakatipu   Cromwell   C. Wanbrow   Oamaru
Te Anau   Alexandra   Kakanui
Lake Te Anau   Clyde   Hampden
Lake Manapouri   Roxburgh   Palmerston   Moeraki Pt
The Key   Lumsden   Middlemarch   Shag Pt
Resolution I.   Athol   Warrington   Waikouaiti
Kingston   Mosgiel   Port Chalmers   Otago Peninsula
Caroline Pk   Gore   Dunedin
Lumsden   Mataura   Brighton
Balfour   Waipahi
Beaumont   Clinton   Balclutha
Ohai   Dipton   Kaitangata
Winton   Mandeville   Nugget Pt
Waimahaka   Henley
Riverton   Invercargill   Owaka
Orepuki   Otautau   Makarewa   Chaslands Mistake
Te Waewae Bay   Edendale   Mt Rae
Pahia   Otatara   Balfour
Waipapa Pt   Fortrose   Long Pt
Codfish I.   Ruapuke   Takanui   Papatowai
Foveaux Strait   Halfmoon Bay   Mason B.
Solander I.   Shelter Pt
Stewart Island   Muttonbird Is
South West Cape

Equidistant Projection   © Collins

METRES	FEET
6000	19686
5000	16409
4000	13124
3000	9843
2000	6562
1000	3281
500	1640
200	656
SEA	LEVEL
200	656
2000	6562
4000	13124
6000	19686

1:5M

KM	MILES
300	200
250	150
200	100
150	
100	50
50	
0	0

NORTH AMERICA Relief

52

Pt Barrow
Brooks Range
Alaska Range
Mt McKinley
Mt Logan
Yukon
Gulf of Alaska
Kodiak I.
Alaska Pen.
Iliamna L.
Nunivak I.
St Lawrence I.
Bering Str.
Seward Pen.
Norton Sound

Beaufort Sea
Porcupine
Mackenzie Mts
Selwyn Mts
Mackenzie
Great Bear L.
Liard
Great Slave Lake
Cassiar Mts
Coast Mountains
Dixon Entrance
Alexander Archipelago
Queen Charlotte Islands
Hecate Str.
Vancouver Island
C. Blanco
Cascade Ra.
Columbia
Fraser
ROCKY MOUNTAINS
F. D. Roosevelt Lake
Bitterroot Ra.
Fort Peck Res.
Yellowstone
Snake
Great Salt L.
Great Basin
Sierra Nevada
Coast Range
Colorado Plateau
Grand Canyon
Colorado
Rio Grande
Sierra Madre Occidental
Baja California
Golfo de California
C. Corrientes
Is. Revillagigedo
Sa Madre del Sur
Golfo de Tehuantepec
Sierra Madre Oriental
Padre Island
Edwards Plateau
Llano Estacado
Red
Ozark Plateau
Arkansas
Platte
Missouri
L. Oahe
L. Sakakawea
Lake of the Woods
L. Winnipegosis
Lake Winnipeg
Nelson
Churchill
Reindeer L.
Wollaston L.
Southern Indian L.
Lake Athabasca
Caribou Mts
Peace
Dubawnt L.
Severn
Bahía de Campeche
Yucatán
Yucatán Channel
Cayman Is.
Golfo de Fonseca
Lago de Nicaragua
Pen. de Nicoya
Panama Canal
Cordillera Central
Golfo del Darién
Sierra Madre
Ilhas de la Bahía

PACIFIC OCEAN

Gulf of Mexico
Mississippi Delta
Mississippi
Ohio
Illinois
L. Erie
L. Michigan
Huron
L. Ontario
Allegheny Mts
Appalachian Mts
Chesapeake B.
C. Hatteras
C. Fear
C. Canaveral
Str. of Florida
Andros
Grand Bahama
Great Abaco
Acklins I.
Turks & Caicos Is
Gt Inagua
Cuba
Greater Antilles
Hispaniola
Jamaica
Puerto Rico
Virgin Is
Guadelo
Dominica
Martinique
Aruba
Neth. Antilles
Lesser Antilles
St L
Anguilla

CARIBBEAN SEA

Lake Superior
L. Nipigon
James Bay
La Grande Res.
L. Bienville
Caniapiscau Res.
Smallwood Res.
Labrador
Ungava Bay
Hudson Bay
Belcher Is
Coats I.
Mansel I.
Southampton I.
Foxe Basin
Nettilling L.
Melville Peninsula
Prince Charles I.
Baffin Island
Cumberland Pen.
Cumberland Sd
Frobisher B.
Hudson Strait
C. Chidley
Labrador Sea
Davis Strait
Baffin Bay
Bylot I.
Home B.
Boothia Pen.
Gulf of Boothia
Brodeur Pen.
Somerset I.
Prince of Wales I.
King William I.
Queen Maud Gulf
Victoria Island
Banks Island
McClure Str.
Prince Patrick I.
Borden I.
Parry Islands
Queen Elizabeth Islands
Axel Heiberg Island
Ellef Ringnes I.
Melville I.
Devon I.
GREENLAND
Kong Frederik VIII Land
Shannon
Oscar Fj.
Scoresby Sd
Kong Oscar Fj.
Kong Christian X Land
Kong Frederik VI Kyst
Kong Christian IX Land
Arctic Circle

Newfoundland
St Lawrence
Anticosti I.
Str. of Belle Isle
Gulf of St Lawrence
Cabot Str.
Cape Breton I.
Sable I.
B. of Fundy
C. Sable
Massachusetts Bay
C. Cod
Long I.
Bermuda

ATLANTIC OCEAN

SOUTH AMERICA

1:30M

METRES	FEET
5000	16409
3000	9843
2000	6562
1000	3281
500	1640
200	656
SEA	LEVEL
200	656
3000	9843
5000	16409
6000	19686

KM	MILES
1800	
1500	900
1200	600
900	
600	300
300	
0	0

Bi-Polar Oblique Projection

CANADA
UNITED STATES OF AMERICA
MEXICO
Greenland (Denmark)
ALASKA
YUKON TERRITORY
NORTHWEST TERRITORIES
NUNAVUT
BRITISH COLUMBIA
ALBERTA
SASKATCHEWAN
MANITOBA
ONTARIO
QUÉBEC
NEWFOUNDLAND
LABRADOR
NEW BRUNSWICK
NOVA SCOTIA
P.E.I.
WASHINGTON
OREGON
CALIFORNIA
NEVADA
IDAHO
MONTANA
WYOMING
UTAH
COLORADO
ARIZONA
NEW MEXICO
NORTH DAKOTA
SOUTH DAKOTA
NEBRASKA
KANSAS
OKLAHOMA
TEXAS
MINNESOTA
IOWA
MISSOURI
ARKANSAS
LOUISIANA
WISCONSIN
ILLINOIS
MICHIGAN
INDIANA
OHIO
KENTUCKY
TENNESSEE
MISS.
ALABAMA
GEORGIA
FLORIDA
S. CAROLINA
N. CAROLINA
VIRGINIA
W.V.
PENNS.
NEW YORK
MAINE
VT.
N.H.
MASS.
R.I.
C.T.
N.J.
DEL.
MD.
Washington D.C.
New York
Philadelphia
Boston
Chicago
Detroit
Los Angeles
San Diego
Seattle
Houston
Dallas
New Orleans
Atlanta
Miami
Montréal
Ottawa
Toronto
Vancouver
Québec
México
Guadalajara
Monterrey
Hudson Bay
Baffin Bay
Davis Strait
Hudson Strait
Foxe Basin
Beaufort Sea
Gulf of Alaska
Gulf of Mexico
Bahía de Campeche
Yucatan Channel
Golfo de California
Golfo de Tehuantepec
ATLANTIC OCEAN
PACIFIC OCEAN
CARIBBEAN SEA
Tropic of Cancer
THE BAHAMAS
CUBA
Havana
JAMAICA
Kingston
HAITI
Port-au-Prince
DOMINICAN REP.
Santo Domingo
PUERTO RICO (U.S.A.)
San Juan
BELIZE
Belmopan
GUATEMALA
Guatemala
HONDURAS
Tegucigalpa
EL SALVADOR
San Salvador
NICARAGUA
Managua
COSTA RICA
San José
PANAMA
Panamá
ANTIGUA & BARBUDA
ST KITTS-NEVIS
DOMINICA
ST LUCIA
ST VINCENT & THE GRENADINES
BARBADOS
GRENADA
TRINIDAD & TOBAGO
Port of Spain
Bermuda (U.K.)
SOUTH AMERICA
1:30M
KM
MILES
1800
1500
1200
900
600
300
0
Oblique Projection
© Collins

3 60° 180° 170° 70° **A** 170° **2** 160° 80° 140°

A R C T I C   O C E A N

B E A U F O R T   S E A

RUS. FED.

Chukchi Sea

Bering Strait

Seward Peninsula

Brooks Range

U.S.A.

A L A S K A

Alaska Range

Kuskokwim Mountains

Bristol Bay

Aleutian Range

GULF OF ALASKA

Alexander Archipelago

YUKON TERRITORY

Mackenzie Mountains

NORTHWEST TERRITORIES

Great Bear Lake

Banks Island

Viscount

Victoria Island

Amundsen Gulf

Great Slave Lake

C A N A D A

Yellowknife

BRITISH COLUMBIA

ALBERTA

R O C K Y   M O U N T A I N S

Coast Mountains

Queen Charlotte Islands

Prince of Wales Island

Dixon Entrance

Vancouver Island

P A C I F I C

O C E A N

Edmonton

Calgary

SASKATCHEWAN

Saskatoon

Regina

Vancouver

Victoria

Seattle

Tacoma

Olympia

WASHINGTON

Spokane

Portland

Salem

Eugene

O R E G O N

Lethbridge

M O N T A N A

Great Falls

Helena

Billings

WYOMING

NORTH DA.

SOUTH DA.

IDAHO

Boise

NEVADA

Great Basin

UTAH

Salt Lake City

NEBRA.

San Francisco

San Jose

Sacramento

Oakland

Stockton

C A L I F O R N I A

Reno

METRES FEET
6000 19686
5000 16409
4000 13124
3000 9843
2000 6562
1000 3281
500 1640
200 656
SEA LEVEL
200 656
2000 6562
4000 13124
6000 19686

Chamberlin Trimetric Projection

4 **5** **6** **E** 130°W **F** **G** 120° **H** 100°

50° 150° 40°N 140°

1:17M

A B C D E F

Great Bear Lake
Echo Bay

YUKON TERRITORY

McQuesten
Elsa
Mt Patterson 2088
Wernecke Mts
Norman Wells
Déline
Keith Arm
McVicar Arm

Beaver Creek
White
Dawson
Stewart
Stewart Crossing
Mayo Keno
Lansing
Great Bear
Fort Norman
Hottah L.
Dawson Range
McArthur Wildlife Sanctuary
Hess
Keele Pk 2972
MACKENZIE MOUNTAINS
Blackwater
Hardisty L.
Digray L.
Rae

Kluane Game Sanctuary
Destruction Bay
Burwash Landing
Carmacks
Macmillan
Tay
Mt Sir James McBrien 2914
Keele
Backbone Ranges
Redstone
Keller Lake
NORTH

Mt Logan 5959
S. Elias Mountains
Mt Vancouver 4785
Kluane National Park
Kluane Lake
Aishihik
Aishihik L.
Pelly Mountains
Big Salmon
Faro
Ross River
Pelly
Ross
Canyon Ranges
Wrigley
Fish Lake
Fort Simpson
Willow L.
Yellowknife

Mt Hubbard
Haines Junction
Alaska Highway
Champagne
Whitehorse
Marsh Lake
Mt Skukum 2382
Tagish
Teslin
Swift River
Frances
Frances Lake
Tungsten
Dome Pk
N. Nahanni
Nahanni National Park
Root
Mackenzie
Fort Providence

Malaspina Gl.
Yakutat Bay
Ocean Cape
Dry Bay
Fairweather
Cape Fairweather
Lituya Bay
Icy Pt
Cape Spencer
Cross Sound
Chichagof Island

ALASKA

COAST MOUNTAINS

BRITISH COLUMBIA

ALBERTA

PACIFIC OCEAN

WASHINGTON

IDAHO

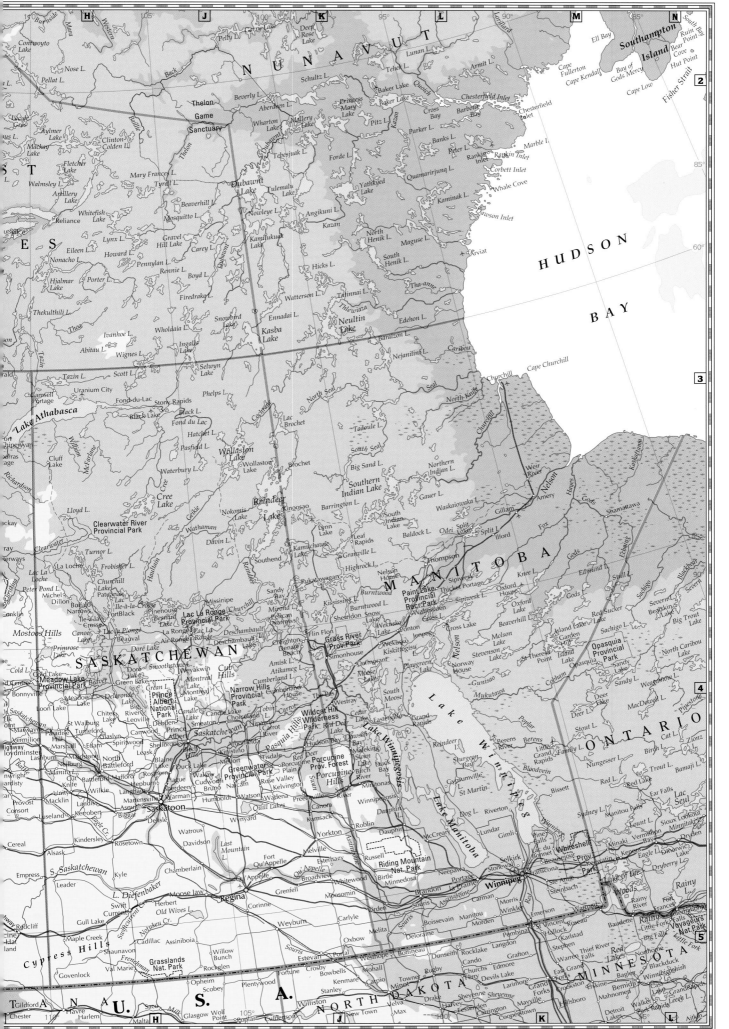

1:7M

KM MILES
350
300 200
250 150
200
150 100
100
50   50
0   0

© Collins

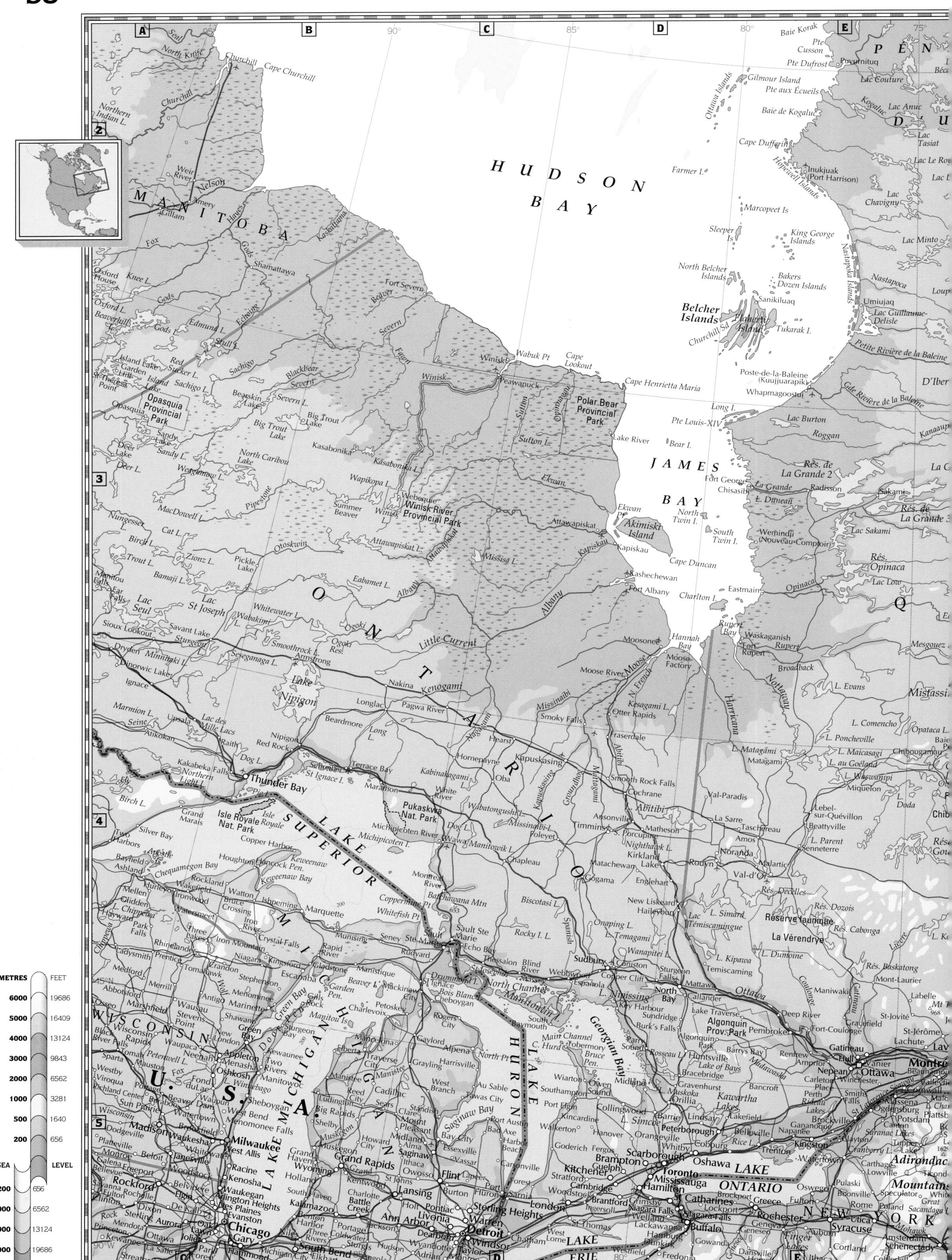

Transverse Mercator Projection

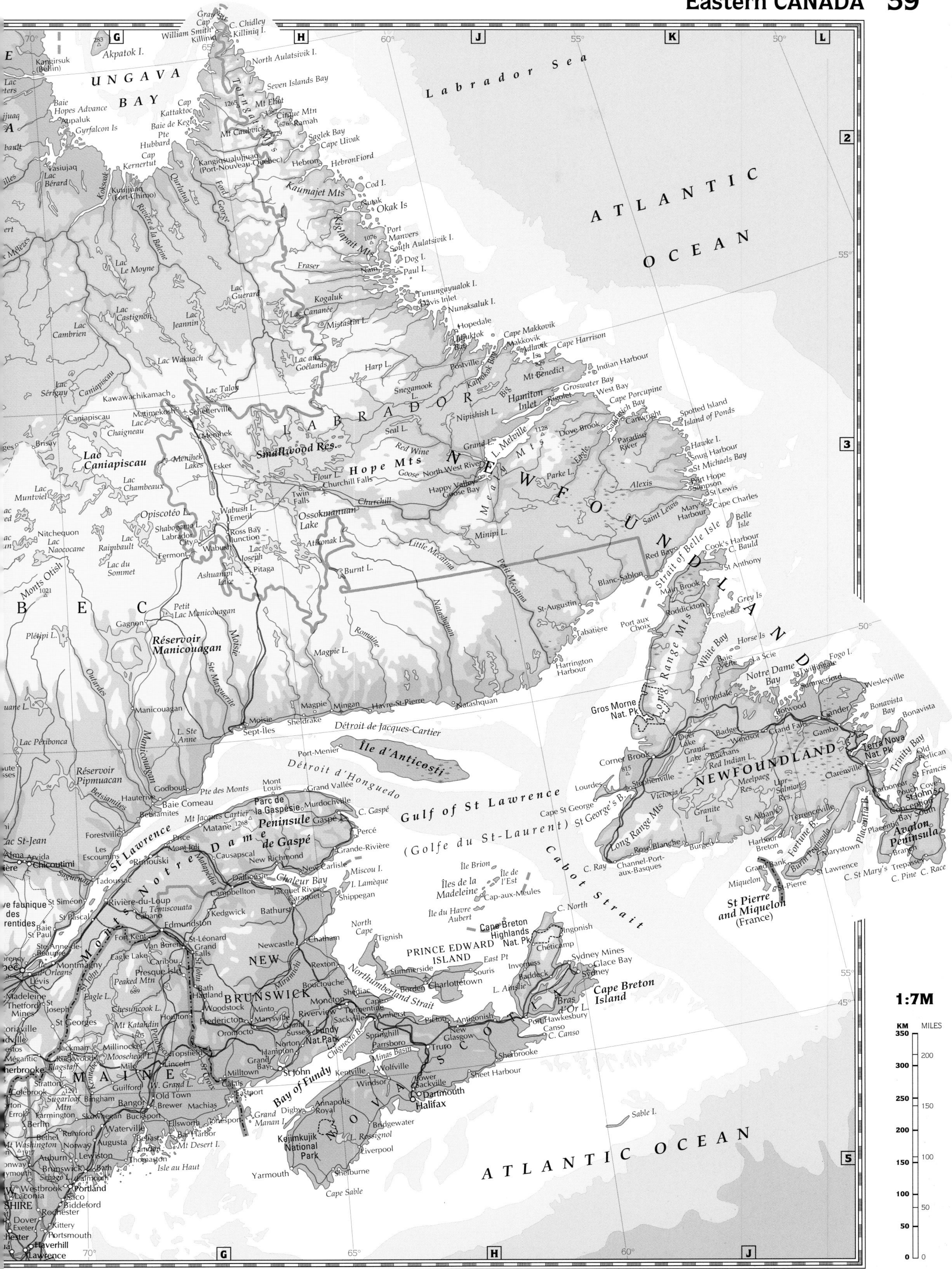

Labrador Sea
ATLANTIC OCEAN
UNGAVA BAY
LABRADOR
NEWFOUNDLAND
Gulf of St Lawrence
(Golfe du St-Laurent)
Cabot Strait
Strait of Belle Isle
Détroit de Jacques-Cartier
Détroit d'Honguedo
Île d'Anticosti
Smallwood Res.
Réservoir Manicouagan
Lac Caniapiscau
Hope Mts
Long Range Mts
Torngat Mts
Kaumajet Mts
Kiglapait Mts
Mealy Mts
Monts Notre Dame
Péninsule de Gaspé
Parc de la Gaspésie
Chaleur Bay
Bay of Fundy
Northumberland Strait
NEW BRUNSWICK
NOVA SCOTIA
PRINCE EDWARD ISLAND
MAINE
Cape Breton Island
Cape Breton Highlands Nat. Pk
Fundy Nat. Park
Kejimkujik National Park
Gros Morne Nat. Pk
Terra Nova Nat. Pk
Avalon Peninsula
St Pierre and Miquelon (France)
Îles de la Madeleine
Halifax
Dartmouth
St John's
Corner Brook
Gander
Fredericton
Moncton
Charlottetown
Sydney
Goose Bay
Happy Valley
Churchill Falls
Labrador City
Wabush
Sept-Îles
Chicoutimi
Rimouski
Campbellton
Bangor
Portland
Augusta
Yarmouth
Sable I.
C. Chidley
Akpatok I.
Kangirsuk (Bellin)
Kuujjuaq (Fort-Chimo)
Kangiqsualujjuaq (Port-Nouveau-Québec)
Hebron
Nain
Hopedale
Makkovik
Postville
Rigolet
Cartwright
Red Bay
Blanc-Sablon
St Anthony
Port aux Basques
Stephenville
Grand Falls
Botwood
Clarenville
Placentia
Marystown
Burin Peninsula
Schefferville
Fermont
Gagnon
Baie Comeau
Havre-St-Pierre
Natashquan
Gaspé
Percé
Matane
Edmundston
Bathurst
Chatham
Newcastle
Truro
New Glasgow
Antigonish
Sherbrooke
Kentville
Wolfville
Windsor
Liverpool
Shelburne
Cape Sable
Digby
Annapolis Royal
Bridgewater
1:7M
KM MILES
© Collins

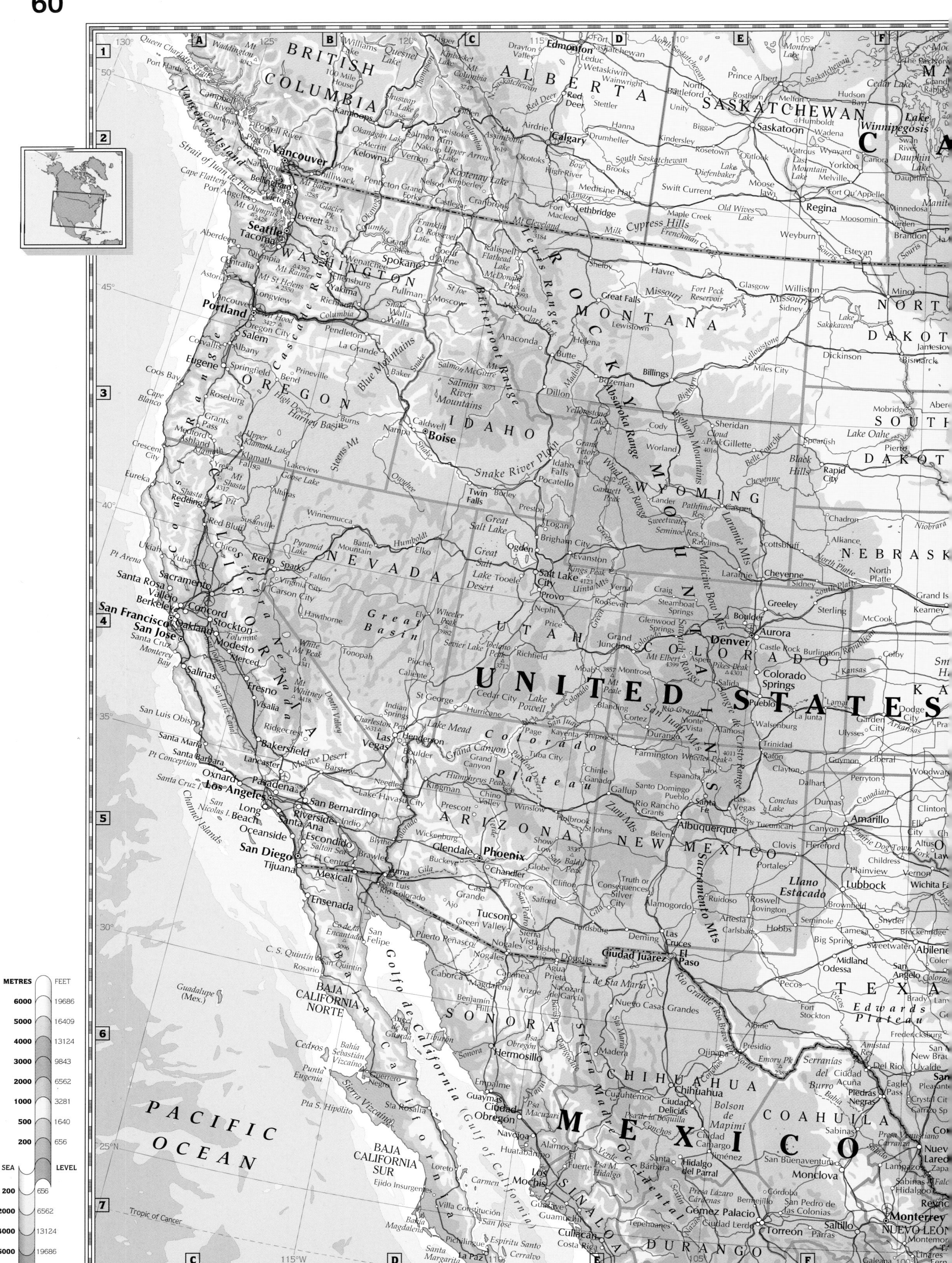
BRITISH COLUMBIA
ALBERTA
SASKATCHEWAN
WASHINGTON
OREGON
IDAHO
MONTANA
WYOMING
NEVADA
UTAH
COLORADO
CALIFORNIA
ARIZONA
NEW MEXICO
NORTH DAKOTA
SOUTH DAKOTA
NEBRASKA
KANSAS
TEXAS
UNITED STATES
MEXICO
BAJA CALIFORNIA NORTE
BAJA CALIFORNIA SUR
SONORA
CHIHUAHUA
COAHUILA
SINALOA
DURANGO
NUEVO LEON
PACIFIC OCEAN
Golfo de California (Gulf of California)
ROCKY MOUNTAINS
Cascade Range
Sierra Nevada
Coast Ranges
Great Basin
Colorado Plateau
Snake River Plain
Sierra Madre Occidental
Llano Estacado
Edwards Plateau
Bolson de Mapimí
Vancouver Island
Strait of Juan de Fuca
Channel Islands
Tropic of Cancer
Edmonton
Calgary
Vancouver
Seattle
Tacoma
Spokane
Portland
Salem
Eugene
Boise
Salt Lake City
Sacramento
San Francisco
Oakland
San Jose
Los Angeles
San Diego
Las Vegas
Phoenix
Tucson
Albuquerque
Denver
El Paso
Ciudad Juárez
Tijuana
Mexicali
Hermosillo
Chihuahua
Monterrey
Regina
Saskatoon
Billings
Cheyenne
Lambert Conformal Conic Projection
METRES
FEET
6000
19686
5000
16409
4000
13124
3000
9843
2000
6562
1000
3281
500
1640
200
656
SEA
LEVEL
200
656
2000
6562
4000
13124
6000
19686

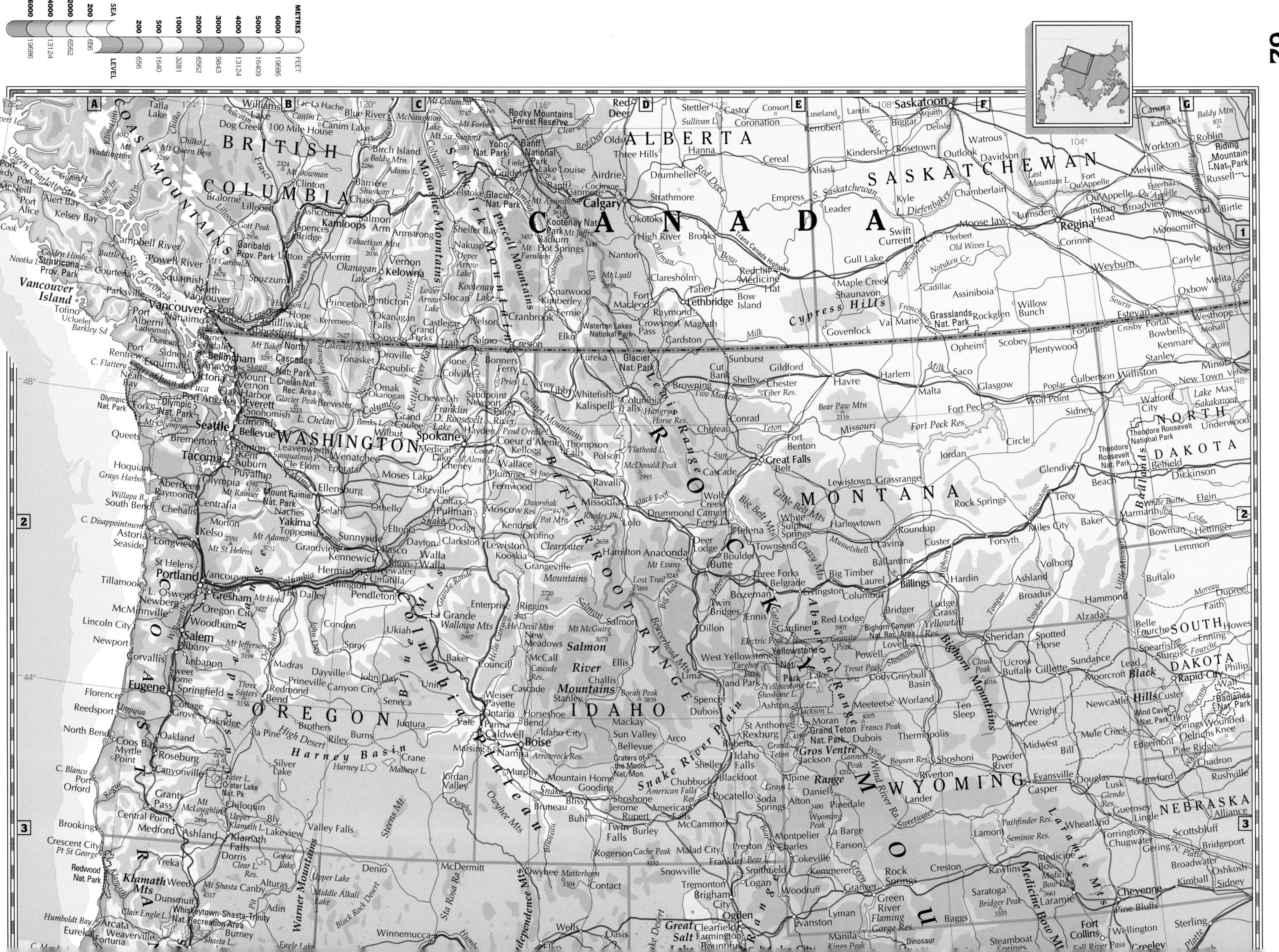

Lambert Conformal Conic Projection

METRES	FEET
6000	19686
5000	16409
4000	13124
3000	9843
2000	6562
1000	3281
500	1640
200	656
SEA	LEVEL
200	656
2000	6562
4000	13124
6000	19686

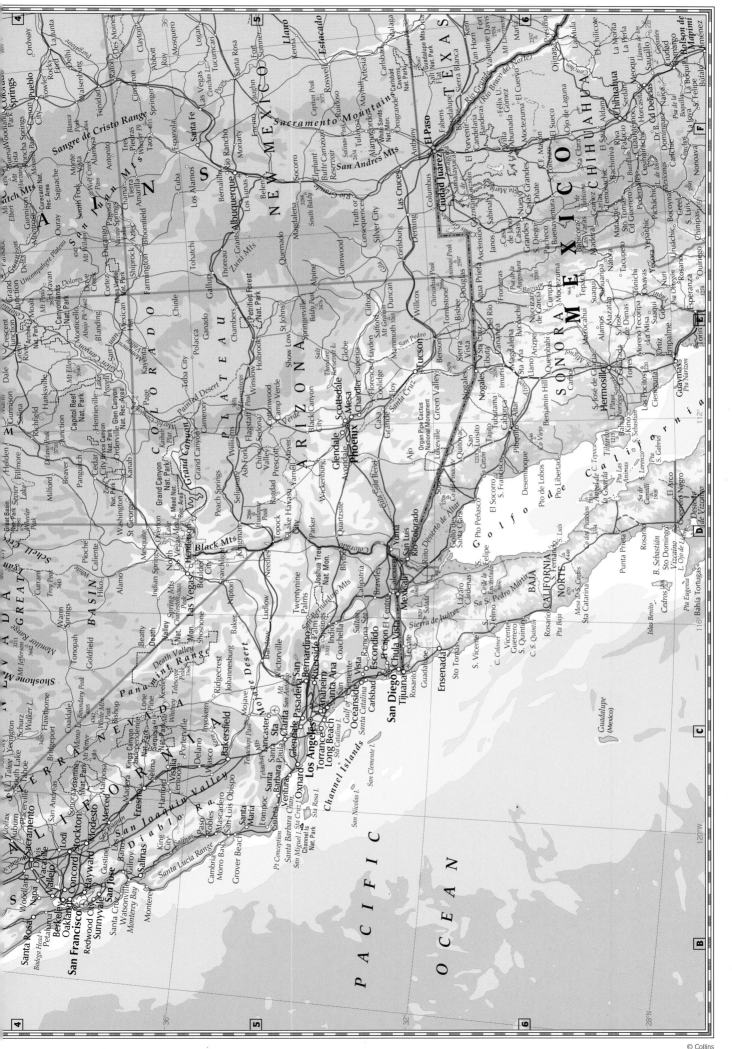

1:7M

KM   MILES
350 ─ 200
300
250 ─ 150
200 ─ 100
150
100 ─ 50
50
0 ─ 0

© Collins

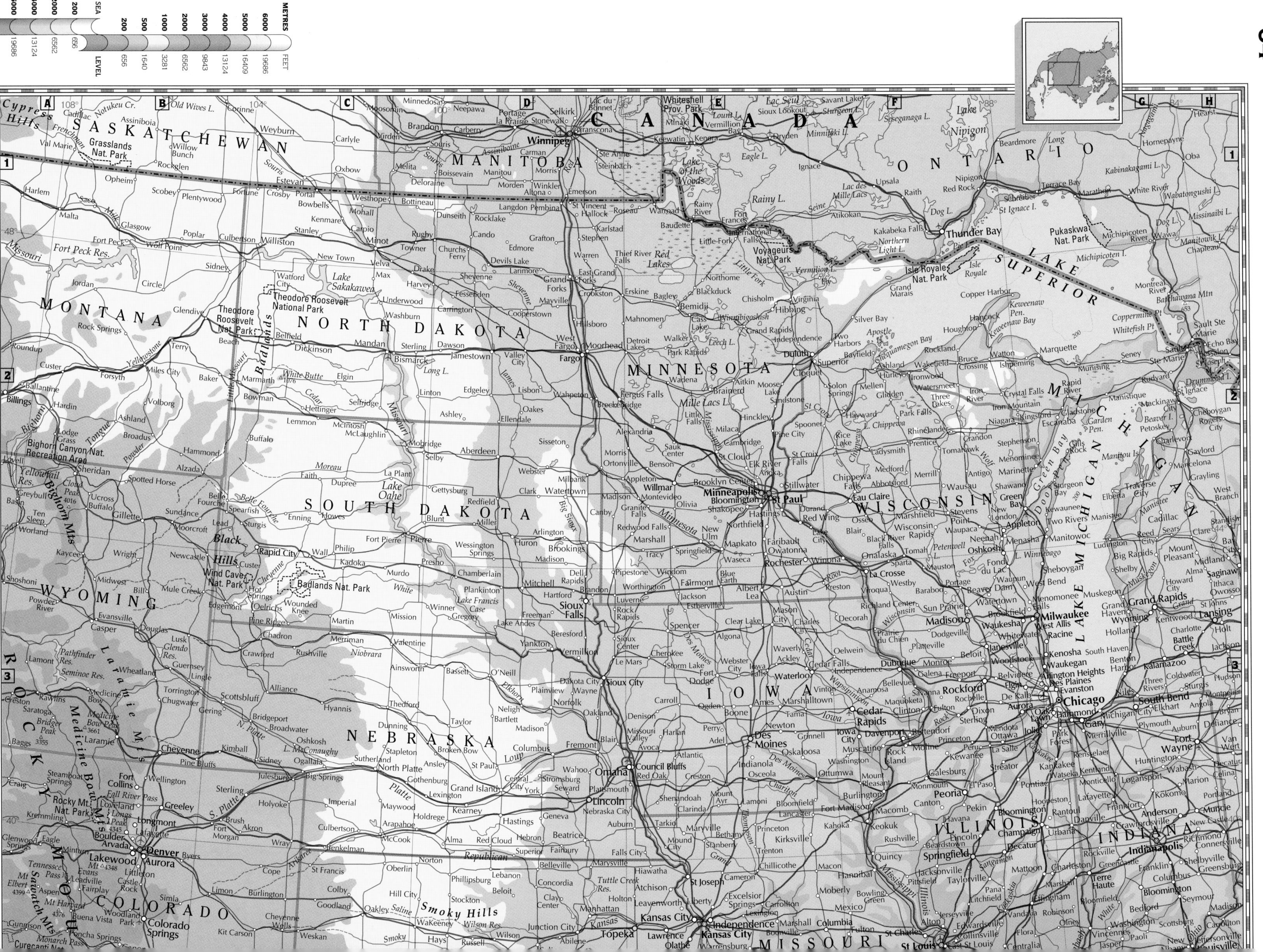

Lambert Conformal Conic Projection

METRES / FEET

METRES	FEET
6000	19686
5000	16409
4000	13124
3000	9843
2000	6562
1000	3281
500	1640
200	656
SEA	LEVEL
200	656
2000	6562
4000	13124
6000	19686

1:7M

Lambert Conformal Conic Projection

METRES	FEET
6000	19686
5000	16409
4000	13124
3000	9843
2000	6562
1000	3281
500	1640
200	656
SEA	LEVEL
200	656
2000	6562
4000	13124
6000	19686

ATLANTIC

OCEAN

THE BAHAMAS

GULF

OF

MEXICO

1:7M

KM   MILES
350
300   200
250
200   150
150
100   100
50
50
0   0

© Collins

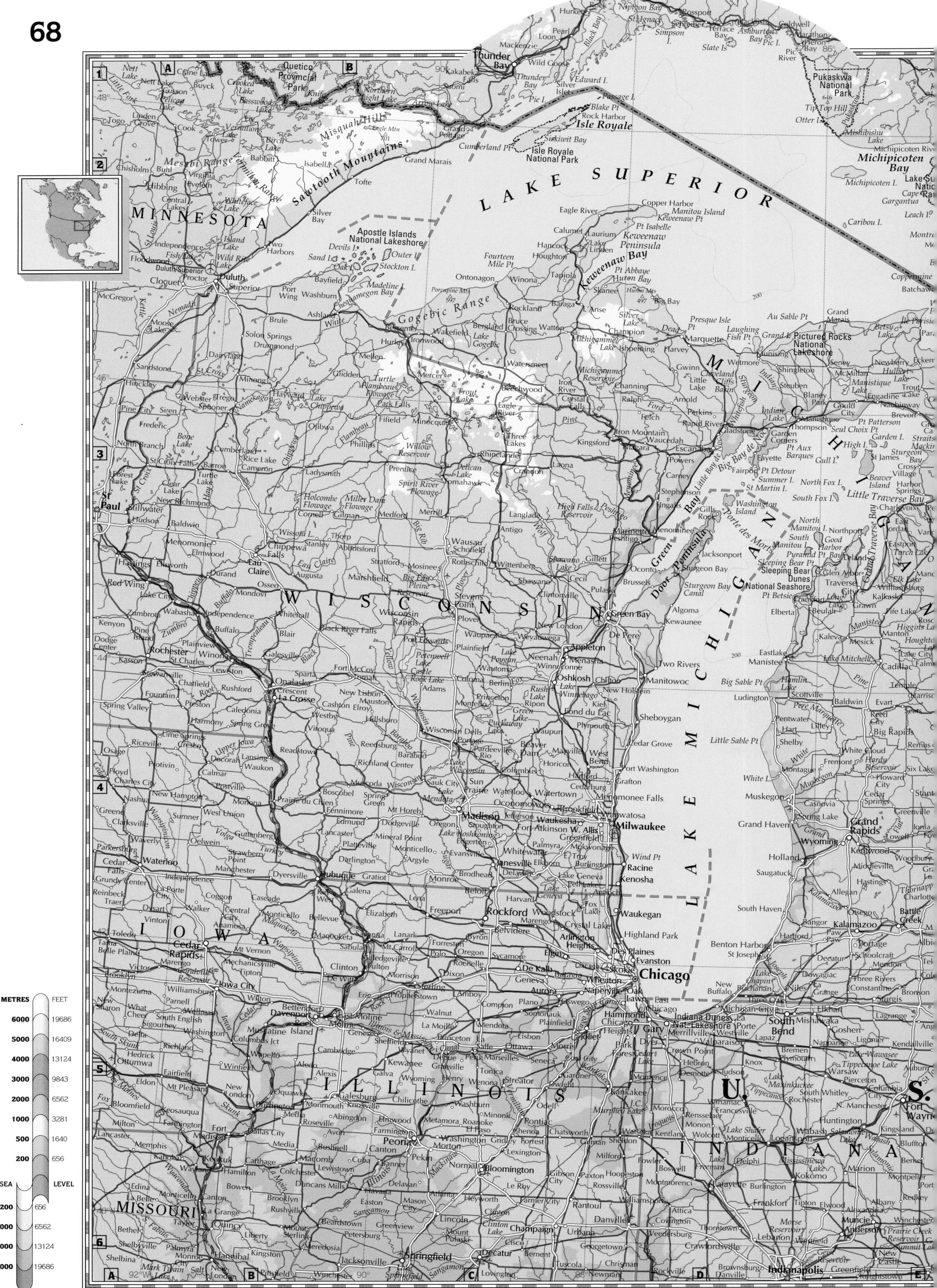

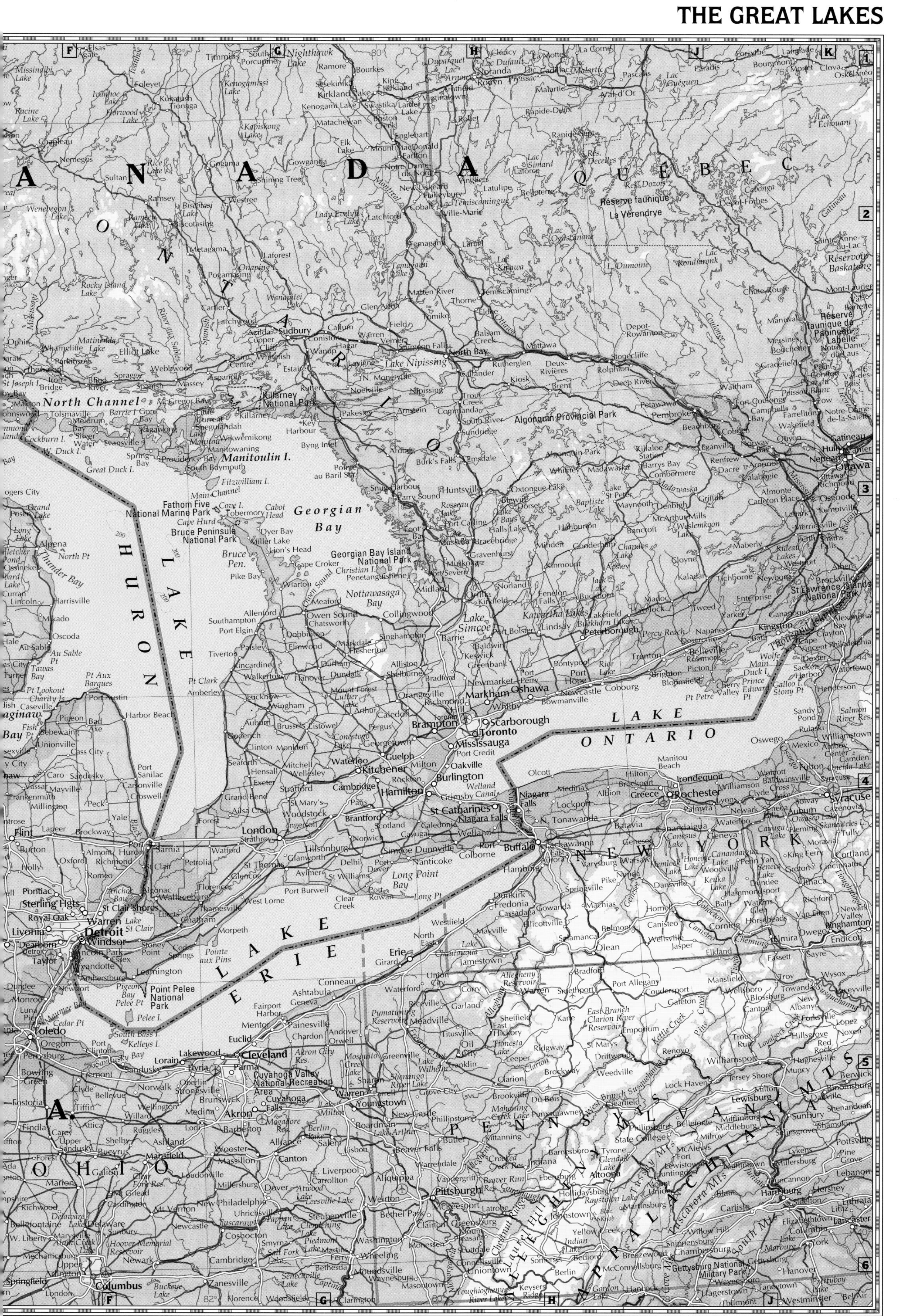

1:3.5M

KM	MILES
175	
	100
150	
125	75
100	
	50
75	
	25
50	
25	
0	0

70

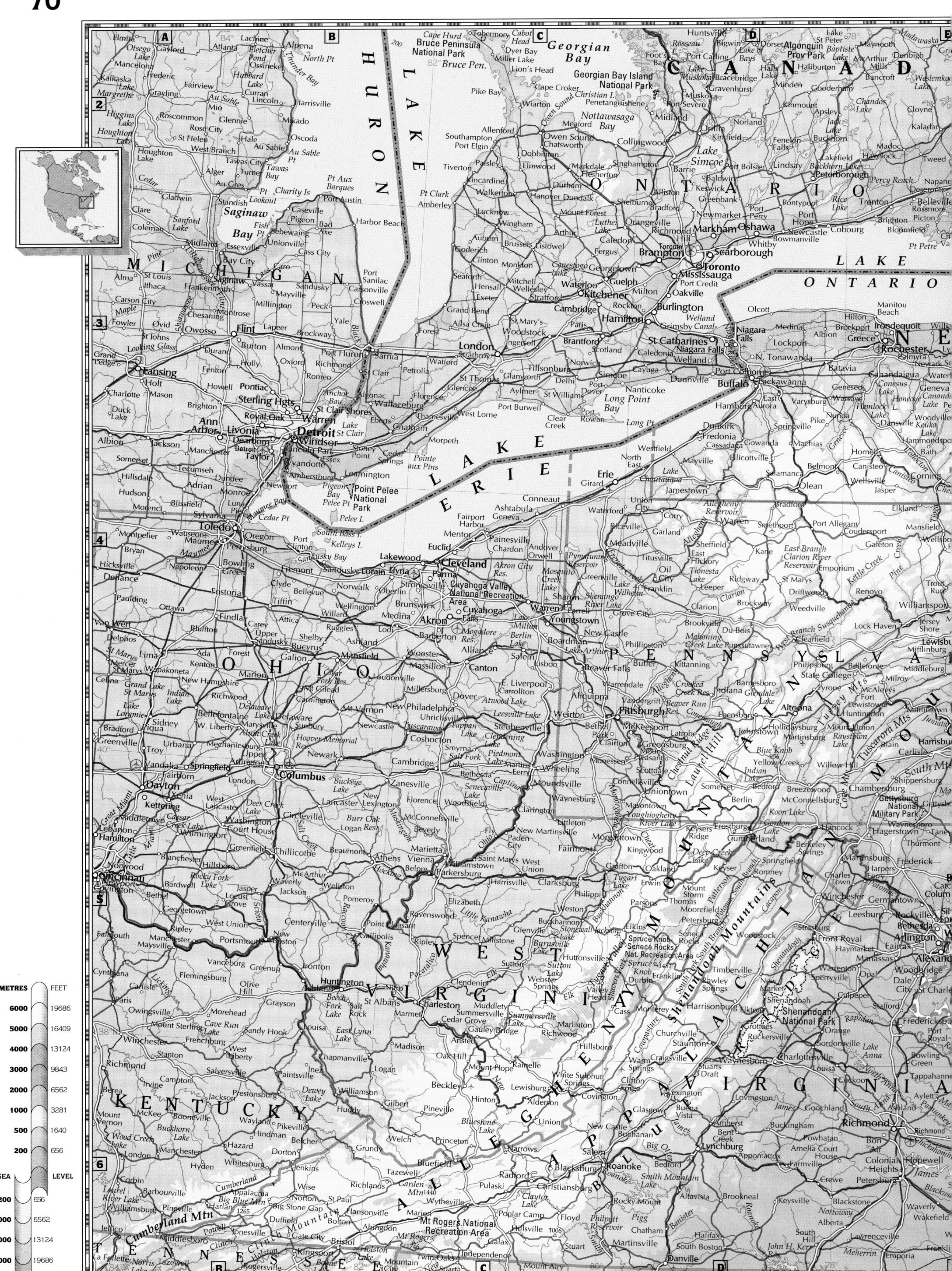

Lambert Conformal Conic Projection

1:3.5M

KM   MILES
175
          100
150
125   75
100
          50
75
50   25
25
0

continuation at the same scale

© Collins

PACIFIC OCEAN

CALIFORNIA

NEVADA

OR

Mojave Desert

OAHU
(Hawaii)
1:1.5M

HAWAIIAN ISLANDS
(Main group)
(U.S.A.) 1:6M

PACIFIC OCEAN

METRES	FEET
6000	19686
5000	16409
4000	13124
3000	9843
2000	6562
1000	3281
500	1640
200	656
SEA	LEVEL
200	656
2000	6562
4000	13124
6000	19686

Lambert Conformal Conic Projection

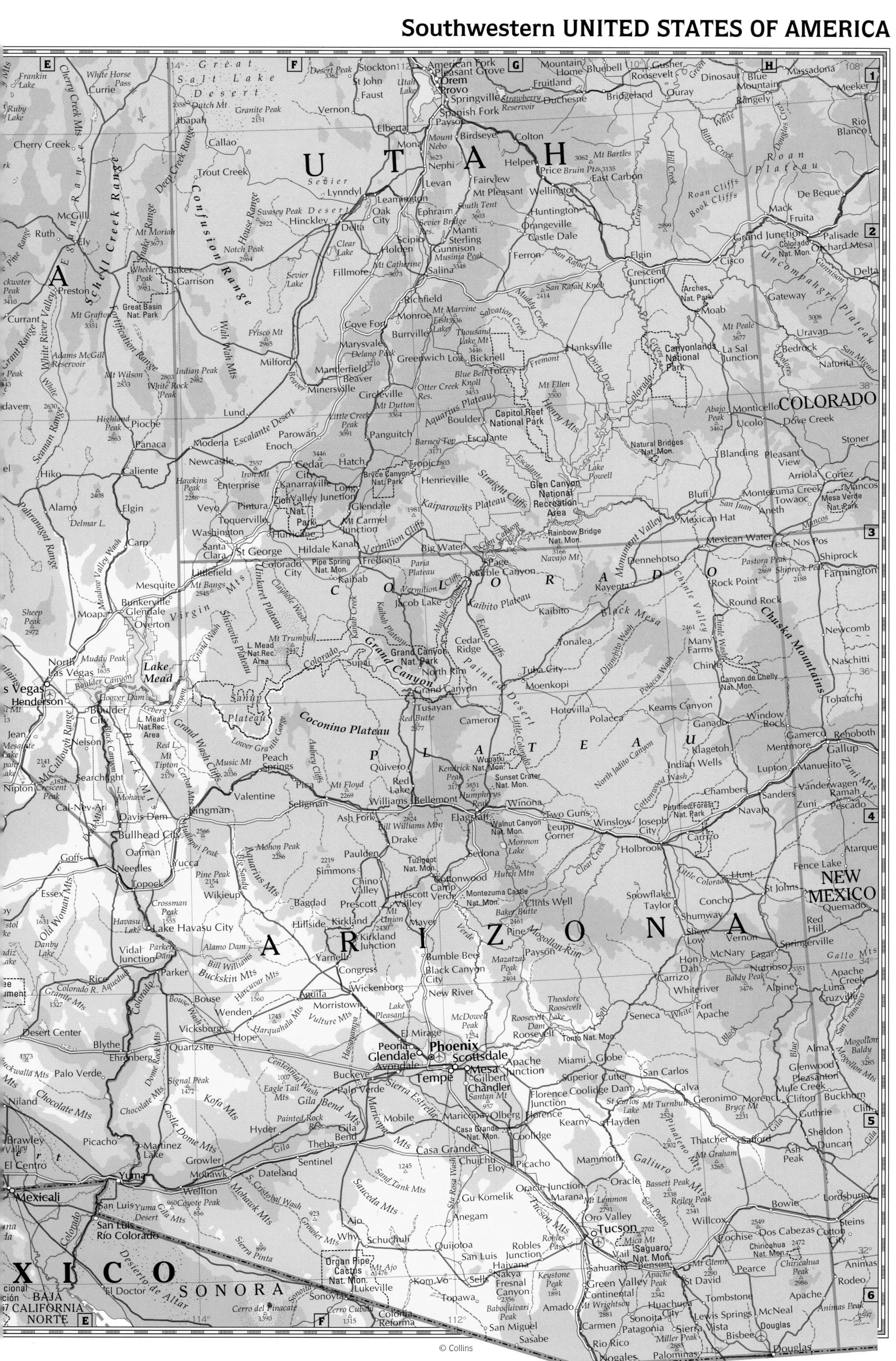

1:3.5M

KM	MILES
175	100
150	
125	75
100	
75	50
50	
25	25
0	0

© Collins

A
B
C
D
E
F
ARIZONA
NEW MEXICO
OKLAHOMA
ARKANSAS
U. S.
TEXAS
LOUISIANA
MISSISSIPPI
MEXICO
GUATEMALA
EL SALVADOR
GULF OF ME
PACIFIC OCEAN
Golfo de California
Baja California
SIERRA MADRE OCCIDENTAL
Sierra Madre Oriental
Sierra Madre del Sur
Sierra Vizcaíno
Edwards Plateau
Llano Estacado
Bolson de Mapimí
Sacramento Mts
Ouachita Mts
Boston Mts
Bahía de Campeche
Golfo de Tehuantepec
Yucatán
Laguna Madre
Islas Marías
Islas Revillagigedo (Mex.)
I. San Benedicto
I. Socorro
Clipperton Island (France)
Isla Cedros
Tiburón
Albuquerque
Amarillo
Oklahoma City
Tulsa
Fort Smith
Memphis
Little Rock
Phoenix
Tucson
Tijuana
Mexicali
Ensenada
Yuma
El Paso
Ciudad Juárez
Lubbock
Midland
Abilene
Fort Worth
Dallas
Shreveport
Jackson
Waco
Austin
San Antonio
Houston
Beaumont
Baton Rouge
New Orleans
Galveston
Corpus Christi
Brownsville
Matamoros
Nuevo Laredo
Hermosillo
Guaymas
Ciudad Obregón
Los Mochis
Chihuahua
Torreón
Gómez Palacio
Monterrey
Saltillo
Culiacán
La Paz
Mazatlán
Durango
Zacatecas
Ciudad Victoria
Tampico
San Luis Potosí
Aguascalientes
Tepic
Guadalajara
León
Querétaro
Morelia
Pachuca
México
Puebla
Toluca
Cuernavaca
Veracruz
Orizaba
Córdoba
Acapulco
Oaxaca
Coatzacoalcos
Villahermosa
Tuxtla Gutiérrez
Tapachula
Mérida
Campeche
Chetumal
Guatemala
San Salvador
Lambert Azimuthal Equal Area Projection
METRES
FEET
6000
19686
5000
16409
4000
13124
3000
9843
2000
6562
1000
3281
500
1640
200
656
SEA
LEVEL
200
656
2000
6562
4000
13124
6000
19686

ATLANTIC

OCEAN

BERMUDA
(U.K.) Hamilton

Tropic of Cancer

THE BAHAMAS

Grand Bahama
Freeport
Little Abaco
Great Abaco
Eleuthera
Governor's Harbour
Nassau
Andros
Cat Island
San Salvador (Watling)
Rum Cay
Great Exuma
Long Island
Crooked Island
Acklins Island
Mayaguana
Crooked I. Passage

TURKS AND CAICOS ISLANDS
(U.K.)
Caicos Is
Cockburn Town
Turks Is

Matthew Town
Great Inagua

HISPANIOLA

LEEWARD ISLANDS

ANGUILLA (U.K.)
Anegada (U.K.)
VIRGIN IS (U.K.)
VIRGIN IS (U.S.A.)
Saint Martin (Fr.)
St Maarten (Neth.)
St Barthélemy (Fr.)
ANTIGUA AND BARBUDA
St Eustatius (Neth.)
Basseterre
St John's
Antigua
ST KITTS-NEVIS
MONTSERRAT (U.K.)
Plymouth
GUADELOUPE (Fr.)
Basse-Terre
Pointe-à-Pitre
Marie Galante
Roseau
DOMINICA

CUBA

Arch. de Sabana
Matanzas
Colon
Güines
Sagua la Grande
Santa Clara
Cienfuegos
G. de Batabanó
Placetas
Caibarién
Arch. de Camagüey
Morón
Ciego de Ávila
Sancti Spíritus
Trinidad
Nuevitas
Camagüey
Victoria de las Tunas
Holguín
Banes
Bayamo
Manzanillo
Arch. de los Jardines de la Reina
Golfo de Guacanayabo
Sierra Maestra
Turquino 2005
Santiago de Cuba
Baracoa
Cabo Cruz
Guantánamo
Port-de-Paix
Cap-Haïtien
Monte Cristi
Puerto Plata
Santiago
San Francisco de Macorís
La Romana

Isla de la Juventud

GREATER

CAYMAN ISLANDS
(U.K.) Cayman Brac
Little Cayman
Grand Cayman

Jamaica Channel
Windward Passage
Île de la Gonâve
Gonaïves
Pico Duarte 3175
HAITI
Port-au-Prince
Jérémie
M. de la Hotte
Les Cayes
La Selle
Jacmel
Barahona
Isla Beata
C. Beata

DOMINICAN REPUBLIC
Santo Domingo

Aguadilla
San Juan
Mayagüez
Ponce
Isla Mona
PUERTO RICO
(U.S.A.)
Co de Punta
St Jago
Vieques
St Croix
Mona Passage
Nona Passage

MARTINIQUE (Fr.)
Fort-de-France
Castries
ST LUCIA
Kingstown
ST VINCENT & THE GRENADINES
Bridgetown
BARBADOS
GRENADA
St George's

JAMAICA
Montego Bay
St Ann's Bay
Savanna la Mar
Mandeville
Kingston
Spanish Town

ANTILLES

WINDWARD ISLANDS

CARIBBEAN SEA

Lesser Antilles

Lesser Antilles

GRENADA
St George's
TRINIDAD AND TOBAGO
Tobago
Scarborough
Trinidad
Port of Spain
Arima

GEORGIA

Macon
Dublin
Cordele
Tifton
Valdosta
Waycross
Brunswick

SOUTH CAROLINA
Columbia
Orangeburg
Charleston
Hilton Head Island
Savannah

NORTH CAROLINA
Winston-Salem
Greensboro
Durham
Raleigh
High Point
Charlotte
Gastonia
Rock Hill
Fayetteville
Kinston
New Bern
Wilmington
Cape Fear
Cape Lookout
Cape Hatteras
Pamlico Sd
Albemarle Sd
Sumter
Suffolk

Knoxville
Asheville
Greenville
Spartanburg
Clark Hill Res.
Florence
Lumberton
Jacksonville

Blue Ridge
Great Smoky Mts
2037

Middlesboro
Kingsport
Bristol
Johnson City
Martinsville
Danville

Athens
Anderson
Greenwood
Augusta
Griffin
Atlanta

Tallahassee
Thomasville
Bainbridge

Lake City
St Augustine
Gainesville
Ocala
Sanford
Orlando
Daytona Beach
Cape Canaveral
Melbourne
Winter Haven
Lakeland
Fort Pierce
West Palm Beach
Fort Lauderdale
Hollywood
Miami Beach
Miami

Jacksonville

Tampa
Clearwater
St Petersburg
Sarasota
Port Charlotte
Fort Myers

L. Okeechobee
The Everglades
Big Cypress Nat. Reserve
Everglades Nat. Park
Cape Sable
Key West

Straits of Florida
Great Bahama Bank

del Río
La Habana (Habana)

NICARAGUA

Cayos Miskitos (Nic.)
Puerto Cabezas
Prinzapolca
Bluefields
Swan Islands (Hond.)
Isla de Providencia (Col.)
Isla de San Andrés (Col.)

COSTA RICA
Limón
Cartago
Chirripó 3819
Puerto Cortés
Volcán Barú 3475
David
Concepción
Golfo de Chiriquí
Isla Coiba
Punta Mariato

PANAMA
Bocas del Toro
Golfo de los Mosquitos
Colón
Panama Canal
Panamá
G. de Panamá
La Chorrera
Aguadulce
Chitré
Las Tablas
Península de Azuero
Pta Mala

Laguna Caratasca
Segovia

Pta de Perlas

VENEZUELA

Punta Gallinas
Península de la Guajira
Riohacha
ARUBA (Neth.)
Curaçao
NETHERLANDS ANTILLES
Bonaire
Punto Fijo
Coro
I. Orchila (Ven.)
Islas Los Roques (Ven.)
Los Testigos (Ven.)
I. Blanquilla (Ven.)
I. La Tortuga (Ven.)
I. de Margarita (Ven.)
Porlamar
Cumaná
Carúpano
Güiria
Pto de Cabello
San Fernando
Maiquetía
Caracas
Los Teques
Barcelona
Maturín
Tucupita
Boca de Macareo

G. de Venezuela
Maracaibo
Mene de Mauroa
Cabimas
Puerto Cabello
San Felipe
Valencia
Maracay
Barquisimeto
San Carlos
Acarigua
San Juan de los Morros
Zaraza
Ciudad Guayana

L. de Maracaibo
Trujillo
Valera
Mérida
Pico Bolívar 5007
Barinas
Libertad
San Fernando de Apure
El Baúl
Calabozo
Valle de la Pascua
El Tigre
Ciudad Bolívar

Machiques
Parque Nacional Sierra Nevada
Guanare
Cabruta
Maripa
Upata
El Callao
El Dorado

COLOMBIA

Santa Marta
Barranquilla
Cartagena
Pico Cristóbal Colón 5775
Sierra Nevada de Santa Marta
Parque Nacional Sierra Nevada de Santa Marta
Valledupar
Calamar
Rosario
Sincelejo
El Banco
Mompós
Golfo de Morrosquillo
Golfo del Darién
Montería
Turbo
Cúcuta
San Cristóbal
Pamplona
Arauca
Guasdualito
Puerto Carreño
Co Yaví 2285

Parque Nacional Paramillo
Parque Nacional de Darién
Golfo de Cupica
Cabo Corrientes
Quibdó
Medellín
Bucaramanga
Barrancabermeja
Socorro
Yopal
Puerto Ayacucho

Manizales
Pereira
Cartago
Armenia
Ibagué
Buga
Tuluá
Sevilla
Palmira
Cali
Buenaventura
Honda
Tunja
Villavicencio
Bogotá
Chiquinquirá
Nevado del Ruiz 5321
Cerro El Nevado 5750
Parque Nacional Sumapaz
Puerto Inírida
Guaviare

Quibdó
I. de Malpelo (Col.)
Popayán
Sanquianga
Tumaco
Volcán de Purace 4580
Neiva
La Macarena
Campoalegre
Garzón
Parque Nacional Cord. de los Picachos
Florencia
Nevado de Huila 5750
Parque Nacional
San José del Guaviare
Parque Nacional El Tuparro
Parque Nacional Jaua Sarisariñama
Parque Nacional Duida-Marahuaca
La Gran Sabana
Parque Nacional Canaima
Parque Nacional Jaua Sarisariñama
Serra Pacaraima
Parque Nacional Serranía de la Neblina
Parque Nacional Parima-Tapirapeco
Negro
Orinoco
Cucuí

Cordillera Central
Cordillera Oriental

1:14M

KM	MILES
700	
	400
600	
	300
500	
400	200
300	
	100
200	
100	
0	0

© Collins

NORTH AMERICA

CARIBBEAN SEA

ATLANTIC OCEAN

Punta Gallinas
G. de Venezuela
Isla de Margarita
Golfo del Darién
Maracaibo
Orinoco Delta
Waini Point
Cabo Corrientes
I. de Malpelo
Cerro Yavi 2285
La Gran Sabana
Sa Pacaraima
Essequibo
Pointe Isère
Cabo Orange
Orinoco
Meta
Guaviare
Guainía
LLANOS
Ilha de Maracá
Cordillera Occidental
Cordillera Central
Cordillera Oriental
Cotopaxi 5896
Chimborazo 6310
Caquetá
Japurá
Putumayo
Negro
Branco
Represa de Balbina
Amazon
I. de Marajó
Mouths of the Amazon
Baía de São Marcos
Equator
Golfo de Guayaquil
Marañón
Amazon
Ucayali
Juruá
Purus
Madeira
Tapajós
Iriri
Xingu
Tocantins
Represa Tucuruí
Parnaíba
Ponta do Calcanhar
SELVAS
Cordillera Central 6768
Nevado de Huascarán
Bahia de Pisco
Beni
Guaporé
Jiparaná
Guaporé
Lago de San Luis
San Miguel
Teles Pires
Juruena
Arinos
Araguaia
Tocantins
São Francisco
Chapada Diamantina
Cabo Santo Antônio
Cordillera Oriental
Cordillera Occidental
Yungas
Altiplano
ANDES
Lago Titicaca
L. de Poopó
Bañados del Izozog
Desierto de Atacama
Ponta da Baleia
Pta Tetas
Gran Chaco
Pilcomayo
Teuco
Paraguai
Paraguaçu
Grande
Paraná
Paranapanema
Cabo de São Tomé
Tropic of Capricorn
Islas de los Desventurados
Pta Ballena
Pta Morro
Cerro Bonete 6872
Salinas Grandes
Saladó
Desaguadero
Sierras de Córdoba
PAMPAS
Iguaçu Falls
Uruguay
Paraná
Ilha de São Sebastião
Juan Fernandez Islands
Aconcagua 6960
Lagoa dos Patos
Lagoa Mirim
Rio de la Plata
PACIFIC OCEAN
Colorado
Negro
Bahía Blanca
Pta Galera
Golfo San Matías
Península Valdés
Isla de Chiloé
Patagonia
Golfo de San Jorge
Archipiélago de los Chonos
Golfo de Penas
Pta Medanosa
L. San Martín
ATLANTIC OCEAN
L. Argentino
Bahía Grande
Est. de Magallanes
Falkland Islands
West Falkland
East Falkland
Tierra del Fuego
I. de los Estados
South Georgia
Cape Horn

METRES / FEET
5000 / 16409
3000 / 9843
2000 / 6562
1000 / 3281
500 / 1640
200 / 656
SEA LEVEL
200 / 656
3000 / 9843
5000 / 16409
6000 / 19686

1:30M

KM / MILES
1800
1500 / 900
1200 / 600
900 / 600
600 / 300
300
0 / 0

Sinusoidal Projection

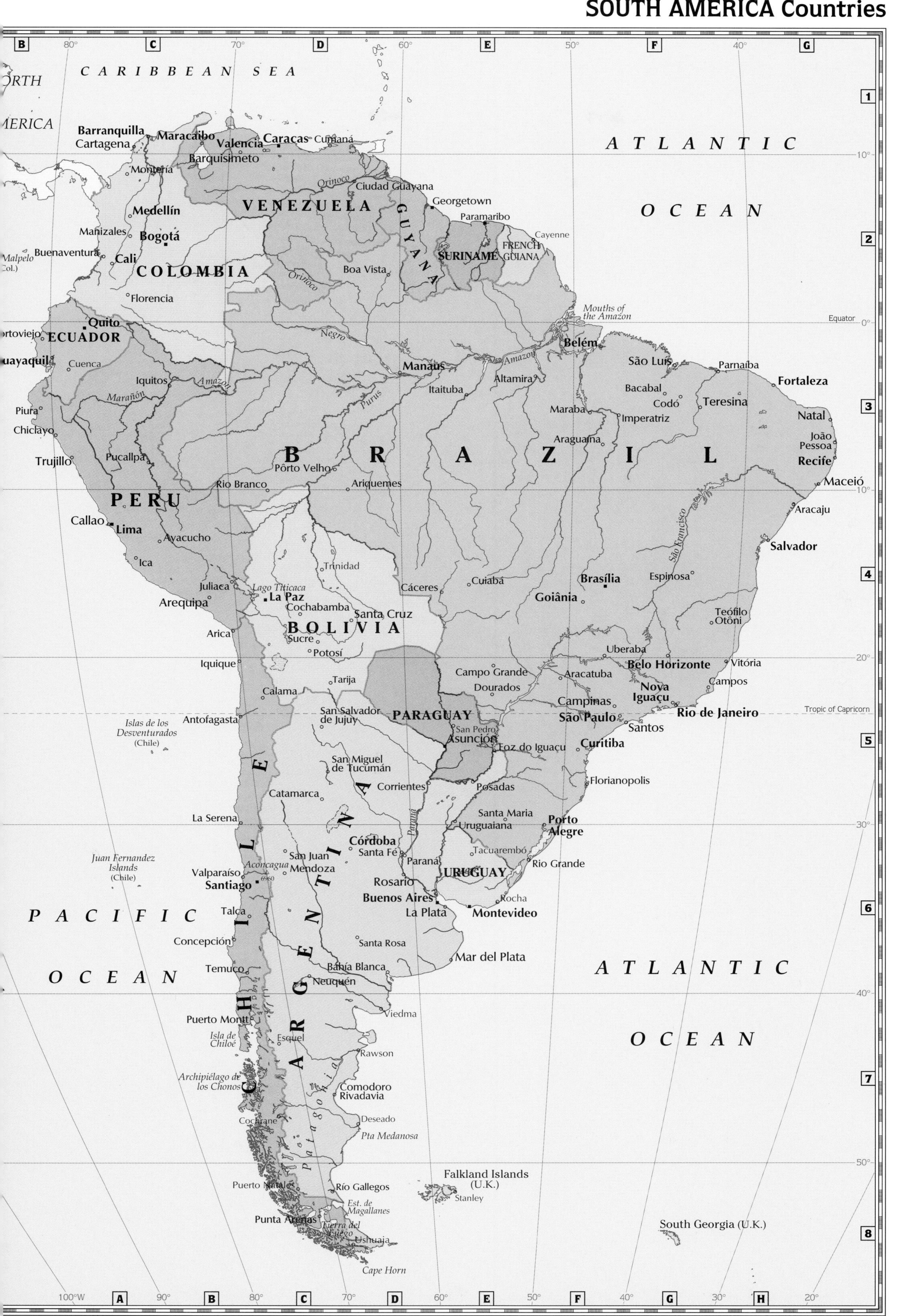

CARIBBEAN SEA

NORTH AMERICA

ATLANTIC

OCEAN

Barranquilla
Cartagena
Montería
Maracaibo
Valencia
Barquisimeto
Caracas
Cumaná
Orinoco
Ciudad Guayana
Georgetown
Paramaribo
Cayenne
FRENCH GUIANA

Medellín
Manizales
Bogotá
Buenaventura
Cali
VENEZUELA
GUYANA
SURINAME

Malpelo (Col.)

COLOMBIA
Florencia
Orinoco
Boa Vista

Quito
Portoviejo
ECUADOR
Guayaquil
Cuenca
Negro
Mouths of the Amazon
Equator 0°

Iquitos
Amazon
Manaus
Altamira
Belém
São Luís
Parnaíba
Fortaleza

Piura
Marañón
Itaituba
Purus
Maraba
Bacabal
Codó
Teresina
Natal

Chiclayo
Pucallpa
Araguaína
Imperatriz
João Pessoa

Trujillo
BRAZIL
Recife

Callao
Lima
Rio Branco
Ariquemes
10°
Maceió

PERU
Pôrto Velho
Aracaju

Ayacucho

Ica
Salvador

Juliaca
Trinidad
Cáceres
Cuiabá
Brasília
Espinosa

Arequipa
Lago Titicaca
La Paz
Goiânia
Teófilo Otôni

Arica
Cochabamba
Santa Cruz
BOLIVIA
Sucre
Uberaba
Belo Horizonte
Vitória
20°

Iquique
Potosí
Campo Grande
Aracatuba
Nova Iguaçu
Campos

Calama
Tarija
Dourados
Campinas
São Paulo
Rio de Janeiro
Tropic of Capricorn

Antofagasta
San Salvador de Jujuy
PARAGUAY
San Pedro
Asunción
Foz do Iguaçu
Santos
Curitiba

Islas de los Desventurados (Chile)
San Miguel de Tucumán
Corrientes
Posadas
Florianopolis

Catamarca
Santa Maria
Uruguaiana
Porto Alegre

La Serena
CHILE
Paraná
Tacuarembó
Rio Grande
30°

Juan Fernandez Islands (Chile)
San Juan
Aconcagua
Mendoza
Córdoba
Santa Fé
Paraná
URUGUAY

Valparaíso
Santiago
ARGENTINA
Rosario
Buenos Aires
La Plata
Rocha
Montevideo

PACIFIC
Talca
Santa Rosa
Mar del Plata

Concepción

OCEAN
Temuco
Bahía Blanca
Neuquén
ATLANTIC
40°

Puerto Montt
Viedma
OCEAN

Isla de Chiloé
Esquel
Rawson

Archipiélago de los Chonos
Comodoro Rivadavia

Patagonia
Deseado
Pta Medanosa

Cochrane
50°

Puerto Natales
Río Gallegos
Falkland Islands (U.K.)
Stanley

Punta Arenas
Est. de Magallanes
Tierra del Fuego
Ushuaia
South Georgia (U.K.)

Cape Horn

1:30M

KM   MILES
1800
1500   900
1200   600
900
600   300
300
0

I Projection

© Collins

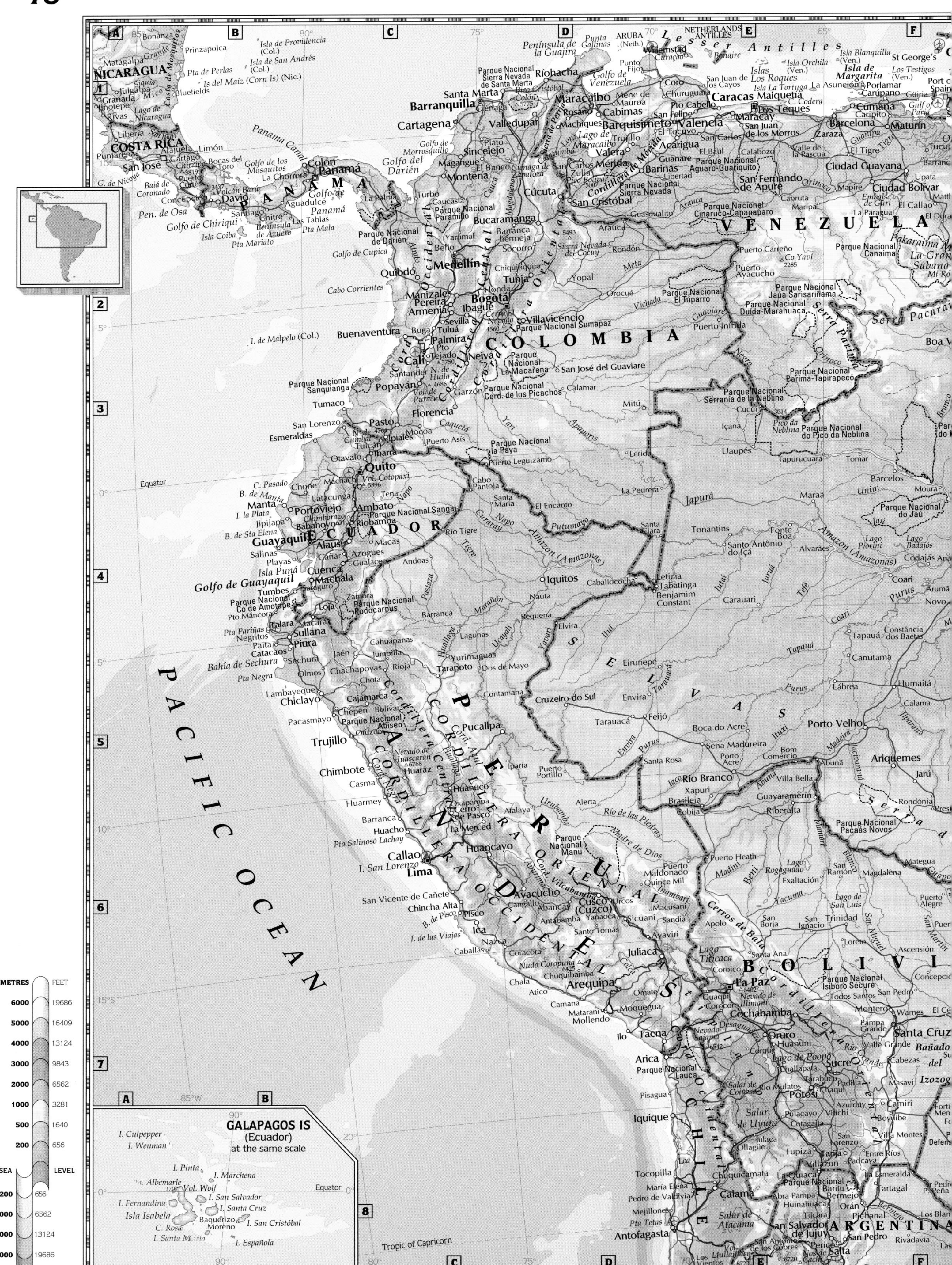

ATLANTIC

OCEAN

1:15M

KM	MILES
	600
900	
	450
750	
600	300
450	
	150
300	
150	
0	0

© Collins

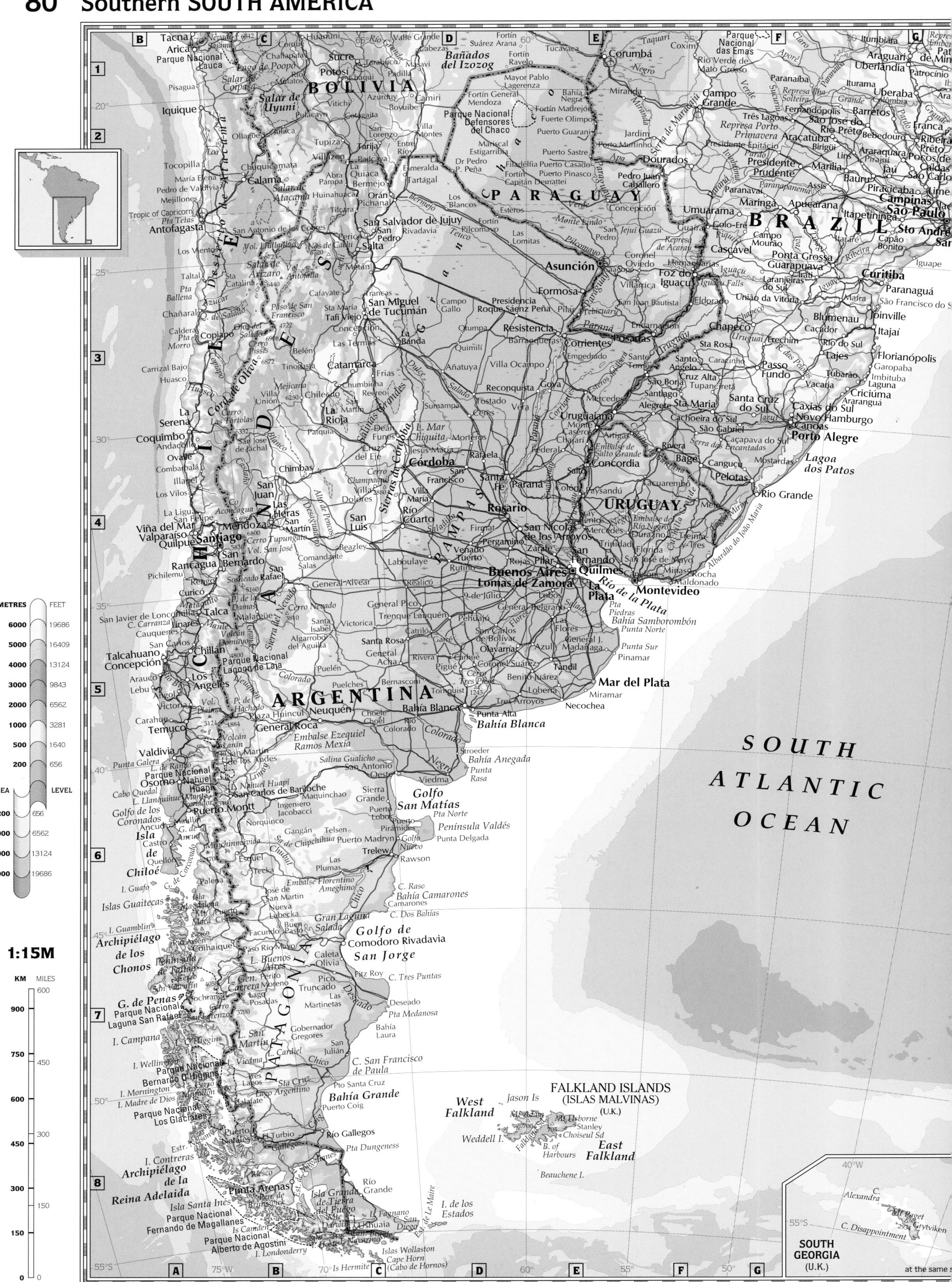
BOLIVIA
PARAGUAY
BRAZIL
URUGUAY
ARGENTINA
PATAGONIA
ANDES
PAMPAS
Gran Chaco
SOUTH ATLANTIC OCEAN
FALKLAND ISLANDS (ISLAS MALVINAS) (U.K.)
West Falkland
East Falkland
SOUTH GEORGIA (U.K.)
Tropic of Capricorn
Desierto de Atacama
Golfo San Matías
Golfo San Jorge
Bahía Grande
Bahía Blanca
Río de la Plata
Lagoa dos Patos
Isla de Chiloé
Archipiélago de los Chonos
Archipiélago de la Reina Adelaida
Isla Grande de Tierra del Fuego
I. de los Estados
Cape Horn (Cabo de Hornos)
Península Valdés
Buenos Aires
Montevideo
Santiago
Asunción
São Paulo
Córdoba
Rosario
Mendoza
Valparaíso
Concepción
Porto Alegre
Curitiba
Mar del Plata
Punta Arenas
Río Gallegos
Ushuaia
Comodoro Rivadavia
Antofagasta
Iquique
Sucre
Potosí
Salar de Uyuni
Corumbá
Campinas
Florianópolis
METRES
FEET
6000
19686
5000
16409
4000
13124
3000
9843
2000
6562
1000
3281
500
1640
200
656
SEA
LEVEL
1:15M
KM
MILES
900
750
600
450
300
150
0
Lambert Azimuthal Equal Area Projection

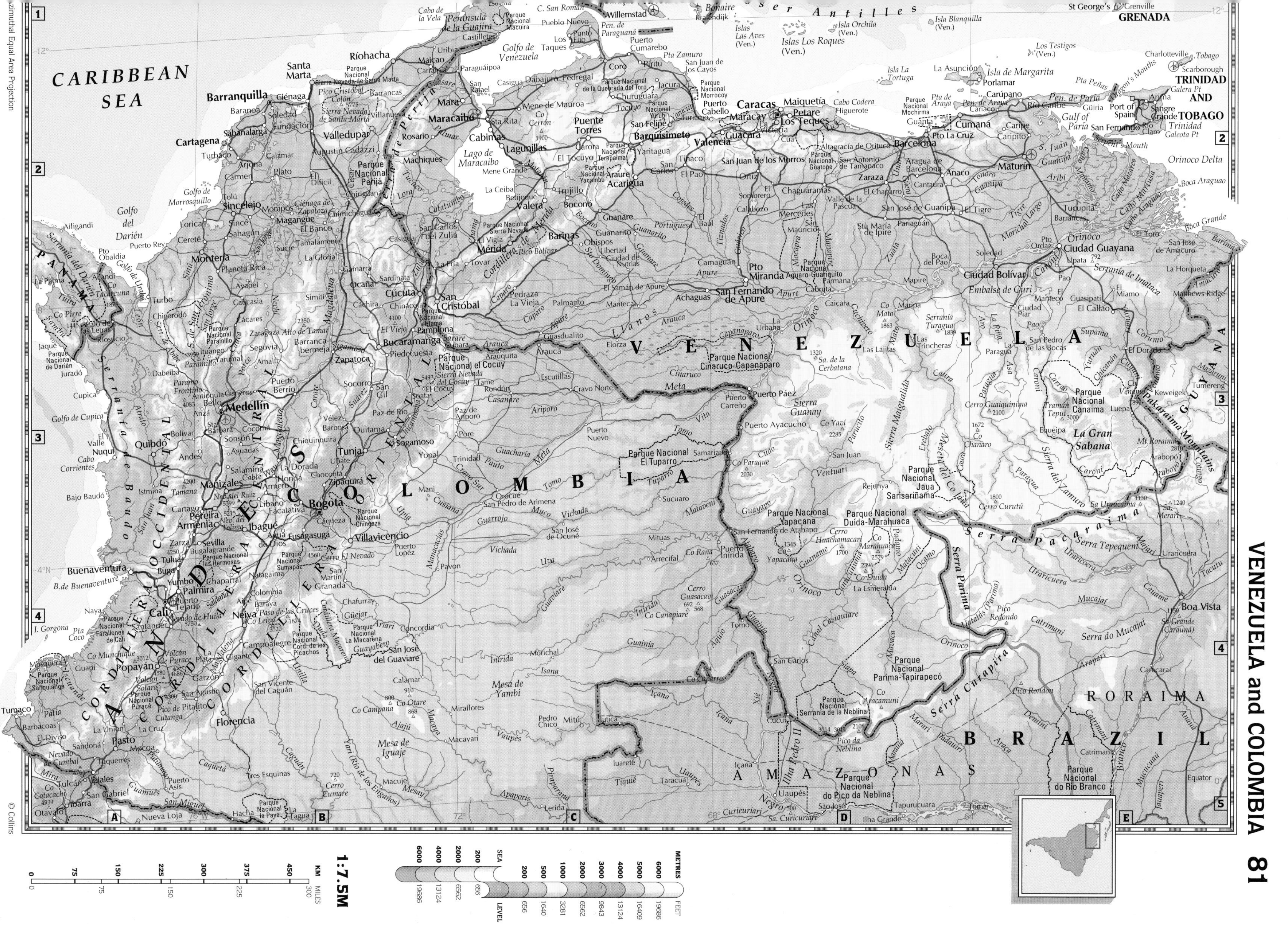

METRES	FEET
6000	19686
5000	16409
4000	13124
3000	9843
2000	6562
1000	3281
500	1640
200	656
SEA	LEVEL
200	656
2000	6562
4000	13124
6000	19686

1:7.5M

KM	MILES
300
450	225
375
300	150
225
75
150
75
0	0

Azimuthal Equal Area Projection

© Collins

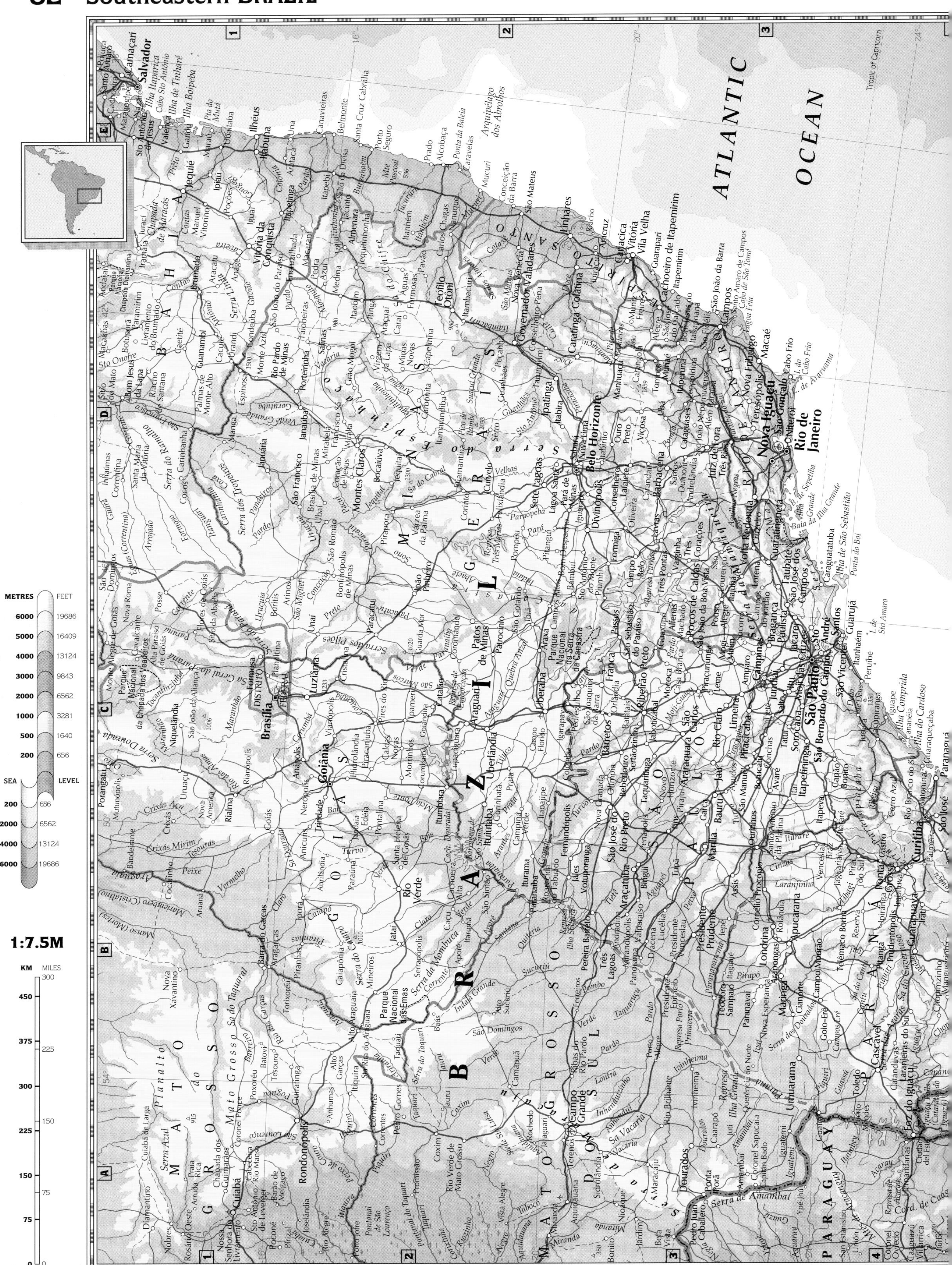

Lambert Azimuthal Equal Area Projection

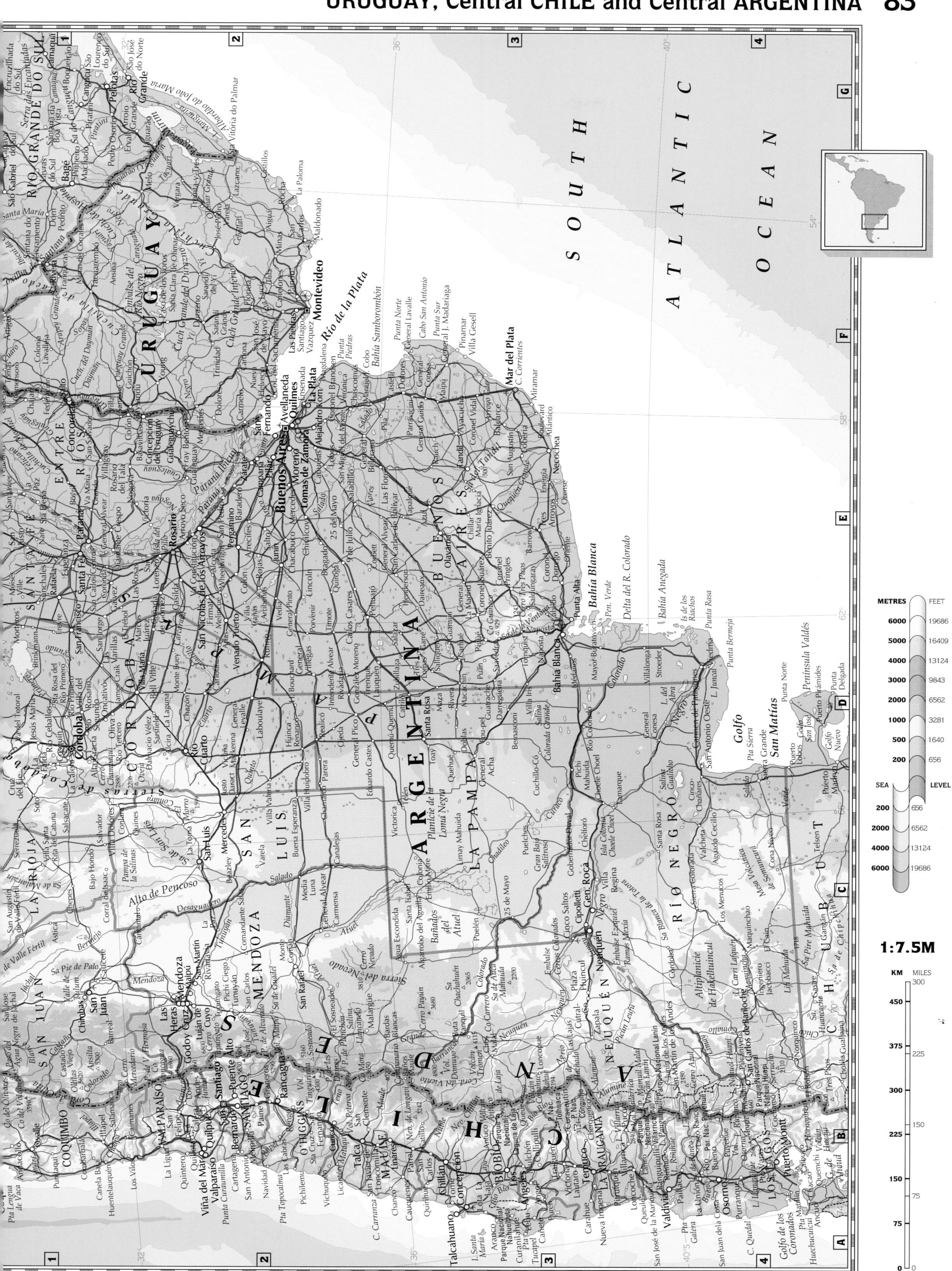
SOUTH ATLANTIC OCEAN
URUGUAY
ARGENTINA
CHILE
BUENOS AIRES
LA PAMPA
MENDOZA
SAN LUIS
CÓRDOBA
SANTA FE
ENTRE RÍOS
NEUQUÉN
RÍO NEGRO
RIO GRANDE DO SUL
Montevideo
Buenos Aires
Río de la Plata
Mar del Plata
Bahía Blanca
Rosario
Córdoba
Mendoza
Santiago
Valparaíso
Concepción
Neuquén
Golfo San Matías
Península Valdés
METRES
FEET
6000
19686
5000
16409
4000
13124
3000
9843
2000
6562
1000
3281
500
1640
200
656
SEA
LEVEL
200
656
2000
6562
4000
13124
6000
19686
1:7.5M
KM
MILES
450
375
300
225
150
75
0
300
225
150
75
0

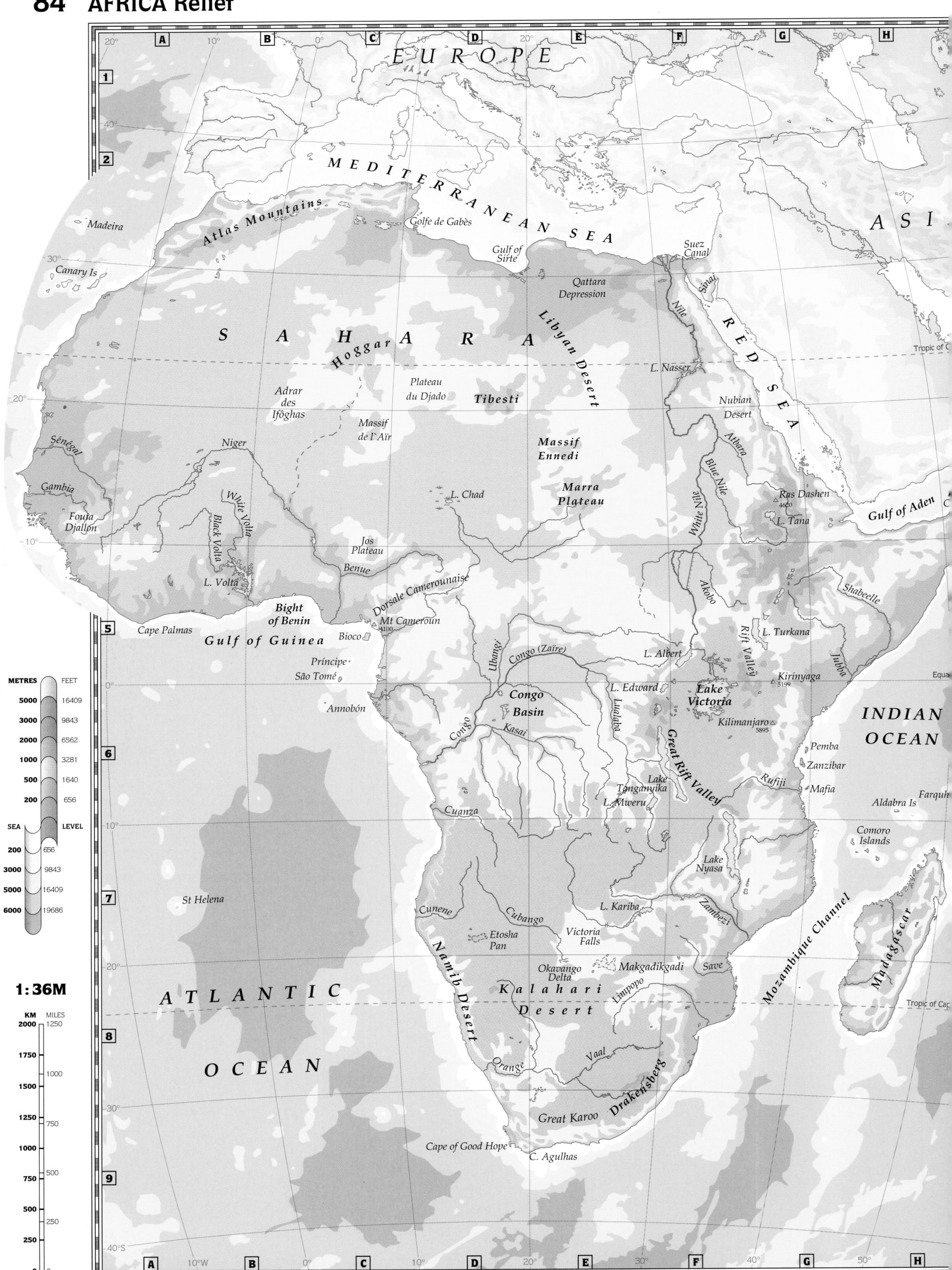

EUROPE

ASI

A

MEDITERRANEAN SEA

Madeira

Atlas Mountains

Golfe de Gabès

Gulf of Sirte

Suez Canal

Canary Is

Qattara Depression

Nile

Sinai

RED SEA

Tropic of C

S A H A R A

Hoggar

Libyan Desert

L. Nasser

Adrar des Ifôghas

Plateau du Djado

Tibesti

Nubian Desert

Massif de l'Aïr

Massif Ennedi

Athara

Blue Nile

Ras Dashen
4620

Sénégal

Niger

White Volta

Marra Plateau

L. Chad

White Nile

L. Tana

Gulf of Aden

Gambia

Fouta Djallon

Black Volta

Jos Plateau

Benue

Akobo

Shabeelle

L. Volta

Dorsale Camerounaise

Bight of Benin

Mt Cameroun
4100

Ubangi

Congo (Zaïre)

L. Albert

Rift Valley

L. Turkana

Jubba

Cape Palmas

Gulf of Guinea

Bioco

Príncipe
São Tomé

Congo

Congo Basin

Kasai

L. Edward

Lake Victoria

Kirinyaga
5199

Equa

INDIAN OCEAN

Annobón

Kilimanjaro
5895

Pemba

Zanzibar

Great Rift Valley

Lualaba

Mafia

Cuanza

Lake Tanganyika

L. Mweru

Rufiji

Aldabra Is

Farqu

Comoro Islands

St Helena

Cunene

Cubango

L. Kariba

Lake Nyasa

Zambezi

Victoria Falls

Madagascar

Namib Desert

Etosha Pan

Okavango Delta

Makgadikgadi

Save

Mozambique Channel

ATLANTIC

Kalahari Desert

Limpopo

Tropic of Cap

OCEAN

Vaal

Drakensberg

Great Karoo

Orange

Cape of Good Hope

C. Agulhas

METRES **FEET**

5000 — 16409
3000 — 9843
2000 — 6562
1000 — 3281
500 — 1640
200 — 656

SEA **LEVEL**

200 — 656
3000 — 9843
5000 — 16409
6000 — 19686

1:36M

KM **MILES**

2000 — 1250
1750 — 1000
1500 — 750
1250 — 500
1000 —
750 — 250
500 —
250 —
0 — 0

Lambert Azimuthal Equal Area Projection

1:36M

EUROPE

ASIA

MEDITERRANEAN SEA

Tangier Oran **Algiers** Annaba **Tunis**
Rabat Fès Constantine **TUNISIA**
Casablanca
Marrakech Tripoli Banghazi

Gulf of Sirte **Alexandria** Port Said
Cairo
El Gîza Suez

MOROCCO

Laâyoune

WESTERN SAHARA

ALGERIA **LIBYA** **EGYPT**

Aswân
L. Nasser

Tropic of Cancer

MAURITANIA **MALI** Port Sudan

Nouakchott *Niger*
Sénégal **SUDAN**
St Louis **NIGER** **CHAD** Omdurman **ERITREA**
Dakar Khartoum Asmara
SENEGAL Bamako Niamey *L. Chad* El Obeid *Blue Nile* *L. Tana* **DJIBOUTI**
THE GAMBIA Banjul Ouagadougou Kano Ndjamena Djibouti *Gulf of Aden*
GUINEA-BISSAU **BURKINA** Berbera
GUINEA *L. Volta* Abuja Sarh Dirê Dawa
Conakry **CÔTE** **BENIN** **NIGERIA** *White Nile* **Addis Ababa**
reetown **SIERRA LEONE** Yamoussoukro **GHANA** Ibadan **CENTRAL** **ETHIOPIA**
D'IVOIRE Porto-Novo **AFRICAN REPUBLIC**
Monrovia Accra Lomé Lagos
Abidjan Uyo **CAMEROON** Bangui *L. Turkana*
LIBERIA Malabo **SOMALIA**
Gulf of Guinea Yaoundé *Congo (Zaïre)* **UGANDA** **KENYA** Mogadishu
EQUATORIAL GUINEA Kisangani Kampala
SÃO TOMÉ & PRÍNCIPE Libreville **DEMOCRATIC** *Lake Victoria* Equator
Port-Gentil **GABON** **REPUBLIC** **RWANDA** Nairobi
Ascension I. (U.K.) **CONGO** *Kasai* **OF** Bukavu Kigali *Kilimanjaro 5895*
Brazzaville **CONGO** **BURUNDI** Bujumbura Arusha **INDIAN**
CABINDA Kinshasa Kananga Bujumbura **TANZANIA** Mombasa **OCEAN**
(Angola) *Lake Tanganyika* Dodoma Zanzibar
Luanda *Cuanza* Likasi *Rufiji* Dar es Salaam
St Helena (U.K.) Aldabra Is. (Sey.)
ANGOLA *Lake Nyasa* Moroni **COMOROS**
Benguela Huambo Ndola Lilongwe Nampula Mahajanga
Zambezi Lusaka **MALAWI** Blantyre
ZAMBIA Harare **MOZAMBIQUE** Antananarivo
Cubango **ZIMBABWE**
Etosha Pan Bulawayo Beira Fianarantsoa **MADAGASCAR**
NAMIBIA Windhoek **BOTSWANA**
ATLANTIC Gaborone Pretoria Maputo
Johannesburg Mbabane **SWAZILAND**
OCEAN Soweto
Maseru **LESOTHO**
REPUBLIC OF Durban
SOUTH AFRICA
Cape Town Port Elizabeth
Cape of Good Hope *C. Agulhas*

ic of Capricorn

KM **MILES**
2000 1250
1750 1000
1500
1250 750
1000
750 500
500
250 250
0 0

Azimuthal Equal Area Projection

© Collins

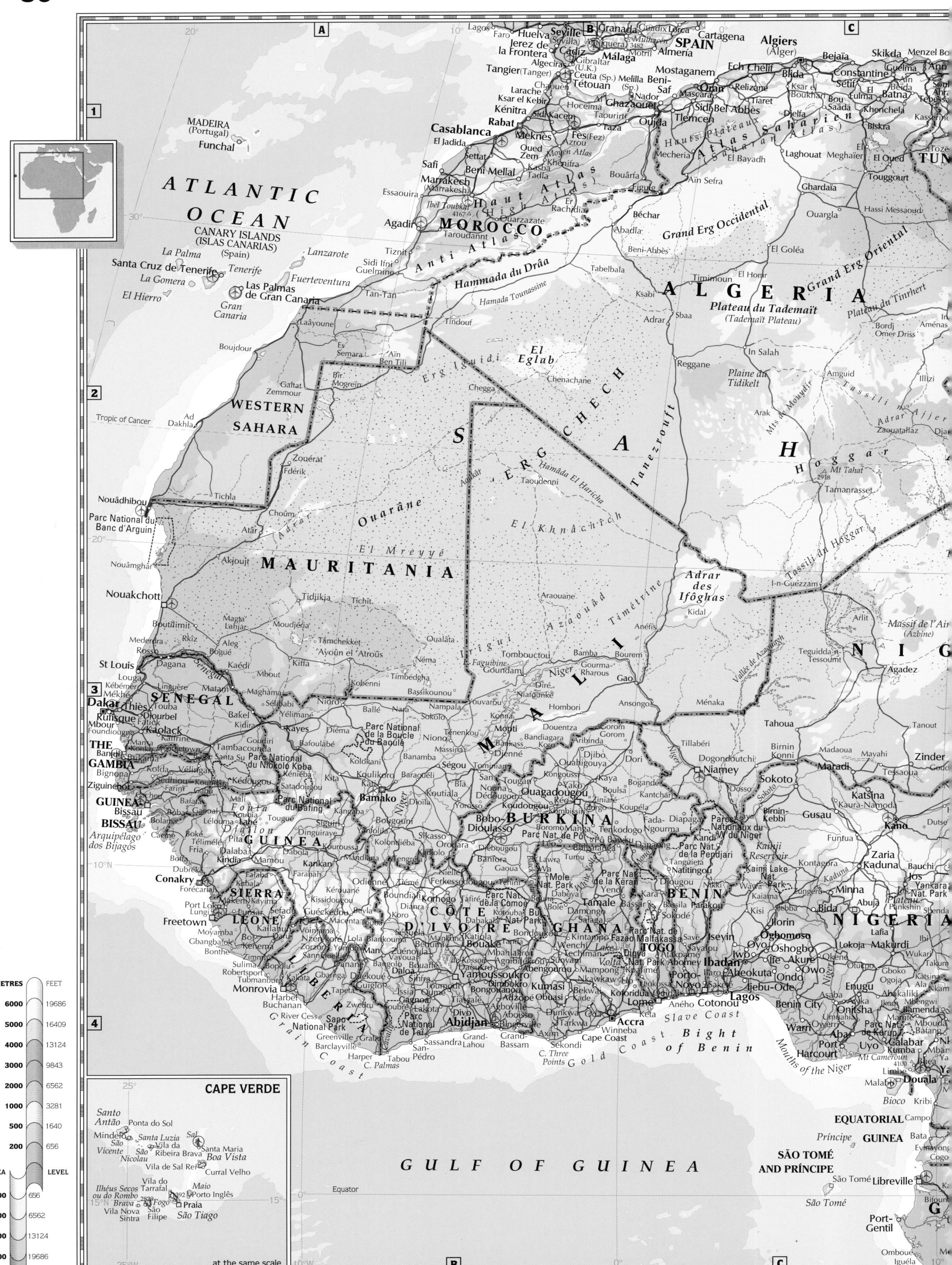

ATLANTIC OCEAN

CANARY ISLANDS
(ISLAS CANARIAS)
(Spain)

MADEIRA
(Portugal)

SPAIN

MOROCCO

WESTERN SAHARA

ALGERIA

MAURITANIA

MALI

SENEGAL

THE GAMBIA

GUINEA BISSAU

GUINEA

SIERRA LEONE

LIBERIA

CÔTE D'IVOIRE

GHANA

BURKINA

TOGO

BENIN

NIGER

NIGERIA

S A H A R A

GULF OF GUINEA

EQUATORIAL GUINEA

SÃO TOMÉ AND PRÍNCIPE

CAPE VERDE

at the same scale

METRES		FEET
6000		19686
5000		16409
4000		13124
3000		9843
2000		6562
1000		3281
500		1640
200		656
SEA		LEVEL
200		656
2000		6562
4000		13124
6000		19686

Lambert Azimuthal Equal Area Projection

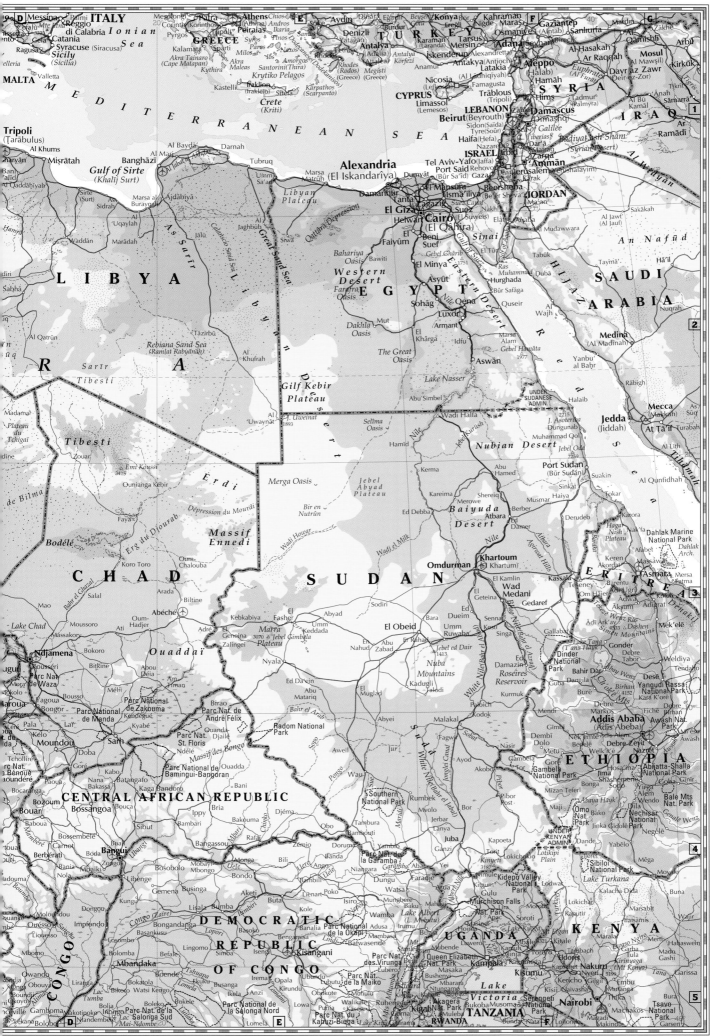

1:16M

KM MILES
1000
600
800
500
600
400
400
300
200
200
100
0

© Collins

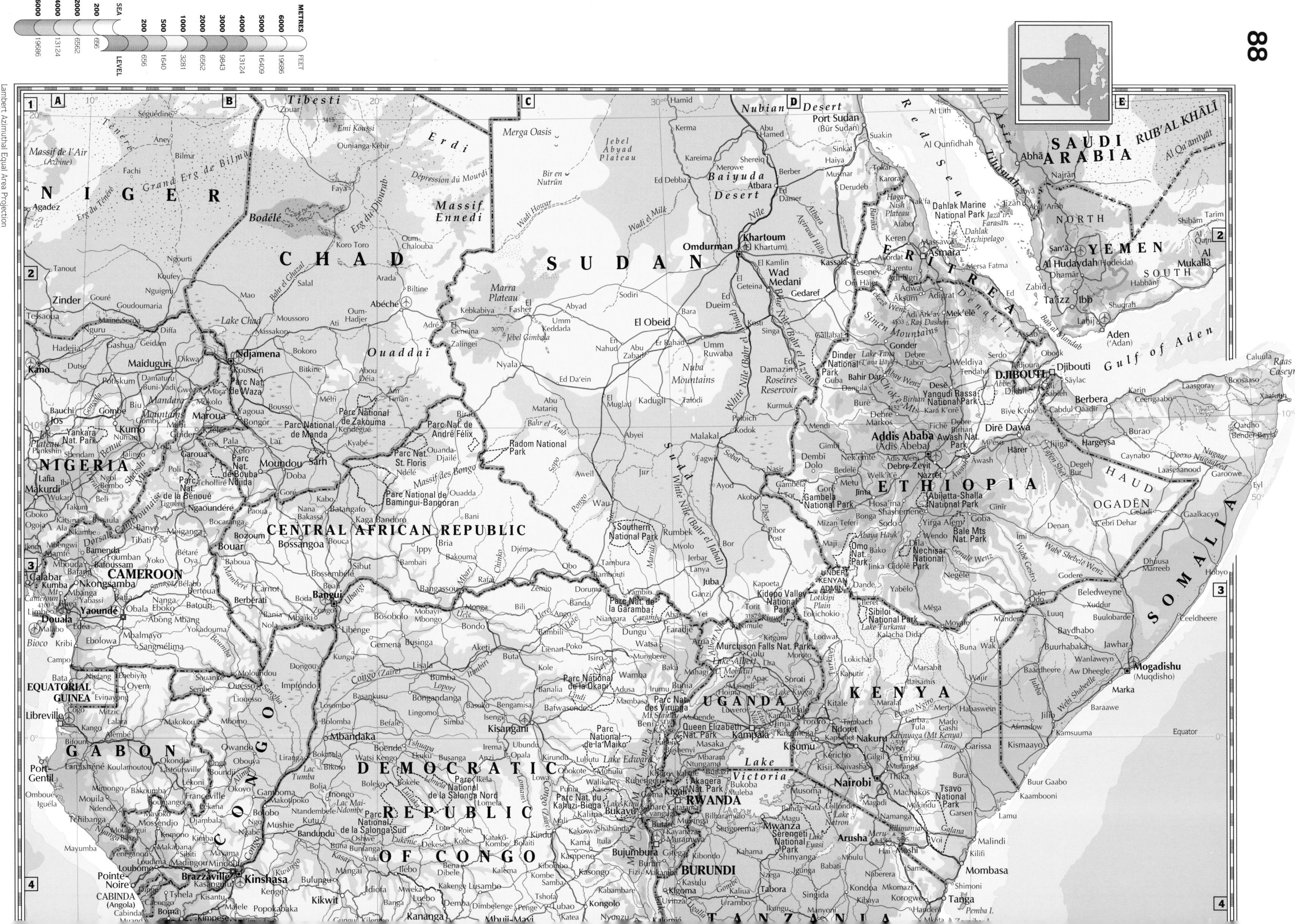

Lambert Azimuthal Equal Area Projection

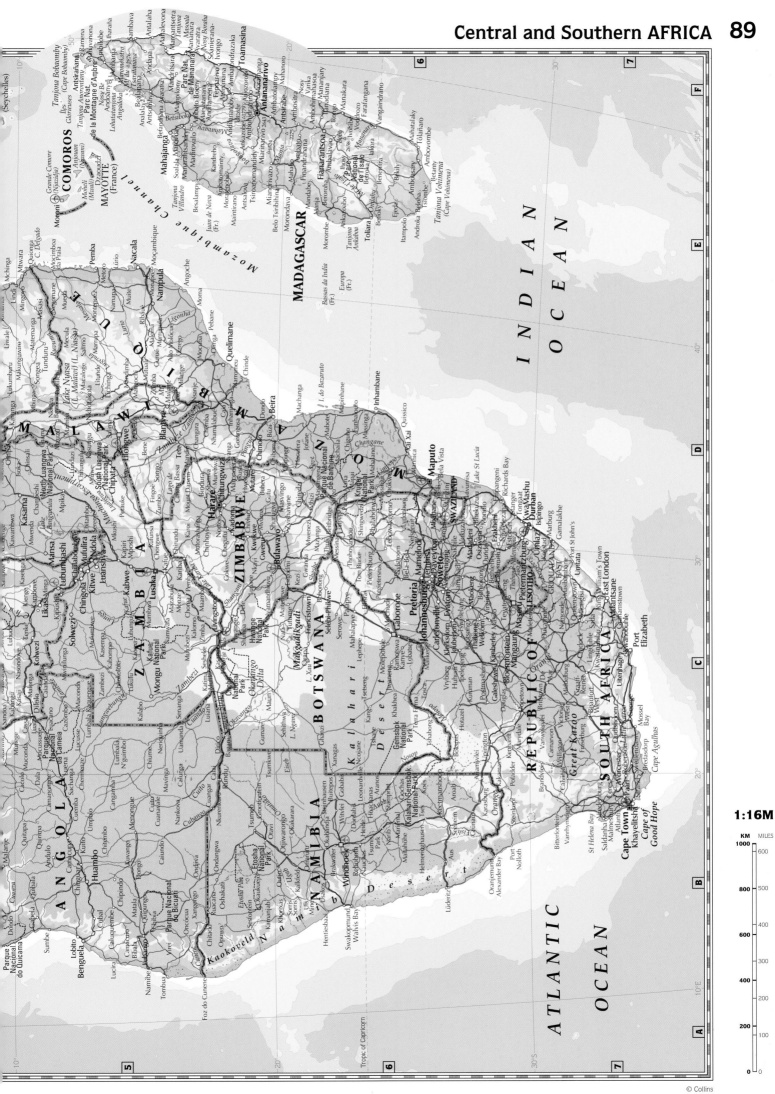

© Collins

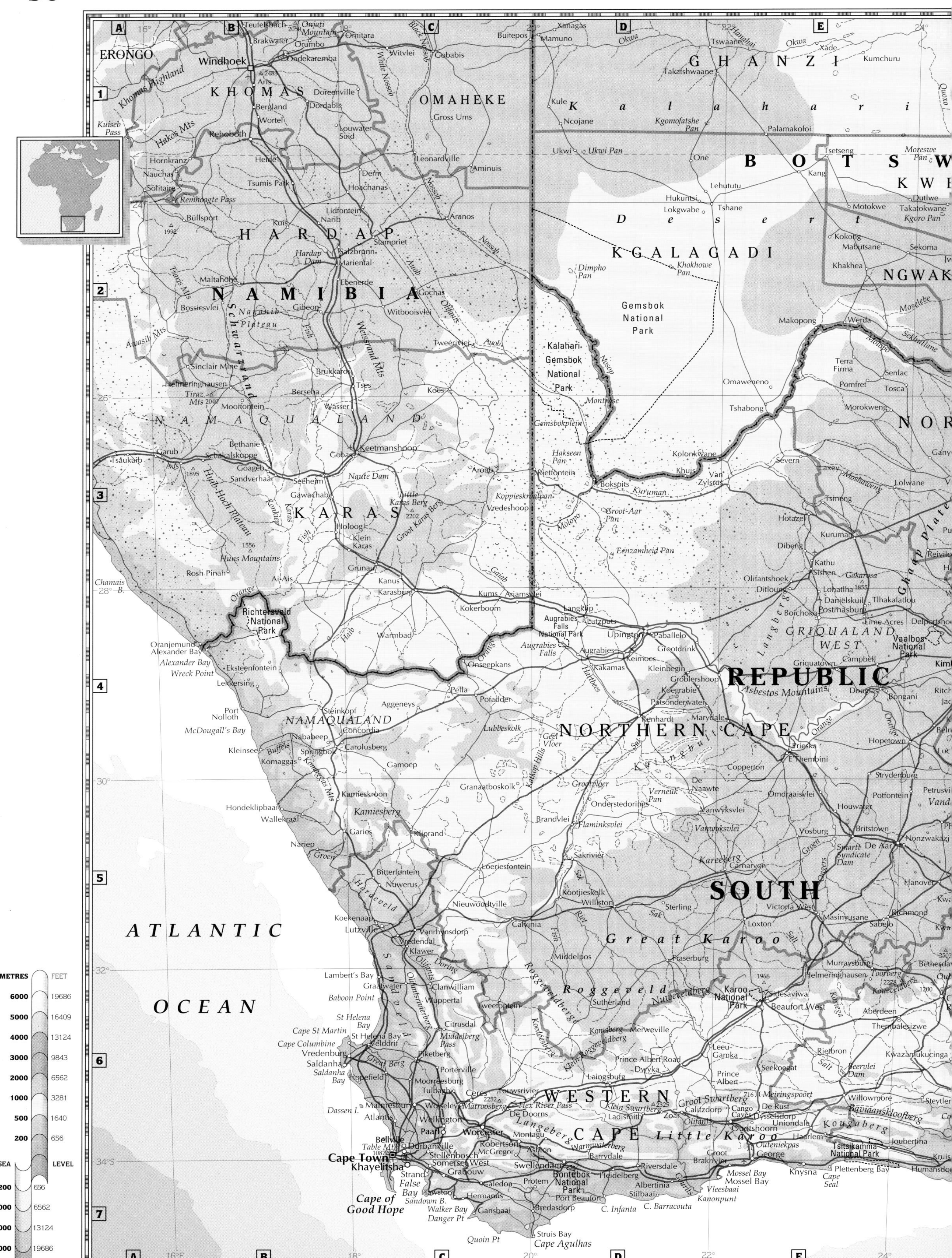

Lambert Azimuthal Equal Area Projection

1:5M

KM MILES
200
300
250 150
200
100
150
100
50
50
0 0

© Collins

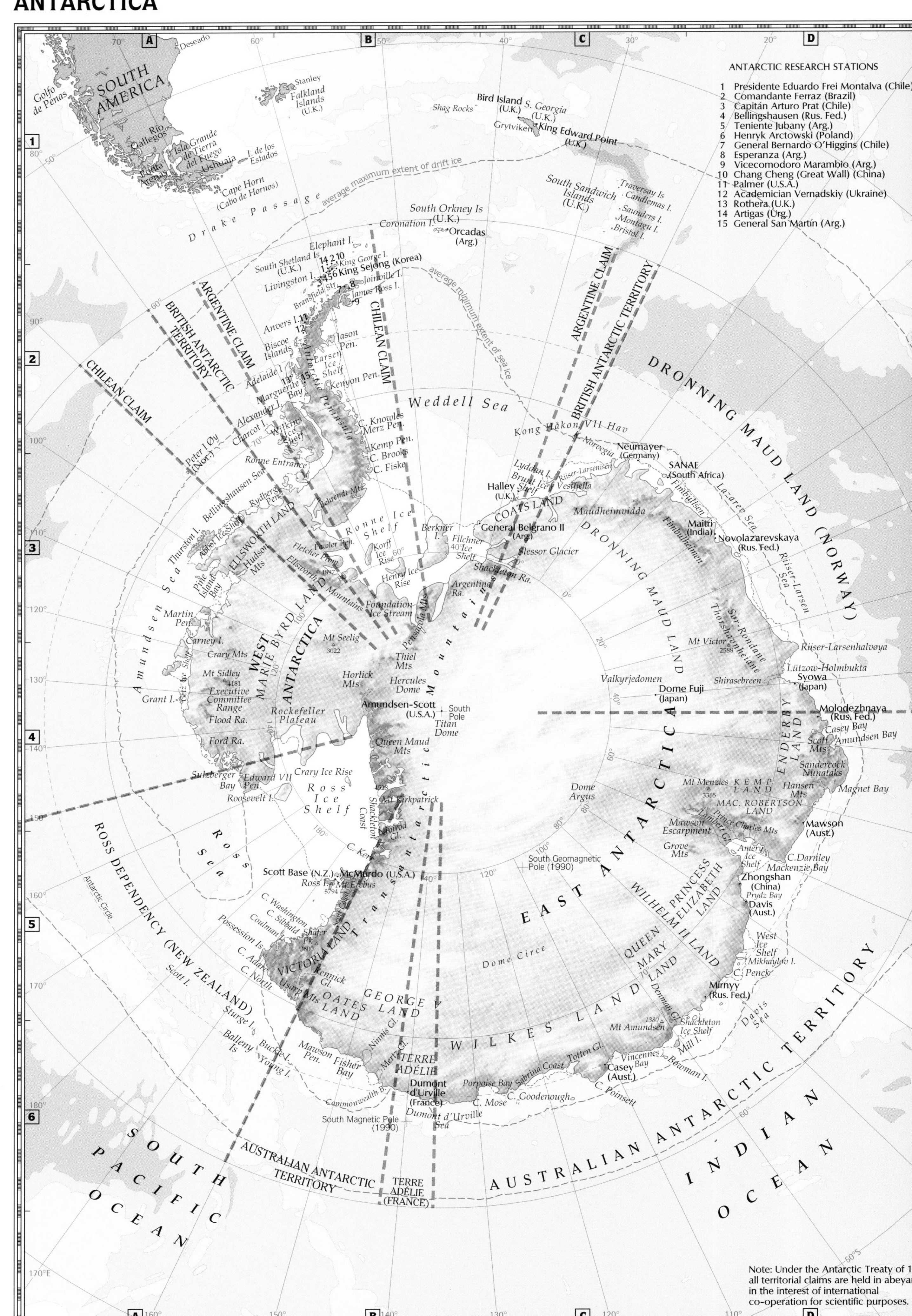

METRES / FEET
SEA LEVEL
200 — 656
3000 — 9843
5000 — 16409
6000 — 19686

1:32M

KM / MILES
1400, 1200, 1000, 800, 600, 400, 200, 0
800, 600, 400, 200, 0

Polar Stereographic Projection

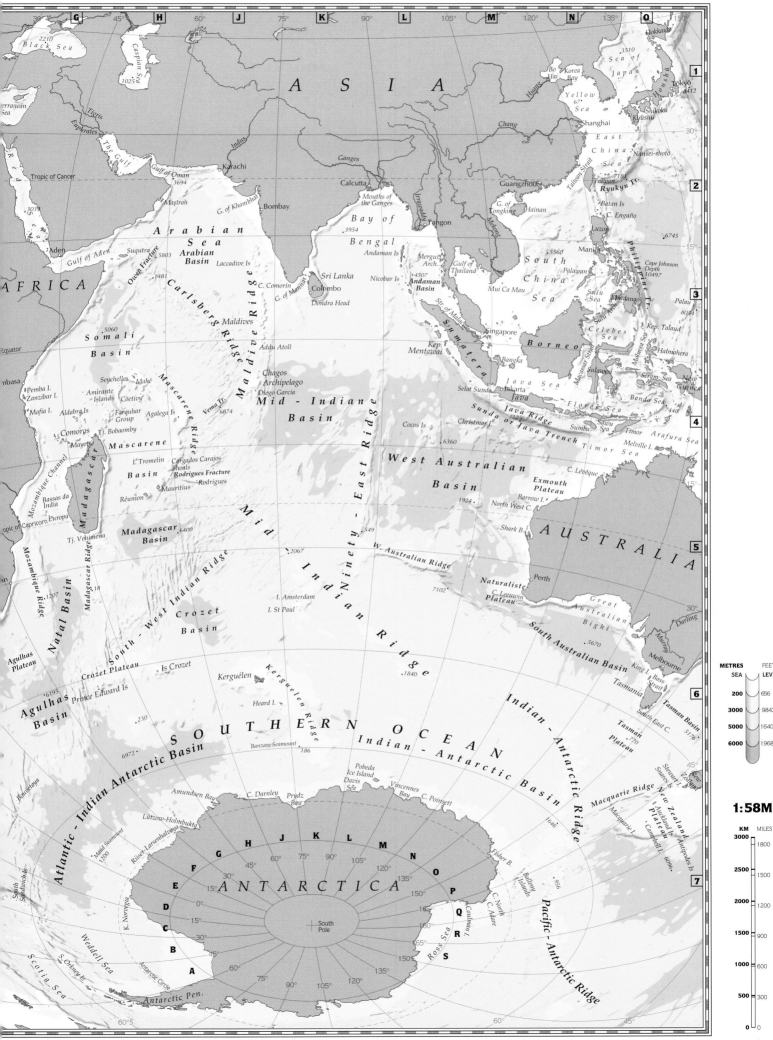

G   H   J   K   L   M   N   O
30° 45° 60° 75° 90° 105° 120° 135° 150°

2210
Black Sea
Caspian Sea
1025
3039
Mediterranean Sea
Tropic of Cancer

A S I A

Sea of Japan
Hokkaido
3510
Honshu
Tokyo
8412
Kyushu
Shikoku

1

Red Sea
Tigris
Euphrates
The Gulf
Gulf of Oman
3694
Karachi
Indus
Ganges
Calcutta

Huang
Chang
Shanghai
East China Sea
Nansei-shoto
Taiwan Strait
Taiwan
Ryukyu Tr.
7181

2

AFRICA
Aden
Gulf of Aden
Suqutra
Owen Fracture
5803
1481
Arabian Basin
Laccadive Is
C. Comorin
G. of Mannar
Sri Lanka
Colombo
Dondra Head
Maṣīrah

Bombay
Mouths of the Ganges
3954
Bay of Bengal
Yangon
Andaman Is
Mergui Arch...
Gulf of Thailand
Nicobar Is
Andaman Basin
4507

Guangzhou
G. of Tongking
Hainan
5560
South China Sea
Mui Ca Mau
Manila
Luzon
6745
Palawan
Cape Johnson Depth 10497
Batan Is
C. Engaño
Mindanao
Palau
8054

3

Somali Basin
5060
Seychelles
Mahé
Amirante Islands
Cöetivy
Farquhar Group
Agalega Is
8°
Comoros
Tj. Bobaomby
Equator
Pemba I.
Zanzibar I.
Mafia I.
Aldabra Is
Mombasa
Mayotte

Carlsberg Ridge
Maldives
Addu Atoll
Maldive Ridge
Chagos Archipelago
Diego Garcia
Mid - Indian Basin
Mascarene Ridge
Vema Tr.
6874
Cargados Carajos Shoals
Rodrigues Fracture
Rodrigues
I. Tromelin
Mascarene Basin
Réunion
Mauritius

Str. of Malacca
Sumatera
Singapore
Kep. Mentawai
Java Sea
Selat Sunda
Jakarta
Java
Sunda Ridge
Java Ridge
Sunda or Java Trench
Christmas I.
Cocos Is
6360
West Australian Basin

Borneo
Sulawesi
Celebes Sea
Kep. Talaud
Halmahera
Makasar Strait
Maluku Sea
Seram Sea
New Guinea
Banda Sea
7440
Flores Sea
Sawu Sea
Sumba
Timor
Arafura Sea
Melville I.
Timor Sea

4

Madagascar Ridge
Madagascar Basin
6400
Bassas da India
Tropic of Capricorn
Europa
Tj. Volimena
2067
Mozambique Channel

Ninety - East Ridge
549
I. Amsterdam
I. St Paul
Mid Indian Ridge
1840

Exmouth Plateau
Barrow I.
North West C.
1924
Shark B.
W. Australian Ridge
7102

AUSTRALIA

5

Mozambique Ridge
1207
Natal Basin
18

South - West Indian Ridge
Crozet Basin
Crozet Plateau
Is Crozet
230
6972

Naturaliste Plateau
C. Leeuwin
5670
Perth
Great Australian Bight
Darling

6

Agulhas Plateau
Agulhas Basin
6195
Prince Edward Is

Kerguélen
Kerguelen Ridge
Heard I.
Banzare Seamount
186

South Australian Basin
South - East Indian Ridge
Indian - Antarctic Basin
Indian - Antarctic Ridge

Murray
Melbourne
King I.
Bass Strait
Tasmania
Tasman Basin
5176
Stewart I.
South East C.
Tasman Plateau
770

6

Atlantic - Indian Antarctic Basin
S O U T H E R N   O C E A N

SEA LEVEL
METRES | FEET
200 | 656
3000 | 9843
5000 | 16409
6000 | 19686

7

Bouvetøya
K. Norvegia
Maud Seamount
1200
Riiser-Larsenhalvøya
Lützow-Holmbukta
Amundsen Bay
C. Darnley
Prydz Bay
Pobeda Ice Island
Davis Sea
Vincennes Bay
C. Poinsett
956
1646

New Zealand Plateau
Auckland Is
Antipodes Is
Campbell I. 6098
Snares Is
Macquarie I.
Macquarie Ridge
Fisher B.

1:58M

South Georgia
South Sandwich Is
Scotia Sea
S. Orkney Is
Weddell Sea
Antarctic Circle
Antarctic Pen.

H   J   K
G
F
E
D
C
B
A
A N T A R C T I C A
South Pole
30° 45° 60° 75° 90° 105° 120° 135° 150° 165° 180° 165° 150° 135° 120° 105° 90° 75° 60°
L   M   N   O
P
Q
R
S
Ross Sea
Balleny Islands
C. North
C. Adare
Coulman I.

Pacific - Antarctic Ridge

KM MILES
3000 | 1800
2500 | 1500
2000 | 1200
1500 | 900
1000 | 600
500 | 300
0

Azimuthal Equal Area Projection
© Collins

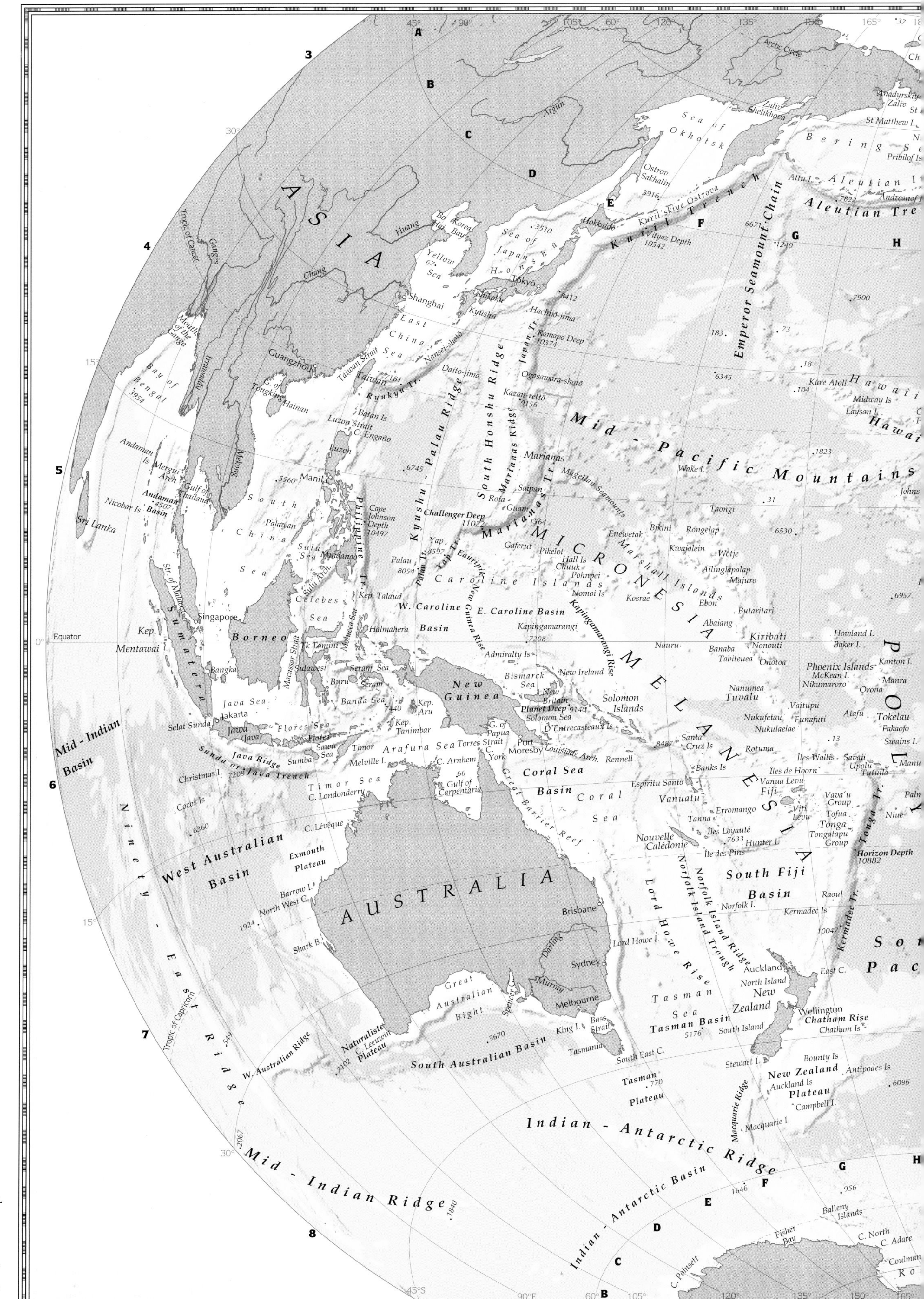

Lambert Azimuthal Equal Area Projection

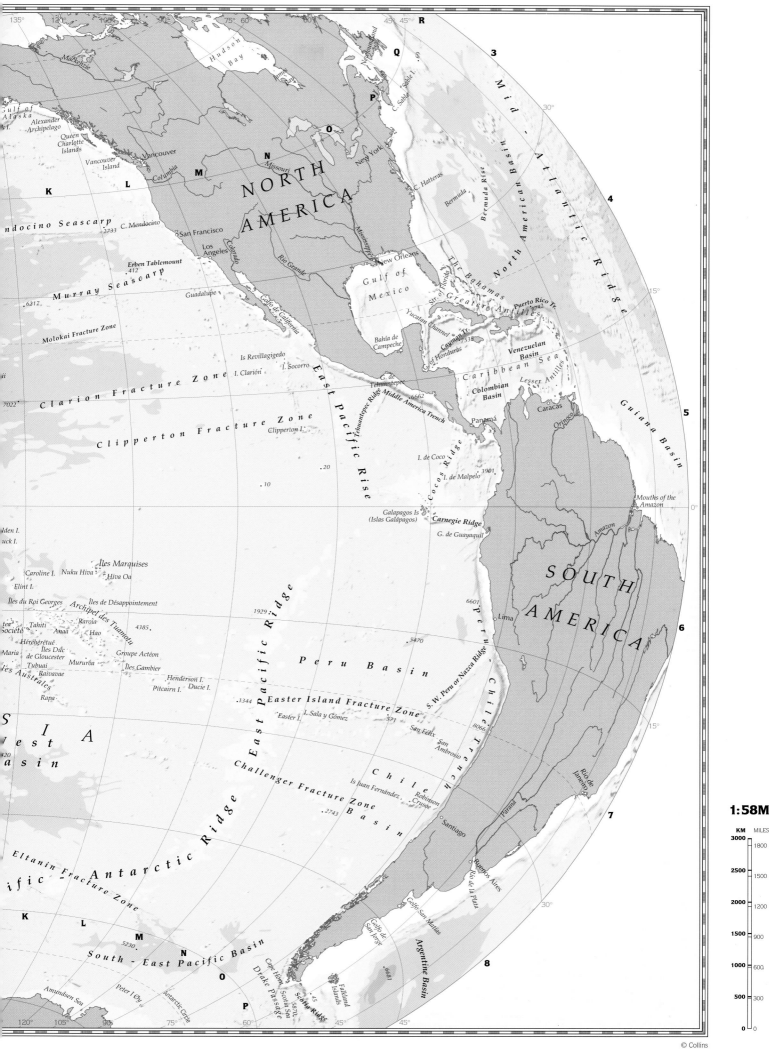

NORTH AMERICA

SOUTH AMERICA

A S I A

West
Basin

Mid - Atlantic Ridge

North American Basin

Bermuda Rise

Bermuda

The Bahamas

Greater Antilles

Puerto Rico Tr.

8742

Cayman Tr.

7535

Venezuelan Basin

Caribbean Sea

Lesser Antilles

Colombian Basin

Guiana Basin

Gulf of Alaska

Alexander Archipelago

Queen Charlotte Islands

Vancouver Island

Vancouver

Columbia

Mackenzie

Hudson Bay

James Bay

C. Sable I.

C. Sable

Newfoundland

New York

C. Hatteras

Missouri

Mississippi

New Orleans

Gulf of Mexico

Bahía de Campeche

Yucatan Channel

of Honduras

G. de Tehuantepec

Tehuantepec Ridge

Middle America Trench

6662

Panamá

Caracas

Orinoco

Rio Grande

Colorado

Guadalupe

Golfo de California

Los Angeles

San Francisco

C. Mendocino

2733

Erben Tablemount

412

Murray Seascarp

ndocino Seascarp

.6217

Molokai Fracture Zone

Is Revillagigedo

I. Clarión

I. Socorro

Clarion Fracture Zone

7022

Clipperton Fracture Zone

Clipperton I.

.20

.10

East Pacific Rise

Cocos Ridge

I. de Coco

I. de Malpelo

3901

Galapagos Is (Islas Galápagos)

Carnegie Ridge

G. de Guayaquil

Mouths of the Amazon

Amazon

Lima

K   L   M   N   O

P

Q

R

3

4

5

6

7

8

Îles Marquises

Nuku Hiva

Hiva Oa

Caroline I.

Flint I.

Îles du Roi Georges

Archipel des Tuamotu

Îles de Désappointement

Tahiti

Raroia

4385.

tea

Société

Anaa

Hao

Héréhérétué

Îles Duc de Gloucester

Maria

Tubuai

Mururoa

Raivavae

Îles Gambier

Groupe Actéon

Îles Australes

Rapa

1929.

East Pacific Ridge

Henderson I.

Pitcairn I.

Ducie I.

.1344

Easter Island Fracture Zone

Easter I.

I. Sala y Gómez

.521

San Félix

San Ambrosio

Peru Basin

.5470

6601

Peru or Nazca Ridge

S.W.

8066

Peru - Chile Trench

Challenger Fracture Zone

Is Juan Fernández

Robinson Crusoe

.2743

Chile Basin

Santiago

Buenos Aires

Rio de la Plata

Río de Janeiro

Paraná

SOUTH AMERICA

Pacific - Antarctic Ridge

Eltanin Fracture Zone

ific

Basin

.5230

South - East Pacific Basin

Amundsen Sea

Peter I Øy

Antarctic Circle

Cape Horn

Drake Passage

Scotia Sea

Sctia Ridge

5870

Falkland Islands

6681

Argentine Basin

Golfo de San Matías

Golfo de San Jorge

K   L   M   N   O   P

120°   105°   90°   75°   60°   45°

135°   120°   105°   90°   75°   60°   45°   45°

30°

15°

0°

15°

30°

69°

1:58M

KM	MILES
3000	1800
2500	1500
2000	1200
1500	900
1000	600
500	300
0	0

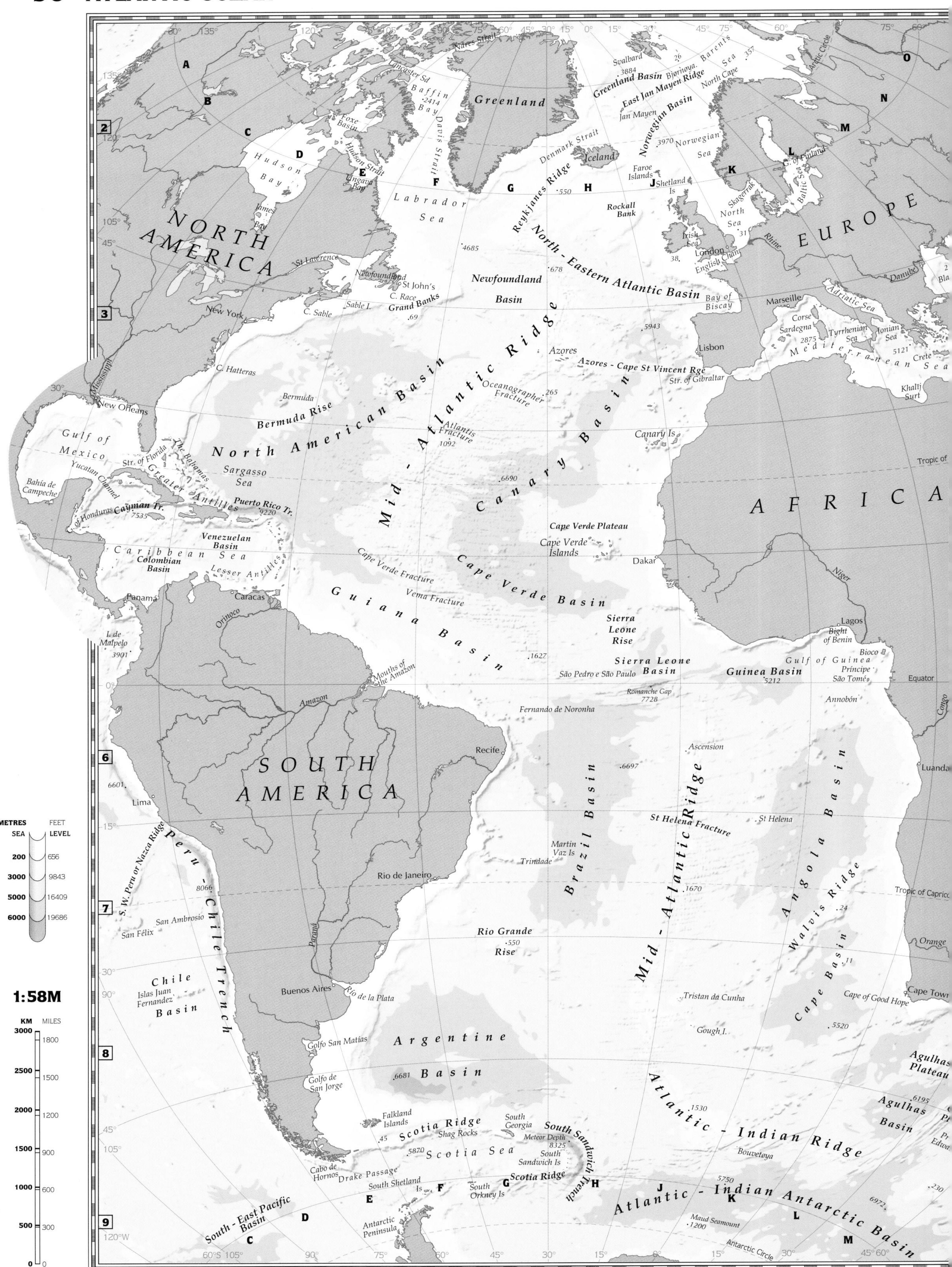

Map labels

NORTH AMERICA
SOUTH AMERICA
EUROPE
AFRICA
Greenland

Hudson Bay
James Bay
Baffin Bay .2414
Foxe Basin
Lancaster Sd
Nares Strait
Hudson Strait
Ungava Bay
Davis Strait
Labrador Sea
St Lawrence
New York
Newfoundland
St John's
C. Race
Grand Banks .69
Sable I.
C. Sable
.4685
Newfoundland Basin
.678
C. Hatteras
Bermuda
Bermuda Rise
New Orleans
Mississippi
Gulf of Mexico
Bahía de Campeche
Yucatan Channel
Str. of Florida
The Bahamas
Greater Antilles
Sargasso Sea
Cayman Tr. 7535
G. of Honduras
Panama
Venezuelan Basin
Colombian Basin
Caribbean Sea
Lesser Antilles
Puerto Rico Tr. 9220
Caracas
Orinoco
I. de Malpelo 3901
Amazon
Mouths of the Amazon
Lima
6601
Recife
S.W. Peru or Nazca Ridge
Peru - Chile Trench
8066
San Ambrosio
San Félix
Chile Basin
Islas Juan Fernandez
Buenos Aires
Rio de la Plata
Paraná
Golfo San Matías
Golfo de San Jorge
Falkland Islands
Cabo de Hornos
Drake Passage
5870
South Shetland Is
Antarctic Peninsula

NORTH - EASTERN ATLANTIC BASIN
Mid - Atlantic Ridge
North American Basin
Canary Basin
Guiana Basin
Cape Verde Basin
Brazil Basin
Angola Basin
Cape Basin
Argentine Basin

Greenland Basin .3884
Svalbard
Bjørnøya .26
Barents Sea .357
North Cape
East Jan Mayen Ridge
Jan Mayen
Norwegian Basin .3970
Norwegian Sea
Reykjanes Ridge
Denmark Strait
Iceland
Faroe Islands
Rockall Bank
Shetland Is
North Sea .31
Irish Sea .38
London
English Chan.
Bay of Biscay
Marseille
Lisbon
Str. of Gibraltar
Corse
Sardegna 2875
Mediterranean Sea
Tyrrhenian Sea
Ionian Sea .5121
Crete
Adriatic Sea
Rhine
Danube
Skagerrak
G. of Finland
Baltic Sea
Khalīj Surt
.550
Azores
Azores - Cape St Vincent Rge
Oceanographer Fracture .265
Atlantis Fracture 1092
.5943
.6690
Canary Is
Cape Verde Plateau
Cape Verde Islands
Dakar
Cape Verde Fracture
Vema Fracture
Cape Verde Basin
.1627
Sierra Leone Rise
Sierra Leone Basin
São Pedro e São Paulo
Guinea Basin
Gulf of Guinea
Lagos
Bight of Benin
Bioco
Príncipe
São Tomé .5212
Annobón
Niger
Luanda
Congo
Fernando de Noronha
Romanche Gap 7728
Ascension .6697
St Helena Fracture
St Helena
Martin Vaz Is
Trindade
Rio de Janeiro
.1670
Rio Grande Rise .550
Walvis Ridge
.24
.11
Orange
Cape Town
Cape of Good Hope
.5520
Tristan da Cunha
Gough I.

South - East Pacific Basin
Scotia Ridge
Scotia Sea
South Sandwich Trench
Atlantic - Indian Ridge
Atlantic - Indian Antarctic Basin
Mid - Atlantic Ridge
Agulhas Plateau
Agulhas Basin

Scotia Ridge .45
South Georgia
Shag Rocks
Meteor Depth 8325
South Sandwich Is
South Orkney Is
.6681
.1530
Bouvetøya
.5750
.6972
Maud Seamount .1200
Antarctic Circle
.6195
.230
Pr. Edw
Prince Edward

Scale legend

METRES
SEA LEVEL
FEET

METRES	FEET
200	656
3000	9843
5000	16409
6000	19686

1:58M

KM	MILES
3000	1800
2500	1500
2000	1200
1500	900
1000	600
500	300
0	0

Tropic of Cancer
Tropic of Capricorn
Equator
Arctic Circle

Lambert Azimuthal Equal Area Projection

THE INDEX includes the names on the maps in the ATLAS. The names are generally indexed to the largest scale map on which they appear, and can be located using the grid reference letters and numbers around the map frame. Names on insets have a symbol: □, followed by the inset number.

Abbreviations used to describe features in the index and on the maps are explained below.

ABBREVIATIONS AND GLOSSARY

A. Alp Alpen Alpi *alp*
Alt *upper*
A.C.T. Australian Capital Territory
Afgh. Afghanistan
Afr. Africa African
Aig. Aiguille *peak*
AK Alaska
AL Alabama
Alg. Algeria
Alta Alberta
Ant. Antarctica
AR Arkansas
Arch. Archipelago
Arg. Argentina
Arr. Arrecife *reef*
Atl. Atlantic
Austr. Australia
AZ Arizona
Azer. Azerbaijan

B. Bad *spa*
Ban *village*
Bay
Bngla. Bangladesh
B.C. British Columbia
Bg Berg *mountain*
Bge. Barragem *reservoir*
Bgt Bight Bugt *bay*
Bj Burj *hills*
Bol. Bolivia
Herz. Bosnia Herzegovina
Br. Burun Burnu *point, cape*
Bt Bukit *bay*
Bü. Büyük *big*
Bulg. Bulgaria

C. Cape
Col *high pass*
CA California
Cabo Cabeço *summit*
Can. Canada
Canal Canale *canal*
Cañon Canyon *canyon*
C.A.R. Central African Republic
Cat. Cataract
Catena *mountains*
Cd Ciudad *town city*
Ch. Chaung *stream*
Chott *salt lake, marsh*
Chan. Channel
Che Chaîne *mountain chain*
Cma Cima *summit*
Cno Corno *peak*
Co Cerro *hill, peak*
CO Colorado
Co. County
Col. Colombia
Cord. Cordillera *mountain chain*
Cr. Creek
CT Connecticut
Cuch. Cuchilla *mountain chain*
Czo Cozzo *mountain*

D. Da *big, river*
Dag Dagh Daği *mountain*
Dağlari *mountains*
-d. -dake *peak*
DC District of Columbia
DE Delaware
Des. Desert
Div. Division
Dj. Djebel *mountain*
Rep. Dominican Republic

Eil. Eiland *island*
Eilanden *islands*
Emb. Embalse *reservoir*
Eng. England
Equat. Equatorial
Escarp. Escarpment

Est. Estuary
Eth. Ethiopia
Etg Etang *lake, lagoon*

F. Firth
Fin. Finland
Fj. Fjell *mountain*
Fjord Fjördur *fjord*
Fl. Fleuve *river*
FL Florida
Fr. Guiana French Guiana

G. Gebel *mountain*
Göl Gölö Gõl *lake*
G. Golfe Golfo Gulf *gulf, bay*
Góra *mountain*
Gunung *mountain*
-g. -gawa *river*
GA Georgia
Gd Grand *big*
Gde Grande *big*
Geb. Gebergte *mountain range*
Gebirge *mountains*
Gl. Glacier
Ger. Germany
Gr. Graben *trench, ditch*
Gross Grosse Grande *big*
Grp Group
Gt Great Groot Groote *big*
Gy Góry Gory *mountains*

H. Hawr *lake*
Hill Hills
Hoch *high*
Hora *mountain*
Hory *mountains*
Halv. Halvøy *peninsula*
Harb. Harbour
Hd Head Headland
Hg. Hegység *mountains*
Hgts Heights
HI Hawaii
Ht Haut *high*
Hte Haute *high*

I. Île Ilha Insel Isla *island, isle*
Island Isle *island, isle*
Isola Isole *island*
IA Iowa
ID Idaho
IL Illinois
IN Indiana
In. Inlet
Indon. Indonesia
Is Islas Îles Ilhas *islands*
Islands Isles *islands, isles*
Isr. Israel
Isth. Isthmus

J. Jabal Jebel *mountain*
Jibãl *mountains*
Jrvi Jaure Jezero *lake*
Jezioro *lake*
Jökull *glacier*

K. Kaap Kap Kapp *cape*
Kaikyõ *strait*
Kato Káto *lower*
Kiang *river or stream*
Ko *island, lake, inlet*
Koh Küh Kühha *island*
Kolpos *gulf*
Kopf *hill*
Kuala *estuary*
Kyst *coast*
Küçük *small*
Kan. Kanal Kanaal *canal*
Kazak. Kazakstan
Kep. Kepulauan *archipelago, islands*
Kg Kampong *village*
Khr Khrebet *mountain range*
Kl. Klein Kleine *small*
Kör. Körfez Körfezi *bay, gulf*
KS Kansas
KY Kentucky
Kyrg. Kyrgyzstan

L. Lac Lago Lake
Liqen Loch Lough *lake, loch*
Lam *stream*
LA Louisiana
Lag. Lagoon Laguna
Lagôa *lagoon*
Lith. Lithuania
Lux. Luxembourg

M. Mae *river*
Me *great, chief, mother*
Meer *lake, sea*
Muang *kingdom, province, town*
Muong *town*
Mys *cape*
Maloye *small*
MA Massachusetts
Madag. Madagascar
Man. Manitoba
Maur. Mauritania
MD Maryland
ME Maine
Mex. Mexico
Mf Massif *mountains, upland*
Mgna Montagna *mountain*
Mgne Montagne *mountain*
Mgnes Montagnes *mountains*
MI Michigan
MN Minnesota
MO Missouri
Mon. Monasterio Monastery *monastery*
Monument *monument*
Moz. Mozambique
MS Mississippi
Mt Mont Mount *mountain*
Mt. Mountain
MT Montana
Mte Monte *mountain*
Mtes Montes *mountains*
Mti Monti Munţi *mountains*
Mtii Munţii *mountains*
Mth Mouth
Mths Mouths
Mtn Mountain
Mts Monts Mountains

N. Nam *south(ern), river*
Neu Ny *new*
Nevado *peak*
Nudo *mountain*
Noord Nord Nörre
Nørre North *north(ern)*
Nos *spit, point*
Nac. Nacional *national*
Nat. National
N.B. New Brunswick
NC North Carolina
ND North Dakota
NE Nebraska
Neth. Netherlands
Neth. Ant. Netherlands Antilles
Nfld Newfoundland
NH New Hampshire
Nic. Nicaragua
Nizh. Nizhneye Nizhniy
Nizhnyaya *lower*
Nizm. Nizmennost' *lowland*
NJ New Jersey
NM New Mexico
N.O. Noord Oost Nord Ost *northeast*
Nov. Novyy Novaya
Noviye Novoye *new*
N.S. Nova Scotia
N.S.W. New South Wales
N.T. Northern Territory
NV Nevada
Nva Nueva *new*
N.W.T. Northwest Territories
NY New York
N.Z. New Zealand

O. Oost Ost *east*
Ostrov *island*
Ø Østre *east*
Ob. Ober *upper, higher*
Oc. Ocean
Ode Oude *old*
Ogl. Oglat *well*
OH Ohio
OK Oklahoma
Ont. Ontario
Or. Óri Óros Ori *mountains*
Oros *mountain*
OR Oregon
Orm. Ormos *bay*
O-va Ostrova *islands*

Ot Olet *mountain*
Öv. Över Övre *upper*
Oz. Ozero *lake*
Ozera *lakes*

P. Pass
Pic Pico Piz *peak*
Pou *mountain*
Pulau *island*
PA Pennsylvania
Pac. Pacific
Pak. Pakistan
Para. Paraguay
Pass. Passage
Peg. Pegunungan *mountain range*
P.E.I. Prince Edward Island
Pen. Peninsula Penisola *peninsula*
Per. Pereval *pass*
Phil. Philippines
Phn. Phnom *hill, mountain*
Pgio Poggio *hill*
Pl. Planina Planinski *mountain(s)*
Pla Playa *beach*
Plat. Plateau
Plosk. Ploskogor'ye *plateau*
P.N.G. Papua New Guinea
Pno Pantano *reservoir, swamp*
Pol. Poland
Por. Porog *rapids*
Port. Portugal
P-ov Poluostrov *peninsula*
P.P. Pulau-pulau *islands*
Pr. Proliv *strait*
Przylądek *cape*
Presq. Presqu'île *peninsula*
Prom. Promontory
Prov. Province Provincial
Psa Presa *dam*
Pso Passo *dam*
Pt Point
Pont *bridge*
Petit *small*
Pta Ponta Punta *cape, point*
Puerta *narrow pass*
Pte Pointe *cape, point*
Ponte Puente *bridge*
Pto Porto Puerto *harbour, port*
Pzo Pizzo *peak, mountain*

Qld. Queensland
Que. Quebec

R. Reshteh *mountain range*
Rüd River *river*
Ra. Range
Rca Rocca *rock, fortress*
Reg. Region
Rep. Republic
Res. Reserve
Resr Reservoir
Resp. Respublika *republic*
Rf Reef
Rge Ridge
RI Rhode Island
Riba Ribeira *coast, bottom of the river valley*
Rte Route
Rus. Fed. Russian Federation

S. Salar Salina *salt pan*
San São *saint*
See *lake*
Seto *strait, channel*
Sjö *lake*
Sör Süd Sud Syd South *south(ern)*
Sa Serra Sierra *mountain range*
S.A. South Australia
Sab. Sabkhat *salt flat*
Sask. Saskatchewan
S. Arabia Saudi Arabia
SC South Carolina
Sc. Scoglio *rock, reef*
Sd Sound Sund *sound*
SD South Dakota
Seb. Sebjet Sebkhat Sebkra *salt flat*
Serr. Serranía *mountain range*
Sev. Severnaya Severnyy *north(ern)*
Sh. Shā'ib *watercourse*
Shaṭṭ *river (-mouth)*
Shima *island*
Shankou *pass*

Si Sidi *lord, master*
Sing. Singapore
Sk. Shuiku *reservoir*
Skt Sankt *saint*
Smt Seamount
Snra Senhora *Mrs, lady*
Snro Senhoro *Mr, gentleman*
Sp. Spain Spanish
Spitze *peak*
Sr Sönder Sønder *southern*
Sr. Sredniy Srednyaya *middle*
St Saint Sint
Staryy *old*
St. Stor Store *big*
Stung *river*
Sta Santa *saint*
Ste Sainte *saint*
Store *big*
Sto Santo *saint*
Str. Strait Stretta *strait*
Sv. Sväty Sveti *holy, saint*
Switz. Switzerland

T. Tal *valley*
Tall Tell *hill*
Tepe Tepesi *hill, peak*
Tajik. Tajikistan
Tanz. Tanzania
Tas. Tasmania
Terr. Territory
Tg Tanjung Tanjong *cape, point*
Thai. Thailand
Tk Teluk *bay*
Tmt Tablemount
TN Tennessee
Tr. Trench Trough
Tre Torre *tower, fortress*
Tte Teniente *lieutenant*
Turk. Turkmenistan
TX Texas

U.A.E. United Arab Emirates
Ug Ujung *point, cape*
U.K. United Kingdom
Ukr. Ukraine
Unt. Unter *lower*
Upr Upper
Uru. Uruguay
U.S.A. United States of America
UT Utah
Uzbek. Uzbekistan

V. Val Valle Valley *valley*
Väster Vest Vester *west(ern)*
Vatn *lake*
Ville *town*
Va Vila *small town*
VA Virginia
Venez. Venezuela
Vic. Victoria
Volc. Volcán Volcan *volcano*
Vdkhr. Vodokhranilishche *reservoir*
Vdskh. Vodoskhovshche Vodaskhovishcha *reservoir*
Vel. Velikiy Velikaya Velikiye *big*
Verkh. Verkhniy Verkhneye Verkhne *upper* Verkhnyaya *upper*
Vost. Vostochnyy *eastern*
Vozv. Vozvyshennost' *hills, upland*
VT Vermont

W. Wadi *watercourse*
Wald *forest*
Wan *bay*
Water *water*
WA Washington
W.A. Western Australia
Wr Wester
WV West Virginia
WY Wyoming

-y -yama *mountain*
Y.T. Yukon Territory
Yt. Ytre Ytter Ytri *outer*
Yugo. Yugoslavia
Yuzh. Yuzhnaya Yuzhno Yuzhnyy *southern*

Zal. Zaliv *bay*
Zap. Zapadnyy Zapadnaya Zapadno Zapadnoye *western*
Zem. Zemlya *land*

A

12 E4 Aachen Ger.
16 E6 Aalen Ger.
12 C4 Aalst Belgium
12 C4 Aarschot Belgium
38 A3 Aba China
88 D3 Aba Congo(Zaire)
86 C4 Aba Nigeria
30 B5 Abā ad Dūd S. Arabia
30 C4 Ābādān Iran
30 D4 Ābādeh Iran
86 B1 Abadla Alg.
82 D2 Abaeté r. Brazil
79 J4 Abaetetuba Brazil
38 E1 Abag Qi China
94 G5 Abaiang i. Pac. Oc.
63 E4 Abajo Pk summit U.S.A.
86 C4 Abakaliki Nigeria
36 B1 Abakan Rus. Fed.
36 A1 Abakanskiy Khrebet mts Rus. Fed.
21 E7 Abana Turkey
30 D4 Āb Anbār Iran
78 D6 Abancay Peru
30 D4 Abarqū Iran
40 J2 Abashiri Japan
40 J2 Abashiri-wan b. Japan
48 E3 Abau P.N.G.
88 D3 Ābaya Hāyk' l. Eth.
Ābay Wenz r. see Blue Nile
24 L4 Abaza Rus. Fed.
31 E3 Abbāsābād Iran
18 C4 Abbasanta Sardinia Italy
68 C2 Abbaye, Pt pt U.S.A.
88 E2 Abbe, L. l. Eth.
14 E1 Abbeville France
65 E6 Abbeville LA U.S.A.
67 D5 Abbeville SC U.S.A.
11 B5 Abbeyfeale Rep. of Ireland
10 E6 Abbey Head hd U.K.
11 D5 Abbeyleix Rep. of Ireland
8 D3 Abbeytown U.K.
6 Q4 Abborrträsk Sweden
92 A3 Abbot Ice Shelf ice feature Ant.
56 E5 Abbotsford Can.
68 B3 Abbotsford U.S.A.
63 F4 Abbott U.S.A.
34 C2 Abbottabad Pak.
29 H3 'Abd al 'Azīz, J. h. Syria
29 L5 Abdanan Iran
87 E3 Abéché Chad
31 E4 Āb-e Garm Iran
51 D4 Abel Tasman National Park N.Z.
86 B4 Abengourou Côte d'Ivoire
7 L9 Åbenrå Denmark
13 K6 Abensberg Ger.
86 C4 Abeokuta Nigeria
9 C5 Aberaeron U.K.
10 F3 Aberchirder U.K.
50 G2 Abercrombie r. Austr.
9 D6 Aberdare U.K.
9 C5 Aberdaron U.K.
50 H2 Aberdeen Austr.
57 H4 Aberdeen Can.
39 Aberdeen H.K. China
90 F6 Aberdeen S. Africa
10 F3 Aberdeen U.K.
71 E5 Aberdeen MD U.S.A.
65 F5 Aberdeen MS U.S.A.
64 D2 Aberdeen SD U.S.A.
62 B2 Aberdeen WA U.S.A.
57 J2 Aberdeen Lake l. Can.
9 C5 Aberdyfi U.K.
10 E4 Aberfeldy U.K.
8 F4 Aberford U.K.
10 D4 Aberfoyle U.K.
9 D6 Abergavenny U.K.
65 C5 Abernathy U.S.A.
9 C5 Aberporth U.K.
9 C5 Abersoch U.K.
9 C5 Aberystwyth U.K.
32 B6 Abhā S. Arabia
30 C2 Abhar Iran
30 C2 Abhar r. Iran
Abiad, Bahr el r. see White Nile
30 C3 Ab-i Bazuft r. Iran
81 A2 Abibe, Serrania de mts Col.
86 B4 Abidjan Côte d'Ivoire
31 H3 Ab-i-Istada l. Afgh.
88 D3 Abijatta-Shalla National Park Eth.
30 E3 Ab-i-Kavir salt flat Iran
64 D4 Abilene KS U.S.A.
65 D5 Abilene TX U.S.A.
9 F6 Abingdon U.K.
68 B5 Abingdon IL U.S.A.
70 C6 Abingdon VA U.S.A.
21 F6 Abinsk Rus. Fed.
31 G2 Ab-i-Safed r. Afgh.
78 C5 Abiseo, Parque Nacional nat. park Peru
57 H2 Abitau Lake l. Can.
58 D4 Abitibi r. Can.
58 E4 Abitibi, Lake l. Can.
86 B4 Aboisso Côte d'Ivoire
86 C4 Abomey Benin
34 C3 Abonar India
87 D4 Abong Mbang Cameroon
43 A4 Aborlan Phil.
87 D3 Abou Déia Chad
29 K1 Abovyan Armenia
10 F3 Aboyne U.K.
83 D4 Abra, L. del l. Arg.
15 B3 Abrantes Port.
80 C2 Abra Pampa Arg.
82 E2 Abrolhos, Arquipélago dos is Brazil
62 E2 Absaroka Range mts U.S.A.
13 H6 Abtsgmünd Ger.
30 C5 Abū'Alī i. S. Arabia
30 D5 Abual Jirab i. U.A.E.
32 B6 Abū 'Arīsh S. Arabia
30 D5 Abu Dhabi U.A.E.
87 F3 Abu Hamed Sudan
86 C4 Abuja Nigeria
87 E3 Abu Matariq Sudan
30 D5 Abū Mūsá i. U.A.E.
78 E5 Abunã Brazil
78 E6 Abunã r. Bol.
32 A7 Ābune Yosēf mt Eth.
28 C6 Abu Qīr, Khalīg b. Egypt
27 F4 Abu Road India
87 F2 Abu Simbel Egypt
29 K6 Abū Şukhayr Iraq
51 C5 Abut Head hd N.Z.
43 C4 Abuyog Phil.
87 E3 Abu Zabad Sudan
Abū Zabī see Abu Dhabi
29 M6 Abūzam Iran
87 E3 Abyad Sudan
87 E4 Abyei Sudan
30 C2 Ābyek Iran
71 J2 Acadia Nat. Park U.S.A.
74 D4 Acambaro Mex.
81 A2 Acandí Col.
15 B1 A Cañiza Spain
74 C4 Acaponeta Mex.
74 E5 Acapulco Mex.
79 J4 Acará Brazil
79 K4 Acaraú r. Brazil
82 A4 Acaray r. Para.
80 E3 Acaray, Represa de resr Para.
81 C2 Acarigua Venez.
74 F5 Acayucán Mex.
86 B4 Accra Ghana
8 E4 Accrington U.K.
81 C3 Achaguas Venez.
34 D5 Achalpur India
33 B2 Achampet India
25 T3 Achayvayam Rus. Fed.
42 D1 Acheng China
12 A4 Achicourt France
11 B4 Achill Rep. of Ireland
11 A4 Achill Island i. Rep. of Ireland
10 C2 Achiltibuie U.K.
13 H1 Achim Ger.
36 B1 Achinsk Rus. Fed.
10 C3 Achnasheen U.K.
10 C3 A'Chralaig mt U.K.
21 F6 Achuyevo Rus. Fed.
28 B3 Acıgöl l. Turkey
28 B3 Acıpayam Turkey
18 F6 Acireale Sicily Italy
64 E3 Ackley U.S.A.
75 K4 Acklins Island i. Bahamas
9 J5 Acle U.K.
83 B2 Aconcagua r. Chile
79 L5 Acopiara Brazil
15 B1 A Coruña Spain
18 C2 Acqui Terme Italy
28 E5 Acre Israel
18 G5 Acri Italy
16 J7 Ács Hungary
46 O6 Actéon, Groupe is Fr. Polynesia Pac. Oc.
70 B4 Ada OH U.S.A.
65 D5 Ada OK U.S.A.
15 D2 Adaja r. Spain
50 G4 Adaminaby Austr.
80 E8 Adam, Mt h. Falkland Is
63 G4 Adams MA U.S.A.
71 G3 Adams MA U.S.A.
68 C4 Adams WV U.S.A.
33 B4 Adam's Bridge rf India/Sri Lanka
56 F4 Adams L. l. Can.
73 E2 Adams McGill Reservoir U.S.A.
62 B2 Adams, Mt mt U.S.A.
56 C3 Adams Mt. mt U.S.A.
62 B2 Adams Peak mt U.S.A.
33 C5 Adam's Pk Sri Lanka
'Adan see Aden
28 E3 Adana Turkey
11 C5 Adare Rep. of Ireland
92 A5 Adare, C. c. Ant.
73 E2 Adaven U.S.A.
32 C5 Ad Dahnā' des. S. Arabia
86 A2 Ad Dakhla Western Sahara
32 D4 Ad Dammām S. Arabia
30 B5 Ad Dawādimī S. Arabia
Ad Dawḩah see Doha
29 J4 Ad Dawr Iraq
30 B5 Ad Dibdibah plain S. Arabia
30 B6 Ad Dilam S. Arabia
30 A5 Ad Dir'īyah S. Arabia
88 D3 Addis Ababa Eth.
72 K2 Addison U.S.A.
29 K6 Ad Dīwānīyah Iraq
9 G6 Addlestone U.K.
93 J4 Addu Atoll atoll Maldives
29 J6 Ad Duwayd well S. Arabia
67 D6 Adel GA U.S.A.
64 E3 Adel IA U.S.A.
50 B3 Adelaide Austr.
67 E7 Adelaide Bahamas
91 G6 Adelaide S. Africa
92 B2 Adelaide I i. Ant.
48 D3 Adelaide River Austr.
72 D4 Adelanto U.S.A.
50 G3 Adelong Austr.
32 C7 Aden Yemen
12 E4 Adenau Ger.
13 J1 Adendorf Ger.
32 C7 Aden, Gulf of g. Somalia/Yemen
30 D5 Adh Dhayd U.A.E.
37 F7 Adi i. Indon.
88 D2 Ādī Ārk'ay Eth.
88 D2 Ādīgrat Eth.
34 D6 Adilabad India
29 J2 Adilcevaz Turkey
62 B3 Adin U.S.A.
87 D2 Adīrī Libya
71 F2 Adirondack Mountains U.S.A.
Ādīs Ābeba see Addis Ababa
88 D3 Ādīs Alem Eth.
88 D2 Adi Ugri Eritrea
28 G3 Adıyaman Turkey
17 N7 Adjud Romania
59 J3 Adlavik Islands is Can.
48 C3 Admiralty Gulf b. Austr.
42 K2 Admiralty Inlet in. Can.
56 C3 Admiralty Island i. U.S.A.
56 C3 Admiralty Island Nat. Monument res. U.S.A.
48 E2 Admiralty Islands is P.N.G.
33 B3 Adoni India
13 L4 Adorf Ger.
13 G3 Adorf (Diemelsee) Ger.
14 D5 Adour r. France
15 E4 Adra Spain
18 F6 Adrano Sicily Italy
86 B2 Adrar Alg.
86 A2 Adrar mts Alg.
86 C3 Adrar des Ifôghas reg. Mali
86 A2 Adrar Maur
31 F3 Adraskand r. Afgh.
87 E3 Adré Chad
69 E5 Adrian MI U.S.A.
65 C5 Adrian TX U.S.A.
18 E2 Adriatic Sea sea Europe
33 B4 Adur India
88 C3 Adusa Congo(Zaire)
88 D2 Ādwa Eth.
25 P3 Adycha r. Rus. Fed.
21 F6 Adygeya, Respublika div. Rus. Fed.
21 F6 Adygeysk Rus. Fed.
21 H6 Adyk Rus. Fed.
86 B4 Adzopé Côte d'Ivoire
19 L5 Aegean Sea sea Greece/Turkey
13 H2 Aerzen Ger.
15 B1 A Estrada Spain
88 D2 Afabet Eritrea
29 K3 Afan Iran
23 F6 Afghanistan country Asia
6 M5 Åfjord Norway
88 E3 Afmadow Somalia
54 C4 Afognak I. i. U.S.A.
15 C1 A Fonsagrada Spain
28 F3 'Afrīn r. Syria/Turkey
28 F2 Afşin Turkey
12 D2 Afsluitdijk barrage Neth.
62 E3 Afton U.S.A.
79 H4 Afuá Brazil
28 E5 'Afula Israel
28 C2 Afyon Turkey
13 L4 Aga Ger.
86 C3 Agadez Niger
86 B1 Agadir Morocco
27 F2 Agadyr' Kazak.
93 H4 Agalega Islands is Mauritius
35 G5 Agartala India
34 C6 Agashi India
69 F2 Agate Can.
19 M6 Agathonisi i. Greece
86 B4 Agboville Côte d'Ivoire
29 L1 Ağcabädi Azer.
29 L2 Ağdam Azer.
14 F5 Agde France
14 E4 Agen France
90 C4 Aggeneys S. Africa
12 F4 Agger r. Ger.
34 D1 Aghil Pass China
11 C3 Aghla Mountain h. Rep. of Ireland
19 L7 Agia Vervara Greece
28 G2 Ağın Turkey
19 K6 Agios Dimitrios Greece
19 L5 Agios Efstratios i. Greece
19 M5 Agios Fokas, Akra pt Greece
19 K5 Agios Konstantinos Greece
19 L7 Agios Nikolaos Greece
19 K4 Agiou Orous, Kolpos b. Greece
87 F3 Agirwat Hills h. Sudan
91 F3 Agisanang S. Africa
86 B4 Agnibilékrou Côte d'Ivoire
19 L2 Agnita Romania
38 A2 Agong China
34 D4 Agra India
21 H7 Agrakhanskiy Poluostrov pen. Rus. Fed.
15 F2 Agreda Spain
29 J2 Ağrı Turkey
19 K7 Agria Gramvousa i. Greece
18 E6 Agrigento Sicily Italy
19 J5 Agrinio Greece
83 B3 Agrio r. Arg.
18 F4 Agropoli Italy
29 K1 Ağstafa Azer.
29 M1 Ağsu Azer.
81 B3 Aguadas Col.
81 B3 Agua de Dios Col.
75 L5 Aguadilla Puerto Rico
83 D4 Aguado Cecilio Arg.
75 H7 Aguadulce Panama
83 C3 Agua Escondida Arg.
74 D4 Aguanaval r. Mex.
83 C1 Agua Negra, Paso del pass Arg./Chile
82 B3 Aguapeí r. Brazil
74 C2 Agua Prieta Mex.
82 A3 Aguaray Guazú r. Para.
81 D2 Aguaro-Guariquito, Parque Nacional nat. park Venez.
74 D4 Aguascalientes Mex.
82 E2 Águas Formosas Brazil
82 C3 Agudos Brazil
73 F5 Aguila U.S.A.
15 D1 Aguilar de Campóo Spain
15 F4 Águilas Spain
43 B4 Aguisan Phil.
93 F7 Agulhas Basin sea feature Ind. Ocean
90 D7 Agulhas, Cape c. S. Africa
82 D3 Agulhas Negras mt Brazil
93 F6 Agulhas Plateau sea feature Ind. Ocean
45 E4 Agung, G. volc. Indon.
43 C4 Agusan r. Phil.
43 B4 Agutaya Phil.
30 B2 Ahar Iran
51 C5 Ahaura N.Z.
12 F2 Ahaus Ger.
51 F3 Ahimanawa Ra. mts N.Z.
51 D1 Ahipara N.Z.
51 D1 Ahipara Bay b. N.Z.
54 B4 Ahklun Mts mts U.S.A.
29 J2 Ahlat Turkey
13 F3 Ahlen Ger.
34 C5 Ahmadabad India
30 E4 Ahmadī Iran
33 A2 Ahmadnagar India
34 B3 Ahmadpur East Pak.
13 J4 Ahorn Ger.
30 C4 Ahram Iran
13 J1 Ahrensburg Ger.
29 J2 Ahta D. mt Turkey
6 T5 Ähtäri Fin.
7 U7 Ahtme Estonia
29 M6 Āhū Iran
14 F3 Ahun France
51 B6 Ahuriri r. N.Z.
30 C4 Ahvāz Iran
34 C5 Ahwa India
Ahwāz see Ahvāz
42 C3 Ai r. China
90 B3 Ai-Ais Namibia
38 D1 Aibag Gol r. China
30 D2 Aidin Turkm.
72 1 Aiea U.S.A.
28 E4 Aigialousa Cyprus
19 K6 Aigina i. Greece
19 K5 Aigio Greece
14 H4 Aigle de Chambeyron mt France
83 F2 Aiguá Uru.
41 F5 Aikawa Japan
67 D5 Aiken U.S.A.
81 A2 Ailigandi Panama
94 G5 Ailinglapalap i. Pac. Oc.
12 A5 Ailly-sur-Noye France
69 G4 Ailsa Craig Can.
10 C5 Ailsa Craig i. U.K.
82 E2 Aimorés, Sa dos h. Brazil
86 C1 Aïn Beïda Alg.
86 B2 'Aïn Ben Tili Maur.
15 H4 Aïn Defla Alg.
15 H5 Aïn el Hadjel Alg.
86 B1 Aïn Sefra Alg.
59 H4 Ainslie, Lake l. Can.
64 D3 Ainsworth U.S.A.
Aintab see Gaziantep
15 H4 Aïn Taya Alg.
15 G5 Aïn Tédélès Alg.
81 B4 Aipe Col.
44 C5 Air i. Indon.
56 G4 Airdrie Can.
10 E5 Airdrie U.K.
12 D6 Aire r. France
14 D5 Aire-sur-l'Adour France
55 L3 Air Force I. i. Can.
38 D1 Airgin Sum China
86 C3 Aïr, Massif de l' mts Niger
57 H3 Air Ronge Can.
80 B7 Aisén, Pto Chile
38 F2 Ai Shan h. China
56 B2 Aishihik Can.
56 B2 Aishihik Lake l. Can.
14 G2 Aisne r. France
15 F3 Aitana mt Spain
48 E2 Aitape P.N.G.
64 E2 Aitkin U.S.A.
46 M5 Aitutaki i. Cook Is Pac. Oc.
17 L7 Aiud Romania
14 G5 Aix-en-Provence France
14 G4 Aix-les-Bains France
56 D3 Aiyansh Can.
35 F5 Aiyar Res. resr India
35 H5 Aizawl India
7 T8 Aizkraukle Latvia
7 R8 Aizpute Latvia
41 F6 Aizu-wakamatsu Japan
18 C4 Ajaccio Corsica France
81 B4 Ajajú r. Col.
33 A1 Ajanta India
Ajanta Range h. see Sahyadriparvat Range
6 O4 Ajaureforsen Sweden
51 D5 Ajax, Mt mt N.Z.
87 E1 Ajdābiyā Libya
a-Jiddét gravel area see Jiddat al Ḩarāsīs
40 G4 Ajigasawa Japan
28 E5 'Ajlūn Jordan
30 D5 Ajman U.A.E.
34 C4 Ajmer India
73 F5 Ajo U.S.A.
73 F5 Ajo, Mt mt U.S.A.
43 B4 Ajuy Phil.
40 H3 Akabira Japan
88 D4 Akagera National Park Rwanda
33 B2 Akalkot India
40 J3 Akan National Park Japan
28 D4 Akanthou Cyprus
51 D5 Akaroa N.Z.
51 D5 Akaroa Har in. N.Z.
35 H4 Akas reg. India
31 H3 Akbar Afgh.
35 E4 Akbarpur India
15 J4 Akbou Alg.
24 G4 Akbulak Rus. Fed.
28 F2 Akçadağ Turkey
29 G3 Akçakale Turkey
28 C1 Akçakoca Turkey
28 D3 Akçali D. mt Turkey
28 C3 Ak D. mt Turkey
29 H2 Ak D. mts Turkey
28 C3 Akdağ mt Turkey
28 E2 Akdağmadeni Turkey
7 Q7 Åkersberga Sweden
12 C2 Akersloot Neth.
88 C3 Aketi Congo(Zaire)
29 J1 Akhalk'alak'i Georgia
21 G7 Akhalts'ikhe Georgia
35 G5 Akhaura Bangl.
32 E5 Akhḑar, Jabal mts Oman
28 A2 Akhisar Turkey
28 F3 Akhtarīn Syria
21 H5 Akhtubinsk Rus. Fed.
29 J1 Akhuryan Armenia
41 C8 Aki Japan
58 D3 Akimiski Island i. Can.
28 E3 Akıncı Burun pt Turkey
28 G1 Akıncılar Turkey
40 G5 Akita Japan
86 A3 Akjoujt Maur.
6 P3 Akkajaure l. Sweden
40 J3 Akkeshi Japan
'Akko see Acre
28 F1 Akkuş Turkey
30 D1 Akkyr, Gory h. Turkm.
34 D4 Aklera India
7 R8 Akmeņrags pt Latvia
34 D1 Akmeqit China
41 D7 Akō Japan
87 F4 Akobo Sudan
34 D5 Akola India
88 D2 Akordat Eritrea
28 D3 Akören Turkey
34 D5 Akot India
55 M3 Akpatok Island i. Que. Can.
59 G1 Akpatok Island i. Can.
6 B4 Akranes Iceland
21 C7 Akrathos, Akra pt Greece
7 J7 Åkrehamn Norway
31 G3 Ak Robat Pass Afgh.
62 G3 Akron CO U.S.A.
70 C4 Akron OH U.S.A.
70 C4 Akron City Reservoir U.S.A.
34 D2 Aksai Chin terr. China/India
28 E2 Aksaray Turkey
21 F6 Aksay Rus. Fed.
34 D2 Aksayqin Hu l. China/Jammu and Kashmir
28 C2 Akşehir Turkey
28 C2 Akşehir Gölü l. Turkey
28 C3 Akseki Turkey
30 D4 Aks-e Rostam r. Iran
26 E2 Akshiganak Kazak.
27 G2 Aksu China
28 C3 Aksu r. Turkey
88 D2 Āksum Eth.
35 F1 Aktag mt China
29 K2 Aktas D. mt Turkey
31 G2 Aktash Uzbek.
26 D2 Aktau Kazak.
27 F2 Aktogay Kazak.
17 O4 Aktsyabrski Belarus
26 D1 Aktyubinsk Kazak.
41 B8 Akune Japan
86 C4 Akure Nigeria
6 D4 Akureyri Iceland
35 G1 Akxokesay China
Akyab see Sittwe
28 G3 Akziyaret Turkey
7 L6 Ål Norway
30 C5 Al 'Abā S. Arabia
67 C5 Alabama div. U.S.A.
67 C6 Alabama r. U.S.A.
67 C5 Alabaster U.S.A.
43 B3 Alabat i. Phil.
29 K7 Al 'Abţīyah well Iraq
28 E1 Alaca Turkey
28 F2 Alacahan Turkey
28 E1 Alaçam Turkey
28 B2 Alaçam Dağları mts Turkey
29 J2 Ala Dag mt Turkey
28 E3 Ala Dağlar mts Turkey
29 J2 Ala Dağlar mts Turkey
21 H7 Alagir Rus. Fed.
79 L6 Alagoinhas Brazil
15 F2 Alagón Spain
43 C5 Alah r. Phil.
6 S5 Alahärmä Fin.
29 L7 Al Ahmadī Kuwait
31 H2 Alai Range mts Asia
6 S5 Alajärvi Fin.
75 H6 Alajuela Costa Rica
29 L2 Alajujeh Iran
34 D3 Alaknanda r. India
27 G2 Alakol', Ozero l. Kazak.
6 W3 Alakurtti Rus. Fed.
78 F4 Alalaú r. Brazil
29 J3 Al 'Amādīyah Iraq
30 B5 Al'Amār S. Arabia
29 L6 Al 'Amārah Iraq
35 H3 Alamdo China
29 K7 Al Amghar waterhole Iraq
43 A2 Alaminos Phil.
65 C7 Alamítos, Sa de los mt Mex.
73 E3 Alamo U.S.A.
73 F4 Alamo Dam dam U.S.A.
63 F5 Alamogordo U.S.A.
65 D6 Alamo Heights U.S.A.
63 E6 Alamos Mex.
60 E6 Alamos Mex.
63 F4 Alamosa U.S.A.
33 B3 Alampur India
6 O4 Alanäs Sweden
33 B2 Aland India
7 Q6 Åland is Fin.
13 K1 Aland r. Ger.
30 B2 Aland r. Iran
44 B5 Alang Besar i. Indon.
68 E3 Alanson U.S.A.
28 D3 Alanya Turkey
28 C1 Alaplı Turkey
Alappuzha see Alleppey
30 C6 Al 'Āqūlah well S. Arabia
15 E3 Alarcón, Embalse de resr Spain
32 C4 Al Arţāwīyah S. Arabia
45 E4 Alas Indon.
28 B2 Alaşehir Turkey
29 J6 Al 'Āshūrīyah well Iraq
54 D3 Alaska div. U.S.A.
54 D4 Alaska, Gulf of g. U.S.A.
56 E3 Alaska Highway Can./U.S.A.
54 B4 Alaska Peninsula U.S.A.
54 D3 Alaska Range mts U.S.A.
29 M2 Älät Azer.
31 F2 Alat Uzbek.
29 J6 Al 'Athāmīn h. Iraq
20 H4 Alatyr' Rus. Fed.
20 H4 Alatyr' r. Rus. Fed.
78 C4 Alausí Ecuador
29 K1 Alaverdi Armenia
6 T4 Alavieska Fin.
6 S5 Alavus Fin.
50 C3 Alawoona Austr.
29 L1 Alazani r. Azer./Georgia
29 K5 Al 'Azīzīyah Iraq
18 C2 Alba Italy
28 F3 Al Bāb Syria
15 F3 Albacete Spain
50 C3 Albacutya, L. l. Austr.
29 K6 Al Baghdādī al Janūbīyah h. Iraq
19 K1 Alba Iulia Romania
58 F3 Albanel, L. l. Can.
5 E4 Albania country Europe
48 B5 Albany Austr.
67 C6 Albany GA U.S.A.
68 E5 Albany IN U.S.A.
66 C4 Albany KY U.S.A.
71 G3 Albany NY U.S.A.
62 B2 Albany OR U.S.A.
58 C3 Albany r. Can.
83 G2 Albardão do João Maria coastal area Brazil
30 B5 Al Barrah S. Arabia
Al Başrah see Basra
29 K6 Al Baṭḩa' marsh Iraq
29 L7 Al Bāţin, Wādī watercourse Asia
48 E3 Albatross Bay b. Austr.
87 E1 Al Bayḑā' Libya
78 Albemarle, Pta pt Galapagos Is Ecuador
67 E5 Albemarle Sd chan. U.S.A.
18 C2 Albenga Italy
15 D3 Alberche r. Spain
48 D4 Alberga watercourse Austr.
15 B2 Albergaria-a-Velha Port.
50 F2 Albert Austr.
14 F2 Albert France
70 E6 Alberta U.S.A.
56 F4 Alberta div. Can.
56 F4 Alberta, Mt mt Can.
90 D7 Albertinia S. Africa
12 D4 Albert Kanaal canal Belgium
50 B3 Albert, Lake l. Austr.
88 D3 Albert, Lake l. Congo(Zaire)/Uganda
64 E3 Albert Lea U.S.A.
88 D3 Albert Nile r. Sudan/Uganda
80 B8 Alberto de Agostini, Parque Nacional nat. park Chile
91 H3 Alberton S. Africa
14 H4 Albertville France
12 E6 Albestroff France
14 F5 Albi France
79 H2 Albina Suriname
72 A2 Albion CA U.S.A.
71 J2 Albion ME U.S.A.
68 E4 Albion MI U.S.A.
70 D3 Albion NY U.S.A.
15 E5 Alborán, Isla de i. Spain
7 L8 Ålborg Denmark
7 M8 Ålborg Bugt b. Denmark
56 F4 Albreda Can.
30 C5 Al Budayyi Bahrain
30 C6 Al Budū', Sabkhat salt pan S. Arabia
15 B4 Albufeira Port.
29 H4 Āl Bū Kamāl Syria
63 F5 Albuquerque U.S.A.
32 E5 Al Buraymī Oman
15 C3 Alburquerque Spain
50 F4 Albury Austr.
29 H4 Al Buşayrah Syria
28 G7 Al Busayṭā' plain S. Arabia
30 B4 Al Buşayyah Iraq
30 B4 Al Bushūk well S. Arabia
15 B3 Alcácer do Sal Port.
15 E2 Alcalá de Henares Spain
15 E4 Alcalá la Real Spain
18 E6 Alcamo Sicily Italy
15 F2 Alcañiz Spain
15 C3 Alcántara Spain
15 E3 Alcaraz Spain
15 D4 Alcaudete Spain
15 E3 Alcázar de San Juan Spain
21 F5 Alchevs'k Ukr.
83 D2 Alcira Arg.
82 E2 Alcobaça Brazil
15 F2 Alcora Spain
83 E2 Alcorta Arg.
15 F3 Alcoy Spain
15 H3 Alcúdia Spain
89 E4 Aldabra Islands is Seychelles
29 K5 Al Daghghārah Iraq
25 O4 Aldan Rus. Fed.
25 P3 Aldan r. Rus. Fed.
9 J5 Aldeburgh U.K.
51 F2 Aldermen Is, The is N.Z.
14 D2 Alderney i. Channel Is U.K.
72 B4 Alder Peak summit U.S.A.
9 G6 Aldershot U.K.
70 C6 Alderson U.S.A.
30 D6 Al Dhafrah reg. U.A.E.
8 D3 Aldingham U.K.
9 F5 Aldridge U.K.
68 B5 Aledo U.S.A.
86 A3 Aleg Maur.
82 E3 Alegre Brazil
80 E3 Alegrete Brazil
83 E2 Alejandro Korn Arg.
20 E2 Alekhovshchina Rus. Fed.
20 F3 Aleksandrov Rus. Fed.
21 J5 Aleksandrov Gay Rus. Fed.
21 H6 Aleksandrovskoye Rus. Fed.
25 Q4 Aleksandrovsk-Sakhalinskiy Rus. Fed.
26 F1 Alekseyevka Kazak.
21 F5 Alekseyevka Belgorod. Obl. Rus. Fed.
21 F5 Alekseyevka Belgorod. Obl. Rus. Fed.
21 G5 Alekseyevskaya Rus. Fed.
20 F4 Aleksin Rus. Fed.
19 J3 Aleksinac Yugo.
74 E5 Alemán, Presa Miguel resr Mex.
88 B4 Alèmbé Gabon
28 E1 Alembeyli Turkey
82 D3 Além Paraíba Brazil
6 M5 Ålen Norway
14 E2 Alençon France
79 H4 Alenquer Brazil
72 2 Alenuihaha Channel U.S.A.
28 F3 Aleppo Syria
78 D6 Alerta Peru
56 D4 Alert Bay Can.
14 G4 Alès France
17 L7 Aleşd Romania
18 C2 Alessandria Italy
6 K5 Ålesund Norway
53 A4 Aleutian Islands is U.S.A.

54 C4 Aleutian Range *mts* U.S.A.
94 H2 Aleutian Trench *sea feature* Pac. Oc.
25 R4 Alevina, Mys *c.* Rus. Fed.
Alevişik *see* Samandağı
71 K2 Alexander U.S.A.
56 B3 Alexander Archipelago *is* U.S.A.
90 B4 Alexander Bay S. Africa
90 B4 Alexander Bay *b.* Namibia/S. Africa
67 C5 Alexander City U.S.A.
92 A2 Alexander I. *i.* Ant.
50 E4 Alexandra Austr.
51 B6 Alexandra N.Z.
80 □ Alexandra, C. *c.* Atl. Ocean
19 K4 Alexandreia Greece
Alexandretta *see* İskenderun
71 F2 Alexandria Can.
87 E1 Alexandria Egypt
19 L3 Alexandria Romania
91 G6 Alexandria S. Africa
10 D5 Alexandria U.K.
68 E5 Alexandria *IN* U.S.A.
65 E6 Alexandria *LA* U.S.A.
64 E2 Alexandria *MN* U.S.A.
70 E5 Alexandria *VA* U.S.A.
71 F2 Alexandria Bay U.S.A.
50 B3 Alexandrina, L. *l.* Austr.
19 L4 Alexandroupoli Greece
68 B5 Alexis U.S.A.
59 J3 Alexis *r.* Can.
56 E4 Alexis Creek Can.
24 K4 Aleysk Rus. Fed.
12 F4 Alf Ger.
15 F1 Alfaro Spain
29 L7 Al Farwānīyah Kuwait
29 J4 Al Fatḥah Iraq
29 M7 Al Fāw Iraq
13 H3 Alfeld (Leine) Ger.
82 D3 Alfenas Brazil
29 M7 Al Fințās Kuwait
17 K7 Alföld *plain* Hungary
9 H4 Alford U.K.
71 F2 Alfred Can.
71 H3 Alfred U.S.A.
29 M7 Al Fuḥayḥīl Kuwait
Al-Fujayrah *see* Fujairah
30 B4 Al Fulayi *watercourse* S. Arabia
Al Furāt *r. see* Euphrates
7 J7 Algård Norway
83 C3 Algarrobo del Aguilla Arg.
15 B4 Algarve *reg.* Port.
20 G4 Algasovo Rus. Fed.
15 D4 Algeciras Spain
15 F3 Algemesí Spain
Alger *see* Algiers
69 E3 Alger U.S.A.
85 C3 Algeria *country* Africa
13 H2 Algermissen Ger.
29 K6 Al Ghammas Iraq
30 B5 Al Ghāṭ S. Arabia
32 D6 Al Ghayḍah Yemen
18 C4 Alghero *Sardinia* Italy
86 C1 Algiers Alg.
91 F6 Algoa Bay *b.* S. Africa
68 D3 Algoma U.S.A.
64 E3 Algona U.S.A.
69 F4 Algonac U.S.A.
69 H3 Algonquin Park Can.
69 H3 Algonquin Provincial Park *res.* Can.
29 J7 Al Habakah *well* S. Arabia
30 B4 Al Ḥadaqah *well* S. Arabia
30 C5 Al Ḥadd Bahrain
30 A4 Al Hadhālīl *plat.* S. Arabia
29 J4 Al Ḥadīthah Iraq
29 J4 Al Ḥaḍr Iraq
28 F4 Al Ḥaffah Syria
30 B5 Al Ḥā'ir S. Arabia
31 E6 Al Hajar Oman
30 E5 Al Ḥajar al Gharbī *mts* Oman
29 G6 Al Hamad *reg.* Jordan/S. Arabia
87 D2 Al Ḥamādah al Ḥamrā' *plat.* Libya
15 F4 Alhama de Murcia Spain
29 J6 Al Hammām *well* Iraq
29 K7 Al Haniyah *esc.* Iraq
30 B6 Al Hariq S. Arabia
29 G6 Al Ḥarrah *reg.* S. Arabia
29 H3 Al Ḥasakah Syria
29 K5 Al Hāshimīyah Iraq
29 L5 Al Ḥayy Iraq
29 K5 Al Ḥillah Iraq
30 B6 Al Ḥillah S. Arabia
30 B6 Al Ḥilwah S. Arabia
30 C5 Al Ḥinnāh S. Arabia
86 B1 Al Hoceima Morocco
32 B7 Al Hudaydah Yemen
32 C4 Al Hufūf S. Arabia
30 D6 Al Ḥumrah *reg.* U.A.E.
30 C5 Al Ḥunayy S. Arabia
30 B6 Al Huwwah S. Arabia
30 D2 'Alīābād Iran
31 F4 'Alīābād Iran
31 E3 'Alīābād Iran
29 L4 'Alīābād Iran
19 M5 Aliağa Turkey
19 K4 Aliakmonas *r.* Greece
29 L5 'Alī al Gharbī Iraq
33 A2 Alībāg India
34 B4 Ali Bandar Pak.
29 M2 Äli Bayramlı Azer.
15 F3 Alicante Spain
91 G6 Alice S. Africa
65 D7 Alice U.S.A.
56 D3 Alice Arm Can.
48 D4 Alice Springs Austr.
67 E7 Alice Town Bahamas
43 B5 Alicia Phil.
34 D4 Aligarh India
30 C3 Alīgūdarz Iran
88 B4 Alima *r.* Congo
7 N8 Alingsås Sweden
28 B2 Aliova *r.* Turkey
34 B3 Alipur Pak.
35 G4 Alipur Duar India
70 C4 Aliquippa U.S.A.
88 E2 Ali Sabieh Djibouti
28 F6 'Al 'Īsāwīyah S. Arabia
29 K2 Alī Shah Iran
29 K5 Al Iskandarīyah Iraq
63 E6 Alisos *r.* Mex.
19 L5 Aliveri Greece
91 G5 Aliwal North S. Africa
56 G4 Alix Can.
87 E1 Al Jabal al Akhḍar *mts* Libya
30 C5 Al Jāfūrah *des.* S. Arabia
87 E2 Al Jaghbūb Libya
29 L7 Al Jahrah Kuwait
30 C5 Al Jamalīyah Qatar
30 C6 Al Jawb *reg.* S. Arabia
32 A4 Al Jawf S. Arabia
87 D1 Al Jawsh Libya
29 G3 Al Jazīrah *reg.* Iraq/Syria
15 B4 Aljezur Port.
30 C5 Al Jībān *reg.* S. Arabia
30 B6 Al Jifārah S. Arabia
29 J6 Al Jil *well* Iraq
30 B5 Al Jilh *esc.* S. Arabia
30 C5 Al Jishshah S. Arabia
28 E6 Al Jīzah Jordan
32 C4 Al Jubayl S. Arabia
30 B5 Al Jubaylah S. Arabia
30 B5 Al Jufayr S. Arabia
30 C5 Al Jurayd *i.* S. Arabia
30 B5 Al Jurayfah S. Arabia
15 B4 Aljustrel Port.
32 E5 Al Khābūrah Oman
29 K5 Al Khāliṣ Iraq
32 E4 Al Khaṣab Oman
30 A6 Al Khāṣirah S. Arabia
30 D6 Al Khatam *reg.* U.A.E.
30 C5 Al Khawr Qatar
30 C5 Al Khīṣah *well* S. Arabia
30 C5 Al Khobar S. Arabia
30 B5 Al Khuff *reg.* S. Arabia
87 E2 Al Khufrah Libya
87 D1 Al Khums Libya
29 K5 Al Kifl Iraq
30 C5 Al Kir'ānah Qatar
12 C2 Alkmaar Neth.
29 K5 Al Kūfah Iraq
29 L5 Al Kumayt Iraq
29 K5 Al Kūt Iraq
Al Kuwayt *see* Kuwait
29 H7 Al Labbah *plain* S. Arabia
Al Lādhiqīyah *see* Latakia
71 J1 Allagash *ME* U.S.A.
71 J1 Allagash *r. ME* U.S.A.
71 J1 Allagash Lake *l.* U.S.A.
35 E4 Allahabad India
29 F5 Al Lajā *lava* Syria
25 P3 Allakh-Yun' Rus. Fed.
91 G3 Allanridge S. Africa
91 H1 Alldays S. Africa
68 E4 Allegan U.S.A.
70 D4 Allegheny *r.* U.S.A.
70 C6 Allegheny Mountains U.S.A.
70 D4 Allegheny Reservoir U.S.A.
67 D5 Allendale U.S.A.
8 E3 Allendale Town U.K.
13 G4 Allendorf (Lumda) Ger.
69 G3 Allenford Can.
11 C3 Allen, Lough *l.* Rep. of Ireland
71 F4 Allentown U.S.A.
33 B4 Alleppey India
13 J2 Aller *r.* Ger.
64 C3 Alliance *NE* U.S.A.
70 C4 Alliance *OH* U.S.A.
29 J6 Al Līfīyah *well* Iraq
7 O9 Allinge-Sandvig Denmark
69 H3 Alliston Can.
32 B5 Al Līth S. Arabia
10 E4 Alloa U.K.
33 C3 Allur India
33 C3 Alluru Kottapatnam India
29 J6 Al Lussuf *well* Iraq
59 F4 Alma Can.
68 E4 Alma *MI* U.S.A.
64 D3 Alma *NE* U.S.A.
73 H5 Alma *NM* U.S.A.
29 J6 Al Ma'ānīyah Iraq
15 B3 Almada Port.
29 K7 Al Ma'danīyāt *well* Iraq
15 D3 Almadén Spain
Al Madīnah *see* Medina
29 K5 Al Maḥmūdīyah Iraq
30 B5 Al Majma'ah S. Arabia
29 L1 Almalı Azer.
30 C5 Al Malsūnīyah *reg.* S. Arabia
30 C5 Al Manāmah Bahrain
72 B1 Almanor, Lake *l.* U.S.A.
15 F3 Almansa Spain
15 D2 Almanzor *mt* Spain
29 L6 Al Ma'qil Iraq
30 D6 Al Mariyyah U.A.E.
87 E1 Al Marj Libya
82 C1 Almas, Rio das *r.* Brazil
27 F2 Almaty Kazak.
Al Mawṣil *see* Mosul
29 H4 Al Mayādīn Syria
30 B5 Al Mazāḥimīyah S. Arabia
15 E2 Almazán Spain
25 N3 Almaznyy Rus. Fed.
79 H4 Almeirim Brazil
15 B3 Almeirim Port.
12 E2 Almelo Neth.
82 E2 Almenara Brazil
15 C2 Almendra, Embalse de *resr* Spain
15 C3 Almendralejo Spain
12 D2 Almere Neth.
15 E4 Almería Spain
15 E4 Almería, Golfo de *b.* Spain
24 G4 Al'met'yevsk Rus. Fed.
7 O8 Älmhult Sweden
30 B5 Al Midhnab S. Arabia
15 D5 Almina, Pta *pt* Morocco
32 C4 Al Mish'āb S. Arabia
28 F5 Al Mismīyah Syria
15 B4 Almodôvar Port.
69 F4 Almont U.S.A.
69 J3 Almonte Can.
15 C4 Almonte Spain
32 C4 Al Mubarrez S. Arabia
28 E7 Al Mudawwara Jordan
30 C5 Al Muharraq Bahrain
32 C7 Al Mukallā Yemen
32 B7 Al Mukhā Yemen
15 E4 Almuñécar Spain
29 K5 Al Muqdādīyah Iraq
30 B5 Al Murabba S. Arabia
28 F1 Almus Turkey
30 B4 Al Musannāh *ridge* S. Arabia
29 K5 Al Musayyib Iraq
19 L7 Almyrou, Ormos *b.* Greece
72 □1 Alna Haina U.S.A.
8 F2 Alnwick U.K.
35 H5 Alon Myanmar
35 H3 Along India
19 K5 Alonnisos *i.* Greece
37 E7 Alor *i.* Indon.
37 E7 Alor, Kepulauan *is* Indon.
45 B1 Alor Setar Malaysia
Alost *see* Aalst
34 C5 Alot India
6 W4 Alozero Rus. Fed.
72 C4 Alpaugh U.S.A.
12 E3 Alpen Ger.
69 F3 Alpena U.S.A.
18 D1 Alpi Dolomitiche *mts* Italy
73 H5 Alpine *AZ* U.S.A.
65 C6 Alpine *TX* U.S.A.
62 E3 Alpine *WY* U.S.A.
4 D4 Alps *mts* Europe
32 C6 Al Qa'āmīyāt *reg.* S. Arabia
87 D1 Al Qaddāḥīyah Libya
28 F4 Al Qadmūs Syria
30 B5 Al Qā'īyah *well* S. Arabia
30 C6 Al Qalībah S. Arabia
29 H3 Al Qāmishlī Syria
30 B5 Al Qar'ah *well* S. Arabia
28 F4 Al Qaryatayn Syria
30 B5 Al Qaṣab S. Arabia
32 C6 Al Qaṭn Yemen
87 D2 Al Qaṭrūn Libya
30 B4 Al Qayṣūmah S. Arabia
28 E5 Al Qunayṭirah Syria
32 B6 Al Qunfidhah S. Arabia
30 A5 Al Qurayn S. Arabia
29 L6 Al Qurnah Iraq
29 K6 Al Qusayr Iraq
30 B6 Al Qūṣūrīyah S. Arabia
28 F5 Al Quṭayfah Syria
30 A5 Al Quwārah S. Arabia
30 B5 Al Quwayīyah S. Arabia
14 H2 Alsace *reg.* France
9 E4 Alsager U.K.
29 J6 Al Samīt *well* Iraq
57 H4 Alsask Can.
13 H4 Alsfeld Ger.
13 K3 Alsleben (Saale) Ger.
8 E3 Alston U.K.
7 R8 Alsunga Latvia
6 S2 Alta Norway
6 S2 Altaelva *r.* Norway
83 D1 Alta Gracia Arg.
81 D2 Altagracia de Orituco Venez.
22 F5 Altai Mountains China/Mongolia
67 D6 Altamaha *r.* U.S.A.
79 H4 Altamira Brazil
51 B6 Alta, Mt *mt* N.Z.
18 G4 Altamura Italy
82 C1 Alta Paraiso de Goiás Brazil
70 D6 Altavista U.S.A.
27 G2 Altay China
36 B2 Altay Mongolia
15 F3 Altea Spain
6 S1 Alteidet Norway
12 E4 Altenahr Ger.
12 F4 Altenberge Ger.
13 L4 Altenburg Ger.
12 F4 Altenkirchen (Westerwald) Ger.
35 H1 Altenqoke China
13 M1 Altentreptow Ger.
29 M1 Altıağaç Azer.
31 H3 Altimur Pass Afgh.
29 K4 Altin Köprü Iraq
19 M5 Altınoluk Turkey
28 C2 Altıntaş Turkey
78 E7 Altiplano *plain* Bol.
13 K2 Altmark *reg.* Ger.
13 J5 Altmühl *r.* Ger.
82 B2 Alto Araguaia Brazil
83 C2 Alto de Pencoso *h.* Arg.
81 B3 Alto de Tamar *mt* Col.
82 B2 Alto Garças Brazil
89 D5 Alto Molócuè Moz.
66 B4 Alton *IL* U.S.A.
65 F4 Alton *MO* U.S.A.
71 H3 Alton *NH* U.S.A.
64 D1 Altona Can.
70 D4 Altoona U.S.A.
82 B2 Alto Sucuriú Brazil
16 F6 Altötting Ger.
9 E4 Altrincham U.K.
13 L1 Alt Schwerin Ger.
36 A1 Altun Shan *mts* China
62 B3 Alturas U.S.A.
65 D5 Altus U.S.A.
28 G1 Alucra Turkey
7 U8 Alūksne Latvia
29 M5 Alūm Iran
70 B4 Alum Creek Lake *l.* U.S.A.
83 B3 Aluminé *r.* Arg.
83 B3 Aluminé, L. *l.* Arg.
21 E6 Alupka Ukr.
87 D1 Al 'Uqaylah Libya
30 C5 Al 'Uqayr S. Arabia
21 E6 Alushta Ukr.
29 K4 'Alut Iran
32 C4 Al 'Uthmānīyah S. Arabia
87 E2 Al 'Uwaynāt Libya
29 J6 Al 'Uwayqīlah S. Arabia
30 A5 Al 'Uyūn S. Arabia
29 L6 Al 'Uzayr Iraq
65 D4 Alva U.S.A.
83 C2 Alvarado, P. de *pass* Chile
78 F4 Alvarães Brazil
7 M5 Alvdal Norway
7 O6 Älvdalen Sweden
7 O8 Alvesta Sweden
7 K6 Ålvik Norway
65 E6 Alvin U.S.A.
6 R4 Älvsbyn Sweden
26 B4 Al Wajh S. Arabia
30 C5 Al Wakrah Qatar
30 C5 Al Wannān S. Arabia
34 D4 Alwar India
30 B5 Al Warī'ah S. Arabia
33 B4 Alwaye India
29 H5 Al Widyān *plat.* Iraq/S. Arabia
30 B4 'Al Wusayṭ *well* S. Arabia
38 A2 Alxa Youqi China
38 B2 Alxa Zuoqi China
48 D3 Alyangula Austr.
10 E4 Alyth U.K.
7 T9 Alytus Lith.
62 F2 Alzada U.S.A.
12 E5 Alzette *r.* Lux.
13 G5 Alzey Ger.
81 E3 Amacuro *r.* Guyana/Venez.
48 D4 Amadeus, Lake *salt flat* Austr.
55 L3 Amadjuak Lake *l.* Can.
73 G6 Amado U.S.A.
15 B3 Amadora Port.
41 A8 Amakusa-nada *b.* Japan
7 N7 Åmal Sweden
33 C2 Amalapuram India
36 D1 Amalat *r.* Rus. Fed.
81 B3 Amalfi Col.
90 F3 Amalia S. Africa
19 J6 Amaliada Greece
34 C5 Amalner India
37 F7 Amamapare Indon.
82 A3 Amambaí Brazil
82 A3 Amambaí *r.* Brazil
82 A3 Amambaí, Serra de *h.* Brazil/Para.
36 E4 Amami-guntō *is* Japan
36 E4 Amami-Ōshima *i.* Japan
26 E1 Amangel'dy Kazak.
18 G5 Amantea Italy
91 J5 Amanzimtoti S. Africa
79 H3 Amapá Brazil
15 C3 Amareleja Port.
72 D3 Amargosa Desert U.S.A.
72 D3 Amargosa Range *mts* U.S.A.
72 D3 Amargosa Valley U.S.A.
65 C5 Amarillo U.S.A.
18 F3 Amaro, Monte *mt* Italy
34 E4 Amarpatan India
28 E1 Amasya Turkey
12 D4 Amay Belgium
79 H4 Amazon *r.* S. America
81 D4 Amazonas *div.* Brazil
Amazonas *r. see* Amazon
79 G4 Amazónia, Parque Nacional *nat. park* Brazil
79 J3 Amazon, Mouths of the *est.* Brazil
34 C6 Ambad India
33 B2 Ambajogai India
34 D3 Ambala India
33 C5 Ambalangoda Sri Lanka
89 E6 Ambalavao Madag.
89 E5 Ambanja Madag.
31 E4 Ambar Iran
25 S3 Ambarchik Rus. Fed.
33 B4 Ambasamudram India
78 C4 Ambato Ecuador
89 E5 Ambato Boeny Madag.
89 E6 Ambato Finandrahana Madag.
89 E5 Ambatolampy Madag.
89 E5 Ambatomainty Madag.
89 E5 Ambatondrazaka Madag.
13 K5 Amberg Ger.
74 G5 Ambergris Cay *i.* Belize
14 G4 Ambérieu-en-Bugey France
69 G3 Amberley Can.
35 E5 Ambikapur India
89 E5 Ambilobe Madag.
56 C3 Ambition, Mt *mt* Can.
8 F2 Amble U.K.
8 E3 Ambleside U.K.
12 D4 Amblève *r.* Belgium
89 E6 Amboasary Madag.
89 E5 Ambohidratrimo Madag.
89 E6 Ambohimahasoa Madag.
Amboina *see* Ambon
37 E7 Ambon Indon.
37 E7 Ambon *i.* Indon.
89 E6 Ambositra Madag.
89 E6 Ambovombe Madag.
73 E4 Amboy *CA* U.S.A.
68 C5 Amboy *IL* U.S.A.
71 F3 Amboy Center U.S.A.
89 B4 Ambriz Angola
49 G3 Ambrym *i.* Vanuatu
33 B3 Ambur India
35 G2 Amdo China
12 D1 Ameland *i.* Neth.
70 E6 Amelia Court House U.S.A.
71 G4 Amenia U.S.A.
62 D3 American Falls U.S.A.
62 D3 American Falls Res. *resr* U.S.A.
73 G1 American Fork U.S.A.
47 K5 American Samoa *terr.* Pac. Oc.
67 C5 Americus U.S.A.
12 D2 Amersfoort Neth.
91 H3 Amersfoort S. Africa
9 G6 Amersham U.K.
57 L3 Amery Can.
92 D5 Amery Ice Shelf *ice feature* Ant.
64 E3 Ames U.S.A.
9 F6 Amesbury U.K.
71 H3 Amesbury U.S.A.
35 E4 Amethi India
19 K5 Amfissa Greece
25 P3 Amga Rus. Fed.
36 F2 Amgu Rus. Fed.
86 C2 Amguid Alg.
36 F1 Amgun' *r.* Rus. Fed.
59 H4 Amherst Can.
71 G3 Amherst *MA* U.S.A.
71 J2 Amherst *ME* U.S.A.
70 D6 Amherst *VA* U.S.A.
69 F4 Amherstburg Can.
18 D3 Amiata, Monte *mt* Italy
14 F2 Amiens France
29 H5 Amij, Wādī *watercourse* Iraq
33 A4 Amindivi Islands *is* India
41 D7 Amino Japan
90 C1 Aminuis Namibia
30 B3 Amīrābād Iran
Amirabad *see* Fūlād Maīalleh
93 H4 Amirante Islands *is* Seychelles
31 F4 Amir Chah Pak.
57 J4 Amisk L. *l.* Can.
65 C6 Amistad Res. *resr* Mex./U.S.A.
34 D5 Amla *Madhya Pradesh* India
34 D5 Amla *Madhya Pradesh* India
7 L7 Åmli Norway
9 C4 Amlwch U.K.
28 E6 'Ammān Jordan
9 D6 Ammanford U.K.
6 V4 Ämmänsaari Fin.
6 P4 Ammarnäs Sweden
13 F1 Ammerland *reg.* Ger.
13 J3 Ammern Ger.
16 E7 Ammersee *l.* Ger.
Ammochostos *see* Famagusta
42 D4 Amnyong-dan *hd* N. Korea
34 C5 Amod India
39 B6 Amo Jiang *r.* China
30 D2 Amol Iran
13 H5 Amorbach Ger.
19 L6 Amorgos *i.* Greece
58 E4 Amos Can.
Amoy *see* Xiamen
33 C5 Amparai India
82 C3 Amparo Brazil
16 E6 Amper *r.* Ger.
15 G2 Amposta Spain
34 D5 Amravati India
34 B5 Amreli India
34 B4 Amri Pak.
28 E4 'Amrit Syria
34 C3 Amritsar India
34 D3 Amroha India
6 Q4 Åmsele Sweden
12 C2 Amstelveen Neth.
12 C2 Amsterdam Neth.
91 J3 Amsterdam S. Africa
71 F3 Amsterdam U.S.A.
93 K6 Amsterdam, Île *i.* Ind. Ocean
16 G6 Amstetten Austria
87 E3 Am Timan Chad
31 F1 Amudar'ya *r.* Turkm./Uzbek.
55 J2 Amund Ringnes I. Can.
92 D4 Amundsen Bay *b.* Ant.
92 B4 Amundsen Gl. *gl.* Ant.
54 F2 Amundsen Gulf *g.* Can.
92 C5 Amundsen, Mt *mt* Ant.
92 B4 Amundsen-Scott *U.S.A. Base* Ant.
92 A3 Amundsen Sea *sea* Ant.
45 E3 Amuntai Indon.
Amur *r. see* Heilong Jiang
25 P4 Amursk Rus. Fed.
21 F6 Amvrosiyivka Ukr.
68 E1 Amyot Can.
35 H6 An Myanmar
46 N5 Anaa *i. Fr. Polynesia* Pac. Oc.
37 E7 Anabanua Indon.
25 N2 Anabar *r.* Rus. Fed.
25 N2 Anabarskiy Zaliv *b.* Rus. Fed.
50 C2 Ana Branch *r.* Austr.
72 C4 Anacapa Is *is* U.S.A.
81 D2 Anaco Venez.
62 D2 Anaconda U.S.A.
62 B1 Anacortes U.S.A.
65 D5 Anadarko U.S.A.
28 F1 Anadolu Dağları *mts* Turkey
25 T3 Anadyr' *r.* Rus. Fed.
25 U3 Anadyrskiy Zaliv *b.* Rus. Fed.
19 L6 Anafi *i.* Greece
82 E1 Anagé Brazil
29 H4 'Ānah Iraq
72 D5 Anaheim U.S.A.
56 D4 Anahim Lake Can.
65 C7 Anáhuac Mex.
33 B4 Anaimalai Hills *mts* India
33 B4 Anai Mudi Pk *mt* India
33 C2 Anakapalle India
89 E5 Analalava Madag.
78 F4 Anamã Brazil
45 C2 Anambas, Kepulauan *is* Indon.
68 B4 Anamosa U.S.A.
28 D3 Anamur Turkey
28 D3 Anamur Burnu *pt* Turkey
41 D8 Anan Japan
34 C5 Anand India
35 F5 Ānandapur India
35 F5 Anandpur *r.* India
33 B3 Anantapur India
34 C2 Anantnag Jammu and Kashmir
21 D6 Anan'yiv Ukr.
21 F6 Anapa Rus. Fed.
82 C2 Anápolis Brazil
30 D4 Anār Iran
30 D3 Anārak Iran
30 C3 Anarbar *r.* Iran
31 F3 Anardara Afgh.
28 D2 Anatolia *reg.* Turkey
49 G4 Anatom *i.* Vanuatu
80 D3 Añatuya Arg.
81 E4 Anauá *r.* Brazil
30 C2 Anbūh Iran
42 D4 Anbyon N. Korea
14 D3 Ancenis France
54 D3 Anchorage U.S.A.
69 F4 Anchor Bay *b.* U.S.A.
18 E3 Ancona Italy
80 B6 Ancud Chile
83 B4 Ancud, Golfo de *g.* Chile
83 B1 Andacollo Chile
35 F5 Andal India
6 K5 Åndalsnes Norway
15 D4 Andalucía *div.* Spain
65 G6 Andalusia U.S.A.
93 L3 Andaman Basin *sea feature* Ind. Ocean
27 H5 Andaman Islands Andaman and Nicobar Is
45 A1 Andaman Sea *sea* Asia
89 E5 Andapa Madag.
82 E1 Andaraí Brazil
6 P2 Andenes Norway
12 D4 Andenne Belgium
12 C4 Anderlecht Belgium
14 D4 Andernos-les-Bains France
54 D3 Anderson *AK* U.S.A.
68 E5 Anderson *IN* U.S.A.
65 E4 Anderson *MO* U.S.A.
67 D5 Anderson *SC* U.S.A.
54 F3 Anderson *r. N.W.T.* Can.
81 B3 Andes Col.
76 C6 Andes *mts* S. America
64 D3 Andes, Lake U.S.A.
6 P2 Andfjorden *chan.* Norway
33 B2 Andhra Pradesh *div.* India
89 E5 Andilamena Madag.
89 E5 Andilanatoby Madag.
30 C3 Andīmeshk Iran
28 F3 Andırın Turkey
21 H7 Andiyskoye Koysu *r.* Rus. Fed.
26 F2 Andizhan Uzbek.
31 G2 Andkhui *r.* Afgh.
31 G2 Andkhvoy Afgh.
89 E5 Andoany Madag.
78 C4 Andoas Peru
33 B2 Andol India
42 E5 Andong S. Korea
42 E5 Andong-ho *l.* S. Korea
5 D4 Andorra *country* Europe
15 G1 Andorra la Vella Andorra
9 F6 Andover U.K.
71 H2 Andover *ME* U.S.A.
70 C4 Andover *OH* U.S.A.
6 O2 Andøya *i.* Norway
82 B3 Andradina Brazil
20 E3 Andreapol' Rus. Fed.
8 C3 Andreas U.K.
88 C3 André Félix, Parc National de *nat. park* C.A.R.
82 D3 Andrelândia Brazil
65 C5 Andrews U.S.A.
18 G4 Andria Italy
89 E6 Androka Madag.
67 E7 Andros *i.* Bahamas
19 L6 Andros *i.* Greece
71 H2 Androscoggin *r.* U.S.A.
67 E7 Andros Town Bahamas
33 A4 Āndrott *i.* India
21 D5 Andrushivka Ukr.
6 Q2 Andselv Norway
15 D3 Andújar Spain
89 B5 Andulo Angola
86 C3 Anéfis Mali
75 M5 Anegada *i.* Virgin Is
83 D4 Anegada, Bahía *b.* Arg.
73 F5 Anegam U.S.A.
86 C4 Aného Togo
'Aneiza, Jabal *h. see* 'Unayzah, Jabal
73 H3 Aneth U.S.A.
15 G1 Aneto *mt* Spain
87 D3 Aney Niger
39 E5 Anfu China
89 E5 Angadoka, Lohatanjona *hd* Madag.
36 B1 Angara *r.* Rus. Fed.
36 C1 Angarsk Rus. Fed.
43 B3 Angat Phil.
7 O5 Ånge Sweden
74 B3 Ángel de la Guarda *i.* Mex.
43 B3 Angeles Phil.
7 N8 Ängelholm Sweden
72 B2 Angels Camp U.S.A.
6 P4 Ångermanälven *r.* Sweden
14 D3 Angers France
57 K2 Angikuni Lake *l.* Can.
44 B2 Angkor Cambodia
9 C4 Anglesey *i.* U.K.
65 E6 Angleton U.S.A.
69 H2 Angliers Can.
Angmagssalik *see* Tasiilaq
44 □ Ang Mo Kio Sing.
88 C3 Ango Congo(Zaire)
89 D5 Angoche Moz.
31 E5 Angohrān Iran
83 B3 Angol Chile
68 E5 Angola U.S.A.
85 E7 Angola *country* Africa
96 K7 Angola Basin *sea feature* Atl. Ocean
74 F5 Angostura, Presa de la *resr* Mex.
14 E4 Angoulême France
24 J5 Angren Uzbek.
44 B2 Ang Thong Thai.
53 K8 Anguilla *terr.* Caribbean Sea
38 E1 Anguli Nur *l.* China
38 E2 Anguo China
82 A3 Anhanduí *r.* Brazil
7 M8 Anholt *i.* Denmark
39 D4 Anhua China
38 E3 Anhui *div.* China
82 A2 Anhumas Brazil
42 D5 Anhŭng S. Korea
82 C2 Anicuns Brazil
20 G3 Anikovo Rus. Fed.
73 H6 Animas U.S.A.
73 H6 Animas Peak *summit* U.S.A.
44 A2 Anin Myanmar
40 H1 Aniva Rus. Fed.
40 H1 Aniva, Mys *c.* Rus. Fed.
36 G2 Aniva, Zaliv *b.* Rus. Fed.
49 G3 Aniwa *i.* Vanuatu
12 B5 Anizy-le-Château France
7 U6 Anjalankoski Fin.
33 B4 Anjengo India
39 F4 Anji China
34 D5 Anji India
31 E3 Anjoman Iran
14 D3 Anjou *reg.* France
89 E5 Anjouan *i.* Comoros
89 E5 Anjozorobe Madag.
42 C4 Anjŭ N. Korea

32 C5 As Sulayyil S. Arabia
30 C5 Aş Şulb reg. S. Arabia
30 B5 Aş Şummān plat. S. Arabia
32 B5 As Sūq S. Arabia
29 H4 Aş Şuwār Syria
28 F5 As Suwaydā' Syria
31 E6 As Suwayq Oman
29 K5 Aş Şuwayrah Iraq
10 C2 Assynt, Loch l. U.K.
19 M7 Astakida i. Greece
Astalu Island i. see Astola Island
26 F1 Astana Kazak.
29 M3 Astaneh Iran
29 M2 Astara Azer.
Asterabad see Gorgān
18 C2 Asti Italy
72 A2 Asti U.S.A.
83 C1 Astica Arg.
31 F5 Astola Island i. Pak.
34 C2 Astor Jammu and Kashmir
34 C2 Astor r. Pak.
15 C1 Astorga Spain
62 B2 Astoria U.S.A.
7 N8 Åstorp Sweden
26 C2 Astrakhan' Rus. Fed.
Astrakhan' Bazar see Cälilabad
21 H6 Astrakhanskaya Oblast' div. Rus. Fed.
20 C4 Astravyets Belarus
92 D3 Astrid Ridge sea feature Ant.
15 C1 Asturias div. Spain
19 M6 Astypalaia i. Greece
80 E3 Asunción Para.
87 F2 Aswân Egypt
87 F2 Asyût Egypt
49 J4 Ata i. Tonga
81 D4 Atabapo r. Col./Venez.
80 C2 Atacama, Desierto de des. Chile
49 J2 Atafu i. Tokelau
86 C4 Atakpamé Togo
19 K5 Atalanti Greece
78 D6 Atalaya Peru
86 A2 Atâr Maur.
44 A1 Ataran r. Myanmar
73 H4 Atarque U.S.A.
72 B4 Atascadero U.S.A.
24 J5 Atasu Kazak.
37 E7 Atauro i. Indon.
87 F3 Atbara Sudan
87 F3 Atbara r. Sudan
26 E1 Atbasar Kazak.
65 F6 Atchafalaya Bay b. U.S.A.
64 E4 Atchison U.S.A.
18 E3 Aterno r. Italy
18 F3 Atessa Italy
12 B4 Ath Belgium
56 G4 Athabasca Can.
54 G4 Athabasca r. U.S.A.
57 G3 Athabasca, Lake l. Can.
11 E4 Athboy Rep. of Ireland
11 C4 Athenry Rep. of Ireland
69 K3 Athens Can.
19 K6 Athens Greece
67 C5 Athens AL U.S.A.
67 D5 Athens GA U.S.A.
70 B5 Athens OH U.S.A.
67 C5 Athens TN U.S.A.
65 E5 Athens TX U.S.A.
9 F5 Atherstone U.K.
12 A5 Athies France
Athina see Athens
11 C4 Athleague Rep. of Ireland
11 D4 Athlone Rep. of Ireland
33 A2 Athni India
51 B6 Athol N.Z.
71 G3 Athol U.S.A.
10 E4 Atholl, Forest of reg. U.K.
19 L4 Athos mt Greece
29 J6 Ath Thārthār, Wādī r. Iraq
11 E5 Athy Rep. of Ireland
87 D3 Ati Chad
78 D7 Atico Peru
57 J4 Atikameg L. l. Can.
58 B4 Atikokan Can.
59 H3 Atikonak L. l. Can.
43 B3 Atimonan Phil.
33 B4 Atirampattinam India
46 M6 Atiu Mauke i. Cook Islands Pac. Oc.
25 R3 Atka Rus. Fed.
21 H5 Atkarsk Rus. Fed.
30 B5 'Atk, W. al watercourse S. Arabia
67 C5 Atlanta GA U.S.A.
68 C5 Atlanta IL U.S.A.
69 E3 Atlanta MI U.S.A.
28 D2 Atlantı Turkey
64 E3 Atlantic U.S.A.
71 F5 Atlantic City U.S.A.
96 J9 Atlantic-Indian Antarctic Basin sea feature Atl. Ocean
96 J9 Atlantic-Indian Ridge sea feature Ind. Ocean
90 C6 Atlantis S. Africa
96 G3 Atlantis Fracture sea feature Atl. Ocean
84 B2 Atlas Mountains mts Alg./Morocco
86 C1 Atlas Saharien mts Alg.
56 C3 Atlin Can.
56 C3 Atlin Lake l. Can.
56 C3 Atlin Prov. Park Can.
28 E5 'Atlit Israel
33 B3 Atmakur India
33 B3 Atmakur India
65 G6 Atmore U.S.A.
65 D5 Atoka U.S.A.
44 C1 Atouat mt Laos
35 G4 Atrai r. India
30 E2 Atrak r. Iran
81 A3 Atrato r. Col.
30 D2 Atrek r. Iran/Turkm.
71 F5 Atsion U.S.A.
32 B5 Aţ Ţā'if S. Arabia
67 C5 Attalla U.S.A.
44 C2 Attapu Laos
19 M6 Attavyros mt Greece
58 D3 Attawapiskat Can.
58 C3 Attawapiskat r. Can.
58 C3 Attawapiskat L. l. Can.
29 G7 Aţ Ţawīl mts S. Arabia
30 A4 At Taysīyah plat. S. Arabia
13 F3 Attendorn Ger.
16 F7 Attersee l. Austria
68 D5 Attica IN U.S.A.
70 B4 Attica OH U.S.A.
12 C5 Attigny France
71 H3 Attleboro U.S.A.
9 J5 Attleborough U.K.
28 F7 Aţ Ţubayq reg. S. Arabia
94 G2 Attu Island i. U.S.A.
30 B5 Aţ Ţulayḩī well S. Arabia
33 B4 Attur India
10 B2 a' Tuath, Loch b. U.K.
83 C2 Atuel r. Arg.
7 O7 Åtvidaberg Sweden
70 C4 Atwood Lake l. U.S.A.
26 D2 Atyrau Kazak.
13 J5 Aub Ger.
14 G5 Aubagne France
12 D5 Aubange Belgium
43 B2 Aubarede Point pt Phil.
14 G4 Aubenas France
12 D5 Auboué France
73 F4 Aubrey Cliffs cliff U.S.A.
54 F3 Aubry Lake l. Can.
50 B3 Auburn Austr.
69 G4 Auburn Can.
67 C5 Auburn AL U.S.A.
72 B2 Auburn CA U.S.A.
68 E5 Auburn IN U.S.A.
71 H2 Auburn ME U.S.A.
64 E3 Auburn NE U.S.A.
70 E3 Auburn NY U.S.A.
62 B2 Auburn WA U.S.A.
14 F4 Aubusson France
83 C3 Auca Mahuida, Sa de mt Arg.
14 E5 Auch France
10 E4 Auchterarder U.K.
51 E2 Auckland N.Z.
49 G7 Auckland Islands is N.Z.
71 H2 Audet Can.
9 J7 Audresselles France
12 A4 Audruicq France
13 L4 Aue Ger.
13 G2 Aue r. Ger.
13 L4 Auerbach Ger.
13 K5 Auerbach in der Oberpfalz Ger.
13 L4 Auersberg mt Ger.
11 D3 Augher U.K.
11 E3 Aughnacloy U.K.
11 E5 Aughrim Rep. of Ireland
90 D4 Augrabies S. Africa
90 D4 Augrabies Falls waterfall S. Africa
90 D4 Augrabies Falls National Park S. Africa
69 F3 Au Gres U.S.A.
16 E6 Augsburg Ger.
18 F6 Augusta Sicily Italy
67 D5 Augusta GA U.S.A.
65 D4 Augusta KS U.S.A.
71 J2 Augusta ME U.S.A.
68 B3 Augusta WV U.S.A.
81 B2 Augustin Cadazzi Col.
48 B4 Augustus, Mt mt Austr.
12 B4 Aulnoye-Aymeries France
9 J7 Ault France
89 B6 Auob r. Namibia
59 G2 Aupaluk Can.
44 C5 Aur i. Malaysia
7 S6 Aura Fin.
34 D4 Auraiya India
34 C6 Aurangābād India
12 F1 Aurich Ger.
82 B2 Aurilândia Brazil
14 F4 Aurillac France
45 D3 Aurkuning Indon.
43 B5 Aurora Phil.
62 F4 Aurora CO U.S.A.
68 C5 Aurora IL U.S.A.
71 J2 Aurora ME U.S.A.
65 E4 Aurora MO U.S.A.
89 B6 Aus Namibia
69 F3 Au Sable U.S.A.
69 E3 Au Sable r. U.S.A.
71 G2 Ausable r. U.S.A.
71 G2 Ausable Forks U.S.A.
68 D2 Au Sable Pt pt MI U.S.A.
69 F3 Au Sable Pt pt MI U.S.A.
10 F1 Auskerry i. U.K.
6 D4 Austari-Jökulsá r. Iceland
64 E3 Austin MN U.S.A.
72 D2 Austin NV U.S.A.
65 D6 Austin TX U.S.A.
46 M6 Australes, Îles is French Polynesia Pac. Oc.
47 D6 Australia country Oceania
92 B6 Australian Antarctic Territory reg. Ant.
50 G3 Australian Capital Territory div. Austr.
5 E4 Austria country Europe
6 O2 Austvågøy i. Norway
13 G5 Autti Fin.
14 G3 Autun France
14 F4 Auvergne reg. France
14 F3 Auxerre France
12 A4 Auxi-le-Château France
14 G3 Auxonne France
71 F3 Ava U.S.A.
14 F3 Avallon France
72 C5 Avalon U.S.A.
59 K4 Avalon Peninsula Can.
30 B2 Avān Iran
28 E2 Avanos Turkey
82 C3 Avaré Brazil
29 L2 Ävärsin Iran
72 D4 Avawatz Mts mts U.S.A.
31 F3 Avaz Iran
79 G4 Aveiro Brazil
15 B2 Aveiro Port.
15 B2 Aveiro, Ria de est. Port.
29 M4 Āvej Iran
83 E2 Avellaneda Arg.
18 F4 Avellino Italy
72 B3 Avenal U.S.A.
50 E4 Avenel Austr.
12 C2 Avenhorn Neth.
18 F4 Aversa Italy
12 B4 Avesnes-sur-Helpe France
7 P6 Avesta Sweden
14 F4 Aveyron r. France
18 E3 Avezzano Italy
10 E3 Aviemore U.K.
18 F4 Avigliano Italy
14 G5 Avignon France
15 D2 Ávila Spain
15 D1 Avilés Spain
12 A4 Avion France
33 C5 Avissawella Sri Lanka
20 H2 Avnyugskiy Rus. Fed.
50 D4 Avoca Vic. Austr.
11 E5 Avoca Rep. of Ireland
64 E3 Avoca U.S.A.
50 D4 Avoca r. Vic. Austr.
18 F6 Avola Sicily Italy
68 B5 Avon U.S.A.
9 F5 Avon r. Eng. U.K.
9 E6 Avon r. Eng. U.K.
9 F7 Avon r. Eng. U.K.
73 F5 Avondale U.S.A.
9 E6 Avonmouth U.K.
67 D7 Avon Park U.S.A.
14 D2 Avranches France
12 A5 Avre r. France
49 G2 Avuavu Solomon Is
41 D7 Awaji-shima i. Japan
51 E3 Awakino N.Z.
30 C5 Awālī Bahrain
51 D1 Awanui N.Z.
51 B6 Awarua Pt pt N.Z.
88 E3 Āwash Eth.
88 D3 Āwash r. Eth.
40 F5 Awa-shima i. Japan
88 D3 Awash National Park Eth.
90 A2 Awasib Mts mts Namibia
51 D4 Awatere r. N.Z.
87 D2 Awbārī Libya
11 C5 Awbeg r. Rep. of Ireland
29 L6 'Awdah, Hawr al l. Iraq
88 E3 Aw Dheegle Somalia
87 E4 Aweil Sudan
10 C4 Awe, Loch l. U.K.
86 C4 Awka Nigeria
43 C6 Awu mt Indon.
50 E4 Axedale Austr.
55 J2 Axel Heiburg I. Can.
86 B4 Axim Ghana
9 E7 Axminster U.K.
12 C5 Ay France
41 D7 Ayabe Japan
83 E3 Ayacucho Arg.
78 D6 Ayacucho Peru
27 G2 Ayaguz Kazak.
36 A3 Ayakkum Hu l. China
15 C4 Ayamonte Spain
36 F1 Ayan Rus. Fed.
21 E7 Ayancık Turkey
42 C4 Ayang N. Korea
81 B2 Ayapel Col.
28 D1 Ayaş Turkey
78 D6 Ayaviri Peru
31 H2 Āybak Afgh.
21 F5 Aydar r. Ukr.
26 E2 Aydarkul', Ozero l. Uzbek.
28 A3 Aydın Turkey
28 A2 Aydın Dağları mts Turkey
44 Ayer Chawan, P. i. Sing.
44 Ayer Merbau, P. i. Sing.
48 D4 Ayers Rock h. Austr.
25 N3 Aykhal Rus. Fed.
20 J2 Aykino Rus. Fed.
51 D5 Aylesbury N.Z.
9 G6 Aylesbury U.K.
70 E6 Aylett U.S.A.
15 E2 Ayllón Spain
69 G4 Aylmer Can.
57 H2 Aylmer Lake l. Can.
30 C4 'Ayn al 'Abd well S. Arabia
31 H2 Ayni Tajik.
28 G3 'Ayn 'Īsá Syria
87 F4 Ayod Sudan
25 S3 Ayon, O. i. Rus. Fed.
86 B3 'Ayoûn el 'Atroûs Maur.
48 E3 Ayr Austr.
10 D5 Ayr U.K.
10 D5 Ayr r. U.K.
28 D3 Ayrancı Turkey
8 C3 Ayre, Point of pt Isle of Man
19 M3 Aytos Bulg.
44 B2 Ayutthaya Thai.
19 M5 Ayvacık Turkey
28 F2 Ayvalı Turkey
19 M5 Ayvalık Turkey
35 E4 Azamgarh India
86 B3 Azaouâd reg. Mali
86 C3 Azaouagh, Vallée de watercourse Mali/Niger
30 B2 Āzarān Iran
Azbine mts see Aïr, Massif de l'
28 D1 Azdavay Turkey
23 D5 Azerbaijan country Asia
30 B2 Azghān Iran
69 G2 Azilda Can.
71 H2 Aziscohos Lake l. U.S.A.
78 C4 Azogues Ecuador
24 F3 Azopol'ye Rus. Fed.
2 Azores terr. Europe
96 H3 Azores - Cape St Vincent Ridge sea feature Atl. Ocean
21 F6 Azov Rus. Fed.
21 F6 Azov, Sea of sea Rus. Fed./Ukr.
86 B1 Azrou Morocco
63 F4 Aztec U.S.A.
15 D3 Azuaga Spain
80 B3 Azucar r. Chile
75 H7 Azuero, Peninsula de pen. Panama
83 E3 Azul Arg.
83 B4 Azul, Cerro mt Arg.
78 C5 Azul, Cordillera mts Peru
82 A1 Azul, Serra h. Brazil
41 G6 Azuma-san volc. Japan
78 F8 Azurduy Bol.
18 B6 Azzaba Alg.
28 F5 Az Zabadānī Syria
29 J6 Az Zafīrī reg. Iraq
Az Zahrān see Dhahran
30 B5 Az Zilfī S. Arabia
29 L6 Az Zubayr Iraq

B

28 E5 Ba'abda Lebanon
28 F4 Ba'albek Lebanon
88 E3 Baardheere Somalia
19 M5 Baba Burnu pt Turkey
19 N2 Babadag Romania
29 M1 Babadağ mt Azer.
31 E2 Babadurmaz Turkm.
21 C7 Babaeski Turkey
78 C4 Babahoyo Ecuador
33 B1 Babai India
35 E3 Babai r. Nepal
38 B1 Babai Gaxun China
29 L2 Bābā Jān Iran
43 C5 Babak Phil.
31 H3 Bābā, Kūh-e mts Afgh.
32 B7 Bāb al Mandab str. Africa/Asia
37 E7 Babar i. Indon.
88 D4 Babati Tanz.
20 E3 Babayevo Rus. Fed.
21 H7 Babayurt Rus. Fed.
68 B2 Babbitt U.S.A.
60 F6 Babia r. Mex.
54 F4 Babine r. Can.
56 D4 Babine Lake l. Can.
37 F7 Babo Indon.
30 D2 Bābol Iran
90 C6 Baboon Point pt S. Africa
73 G6 Baboquivari Peak summit U.S.A.
88 B3 Baboua C.A.R.
20 D4 Babruysk Belarus
34 B4 Babuhri India
34 C2 Babusar Pass Pak.
43 A4 Babuyan Phil.
43 B2 Babuyan i. Phil.
39 F7 Babuyan Channel Phil.
43 B2 Babuyan Islands is Phil.
29 K5 Babylon Iraq
79 K4 Bacabal Brazil
28 C1 Bacakliyayla T. mt Turkey
37 E6 Bacan i. Indon.
43 B2 Bacarra Phil.
17 N7 Bacău Romania
50 E4 Bacchus Marsh Austr.
39 C6 Băc Giang Vietnam
63 F6 Bachiniva Mex.
27 F3 Bachu China
57 J1 Back r. Can.
19 H2 Bačka Palanka Yugo.
56 D2 Backbone Ranges mts Can.
6 P5 Backe Sweden
10 E4 Backwater Reservoir U.K.
39 B6 Bac Lac Vietnam
44 C3 Bac Liêu Vietnam
39 C6 Băc Ninh Vietnam
43 B4 Bacolod Phil.
43 B3 Baco, Mt mt Phil.
39 B6 Băc Quang Vietnam
58 F2 Bacqueville, Lac l. Can.
13 L6 Bad Abbach Ger.
33 A4 Badagara India
38 A1 Badain Jaran Shamo des. China
78 F4 Badajós, Lago l. Brazil
15 C3 Badajoz Spain
33 A3 Badami India
29 H6 Badanah S. Arabia
35 H4 Badarpur India
69 F4 Bad Axe U.S.A.
13 F5 Bad Bergzabern Ger.
13 G3 Bad Berleburg Ger.
13 J1 Bad Bevensen Ger.
13 K4 Bad Blankenburg Ger.
13 G4 Bad Camberg Ger.
59 H4 Baddeck Can.
31 G4 Baddo r. Pak.
13 H3 Bad Driburg Ger.
13 L3 Bad Düben Ger.
13 G5 Bad Dürkheim Ger.
13 L3 Bad Dürrenberg Ger.
28 C3 Bademli Geçidi pass Turkey
13 F4 Bad Ems Ger.
16 H6 Baden Austria
16 D7 Baden Switz.
16 D6 Baden-Baden Ger.
10 D4 Badenoch reg. U.K.
13 G5 Baden-Württemberg div. Ger.
13 G2 Bad Essen Ger.
13 F3 Badger Can.
13 J3 Bad Grund (Harz) Ger.
13 J3 Bad Harzburg Ger.
13 H4 Bad Hersfeld Ger.
16 F7 Bad Hofgastein Austria
13 G4 Bad Homburg vor der Höhe Ger.
18 D2 Badia Polesine Italy
34 B4 Badin Pak.
16 F7 Bad Ischl Austria
Bādiyat ash Shām des. see Syrian Desert
13 J4 Bad Kissingen Ger.
13 K3 Bad Kösen Ger.
13 F5 Bad Kreuznach Ger.
13 G4 Bad Laasphe Ger.
64 C2 Badlands reg. U.S.A.
64 C3 Badlands Nat. Park U.S.A.
13 J3 Bad Langensalza Ger.
13 J3 Bad Lauterberg im Harz Ger.
13 G3 Bad Lippspringe Ger.
13 F4 Bad Marienberg Ger.
13 H5 Bad Mergentheim Ger.
13 G4 Bad Nauheim Ger.
12 F4 Bad Neuenahr-Ahrweiler Ger.
13 J4 Bad Neustadt an der Saale Ger.
13 J1 Bad Oldesloe Ger.
38 D4 Badong China
44 C3 Ba Đông Vietnam
13 H3 Bad Pyrmont Ger.
29 K5 Badrah Iraq
16 F7 Bad Reichenhall Ger.
34 D3 Badrinath Peaks mts India
13 J3 Bad Sachsa Ger.
13 J2 Bad Salzdetfurth Ger.
13 G2 Bad Salzuflen Ger.
13 J4 Bad Salzungen Ger.
13 G4 Bad Schwalbach Ger.
16 E4 Bad Schwartau Ger.
16 E4 Bad Segeberg Ger.
48 E3 Badu I. i. Austr.
33 C5 Badulla Sri Lanka
13 G4 Bad Vilbel Ger.
13 K2 Bad Wilsnack Ger.
13 J5 Bad Windsheim Ger.
13 G1 Bad Zwischenahn Ger.
6 B3 Bæir Iceland
50 H2 Baerami Austr.
12 E4 Baesweiler Ger.
15 E4 Baeza Spain
86 D4 Bafang Cameroon
86 A3 Bafatá Guinea-Bissau
55 M2 Baffin Bay b. Can./Greenland
55 L2 Baffin Island i. Can.
86 D4 Bafia Cameroon
86 A3 Bafing, Parc National du nat. park Mali
86 A3 Bafoulabé Mali
86 D4 Bafoussam Cameroon
30 D4 Bāfq Iran
28 E1 Bafra Turkey
21 E7 Bafra Burnu pt Turkey
30 E4 Bāft Iran
88 C3 Bafwasende Congo(Zaire)
35 F4 Bagaha India
43 A5 Bagahak, Mt h. Malaysia
33 A2 Bagalkot India
88 D4 Bagamoyo Tanz.
45 B2 Bagan Datuk Malaysia
89 C5 Bagani Namibia
44 B4 Bagan Serai Malaysia
44 B5 Bagansiapiapi Indon.
73 F4 Bagdad U.S.A.
83 F1 Bagé Brazil
34 D3 Bageshwar India
62 F3 Baggs U.S.A.
9 C6 Baggy Point pt U.K.
34 C5 Bagh India
31 F2 Baghbaghū Iran
29 K5 Baghdād Iraq
30 C4 Bāgh-e Malek Iran
31 H2 Baghlān Afgh.
31 G3 Baghrān Afgh.
64 E2 Bagley U.S.A.
35 E3 Baglung Nepal
15 G1 Bagnères-de-Luchon France
14 G4 Bagnols-sur-Cèze France
35 F4 Bagnuiti r. Nepal
38 C2 Bag Nur l. China
Bago see Pegu
43 B4 Bago Phil.
17 K3 Bagrationovsk Rus. Fed.
43 C5 Baguio Phil.
43 B2 Baguio Phil.
34 D3 Bahadurgarh India
Bahāmabād see Rafsanjān
53 J7 Bahamas, The country Caribbean Sea
35 G4 Baharampur India
87 E2 Bahariya Oasis oasis Egypt
45 B2 Bahau Malaysia
34 C3 Bahawalnagar Pak.
34 B3 Bahawalpur Pak.
28 F3 Bahçe Turkey
38 C4 Ba He r. China
34 D3 Baheri India
88 D4 Bahi Tanz.
82 E1 Bahia div. Brazil
83 D3 Bahía Blanca Arg.
74 G5 Bahía, Islas de la is Honduras
80 C7 Bahía Laura Arg.
80 E2 Bahía Negra Para.
88 D2 Bahir Dar Eth.
30 C4 Bahmanyārī ye Pā'īn Iran
35 E4 Bahraich India
23 E7 Bahrain country Asia
30 C5 Bahrain, Gulf of g. Asia
29 M3 Bahrāmābād Iran
30 E4 Bahrāmjerd Iran
Bahr el Azraq r. see Blue Nile
31 F5 Bāhū Kālāt Iran
17 L7 Baia Mare Romania
30 D3 Baiazeh Iran
36 E2 Baicheng China
59 G4 Baie Comeau Can.
58 F3 Baie du Poste Can.
59 F4 Baie Saint Paul Can.
59 J3 Baie Verte Can.
38 E2 Baigou r. China
34 E5 Baihar India
38 D3 Baihe Shaanxi China
42 E2 Baihe China
29 J4 Baiji Iraq
36 C1 Baikal, Lake l. Rus. Fed.
19 K2 Băileşti Romania
19 K2 Băileştilor, Câmpia plain Romania
12 A4 Bailleul France
57 H2 Baillie r. Can.
11 E4 Baillieborough Rep. of Ireland
38 B3 Bailong Jiang r. China
36 C3 Baima China
9 G4 Bain r. U.K.
67 C6 Bainbridge GA U.S.A.
71 F3 Bainbridge NY U.S.A.
35 G3 Baingoin China
35 E2 Bairab Co l. China
35 F4 Bairagnia India
54 C3 Baird Mountains U.S.A.
47 J3 Bairiki Kiribati
38 F1 Bairing Qiao China
38 F1 Bairin Youqi China
38 F1 Bairin Zuoqi China
50 F4 Bairnsdale Austr.
28 F6 Bā'ir, Wādī watercourse Jordan
43 B4 Bais Phil.
39 C7 Baisha Hainan China
39 E5 Baisha Jiangxi China
38 C4 Baisha Sichuan China
42 D2 Baishan China
38 B3 Baishui Jiang r. China
39 B7 Bai Thường Vietnam
38 E1 Baitle r. China
42 A2 Baixingt China
38 B2 Baiyin China
87 F3 Baiyuda Desert Sudan
19 H1 Baja Hungary
74 A2 Baja California pen. Mex.
60 C6 Baja California Norte div. Mex.
60 D6 Baja California Sur div. Mex.
29 M3 Bājalān Iran
34 E3 Bajang Nepal
35 G5 Baj Baj India
31 E2 Bājgīrān Iran
81 A3 Bajo Baudó Col.
83 D1 Bajo Hondo Arg.
86 A3 Bakel Senegal
72 D4 Baker CA U.S.A.
62 F2 Baker MT U.S.A.
73 E2 Baker NV U.S.A.
62 C2 Baker OR U.S.A.
73 G4 Baker Butte summit U.S.A.
56 C3 Baker I. i. U.S.A.
49 J1 Baker Island i. Pac. Oc.
57 K2 Baker Lake Can.
57 K2 Baker Lake l. Can.
62 B1 Baker, Mt volc. U.S.A.
58 E2 Bakers Dozen Islands is Can.
72 C4 Bakersfield U.S.A.
44 C2 Bâ Kêv Cambodia
30 E2 Bakharden Turkm.
31 E2 Bakhardok Turkm.
31 F3 Bākharz mts Iran
34 B4 Bakhasar India
21 E6 Bakhchysaray Ukr.
21 E5 Bakhmach Ukr.
30 D4 Bakhtegan, Daryācheh-ye l. Iran
Bakı see Baku
28 B1 Bakırköy Turkey
88 D3 Bako Eth.
88 C3 Bakouma C.A.R.
88 B4 Bakoumba Gabon
21 G7 Baksan Rus. Fed.
29 M1 Baku Azer.
88 D3 Baku Congo(Zaire)
92 A4 Bakutis Coast coastal area Ant.
28 D2 Balâ Turkey
9 D5 Bala U.K.
43 A4 Balabac Phil.
43 A5 Balabac i. Phil.
45 E1 Balabac Strait str. Malaysia/Phil.
78 E6 Bala, Cerros de mts Bol.
29 K4 Balad Iraq
30 C2 Baladeh Iran
30 C4 Bālādeh Iran
34 E5 Balaghat India
33 A2 Balaghat Range h. India
31 E4 Bālā Ḩowz Iran
29 L1 Balakän Azer.
20 G3 Balakhna Rus. Fed.
50 B3 Balaklava Austr.
21 E6 Balaklava Ukr.
21 F5 Balakliya Ukr.
21 H4 Balakovo Rus. Fed.
45 E1 Balambangan i. Malaysia
31 F3 Bālā Morghāb Afgh.
34 B4 Bālān India
21 H5 Balanda r. Rus. Fed.
28 B3 Balan Dağı mt Turkey
43 B3 Balanga Phil.
35 E5 Bālāngīr India
33 C5 Balangoda Sri Lanka
21 G5 Balashov Rus. Fed.
34 C5 Balasinor India
16 H7 Balaton l. Hungary
16 H7 Balatonboglár Hungary
16 H7 Balatonfüred Hungary
79 G4 Balbina, Represa de resr Brazil
11 E4 Balbriggan Rep. of Ireland
83 E3 Balcarce Arg.
19 N3 Balchik Bulg.
51 B7 Balclutha N.Z.
65 F5 Bald Knob U.S.A.
73 E3 Bald Mtn mt U.S.A.
57 K3 Baldock Lake l. Can.
69 H3 Baldwin Can.
67 D6 Baldwin FL U.S.A.
68 E4 Baldwin MI U.S.A.
68 A3 Baldwin WV U.S.A.
71 E3 Baldwinsville U.S.A.
73 H5 Baldy Peak mt U.S.A.
Baleares, Islas is see Balearic Islands
15 H3 Balearic Islands is Spain
45 D2 Baleh r. Malaysia
82 E2 Baleia, Ponta da pt Brazil
59 G2 Baleine, Rivière à la r. Can.
88 D3 Bale Mts National Park Eth.
43 B3 Baler Phil.
43 B3 Baler Bay b. Phil.
35 F5 Bāleshwar India
7 K6 Balestrand Norway
51 B6 Balfour N.Z.
45 E4 Bali i. Indon.
45 A2 Balige Indon.
35 E5 Baliguda India
38 F1 Balihan China
28 A2 Balıkesir Turkey
45 E3 Balikpapan Indon.
43 A5 Balimbing Phil.
33 C2 Balimila Reservoir India
48 E2 Balimo P.N.G.
16 D6 Balingen Ger.
43 B2 Balintang Channel Phil.
10 E3 Balintore U.K.
45 E4 Bali Sea g. Indon.
43 B5 Baliungan i. Phil.
31 H2 Baljuvon Tajik.
12 D2 Balk Neth.

4 F4 Balkan Mountains mts Bulg./Yugo.
31 G2 Balkhab r. Afgh.
27 F2 Balkhash Kazak.
27 F2 Balkhash, Ozero l. Kazak.
21 H6 Balkuduk Kazak.
10 C4 Ballachulish U.K.
48 C5 Balladonia Austr.
50 G1 Balladoran Austr.
11 C4 Ballaghaderreen Rep. of Ireland
50 E4 Ballan Austr.
6 P2 Ballangen Norway
62 E2 Ballantine U.S.A.
10 D5 Ballantrae U.K.
50 D4 Ballarat Austr.
48 C4 Ballard, L. salt flat Austr.
34 D6 Ballarpur India
10 E3 Ballater U.K.
86 B3 Ballé Mali
80 B3 Ballena, Pta pt Chile
92 A6 Balleny Is is Ant.
35 F4 Ballia India
49 F4 Ballina Austr.
11 B3 Ballina Rep. of Ireland
11 C3 Ballinafad Rep. of Ireland
11 D4 Ballinalack Rep. of Ireland
11 D3 Ballinamore Rep. of Ireland
11 C4 Ballinasloe Rep. of Ireland
11 C4 Ballindine Rep. of Ireland
65 D6 Ballinger U.S.A.
10 E4 Ballinluig U.K.
11 B4 Ballinrobe Rep. of Ireland
71 G3 Ballston Spa U.S.A.
11 E3 Ballybay Rep. of Ireland
11 A6 Ballybrack Rep. of Ireland
11 B5 Ballybunnion Rep. of Ireland
11 E5 Ballycanew Rep. of Ireland
11 B3 Ballycastle Rep. of Ireland
11 E2 Ballycastle U.K.
11 F3 Ballyclare U.K.
11 A4 Ballyconneely Bay b. Rep. of Ireland
11 D3 Ballyconnell Rep. of Ireland
11 C4 Ballygar Rep. of Ireland
11 D3 Ballygawley U.K.
11 D2 Ballygorman Rep. of Ireland
11 C4 Ballyhaunis Rep. of Ireland
11 B5 Ballyheigue Rep. of Ireland
11 C5 Ballyhoura Mts h. Rep. of Ireland
11 D2 Ballykelly U.K.
11 D5 Ballylynan Rep. of Ireland
11 D5 Ballymacmague Rep. of Ireland
11 D4 Ballymahon Rep. of Ireland
11 E3 Ballymena U.K.
11 E2 Ballymoney U.K.
11 C3 Ballymote Rep. of Ireland
11 F3 Ballynahinch U.K.
11 C3 Ballyshannon Rep. of Ireland
11 E5 Ballyteige Bay b. Rep. of Ireland
11 B4 Ballyvaughan Rep. of Ireland
11 E3 Ballyward U.K.
10 A3 Balmartin U.K.
Balmer see Barmer
50 C4 Balmoral Austr.
65 C6 Balmorhea U.S.A.
31 G4 Balochistān div. Pak.
26 E4 Balochistān reg. Pak.
34 E5 Balod India
35 E5 Baloda Bazar India
48 E4 Balonne r. Austr.
34 C4 Balotra India
35 E4 Balrampur India
50 D3 Balranald Austr.
19 L2 Balş Romania
69 H2 Balsam Creek Can.
79 J5 Balsas Brazil
21 D6 Balta Ukr.
20 J3 Baltasi Rus. Fed.
10 □ Baltasound U.K.
34 D2 Baltero Gl. gl. Pak.
21 C6 Bălţi Moldova
7 P9 Baltic Sea g. Europe
28 C6 Baltîm Egypt
91 H1 Baltimore S. Africa
70 E5 Baltimore U.S.A.
11 E5 Baltinglass Rep. of Ireland
34 C2 Baltistan reg. Jammu and Kashmir
17 J3 Baltiysk Rus. Fed.
31 E4 Baluch Ab well Iran
35 G4 Balurghat India
43 C5 Balut i. Phil.
13 F3 Balve Ger.
7 U8 Balvi Latvia
19 M5 Balya Turkey
26 D2 Balykshi Kazak.
31 E4 Bam Iran
31 E2 Bām Iran
39 C5 Bama China
48 E3 Bamaga Austr.
58 B3 Bamaji L. l. Can.
86 B3 Bamako Mali
86 B3 Bamba Mali
43 B2 Bambang Phil.
88 C3 Bambari C.A.R.
44 A5 Bambel Indon.
13 J5 Bamberg Ger.
67 D5 Bamberg U.S.A.
88 C3 Bambili Congo(Zaire)
91 G5 Bamboesberg mts S. Africa
88 C3 Bambouti C.A.R.
82 D3 Bambuí Brazil
29 M6 Bāmdezh Iran
86 D4 Bamenda Cameroon
30 E2 Bami Turkm.
31 G3 Bāmīān Afgh.
42 C2 Bamiancheng China
88 C3 Bamingui-Bangoran, Parc National de nat. park C.A.R.
31 F5 Bam Posht reg. Iran
31 F5 Bam Posht, Kūh-e mts Iran
9 D7 Bampton U.K.
31 F5 Bampūr Iran
31 E5 Bampūr watercourse Iran
31 F3 Bamrūd Iran
49 G2 Banaba i. Kiribati
79 L5 Banabuiu, Açude resr Brazil
83 C3 Bañados del Atuel marsh Arg.
78 F7 Bañados del Izozog swamp Bol.
11 D4 Banagher Rep. of Ireland
88 C3 Banalia Congo(Zaire)
91 K1 Banamana, Lagoa l. Moz.
86 B3 Banamba Mali
79 H6 Bananal, Ilha do i. Brazil
35 F6 Bānapur India
44 B2 Ban Aranyaprathet Thai.
34 D4 Banas r. India
28 B2 Banaz Turkey
44 B1 Ban Ban Laos
35 H3 Banbar China
44 B4 Ban Betong Thai.
11 E3 Banbridge U.K.
44 B2 Ban Bua Yai Thai.
9 F5 Banbury U.K.
43 A4 Bancalan i. Phil.
86 A2 Banc d'Arguin, Parc National du nat. park Maur.
44 A1 Ban Chiang Dao Thai.
10 F3 Banchory U.K.
74 G5 Banco Chinchorro is Mex.
43 A5 Bancoran i. Phil.
69 J3 Bancroft Can.
31 E3 Band Iran
88 C3 Banda Congo(Zaire)
34 E4 Banda India
45 A1 Banda Aceh Indon.
34 B2 Banda Daud Shah Pak.
44 A5 Bandahara, G. mt Indon.
41 F6 Bandai-Asahi National Park Japan
37 E7 Banda, Kepulauan is Indon.
31 F4 Bandān Iran
31 F4 Bandān Kūh mts Iran
Bandar see Machilipatnam
35 H5 Bandarban Bangl.
30 E5 Bandar-e 'Abbās Iran
30 C2 Bandar-e Anzalī Iran
30 C4 Bandar-e Deylam Iran
30 D5 Bandar-e Khoemir Iran
30 D5 Bandar-e Lengeh Iran
30 D5 Bandar-e Māqām Iran
30 C4 Bandar-e Ma'shur Iran
30 C4 Bandar-e Rīg Iran
Bandar-e Shāhpūr see Bandar Khomeynī
30 D2 Bandar-e Torkeman Iran
30 C4 Bandar Khomeynī Iran
34 D3 Bandarpunch mt India
45 D1 Bandar Seri Begawan Brunei
37 F7 Banda Sea Indon.
31 E5 Band Bonī Iran
30 D5 Band-e Chārak Iran
82 B1 Bandeirante Brazil
82 E3 Bandeiras, Pico de mt Brazil
91 H1 Bandelierkop S. Africa
30 D5 Band-e Moghūyeh Iran
74 C4 Banderas, Bahía de b. Mex.
30 D3 Band-e Sar Qom Iran
34 C4 Bandi r. Rajasthan India
34 C4 Bandi r. Rajasthan India
34 E6 Bandia r. India
86 B3 Bandiagara Mali
31 G3 Band-i-Amir r. Afgh.
31 F3 Band-i-Baba mts Afgh.
28 A1 Bandırma Turkey
31 F3 Band-i-Turkestan mts Afgh.
11 C6 Bandon Rep. of Ireland
Ban Don see Surat Thani
11 C6 Bandon r. Rep. of Ireland
29 M2 Bändovan Burnu pt Azer.
29 M6 Band Qīr Iran
88 B4 Bandundu Congo(Zaire)
45 C4 Bandung Indon.
30 B3 Bāneh Iran
75 J4 Banes Cuba
56 F4 Banff Can.
10 F3 Banff U.K.
56 F4 Banff National Park Can.
86 B3 Banfora Burkina
88 C4 Banga Congo(Zaire)
43 C5 Banga Phil.
43 C5 Bangai Point pt Phil.
33 B3 Bangalore India
34 D4 Banganga r. India
35 G5 Bangaon India
43 B2 Bangar Phil.
88 C3 Bangassou C.A.R.
35 E2 Bangdag Co salt l. China
44 C1 Bangfai, Xée r. Laos
37 E7 Banggai Indon.
37 E7 Banggai, Kepulauan is Indon.
45 E1 Banggi i. Malaysia
87 E1 Banghāzī Libya
44 C1 Banghiang, Xé r. Laos
45 C3 Bangka i. Indon.
45 D4 Bangkalan Indon.
44 A5 Bangkaru i. Indon.
45 B3 Bangko Indon.
35 G3 Bangkog Co salt l. China
44 B2 Bangkok Thai.
44 B2 Bangkok, Bight of b. Thai.
23 H7 Bangladesh country Asia
86 B4 Bangolo Côte d'Ivoire
34 D2 Bangong Co l. China
11 F3 Bangor N. Ireland U.K.
9 C4 Bangor Wales U.K.
71 J2 Bangor ME U.S.A.
70 B4 Bangor MI U.S.A.
71 F4 Bangor PA U.S.A.
11 B3 Bangor Erris Rep. of Ireland
44 A3 Bang Saphan Yai Thai.
73 F3 Bangs, Mt mt U.S.A.
6 M4 Bangsund Norway
43 B2 Bangued Phil.
88 B3 Bangui C.A.R.
43 B2 Bangui Phil.
44 A5 Bangunpurba Indon.
89 C5 Bangweulu, Lake l. Zambia
44 B4 Ban Hat Yai Thai.
89 D6 Banhine, Parque Nacional de nat. park Moz.
44 B1 Ban Hin Heup Laos
44 A3 Ban Hua Hin Thai.
88 C3 Bani C.A.R.
43 A2 Bani Phil.
88 B3 Bania C.A.R.
30 D5 Banī Forūr, Jazīrah-ye i. Iran
34 C2 Banihal Pass and Tunnel Jammu and Kashmir
70 D6 Banister r. U.S.A.
87 D1 Banī Walīd Libya
30 C5 Banī Wuṭayfān well S. Arabia
28 E4 Bāniyās Syria
28 E5 Bāniyās Syria
18 G2 Banja Luka Bos.-Herz.
34 D3 Banjar India
45 D3 Banjarmasin Indon.
86 A3 Banjul The Gambia
29 M2 Bankä Azer.
35 F4 Banka India
44 A4 Ban Kantang Thai.
33 A3 Bankapur India
86 B3 Bankass Mali
44 A2 Ban Khao Yoi Thai.
44 C1 Ban Khemmarat Thai.
44 A3 Ban Khok Kloi Thai.
44 A1 Ban Khun Yuam Thai.
35 F5 Banki India
54 F2 Banks Island N.W.T. Can.
54 E4 Banks Island i. B.C. Can.
49 G3 Banks Islands is Vanuatu
62 C2 Banks L. l. U.S.A.
57 L2 Banks Lake l. Can.
51 D5 Banks Peninsula N.Z.
44 A2 Ban Kui Nua Thai.
35 F5 Bankura India
44 A1 Ban Mae Sariang Thai.
44 A1 Ban Mae Sot Thai.
44 B1 Ban Mouang Laos
44 B2 Ban Muang Phon Thai.
11 E5 Bann r. Rep. of Ireland
11 E3 Bann r. U.K.
44 C1 Ban Na Kae Thai.
44 C1 Ban Nakham Laos
44 B1 Ban Na Noi Thai.
44 A3 Ban Na San Thai.
44 B4 Ban Na Thawi Thai.
68 C5 Banner U.S.A.
67 E7 Bannerman Town Bahamas
72 D5 Banning U.S.A.
83 B3 Baños Maule Chile
44 B1 Ban Pak-Leng Laos
44 B3 Ban Pak Phanang Thai.
44 B2 Ban Pak Thong Chai Thai.
44 C1 Ban Phaeng Thai.
44 B1 Ban Phai Thai.
44 B2 Ban Phanat Nikhom Thai.
44 C2 Ban Phon Laos
44 B1 Ban Phon Thong Thai.
44 A2 Banphot Phisai Thai.
44 A2 Ban Pong Thai.
44 B1 Ban Pua Thai.
44 A1 Ban Saraphi Thai.
44 B2 Ban Sattahip Thai.
44 A3 Ban Sawi Thai.
35 E4 Bansi India
44 A3 Ban Sichon Thai.
44 B2 Ban Si Racha Thai.
17 J6 Banská Bystrica Slovakia
44 A1 Ban Sut Ta Thai.
33 B2 Banswada India
34 C5 Banswara India
44 A3 Ban Takua Pa Thai.
43 B4 Bantayan i. Phil.
11 C5 Banteer Rep. of Ireland
44 A3 Ban Tha Chang Thai.
44 A1 Ban Tha Don Thai.
44 A3 Ban Thai Muang Thai.
44 A3 Ban Tha Kham Thai.
44 A1 Ban Tha Song Yang Thai.
44 B2 Ban Tha Tako Thai.
44 B2 Ban Tha Tum Thai.
44 C1 Ban Tha Uthen Thai.
44 A2 Ban Thung Luang Thai.
43 B3 Banton i. Phil.
44 C1 Ban Tôp Laos
11 B6 Bantry Rep. of Ireland
11 B6 Bantry Bay b. Rep. of Ireland
33 A3 Bantval India
44 B1 Ban Woen Laos
45 A2 Banyak, Pulau Pulau is Indon.
86 D4 Banyo Cameroon
15 H1 Banyoles Spain
45 D4 Banyuwangi Indon.
92 C6 Banzare Coast coastal area Ant.
93 J7 Banzare Seamount sea feature Ind. Ocean
13 K1 Banzkow Ger.
38 B3 Bao'an China
38 E2 Baoding China
38 D3 Baofeng China
38 C3 Baoji China
39 C4 Baojing China
38 D4 Baokang China
42 E1 Baolin China
42 B2 Baolizhen China
44 C3 Bao Lôc Vietnam
40 C1 Baoqing China
36 B4 Baoshan China
38 D1 Baotou China
39 B4 Baoxing China
38 F3 Baoying China
34 C4 Bap India
33 C3 Bapatla India
12 A4 Bapaume France
69 H3 Baptiste Lake l. Can.
35 H2 Baqên China
35 H3 Baqên China
29 K5 Ba'qūbah Iraq
78 □ Baquerizo Moreno Galapagos Is Ecuador
19 H3 Bar Yugo.
87 F3 Bara Sudan
88 E3 Baraawe Somalia
35 F4 Barabar Hills h. India
68 C4 Baraboo U.S.A.
68 B4 Baraboo r. U.S.A.
75 K4 Baracoa Cuba
83 E2 Baradero Arg.
50 G1 Baradine Austr.
50 G1 Baradine r. Austr.
68 C2 Baraga U.S.A.
35 E5 Baragarh India
75 K5 Barahona Dom. Rep.
35 H4 Barail Range mts India
35 H4 Barak r. India
88 D2 Baraka watercourse Eritrea/Sudan
15 E1 Barakaldo Spain
31 H3 Barakī Barak Afgh.
35 F5 Bārākot India
34 D2 Bara Lacha Pass India
29 J5 Baṛ al Milḥ l. Iraq
57 K3 Baralzon Lake l. Can.
33 A2 Baramati India
34 D4 Baran India
34 B4 Baran r. Pak.
20 C4 Baranavichy Belarus
25 S3 Baranikha Rus. Fed.
21 C5 Baranivka Ukr.
31 F3 Bārān, Kūh-e mts Iran
81 B2 Baranoa Col.
56 B3 Baranof Island i. U.S.A.
82 A2 Barão de Melgaço Brazil
86 B3 Baraouéli Mali
12 D4 Baraque de Fraiture h. Belgium
37 E7 Barat Daya, Kepulauan is Indon.
50 B2 Baratta Austr.
34 D3 Baraut India
81 B4 Baraya Col.
82 D3 Barbacena Brazil
81 A4 Barbacoas Col.
53 K8 Barbados country Caribbean Sea
15 G1 Barbastro Spain
15 D4 Barbate de Franco Spain
72 □1 Barbers Pt pt U.S.A.
91 J2 Barberton S. Africa
70 C4 Barberton U.S.A.
14 D4 Barbezieux-St-Hilaire France
81 B3 Barbosa Col.
57 L2 Barbour Bay b. Can.
70 B6 Barbourville U.S.A.
43 B4 Barboza Phil.
75 M5 Barbuda i. Antigua
13 K3 Barby (Elbe) Ger.
48 E4 Barcaldine Austr.
15 H2 Barcelona Spain
81 D2 Barcelona Venez.
78 F4 Barcelos Brazil
13 J4 Barchfeld Ger.
86 B4 Barclayville Liberia
18 G2 Barcs Hungary
29 L1 Bärdä Azer.
6 E4 Bárðarbunga mt Iceland
83 C2 Bardas Blancas Arg.
35 F5 Barddhamān India
17 K6 Bardejov Slovakia
30 C5 Bardestān Iran
44 C2 Bar Đôn Vietnam
9 C5 Bardsey Island i. U.K.
66 C4 Bardstown U.S.A.
70 B5 Bardwell U.S.A.
34 D3 Bareilly India
24 C2 Barentsburg Svalbard
24 D2 Barentsøya i. Svalbard
24 F2 Barents Sea sea Arctic Ocean
88 D2 Barentu Eritrea
34 E3 Barga China
34 D5 Bargi India
10 D5 Bargrennan U.K.
13 J1 Bargteheide Ger.
35 G5 Barguna Bangl.
71 J2 Bar Harbor U.S.A.
18 G4 Bari Italy
44 C3 Ba Ria Vietnam
34 C3 Bari Doab lowland Pak.
35 E3 Barikot Nepal
81 E2 Barima r. Venez.
81 C2 Barinas Venez.
35 G5 Barisal Bangl.
45 B3 Barisan, Pegunungan mts Indon.
45 D3 Barito r. Indon.
78 F8 Baritu, Parque Nacional nat. park Arg.
31 E6 Barkā Oman
38 B4 Barkam China
30 C4 Barkan, Ra's-e pt Iran
7 U8 Barkava Latvia
56 E4 Barkerville Can.
66 C4 Barkley, L. l. U.S.A.
56 D5 Barkley Sd in. Can.
91 G5 Barkly East S. Africa
48 D3 Barkly Tableland reg. Austr.
90 F4 Barkly West S. Africa
36 B2 Barkol China
34 D3 Barkot India
30 E4 Barkūh Iran
17 N7 Bârlad Romania
14 G2 Bar-le-Duc France
48 B4 Barlee, L. salt flat Austr.
18 G4 Barletta Italy
50 F3 Barmedman Austr.
34 B4 Barmer India
50 C3 Barmera Austr.
9 C5 Barmouth U.K.
34 C3 Barnala India
8 F3 Barnard Castle U.K.
50 E1 Barnato Austr.
24 K4 Barnaul Rus. Fed.
71 F5 Barnegat U.S.A.
71 F5 Barnegat Bay b. U.S.A.
70 D4 Barnesboro U.S.A.
55 L2 Barnes Icecap ice cap Can.
12 D2 Barneveld Neth.
50 E2 Barneys Lake l. Austr.
73 G3 Barney Top mt U.S.A.
65 C6 Barnhart U.S.A.
8 F4 Barnsley U.K.
9 C6 Barnstaple U.K.
Barnstaple Bay b. see Bideford Bay
13 G2 Barnstorf Ger.
67 D5 Barnwell U.S.A.
Baroda see Vadodara
34 C1 Baroghil Pass Afgh.
35 H4 Barpathar India
35 G4 Barpeta India
68 D3 Barques, Pt Aux pt MI U.S.A.
69 F3 Barques, Pt Aux pt MI U.S.A.
81 C2 Barquisimeto Venez.
79 K6 Barra Brazil
10 A4 Barra i. U.K.
90 D7 Barracouta, Cape hd S. Africa
79 G6 Barra do Bugres Brazil
79 J5 Barra do Corda Brazil
82 B1 Barra do Garças Brazil
79 G5 Barra do São Manuel Brazil
78 C6 Barranca Lima Peru
78 C4 Barranca Loreto Peru
81 B3 Barrancabermeja Col.
81 B2 Barrancas Col.
81 E2 Barrancas Venez.
83 B3 Barrancas r. Mendoza/Neuquén Arg.
80 E3 Barranqueras Arg.
81 B2 Barranquilla Col.
10 A3 Barra, Sound of chan. U.K.
71 G2 Barre U.S.A.
83 C1 Barreal Arg.
79 K6 Barreiras Brazil
79 G4 Barreirinha Brazil
79 K4 Barreirinhas Brazil
15 B3 Barreiro Port.
82 B1 Barreiro r. Brazil
79 L5 Barreiros Brazil
82 C3 Barretos Brazil
56 G4 Barrhead Can.
10 D5 Barrhead U.K.
69 H3 Barrie Can.
69 F3 Barrie I i. Can.
56 E4 Barrière Can.
50 C1 Barrier Range h. Austr.
57 J3 Barrington Lake l. Can.
50 H2 Barrington, Mt Austr.
68 B3 Barron U.S.A.
65 C7 Barroterán Mex.
83 E3 Barrow Arg.
54 C2 Barrow AK U.S.A.
11 E5 Barrow r. Rep. of Ireland
48 D4 Barrow Creek Austr.
48 B4 Barrow I. i. Austr.
8 D3 Barrow-in-Furness U.K.
54 C2 Barrow, Point c. U.S.A.
55 J2 Barrow Strait str. Can.
9 D6 Barry U.K.
90 D6 Barrydale S. Africa
69 J3 Barrys Bay Can.
34 C3 Barsalpur India
33 A2 Barsi India
34 D5 Barsi Takli India
13 H2 Barsinghausen Ger.
72 D4 Barstow U.S.A.
14 G2 Bar-sur-Aube France
16 F3 Barth Ger.
79 G2 Bartica Guyana
28 D1 Bartın Turkey
48 E3 Bartle Frere, Mt mt Austr.
73 G2 Bartles, Mt mt U.S.A.
61 G4 Bartlesville OK U.S.A.
64 D3 Bartlett NE U.S.A.
71 H2 Bartlett NH U.S.A.
56 F2 Bartlett Lake l. Can.
71 G2 Barton U.S.A.
8 G4 Barton-upon-Humber U.K.
17 K3 Bartoszyce Pol.
45 B2 Barumun r. Indon.
45 D4 Barung i. Indon.
44 A5 Barus Indon.
38 B1 Baruunsuu Mongolia
36 D2 Baruun Urt Mongolia
75 H7 Barú, Volcán volc. Panama
34 D5 Barwah India
34 C3 Barwala India
34 C5 Barwani India
48 E5 Barwon r. Austr.
20 D4 Barysaw Belarus
20 H4 Barysh Rus. Fed.
20 H4 Barysh r. Rus. Fed.
30 C3 Barzūk Iran
30 D5 Basaidu Iran
72 C2 Basalt U.S.A.
39 □ Basalt I. i. H.K. China
88 B3 Basankusu Congo(Zaire)
33 B2 Basar India
19 N2 Basarabi Romania
83 E2 Basavilbaso Arg.
43 B4 Basay Phil.
43 B1 Basco Phil.
16 C7 Basel Switz.
68 B1 Basewood Lake l. U.S.A.
31 E5 Bashākerd, Kūhhā-ye mts Iran
56 G4 Bashaw Can.
91 H6 Bashee r. S. Africa
31 H3 Bashgul r. Afgh.
20 G4 Bashmakovo Rus. Fed.
30 C4 Bāsht Iran
21 E6 Bashtanka Ukr.
34 D4 Basi India
35 F5 Basia India
43 B5 Basilan i. Phil.
43 B5 Basilan Strait chan. Phil.
9 H6 Basildon U.K.
62 E2 Basin U.S.A.
9 F6 Basingstoke U.K.
29 K4 Bāsīra r. Iraq
35 G5 Basirhat India
71 K2 Baskahegan Lake l. U.S.A.
29 K2 Başkale Turkey
69 K2 Baskatong, Réservoir resr Can.
21 H5 Baskunchak, Ozero l. Rus. Fed.
Basle see Basel
34 D5 Basoda India
88 C3 Basoko Congo(Zaire)
29 L6 Basra Iraq
18 D2 Bassano del Grappa Italy
86 C4 Bassar Togo
89 D6 Bassas da India i. Ind. Ocean
37 B5 Bassein Myanmar
8 D3 Bassenthwaite Lake l. U.K.
86 A3 Basse Santa Su The Gambia
75 M5 Basse Terre Guadeloupe
75 M5 Basseterre St Kitts-Nevis
64 D3 Bassett U.S.A.
73 G5 Bassett Peak summit U.S.A.
71 J2 Bass Harbor U.S.A.
86 B3 Bassikounou Maur.
86 C4 Bassila Benin
10 F4 Bass Rock i. U.K.
48 E5 Bass Strait str. Austr.
13 G2 Bassum Ger.
7 N8 Båstad Sweden
30 D5 Bastak Iran
30 B2 Bastānābād Iran
13 J4 Bastheim Ger.
35 E4 Basti India
18 C3 Bastia Corsica France
12 D4 Bastogne Belgium
65 F5 Bastrop LA U.S.A.
65 D6 Bastrop TX U.S.A.
31 G5 Basul r. Pak.
86 C4 Bata Equatorial Guinea
75 H4 Batabanó, Golfo de b. Cuba
43 B2 Batac Phil.
43 C3 Batag i. Phil.
25 P3 Batagay Rus. Fed.
34 B2 Batai Pass Pak.
34 C3 Batala India
15 B3 Batalha Port.
44 C5 Batam i. Indon.
25 O3 Batamay Rus. Fed.
43 B1 Batan i. Phil.
88 B3 Batangafo C.A.R.
43 B3 Batangas Phil.
45 B3 Batanghari r. Indon.
44 A5 Batangtoru Indon.
43 B1 Batan Islands is Phil.
82 C3 Batatais Brazil
68 C5 Batavia IL U.S.A.
70 D3 Batavia NY U.S.A.
21 F6 Bataysk Rus. Fed.
69 E2 Batchawana r. Can.
69 E2 Batchawana Bay Can.
58 D4 Batchawana Mtn h. Can.
48 D3 Batchelor Austr.
69 E2 Batchewana Can.
44 B2 Bătdâmbâng Cambodia
50 H3 Batemans B. b. Austr.
50 H3 Batemans Bay Austr.
65 F5 Batesville AR U.S.A.
65 F5 Batesville MS U.S.A.
20 D3 Batetskiy Rus. Fed.
59 G4 Bath N.B. Can.
69 J3 Bath Ont. Can.
9 E6 Bath U.K.
71 J3 Bath ME U.S.A.
70 E3 Bath NY U.S.A.
10 E5 Bathgate U.K.
34 C3 Bathinda India
50 G2 Bathurst Austr.
59 G4 Bathurst Can.
91 G6 Bathurst S. Africa
55 J2 Bathurst I. i. Can.
54 H3 Bathurst Inlet N.W.T. Can.
54 H3 Bathurst Inlet in. N.W.T. Can.
48 D3 Bathurst Island i. Austr.
50 G3 Bathurst, L. l. Austr.
30 D3 Bāṭlāq-e Gavkhūnī marsh Iran
8 F4 Batley U.K.
50 G3 Batlow Austr.
29 H3 Batman Turkey
86 C1 Batna Alg.
30 C6 Baṭn aṭ Ṭarfā' depression S. Arabia
65 F6 Baton Rouge U.S.A.
87 D4 Batouri Cameroon
82 B1 Batovi Brazil
28 E4 Batroûn Lebanon
6 V1 Båtsfjord Norway
33 C5 Batticaloa Sri Lanka
18 F4 Battipaglia Italy
57 G4 Battle r. Can.
68 E4 Battle Creek U.S.A.
57 H4 Battleford Can.
62 C3 Battle Mountain U.S.A.
34 C1 Battura Glacier gl. Jammu and Kashmir
44 B4 Batu Gajah Malaysia
43 C5 Batulaki Phil.
29 H1 Bat'umi Georgia
45 B2 Batu Pahat Malaysia
45 A3 Batu, Pulau Pulau is Indon.
44 B4 Batu Puteh, Gunung mt Malaysia
37 E7 Baubau Indon.
86 C3 Bauchi Nigeria
64 E1 Baudette U.S.A.
81 A3 Baudo, Serranía de mts Col.
14 D3 Baugé France
13 H5 Bauland reg. Ger.
59 K3 Bauld, C. hd Can.
14 H3 Baume-les-Dames France
34 C2 Baundal India
82 C3 Bauru Brazil
82 B2 Baús Brazil
12 E4 Bausendorf Ger.
7 T8 Bauska Latvia
16 G5 Bautzen Ger.
90 E6 Baviaanskloofberg mts S. Africa
60 E6 Bavispe r. Mex.
9 J5 Bawdeswell U.K.
45 D4 Bawean i. Indon.
12 F2 Bawinkel Ger.
87 E2 Bawiti Egypt
86 B3 Bawku Ghana
44 A1 Bawlake Myanmar
39 A4 Bawolung China
38 B3 Baxi China
38 E2 Ba Xian Hebei China
39 C4 Ba Xian Sichuan China
67 D6 Baxley U.S.A.
75 J4 Bayamo Cuba
34 D4 Bayana India
36 B3 Bayan Har Shan mts China

36 C2 Bayanhongor Mongolia
38 B1 Bayan Mod China
38 C1 Bayan Obo China
42 A1 Bayan Qagan China
30 D4 Bayāz Iran
43 C4 Baybay Phil.
29 H1 Bayburt Turkey
69 F4 Bay City *MI* U.S.A.
65 D6 Bay City *TX* U.S.A.
24 H3 Baydaratskaya Guba *b.* Rus. Fed.
88 E3 Baydhabo Somalia
13 L5 Bayerischer Wald *mts* Ger.
13 J5 Bayern *div.* Ger.
68 B2 Bayfield U.S.A.
19 M5 Bayındır Turkey
28 F6 Bāyir Jordan
Baykal, Ozero *l. see* Baikal, Lake
Baykal Range *mts see* Baykal'sky Khrebet
36 C1 Baykal'sky Khrebet *mts* Rus. Fed.
29 H2 Baykan Turkey
43 B3 Bay, Laguna de *lag.* Phil.
24 G4 Baymak Rus. Fed.
30 D6 Baynūna'h *reg.* U.A.E.
43 B2 Bayombong Phil.
14 D5 Bayonne France
43 B4 Bayo Point *pt* Phil.
31 F2 Bayramaly Turkm.
19 M5 Bayramiç Turkey
13 K5 Bayreuth Ger.
65 F6 Bay St Louis U.S.A.
71 G4 Bay Shore U.S.A.
9 E5 Bayston Hill U.K.
31 G2 Baysun Uzbek.
31 G2 Baysuntau, Gory *mts* Uzbek.
65 E6 Baytown U.S.A.
51 F3 Bay View N.Z.
15 E4 Baza Spain
29 L1 Bazardyuzi, Gora *mt* Azer./Rus. Fed.
30 C2 Bāzār-e Māsāl Iran
29 K2 Bāzargān Iran
21 H4 Bazarnyy Karabulak Rus. Fed.
89 D6 Bazaruto, Ilha do *i.* Moz.
31 G5 Bazdar Pak.
38 C4 Bazhong China
31 F5 Bazman Iran
31 F4 Bazmān, Kūh-e *mt* Iran
44 C3 Be *r.* Vietnam
64 C2 Beach U.S.A.
69 J3 Beachburg Can.
71 F5 Beach Haven U.S.A.
50 C4 Beachport Austr.
71 F5 Beachwood U.S.A.
9 H7 Beachy Head *hd* U.K.
71 G4 Beacon U.S.A.
91 G6 Beacon Bay S. Africa
39 □ Beacon Hill *h.* *H.K.* China
9 G6 Beaconsfield U.K.
80 C8 Beagle, Canal *chan.* Arg.
48 C3 Beagle Gulf *b.* Austr.
89 E5 Bealanana Madag.
9 E7 Beaminster U.K.
62 E3 Bear *r.* U.S.A.
57 N2 Bear Cove *b.* Can.
58 C4 Beardmore Can.
92 B4 Beardmore Gl. *gl.* Ant.
68 B5 Beardstown U.S.A.
58 D3 Bear Island *i.* Can.
24 C2 Bear Island *i.* Svalbard
62 E3 Bear L. *l.* U.S.A.
56 D3 Bear Lake Can.
34 D4 Bearma *r.* India
10 A4 Bearnaraigh *i.* U.K.
62 E1 Bear Paw Mtn *mt* U.S.A.
92 A3 Bear Pen. *pen.* Ant.
58 B3 Bearskin Lake Can.
72 B2 Bear Valley U.S.A.
34 C3 Beas *r.* India
34 C3 Beas Dam *dam* India
75 K5 Beata, Cabo *c.* Dom. Rep.
75 K5 Beata, I. *i.* Dom. Rep.
64 D3 Beatrice U.S.A.
56 E3 Beatton *r.* Can.
56 E3 Beatton River Can.
72 D3 Beatty U.S.A.
58 E4 Beattyville Can.
14 G5 Beaucaire France
80 E8 Beauchene I. *i.* Falkland Is
50 D4 Beaufort Austr.
45 E1 Beaufort Malaysia
67 D5 Beaufort U.S.A.
54 D2 Beaufort Sea Can./U.S.A.
90 E6 Beaufort West S. Africa
58 F4 Beauharnois Can.
10 D3 Beauly U.K.
10 D3 Beauly Firth *est.* U.K.
9 C4 Beaumaris U.K.
12 C4 Beaumont Belgium
51 B6 Beaumont N.Z.
65 F6 Beaumont *MS* U.S.A.
70 B5 Beaumont *OH* U.S.A.
65 E6 Beaumont *TX* U.S.A.
14 G3 Beaune France
14 D3 Beaupréau France
12 A4 Beauquesne France
12 C4 Beauraing Belgium
57 K4 Beausejour Can.
14 F2 Beauvais France
57 H3 Beauval Can.
12 A4 Beauval France
73 F2 Beaver U.S.A.
54 H4 Beaver *r.* *Alta.* Can.
56 D2 Beaver *r.* *B.C./Y.T.* Can.
58 C2 Beaver *r.* *Ont.* Can.
73 F2 Beaver *r.* U.S.A.
56 A2 Beaver Creek Can.
66 C4 Beaver Dam *KY* U.S.A.
68 C4 Beaver Dam *WI* U.S.A.
70 C4 Beaver Falls U.S.A.
62 D2 Beaverhead Mts *mts* U.S.A.
57 K4 Beaverhill L. *l.* *Man.* Can.
57 J2 Beaverhill L. *l.* *N.W.T.* Can.
68 E3 Beaver Island *i.* U.S.A.
65 E4 Beaver L. *resr* U.S.A.
56 F3 Beaverlodge Can.
70 D4 Beaver Run Reservoir U.S.A.
34 C4 Beawar India
83 C2 Beazley Arg.
82 C3 Bebedouro Brazil
9 D4 Bebington U.K.
13 H4 Bebra Ger.
58 F1 Bécard, Lac *l.* Can.
9 J5 Beccles U.K.
19 J2 Bečej Yugo.
15 C1 Becerreá Spain
86 B1 Béchar Alg.
13 J5 Bechhofen Ger.
70 C6 Beckley U.S.A.
13 G3 Beckum Ger.
13 L4 Bečov nad Teplou Czech Rep.
8 F3 Bedale U.K.
12 E4 Bedburg Ger.
71 J2 Beddington U.S.A.
88 D3 Bedelē Eth.
13 G1 Bederkesa Ger.
71 G2 Bedford Can.
91 J4 Bedford S. Africa
9 G5 Bedford U.K.
66 C4 Bedford *IN* U.S.A.
71 H3 Bedford *MA* U.S.A.
70 D4 Bedford *PA* U.S.A.
70 D6 Bedford *VA* U.S.A.
9 G5 Bedford Level *lowland* U.K.
50 F2 Bedgerebong Austr.
8 F2 Bedlington U.K.
44 □ Bedok Sing.
44 □ Bedok Res. *resr* Sing.
73 H2 Bedrock U.S.A.
12 E1 Bedum Neth.
9 F5 Bedworth U.K.
70 B5 Beech Fork Lake *l.* U.S.A.
68 C2 Beechwood U.S.A.
50 F4 Beechworth Austr.
50 H3 Beecroft Pen. *pen.* Austr.
13 L2 Beelitz Ger.
49 F4 Beenleigh Austr.
11 A5 Beenoskee *h.* Rep. of Ireland
12 B3 Beernem Belgium
28 E6 Beersheba Israel
Be'ér Sheva' *see* Beersheba
90 E6 Beervlei Dam *dam* S. Africa
13 L2 Beetzsee *l.* Ger.
65 D6 Beeville U.S.A.
88 C3 Befale Congo(Zaire)
89 E5 Befandriana Avaratra Madag.
50 G4 Bega Austr.
34 B3 Begari *r.* Pak.
15 H2 Begur, Cap de *pt* Spain
35 F4 Begusarai India
31 E3 Behābād Iran
79 H3 Béhague, Pointe *pt* Fr. Guiana
30 C4 Behbehān Iran
56 C3 Behm Canal *in.* U.S.A.
92 B3 Behrendt Mts *mts* Ant.
30 D2 Behshahr Iran
31 G3 Behsūd Afgh.
36 E2 Bei'an China
39 C4 Beibei China
38 B4 Beichuan China
39 C6 Beihai China
39 D6 Bei Jiang *r.* China
38 E2 Beijing China
38 E1 Beijing *div.* China
12 E2 Beilen Neth.
39 C7 Beili China
39 D6 Beiliu China
13 K5 Beilngries Ger.
10 C5 Beinn an Oir *h.* U.K.
10 D3 Beinn Dearg *mt* U.K.
42 A3 Beipiao China
89 D5 Beira Moz.
38 E3 Beiru *r.* China
28 E5 Beirut Lebanon
89 C6 Beitbridge Zimbabwe
10 D5 Beith U.K.
17 L7 Beiuş Romania
42 A3 Beizhen China
15 C3 Beja Port.
86 C1 Béja Tunisia
86 C1 Bejaïa Alg.
15 D2 Béjar Spain
31 E3 Bejestān Iran
34 B3 Beji *r.* Pak.
17 K7 Békés Hungary
17 K7 Békéscsaba Hungary
89 E6 Bekily Madag.
40 J3 Bekkai Japan
86 B4 Bekwai Ghana
35 E4 Bela India
31 G5 Bela Pak.
34 B3 Belab *r.* Pak.
91 H2 Bela-Bela S. Africa
87 D4 Bélabo Cameroon
19 J2 Bela Crkva Yugo.
71 E5 Bel Air U.S.A.
15 D3 Belalcázar Spain
13 L5 Bělá nad Radbuzou Czech Rep.
50 E2 Belaraboon Austr.
5 F3 Belarus *country* Europe
82 A3 Bela Vista Brazil
89 D6 Bela Vista Moz.
44 A5 Belawan Indon.
25 T3 Belaya *r.* Rus. Fed.
21 G6 Belaya Glina Rus. Fed.
21 G5 Belaya Kalitva Rus. Fed.
20 J3 Belaya Kholunitsa Rus. Fed.
17 J5 Bełchatów Pol.
70 B6 Belcher U.S.A.
55 K4 Belcher Islands *is* Can.
31 G3 Belchiragh Afgh.
28 F2 Belcik Turkey
11 D3 Belcoo U.K.
69 J1 Belcourt Can.
72 B1 Belden U.S.A.
88 E3 Beledweyne Somalia
30 D2 Belek Turkm.
79 J4 Belém Brazil
80 C3 Belén Arg.
28 F3 Belen Turkey
63 F5 Belen U.S.A.
49 G3 Bélep, Îles *is* New Caledonia
20 F4 Belev Rus. Fed.
51 D5 Belfast N.Z.
91 J2 Belfast S. Africa
11 F3 Belfast U.K.
71 J2 Belfast U.S.A.
11 F3 Belfast Lough *in.* U.K.
64 C2 Belfield U.S.A.
8 F2 Belford U.K.
14 H3 Belfort France
33 A3 Belgaum India
13 M3 Belgern Ger.
5 D3 Belgium *country* Europe
21 F5 Belgorod Rus. Fed.
21 F5 Belgorodskaya Oblast' *div.* Rus. Fed.
62 E2 Belgrade U.S.A.
19 J2 Belgrade Yugo.
86 D4 Beli Nigeria
18 E6 Belice *r.* *Sicily* Italy
20 G4 Belinskiy Rus. Fed.
45 C3 Belinyu Indon.
45 C3 Belitung *i.* Indon.
74 G5 Belize Belize
53 H8 Belize *country* Central America
40 E2 Belkina, Mys *pt* Rus. Fed.
25 P2 Bel'kovskiy, O. *i.* Rus. Fed.
50 G2 Bell *r.* Austr.
56 D4 Bella Bella Can.
14 E3 Bellac France
56 D4 Bella Coola Can.
65 E6 Bellaire U.S.A.
33 B3 Bellary India
83 F1 Bella Unión Uru.
70 B4 Bellefontaine U.S.A.
70 E4 Bellefonte U.S.A.
64 C2 Belle Fourche U.S.A.
64 C2 Belle Fourche *r.* U.S.A.
14 G3 Bellegarde-sur-Valserine France
67 D7 Belle Glade U.S.A.
14 C3 Belle-Île *i.* France
59 K3 Belle Isle *i.* Can.
55 N4 Belle Isle, Strait of *Nfld* Can.
59 J3 Belle Isle, Strait of *str.* Can.
73 G4 Bellemont U.S.A.
68 A5 Belle Plaine U.S.A.
69 H2 Belleterre Can.
69 J3 Belleville Can.
64 D4 Belleville U.S.A.
68 B4 Bellevue *IA* U.S.A.
62 D3 Bellevue *ID* U.S.A.
70 B4 Bellevue *OH* U.S.A.
62 B2 Bellevue *WA* U.S.A.
Bellin *see* Kangirsuk
8 E2 Bellingham U.K.
62 B1 Bellingham U.S.A.
92 B2 Bellingshausen *Rus. Fed. Base* Ant.
92 A3 Bellingshausen Sea *sea* Ant.
16 D7 Bellinzona Switz.
81 B3 Bello Col.
71 G3 Bellows Falls U.S.A.
34 B3 Bellpat Pak.
71 F5 Belltown U.S.A.
18 E1 Belluno Italy
33 B3 Belluru India
83 D2 Bell Ville Arg.
90 C6 Bellville S. Africa
13 G2 Belm Ger.
90 F4 Belmont S. Africa
10 □ Belmont U.K.
70 D3 Belmont U.S.A.
82 E1 Belmonte Brazil
74 G5 Belmopan Belize
11 B3 Belmullet Rep. of Ireland
12 B4 Belœil Belgium
71 G2 Beloeil Can.
36 E1 Belogorsk Rus. Fed.
89 E6 Beloha Madag.
82 D2 Belo Horizonte Brazil
64 D4 Beloit *KS* U.S.A.
68 C4 Beloit *WI* U.S.A.
20 E1 Belomorsk Rus. Fed.
35 G5 Belonia India
21 F6 Belorechensk Rus. Fed.
28 F3 Belören Turkey
24 G4 Beloretsk Rus. Fed.
Belorussia *country see* Belarus
89 E5 Belo Tsiribihina Madag.
20 F1 Beloye Rus. Fed.
Beloye More *g. see* White Sea
20 F2 Beloye, Ozero *l.* Rus. Fed.
20 F2 Belozersk Rus. Fed.
70 C5 Belpre U.S.A.
62 E2 Belt U.S.A.
72 D3 Belted Range *mts* U.S.A.
65 D6 Belton U.S.A.
33 A3 Belur India
43 A5 Beluran Malaysia
68 C4 Belvidere U.S.A.
20 H3 Belyshevo Rus. Fed.
20 E4 Belyy Rus. Fed.
24 J2 Belyy, O. *i.* Rus. Fed.
13 L2 Belzig Ger.
68 C6 Bement U.S.A.
64 E2 Bemidji U.S.A.
88 C4 Bena Dibele Congo(Zaire)
10 D4 Ben Alder *mt* U.K.
50 E4 Benalla Austr.
18 D6 Ben Arous Tunisia
15 D1 Benavente Spain
10 E3 Ben Avon *mt* U.K.
11 B4 Benbaun *h.* Rep. of Ireland
10 A3 Benbecula *i.* U.K.
11 C3 Benbulben *h.* Rep. of Ireland
11 E3 Benburb U.K.
10 C4 Ben Cruachan *mt* U.K.
62 B2 Bend U.S.A.
91 G5 Bendearg *mt* S. Africa
50 H1 Bendemeer Austr.
88 E3 Bender-Bayla Somalia
50 E4 Bendigo Austr.
50 G4 Bendoc Austr.
89 D5 Bene Moz.
71 J2 Benedicta U.S.A.
59 J3 Benedict, Mount *h.* Can.
89 E6 Benenitra Madag.
16 G6 Benešov Czech Rep.
12 E6 Bénestroff France
18 F4 Benevento Italy
13 F3 Beng *r.* China
22 F8 Bengal, Bay of Asia
88 C3 Bengamisa Congo(Zaire)
38 E3 Bengbu China
44 B5 Bengkalis Indon.
45 B3 Bengkulu Indon.
7 N7 Bengtsfors Sweden
89 B5 Benguela Angola
28 C6 Benha Egypt
10 B4 Ben Hiant *h.* U.K.
10 D2 Ben Hope *mt* U.K.
88 C3 Beni Congo(Zaire)
78 E6 Beni *r.* Bol.
86 B1 Beni-Abbès Alg.
15 F3 Benidorm Spain
86 B1 Beni Mellal Morocco
85 D5 Benin *country* Africa
86 C4 Benin, Bight of *g.* Africa
86 C4 Benin City Nigeria
86 B1 Beni-Saf Alg.
87 F2 Beni Suef Egypt
83 E3 Benito Juárez Arg.
43 B2 Benito Soliven Phil.
78 E4 Benjamim Constant Brazil
74 B2 Benjamín Hill Mex.
40 D2 Benjina Indon.
64 C3 Benkelman U.S.A.
10 D2 Ben Klibreck *mt* U.K.
10 D4 Ben Lawers *mt* U.K.
10 D4 Ben Lomond *mt* U.K.
10 D2 Ben Loyal *h.* U.K.
10 D4 Ben Lui *mt* U.K.
10 E3 Ben Macdui *mt* U.K.
10 D4 Ben More *mt* *Scot.* U.K.
10 B4 Ben More *mt* *Scot.* U.K.
10 D2 Ben More Assynt *mt* U.K.
51 C6 Benmore, L. *l.* N.Z.
25 Q2 Bennetta, O. *i.* Rus. Fed.
10 C4 Ben Nevis *mt* U.K.
71 G3 Bennington U.S.A.
91 H3 Benoni S. Africa
87 D4 Bénoué, Parc National de la *nat. park* Cameroon
13 G5 Bensheim Ger.
73 G6 Benson *AZ* U.S.A.
64 E2 Benson *MN* U.S.A.
31 E5 Bent Iran
45 B2 Benta Seberang Malaysia
70 D6 Bent Creek U.S.A.
37 E7 Benteng Indon.
50 C3 Bentinck I. *i.* Austr.
44 A3 Bentinck I. *i.* Myanmar
8 F4 Bentley U.K.
71 K2 Benton Can.
65 E5 Benton *AR* U.S.A.
72 C3 Benton *CA* U.S.A.
66 B4 Benton *IL* U.S.A.
68 D4 Benton Harbor U.S.A.
44 C3 Bên Tre Vietnam
44 B5 Bentung Malaysia
86 D4 Benue *r.* Nigeria
10 D4 Ben Vorlich *mt* U.K.
11 B4 Benwee *h.* Rep. of Ireland
11 B3 Benwee Head *hd* Rep. of Ireland
10 D3 Ben Wyvis *mt* U.K.
42 C3 Benxi *Liaoning* China
42 B3 Benxi *Liaoning* China
43 C5 Beo Indon.
Beograd *see* Belgrade
34 E5 Beohari India
86 B4 Béoumi Côte d'Ivoire
39 C5 Bepian Jiang *r.* China
41 B8 Beppu Japan
49 H3 Beqa *i.* Fiji
34 C4 Berach *r.* India
59 G2 Bérard, Lac *l.* Can.
34 D5 Berasia India
44 A5 Berastagi Indon.
19 H4 Berat Albania
45 E3 Beratus, Gunung *mt* Indon.
37 F7 Berau, Teluk *b.* Indon.
87 F3 Berber Sudan
88 E2 Berbera Somalia
88 B3 Berbérati C.A.R.
14 E1 Berck France
29 K1 Berd Armenia
25 O3 Berdigestyakh Rus. Fed.
36 A1 Berdsk Rus. Fed.
21 F6 Berdyans'k Ukr.
21 D5 Berdychiv Ukr.
70 A6 Berea U.S.A.
21 B5 Berehove Ukr.
48 E2 Bereina P.N.G.
57 K4 Berens *r.* Can.
57 K4 Berens River Can.
64 D3 Beresford U.S.A.
21 C5 Berezhany Ukr.
21 D6 Berezivka Ukr.
21 C5 Berezne Ukr.
20 G2 Bereznik Rus. Fed.
24 H3 Berezovo Rus. Fed.
13 K3 Berga Ger.
15 G1 Berga Spain
19 M5 Bergama Turkey
18 C2 Bergamo Italy
7 P6 Bergby Sweden
13 H2 Bergen Ger.
16 F3 Bergen Ger.
7 J6 Bergen Norway
12 C3 Bergen op Zoom Neth.
14 E4 Bergerac France
12 C6 Bergères-lès-Vertus France
12 E4 Bergheim Ger.
12 F4 Bergisches Land *reg.* Ger.
12 F4 Bergisch Gladbach Ger.
90 B1 Bergland Namibia
68 C2 Bergland U.S.A.
7 P6 Bergsjö Sweden
6 R4 Bergsviken Sweden
13 J5 Bergtheim Ger.
12 A4 Bergues France
12 E1 Bergum Neth.
91 H4 Bergville S. Africa
45 B3 Berhala, Selat *chan.* Indon.
25 S4 Beringa, O. *i.* Rus. Fed.
12 D3 Beringen Belgium
25 T3 Beringovskiy Rus. Fed.
25 T4 Bering Sea *sea* Pac. Oc.
54 B3 Bering Strait *str.* Rus. Fed./U.S.A.
30 E5 Berīzak Iran
6 M5 Berkåk Norway
12 E2 Berkel *r.* Neth.
72 A3 Berkeley U.S.A.
70 D5 Berkeley Springs U.S.A.
12 D2 Berkhout Neth.
92 B3 Berkner I. *i.* Ant.
19 K3 Berkovitsa Bulg.
9 F6 Berkshire Downs *h.* U.K.
12 C3 Berlare Belgium
6 V1 Berlevåg Norway
13 M2 Berlin Ger.
71 F5 Berlin *MD* U.S.A.
71 H2 Berlin *NH* U.S.A.
70 D5 Berlin *PA* U.S.A.
68 C4 Berlin *WI* U.S.A.
55 K2 Berlinguet Inlet *in.* Can.
70 C4 Berlin Lake *l.* U.S.A.
50 H4 Bermagui Austr.
83 D4 Bermeja, Pta *pt* Arg.
65 C7 Bermejillo Mex.
78 F8 Bermejo Bol.
83 C1 Bermejo *r.* *San Juan* Arg.
80 D2 Bermejo *r.* *Chaco/Formosa* Arg./Bol.
53 K6 Bermuda *terr.* Atl. Ocean
96 E3 Bermuda Rise *sea feature* Atl. Ocean
16 C7 Bern Switz.
63 F5 Bernalillo U.S.A.
80 A7 Bernardo O'Higgins, Parque Nacional *nat. park* Chile
83 D3 Bernasconi Arg.
13 K3 Bernburg (Saale) Ger.
13 G1 Berne Ger.
68 E5 Berne U.S.A.
16 C7 Berner Alpen *mts* Switz.
10 A3 Berneray *i.* U.K.
55 K2 Bernier Bay *b.* Can.
48 B4 Bernier I. *i.* Austr.
16 E7 Bernina Pass Switz.
12 F5 Bernkastel-Kues Ger.
89 E6 Beroroha Madag.
16 G6 Beroun Czech Rep.
16 F5 Berounka *r.* Czech Rep.
50 C3 Berri Austr.
10 E2 Berriedale U.K.
50 E3 Berrigan Austr.
50 H3 Berrima Austr.
15 H4 Berrouaghia Alg.
50 H3 Berry Austr.
14 E3 Berry *reg.* France
72 A2 Berryessa, Lake *l.* U.S.A.
67 E7 Berry Islands *is* Bahamas
90 B3 Berseba Namibia
13 F2 Bersenbrück Ger.
21 D5 Bershad' Ukr.
45 B1 Bertam Malaysia
79 K5 Bertolínia Brazil
87 D4 Bertoua Cameroon
11 B4 Bertraghboy Bay *b.* Rep. of Ireland
49 H2 Beru *i.* Kiribati
78 F4 Beruri Brazil
50 E5 Berwick Austr.
71 E4 Berwick U.S.A.
8 E2 Berwick-upon-Tweed U.K.
56 F3 Berwyn Can.
9 D5 Berwyn *h.* U.K.
21 E6 Beryslav Ukr.
89 E5 Besalampy Madag.
14 H3 Besançon France
31 G2 Beshir Turkm.
31 G2 Beshkent Uzbek.
30 D4 Beshneh Iran
29 H3 Beşiri Turkey
21 H7 Beslan Rus. Fed.
57 H3 Besnard Lake *l.* Can.
28 F3 Besni Turkey
11 E3 Bessbrook U.K.
67 C5 Bessemer *AL* U.S.A.
68 B2 Bessemer *MI* U.S.A.
89 E6 Betanty Madag.
15 B1 Betanzos Spain
87 D4 Bétaré Oya Cameroon
91 H3 Bethal S. Africa
90 B3 Bethanie Namibia
64 E3 Bethany *MO* U.S.A.
65 D5 Bethany *OK* U.S.A.
54 B3 Bethel *AK* U.S.A.
71 H2 Bethel *ME* U.S.A.
68 A6 Bethel *MO* U.S.A.
70 A5 Bethel *OH* U.S.A.
70 D4 Bethel Park U.S.A.
9 C4 Bethesda U.K.
70 E5 Bethesda *MD* U.S.A.
70 C4 Bethesda *OH* U.S.A.
90 F5 Bethesdaweg S. Africa
91 H4 Bethlehem S. Africa
71 F4 Bethlehem U.S.A.
28 E6 Bethlehem West Bank
91 F5 Bethulie S. Africa
12 A4 Béthune France
81 C2 Betijoque Venez.
89 E6 Betioky Madag.
26 F2 Betpak-Dala *plain* Kazak.
89 E6 Betroka Madag.
28 E5 Bet She'an Israel
59 G4 Betsiamites Can.
59 G4 Betsiamites *r.* Can.
89 E5 Betsiboka *r.* Madag.
68 D3 Betsie, Pt *pt* U.S.A.
68 E2 Betsy Lake *l.* U.S.A.
68 B5 Bettendorf U.S.A.
35 F4 Bettiah India
10 D2 Bettyhill U.K.
11 E4 Bettystown Rep. of Ireland
34 D5 Betul India
12 D3 Betuwe *reg.* Neth.
34 D4 Betwa *r.* India
9 D4 Betws-y-coed U.K.
13 F4 Betzdorf Ger.
50 D3 Beulah Austr.
68 D3 Beulah U.S.A.
8 H6 Beult *r.* U.K.
8 G4 Beverley U.K.
54 C4 Beverley, L. *l.* U.S.A.
71 H3 Beverly *MA* U.S.A.
70 C5 Beverly *OH* U.S.A.
72 C4 Beverly Hills U.S.A.
57 J2 Beverly Lake *l.* Can.
13 G1 Beverstedt Ger.
13 H3 Beverungen Ger.
12 C2 Beverwijk Neth.
12 F5 Bexbach Ger.
9 H7 Bexhill U.K.
30 B3 Beyānlū Iran
28 C3 Bey Dağları *mts* Turkey
28 B1 Beykoz Turkey
86 B4 Beyla Guinea
29 L2 Beyläqan Azer.
28 C1 Beypazarı Turkey
28 F2 Beypınarı Turkey
33 A4 Beypore India
Beyrouth *see* Beirut
28 C3 Beyşehir Turkey
28 C3 Beyşehir Gölü *l.* Turkey
21 F6 Beysug *r.* Rus. Fed.
29 J3 Beytüşşebap Turkey
30 E3 Bezameh Iran
20 J3 Bezbozhnik Rus. Fed.
20 D3 Bezhanitsy Rus. Fed.
20 F3 Bezhetsk Rus. Fed.
14 F5 Béziers France
Bezwada *see* Vijayawada
34 B4 Bhabhar India
35 E4 Bhabua India
34 B5 Bhadar *r.* India
35 F4 Bhadgaon Nepal
35 E4 Bhadohi India
34 C3 Bhadra India
33 C2 Bhadrachalam India
Bhadrachalam Road Sta. *see* Kottagudem
35 F5 Bhadrakh India
33 A3 Bhadra Reservoir India
33 A3 Bhadravati India
34 A3 Bhag Pak.
34 D2 Bhaga *r.* India
35 F4 Bhagalpur India
35 G5 Bhagirathi *r.* India
34 D5 Bhainsdehi India
35 G4 Bhairab Bazar Bangl.
35 E4 Bhairawa Nepal
33 B2 Bhalki India
36 B4 Bhamo Myanmar
33 C2 Bhamragarh India
34 D4 Bhander India
35 F6 Bhanjanagar India
34 C4 Bhanpura India
34 D5 Bhanrer Range *h.* India
34 D4 Bharatpur India
35 H4 Bhareli *r.* India
31 F5 Bhari *r.* Pak.
34 C5 Bharuch India
35 E5 Bhatapara India
33 A3 Bhatkal India
35 G5 Bhatpara India
33 B4 Bhavani India
33 B4 Bhavani *r.* India
34 C5 Bhavnagar India
34 C3 Bhawana Pak.
35 E6 Bhawanipatna India
91 J3 Bhekuzulu S. Africa
35 E3 Bheri *r.* Nepal
34 C4 Bhilwara India
33 B2 Bhima *r.* India
33 C2 Bhīmavaram India
34 D4 Bhind India
34 C4 Bhindar India
35 E4 Bhinga India
34 C4 Bhinmal India
34 D3 Bhiwani India
35 F4 Bhojpur Nepal
33 B2 Bhongir India
91 H5 Bhongweni S. Africa
34 D5 Bhopal India
33 C2 Bhopalpatnam India
33 A2 Bhor India
35 F5 Bhuban India
35 F5 Bhubaneshwar India
34 B5 Bhuj India
34 C5 Bhusawal India
23 J7 Bhutan *country* Asia
34 B4 Bhuttewala India
30 E5 Bīābān *mts* Iran
34 C2 Biafo Gl. *gl.* Pak.
37 F7 Biak Indon.
37 F7 Biak *i.* Indon.
17 L4 Biała Podlaska Pol.
16 G4 Białogard Pol.
17 L4 Białystok Pol.
86 B4 Biankouma Côte d'Ivoire
42 B1 Bianzhao China
30 D2 Bīārjmand Iran
14 D5 Biarritz France
30 B5 Bi'ār Tabrāk *well* S. Arabia
16 D7 Biasca Switz.
40 G3 Bibai Japan
89 B5 Bibala Angola
50 G4 Bibbenluke Austr.
18 D3 Bibbiena Italy
16 D6 Biberach an der Riß Ger.
35 G4 Bibiyana *r.* Bangl.
13 G5 Biblis Ger.
28 C2 Biçer Turkey
9 F6 Bicester U.K.
57 G4 Biche, Lac la *l.* Can.
21 G7 Bichvint'a Georgia
48 D3 Bickerton I. *i.* Austr.
9 D7 Bickleigh U.K.
73 G2 Bicknell U.S.A.
89 B5 Bicuari, Parque Nacional do *nat. park* Angola
86 C4 Bida Nigeria
43 A5 Bidadari, Tg *pt* Malaysia
30 D4 Bida Khabit Iran
33 B2 Bidar India
31 E6 Bidbid Oman
71 H3 Biddeford U.S.A.
12 D2 Biddinghuizen Neth.
10 C4 Bidean Nam Bian *mt* U.K.
9 C6 Bideford U.K.
9 C6 Bideford Bay *b.* U.K.
17 L4 Biebrza *r.* Pol.
13 G4 Biedenkopf Ger.
16 C7 Biel Switz.
16 H5 Bielawa Pol.
13 G2 Bielefeld Ger.

18 C2 Biella Italy
17 J6 Bielsko-Biała Pol.
17 L4 Bielsk Podlaski Pol.
13 J1 Bienenbüttel Ger.
44 C3 Biên Hoa Vietnam
Bienne *see* Biel
58 F2 Bienville, Lac *l.* Can.
12 C3 Biesbosch, Nationaal Park de *nat. park* Neth.
91 F3 Biesiesvlei S. Africa
13 H6 Bietigheim-Bissingen Ger.
12 D5 Bièvre Belgium
88 B4 Bifoun Gabon
59 J3 Big *r.* Can.
72 A2 Big *r.* U.S.A.
21 C7 Biga Turkey
28 B2 Bigadiç Turkey
19 M5 Biga Yarımadası *pen.* Turkey
68 D2 Big Bay U.S.A.
68 D3 Big Bay de Noc *b.* U.S.A.
72 D4 Big Bear Lake U.S.A.
62 E2 Big Belt Mts *mts* U.S.A.
91 J3 Big Bend Swaziland
65 C6 Big Bend Nat. Park U.S.A.
65 F5 Big Black *r.* U.S.A.
9 D7 Bigbury-on-Sea U.K.
67 D7 Big Cypress Nat. Preserve *res.* U.S.A.
68 C3 Big Eau Pleine Reservoir U.S.A.
57 L5 Big Falls U.S.A.
57 H4 Biggar Can.
10 E5 Biggar U.K.
56 B3 Bigger, Mt *mt* Can.
9 G5 Biggleswade U.K.
62 D2 Big Hole *r.* U.S.A.
62 F2 Bighorn *r.* U.S.A.
62 E2 Bighorn Canyon Nat. Recreation Area *res.* U.S.A.
62 F2 Bighorn Mountains U.S.A.
67 F7 Bight, The Bahamas
55 L3 Big Island *i.* *N.W.T.* Can.
56 F2 Big Island *i.* Can.
71 K2 Big Lake *l.* U.S.A.
86 A3 Bignona Senegal
70 D6 Big Otter *r.* U.S.A.
72 C3 Big Pine U.S.A.
68 E4 Big Rapids U.S.A.
68 C3 Big Rib *r.* U.S.A.
57 H4 Big River Can.
68 D3 Big Sable Pt *pt* U.S.A.
56 C2 Big Salmon *r.* Can.
57 K3 Big Sand Lake *l.* Can.
73 F4 Big Sandy *r.* U.S.A.
64 D2 Big Sioux *r.* U.S.A.
72 D2 Big Smokey Valley *v.* U.S.A.
65 C5 Big Spring U.S.A.
64 C3 Big Springs U.S.A.
70 B6 Big Stone Gap U.S.A.
72 B3 Big Sur U.S.A.
62 E2 Big Timber U.S.A.
58 C3 Big Trout Lake Can.
58 C3 Big Trout Lake *l.* Can.
73 G3 Big Water U.S.A.
69 H3 Bigwin Can.
18 F2 Bihać Bos.-Herz.
35 F4 Bihar *div.* India
35 F4 Bihar Sharif India
40 J3 Bihoro Japan
17 L7 Bihor, Vârful *mt* Romania
86 A3 Bijagós, Arquipélago dos *is* Guinea-Bissau
34 C4 Bijainagar India
33 A2 Bijapur India
30 B3 Bījār Iran
33 C2 Bijārpur India
19 H2 Bijeljina Bos.-Herz.
19 H3 Bijelo Polje Yugo.
39 B5 Bijie China
31 E5 Bījnābād Iran
35 G4 Bijni India
34 D3 Bijnor India
34 B3 Bijnot Pak.
34 C3 Bikaner India
36 F2 Bikin Rus. Fed.
40 D1 Bikin *r.* Rus. Fed.
46 H3 Bikini *i.* Marshall Islands
88 B4 Bikoro Congo(Zaire)
38 B3 Bikou China
34 C4 Bilara India
35 E5 Bilaspur India
29 M2 Biläsuvar Azer.
21 D5 Bila Tserkva Ukr.
44 A2 Bilauktaung Range *mts* Myanmar/Thai.
15 E1 Bilbao Spain
28 C6 Bilbeis Egypt
19 H3 Bileća Bos.-Herz.
28 B1 Bilecik Turkey
17 L5 Biłgoraj Pol.
88 D4 Bilharamulo Tanz.
21 D6 Bilhorod-Dnistrovs'kyy Ukr.
88 C3 Bili Congo(Zaire)
25 S3 Bilibino Rus. Fed.
43 C4 Biliran *i.* Phil.
42 B4 Biliu *r.* China
62 F3 Bill U.S.A.
9 H6 Billericay U.K.
8 F3 Billingham U.K.
62 E2 Billings U.S.A.
9 E7 Bill of Portland *hd* U.K.
73 F4 Bill Williams *r.* U.S.A.
73 F4 Bill Williams Mtn *mt* U.S.A.
87 D3 Bilma Niger
48 F4 Biloela Austr.
21 E6 Bilohirs'k Ukr.
17 N5 Bilohir"ya Ukr.
33 B2 Biloli India
21 F5 Biloluts'k Ukr.
21 E5 Bilopillya Ukr.
21 F5 Bilovods'k Ukr.
67 B6 Biloxi U.S.A.
48 D4 Bilpa Morea Claypan *salt flat* Austr.
10 E5 Bilston U.K.
87 E3 Biltine Chad
44 A1 Bilugyun I. *i.* Myanmar
20 J4 Bilyarsk Rus. Fed.
21 D6 Bilyayivka Ukr.
12 D4 Bilzen Belgium
50 G3 Bimberi, Mt *mt* Austr.
67 E7 Bimini Is *is* Bahamas
29 M3 Binab Iran
34 D4 Bina-Etawa India
37 E7 Binaija, G. *mt* Indon.
28 F2 Binboğa Daği *mt* Turkey
34 E4 Bindki India
89 B4 Bindu Congo(Zaire)
89 D5 Bindura Zimbabwe
15 G2 Binefar Spain
38 B2 Bingcaowan China
13 F5 Bingen am Rhein Ger.
86 B4 Bingerville Côte d'Ivoire
71 J2 Bingham U.S.A.
71 F3 Binghamton U.S.A.
29 H2 Bingöl Turkey
29 H2 Bingol D. *mt* Turkey
39 C6 Binh Gia Vietnam
44 D2 Binh Sơn Vietnam
35 H4 Bini India
35 E5 Binika India
44 A5 Binjai Indon.
30 D5 Bin Mürkhan *well* U.A.E.
50 G1 Binnaway Austr.
44 C5 Bintan *i.* Indon.
43 B3 Bintuan Phil.
45 B3 Bintuhan Indon.
45 D2 Bintulu Malaysia
38 C3 Bin Xian China
53 F5 Binya Austr.
39 C6 Binyang China
38 F2 Binzhou China
83 B3 Bíobío *div.* Chile
83 B3 Bío Bío *r.* Chile
86 C4 Bioco *i.* Equatorial Guinea
18 F3 Biograd na Moru Croatia
18 G3 Biokovo *mts* Croatia
33 A2 Bir India
31 F5 Bīrag, Kūh-e *mts* Iran
29 H5 Bi'r al Mulūsi Iraq
20 F2 Birandozero Rus. Fed.
88 C2 Birao C.A.R.
35 F4 Biratnagar Nepal
29 G3 Bi'r Buţaymān Syria
56 G3 Birch *r.* Can.
57 G3 Birch Hills Can.
50 D3 Birchip Austr.
56 F4 Birch Island Can.
57 K4 Birch L. *l.* Can.
68 B2 Birch Lake *l.* U.S.A.
56 G3 Birch Mountains *h.* Can.
57 J4 Birch River Can.
12 D1 Birdaard Neth.
92 C1 Bird Island *U.K. Base* Ant.
73 G2 Birdseye U.S.A.
48 D4 Birdsville Austr.
28 F3 Birecik Turkey
87 E3 Bir en Nutrûn *well* Sudan
45 A1 Bireun Indon.
30 B6 Bi'r Ghawdah *well* S. Arabia
88 D2 Birhan *mt* Eth.
82 B3 Birigüi Brazil
31 E3 Bīrjand Iran
29 J6 Birkat al 'Aqabah *well* Iraq
29 J6 Birkat al 'Athāmīn *well* Iraq
29 K6 Birkát Hamad *well* Iraq
30 A4 Birkat Zubālah *waterhole* S. Arabia
12 F5 Birkenfeld Ger.
9 D4 Birkenhead U.K.
28 C7 Birket Qârûn *l.* Egypt
29 K3 Bīrkim Iraq
18 F7 Birkirkara Malta
9 F5 Birmingham U.K.
67 C5 Birmingham U.S.A.
86 A2 Bîr Mogreïn Maur.
28 B6 Bîr Nâḩid *oasis* Egypt
86 C3 Birnin-Kebbi Nigeria
86 C3 Birnin Konni Niger
36 F2 Birobidzhan Rus. Fed.
11 D4 Birr Rep. of Ireland
29 J5 Bi'r Sābil Iraq
10 E1 Birsay U.K.
9 F5 Birstall U.K.
13 H4 Birstein Ger.
28 F7 Bîr Tâba Egypt
57 J4 Birtle Can.
35 H3 Biru China
33 A3 Birur India
7 T8 Biržai Lith.
73 H6 Bisbee U.S.A.
4 C4 Biscay, Bay of *sea* France/Spain
67 D7 Biscayne Nat. Park U.S.A.
16 F7 Bischofshofen Austria
92 B2 Biscoe Islands *is* Ant.
69 F2 Biscotasi Lake *l.* Can.
69 F2 Biscotasing Can.
39 C4 Bishan China
29 M5 Bīsheh Iran
27 F2 Bishkek Kyrg.
35 F5 Bishnupur India
91 G6 Bisho S. Africa
72 C3 Bishop U.S.A.
8 F3 Bishop Auckland U.K.
9 H6 Bishop's Stortford U.K.
29 G4 Bishrī, Jabal *h.* Syria
36 E1 Bishui China
86 C1 Biskra Alg.
43 C4 Bislig Phil.
64 C2 Bismarck U.S.A.
48 E2 Bismarck Archipelago *is* P.N.G.
48 E2 Bismarck Range *mts* P.N.G.
48 E2 Bismarck Sea *sea* P.N.G.
13 K2 Bismark (Altmark) Ger.
29 H3 Bismil Turkey
7 L6 Bismo Norway
29 L4 Bīsotūn Iran
6 P5 Bispgården Sweden
13 J1 Bispingen Ger.
15 G4 Bissa, Djebel *mt* Alg.
33 C2 Bissamcuttak India
86 A3 Bissau Guinea-Bissau
86 D4 Bissaula Nigeria
57 K4 Bissett Can.
56 F3 Bistcho Lake *l.* Can.
17 M7 Bistrița Romania
17 N7 Bistrița *r.* Romania
12 E5 Bitburg Ger.
12 F5 Bitche France
87 D3 Bitkine Chad
29 J2 Bitlis Turkey
19 J4 Bitola Macedonia
18 G4 Bitonto Italy
30 B6 Bitrān, J. *h.* S. Arabia
73 H2 Bitter Creek *r.* U.S.A.
13 L3 Bitterfeld Ger.
90 C5 Bitterfontein S. Africa
28 D6 Bitter Lakes *l.* Egypt
62 D2 Bitterroot Range *mts* U.S.A.
13 K2 Bittkau Ger.
21 G5 Bityug *r.* Rus. Fed.
87 D3 Biu Nigeria
41 D7 Biwa-ko *l.* Japan
38 D3 Biyang China
34 D5 Biyāvra India
88 E2 Bīye K'obē Eth.
24 K4 Biysk Rus. Fed.
91 H5 Bizana S. Africa
86 C1 Bizerte Tunisia
6 A4 Bjargtangar *hd* Iceland
6 Q5 Bjästa Sweden
18 G2 Bjelovar Croatia
6 P2 Bjerkvik Norway
7 L8 Bjerringbro Denmark
7 P6 Björklinge Sweden
7 L5 Bjorli Norway
6 Q5 Björna Sweden
Bjørnøya *i.* *see* Bear Island
6 Q5 Bjurholm Sweden
86 B3 Bla Mali
10 B3 Bla Bheinn *mt* U.K.
65 F5 Black *r.* *AR* U.S.A.
73 H5 Black *r.* *AZ* U.S.A.
69 F4 Black *r.* *MI* U.S.A.
68 B3 Black *r.* *WV* U.S.A.
48 E4 Blackall Austr.
68 C1 Black Bay *b.* Can.
58 B3 Blackbear *r.* Can.
9 F6 Black Bourton U.K.
8 E4 Blackburn U.K.
72 A2 Black Butte *summit* U.S.A.
72 A2 Black Butte L. *l.* U.S.A.
73 E4 Black Canyon U.S.A.
73 F4 Black Canyon City U.S.A.
64 E2 Blackduck U.S.A.
56 G4 Blackfalds Can.
62 D3 Blackfoot U.S.A.
62 D2 Black Foot *r.* U.S.A.
64 C2 Black Hills *reg.* U.S.A.
10 D3 Black Isle *i.* U.K.
57 H3 Black Lake Can.
57 H3 Black Lake *l.* Can.
69 E3 Black Lake *l.* U.S.A.
73 G3 Black Mesa *plat.* U.S.A.
9 D6 Black Mountain *h.* U.K.
72 D4 Black Mt *mt* U.S.A.
9 D6 Black Mts *h.* U.K.
73 E4 Black Mts *mts* *AZ* U.S.A.
90 C1 Black Nossob *watercourse* Namibia
39 □ Black Point *pt* *H.K.* China
8 D4 Blackpool U.K.
68 B3 Black River Falls U.S.A.
8 A4 Blackrock Rep. of Ireland
62 C3 Black Rock Desert U.S.A.
70 C6 Blacksburg U.S.A.
4 G4 Black Sea *sea* Asia/Europe
11 A3 Blacksod Bay *b.* Rep. of Ireland
11 E5 Blackstairs Mountain *h.* Rep. of Ireland
11 E5 Blackstairs Mountains *h.* Rep. of Ireland
70 E6 Blackstone U.S.A.
50 H1 Black Sugarloaf *mt* Austr.
86 B4 Black Volta *r.* Africa
11 E5 Blackwater Rep. of Ireland
11 E4 Blackwater *r.* Rep. of Ireland
11 D5 Blackwater *r.* Rep. of Ireland
11 E3 Blackwater *r.* Rep. of Ireland/U.K.
9 H6 Blackwater *r.* U.K.
70 E6 Blackwater *r.* U.S.A.
56 E2 Blackwater Lake *l.* Can.
10 D4 Blackwater Reservoir U.K.
65 D4 Blackwell U.S.A.
48 B5 Blackwood *r.* Austr.
21 G6 Blagodarnyy Rus. Fed.
40 D2 Blagodatnyy Rus. Fed.
19 K3 Blagoevgrad Bulg.
36 E1 Blagoveshchensk Rus. Fed.
70 E4 Blain U.S.A.
62 B1 Blaine U.S.A.
57 H4 Blaine Lake Can.
64 D3 Blair *NE* U.S.A.
68 B3 Blair *WV* U.S.A.
10 E4 Blair Atholl U.K.
10 E4 Blairgowrie U.K.
67 C6 Blakely U.S.A.
9 J5 Blakeney U.K.
68 C1 Blake Pt *pt* U.S.A.
83 E3 Blanca, Bahía *b.* Arg.
83 C3 Blanca de la Totora, Sa *h.* Arg.
63 F4 Blanca Peak *summit* U.S.A.
48 D4 Blanche, L. *salt flat* Austr.
70 B5 Blanchester U.S.A.
50 B3 Blanchetown Austr.
14 H4 Blanc, Mont *mt* France/Italy
83 C1 Blanco *r.* Arg.
78 F6 Blanco *r.* Bol.
62 A3 Blanco, C. *c.* U.S.A.
59 J3 Blanc-Sablon Can.
50 F2 Bland *r.* Austr.
6 D4 Blanda *r.* Iceland
9 E7 Blandford Forum U.K.
73 H3 Blanding U.S.A.
15 H2 Blanes Spain
68 E2 Blaney Park U.S.A.
44 A5 Blangkejeren Indon.
12 B3 Blankenberge Belgium
12 E4 Blankenheim Ger.
81 D2 Blanquilla, Isla *i.* Venez.
16 H6 Blansko Czech Rep.
89 D5 Blantyre Malawi
11 C6 Blarney Rep. of Ireland
13 H5 Blaufelden Ger.
6 Q4 Blåviksjön Sweden
50 G2 Blayney Austr.
13 J1 Bleckede Ger.
51 D4 Blenheim N.Z.
12 E3 Blerick Neth.
11 E4 Blessington Lakes *l.* Rep. of Ireland
9 G5 Bletchley U.K.
86 C1 Blida Alg.
12 F5 Blies *r.* Ger.
49 H3 Bligh Water *b.* Fiji
69 F2 Blind River Can.
62 D3 Bliss U.S.A.
69 F5 Blissfield U.S.A.
71 H4 Block I. *i.* U.S.A.
71 H4 Block Island Sound *chan.* U.S.A.
91 G4 Bloemfontein S. Africa
91 F3 Bloemhof S. Africa
91 F3 Bloemhof Dam *dam* S. Africa
13 H3 Blomberg Ger.
6 C4 Blönduós Iceland
71 E5 Bloodsworth I. *i.* U.S.A.
57 K4 Bloodvein *r.* Can.
11 C2 Bloody Foreland *pt* Rep. of Ireland
69 J4 Bloomfield Can.
68 A5 Bloomfield *IA* U.S.A.
66 C4 Bloomfield *IN* U.S.A.
63 E4 Bloomfield *NM* U.S.A.
68 C5 Bloomington *IL* U.S.A.
66 C4 Bloomington *IN* U.S.A.
64 E2 Bloomington *MN* U.S.A.
71 E4 Bloomsburg U.S.A.
70 E4 Blossburg U.S.A.
55 Q3 Blosseville Kyst Greenland
91 H1 Blouberg S. Africa
9 F5 Bloxham U.K.
73 H5 Blue *r.* U.S.A.
73 G1 Bluebell U.S.A.
73 G2 Blue Bell Knoll *summit* U.S.A.
64 E3 Blue Earth U.S.A.
70 C6 Bluefield U.S.A.
75 H6 Bluefields Nic.
71 J2 Blue Hill U.S.A.
69 H5 Blue Knob *h.* U.S.A.
73 H1 Blue Mountain U.S.A.
35 H5 Blue Mountain *mt* India
71 F3 Blue Mountain Lake U.S.A.
91 G4 Blue Mountain Pass Lesotho
50 G2 Blue Mountains *N.S.W.* Austr.
62 C2 Blue Mountains U.S.A.
50 H2 Blue Mountains Nat. Park Austr.
87 F3 Blue Nile *r.* Sudan
54 G3 Bluenose Lake *l.* Can.
67 C5 Blue Ridge U.S.A.
70 D6 Blue Ridge *mts* U.S.A.
56 F4 Blue River Can.
72 D2 Blue Springs U.S.A.
11 C3 Blue Stack *mt* Rep. of Ireland
11 C3 Blue Stack Mts *h.* Rep. of Ireland
70 C6 Bluestone Lake *l.* U.S.A.
51 B7 Bluff N.Z.
73 H3 Bluff U.S.A.
39 □ Bluff I. *i.* *H.K.* China
67 E7 Bluff, The Bahamas
68 E5 Bluffton *IN* U.S.A.
70 B4 Bluffton *OH* U.S.A.
80 G3 Blumenau Brazil
64 C2 Blunt U.S.A.
62 B3 Bly U.S.A.
50 B2 Blyth Austr.
8 F2 Blyth *Eng.* U.K.
9 F4 Blyth *Eng.* U.K.
73 E5 Blythe U.S.A.
65 F5 Blytheville U.S.A.
7 L7 Bø Norway
86 A4 Bo Sierra Leone
43 B3 Boac Phil.
79 K5 Boa Esperança, Açude *resr* Brazil
38 D3 Bo'ai *Henan* China
39 C6 Bo'ai *Yunnan* China
88 B3 Boali C.A.R.
91 K3 Boane Moz.
70 C4 Boardman U.S.A.
91 F1 Boatlaname Botswana
79 L5 Boa Viagem Brazil
81 E4 Boa Vista Brazil
86 □ Boa Vista *i.* Cape Verde
50 F2 Bobadah Austr.
39 D6 Bobai China
89 E5 Bobaomby, Tanjona *c.* Madag.
33 C2 Bobbili India
86 B3 Bobo-Dioulasso Burkina
89 C6 Bobonong Botswana
21 G5 Bobrov Rus. Fed.
21 D5 Bobrovytsya Ukr.
21 E5 Bobrynets' Ukr.
89 E6 Boby *mt* Madag.
81 E2 Boca Araguao *est.* Venez.
81 D2 Boca del Pao Venez.
75 M7 Boca de Macareo Venez.
78 E5 Boca do Acre Brazil
79 H4 Boca do Jari Brazil
81 E2 Boca Grande *est.* Venez.
82 D2 Bocaiúva Brazil
81 C2 Bocanó *r.* Venez.
88 B3 Bocaranga C.A.R.
67 D7 Boca Raton U.S.A.
75 H7 Bocas del Toro Panama
17 K6 Bochnia Pol.
12 E3 Bocholt Ger.
12 F3 Bochum Ger.
91 H1 Bochum S. Africa
13 J2 Bockenem Ger.
81 C2 Boconó Venez.
88 B3 Boda C.A.R.
50 H4 Bodalla Austr.
36 D1 Bodaybo Rus. Fed.
65 E5 Bodcau Lake *l.* U.S.A.
10 G3 Boddam U.K.
13 K3 Bode *r.* Ger.
72 A2 Bodega Head *hd* U.S.A.
87 D3 Bodélé *reg.* Chad
6 R4 Boden Sweden
9 E5 Bodenham U.K.
Bodensee *l.* *see* Constance, Lake
13 J2 Bodenteich Ger.
13 H3 Bodenwerder Ger.
33 B2 Bodhan India
33 B4 Bodinayakkanur India
9 C7 Bodmin U.K.
9 C7 Bodmin Moor *reg.* U.K.
6 O3 Bodø Norway
19 M6 Bodrum Turkey
12 C3 Boechout Belgium
88 C4 Boende Congo(Zaire)
86 A3 Boffa Guinea
35 H3 Boga India
65 F6 Bogalusa U.S.A.
50 F1 Bogan *r.* Austr.
86 B3 Bogandé Burkina
50 F2 Bogan Gate Austr.
20 J3 Bogatye Saby Rus. Fed.
28 E2 Boğazlıyan Turkey
35 F3 Bogcang Zangbo *r.* China
36 A2 Bogda Shan *mts* China
11 B5 Boggeragh Mts *h.* Rep. of Ireland
15 H5 Boghar Alg.
9 G7 Bognor Regis U.K.
43 C4 Bogo Phil.
11 D4 Bog of Allen *reg.* Rep. of Ireland
20 E4 Bogolyubovo Rus. Fed.
50 F4 Bogong, Mt *mt* Austr.
40 D2 Bogopol' Rus. Fed.
45 C4 Bogor Indon.
20 G3 Bogorodsk Rus. Fed.
20 J3 Bogorodskoye Rus. Fed.
81 B3 Bogotá Col.
36 A1 Bogotol Rus. Fed.
35 G4 Bogra Bangl.
25 L4 Boguchany Rus. Fed.
21 G5 Boguchar Rus. Fed.
86 A3 Bogué Maur.
38 F2 Bo Hai *g.* China
42 A4 Bohai Haixia *chan.* China
14 F2 Bohain-en-Vermandois France
38 E2 Bohai Wan *b.* China
13 L3 Böhlen Ger.
91 H4 Bohlokong S. Africa
13 L5 Böhmer Wald *mts* Ger.
13 G2 Bohmte Ger.
21 E5 Bohodukhiv Ukr.
43 C4 Bohol *i.* Phil.
43 C4 Bohol Sea *sea* Phil.
43 B4 Bohol Str. *chan.* Phil.
27 G2 Bohu China
21 D5 Bohuslav Ukr.
71 F4 Boiceville U.S.A.
90 E4 Boichoko S. Africa
91 G3 Boikhutso S. Africa
79 G4 Boim Brazil
35 H5 Boinu *r.* Myanmar
82 E1 Boipeba, Ilha *i.* Brazil
82 D4 Boi, Ponta do *pt* Brazil
82 C2 Bois *r.* Brazil
69 E3 Bois Blanc I. *i.* U.S.A.
12 C4 Bois de Chimay *woodland* Belgium
62 C3 Boise U.S.A.
65 C4 Boise City U.S.A.
57 J5 Boissevain Can.
91 F3 Boitumelong S. Africa
13 J1 Boizenburg Ger.
43 B2 Bojeador, Cape *c.* Phil.
30 E2 Bojnūrd Iran
35 G1 Bokadaban Feng *mt* China
35 H4 Bokajan India
35 F5 Bokaro India
88 B4 Bokatola Congo(Zaire)
86 A3 Boké Guinea
88 C4 Bokele Congo(Zaire)
7 J7 Boknafjorden *chan.* Norway
87 D3 Bokoro Chad
21 G5 Bokovskaya Rus. Fed.
20 E3 Boksitogorsk Rus. Fed.
90 D3 Bokspits Botswana
88 C4 Bolaiti Congo(Zaire)
86 A3 Bolama Guinea-Bissau
34 A3 Bolan *r.* Pak.
34 A3 Bolan Pass Pak.
14 E2 Bolbec France
30 C4 Boldājī Iran
13 M1 Boldekow Ger.
27 G2 Bole China
86 B4 Bole Ghana
88 B4 Boleko Congo(Zaire)
86 B3 Bolgatanga Ghana
21 D6 Bolhrad Ukr.
42 B1 Boli China
88 B4 Bolia Congo(Zaire)
6 R4 Boliden Sweden
43 A2 Bolinao Phil.
19 L2 Bolintin-Vale Romania
81 A3 Bolívar Col.
78 C5 Bolívar Peru
65 E4 Bolivar *MO* U.S.A.
67 B5 Bolivar *TN* U.S.A.
77 D4 Bolivia *country* S. America
28 E3 Bolkar Dağları *mts* Turkey
20 F4 Bolkhov Rus. Fed.
69 F1 Bolkow Can.
14 G4 Bollène France
7 P6 Bollnäs Sweden
6 P5 Bollstabruk Sweden
7 N8 Bolmen *l.* Sweden
21 H7 Bolnisi Georgia
88 B4 Bolobo Congo(Zaire)
43 B5 Bolod Islands *is* Phil.
18 D2 Bologna Italy
20 F3 Bologovo Rus. Fed.
20 E3 Bologoye Rus. Fed.
91 F4 Bolokanang S. Africa
88 B5 Bolomba Congo(Zaire)
43 B5 Bolong Phil.
24 K4 Bolotnoye Rus. Fed.
44 C2 Bolovens, Plateau des *plat.* Laos
35 F5 Bolpur India
18 D3 Bolsena, Lago di *l.* Italy
17 K3 Bol'shakovo Rus. Fed.
6 X3 Bol'shaya Imandra, Oz. *l.* Rus. Fed.
21 G6 Bol'shaya Martinovka Rus. Fed.
25 M2 Bolshevik, O. *i.* Rus. Fed.
20 H2 Bol'shiye Chirki Rus. Fed.
25 S3 Bol'shoy Aluy *r.* Rus. Fed.
40 C3 Bol'shoy Kamen' Rus. Fed.
Bol'shoy Kavkaz *mts* *see* Caucasus
21 J5 Bol'shoy Uzen' *r.* Rus. Fed.
74 D3 Bolson de Mapimí *des.* Mex.
12 D1 Bolsward Neth.
8 E4 Bolton U.K.
70 B6 Bolton U.S.A.
28 C1 Bolu Turkey
6 B3 Bolungarvík Iceland
39 E6 Boluo China
28 C2 Bolvadin Turkey
18 D1 Bolzano Italy
88 B4 Boma Congo(Zaire)
50 H3 Bomaderry Austr.
50 G4 Bombala Austr.
Bombay *see* Mumbai
37 F7 Bomberai Peninsula Indon.
78 E5 Bom Comércio Brazil
82 D2 Bom Despacho Brazil
35 H4 Bomdila India
35 H3 Bomi China
82 D1 Bom Jesus da Lapa Brazil
82 E3 Bom Jesus do Itabapoana Brazil
7 J7 Bømlo *i.* Norway
30 B2 Bonāb Iran
70 E6 Bon Air U.S.A.
75 L6 Bonaire *i.* Neth. Ant.
75 H6 Bonanza Nic.
48 C3 Bonaparte Archipelago *is* Austr.
10 D3 Bonar Bridge U.K.
59 K4 Bonavista Can.
59 K4 Bonavista Bay *b.* Can.
87 D1 Bon, Cap *c.* Tunisia
10 F5 Bonchester Bridge U.K.
88 C3 Bondo Congo(Zaire)
43 B3 Bondoc Peninsula Phil.
86 B4 Bondoukou Côte d'Ivoire
68 A3 Bone Lake *l.* U.S.A.
13 F3 Bönen Ger.
37 E7 Bonerate, Kepulauan *is* Indon.
10 E4 Bo'ness U.K.
37 E7 Bone, Teluk *b.* Indon.
82 D2 Bonfinópolis de Minas Brazil
88 D3 Bonga Eth.
43 B3 Bongabong Phil.
35 G4 Bongaigaon India
88 C3 Bongandanga Congo(Zaire)
90 E4 Bongani S. Africa
43 A5 Bongao Phil.
35 G3 Bong Co *l.* China
43 C5 Bongo *i.* Phil.
89 E5 Bongolava *mts* Madag.
88 C3 Bongo, Massif des *mts* C.A.R.
87 D3 Bongor Chad
86 B4 Bongouanou Côte d'Ivoire
44 D2 Bông Sơn Vietnam
13 C3 Bonheiden Belgium
18 C4 Bonifacio *Corsica* France
18 C4 Bonifacio, Strait of *str.* France/Italy
Bonin Is *is* *see* Ogasawara-shotō
82 A3 Bonito Brazil
12 F4 Bonn Ger.
6 O3 Bonnåsjøen Norway
62 C1 Bonners Ferry U.S.A.
14 H3 Bonneville France
50 C4 Bonney, L. *l.* Austr.
48 B5 Bonnie Rock Austr.
10 E5 Bonnyrigg U.K.
57 G4 Bonnyville Can.
43 A4 Bonobono Phil.
44 C3 Bonom Mhai *mt* Vietnam
18 C4 Bonorva *Sardinia* Italy
90 D7 Bontebok National Park S. Africa
86 A4 Bonthe Sierra Leone
43 B2 Bontoc Phil.
45 E4 Bontosunggu Indon.
91 F6 Bontrug S. Africa
91 G1 Bonwapitse Botswana
73 H2 Book Cliffs *cliff* U.S.A.
50 D2 Boolaboolka L. *l.* Austr.
50 B2 Booleroo Centre Austr.
11 D5 Booley Hills *h.* Rep. of Ireland
50 E2 Booligal Austr.
64 E3 Boone *IA* U.S.A.
67 D4 Boone *NC* U.S.A.
70 B6 Boone Lake *l.* U.S.A.
70 B6 Booneville *KY* U.S.A.
65 F5 Booneville *MS* U.S.A.
72 A2 Boonville *CA* U.S.A.
66 C4 Boonville *IN* U.S.A.
64 E4 Boonville *MO* U.S.A.
71 F3 Boonville *NY* U.S.A.
50 F3 Booroorban Austr.
50 G3 Boorowa Austr.
50 D4 Boort Austr.
88 E2 Boosaaso Somalia
71 J3 Boothbay Harbor U.S.A.
55 J2 Boothia, Gulf of Can.
55 J2 Boothia Peninsula Can.
9 E4 Bootle U.K.
86 A4 Bopolu Liberia
12 F4 Boppard Ger.
83 G1 Boqueirão Brazil
60 E6 Boquilla, Presa de la *resr* Mex.
13 L5 Bor Czech Rep.
87 F4 Bor Sudan
28 E3 Bor Turkey
19 K2 Bor Yugo.
62 D2 Borah Peak *summit* U.S.A.
7 N8 Borås Sweden
30 C4 Borāzjān Iran
79 G4 Borba Brazil

79 L5 Borborema, Planalto da plat. Brazil
13 G3 Borchen Ger.
92 B5 Borchgrevink Coast coastal area Ant.
29 H1 Borçka Turkey
28 B3 Bor D. mt Turkey
14 D4 Bordeaux France
59 H4 Borden Can.
54 G2 Borden I. i. Can.
55 K2 Borden Peninsula Can.
50 C4 Bordertown Austr.
6 C4 Borðeyri Iceland
15 J4 Bordj Bou Arréridj Alg.
15 G5 Bordj Bounaama Alg.
86 C2 Bordj Omer Driss Alg.
6 □ Borðoy i. Faroe Is
10 A3 Boreray i. U.K.
6 G4 Borgarfjörður Iceland
6 C4 Borgarnes Iceland
6 N4 Børgefjell Nasjonalpark nat. park Norway
65 C5 Borger U.S.A.
7 P8 Borgholm Sweden
18 B2 Borgo San Dalmazzo Italy
18 D3 Borgo San Lorenzo Italy
18 C2 Borgosesia Italy
12 B4 Borinage reg. Belgium
21 G5 Borisoglebsk Rus. Fed.
21 F5 Borisovka Rus. Fed.
20 F3 Borisovo-Sudskoye Rus. Fed.
30 C4 Borj-e Chīn Iran
21 G7 Borjomi Georgia
12 E3 Borken Ger.
6 P2 Borkenes Norway
12 E1 Borkum Ger.
12 E1 Borkum i. Ger.
7 O6 Borlänge Sweden
28 B2 Borlu Turkey
13 L3 Borna Ger.
12 D1 Borndiep chan. Neth.
12 E2 Borne Neth.
45 D2 Borneo i. Asia
7 O9 Bornholm i. Denmark
19 M5 Bornova Turkey
43 B4 Borocay i. Phil.
24 K3 Borodino Rus. Fed.
7 V6 Borodinskoye Rus. Fed.
21 D5 Borodyanka Ukr.
25 P3 Borogontsy Rus. Fed.
20 F3 Borok Rus. Fed.
86 B3 Boromo Burkina
43 C4 Borongan Phil.
8 F3 Boroughbridge U.K.
20 E3 Borovichi Rus. Fed.
20 J3 Borovoy Kirovsk. Rus. Fed.
20 K2 Borovoy Komi Rus. Fed.
20 E1 Borovoy Korel. Rus. Fed.
11 C5 Borrisokane Rep. of Ireland
48 D3 Borroloola Austr.
6 M5 Børsa Norway
17 M7 Borşa Romania
21 C5 Borshchiv Ukr.
36 C2 Borshchovochnyy Khrebet mts Rus. Fed.
30 C4 Borūjen Iran
30 C3 Borūjerd Iran
10 B3 Borve U.K.
21 B5 Boryslav Ukr.
21 D5 Boryspil' Ukr.
21 E5 Borzna Ukr.
36 D1 Borzya Rus. Fed.
18 G2 Bosanska Dubica Bos.-Herz.
18 G2 Bosanska Gradiška Bos.-Herz.
18 G2 Bosanska Krupa Bos.-Herz.
18 G2 Bosanski Novi Bos.-Herz.
18 G2 Bosansko Grahovo Bos.-Herz.
68 B4 Boscobel U.S.A.
39 C6 Bose China
91 F4 Boshof S. Africa
5 E4 Bosnia-Herzegovina country Europe
88 B3 Bosobolo Congo(Zaire)
41 G7 Bōsō-hantō pen. Japan
28 B1 Bosporus str. Turkey
88 B3 Bossangoa C.A.R.
88 B3 Bossembélé C.A.R.
65 E5 Bossier City U.S.A.
90 B2 Bossiesvlei Namibia
35 F1 Bostan China
29 L6 Bostan Iran
34 A2 Bosten Hu l. China
9 G5 Boston U.K.
71 H3 Boston U.S.A.
69 H1 Boston Creek Can.
71 H3 Boston-Logan International airport U.S.A.
65 E5 Boston Mts mts U.S.A.
8 F4 Boston Spa U.K.
68 D5 Boswell U.S.A.
34 B5 Botad India
50 H2 Botany Bay b. Austr.
6 P5 Boteå Sweden
19 L3 Botev mt Bulg.
19 K3 Botevgrad Bulg.
91 G3 Bothaville S. Africa
6 Q6 Bothnia, Gulf of g. Fin./Sweden
21 H5 Botkul', Ozero l. Kazak./Rus. Fed.
17 N7 Botoşani Romania
38 E2 Botou China
44 C1 Bô Trach Vietnam
91 G4 Botshabelo S. Africa
85 F8 Botswana country Africa
18 G5 Botte Donato, Monte mt Italy
6 S4 Bottenviken g. Fin./Sweden
8 G4 Bottesford U.K.
64 C1 Bottineau U.S.A.
12 E3 Bottrop Ger.
82 C3 Botucatu Brazil
82 D1 Botuporã Brazil
59 K4 Botwood Can.
86 B4 Bouaflé Côte d'Ivoire
86 B4 Bouaké Côte d'Ivoire
88 B3 Bouar C.A.R.
86 B1 Bouârfa Morocco
87 D4 Bouba Ndjida, Parc National de nat. park Cameroon
88 B3 Bouca C.A.R.
12 B4 Bouchain France
83 D2 Bouchard, H. Arg.
71 G2 Boucherville Can.
69 K2 Bouchette Can.
86 B3 Boucle du Baoulé, Parc National de la nat. park Mali
59 H4 Bouctouche Can.
49 F2 Bougainville Island i. P.N.G.
86 B3 Bougouni Mali
12 D5 Bouillon Belgium
15 H4 Bouira Alg.
86 A2 Boujdour Western Sahara
62 F3 Boulder CO U.S.A.
62 D2 Boulder MT U.S.A.
73 G3 Boulder UT U.S.A.
73 E3 Boulder Canyon U.S.A.
73 E4 Boulder City U.S.A.
72 D5 Boulevard U.S.A.
83 E3 Boulevard Atlántico Arg.
48 D4 Boulia Austr.
14 F2 Boulogne-Billancourt France
14 E1 Boulogne-sur-Mer France
86 B3 Boulsa Burkina
88 B4 Boumango Gabon
87 D4 Boumba r. Cameroon
15 H4 Boumerdes Alg.
86 B4 Bouna Côte d'Ivoire
71 H2 Boundary Mountains U.S.A.
72 C3 Boundary Peak summit U.S.A.
86 B4 Boundiali Côte d'Ivoire
88 B4 Boundji Congo
44 D1 Boung r. Vietnam
39 A6 Boun Nua Laos
62 E3 Bountiful U.S.A.
49 H6 Bounty Islands is N.Z.
86 B3 Bourem Mali
14 E4 Bourganeuf France
14 G3 Bourg-en-Bresse France
14 F3 Bourges France
71 F2 Bourget Can.
69 K1 Bourgmont Can.
14 G3 Bourgogne reg. France
48 E5 Bourke Austr.
69 G1 Bourkes Can.
9 G5 Bourne U.K.
9 F7 Bournemouth U.K.
12 F2 Bourtanger Moor reg. Ger.
86 C1 Bou Saâda Alg.
18 C6 Bou Salem Tunisia
73 E5 Bouse U.S.A.
73 E5 Bouse Wash r. U.S.A.
87 D3 Bousso Chad
12 B4 Boussu Belgium
86 A3 Boutilimit Maur.
96 K9 Bouvetøya i. Atl. Ocean
14 C5 Bouy France
13 H3 Bovenden Ger.
45 D2 Boven Kapuas Mts mts Malaysia
83 E1 Bovril Arg.
57 G4 Bow r. Can.
64 C1 Bowbells U.S.A.
48 E4 Bowen Austr.
68 B5 Bowen U.S.A.
50 G4 Bowen, Mt mt Austr.
73 H5 Bowie AZ U.S.A.
65 D5 Bowie TX U.S.A.
57 G5 Bow Island Can.
30 B2 Bowkan Iran
66 C4 Bowling Green KY U.S.A.
64 F4 Bowling Green MO U.S.A.
70 B4 Bowling Green OH U.S.A.
70 E5 Bowling Green VA U.S.A.
64 C2 Bowman U.S.A.
92 C6 Bowman I. i. Ant.
56 E4 Bowman, Mt mt Can.
92 B3 Bowman Pen. pen. Ant.
69 H4 Bowmanville Can.
10 B5 Bowmore U.K.
50 H3 Bowral Austr.
56 E4 Bowron r. Can.
56 E4 Bowron Lake Provincial Park res. Can.
13 H5 Boxberg Ger.
38 E3 Bo Xian China
38 F2 Boxing China
12 D3 Boxtel Neth.
28 E1 Boyabat Turkey
39 E4 Boyang China
57 J2 Boyd Lake l. Can.
56 G4 Boyle Can.
11 C4 Boyle Rep. of Ireland
11 E4 Boyne r. Rep. of Ireland
31 G2 Boyni Qara Afgh.
67 D7 Boynton Beach U.S.A.
62 E3 Boysen Res. resr U.S.A.
78 F8 Boyuibe Bol.
29 K1 Böyük Hinaldağ mt Azer.
19 M5 Bozcaada i. Turkey
19 M5 Bozdağ mt Turkey
28 A2 Boz Dağları mts Turkey
28 B3 Bozdoğan Turkey
9 G5 Bozeat U.K.
62 E2 Bozeman U.S.A.
28 D3 Bozkır Turkey
88 B3 Bozoum C.A.R.
28 G3 Bozova Turkey
30 B2 Bozqūsh, Kūh-e mts Iran
28 C2 Bozüyük Turkey
18 B2 Bra Italy
92 B2 Brabant I. i. Ant.
18 G3 Brač i. Croatia
10 B3 Bracadale U.K.
10 B3 Bracadale, Loch b. U.K.
18 E3 Bracciano, Lago di l. Italy
69 H3 Bracebridge Can.
6 O5 Bracke Sweden
13 H5 Brackenheim Ger.
9 G6 Bracknell U.K.
18 G4 Bradano r. Italy
67 D7 Bradenton U.S.A.
69 H3 Bradford Can.
8 F4 Bradford U.K.
70 A4 Bradford OH U.S.A.
70 D4 Bradford PA U.S.A.
71 G3 Bradford VT U.S.A.
65 D6 Brady U.S.A.
56 B3 Brady Gl. gl. U.S.A.
10 □ Brae U.K.
50 B2 Braemar Austr.
10 E3 Braemar U.K.
15 B2 Braga Port.
83 E2 Bragado Arg.
79 J4 Bragança Brazil
15 C2 Bragança Port.
82 C3 Bragança Paulista Brazil
21 D5 Brahin Belarus
13 J1 Brahlstorf Ger.
35 G5 Brahmanbaria Bangl.
35 F5 Brahmani r. India
33 D2 Brahmapur India
35 G4 Brahmaputra r. Asia
19 M2 Brăila Romania
12 B5 Braine France
12 C4 Braine-le-Comte Belgium
64 E2 Brainerd U.S.A.
9 H6 Braintree U.K.
91 H1 Brak r. S. Africa
12 B4 Brakel Belgium
13 H3 Brakel Ger.
13 G1 Brake (Unterweser) Ger.
89 B6 Brakwater Namibia
56 E4 Bralorne Can.
7 L9 Bramming Denmark
7 P5 Brämön i. Sweden
69 H4 Brampton Can.
8 E3 Brampton Eng. U.K.
9 J5 Brampton Eng. U.K.
13 G2 Bramsche Ger.
9 H5 Brancaster U.K.
59 K4 Branch Can.
81 E4 Branco r. Brazil
7 M6 Brandbu Norway
7 L9 Brande Denmark
13 L2 Brandenburg Ger.
13 L2 Brandenburg div. Ger.
91 G4 Brandfort S. Africa
13 M3 Brandis Ger.
57 K5 Brandon Can.
9 H5 Brandon U.K.
64 D3 Brandon SD U.S.A.
71 G3 Brandon VT U.S.A.
11 A5 Brandon Head hd Rep. of Ireland
11 E5 Brandon Hill h. Rep. of Ireland
11 A5 Brandon Mountain mt Rep. of Ireland
90 D5 Brandvlei S. Africa
67 D6 Branford U.S.A.
17 J3 Braniewo Pol.
92 B2 Bransfield Str. str. Ant.
69 G4 Brantford Can.
50 C4 Branxholme Austr.
59 H4 Bras d'Or L. l. Can.
78 E6 Brasileia Brazil
82 C1 Brasília Brazil
82 D2 Brasília de Minas Brazil
79 G4 Brasília Legal Brazil
17 N3 Braslaw Belarus
19 L2 Braşov Romania
43 A5 Brassey Range mts Malaysia
71 J2 Brassua Lake l. U.S.A.
16 H6 Bratislava Slovakia
36 C1 Bratsk Rus. Fed.
36 C1 Bratskoye Vdkhr. resr Rus. Fed.
71 G3 Brattleboro U.S.A.
16 F6 Braunau am Inn Austria
13 G4 Braunfels Ger.
13 J3 Braunlage Ger.
13 K3 Braunsbedra Ger.
13 J2 Braunschweig Ger.
86 □ Brava i. Cape Verde
7 P7 Bråviken in. Sweden
Bravo del Norte, Rio r. see Rio Grande r. Mexico/U.S.A.
73 E5 Brawley U.S.A.
11 E4 Bray Rep. of Ireland
56 F4 Brazeau Can.
56 F4 Brazeau r. Can.
77 D3 Brazil country S. America
96 H7 Brazil Basin sea feature Atl. Ocean
65 D5 Brazos r. U.S.A.
88 B4 Brazzaville Congo
19 H2 Brčko Bos.-Herz.
51 A6 Breaksea Sd in. N.Z.
51 E1 Bream Bay b. N.Z.
51 E1 Bream Head hd N.Z.
9 C6 Brechfa U.K.
10 F4 Brechin U.K.
12 C3 Brecht Belgium
64 D2 Breckenridge MN U.S.A.
65 D5 Breckenridge TX U.S.A.
16 H6 Břeclav Czech Rep.
9 D6 Brecon U.K.
9 D6 Brecon Beacons h. U.K.
9 D6 Brecon Beacons National Park U.K.
12 C3 Breda Neth.
90 D7 Bredasdorp S. Africa
50 G3 Bredbo Austr.
13 L2 Breddin Ger.
12 E3 Bredevoort Neth.
6 O3 Bredviken Norway
12 D3 Bree Belgium
70 D5 Breezewood U.S.A.
16 D7 Bregenz Austria
6 B4 Breiðafjörður b. Iceland
6 F4 Breiðdalsvík Iceland
13 G4 Breidenbach Ger.
16 C6 Breisach am Rhein Ger.
13 J1 Breitenfelde Ger.
13 J5 Breitengüßbach Ger.
6 S1 Breivikbotn Norway
79 J6 Brejinho de Nazaré Brazil
6 L5 Brekstad Norway
13 G1 Bremen Ger.
67 C5 Bremen GA U.S.A.
68 D5 Bremen IN U.S.A.
13 G1 Bremerhaven Ger.
62 B2 Bremerton U.S.A.
13 H1 Bremervörde Ger.
12 F4 Bremm Ger.
65 D6 Brenham U.S.A.
6 N4 Brenna Norway
16 E7 Brenner Pass Austria/Italy
69 H2 Brent Can.
18 D2 Brenta r. Italy
9 H6 Brentwood U.K.
72 B3 Brentwood CA U.S.A.
71 G4 Brentwood NY U.S.A.
18 D2 Brescia Italy
18 D1 Bressanone Italy
10 □ Bressay i. U.K.
14 D3 Bressuire France
21 B4 Brest Belarus
14 B2 Brest France
14 C2 Bretagne reg. France
12 A5 Breteuil France
65 F6 Breton Sound b. U.S.A.
51 E1 Brett, Cape c. N.Z.
13 G5 Bretten Ger.
9 E4 Bretton U.K.
67 D5 Brevard U.S.A.
79 H4 Breves Brazil
68 E2 Brevort U.S.A.
48 E4 Brewarrina Austr.
71 J2 Brewer U.S.A.
62 C1 Brewster U.S.A.
65 G6 Brewton U.S.A.
91 H3 Breyten S. Africa
Brezhnev see Naberezhnyye Chelny
17 J6 Brezno Slovakia
18 G2 Brezovo Polje h. Croatia
88 C3 Bria C.A.R.
14 H4 Briançon France
50 F3 Bribbaree Austr.
21 C5 Briceni Moldova
14 H4 Bric Froid mt France/Italy
11 C5 Bride r. Rep. of Ireland
73 G1 Bridgeland U.S.A.
9 D6 Bridgend U.K.
10 D4 Bridge of Orchy U.K.
72 C2 Bridgeport CA U.S.A.
71 G4 Bridgeport CT U.S.A.
64 C3 Bridgeport NE U.S.A.
62 E2 Bridger U.S.A.
62 F3 Bridger Peak summit U.S.A.
71 F5 Bridgeton U.S.A.
75 N6 Bridgetown Barbados
59 H5 Bridgewater Can.
71 K1 Bridgewater U.S.A.
50 C5 Bridgewater, C. hd Austr.
9 E5 Bridgnorth U.K.
71 H2 Bridgton U.S.A.
9 D6 Bridgwater U.K.
9 D6 Bridgwater Bay b. U.K.
8 G3 Bridlington U.K.
8 G3 Bridlington Bay b. U.K.
9 E7 Bridport U.K.
16 C7 Brig Switz.
8 G4 Brigg U.K.
62 D3 Brigham City U.S.A.
50 F4 Bright Austr.
9 J6 Brightlingsea U.K.
69 J3 Brighton Can.
51 C6 Brighton N.Z.
9 G7 Brighton U.K.
69 F4 Brighton U.S.A.
14 H5 Brignoles France
86 A3 Brikama The Gambia
13 G3 Brilon Ger.
18 G4 Brindisi Italy
83 D1 Brinkmann Arg.
50 B2 Brinkworth Austr.
59 H4 Brion, Île i. Can.
14 F4 Brioude France
59 F3 Brisay Can.
49 F4 Brisbane Austr.
71 K1 Bristol Can.
9 E6 Bristol U.K.
71 G4 Bristol CT U.S.A.
71 F4 Bristol PA U.S.A.
70 B6 Bristol TN U.S.A.
54 B4 Bristol Bay b. U.S.A.
9 C6 Bristol Channel est. U.K.
92 C1 Bristol I. i. Atl. Ocean
73 E4 Bristol Lake l. U.S.A.
73 E4 Bristol Mts mts U.S.A.
92 A2 British Antarctic Territory reg. Ant.
56 D3 British Columbia div. Can.
55 K1 British Empire Range mts Can.
3 □ British Indian Ocean Territory terr. Ind. Ocean
91 G2 Brits S. Africa
90 E5 Britstown S. Africa
Brittany reg. see Bretagne
14 E4 Brive-la-Gaillarde France
15 E1 Briviesca Spain
9 D7 Brixham U.K.
16 H6 Brno Czech Rep.
67 D5 Broad r. U.S.A.
71 F3 Broadalbin U.S.A.
58 E3 Broadback r. Can.
50 E4 Broadford Austr.
11 C5 Broadford Rep. of Ireland
10 C3 Broadford U.K.
10 E5 Broad Law h. U.K.
9 J6 Broadstairs U.K.
62 F2 Broadus U.S.A.
57 J4 Broadview Can.
64 C3 Broadwater U.S.A.
51 D1 Broadwood N.Z.
7 S8 Broceni Latvia
57 J3 Brochet Can.
57 J3 Brochet, Lac l. Can.
13 J3 Brocken mt Ger.
54 G2 Brock I. i. Can.
70 E3 Brockport U.S.A.
71 H3 Brockton U.S.A.
69 K3 Brockville Can.
69 F4 Brockway MI U.S.A.
70 D4 Brockway PA U.S.A.
55 K2 Brodeur Peninsula Can.
68 C4 Brodhead U.S.A.
10 C5 Brodick U.K.
17 J4 Brodnica Pol.
21 C5 Brody Ukr.
65 E4 Broken Arrow U.S.A.
50 H2 Broken B. b. Austr.
64 D3 Broken Bow NE U.S.A.
65 E5 Broken Bow OK U.S.A.
50 C1 Broken Hill Austr.
13 J2 Brome Ger.
9 G6 Bromley U.K.
9 E5 Bromsgrove U.K.
7 L8 Brønderslev Denmark
91 H2 Bronkhorstspruit S. Africa
6 N4 Brønnøysund Norway
68 E5 Bronson U.S.A.
9 J5 Brooke U.K.
43 A4 Brooke's Point Phil.
68 C4 Brookfield U.S.A.
65 F6 Brookhaven U.S.A.
62 A3 Brookings OR U.S.A.
64 D2 Brookings SD U.S.A.
71 H3 Brookline U.S.A.
68 A5 Brooklyn IA U.S.A.
68 B5 Brooklyn IL U.S.A.
64 E2 Brooklyn Center U.S.A.
70 D6 Brookneal U.S.A.
57 G4 Brooks Can.
72 A2 Brooks CA U.S.A.
71 J2 Brooks ME U.S.A.
92 B3 Brooks, C. c. Ant.
54 D3 Brooks Range mts U.S.A.
67 D6 Brooksville U.S.A.
70 D4 Brookville U.S.A.
48 C3 Broome Austr.
10 C3 Broom, Loch in. U.K.
10 E2 Brora U.K.
7 O9 Brösarp Sweden
11 D4 Brosna r. Rep. of Ireland
62 B3 Brothers U.S.A.
39 □ Brothers, The is H.K. China
8 E3 Brough U.K.
10 E1 Brough Head hd U.K.
11 E3 Broughshane U.K.
50 B2 Broughton r. Austr.
55 M3 Broughton Island Can.
17 P5 Brovary Ukr.
7 L8 Brovst Denmark
65 C5 Brownfield U.S.A.
62 D1 Browning U.S.A.
50 B2 Brown, Mt mt Austr.
68 D6 Brownsburg U.S.A.
71 F5 Browns Mills U.S.A.
67 B5 Brownsville TN U.S.A.
65 D7 Brownsville TX U.S.A.
71 J2 Brownville U.S.A.
71 J2 Brownville Junction U.S.A.
65 D6 Brownwood U.S.A.
17 O4 Brozha Belarus
14 F1 Bruay-en-Artois France
68 C2 Bruce Crossing U.S.A.
58 D4 Bruce Pen. pen. Can.
69 G3 Bruce Peninsula National Park Can.
13 G5 Bruchsal Ger.
13 L2 Brück Ger.
16 G7 Bruck an der Mur Austria
9 E6 Brue r. U.K.
12 B3 Bruges Belgium
Brugge see Bruges
13 G5 Brühl Baden-Württemberg Ger.
12 E4 Brühl Nordrhein-Westfalen Ger.
73 G2 Bruin Pt summit U.S.A.
35 J3 Bruint India
90 C2 Brukkaros Namibia
68 B2 Brule U.S.A.
12 C5 Brûly Belgium
82 E1 Brumado Brazil
7 M6 Brumunddal Norway
13 K2 Brunau Ger.
62 D3 Bruneau U.S.A.
62 D3 Bruneau r. U.S.A.
23 L9 Brunei country Asia
6 O5 Brunflo Sweden
18 D1 Brunico Italy
51 C5 Brunner, L. l. N.Z.
57 H4 Bruno Can.
16 D4 Brunsbüttel Ger.
67 D6 Brunswick GA U.S.A.
71 J3 Brunswick ME U.S.A.
70 C4 Brunswick OH U.S.A.
80 B8 Brunswick, Península de pen. Chile
16 H6 Bruntál Czech Rep.
92 C3 Brunt Ice Shelf ice feature Ant.
91 J4 Bruntville S. Africa
48 E6 Bruny I. i. Austr.
62 G3 Brush U.S.A.
12 C4 Brussels Belgium
69 G4 Brussels Can.
68 D3 Brussels U.S.A.
17 O5 Brusyliv Ukr.
50 F4 Bruthen Austr.
Bruxelles see Brussels
70 A4 Bryan OH U.S.A.
65 D6 Bryan TX U.S.A.
92 A3 Bryan Coast coastal area Ant.
50 B2 Bryan, Mt h. Austr.
20 E4 Bryansk Rus. Fed.
20 E4 Bryanskaya Oblast' div. Rus. Fed.
21 H6 Bryanskoye Rus. Fed.
73 F3 Bryce Canyon Nat. Park U.S.A.
73 H5 Bryce Mt mt U.S.A.
7 J7 Bryne Norway
21 F6 Bryukhovetskaya Rus. Fed.
16 H5 Brzeg Pol.
49 F2 Buala Solomon Is
86 A3 Buba Guinea-Bissau
29 M7 Būbīyān I. i. Kuwait
43 B5 Bubuan i. Phil.
28 C3 Bucak Turkey
81 B3 Bucaramanga Col.
43 C4 Bucas Grande i. Phil.
50 G4 Buchan Austr.
86 A4 Buchanan Liberia
68 D5 Buchanan MI U.S.A.
70 D6 Buchanan VA U.S.A.
65 D6 Buchanan, L. l. U.S.A.
55 L2 Buchan Gulf b. Can.
59 J4 Buchans Can.
19 M2 Bucharest Romania
13 J1 Büchen Ger.
13 H5 Buchen (Odenwald) Ger.
13 L1 Buchholz Ger.
13 H1 Buchholz in der Nordheide Ger.
72 B4 Buchon, Point pt U.S.A.
17 M7 Bucin, Pasul pass Romania
50 E1 Buckambool Mt h. Austr.
13 H2 Bückeburg Ger.
13 H2 Bücken Ger.
73 F5 Buckeye U.S.A.
70 B5 Buckeye Lake l. U.S.A.
70 C5 Buckhannon U.S.A.
70 C5 Buckhannon r. U.S.A.
10 E4 Buckhaven U.K.
69 H3 Buckhorn Can.
73 H5 Buckhorn U.S.A.
69 H3 Buckhorn Lake l. Can.
70 B6 Buckhorn Lake l. U.S.A.
10 F3 Buckie U.K.
69 K3 Buckingham Can.
9 G5 Buckingham U.K.
70 D6 Buckingham U.S.A.
48 D3 Buckingham Bay b. Austr.
48 E4 Buckland Tableland reg. Austr.
92 A6 Buckle I. i. Ant.
73 F4 Buckskin Mts mts U.S.A.
72 B2 Bucks Mt mt U.S.A.
71 J2 Bucksport U.S.A.
13 L2 Bückwitz Ger.
Bucureşti see Bucharest
70 B4 Bucyrus U.S.A.
17 P4 Buda-Kashalyova Belarus
17 J7 Budapest Hungary
34 D3 Budaun India
50 E1 Budda Austr.
92 C6 Budd Coast coastal area Ant.
10 F4 Buddon Ness pt U.K.
18 C4 Buddusò Sardinia Italy
9 C7 Bude U.K.
65 F6 Bude U.S.A.
21 H6 Budennovsk Rus. Fed.
13 H4 Büdingen Ger.
34 D5 Budni India
20 E3 Budogoshch' Rus. Fed.
35 H2 Budongquan China
18 C4 Budoni Sardinia Italy
86 C4 Buea Cameroon
72 B4 Buellton U.S.A.
83 D2 Buena Esperanza Arg.
81 A4 Buenaventura Col.
74 C3 Buenaventura Mex.
81 A4 Buenaventure, B. de b. Col.
63 F4 Buena Vista CO U.S.A.
70 D6 Buena Vista VA U.S.A.
15 E2 Buendia, Embalse de resr Spain
83 B4 Bueno r. Chile
83 E2 Buenos Aires Arg.
83 E3 Buenos Aires div. Arg.
80 B7 Buenos Aires, L. l. Arg./Chile
80 C7 Buen Pasto Arg.
70 D3 Buffalo NY U.S.A.
65 D4 Buffalo OK U.S.A.
64 C2 Buffalo SD U.S.A.
65 D6 Buffalo TX U.S.A.
68 B3 Buffalo WV U.S.A.
62 F2 Buffalo WY U.S.A.
56 G3 Buffalo r. Can.
68 B3 Buffalo r. U.S.A.
56 F3 Buffalo Head Hills h. Can.
56 F2 Buffalo Lake l. Can.
50 F4 Buffalo, Mt mt Austr.
57 H3 Buffalo Narrows Can.
90 B4 Buffels watercourse S. Africa
91 G1 Buffels Drift S. Africa
67 D5 Buford U.S.A.
19 L2 Buftea Romania
17 K4 Bug r. Pol.
81 A4 Buga Col.
81 A3 Bugalagrande Col.
50 G1 Bugaldie Austr.
30 D2 Bugdayli Turkm.
45 D4 Bugel, Tanjung pt Indon.
12 C3 Buggenhout Belgium
18 G2 Bugojno Bos.-Herz.
43 A4 Bugsuk i. Phil.
43 B2 Buguey Phil.
30 D4 Būhābād Iran
29 J5 Buḩayrat ath Tharthār l. Iraq
29 K4 Buḩayrat Shārī l. Iraq
89 D5 Buhera Zimbabwe
43 B3 Buhi Phil.
62 D3 Buhl ID U.S.A.
68 A2 Buhl MN U.S.A.
29 J3 Bühtan r. Turkey
17 N7 Buhuşi Romania
9 D5 Builth Wells U.K.
86 B4 Bui National Park Ghana
20 J4 Buinsk Rus. Fed.
29 L4 Bu'in Soflā Iran
36 D2 Buir Nur l. Mongolia
89 B6 Buitepos Namibia
19 J3 Bujanovac Yugo.
88 C4 Bujumbura Burundi
36 D1 Bukachacha Rus. Fed.
49 F2 Buka I. i. P.N.G.
30 D4 Būkand Iran
88 C4 Bukavu Congo(Zaire)
31 G2 Bukhara Uzbek.
43 C6 Bukide i. Indon.
44 □ Bukit Batok Sing.
44 B5 Bukit Fraser Malaysia
44 □ Bukit Panjang Sing.
44 □ Bukit Timah Sing.
45 B3 Bukittinggi Indon.
88 D4 Bukoba Tanz.
44 □ Bukum, P. i. Sing.
37 F7 Bula Indon.
20 J4 Bula r. Rus. Fed.
16 D7 Bülach Switz.
50 J2 Bulahdelal Austr.
43 B3 Bulan Phil.
28 G1 Bulancak Turkey
34 D3 Bulandshahr India
29 J2 Bulanık Turkey
89 C6 Bulawayo Zimbabwe
28 F3 Bulbul Syria
28 B2 Buldan Turkey
34 D5 Buldana India
91 J2 Bulembu Swaziland
36 C2 Bulgan Mongolia
38 B1 Bulgan Mongolia
5 F4 Bulgaria country Europe
51 D4 Buller r. N.Z.

50 F4 **Buller, Mt** *mt* Austr.
73 E4 **Bullhead City** U.S.A.
72 D4 **Bullion Mts** *mts* U.S.A.
90 B2 **Büllsport** Namibia
44 □ **Buloh, P.** *i.* Sing.
50 D4 **Buloke, Lake** *l.* Austr.
91 G4 **Bultfontein** S. Africa
43 C5 **Buluan** Phil.
48 C2 **Bulukumba** Indon.
25 O2 **Bulun** Rus. Fed.
88 B4 **Bulungu** *Bandundu* Congo(Zaire)
88 C4 **Bulungu** *Kasai-Occidental* Congo(Zaire)
31 G2 **Bulungur** Uzbek.
43 C3 **Bulusan** Phil.
88 C3 **Bumba** Congo(Zaire)
38 B1 **Bumbat Sum** China
73 F4 **Bumble Bee** U.S.A.
43 A5 **Bum-Bum** *i.* Malaysia
88 B4 **Buna** Congo(Zaire)
88 D3 **Buna** Kenya
88 D4 **Bunazi** Tanz.
11 C2 **Bunbeg** Rep. of Ireland
48 B5 **Bunbury** Austr.
11 E5 **Bunclody** Rep. of Ireland
11 D2 **Buncrana** Rep. of Ireland
88 D4 **Bunda** Tanz.
48 F4 **Bundaberg** Austr.
34 C4 **Bundi** India
11 C3 **Bundoran** Rep. of Ireland
35 F5 **Bundu** India
9 J5 **Bungay** U.K.
44 B2 **Bung Boraphet** *l.* Thai.
50 G3 **Bungendore** Austr.
92 C6 **Bunger Hills** *h.* Ant.
41 C8 **Bungo-suidō** *chan.* Japan
88 D3 **Bunia** Congo(Zaire)
88 C4 **Bunianga** Congo(Zaire)
50 D4 **Buninyong** Austr.
86 D3 **Buni-Yadi** Nigeria
34 C2 **Bunji** Jammu and Kashmir
73 E3 **Bunkerville** U.S.A.
65 E6 **Bunkie** U.S.A.
67 D6 **Bunnell** U.S.A.
28 E2 **Bünyan** Turkey
43 A6 **Bunyu** *i.* Indon.
30 C4 **Bu ol Kheyr** Iran
44 D2 **Buôn Hô** Vietnam
44 D2 **Buôn Mê Thuôt** Vietnam
25 P2 **Buorkhaya, Guba** *b.* Rus. Fed.
32 C4 **Buqayq** S. Arabia
88 D4 **Bura** Kenya
34 E3 **Burang** China
82 E2 **Buranhaém** *r.* Brazil
88 E3 **Burao** Somalia
43 C4 **Burauen** Phil.
32 B4 **Buraydah** S. Arabia
13 G4 **Burbach** Ger.
72 C4 **Burbank** U.S.A.
50 F2 **Burcher** Austr.
31 G2 **Burdalyk** Turkm.
28 C3 **Burdur** Turkey
88 D2 **Burē** Eth.
9 J5 **Bure** *r.* U.K.
6 R4 **Bureå** Sweden
36 F1 **Bureinskiy Khrebet** *mts* Rus. Fed.
28 D6 **Bûr Fu'ad** Egypt
19 M3 **Burgas** Bulg.
67 E5 **Burgaw** U.S.A.
13 K2 **Burg bei Magdeburg** Ger.
13 J5 **Burgbernheim** Ger.
13 J2 **Burgdorf** Ger.
59 J4 **Burgeo** Can.
91 G5 **Burgersdorp** S. Africa
91 J2 **Burgersfort** S. Africa
9 G7 **Burgess Hill** U.K.
13 H4 **Burghaun** Ger.
16 F6 **Burghausen** Ger.
10 E3 **Burghead** U.K.
12 B3 **Burgh-Haamstede** Neth.
18 F6 **Burgio, Serra di** *h. Sicily* Italy
13 L5 **Burglengenfeld** Ger.
15 E1 **Burgos** Spain
13 L4 **Burgstädt** Ger.
7 Q8 **Burgsvik** Sweden
Burgundy *reg. see* **Bourgogne**
36 B3 **Burhan Budai Shan** *mts* China
19 M5 **Burhaniye** Turkey
34 D5 **Burhanpur** India
35 E5 **Burhar-Dhanpuri** India
35 F4 **Burhi Gandak** *r.* India
43 B3 **Burias** *i.* Phil.
35 H4 **Buri Dihing** *r.* India
35 E4 **Buri Gandak** *r.* Nepal
59 J4 **Burin Peninsula** Can.
44 B2 **Buriram** Thai.
79 K5 **Buriti Bravo** Brazil
82 C1 **Buritis** Brazil
31 G4 **Burj** Pak.
92 A3 **Burke I.** *i.* Ant.
51 C6 **Burke Pass** N.Z.
48 D3 **Burketown** Austr.
85 C4 **Burkina** *country* Africa
69 H3 **Burk's Falls** Can.
62 D3 **Burley** U.S.A.
69 H4 **Burlington** Can.
64 C4 **Burlington** *CO* U.S.A.
68 B5 **Burlington** *IA* U.S.A.
68 D5 **Burlington** *IN* U.S.A.
71 J2 **Burlington** *ME* U.S.A.
71 G2 **Burlington** *VT* U.S.A.
68 C4 **Burlington** *WV* U.S.A.
Burma *country see* **Myanmar**
65 D6 **Burnet** U.S.A.
62 B3 **Burney** U.S.A.
71 J2 **Burnham** U.S.A.
48 E6 **Burnie** Austr.
8 G3 **Burniston** U.K.
8 E4 **Burnley** U.K.
62 C3 **Burns** U.S.A.
57 H1 **Burnside** *r.* Can.
54 F4 **Burns Lake** Can.
70 C5 **Burnsville Lake** *l.* U.S.A.
67 F7 **Burnt Ground** Bahamas
10 E4 **Burntisland** U.K.
59 H3 **Burnt Lake** *l.* Can.
57 K3 **Burntwood** *r.* Can.
57 J3 **Burnt Wood Lake** *l.* Can.
50 D3 **Buronga** Austr.
24 K5 **Burqin** China
28 G5 **Burqu'** Jordan
50 B2 **Burra** Austr.
10 □ **Burravoe** U.K.
10 F2 **Burray** *i.* U.K.
19 J4 **Burrel** Albania
50 G2 **Burrendong Reservoir** Austr.
50 H3 **Burrewarra Pt** *pt* Austr.
15 F3 **Burriana** Spain
50 G3 **Burrinjuck** Austr.
50 G3 **Burrinjuck Reservoir** Austr.
70 B5 **Burr Oak Reservoir** U.S.A.
74 D3 **Burro, Serranías del** *mts* Mex.
10 D6 **Burrow Head** *hd* U.K.
73 G2 **Burrville** U.S.A.
28 B1 **Bursa** Turkey
87 F2 **Bûr Safâga** Egypt
Bûr Sa'îd *see* **Port Said**
13 G5 **Bürstadt** Ger.
Būr Sudan *see* **Port Sudan**
50 C2 **Burta** Austr.
68 E3 **Burt Lake** *l.* U.S.A.
69 F4 **Burton** U.S.A.
58 E3 **Burton, Lac** *l.* Can.
11 C3 **Burtonport** Rep. of Ireland
9 F5 **Burton upon Trent** U.K.
6 R4 **Burträsk** Sweden
71 K1 **Burtts Corner** Can.
50 D2 **Burtundy** Austr.
37 E7 **Buru** *i.* Indon.
28 C6 **Burullus, Bahra el** *lag.* Egypt
85 F6 **Burundi** *country* Africa
88 C4 **Bururi** Burundi
56 B2 **Burwash Landing** Can.
10 F2 **Burwick** U.K.
21 E5 **Buryn'** Ukr.
9 H5 **Bury St Edmunds** U.K.
34 C2 **Burzil Pass** Jammu and Kashmir
88 C4 **Busanga** Congo(Zaire)
11 E2 **Bush** *r.* U.K.
30 C4 **Būshehr** Iran
35 E2 **Bushêngcaka** China
88 D4 **Bushenyi** Uganda
Bushire *see* **Būshehr**
11 E2 **Bushmills** U.K.
68 B5 **Bushnell** U.S.A.
88 C3 **Businga** Congo(Zaire)
44 □ **Busing, P.** *i.* Sing.
28 F5 **Buşrá ash Shām** Syria
48 B5 **Busselton** Austr.
12 D2 **Bussum** Neth.
65 C7 **Bustamante** Mex.
18 C2 **Busto Arsizio** Italy
43 A3 **Busuanga** Phil.
43 A3 **Busuanga** *i.* Phil.
88 C3 **Buta** Congo(Zaire)
44 A4 **Butang Group** *is* Thai.
83 C3 **Buta Ranquil** Arg.
88 C4 **Butare** Rwanda
94 G5 **Butaritari** *i.* Pac. Oc.
50 A2 **Bute** Austr.
10 C5 **Bute** *i.* U.K.
56 D4 **Butedale** Can.
56 D4 **Bute In.** *in.* Can.
10 C5 **Bute, Sound of** *chan.* U.K.
91 H4 **Butha Buthe** Lesotho
13 G1 **Butjadingen** *reg.* Ger.
68 E5 **Butler** *IN* U.S.A.
70 D4 **Butler** *PA* U.S.A.
11 D3 **Butlers Bridge** Rep. of Ireland
37 E7 **Buton** *i.* Indon.
13 L1 **Bützow** Ger.
62 D2 **Butte** U.S.A.
13 K3 **Buttelstedt** Ger.
72 B1 **Butte Meadows** U.S.A.
45 B1 **Butterworth** Malaysia
91 H6 **Butterworth** S. Africa
11 C5 **Buttevant** Rep. of Ireland
56 D5 **Buttle L.** *l.* Can.
10 B2 **Butt of Lewis** *hd* U.K.
55 J4 **Button Bay** *b.* Can.
72 C4 **Buttonwillow** U.S.A.
43 C4 **Butuan** Phil.
39 B5 **Butuo** China
21 G5 **Buturlinovka** Rus. Fed.
35 E4 **Butwal** Nepal
13 G4 **Butzbach** Ger.
88 E3 **Buulobarde** Somalia
88 E4 **Buur Gaabo** Somalia
88 E3 **Buurhabaka** Somalia
35 F4 **Buxar** India
13 H1 **Buxtehude** Ger.
9 F4 **Buxton** U.K.
20 G3 **Buy** Rus. Fed.
68 A1 **Buyck** U.S.A.
21 H7 **Buynaksk** Rus. Fed.
Büyük Ağri *mt see* **Ararat, Mt**
28 A3 **Büyükmenderes** *r.* Turkey
42 B3 **Buyun Shan** *mt* China
12 C5 **Buzancy** France
19 M2 **Buzău** Romania
89 D5 **Búzi** Moz.
24 G4 **Buzuluk** Rus. Fed.
21 G5 **Buzuluk** *r.* Rus. Fed.
71 H4 **Buzzards Bay** *b.* U.S.A.
35 G4 **Byakar** Bhutan
19 L3 **Byala** Bulg.
19 K3 **Byala Slatina** Bulg.
17 O4 **Byalynichy** Belarus
54 H2 **Byam Martin I.** *i.* Can.
20 D4 **Byarezina** *r.* Belarus
20 C4 **Byaroza** Belarus
28 E4 **Byblos** Lebanon
16 J4 **Bydgoszcz** Pol.
20 D4 **Byerazino** Belarus
62 F4 **Byers** U.S.A.
17 O3 **Byeshankovichy** Belarus
7 K7 **Bygland** Norway
20 D4 **Bykhaw** Belarus
7 K7 **Bykle** Norway
55 L2 **Bylot Island** *i.* Can.
69 G3 **Byng Inlet** Can.
92 B5 **Byrd Gl.** *gl.* Ant.
7 K6 **Byrkjelo** Norway
68 C4 **Byron** *IL* U.S.A.
71 H2 **Byron** *ME* U.S.A.
49 F4 **Byron Bay** Austr.
25 M2 **Byrranga, Gory** *mts* Rus. Fed.
6 R4 **Byske** Sweden
25 P3 **Bytantay** *r.* Rus. Fed.
17 J5 **Bytom** Pol.
16 H3 **Bytów** Pol.
31 E2 **Byuzmeyin** Turkm.

C

80 E3 **Caacupé** Para.
82 A4 **Caagazú, Cordillera de** *h.* Para.
82 A4 **Caaguazú** Para.
82 A3 **Caarapó** Brazil
82 A4 **Caazapá** Para.
78 C6 **Caballas** Peru
78 D4 **Caballococha** Peru
43 B3 **Cabanatuan** Phil.
59 G4 **Cabano** Can.
88 E2 **Cabdul Qaadir** Somalia
82 A1 **Cabeceira Rio Manso** Brazil
79 M5 **Cabedelo** Brazil
15 D3 **Cabeza del Buey** Spain
78 F7 **Cabezas** Bol.
83 E3 **Cabildo** Arg.
81 C2 **Cabimas** Venez.
88 B4 **Cabinda** Angola
88 B4 **Cabinda** *div.* Angola
62 C1 **Cabinet Mts** *mts* U.S.A.
81 B3 **Cable Way** *pass* Col.
82 D3 **Cabo Frio** Brazil
82 E3 **Cabo Frio, Ilha do** *i.* Brazil
58 E4 **Cabonga, Réservoir** *resr* Can.
65 E4 **Cabool** U.S.A.
49 F4 **Caboolture** Austr.
79 H3 **Cabo Orange, Parque Nacional de** *nat. park* Brazil
78 C4 **Cabo Pantoja** Peru
74 B2 **Caborca** Mex.
69 G3 **Cabot Head** *pt* Can.
59 J4 **Cabot Strait** *str.* Can.
82 D2 **Cabral, Serra do** *mts* Brazil
29 L2 **Cäbrayıl** Azer.
15 H3 **Cabrera** *i.* Spain
15 C1 **Cabrera, Sierra de la** *mts* Spain
15 F3 **Cabriel** *r.* Spain
81 D3 **Cabruta** Venez.
43 B2 **Cabugao** Phil.
80 F3 **Caçador** Brazil
19 J3 **Čačak** Yugo.
83 G1 **Caçapava do Sul** Brazil
70 D5 **Cacapon** *r.* U.S.A.
81 B3 **Cácares** Col.
18 C4 **Caccia, Capo** *pt Sardinia* Italy
79 G7 **Cáceres** Brazil
15 C3 **Cáceres** Spain
62 D3 **Cache Peak** *summit* U.S.A.
86 A3 **Cacheu** Guinea-Bissau
80 C3 **Cachi** *r.* Arg.
79 H5 **Cachimbo, Serra do** *h.* Brazil
81 B3 **Cáchira** Col.
82 E1 **Cachoeira** Brazil
82 B2 **Cachoeira Alta** Brazil
83 G1 **Cachoeira do Sul** Brazil
82 E3 **Cachoeiro de Itapemirim** Brazil
86 A3 **Cacine** Guinea-Bissau
79 H3 **Caciporé, Cabo** *pt* Brazil
89 B5 **Cacolo** Angola
88 B4 **Cacongo** Angola
72 D3 **Cactus Range** *mts* U.S.A.
82 B2 **Caçu** Brazil
82 D1 **Caculé** Brazil
17 J6 **Čadca** Slovakia
13 H1 **Cadenberge** Ger.
43 B3 **Cadig Mountains** Phil.
69 H1 **Cadillac** *Que.* Can.
57 H5 **Cadillac** *Sask.* Can.
68 E3 **Cadillac** U.S.A.
43 B4 **Cadiz** Phil.
15 C4 **Cádiz** Spain
15 C4 **Cádiz, Golfo de** *g.* Spain
73 E4 **Cadiz Lake** *l.* U.S.A.
14 D2 **Caen** France
9 C4 **Caernarfon** U.K.
9 C4 **Caernarfon Bay** *b.* U.K.
9 D6 **Caerphilly** U.K.
70 B5 **Caesar Creek Lake** *l.* U.S.A.
28 E5 **Caesarea** Israel
82 D1 **Caetité** Brazil
80 C3 **Cafayate** Arg.
43 B4 **Cagayan** *i.* Phil.
43 B2 **Cagayan** *r.* Phil.
43 C4 **Cagayan de Oro** Phil.
43 B4 **Cagayan Islands** *is* Phil.
18 E3 **Cagli** Italy
18 C5 **Cagliari** *Sardinia* Italy
18 C5 **Cagliari, Golfo di** *b. Sardinia* Italy
81 B4 **Caguán** *r.* Col.
11 B6 **Caha** *h.* Rep. of Ireland
67 C5 **Cahaba** *r.* U.S.A.
11 B6 **Caha Mts** *h.* Rep. of Ireland
11 A6 **Cahermore** Rep. of Ireland
11 D5 **Cahir** Rep. of Ireland
11 A6 **Cahirciveen** Rep. of Ireland
89 D5 **Cahora Bassa, Lago de** *resr* Moz.
11 E5 **Cahore Point** *pt* Rep. of Ireland
14 E4 **Cahors** France
78 C5 **Cahuapanas** Peru
21 D6 **Cahul** Moldova
89 D5 **Caia** Moz.
79 G6 **Caiabis, Serra dos** *h.* Brazil
89 C5 **Caianda** Angola
82 B2 **Caiapó** *r.* Brazil
82 B2 **Caiapônia** Brazil
82 B2 **Caiapó, Serra do** *mts* Brazil
75 J4 **Caibarién** Cuba
44 C3 **Cai Be** Vietnam
81 D3 **Caicara** Venez.
75 K4 **Caicos Is** *is* Turks and Caicos Is
83 B1 **Caimanes** Chile
43 A3 **Caiman Point** *pt* Phil.
15 F2 **Caimodorro** *mt* Spain
44 C3 **Cai Nước** Vietnam
10 E3 **Cairn Gorm** *mt* U.K.
10 E3 **Cairngorm Mountains** U.K.
10 C6 **Cairnryan** U.K.
48 E3 **Cairns** Austr.
10 E3 **Cairn Toul** *mt* U.K.
87 F1 **Cairo** Egypt
67 C6 **Cairo** U.S.A.
18 C2 **Cairo Montenotte** Italy
89 B5 **Caiundo** Angola
78 C5 **Cajamarca** Peru
43 B3 **Cajidiocan** Phil.
18 G1 **Čakovec** Croatia
28 B2 **Çal** Turkey
91 G5 **Cala** S. Africa
86 C4 **Calabar** Nigeria
69 J3 **Calabogie** Can.
81 D2 **Calabozo** Venez.
19 K3 **Calafat** Romania
80 B8 **Calafate** Arg.
43 B3 **Calagua Islands** *is* Phil.
15 F1 **Calahorra** Spain
89 B5 **Calai** Angola
14 E1 **Calais** France
71 K2 **Calais** U.S.A.
78 F5 **Calama** Brazil
80 C2 **Calama** Chile
81 B2 **Calamar** *Bolívar* Col.
81 B4 **Calamar** *Guaviare* Col.
43 A4 **Calamian Group** *is* Phil.
15 F2 **Calamocha** Spain
89 B4 **Calandula** Angola
87 E2 **Calanscio Sand Sea** *des.* Libya
43 B3 **Calapan** Phil.
19 M2 **Călărași** Romania
15 F2 **Calatayud** Spain
43 B3 **Calauag** Phil.
43 B3 **Calavite, Cape** *pt* Phil.
43 A3 **Calawit** *i.* Phil.
43 B2 **Calayan** *i.* Phil.
43 C3 **Calbayog** Phil.
13 K3 **Calbe (Saale)** Ger.
43 C4 **Calbiga** Phil.
83 B4 **Calbuco** Chile
79 L5 **Calcanhar, Ponta do** *pt* Brazil
65 E6 **Calcasieu L.** *l.* U.S.A.
79 H3 **Calçoene** Brazil
35 G5 **Calcutta** India
15 B3 **Caldas da Rainha** Port.
82 C2 **Caldas Novas** Brazil
13 H3 **Calden** Ger.
80 B3 **Caldera** Chile
29 J2 **Çaldıran** Turkey
62 C3 **Caldwell** U.S.A.
70 D3 **Caledon** Can.
90 C7 **Caledon** S. Africa
91 G5 **Caledon** *r.* Lesotho/S. Africa
69 H4 **Caledonia** Can.
68 B4 **Caledonia** U.S.A.
80 C7 **Caleta Olivia** Arg.
73 E5 **Calexico** U.S.A.
8 C3 **Calf of Man** *i.* U.K.
56 G4 **Calgary** Can.
67 C5 **Calhoun** U.S.A.
81 A4 **Cali** Col.
43 C4 **Calicoan** *i.* Phil.
33 A4 **Calicut** India
72 C4 **Caliente** *CA* U.S.A.
73 E3 **Caliente** *NV* U.S.A.
72 B3 **California** *div.* U.S.A.
72 B3 **California Aqueduct** *canal* U.S.A.
74 B2 **California, Golfo de** *g.* Mex.
72 C4 **California Hot Springs** U.S.A.
29 M2 **Cälilabad** Azer.
63 D5 **Calipatria** U.S.A.
72 A2 **Calistoga** U.S.A.
90 D6 **Calitzdorp** S. Africa
72 D2 **Callaghan, Mt** *mt* U.S.A.
67 D6 **Callahan** U.S.A.
11 D5 **Callan** Rep. of Ireland
69 H2 **Callander** Can.
10 D4 **Callander** U.K.
78 C6 **Callao** Peru
73 F2 **Callao** U.S.A.
71 F4 **Callicoon** U.S.A.
9 C7 **Callington** U.K.
69 G2 **Callum** Can.
56 G4 **Calmar** Can.
68 B4 **Calmar** U.S.A.
73 E4 **Cal-Nev-Ari** U.S.A.
67 D7 **Caloosahatchee** *r.* U.S.A.
72 B2 **Calpine** U.S.A.
18 F6 **Caltanissetta** *Sicily* Italy
68 C2 **Calumet** U.S.A.
89 B5 **Calunga** Angola
89 B5 **Caluquembe** Angola
43 B4 **Calusa** *i.* Phil.
88 F2 **Caluula** Somalia
73 G5 **Calva** U.S.A.
56 D4 **Calvert I.** *i.* Can.
18 C3 **Calvi** *Corsica* France
15 H3 **Calvià** Spain
90 C5 **Calvinia** S. Africa
18 F4 **Calvo, Monte** *mt* Italy
9 H5 **Cam** *r.* U.K.
82 E1 **Camaçari** Brazil
72 B2 **Camache Reservoir** U.S.A.
89 B5 **Camacuio** Angola
89 B5 **Camacupa** Angola
81 D2 **Camaguán** Venez.
75 J4 **Camagüey** Cuba
75 J4 **Camagüey, Arch. de** *is* Cuba
45 B1 **Camah, Gunung** *mt* Malaysia
Çamalan *see* **Gülek**
78 D7 **Camana** Peru
89 C5 **Camanongue** Angola
82 B2 **Camapuã** Brazil
83 G1 **Camaquã** Brazil
83 G1 **Camaquã** *r.* Brazil
28 E3 **Çamardı** Turkey
65 D7 **Camargo** Mex.
80 C6 **Camarones** Arg.
80 C6 **Camarones, Bahía** *b.* Arg.
62 B2 **Camas** U.S.A.
44 C3 **Ca Mau** Vietnam
Cambay *see* **Khambhat**
Cambay, Gulf of *g. see* **Khambhat, Gulf of**
9 G6 **Camberley** U.K.
23 K8 **Cambodia** *country* Asia
9 B7 **Camborne** U.K.
14 F1 **Cambrai** France
72 B4 **Cambria** U.S.A.
9 D5 **Cambrian Mountains** *reg.* U.K.
69 G4 **Cambridge** Can.
51 E2 **Cambridge** N.Z.
9 H5 **Cambridge** U.K.
68 B5 **Cambridge** *IL* U.S.A.
71 H3 **Cambridge** *MA* U.S.A.
71 E5 **Cambridge** *MD* U.S.A.
64 E2 **Cambridge** *MN* U.S.A.
71 G3 **Cambridge** *NY* U.S.A.
70 C4 **Cambridge** *OH* U.S.A.
59 G2 **Cambrien, Lac** *l.* Can.
50 H3 **Camden** Austr.
67 C5 **Camden** *AL* U.S.A.
65 E5 **Camden** *AR* U.S.A.
71 J2 **Camden** *ME* U.S.A.
71 F5 **Camden** *NJ* U.S.A.
71 F3 **Camden** *NY* U.S.A.
67 D5 **Camden** *SC* U.S.A.
80 B8 **Camden, Isla** *i.* Chile
89 C5 **Cameia, Parque Nacional da** *nat. park* Angola
73 G4 **Cameron** *AZ* U.S.A.
65 E6 **Cameron** *LA* U.S.A.
64 E4 **Cameron** *MO* U.S.A.
65 D6 **Cameron** *TX* U.S.A.
68 B3 **Cameron** *WV* U.S.A.
44 B4 **Cameron Highlands** Malaysia
56 F3 **Cameron Hills** *h.* Can.
72 B2 **Cameron Park** U.S.A.
85 E5 **Cameroon** *country* Africa
86 C4 **Cameroun, Mt** *mt* Cameroon
79 J4 **Cametá** Brazil
43 B2 **Camiguin** *i.* Phil.
43 C4 **Camiguin** *i.* Phil.
43 B3 **Camiling** Phil.
67 C6 **Camilla** U.S.A.
78 F8 **Camiri** Bol.
79 K4 **Camocim** Brazil
48 D3 **Camooweal** Austr.
43 C4 **Camotes Sea** *g.* Phil.
83 E2 **Campana** Arg.
81 B4 **Campana, Co** *h.* Col.
80 A7 **Campana, I.** *i.* Chile
83 B2 **Campanario** *mt* Arg./Chile
56 D4 **Campania I.** *i.* Can.
90 E4 **Campbell** S. Africa
51 E4 **Campbell, Cape** *c.* N.Z.
46 H9 **Campbell Island** *i.* N.Z.
56 D4 **Campbell River** Can.
69 J3 **Campbells Bay** Can.
66 C4 **Campbellsville** U.S.A.
59 G4 **Campbellton** Can.
10 C5 **Campbeltown** U.K.
74 F5 **Campeche** Mex.
74 F5 **Campeche, Bahía de** *g.* Mex.
50 D5 **Camperdown** Austr.
19 L2 **Câmpina** Romania
79 L5 **Campina Grande** Brazil
82 C3 **Campinas** Brazil
82 C2 **Campina Verde** Brazil
86 C4 **Campo** Cameroon
81 B4 **Campoalegre** Col.
18 F4 **Campobasso** Italy
82 D3 **Campo Belo** Brazil
79 H6 **Campo de Diauarum** Brazil
82 C2 **Campo Florido** Brazil
80 D3 **Campo Gallo** Arg.
82 A3 **Campo Grande** Brazil
79 K4 **Campo Maior** Brazil
15 C3 **Campo Maior** Port.
82 B4 **Campo Mourão** Brazil
82 E3 **Campos** Brazil
82 C2 **Campos Altos** Brazil
82 D3 **Campos do Jordão** Brazil
82 B4 **Campos Eré** *reg.* Brazil
10 D4 **Campsie Fells** *h.* U.K.
70 B6 **Campton** *KY* U.S.A.
71 H3 **Campton** *NH* U.S.A.
19 L2 **Câmpulung** Romania
17 M7 **Câmpulung Moldovenesc** Romania
73 G4 **Camp Verde** U.S.A.
44 D3 **Cam Ranh** Vietnam
56 G4 **Camrose** Can.
9 B6 **Camrose** U.K.
57 G2 **Camsell Lake** *l.* Can.
57 H3 **Camsell Portage** Can.
21 C7 **Çan** Turkey
71 G3 **Canaan** U.S.A.
53 E4 **Canada** N. America
83 E2 **Cañada de Gómez** Arg.
71 H2 **Canada Falls Lake** *l.* U.S.A.
65 C5 **Canadian** *r.* U.S.A.
81 E3 **Canaima, Parque Nacional** *nat. park* Venez.
71 F3 **Canajoharie** U.S.A.
21 C7 **Çanakkale** Turkey
Çanakkale Boğazı *str. see* **Dardanelles**
83 C2 **Canalejas** Arg.
70 E3 **Canandaigua** U.S.A.
70 E3 **Canandaigua Lake** *l.* U.S.A.
74 B2 **Cananea** Mex.
59 H2 **Cananée, Lac** *l.* Can.
82 C4 **Cananéia** Brazil
81 C4 **Canapiare, Co** *h.* Col.
78 C4 **Cañar** Ecuador
Canarias, Islas *is see* **Canary Islands**
96 G4 **Canary Basin** *sea feature* Atl. Ocean
84 A3 **Canary Islands** *is* Atlantic Ocean
71 F3 **Canastota** U.S.A.
82 C2 **Canastra, Serra da** *mts* Brazil
67 D6 **Canaveral, Cape** *c.* U.S.A.
15 E2 **Cañaveras** Spain
82 E1 **Canavieiras** Brazil
50 F1 **Canbelego** Austr.
50 G3 **Canberra** Austr.
62 B3 **Canby** *CA* U.S.A.
64 D2 **Canby** *MN* U.S.A.
74 G4 **Cancún** Mex.
63 F6 **Candelaria** *Chihuahua* Mex.
15 D2 **Candeleda** Spain
50 G4 **Candelo** Austr.
79 J4 **Cândido Mendes** Brazil
28 D1 **Çandır** Turkey
57 H4 **Candle Lake** Can.
57 H4 **Candle Lake** *l.* Can.
92 C1 **Candlemas I.** *i.* Atl. Ocean
71 G4 **Candlewood, Lake** *l.* U.S.A.
64 D1 **Cando** U.S.A.
43 B2 **Candon** Phil.
83 B1 **Canela Baja** Chile
83 F2 **Canelones** Uru.
83 B3 **Cañete** Chile
15 F2 **Cañete** Spain
78 D6 **Cangallo** Peru
89 B5 **Cangamba** Angola
15 C1 **Cangas del Narcea** Spain
90 E6 **Cango Caves** *caves* S. Africa
79 L5 **Canguaretama** Brazil
83 G1 **Canguçu** Brazil
83 G1 **Canguçu, Sa do** *h.* Brazil
39 D6 **Cangwu** China
38 E2 **Cangzhou** China
59 G3 **Caniapiscau** Can.
59 G2 **Caniapiscau** *r.* Can.
59 G3 **Caniapiscau, Lac** *l.* Can.
18 E6 **Canicattì** *Sicily* Italy
56 E4 **Canim Lake** Can.
56 E4 **Canim Lake** *l.* Can.
79 L4 **Canindé** Brazil
79 K5 **Canindé** *r.* Brazil
10 C2 **Canisp** *h.* U.K.
70 E3 **Canisteo** U.S.A.
70 E3 **Canisteo** *r.* U.S.A.
28 D1 **Çankırı** Turkey
43 B4 **Canlaon** Phil.
56 F4 **Canmore** Can.
10 B3 **Canna** *i.* U.K.
33 A4 **Cannanore** India
33 A4 **Cannanore Islands** *is* India
14 H5 **Cannes** France
9 E5 **Cannock** U.K.
50 G4 **Cann River** Austr.
81 E2 **Caño Araguao** *r.* Venez.
80 F3 **Canõas** Brazil
57 H3 **Canoe L.** *l.* Can.
82 B4 **Canoinhas** Brazil
81 E2 **Caño Macareo** *r.* Venez.
81 E2 **Caño Manamo** *r.* Venez.
81 E2 **Caño Mariusa** *r.* Venez.
63 F4 **Canon City** U.S.A.
50 C2 **Canopus** Austr.
57 J4 **Canora** Can.
50 G2 **Canowindra** Austr.
59 H4 **Canso, C.** *hd* Can.
15 D1 **Cantábrica, Cordillera** *mts* Spain
Cantábrico, Mar *sea see* **Biscay, Bay of**
83 C2 **Cantantal** Arg.
81 D2 **Cantaura** Venez.
71 K2 **Canterbury** Can.
9 J6 **Canterbury** U.K.
51 C6 **Canterbury Bight** *b.* N.Z.
51 C5 **Canterbury Plains** *plain* N.Z.
44 C3 **Cân Thơ** Vietnam
43 C4 **Cantilan** Phil.
79 K5 **Canto do Buriti** Brazil
Canton *see* **Guangzhou**
68 B5 **Canton** *IL* U.S.A.
71 H2 **Canton** *ME* U.S.A.
68 B5 **Canton** *MO* U.S.A.
65 F5 **Canton** *MS* U.S.A.
71 F2 **Canton** *NY* U.S.A.
70 C4 **Canton** *OH* U.S.A.
70 E4 **Canton** *PA* U.S.A.
82 B4 **Cantu** *r.* Brazil
82 B4 **Cantu, Serra do** *h.* Brazil
83 E2 **Cañuelas** Arg.
79 G4 **Canumã** Brazil
78 F5 **Canutama** Brazil
51 D4 **Canvastown** N.Z.
9 H6 **Canvey Island** U.K.
65 C5 **Canyon** U.S.A.
62 C2 **Canyon City** U.S.A.
73 H3 **Canyon de Chelly National Monument** *res.* U.S.A.
62 D2 **Canyon Ferry L.** *l.* U.S.A.
73 H2 **Canyonlands National Park** U.S.A.
56 D2 **Canyon Ranges** *mts* Can.
62 B3 **Canyonville** U.S.A.
42 C3 **Cao** *r.* China
39 C6 **Cao Băng** Vietnam
44 D2 **Cao Nguyên Đắc Lắc** *plat.* Vietnam
42 C2 **Caoshi** China
38 E3 **Cao Xian** China
43 B5 **Cap** *i.* Phil.
81 D3 **Capanaparo** *r.* Venez.
79 J4 **Capanema** Brazil
82 B4 **Capanema** *r.* Brazil
82 C4 **Capão Bonito** Brazil
81 C3 **Caparo** *r.* Venez.
81 C4 **Caparro, Co** *h.* Brazil
43 B3 **Capas** Phil.
59 H4 **Cap-aux-Meules** Can.
59 F4 **Cap-de-la-Madeleine** Can.
48 E6 **Cape Barren Island** *i.* Austr.
96 K8 **Cape Basin** *sea feature* Atl. Ocean
59 H4 **Cape Breton Highlands Nat. Park** *nat. park* Can.
59 H4 **Cape Breton Island** *i.* Can.

59 J3 Cape Charles Can.
71 E6 Cape Charles U.S.A.
86 B4 Cape Coast Ghana
71 H4 Cape Cod Bay b. U.S.A.
71 J4 Cape Cod National Seashore res. U.S.A.
67 D7 Cape Coral U.S.A.
69 G3 Cape Croker Can.
55 L3 Cape Dorset Can.
67 E5 Cape Fear r. U.S.A.
65 F4 Cape Girardeau U.S.A.
94 D5 Cape Johnson Depth depth Pac. Oc.
82 D2 Capelinha Brazil
12 C3 Capelle aan de IJssel Neth.
71 F5 Cape May U.S.A.
71 F5 Cape May Court House U.S.A.
71 F5 Cape May Pt pt U.S.A.
89 B4 Capenda-Camulemba Angola
55 M5 Cape Sable c. Can.
59 J4 Cape St George Can.
59 H4 Cape Tormentine Can.
90 C6 Cape Town S. Africa
3 □ Cape Verde country Africa
96 G5 Cape Verde Basin sea feature Atl. Ocean
96 F5 Cape Verde Fracture sea feature Atl. Ocean
96 H4 Cape Verde Plateau sea feature Atl. Ocean
71 E2 Cape Vincent U.S.A.
48 E3 Cape York Peninsula Austr.
75 K5 Cap-Haïtien Haiti
79 J4 Capim r. Brazil
92 B2 Capitán Arturo Prat Chile Base Ant.
82 A3 Capitán Bado Para.
63 F5 Capitan Peak mt U.S.A.
73 G2 Capitol Reef National Park U.S.A.
18 G3 Čapljina Bos.-Herz.
18 F5 Capo d'Orlando Sicily Italy
11 D5 Cappoquin Rep. of Ireland
18 C3 Capraia, Isola di i. Italy
48 F4 Capricorn Channel Austr.
18 F4 Capri, Isola di i. Italy
89 C5 Caprivi Strip reg. Namibia
Cap St Jacques see Vung Tau
72 □2 Captain Cook U.S.A.
50 G3 Captain's Flat Austr.
70 C5 Captina r. U.S.A.
43 C3 Capul i. Phil.
78 C3 Caquetá r. Col.
81 B3 Cáqueza Col.
43 B3 Carabao i. Phil.
19 L2 Caracal Romania
81 E4 Caracarai Brazil
81 D2 Caracas Venez.
79 K5 Caracol Brazil
43 C5 Caraga Phil.
83 F2 Caraguatá r. Uru.
82 D3 Caraguatatuba Brazil
83 B3 Carahue Chile
82 E2 Caraí Brazil
82 D3 Carandaí Brazil
82 D3 Carangola Brazil
19 K2 Caransebeş Romania
59 H4 Caraquet Can.
81 B3 Carare r. Col.
75 H5 Caratasca, Laguna lag. Honduras
82 D2 Caratinga Brazil
78 E4 Carauari Brazil
Carauná mt see Grande, Serra
15 F3 Caravaca de la Cruz Spain
82 E2 Caravelas Brazil
80 F3 Carazinho Brazil
64 D1 Carberry Can.
18 C5 Carbonara, Capo pt Sardinia Italy
66 B4 Carbondale IL U.S.A.
71 F4 Carbondale PA U.S.A.
59 K4 Carbonear Can.
18 C5 Carbonia Sardinia Italy
82 D2 Carbonita Brazil
15 F3 Carcaixent Spain
43 B4 Carcar Phil.
83 E2 Carcaraña r. Arg.
14 F5 Carcassonne France
56 C2 Carcross Can.
48 B4 Cardabia Austr.
33 B4 Cardamon Hills mts India
74 E4 Cárdenas Mex.
80 B7 Cardiel, L. l. Arg.
9 D6 Cardiff U.K.
9 C5 Cardigan U.K.
9 C5 Cardigan Bay b. U.K.
71 F2 Cardinal Can.
70 B4 Cardington U.S.A.
83 F2 Cardona Uru.
82 C4 Cardoso, Ilha do i. Brazil
51 B6 Cardrona N.Z.
56 G5 Cardston Can.
17 L7 Carei Romania
14 D2 Carentan France
70 B4 Carey U.S.A.
48 C4 Carey, L. salt flat Austr.
57 J2 Carey Lake l. Can.
93 J5 Cargados Carajos is Mauritius
14 C2 Carhaix-Plouguer France
83 D3 Carhué Arg.
82 E3 Cariacica Brazil
81 E2 Cariaco Venez.
52 J8 Caribbean Sea sea Atl. Ocean
56 E4 Cariboo Mts mts Can.
71 K1 Caribou U.S.A.
57 K3 Caribou r. Man. Can.
56 D2 Caribou r. N.W.T. Can.
68 E2 Caribou I. i. Can.
55 K4 Caribou Lake l. Can.
56 F3 Caribou Mountains Can.
43 C4 Carigara Phil.
12 D5 Carignan France
15 F2 Cariñena Spain
82 D1 Carinhanha Brazil
82 D1 Carinhanha r. Brazil
81 E2 Caripe Venez.
81 E2 Caripito Venez.
11 D3 Cark Mountain h. Rep. of Ireland
69 J3 Carleton Place Can.
91 G3 Carletonville S. Africa
62 C3 Carlin U.S.A.
11 E3 Carlingford Lough in. Rep. of Ireland/U.K.
8 E3 Carlisle U.K.
70 A5 Carlisle KY U.S.A.
70 E4 Carlisle PA U.S.A.
14 E5 Carlit, Pic mt France
83 E2 Carlos Casares Arg.
82 E2 Carlos Chagas Brazil
11 E5 Carlow Rep. of Ireland
10 B2 Carloway U.K.
72 D5 Carlsbad CA U.S.A.
63 F5 Carlsbad NM U.S.A.
65 C6 Carlsbad TX U.S.A.
63 F5 Carlsbad Caverns Nat. Park U.S.A.
93 J3 Carlsberg Ridge sea feature Ind. Ocean
92 B3 Carlson In. in Ant.
10 E5 Carluke U.K.
57 J5 Carlyle Can.
56 B2 Carmacks Can.
18 B2 Carmagnola Italy
57 K5 Carman Can.
9 C6 Carmarthen U.K.
9 C6 Carmarthen Bay b. U.K.
14 F4 Carmaux France
71 J2 Carmel U.S.A.
9 C4 Carmel Head hd U.K.
83 F2 Carmelo Uru.
81 B2 Carmen Col.
43 C4 Carmen Phil.
73 G6 Carmen U.S.A.
74 B3 Carmen i. Mex.
83 D4 Carmen de Patagones Arg.
83 C2 Carmensa Arg.
66 B4 Carmi U.S.A.
72 B2 Carmichael U.S.A.
15 D4 Carmona Spain
14 C3 Carnac France
90 E5 Carnarvon S. Africa
11 D2 Carndonagh Rep. of Ireland
9 D4 Carnedd Llywelyn mt U.K.
48 C4 Carnegie, L. salt flat Austr.
95 O6 Carnegie Ridge sea feature Pac. Oc.
10 C3 Carn Eighe mt U.K.
68 D3 Carney U.S.A.
92 A3 Carney I. i. Ant.
8 E3 Carnforth U.K.
11 F3 Carnlough U.K.
10 C3 Carn nan Gabhar mt U.K.
88 B3 Carnot C.A.R.
48 D5 Carnot, C. hd Austr.
10 F4 Carnoustie U.K.
11 E5 Carnsore Point pt Rep. of Ireland
10 E5 Carnwath U.K.
57 H4 Carnwood Can.
69 F4 Caro U.S.A.
67 D7 Carol City U.S.A.
79 J5 Carolina Brazil
91 J3 Carolina S. Africa
46 M4 Caroline Island i. Kiribati
46 E3 Caroline Islands is Pac. Oc.
51 A6 Caroline Pk summit N.Z.
90 B4 Carolusberg S. Africa
81 E2 Caroní r. Venez.
81 C2 Carora Venez.
73 E3 Carp U.S.A.
4 F4 Carpathian Mountains Romania/Ukr.
Carpaţii Meridionali mts see Transylvanian Alps
48 D3 Carpentaria, Gulf of g. Austr.
14 G4 Carpentras France
18 D2 Carpi Italy
79 L5 Carpina Brazil
72 C4 Carpinteria U.S.A.
57 J5 Carpio U.S.A.
56 E4 Carp Lake Prov. Park res. Can.
71 H2 Carrabassett Valley U.S.A.
67 C6 Carrabelle U.S.A.
81 B2 Carraipía Col.
11 B4 Carra, Lough l. Rep. of Ireland
11 B6 Carran h. Rep. of Ireland
11 B6 Carrantuohill mt Rep. of Ireland
83 B2 Carranza, C. pt Chile
74 D3 Carranza, Presa V. l. Mex.
81 E3 Carrao r. Venez.
18 D2 Carrara Italy
50 E3 Carrathool Austr.
83 C3 Carrero, Co mt Arg.
81 E1 Carriacou i. Grenada
10 D5 Carrick reg. U.K.
11 F3 Carrickfergus U.K.
11 E4 Carrickmacross Rep. of Ireland
11 C4 Carrick-on-Shannon Rep. of Ireland
11 D5 Carrick-on-Suir Rep. of Ireland
50 B2 Carrieton Austr.
11 D4 Carrigallen Rep. of Ireland
11 C6 Carrigtwohill Rep. of Ireland
83 C4 Carri Lafquén, L. l. Arg.
64 D2 Carrington U.S.A.
80 B3 Carrizal Bajo Chile
73 G4 Carrizo AZ U.S.A.
73 H4 Carrizo AZ U.S.A.
72 D5 Carrizo Cr. r. U.S.A.
65 D6 Carrizo Springs U.S.A.
63 F5 Carrizozo U.S.A.
64 E3 Carroll U.S.A.
67 C5 Carrollton GA U.S.A.
66 C4 Carrollton KY U.S.A.
64 E4 Carrollton MO U.S.A.
70 C4 Carrollton OH U.S.A.
57 J4 Carrot r. Can.
57 J4 Carrot River Can.
8 B3 Carrowdore U.K.
11 B3 Carrowmore Lake l. Rep. of Ireland
71 F2 Carry Falls Reservoir U.S.A.
28 F1 Çarşamba Turkey
68 E4 Carson City MI U.S.A.
72 C2 Carson City NV U.S.A.
72 C2 Carson Lake l. U.S.A.
72 C2 Carson Sink l. U.S.A.
69 F4 Carsonville U.S.A.
83 B2 Cartagena Chile
81 B2 Cartagena Col.
15 F4 Cartagena Spain
81 B3 Cartago Col.
75 H7 Cartago Costa Rica
67 C5 Cartersville U.S.A.
68 B5 Carthage IL U.S.A.
65 E4 Carthage MO U.S.A.
71 F2 Carthage NY U.S.A.
65 E5 Carthage TX U.S.A.
69 G2 Cartier Can.
8 E3 Cartmel U.K.
59 J3 Cartwright Can.
79 L5 Caruarú Brazil
81 E2 Carúpano Venez.
72 D2 Carvers U.S.A.
12 A4 Carvin France
67 E5 Cary U.S.A.
86 B1 Casablanca Morocco
82 C3 Casa Branca Brazil
63 E6 Casa de Janos Mex.
73 G5 Casa Grande U.S.A.
73 G5 Casa Grande National Monument res. U.S.A.
18 C2 Casale Monferrato Italy
18 D2 Casalmaggiore Italy
81 C3 Casanare r. Col.
19 H4 Casarano Italy
68 B4 Cascade IA U.S.A.
62 C2 Cascade ID U.S.A.
62 E2 Cascade MT U.S.A.
51 B6 Cascade r. N.Z.
51 B6 Cascade Pt pt N.Z.
62 B3 Cascade Range mts U.S.A.
62 D2 Cascade Res. resr U.S.A.
15 B3 Cascais Port.
82 B4 Cascavel Brazil
71 J3 Casco Bay b. U.S.A.
18 F4 Caserta Italy
69 F4 Caseville U.S.A.
92 C6 Casey Austr. Base Ant.
92 D4 Casey Bay b. Ant.
11 D5 Cashel Rep. of Ireland
68 B4 Cashton U.S.A.
81 C2 Casigua Falcón Venez.
81 B2 Casigua Zulia Venez.
43 B2 Casiguran Phil.
83 E2 Casilda Arg.
49 F4 Casino Austr.
81 D4 Casiquiare, Canal r. Venez.
78 C5 Casma Peru
68 E4 Casnovia U.S.A.
72 A2 Caspar U.S.A.
15 F2 Caspe Spain
62 F3 Casper U.S.A.
Caspian Lowland lowland see Prikaspiyskaya Nizmennost'
22 B5 Caspian Sea sea Asia/Europe
70 D5 Cass U.S.A.
69 F4 Cass r. U.S.A.
70 D3 Cassadaga U.S.A.
89 C5 Cassai Angola
69 F4 Cass City U.S.A.
12 A4 Cassel France
71 F2 Casselman Can.
56 D3 Cassiar Can.
56 C3 Cassiar Mountains Can.
50 G2 Cassilis Austr.
18 E4 Cassino Italy
64 E2 Cass Lake U.S.A.
79 J4 Castanhal Brazil
83 C1 Castaño r. Arg.
65 C7 Castaños Mex.
83 C1 Castaño Viejo Arg.
18 D2 Castelfranco Veneto Italy
14 E4 Casteljaloux France
18 F4 Castellammare di Stabia Italy
83 F3 Castelli Arg.
15 F3 Castelló de la Plana Spain
15 C3 Castelo Branco Port.
15 C3 Castelo de Vide Port.
18 C4 Castelsardo Sardinia Italy
18 E6 Casteltermini Sicily Italy
18 E6 Castelvetrano Sicily Italy
50 C4 Casterton Austr.
59 G2 Castignon, Lac l. Can.
15 E3 Castilla - La Mancha div. Spain
15 D2 Castilla y León div. Spain
81 C2 Castilletes Col.
83 G2 Castillos Uru.
11 B4 Castlebar Rep. of Ireland
10 A4 Castlebay U.K.
11 E4 Castlebellingham Rep. of Ireland
11 E3 Castleblayney Rep. of Ireland
11 E5 Castlebridge Rep. of Ireland
8 E3 Castle Carrock U.K.
9 E6 Castle Cary U.K.
73 G2 Castle Dale U.S.A.
11 D3 Castlederg U.K.
11 E5 Castledermot Rep. of Ireland
73 E5 Castle Dome Mts mts U.S.A.
9 F5 Castle Donnington U.K.
10 E6 Castle Douglas U.K.
8 F4 Castleford U.K.
56 F5 Castlegar Can.
11 A5 Castlegregory Rep. of Ireland
11 B5 Castleisland Rep. of Ireland
50 E4 Castlemaine Austr.
11 B5 Castlemaine Rep. of Ireland
11 C6 Castlemartyr Rep. of Ireland
72 B4 Castle Mt mt U.S.A.
39 □ Castle Peak h. H.K. China
39 □ Castle Peak Bay b. H.K. China
51 F4 Castlepoint N.Z.
11 D4 Castlepollard Rep. of Ireland
11 C4 Castlerea Rep. of Ireland
50 G1 Castlereagh r. Austr.
63 F4 Castle Rock U.S.A.
68 B4 Castle Rock Lake l. U.S.A.
8 C3 Castletown Isle of Man
11 D5 Castletown Rep. of Ireland
57 G4 Castor Can.
14 F5 Castres France
12 C2 Castricum Neth.
75 M6 Castries St Lucia
82 C4 Castro Brazil
80 B6 Castro Chile
15 D4 Castro del Río Spain
15 E1 Castro-Urdiales Spain
15 B4 Castro Verde Port.
18 G5 Castrovillari Italy
72 B3 Castroville U.S.A.
51 A6 Caswell Sd in. N.Z.
29 H2 Çat Turkey
78 B5 Catacaos Peru
82 D3 Cataguases Brazil
65 E6 Catahoula L. l. U.S.A.
43 B3 Cataiñgan Phil.
29 J3 Çatak Turkey
82 C2 Catalão Brazil
15 G2 Cataluña div. Spain
80 C3 Catamarca Arg.
43 C3 Catanduanes i. Phil.
82 B4 Catanduvas Brazil
18 F6 Catania Sicily Italy
18 G5 Catanzaro Italy
65 D6 Catarina U.S.A.
43 C3 Catarman Phil.
15 F3 Catarroja Spain
81 B2 Catatumbo r. Venez.
43 C4 Catbalogan Phil.
67 E7 Cat Cays is Bahamas
43 C5 Cateel Phil.
43 C5 Cateel Bay b. Phil.
91 K3 Catembe Moz.
50 G4 Cathcart Austr.
91 G6 Cathcart S. Africa
91 H4 Cathedral Peak mt S. Africa
11 A6 Catherdaniel Rep. of Ireland
73 F2 Catherine, Mt mt U.S.A.
83 B3 Catillo Chile
67 E7 Cat Island i. Bahamas
58 B3 Cat L. l. Can.
74 G4 Catoche, C. c. Mex.
70 E5 Catonsville U.S.A.
83 D3 Catriló Arg.
81 E4 Catrimani Brazil
81 E4 Catrimani r. Brazil
71 G3 Catskill U.S.A.
71 F4 Catskill Mts mts U.S.A.
12 A4 Cats, Mont des h. France
91 K3 Catuane Moz.
81 E4 Cauamé r. Brazil
43 B4 Cauayan Phil.
59 H2 Caubvick, Mount mt Can.
81 B3 Cauca r. Col.
79 L4 Caucaia Brazil
81 B3 Caucasia Col.
4 H4 Caucasus mts Asia/Europe
83 C1 Caucete Arg.
71 J1 Caucomgomoc Lake l. U.S.A.
12 B4 Caudry France
43 C4 Cauit Point pt Phil.
83 B2 Cauquenes Chile
81 D3 Caura r. Venez.
59 G4 Causapscal Can.
14 G5 Cavaillon France
82 C1 Cavalcante Brazil
86 B4 Cavally r. Côte d'Ivoire
11 D4 Cavan Rep. of Ireland
65 F4 Cave City U.S.A.
82 E1 Caveira r. Brazil
50 D4 Cavendish Austr.
82 B4 Cavernoso, Serra do mts Brazil
70 B5 Cave Run Lake l. U.S.A.
43 B4 Cavili rf Phil.
43 B3 Cavite Phil.
10 E3 Cawdor U.K.
50 C2 Cawndilla Lake l. Austr.
9 J5 Cawston U.K.
79 K4 Caxias Brazil
80 F3 Caxias do Sul Brazil
89 B4 Caxito Angola
28 C2 Çay Turkey
67 D5 Cayce U.S.A.
28 D1 Çaycuma Turkey
29 H1 Çayeli Turkey
79 H3 Cayenne Fr. Guiana
28 E3 Çayhan Turkey
28 C1 Çayırhan Turkey
75 J5 Cayman Brac i. Cayman Is
53 H8 Cayman Islands terr. Caribbean Sea
96 D4 Cayman Trench sea feature Atl. Ocean
88 E3 Caynabo Somalia
69 H4 Cayuga Can.
70 E3 Cayuga Lake l. U.S.A.
71 F3 Cazenovia U.S.A.
89 C5 Cazombo Angola
83 F2 Cebollatí r. Uru.
43 B4 Cebu Phil.
43 B4 Cebu i. Phil.
68 C3 Cecil U.S.A.
18 D3 Cecina Italy
68 A4 Cedar r. IA U.S.A.
64 C2 Cedar r. ND U.S.A.
68 D4 Cedarburg U.S.A.
73 F3 Cedar City U.S.A.
65 D5 Cedar Creek Res. resr U.S.A.
68 A4 Cedar Falls U.S.A.
68 D4 Cedar Grove WI U.S.A.
70 C5 Cedar Grove WV U.S.A.
71 F6 Cedar I. i. U.S.A.
57 J4 Cedar L. l. Can.
68 D5 Cedar Lake l. U.S.A.
70 B4 Cedar Pt pt U.S.A.
68 B5 Cedar Rapids U.S.A.
73 G3 Cedar Ridge U.S.A.
71 F5 Cedar Run U.S.A.
69 F4 Cedar Springs Can.
68 E4 Cedar Springs U.S.A.
67 C5 Cedartown U.S.A.
91 H5 Cedarville S. Africa
68 E3 Cedarville U.S.A.
74 A3 Cedros i. Mex.
48 D5 Ceduna Austr.
88 E3 Ceeldheere Somalia
88 E2 Ceerigaabo Somalia
18 F5 Cefalù Sicily Italy
17 J7 Cegléd Hungary
39 B5 Ceheng China
28 E1 Çekerek Turkey
44 B4 Celah, Gunung mt Malaysia
74 D4 Celaya Mex.
11 E4 Celbridge Rep. of Ireland
Celebes i. see Sulawesi
45 E2 Celebes Sea sea Indon./Phil.
70 A4 Celina U.S.A.
18 F1 Celje Slovenia
13 J2 Celle Ger.
28 E1 Cemilbey Turkey
28 G2 Çemişgezek Turkey
37 F7 Cenderawasih, Teluk b. Indon.
39 C5 Cengong China
73 F5 Centennial Wash r. U.S.A.
65 E6 Center U.S.A.
71 G4 Centereach U.S.A.
67 C5 Center Point U.S.A.
70 B5 Centerville U.S.A.
91 G1 Central div. Botswana
85 E5 Central African Republic country Africa
31 G4 Central Brahui Range mts Pak.
68 B4 Central City IA U.S.A.
64 D3 Central City NE U.S.A.
81 A4 Central, Cordillera mts Col.
78 C5 Central, Cordillera mts Peru
43 B2 Central, Cordillera mts Phil.
39 □ Central District H.K. China
66 B4 Centralia IL U.S.A.
62 B2 Centralia WA U.S.A.
68 A2 Central Lakes U.S.A.
31 G5 Central Makran Range mts Pak.
62 B3 Central Point U.S.A.
48 E2 Central Ra. mts P.N.G.
67 C5 Centreville U.S.A.
39 D6 Cenxi China
Cephalonia i. see Kefallonia
81 D3 Cerbatana, Sa de la mt Venez.
73 E4 Cerbat Mts mts U.S.A.
57 G4 Cereal Can.
80 D3 Ceres Arg.
90 C6 Ceres S. Africa
81 B2 Cereté Col.
15 E2 Cerezo de Abajo Spain
18 F4 Cerignola Italy
28 D2 Çerikli Turkey
28 D1 Çerkeş Turkey
28 G3 Çermelik r. Syria
29 G2 Çermik Turkey
19 N2 Cernavodă Romania
65 D7 Cerralvo Mex.
74 C4 Cerralvo i. Mex.
19 H4 Cërrik Albania
74 D4 Cerritos Mex.
82 C4 Cerro Azul Brazil
78 B4 Cerro de Amotape, Parque Nacional nat. park Peru
78 C6 Cerro de Pasco Peru
81 D3 Cerro Jáua, Meseta del plat. Venez.
81 C2 Cerrón, Co mt Venez.
83 C3 Cerros Colorados, Embalse resr Arg.
18 F4 Cervati, Monte mt Italy
18 C3 Cervione Corsica France
15 C1 Cervo Spain
81 B2 César r. Col.
18 E2 Cesena Italy
7 T8 Cēsis Latvia
16 G6 České Budějovice Czech Rep.
16 G6 Český Krumlov Czech Rep.
13 L5 Český Les mts Czech Rep./Ger.
19 M5 Çeşme Turkey
50 H2 Cessnock Austr.
19 H3 Cetinje Yugo.
18 F5 Cetraro Italy
15 D5 Ceuta Spain
14 F4 Cévennes mts France
28 E3 Ceyhan Turkey
28 E3 Ceyhan r. Turkey
29 H3 Ceylanpınar Turkey
31 F2 Chaacha Turkm.
12 A5 Chaalis, Abbaye de France
83 E2 Chacabuco Arg.
83 B4 Chacao Chile
83 C3 Chachahuén, Sa mt Arg.
78 C5 Chachapoyas Peru
20 D4 Chachersk Belarus
82 B2 Chachoengsao Thai.
34 B4 Chachro Pak.
56 C4 Chacon, C. c. U.S.A.
85 E4 Chad country Africa
27 H1 Chadan Rus. Fed.
91 G1 Chadibe Botswana
83 C3 Chadileo r. Arg.
87 D3 Chad, Lake l. Africa
64 C3 Chadron U.S.A.
44 A1 Chae Hom Thai.
42 C4 Chaeryŏng N. Korea
81 B4 Chafurray Col.
31 G4 Chagai Pak.
31 F4 Chagai Hills mts Afgh./Pak.
35 F2 Chagdo Kangri reg. China
31 G3 Chaghcharān Afgh.
14 G3 Chagny France
93 J4 Chagos Archipelago is British Indian Ocean Terr.
20 J4 Chagra r. Rus. Fed.
81 D2 Chaguaramas Venez.
35 G3 Cha'gyüngoinba China
31 F4 Chahah Burjal Afgh.
31 E3 Chāh Ākhvor Iran
31 E3 Chahār Takāb Iran
30 D3 Chāh Badam Iran
31 F5 Chāh Bahār Iran
30 D4 Chāh-e Bāgh well Iran
30 E3 Chāh-e Kavīr well Iran
30 D3 Chāh-e Khorāsān well Iran
31 E3 Chāh-e Khoshāb Iran
31 E4 Chāh-e Malek Iran
30 D3 Chāh-e Mirzā well Iran
30 D3 Chāh-e Mūjān well Iran
30 D3 Chāh-e Nūklok Iran
30 D3 Chāh-e Nūklok well Iran
30 D4 Chāh-e Qeyşar well Iran
30 D3 Chāh-e Qobād well Iran
30 D4 Chāh-e Rāh Iran
31 E4 Chāh-e-Raḩmān well Iran
30 D3 Chāh-e Shūr Iran
30 D3 Chāh-e Shur well Iran
30 D3 Chah Haji Abdulla well Iran
30 D4 Chāh Ḩaqq Iran
31 H2 Chah-i-Ab Afgh.
29 K4 Chah-i-Shurkh Iraq
30 D3 Chāh Pās well Iran
30 C4 Chāh Rūstā'ī Iran
31 F4 Chah Sandan Pak.
42 C2 Chai r. China
35 F5 Chāībāsa India
59 G3 Chaigneau, Lac l. Can.
44 B2 Chai Si r. Thai.
39 □ Chai Wan H.K. China
44 A3 Chaiya Thai.
44 B2 Chaiyaphum Thai.
83 F1 Chajarí Arg.
34 B3 Chakar r. Pak.
35 H5 Chakaria Bangl.
31 F4 Chakhānsūr Afgh.
35 E4 Chakia India
31 G5 Chakku Pak.
78 D7 Chala Peru
31 G3 Chalap Dalan mts Afgh.
74 G6 Chalatenango El Salvador
59 G4 Chaleur Bay in. Can.
39 D5 Chaling China
34 C5 Chalisgaon India
19 K5 Chalkida Greece
51 A7 Chalky Inlet in. N.Z.
14 D3 Challans France
78 E7 Challapata Bol.
94 E5 Challenger Deep depth Pac. Oc.
95 M8 Challenger Fracture Zone sea feature Pac. Oc.
62 D2 Challis U.S.A.
14 G2 Châlons-en-Champagne France
14 G3 Chalon-sur-Saône France
42 C2 Chaluhe China
30 C2 Chālūs Iran
13 L5 Cham Ger.
63 F4 Chama U.S.A.
89 D5 Chama Zambia
81 C2 Chama r. Venez.
83 D2 Chamaico Arg.
90 A3 Chamais Bay b. Namibia
31 G4 Chaman Pak.
34 D4 Chambal r. India
59 G3 Chambeaux, Lac l. Can.
57 H4 Chamberlain Can.
64 D3 Chamberlain U.S.A.
71 J1 Chamberlain Lake l. U.S.A.
73 H4 Chambers U.S.A.
70 E5 Chambersburg U.S.A.
14 G4 Chambéry France
89 D5 Chambeshi Zambia
18 C7 Chambi, Jebel mt Tunisia
14 G4 Chamechaude mt France
30 C3 Chame-ye Ḩannā Iran
30 C3 Chameshk Iran
83 C1 Chamical Arg.
35 F4 Chamlang mt Nepal
44 B3 Châmnar Cambodia
58 F4 Chamouchouane r. Can.
35 E5 Champa India
56 B2 Champagne Can.
14 G2 Champagne reg. France
91 H4 Champagne Castle mt S. Africa
14 G3 Champagnole France
68 C5 Champaign U.S.A.
83 D1 Champaqui, Cerro mt Arg.
44 C2 Champasak Laos
35 H5 Champhai India
68 D2 Champion U.S.A.
71 G2 Champlain U.S.A.
71 G2 Champlain, L. l. Can./U.S.A.
74 F5 Champotón Mex.
33 B4 Chamrajnagar India
20 H4 Chamzinka Rus. Fed.
44 B4 Chana Thai.
80 B3 Chañaral Chile
81 E3 Chanaro, Co mt Venez.
83 B2 Chanco Chile
Chanda see Chandrapur
54 D3 Chandalar r. U.S.A.
35 E5 Chandarpur India
34 D3 Chandausi India
65 F6 Chandeleur Islands is U.S.A.
34 E5 Chandia India
34 D3 Chandigarh India
73 G5 Chandler U.S.A.
69 J3 Chandos Lake l. Can.
35 G5 Chandpur Bangl.
34 D3 Chandpur India
35 H5 Chandraghona Bangl.
34 D6 Chandrapur India
34 D5 Chandur India
89 D6 Changane r. Moz.
89 D5 Changara Moz.
42 E3 Changbai China
42 D3 Changbai Shan mts China/N. Korea
39 C7 Changcheng China
92 B1 Chang Cheng (Great Wall) China Base Ant.
42 C2 Changchun China
42 C1 Changchunling China
38 F2 Changdao China
39 D4 Changde China
42 D4 Changdo N. Korea
38 E3 Changfeng China
42 E5 Changgi Gap pt S. Korea

42 B4 Changhai China
42 D6 Changhang S. Korea
42 D5 Changhowan S. Korea
39 F5 Chang-hua Taiwan
44 D1 Changhua Jiang *r.* China
42 D6 Changhung S. Korea
44 □ Changi Sing.
39 C7 Changjiang China
Chang Jiang *r.* *see* Yangtze
Changjiang Kou *est.* *see* Yangtze, Mouth of the
42 D3 Changjin N. Korea
42 D3 Changjin Reservoir N. Korea
39 F5 Changle China
38 F2 Changli China
42 B1 Changling China
39 D5 Changning China
42 C4 Changnyŏn N. Korea
38 E1 Changping China
42 E5 Changp'yŏng S. Korea
42 C4 Changsan-got *pt* N. Korea
39 D4 Changsha China
39 F4 Changshan China
42 B4 Changshan Qundao *is* China
39 C4 Changshou China
39 D4 Changshoujie China
38 F4 Changshu China
39 C5 Changshun China
42 D6 Changsŏng S. Korea
39 E5 Changtai China
39 E5 Changting *Fujian* China
42 E1 Changting *Heilongjiang* China
42 C2 Changtu China
42 E6 Ch'angwŏn S. Korea
38 C3 Changwu China
42 A4 Changxing Dao *i.* China
39 D4 Changyang China
38 F2 Changyi China
42 C4 Changyŏn N. Korea
38 E3 Changyuan China
38 D2 Changzhi China
38 F4 Changzhou China
19 L7 Chania Greece
42 D3 Chanjin *r.* N. Korea
38 B3 Chankou China
33 B3 Channapatna India
72 C5 Channel Islands *is* U.S.A.
4 C4 Channel Islands *terr.* English Channel
72 B5 Channel Is Nat. Park U.S.A.
59 J4 Channel-Port-aux-Basques Can.
9 J6 Channel Tunnel *tunnel* France/U.K.
68 C2 Channing U.S.A.
15 C1 Chantada Spain
44 B2 Chanthaburi Thai.
14 F2 Chantilly France
65 E4 Chanute U.S.A.
24 J4 Chany, Ozero *salt l.* Rus. Fed.
38 E2 Chaobai Xinhe *r.* China
38 E4 Chao Hu *l.* China
44 B2 Chao Phraya *r.* Thai.
86 B1 Chaouèn Morocco
35 H2 Chaowula Shan *mts* China
38 E4 Chao Xian China
39 E6 Chaoyang *Guangdong* China
38 F1 Chaoyang *Liaoning* China
39 E6 Chaozhou China
82 E1 Chapada Diamantina, Parque Nacional *nat. park* Brazil
82 A1 Chapada dos Guimarães Brazil
82 C1 Chapada dos Veadeiros, Parque Nacional da *nat. park* Brazil
74 D4 Chapala, L. de *l.* Mex.
81 B4 Chaparral Col.
26 D1 Chapayev Kazak.
20 J4 Chapayevsk Rus. Fed.
80 F3 Chapecó Brazil
80 F3 Chapecó *r.* Brazil
9 F4 Chapel-en-le-Frith U.K.
67 E5 Chapel Hill U.S.A.
12 C4 Chapelle-lez-Herlaimont Belgium
9 F4 Chapeltown U.K.
68 D5 Chapin, Lake *l.* U.S.A.
69 F2 Chapleau Can.
20 F4 Chaplygin Rus. Fed.
21 E6 Chaplynka Ukr.
70 B6 Chapmanville U.S.A.
31 G3 Chapri Pass Afgh.
78 E7 Chaqui Bol.
34 D2 Char Jammu and Kashmir
35 H3 Char Chu *r.* China
92 A2 Charcot I. *i.* Ant.
57 G3 Chard Can.
9 E7 Chard U.K.
29 L3 Chārdagh Iran
29 L5 Chardāvol Iran
70 C4 Chardon U.S.A.
31 F2 Chardzhev Turkm.
14 E3 Charente *r.* France
31 H3 Chārīkār Afgh.
68 E5 Chariton *r.* U.S.A.
69 F3 Charity Is *i.* U.S.A.
24 G3 Charkayuvom Rus. Fed.
34 D4 Charkhari India
12 C4 Charleroi Belgium
61 L4 Charles, Cape *pt* *VA* U.S.A.
68 A4 Charles City U.S.A.
12 A5 Charles de Gaulle *airport* France
65 E6 Charles, Lake U.S.A.
51 C4 Charleston N.Z.
68 B4 Charleston *IL* U.S.A.
71 J2 Charleston *ME* U.S.A.
65 F4 Charleston *MO* U.S.A.
67 E5 Charleston *SC* U.S.A.
70 C5 Charleston *WV* U.S.A.
73 E3 Charleston Peak *summit* U.S.A.
11 C4 Charlestown Rep. of Ireland
71 G3 Charlestown *NH* U.S.A.
71 H4 Charlestown *RI* U.S.A.
70 E5 Charles Town U.S.A.
48 E4 Charleville Austr.
14 G2 Charleville-Mézières France
68 E3 Charlevoix U.S.A.
56 E3 Charlie Lake Can.
68 E4 Charlotte *MI* U.S.A.
67 D5 Charlotte *NC* U.S.A.
67 D7 Charlotte Harbor *b.* U.S.A.
70 D5 Charlottesville U.S.A.
59 H4 Charlottetown Can.
81 E2 Charlotteville Trinidad and Tobago
50 D4 Charlton Austr.
58 E3 Charlton I. *i.* Can.
20 F2 Charozero Rus. Fed.
34 B2 Charsadda Pak.
48 E4 Charters Towers Austr.
14 E2 Chartres France
83 E2 Chascomús Arg.
56 F4 Chase Can.
31 F2 Chashkent Turkm.
29 L4 Chashmeh Iran
30 E3 Chashmeh Nūrī Iran
30 D3 Chashmeh ye Palasi Iran
30 D3 Chashmeh ye Shotoran *well* Iran
20 D4 Chashniki Belarus
51 B7 Chaslands Mistake *c.* N.Z.
42 D3 Chasŏng N. Korea
30 D3 Chastab, Kūh-e *mts* Iran
14 D3 Châteaubriant France
14 E3 Château-du-Loir France
14 E2 Châteaudun France
71 F2 Chateaugay U.S.A.
71 G2 Châteauguay Can.
14 B2 Châteaulin France
14 F3 Châteauneuf-sur-Loire France
14 E3 Châteauroux France
12 E6 Château-Salins France
14 F2 Château-Thierry France
12 C4 Châtelet Belgium
14 E3 Châtellerault France
68 A4 Chatfield U.S.A.
68 G4 Chatham *N.B.* Can.
69 F4 Chatham *Ont.* Can.
9 H6 Chatham U.K.
71 H4 Chatham *MA* U.S.A.
71 G3 Chatham *NY* U.S.A.
70 D6 Chatham *VA* U.S.A.
49 J6 Chatham Islands *is* N.Z.
94 G8 Chatham Rise *sea feature* Pac. Oc.
56 C4 Chatham Sd *chan.* Can.
56 C3 Chatham Strait *chan.* U.S.A.
35 F4 Chatra India
69 G3 Chatsworth Can.
68 C5 Chatsworth U.S.A.
67 C5 Chattanooga U.S.A.
9 H5 Chatteris U.K.
44 B2 Chatturat Thai.
44 C3 Châu Đôc Vietnam
34 B4 Chauhtan India
35 H5 Chauk Myanmar
34 E4 Chauka *r.* India
14 G2 Chaumont France
44 A2 Chaungwabyin Myanmar
25 S3 Chaunskaya Guba *b.* Rus. Fed.
14 F2 Chauny France
35 F4 Chauparan India
70 D3 Chautauqua, Lake *l.* U.S.A.
33 C4 Chavakachcheri Sri Lanka
28 D4 Chavār Iran
79 J4 Chaves Brazil
15 C2 Chaves Port.
58 E2 Chavigny, Lac *l.* Can.
20 D4 Chavusy Belarus
34 A3 Chawal *r.* Pak.
39 B6 Chây *r.* Vietnam
Chāyul *see* Qayü
83 D2 Chazón Arg.
71 G2 Chazy U.S.A.
9 F5 Cheadle U.K.
70 D5 Cheat *r.* U.S.A.
16 F5 Cheb Czech Rep.
18 D7 Chebba Tunisia
20 H3 Cheboksary Rus. Fed.
68 E3 Cheboygan U.S.A.
21 H7 Chechen', Ostrov *i.* Rus. Fed.
21 H7 Chechenskaya Respublika *div.* Rus. Fed.
42 E5 Chech'ŏn S. Korea
65 E5 Checotah U.S.A.
42 A5 Chedao China
9 E6 Cheddar U.K.
57 G3 Cheecham Can.
85 B5 Cheetham, C. *c.* Ant.
54 B3 Chefornak *AK* U.S.A.
91 K1 Chefu Moz.
86 B2 Chegga Maur.
89 D5 Chegutu Zimbabwe
62 B2 Chehalis U.S.A.
31 H3 Chehardar Pass Afgh.
29 L5 Cheharīz Iraq
30 E4 Chehell'āyeh Iran
42 D7 Cheju S. Korea
42 D7 Cheju-do *i.* S. Korea
42 D7 Cheju-haehyŏp *chan.* S. Korea
20 F4 Chekhov Rus. Fed.
62 B2 Chelan, L. *l.* U.S.A.
30 D2 Cheleken Turkm.
83 C3 Chelforó Arg.
15 G4 Chélif *r.* Alg.
26 D2 Chelkar Kazak.
17 L5 Chełm Pol.
9 H6 Chelmer *r.* U.K.
17 J4 Chełmno Pol.
9 H6 Chelmsford U.K.
71 H3 Chelmsford U.S.A.
9 E6 Cheltenham U.K.
15 F3 Chelva Spain
24 H4 Chelyabinsk Rus. Fed.
89 D5 Chemba Moz.
34 D2 Chem Co *l.* China
13 L4 Chemnitz Ger.
70 E3 Chemung *r.* U.S.A.
34 B3 Chenab *r.* Pak.
86 B2 Chenachane Alg.
71 F3 Chenango *r.* U.S.A.
62 C2 Cheney U.S.A.
65 D4 Cheney Res. *resr* U.S.A.
33 C3 Chengalpattu India
38 E2 Cheng'an China
39 D5 Chengbu China
38 E1 Chengde China
39 B4 Chengdu China
38 C3 Chengguo China
39 E6 Chenghai China
38 C4 Chengkou China
37 D5 Chengmai China
42 B4 Chengzitan China
38 F3 Cheniu Shan *i.* China
33 C3 Chennai India
68 C5 Chenoa U.S.A.
39 D5 Chenxi China
39 D5 Chenzhou China
44 D2 Cheo Reo Vietnam
78 C5 Chepén Peru
83 C1 Chepes Arg.
9 E6 Chepstow U.K.
20 J3 Cheptsa *r.* Rus. Fed.
29 L5 Cheqad Kabūd Iran
68 B2 Chequamegon Bay *b.* U.S.A.
14 F3 Cher *r.* France
67 E5 Cheraw U.S.A.
14 D2 Cherbourg France
15 H4 Cherchell Alg.
20 J4 Cherdakly Rus. Fed.
36 C1 Cheremkhovo Rus. Fed.
40 D2 Cheremshany Rus. Fed.
20 F3 Cherepovets Rus. Fed.
20 H2 Cherevkovo Rus. Fed.
18 B7 Chéria Alg.
21 E5 Cherkasy Ukr.
21 G6 Cherkessk Rus. Fed.
33 C2 Cherla India
89 C5 Chermenze Angola
24 K2 Chernaya Rus. Fed.
20 J3 Chernaya Kholunitsa Rus. Fed.
40 C2 Chernigovka Rus. Fed.
21 D5 Chernihiv Ukr.
21 F6 Cherninivka Ukr.
21 C5 Chernivtsi Ukr.
36 B1 Chernogorsk Rus. Fed.
20 H3 Chernovskoye Rus. Fed.
21 D5 Chernyakhiv Ukr.
17 K3 Chernyakhovsk Rus. Fed.
21 F5 Chernyanka Rus. Fed.
25 N3 Chernyshevskiy Rus. Fed.
21 H6 Chernyye Zemli *reg.* Rus. Fed.
21 H5 Chernyy Yar Rus. Fed.
64 E3 Cherokee *IA* U.S.A.
65 D4 Cherokee *OK* U.S.A.
65 E4 Cherokees, Lake o' the *l.* U.S.A.
67 E7 Cherokee Sound Bahamas
83 B3 Cherquenco Chile
35 G4 Cherrapunji India
73 E2 Cherry Creek U.S.A.
73 E1 Cherry Creek Mts *mts* U.S.A.
71 K2 Cherryfield U.S.A.
49 G3 Cherry Island *i.* Solomon Is
69 J4 Cherry Valley Can.
71 F3 Cherry Valley U.S.A.
25 Q3 Cherskogo, Khrebet *mts* Rus. Fed.
21 G5 Chertkovo Rus. Fed.
20 J2 Cherva Rus. Fed.
19 L3 Cherven Bryag Bulg.
21 C5 Chervonohrad Ukr.
21 E5 Chervonozavods'ke Ukr.
20 D4 Chervyen' Belarus
9 F6 Cherwell *r.* U.K.
20 D4 Cherykaw Belarus
69 E4 Chesaning U.S.A.
71 E6 Chesapeake U.S.A.
71 E5 Chesapeake Bay *b.* U.S.A.
9 G6 Chesham U.K.
71 G3 Cheshire U.S.A.
9 E4 Cheshire Plain *lowland* U.K.
31 F2 Cheshme 2-y Turkm.
24 F3 Cheshskaya Guba *b.* Rus. Fed.
31 F3 Chesht-e Sharīf Afgh.
9 G6 Cheshunt U.K.
9 E4 Chester U.K.
72 B1 Chester *CA* U.S.A.
66 B4 Chester *IL* U.S.A.
62 E1 Chester *MT* U.S.A.
71 F5 Chester *PA* U.S.A.
67 D5 Chester *SC* U.S.A.
71 E5 Chester *r.* U.S.A.
9 F4 Chesterfield U.K.
49 F3 Chesterfield, Îles *is* New Caledonia
55 J3 Chesterfield Inlet *N.W.T.* Can.
57 L2 Chesterfield Inlet Can.
57 L2 Chesterfield Inlet *in.* Can.
8 F3 Chester-le-Street U.K.
71 E5 Chestertown *MD* U.S.A.
71 G3 Chestertown *NY* U.S.A.
71 F2 Chesterville Can.
70 D4 Chestnut Ridge *ridge* U.S.A.
71 J1 Chesuncook U.S.A.
71 J1 Chesuncook Lake *l.* U.S.A.
18 B6 Chetaïbi Alg.
59 H4 Chéticamp Can.
33 A4 Chetlat *i.* India
74 G5 Chetumal Mex.
56 E3 Chetwynd Can.
39 □ Cheung Chau *H.K.* China
39 □ Cheung Chau *i.* *H.K.* China
51 D5 Cheviot N.Z.
8 E2 Cheviot Hills *h.* U.K.
8 E2 Cheviot, The *h.* U.K.
62 C1 Chewelah U.S.A.
65 D5 Cheyenne *OK* U.S.A.
62 F3 Cheyenne *WY* U.S.A.
64 C3 Cheyenne *r.* U.S.A.
64 C4 Cheyenne Wells U.S.A.
56 E4 Chezacut Can.
34 C4 Chhapar India
35 F4 Chhapra India
34 D4 Chhatarpur India
34 B3 Chhatr Pak.
34 D5 Chhindwara India
35 C4 Chhota Udepur India
34 C4 Chhoti Sadri India
35 G4 Chhukha Bhutan
39 F6 Chia-i Taiwan
44 B1 Chiang Kham Thai.
44 B1 Chiang Khan Thai.
44 A1 Chiang Mai Thai.
18 C2 Chiari Italy
41 G7 Chiba Japan
89 B5 Chibia Angola
89 D6 Chiboma Moz.
58 F4 Chibougamau Can.
58 F4 Chibougamau L. *l.* Can.
58 F4 Chibougamau, Parc de *res.* Can.
41 E6 Chibu-Sangaku Nat. Park Japan
91 K2 Chibuto Moz.
35 G2 Chibuzhang Hu *l.* China
Chicacole *see* Srikakulam
68 D5 Chicago U.S.A.
68 D5 Chicago *airport* *IL* U.S.A.
68 D5 Chicago Heights U.S.A.
68 C5 Chicago Ship Canal *canal* U.S.A.
81 B3 Chicamocha *r.* Col.
81 E3 Chicanán *r.* Venez.
56 B3 Chichagof U.S.A.
56 B3 Chichagof Island *i.* U.S.A.
38 E1 Chicheng China
9 G7 Chichester U.K.
48 B4 Chichester Range *mts* Austr.
41 F7 Chichibu Japan
41 F7 Chichibu-Tama National Park Japan
70 E6 Chickahominy *r.* U.S.A.
67 C5 Chickamauga L. *l.* U.S.A.
65 D5 Chickasha U.S.A.
15 C4 Chiclana de la Frontera Spain
78 C5 Chiclayo Peru
72 B2 Chico U.S.A.
80 C6 Chico *r.* *Chubut* Arg.
83 B4 Chico *r.* *Chubut/Río Negro* Arg.
80 C7 Chico *r.* *Santa Cruz* Arg.
91 L2 Chicomo Moz.
71 G3 Chicopee U.S.A.
43 B2 Chico Sapocoy, Mt *mt* Phil.
59 F4 Chicoutimi Can.
91 J1 Chicualacuala Moz.
33 B4 Chidambaram India
91 L2 Chidenguele Moz.
59 H1 Chidley, C. *c.* Can.
42 D6 Chido S. Korea
91 L2 Chiducuane Moz.
67 D6 Chiefland U.S.A.
16 F7 Chiemsee *l.* Ger.
12 D5 Chiers *r.* France
18 F3 Chieti Italy
38 F1 Chifeng China
82 E2 Chifre, Serra do *mts* Brazil
24 J5 Chiganak Kazak.
59 G4 Chignecto B. *b.* Can.
81 A3 Chigorodó Col.
89 D6 Chigubo Moz.
35 G3 Chigu Co *l.* China
74 C3 Chihuahua Mex.
65 B6 Chihuahua *div.* Mex.
39 D6 Chikan China
33 B3 Chik Ballapur India
20 D3 Chikhachevo Rus. Fed.
34 D5 Chikhali Kalan Parasia India
34 D5 Chikhli India
33 A3 Chikmagalur India
41 F6 Chikuma-gawa *r.* Japan
56 E4 Chilanko Forks Can.
27 F3 Chilas Jammu and Kashmir
33 B5 Chilaw Sri Lanka
72 B2 Chilcoot U.S.A.
56 E4 Chilcotin *r.* Can.
65 C5 Childress U.S.A.
77 C7 Chile *country* S. America
95 O8 Chile Basin *sea feature* Pac. Oc.
80 C3 Chilecito Arg.
21 H6 Chilgir Rus. Fed.
68 C5 Chilicothe *IL* U.S.A.
35 F6 Chilika Lake *l.* India
89 C5 Chililabombwe Zambia
56 E4 Chilko *r.* Can.
56 E4 Chilko L. *l.* Can.
56 B2 Chilkoot Trail National Historic Site U.S.A.
83 B3 Chillán Chile
83 B3 Chillán, Nevado *mts* Chile
83 E3 Chillar Arg.
64 E4 Chillicothe *MO* U.S.A.
70 B5 Chillicothe *OH* U.S.A.
34 C1 Chillinji Pak.
56 E5 Chilliwack Can.
30 D1 Chil'mamedkum, Peski *des.* Turkm.
80 B6 Chiloé, Isla de *i.* Chile
62 B3 Chiloquin U.S.A.
74 E5 Chilpancingo Mex.
50 F4 Chiltern Austr.
9 G6 Chiltern Hills *h.* U.K.
68 C3 Chilton U.S.A.
39 F5 Chi-lung Taiwan
34 D2 Chilung Pass India
89 D4 Chimala Tanz.
12 C4 Chimay Belgium
83 C1 Chimbas Arg.
78 C4 Chimborazo *mt* Ecuador
78 C5 Chimbote Peru
81 B2 Chimichaguá Col.
89 D5 Chimoio Moz.
65 D7 China Mex.
36 C4 China *country* Asia
23 H6 China Lake Pak.
81 B3 Chinácota Col.
72 D4 China Lake *l.* *CA* U.S.A.
71 J2 China Lake *l.* *ME* U.S.A.
74 G6 Chinandega Nic.
72 C5 China Pt *pt* U.S.A.
78 C6 Chincha Alta Peru
56 F3 Chinchaga *r.* Can.
71 F6 Chincoteague B. *b.* U.S.A.
89 D5 Chinde Moz.
42 D6 Chindo S. Korea
42 D6 Chin-do *i.* S. Korea
36 B3 Chindu China
35 H5 Chindwin *r.* Myanmar
34 C2 Chineni Jammu and Kashmir
81 B3 Chingaza, Parque Nacional *nat. park* Col.
42 C4 Chinghwa N. Korea
89 C5 Chingola Zambia
89 B5 Chinguar Angola
42 E6 Chinhae S. Korea
89 D5 Chinhoyi Zimbabwe
34 C3 Chiniot Pak.
42 E6 Chinju S. Korea
88 C3 Chinko *r.* C.A.R.
73 H3 Chinle U.S.A.
73 H3 Chinle Valley *v.* U.S.A.
73 H3 Chinle Wash *r.* U.S.A.
39 F5 Chinmen Taiwan
39 F5 Chinmen Tao *i.* Taiwan
33 B2 Chinnur India
41 F7 Chino Japan
14 E3 Chinon France
73 F4 Chino Valley U.S.A.
89 D5 Chinsali Zambia
33 B3 Chintamani India
18 E2 Chioggia Italy
19 M5 Chios Greece
19 L5 Chios *i.* Greece
89 D5 Chipata Zambia
83 C4 Chipchihua, Sa de *mts* Arg.
89 B5 Chipindo Angola
89 D6 Chipinge Zimbabwe
33 A2 Chiplun India
9 E6 Chippenham U.K.
68 B3 Chippewa *r.* U.S.A.
68 B3 Chippewa Falls U.S.A.
68 B3 Chippewa, Lake *l.* U.S.A.
9 F6 Chipping Norton U.K.
9 E6 Chipping Sodbury U.K.
71 K2 Chiputneticook Lakes *l.* U.S.A.
74 G6 Chiquimula Guatemala
81 B3 Chiquinquira Col.
21 G5 Chir *r.* Rus. Fed.
33 C3 Chirada India
33 A4 Chirakkal India
33 C3 Chirala India
31 G3 Chiras Afgh.
34 C3 Chirāwa India
89 D6 Chiredzi Zimbabwe
73 H5 Chiricahua National Monument *res.* U.S.A.
73 H6 Chiricahua Peak *summit* U.S.A.
81 B2 Chiriguaná Col.
54 C4 Chirikof I. *i.* U.S.A.
75 H7 Chiriquí, Golfo de *b.* Panama
9 D5 Chirk U.K.
10 F5 Chirnside U.K.
19 L3 Chirpan Bulg.
75 H7 Chirripo *mt* Costa Rica
89 C5 Chirundu Zambia
58 E3 Chisasibi Can.
68 A2 Chisholm U.S.A.
34 C3 Chishtian Mandi Pak.
39 B4 Chishur China
21 D6 Chişinău Moldova
17 K7 Chişineu-Criş Romania
20 J4 Chistopol' Rus. Fed.
36 D1 Chita Rus. Fed.
89 B5 Chitado Angola
89 D5 Chitambo Zambia
88 C4 Chitato Angola
57 H4 Chitek Lake Can.
89 B5 Chitembo Angola
89 D4 Chitipa Malawi
89 C5 Chitokoloki Zambia
40 G3 Chitose Japan
33 B3 Chitradurga India
34 B2 Chitral Pak.
34 B2 Chitral *r.* Pak.
75 H7 Chitré Panama
35 G5 Chittagong Bangl.
35 F5 Chittaranjan India
34 C4 Chittaurgarh India
33 B3 Chittoor India
33 B4 Chittur India
89 D5 Chitungulu Zambia
89 D5 Chitungwiza Zimbabwe
89 C5 Chiume Angola
89 D5 Chivhu Zimbabwe
83 E2 Chivilcoy Arg.
39 D6 Chixi China
29 J3 Chiya-e Linik *h.* Iraq
41 D7 Chizu Japan
20 G3 Chkalovsk Rus. Fed.
40 C2 Chkalovskoye Rus. Fed.
42 D6 Ch'o *i.* S. Korea
44 □ Choa Chu Kang Sing.
44 □ Choa Chu Kang *h.* Sing.
44 C2 Chŏâm Khsant Cambodia
83 B1 Choapa *r.* Chile
89 C5 Chobe National Park Botswana
42 D5 Choch'iwŏn S. Korea
73 E5 Chocolate Mts *mts* U.S.A.
83 B3 Chocontá Col.
42 C4 Cho Do *i.* N. Korea
13 L4 Chodov Czech Rep.
83 D3 Choele Choel Arg.
34 C2 Chogo Lungma Gl. *gl.* Pak.
21 H6 Chograyskoye Vdkhr. *resr* Rus. Fed.
57 J4 Choiceland Can.
49 F2 Choiseul *i.* Solomon Is
80 E8 Choiseul Sound *chan.* Falkland Is
16 H4 Chojnice Pol.
40 G5 Chōkai-san *volc.* Japan
65 D6 Choke Canyon L. *l.* U.S.A.
88 D2 Ch'ok'ē Mts *mts* Eth.
35 F3 Choksum China
25 Q2 Chokurdakh Rus. Fed.
89 D6 Chókwè Moz.
14 D3 Cholet France
83 B4 Cholila Arg.
74 G6 Choluteca Honduras
89 C5 Choma Zambia
42 E5 Chŏmch'ŏn S. Korea
35 G4 Chomo Lhari *mt* Bhutan
44 A1 Chom Thong Thai.
16 F5 Chomutov Czech Rep.
25 M3 Chona *r.* Rus. Fed.
42 D5 Ch'ŏnan S. Korea
44 B2 Chon Buri Thai.
42 D3 Ch'ŏnch'ŏn N. Korea
78 B4 Chone Ecuador
39 F5 Chong'an China
42 C4 Chŏngchon *r.* N. Korea
42 E6 Chongdo S. Korea
42 E3 Ch'ŏngjin N. Korea
42 C4 Chŏngju N. Korea
42 D6 Chŏngju S. Korea
42 D5 Ch'ŏngju S. Korea
44 B2 Chông Kal Cambodia
42 D4 Chŏngp'yŏng N. Korea
39 C4 Chongqing China
39 E5 Chongren China
91 K2 Chonguene Moz.
89 C5 Chongwe Zambia
39 D4 Chongyang China
39 F5 Chongyang Xi *r.* China
39 E5 Chongyi China
39 C6 Chongzuo China
42 D6 Ch'ŏnju S. Korea
35 F3 Cho Oyu *mt* China
44 C3 Chơ Phước Hai Vietnam
82 B4 Chopim *r.* Brazil
82 B4 Chopimzinho Brazil
71 F5 Choptank *r.* U.S.A.
34 B4 Chor Pak.
8 E4 Chorley U.K.
21 D5 Chornobyl' Ukr.
21 E6 Chornomors'ke Ukr.
21 C5 Chortkiv Ukr.
42 D4 Ch'ŏrwŏn S. Korea
42 C3 Ch'osan N. Korea
41 G7 Chōshi Japan
83 B3 Chos Malal Arg.
16 G4 Choszczno Pol.
78 C5 Chota Peru
62 D2 Choteau U.S.A.
34 B3 Choti Pak.
86 A2 Choûm Maur.
72 B3 Chowchilla U.S.A.
56 F4 Chown, Mt *mt* Can.
36 D2 Choybalsan Mongolia
36 C2 Choyr Mongolia
16 H6 Chřiby *h.* Czech Rep.
68 D6 Chrisman U.S.A.
91 J3 Chrissiesmeer S. Africa
51 D5 Christchurch N.Z.
9 F7 Christchurch U.K.
91 F3 Christiana S. Africa
55 M2 Christian, C. *pt* Can.
69 G3 Christian I. *i.* Can.
Christiansåb *see* Qasigiannguit
70 C6 Christiansburg U.S.A.
56 C3 Christian Sound *chan.* U.S.A.
57 G3 Christina *r.* Can.
49 G6 Christina, Mt *mt* N.Z.
Christmas Island *i.* *see* Kiritimati
37 C8 Christmas Island *terr.* Ind. Ocean
16 G6 Chrudim Czech Rep.
19 L7 Chrysi *i.* Greece
27 F2 Chu Kazak.
24 H5 Chu *r.* Kazak.
35 G5 Chuadanga Bangl.
91 K2 Chuali, L. *l.* Moz.
38 F4 Chuansha China
62 D3 Chubbuck U.S.A.
83 C4 Chubut *div.* Arg.
80 C6 Chubut *r.* Arg.
73 E5 Chuckwalla Mts *mts* U.S.A.
21 D5 Chudniv Ukr.
20 D3 Chudovo Rus. Fed.
Chudskoye Ozero *l.* *see* Peipus, Lake
54 C4 Chugach Mountains U.S.A.
41 C7 Chūgoku-sanchi *mts* Japan
40 C2 Chuguyevka Rus. Fed.
62 F3 Chugwater U.S.A.
21 F5 Chuhuyiv Ukr.
73 G5 Chuichu U.S.A.
36 F1 Chukchagirskoye, Ozero *l.* Rus. Fed.
25 V3 Chukchi Sea *sea* Rus. Fed./U.S.A.
20 G3 Chukhloma Rus. Fed.
25 U3 Chukotskiy Poluostrov *pen.* Rus. Fed.
20 H1 Chulasa Rus. Fed.
72 D5 Chula Vista U.S.A.
24 K4 Chulym Rus. Fed.
35 G4 Chumbi China
80 C3 Chumbicha Arg.
36 F1 Chumikan Rus. Fed.
44 B1 Chum Phae Thai.
44 A3 Chumphon Thai.
44 B2 Chum Saeng Thai.
25 L4 Chuna *r.* Rus. Fed.
39 F4 Chun'an China
42 D5 Ch'unch'ŏn S. Korea
42 D5 Ch'ungju S. Korea
Chungking *see* Chongqing
42 E6 Ch'ungmu S. Korea
42 C4 Chŭngsan N. Korea
31 H3 Chungur, Koh-i- *h.* Afgh.
42 F2 Chunhua China
35 F3 Chunit Tso *salt l.* China
25 M3 Chunya *r.* Rus. Fed.
44 C3 Chuŏr Phnum Dâmrei *mts* Cambodia
44 C2 Chuŏr Phnum Dângrêk *mts* Cambodia/Thai.
44 B2 Chuŏr Phnum Krâvanh *mts* Cambodia
38 A4 Chuosijia China
29 L3 Chūplū Iran
78 D7 Chuquibamba Peru
80 C2 Chuquicamata Chile
16 D7 Chur Switz.
25 P3 Churapcha Rus. Fed.
57 L3 Churchill Can.
57 K3 Churchill *r.* *Man./Sask.* Can.
59 H3 Churchill *r.* *Nfld* Can.
55 J4 Churchill *r.* *Sask.* Can.
57 L3 Churchill, Cape *c.* Can.
59 H3 Churchill Falls Can.
57 H3 Churchill Lake *l.* Can.

56 D3 Churchill Peak *summit* Can.
58 E2 Churchill Sound *chan.* Can.
64 D1 Churchs Ferry U.S.A.
70 D5 Churchville U.S.A.
35 F4 Churia Ghati Hills *mts* Nepal
20 H3 Churov Rus. Fed.
34 C3 Churu India
81 C2 Churuguara Venez.
34 D2 Chushul Jammu and Kashmir
73 H3 Chuska Mountains U.S.A.
59 F4 Chute-des-Passes Can.
69 J2 Chute-Rouge Can.
69 K2 Chute-St-Philippe Can.
39 F5 Chu-tung Taiwan
46 G3 Chuuk *i.* Micronesia
20 H4 Chuvashskaya Respublika *div.* Rus. Fed.
38 F3 Chu Xian China
39 A5 Chuxiong China
44 D2 Chư Yang Sin *mt* Vietnam
29 K4 Chwārtā Iraq
21 D6 Ciadâr-Lunga Moldova
45 C4 Ciamis Indon.
45 C4 Cianjur Indon.
82 B3 Cianorte Brazil
63 E6 Cibuta Mex.
18 F2 Čičarija *mts* Croatia
28 E2 Çiçekdağı Turkey
21 E7 Cide Turkey
17 K4 Ciechanów Pol.
75 J4 Ciego de Avila Cuba
81 B2 Ciénaga Col.
81 B2 Ciénaga de Zapatoza *l.* Col.
65 C7 Ciénega de Flores Mex.
63 E6 Cieneguita Mex.
75 H4 Cienfuegos Cuba
15 F3 Cieza Spain
15 E2 Cifuentes Spain
29 M2 Çigil Adası *i.* Azer.
15 E3 Cigüela *r.* Spain
28 D2 Cihanbeyli Turkey
15 D3 Cijara, Embalse de *resr* Spain
45 C4 Cilacap Indon.
29 J1 Çıldır Turkey
29 J1 Çıldır Gölü *l.* Turkey
39 D4 Cili China
29 K3 Cilo D. *mt* Turkey
29 N1 Çiloy Adası *i.* Azer.
73 E4 Cima U.S.A.
63 F4 Cimarron U.S.A.
65 D4 Cimarron *r.* U.S.A.
12 D5 Cimetière d'Ossuaire France
21 D6 Cimişlia Moldova
18 D2 Cimone, Monte *mt* Italy
29 H3 Çınar Turkey
81 C3 Cinaruco *r.* Venez.
81 D3 Cinaruco-Capanaparo, Parque Nacional *nat. park* Venez.
15 G2 Cinca *r.* Spain
70 A5 Cincinnati U.S.A.
71 F3 Cincinnatus U.S.A.
83 D4 Cinco Chañares Arg.
83 C3 Cinco Saltos Arg.
9 E6 Cinderford U.K.
28 B3 Çine Turkey
12 D4 Ciney Belgium
14 J5 Cinto, Monte *mt* France
83 B2 Cinzas *r.* Brazil
83 C3 Cipolletti Arg.
54 D3 Circle *AK* U.S.A.
62 F2 Circle U.S.A.
70 B5 Circleville *OH* U.S.A.
73 F2 Circleville *UT* U.S.A.
45 C4 Cirebon Indon.
9 F6 Cirencester U.K.
18 B2 Ciriè Italy
18 G5 Cirò Marina Italy
59 H2 Cirque Mtn *mt* Can.
68 C6 Cisco *IL* U.S.A.
65 D5 Cisco *TX* U.S.A.
73 H2 Cisco *UT* U.S.A.
81 B3 Cisneros Col.
74 E5 Citlaltépetl, Vol. *volc.* Mex.
18 G3 Čitluk Bos.-Herz.
90 C6 Citrusdal S. Africa
18 E3 Città di Castello Italy
19 L2 Ciucaş, Vârful *mt* Romania
74 D3 Ciudad Acuña Mex.
74 D5 Ciudad Altamirano Mex.
81 E3 Ciudad Bolívar Venez.
74 C3 Ciudad Camargo Mex.
74 F5 Ciudad del Carmen Mex.
82 A4 Ciudad del Este Para.
74 C3 Ciudad Delicias Mex.
81 C2 Ciudad de Nutrias Venez.
74 E4 Ciudad de Valles Mex.
81 E2 Ciudad Guayana Venez.
74 D5 Ciudad Guzmán Mex.
74 E5 Ciudad Ixtepec Mex.
74 C2 Ciudad Juárez Mex.
65 C7 Ciudad Lerdo Mex.
74 E4 Ciudad Mante Mex.
65 D7 Ciudad Mier Mex.
74 C3 Ciudad Obregón Mex.
81 E3 Ciudad Piar Venez.
15 E3 Ciudad Real Spain
65 D7 Ciudad Río Bravo Mex.
15 C2 Ciudad Rodrigo Spain
74 E4 Ciudad Victoria Mex.
15 H2 Ciutadella de Menorca Spain
28 F1 Cıva Burnu *pt* Turkey
28 B2 Civan Dağ *mt* Turkey
18 E1 Cividale del Friuli Italy
18 E3 Civita Castellana Italy
18 E3 Civitanova Marche Italy
18 D3 Civitavecchia Italy
28 B2 Çivril Turkey
39 F4 Cixi China
38 E2 Ci Xian China
29 J3 Cizre Turkey
9 J6 Clacton-on-Sea U.K.
11 D3 Clady U.K.
57 G3 Claire, Lake *l.* Can.
62 B3 Clair Engle L. *resr* U.S.A.
70 D4 Clairton U.S.A.
14 F3 Clamecy France
72 D2 Clan Alpine Mts *mts* U.S.A.
11 E4 Clane Rep. of Ireland
67 C5 Clanton U.S.A.
90 C6 Clanwilliam S. Africa
11 D4 Clara Rep. of Ireland
44 A3 Clara I. *i.* Myanmar
50 D2 Clare *N.S.W.* Austr.
50 B2 Clare *S.A.* Austr.
68 E4 Clare U.S.A.
11 C4 Clare *r.* Rep. of Ireland
11 C5 Clarecastle Rep. of Ireland
11 A4 Clare Island *i.* Rep. of Ireland
71 G3 Claremont U.S.A.
65 E4 Claremore U.S.A.
11 C4 Claremorris Rep. of Ireland
51 D5 Clarence N.Z.
92 B1 Clarence I. *i.* Ant.
56 C3 Clarence Str. *chan.* U.S.A.
67 F7 Clarence Town Bahamas
65 C5 Clarendon U.S.A.
59 K4 Clarenville Can.
56 G5 Claresholm Can.
64 E3 Clarinda U.S.A.
70 C5 Clarington U.S.A.
70 D4 Clarion U.S.A.
70 D4 Clarion *r.* U.S.A.
95 L4 Clarion Fracture Zone *sea feature* Pac. Oc.
64 D2 Clark U.S.A.
91 H5 Clarkebury S. Africa
48 E6 Clarke I. *i.* Austr.
60 D2 Clark Fork *r.* *MT* U.S.A.
67 D5 Clark Hill Res. *resr* U.S.A.
73 E4 Clark Mt *mt* U.S.A.
69 G3 Clark, Pt *pt* Can.
70 C5 Clarksburg U.S.A.
65 F5 Clarksdale U.S.A.
71 F4 Clarks Summit U.S.A.
62 C2 Clarkston U.S.A.
65 E5 Clarksville *AR* U.S.A.
68 A4 Clarksville *IA* U.S.A.
67 C4 Clarksville *TN* U.S.A.
82 B1 Claro *r.* *Goiás* Brazil
82 B2 Claro *r.* *Goiás* Brazil
11 D5 Clashmore Rep. of Ireland
11 D3 Claudy U.K.
43 B2 Claveria Phil.
12 D4 Clavier Belgium
71 G2 Clayburg U.S.A.
64 D4 Clay Center U.S.A.
73 F3 Clayhole Wash *r.* U.S.A.
67 D5 Clayton *GA* U.S.A.
63 G4 Clayton *NM* U.S.A.
71 E2 Clayton *NY* U.S.A.
71 J1 Clayton Lake U.S.A.
70 C6 Claytor Lake *l.* U.S.A.
11 B6 Clear, Cape *c.* Rep. of Ireland
69 G4 Clear Creek Can.
73 G4 Clear Creek *r.* U.S.A.
54 D4 Cleare, C. *c.* U.S.A.
70 D4 Clearfield *PA* U.S.A.
62 E3 Clearfield *UT* U.S.A.
70 B4 Clear Fork Reservoir U.S.A.
56 F3 Clear Hills *mts* Can.
64 E3 Clear Lake *IA* U.S.A.
68 A3 Clear Lake *WV* U.S.A.
72 A2 Clear Lake *l.* *CA* U.S.A.
73 F2 Clear Lake *l.* *UT* U.S.A.
62 B3 Clear L. Res. *resr* U.S.A.
67 D7 Clearwater U.S.A.
56 F4 Clearwater *r.* *Alta.* Can.
57 H3 Clearwater *r.* *Sask.* Can.
39 □ Clear Water Bay *b.* *H.K.* China
62 D2 Clearwater Mountains U.S.A.
57 H3 Clearwater River Provincial Park *res.* Can.
65 D5 Cleburne U.S.A.
62 B2 Cle Elum U.S.A.
8 G4 Cleethorpes U.K.
44 □ Clementi Sing.
70 C5 Clendenin U.S.A.
70 C4 Clendening Lake *l.* U.S.A.
43 A4 Cleopatra Needle *mt* Phil.
69 H1 Cléricy Can.
48 E4 Clermont Austr.
12 A5 Clermont France
67 D6 Clermont U.S.A.
12 D5 Clermont-en-Argonne France
14 F4 Clermont-Ferrand France
12 E4 Clervaux Lux.
18 D1 Cles Italy
9 E6 Clevedon U.K.
65 F5 Cleveland *MS* U.S.A.
70 C4 Cleveland *OH* U.S.A.
67 C5 Cleveland *TN* U.S.A.
68 D2 Cleveland Cliffs Basin *l.* U.S.A.
8 F3 Cleveland Hills *h.* U.K.
56 G5 Cleveland, Mt *mt* U.S.A.
8 D4 Cleveleys U.K.
11 B4 Clew Bay *b.* Rep. of Ireland
67 D7 Clewiston U.S.A.
11 A4 Clifden Rep. of Ireland
73 H5 Cliff U.S.A.
11 C3 Cliffoney Rep. of Ireland
51 E4 Clifford Bay *b.* N.Z.
73 H5 Clifton U.S.A.
70 D6 Clifton Forge U.S.A.
70 B6 Clinch *r.* U.S.A.
70 B6 Clinch Mountain *mts* U.S.A.
56 E4 Clinton *B.C.* Can.
69 G4 Clinton *Ont.* Can.
71 G4 Clinton *CT* U.S.A.
68 B5 Clinton *IA* U.S.A.
68 C5 Clinton *IL* U.S.A.
71 H3 Clinton *MA* U.S.A.
71 J2 Clinton *ME* U.S.A.
64 E4 Clinton *MO* U.S.A.
65 F5 Clinton *MS* U.S.A.
67 E5 Clinton *NC* U.S.A.
65 D5 Clinton *OK* U.S.A.
57 H2 Clinton-Colden Lake *l.* Can.
68 C5 Clinton Lake *l.* U.S.A.
68 C3 Clintonville U.S.A.
73 G4 Clints Well U.S.A.
95 L5 Clipperton Fracture Zone *sea feature* Pac. Oc.
74 C6 Clipperton Island *terr.* Pac. Oc.
10 B3 Clisham *h.* U.K.
8 E4 Clitheroe U.K.
91 G4 Clocolan S. Africa
11 D4 Cloghan Rep. of Ireland
11 C6 Clonakilty Rep. of Ireland
11 C6 Clonakilty Bay *b.* Rep. of Ireland
11 C4 Clonbern Rep. of Ireland
48 E4 Cloncurry Austr.
11 D3 Clones Rep. of Ireland
11 D5 Clonmel Rep. of Ireland
11 D4 Clonygowan Rep. of Ireland
11 B5 Cloonbannin Rep. of Ireland
11 D4 Clooneagh Rep. of Ireland
13 G2 Cloppenburg Ger.
68 A2 Cloquet U.S.A.
62 F2 Cloud Peak *summit* U.S.A.
51 E4 Cloudy Bay *b.* N.Z.
39 □ Cloudy Hill *h.* *H.K.* China
69 K1 Clova Can.
72 A2 Cloverdale U.S.A.
65 C5 Clovis U.S.A.
69 J3 Cloyne Can.
10 C3 Cluanie, Loch *l.* U.K.
57 H3 Cluff Lake Can.
17 L7 Cluj-Napoca Romania
9 D5 Clun U.K.
50 D4 Clunes Austr.
14 H3 Cluses France
9 D4 Clwydian Range *h.* U.K.
56 G4 Clyde Can.
70 E3 Clyde *NY* U.S.A.
70 B4 Clyde *OH* U.S.A.
10 D5 Clyde *r.* U.K.
10 D5 Clydebank U.K.
10 D5 Clyde, Firth of *est.* U.K.
55 M2 Clyde River Can.
63 C5 Coachella U.S.A.
83 B2 Co Aconcagua *mt* Arg.
65 C7 Coahuila *div.* Mex.
56 D2 Coal *r.* Can.
68 C5 Coal City U.S.A.
72 D3 Coaldale U.S.A.
65 D5 Coalgate U.S.A.
72 B3 Coalinga U.S.A.
56 D3 Coal River Can.
9 F5 Coalville U.K.
78 F4 Coari Brazil
78 F5 Coari *r.* Brazil
67 C6 Coastal Plain *plain* U.S.A.
56 D4 Coast Mountains Can.
62 B2 Coast Range *mts* U.S.A.
83 B2 Coast Ranges *mts* U.S.A.
10 E5 Coatbridge U.K.
71 F5 Coatesville U.S.A.
59 F4 Coaticook Can.
55 K3 Coats Island *i.* Can.
92 C3 Coats Land *coastal area* Ant.
74 F5 Coatzacoalcos Mex.
69 H2 Cobalt Can.
74 F5 Cobán Guatemala
50 E1 Cobar Austr.
50 G4 Cobargo Austr.
50 G4 Cobberas, Mt *mt* Austr.
50 D5 Cobden Austr.
69 J3 Cobden Can.
11 C6 Cóbh Rep. of Ireland
57 K4 Cobham *r.* Can.
78 E6 Cobija Bol.
71 F3 Cobleskill U.S.A.
69 H4 Cobourg Can.
48 D3 Cobourg Penina *pen.* Austr.
50 E3 Cobram Austr.
13 J4 Coburg Ger.
15 D2 Coca Spain
82 B1 Cocalinho Brazil
Cocanada *see* Kākināda
78 E7 Cochabamba Bol.
84 B4 Cochamó Chile
12 F4 Cochem Ger.
33 B4 Cochin India
73 H5 Cochise U.S.A.
56 G4 Cochrane *Alta.* Can.
58 D4 Cochrane *Ont.* Can.
80 B7 Cochrane Chile
57 J3 Cochrane *r.* Can.
50 C2 Cockburn Austr.
69 F3 Cockburn I. *i.* Can.
10 F5 Cockburnspath U.K.
67 F7 Cockburn Town Bahamas
75 K4 Cockburn Town Turks and Caicos Is
8 D3 Cockermouth U.K.
90 F6 Cockscomb *summit* S. Africa
75 H6 Coco *r.* Honduras/Nic.
74 G7 Coco, Isla de *i.* Col.
73 F4 Coconino Plateau *plat.* U.S.A.
50 F2 Cocoparra Range *h.* Austr.
81 A4 Coco, Pta *pt* Col.
81 B3 Cocorná Col.
82 D1 Cocos Brazil
93 L4 Cocos Is *is* Ind. Ocean
95 O5 Cocos Ridge *sea feature* Pac. Oc.
81 B3 Cocuy, Parque Nacional el *nat. park* Col.
81 B3 Cocuy, Sierra Nevada del *mt* Col.
78 F4 Codajás Brazil
71 H4 Cod, Cape *c.* U.S.A.
81 D2 Codera, C. *pt* Venez.
51 A7 Codfish I. *i.* N.Z.
18 E2 Codigoro Italy
59 H2 Cod Island *i.* Can.
19 L2 Codlea Romania
79 K4 Codó Brazil
9 E5 Codsall U.K.
11 A6 Cod's Head *hd* Rep. of Ireland
62 E2 Cody U.S.A.
48 E3 Coen Austr.
12 F3 Coesfeld Ger.
93 H4 Coëtivy *i.* Seychelles
62 C2 Coeur d'Alene U.S.A.
62 C2 Coeur d'Alene L. *l.* U.S.A.
12 E2 Coevorden Neth.
91 H5 Coffee Bay S. Africa
65 E4 Coffeyville U.S.A.
49 F5 Coffs Harbour Austr.
91 G6 Cofimvaba S. Africa
68 B4 Coggon U.S.A.
14 D4 Cognac France
86 C4 Cogo Equatorial Guinea
70 E3 Cohocton *r.* U.S.A.
71 G3 Cohoes U.S.A.
50 E3 Cohuna Austr.
75 H7 Coiba, Isla *i.* Panama
80 C8 Coig *r.* Arg.
80 B7 Coihaique Chile
33 B4 Coimbatore India
15 B2 Coimbra Port.
15 D4 Coín Spain
78 E7 Coipasa, Salar de *salt flat* Bol.
81 C2 Cojedes *r.* Venez.
62 E3 Cokeville U.S.A.
50 D5 Colac Austr.
Colair L. *l. see* Kolleru L.
82 E2 Colatina Brazil
12 K2 Colbitz Ger.
64 C4 Colby U.S.A.
78 D7 Colca *r.* Peru
9 H6 Colchester U.K.
68 B5 Colchester U.S.A.
10 F5 Coldingham U.K.
13 L3 Colditz Ger.
57 G4 Cold L. *l.* Can.
57 G4 Cold Lake Can.
10 F5 Coldstream U.K.
65 D4 Coldwater *KS* U.S.A.
68 E5 Coldwater *MI* U.S.A.
68 D1 Coldwell Can.
71 H2 Colebrook U.S.A.
68 E4 Coleman *MI* U.S.A.
65 D6 Coleman *TX* U.S.A.
91 H4 Colenso S. Africa
50 C4 Coleraine Austr.
11 E2 Coleraine U.K.
51 C5 Coleridge, L. *l.* N.Z.
33 B4 Coleroon *r.* India
90 F5 Colesberg S. Africa
72 B2 Colfax *CA* U.S.A.
62 C2 Colfax *WA* U.S.A.
10 □ Colgrave Sound *chan.* U.K.
91 G3 Coligny S. Africa
74 D5 Colima Mex.
10 B4 Coll *i.* U.K.
15 E2 Collado Villalba Spain
67 C5 College Park U.S.A.
65 D6 College Station U.S.A.
50 G1 Collie Austr.
48 C3 Collier Bay *b.* Austr.
69 G3 Collingwood Can.
51 D4 Collingwood N.Z.
65 F6 Collins U.S.A.
66 B4 Collinsville U.S.A.
83 B3 Collipulli Chile
11 C3 Collooney Rep. of Ireland
14 H2 Colmar France
15 E2 Colmenar Viejo Spain
10 D5 Colmonell U.K.
9 H6 Colne *r.* U.K.
50 H2 Colo *r.* Austr.
12 F4 Cologne Ger.
68 C3 Coloma U.S.A.
82 C3 Colômbia Brazil
81 B4 Colombia Col.
65 D7 Colombia Mex.
77 C2 Colombia *country* S. America
96 D5 Colombian Basin *sea feature* Atl. Ocean
33 B5 Colombo Sri Lanka
15 E5 Colomiers France
83 E2 Colón *Buenos Aires* Arg.
83 E2 Colón *Entre Ríos* Arg.
75 H4 Colón Cuba
75 J7 Colón Panama
63 C6 Colonet, C. *c.* Mex.
82 E1 Colônia *r.* Brazil
83 D3 Colonia Choele Choel, Isla *i.* Arg.
83 F2 Colonia del Sacramento Uru.
83 C3 Colonia Emilio Mitre Arg.
83 F1 Colonia Lavalleja Uru.
70 E6 Colonial Heights U.S.A.
74 F6 Colonia Reforma Mex.
18 G5 Colonna, Capo *pt* Italy
10 B4 Colonsay *i.* U.K.
83 D3 Colorada Grande, Salina *l.* Arg.
63 F4 Colorado *div.* U.S.A.
83 D3 Colorado *r.* *La Pampa/Río Negro* Arg.
83 C1 Colorado *r.* *San Juan* Arg.
73 E5 Colorado *r.* Mex./U.S.A.
65 D6 Colorado *r.* U.S.A.
73 F3 Colorado City *AZ* U.S.A.
65 C5 Colorado City *TX* U.S.A.
83 D3 Colorado, Delta del Río *delta* Arg.
72 D5 Colorado Desert U.S.A.
73 H2 Colorado National Monument *res.* U.S.A.
73 G3 Colorado Plateau *plat.* U.S.A.
73 E4 Colorado River Aqueduct *canal* U.S.A.
63 F4 Colorado Springs U.S.A.
13 M1 Cölpin Ger.
9 G5 Colsterworth U.K.
9 J5 Coltishall U.K.
72 D4 Colton *CA* U.S.A.
71 F2 Colton *NY* U.S.A.
73 G2 Colton *UT* U.S.A.
70 E5 Columbia *MD* U.S.A.
64 E4 Columbia *MO* U.S.A.
65 F6 Columbia *MS* U.S.A.
70 E4 Columbia *PA* U.S.A.
67 D5 Columbia *SC* U.S.A.
67 C5 Columbia *TN* U.S.A.
62 B2 Columbia *r.* Can./U.S.A.
55 L1 Columbia, C. *c.* Can.
68 E5 Columbia City U.S.A.
70 E5 Columbia, District of *div.* U.S.A.
71 K2 Columbia Falls *ME* U.S.A.
62 D1 Columbia Falls *MT* U.S.A.
56 F4 Columbia Mountains Can.
56 F4 Columbia, Mt *mt* Can.
62 C2 Columbia Plateau *plat.* U.S.A.
90 B6 Columbine, Cape *pt* S. Africa
67 C5 Columbus *GA* U.S.A.
66 C4 Columbus *IN* U.S.A.
65 F5 Columbus *MS* U.S.A.
62 E2 Columbus *MT* U.S.A.
64 D3 Columbus *NE* U.S.A.
63 F6 Columbus *NM* U.S.A.
70 B5 Columbus *OH* U.S.A.
65 D6 Columbus *TX* U.S.A.
68 C4 Columbus *WV* U.S.A.
68 B5 Columbus Jct U.S.A.
67 F7 Columbus Pt *pt* Bahamas
72 D2 Columbus Salt Marsh *salt marsh* U.S.A.
72 A2 Colusa U.S.A.
51 E2 Colville N.Z.
62 C1 Colville U.S.A.
54 C3 Colville *r.* *AK* U.S.A.
51 E2 Colville Channel N.Z.
54 F3 Colville Lake Can.
9 D4 Colwyn Bay U.K.
18 E2 Comacchio Italy
18 E2 Comacchio, Valli di *lag.* Italy
35 G3 Comai China
83 B4 Comallo *r.* Arg.
65 D6 Comanche U.S.A.
92 B1 Comandante Ferraz *Brazil Base* Ant.
83 C2 Comandante Salas Arg.
17 N7 Comănești Romania
83 B1 Combarbalá Chile
11 F3 Comber U.K.
69 J3 Combermere Can.
35 H6 Combermere Bay *b.* Myanmar
12 A4 Combles France
91 K1 Combomune Moz.
58 E3 Comencho, L. *l.* Can.
11 D5 Comeragh Mountains *h.* Rep. of Ireland
65 D6 Comfort U.S.A.
35 G5 Comilla Bangl.
12 A4 Comines Belgium
18 C4 Comino, Capo *pt* *Sardinia* Italy
74 F5 Comitán de Domínguez Mex.
71 G4 Commack U.S.A.
69 H3 Commanda Can.
55 K3 Committee Bay *b.* Can.
92 B6 Commonwealth B. *b.* Ant.
18 C2 Como Italy
35 G3 Como Chamling *l.* China
80 C7 Comodoro Rivadavia Arg.
86 B4 Comoé, Parc National de la *nat. park* Côte d'Ivoire
18 C2 Como, Lago di *l.* Italy
33 B4 Comorin, Cape *c.* India
85 H7 Comoros *country* Africa
14 F2 Compiègne France
74 D4 Compostela Mex.
43 C5 Compostela Phil.
82 C4 Comprida, Ilha *i.* Brazil
68 C5 Compton U.S.A.
21 D6 Comrat Moldova
10 E4 Comrie U.K.
65 C6 Comstock U.S.A.
35 H4 Cona China
86 A4 Conakry Guinea
83 C4 Cona Niyeo Arg.
82 C2 Conceição *r.* Brazil
82 E2 Conceição da Barra Brazil
79 J5 Conceição do Araguaia Brazil
80 C3 Concepción Arg.
78 F7 Concepción Bol.
83 B3 Concepción Chile
75 H7 Concepción Panama
80 E2 Concepción Para.
83 E2 Concepción del Uruguay Arg.
59 K4 Conception Bay South Can.
67 F7 Conception I. *i.* Bahamas
72 B4 Conception, Pt *pt* U.S.A.
82 C3 Conchas Brazil
63 F5 Conchas L. *l.* U.S.A.
73 H4 Concho U.S.A.
74 E3 Conchos *r.* *Tamaulipas* Mex.
74 D3 Conchos *r.* *Chihuahua* Mex.
72 A3 Concord *CA* U.S.A.
67 D5 Concord *NC* U.S.A.
71 H3 Concord *NH* U.S.A.
83 F1 Concordia Arg.
81 B4 Concordia Col.
90 B4 Concordia S. Africa
64 D4 Concordia U.S.A.
44 C3 Côn Đao Vietnam
82 E1 Condeúba Brazil
50 F2 Condobolin Austr.
14 E5 Condom France
62 B2 Condon U.S.A.
12 D4 Condroz *reg.* Belgium
67 C6 Conecuh *r.* U.S.A.
18 E2 Conegliano Italy
70 D4 Conemaugh *r.* U.S.A.
69 G4 Conestogo Lake *l.* Can.
70 E3 Conesus Lake *l.* U.S.A.
71 G4 Coney I. *i.* U.S.A.
48 F3 Conflict Group *is* P.N.G.
14 E3 Confolens France
73 F2 Confusion Range *mts* U.S.A.
39 D6 Conghua China
39 C5 Congjiang China
9 E4 Congleton U.K.
85 E6 Congo *country* Africa
85 F5 Congo *country* Africa
88 B4 Congo *r.* Africa
84 D6 Congo Basin *basin* Africa
73 F4 Congress U.S.A.
83 B3 Conguillo, Parque Nacional *nat. park* Chile
9 G4 Coningsby U.K.
58 D4 Coniston Can.
8 D3 Coniston U.K.
57 G3 Conklin Can.
83 D2 Conlara Arg.
83 D2 Conlara *r.* Arg.
70 C4 Conneaut U.S.A.
71 G4 Connecticut *div.* U.S.A.
66 F3 Connecticut *r.* U.S.A.
70 D4 Connellsville U.S.A.
11 B4 Connemara *reg.* Rep. of Ireland
71 J1 Conners Can.
66 C4 Connersville U.S.A.
11 B3 Conn, Lough *l.* Rep. of Ireland
50 E2 Conoble Austr.
39 B6 Co Nôi Vietnam
71 E5 Conowingo U.S.A.
62 E1 Conrad U.S.A.
65 E6 Conroe U.S.A.
82 D3 Conselheiro Lafaiete Brazil
82 E2 Conselheiro Pena Brazil
8 F3 Consett U.K.
44 C3 Côn Sơn *i.* Vietnam
57 G4 Consort Can.
16 D7 Constance, Lake *l.* Ger./Switz.
78 F5 Constância dos Baetas Brazil
19 N2 Constanţa Romania
15 D4 Constantina Spain
86 C1 Constantine Alg.
68 E5 Constantine U.S.A.
73 E6 Constitución de 1857, Parque Nacional *nat. park* Mex.
62 D3 Contact U.S.A.
78 C5 Contamana Peru
82 E1 Contas *r.* Brazil
73 G6 Continental U.S.A.
71 H3 Contoocook *r.* U.S.A.
80 B8 Contreras, I. *i.* Chile
57 G1 Contwoyto Lake *l.* Can.
65 E5 Conway *AR* U.S.A.
71 H3 Conway *NH* U.S.A.
67 E5 Conway *SC* U.S.A.
49 H4 Conway Reef *rf* Fiji
9 D4 Conwy U.K.
9 D4 Conwy *r.* U.K.
48 D4 Coober Pedy Austr.
68 A2 Cook U.S.A.
56 D4 Cook, C. *c.* Can.
67 C4 Cookeville U.S.A.
91 F6 Cookhouse S. Africa
54 C3 Cook Inlet *chan.* U.S.A.
47 L5 Cook Islands *is* N.Z.
51 C5 Cook, Mt *mt* N.Z.
71 F3 Cooksburg U.S.A.
59 J3 Cook's Harbour Can.
11 E3 Cookstown U.K.
51 E4 Cook Strait *str.* N.Z.
48 E3 Cooktown Austr.
50 F1 Coolabah Austr.
50 G1 Coolah Austr.
50 F3 Coolamon Austr.
48 C5 Coolgardie Austr.
73 G5 Coolidge U.S.A.
73 G5 Coolidge Dam U.S.A.
50 G4 Cooma Austr.
11 A6 Coomacarrea *h.* Rep. of Ireland
50 C2 Coombah Austr.
50 B3 Coonalpyn Austr.
50 G1 Coonamble Austr.
50 C4 Coonawarra Austr.
Coondapoor *see* Kundāpura
48 D4 Cooper Creek *watercourse* Austr.
71 J2 Coopers Mills U.S.A.
67 E7 Coopers Town Bahamas
64 D2 Cooperstown *ND* U.S.A.
71 F3 Cooperstown *NY* U.S.A.
50 B3 Coorong, The *in.* Austr.
62 A3 Coos Bay U.S.A.
50 G3 Cootamundra Austr.
11 D3 Cootehill Rep. of Ireland
83 B3 Copahue, Volcán *mt* Chile
62 G4 Cope U.S.A.
7 N9 Copenhagen Denmark
80 B3 Copiapo Chile
80 B3 Copiapo *r.* Chile
18 D2 Copparo Italy
69 G2 Copper Cliff Can.
68 D2 Copper Harbor U.S.A.
54 G3 Coppermine *N.W.T.* Can.
54 G3 Coppermine *r.* *N.W.T.* Can.
68 E2 Coppermine Pt *pt* Can.
90 E4 Copperton S. Africa
35 F3 Coqên China
57 E5 Coquihalla Highway Can.
83 B1 Coquimbo Chile
83 B1 Coquimbo *div.* Chile
19 L3 Corabia Romania
82 D2 Coração de Jesus Brazil
Coracesium *see* Alanya
78 D7 Coracora Peru
67 D7 Coral Gables U.S.A.
55 K3 Coral Harbour Can.
49 F3 Coral Sea *sea* Coral Sea Is Terr.
94 E6 Coral Sea Basin *sea feature* Pac. Oc.
47 G5 Coral Sea Islands Territory *terr.* Pac. Oc.
68 B5 Coralville Reservoir U.S.A.
50 D5 Corangamite, L. *l.* Austr.
79 G3 Corantijn *r.* Suriname
29 M1 Corat Azer.
12 B5 Corbeny France
83 E2 Corbett Arg.
57 L2 Corbett Inlet *in.* Can.
12 A5 Corbie France
70 A6 Corbin U.S.A.
9 G5 Corby U.K.
72 C3 Corcoran U.S.A.
80 B6 Corcovado, G. de *b.* Chile
67 D6 Cordele U.S.A.
81 B4 Cordillera de los Picachos, Parque Nacional *nat. park* Col.
43 B4 Cordilleras Range *mts* Phil.
83 C4 Córdoba *Río Negro* Arg.
83 D1 Córdoba Arg.

13 G2 Damme Ger.
34 D5 Damoh India
86 B4 Damongo Ghana
48 E2 Dampier Strait chan. P.N.G.
37 F7 Dampir, Selat chan. Indon.
Damqoq Kanbab r. see Maquan He
35 H2 Dam Qu r. China
35 H3 Damroh India
12 E1 Damwoude Neth.
86 B4 Danané Côte d'Ivoire
44 D1 Đa Năng Vietnam
43 C4 Danao Phil.
38 A4 Danba China
71 G4 Danbury CT U.S.A.
71 H3 Danbury NH U.S.A.
71 G3 Danby U.S.A.
73 E4 Danby Lake l. U.S.A.
38 E3 Dancheng China
88 D3 Dande Eth.
33 A3 Dandeli India
50 E4 Dandenong Austr.
42 C3 Dandong China
9 E4 Dane r. U.K.
55 Q2 Daneborg Greenland
71 K2 Danforth U.S.A.
39 E6 Dangan Liedao is China
33 G3 Dangbe La pass China
40 B2 Dangbizhen Rus. Fed.
38 B3 Dangchang China
46 L5 Danger Islands is Cook Islands Pac. Oc.
90 C7 Danger Pt pt S. Africa
88 D2 Dangila Eth.
Dangla mts see Tanggula Shan
35 G3 Dangqên China
74 G5 Dangriga Belize
38 E3 Dangshan China
38 F4 Dangtu China
39 D4 Dangyang China
62 E3 Daniel U.S.A.
90 E4 Daniëlskuil S. Africa
20 G3 Danilov Rus. Fed.
21 H5 Danilovka Rus. Fed.
20 G3 Danilovskaya Vozvyshennost' reg. Rus. Fed.
38 D2 Daning China
29 M1 Dänizkänarı Azer.
38 D3 Danjiangkou Sk. resr China
30 E6 Đank Oman
34 D2 Dankhar India
20 F4 Dankov Rus. Fed.
39 B4 Danleng China
74 G6 Danlí Honduras
Dannebrogsø i. see Qillak
71 G2 Dannemora U.S.A.
13 K1 Dannenberg (Elbe) Ger.
13 M1 Dannenwalde Ger.
51 F4 Dannevirke N.Z.
91 J4 Dannhauser S. Africa
44 B1 Dan Sai Thai.
70 E3 Dansville U.S.A.
34 C4 Danta India
33 C2 Dantewara India
19 M3 Danube r. Europe
68 D5 Danville IL U.S.A.
68 D6 Danville IN U.S.A.
66 C4 Danville KY U.S.A.
69 J5 Danville PA U.S.A.
70 D6 Danville VA U.S.A.
39 C7 Dan Xian China
38 F4 Danyang China
39 C5 Danzhai China
43 B4 Dao Phil.
39 C6 Đao Bach Long Vi i. Vietnam
39 C6 Đao Cai Bâu i. Vietnam
39 C6 Đao Cat Ba i. Vietnam
44 B3 Đao Phu Quôc i. Vietnam
39 B6 Đao Thô Chu' i. Vietnam
86 B4 Daoukro Côte d'Ivoire
44 B3 Đao Vây i. Vietnam
39 D5 Dao Xian China
39 C4 Daozhen China
43 C4 Dapa Phil.
86 C3 Dapaong Togo
35 J4 Daphabum mt India
43 B4 Dapiak, Mt mt Phil.
43 B4 Dapitan Phil.
27 H3 Da Qaidam China
36 E2 Daqing China
38 D1 Daqing Shan mts China
30 D3 Daqq-e Dombūn Iran
31 F3 Daqq-e-Tundi, Dasht-e l. Afgh.
29 K4 Dāqūq Iraq
39 G4 Daqu Shan i. China
28 F5 Dar'ā Syria
30 D4 Dārāb Iran
43 B3 Daraga Phil.
17 O4 Darahanava Belarus
86 D1 Daraj Libya
30 D4 Dārākūyeh Iran
43 C4 Daram i. Phil.
30 D3 Darang, Kūh-e h. Iran
25 N4 Darasun Rus. Fed.
30 E4 Darband Iran
35 F4 Darbhanga India
72 C2 Dardanelle U.S.A.
65 E5 Dardanelle, Lake l. U.S.A.
19 M4 Dardanelles str. Turkey
13 J3 Dardesheim Ger.
28 F2 Darende Turkey
88 D4 Dar es Salaam Tanz.
18 D2 Darfo Boario Terme Italy
34 B2 Dargai Pak.
31 F1 Dargan-Ata Turkm.
51 D1 Dargaville N.Z.
50 F4 Dargo Austr.
36 C2 Darhan Mongolia
38 D1 Darhan Muminggan Lianheqi China
67 D6 Darien U.S.A.
81 A2 Darién, Golfo del g. Col.
75 J7 Darién, Parque Nacional de nat. park Panama
81 A2 Darién, Serranía del mts Panama
35 G4 Darjiling India
30 C4 Darkhazīneh Iran
36 B3 Darlag China
50 D2 Darling r. Austr.
48 E4 Darling Downs reg. Austr.
48 B5 Darling Range h. Austr.
8 F3 Darlington U.K.
68 B4 Darlington U.S.A.
50 F3 Darlington Point Austr.
16 H3 Darłowo Pol.
30 B5 Darmā S. Arabia
34 E3 Darma Pass China/India
33 B2 Darmaraopet India
30 E4 Dar Mazār Iran
13 G5 Darmstadt Ger.
34 C5 Darna r. India
87 E1 Darnah Libya
91 J4 Darnall S. Africa
50 D2 Darnick Austr.
54 F3 Darnley Bay b. Can.
92 D5 Darnley, C. c. Ant.
15 F2 Daroca Spain
20 G3 Darovka Rus. Fed.
20 H3 Darovskoy Rus. Fed.
83 D3 Darregueira Arg.
30 E3 Darreh Bīd Iran
31 E2 Darreh Gaz Iran
29 L4 Darreh Gozaru r. Iran
31 H3 Darreh-ye Shekārī r. Afgh.
33 B3 Darsi India
29 M6 Darsīyeh Iran
9 D7 Dart r. U.K.
9 H6 Dartford U.K.
50 C4 Dartmoor Austr.
9 C7 Dartmoor reg. U.K.
9 D7 Dartmoor National Park U.K.
59 H5 Dartmouth Can.
9 D7 Dartmouth U.K.
8 F4 Darton U.K.
11 C3 Darty Mts h. Rep. of Ireland
48 E2 Daru P.N.G.
86 A4 Daru Sierra Leone
35 G3 Darum Tso l. China
18 G2 Daruvar Croatia
31 E1 Darvaza Turkm.
30 C4 Darvīsla Iran
31 G4 Darwazgai Afgh.
8 E4 Darwen U.K.
31 G4 Darweshan Afgh.
48 D3 Darwin Austr.
80 C8 Darwin, Mte mt Chile
34 B3 Darya Khan Pak.
31 E4 Dārzīn Iran
30 D5 Dās i. U.A.E.
38 D4 Dashennongjia mt China
32 E1 Dashkhovuz Turkm.
30 E2 Dasht Iran
31 F5 Dasht r. Pak.
30 E4 Dasht Āb Iran
30 C4 Dasht-e Palang r. Iran
31 F5 Dashtiari Iran
31 H2 Dashtiobburdon Tajik.
38 C2 Dashuikeng China
38 B2 Dashuitou China
34 C2 Daska Pak.
29 L1 Daşkäsän Azer.
34 C1 Daspar mt Pak.
13 H3 Dassel Ger.
90 C6 Dassen Island i. S. Africa
29 L2 Dastakert Armenia
30 E3 Dastgardān Iran
42 F2 Da Suifen r. China
19 M6 Datça Turkey
40 G3 Date Japan
73 F5 Dateland U.S.A.
34 D4 Datia India
39 E5 Datian China
38 A2 Datong Qinghai China
38 D1 Datong Shanxi China
38 B2 Datong He r. China
38 A2 Datong Shan mts China
43 C5 Datu Piang Phil.
45 C2 Datu, Tanjung c. Indon./Malaysia
20 C3 Daugava r. Belarus/Latvia
7 U9 Daugavpils Latvia
31 G2 Daulatabad Afgh.
34 C6 Daulatabad India
Daulatabad see Malāyer
12 E4 Daun Ger.
33 A2 Daund India
44 A2 Daung Kyun i. Myanmar
57 J4 Dauphin Can.
14 G4 Dauphiné reg. France
65 F6 Dauphin I. i. U.S.A.
57 K4 Dauphin L. l. Can.
34 D4 Dausa India
10 E3 Dava U.K.
29 M1 Däväçi Azer.
33 A3 Davangere India
43 C5 Davao Phil.
43 C5 Davao Gulf b. Phil.
31 F5 Dāvar Panāh Iran
91 H3 Davel S. Africa
72 A3 Davenport CA U.S.A.
68 B5 Davenport IA U.S.A.
9 F5 Daventry U.K.
91 H3 Daveyton S. Africa
75 H7 David Panama
57 H4 Davidson Can.
57 J3 Davin Lake l. Can.
72 B2 Davis U.S.A.
92 D5 Davis Austr. Base Ant.
73 E4 Davis Dam U.S.A.
59 H2 Davis Inlet Can.
92 D5 Davis Sea sea Ant.
55 N3 Davis Strait str. Can./Greenland
16 D7 Davos Switz.
42 B3 Dawa China
38 A1 Dawan China
35 F3 Dawaxung China
38 B4 Dawe China
Dawei see Tavoy
38 E3 Dawen r. China
30 C5 Dawḥat Salwah b. Qatar/S. Arabia
44 A1 Dawna Range mts Myanmar/Thai.
32 D6 Dawqah Oman
54 E3 Dawson Y.T. Can.
67 C6 Dawson GA U.S.A.
64 D2 Dawson ND U.S.A.
57 J4 Dawson Bay b. Can.
56 E3 Dawson Creek Can.
57 L2 Dawson Inlet in. Can.
56 B2 Dawson Range mts Can.
28 E4 Dawu Hubei China
36 C3 Dawu Sichuan China
14 D5 Dax France
38 C4 Daxian China
39 C6 Daxin China
38 E2 Daxing China
39 A4 Daxue Shan mts China
84 B4 Dayang r. China
35 H4 Dayang r. India
39 D6 Dayao Shan mts China
39 E4 Daye China
39 B4 Dayi China
50 E4 Daylesford Austr.
72 D3 Daylight Pass U.S.A.
83 F1 Daymán r. Uru.
83 F1 Daymán, Cuchilla del h. Uru.
39 D4 Dayong China
29 H4 Dayr az Zawr Syria
70 A5 Dayton OH U.S.A.
67 C5 Dayton TN U.S.A.
62 C2 Dayton WA U.S.A.
67 D6 Daytona Beach U.S.A.
39 E5 Dayu China
39 D5 Dayu Ling mts China
38 F3 Da Yunhe r. China
62 C2 Dayville U.S.A.
39 D7 Dazhou Dao i. China
38 C4 Dazhu China
39 B4 Dazu China
90 E5 De Aar S. Africa
68 D2 Dead r. U.S.A.
67 F7 Deadman's Cay Bahamas
73 E4 Dead Mts mts U.S.A.
71 H2 Dead River r. U.S.A.
28 E6 Dead Sea salt l. Asia
9 J6 Deal U.K.
91 F4 Dealesville S. Africa
39 E4 De'an China
56 D4 Dean r. Can.
9 E6 Dean, Forest of forest U.K.
83 D1 Deán Funes Arg.
69 F4 Dearborn U.S.A.
56 D3 Dease r. Can.
56 C3 Dease Lake Can.
54 H3 Dease Strait chan. Can.
72 D3 Death Valley v. U.S.A.
72 D3 Death Valley Junction U.S.A.
72 D3 Death Valley National Monument res. U.S.A.
14 E2 Deauville France
45 D2 Debak Malaysia
39 C6 Debao China
19 J4 Debar Macedonia
57 H4 Debden Can.
9 J5 Debenham U.K.
73 H2 De Beque U.S.A.
71 J2 Deblois U.S.A.
88 D3 Debre Birhan Eth.
17 K7 Debrecen Hungary
88 D2 Debre Markos Eth.
88 D2 Debre Tabor Eth.
88 D3 Debre Zeyit Eth.
67 C5 Decatur AL U.S.A.
67 C5 Decatur GA U.S.A.
68 C6 Decatur IL U.S.A.
68 E5 Decatur IN U.S.A.
68 E4 Decatur MI U.S.A.
33 B2 Deccan plat. India
69 H2 Decelles, Réservoir resr Can.
16 G5 Děčín Czech Rep.
68 B4 Decorah U.S.A.
9 F6 Deddington U.K.
13 J2 Dedeleben Ger.
13 J2 Dedelstorf Ger.
12 E2 Dedemsvaart Neth.
82 C4 Dedo de Deus mt Brazil
90 C6 De Doorns S. Africa
29 L1 Dedoplis Tsqaro Georgia
86 B3 Dédougou Burkina
20 D3 Dedovichi Rus. Fed.
89 D5 Dedza Malawi
9 D4 Dee est. Wales U.K.
9 E4 Dee r. Eng./Wales U.K.
10 F3 Dee r. Scot. U.K.
11 C5 Deel r. Rep. of Ireland
11 D3 Deele r. Rep. of Ireland
39 □ Deep Bay b. H.K. China
70 D5 Deep Creek Lake l. U.S.A.
72 F2 Deep Creek Range mts U.S.A.
69 J2 Deep River Can.
71 G4 Deep River U.S.A.
57 K1 Deep Rose Lake l. Can.
72 D3 Deep Springs U.S.A.
70 B5 Deer Creek Lake l. U.S.A.
71 K2 Deer I. i. Can.
71 J2 Deer I. i. U.S.A.
71 J2 Deer Isle U.S.A.
58 B3 Deer L. l. Can.
59 J4 Deer Lake Nfld Can.
58 B3 Deer Lake Ont. Can.
62 D2 Deer Lodge U.S.A.
80 D2 Defensores del Chaco, Parque Nacional nat. park Para.
70 A4 Defiance U.S.A.
67 C6 De Funiak Springs U.S.A.
36 B3 Dêgê China
88 E3 Degeh Bur Eth.
35 G3 Dêgên China
13 L6 Deggendorf Ger.
33 C3 Degh r. Pak.
12 B3 De Haan Belgium
30 D4 Dehaj Iran
31 F4 Dehak Iran
31 F5 Dehak Iran
30 D4 Deh Bīd Iran
30 C4 Deh-Dasht Iran
30 C4 Deh-e Khalīfeh Iran
30 C3 Deheq Iran
30 C2 Dehgāh Iran
30 B3 Dehgolān Iran
33 B5 Dehiwala-Mount Lavinia Sri Lanka
30 D5 Dehkūyeh Iran
30 B3 Dehlonān Iran
34 D3 Dehra Dun India
35 F4 Dehri India
31 E4 Deh Salm Iran
30 E4 Deh Sard Iran
29 K4 Deh Sheykh Iran
31 F4 Deh Shū Afgh.
39 F5 Dehua China
42 C1 Dehui China
12 B4 Deinze Belgium
28 E5 Deir el Qamer Lebanon
Deir-ez-Zor see Dayr az Zawr
17 L7 Dej Romania
39 C4 Dejiang China
68 C5 De Kalb IL U.S.A.
65 E5 De Kalb TX U.S.A.
71 F2 De Kalb Junction U.S.A.
32 A6 Dekemhare Eritrea
88 C4 Dekese Congo(Zaire)
31 G2 Dekhkanabad Uzbek.
12 C1 De Koog Neth.
12 C2 De Kooy Neth.
72 C4 Delano U.S.A.
73 F2 Delano Peak summit U.S.A.
31 F3 Delārām Afgh.
91 F3 Delareyville S. Africa
57 H4 Delaronde Lake l. Can.
68 C5 Delavan IL U.S.A.
68 C4 Delavan WV U.S.A.
70 B4 Delaware U.S.A.
71 F5 Delaware div. U.S.A.
71 F4 Delaware r. U.S.A.
71 F5 Delaware Bay b. U.S.A.
70 B4 Delaware Lake l. U.S.A.
71 F4 Delaware Water Gap National Recreational Area res. U.S.A.
13 G3 Delbrück Ger.
50 G4 Delegate Austr.
16 C7 Delémont Switz.
12 C2 Delft Neth.
33 B4 Delft I. i. Sri Lanka
12 E1 Delfzijl Neth.
89 E5 Delgado, Cabo pt Moz.
69 G4 Delhi Can.
34 D3 Delhi India
63 F4 Delhi CO U.S.A.
71 F3 Delhi NY U.S.A.
29 J2 Deli r. Turkey
28 E2 Delice Turkey
28 E1 Delice r. Turkey
30 C3 Delījān Iran
56 E1 Déline Can.
36 B3 Delingha China
57 H4 Delisle Can.
13 L3 Delitzsch Ger.
13 H3 Delligsen Ger.
64 D3 Dell Rapids U.S.A.
15 H4 Dellys Alg.
72 D5 Del Mar U.S.A.
73 E3 Delmar L. l. U.S.A.
13 G1 Delmenhorst Ger.
25 R2 De-Longa, O-va is Rus. Fed.
54 B3 De Long Mts mts U.S.A.
57 J5 Deloraine Can.
68 D5 Delphi U.S.A.
70 A4 Delphos U.S.A.
90 F4 Delportshoop S. Africa
67 D7 Delray Beach U.S.A.
63 E6 Del Río Mex.
65 C6 Del Rio U.S.A.
7 P6 Delsbo Sweden
73 H2 Delta CO U.S.A.
68 A5 Delta IA U.S.A.
73 F2 Delta UT U.S.A.
54 D3 Delta Junction U.S.A.
71 F3 Delta Reservoir U.S.A.
67 D6 Deltona U.S.A.
11 D4 Delvin Rep. of Ireland
19 J5 Delvinë Albania
15 E1 Demanda, Sierra de la mts Spain
88 C4 Demba Congo(Zaire)
88 D3 Dembī Dolo Eth.
20 D4 Demidov Rus. Fed.
63 F5 Deming U.S.A.
28 E4 Demini r. Brazil
28 B2 Demirci Turkey
19 M4 Demirköy Turkey
16 F4 Demmin Ger.
67 C5 Demopolis U.S.A.
68 D5 Demotte U.S.A.
45 B3 Dempo, G. volc. Indon.
34 D2 Dêmqog China/India
20 H2 Dem'yanovo Rus. Fed.
17 Q2 Demyansk Rus. Fed.
90 D5 De Naawte S. Africa
88 E2 Denakil reg. Eritrea
88 E3 Denan Eth.
57 J4 Denare Beach Can.
31 G2 Denau Uzbek.
69 J3 Denbigh Can.
9 D4 Denbigh U.K.
12 C1 Den Burg Neth.
44 B1 Den Chai Thai.
45 C3 Dendang Indon.
12 C3 Dendermonde Belgium
91 H1 Dendron S. Africa
38 C1 Dengkou China
35 H3 Dêngqên China
38 D3 Deng Xian China
Den Haag see The Hague
48 B4 Denham Austr.
12 D2 Den Ham Neth.
12 C2 Den Helder Neth.
15 G3 Denia Spain
50 E3 Deniliquin Austr.
62 C3 Denio U.S.A.
64 E3 Denison IA U.S.A.
65 D5 Denison TX U.S.A.
28 B3 Denizli Turkey
50 H2 Denman Austr.
92 C5 Denman Glacier gl. Ant.
48 B5 Denmark Austr.
5 D3 Denmark country Europe
55 Q3 Denmark Strait Greenland/Iceland
73 H3 Dennehotso U.S.A.
71 H4 Dennis Port U.S.A.
10 E4 Denny U.K.
71 K2 Dennysville U.S.A.
45 E4 Denpasar Indon.
71 F5 Denton MD U.S.A.
65 D5 Denton TX U.S.A.
48 F2 D'Entrecasteaux Islands is P.N.G.
48 B5 d'Entrecasteaux, Pt pt Austr.
49 G3 d'Entrecasteaux, Récifs rf New Caledonia
62 F4 Denver U.S.A.
35 F4 Deo India
34 D3 Deoband India
35 F5 Deogarh India
35 E5 Deogarh mt India
35 F4 Deoghar India
34 D5 Deori India
35 E4 Deoria India
34 C2 Deosai, Plains of plain Pak.
35 E5 Deosil India
12 A3 De Panne Belgium
12 D3 De Peel reg. Neth.
68 C3 De Pere U.S.A.
71 F3 Deposit U.S.A.
69 J2 Depot-Forbes Can.
69 J2 Depot-Rowanton Can.
68 C5 Depue U.S.A.
25 P3 Deputatskiy Rus. Fed.
36 B4 Dêqên China
39 D6 Deqing Guangdong China
39 F4 Deqing Zhejiang China
39 F5 Deqiu China
65 E5 De Queen U.S.A.
34 B3 Dera Bugti Pak.
34 B3 Dera Ghazi Khan Pak.
34 B3 Dera Ismail Khan Pak.
34 B3 Derawar Fort Pak.
21 J7 Derbent Rus. Fed.
31 G2 Derbent Uzbek.
48 C3 Derby Austr.
9 F5 Derby U.K.
71 G4 Derby CT U.S.A.
65 D4 Derby KS U.S.A.
11 D3 Derg r. Rep. of Ireland/U.K.
21 J5 Dergachi Rus. Fed.
11 C5 Derg, Lough l. Rep. of Ireland
21 F5 Derhachi Ukr.
65 E6 De Ridder U.S.A.
29 H3 Derik Turkey
28 E2 Derinkuyu Turkey
21 F5 Derkul r. Rus. Fed./Ukr.
90 C1 Derm Namibia
11 D4 Derravaragh, Lough l. Rep. of Ireland
71 H3 Derry U.S.A.
11 E5 Derry r. Rep. of Ireland
11 C3 Derryveagh Mts h. Rep. of Ireland
38 A1 Derstei China
87 F3 Derudeb Sudan
90 E6 De Rust S. Africa
18 G2 Derventa Bos.-Herz.
48 E6 Derwent r. Austr.
8 G4 Derwent r. U.K.
10 G6 Derwent Reservoir U.K.
8 D3 Derwent Water l. U.K.
26 E1 Derzhavinsk Kazak.
83 C2 Desaguadero r. Arg.
78 E7 Desaguadero r. Bol.
46 N5 Désappointement, Îles de is Pac. Oc.
72 D2 Desatoya Mts mts U.S.A.
69 F2 Desbarats Can.
54 F3 Des Bois, Lac l. Can.
57 J3 Deschambault L. l. Can.
57 J4 Deschambault Lake Can.
62 B2 Deschutes r. U.S.A.
88 D2 Desē Eth.
80 C7 Deseado Arg.
80 C7 Deseado r. Arg.
69 J3 Deseronto Can.
34 B3 Desert Canal canal Pak.
73 E5 Desert Center U.S.A.
73 F1 Desert Peak summit U.S.A.
56 G3 Desmarais Can.
64 E3 Des Moines IA U.S.A.
63 G4 Des Moines NM U.S.A.
68 A5 Des Moines r. IA U.S.A.
21 D5 Desna Ukr.
20 E5 Desna r. Rus. Fed.
20 E4 Desnogorsk Rus. Fed.
43 C4 Desolation Point pt Phil.
68 D4 Des Plaines U.S.A.
13 L3 Dessau Ger.
12 B3 Destelbergen Belgium
69 H1 Destor Can.
56 B2 Destruction Bay Can.
76 C5 Desventurados, Islas de los is Chile
19 J2 Deta Romania
56 G2 Detah Can.
89 C5 Dete Zimbabwe
13 G3 Detmold Ger.
68 D3 Detour, Pt pt U.S.A.
69 F3 De Tour Village U.S.A.
69 F4 Detroit U.S.A.
69 F4 Detroit airport MI U.S.A.
64 E2 Detroit Lakes U.S.A.
50 G3 Deua Nat. Park Austr.
13 L3 Deuben Ger.
12 D3 Deurne Neth.
18 F1 Deutschlandsberg Austria
13 L3 Deutzen Ger.
19 H2 Deux-Rivières Can.
19 K2 Deva Romania
33 B2 Devarkonda India
28 F2 Develi Turkey
12 E2 Deventer Neth.
16 H6 Devět Skal h. Czech Rep.
34 B4 Devikot India
11 D5 Devils Bit Mountain h. Rep. of Ireland
9 D5 Devil's Bridge U.K.
71 G5 Devils Den U.S.A.
72 C2 Devils Gate pass U.S.A.
68 B2 Devils I. i. U.S.A.
64 D1 Devils Lake U.S.A.
72 C3 Devils Peak summit U.S.A.
72 C3 Devils Postpile National Monument res. U.S.A.
67 F7 Devil's Pt Bahamas
9 F6 Devizes U.K.
34 C4 Devli India
19 M3 Devnya Bulg.
56 G4 Devon Can.
9 G5 Devon r. U.K.
55 J2 Devon Island i. Can.
48 E6 Devonport Austr.
28 C1 Devrek Turkey
28 D1 Devrekâni Turkey
28 E1 Devrez r. Turkey
33 A2 Devrukh India
34 D5 Dewas India
45 A2 Dewa, Tanjung pt Indon.
91 G4 Dewetsdorp S. Africa
70 B6 Dewey Lake l. U.S.A.
65 F5 De Witt AR U.S.A.
68 B5 De Witt IA U.S.A.
8 F4 Dewsbury U.K.
39 E4 Dexing China
71 J2 Dexter ME U.S.A.
65 F4 Dexter MO U.S.A.
71 E2 Dexter NY U.S.A.
38 B4 Deyang China
30 E3 Deyhuk Iran
29 M3 Deylaman Iran
31 F2 Deynau Turkm.
48 D2 Deyong, Tg pt Indon.
30 C5 Deyyer Iran
29 M6 Dez r. Iran
30 C3 Dezfūl Iran
30 C4 Dez Gerd Iran
38 E2 Dezhou China
30 B5 Dhahlān, J. h. S. Arabia
32 D4 Dhahran S. Arabia
35 G5 Dhaka Bangl.
35 G5 Dhaleswari r. Bangl.
35 H4 Dhaleswari r. India
32 B7 Dhamār Yemen
35 F5 Dhāmara India
34 C5 Dhamnod India
35 E5 Dhamtari India
34 B3 Dhana Sar Pak.
35 F5 Dhanbad India
34 C5 Dhandhuka India
35 E3 Dhang Ra. mts Nepal
34 C5 Dhar India
35 F4 Dharan Bazar Nepal
33 B4 Dharapuram India
34 B5 Dhari India
33 B3 Dharmapuri India
33 B3 Dharmavaram India
34 D2 Dharmshala India
33 A3 Dhārwād India
34 D4 Dhasan r. India
35 E3 Dhaulagiri mt Nepal
34 D4 Dhaulpur India
34 C4 Dhebar L. l. India
35 H4 Dhekiajuli India
28 E6 Dhībān Jordan
35 H4 Dhing India
33 B3 Dhone India
34 B5 Dhoraji India
34 B5 Dhrangadhra India
34 C5 Dhule India
35 F4 Dhulian India
35 F4 Dhunche Nepal
34 D4 Dhund r. India
88 E3 Dhuusa Marreeb Somalia
19 L7 Dia i. Greece
72 B3 Diablo, Mt mt U.S.A.
72 B3 Diablo Range mts U.S.A.
83 E2 Diamante Arg.
83 C2 Diamante r. Arg.
82 D2 Diamantina Brazil
48 D4 Diamantina watercourse Austr.
79 K6 Diamantina, Chapada plat. Brazil
82 A1 Diamantino Brazil
72 □1 Diamond Head hd U.S.A.
73 E2 Diamond Peak summit U.S.A.
39 D6 Dianbai China
39 B5 Dian Chi l. China
39 C4 Dianjiang China
79 J6 Dianópolis Brazil
86 B4 Dianra Côte d'Ivoire
40 B2 Diaoling China
86 C3 Diapaga Burkina
31 E6 Đibab Oman
35 H4 Dibang r. India
88 C4 Dibaya Congo(Zaire)
90 E3 Dibeng S. Africa
58 F2 D'Iberville, Lac l. Can.
91 G1 Dibete Botswana
35 H4 Dibrugarh India
65 C5 Dickens U.S.A.
71 J1 Dickey U.S.A.
64 C2 Dickinson U.S.A.
67 C4 Dickson U.S.A.
71 F4 Dickson City U.S.A.
Dicle r. see Tigris
43 B2 Didicas i. Phil.
34 C4 Didwana India
19 M4 Didymoteicho Greece
14 G4 Die France
12 F4 Dieblich Ger.
86 B3 Diébougou Burkina
13 G5 Dieburg Ger.
57 H4 Diefenbaker, L. l. Can.
93 J4 Diego Garcia i. British Indian Ocean Terr.
12 E5 Diekirch Lux.
86 B3 Diéma Mali
13 H3 Diemel r. Ger.
39 B6 Điên Biên Vietnam
44 C1 Diên Châu Vietnam
44 D2 Diên Khanh Vietnam
13 G2 Diepholz Ger.
14 E2 Dieppe France
38 C2 Di'er Nonchang Qu r. China
42 C1 Di'er Songhua Jiang r. China
12 D3 Diessen Neth.
12 D4 Diest Belgium
16 D7 Dietikon Switz.
13 G4 Diez Ger.
87 D3 Diffa Niger
33 D2 Digapahandi India
59 G5 Digby Can.

68 B3 Durand *WV* U.S.A.
74 D4 Durango Mex.
15 E1 Durango Spain
63 F4 Durango U.S.A.
65 B7 Durango *div.* Mex.
65 D5 Durant U.S.A.
83 F2 Durazno Uru.
83 F1 Durazno, Cuchilla Grande del *h.* Uru.
91 J4 Durban S. Africa
14 F5 Durban-Corbières France
90 C6 Durbanville S. Africa
70 D5 Durbin U.S.A.
12 D4 Durbuy Belgium
12 E4 Düren Ger.
34 E5 Durg India
35 F5 Durgapur India
69 G3 Durham Can.
8 F3 Durham U.K.
72 B2 Durham *CA* U.S.A.
67 E4 Durham *NC* U.S.A.
71 H3 Durham *NH* U.S.A.
21 D6 Durleşti Moldova
13 G6 Durmersheim Ger.
19 H3 Durmitor *mt* Yugo.
10 D2 Durness U.K.
19 H4 Durrës Albania
9 F6 Durrington U.K.
11 A6 Dursey Island *i.* Rep. of Ireland
28 B2 Dursunbey Turkey
31 F3 Dūruḩ Iran
28 F5 Durūz, Jabal ad *mt* Syria
51 D4 D'Urville Island *i.* N.Z.
48 D2 d'Urville, Tanjung *pt* Indon.
31 G3 Durzab Afgh.
31 G4 Dushai Pak.
31 E2 Dushak Turkm.
39 C5 Dushan China
31 H2 Dushanbe Tajik.
21 H7 Dushet'i Georgia
51 A6 Dusky Sound *in.* N.Z.
12 E3 Düsseldorf Ger.
73 F1 Dutch Mt *mt* U.S.A.
90 E1 Dutlwe Botswana
86 C3 Dutse Nigeria
73 F2 Dutton, Mt *mt* U.S.A.
13 H3 Duvannoye Rus. Fed.
59 F2 Duvert, Lac *l.* Can.
39 C5 Duyun China
31 F5 Duzab Pak.
28 C1 Düzce Turkey
Duzdab *see* Zāhedān
20 D4 Dvina, Western *r.* Rus. Fed.
21 F5 Dvorichna Ukr.
40 B2 Dvoryanka Rus. Fed.
34 B5 Dwarka India
91 G2 Dwarsberg S. Africa
68 C5 Dwight U.S.A.
12 E2 Dwingelderveld, Nationaal Park *nat. park* Neth.
62 C2 Dworshak Res. *resr* U.S.A.
90 D6 Dwyka S. Africa
20 E4 Dyat'kovo Rus. Fed.
10 F3 Dyce U.K.
68 D5 Dyer *IN* U.S.A.
72 C3 Dyer *NV* U.S.A.
69 G3 Dyer Bay Can.
55 M3 Dyer, C. *c.* Can.
67 B4 Dyersburg U.S.A.
68 B4 Dyersville U.S.A.
9 D5 Dyfi *r.* U.K.
10 E3 Dyke U.K.
21 G7 Dykh Tau *mt* Georgia/Rus. Fed.
13 L5 Dyleň *h.* Czech Rep.
17 J4 Dylewska Góra *h.* Pol.
91 H5 Dyoki S. Africa
68 A4 Dysart U.S.A.
90 E6 Dysselsdorp S. Africa
20 D2 Dzamïn Üüd Mongolia
89 E5 Dzaoudzi *Mayotte* Africa
20 G3 Dzerzhinsk Rus. Fed.
17 N5 Dzerzhyns'k Ukr.
30 D1 Dzhanga Turkm.
21 E6 Dzhankoy Ukr.
21 H5 Dzhanybek Rus. Fed.
31 G2 Dzharkurgan Uzbek.
30 D2 Dzhebel Turkm.
26 E1 Dzhetygara Kazak.
26 E2 Dzhezkazgan Kazak.
25 R3 Dzhigudzhak Rus. Fed.
31 G1 Dzhizak Uzbek.
36 F1 Dzhugdzhur, Khrebet *mts* Rus. Fed.
Dzhul'fa *see* Culfa
31 G2 Dzhuma Uzbek.
27 F2 Dzhungarskiy Alatau, Khr. *mts* China/Kazak.
24 H5 Dzhusaly Kazak.
17 K4 Działdowo Pol.
36 C2 Dzuunmod Mongolia
20 C4 Dzyaniskavichy Belarus
20 C4 Dzyarzhynsk Belarus
17 N4 Dzyatlavichy Belarus

E

58 C3 Eabamet L. *l.* Can.
73 H4 Eagar U.S.A.
63 F4 Eagle U.S.A.
59 J3 Eagle *r.* Can.
71 F3 Eagle Bay U.S.A.
57 H4 Eagle Cr. *r.* Can.
72 D4 Eagle Crags *summit* U.S.A.
57 L5 Eagle L. *l.* Can.
62 B3 Eagle L. *l.* *CA* U.S.A.
71 J1 Eagle Lake *ME* U.S.A.
71 J1 Eagle Lake *l.* *ME* U.S.A.
68 B2 Eagle Mtn *h.* U.S.A.
65 C6 Eagle Pass U.S.A.
54 D3 Eagle Plain *plain* Can.
68 C2 Eagle River *MI* U.S.A.
68 C3 Eagle River *WV* U.S.A.
56 F3 Eaglesham Can.
73 F5 Eagle Tail Mts *mts* U.S.A.
58 B3 Ear Falls Can.
72 C4 Earlimart U.S.A.
10 F5 Earlston U.K.
69 H2 Earlton Can.
10 E4 Earn *r.* U.K.
10 D4 Earn, L. *l.* U.K.
65 C5 Earth U.S.A.
8 H4 Easington U.K.
67 D5 Easley U.S.A.
92 C5 East Antarctica *reg.* Ant.
71 F4 East Ararat U.S.A.
70 D3 East Aurora U.S.A.
65 F6 East Bay *b.* U.S.A.
71 G2 East Berkshire U.S.A.
9 H7 Eastbourne U.K.
70 D4 East Branch Clarion River Reservoir U.S.A.
71 H4 East Brooklyn U.S.A.
51 G2 East Cape *c.* N.Z.
73 G2 East Carbon U.S.A.
94 E5 East Caroline Basin *sea feature* Pac. Oc.
68 D5 East Chicago U.S.A.
36 E3 East China Sea Asia
51 E2 East Coast Bays N.Z.
71 G2 East Corinth U.S.A.
9 H5 East Dereham U.K.
95 M7 Easter Island *i.* Pac. Oc.
95 M7 Easter Island Fracture Zone *sea feature* Pac. Oc.
91 G5 Eastern Cape *div.* S. Africa
87 F2 Eastern Desert Egypt
35 E6 Eastern Ghats *mts* India
34 B4 Eastern Nara *canal* Pak.
Eastern Transvaal *div. see* Mpumalanga
57 K4 Easterville Can.
80 E8 East Falkland *i.* Falkland Is
71 H4 East Falmouth U.S.A.
12 E1 East Frisian Islands *is* Ger.
72 D2 Eastgate U.S.A.
64 D2 East Grand Forks U.S.A.
9 G6 East Grinstead U.K.
71 G4 East Hampton U.S.A.
71 G3 Easthampton U.S.A.
70 D4 East Hickory U.S.A.
71 G3 East Jamaica U.S.A.
96 K1 East Jan Mayen Ridge *sea feature* Atl. Ocean
68 E3 East Jordan U.S.A.
10 D5 East Kilbride U.K.
68 D3 Eastlake U.S.A.
39 □ East Lamma Channel *H.K.* China
9 F7 Eastleigh U.K.
70 C4 East Liverpool U.S.A.
10 B3 East Loch Tarbert *b.* U.K.
91 G6 East London S. Africa
70 B5 East Lynn Lake *l.* U.S.A.
58 E3 Eastmain *Que.* Can.
58 F3 Eastmain *r.* *Que.* Can.
71 G2 Eastman Can.
67 D5 Eastman U.S.A.
71 J2 East Millinocket U.S.A.
68 B5 East Moline U.S.A.
68 C5 Easton *IL* U.S.A.
71 E5 Easton *MD* U.S.A.
71 F4 Easton *PA* U.S.A.
95 M8 East Pacific Ridge *sea feature* Pac. Oc.
95 N5 East Pacific Rise *sea feature* Pac. Oc.
72 A2 East Park Res. *resr* U.S.A.
67 C5 East Point U.S.A.
59 H4 East Point *pt* *P.E.I.* Can.
71 K2 Eastport *ME* U.S.A.
68 E3 Eastport *MI* U.S.A.
72 D1 East Range *mts* U.S.A.
East Retford *see* Retford
66 B4 East St Louis U.S.A.
25 R2 East Siberian Sea *sea* Rus. Fed.
23 M10 East Timor *terr.* Asia
35 F4 East Tons *r.* India
68 C4 East Troy U.S.A.
71 F6 Eastville U.S.A.
72 C2 East Walker *r.* U.S.A.
71 G3 East Wallingford U.S.A.
67 D5 Eatonton U.S.A.
68 B3 Eau Claire U.S.A.
68 B3 Eau Claire *r.* U.S.A.
58 F2 Eau Claire, Lac à l' *l.* Can.
37 G6 Eauripik Atoll Micronesia
94 E5 Eauripik - New Guinea Rise *sea feature* Pac. Oc.
74 E4 Ebano Mex.
9 D6 Ebbw Vale U.K.
86 D4 Ebebiyin Equatorial Guinea
90 B2 Ebenerde Namibia
70 D4 Ebensburg U.S.A.
28 C2 Eber Gölü *l.* Turkey
13 J3 Ebergötzen Ger.
16 F4 Eberswalde-Finow Ger.
69 F4 Eberts Can.
40 G3 Ebetsu Japan
39 B4 Ebian China
18 F4 Eboli Italy
86 D4 Ebolowa Cameroon
94 G5 Ebon *i.* Pac. Oc.
29 K3 Ebrāhim Ḩeşār Iran
15 G2 Ebro *r.* Spain
13 J1 Ebstorf Ger.
19 M4 Eceabat Turkey
43 B2 Echague Phil.
15 E1 Echarri-Aranaz Spain
86 C1 Ech Chélif Alg.
15 E1 Echegárate, Puerto *pass* Spain
39 E4 Echeng China
56 F1 Echo Bay *N.W.T.* Can.
69 E2 Echo Bay *Ont.* Can.
73 G3 Echo Cliffs *cliff* U.S.A.
58 B3 Echoing *r.* Can.
69 K2 Échouani, Lac *l.* Can.
12 D3 Echt Neth.
12 E5 Echternach Lux.
50 E4 Echuca Austr.
13 G4 Echzell Ger.
15 D4 Écija Spain
13 K5 Eckental Ger.
68 E2 Eckerman U.S.A.
16 D3 Eckernförde Ger.
55 L2 Eclipse Sound *chan.* Can.
77 C3 Ecuador *country* S. America
58 E2 Écueils, Pte aux *pt* Can.
88 E2 Ed Eritrea
7 M7 Ed Sweden
57 H4 Edam Can.
12 D2 Edam Neth.
10 F1 Eday *i.* U.K.
87 E3 Ed Da'ein Sudan
87 F3 Ed Damazin Sudan
87 F3 Ed Damer Sudan
87 F3 Ed Debba Sudan
87 F3 Ed Dueim Sudan
48 E6 Eddystone Pt *pt* Austr.
12 D2 Ede Neth.
86 D4 Edéa Cameroon
57 K2 Edehon Lake *l.* Can.
82 C2 Edéia Brazil
50 G4 Eden Austr.
65 D6 Eden *TX* U.S.A.
8 E3 Eden *r.* U.K.
91 F4 Edenburg S. Africa
51 B7 Edendale N.Z.
11 D4 Edenderry Rep. of Ireland
50 C4 Edenhope Austr.
67 E4 Edenton U.S.A.
91 G3 Edenville S. Africa
19 K4 Edessa Greece
13 F1 Edewecht Ger.
71 H4 Edgartown U.S.A.
64 D2 Edgeley U.S.A.
64 C3 Edgemont U.S.A.
68 C4 Edgerton U.S.A.
11 D4 Edgeworthstown Rep. of Ireland
68 A5 Edina U.S.A.
65 D7 Edinburg U.S.A.
10 E5 Edinburgh U.K.
21 C7 Edirne Turkey
56 F4 Edith Cavell, Mt *mt* Can.
62 B2 Edmonds U.S.A.
56 G4 Edmonton Can.
57 K5 Edmore U.S.A.
68 B4 Edmund U.S.A.
57 L4 Edmund L. *l.* Can.
59 G4 Edmundston Can.
65 D6 Edna U.S.A.
56 C3 Edna Bay U.S.A.
19 M5 Edremit Turkey
7 O6 Edsbyn Sweden
56 F4 Edson Can.
83 D2 Eduardo Castex Arg.
50 E3 Edward *r.* Austr.
68 C1 Edward I. *i.* Can.
88 C4 Edward, Lake *l.* Congo(Zaire)/Uganda
71 F2 Edwards U.S.A.
65 C6 Edwards Plateau *plat.* U.S.A.
66 B4 Edwardsville U.S.A.
92 D4 Edward VIII Ice Shelf *ice feature* Ant.
92 A4 Edward VII Pen. *pen.* Ant.
56 C3 Edziza Pk *mt* Can.
12 B3 Eeklo Belgium
72 A1 Eel *r.* U.S.A.
12 E1 Eemshaven *pt* Neth.
12 E1 Eenrum Neth.
90 D3 Eenzamheid Pan *salt pan* S. Africa
49 G3 Éfaté *i.* Vanuatu
66 B4 Effingham U.S.A.
28 D1 Eflâni Turkey
72 E2 Egan Range *mts* U.S.A.
69 J3 Eganville Can.
17 K7 Eger Hungary
7 K7 Egersund Norway
13 G3 Eggegebirge *h.* Ger.
13 K5 Eggolsheim Ger.
12 C4 Eghezée Belgium
6 F4 Egilsstaðir Iceland
28 C3 Eğirdir Turkey
28 C3 Eğirdir Gölü *l.* Turkey
14 F4 Égletons France
11 D2 Eglinton U.K.
54 F2 Eglinton I. *i.* Can.
12 C2 Egmond aan Zee Neth.
51 D3 Egmont, Cape *c.* N.Z.
51 E3 Egmont, Mt *volc.* N.Z.
51 E3 Egmont National Park N.Z.
28 B2 Eğrigöz Dağı *mts* Turkey
8 G3 Egton U.K.
82 D1 Éguas *r.* Brazil
25 V3 Egvekinot Rus. Fed.
85 F3 Egypt *country* Africa
16 D6 Ehingen (Donau) Ger.
13 J2 Ehra-Lessien Ger.
73 E5 Ehrenberg U.S.A.
13 J5 Eibelstadt Ger.
12 E2 Eibergen Neth.
13 H4 Eichenzell Ger.
13 K6 Eichstätt Ger.
7 K6 Eidfjord Norway
7 M6 Eidsvoll Norway
12 E4 Eifel *reg.* Ger.
10 B4 Eigg *i.* U.K.
33 A4 Eight Degree Chan. India/Maldives
92 A3 Eights Coast *coastal area* Ant.
48 C3 Eighty Mile Beach *beach* Austr.
50 E4 Eildon Austr.
50 F4 Eildon, Lake *l.* Austr.
10 C4 Eilean Shona *i.* U.K.
57 H2 Eileen Lake *l.* Can.
13 L3 Eilenburg Ger.
13 J2 Eimke Ger.
13 H3 Einbeck Ger.
12 D3 Eindhoven Neth.
16 D7 Einsiedeln Switz.
78 E5 Eirunepé Brazil
13 H3 Eisberg *h.* Ger.
89 C5 Eiseb *watercourse* Namibia
13 J4 Eisenach Ger.
13 K4 Eisenberg Ger.
16 G4 Eisenhüttenstadt Ger.
16 H7 Eisenstadt Austria
13 J4 Eisfeld Ger.
10 C3 Eishort, Loch *in.* U.K.
13 K3 Eisleben Lutherstadt Ger.
13 H4 Eiterfeld Ger.
Eivissa *see* Ibiza
Eivissa *i. see* Ibiza
15 F1 Ejea de los Caballeros Spain
89 E6 Ejeda Madag.
74 B3 Ejido Insurgentes Mex.
38 C2 Ejin Horo Qi China
38 A1 Ejin Qi China
29 K1 Ejmiatsin Armenia
7 S7 Ekenäs Fin.
12 C3 Ekeren Belgium
51 E4 Eketahuna N.Z.
27 F1 Ekibastuz Kazak.
25 M3 Ekonda Rus. Fed.
7 N6 Ekshärad Sweden
7 O8 Eksjö Sweden
90 B4 Eksteenfontein S. Africa
88 C4 Ekuku Congo(Zaire)
58 D3 Ekwan *r.* Can.
58 D3 Ekwan Point *pt* Can.
19 K6 Elafonisou, Steno *chan.* Greece
28 B6 El 'Alamein Egypt
28 B6 El 'Amirîya Egypt
91 H2 Elands *r.* S. Africa
91 H2 Elandsdoorn S. Africa
18 B7 El Aouinet Alg.
28 B6 El 'Arab, Khalîg *b.* Egypt
28 D6 El 'Arîsh Egypt
19 K5 Elassona Greece
28 E7 Elat Israel
29 G2 Elazığ Turkey
18 D3 Elba, Isola d' *i.* Italy
36 F1 El'ban Rus. Fed.
81 B2 El Banco Col.
28 D6 El Bardawîl, Sabkhet *lag.* Egypt
19 J4 Elbasan Albania
28 E2 Elbaşı Turkey
81 C2 El Baúl Venez.
86 C1 El Bayadh Alg.
13 J1 Elbe *r.* Ger.
68 D3 Elberta *MI* U.S.A.
73 G2 Elberta *UT* U.S.A.
63 F4 Elbert, Mount *mt* U.S.A.
67 D5 Elberton U.S.A.
14 E2 Elbeuf France
28 F2 Elbistan Turkey
17 J3 Elbląg Pol.
83 B4 El Bolsón Arg.
67 E7 Elbow Cay *i.* Bahamas
21 G7 Elbrus *mt* Rus. Fed.
12 D2 Elburg Neth.
15 E2 El Burgo de Osma Spain
83 C4 El Cain Arg.
72 D5 El Cajon U.S.A.
81 E3 El Callao Venez.
65 D6 El Campo U.S.A.
73 E5 El Centro U.S.A.
78 F7 El Cerro Bol.
81 D2 El Chaparro Venez.
15 F3 Elche Spain
48 D3 Elcho I. *i.* Austr.
81 B3 El Cocuy Col.
15 F3 Elda Spain
13 K1 Elde *r.* Ger.
69 H2 Eldee Can.
72 D5 El Descanso Mex.
81 B2 El Difícil Col.
25 P3 El'dikan Rus. Fed.
81 A4 El Diviso Col.
73 E6 El Doctor Mex.
68 A5 Eldon *IA* U.S.A.
64 E4 Eldon *MO* U.S.A.
80 F3 Eldorado Arg.
74 C4 El Dorado Mex.
65 E5 El Dorado *AR* U.S.A.
65 D4 El Dorado *KS* U.S.A.
65 C6 Eldorado U.S.A.
81 E3 El Dorado Venez.
88 D3 Eldoret Kenya
62 E2 Electric Peak *summit* U.S.A.
86 B2 El Eglab *plat.* Alg.
15 E4 El Ejido Spain
20 F4 Elektrostal' Rus. Fed.
78 D4 El Encanto Col.
13 J3 Elend Ger.
63 F5 Elephant Butte Res. *resr* U.S.A.
92 B1 Elephant I. *i.* Ant.
35 H5 Elephant Point *pt* Bangl.
29 J2 Eleşkirt Turkey
86 C1 El Eulma Alg.
67 E7 Eleuthera *i.* Bahamas
18 C6 El Fahs Tunisia
87 F2 El Faiyûm Egypt
87 E3 El Fasher Sudan
13 H4 Elfershausen Ger.
60 E6 El Fuerte Mex.
87 E3 El Geneina Sudan
87 F3 El Geteina Sudan
10 E3 Elgin U.K.
68 C4 Elgin *IL* U.S.A.
64 C2 Elgin *ND* U.S.A.
73 E3 Elgin *NV* U.S.A.
73 G2 Elgin *UT* U.S.A.
25 Q3 El'ginskiy Rus. Fed.
87 F2 El Gîza Egypt
86 C1 El Goléa Alg.
87 F4 Elgon, Mount *mt* Uganda
18 B6 El Hadjar Alg.
28 B6 El Hammâm Egypt
28 F6 El Hazim Jordan
86 A2 El Hierro *i.* Canary Is
86 C2 El Homr Alg.
79 F4 Elie U.K.
51 C5 Elie de Beaumont *mt* N.Z.
54 B3 Elim *AK* U.S.A.
59 H2 Eliot, Mount *mt* Can.
15 F1 Elizondo Spain
El Iskandarîya *see* Alexandria
21 H6 Elista Rus. Fed.
68 B4 Elizabeth *IL* U.S.A.
71 F4 Elizabeth *NJ* U.S.A.
70 C5 Elizabeth *WV* U.S.A.
67 E4 Elizabeth City U.S.A.
71 H4 Elizabeth Is *is* U.S.A.
70 B6 Elizabethton U.S.A.
66 C4 Elizabethtown *KY* U.S.A.
67 E5 Elizabethtown *NC* U.S.A.
71 G2 Elizabethtown *NY* U.S.A.
70 E4 Elizabethtown *PA* U.S.A.
86 B1 El Jadida Morocco
28 F6 El Jafr Jordan
65 B7 El Jaralito Mex.
18 D7 El Jem Tunisia
17 L4 Ełk Pol.
72 A2 Elk U.S.A.
56 G4 Elk *r.* Can.
70 C5 Elk *r.* U.S.A.
28 F4 El Kaa Lebanon
18 C6 El Kala Alg.
87 F3 El Kamlin Sudan
65 D5 Elk City U.S.A.
72 A2 Elk Creek U.S.A.
72 B2 Elk Grove U.S.A.
87 F2 El Khârga Egypt
68 E5 Elkhart U.S.A.
El Khartum *see* Khartoum
86 B2 El Khnâchîch *esc.* Mali
68 C4 Elkhorn U.S.A.
64 D3 Elkhorn *r.* U.S.A.
32 B1 El'khotovo Rus. Fed.
19 M3 Elkhovo Bulg.
70 D5 Elkins U.S.A.
56 G4 Elk Island Nat. Park Can.
69 G2 Elk Lake Can.
68 E3 Elk Lake *l.* U.S.A.
70 E4 Elkland U.S.A.
56 F5 Elko Can.
62 D3 Elko U.S.A.
57 G4 Elk Point Can.
64 E2 Elk River U.S.A.
71 F5 Elkton *MD* U.S.A.
70 D5 Elkton *VA* U.S.A.
29 G4 El Kubar Syria
57 M2 Ell Bay *b.* Can.
55 H2 Ellef Ringnes I. *i.* Can.
34 C3 Ellenabad India
64 D2 Ellendale U.S.A.
73 G2 Ellen, Mt *mt* U.S.A.
62 B2 Ellensburg U.S.A.
71 F4 Ellenville U.S.A.
50 G4 Ellery, Mt *mt* Austr.
55 K2 Ellesmere Island *i.* Can.
51 D5 Ellesmere, Lake *l.* N.Z.
9 E4 Ellesmere Port U.K.
54 H3 Ellice *r.* Can.
70 D3 Ellicottville U.S.A.
13 J5 Ellingen Ger.
91 G5 Elliot S. Africa
91 H5 Elliotdale S. Africa
69 F2 Elliot Lake Can.
62 D2 Ellis U.S.A.
91 G1 Ellisras S. Africa
10 F3 Ellon U.K.
71 J2 Ellsworth *ME* U.S.A.
68 A3 Ellsworth *WV* U.S.A.
92 A3 Ellsworth Land *reg.* Ant.
92 B3 Ellsworth Mountains Ant.
13 J6 Ellwangen (Jagst) Ger.
28 B3 Elmalı Turkey
87 F1 El Mansûra Egypt
81 E3 El Manteco Venez.
86 C1 El Meghaïer Alg.
81 E3 El Miamo Venez.
28 E4 El Mîna Lebanon
87 F2 El Minya Egypt
68 E3 Elmira *MI* U.S.A.
70 E3 Elmira *NY* U.S.A.
73 F5 El Mirage U.S.A.
15 E4 El Moral Spain
50 E4 Elmore Austr.
83 D2 El Morro *mt* Arg.
86 B2 El Mreyyé *reg.* Maur.
13 H1 Elmshorn Ger.
87 E3 El Muglad Sudan
69 G3 Elmwood Can.
68 C5 Elmwood *IL* U.S.A.
68 A3 Elmwood *WV* U.S.A.
6 K5 Elnesvågen Norway
81 B3 El Nevado, Cerro *mt* Col.
43 A4 El Nido Phil.
87 F3 El Obeid Sudan
81 C3 Elorza Venez.
86 C1 El Oued Alg.
73 G5 Eloy U.S.A.
65 B7 El Palmito Mex.
81 E2 El Pao *Bolívar* Venez.
81 C2 El Pao *Cojedes* Venez.
68 C5 El Paso *IL* U.S.A.
63 F6 El Paso *TX* U.S.A.
10 C2 Elphin U.K.
72 C3 El Portal U.S.A.
15 H2 El Prat de Llobregat Spain
15 C4 El Puerto de Santa María Spain
El Qâhira *see* Cairo
28 D6 El Qantara Egypt
28 E7 El Quweira Jordan
65 D5 El Reno U.S.A.
68 B4 Elroy U.S.A.
56 B2 Elsa Can.
28 C7 El Saff Egypt
28 D6 El Sâlhîya Egypt
74 C4 El Salto Mex.
43 C4 El Salvador Phil.
53 H8 El Salvador *country* Central America
81 C3 El Samán de Apure Venez.
69 F1 Elsas Can.
13 G2 Else *r.* Ger.
35 H2 Elsen Nur *l.* China
28 D7 El Shatt Egypt
81 D2 El Sombrero Venez.
83 C2 El Sosneado Arg.
El Suweis *see* Suez
95 L9 Eltanin Fracture Zone *sea feature* Pac. Oc.
18 C6 El Tarf Alg.
15 C1 El Teleno *mt* Spain
28 E7 El Thamad Egypt
81 D2 El Tigre Venez.
13 J5 Eltmann Ger.
81 C2 El Tocuyo Venez.
21 H5 El'ton Rus. Fed.
21 H5 El'ton, Ozero *l.* Rus. Fed.
62 C2 Eltopia U.S.A.
81 E2 El Toro Venez.
83 E2 El Trébol Arg.
81 C3 El Tuparro, Parque Nacional *nat. park* Col.
87 F2 El Tur Egypt
80 B8 El Turbio Chile
33 C2 Eluru India
7 U7 Elva Estonia
81 A3 El Valle Col.
10 E5 Elvanfoot U.K.
15 C3 Elvas Port.
7 M6 Elverum Norway
81 B3 El Viejo *mt* Col.
81 C2 El Vigía Venez.
78 D5 Elvira Brazil
88 E3 El Wak Kenya
68 E5 Elwood U.S.A.
13 J3 Elxleben Ger.
9 H5 Ely U.K.
68 B2 Ely *MN* U.S.A.
73 E2 Ely *NV* U.S.A.
70 B4 Elyria U.S.A.
13 G4 Elz Ger.
13 H2 Elze Ger.
49 G3 Émaé *i.* Vanuatu
30 D2 Emāmrūd Iran
31 H2 Emām Şaḩēb Afgh.
29 L5 Emāmzadeh Naşrod Dīn Iran
7 O8 Emån *r.* Sweden
82 B2 Emas, Parque Nacional das *nat. park* Brazil
26 D2 Emba Kazak.
91 H3 Embalenhle S. Africa
57 G3 Embarras Portage Can.
82 C2 Emborcação, Represa de *resr* Brazil
71 F2 Embrun Can.
88 D4 Embu Kenya
12 F1 Emden Ger.
39 B4 Emei China
39 B4 Emei Shan *mt* China
50 E4 Emerald *Vic.* Austr.
48 E4 Emerald Austr.
59 G3 Emeril Can.
57 K5 Emerson Can.
28 B2 Emet Turkey
91 J2 eMgwenya S. Africa
73 E3 Emigrant Valley *v.* U.S.A.
91 J2 eMijindini S. Africa
87 D3 Emi Koussi *mt* Chad
19 M3 Eminska Planina *h.* Bulg.
28 C2 Emir D. *mt* Turkey
28 C2 Emirdağ Turkey
7 O8 Emmaboda Sweden
7 S7 Emmaste Estonia
12 D2 Emmeloord Neth.
12 F4 Emmelshausen Ger.
12 E2 Emmen Neth.
16 D7 Emmen Switz.
12 E3 Emmerich Ger.
33 B3 Emmiganuru India
65 C6 Emory Pk *summit* U.S.A.
74 B3 Empalme Mex.
91 J4 Empangeni S. Africa
80 E3 Empedrado Arg.
94 G3 Emperor Seamount Chain *sea feature* Pac. Oc.
18 D3 Empoli Italy
64 D4 Emporia *KS* U.S.A.
70 E6 Emporia *VA* U.S.A.
70 D4 Emporium U.S.A.
57 G4 Empress Can.
31 E3 'Emrānī Iran
12 F2 Ems *r.* Ger.
69 H3 Emsdale Can.
12 F2 Emsdetten Ger.
12 F1 Ems-Jade-Kanal *canal* Ger.
12 F2 Emsland *reg.* Ger.
91 H3 Emzinoni S. Africa
6 N5 Enafors Sweden
37 F7 Enarotali Indon.
41 E7 Ena-san *mt* Japan
74 A2 Encantada, Co de la *mt* Mex.
83 G1 Encantadas, Serra das *h.* Brazil
43 B3 Encanto, Cape *pt* Phil.
80 E3 Encarnación Para.
65 D6 Encinal U.S.A.
72 D5 Encinitas U.S.A.
63 F5 Encino U.S.A.
50 B3 Encounter Bay *b.* Austr.
82 E1 Encruzilhada Brazil
83 G1 Encruzilhada do Sul Brazil
56 D4 Endako Can.
44 B5 Endau Malaysia
48 E3 Endeavour Strait *chan.* Austr.
37 E7 Endeh Indon.
92 D4 Enderby Land *reg.* Ant.
71 E3 Endicott U.S.A.
56 C3 Endicott Arm *in.* U.S.A.
54 C3 Endicott Mts *mts* U.S.A.
83 E3 Energía Arg.
21 E6 Enerhodar Ukr.
94 F5 Enewetak *i.* Pac. Oc.
18 D6 Enfidaville Tunisia
71 G3 Enfield U.S.A.
68 E2 Engadine U.S.A.
6 L5 Engan Norway
43 B2 Engaño, Cape *c.* Phil.
Engaños, Río de los *r. see* Yari
40 H2 Engaru Japan
91 G5 Engcobo S. Africa
21 H5 Engel's Rus. Fed.
12 C1 Engelschmangat *chan.* Neth.
45 B4 Enggano *i.* Indon.
12 C4 Enghien Belgium
9 E5 England *div.* U.K.
59 J3 Englee Can.
67 F5 Englehard U.S.A.
69 H2 Englehart Can.
9 D7 English Channel *str.* France/U.K.
21 G7 Enguri *r.* Georgia
91 J4 Enhlalakahle S. Africa
65 D4 Enid U.S.A.
40 G3 Eniwa Japan
12 D2 Enkhuizen Neth.
7 P7 Enköping Sweden
18 F6 Enna *Sicily* Italy
57 J2 Ennadai Lake *l.* Can.
87 E3 En Nahud Sudan
87 E3 Ennedi, Massif *mts* Chad
11 D4 Ennell, Lough *l.* Rep. of Ireland
64 C2 Enning U.S.A.

92 B3 Filchner Ice Shelf *ice feature* Ant.
8 G3 Filey U.K.
19 J5 Filippiada Greece
7 O7 Filipstad Sweden
6 L5 Fillan Norway
72 C4 Fillmore *CA* U.S.A.
73 F2 Fillmore *UT* U.S.A.
92 C3 Fimbulheimen *mts* Ant.
92 C3 Fimbulisen *ice feature* Ant.
71 F2 Finch Can.
10 E3 Findhorn *r.* U.K.
29 H3 Fındık Turkey
70 B4 Findlay U.S.A.
48 E6 Fingal Austr.
58 E5 Finger Lakes *l.* U.S.A.
89 D5 Fingoè Moz.
28 C3 Finike Turkey
28 C3 Finike Körfezi *b.* Turkey
Finisterre, Cape *c. see* Fisterra, Cabo
5 F2 Finland *country* Europe
7 S7 Finland, Gulf of *g.* Europe
56 D3 Finlay *r.* Can.
56 D3 Finlay, Mt *mt* Can.
50 E3 Finley Austr.
13 K3 Finne *ridge* Ger.
6 P2 Finnsnes Norway
7 O7 Finspång Sweden
11 D3 Fintona U.K.
11 C3 Fintown Rep. of Ireland
10 C3 Fionn Loch *l.* U.K.
10 B4 Fionnphort U.K.
51 A6 Fiordland National Park N.Z.
Fırat *r. see* Euphrates
72 B3 Firebaugh U.S.A.
57 J2 Firedrake Lake *l.* Can.
71 G4 Fire Island National Seashore *res.* U.S.A.
Firenze *see* Florence
29 K6 Firk, Sha'īb *watercourse* Iraq
83 E2 Firmat Arg.
14 G4 Firminy France
13 J6 Firngrund *reg.* Ger.
17 Q2 Firovo Rus. Fed.
34 B3 Firoza Pak.
34 D4 Firozabad India
31 G3 Firozkoh *reg.* Afgh.
34 C3 Firozpur India
71 H2 First Connecticut L. *l.* U.S.A.
30 D4 Fīrūzābād Iran
Firuzabad *see* Rāsk
12 F5 Fischbach Ger.
89 B6 Fish *r.* Namibia
90 D5 Fish *r.* S. Africa
92 B6 Fisher Bay *b.* Ant.
71 F6 Fisherman I. *i.* U.S.A.
71 H4 Fishers I. *i.* U.S.A.
57 N2 Fisher Strait *chan.* Can.
9 C6 Fishguard U.K.
56 E2 Fish Lake *l.* Can.
68 A2 Fish Lake *l. MN* U.S.A.
73 G2 Fish Lake *l. UT* U.S.A.
39 □ Fish Ponds *l. H.K.* China
69 F4 Fish Pt *pt* U.S.A.
92 B3 Fiske, C. *c.* Ant.
Fiskenæsset *see* Qeqertarsuatsiaat
12 B5 Fismes France
15 B1 Fisterra Spain
15 B1 Fisterra, Cabo *c.* Spain
71 H3 Fitchburg U.S.A.
57 G3 Fitzgerald Can.
67 D6 Fitzgerald U.S.A.
80 C7 Fitz Roy Arg.
48 C3 Fitzroy Crossing Austr.
69 G3 Fitzwilliam I. *i.* Can.
11 D3 Fivemiletown U.K.
18 D2 Fivizzano Italy
88 C4 Fizi Congo(Zaire)
7 L6 Flå Norway
91 H5 Flagstaff S. Africa
73 G4 Flagstaff U.S.A.
71 H2 Flagstaff Lake *l.* U.S.A.
58 E2 Flaherty Island *i.* Can.
68 B3 Flambeau *r.* U.S.A.
8 G3 Flamborough Head *hd* U.K.
13 L2 Fläming *h.* Ger.
62 E3 Flaming Gorge Res. *l.* U.S.A.
90 D5 Flaminksvlei *salt pan* S. Africa
12 A4 Flandre *reg.* France
10 A2 Flannan Isles *is* U.K.
6 O4 Flåsjön *l.* Sweden
68 E4 Flat *r.* U.S.A.
62 D2 Flathead L. *l.* U.S.A.
60 D2 Flathead Lake *l.* U.S.A.
51 E4 Flat Point *pt* N.Z.
62 A1 Flattery, C. *c.* U.S.A.
48 E3 Flattery, C. *pt* Austr.
13 K2 Fleetmark Ger.
8 D4 Fleetwood U.K.
71 F4 Fleetwood U.S.A.
7 K7 Flekkefjord Norway
70 E3 Fleming U.S.A.
70 B5 Flemingsburg U.S.A.
7 P7 Flen Sweden
16 D3 Flensburg Ger.
14 D2 Flers France
69 G3 Flesherton Can.
57 H2 Fletcher Lake *l.* Can.
69 F3 Fletcher Pond *l.* U.S.A.
92 B3 Fletcher Prom. *hd* Ant.
48 E3 Flinders *r.* Austr.
48 B5 Flinders Bay *b.* Austr.
48 E5 Flinders I. *i.* Austr.
50 A2 Flinders Ranges *mts* Austr.
50 B1 Flinders Ranges Nat. Park Austr.
57 J4 Flin Flon Can.
9 D4 Flint U.K.
69 F4 Flint U.S.A.
67 C6 Flint *r. GA* U.S.A.
69 F4 Flint *r. MI* U.S.A.
46 M5 Flint Island *i.* Kiribati
7 N6 Flisa Norway
8 E2 Flodden U.K.
13 M4 Flöha Ger.
13 M4 Flöha *r.* Ger.
92 A4 Flood Ra. *mts* Ant.
68 A2 Floodwood U.S.A.
66 B4 Flora U.S.A.
14 F4 Florac France
12 E5 Florange France
69 F4 Florence Can.
18 D3 Florence Italy
67 C5 Florence *AL* U.S.A.
73 G5 Florence *AZ* U.S.A.
64 D4 Florence *KS* U.S.A.
70 C5 Florence *OH* U.S.A.
62 A3 Florence *OR* U.S.A.
67 E5 Florence *SC* U.S.A.
73 G5 Florence Junction U.S.A.
71 K1 Florenceville Can.
81 B4 Florencia Col.
12 C4 Florennes Belgium
80 C6 Florentino Ameghino, Embalse *resr* Arg.
74 G5 Flores Guatemala
37 E7 Flores *i.* Indon.
83 E2 Flores *r.* Arg.
82 C1 Flores de Goiás Brazil
37 D7 Flores Sea Indon.
79 L5 Floresta Brazil
79 K5 Floriano Brazil
80 G3 Florianópolis Brazil
83 F2 Florida Uru.
67 D6 Florida *div.* U.S.A.
67 D7 Florida Bay *b.* U.S.A.
67 D7 Florida City U.S.A.
49 G2 Florida Is *is* Solomon Is
61 K7 Florida Keys *is FL* U.S.A.
75 H4 Florida, Straits of *str.* Bahamas/U.S.A.
19 J4 Florina Greece
7 J6 Florø Norway
59 H3 Flour Lake *l.* Can.
68 A4 Floyd *IA* U.S.A.
70 C6 Floyd *VA* U.S.A.
65 C5 Floydada U.S.A.
73 F4 Floyd, Mt *mt* U.S.A.
12 D2 Fluessen *l.* Neth.
70 C5 Fly U.S.A.
48 E2 Fly *r.* P.N.G.
19 H3 Foča Bos.-Herz.
10 E3 Fochabers U.K.
91 G3 Fochville S. Africa
19 M2 Focşani Romania
39 D6 Fogang China
18 F4 Foggia Italy
86 □ Fogo *i.* Cape Verde
59 K4 Fogo I. *i.* Can.
10 D2 Foinaven *h.* U.K.
14 E5 Foix France
6 O3 Folda *chan.* Norway
6 N4 Foldereid Norway
6 M4 Foldfjorden *chan.* Norway
19 L6 Folegandros *i.* Greece
69 F1 Foleyet Can.
18 E3 Foligno Italy
9 J6 Folkestone U.K.
9 G5 Folkingham U.K.
67 D6 Folkston U.S.A.
7 M5 Folldal Norway
18 D3 Follonica Italy
72 B2 Folsom Lake *l.* U.S.A.
21 G6 Fomin Rus. Fed.
20 J2 Fominskiy Rus. Fed.
57 H3 Fond-du-Lac Can.
68 C4 Fond du Lac U.S.A.
57 J3 Fond du Lac *r.* Can.
15 B2 Fondevila Spain
18 E4 Fondi Italy
49 H2 Fongafale Tuvalu
18 C4 Fonni *Sardinia* Italy
74 G6 Fonseca, G. de *b.* Central America
59 F3 Fontanges Can.
56 E3 Fontas Can.
56 E3 Fontas *r.* Can.
78 E4 Fonte Boa Brazil
14 D3 Fontenay-le-Comte France
6 F3 Fontur *pt* Iceland
69 H3 Foot's Bay Can.
38 C3 Foping China
50 G2 Forbes Austr.
62 C1 Forbes, Mt *mt* Can.
13 K5 Forchheim Ger.
59 G2 Ford *r.* Can.
68 D2 Ford *r.* U.S.A.
7 J6 Førde Norway
57 K2 Forde Lake *l.* Can.
9 H5 Fordham U.K.
9 F7 Fordingbridge U.K.
92 A4 Ford Ra. *mts* Ant.
65 E5 Fordyce U.S.A.
86 A4 Forécariah Guinea
9 F7 Foreland *hd* U.K.
9 D6 Foreland Point *pt* U.K.
56 D4 Foresight Mtn *mt* Can.
69 G4 Forest Can.
65 F5 Forest *MS* U.S.A.
70 B4 Forest *OH* U.S.A.
71 G3 Forest Dale U.S.A.
50 F3 Forest Hill Austr.
72 B2 Foresthill U.S.A.
68 A3 Forest Lake U.S.A.
67 C5 Forest Park U.S.A.
59 G4 Forestville Can.
10 F4 Forfar U.K.
62 A2 Forks U.S.A.
71 J2 Forks, The U.S.A.
70 E4 Forksville U.S.A.
18 E2 Forlì Italy
8 D4 Formby U.K.
15 G3 Formentera *i.* Spain
15 H3 Formentor, Cap de *pt* Spain
82 D3 Formiga Brazil
80 E3 Formosa Arg.
82 C1 Formosa Brazil
Formosa *country see* Taiwan
79 G6 Formosa, Serra *h.* Brazil
82 D1 Formoso *r.* Brazil
10 E3 Forres U.K.
50 D5 Forrest *Vic.* Austr.
68 C5 Forrest U.S.A.
65 F5 Forrest City U.S.A.
68 C4 Forreston U.S.A.
6 P5 Fors Sweden
48 E3 Forsayth Austr.
6 S3 Forsnäs Sweden
7 S6 Forssa Fin.
65 E4 Forsyth *MO* U.S.A.
62 F2 Forsyth *MT* U.S.A.
69 J1 Forsythe Can.
34 C3 Fort Abbas Pak.
58 D3 Fort Albany Can.
79 L4 Fortaleza Brazil
73 H5 Fort Apache U.S.A.
56 G4 Fort Assiniboine Can.
68 C4 Fort Atkinson U.S.A.
10 D3 Fort Augustus U.K.
91 G6 Fort Beaufort S. Africa
62 E2 Fort Benton U.S.A.
57 H3 Fort Black Can.
72 A2 Fort Bragg U.S.A.
Fort-Chimo *see* Kuujjuaq
57 G3 Fort Chipewyan Can.
65 D5 Fort Cobb Res. *resr* U.S.A.
62 F3 Fort Collins U.S.A.
69 J3 Fort-Coulonge Can.
71 F2 Fort Covington U.S.A.
65 C6 Fort Davis U.S.A.
75 M6 Fort-de-France Martinique
67 C5 Fort Deposit U.S.A.
64 E3 Fort Dodge U.S.A.
64 E1 Fort Frances U.S.A.
58 E3 Fort George Can.
54 F3 Fort Good Hope Can.
10 D4 Forth *r.* U.K.
10 F4 Forth, Firth of *est.* U.K.
73 E2 Fortification Range *mts* U.S.A.
80 D2 Fortín Capitán Demattei Para.
80 D2 Fortín General Mendoza Para.
80 E2 Fortín Madrejón Para.
80 D2 Fortín Pilcomayo Arg.
78 F7 Fortín Ravelo Bol.
78 F7 Fortín Suárez Arana Bol.
71 J1 Fort Kent U.S.A.
67 D7 Fort Lauderdale U.S.A.
56 E2 Fort Liard Can.
57 G3 Fort Mackay Can.
56 G5 Fort Macleod Can.
68 B5 Fort Madison U.S.A.
68 B3 Fort McCoy U.S.A.
57 G3 Fort McMurray Can.
54 E3 Fort McPherson Can.
62 G3 Fort Morgan U.S.A.
67 D7 Fort Myers U.S.A.
56 E3 Fort Nelson Can.
56 E3 Fort Nelson *r.* Can.
56 D2 Fort Norman Can.
67 C5 Fort Payne U.S.A.
62 F1 Fort Peck U.S.A.
62 F2 Fort Peck Res. *resr* U.S.A.
67 D7 Fort Pierce U.S.A.
64 C2 Fort Pierre U.S.A.
56 F2 Fort Providence Can.
57 J4 Fort Qu'Appelle Can.
56 G2 Fort Resolution Can.
51 B7 Fortrose N.Z.
10 D3 Fortrose U.K.
72 A2 Fort Ross U.S.A.
58 E3 Fort Rupert Can.
56 E4 Fort St James Can.
56 E3 Fort St John Can.
56 G4 Fort Saskatchewan Can.
65 E4 Fort Scott U.S.A.
58 C2 Fort Severn Can.
26 D2 Fort-Shevchenko Rus. Fed.
56 E2 Fort Simpson Can.
57 G2 Fort Smith Can.
65 E5 Fort Smith U.S.A.
65 C6 Fort Stockton U.S.A.
63 F5 Fort Sumner U.S.A.
62 A3 Fortuna U.S.A.
64 C1 Fortune U.S.A.
59 J4 Fortune B. *b.* Can.
56 F3 Fort Vermilion Can.
67 C6 Fort Walton Beach U.S.A.
68 E5 Fort Wayne U.S.A.
10 C4 Fort William U.K.
65 D5 Fort Worth U.S.A.
54 D3 Fort Yukon U.S.A.
30 D5 Forūr, Jazīreh-ye *i.* Iran
6 N4 Forvik Norway
39 D6 Foshan China
18 B2 Fossano Italy
50 F5 Foster Austr.
55 Q2 Foster B. *b.* Greenland
53 B3 Foster, Mt *mt* Can./U.S.A.
70 B4 Fostoria U.S.A.
9 G4 Fotherby U.K.
14 D2 Fougères France
10 □ Foula *i.* U.K.
9 H6 Foulness Point *pt* U.K.
33 C4 Foul Pt *pt* Sri Lanka
51 C4 Foulwind, Cape *c.* N.Z.
86 D4 Foumban Cameroon
92 B3 Foundation Ice Stream *ice feature* Ant.
86 A3 Foundiougne Senegal
84 A3 Fountain U.S.A.
14 G2 Fourches, Mont des *h.* France
72 D4 Four Corners U.S.A.
91 H4 Fouriesburg S. Africa
12 C4 Fourmies France
19 M6 Fournoi *i.* Greece
68 C2 Fourteen Mile Pt *pt* U.S.A.
86 A3 Fouta Djallon *reg.* Guinea
51 A7 Foveaux Strait *str.* N.Z.
67 E7 Fowl Cay *i.* Bahamas
63 F4 Fowler *CO* U.S.A.
68 D5 Fowler *IN* U.S.A.
68 E4 Fowler *MI* U.S.A.
92 B3 Fowler Pen. *pen.* Ant.
48 D5 Fowlers Bay Austr.
29 M3 Fowman Iran
57 L3 Fox *r.* Can.
68 C4 Fox *r.* U.S.A.
56 F4 Fox Creek Can.
8 C3 Foxdale U.K.
55 K3 Foxe Basin *g.* Can.
55 K3 Foxe Channel *str.* Can.
55 L3 Foxe Peninsula Can.
51 C5 Fox Glacier N.Z.
56 G3 Fox Lake Can.
68 C4 Fox Lake U.S.A.
51 E4 Foxton N.Z.
10 D3 Foyers U.K.
11 D3 Foyle *r.* Rep. of Ireland/U.K.
11 D2 Foyle, Lough *b.* Rep. of Ireland/U.K.
11 B5 Foynes Rep. of Ireland
89 B5 Foz do Cunene Angola
82 A4 Foz do Iguaçu Brazil
15 G2 Fraga Spain
92 D4 Framnes Mts *mts* Ant.
82 C3 Franca Brazil
49 G3 Français, Récif des *rf* New Caledonia
5 D4 France *country* Europe
50 C4 Frances Austr.
56 D2 Frances *r.* Can.
56 D2 Frances Lake Can.
56 D2 Frances Lake *l.* Can.
68 D5 Francesville U.S.A.
88 B4 Franceville Gabon
64 D3 Francis Case, Lake *l.* U.S.A.
65 C7 Francisco I. Madero *Coahuila* Mex.
82 D2 Francisco Sá Brazil
71 H2 Francis, Lake *l.* U.S.A.
89 C6 Francistown Botswana
56 D4 François Lake *l.* Can.
62 E3 Francs Peak *summit* U.S.A.
12 D1 Franeker Neth.
13 M4 Frankenberg Ger.
13 G3 Frankenberg (Eder) Ger.
69 F4 Frankenmuth U.S.A.
13 G5 Frankenthal (Pfalz) Ger.
13 K4 Frankenwald *forest* Ger.
91 H3 Frankfort S. Africa
68 D5 Frankfort *IN* U.S.A.
66 C4 Frankfort *KY* U.S.A.
68 D3 Frankfort *MI* U.S.A.
13 G4 Frankfurt am Main Ger.
16 G4 Frankfurt an der Oder Ger.
73 E1 Frankin Lake *l.* U.S.A.
13 K5 Fränkische Alb *reg.* Ger.
13 K5 Fränkische Schweiz *reg.* Ger.
62 E3 Franklin *ID* U.S.A.
66 C4 Franklin *IN* U.S.A.
65 F6 Franklin *LA* U.S.A.
71 H3 Franklin *MA* U.S.A.
67 D5 Franklin *NC* U.S.A.
71 H3 Franklin *NH* U.S.A.
71 F4 Franklin *NJ* U.S.A.
70 D4 Franklin *PA* U.S.A.
67 C5 Franklin *TN* U.S.A.
70 E6 Franklin *VA* U.S.A.
70 D5 Franklin *WV* U.S.A.
54 F3 Franklin Bay *b.* Can.
62 C1 Franklin D. Roosevelt Lake *l.* U.S.A.
92 B5 Franklin I. *i.* Ant.
56 E2 Franklin Mountains Can.
51 A6 Franklin Mts *mts* N.Z.
55 J2 Franklin Str. Can.
50 E5 Frankston Austr.
7 P5 Fränsta Sweden
68 E1 Franz Can.
51 C5 Franz Josef Glacier N.Z.
24 G2 Franz Josef Land *is* Rus. Fed.
18 C5 Frasca, Capo della *pt Sardinia* Italy
18 E4 Frascati Italy
56 E4 Fraser *r. B.C.* Can.
59 H2 Fraser *r. Nfld* Can.
90 D5 Fraserburg S. Africa
10 F3 Fraserburgh U.K.
58 D4 Fraserdale Can.
49 F4 Fraser Island *i.* Austr.
56 E4 Fraser Lake Can.
56 E4 Fraser Plateau *plat.* Can.
51 F3 Frasertown N.Z.
68 E2 Frater Can.
16 D7 Frauenfeld Switz.
83 E2 Fray Bentos Uru.
12 E4 Frechen Ger.
8 E4 Freckleton U.K.
68 E3 Frederic *MI* U.S.A.
68 A3 Frederic *WI* U.S.A.
7 L9 Fredericia Denmark
70 E5 Frederick *MD* U.S.A.
65 D5 Frederick *OK* U.S.A.
65 D6 Fredericksburg *TX* U.S.A.
70 E5 Fredericksburg *VA* U.S.A.
56 C3 Frederick Sound *chan.* U.S.A.
65 F4 Fredericktown U.S.A.
59 G4 Fredericton Can.
Frederikshåb *see* Paamiut
7 M8 Frederikshavn Denmark
7 N9 Frederiksværk Denmark
73 F3 Fredonia *AZ* U.S.A.
70 D3 Fredonia *NY* U.S.A.
6 Q4 Fredrika Sweden
7 M7 Fredrikstad Norway
71 F4 Freehold U.S.A.
71 F4 Freeland U.S.A.
72 C2 Freel Peak *summit* U.S.A.
64 D3 Freeman U.S.A.
68 D5 Freeman, Lake *l.* U.S.A.
68 C4 Freeport *IL* U.S.A.
71 H3 Freeport *ME* U.S.A.
71 G4 Freeport *NY* U.S.A.
65 E6 Freeport *TX* U.S.A.
67 E7 Freeport City Bahamas
65 D7 Freer U.S.A.
91 G4 Free State *div.* S. Africa
86 A4 Freetown Sierra Leone
15 C3 Fregenal de la Sierra Spain
14 C2 Fréhel, Cap *pt* France
16 C6 Freiburg im Breisgau Ger.
12 F5 Freisen Ger.
16 E6 Freising Ger.
16 G6 Freistadt Austria
14 H5 Fréjus France
48 B5 Fremantle Austr.
68 E4 Fremont *MI* U.S.A.
64 D3 Fremont *NE* U.S.A.
70 B4 Fremont *OH* U.S.A.
73 G2 Fremont *r.* U.S.A.
70 B6 Frenchburg U.S.A.
70 C4 French Creek *r.* U.S.A.
77 E2 French Guiana *terr.* S. America
50 E5 French I. *i.* Austr.
72 C2 Frenchman U.S.A.
57 H5 Frenchman *r.* Can./U.S.A.
72 B2 Frenchman L. *l. CA* U.S.A.
73 E3 Frenchman L. *l. NV* U.S.A.
11 C4 Frenchpark Rep. of Ireland
51 D4 French Pass N.Z.
47 N5 French Polynesia *terr.* Pac. Oc.
3 □ French Southern and Antarctic Lands *terr.* Southern Ocean
71 J1 Frenchville U.S.A.
12 F2 Freren Ger.
11 D5 Freshford Rep. of Ireland
73 G6 Fresnal Canyon U.S.A.
74 D4 Fresnillo Mex.
72 C3 Fresno U.S.A.
72 C3 Fresno *r.* U.S.A.
15 H3 Freu, Cap des *pt* Spain
13 F4 Freudenberg Ger.
16 D6 Freudenstadt Ger.
12 A4 Frévent France
13 L1 Freyenstein Ger.
14 H2 Freyming-Merlebach France
83 D1 Freyre Arg.
86 A3 Fria Guinea
72 C3 Friant U.S.A.
80 C3 Frias Arg.
16 C7 Fribourg Switz.
13 F1 Friedeburg Ger.
13 M1 Friedland Ger.
16 D7 Friedrichshafen Ger.
71 J3 Friendship U.S.A.
13 L2 Friesack Ger.
12 D1 Friese Wad *tidal flats* Neth.
13 F1 Friesoythe Ger.
9 J6 Frinton-on-Sea U.K.
65 D6 Frio *r.* U.S.A.
10 B4 Frisa, Loch *l.* U.K.
73 F2 Frisco Mt *mt* U.S.A.
13 H3 Fritzlar Ger.
55 M3 Frobisher Bay *b.* Can.
57 H3 Frobisher Lake *l.* Can.
6 L5 Frohavet *b.* Norway
13 L3 Frohburg Ger.
12 A5 Froissy France
21 G5 Frolovo Rus. Fed.
20 K2 Frolovskaya Rus. Fed.
9 E6 Frome U.K.
50 B1 Frome Downs Austr.
48 D5 Frome, Lake *salt flat* Austr.
13 F3 Fröndenberg Ger.
74 F5 Frontera Mex.
70 D5 Front Royal U.S.A.
18 E4 Frosinone Italy
70 D5 Frostburg U.S.A.
6 L5 Frøya *i.* Norway
12 A4 Fruges France
73 H2 Fruita U.S.A.
73 G1 Fruitland U.S.A.
16 C7 Frutigen Switz.
17 J6 Frýdek-Místek Czech Rep.
71 H2 Fryeburg U.S.A.
39 F5 Fu'an China
39 D5 Fuchuan China
39 F4 Fuchun Jiang *r.* China
10 A3 Fuday *i.* U.K.
39 E5 Fude China
39 F5 Fuding China
15 E2 Fuenlabrada Spain
15 D3 Fuente Obejuna Spain
80 E2 Fuerte Olimpo Para.
86 A2 Fuerteventura *i.* Canary Is
43 B2 Fuga *i.* Phil.
38 E3 Fugou China
38 D2 Fugu China
29 J4 Fuḩaymī Iraq
32 E4 Fujairah U.A.E.
41 F7 Fuji Japan
39 E5 Fujian *div.* China
38 C4 Fu Jiang *r.* China
41 F7 Fuji-Hakone-Izu National Park Japan
40 B1 Fujin China
41 F7 Fujinomiya Japan
41 F7 Fuji-san *volc.* Japan
40 H3 Fukagawa Japan
41 D7 Fukuchiyama Japan
41 A8 Fukue Japan
41 A8 Fukue-jima *i.* Japan
41 E6 Fukui Japan
41 B8 Fukuoka Japan
41 G6 Fukushima Japan
41 B9 Fukuyama Japan
30 D2 Fūlād Maīalleh Iran
13 H4 Fulda Ger.
13 H3 Fulda *r.* Ger.
9 G6 Fulham U.K.
38 E3 Fuliji China
39 C4 Fuling China
57 M2 Fullerton, Cape *hd* Can.
68 B5 Fulton *IL* U.S.A.
66 B4 Fulton *KY* U.S.A.
64 F4 Fulton *MO* U.S.A.
71 E3 Fulton *NY* U.S.A.
91 K2 Fumane Moz.
12 C5 Fumay France
41 F7 Funabashi Japan
49 H2 Funafuti *i.* Tuvalu
86 A1 Funchal Port.
81 B2 Fundación Col.
15 C2 Fundão Port.
59 G5 Fundy, Bay of *g.* Can.
59 G4 Fundy Nat. Park Can.
72 D3 Funeral Peak *summit* U.S.A.
89 D6 Funhalouro Moz.
38 F3 Funing *Jiangsu* China
39 B6 Funing *Yunnan* China
38 D3 Funiu Shan *mts* China
86 C3 Funtua Nigeria
10 □ Funzie U.K.
39 F5 Fuqing China
42 D2 Fur *r.* China
40 H3 Furano Japan
30 E5 Fürgun, Kūh-e *mt* Iran
20 G3 Furmanov Rus. Fed.
40 D3 Furmanovo Rus. Fed.
72 D3 Furnace Creek U.S.A.
82 C3 Furnas, Represa *resr* Brazil
48 E6 Furneaux Group *is* Austr.
13 F2 Fürstenau Ger.
13 M1 Fürstenberg Ger.
16 G4 Fürstenwalde Ger.
13 J5 Fürth Ger.
13 L5 Furth im Wald Ger.
40 G3 Furubira Japan
40 G5 Furukawa Japan
55 K3 Fury and Hecla Strait *str.* Can.
81 B3 Fusagasugá Col.
39 C7 Fushan *Hainan* China
42 A5 Fushan *Shandong* China
42 B3 Fushun *Liaoning* China
42 B3 Fushun *Liaoning* China
39 B4 Fushun *Sichuan* China
42 B3 Fushuncheng China
42 D2 Fusong China
39 C6 Fusui China
41 B8 Futago-san *volc.* Japan
49 H3 Futuna *i.* Vanuatu
39 E5 Futun Xi *r.* China
38 C3 Fu Xian China
42 A2 Fuxin *Liaoning* China
42 A2 Fuxin *Liaoning* China
40 F5 Fuya Japan
38 E3 Fuyang *Anhui* China
39 F4 Fuyang *Zhejiang* China
38 E2 Fuyang *r.* China
36 E2 Fuyu *Heilongjiang* China
42 C1 Fuyu China
39 B5 Fuyuan China
39 F5 Fuzhou *Fujian* China
39 E5 Fuzhou *Jiangxi* China
42 A4 Fuzhou Wan *b.* China
29 L2 Füzuli Azer.
7 M9 Fyn *i.* Denmark
10 C5 Fyne, Loch *in.* U.K.
F.Y.R.O.M. *country see* Macedonia

G

18 C6 Gaâfour Tunisia
88 E3 Gaalkacyo Somalia
91 F2 Gabane Botswana
72 D2 Gabbs U.S.A.
72 C2 Gabbs Valley Range *mts* U.S.A.
89 B5 Gabela Angola
86 D1 Gabès Tunisia
87 D1 Gabès, Golfe de *g.* Tunisia
50 G4 Gabo I. *i.* Austr.
85 E6 Gabon *country* Africa
89 C6 Gaborone Botswana
31 E5 Gābrīk Iran
31 E5 Gābrīk *watercourse* Iran
19 L3 Gabrovo Bulg.
86 A3 Gabú Guinea-Bissau
30 C2 Gach Sār Iran
30 C4 Gach Sārān Iran
33 A3 Gadag India
6 O4 Gäddede Sweden
13 K1 Gadebusch Ger.
34 B5 Gadhra India
34 B4 Gadra Pak.
67 C5 Gadsden U.S.A.
33 B2 Gadwal India
6 S2 Gædnovuoppe Norway
9 D6 Gaer U.K.
19 L2 Găeşti Romania
18 E4 Gaeta Italy
18 E4 Gaeta, Golfo di *g.* Italy
46 F3 Gaferut *i.* Micronesia
67 D5 Gaffney U.S.A.
86 C1 Gafsa Tunisia
20 E4 Gagarin Rus. Fed.
20 H4 Gagino Rus. Fed.
86 B4 Gagnoa Côte d'Ivoire
59 G3 Gagnon Can.
21 G7 Gagra Georgia
29 L4 Gahvāreh Iran
90 C3 Gaiab *watercourse* Namibia
35 G4 Gaibandha Bangl.
13 H6 Gaildorf Ger.
14 E5 Gaillac France
67 D6 Gainesville *FL* U.S.A.
67 D5 Gainesville *GA* U.S.A.
65 D5 Gainesville *TX* U.S.A.
9 G4 Gainsborough U.K.
48 D5 Gairdner, Lake *salt flat* Austr.
10 C3 Gairloch U.K.
10 C3 Gair Loch *in.* U.K.
42 B3 Gai Xian China
33 C2 Gajapatinagaram India
31 G5 Gajar Pak.
90 E3 Gakarosa *mt* S. Africa
34 C1 Gakuch Jammu and Kashmir
35 G3 Gala China
31 G2 Galaasiya Uzbek.
28 C7 Galâla el Baharîya, G. el *plat.* Egypt
88 D4 Galana *r.* Kenya
78 □ Galapagos Islands *is* Ecuador
10 F5 Galashiels U.K.
19 N2 Galaţi Romania
19 H4 Galatina Italy
70 C6 Galax U.S.A.
11 C5 Galbally Rep. of Ireland
7 L6 Galdhøpiggen *summit* Norway
60 F7 Galeana Mex.
30 D5 Galeh Dār Iran
68 B4 Galena U.S.A.
81 E2 Galeota Pt *pt* Trinidad and Tobago
81 E2 Galera Pt *pt* Trinidad and Tobago
83 B4 Galera, Punta *pt* Chile
68 B5 Galesburg U.S.A.
90 F4 Galeshewe S. Africa
68 B3 Galesville U.S.A.
70 E4 Galeton U.S.A.
21 G7 Gali Georgia
20 G3 Galich Rus. Fed.
20 G2 Galichskaya Vozvyshennost' *reg.* Rus. Fed.

15 C1 **Galicia** *div.* Spain
28 E5 **Galilee, Sea of** *l.* Israel
70 B4 **Galion** U.S.A.
18 C6 **Galite, Canal de la** *chan.* Tunisia
73 G5 **Galiuro Mts** *mts* U.S.A.
87 F3 **Gallabat** Sudan
67 C4 **Gallatin** U.S.A.
62 E2 **Gallatin** *r.* U.S.A.
33 C5 **Galle** Sri Lanka
80 B8 **Gallegos** *r.* Arg.
81 C1 **Gallinas, Pta** *pt* Col.
18 G4 **Gallipoli** Italy
70 B5 **Gallipolis** U.S.A.
6 R3 **Gällivare** Sweden
6 O5 **Gällö** Sweden
71 E3 **Gallo I.** *i.* U.S.A.
73 H4 **Gallo Mts** *mts* U.S.A.
10 D6 **Galloway, Mull of** *c.* U.K.
73 H4 **Gallup** U.S.A.
31 G1 **Gallyaaral** Uzbek.
10 B4 **Galmisdale** U.K.
50 G3 **Galong** Austr.
33 C4 **Galoya** Sri Lanka
33 C5 **Gal Oya** *r.* Sri Lanka
10 D5 **Galston** U.K.
72 B2 **Galt** U.S.A.
86 A2 **Galtat Zemmour** Western Sahara
11 C5 **Galtee Mountains** *h.* Rep. of Ireland
11 C5 **Galtymore** *h.* Rep. of Ireland
31 E3 **Galūgāh-e Āsīyeh** Iran
68 B5 **Galva** U.S.A.
65 E6 **Galveston** U.S.A.
65 E6 **Galveston Bay** *b.* U.S.A.
83 E2 **Galvez** Arg.
35 E3 **Galwa** Nepal
11 B4 **Galway** Rep. of Ireland
11 B4 **Galway Bay** *g.* Rep. of Ireland
39 B6 **Gâm** *r.* Vietnam
9 J8 **Gamaches** France
91 J5 **Gamalakhe** S. Africa
81 B2 **Gamarra** Col.
35 G3 **Gamba** China
88 D3 **Gambēla** Eth.
88 D3 **Gambela National Park** Eth.
54 A3 **Gambell** U.S.A.
34 D4 **Gambhir** *r.* India
85 B4 **Gambia, The** *country* Africa
46 O6 **Gambier, Îles** *is Fr. Polynesia* Pac. Oc.
59 K4 **Gambo** Can.
88 B4 **Gamboma** Congo
73 H4 **Gamerco** U.S.A.
7 P8 **Gamleby** Sweden
6 S4 **Gammelstaden** Sweden
90 C4 **Gamoep** S. Africa
40 B3 **Gamova, Mys** *pt* Rus. Fed.
33 C5 **Gampola** Sri Lanka
31 F4 **Gamshadzai K.** *mts* Iran
38 A3 **Gana** China
73 H4 **Ganado** U.S.A.
69 J3 **Gananoque** Can.
30 C4 **Ganāveh** Iran
29 L1 **Gäncä** Azer.
39 C7 **Gancheng** China
Gand *see* **Gent**
45 E3 **Gandadiwata, Bukit** *mt* Indon.
35 G3 **Gandaingoin** China
88 C4 **Gandajika** Congo(Zaire)
35 E4 **Gandak Dam** *dam* Nepal
34 B3 **Gandari Mountain** *mt* Pak.
34 A3 **Gandava** Pak.
59 K4 **Gander** Can.
13 G1 **Ganderkesee** Ger.
15 G2 **Gandesa** Spain
34 C5 **Gandevi** India
34 B5 **Gāndhīdhām** India
34 C5 **Gandhinagar** India
34 C4 **Gāndhi Sāgar** *resr* India
34 C4 **Gāndhi Sāgar Dam** *dam* India
15 F3 **Gandía** Spain
31 F4 **Gand-i-Zureh** *plain* Afgh.
82 E1 **Gandu** Brazil
33 C5 **Ganga** *r.* Sri Lanka
83 C4 **Gangán** Arg.
34 C3 **Ganganagar** India
34 D4 **Gangapur** India
35 H5 **Gangaw** Myanmar
33 B3 **Gangawati** India
38 A2 **Gangca** China
34 E3 **Gangdisê Shan** *mts* China
14 F5 **Ganges** France
35 G5 **Ganges, Mouths of the** *est.* Bangl./India
34 D3 **Gangoh** India
34 D3 **Gangotri** *mt* India
35 G4 **Gangtok** India
38 B3 **Gangu** China
33 D2 **Ganjam** India
30 C4 **Ganjgān** Iran
39 E4 **Gan Jiang** *r.* China
39 B4 **Ganluo** China
50 F3 **Ganmain** Austr.
14 F3 **Gannat** France
62 E3 **Gannett Peak** *summit* U.S.A.
34 C5 **Ganora** India
38 C2 **Ganquan** China
90 C7 **Gansbaai** S. Africa
38 B3 **Gansu** *div.* China
38 B2 **Gantang** China
21 G7 **Gant'iadi** Georgia
39 E5 **Gan Xian** China
90 F3 **Ganyesa** S. Africa
38 F3 **Ganyu** China
39 E5 **Ganzhou** China
87 F4 **Ganzi** Sudan
86 B3 **Gao** Mali
39 E4 **Gao'an** China
38 E2 **Gaocheng** China
38 F4 **Gaochun** China
39 E4 **Gaohebu** China
38 B2 **Gaolan** China
38 F2 **Gaomi** China
39 D5 **Gaomutang** China
38 D3 **Gaoping** China
38 A2 **Gaotai** China
38 E2 **Gaotang** China
38 C2 **Gaotouyao** China
86 B3 **Gaoua** Burkina
86 A3 **Gaoual** Guinea
38 B4 **Gao Xian** China
38 E2 **Gaoyang** China
38 E2 **Gaoyi** China
38 F3 **Gaoyou** China
38 F3 **Gaoyou Hu** *l.* China
39 D6 **Gaozhou** China
14 H4 **Gap** France
43 B3 **Gapan** Phil.
15 F5 **Gap Carbon** *hd* Alg.
34 E2 **Gar** China
31 F4 **Garagheh** Iran
11 C4 **Gara, Lough** *l.* Rep. of Ireland
88 C3 **Garamba** *r.* Congo(Zaire)
88 C3 **Garamba, Park National de la** *nat. park* Congo(Zaire)
79 L5 **Garanhuns** Brazil
91 G2 **Ga-Rankuwa** S. Africa
88 D3 **Garba Tula** Kenya
72 A1 **Garberville** U.S.A.
30 C3 **Garbosh, Kūh-e** *mt* Iran
13 H2 **Garbsen** Ger.
82 C3 **Garça** Brazil
82 B1 **Garças, Rio das** *r.* Brazil
35 G2 **Garco** China
29 K1 **Gardabani** Georgia
18 D2 **Garda, Lago di** *l.* Italy
18 B6 **Garde, Cap de** *hd* Alg.
13 K2 **Gardelegen** Ger.
64 C4 **Garden City** U.S.A.
68 D3 **Garden Corners** U.S.A.
72 C5 **Garden Grove** U.S.A.
57 L4 **Garden Hill** Can.
68 E3 **Garden I.** *i.* U.S.A.
66 C2 **Garden Pen.** *pen.* U.S.A.
31 H3 **Gardez** Afgh.
71 J2 **Gardiner** *ME* U.S.A.
62 E2 **Gardiner** *MT* U.S.A.
71 G4 **Gardiners I.** *i.* U.S.A.
68 C5 **Gardner** U.S.A.
71 K2 **Gardner Lake** *l.* U.S.A.
94 H4 **Gardner Pinnacles** *is HI* U.S.A.
72 C2 **Gardnerville** U.S.A.
10 D4 **Garelochhead** U.K.
14 E2 **Gargantua, Cape** *c.* Can.
29 M6 **Gargar** Iran
7 R9 **Gargždai** Lith.
34 D5 **Garhakota** India
34 E5 **Garhchiroli** India
34 A3 **Garhi Khairo** Pak.
34 D4 **Garhi Malehra** India
56 E5 **Garibaldi, Mt** *mt* Can.
56 E5 **Garibaldi Prov. Park** *nat. park* Can.
91 F5 **Gariep Dam** *resr* S. Africa
90 B5 **Garies** S. Africa
18 E4 **Garigliano** *r.* Italy
88 D4 **Garissa** Kenya
7 T8 **Garkalne** Latvia
70 D4 **Garland** *PA* U.S.A.
65 D5 **Garland** *TX* U.S.A.
30 C2 **Garmī** Iran
16 E7 **Garmisch-Partenkirchen** Ger.
30 D3 **Garmsar** Iran
31 F4 **Garmsel** *reg.* Afgh.
64 E4 **Garnett** U.S.A.
50 D2 **Garnpung Lake** *l.* Austr.
35 G4 **Gāro Hills** *h.* India
14 D4 **Garonne** *r.* France
88 E3 **Garoowe** Somalia
82 G3 **Garopaba** Brazil
87 D4 **Garoua** Cameroon
83 D3 **Garré** Arg.
73 E2 **Garrison** U.S.A.
11 F2 **Garron Point** *pt* U.K.
31 G4 **Garruk** Pak.
57 J1 **Garry Lake** *l.* Can.
10 D4 **Garry, Loch** *l.* U.K.
10 B2 **Garrynahine** U.K.
88 E4 **Garsen** Kenya
9 D5 **Garth** U.K.
13 K1 **Gartow** Ger.
90 B3 **Garub** Namibia
45 C4 **Garut** Indon.
11 E3 **Garvagh** U.K.
10 D3 **Garve** U.K.
68 D5 **Gary** U.S.A.
34 E3 **Garyarsa** China
41 C7 **Garyū-zan** *mt* Japan
34 D2 **Gar Zangbo** *r.* China
36 B3 **Garzê** China
81 B4 **Garzón** Col.
14 D5 **Gascogne** *reg.* France
64 E4 **Gasconade** *r.* U.S.A.
14 C5 **Gascony, Gulf of** *g.* France/Spain
48 B4 **Gascoyne** *r.* Austr.
Gascuña, Golfo de *g. see* **Gascony, Gulf of**
34 D2 **Gasherbrum** *mt* China/Jammu and Kashmir
31 F5 **Gasht** Iran
86 D3 **Gashua** Nigeria
31 E3 **Gask** Iran
45 C3 **Gaspar, Selat** *chan.* Indon.
59 H4 **Gaspé** Can.
59 H4 **Gaspé, C.** *c.* Can.
59 G4 **Gaspé, Péninsule de** *pen.* Can.
59 G4 **Gaspésie, Parc de la** *nat. park* Can.
12 E2 **Gasselte** Neth.
67 D5 **Gastonia** U.S.A.
83 C4 **Gastre** Arg.
15 E4 **Gata, Cabo de** *c.* Spain
28 D4 **Gata, Cape** *c.* Cyprus
20 D3 **Gatchina** Rus. Fed.
70 B6 **Gate City** U.S.A.
10 D6 **Gatehouse of Fleet** U.K.
8 F3 **Gateshead** U.K.
65 D6 **Gatesville** U.S.A.
73 H2 **Gateway** U.S.A.
71 F4 **Gateway National Recreational Area** *res.* U.S.A.
69 K3 **Gatineau** Can.
69 K2 **Gatineau** *r.* Can.
30 D4 **Gatrūyeh** Iran
29 M5 **Gatvand** Iran
49 H3 **Gau** *i.* Fiji
57 K3 **Gauer Lake** *l.* Can.
6 M5 **Gaula** *r.* Norway
70 C5 **Gauley Bridge** U.S.A.
12 D5 **Gaume** *reg.* Belgium
35 F4 **Gauri Sankar** *mt* China
91 G3 **Gauteng** *div.* S. Africa
31 G3 **Gauzan** Afgh.
31 F5 **Gavāter** Iran
30 D5 **Gāvbandī** Iran
30 D5 **Gāvbūs, Kūh-e** *mts* Iran
19 L7 **Gavdos** *i.* Greece
30 B3 **Gaveh** *r.* Iran
82 E1 **Gavião** *r.* Brazil
29 L4 **Gāvīleh** Iran
72 B4 **Gaviota** U.S.A.
30 E4 **Gāv Koshī** Iran
7 P6 **Gävle** Sweden
20 F3 **Gavrilov-Yam** Rus. Fed.
90 B3 **Gawachab** Namibia
50 B3 **Gawler** Austr.
38 A1 **Gaxun Nur** *salt l.* China
35 F4 **Gaya** India
86 C3 **Gaya** Niger
42 E2 **Gaya** *r.* China
68 E3 **Gaylord** U.S.A.
28 E6 **Gaza** Gaza
91 K1 **Gaza** *div.* Moz.
28 E6 **Gaza** *terr.* Asia
32 F1 **Gaz-Achak** Turkm.
30 D2 **Gazandzhyk** Turkm.
31 H3 **Gazdarra Pass** Afgh.
28 F3 **Gaziantep** Turkey
31 F3 **Gazīk** Iran
28 D3 **Gazipaşa** Turkey
31 F1 **Gazli** Uzbek.
31 E5 **Gaz Māhū** Iran
31 E4 **Gaz Şāleḩ** Iran
86 A4 **Gbangbatok** Sierra Leone
86 B4 **Gbarnga** Liberia
86 C4 **Gboko** Nigeria
17 J3 **Gdańsk** Pol.
17 J3 **Gdańsk, Gulf of** *g.* Pol./Rus. Fed.
20 C3 **Gdov** Rus. Fed.
17 J3 **Gdynia** Pol.
10 C1 **Gealldruig Mhor** *i.* U.K.
13 J3 **Gebesee** Ger.
87 F3 **Gedaref** Sudan
13 H4 **Gedern** Ger.
12 C5 **Gedinne** Belgium
28 B2 **Gediz** Turkey
28 A2 **Gediz** *r.* Turkey
9 H5 **Gedney Drove End** U.K.
7 M9 **Gedser** Denmark
12 D3 **Geel** Belgium
50 E5 **Geelong** Austr.
90 D4 **Geel Vloer** *salt pan* S. Africa
12 F2 **Geeste** Ger.
13 J1 **Geesthacht** Ger.
38 F4 **Ge Hu** *l.* China
86 D3 **Geidam** Nigeria
13 H5 **Geiersberg** *h.* Ger.
57 J3 **Geikie** *r.* Can.
12 E4 **Geilenkirchen** Ger.
7 L6 **Geilo** Norway
7 K5 **Geiranger** Norway
68 E6 **Geist Reservoir** U.S.A.
13 L3 **Geithain** Ger.
39 B6 **Gejiu** China
18 F6 **Gela** *Sicily* Italy
88 E3 **Geladī** Eth.
44 B4 **Gelang, Tanjung** *pt* Malaysia
12 E3 **Geldern** Ger.
21 F6 **Gelendzhik** Rus. Fed.
17 L3 **Gelgaudiškis** Lith.
21 C7 **Gelibolu** Turkey
28 C2 **Gelincik Dağı** *mt* Turkey
13 G3 **Gelmord** Iran
13 H4 **Gelnhausen** Ger.
12 F3 **Gelsenkirchen** Ger.
44 B5 **Gemas** Malaysia
43 C5 **Gemeh** Indon.
88 B3 **Gemena** Congo(Zaire)
28 F2 **Gemerek** Turkey
28 B1 **Gemlik** Turkey
18 E1 **Gemona del Friuli** Italy
89 C6 **Gemsbok National Park** Botswana
90 D3 **Gemsbokplein** *well* S. Africa
88 E3 **Genalē Wenz** *r.* Eth.
12 C4 **Genappe** Belgium
83 D3 **General Acha** Arg.
83 E3 **General Alvear** *Buenos Aires* Arg.
83 E1 **General Alvear** *Entre Rios* Arg.
83 C2 **General Alvear** *Mendoza* Arg.
83 E2 **General Belgrano** Arg.
92 B3 **General Belgrano II** *Arg. Base* Ant.
92 B2 **General Bernardo O'Higgins** *Chile Base* Ant.
65 D7 **General Bravo** Mex.
80 B7 **General Carrera, L.** *l.* Chile
83 F3 **General Conesa** *Buenos Aires* Arg.
83 D4 **General Conesa** *Rio Negro* Arg.
83 F3 **General Guido** Arg.
83 F3 **General J. Madariaga** Arg.
83 E3 **General La Madrid** Arg.
83 F3 **General Lavalle** Arg.
83 D2 **General Levalle** Arg.
43 C4 **General Luna** Phil.
43 C4 **General MacArthur** Phil.
83 D2 **General Pico** Arg.
83 E2 **General Pinto** Arg.
83 C3 **General Roca** Arg.
92 B2 **General San Martín** *Arg. Base* Ant.
43 C5 **General Santos** Phil.
83 D2 **General Villegas** Arg.
70 D3 **Genesee** *r.* U.S.A.
68 B5 **Geneseo** *IL* U.S.A.
70 E3 **Geneseo** *NY* U.S.A.
91 G3 **Geneva** S. Africa
Geneva *see* **Genève**
68 C5 **Geneva** *IL* U.S.A.
64 D3 **Geneva** *NE* U.S.A.
70 E3 **Geneva** *NY* U.S.A.
70 C4 **Geneva** *OH* U.S.A.
Geneva, Lake *l. see* **Léman, Lac**
68 C4 **Geneva, Lake** *l.* U.S.A.
16 C7 **Genève** Switz.
15 D4 **Genil** *r.* Spain
12 D4 **Genk** Belgium
12 D3 **Gennep** Neth.
50 G4 **Genoa** Austr.
18 C2 **Genoa** Italy
Genova *see* **Genoa**
18 C2 **Genova, Golfo di** *g.* Italy
12 B3 **Gent** Belgium
13 L2 **Genthin** Ger.
48 B5 **Geographe Bay** *b.* Austr.
90 E6 **George** S. Africa
59 G2 **George** *r.* Can.
50 G3 **George, L.** *l. N.S.W.* Austr.
50 B4 **George, L.** *l. S.A.* Austr.
67 D6 **George, L.** *l.* U.S.A.
71 G3 **George, Lake** *l.* U.S.A.
51 A6 **George Sd** *in.* N.Z.
50 B2 **Georgetown** *S.A.* Austr.
67 F7 **George Town** Bahamas
69 H4 **Georgetown** Can.
79 G2 **Georgetown** Guyana
45 B1 **George Town** Malaysia
86 A3 **Georgetown** The Gambia
71 F5 **Georgetown** *DE* U.S.A.
68 D6 **Georgetown** *IL* U.S.A.
66 C4 **Georgetown** *KY* U.S.A.
70 B5 **Georgetown** *OH* U.S.A.
67 E5 **Georgetown** *SC* U.S.A.
65 D6 **Georgetown** *TX* U.S.A.
92 B2 **George VI Sd** *chan.* Ant.
92 B5 **George V Land** *reg.* Ant.
65 D6 **George West** U.S.A.
23 D5 **Georgia** *country* Asia
67 D5 **Georgia** *div.* U.S.A.
69 G3 **Georgian Bay** *b.* Can.
69 H3 **Georgian Bay Island National Park** Can.
56 E5 **Georgia, Strait of** *chan.* Can.
48 D4 **Georgina** *watercourse* Austr.
27 G2 **Georgiyevka** Kazak.
21 G6 **Georgiyevsk** Rus. Fed.
20 H3 **Georgiyevskoye** Rus. Fed.
13 L4 **Gera** Ger.
12 B4 **Geraardsbergen** Belgium
79 J6 **Geral de Goiás, Serra** *h.* Brazil
51 C6 **Geraldine** N.Z.
82 C1 **Geral do Paraná, Serra** *h.* Brazil
48 B4 **Geraldton** Austr.
30 D5 **Gerāsh** Iran
29 H3 **Gercüş** Turkey
28 D1 **Gerede** Turkey
28 D1 **Gerede** *r.* Turkey
31 G4 **Gereshk** Afgh.
44 B4 **Gerik** Malaysia
31 E3 **Gerīmenj** Iran
64 C3 **Gering** U.S.A.
62 C3 **Gerlach** U.S.A.
56 E3 **Germansen Landing** Can.
70 E5 **Germantown** U.S.A.
5 D3 **Germany** *country* Europe
13 G5 **Germersheim** Ger.
91 H3 **Germiston** S. Africa
13 G5 **Gernsheim** Ger.
12 E4 **Gerolstein** Ger.
13 J5 **Gerolzhofen** Ger.
73 G5 **Geronimo** U.S.A.
50 H3 **Gerringong** Austr.
13 H4 **Gersfeld** Ger.
13 J4 **Gerstungen** Ger.
13 K2 **Gerwisch** Ger.
35 F2 **Gêrzê** China
21 E7 **Gerze** Turkey
12 F3 **Gescher** Ger.
30 D3 **Getcheh, Kūh-e** *h.* Iran
12 D4 **Gete** *r.* Belgium
70 E5 **Gettysburg** *PA* U.S.A.
64 D2 **Gettysburg** *SD* U.S.A.
70 E5 **Gettysburg National Military Park** *res.* U.S.A.
39 C5 **Getu He** *r.* China
92 A4 **Getz Ice Shelf** *ice feature* Ant.
45 A2 **Geumapang** *r.* Indon.
50 G2 **Geurie** Austr.
29 J2 **Gevaş** Turkey
19 K4 **Gevgelija** Macedonia
15 E1 **Gexto** Spain
Gey *see* **Nikshahr**
44 □ **Geylang** Sing.
91 F3 **Geysdorp** S. Africa
28 C1 **Geyve** Turkey
90 F2 **Ghaap Plateau** *plat.* S. Africa
86 C1 **Ghadāmis** Libya
30 D2 **Ghaem Shahr** Iran
34 C3 **Ghaggar, Dry Bed of** *watercourse* Pak.
34 E4 **Ghaghara** *r.* India
35 F5 **Ghaghra** India
85 C5 **Ghana** *country* Africa
30 D5 **Ghanādah, Rās** *pt* U.A.E.
34 C4 **Ghanliala** India
89 C6 **Ghanzi** Botswana
90 E1 **Ghanzi** *div.* Botswana
28 E6 **Gharandal** Jordan
86 C1 **Ghardaïa** Alg.
31 H2 **Gharm** Tajik.
30 C5 **Ghār, Ras al** *pt* S. Arabia
87 D1 **Gharyān** Libya
86 D2 **Ghāt** Libya
34 B3 **Ghauspur** Pak.
87 D3 **Ghazal, Bahr el** *watercourse* Chad
86 B1 **Ghazaouet** Alg.
34 D3 **Ghaziabad** India
35 E4 **Ghazipur** India
34 A3 **Ghazluna** Pak.
31 H3 **Ghaznī** Afgh.
31 H3 **Ghazni** *r.* Afgh.
31 G3 **Ghazoor** Afgh.
Ghent *see* **Gent**
17 M7 **Gheorgheni** Romania
17 L7 **Gherla** Romania
18 C3 **Ghisonaccia** *Corsica* France
31 G3 **Ghizao** Afgh.
34 C1 **Ghizar** Pak.
33 A2 **Ghod** *r.* India
35 G4 **Ghoraghat** Bangl.
31 H3 **Ghorband** *r.* Afgh.
31 H3 **Ghorband Pass** Afgh.
34 B4 **Ghotāru** India
34 B4 **Ghotki** Pak.
30 D4 **Ghōwrī** Iran
35 F4 **Ghuari** *r.* India
29 J5 **Ghudāf, Wādī al** *watercourse* Iraq
31 J2 **Ghūdara** Tajik.
34 D6 **Ghugus** India
34 B4 **Ghulam Mohammed Barrage** *barrage* Pak.
31 F3 **Ghurian** Afgh.
12 A3 **Ghyvelde** France
44 C3 **Gia Đinh** Vietnam
21 G6 **Giaginskaya** Rus. Fed.
19 K4 **Giannitsa** Greece
91 H4 **Giant's Castle** *mt* S. Africa
11 E2 **Giant's Causeway** U.K.
45 E4 **Gianyar** Indon.
44 C3 **Gia Rai** Vietnam
18 F6 **Giarre** *Sicily* Italy
18 B2 **Giaveno** Italy
90 B2 **Gibeon** Namibia
15 D4 **Gibraltar** *terr.* Europe
15 C5 **Gibraltar, Strait of** *str.* Morocco/Spain
68 C5 **Gibson City** U.S.A.
48 C4 **Gibson Desert** Austr.
36 B2 **Gichgeniyn Nuruu** *mts* Mongolia
33 B3 **Giddalur** India
28 D6 **Giddi, G. el** *h.* Egypt
88 D3 **Gīdolē** Eth.
14 F3 **Gien** France
13 G4 **Gießen** Ger.
13 J2 **Gifhorn** Ger.
56 F3 **Gift Lake** Can.
41 E7 **Gifu** Japan
81 B4 **Gigante** Col.
65 B7 **Gigantes, Llanos de los** *plain* Mex.
10 C5 **Gigha** *i.* U.K.
15 D1 **Gijón** Spain
73 F5 **Gila** *r.* U.S.A.
73 F5 **Gila Bend** U.S.A.
73 F5 **Gila Bend Mts** *mts* U.S.A.
73 E5 **Gila Mts** *mts* U.S.A.
29 K4 **Gilan Garb** Iran
29 M1 **Gilāzi** Azer.
73 G5 **Gilbert** *AZ* U.S.A.
70 C6 **Gilbert** *WV* U.S.A.
48 E3 **Gilbert** *r.* Austr.
49 H2 **Gilbert Islands** *is* Kiribati
79 J5 **Gilbués** Brazil
30 E3 **Gil Chashmeh** Iran
62 E1 **Gildford** U.S.A.
87 E2 **Gilf Kebir Plateau** *plat.* Egypt
56 D4 **Gilford I.** *i.* Can.
50 G1 **Gilgandra** Austr.
88 D4 **Gilgil** Kenya
34 C2 **Gilgit** Jammu and Kashmir
34 C2 **Gilgit** *r.* Jammu and Kashmir
50 F2 **Gilgunnia** Austr.
56 D4 **Gil Island** *i.* Can.
57 L3 **Gillam** Can.
68 C3 **Gillett** U.S.A.
62 F2 **Gillette** U.S.A.
9 H6 **Gillingham** *Eng.* U.K.
9 E6 **Gillingham** *Eng.* U.K.
8 F3 **Gilling West** U.K.
92 D5 **Gillock I.** *i.* Ant.
68 D3 **Gills Rock** U.S.A.
68 D5 **Gilman** *IL* U.S.A.
68 B3 **Gilman** *WV* U.S.A.
58 E2 **Gilmour Island** *i.* Can.
72 B3 **Gilroy** U.S.A.
71 G3 **Gilsum** U.S.A.
87 E3 **Gimbala, Jebel** *mt* Sudan
88 D3 **Gīmbī** Eth.
57 K4 **Gimli** Can.
33 C5 **Gin Ganga** *r.* Sri Lanka
33 B3 **Gingee** India
88 E3 **Gīnīr** Eth.
18 G4 **Ginosa** Italy
18 G4 **Gioia del Colle** Italy
50 E5 **Gippsland** *reg.* Austr.
34 B4 **Girab** India
31 E5 **Giran** Iran
31 E4 **Gīrān Rīg** *mt* Iran
70 C3 **Girard** U.S.A.
34 B3 **Girdao** Pak.
31 G5 **Girdar Dhor** *r.* Pak.
31 F4 **Girdi** Iran
28 G1 **Giresun** Turkey
34 B5 **Gir Forest** *forest* India
35 F4 **Girīdīh** India
50 F1 **Girilambone** Austr.
34 C5 **Girna** *r.* India
15 H2 **Girona** Spain
14 D4 **Gironde** *est.* France
50 F2 **Girral** Austr.
10 D5 **Girvan** U.K.
20 E2 **Girvas** Rus. Fed.
34 E4 **Girwan** India
51 G3 **Gisborne** N.Z.
56 E4 **Giscome** Can.
7 N8 **Gislaved** Sweden
31 G2 **Gissar Range** *mts* Tajik./Uzbek.
88 C4 **Gitarama** Rwanda
88 C4 **Gitega** Burundi
18 E3 **Giulianova** Italy
19 L3 **Giurgiu** Romania
19 L2 **Giuvala, Pasul** *pass* Romania
12 C4 **Givet** France
14 G4 **Givors** France
12 C6 **Givry-en-Argonne** France
91 J1 **Giyani** S. Africa
28 C7 **Giza Pyramids** Egypt
31 G1 **Gizhduvan** Uzbek.
25 S3 **Gizhiga** Rus. Fed.
19 J4 **Gjirokastër** Albania
55 J3 **Gjoa Haven** Can.
6 L5 **Gjøra** Norway
7 M6 **Gjøvik** Norway
59 J4 **Glace Bay** Can.
56 B3 **Glacier B.** *b.* U.S.A.
56 B3 **Glacier Bay National Park and Preserve** U.S.A.
56 F4 **Glacier Nat. Park** Can.
62 D1 **Glacier Nat. Park** U.S.A.
62 B1 **Glacier Peak** *volc.* U.S.A.
6 M4 **Gladstad** Norway
50 B2 **Gladstone** *S.A.* Austr.
48 F4 **Gladstone** Austr.
68 D3 **Gladstone** U.S.A.
68 E4 **Gladwin** U.S.A.
10 E4 **Glamis** U.K.
43 C5 **Glan** Phil.
12 F5 **Glan** *r.* Ger.
11 B5 **Glanaruddery Mts** *h.* Rep. of Ireland
13 G2 **Glandorf** Ger.
8 F2 **Glanton** U.K.
69 G4 **Glanworth** Can.
10 D5 **Glasgow** U.K.
66 C4 **Glasgow** *KY* U.S.A.
62 F1 **Glasgow** *MT* U.S.A.
70 D6 **Glasgow** *VA* U.S.A.
57 H4 **Glaslyn** Can.
72 C3 **Glass Mt** *mt* U.S.A.
9 E6 **Glastonbury** U.K.
13 L4 **Glauchau** Ger.
24 G4 **Glazov** Rus. Fed.
21 F4 **Glazunovka** Rus. Fed.
17 P3 **Glazunovo** Rus. Fed.
71 H2 **Glen** U.S.A.
10 C3 **Glen Affric** *v.* U.K.
69 G2 **Glen Afton** Can.
51 E2 **Glen Afton** N.Z.
54 D3 **Glenallen** U.S.A.
91 H1 **Glen Alpine Dam** *dam* S. Africa
11 C4 **Glenamaddy** Rep. of Ireland
68 E3 **Glen Arbor** U.S.A.
51 C6 **Glenavy** N.Z.
10 C3 **Glen Cannich** *v.* U.K.
63 E4 **Glen Canyon** *gorge* U.S.A.
73 G3 **Glen Canyon National Recreation Area** *res.* U.S.A.
10 E4 **Glen Clova** *v.* U.K.
50 C4 **Glencoe** Austr.
69 G4 **Glencoe** Can.
91 J4 **Glencoe** S. Africa
10 C4 **Glen Coe** *v.* U.K.
69 E2 **Glendale** Can.
73 F5 **Glendale** *AZ* U.S.A.
72 C4 **Glendale** *CA* U.S.A.
73 E3 **Glendale** *NV* U.S.A.
73 F3 **Glendale** *UT* U.S.A.
70 D4 **Glendale Lake** *l.* U.S.A.
50 H2 **Glen Davis** Austr.
62 F2 **Glendive** U.S.A.
57 G4 **Glendon** Can.
62 F3 **Glendo Res.** *l.* U.S.A.
50 C4 **Glenelg** *r.* Austr.
10 F4 **Glen Esk** *v.* U.K.
10 A5 **Glengad Head** *hd* Rep. of Ireland
10 C3 **Glen Garry** *v. Scot.* U.K.
10 D4 **Glen Garry** *v. Scot.* U.K.
11 D3 **Glengavlen** Rep. of Ireland
48 F4 **Glen Innes** Austr.
10 D6 **Glenluce** U.K.
10 D4 **Glen Lyon** *v.* U.K.
10 D3 **Glen More** *v.* U.K.
10 D3 **Glen Moriston** *v.* U.K.
10 C4 **Glen Nevis** *v.* U.K.
69 F3 **Glennie** U.S.A.
73 G6 **Glenn, Mt** *mt* U.S.A.
70 E6 **Glenns** U.S.A.
56 C3 **Glenora** Can.
71 F2 **Glen Robertson** Can.
10 E4 **Glenrothes** U.K.
71 G3 **Glens Falls** U.S.A.
10 E4 **Glen Shee** *v.* U.K.
10 C3 **Glen Shiel** *v.* U.K.
11 C3 **Glenties** Rep. of Ireland
11 D2 **Glenveagh National Park** Rep. of Ireland
70 C5 **Glenville** U.S.A.
65 E5 **Glenwood** *AR* U.S.A.
73 H5 **Glenwood** *NM* U.S.A.
63 F4 **Glenwood Springs** U.S.A.
68 B2 **Glidden** U.S.A.
13 J1 **Glinde** Ger.
17 J5 **Gliwice** Pol.
73 G5 **Globe** U.S.A.
16 H5 **Głogów** Pol.
6 N3 **Glomfjord** Norway
7 M5 **Glomma** *r.* Norway
89 E5 **Glorieuses, Îles** *is* Ind. Ocean
50 H1 **Gloucester** Austr.
9 E6 **Gloucester** U.K.
71 H3 **Gloucester** *MA* U.S.A.
70 E6 **Gloucester** *VA* U.S.A.
71 F3 **Gloversville** U.S.A.
13 L2 **Glöwen** Ger.
40 D1 **Glubinnoye** Rus. Fed.
21 G5 **Glubokiy** Rus. Fed.
27 G1 **Glubokoye** Kazak.
13 H1 **Glückstadt** Ger.
6 □ **Gluggarnir** *h.* Faroe Is
8 F4 **Glusburn** U.K.
21 H5 **Gmelinka** Rus. Fed.
16 G6 **Gmünd** Austria
16 F7 **Gmunden** Austria
7 P5 **Gnarp** Sweden
13 H1 **Gnarrenburg** Ger.
16 H4 **Gniezno** Pol.
19 J3 **Gnjilane** Yugo.
33 A3 **Goa** India
33 A3 **Goa** *div.* India
90 B3 **Goageb** Namibia
50 H4 **Goalen Head** *hd* Austr.

35 G4 Goalpara India
10 C5 Goat Fell h. U.K.
88 E3 Goba Eth.
89 B6 Gobabis Namibia
90 C3 Gobas Namibia
83 E1 Gobernador Crespo Arg.
83 C3 Gobernador Duval Arg.
80 B7 Gobernador Gregores Arg.
22 H5 Gobi des. Mongolia
41 D8 Gobō Japan
12 E3 Goch Ger.
89 B6 Gochas Namibia
44 C3 Go Công Vietnam
9 G6 Godalming U.K.
33 C2 Godavari r. India
33 C2 Godavari, Mouths of the river mouth India
59 G4 Godbout Can.
72 C3 Goddard, Mt mt U.S.A.
88 E3 Godere Eth.
69 G4 Goderich Can.
34 C5 Godhra India
83 C2 Godoy Cruz Arg.
57 L3 Gods r. Can.
57 L4 Gods Lake l. Can.
57 M2 Gods Mercy, Bay of b. Can.
Godwin Austen mt see K2
12 B3 Goedereede Neth.
58 E4 Goéland, Lac au l. Can.
59 H2 Goélands, Lac aux l. Can.
12 B3 Goes Neth.
69 E2 Goetzville U.S.A.
73 E4 Goffs U.S.A.
69 G2 Gogama Can.
68 C2 Gogebic, Lake l. U.S.A.
68 C2 Gogebic Range h. U.S.A.
Gogra r. see Ghaghara
34 D4 Gohad India
79 M5 Goiana Brazil
82 C2 Goiandira Brazil
82 C2 Goiânia Brazil
82 B1 Goiás Brazil
82 B2 Goiás div. Brazil
82 B4 Goio-Erê Brazil
34 C3 Gojra Pak.
33 A2 Gokak India
21 C7 Gökçeada i. Turkey
28 B2 Gökçedağ Turkey
35 G3 Gokhar La pass China
28 E1 Gökirmak r. Turkey
31 F5 Gokprosh Hills mts Pak.
28 F2 Göksun Turkey
28 E3 Göksu Nehri r. Turkey
89 C5 Gokwe Zimbabwe
7 L6 Gol Norway
34 E3 Gola India
35 H4 Golaghat India
28 F3 Gölbaşı Turkey
24 K2 Gol'chikha Rus. Fed.
28 B1 Gölcük Turkey
17 L3 Gołdap Pol.
13 L1 Goldberg Ger.
49 F4 Gold Coast Austr.
86 B4 Gold Coast coastal area Ghana
56 F4 Golden Can.
51 D4 Golden Bay b. N.Z.
13 J3 Goldene Aue reg. Ger.
72 A3 Golden Gate National Recreation Area res. U.S.A.
56 D5 Golden Hinde mt Can.
13 G2 Goldenstedt Ger.
11 C5 Golden Vale lowland Rep. of Ireland
72 D3 Goldfield U.S.A.
72 D3 Gold Point U.S.A.
67 E5 Goldsboro U.S.A.
65 D6 Goldthwaite U.S.A.
29 J1 Göle Turkey
31 F3 Golestān Afgh.
30 D4 Golestānak Iran
72 C4 Goleta U.S.A.
65 D6 Goliad U.S.A.
42 A1 Golin Baixing China
28 F1 Gölköy Turkey
13 L2 Golm Ger.
29 K3 Golmānkhānen Iran
36 B3 Golmud China
35 H1 Golmud He r. China
43 B3 Golo i. Phil.
40 J3 Golovnino Rus. Fed.
30 C3 Golpāyegān Iran
28 C1 Gölpazarı Turkey
10 E3 Golspie U.K.
31 F3 Gol Vardeh Iran
19 L4 Golyama Syutkya mt Bulg.
19 L4 Golyam Persenk mt Bulg.
13 L2 Golzow Ger.
88 C4 Goma Congo(Zaire)
35 G3 Gomang Co salt l. China
34 E4 Gomati r. India
44 □ Gombak, Bukit h. Sing.
86 D3 Gombe Nigeria
88 D4 Gombe r. Tanz.
87 D3 Gombi Nigeria
86 A2 Gomera, La i. Canary Is
65 C7 Gómez Palacio Mex.
65 D7 Gómez, Presa M. R. resr Mex.
30 D2 Gomīshān Iran
13 K2 Gommern Ger.
35 F2 Gomo Co salt l. China
31 E2 Gonābād Iran
Gonabad see Jūymand
75 K5 Gonaïves Haiti
91 J1 Gonarezhou National Park Zimbabwe
75 K5 Gonâve, Île de la i. Haiti
30 D2 Gonbad-e Kavus Iran
35 E4 Gonda India
34 B5 Gondal India
88 D2 Gonder Eth.
34 E5 Gondia India
28 A1 Gönen Turkey
39 D4 Gong'an China
39 D5 Gongcheng China
39 A4 Gongga Shan mt China
38 A2 Gonghe China
38 E1 Gonghui China
82 E1 Gongogi r. Brazil
86 D3 Gongola r. Nigeria
39 B5 Gongwang Shan mts China
38 D3 Gong Xian Henan China
39 B4 Gong Xian Sichuan China
91 H6 Gonubie S. Africa
72 B3 Gonzales CA U.S.A.
65 D6 Gonzales TX U.S.A.
83 D2 González Moreno Arg.
70 E6 Goochland U.S.A.
92 C6 Goodenough, C. c. Ant.
48 F2 Goodenough I. i. P.N.G.
69 H3 Gooderham Can.
68 E3 Good Harbor Bay b. U.S.A.
90 C7 Good Hope, Cape of c. S. Africa
62 D3 Gooding U.S.A.
64 C4 Goodland U.S.A.
8 G4 Goole U.K.
50 E3 Goolgowi Austr.
50 G2 Goolma Austr.
50 G2 Gooloogong Austr.
50 B3 Goolwa Austr.
48 F4 Goondiwindi Austr.
59 H3 Goose r. Can.
62 B3 Goose L. l. U.S.A.
33 B3 Gooty India
16 D6 Göppingen Ger.
35 E4 Gorakhpur India
19 H3 Goražde Bos.-Herz.
20 G3 Gorchukha Rus. Fed.
67 E7 Gorda Cay i. Bahamas
28 B2 Gördes Turkey
17 P4 Gordeyevka Rus. Fed.
10 F5 Gordon U.K.
48 E6 Gordon, L. l. Austr.
56 G2 Gordon Lake l. Can.
70 D5 Gordon Lake l. U.S.A.
70 D5 Gordonsville U.S.A.
87 D4 Goré Chad
88 D3 Gorē Eth.
51 B7 Gore N.Z.
69 F3 Gore Bay Can.
10 E5 Gorebridge U.K.
11 E5 Gorey Rep. of Ireland
31 E4 Gorg Iran
30 D2 Gorgān Iran
81 A4 Gorgona, I. i. Col.
71 H2 Gorham U.S.A.
21 H7 Gori Georgia
12 C3 Gorinchem Neth.
29 L2 Goris Armenia
18 E2 Gorizia Italy
Gor'kiy see Nizhniy Novgorod
21 H5 Gor'ko-Solenoye, Ozero l. Rus. Fed.
20 G3 Gor'kovskoye Vdkhr. resr Rus. Fed.
17 K6 Gorlice Pol.
16 G5 Görlitz Ger.
34 D4 Gormi India
19 L3 Gorna Oryakhovitsa Bulg.
19 J3 Gornji Milanovac Yugo.
18 G3 Gornji Vakuf Bos.-Herz.
36 A1 Gorno-Altaysk Rus. Fed.
40 G1 Gornozavodsk Rus. Fed.
24 K4 Gornyak Rus. Fed.
40 C2 Gornye Klyuchi Rus. Fed.
40 C2 Gornyy Primorskiy Kray Rus. Fed.
21 J5 Gornyy Saratov. Obl. Rus. Fed.
21 H5 Gornyy Balykley Rus. Fed.
20 G3 Gorodets Rus. Fed.
21 H5 Gorodishche Rus. Fed.
21 G6 Gorodovikovsk Rus. Fed.
48 E2 Goroka P.N.G.
50 C4 Goroke Austr.
20 G3 Gorokhovets Rus. Fed.
86 B3 Gorom Gorom Burkina
89 D5 Gorongosa Moz.
37 E6 Gorontalo Indon.
21 F5 Gorshechnoye Rus. Fed.
11 C4 Gort Rep. of Ireland
11 C2 Gortahork Rep. of Ireland
82 D1 Gorutuba r. Brazil
21 F6 Goryachiy Klyuch Rus. Fed.
13 L2 Görzke Ger.
16 G4 Gorzów Wielkopolski Pol.
50 H2 Gosford Austr.
8 F2 Gosforth U.K.
68 E5 Goshen IN U.S.A.
71 F4 Goshen NY U.S.A.
40 G4 Goshogawara Japan
13 J3 Goslar Ger.
18 F2 Gospić Croatia
9 F7 Gosport U.K.
19 J4 Gostivar Macedonia
Göteborg see Gothenburg
7 N7 Götene Sweden
13 J4 Gotha Ger.
7 M8 Gothenburg Sweden
64 C3 Gothenburg U.S.A.
7 Q8 Gotland i. Sweden
19 K4 Gotse Delchev Bulg.
7 Q7 Gotska Sandön i. Sweden
41 C7 Gōtsu Japan
13 H3 Göttingen Ger.
56 E4 Gott Peak summit Can.
Gottwaldow see Zlín
42 A3 Goubangzi China
12 C2 Gouda Neth.
86 A3 Goudiri Senegal
86 D3 Goudoumaria Niger
68 E1 Goudreau Can.
96 J8 Gough Island i. Atl. Ocean
58 F4 Gouin, Réservoir resr Can.
68 E2 Goulais River Can.
50 G3 Goulburn Austr.
50 H2 Goulburn r. N.S.W. Austr.
50 E4 Goulburn r. Vic. Austr.
48 D3 Goulburn Is is Austr.
62 E3 Gould City U.S.A.
92 B4 Gould Coast coastal area Ant.
86 B3 Goundam Mali
15 G4 Gouraya Alg.
86 D3 Gouré Niger
90 D7 Gourits r. S. Africa
86 B3 Gourma-Rharous Mali
14 E2 Gournay-en-Bray France
92 G4 Gourock Range mts Austr.
12 A5 Goussainville France
71 F2 Gouverneur U.S.A.
57 H5 Govenlock Can.
82 E2 Governador Valadares Brazil
43 C5 Governor Generoso Phil.
67 E7 Governor's Harbour Bahamas
36 B2 Govĭ Altayn Nuruu mts Mongolia
35 E4 Govind Ballash Pant Sāgar resr India
34 D3 Govind Sagar resr India
31 G2 Govurdak Turkm.
70 D3 Gowanda U.S.A.
31 G4 Gowārān Afgh.
30 D4 Gowd-e Aḥmad Iran
30 E3 Gowd-e Hasht Tekkeh waterhole Iran
30 D4 Gowd-e Mokh l. Iran
9 C6 Gower pen. U.K.
69 G2 Gowganda Can.
31 E4 Gowk Iran
11 D4 Gowna, Lough l. Rep. of Ireland
80 E3 Goya Arg.
29 L1 Göyçay Azer.
29 H2 Göynük Turkey
40 G5 Goyō-zan mt Japan
29 M2 Göytäpä Azer.
31 F3 Gözareh Afgh.
28 G2 Gözene Turkey
34 E2 Gozha Co salt l. China
18 F6 Gozo i. Malta
90 F6 Graaff-Reinet S. Africa
90 C6 Graafwater S. Africa
13 J4 Grabfeld plain Ger.
86 B4 Grabo Côte d'Ivoire
90 C7 Grabouw S. Africa
13 K1 Grabow Ger.
18 F2 Gračac Croatia
69 J2 Gracefield Can.
13 L3 Gräfenhainichen Ger.
13 K5 Grafenwöhr Ger.
49 F4 Grafton Austr.
64 D1 Grafton ND U.S.A.
68 D4 Grafton WI U.S.A.
70 C5 Grafton WV U.S.A.
73 E2 Grafton, Mt mt U.S.A.
65 D5 Graham U.S.A.
Graham Bell Island i. see Greem-Bell, Ostrov
55 J2 Graham I. i. Can.
56 C4 Graham Island i. Can.
71 J2 Graham Lake l. U.S.A.
92 B2 Graham Land reg. Ant.
73 H5 Graham, Mt mt U.S.A.
91 G6 Grahamstown S. Africa
11 E5 Graigue Rep. of Ireland
86 A4 Grain Coast coastal area Liberia
79 J5 Grajaú Brazil
10 B2 Gralisgeir i. U.K.
19 J4 Grámmos mt Greece
10 D4 Grampian Mountains U.K.
50 D4 Grampians mts Austr.
90 C5 Granaatboskolk S. Africa
81 B4 Granada Col.
75 G6 Granada Nic.
15 E4 Granada Spain
64 C4 Granada U.S.A.
11 D4 Granard Rep. of Ireland
83 C1 Gran Bajo Salitroso salt flat Arg.
58 F4 Granby Can.
86 A2 Gran Canaria i. Canary Is
80 D3 Gran Chaco reg. Arg./Para.
66 C3 Grand r. MI U.S.A.
64 E3 Grand r. MO U.S.A.
67 E7 Grand Bahama i. Bahamas
59 J4 Grand Bank Can.
96 F2 Grand Banks sea feature Atl. Ocean
86 B4 Grand-Bassam Côte d'Ivoire
59 G4 Grand Bay Can.
69 G4 Grand Bend Can.
11 D4 Grand Canal canal Rep. of Ireland
73 F3 Grand Canyon U.S.A.
73 F3 Grand Canyon gorge U.S.A.
73 F3 Grand Canyon Nat. Park U.S.A.
75 H5 Grand Cayman i. Cayman Is
57 G4 Grand Centre Can.
62 C2 Grand Coulee U.S.A.
83 C3 Grande r. Arg.
79 J6 Grande r. Bahia Brazil
82 B2 Grande r. São Paulo Brazil
80 C8 Grande, Bahía b. Arg.
56 F4 Grande Cache Can.
14 H4 Grande Casse, Pointe de la mt France
89 E5 Grande Comore i. Comoros
83 F1 Grande, Cuchilla h. Uru.
82 D3 Grande, Ilha i. Brazil
56 F3 Grande Prairie Can.
87 D3 Grand Erg de Bilma sand dunes Niger
86 B1 Grand Erg Occidental des. Alg.
86 C2 Grand Erg Oriental des. Alg.
59 H4 Grande-Rivière Can.
58 F3 Grande Rivière de la Baleine r. Can.
62 C2 Grande Ronde r. U.S.A.
81 E4 Grande, Serra mt Brazil
59 G4 Grand Falls N.B. Can.
59 J4 Grand Falls Nfld Can.
56 F5 Grand Forks Can.
64 D2 Grand Forks U.S.A.
71 F3 Grand Gorge U.S.A.
71 K2 Grand Harbour Can.
68 D4 Grand Haven U.S.A.
56 F2 Grandin, Lac l. Can.
64 D3 Grand Island U.S.A.
68 D2 Grand Island i. U.S.A.
65 F6 Grand Isle LA U.S.A.
71 J1 Grand Isle ME U.S.A.
73 H2 Grand Junction U.S.A.
86 B4 Grand-Lahou Côte d'Ivoire
59 G4 Grand Lake l. N.B. Can.
59 J4 Grand Lake l. Nfld Can.
59 H3 Grand Lake l. Nfld Can.
65 E6 Grand Lake l. LA U.S.A.
71 K2 Grand Lake l. ME U.S.A.
69 F3 Grand Lake l. MI U.S.A.
71 J1 Grand Lake Matagamon l. U.S.A.
70 A4 Grand Lake St Marys l. U.S.A.
71 J1 Grand Lake Seboeis l. U.S.A.
71 K2 Grand Lake Stream U.S.A.
68 E4 Grand Ledge U.S.A.
59 G5 Grand Manan I. i. Can.
68 E2 Grand Marais MI U.S.A.
68 B2 Grand Marais MN U.S.A.
59 F4 Grand-Mère Can.
15 B3 Grândola Port.
49 G3 Grand Passage chan. New Caledonia
68 C2 Grand Portage U.S.A.
57 K4 Grand Rapids Can.
68 E4 Grand Rapids MI U.S.A.
64 E2 Grand Rapids MN U.S.A.
49 G3 Grand Récif de Cook rf New Caledonia
49 G4 Grand Récif du Sud rf New Caledonia
62 E3 Grand Teton mt U.S.A.
62 E3 Grand Teton Nat. Park U.S.A.
68 E3 Grand Traverse Bay b. U.S.A.
59 G4 Grand Vallée Can.
62 C2 Grandview U.S.A.
73 F3 Grand Wash r. U.S.A.
73 E4 Grand Wash Cliffs cliff U.S.A.
83 B2 Graneros Chile
11 D6 Grange Rep. of Ireland
63 E3 Granger U.S.A.
7 O6 Grängesberg Sweden
62 C2 Grangeville U.S.A.
56 D3 Granisle Can.
64 E2 Granite Falls U.S.A.
59 J4 Granite Lake l. Can.
73 E4 Granite Mts mts U.S.A.
62 E2 Granite Peak summit MT U.S.A.
73 F1 Granite Peak summit UT U.S.A.
18 E6 Granitola, Capo c. Sicily Italy
80 C6 Gran Laguna Salada l. Arg.
7 O7 Gränna Sweden
18 B2 Gran Paradiso mt Italy
16 E7 Gran Pilastro mt Austria/Italy
13 L3 Granschütz Ger.
13 M1 Gransee Ger.
9 G5 Grantham U.K.
92 A4 Grant I. i. Ant.
72 D2 Grant, Mt mt NV U.S.A.
72 C2 Grant, Mt mt NV U.S.A.
10 E3 Grantown-on-Spey U.K.
73 E2 Grant Range mts U.S.A.
63 F5 Grants U.S.A.
62 B3 Grants Pass U.S.A.
14 D2 Granville France
68 C5 Granville IL U.S.A.
71 G3 Granville NY U.S.A.
57 J3 Granville Lake l. Can.
82 D2 Grão Mogol Brazil
72 C4 Grapevine U.S.A.
72 D3 Grapevine Mts mts U.S.A.
73 G3 Graphite U.S.A.
91 J2 Graskop S. Africa
57 G2 Gras, Lac de l. Can.
71 F2 Grass r. U.S.A.
14 H5 Grasse France
8 F3 Grassington U.K.
57 H5 Grasslands Nat. Park Can.
62 E2 Grassrange U.S.A.
57 J4 Grass River Prov. Park res. Can.
72 B2 Grass Valley U.S.A.
67 E7 Grassy Cr. r. Bahamas
7 N7 Grästorp Sweden
68 B4 Gratiot U.S.A.
15 G1 Graus Spain
57 J2 Gravel Hill Lake l. Can.
12 A4 Gravelines France
91 J1 Gravelotte S. Africa
69 H3 Gravenhurst Can.
9 H6 Gravesend U.K.
18 G4 Gravina in Puglia Italy
68 E3 Grawn U.S.A.
14 G3 Gray France
71 H3 Gray U.S.A.
68 E3 Grayling U.S.A.
9 H6 Grays U.K.
62 A2 Grays Harbor in. U.S.A.
62 E3 Grays L. l. U.S.A.
70 B5 Grayson U.S.A.
59 H1 Gray Strait chan. Can.
66 B4 Grayville U.S.A.
16 G7 Graz Austria
67 E7 Great Abaco i. Bahamas
48 C5 Great Australian Bight g. Austr.
9 H6 Great Baddow U.K.
75 J3 Great Bahama Bank sea feature Bahamas
51 E2 Great Barrier Island i. N.Z.
48 E3 Great Barrier Reef rf Austr.
71 G3 Great Barrington U.S.A.
63 C4 Great Basin basin U.S.A.
73 E2 Great Basin Nat. Park U.S.A.
71 F5 Great Bay b. U.S.A.
56 E1 Great Bear r. Can.
56 E1 Great Bear Lake l. Can.
64 D4 Great Bend U.S.A.
90 C6 Great Berg r. S. Africa
10 B2 Great Bernera i. U.K.
11 A5 Great Blasket I. i. Rep. of Ireland
8 D3 Great Clifton U.K.
10 D5 Great Cumbrae i. U.K.
50 F4 Great Dividing Range mts Austr.
8 G3 Great Driffield U.K.
69 F3 Great Duck I. i. Can.
71 F5 Great Egg Harbor in. U.S.A.
75 H4 Greater Antilles is Caribbean Sea
75 J4 Great Exuma i. Bahamas
62 E2 Great Falls U.S.A.
91 G6 Great Fish r. S. Africa
91 G6 Great Fish Point pt S. Africa
35 F4 Great Gandak r. India
67 E7 Great Guana Cay i. Bahamas
67 E7 Great Harbour Cay i. Bahamas
75 K4 Great Inagua i. Bahamas
90 D5 Great Karoo plat. S. Africa
91 H6 Great Kei r. S. Africa
48 E6 Great Lake l. Austr.
9 E5 Great Malvern U.K.
70 A5 Great Miami r. U.S.A.
87 F2 Great Oasis, The oasis Egypt
9 D4 Great Ormes Head hd U.K.
9 H5 Great Ouse r. U.K.
71 G4 Great Peconic Bay b. U.S.A.
71 H4 Great Pt pt U.S.A.
9 D5 Great Rhos h. U.K.
88 D4 Great Ruaha r. Tanz.
71 F3 Great Sacandaga L. l. U.S.A.
18 B2 Great St Bernard Pass Italy/Switz.
67 E7 Great Sale Cay i. Bahamas
62 D3 Great Salt Lake l. U.S.A.
62 D3 Great Salt Lake Desert U.S.A.
87 E2 Great Sand Sea des. Egypt/Libya
48 C4 Great Sandy Desert Austr.
49 H3 Great Sea Reef rf Fiji
54 G3 Great Slave Lake N.W.T. Can.
56 G2 Great Slave Lake l. Can.
67 D5 Great Smoky Mts mts U.S.A.
67 D5 Great Smoky Mts Nat. Park U.S.A.
56 E3 Great Snow Mtn mt Can.
71 G4 Great South Bay b. U.S.A.
9 H7 Greatstone-on-Sea U.K.
9 J6 Great Stour r. U.K.
9 C7 Great Torrington U.K.
48 C4 Great Victoria Desert Austr.
38 F1 Great Wall China
9 H6 Great Waltham U.K.
71 K2 Great Wass I. i. U.S.A.
8 F3 Great Whernside h. U.K.
9 J5 Great Yarmouth U.K.
29 J3 Great Zab r. Iraq
18 E4 Greco, Monte mt Italy
15 D2 Gredos, Sa de mts Spain
5 F5 Greece country Europe
62 F3 Greeley U.S.A.
55 K1 Greely Fiord in. Can.
24 H1 Greem-Bell, Ostrov i. Rus. Fed.
66 C4 Green r. KY U.S.A.
73 H2 Green r. UT/WY U.S.A.
69 H3 Greenbank Can.
68 C3 Green Bay U.S.A.
68 D3 Green Bay b. U.S.A.
50 H4 Green C. hd Austr.
11 E3 Greencastle U.K.
66 C4 Greencastle U.S.A.
67 E7 Green Cay i. Bahamas
67 D6 Green Cove Springs U.S.A.
68 A4 Greene IA U.S.A.
71 F3 Greene NY U.S.A.
67 D4 Greeneville U.S.A.
72 B3 Greenfield CA U.S.A.
68 E6 Greenfield IN U.S.A.
71 G3 Greenfield MA U.S.A.
70 B5 Greenfield OH U.S.A.
68 C4 Greenfield WI U.S.A.
43 A4 Green Island Bay b. Phil.
57 H4 Green Lake Can.
68 C4 Green Lake l. U.S.A.
53 M2 Greenland terr. Arctic Ocean
96 J1 Greenland Basin sea feature Arctic Ocean
10 F5 Greenlaw U.K.
71 G2 Green Mountains U.S.A.
10 D5 Greenock U.K.
11 E3 Greenore Rep. of Ireland
71 G4 Greenport U.S.A.
63 E4 Green River UT U.S.A.
62 E3 Green River WY U.S.A.
67 E4 Greensboro U.S.A.
66 C4 Greensburg IN U.S.A.
65 D4 Greensburg KS U.S.A.
70 D4 Greensburg PA U.S.A.
10 C3 Greenstone Point pt U.K.
61 L5 Green Swamp swamp NC U.S.A.
70 B5 Greenup U.S.A.
71 F2 Green Valley Can.
73 G6 Green Valley U.S.A.
68 C5 Greenview U.S.A.
86 B4 Greenville Liberia
67 C6 Greenville AL U.S.A.
72 B1 Greenville CA U.S.A.
67 D6 Greenville FL U.S.A.
71 J2 Greenville ME U.S.A.
68 E4 Greenville MI U.S.A.
65 F5 Greenville MS U.S.A.
67 E5 Greenville NC U.S.A.
71 H3 Greenville NH U.S.A.
70 A4 Greenville OH U.S.A.
70 C4 Greenville PA U.S.A.
67 D5 Greenville SC U.S.A.
65 D5 Greenville TX U.S.A.
57 J4 Greenwater Provincial Park res. Can.
50 H3 Greenwell Point Austr.
71 G4 Greenwich CT U.S.A.
71 G3 Greenwich NY U.S.A.
73 G2 Greenwich UT U.S.A.
65 F5 Greenwood MS U.S.A.
67 D5 Greenwood SC U.S.A.
65 E5 Greers Ferry Lake l. U.S.A.
64 D3 Gregory U.S.A.
48 C4 Gregory Lake salt flat Austr.
48 E3 Gregory Range h. Austr.
16 F3 Greifswald Ger.
13 L4 Greiz Ger.
28 E4 Greko, Cape c. Cyprus
7 M8 Grenå Denmark
65 F5 Grenada U.S.A.
53 K8 Grenada country Caribbean Sea
14 E5 Grenade France
7 M8 Grenen spit Denmark
50 G2 Grenfell Austr.
57 J4 Grenfell Can.
14 G4 Grenoble France
81 E1 Grenville Grenada
48 E3 Grenville, C. hd Austr.
62 B2 Gresham U.S.A.
8 F3 Greta r. U.K.
10 E6 Gretna U.K.
65 F6 Gretna U.S.A.
13 J3 Greußen Ger.
12 B3 Grevelingen chan. Neth.
12 F2 Greven Ger.
19 J4 Grevena Greece
12 D3 Grevenbicht Neth.
12 E3 Grevenbroich Ger.
12 E5 Grevenmacher Lux.
16 E4 Grevesmühlen Ger.
51 C5 Grey r. N.Z.
62 E2 Greybull U.S.A.
56 B2 Grey Hunter Pk summit Can.
59 J3 Grey Is is Can.
51 C5 Greymouth N.Z.
48 E4 Grey Range h. Austr.
91 J4 Greytown S. Africa
12 C4 Grez-Doiceau Belgium
21 G5 Gribanovskiy Rus. Fed.
72 B2 Gridley CA U.S.A.
68 C5 Gridley IL U.S.A.
67 C5 Griffin U.S.A.
50 F3 Griffith Austr.
69 J3 Griffith Can.
54 F2 Griffiths Point pt Can.
13 L3 Grimma Ger.
16 F3 Grimmen Ger.
69 H4 Grimsby Can.
8 G4 Grimsby U.K.
6 E3 Grímsey i. Iceland
56 F3 Grimshaw Can.
6 E4 Grímsstaðir Iceland
7 L7 Grimstad Norway
6 B5 Grindavík Iceland
7 L9 Grindsted Denmark
19 N2 Grindul Chituc spit Romania
64 E3 Grinnell U.S.A.
91 H5 Griqualand East reg. S. Africa
90 E4 Griqualand West reg. S. Africa
90 E4 Griquatown S. Africa
55 K2 Grise Fiord Can.
45 B3 Grisik Indon.
9 J7 Gris Nez, Cap pt France
10 F2 Gritley U.K.
18 G2 Grmeč mts Bos.-Herz.
12 C3 Grobbendonk Belgium
91 H2 Groblersdal S. Africa
90 E4 Groblershoop S. Africa
40 B2 Grodekovo Rus. Fed.
Grodno see Hrodna
90 B5 Groen watercourse Northern Cape S. Africa
90 E5 Groen watercourse Northern Cape S. Africa
14 C3 Groix, Île de i. France
18 D6 Grombalia Tunisia
12 F2 Gronau (Westfalen) Ger.
6 N4 Grong Norway
12 E1 Groningen Neth.
12 E1 Groninger Wad tidal flats Neth.
73 E3 Groom L. l. U.S.A.
90 D3 Groot-Aar Pan salt pan S. Africa
90 E7 Groot Brakrivier S. Africa
91 H3 Grootdraaidam dam S. Africa
90 D4 Grootdrink S. Africa
48 D3 Groote Eylandt i. Austr.
89 B5 Grootfontein Namibia
90 C3 Groot Karas Berg plat. Namibia
91 J1 Groot Letaba r. S. Africa
91 G2 Groot Marico S. Africa
90 D6 Groot Swartberg mts S. Africa
90 D5 Grootvloer salt pan S. Africa
91 G6 Groot Winterberg mt S. Africa
68 E3 Gros Cap U.S.A.
59 J4 Gros Morne Nat. Pk nat. park Can.
13 J3 Großengottern Ger.
13 G2 Großenkneten Ger.
13 H4 Großenlüder Ger.
13 J4 Großer Beerberg h. Ger.
13 J4 Großer Gleichberg h. Ger.
16 G7 Grosser Speikkogel mt Austria
18 D3 Grosseto Italy
13 G5 Groß-Gerau Ger.
18 E1 Großglockner mt Austria
13 J2 Groß Oesingen Ger.
13 K3 Großrudestedt Ger.
13 M2 Groß Schönebeck Ger.
90 C1 Gross Ums Namibia
62 E3 Gros Ventre Range mts U.S.A.
59 J3 Groswater Bay b. Can.
71 E3 Groton U.S.A.
70 D5 Grottoes U.S.A.
56 F3 Grouard Can.
58 D4 Groundhog r. Can.
12 D1 Grouw Neth.
70 C4 Grove City U.S.A.
67 C6 Grove Hill U.S.A.
72 B3 Groveland U.S.A.
92 D5 Grove Mts mts Ant.
72 B4 Grover Beach U.S.A.
71 H2 Groveton U.S.A.

73 F5 **Growler** U.S.A.
73 F5 **Growler Mts** *mts* U.S.A.
21 H7 **Groznyy** Rus. Fed.
19 M3 **Grudovo** Bulg.
17 J4 **Grudziądz** Pol.
10 C3 **Gruinard Bay** *b.* U.K.
89 B6 **Grünau** Namibia
6 B4 **Grundarfjörður** Iceland
70 B6 **Grundy** U.S.A.
68 A4 **Grundy Center** U.S.A.
13 G5 **Grünstadt** Ger.
21 F4 **Gryazi** Rus. Fed.
20 G3 **Gryazovets** Rus. Fed.
16 G4 **Gryfice** Pol.
16 G4 **Gryfino** Pol.
16 G5 **Gryfów Śląski** Pol.
6 P2 **Gryllefjord** Norway
80 □ **Grytviken** Atl. Ocean
35 F5 **Gua** India
75 J4 **Guacanayabo, Golfo de** *b.* Cuba
81 D2 **Guacara** Venez.
81 C3 **Guacharía** *r.* Col.
15 D4 **Guadajoz** *r.* Spain
74 D4 **Guadalajara** Mex.
15 E2 **Guadalajara** Spain
15 F2 **Guadalaviar** *r.* Spain
49 G2 **Guadalcanal** *i.* Solomon Is
15 C4 **Guadalete** *r.* Spain
15 F2 **Guadalope** *r.* Spain
15 D4 **Guadalquivir** *r.* Spain
65 C7 **Guadalupe** *Nuevo León* Mex.
72 B4 **Guadalupe** U.S.A.
60 C6 **Guadalupe** *i.* Mex.
65 D6 **Guadalupe** *r.* U.S.A.
65 B6 **Guadalupe Mts Nat. Park** U.S.A.
65 B6 **Guadalupe Pk** *mt* U.S.A.
15 D3 **Guadalupe, Sierra de** *mts* Spain
15 D2 **Guadarrama, Sierra de** *mts* Spain
53 K8 **Guadeloupe** *terr.* Caribbean Sea
83 C2 **Guadel, Sa de** *mts* Arg.
15 C4 **Guadiana** *r.* Port./Spain
15 E4 **Guadix** Spain
80 B6 **Guafo, I.** *i.* Chile
81 D4 **Guainía** *r.* Col./Venez.
81 E3 **Guaiquinima, Cerro** *mt* Venez.
82 A4 **Guaíra** Brazil
80 B6 **Guaitecas, Islas** *is* Chile
81 C1 **Guajira, Península de** *pen.* Col.
78 C4 **Gualaceo** Ecuador
72 A2 **Gualala** U.S.A.
83 E2 **Gualeguay** Arg.
83 E2 **Gualeguay** *r.* Arg.
83 E2 **Gualeguaychu** Arg.
83 B4 **Gualjaina** Arg.
46 F2 **Guam** *terr.* Pac. Oc.
80 A6 **Guamblin, I.** *i.* Chile
83 D3 **Guaminí** Arg.
60 E6 **Guamúchil** Mex.
81 A4 **Guamués** *r.* Col.
44 B4 **Gua Musang** Malaysia
83 D3 **Guanaco, Co** *h.* Arg.
74 D4 **Guanajuato** Mex.
82 D1 **Guanambi** Brazil
81 D4 **Guaname** *r.* Venez.
81 C2 **Guanare** Venez.
81 C2 **Guanare** *r.* Venez.
81 C2 **Guanarito** Venez.
81 C2 **Guanarito** *r.* Venez.
81 D3 **Guanay, Sierra** *mts* Venez.
38 D2 **Guandi Shan** *mt* China
75 H4 **Guane** Cuba
39 C4 **Guang'an** China
39 D6 **Guangdong** *div.* China
39 F4 **Guangfeng** China
39 D6 **Guanghai** China
38 B4 **Guanghan** China
39 E5 **Guanghang** China
38 B3 **Guanghe** China
39 E4 **Guangji** China
38 E2 **Guangling** China
42 B4 **Guanglu Dao** *i.* China
39 B5 **Guangnan** China
39 D6 **Guangning** China
38 F2 **Guangrao** China
38 E4 **Guangshan** China
38 D4 **Guangshui** China
39 C6 **Guangxi** *div.* China
38 B3 **Guangyuan** China
39 E5 **Guangze** China
39 D6 **Guangzhou** China
82 D2 **Guanhães** Brazil
82 D2 **Guanhães** *r.* Brazil
81 E2 **Guanipa** *r.* Venez.
39 B5 **Guanling** China
38 C4 **Guanmian Shan** *mts* China
38 D3 **Guanpo** China
42 C3 **Guanshui** China
81 D2 **Guanta** Venez.
75 J4 **Guantánamo** Cuba
38 E1 **Guanting Sk.** *resr* China
38 B4 **Guan Xian** China
39 D5 **Guanyang** China
38 F3 **Guanyun** China
81 A4 **Guapí** Col.
78 F6 **Guaporé** *r.* Bol./Brazil
78 E7 **Guaqui** Bol.
82 D1 **Guará** *r.* Brazil
79 L5 **Guarabira** Brazil
82 E3 **Guarapari** Brazil
82 B4 **Guarapuava** Brazil
82 C4 **Guaraqueçaba** Brazil
82 C3 **Guaratinguetá** Brazil
82 C4 **Guaratuba, Baía de** *b.* Brazil
15 C2 **Guarda** Port.
82 C2 **Guarda Mor** Brazil
15 D1 **Guardo** Spain
81 D2 **Guárico** *r.* Venez.
81 C3 **Guarrojo** *r.* Col.
82 C4 **Guarujá** Brazil
81 D4 **Guasacavi** *r.* Col.
81 C4 **Guasacavi, Cerro** *h.* Col.
81 B2 **Guasare** *r.* Venez.
74 C3 **Guasave** Mex.
81 C3 **Guasdualito** Venez.
81 E3 **Guasipati** Venez.
82 B4 **Guassú** *r.* Brazil
74 F6 **Guatemala** Guatemala
53 G8 **Guatemala** *country* Central America
81 D2 **Guatope, Parque Nacional** *nat. park* Venez.
83 D3 **Guatrache** Arg.
81 C4 **Guaviare** *r.* Col.
82 C3 **Guaxupé** Brazil
81 B4 **Guayabero** *r.* Col.
81 D3 **Guayapo** *r.* Venez.
78 C4 **Guayaquil** Ecuador
78 B4 **Guayaquil, Golfo de** *g.* Ecuador
78 E6 **Guayaramerín** Bol.
74 B3 **Guaymas** Mex.
88 D2 **Guba** Eth.
33 B3 **Gubbi** India
18 E3 **Gubbio** Italy
21 F5 **Gubkin** Rus. Fed.
38 D3 **Gucheng** China
21 G7 **Gudaut'a** Georgia
7 M6 **Gudbrandsdalen** *v.* Norway
21 H7 **Gudermes** Rus. Fed.
33 C2 **Gudivada** India
33 B3 **Gudiyattam** India
42 E2 **Gudong** *r.* China
31 G5 **Gudri** *r.* Pak.
28 D1 **Güdül** Turkey
33 B3 **Gudur** *Andhra Pradesh* India
33 B3 **Gudur** *Andhra Pradesh* India
7 K6 **Gudvangen** Norway
86 A4 **Guéckédou** Guinea
69 J1 **Guéguen, Lac** *l.* Can.
81 B4 **Güejar** *r.* Col.
86 C1 **Guelma** Alg.
86 A2 **Guelmine** Morocco
69 G4 **Guelph** Can.
12 E5 **Guénange** France
81 D2 **Güera** *r.* Venez.
59 G2 **Guerard, Lac** *l.* Can.
14 E3 **Guéret** France
62 F3 **Guernsey** U.S.A.
14 C2 **Guernsey** *i.* *Channel Is* U.K.
74 B3 **Guerrero Negro** Mex.
55 M4 **Guers, Lac** *l.* Can.
30 D3 **Gügerd, Kūh-e** *mts* Iran
96 F5 **Guiana Basin** *sea feature* Atl. Ocean
50 B4 **Guichen B.** *b.* Austr.
39 E4 **Guichi** China
83 F2 **Guichón** Uru.
38 A3 **Guide** China
87 D4 **Guider** Cameroon
39 C5 **Guiding** China
18 E4 **Guidonia-Montecelio** Italy
86 B4 **Guiglo** Côte d'Ivoire
12 B5 **Guignicourt** France
91 K2 **Guija** Moz.
39 D6 **Gui Jiang** *r.* China
39 F4 **Guiji Shan** *mts* China
9 G6 **Guildford** U.K.
71 J2 **Guilford** U.S.A.
39 D5 **Guilin** China
58 E2 **Guillaume-Delisle, Lac** *l.* Can.
15 B2 **Guimarães** Port.
43 B4 **Guimaras Str.** *chan.* Phil.
38 E3 **Guimeng Ding** *mt* China
38 A3 **Guinan** China
72 A2 **Guinda** U.S.A.
43 C4 **Guindulman** Phil.
85 B4 **Guinea** *country* Africa
96 J5 **Guinea Basin** *sea feature* Atl. Ocean
85 B4 **Guinea-Bissau** *country* Africa
84 B5 **Guinea, Gulf of** *g.* Africa
75 H4 **Güines** Cuba
14 C2 **Guingamp** France
14 B2 **Guipavas** France
39 D6 **Guiping** China
82 B2 **Guiratinga** Brazil
81 E2 **Güiria** Venez.
12 B5 **Guiscard** France
12 B5 **Guise** France
43 C4 **Guiuan** Phil.
39 E4 **Guixi** China
39 C6 **Gui Xian** China
39 C5 **Guiyang** *Guizhou* China
39 D5 **Guiyang** *Hunan* China
39 C5 **Guizhou** *div.* China
34 B5 **Gujarat** *div.* India
34 C2 **Gujar Khan** Pak.
34 C2 **Gujranwala** Pak.
34 C2 **Gujrat** Pak.
73 G5 **Gu Komelik** U.S.A.
21 F5 **Gukovo** Rus. Fed.
34 K3 **Gük Tappeh** Iran
34 D2 **Gulabgarh** Jammu and Kashmir
38 B2 **Gulang** China
50 G1 **Gulargambone** Austr.
33 B2 **Gulbarga** India
7 U8 **Gulbene** Latvia
28 E3 **Gülek** Turkey
65 F6 **Gulfport** U.S.A.
30 C4 **Gulf, The** *g.* Asia
50 G2 **Gulgong** Austr.
36 E1 **Gulian** China
39 B5 **Gulin** China
31 G4 **Gulistan** Pak.
26 E2 **Gulistan** Uzbek.
13 K1 **Gülitz** Ger.
68 E3 **Gull I.** *i.* U.S.A.
57 H4 **Gull Lake** Can.
6 R3 **Gullträsk** Sweden
28 D3 **Gülnar** Turkey
31 F3 **Gulran** Afgh.
21 G7 **Gulrip'sh** Georgia
28 E2 **Gülşehir** Turkey
88 D3 **Gulu** Uganda
34 B3 **Gumal** *r.* Pak.
89 C5 **Gumare** Botswana
30 D2 **Gumdag** Turkm.
35 F5 **Gumia** India
35 F5 **Gumla** India
12 F3 **Gummersbach** Ger.
28 E1 **Gümüşhacıköy** Turkey
29 G1 **Gümüşhane** Turkey
34 D4 **Guna** India
50 E3 **Gunbar** Austr.
50 G3 **Gundagai** Austr.
13 H5 **Gundelsheim** Ger.
28 D3 **Gündoğmuş** Turkey
28 B2 **Güney** Turkey
88 B4 **Gungu** Congo(Zaire)
21 H7 **Gunib** Rus. Fed.
57 K4 **Gunisao** *r.* Can.
50 H1 **Gunnedah** Austr.
92 D3 **Gunnerus Ridge** *sea feature* Ant.
50 G3 **Gunning** Austr.
63 F4 **Gunnison** *CO* U.S.A.
73 G2 **Gunnison** *UT* U.S.A.
63 E4 **Gunnison** *r.* U.S.A.
33 B3 **Guntakal** India
13 J3 **Güntersberge** Ger.
67 C5 **Guntersville** U.S.A.
67 C5 **Guntersville L.** *l.* U.S.A.
33 C2 **Guntur** India
45 A2 **Gunungsitoli** Indon.
44 A5 **Gunungtua** Indon.
33 C2 **Gunupur** India
16 E6 **Günzburg** Ger.
13 J5 **Gunzenhausen** Ger.
38 E1 **Guojiatun** China
38 E3 **Guoyang** China
38 A2 **Gurban Hudag** China
38 D1 **Gurban Obo** China
31 F5 **Gurdim** Iran
28 B2 **Güre** Turkey
34 D3 **Gurgaon** India
79 K5 **Gurgueia** *r.* Brazil
34 B4 **Gurha** India
81 E3 **Guri, Embalse de** *resr* Venez.
82 C2 **Gurinhatã** Brazil
21 H7 **Gurjaani** Georgia
31 E4 **Gur Khar** Iran
29 J2 **Gürpınar** Turkey
35 G3 **Guru** China
89 D5 **Guruè** Moz.
28 F2 **Gürün** Turkey
79 J4 **Gurupi** *r.* Brazil
34 C4 **Guru Sikhar** *mt* India
20 B4 **Gur'yevsk** Rus. Fed.
86 C3 **Gusau** Nigeria
13 K2 **Güsen** Ger.
20 B4 **Gusev** Rus. Fed.
42 B4 **Gushan** China
73 H1 **Gusher** U.S.A.
31 F3 **Gushgy** Turkm.
38 E3 **Gushi** China
43 A5 **Gusi** Malaysia
25 M2 **Gusikha** Rus. Fed.
20 D4 **Gusino** Rus. Fed.
25 M4 **Gusinoozersk** Rus. Fed.
35 F5 **Guskara** India
20 G4 **Gus'-Khrustal'nyy** Rus. Fed.
18 C5 **Guspini** *Sardinia* Italy
56 B3 **Gustavus** U.S.A.
13 K3 **Güsten** Ger.
72 B3 **Gustine** U.S.A.
13 L1 **Güstrow** Ger.
35 H3 **Gutang** China
13 M2 **Güterfelde** Ger.
13 G3 **Gütersloh** Ger.
73 H5 **Guthrie** *AZ* U.S.A.
66 C4 **Guthrie** *KY* U.S.A.
65 D5 **Guthrie** *OK* U.S.A.
65 C5 **Guthrie** *TX* U.S.A.
39 E5 **Gutian** *Fujian* China
39 F5 **Gutian** *Fujian* China
12 E5 **Gutland** *reg.* Ger./Lux.
35 F3 **Gutsuo** China
68 B4 **Guttenberg** U.S.A.
89 D5 **Gutu** Zimbabwe
35 G4 **Guwahati** India
29 J3 **Guwēr** Iraq
13 H3 **Guxhagen** Ger.
77 E2 **Guyana** *country* S. America
38 D1 **Guyang** China
65 C4 **Guymon** U.S.A.
30 D4 **Güyom** Iran
50 H1 **Guyra** Austr.
38 E1 **Guyuan** *Hebei* China
38 C3 **Guyuan** *Ningxia* China
31 G2 **Guzar** Uzbek.
39 C4 **Guzhang** China
38 E3 **Guzhen** China
17 K3 **Gvardeysk** Rus. Fed.
50 G1 **Gwabegar** Austr.
31 F5 **Gwadar** Pak.
31 F5 **Gwadar West Bay** *b.* Pak.
34 D4 **Gwalior** India
89 C6 **Gwanda** Zimbabwe
31 G4 **Gwash** Pak.
31 F5 **Gwatar Bay** *b.* Pak.
11 C3 **Gweebarra Bay** *b.* Rep. of Ireland
11 C2 **Gweedore** Rep. of Ireland
89 C5 **Gweru** Zimbabwe
68 D2 **Gwinn** U.S.A.
87 D3 **Gwoza** Nigeria
50 H1 **Gwydir** *r.* Austr.
35 H3 **Gyaca** China
38 B3 **Gyagartang** China
35 F3 **Gyangrang** China
35 G3 **Gyangzê** China
35 G3 **Gyaring Co** *l.* China
36 B3 **Gyaring Hu** *l.* China
19 L6 **Gyaros** *i.* Greece
35 H3 **Gyarubtang** China
24 J2 **Gydanskiy Poluostrov** *pen.* Rus. Fed.
35 H3 **Gyimda** China
35 F3 **Gyirong** *Xizang* China
35 F3 **Gyirong** *Xizang* China
35 H2 **Gyiza** China
55 O3 **Gyldenløves Fjord** *in.* Greenland
49 F4 **Gympie** Austr.
17 J7 **Gyöngyös** Hungary
16 H7 **Győr** Hungary
57 K4 **Gypsumville** Can.
59 G2 **Gyrfalcon Is** *i.* Can.
19 K6 **Gytheio** Greece
17 K7 **Gyula** Hungary
29 J1 **Gyumri** Armenia
30 E2 **Gyzylarbat** Turkm.

H

6 T5 **Haapajärvi** Fin.
6 T4 **Haapavesi** Fin.
7 S7 **Haapsalu** Estonia
12 C2 **Haarlem** Neth.
90 E6 **Haarlem** S. Africa
13 G3 **Haarstrang** *ridge* Ger.
51 B5 **Haast** N.Z.
31 G5 **Hab** *r.* Pak.
Habana *see* **Havana**
33 C4 **Habarane** Sri Lanka
88 D3 **Habaswein** Kenya
56 F3 **Habay** Can.
32 C7 **Habbān** Yemen
29 J5 **Habbānīyah** Iraq
29 J5 **Ḥabbānīyah, Hawr al** *l.* Iraq
31 G5 **Hab Chauki** Pak.
35 G4 **Habiganj** Bangl.
38 E1 **Habirag** China
35 G5 **Habra** India
81 B5 **Hacha** Col.
83 B3 **Hachado, P. de** *pass* Arg./Chile
41 F8 **Hachijō-jima** *i.* Japan
40 G4 **Hachinohe** Japan
41 F7 **Hachiōji** Japan
28 E2 **Hacıbektaş** Turkey
29 H2 **Hacıömer** Turkey
89 D6 **Hacufera** Moz.
30 C6 **Hadabat al Budū** *plain* S. Arabia
33 A3 **Hadagalli** India
10 F5 **Haddington** U.K.
86 D3 **Hadejia** Nigeria
28 E5 **Hadera** Israel
7 L9 **Haderslev** Denmark
32 C6 **Ḥaḍhramaut** *reg.* Yemen
28 D3 **Hadım** Turkey
9 H5 **Hadleigh** U.K.
54 H2 **Hadley Bay** *b.* Can.
42 D6 **Hadong** S. Korea
28 F6 **Ḥadraj, Wādī** *watercourse* S. Arabia
7 M8 **Hadsund** Denmark
21 E5 **Hadyach** Ukr.
83 F1 **Haedo, Cuchilla de** *h.* Uru.
42 C4 **Haeju** N. Korea
42 C5 **Haeju-man** *b.* N. Korea
42 D6 **Haenam** S. Korea
91 H1 **Haenertsburg** S. Africa
30 B4 **Hafar al Bāṭin** S. Arabia
57 H4 **Hafford** Can.
28 F2 **Hafik** Turkey
34 C2 **Hafizabad** Pak.
35 H4 **Hāflong** India
6 C4 **Hafnarfjörður** Iceland
30 C4 **Haft Gel** Iran
6 B4 **Hafursfjörður** *b.* Iceland
69 G2 **Hagar** Can.
33 B3 **Hagari** *r.* India
88 D2 **Hagar Nish Plateau** *plat.* Eritrea
12 C4 **Hageland** *reg.* Belgium
12 F3 **Hagen** Ger.
48 E2 **Hagen, Mount** *mt* P.N.G.
13 K1 **Hagenow** Ger.
70 E5 **Hagerstown** U.S.A.
14 D5 **Hagetmau** France
7 N6 **Hagfors** Sweden
41 B7 **Hagi** Japan
39 B6 **Ha Giang** Vietnam
9 E5 **Hagley** U.K.
11 B5 **Hag's Head** *hd* Rep. of Ireland
57 H4 **Hague** Can.
14 D2 **Hague, Cap de la** *pt* France
14 H2 **Haguenau** France
36 G4 **Hahajima-rettō** *is* Japan
88 D4 **Hai** Tanz.
38 E2 **Hai** *r.* China
38 F3 **Hai'an** China
90 B4 **Haib** *watercourse* Namibia
42 B3 **Haicheng** China
13 K5 **Haidenaab** *r.* Ger.
39 C6 **Hai Dương** Vietnam
28 E5 **Haifa** Israel
28 E5 **Haifa, Bay of** *b.* Israel
39 E6 **Haifeng** China
13 G4 **Haiger** Ger.
39 D6 **Haikang** China
39 D6 **Haikou** China
32 B4 **Ḥā'il** S. Arabia
36 D2 **Hailar** China
69 H2 **Haileybury** Can.
42 E1 **Hailin** China
42 C2 **Hailong** China
9 H7 **Hailsham** U.K.
6 T4 **Hailuoto** Fin.
38 F4 **Haimen** China
39 C7 **Hainan** *div.* China
39 D7 **Hainan** *i.* China
56 B3 **Haines** U.S.A.
56 B2 **Haines Junction** Can.
13 J3 **Hainich** *ridge* Ger.
13 M4 **Hainichen** Ger.
13 J3 **Hainleite** *ridge* Ger.
39 C6 **Hai Phong** Vietnam
38 A2 **Hairag** China
38 B1 **Hairhan Namag** China
39 F5 **Haitan Dao** *i.* China
53 J8 **Haiti** *country* Caribbean Sea
39 C7 **Haitou** China
73 G5 **Haivana Nakya** U.S.A.
72 D3 **Haiwee Reservoir** U.S.A.
38 E2 **Haixing** China
87 F3 **Haiya** Sudan
38 A2 **Haiyan** *Qinghai* China
39 F4 **Haiyan** *Zhejiang* China
42 A5 **Haiyang** China
42 B4 **Haiyang Dao** *i.* China
38 B2 **Haiyuan** China
38 F3 **Haizhou Wan** *b.* China
17 K7 **Hajdúböszörmény** Hungary
18 C7 **Hajeb El Ayoun** Tunisia
32 D7 **Ḥajhir** *mt* Yemen
40 F5 **Hajiki-zaki** *pt* Japan
35 F4 **Hajipur** India
30 D4 **Hājjīābād** Iran
30 D4 **Ḥājjīābād** Iran
32 E6 **Ḥajmah** Oman
35 H5 **Haka** Myanmar
72 □2 **Hakalau** U.S.A.
83 C4 **Hakelhuincul, Altiplanicie de** *plat.* Arg.
Hakha *see* **Haka**
29 J3 **Hakkârı** Turkey
6 R3 **Hakkas** Sweden
41 D7 **Hakken-zan** *mt* Japan
40 H2 **Hako-dake** *mt* Japan
40 G4 **Hakodate** Japan
90 B1 **Hakos Mts** *mts* Namibia
90 D3 **Hakseen Pan** *salt pan* S. Africa
41 E6 **Hakui** Japan
41 E6 **Haku-san** *volc.* Japan
41 E6 **Haku-san National Park** Japan
34 B4 **Hala** Pak.
Ḥalab *see* **Aleppo**
30 B6 **Halabān** S. Arabia
29 K4 **Ḥalabja** Iraq
42 C1 **Halaha** China
42 C1 **Halahai** China
87 F2 **Halaib** Sudan
32 E6 **Ḥalāniyāt, Juzur al** *is* Oman
72 □2 **Halawa** U.S.A.
28 F4 **Halba** Lebanon
36 B2 **Halban** Mongolia
13 K3 **Halberstadt** Ger.
43 B3 **Halcon, Mt** *mt* Phil.
6 □ **Haldarsvik** Faroe Is
7 M7 **Halden** Norway
13 K2 **Haldensleben** Ger.
35 G5 **Haldi** *r.* India
35 G5 **Haldia** India
35 G4 **Haldibari** India
34 D3 **Haldwani** India
69 F3 **Hale** U.S.A.
29 G4 **Halebiye** Syria
72 □1 **Haleiwa** U.S.A.
9 E5 **Halesowen** U.K.
9 J5 **Halesworth** U.K.
28 F3 **Halfeti** Turkey
51 B7 **Halfmoon Bay** N.Z.
11 C6 **Halfway** Rep. of Ireland
56 E3 **Halfway** *r.* Can.
12 C2 **Halfweg** Neth.
35 E4 **Halia** India
69 H3 **Haliburton** Can.
59 H5 **Halifax** Can.
8 F4 **Halifax** U.K.
70 D6 **Halifax** U.S.A.
10 E2 **Halkirk** U.K.
6 P5 **Hälla** Sweden
42 D7 **Halla-san** *mt* S. Korea
55 K3 **Hall Beach** Can.
12 C4 **Halle** Belgium
12 E3 **Halle** Neth.
7 O7 **Hällefors** Sweden
16 F7 **Hallein** Austria
13 K3 **Halle-Neustadt** Ger.
13 K3 **Halle (Saale)** Ger.
92 A5 **Hallett, C.** *c.* Ant.
92 C3 **Halley** *U.K. Base* Ant.
46 G3 **Hall Islands** *is* Micronesia
6 Q4 **Hällnäs** Sweden
64 D1 **Hallock** U.S.A.
55 M3 **Hall Peninsula** Can.
7 O7 **Hallsberg** Sweden
48 C3 **Halls Creek** Austr.
69 H3 **Halls Lake** Can.
12 B4 **Halluin** France
6 O5 **Hallviken** Sweden
37 E6 **Halmahera** *i.* Indon.
7 N8 **Halmstad** Sweden
34 C5 **Halol** India
7 M8 **Hals** Denmark
6 T5 **Halsua** Fin.
12 F3 **Haltern** Ger.
8 E3 **Haltwhistle** U.K.
30 D5 **Ḥālūl** *i.* Qatar
12 F3 **Halver** Ger.
12 B5 **Ham** France
41 C7 **Hamada** Japan
86 B2 **Ḥamâda El Ḥaricha** *des.* Mali
30 C3 **Hamadān** Iran
86 B2 **Hamada Tounassine** *des.* Alg.
28 F4 **Ḥamāh** Syria
40 G3 **Hamamasu** Japan
41 E7 **Hamamatsu** Japan
7 M6 **Hamar** Norway
6 O2 **Hamarøy** Norway
40 H2 **Hamatonbetsu** Japan
33 C5 **Hambantota** Sri Lanka
13 G1 **Hambergen** Ger.
8 F3 **Hambleton Hills** *h.* U.K.
13 H1 **Hamburg** Ger.
91 G6 **Hamburg** S. Africa
65 F5 **Hamburg** *AR* U.S.A.
70 D3 **Hamburg** *NY* U.S.A.
71 F4 **Hamburg** *PA* U.S.A.
13 G1 **Hamburgisches Wattenmeer, Nationalpark** *nat. park* Ger.
71 G4 **Hamden** U.S.A.
7 T6 **Hämeenlinna** Fin.
13 H2 **Hameln** Ger.
48 B4 **Hamersley Range** *mts* Austr.
42 D4 **Hamhŭng** N. Korea
36 B2 **Hami** China
30 C4 **Ḥamīd** Iran
87 F2 **Hamīd** Sudan
50 D4 **Hamilton** Austr.
75 M2 **Hamilton** Bermuda
69 H4 **Hamilton** Can.
51 E2 **Hamilton** N.Z.
10 D5 **Hamilton** U.K.
67 C5 **Hamilton** *AL* U.S.A.
68 B5 **Hamilton** *IL* U.S.A.
62 D2 **Hamilton** *MT* U.S.A.
71 F3 **Hamilton** *NY* U.S.A.
70 A5 **Hamilton** *OH* U.S.A.
72 A2 **Hamilton City** U.S.A.
72 B3 **Hamilton, Mt** *mt* *CA* U.S.A.
73 E2 **Hamilton, Mt** *mt* *NV* U.S.A.
7 U6 **Hamina** Fin.
34 D3 **Hamirpur** India
29 H6 **Ḥāmir, W.** *watercourse* S. Arabia
59 J3 **Hamiton Inlet** *in.* Can.
42 D4 **Hamju** N. Korea
50 B3 **Hamley Bridge** Austr.
68 D3 **Hamlin Lake** *l.* U.S.A.
13 F3 **Hamm** Ger.
86 B2 **Hammada du Drâa** *plat.* Alg.
29 J3 **Hammam Ali** Iraq
18 D6 **Hammamet** Tunisia
87 D1 **Hammamet, Golfe de** *b.* Tunisia
29 L6 **Ḥammār, Hawr al** *l.* Iraq
6 P5 **Hammarstrand** Sweden
13 H4 **Hammelburg** Ger.
6 O5 **Hammerdal** Sweden
6 S1 **Hammerfest** Norway
12 E3 **Hamminkeln** Ger.
50 B2 **Hammond** Austr.
68 D5 **Hammond** *IN* U.S.A.
65 F6 **Hammond** *LA* U.S.A.
62 F2 **Hammond** *MT* U.S.A.
69 E3 **Hammond Bay** *b.* U.S.A.
70 E3 **Hammondsport** U.S.A.
71 F5 **Hammonton** U.S.A.
12 D4 **Hamoir** Belgium
51 C6 **Hampden** N.Z.
9 F6 **Hampshire Downs** *h.* U.K.
59 G4 **Hampton** Can.
65 E5 **Hampton** *AR* U.S.A.
71 H3 **Hampton** *NH* U.S.A.
71 E6 **Hampton** *VA* U.S.A.
29 K4 **Ḥamrīn, Jabal** *h.* Iraq
44 C3 **Ham Tân** Vietnam
34 D2 **Hamta Pass** India
31 E5 **Hāmūn-e Jaz Mūrīān** *salt marsh* Iran
31 F4 **Hāmūn Helmand** *salt flat* Afgh./Iran
31 G4 **Hamun-i-Lora** *l.* Pak.
31 F4 **Hāmūn Pu** *marsh* Afgh.
29 J2 **Hamur** Turkey
72 □2 **Hana** U.S.A.
90 E1 **Hanahai** *watercourse* Botswana/Namibia
72 □2 **Hanalei** U.S.A.
40 G5 **Hanamaki** Japan
13 G4 **Hanau** Ger.
38 D3 **Hancheng** China
70 D5 **Hancock** *MD* U.S.A.
68 C2 **Hancock** *MI* U.S.A.
71 F4 **Hancock** *NY* U.S.A.
10 C2 **Handa Island** *i.* U.K.
38 E2 **Handan** China
88 D4 **Handeni** Tanz.
72 C3 **Hanford** U.S.A.
33 A3 **Hangal** India
36 B2 **Hangayn Nuruu** *mts* Mongolia
38 C1 **Hanggin Houqi** China
38 C2 **Hanggin Qi** China
12 D4 **Han, Grotte de** Belgium
38 E2 **Hangu** China
34 B2 **Hangu** Pak.
39 D5 **Hanguang** China
39 F4 **Hangzhou** China
39 F4 **Hangzhou Wan** *b.* China
29 H2 **Hani** Turkey
30 C5 **Ḥanīdh** S. Arabia
38 B2 **Hanjiaoshui** China
13 J2 **Hankensbüttel** Ger.
90 F6 **Hankey** S. Africa
7 S7 **Hanko** Fin.
73 G2 **Hanksville** U.S.A.
34 D2 **Hanle** Jammu and Kashmir
51 D5 **Hanmer Springs** N.Z.
31 F4 **Hanmi Mashkel** *salt flat* Pak.
57 G4 **Hanna** Can.
58 D3 **Hannah Bay** *b.* Can.
68 B6 **Hannibal** U.S.A.
13 H2 **Hannover** Ger.
13 H3 **Hannoversch Münden** Ger.
12 D4 **Hannut** Belgium
7 O9 **Hanöbukten** *b.* Sweden
39 B6 **Ha Nôi** Vietnam
Hanoi *see* **Ha Nôi**
69 G3 **Hanover** Can.
90 F5 **Hanover** S. Africa
71 G3 **Hanover** *NH* U.S.A.
70 E5 **Hanover** *PA* U.S.A.
92 D4 **Hansen Mts** *mts* Ant.
39 D4 **Hanshou** China
38 E4 **Han Shui** *r.* China
34 D3 **Hansi** India
6 Q2 **Hansnes** Norway
70 B6 **Hansonville** U.S.A.
7 L8 **Hanstholm** Denmark
12 E6 **Han-sur-Nied** France
20 C4 **Hantsavichy** Belarus
34 C3 **Hanumangarh** India
50 F3 **Hanwwood** Austr.
39 E4 **Hanyang** China
38 C3 **Hanyin** China
39 B4 **Hanyuan** China
38 C3 **Hanzhong** China
46 N5 **Hao** *atoll* *Fr. Polynesia* Pac. Oc.
35 G5 **Hāora** India
6 T4 **Haparanda** Sweden
35 H4 **Hāpoli** India
59 H3 **Happy Valley-Goose Bay** Can.
42 E3 **Hapsu** N. Korea
34 D3 **Hapur** India
33 C5 **Haputale** Sri Lanka
30 C5 **Ḥaraḍ** *well* S. Arabia
30 C5 **Ḥaraḍh** S. Arabia
20 D4 **Haradok** Belarus
41 G6 **Haramachi** Japan
34 C2 **Haramukh** *mt* India
34 C3 **Harappa Road** Pak.
89 D5 **Harare** Zimbabwe
36 C2 **Har-Ayrag** Mongolia
86 A4 **Harbel** Liberia
36 E2 **Harbin** China
69 F4 **Harbor Beach** U.S.A.
68 E3 **Harbor Springs** U.S.A.
59 J4 **Harbour Breton** Can.
80 E8 **Harbours, B. of** *b.* Falkland Is

73 F5 Harcuvar Mts *mts* U.S.A.
34 D5 Harda Khās India
7 K6 Hardangervidda *plat.* Norway
7 K6 Hardangervidda Nasjonalpark *nat. park* Norway
90 B2 Hardap *div.* Namibia
90 B2 Hardap Dam *dam* Namibia
12 E2 Hardenberg Neth.
45 E2 Harden, Bukit *mt* Indon.
12 D2 Harderwijk Neth.
90 C5 Hardeveld *mts* S. Africa
13 H5 Hardheim Ger.
62 F2 Hardin U.S.A.
91 H5 Harding S. Africa
57 G4 Hardisty Can.
56 F2 Hardisty Lake *l.* Can.
34 E4 Hardoi India
71 G2 Hardwick U.S.A.
65 F4 Hardy U.S.A.
68 E4 Hardy Reservoir U.S.A.
28 D6 Hareidîn, W. *watercourse* Egypt
12 B4 Harelbeke Belgium
12 E1 Haren Neth.
12 F2 Haren (Ems) Ger.
88 E3 Hārer Eth.
71 F4 Harford U.S.A.
88 E3 Hargeysa Somalia
17 M7 Harghita-Mădăraş, Vârful *mt* Romania
29 H2 Harhal D. *mts* Turkey
38 C2 Harhatan China
36 B3 Har Hu *l.* China
34 D3 Haridwar India
33 A3 Harihar India
51 C5 Harihari N.Z.
41 D7 Harima-nada *b.* Japan
35 G5 Haringhat *r.* Bangl.
12 C3 Haringvliet *est.* Neth.
31 G3 Hari Rūd *r.* Afgh./Iran
7 S6 Harjavalta Fin.
64 E3 Harlan *IA* U.S.A.
70 B6 Harlan *KY* U.S.A.
9 C5 Harlech U.K.
62 E1 Harlem U.S.A.
9 J5 Harleston U.K.
12 D1 Harlingen Neth.
65 D7 Harlingen U.S.A.
9 H6 Harlow U.K.
62 E2 Harlowtown U.S.A.
12 B5 Harly France
71 J2 Harmony *ME* U.S.A.
68 A4 Harmony *MN* U.S.A.
13 J1 Harmsdorf Ger.
34 A3 Harnai Pak.
12 A4 Harnes France
62 B3 Harney Basin *basin* U.S.A.
62 C3 Harney L. *l.* U.S.A.
7 P5 Härnösand Sweden
36 E2 Har Nur China
36 B2 Har Nuur *l.* Mongolia
10 □ Haroldswick U.K.
86 B4 Harper Liberia
72 D4 Harper Lake *l.* U.S.A.
70 E5 Harpers Ferry U.S.A.
59 H2 Harp Lake *l.* Can.
13 G2 Harpstedt Ger.
29 G2 Harput Turkey
38 F1 Harqin China
38 F1 Harqin Qi China
73 F5 Harquahala Mts *mts* U.S.A.
29 G3 Harran Turkey
28 F5 Harrat er Rujeila *lava* Jordan
58 E3 Harricana *r.* Can.
67 C5 Harriman U.S.A.
71 G3 Harriman Reservoir U.S.A.
71 F5 Harrington U.S.A.
59 J3 Harrington Harbour Can.
10 B3 Harris U.K.
66 B4 Harrisburg *IL* U.S.A.
70 E4 Harrisburg *PA* U.S.A.
91 H4 Harrismith S. Africa
65 E4 Harrison *AR* U.S.A.
68 E3 Harrison *MI* U.S.A.
54 C2 Harrison Bay *b.* U.S.A.
70 D5 Harrisonburg U.S.A.
59 J3 Harrison, Cape *c.* Can.
56 E5 Harrison L. *l.* Can.
64 E4 Harrisonville U.S.A.
10 A3 Harris, Sound of *chan.* U.K.
69 F3 Harrisville *MI* U.S.A.
71 F2 Harrisville *NY* U.S.A.
70 C5 Harrisville *WV* U.S.A.
8 F4 Harrogate U.K.
13 H1 Harsefeld Ger.
30 B3 Harsin Iran
28 G1 Harşit *r.* Turkey
19 M2 Hârşova Romania
6 P2 Harstad Norway
13 H2 Harsum Ger.
68 D4 Hart U.S.A.
42 B2 Hartao China
90 D4 Hartbees *watercourse* S. Africa
16 G7 Hartberg Austria
7 K6 Harteigan *mt* Norway
10 E5 Hart Fell *h.* U.K.
71 G4 Hartford *CT* U.S.A.
68 D4 Hartford *MI* U.S.A.
64 D3 Hartford *SD* U.S.A.
68 C4 Hartford *WV* U.S.A.
56 E3 Hart Highway Can.
59 G4 Hartland Can.
9 C7 Hartland U.K.
71 J2 Hartland U.S.A.
9 C6 Hartland Point *pt* U.K.
8 F3 Hartlepool U.K.
65 C5 Hartley U.S.A.
56 D4 Hartley Bay Can.
7 U6 Hartola Fin.
56 E4 Hart Ranges *mts* Can.
16 E6 Härtsfeld *h.* Ger.
90 F3 Hartswater S. Africa
67 D5 Hartwell Res. *resr* U.S.A.
36 B2 Har Us Nuur *l.* Mongolia
31 F3 Harut *watercourse* Afgh.
68 C4 Harvard U.S.A.
63 F4 Harvard, Mt *mt* U.S.A.
71 K2 Harvey Can.
68 D2 Harvey *MI* U.S.A.
64 C2 Harvey *ND* U.S.A.
9 J6 Harwich U.K.
34 C3 Haryana *div.* India
28 F6 Ḥaṣāh, Wādī al *watercourse* Jordan
30 B2 Hasan Iran
34 C2 Hasan Abdal Pak.
28 E2 Hasan Dağı *mts* Turkey
29 H3 Hasankeyf Turkey
30 E5 Ḥasan Langī Iran
33 B2 Hasanparti India
28 E5 Hasbani *r.* Lebanon
28 E2 Hasbek Turkey
29 K6 Ḥasb, Sha'īb *watercourse* Iraq
35 E5 Hasdo *r.* India
13 F2 Hase *r.* Ger.
12 F2 Haselünne Ger.
13 J4 Hasenkopf *h.* Ger.
30 C3 Hashtgerd Iran
30 C2 Hashtpar Iran
65 D5 Haskell U.S.A.
9 G6 Haslemere U.K.
17 M7 Hăşmaşul Mare *mt* Romania
33 B3 Hassan India
29 K4 Hassan Iraq
73 F5 Hassayampa *r.* U.S.A.
13 J4 Haßberge *reg.* Ger.
12 D4 Hasselt Belgium
12 E2 Hasselt Neth.
86 C1 Hassi Messaoud Alg.
7 N8 Hässleholm Sweden
50 E5 Hastings Austr.
51 F3 Hastings N.Z.
9 H7 Hastings U.K.
68 E4 Hastings *MI* U.S.A.
68 A3 Hastings *MN* U.S.A.
64 D3 Hastings *NE* U.S.A.
Hatay *see* Antakya
73 F3 Hatch U.S.A.
67 E7 Hatchet Bay Bahamas
57 J3 Hatchet Lake *l.* Can.
67 B5 Hatchie *r.* U.S.A.
50 D2 Hatfield Austr.
8 G4 Hatfield U.K.
36 C1 Hatgal Mongolia
34 D4 Hathras India
35 F4 Hatia Nepal
44 C3 Ha Tiên Vietnam
44 C1 Ha Tĩnh Vietnam
50 D3 Hattah Austr.
67 F5 Hatteras, Cape *c.* U.S.A.
6 N4 Hattfjelldal Norway
35 E6 Hatti *r.* India
67 B6 Hattiesburg U.S.A.
12 F3 Hattingen Ger.
88 E3 Haud *reg.* Eth.
7 K7 Hauge Norway
7 J7 Haugesund Norway
51 E3 Hauhungaroa *mt* N.Z.
7 K7 Haukeligrend Norway
6 T4 Haukipudas Fin.
7 V5 Haukivesi *l.* Fin.
57 H3 Haultain *r.* Can.
51 E2 Hauraki Gulf *g.* N.Z.
51 A7 Hauroko, L. *l.* N.Z.
86 B1 Haut Atlas *mts* Morocco
59 G4 Hauterive Can.
71 J3 Haut, Isle au *i.* U.S.A.
86 B1 Hauts Plateaux *plat.* Alg.
72 □1 Hauula U.S.A.
75 H4 Havana Cuba
68 B5 Havana U.S.A.
9 G7 Havant U.K.
73 E4 Havasu Lake *l.* U.S.A.
13 L2 Havel *r.* Ger.
12 D4 Havelange Belgium
13 L2 Havelberg Ger.
13 L2 Havelländisches Luch *marsh* Ger.
69 J3 Havelock Can.
67 E5 Havelock U.S.A.
51 F3 Havelock North N.Z.
9 C6 Haverfordwest U.K.
71 H3 Haverhill U.S.A.
33 A3 Haveri India
12 D4 Haversin Belgium
12 F3 Havixbeck Ger.
16 G6 Havlíčkův Brod Czech Rep.
6 T1 Havøysund Norway
19 M5 Havran Turkey
62 E1 Havre U.S.A.
59 H4 Havre Aubert, Île du *i.* Can.
71 E5 Havre de Grace U.S.A.
59 H3 Havre-St-Pierre Can.
19 M4 Havsa Turkey
28 E1 Havza Turkey
72 □2 Hawaii *i.* U.S.A.
46 M2 Hawaii *is* Pac. Oc.
94 H4 Hawaiian Ridge *sea feature* Pac. Oc.
72 □2 Hawaii Volcanoes National Park U.S.A.
29 L7 Ḥawallī Kuwait
9 D4 Hawarden U.K.
51 B6 Hawea, L. *l.* N.Z.
51 E3 Hawera N.Z.
8 E3 Hawes U.K.
72 □2 Hawi U.S.A.
10 F5 Hawick U.K.
29 L6 Ḥawīzah, Hawr al *l.* Iraq
51 B6 Hawkdun Range *mts* N.Z.
51 F3 Hawke Bay *b.* N.Z.
59 J3 Hawke Island *i.* Can.
50 B1 Hawker Austr.
71 F2 Hawkesbury Can.
73 F3 Hawkins Peak *summit* U.S.A.
69 F3 Hawks U.S.A.
71 K2 Hawkshaw Can.
71 F4 Hawley U.S.A.
29 J5 Ḥawrān, Wādī *watercourse* Iraq
90 C7 Hawston S. Africa
72 C2 Hawthorne U.S.A.
42 C1 Haxat China
8 F3 Haxby U.K.
50 E3 Hay Austr.
56 F2 Hay *r.* Can.
68 B3 Hay *r.* U.S.A.
38 B1 Haya China
40 G5 Hayachine-san *mt* Japan
30 B2 Haydarābad Iran
73 G5 Hayden *AZ* U.S.A.
62 C2 Hayden *ID* U.S.A.
57 L3 Hayes *r.* Can.
55 M2 Hayes Halvø *pen.* Greenland
9 B7 Hayle U.K.
28 D2 Haymana Turkey
70 E5 Haymarket U.S.A.
55 J3 Haynes *r.* Can.
71 J2 Haynesville U.S.A.
9 D5 Hay-on-Wye U.K.
21 C7 Hayrabolu Turkey
56 F2 Hay River Can.
64 D4 Hays U.S.A.
21 D5 Haysyn Ukr.
72 A3 Hayward *CA* U.S.A.
68 B2 Hayward *WV* U.S.A.
9 G7 Haywards Heath U.K.
31 G3 Hazarajat *reg.* Afgh.
70 B6 Hazard U.S.A.
35 F5 Hazārībāg India
35 E5 Hazaribagh Range *mts* India
12 A4 Hazebrouck France
56 D3 Hazelton Can.
71 F4 Hazelton U.S.A.
54 G2 Hazen Strait *chan.* Can.
12 C2 Hazerswoude-Rijndijk Neth.
29 G6 Ḥazm al Jalāmid *ridge* S. Arabia
31 G2 Hazrat Sultan Afgh.
29 H2 Hazro Turkey
11 B4 Headford Rep. of Ireland
72 A2 Healdsburg U.S.A.
50 E4 Healesville Austr.
9 F4 Heanor U.K.
93 J7 Heard Island *i.* Ind. Ocean
65 D6 Hearne U.S.A.
58 D4 Hearst Can.
92 B2 Hearst I. *i.* Ant.
9 H7 Heathfield U.K.
71 E6 Heathsville U.S.A.
65 D7 Hebbronville U.S.A.
38 E2 Hebei *div.* China
65 E5 Heber Springs U.S.A.
38 E3 Hebi China
59 H2 Hebron Can.
68 D5 Hebron *IN* U.S.A.
64 D3 Hebron *NE* U.S.A.
71 G3 Hebron *NY* U.S.A.
28 E6 Hebron West Bank
59 H2 Hebron Fiord *in.* Can.
54 E4 Hecate Strait *B.C.* Can.
56 C4 Hecate Strait *chan.* Can.
56 C3 Heceta I. *i.* U.S.A.
39 C5 Hechi China
39 C4 Hechuan China
7 N5 Hede Sweden
7 O6 Hedemora Sweden
39 D6 Hede Sk. *resr* China
62 C2 He Devil Mt. *mt* U.S.A.
68 A5 Hedrick U.S.A.
12 D2 Heeg Neth.
12 F2 Heek Ger.
12 C4 Heer Belgium
12 E2 Heerde Neth.
12 D2 Heerenveen Neth.
12 C2 Heerhugowaard Neth.
12 D4 Heerlen Neth.
Ḥefa *see* Haifa
38 E4 Hefei China
39 D4 Hefeng China
40 B1 Hegang China
41 E6 Hegura-jima *i.* Japan
13 K3 Heidberg *h.* Ger.
13 D3 Heide Ger.
89 B6 Heide Namibia
13 G5 Heidelberg Ger.
91 H3 Heidelberg *Gauteng* S. Africa
90 D7 Heidelberg *Western Cape* S. Africa
91 G3 Heilbron S. Africa
13 H5 Heilbronn Ger.
13 E3 Heiligenhafen Ger.
39 □ Hei Ling Chau *i. H.K.* China
42 E1 Heilongjiang *div.* China
36 E2 Heilong Jiang *r.* China/Rus. Fed.
13 J5 Heilsbronn Ger.
6 M5 Heimdal Norway
7 U6 Heinola Fin.
44 A2 Heinze Is *is* Myanmar
42 B3 Heishan China
12 C3 Heist-op-den-Berg Belgium
38 E2 Hejian China
39 B4 Hejiang China
39 D6 He Jiang *r.* China
38 D3 Hejin China
28 F2 Hekimhan Turkey
6 D5 Hekla *volc.* Iceland
38 B2 Hekou *Gansu* China
39 B6 Hekou *Yunnan* China
6 N5 Helagsfjället *mt* Sweden
38 B2 Helan Shan *mts* China
13 K3 Helbra Ger.
35 H4 Helem India
65 F5 Helena *AR* U.S.A.
62 E2 Helena *MT* U.S.A.
72 D3 Helen, Mt *mt* U.S.A.
10 D4 Helensburgh U.K.
28 E6 Ḥeleẓ Israel
16 C3 Helgoland *i.* Ger.
16 D3 Helgoländer Bucht *b.* Ger.
6 C5 Hella Iceland
6 P2 Helland Norway
30 C4 Helleh *r.* Iran
12 C3 Hellevoetsluis Neth.
6 R2 Helligskogen Norway
15 F3 Hellín Spain
62 C2 Hells Canyon *gorge* U.S.A.
31 F4 Helmand *r.* Afgh.
13 K4 Helmbrechts Ger.
13 J3 Helme *r.* Ger.
89 B6 Helmeringhausen Namibia
90 E6 Helmeringhausen S. Africa
12 D3 Helmond Neth.
10 E2 Helmsdale U.K.
10 E2 Helmsdale *r.* U.K.
13 K2 Helmstedt Ger.
42 E2 Helong China
73 G2 Helper U.S.A.
7 N8 Helsingborg Sweden
7 N8 Helsingør Denmark
7 T6 Helsinki Fin.
9 B7 Helston U.K.
8 D3 Helvellyn *mt* U.K.
11 D5 Helvick Head *hd* Rep. of Ireland
87 F2 Helwân Egypt
9 G6 Hemel Hempstead U.K.
72 D5 Hemet U.S.A.
70 E3 Hemlock Lake *l.* U.S.A.
13 H2 Hemmingen Ger.
71 G2 Hemmingford Can.
13 H1 Hemmoor Ger.
65 D6 Hempstead U.S.A.
9 J5 Hemsby U.K.
7 Q8 Hemse Sweden
38 A3 Henan *Qinghai* China
38 D3 Henan *div.* China
15 E2 Henares *r.* Spain
40 F4 Henashi-zaki *pt* Japan
28 C1 Hendek Turkey
83 E3 Henderson Arg.
66 C4 Henderson *KY* U.S.A.
67 E4 Henderson *NC* U.S.A.
73 E3 Henderson *NV* U.S.A.
71 E3 Henderson *NY* U.S.A.
65 E5 Henderson *TX* U.S.A.
46 P6 Henderson Island *i. Pitcairn Is* Pac. Oc.
67 D5 Hendersonville *NC* U.S.A.
67 C4 Hendersonville *TN* U.S.A.
30 C4 Hendījān Iran
9 G6 Hendon U.K.
30 D5 Hendorābī *i.* Iran
36 B4 Hengduan Shan *mts* China
12 E2 Hengelo Neth.
39 D5 Hengshan *Hunan* China
38 C2 Hengshan *Shaanxi* China
42 F1 Hengshan China
39 D5 Heng Shan *mt Hunan* China
38 D2 Heng Shan *mt* China
38 E2 Hengshui China
39 C6 Heng Xian China
39 D5 Hengyang *Hunan* China
39 D5 Hengyang *Hunan* China
21 E6 Heniches'k Ukr.
51 C6 Henley N.Z.
9 G6 Henley-on-Thames U.K.
71 F5 Henlopen, Cape *pt* U.S.A.
12 F4 Hennef (Sieg) Ger.
91 G3 Hennenman S. Africa
13 M2 Hennigsdorf Berlin Ger.
71 H3 Henniker U.S.A.
65 D5 Henrietta U.S.A.
58 D2 Henrietta Maria, Cape *c.* Can.
73 G3 Henrieville U.S.A.
68 C5 Henry U.S.A.
92 B3 Henry Ice Rise *ice feature* Ant.
55 M3 Henry Kater, C. *hd* Can.
73 G2 Henry Mts *mts* U.S.A.
69 G4 Hensall Can.
13 H1 Henstedt-Ulzburg Ger.
89 B6 Hentiesbaai Namibia
50 F3 Henty Austr.
37 B5 Henzada Myanmar
57 H4 Hepburn Can.
39 E5 Heping China
39 C6 Hepu China
38 D2 Hequ China
31 F3 Herāt Afgh.
14 F5 Hérault *r.* France
57 H4 Herbert Can.
13 G4 Herborn Ger.
13 H4 Herbstein Ger.
92 B4 Hercules Dome *ice feature* Ant.
12 F3 Herdecke Ger.
13 F4 Herdorf Ger.
9 E5 Hereford U.K.
65 C5 Hereford U.S.A.
46 N5 Héréhérétué *i.* Pac. Oc.
12 C4 Herent Belgium
13 G2 Herford Ger.
13 J4 Heringen (Werra) Ger.
64 D4 Herington U.S.A.
30 B2 Herīs Iran
16 D7 Herisau Switz.
92 B3 Heritage Ra. *mts* Ant.
71 F3 Herkimer U.S.A.
13 H3 Herleshausen Ger.
10 □ Herma Ness *hd* U.K.
13 J2 Hermannsburg Ger.
90 C7 Hermanus S. Africa
91 H5 Hermes, Cape *pt* S. Africa
51 F1 Hermidale Austr.
62 C2 Hermiston U.S.A.
80 C9 Hermite, Is *i.* Chile
48 E2 Hermit Is *is* P.N.G.
Hermon, Mount *mt see* Sheikh, Jebel esh
83 B2 Hermosa, P. de V. *pass* Chile
81 B4 Hermosas, Parque Nacional las *nat. park* Col.
74 B3 Hermosillo Mex.
80 F3 Hernandarias Para.
12 F3 Herne Ger.
9 J6 Herne Bay U.K.
7 L8 Herning Denmark
68 D1 Heron Bay Can.
15 D3 Herrera del Duque Spain
65 B7 Herreras Mex.
13 J5 Herrieden Ger.
70 E4 Hershey U.S.A.
9 G6 Hertford U.K.
91 F4 Hertzogville S. Africa
12 D4 Herve Belgium
49 F4 Hervey Bay *b.* Austr.
46 M5 Hervey Is *is* Pac. Oc.
13 L2 Herzberg *Brandenburg* Ger.
13 M3 Herzberg *Brandenburg* Ger.
12 F2 Herzlake Ger.
13 J5 Herzogenaurach Ger.
13 L1 Herzsprung Ger.
29 M4 Ḥeşar Iran
12 C4 Hesbaye *reg.* Belgium
12 F1 Hesel Ger.
39 C6 Heshan China
38 C3 Heshui China
38 D2 Heshun China
72 D4 Hesperia U.S.A.
56 C2 Hess *r.* Can.
13 J5 Heßdorf Ger.
13 J5 Hesselberg *h.* Ger.
13 H4 Hessen *div.* Ger.
13 H3 Hessisch Lichtenau Ger.
39 B6 Het *r.* Laos
72 B3 Hetch Hetchy Aqueduct *canal* U.S.A.
12 D3 Heteren Neth.
64 C2 Hettinger U.S.A.
8 E3 Hetton U.K.
13 K3 Hettstedt Ger.
8 E3 Hexham U.K.
38 F4 He Xian *Anhui* China
39 D5 He Xian *Guangxi* China
38 B2 Hexibao China
38 E1 Hexigten Qi China
90 C6 Hex River Pass S. Africa
38 D3 Heyang China
30 D4 Ḥeydarābād Iran
31 F4 Ḥeydarābād Iran
8 E3 Heysham U.K.
39 E6 Heyuan China
50 C5 Heywood Austr.
8 E4 Heywood U.K.
68 C5 Heyworth U.S.A.
38 E3 Heze China
39 B5 Hezhang China
38 B3 Hezheng China
38 B3 Hezuozhen China
67 D7 Hialeah U.S.A.
64 E4 Hiawatha U.S.A.
68 A2 Hibbing U.S.A.
67 D5 Hickory U.S.A.
51 G2 Hicks Bay N.Z.
57 K2 Hicks L. *l.* Can.
70 A4 Hicksville U.S.A.
65 D5 Hico U.S.A.
40 H3 Hidaka-sanmyaku *mts* Japan
74 C3 Hidalgo del Parral Mex.
74 C3 Hidalgo, Psa M. *resr* Mex.
82 C2 Hidrolândia Brazil
41 C7 Higashi-Hiroshima Japan
40 G5 Higashine Japan
41 D7 Higashi-ōsaka Japan
41 A8 Higashi-suidō *chan.* Japan
71 F3 Higgins Bay U.S.A.
68 E3 Higgins Lake *l.* U.S.A.
High Atlas *mts see* Haut Atlas
62 B3 High Desert U.S.A.
68 C3 High Falls Reservoir U.S.A.
68 E3 High I. *i.* U.S.A.
39 □ High Island Res. *resr H.K.* China
68 D4 Highland Park U.S.A.
72 C2 Highland Peak *summit CA* U.S.A.
73 E3 Highland Peak *summit NV* U.S.A.
56 F3 High Level Can.
35 F5 High Level Canal *canal* India
67 E5 High Point U.S.A.
56 F3 High Prairie Can.
56 G4 High River Can.
67 E7 High Rock Bahamas
57 J3 Highrock Lake *l.* Can.
8 E3 High Seat *h.* U.K.
71 F4 Hightstown U.S.A.
9 G6 High Wycombe U.K.
81 D2 Higuerote Venez.
7 S7 Hiiumaa *i.* Estonia
32 A4 Hijaz *reg.* S. Arabia
73 E3 Hiko U.S.A.
41 E7 Hikone Japan
51 G2 Hikurangi *mt* N.Z.
73 F3 Hildale U.S.A.
13 J4 Hildburghausen Ger.
13 J4 Hilders Ger.
13 H2 Hildesheim Ger.
35 G4 Hili Bangl.
92 B5 Hillary Coast *coastal area* Ant.
64 D4 Hill City U.S.A.
73 H2 Hill Creek *r.* U.S.A.
12 C2 Hillegom Neth.
7 N9 Hillerød Denmark
64 D2 Hillsboro *ND* U.S.A.
71 H3 Hillsboro *NH* U.S.A.
70 B5 Hillsboro *OH* U.S.A.
65 D5 Hillsboro *TX* U.S.A.
70 C5 Hillsboro *WV* U.S.A.
68 B4 Hillsboro *WV* U.S.A.
68 E5 Hillsdale *MI* U.S.A.
71 G3 Hillsdale *NY* U.S.A.
71 E4 Hillsgrove U.S.A.
10 F4 Hillside U.K.
73 F4 Hillside U.S.A.
50 E2 Hillston Austr.
70 C6 Hillsville U.S.A.
50 H3 Hilltop Austr.
72 □2 Hilo U.S.A.
91 J4 Hilton S. Africa
70 E3 Hilton U.S.A.
69 F2 Hilton Beach Can.
67 D5 Hilton Head Island U.S.A.
29 G3 Hilvan Turkey
12 D2 Hilversum Neth.
34 D3 Himachal Pradesh *div.* India
22 F6 Himalaya *mts* Asia
35 F3 Himalchul *mt* Nepal
6 S4 Himanka Fin.
19 H4 Himarë Albania
34 C5 Himatnagar India
41 D7 Himeji Japan
40 G5 Himekami-dake *mt* Japan
91 H4 Himeville S. Africa
41 E6 Himi Japan
28 F4 Ḥimş Syria
28 F4 Ḥimş, Baḥrat *resr* Syria
43 C4 Hinatuan Phil.
48 E3 Hinchinbrook I. *i.* Austr.
9 F5 Hinckley U.K.
68 A2 Hinckley *MN* U.S.A.
73 F2 Hinckley *UT* U.S.A.
71 F3 Hinckley Reservoir U.S.A.
34 D3 Hindan *r.* India
34 D4 Hindaun India
8 G3 Hinderwell U.K.
29 K5 Hindīyah Barrage Iraq
8 E4 Hindley U.K.
70 B6 Hindman U.S.A.
50 C4 Hindmarsh, L. *l.* Austr.
35 F5 Hindola India
31 G3 Hindu Kush *mts* Afgh./Pak.
33 B3 Hindupur India
56 F3 Hines Creek Can.
67 D6 Hinesville U.S.A.
34 D5 Hinganghat India
31 G5 Hinglaj Pak.
31 G5 Hingol *r.* Pak.
34 D6 Hingoli India
29 H2 Hınıs Turkey
72 D4 Hinkley U.S.A.
6 O2 Hinnøya *i.* Norway
43 B4 Hinobaan Phil.
15 D3 Hinojosa del Duque Spain
41 C7 Hino-misaki *pt* Japan
71 G3 Hinsdale U.S.A.
12 F1 Hinte Ger.
56 F4 Hinton Can.
70 C6 Hinton U.S.A.
12 C2 Hippolytushoef Neth.
29 K2 Hirabit Dağ *mt* Turkey
41 A8 Hirado Japan
41 A8 Hirado-shima *i.* Japan
35 E5 Hirakud Reservoir India
40 H3 Hiroo Japan
40 G4 Hirosaki Japan
41 C7 Hiroshima Japan
13 K5 Hirschaid Ger.
13 K4 Hirschberg Ger.
16 E7 Hirschberg *mt* Ger.
14 G2 Hirson France
7 L8 Hirtshals Denmark
29 M3 Hisar Iran
31 G3 Hisar, Koh-i- *mts* Afgh.
28 D1 Hisarönü Turkey
28 E6 Hisban Jordan
31 H2 Hisor Tajik.
75 K4 Hispaniola *i.* Caribbean Sea
34 C3 Hissar India
35 F4 Hisua India
29 J5 Hīt Iraq
41 G6 Hitachi Japan
41 G6 Hitachi-ōta Japan
41 B8 Hitoyoshi Japan
6 L5 Hitra *i.* Norway
13 K1 Hitzacker Ger.
41 C7 Hiuchi-nada *b.* Japan
46 O4 Hiva Oa *i. Fr. Polynesia* Pac. Oc.
56 E4 Hixon Can.
29 J2 Hizan Turkey
7 O7 Hjälmaren *l.* Sweden
57 H2 Hjalmar Lake *l.* Can.
7 L5 Hjerkinn Norway
7 O7 Hjo Sweden
7 M8 Hjørring Denmark
91 J4 Hlabisa S. Africa
35 F3 Hlako Kangri *mt* China
91 J3 Hlatikulu Swaziland
21 E5 Hlobyne Ukr.
91 G4 Hlohlowane S. Africa
91 H4 Hlotse Lesotho
91 K4 Hluhluwe S. Africa
21 E5 Hlukhiv Ukr.
17 O4 Hlusha Belarus
20 C4 Hlybokaye Belarus
86 C4 Ho Ghana
89 B6 Hoachanas Namibia
48 E6 Hobart Austr.
65 D5 Hobart U.S.A.
65 C5 Hobbs U.S.A.
92 A4 Hobbs Coast *coastal area* Ant.
67 D7 Hobe Sound U.S.A.
7 L8 Hobro Denmark
88 E3 Hobyo Somalia
13 H5 Höchberg Ger.
44 C3 Hô Chi Minh Vietnam
16 G7 Hochschwab *mt* Austria
13 G5 Hockenheim Ger.
70 B5 Hocking *r.* U.S.A.
34 D4 Hodal India
8 E4 Hodder *r.* U.K.
9 G6 Hoddesdon U.K.
Hodeida *see* Al Hudaydah
71 K1 Hodgdon U.S.A.
17 K7 Hódmezővásárhely Hungary
15 J5 Hodna, Chott el *salt l.* Alg.
42 D4 Hodo dan *pt* N. Korea
12 C3 Hoek van Holland Neth.
12 D4 Hoensbroek Neth.
42 E2 Hoeryŏng N. Korea
42 D4 Hoeyang N. Korea
13 K4 Hof Ger.
13 J4 Hofheim in Unterfranken Ger.
91 F5 Hofmeyr S. Africa
6 F4 Höfn Iceland
7 P6 Hofors Sweden
6 D4 Hofsjökull *ice cap* Iceland
41 B7 Hōfu Japan
7 N8 Höganäs Sweden
86 C2 Hoggar *plat.* Alg.
71 F6 Hog I. *i.* U.S.A.
7 P8 Högsby Sweden
13 H5 Hohenloher Ebene *plain* Ger.
13 L3 Hohenmölsen Ger.
13 L2 Hohennauen Ger.
13 K4 Hohenwarte-talsperre *resr* Ger.
13 H4 Hohe Rhön *mts* Ger.
16 F7 Hohe Tauern *mts* Austria
12 E4 Hohe Venn *moorland* Belgium
38 D1 Hohhot China
35 G2 Hoh Xil Hu *salt l.* China
35 G2 Hoh Xil Shan *mts* China
44 D2 Hôi An Vietnam
88 D3 Hoima Uganda

39 B6 Hôi Xuân Vietnam
35 H4 Hojai India
41 C8 Hōjo Japan
51 D1 Hokianga Harbour *in.* N.Z.
51 C5 Hokitika N.Z.
40 H3 Hokkaidō *i.* Japan
7 L7 Hokksund Norway
29 K1 Hoktemberyan Armenia
7 L6 Hol Norway
33 B3 Holalkere India
7 M9 Holbæk Denmark
9 H5 Holbeach U.K.
73 G4 Holbrook U.S.A.
68 B3 Holcombe Flowage *resr* U.S.A.
57 G4 Holden Can.
73 F2 Holden U.S.A.
65 D5 Holdenville U.S.A.
64 D3 Holdrege U.S.A.
33 B3 Hole Narsipur India
75 J4 Holguín Cuba
7 N6 Höljes Sweden
68 D4 Holland U.S.A.
70 D4 Hollidaysburg U.S.A.
56 C3 Hollis *AK* U.S.A.
65 D5 Hollis *OK* U.S.A.
72 B3 Hollister U.S.A.
69 F4 Holly U.S.A.
65 F5 Holly Springs U.S.A.
67 D7 Hollywood U.S.A.
6 N4 Holm Norway
54 G2 Holman Can.
6 T2 Holmestrand *Finnmark* Norway
7 M7 Holmestrand *Vestfold* Norway
6 R5 Holmön *i.* Sweden
55 M2 Holms Ø *i.* Greenland
6 R5 Holmsund Sweden
90 B3 Holoog Namibia
7 L8 Holstebro Denmark
67 D4 Holston *r.* U.S.A.
70 C6 Holston Lake *l.* U.S.A.
9 C7 Holsworthy U.K.
9 J5 Holt U.K.
68 E4 Holt U.S.A.
64 E4 Holton U.S.A.
12 D1 Holwerd Neth.
11 D5 Holycross Rep. of Ireland
9 C4 Holyhead U.K.
9 C4 Holyhead Bay *b.* U.K.
8 F2 Holy Island *i. Eng.* U.K.
9 C4 Holy Island *i. Wales* U.K.
71 G3 Holyoke U.S.A.
9 D4 Holywell U.K.
13 L3 Holzhausen Ger.
16 E7 Holzkirchen Ger.
13 H3 Holzminden Ger.
30 C3 Homāyunshahr Iran
13 H3 Homberg (Efze) Ger.
86 B3 Hombori Mali
12 F5 Homburg Ger.
55 M3 Home Bay *b.* Can.
12 D5 Homécourt France
65 E5 Homer U.S.A.
67 D6 Homerville U.S.A.
67 D7 Homestead U.S.A.
67 C5 Homewood U.S.A.
33 B2 Homnabad India
43 C4 Homonhon *pt* Phil.
Homs *see* Ḥimṣ
21 D4 Homyel' Belarus
33 A3 Honavar India
81 B3 Honda Col.
43 A4 Honda Bay *b.* Phil.
73 H4 Hon Dah U.S.A.
90 B5 Hondeklipbaai S. Africa
38 C1 Hondlon Ju China
65 D6 Hondo U.S.A.
12 E1 Hondsrug *reg.* Neth.
53 H8 Honduras *country* Central America
7 M6 Hønefoss Norway
71 F4 Honesdale U.S.A.
72 B1 Honey Lake *l.* U.S.A.
71 E3 Honeyoye Lake *l.* U.S.A.
14 E2 Honfleur France
38 E4 Hong'an China
42 D5 Hongch'ŏn S. Korea
39 C6 Hông Gai Vietnam
39 E6 Honghai Wan *b.* China
39 B6 Honghe China
38 E3 Hong He *r.* China
39 D4 Honghu China
39 C5 Hongjiang China
39 E6 Hong Kong China
39 E6 Hong Kong *div.* China
39 □ Hong Kong Island *i. H.K.* China
38 C2 Hongliu *r.* China
38 B2 Hongliuyuan China
44 C3 Hông Ngư Vietnam
39 C6 Hong or Red River, Mouths of the *est.* Vietnam
39 C7 Hongqizhen China
38 B2 Hongshansi China
42 D2 Hongshi China
39 D6 Hongshui He *r.* China
39 C6 Hông, Sông *r.* Vietnam
38 D2 Hongtong China
59 G4 Honguedo, Détroit d' *chan.* Can.
42 D3 Hongwŏn N. Korea
42 B1 Hongxing China
38 B3 Hongyuan China
38 F3 Hongze China
38 F3 Hongze Hu *l.* China
49 F2 Honiara Solomon Is
9 D7 Honiton U.K.
40 G5 Honjō Japan
7 S6 Honkajoki Fin.
44 C3 Hon Khoai *i.* Vietnam
44 D2 Hon Lớn *i.* Vietnam
44 C1 Hon Mê *i.* Vietnam
33 A3 Honnali India
6 T1 Honningsvåg Norway
72 □2 Honokaa U.S.A.
72 □1 Honolulu U.S.A.
44 C3 Hon Rai *i.* Vietnam
41 C7 Honshū *i.* Japan
62 B2 Hood, Mt *volc.* U.S.A.
48 B5 Hood Pt *pt* Austr.
12 E2 Hoogeveen Neth.
12 E1 Hoogezand-Sappemeer Neth.
65 C4 Hooker U.S.A.
11 E5 Hook Head *hd* Rep. of Ireland
Hook of Holland *see* Hoek van Holland
56 B3 Hoonah U.S.A.
54 B3 Hooper Bay *AK* U.S.A.
71 E5 Hooper I. *i.* U.S.A.
68 D5 Hoopeston U.S.A.
91 F3 Hoopstad S. Africa
7 N9 Höör Sweden
12 D2 Hoorn Neth.
71 G3 Hoosick U.S.A.
73 E3 Hoover Dam *dam* U.S.A.
70 B4 Hoover Memorial Reservoir U.S.A.
29 H1 Hopa Turkey
71 F4 Hop Bottom U.S.A.
56 E5 Hope *B.C.* Can.
65 E5 Hope *AR* U.S.A.
73 F5 Hope *AZ* U.S.A.
51 D5 Hope *r.* N.Z.
59 J2 Hopedale Can.
90 C6 Hopefield S. Africa
59 H3 Hope Mountains Can.
24 D2 Hopen *i.* Svalbard
54 B3 Hope, Point *c.* U.S.A.
51 D4 Hope Saddle *pass* N.Z.
59 G2 Hopes Advance, Baie *b.* Can.
50 D3 Hopetoun Austr.
90 F4 Hopetown S. Africa
70 E6 Hopewell U.S.A.
58 E2 Hopewell Islands *is* Can.
48 C4 Hopkins, L. *salt flat* Austr.
66 C4 Hopkinsville U.S.A.
72 A2 Hopland U.S.A.
62 B2 Hoquiam U.S.A.
38 A3 Hor China
29 L2 Horadiz Azer.
29 J1 Horasan Turkey
7 N9 Hörby Sweden
68 C4 Horeb, Mount U.S.A.
38 B1 Hörh Uul *mts* Mongolia
68 C4 Horicon U.S.A.
38 D1 Horinger China
94 H6 Horizon Depth *depth* Pac. Oc.
20 D4 Horki Belarus
92 B4 Horlick Mts *mts* Ant.
21 F5 Horlivka Ukr.
31 F4 Hormak Iran
30 E5 Hormoz *i.* Iran
30 E5 Hormuz, Strait of *str.* Iran/Oman
16 G6 Horn Austria
6 B3 Horn *c.* Iceland
56 F2 Horn *r.* Can.
6 P3 Hornavan *l.* Sweden
65 E6 Hornbeck U.S.A.
13 J2 Hornburg Ger.
80 C9 Horn, Cape *c.* Chile
9 G4 Horncastle U.K.
7 P6 Horndal Sweden
13 H1 Horneburg Ger.
6 Q5 Hörnefors Sweden
70 E3 Hornell U.S.A.
58 D4 Hornepayne Can.
67 B6 Horn I. *i.* U.S.A.
49 J3 Horn, Îles de *is* Wallis and Futuna Is
90 B1 Hornkranz Namibia
83 B4 Hornopiren, V. *volc.* Chile
65 C7 Hornos Mex.
Hornos, Cabo de *c. see* Horn, Cape
50 H2 Hornsby Austr.
8 G4 Hornsea U.K.
7 P6 Hornslandet *pen.* Sweden
17 M6 Horodenka Ukr.
21 D5 Horodnya Ukr.
21 C5 Horodok *Khmel'nyts'kyy* Ukr.
21 B5 Horodok *L'viv* Ukr.
40 H2 Horokanai Japan
17 M5 Horokhiv Ukr.
40 H3 Horoshiri-dake *mt* Japan
42 A2 Horqin Shadi *reg.* China
36 E2 Horqin Youyi Qianqi China
42 A1 Horqin Youyi Zhongqi China
42 B2 Horqin Zuoyi Houqi China
42 B1 Horqin Zuoyi Zhongqi China
9 C7 Horrabridge U.K.
35 G3 Horru China
56 E4 Horsefly Can.
70 E3 Horseheads U.S.A.
59 J3 Horse Is *is* Can.
11 C4 Horseleap Rep. of Ireland
7 L9 Horsens Denmark
62 C3 Horseshoe Bend U.S.A.
50 D4 Horsham Austr.
9 G6 Horsham U.K.
13 L5 Horšovský Týn Czech Rep.
13 H4 Horst *h.* Ger.
12 F2 Hörstel Ger.
7 M7 Horten Norway
54 F3 Horton *r.* Can.
69 F1 Horwood Lake *l.* Can.
17 N5 Horyn' *r.* Ukr.
35 H2 Ho Sai Hu *l.* China
88 D3 Hosa'ina Eth.
13 H4 Hösbach Ger.
33 B3 Hosdurga India
29 L4 Hoseynābād Iran
30 C4 Ḥoseynīyeh Iran
31 F5 Hoshab Pak.
34 D5 Hoshangabad India
34 C3 Hoshiarpur India
33 B3 Hospet India
11 C5 Hospital Rep. of Ireland
83 F1 Hospital, Cuchilla del *h.* Uru.
80 C9 Hoste, I. *i.* Chile
6 O5 Hotagen *l.* Sweden
27 G3 Hotan China
90 E3 Hotazel S. Africa
73 G4 Hotevilla U.S.A.
50 F4 Hotham, Mt *mt* Austr.
6 P4 Hoting Sweden
65 E5 Hot Springs *AR* U.S.A.
64 C3 Hot Springs *SD* U.S.A.
56 F1 Hottah Lake *l.* Can.
75 K5 Hotte, Massif de la *mts* Haiti
12 D4 Houffalize Belgium
44 □ Hougang Sing.
68 C2 Houghton U.S.A.
68 E3 Houghton Lake U.S.A.
68 E3 Houghton Lake *l.* U.S.A.
8 F3 Houghton le Spring U.K.
71 K1 Houlton U.S.A.
38 D3 Houma China
65 F6 Houma U.S.A.
10 C3 Hourn, Loch *in.* U.K.
71 G3 Housatonic U.S.A.
73 F2 House Range *mts* U.S.A.
56 D4 Houston Can.
65 F4 Houston *MO* U.S.A.
65 F5 Houston *MS* U.S.A.
65 E6 Houston *TX* U.S.A.
91 H1 Hout *r.* S. Africa
48 B4 Houtman Abrolhos *is* Austr.
10 E2 Houton U.K.
90 E5 Houwater S. Africa
36 B2 Hovd Mongolia
9 G7 Hove U.K.
9 J5 Hoveton U.K.
30 C4 Hoveyzeh Iran
7 O8 Hovmantorp Sweden
38 C1 Hövsgöl Mongolia
36 C1 Hövsgöl Nuur *l.* Mongolia
36 C2 Hövüün Mongolia
68 E4 Howard City U.S.A.
57 H2 Howard Lake *l.* Can.
8 G4 Howden U.K.
50 G4 Howe, C. *hd* Austr.
69 F4 Howell U.S.A.
64 C2 Howes U.S.A.
71 G2 Howick Can.
91 J4 Howick S. Africa
50 F4 Howitt, Mt *mt* Austr.
71 J2 Howland U.S.A.
49 J1 Howland Island *i.* Pac. Oc.
50 F3 Howlong Austr.
11 E4 Howth Rep. of Ireland
30 D3 Ḥowz-e Dūmatu Iran
30 E4 Ḥowz-e Panj Iran
13 H3 Höxter Ger.
10 E2 Hoy *i.* U.K.
13 H2 Hoya Ger.
7 K6 Hoyanger Norway
16 G5 Hoyerswerda Ger.
6 N4 Høylandet Norway
13 K3 Hoym Ger.
6 V5 Höytiäinen *l.* Fin.
29 G2 Hozat Turkey
16 G5 Hradec Králové Czech Rep.
13 M4 Hradiště *h.* Czech Rep.
19 H3 Hrasnica Bos.-Herz.
29 K1 Hrazdan Armenia
21 E5 Hrebinka Ukr.
20 B4 Hrodna Belarus
39 F6 Hsi-hsu-p'ing Hsü *i.* Taiwan
39 F5 Hsin-chu Taiwan
39 F5 Hsueh Shan *mt* Taiwan
39 E5 Hua'an China
81 D4 Huachamacari, Cerro *mt* Venez.
38 C2 Huachi China
78 C6 Huacho Peru
40 B1 Huachuan China
73 G6 Huachuca City U.S.A.
83 C1 Huaco Arg.
38 D1 Huade China
42 D2 Huadian China
46 M5 Huahine *i. Fr. Polynesia* Pac. Oc.
38 E1 Huai'an *Hebei* China
38 F3 Huai'an *Jiangsu* China
38 E3 Huaibei China
38 E3 Huaibin China
42 C2 Huaide China
38 C2 Huaidezhen China
38 F3 Huai He *r.* China
39 C5 Huaihua China
39 D6 Huaiji China
38 E1 Huailai China
39 B7 Huai Luang *r.* Thai.
38 E3 Huainan China
39 E4 Huaining China
38 D2 Huairen China
38 E3 Huaiyang China
38 F3 Huaiyin China
38 E3 Huaiyuan *Anhui* China
39 C5 Huaiyuan *Guangxi* China
38 B3 Huajialing China
37 F7 Huaki Indon.
73 F4 Hualapai Peak *summit* U.S.A.
39 F5 Hua-lien Taiwan
78 C5 Huallaga *r.* Peru
38 B2 Hualong China
89 B5 Huambo Angola
40 B1 Huanan China
83 C4 Huancache, Sa *mts* Arg.
78 C6 Huancayo Peru
38 E2 Huangbizhuang Sk. *resr* China
38 A2 Huangcheng China
38 E3 Huangchuan China
39 E4 Huanggang China
Huang Hai *sea see* Yellow Sea
38 E2 Huang He *r.* China
37 F2 Huanghe Kou *est.* China
35 H2 Huanghetan China
38 E2 Huanghua China
38 C3 Huangling China
39 C7 Huangliu China
39 E4 Huangmei China
42 D2 Huangnihe China
39 E4 Huangpi China
39 C5 Huangping China
38 D1 Huangqi Hai *l.* China
39 F4 Huangshan China
39 F4 Huang Shan *mt* China
39 E4 Huangshi China
38 B2 Huang Shui *r.* China
38 C2 Huangtu Gaoyuan *plat.* China
38 F2 Huang Xian China
39 F4 Huangyan China
38 A2 Huangyuan China
39 C5 Huanjiang China
38 C2 Huan Jiang *r.* China
42 C3 Huanren China
38 F2 Huantai China
78 C5 Huanuco Peru
78 E7 Huanuni Bol.
38 C2 Huan Xian China
39 G5 Hua-p'ing Hsü *i.* Taiwan
78 C5 Huaráz Peru
78 C6 Huarmey Peru
39 D4 Huarong China
78 C5 Huascaran, Nevado de *mt* Peru
80 B3 Huasco Chile
80 B3 Huasco *r.* Chile
42 D2 Huashulinzi China
74 C3 Huatabampo Mex.
38 C3 Huating China
42 A3 Huatong China
39 D6 Hua Xian *Guangdong* China
38 E3 Hua Xian *Henan* China
38 D4 Huayuan *Hubei* China
39 C4 Huayuan *Hunan* China
39 C4 Huayun China
39 D6 Huazhou China
69 F3 Hubbard Lake *l.* U.S.A.
56 B2 Hubbard, Mt *mt* Can./U.S.A.
59 G2 Hubbard, Pointe *hd* Can.
38 D4 Hubei *div.* China
33 A3 Hubli India
42 D3 Huch'ang N. Korea
12 E3 Hückelhoven Ger.
9 F4 Hucknall U.K.
8 F4 Huddersfield U.K.
70 B6 Huddy U.S.A.
7 P6 Hudiksvall Sweden
68 E5 Hudson *MI* U.S.A.
71 G3 Hudson *NY* U.S.A.
68 A3 Hudson *WV* U.S.A.
66 F3 Hudson *r.* U.S.A.
57 J4 Hudson Bay *Sask.* Can.
55 K4 Hudson Bay *b.* Can.
71 G3 Hudson Falls U.S.A.
55 Q2 Hudson Land *reg.* Greenland
92 A3 Hudson Mts *mts* Ant.
56 E3 Hudson's Hope Can.
55 L3 Hudson Strait *str.* Can.
44 C1 Huê Vietnam
83 A4 Huechucuicui, Pta *pt* Chile
74 F5 Huehuetenango Guatemala
15 C4 Huelva Spain
83 B1 Huentelauquén Chile
83 B4 Huequi, Volcán *volc.* Chile
15 F4 Huércal-Overa Spain
15 F1 Huesca Spain
15 E4 Huéscar Spain
70 E4 Hughesville U.S.A.
35 F5 Hugli *est.* India
35 G5 Hugli-Chunchura India
65 E5 Hugo U.S.A.
65 C4 Hugoton U.S.A.
38 D2 Huguan China
90 F3 Huhudi S. Africa
39 F5 Hui'an China
38 C2 Hui'anbu China
51 F3 Huiarau Range *mts* N.Z.
90 B3 Huib-Hoch Plateau *plat.* Namibia
39 E5 Huichang China
42 D3 Huich'ŏn N. Korea
39 E6 Huidong *Guangdong* China
39 B5 Huidong *Sichuan* China
42 D2 Huifa *r.* China
12 C3 Huijbergen Neth.
38 E3 Huiji *r.* China
39 E6 Huilai China
81 B4 Huila, Nevado de *mt* Col.
39 B5 Huili China
38 E2 Huimin China
80 C2 Huinahuaca Arg.
42 D2 Huinan China
83 D2 Huinca Renancó Arg.
38 B3 Huining China
39 C5 Huishui China
35 G2 Huiten Nur *l.* China
39 C5 Huitong China
7 S6 Huittinen Fin.
38 C3 Hui Xian *Gansu* China
38 D3 Hui Xian *Henan* China
74 F5 Huixtla Mex.
39 B5 Huize China
39 E6 Huizhou China
36 C2 Hujirt Mongolia
39 E4 Hukou China
90 D1 Hukuntsi Botswana
68 E2 Hulbert Lake *l.* U.S.A.
30 B3 Hulilan Iran
40 C2 Hulin China
69 K3 Hull Can.
7 O8 Hultsfred Sweden
42 A3 Huludao China
36 D2 Hulun Nur *l.* China
21 F6 Hulyaypole Ukr.
36 E1 Huma China
78 F5 Humaitá Brazil
90 F7 Humansdorp S. Africa
30 B5 Humayyān, J. *h.* S. Arabia
8 H4 Humber, Mouth of the *est.* U.K.
57 H4 Humboldt Can.
62 C3 Humboldt *r.* U.S.A.
62 A3 Humboldt Bay *b.* U.S.A.
72 C1 Humboldt Lake *l.* U.S.A.
72 C1 Humboldt Range *mts* U.S.A.
72 D2 Humbolt Salt Marsh *marsh* U.S.A.
31 E5 Hūmedān Iran
39 D6 Hu Men *chan.* China
17 K6 Humenné Slovakia
50 F3 Hume Reservoir Austr.
72 C3 Humphreys, Mt *mt* U.S.A.
73 G4 Humphreys Peak *summit* U.S.A.
42 B3 Hun *r.* China
6 C4 Húnaflói *b.* Iceland
39 D5 Hunan *div.* China
42 F2 Hunchun China
42 F2 Hunchun *r.* China
13 L3 Hundeluft Ger.
7 M9 Hundested Denmark
19 K2 Hunedoara Romania
13 H4 Hünfeld Ger.
5 E4 Hungary *country* Europe
48 E4 Hungerford Austr.
42 D4 Hŭngnam N. Korea
62 D1 Hungry Horse Res. *resr* U.S.A.
39 □ Hung Shui Kiu *H.K.* China
39 C6 Hưng Yên Vietnam
42 D3 Hunjiang China
42 C3 Hun Jiang *r.* China
90 B3 Huns Mountains Namibia
12 F5 Hunsrück *reg.* Ger.
9 H5 Hunstanton U.K.
33 B3 Hunsur India
73 H4 Hunt U.S.A.
13 G2 Hunte *r.* Ger.
71 F3 Hunter U.S.A.
50 H2 Hunter *r.* Austr.
56 D4 Hunter I. *i.* Can.
49 H4 Hunter I. *i.* New Caledonia
48 E6 Hunter Is *is* Austr.
35 H6 Hunter's Bay *b.* Myanmar
51 C6 Hunters Hills, The *h.* N.Z.
71 F2 Huntingdon Can.
9 G5 Huntingdon U.K.
70 E4 Huntingdon U.S.A.
68 E5 Huntington *IN* U.S.A.
73 G2 Huntington *UT* U.S.A.
70 B5 Huntington *WV* U.S.A.
72 D5 Huntington Beach U.S.A.
51 E2 Huntly N.Z.
10 F3 Huntly U.K.
69 H3 Huntsville Can.
67 C5 Huntsville *AL* U.S.A.
65 E6 Huntsville *TX* U.S.A.
38 D2 Hunyuan China
34 C1 Hunza Pak.
34 C2 Hunza *r.* Pak.
42 B1 Huolin *r.* China
38 E2 Huolu China
44 C1 Hương Khê Vietnam
44 C1 Hương Thuy Vietnam
48 E2 Huon Peninsula P.N.G.
38 E3 Huoqiu China
38 E4 Huoshan China
38 E4 Huo Shan *mt* China
39 F6 Huo-shao Tao *i.* Taiwan
38 D2 Huo Xian China
30 E4 Ḥūr Iran
69 G3 Hurd, Cape *hd* Can.
38 C1 Hure Jadgai China
42 A2 Hure Qi China
87 F2 Hurghada Egypt
68 C1 Hurkett Can.
11 C5 Hurler's Cross Rep. of Ireland
68 B2 Hurley U.S.A.
64 D2 Huron U.S.A.
68 C2 Huron Bay *b.* U.S.A.
69 F3 Huron, Lake *l.* Can./U.S.A.
68 D2 Huron Mts *h.* U.S.A.
73 F3 Hurricane U.S.A.
9 F6 Hursley U.K.
9 H6 Hurst Green U.K.
51 D5 Hurunui *r.* N.Z.
6 E3 Húsavík *Norðurland eystra* Iceland
6 C4 Húsavík *Vestfirðir* Iceland
17 O7 Huşi Romania
7 O8 Huskvarna Sweden
54 C3 Huslia U.S.A.
7 J7 Husnes Norway
35 F4 Hussainabad India
16 D3 Husum Ger.
6 Q5 Husum Sweden
36 C2 Hutag Mongolia
64 D4 Hutchinson U.S.A.
73 G4 Hutch Mtn *mt* U.S.A.
44 A1 Huthi Myanmar
40 C2 Hutou China
57 N2 Hut Point *pt* Can.
70 D5 Huttonsville U.S.A.
38 D2 Hutuo *r.* China
28 G3 Hüvek Turkey
38 C3 Hu Xian China
38 F4 Huzhou China
38 A2 Huzhu China
6 E4 Hvannadalshnúkur *mt* Iceland
18 G3 Hvar *i.* Croatia
21 E6 Hvardiys'ke Ukr.
6 C4 Hveragerði Iceland
7 L8 Hvide Sande Denmark
6 C4 Hvíta *r.* Iceland
42 E3 Hwadae N. Korea
89 C5 Hwange Zimbabwe
89 C5 Hwange National Park Zimbabwe
42 C4 Hwangju N. Korea
89 D5 Hwedza Zimbabwe
71 H4 Hyannis *MA* U.S.A.
64 C3 Hyannis *NE* U.S.A.
36 B2 Hyargas Nuur *l.* Mongolia
56 C3 Hydaburg U.S.A.
51 C6 Hyde N.Z.
48 B5 Hyden Austr.
70 B6 Hyden U.S.A.
71 G4 Hyde Park U.S.A.
73 F5 Hyder U.S.A.
33 B2 Hyderabad India
34 B4 Hyderabad Pak.
14 H5 Hyères France
14 H5 Hyères, Îles d' *is* France
42 E3 Hyesan N. Korea
56 D2 Hyland *r.* Can.
7 J6 Hyllestad Norway
7 N8 Hyltebruk Sweden
50 C4 Hynam Austr.
41 D7 Hyōnosen *mt* Japan
6 V4 Hyrynsalmi Fin.
56 F3 Hythe Can.
9 J6 Hythe U.K.
41 B8 Hyūga Japan
7 T6 Hyvinkää Fin.

I

78 E6 Iaco *r.* Brazil
79 K6 Iaçu Brazil
89 E6 Iakora Madag.
19 M2 Ialomiţa *r.* Romania
19 M2 Ianca Romania
17 N7 Iaşi Romania
43 A3 Iba Phil.
86 C4 Ibadan Nigeria
81 B3 Ibagué Col.
73 F1 Ibapah U.S.A.
78 C3 Ibarra Ecuador
32 B7 Ibb Yemen
13 F2 Ibbenbüren Ger.
44 A4 Ibi Indon.
86 C4 Ibi Nigeria
82 C2 Ibiá Brazil
79 K4 Ibiapaba, Serra da *h.* Brazil
83 F1 Ibicuí da Cruz *r.* Brazil
82 E2 Ibiraçu Brazil
15 G3 Ibiza Spain
15 G3 Ibiza *i. Balearic Is* Spain
18 F6 Iblei, Monti *mts Sicily* Italy
30 B5 Ibn Buşayyiş *well* S. Arabia
79 K6 Ibotirama Brazil
32 E5 Ibrā' Oman
32 E5 Ibrī Oman
43 B1 Ibuhos *i.* Phil.
41 B9 Ibusuki Japan
78 C6 Ica Peru
81 D4 Içana Brazil
81 D4 Içana *r.* Brazil
73 E3 Iceberg Canyon U.S.A.
28 E3 İçel Turkey
5 B2 Iceland Europe
33 A2 Ichalkaranji India
33 D2 Ichchapuram India
41 B8 Ichifusa-yama *mt* Japan
40 G5 Ichinoseki Japan
25 R4 Ichinskaya Sopka *mt* Rus. Fed.
21 E5 Ichnya Ukr.
42 D4 Ich'ŏn N. Korea
42 D5 Ich'ŏn S. Korea
12 B3 Ichtegem Belgium
13 J4 Ichtershausen Ger.
56 B3 Icy Pt *pt* U.S.A.
56 B3 Icy Strait *chan.* U.S.A.
65 E5 Idabel U.S.A.
62 D2 Idaho *div.* U.S.A.
62 D3 Idaho City U.S.A.
62 D3 Idaho Falls U.S.A.
12 F5 Idar-Oberstein Ger.
87 F2 Idfu Egypt
86 D2 Idhān Awbārī *des.* Libya
87 D2 Idhān Murzūq *des.* Libya
88 B4 Idiofa Congo(Zaire)
54 C3 Iditarod U.S.A.
6 S2 Idivuoma Sweden
28 C6 Idku Egypt
28 F4 Idlib Syria
7 N6 Idre Sweden
13 G4 Idstein Ger.
91 H6 Idutywa S. Africa
7 T8 Iecava Latvia
82 B3 Iepê Brazil
12 A4 Ieper Belgium
19 L7 Ierapetra Greece
89 D4 Ifakara Tanz.
89 E6 Ifanadiana Madag.
86 C4 Ife Nigeria
6 U1 Ifjord Norway
45 D2 Igan Malaysia
82 C3 Igarapava Brazil
24 K3 Igarka Rus. Fed.
34 C6 Igatpuri India
29 K2 Iğdır Turkey
7 P6 Iggesund Sweden
18 C5 Iglesias *Sardinia* Italy
55 K3 Igloolik Can.
58 B4 Ignace Can.
7 U9 Ignalina Lith.
21 C7 İğneada Turkey
19 N4 İğneada Burnu *pt* Turkey
17 Q3 Igorevskaya Rus. Fed.
19 J5 Igoumenitsa Greece
24 H3 Igrim Rus. Fed.
82 B4 Iguaçu *r.* Brazil
82 A4 Iguaçu Falls *waterfall* Arg./Brazil
82 E1 Iguaí Brazil
81 B4 Iguaje, Mesa de *h.* Col.
74 E5 Iguala Mex.
15 G2 Igualada Spain
82 C4 Iguape Brazil
82 D3 Iguarapé Brazil
82 A3 Iguatemi Brazil
82 A3 Iguatemi *r.* Brazil
79 L5 Iguatu Brazil
Iguazú, Cataratas do *waterfall see* Iguaçu Falls
88 A4 Iguéla Gabon
88 D4 Igunga Tanz.
89 E5 Iharaña Madag.
36 C2 Ihbulag Mongolia
89 E6 Ihosy Madag.
42 B2 Ih Tal China
41 F6 Iide-san *mt* Japan
6 U2 Iijärvi *l.* Fin.
6 T4 Iijoki *r.* Fin.
6 U5 Iisalmi Fin.
41 B8 Iizuka Japan
86 C4 Ijebu-Ode Nigeria
29 K1 Ijevan Armenia
12 C2 IJmuiden Neth.
12 D2 IJssel *r.* Neth.
12 D2 IJsselmeer *l.* Neth.
7 S6 Ikaalinen Fin.
91 G2 Ikageleng S. Africa
91 G3 Ikageng S. Africa
19 M6 Ikaria *i.* Greece
7 L8 Ikast Denmark
40 H3 Ikeda Japan
88 C4 Ikela Congo(Zaire)
19 K3 Ikhtiman Bulg.
90 F4 Ikhutseng S. Africa
41 A8 Iki *i.* Japan
21 H6 Iki-Burul Rus. Fed.
86 C4 Ikom Nigeria

89 E6 Ikongo Madag.
21 H6 Ikryanoye Rus. Fed.
88 D4 Ikungu Tanz.
43 B2 Ilagan Phil.
88 D3 Ilaisamis Kenya
30 B3 Īlām Iran
35 F4 Ilam Nepal
86 C4 Ilaro Nigeria
17 J4 Iława Pol.
57 H3 Île-à-la-Crosse Can.
57 H3 Île-à-la-Crosse, Lac l. Can.
88 C4 Ilebo Congo(Zaire)
88 D3 Ileret Kenya
20 G2 Ileza Rus. Fed.
57 K3 Ilford Can.
9 H6 Ilford U.K.
9 C6 Ilfracombe U.K.
28 D1 Ilgaz Turkey
28 D1 Ilgaz D. mts Turkey
28 C2 Ilgın Turkey
81 D5 Ilha Grande Brazil
82 D3 Ilha Grande, Baía da b. Brazil
82 B3 Ilha Grande, Represa resr Brazil
82 B3 Ilha Solteira, Represa resr Brazil
15 B2 Ílhavo Port.
82 E1 Ilhéus Brazil
86 □ Ilhéus Secos ou do Rombo i. Cape Verde
54 C4 Iliamna Lake l. U.S.A.
28 G2 İliç Turkey
43 C4 Iligan Phil.
43 C4 Iligan Bay b. Phil.
20 H2 Il'insko-Podomskoye Rus. Fed.
71 F3 Ilion U.S.A.
33 B3 Ilkal India
9 F5 Ilkeston U.K.
8 F4 Ilkley U.K.
43 B5 Illana Bay b. Phil.
83 B1 Illapel Chile
83 B1 Illapel r. Chile
16 E7 Iller r. Ger.
21 D6 Illichivs'k Ukr.
78 E7 Illimani, Nevado de mt Bol.
68 C5 Illinois div. U.S.A.
68 C5 Illinois r. U.S.A.
68 B5 Illinois and Mississippi Canal canal U.S.A.
21 D5 Illintsi Ukr.
86 C2 Illizi Alg.
13 K4 Ilm r. Ger.
6 S5 Ilmajoki Fin.
13 J4 Ilmenau Ger.
13 J1 Ilmenau r. Ger.
20 D3 Il'men', Ozero l. Rus. Fed.
9 E7 Ilminster U.K.
78 D7 Ilo Peru
43 B4 Iloc i. Phil.
43 B4 Iloilo Phil.
6 W5 Ilomantsi Fin.
86 C4 Ilorin Nigeria
21 F6 Ilovays'k Ukr.
21 G5 Ilovlya Rus. Fed.
21 H5 Ilovlya r. Rus. Fed.
13 J2 Ilsede Ger.
55 N3 Ilulissat Greenland
41 C7 Imabari Japan
41 F6 Imaichi Japan
29 K6 Imām al Ḩamzah Iraq
28 E3 İmamoğlu Turkey
29 K5 Imām Ḩamīd Iraq
40 D2 Iman r. Rus. Fed.
41 A8 Imari Japan
81 E3 Imataca, Serranía de mts Venez.
7 V6 Imatra Fin.
41 E7 Imazu Japan
80 G3 Imbituba Brazil
82 B4 Imbituva Brazil
20 G3 imeni Babushkina Rus. Fed.
21 F2 imeni Chapayeva Turkm.
88 E3 Īmī Eth.
29 M2 İmişli Azer.
42 D6 Imja-do i. S. Korea
42 D4 Imjin r. N. Korea
18 D2 Imola Italy
91 H4 Impendle S. Africa
79 J5 Imperatriz Brazil
18 C3 Imperia Italy
64 C3 Imperial U.S.A.
72 D5 Imperial Beach U.S.A.
73 E5 Imperial Valley v. U.S.A.
88 B3 Impfondo Congo
35 H4 Imphal India
19 L4 İmroz Turkey
28 F5 Imtān Syria
43 A4 Imuruan Bay b. Phil.
41 E7 Ina Japan
78 E6 Inambari r. Peru
86 C2 In Aménas Alg.
51 C4 Inangahua Junction N.Z.
37 F7 Inanwatan Indon.
6 U2 Inari Fin.
6 U2 Inarijärvi l. Fin.
6 T2 Inarijoki r. Fin./Norway
15 H3 Inca Spain
21 C7 İnce Burnu pt Turkey
21 E7 İnce Burnu pt Turkey
28 D3 İncekum Burnu pt Turkey
28 E2 İncesu Turkey
11 E5 Inch Rep. of Ireland
10 C2 Inchard, Loch b. U.K.
10 E4 Inchkeith i. U.K.
42 D5 Inch'ŏn S. Korea
91 K2 Incomati r. Moz.
10 B5 Indaal, Loch in. U.K.
82 D2 Indaiá r. Brazil
82 B2 Indaiá Grande r. Brazil
6 P5 Indalsälven r. Sweden
7 J6 Indalstø Norway
65 B7 Indé Mex.
72 C3 Independence CA U.S.A.
68 B4 Independence IA U.S.A.
65 E4 Independence KS U.S.A.
68 A2 Independence MN U.S.A.
64 E4 Independence MO U.S.A.
70 C6 Independence VA U.S.A.
68 B3 Independence WV U.S.A.
62 C3 Independence Mts mts U.S.A.
26 D2 Inderborskiy Kazak.
33 B2 Indi India
23 G7 India country Asia
68 D2 Indian r. U.S.A.
70 D4 Indiana U.S.A.
68 D5 Indiana div. U.S.A.
68 D5 Indiana Dunes National Lakeshore res. U.S.A.
93 M7 Indian-Antarctic Basin sea feature Ind. Ocean
93 O7 Indian-Antarctic Ridge sea feature Pac. Oc.
68 D6 Indianapolis U.S.A.
Indian Desert see Thar Desert
59 J3 Indian Harbour Can.
71 F3 Indian Lake NY U.S.A.
68 D3 Indian Lake l. MI U.S.A.
70 B4 Indian Lake l. OH U.S.A.
70 D4 Indian Lake l. PA U.S.A.
64 E3 Indianola IA U.S.A.
65 F5 Indianola MS U.S.A.
73 F2 Indian Peak summit U.S.A.
68 E3 Indian River U.S.A.
73 E3 Indian Springs U.S.A.
73 G4 Indian Wells U.S.A.
25 Q2 Indigirka r. Rus. Fed.
19 J2 Inđija Yugo.
56 F2 Indin Lake l. Can.
72 D5 Indio U.S.A.
49 G3 Indispensable Reefs rf Solomon Is
23 K10 Indonesia country Asia
34 C5 Indore India
45 C4 Indramayu, Tanjung pt Indon.
45 B3 Indrapura Indon.
33 C2 Indravati r. India
14 E3 Indre r. France
Indur see Nizamabad
34 B4 Indus r. Pak.
34 A5 Indus, Mouths of the est. Pak.
91 G5 Indwe S. Africa
21 E7 İnebolu Turkey
28 B1 İnegöl Turkey
70 B6 Inez U.S.A.
90 D7 Infanta, Cape hd S. Africa
74 D5 Infiernillo, L. l. Mex.
68 D3 Ingalls U.S.A.
57 J2 Ingalls Lake l. Can.
72 B2 Ingalls, Mt mt U.S.A.
12 B4 Ingelmunster Belgium
83 C4 Ingeniero Jacobacci Arg.
69 G4 Ingersoll Can.
31 G2 Ingichka Uzbek.
8 E3 Ingleborough h. U.K.
55 L2 Inglefield Land reg. Greenland
8 E3 Ingleton U.K.
50 D4 Inglewood Austr.
9 H4 Ingoldmells U.K.
16 E6 Ingolstadt Ger.
59 H4 Ingonish Can.
35 G4 Ingrāj Bāzār India
56 F2 Ingray Lake l. Can.
92 D5 Ingrid Christensen Coast coastal area Ant.
21 H7 Ingushskaya Respublika div. Rus. Fed.
91 K3 Ingwavuma S. Africa
91 K2 Inhaca Moz.
91 K2 Inhaca e dos Portugueses, Ilhas da S. Africa
91 K3 Inhaca, Península pen. Moz.
89 D6 Inhambane Moz.
91 K1 Inhambane div. Moz.
89 D5 Inhaminga Moz.
83 A3 Inhanduízinho r. Brazil
82 D1 Inhaúmas Brazil
81 C4 Inírida r. Col.
11 A4 Inishark i. Rep. of Ireland
11 A4 Inishbofin i. Rep. of Ireland
11 A3 Inishkea North i. Rep. of Ireland
11 A3 Inishkea South i. Rep. of Ireland
11 B4 Inishmaan i. Rep. of Ireland
11 B4 Inishmore i. Rep. of Ireland
11 C3 Inishmurray i. Rep. of Ireland
11 D2 Inishowen pen. Rep. of Ireland
11 E2 Inishowen Head hd Rep. of Ireland
11 D2 Inishtrahull i. Rep. of Ireland
11 D2 Inishtrahull Sound chan. Rep. of Ireland
11 A4 Inishturk i. Rep. of Ireland
31 F2 Inkylap Turkm.
51 D5 Inland Kaikoura Range mts N.Z.
6 O3 Inndyr Norway
Inner Mongolian Aut. Region div. see Nei Monggol Zizhiqu
10 C3 Inner Sound chan. U.K.
48 E3 Innisfail Austr.
16 E7 Innsbruck Austria
11 D4 Inny r. Rep. of Ireland
88 B4 Inongo Congo(Zaire)
16 J4 Inowrocław Pol.
86 C2 In Salah Alg.
20 H4 Insar Rus. Fed.
10 F3 Insch U.K.
42 D6 Insil S. Korea
24 H3 Inta Rus. Fed.
83 D2 Intendente Alvear Arg.
16 C7 Interlaken Switz.
64 E1 International Falls U.S.A.
41 G7 Inubō-zaki pt Japan
58 E2 Inukjuak Can.
54 E3 Inuvik Can.
10 C4 Inveraray U.K.
10 F4 Inverbervie U.K.
51 B7 Invercargill N.Z.
48 F4 Inverell Austr.
10 D3 Invergordon U.K.
10 E4 Inverkeithing U.K.
59 H4 Inverness Can.
10 D3 Inverness U.K.
67 D6 Inverness U.S.A.
10 F3 Inverurie U.K.
48 D5 Investigator Strait chan. Austr.
27 G1 Inya Rus. Fed.
63 C5 Inyokern U.S.A.
72 C3 Inyo Mts mts U.S.A.
88 D4 Inyonga Tanz.
20 H4 Inza Rus. Fed.
21 G4 Inzhavino Rus. Fed.
19 J5 Ioannina Greece
36 G4 Iō-Jima Japan
65 E4 Iola U.S.A.
10 B4 Iona i. U.K.
62 C1 Ione U.S.A.
68 E4 Ionia U.S.A.
19 H5 Ionian Islands is Greece
18 G6 Ionian Sea sea Greece/Italy
Ionoi Nisoi is see Ionian Islands
36 G1 Iony, Ostrov i. Rus. Fed.
29 L1 Iori r. Georgia
19 L6 Ios i. Greece
41 B9 Iō-shima i. Japan
68 A4 Iowa div. U.S.A.
68 B5 Iowa r. U.S.A.
68 B5 Iowa City U.S.A.
64 E3 Iowa Falls U.S.A.
82 C2 Ipameri Brazil
78 D5 Iparía Peru
82 D2 Ipatinga Brazil
21 G6 Ipatovo Rus. Fed.
91 F3 Ipelegeng S. Africa
81 A4 Ipiales Col.
82 E1 Ipiaú Brazil
82 B4 Ipiranga Brazil
45 B2 Ipoh Malaysia
79 L5 Ipojuca r. Brazil
82 B2 Iporá Brazil
88 C3 Ippy C.A.R.
19 M4 İpsala Turkey
9 J5 Ipswich U.K.
55 M3 Iqaluit Can.
80 B2 Iquique Chile
78 D4 Iquitos Peru
31 F5 Īrafshān reg. Iran
41 E7 Irago-misaki pt Japan
19 L6 Irakleia i. Greece
Irakleio see Iraklion
19 L7 Iraklion Greece
82 E1 Iramaia Brazil
23 E6 Iran country Asia
45 D2 Iran, Pegunungan mts Indon.
30 B2 Īrānshāh Iran
31 F5 Īrānshahr Iran
Iranshahr see Fahraj
74 D4 Irapuato Mex.
23 D6 Iraq country Asia
62 G2 Irasville U.S.A.
82 B4 Irati Brazil
28 E5 Irbid Jordan
24 H4 Irbit Rus. Fed.
79 K6 Irecê Brazil
5 C3 Ireland, Republic of country Europe
88 C4 Irema Congo(Zaire)
26 E2 Irgiz Kazak.
42 D6 Iri S. Korea
37 F7 Irian Jaya reg. Indon.
29 L2 Īrī Dagh mt Iran
43 B3 Iriga Phil.
86 B3 Irîgui reg. Mali/Maur.
89 D4 Iringa Tanz.
33 B4 Irinjalakuda India
79 H4 Iriri r. Brazil
8 B4 Irish Sea sea Rep. of Ireland
79 J4 Irituia Brazil
30 C5 'Irj well S. Arabia
36 C1 Irkutsk Rus. Fed.
28 D2 Irmak Turkey
69 F2 Iron Bridge Can.
70 E3 Irondequoit U.S.A.
68 C3 Iron Mountain MI U.S.A.
73 F3 Iron Mountain mt UT U.S.A.
68 C2 Iron River U.S.A.
65 F4 Ironton MO U.S.A.
70 B5 Ironton OH U.S.A.
68 B2 Ironwood U.S.A.
71 F2 Iroquois Can.
68 D5 Iroquois r. U.S.A.
43 C3 Irosin Phil.
41 F7 Irō-zaki pt Japan
21 D5 Irpin' Ukr.
30 A5 Irq al Mazhūr sand dunes S. Arabia
30 B5 'Irq ath Thāmām sand dunes S. Arabia
30 B5 Irq Jahām sand dunes S. Arabia
35 H Irrawaddy r. China/Myanmar
37 B5 Irrawaddy, Mouths of the est. Myanmar
34 C1 Irshad Pass Afgh./Pak.
20 J2 Irta Rus. Fed.
8 E3 Irthing r. U.K.
27 F1 Irtysh r. Kazak./Rus. Fed.
88 C3 Irumu Congo(Zaire)
15 F1 Irún Spain
10 D5 Irvine U.K.
72 D5 Irvine CA U.S.A.
70 B6 Irvine KY U.S.A.
65 D5 Irving U.S.A.
43 B5 Isabela Phil.
78 □ Isabela, Isla i. Galapagos Is Ecuador
75 G6 Isabelia, Cordillera mts Nic.
68 B2 Isabella U.S.A.
72 C4 Isabella Lake l. U.S.A.
68 D2 Isabelle, Pt pt U.S.A.
6 B3 Ísafjarðardjúp est. Iceland
6 B3 Ísafjörður Iceland
41 B8 Isahaya Japan
34 B2 Isà Khel Pak.
20 G1 Isakogorka Rus. Fed.
89 E6 Isalo, Massif de l' mts Madag.
89 E6 Isalo, Parc National de l' nat. park Madag.
81 C4 Isana r. Col.
10 □ Isbister U.K.
18 E4 Ischia, Isola d' i. Italy
81 A4 Iscuande r. Col.
41 E7 Ise Japan
88 C3 Isengi Congo(Zaire)
14 H4 Isère r. France
13 F3 Iserlohn Ger.
13 H2 Isernhagen Ger.
18 F4 Isernia Italy
41 F6 Isesaki Japan
41 E7 Ise-shima National Park Japan
41 E7 Ise-wan b. Japan
86 C4 Iseyin Nigeria
Isfahan see Eşfahan
31 H2 Isfana Kyrg.
29 K5 Isḩāq Iraq
20 J4 Isheyevka Rus. Fed.
40 G3 Ishikari-gawa r. Japan
40 G3 Ishikari-wan b. Japan
40 G5 Ishinomaki Japan
40 G5 Ishinomaki-wan b. Japan
41 G6 Ishioka Japan
41 C8 Ishizuchi-san mt Japan
34 C1 Ishkuman Pak.
68 D2 Ishpeming U.S.A.
31 G2 Ishtykhan Uzbek.
35 G4 Ishurdi Bangl.
78 E7 Isiboro Sécure, Parque Nacional nat. park Bol.
28 B2 Işıklı Turkey
28 B2 Işıklı Barajı resr Turkey
24 J4 Isil'kul' Rus. Fed.
91 J4 Isipingo S. Africa
88 C3 Isiro Congo(Zaire)
31 G2 Iskabad Canal canal Afgh.
28 F3 İskenderun Turkey
28 E1 İskilip Turkey
36 A1 Iskitim Rus. Fed.
19 L3 Iskŭr r. Bulg.
56 C3 Iskut Can.
56 C3 Iskut r. Can.
28 F3 İslahiye Turkey
34 C2 Islamabad Pak.
34 C3 Islam Barrage barrage Pak.
34 B4 Islamgarh Pak.
34 B4 Islamkot Pak.
67 D7 Islamorada U.S.A.
31 F3 Islam Qala Afgh.
43 A4 Island Bay b. Phil.
71 J1 Island Falls U.S.A.
57 L4 Island L. l. Can.
48 D5 Island Lagoon salt flat Austr.
57 L4 Island Lake Can.
68 A2 Island Lake l. U.S.A.
11 F3 Island Magee pen. U.K.
72 A1 Island Mountain U.S.A.
62 E2 Island Park U.S.A.
71 H2 Island Pond U.S.A.
51 E1 Islands, Bay of b. N.Z.
10 B5 Islay i. U.K.
70 E6 Isle of Wight U.S.A.
68 C2 Isle Royale National Park U.S.A.
87 F1 Ismâ'ilîya Egypt
29 M1 İsmayıllı Azer.
7 R5 Isojoki Fin.
89 D5 Isoka Zambia
6 U3 Isokylä Fin.
18 G5 Isola di Capo Rizzuto Italy
28 C3 Isparta Turkey
19 M3 Isperikh Bulg.
31 F5 Ispikan Pak.
29 H1 İspir Turkey
23 C6 Israel country Asia
20 H4 Issa Rus. Fed.
13 E3 Isselburg Ger.
86 B4 Issia Côte d'Ivoire
29 K6 Issin Iraq
14 F4 Issoire France
29 J4 Iṣṭablāt Iraq
28 B1 İstanbul Turkey
İstanbul Boğazı str. see Bosporus
30 C3 Īstgāh-e Eznā Iran
19 K5 Istiaia Greece
81 A3 Istmina Col.
67 D7 Istokpoga, L. l. U.S.A.
18 E2 Istra pen. Croatia
14 G5 Istres France
Istria pen. see Istra
35 G5 Iswaripur Bangl.
79 L6 Itabaianinha Brazil
79 K6 Itaberaba Brazil
82 D2 Itabira Brazil
82 D3 Itabirito Brazil
82 E1 Itabuna Brazil
79 G4 Itacoatiara Brazil
82 B3 Itaguajé Brazil
82 C3 Itaí Brazil
82 A4 Itaimbey r. Para.
79 G4 Itaituba Brazil
80 G3 Itajaí Brazil
82 D3 Itajubá Brazil
35 F5 Itaki India
5 E4 Italy country Europe
79 L7 Itamaraju Brazil
82 D2 Itamarandiba Brazil
82 E2 Itambacuri Brazil
82 E2 Itambacuri r. Brazil
82 D2 Itambé, Pico de mt Brazil
89 E6 Itampolo Madag.
35 H4 Itanagar India
82 D1 Itanguari r. Brazil
82 C4 Itanhaém Brazil
82 E2 Itanhém Brazil
82 E2 Itanhém r. Brazil
82 E2 Itaobim Brazil
82 C2 Itapajipe Brazil
82 E1 Itaparica, Ilha i. Brazil
82 E1 Itapebi Brazil
82 E3 Itapemirim Brazil
82 E3 Itaperuna Brazil
82 E1 Itapetinga Brazil
82 C3 Itapetininga Brazil
82 C3 Itapeva Brazil
79 L6 Itapicuru r. Bahia Brazil
79 K5 Itapicuru r. Maranhão Brazil
79 K4 Itapicuru Mirim Brazil
79 L4 Itapipoca Brazil
82 C4 Itararé Brazil
82 C3 Itararé r. Brazil
34 D5 Itarsi India
82 B2 Itarumã Brazil
43 B1 Itbayat i. Phil.
56 G1 Itchen Lake l. Can.
19 K5 Itea Greece
68 E4 Ithaca MI U.S.A.
70 E3 Ithaca NY U.S.A.
13 H2 Ith Hils ridge Ger.
28 F6 Ithrah S. Arabia
88 C3 Itimbiri r. Congo(Zaire)
82 E2 Itinga Brazil
82 A2 Itiquira Brazil
82 A2 Itiquira r. Brazil
41 F7 Itō Japan
41 E6 Itoigawa Japan
18 C4 Ittiri Sardinia Italy
82 C3 Itu Brazil
81 B3 Ituango Col.
78 D5 Itui r. Brazil
82 C2 Ituiutaba Brazil
88 C4 Itula Congo(Zaire)
82 C2 Itumbiara Brazil
79 G2 Ituni Guyana
79 J5 Itupiranga Brazil
82 B2 Iturama Brazil
82 A4 Iturbe Para.
36 G2 Iturup, Ostrov i. Rus. Fed.
78 E5 Ituxi r. Brazil
16 D4 Itzehoe Ger.
81 C4 Iuaretê Brazil
25 V3 Iultin Rus. Fed.
81 C4 Iutica Brazil
82 B3 Ivaí r. Brazil
6 U2 Ivalo Fin.
6 U2 Ivalojoki r. Fin.
21 C4 Ivanava Belarus
19 H3 Ivangrad Yugo.
50 E2 Ivanhoe Austr.
69 F1 Ivanhoe r. Can.
57 H2 Ivanhoe Lake l. N.W.T. Can.
69 F1 Ivanhoe Lake l. Ont. Can.
17 O5 Ivankiv Ukr.
21 C5 Ivano-Frankivs'k Ukr.
20 G3 Ivanovo Rus. Fed.
20 G3 Ivanovskaya Oblast' div. Rus. Fed.
73 E4 Ivanpah Lake l. U.S.A.
20 J4 Ivanteyevka Rus. Fed.
20 C4 Ivatsevichy Belarus
19 M4 Ivaylovgrad Bulg.
24 H3 Ivdel' Rus. Fed.
82 B3 Ivinheima Brazil
82 B3 Ivinheima r. Brazil
55 O3 Ivittuut Greenland
89 E6 Ivohibe Madag.
Ivory Coast country see Côte d'Ivoire
18 B2 Ivrea Italy
19 M5 İvrindi Turkey
21 H7 Ivris Ugheltekhili pass Georgia
55 L3 Ivujivik Can.
17 N4 Ivyanyets Belarus
40 G5 Iwaizumi Japan
41 G6 Iwaki Japan
40 G4 Iwaki-san volc. Japan
41 C7 Iwakuni Japan
40 G3 Iwamizawa Japan
40 G5 Iwate-san volc. Japan
86 C4 Iwo Nigeria
Iwo Jima see Iō-Jima
20 C4 Iwye Belarus
12 C4 Ixelles Belgium
74 E4 Ixmiquilpán Mex.
91 J5 Ixopo S. Africa
9 H5 Ixworth U.K.
41 C8 Iyo Japan
41 C8 Iyo-nada b. Japan
74 G5 Izabal, L. de l. Guatemala
40 G3 Izari-dake mt Japan
88 D4 Izazi Tanz.
21 H7 Izberbash Rus. Fed.
17 Q3 Izdeshkovo Rus. Fed.
12 B4 Izegem Belgium
30 C4 Īzeh Iran
24 G4 Izhevsk Rus. Fed.
24 G3 Izhma Rus. Fed.
20 K1 Izhma r. Rus. Fed.
21 F4 Izmalkovo Rus. Fed.
21 D6 Izmayil Ukr.
19 M5 İzmir Turkey
19 M5 İzmir Körfezi g. Turkey
28 B1 İznik Gölü l. Turkey
21 G6 Izobil'nyy Rus. Fed.
41 F7 Izu-hantō pen. Japan
41 A7 Izuhara Japan
41 D7 Izumisano Japan
41 C7 Izumo Japan
41 F7 Izu-shotō is Japan
21 C5 Izyaslav Ukr.
21 F5 Izyum Ukr.

J

30 E3 Jaba watercourse Iran
Jabal, Bahr el r. see White Nile
15 E3 Jabalón r. Spain
34 D5 Jabalpur India
28 F3 Jabbūl Syria
48 D3 Jabiru Austr.
28 E4 Jablah Syria
18 G3 Jablanica Bos.-Herz.
79 M5 Jaboatão Brazil
82 C3 Jaboticabal Brazil
15 F1 Jaca Spain
79 K6 Jacaré r. Brazil
79 G5 Jacareacanga Brazil
82 C3 Jacareí Brazil
83 C1 Jáchal r. Arg.
13 L4 Jáchymov Czech Rep.
82 E2 Jacinto Brazil
78 F5 Jaciparaná r. Brazil
68 D1 Jackfish Can.
69 H3 Jack Lake l. Can.
71 H2 Jackman U.S.A.
65 D5 Jacksboro U.S.A.
65 G6 Jackson AL U.S.A.
72 B2 Jackson CA U.S.A.
70 B6 Jackson KY U.S.A.
68 E4 Jackson MI U.S.A.
64 E3 Jackson MN U.S.A.
65 E4 Jackson MO U.S.A.
65 F5 Jackson MS U.S.A.
70 B5 Jackson OH U.S.A.
67 B5 Jackson TN U.S.A.
62 E3 Jackson WY U.S.A.
51 B5 Jackson Head hd N.Z.
62 E2 Jackson L. l. U.S.A.
65 E6 Jackson, Lake U.S.A.
68 D3 Jacksonport U.S.A.
65 E5 Jacksonville AR U.S.A.
67 D6 Jacksonville FL U.S.A.
68 B6 Jacksonville IL U.S.A.
67 E5 Jacksonville NC U.S.A.
65 E6 Jacksonville TX U.S.A.
67 D6 Jacksonville Beach U.S.A.
75 K5 Jacmel Haiti
34 B3 Jacobabad Pak.
79 K6 Jacobina Brazil
73 F3 Jacob Lake U.S.A.
90 F4 Jacobsdal S. Africa
Jacobshavn see Ilulissat
59 H4 Jacques-Cartier, Détroit de chan. Can.
59 G4 Jacques Cartier, Mt mt Can.
59 G4 Jacquet River Can.
83 G1 Jacuí r. Brazil
79 L6 Jacuípe r. Brazil
79 J4 Jacunda Brazil
82 C4 Jacupiranga Brazil
81 C2 Jacura Venez.
33 B2 Jadcherla India
31 F5 Jaddi, Ras pt Pak.
13 G1 Jadebusen b. Ger.
18 G2 Jadovnik mt Bos.-Herz.
87 D1 Jādū Libya
78 C5 Jaén Peru
43 B3 Jaen Phil.
15 E4 Jaén Spain
30 C3 Ja'farābād Iran
Jaffa see Tel Aviv-Yafo
50 B4 Jaffa, C. pt Austr.
33 B4 Jaffna Sri Lanka
71 G3 Jaffrey U.S.A.
34 D3 Jagadhri India
33 B3 Jagalur India
33 C2 Jagdalpur India
91 F4 Jagersfontein S. Africa
34 D2 Jaggang China
31 E5 Jagīn watercourse Iran
Jagok Tso salt l. see Urru Co
34 C3 Jagraon India
13 H5 Jagst r. Ger.
33 B2 Jagtial India
83 G2 Jaguarão Brazil
83 G2 Jaguarão r. Brazil/Uru.
82 C3 Jaguariaíva Brazil
35 F4 Jahanabad India
29 M3 Jahan Dagh mt Iran
34 C4 Jahazpur India
29 K7 Jahmah well Iraq
30 D4 Jahrom Iran
38 B3 Jainca China
34 C4 Jaipur India
34 B4 Jaisalmer India
34 E5 Jaisinghnagar India
34 D5 Jaitgarh mt India
35 E3 Jajarkot Nepal
30 E2 Jajarm Iran
18 G2 Jajce Bos.-Herz.
45 C4 Jakarta Indon.
56 C2 Jakes Corner Can.
34 B5 Jakhan India
31 G4 Jakin mt Afgh.
6 P3 Jäkkvik Sweden
6 S5 Jakobstad Fin.
65 C5 Jal U.S.A.
31 H3 Jalālābād Afgh.
27 F2 Jalal-Abad Kyrg.
34 C3 Jalandhar India
74 E5 Jalapa Enríquez Mex.
7 S5 Jalasjärvi Fin.
35 G4 Jaldhaka r. Bangl.
33 B2 Jaldrug India
82 B3 Jales Brazil
35 F5 Jaleshwar India
34 D5 Jalgaon Maharashtra India
34 C5 Jalgaon Maharashtra India
29 L6 Jalībah Iraq
86 D4 Jalingo Nigeria
34 C6 Jalna India
31 F5 Jālo Iran
15 F2 Jalón r. Spain
35 G4 Jalpaiguri India
87 E2 Jālū Libya
29 K4 Jalūlā Iraq
31 F3 Jām r. Iran
31 F3 Jām reg. Iran
34 D5 Jamai India
53 J8 Jamaica country Caribbean Sea
75 J5 Jamaica Channel Haiti/Jamaica
30 C3 Jamālābād Iran
29 L3 Jamalabad Iran
35 G4 Jamalpur Bangl.
35 F4 Jamalpur India
79 G5 Jamanxim r. Brazil
45 C3 Jambi Indon.
34 C4 Jambo India
45 A2 Jamboaye r. Indon.
43 A5 Jambongan i. Malaysia
44 A5 Jambuair, Tg pt Indon.
29 K4 Jambur Iraq
33 A1 Jambusar India
64 D2 James r. ND U.S.A.
70 D6 James r. VA U.S.A.
34 B4 Jamesabad Pak.
58 D3 James Bay b. Can.
83 D2 James Craik Arg.
55 Q2 Jameson Land reg. Greenland

51 B6 James Pk mt N.Z.
92 B2 James Ross I. i. Ant.
55 J3 James Ross Strait chan. Can.
50 B2 Jamestown Austr.
91 G5 Jamestown S. Africa
64 D2 Jamestown ND U.S.A.
70 D3 Jamestown NY U.S.A.
29 M4 Jamīlābād Iran
33 A2 Jamkhandi India
33 A2 Jamkhed India
33 B3 Jammalamadugu India
34 C2 Jammu Jammu and Kashmir
34 C2 Jammu and Kashmir terr. Asia
34 B5 Jamnagar India
34 D4 Jamni r. India
45 C4 Jampang Kulon Indon.
34 B3 Jampur Pak.
7 T6 Jämsä Fin.
7 T6 Jämsänkoski Fin.
35 F5 Jamshedpur India
35 G5 Jamuna r. Bangl.
82 D1 Janaúba Brazil
82 B2 Jandaia Brazil
30 D3 Jandaq Iran
34 B2 Jandola Pak.
72 B1 Janesville CA U.S.A.
68 C4 Janesville WI U.S.A.
31 E3 Jangal Iran
35 G4 Jangipur India
29 L2 Jānī Beyglū Iran
13 M2 Jänickendorf Ger.
96 J1 Jan Mayen i. Arctic Ocean
29 L5 Jannah Iraq
31 F3 Jannatabad Iran
90 F6 Jansenville S. Africa
82 D1 Januária Brazil
34 C5 Jaora India
23 O6 Japan country Asia
Japan Alps Nat. Park see Chibu-Sangaku Nat. Park
40 C5 Japan, Sea of sea Pac. Oc.
94 E4 Japan Tr. sea feature Pac. Oc.
78 E4 Japurá r. Brazil
35 H4 Jāpvo Mount mt India
81 A3 Jaqué Panama
28 G3 Jarābulus Syria
82 A3 Jaraguari Brazil
28 E5 Jarash Jordan
82 A3 Jardim Brazil
75 J4 Jardines de la Reina, Archipiélago de los is Cuba
42 B2 Jargalang China
36 D2 Jargalant Mongolia
29 K4 Jarmo Iraq
7 P7 Järna Sweden
16 H5 Jarocin Pol.
17 L5 Jarosław Pol.
6 N5 Järpen Sweden
30 C4 Jarrāhi watercourse Iran
38 B2 Jartai China
78 F6 Jarú Brazil
42 A1 Jarud Qi China
7 T7 Järvakandi Estonia
7 T6 Järvenpää Fin.
46 L4 Jarvis Island i. Pac. Oc.
34 B5 Jasdan India
31 E5 Jāsk Iran
17 K6 Jasło Pol.
80 D8 Jason Is is Falkland Is
92 B2 Jason Pen. pen. Ant.
56 F4 Jasper Can.
67 C5 Jasper AL U.S.A.
65 E4 Jasper AR U.S.A.
67 D6 Jasper FL U.S.A.
66 C4 Jasper IN U.S.A.
70 E3 Jasper NY U.S.A.
70 B5 Jasper OH U.S.A.
65 E6 Jasper TX U.S.A.
56 F4 Jasper Nat. Park Can.
29 K5 Jaṣṣān Iraq
17 J6 Jastrzębie-Zdrój Pol.
34 C4 Jaswantpura India
17 J7 Jászberény Hungary
82 B2 Jataí Brazil
79 G4 Jatapu r. Brazil
33 A2 Jath India
34 B4 Jati Pak.
34 B3 Jatoi Pak.
82 C3 Jaú Brazil
78 F4 Jaú r. Brazil
81 F5 Jauaperi r. Brazil
81 D3 Jaua Sarisariñama, Parque Nacional nat. park Venez.
7 S8 Jaunlutriņi Latvia
7 U8 Jaunpiebalga Latvia
35 E4 Jaunpur India
78 F4 Jaú, Parque Nacional do nat. park Brazil
31 F4 Jauri Iran
82 A2 Jauru Brazil
82 B2 Jauru r. Brazil
21 G7 Java Georgia
45 C4 Java i. Indon.
33 B3 Javadi Hills mts India
31 G3 Javand Afgh.
93 M4 Java Ridge sea feature Ind. Ocean
36 D2 Javarthushuu Mongolia
45 D3 Java Sea sea Indon.
Java Trench sea feature see Sunda Trench
13 K2 Jävenitz Ger.
Jawa i. see Java
34 C4 Jawad India
34 B4 Jawai r. India
28 F3 Jawbān Bayk Syria
34 C6 Jawhar India
88 E3 Jawhar Somalia
16 H5 Jawor Pol.
37 F7 Jaya, Pk mt Indon.
37 G7 Jayapura Indon.
35 F4 Jaynagar India
28 F5 Jayrūd Syria
32 B6 Jazā'ir Farasān is S. Arabia
29 M3 Jazvān Iran
29 G4 Jdaide Syria
73 E4 Jean U.S.A.
56 E2 Jean Marie River Can.
59 G2 Jeannin, Lac l. Can.
31 E4 Jebāl Bārez, Kūh-e mts Iran
86 C4 Jebba Nigeria
87 E3 Jebel Abyad Plateau plat. Sudan
34 C3 Jech Doab lowland Pak.
10 F5 Jedburgh U.K.
32 A5 Jedda S. Arabia
18 C6 Jedeida Tunisia
13 K1 Jeetze r. Ger.
71 F3 Jefferson NY U.S.A.
68 C4 Jefferson WI U.S.A.
62 D2 Jefferson r. U.S.A.
64 E4 Jefferson City U.S.A.
72 D2 Jefferson, Mt mt NV U.S.A.
62 B2 Jefferson, Mt volc. OR U.S.A.
66 C4 Jeffersonville U.S.A.
90 F7 Jeffrey's Bay S. Africa
80 E2 Jejuí Guazú r. Para.
7 T8 Jēkabpils Latvia
16 G5 Jelenia Góra Pol.
35 G4 Jelep La pass China
7 S8 Jelgava Latvia
70 A6 Jellico U.S.A.
44 C5 Jemaja i. Indon.
45 D4 Jember Indon.
45 E3 Jempang, Danau l. Indon.
13 K4 Jena Ger.
86 C1 Jendouba Tunisia
28 E5 Jenin West Bank
86 B6 Jenkins U.S.A.
72 A2 Jenner U.S.A.
65 E6 Jennings U.S.A.
57 K4 Jenpeg Can.
50 D4 Jeparit Austr.
82 E1 Jequié Brazil
82 D2 Jequitaí Brazil
82 D2 Jequitaí r. Brazil
82 E2 Jequitinhonha Brazil
82 E2 Jequitinhonha r. Brazil
44 B5 Jerantut Malaysia
87 F4 Jerbar Sudan
75 K5 Jérémie Haiti
15 C4 Jerez de la Frontera Spain
15 C3 Jerez de los Caballeros Spain
19 J5 Jergucat Albania
28 E6 Jericho West Bank
13 L2 Jerichow Ger.
50 E3 Jerilderie Austr.
29 K2 Jermuk Armenia
62 D3 Jerome U.S.A.
14 C2 Jersey i. Channel Is U.K.
71 F4 Jersey City U.S.A.
70 E4 Jersey Shore U.S.A.
66 B4 Jerseyville U.S.A.
79 K5 Jerumenha Brazil
28 E6 Jerusalem Israel/West Bank
50 H3 Jervis B. b. Austr.
50 H3 Jervis Bay Austr.
50 H3 Jervis Bay Terr. Austr.
18 F1 Jesenice Slovenia
18 E3 Jesi Italy
13 L3 Jessen Ger.
7 M6 Jessheim Norway
35 G5 Jessore Bangl.
13 H1 Jesteburg Ger.
67 D6 Jesup U.S.A.
74 F5 Jesús Carranza Mex.
83 D1 Jesús María Arg.
34 B5 Jetalsar India
64 D4 Jetmore U.S.A.
13 F1 Jever Ger.
35 F4 Jha Jha India
34 D3 Jhajjar India
34 C4 Jhajju India
34 A3 Jhal Pak.
35 G5 Jhalakati Bangl.
31 G5 Jhal Jhao Pak.
34 C3 Jhang Pak.
34 D4 Jhansi India
35 F5 Jharia India
35 F5 Jharsuguda India
34 B3 Jhatpat Pak.
34 C2 Jhelum Pak.
34 C2 Jhelum r. Pak.
35 G5 Jhenida Bangl.
34 B4 Jhudo Pak.
35 F4 Jhumritilaiya India
34 C3 Jhunjhunūn India
38 C3 Jiachuan China
38 F4 Jiading China
39 D5 Jiahe China
39 B4 Jiajiang China
38 B3 Jialing Jiang r. China
40 B1 Jiamusi China
39 E5 Ji'an Jiangxi China
39 E5 Ji'an Jiangxi China
42 D3 Ji'an China
38 F1 Jianchang China
39 F4 Jiande China
39 B4 Jiang'an China
39 C4 Jiangbei China
39 A6 Jiangcheng China
39 B5 Jiangchuan China
38 B4 Jiange China
39 D5 Jianghua China
39 C4 Jiangjin China
39 C5 Jiangkou China
39 E5 Jiangle China
39 D4 Jiangling China
38 B3 Jiangluozhen China
39 D6 Jiangmen China
39 F4 Jiangshan China
38 F3 Jiangsu div. China
39 E5 Jiangxi div. China
38 D3 Jiang Xian China
38 F4 Jiangyin China
39 D5 Jiangyong China
38 B4 Jiangyou China
38 F3 Jianhu China
39 D6 Jian Jiang r. China
39 D4 Jianli China
39 E5 Jianning China
39 F5 Jian'ou China
38 F1 Jianping Liaoning China
38 F1 Jianping Liaoning China
39 C4 Jianshi China
39 B6 Jianshui China
39 F5 Jianyang Fujian China
39 B4 Jianyang Sichuan China
38 D2 Jiaocheng China
38 E2 Jiaohe Hebei China
42 D2 Jiaohe China
39 F4 Jiaojiang China
42 A2 Jiaolai r. Nei Monggol China
38 F2 Jiaolai r. Shandong China
39 E5 Jiaoling China
38 F3 Jiaonan China
38 F2 Jiao Xian China
38 F2 Jiaozhou Wan b. China
38 D3 Jiaozuo China
42 D2 Jiapigou China
38 F3 Jiashan China
38 D2 Jia Xian China
38 F4 Jiaxing China
39 D4 Jiayu China
36 B3 Jiayuguan China
39 E6 Jiazi China
30 B6 Jibāl al Ḩawshah mts S. Arabia
Jiddah see Jedda
32 E6 Jiddat al Ḩarāsīs gravel area Oman
42 F1 Jidong China
38 B2 Jiehebe China
6 Q2 Jiehkkevarri mt Norway
39 E6 Jieshi China
39 E6 Jieshi Wan b. China
38 E3 Jieshou China
6 T2 Iešjávri l. Norway
39 E6 Jiexi China
38 D2 Jiexiu China
39 E6 Jieyang China
7 T9 Jieznas Lith.
38 A3 Jigzhi China
16 G6 Jihlava Czech Rep.
31 F3 Jija Sarai Afgh.
88 E3 Jijiga Eth.
39 A4 Jiju China
31 H3 Jilga r. Afgh.
34 D2 Jilganang Kol, S. salt l. China/Jammu and Kashmir
88 E3 Jilib Somalia
42 D2 Jilin China
42 C2 Jilin div. China
38 A2 Jiling China
42 C2 Jilin Handa Ling mts China
88 D3 Jīma Eth.
74 D3 Jiménez Chihuahua Mex.
74 E3 Jiménez Tamaulipas Mex.
38 F2 Jimo China
71 F4 Jim Thorpe U.S.A.
38 E2 Jinan China
38 B2 Jinchang China
38 D3 Jincheng China
38 B4 Jinchuan China
34 D3 Jind India
50 G4 Jindabyne Austr.
50 F3 Jindera Austr.
16 G6 Jindřichův Hradec Czech Rep.
38 C3 Jing r. China
39 E4 Jing'an China
38 C2 Jingbian China
38 C3 Jingchuan China
39 F4 Jingde China
39 E4 Jingdezhen China
39 E5 Jinggangshan China
39 E4 Jinggongqiao China
38 E2 Jinghai China
37 C4 Jinghong China
38 F3 Jingjiang China
38 D2 Jingle China
38 D4 Jingmen China
38 B3 Jingning China
42 E2 Jingpo China
42 E2 Jingpo Hu resr China
38 B2 Jingtai China
39 C6 Jingxi China
39 F4 Jing Xian Anhui China
39 C5 Jing Xian Hunan China
42 D2 Jingyu China
38 B2 Jingyuan China
38 F3 Jinhu China
39 F4 Jinhua China
38 D1 Jining Nei Monggol China
38 E3 Jining Shandong China
88 D3 Jinja Uganda
39 F5 Jinjiang China
39 E4 Jin Jiang r. China
88 D3 Jinka Eth.
42 A3 Jinlingsi China
39 C7 Jinmu Jiao pt China
74 G6 Jinotepe Nic.
39 C5 Jinping Guizhou China
39 B6 Jinping Yunnan China
39 A5 Jinping Shan mts China
39 C5 Jinsha China
Jinsha Jiang r. see Yangtze
38 F4 Jinshan China
39 D4 Jinshi China
38 B4 Jintang China
43 B4 Jintotolo i. Phil.
43 B4 Jintotolo Channel Phil.
34 D6 Jintur India
39 E5 Jinxi Jiangxi China
42 A3 Jinxi China
42 A3 Jin Xian Liaoning China
42 A4 Jin Xian Liaoning China
39 E4 Jinxian China
38 E3 Jinxiang Shandong China
39 F5 Jinxiang Zhejiang China
39 B5 Jinyang China
39 F4 Jinyun China
38 E4 Jinzhai China
42 A3 Jinzhou China
42 A4 Jinzhou Wan b. China
78 F5 Jiparaná r. Brazil
78 B4 Jipijapa Ecuador
31 H2 Jirgatol Tajik.
31 E4 Jīroft Iran
30 C6 Jirwan well S. Arabia
39 C4 Jishou China
39 E5 Jishui China
28 F4 Jisr ash Shughūr Syria
44 B4 Jitra Malaysia
38 C2 Jiudengkou China
38 B4 Jiuding Shan mt China
38 C3 Jiufoping China
39 E4 Jiujiang Jiangxi China
39 E4 Jiujiang Jiangxi China
39 E4 Jiuling Shan mts China
39 A4 Jiulong China
42 A2 Jiumiao China
42 B5 Jiurongcheng China
42 C1 Jiutai China
39 C5 Jiuxu China
31 F5 Jiwani Pak.
39 F4 Jixi Anhui China
42 F1 Jixi China
38 E2 Ji Xian Hebei China
38 E3 Ji Xian Henan China
40 B1 Jixian China
38 D3 Jiyuan China
32 B6 Jīzān S. Arabia
41 C7 Jizō-zaki pt Japan
79 M5 João Pessoa Brazil
82 C2 João Pinheiro Brazil
72 C2 Job Peak summit U.S.A.
13 L4 Jocketa Ger.
35 F5 Joda India
34 C4 Jodhpur India
6 V5 Joensuu Fin.
41 F6 Jōetsu Japan
89 D6 Jofane Moz.
56 F4 Joffre, Mt mt Can.
7 U7 Jõgeva Estonia
7 U7 Jõgua Estonia
91 G3 Johannesburg S. Africa
72 D4 Johannesburg U.S.A.
34 E5 Johilla r. India
62 C2 John Day U.S.A.
62 B2 John Day r. U.S.A.
56 F3 John d'Or Prairie Can.
70 D6 John H. Kerr Res. resr U.S.A.
10 E2 John o'Groats U.K.
67 D4 Johnson City U.S.A.
56 C2 Johnson's Crossing Can.
67 D5 Johnston U.S.A.
10 D5 Johnstone U.K.
46 L2 Johnston I. i. Pac. Oc.
11 D5 Johnstown Rep. of Ireland
71 F3 Johnstown NY U.S.A.
70 D4 Johnstown PA U.S.A.
69 F3 Johnswood U.S.A.
45 B2 Johor Bahru Malaysia
7 U7 Jõhvi Estonia
80 G3 Joinville Brazil
14 G2 Joinville France
92 B2 Joinville I. i. Ant.
6 Q3 Jokkmokk Sweden
6 F4 Jökulsá á Brú r. Iceland
6 E3 Jökulsá á Fjöllum r. Iceland
6 F4 Jökulsá í Fljótsdal r. Iceland
30 B2 Jolfa Iran
68 C5 Joliet U.S.A.
58 F4 Joliette Can.
43 B5 Jolo Phil.
43 B5 Jolo i. Phil.
43 B3 Jomalig i. Phil.
45 D4 Jombang Indon.
7 T9 Jonava Lith.
38 B3 Jonê China
65 F5 Jonesboro AR U.S.A.
71 K2 Jonesboro ME U.S.A.
92 A3 Jones Mts mts Ant.
71 K2 Jonesport U.S.A.
55 K2 Jones Sound chan. Can.
70 B6 Jonesville U.S.A.
87 F4 Jonglei Canal canal Sudan
35 E5 Jonk r. India
7 O8 Jönköping Sweden
59 F4 Jonquière Can.
65 E4 Joplin U.S.A.
71 E5 Joppatowne U.S.A.
34 D4 Jora India
62 F2 Jordan U.S.A.
23 C6 Jordan country Asia
28 E6 Jordan r. Asia
62 E3 Jordan r. U.S.A.
62 C3 Jordan Valley U.S.A.
82 B4 Jordão r. Brazil
7 N6 Jordet Norway
35 H4 Jorhat India
13 H1 Jork Ger.
6 R4 Jörn Sweden
7 U5 Joroinen Fin.
7 K7 Jørpeland Norway
86 C4 Jos Nigeria
43 C5 Jose Abad Santos Phil.
80 B6 José de San Martin Arg.
82 A2 Joselândia Brazil
83 F2 José Pedro Varela Uru.
48 C3 Joseph Bonaparte Gulf g. Austr.
73 G4 Joseph City U.S.A.
59 G3 Joseph, Lac l. Can.
55 M4 Joseph, Lake l. Can.
41 F6 Jōshinetsu-kōgen National Park Japan
73 E5 Joshua Tree National Monument res. U.S.A.
86 C4 Jos Plateau plat. Nigeria
7 K6 Jostedalsbreen Nasjonalpark nat. park Norway
7 L6 Jotunheimen Nasjonalpark nat. park Norway
90 E6 Joubertina S. Africa
91 G3 Jouberton S. Africa
12 D2 Joure Neth.
7 U6 Joutsa Fin.
7 V6 Joutseno Fin.
12 E5 Jouy-aux-Arches France
35 H4 Jowai India
11 B4 Joyce's Country reg. Rep. of Ireland
62 A1 Juan de Fuca, Str. of chan. U.S.A.
89 E5 Juan de Nova i. Ind. Ocean
76 B6 Juan Fernández, Islas is Chile
6 V5 Juankoski Fin.
79 K5 Juàzeiro Brazil
79 L5 Juàzeiro do Norte Brazil
87 F4 Juba Sudan
88 E3 Jubba r. Somalia
72 D4 Jubilee Pass U.S.A.
15 F3 Júcar r. Spain
74 E5 Juchitán Mex.
82 E2 Jucururu r. Brazil
7 J7 Judaberg Norway
29 H6 Judaidat al Hamir Iraq
29 H6 Judayyidat 'Ar'ar well Iraq
16 G7 Judenburg Austria
7 M9 Juelsminde Denmark
38 C2 Juh China
38 F1 Juhua Dao i. China
75 G6 Juigalpa Nic.
12 F1 Juist i. Ger.
82 D3 Juiz de Fora Brazil
78 E8 Julaca Bol.
64 C3 Julesburg U.S.A.
78 D7 Juliaca Peru
12 C2 Julianadorp Neth.
79 G3 Juliana Top summit Suriname
12 E4 Jülich Ger.
18 E1 Julijske Alpe mts Slovenia
83 E2 Julio, 9 de Arg.
78 C5 Jumbilla Peru
15 F3 Jumilla Spain
35 E3 Jumla Nepal
34 B5 Junagadh India
35 E6 Junagarh India
38 F3 Junan China
83 B2 Juncal mt Chile
83 D4 Juncal, L. l. Arg.
65 D6 Junction TX U.S.A.
63 D4 Junction UT U.S.A.
64 D4 Junction City U.S.A.
82 C3 Jundiaí Brazil
56 C3 Juneau U.S.A.
50 F3 Junee Austr.
16 C7 Jungfrau mt Switz.
36 A2 Junggar Pendi basin China
34 A4 Jungshahi Pak.
70 E4 Juniata r. U.S.A.
83 E2 Junín Arg.
83 B3 Junín de los Andes Arg.
71 K1 Juniper Can.
72 B3 Junipero Serro Peak summit U.S.A.
39 B4 Junlian China
33 A2 Junnar India
6 P5 Junsele Sweden
62 C3 Juntura U.S.A.
38 D3 Jun Xian China
7 T8 Juodupė Lith.
82 C4 Juquiá Brazil
87 E4 Jur r. Sudan
10 C4 Jura i. U.K.
14 H3 Jura mts France/Switz.
82 E1 Juraci Brazil
81 A3 Juradó Col.
10 C5 Jura, Sound of chan. U.K.
7 S9 Jurbarkas Lith.
28 E6 Jurf ed Darāwīsh Jordan
13 L1 Jürgenstorf Ger.
42 A1 Jurh China
42 A1 Jurhe China
35 G2 Jurhen Ul Shan mts China
7 S8 Jūrmala Latvia
6 U4 Jurmu Fin.
38 F4 Jurong China
44 □ Jurong Sing.
78 E4 Juruá r. Brazil
79 G6 Juruena r. Brazil
6 R5 Jurva Fin.
30 E2 Jūshqān Iran
83 D2 Justo Daract Arg.
78 E4 Jutaí r. Brazil
13 M3 Jüterbog Ger.
82 A3 Juti Brazil
74 G6 Jutiapa Guatemala
74 G6 Juticalpa Honduras
6 P3 Jutis Sweden
6 V5 Juuka Fin.
7 U6 Juva Fin.
75 H4 Juventud, Isla de la i. Cuba
31 F4 Juwain Afgh.
38 F3 Ju Xian China
38 A1 Juyan China
38 E3 Juye China
31 E3 Jūymand Iran
30 D4 Jūyom Iran
89 C6 Jwaneng Botswana
7 T5 Jyväskylä Fin.

K

34 D2 K2 mt China/Jammu and Kashmir
42 C4 Ka i. N. Korea
31 E2 Kaakhka Turkm.
72 □1 Kaala mt U.S.A.
88 E4 Kaambooni Kenya
7 S6 Kaarina Fin.
13 K1 Kaarßen Ger.
12 E3 Kaarst Ger.
6 V5 Kaavi Fin.
31 F2 Kabakly Turkm.
86 A4 Kabala Sierra Leone
88 C4 Kabale Uganda
88 C4 Kabalo Congo(Zaire)
88 C4 Kabambare Congo(Zaire)
89 C5 Kabangu Congo(Zaire)
44 A5 Kabanjahe Indon.
21 G7 Kabardino-Balkarskaya Respublika div. Rus. Fed.
88 C4 Kabare Congo(Zaire)
6 R3 Kåbdalis Sweden
68 E1 Kabenung Lake l. Can.
58 D4 Kabinakagami Lake l. Can.
88 C4 Kabinda Congo(Zaire)
30 B3 Kabīrkūh mts Iran
34 B3 Kabirwala Pak.
88 B3 Kabo C.A.R.
89 C5 Kabompo Zambia
88 C4 Kabongo Congo(Zaire)
31 F3 Kabūdeh Iran
31 E2 Kabūd Gonbad Iran
30 C3 Kabūd Rāhang Iran
43 B2 Kabugao Phil.
31 H3 Kābul Afgh.
31 H3 Kabul r. Afgh.
43 C6 Kaburuang i. Indon.
89 C5 Kabwe Zambia
31 F4 Kacha Kuh mts Iran/Pak.
21 H5 Kachalinskaya Rus. Fed.
34 B5 Kachchh, Gulf of g. India
34 C1 Kach Pass Afgh.
36 C1 Kachug Rus. Fed.
29 H1 Kaçkar Dağı mt Turkey
33 B4 Kadaiyanallur India
34 A3 Kadanai r. Afgh./Pak.
44 A2 Kadan Kyun i. Myanmar
49 H3 Kadavu i. Fiji
49 H3 Kadavu Passage chan. Fiji
86 B4 Kade Ghana
29 K5 Kādhimain Iraq
34 C5 Kadi India
28 B1 Kadıköy Turkey
50 A2 Kadina Austr.
28 D2 Kadınhanı Turkey
86 B3 Kadiolo Mali
33 B3 Kadiri India
28 F3 Kadirli Turkey
33 A4 Kadmat i. India
64 C3 Kadoka U.S.A.
89 C5 Kadoma Zimbabwe
87 E3 Kadugli Sudan
86 C3 Kaduna Nigeria
86 C3 Kaduna r. Nigeria
35 J3 Kadusam mt China
20 F3 Kaduy Rus. Fed.
33 A2 Kadwa r. India
20 G3 Kadyy Rus. Fed.
24 G3 Kadzherom Rus. Fed.
42 C4 Kaechon N. Korea
86 A3 Kaédi Maur.
87 D3 Kaélé Cameroon
72 □1 Kaena Pt pt U.S.A.
51 D1 Kaeo N.Z.
42 D5 Kaesŏng N. Korea
28 F6 Kāf S. Arabia
89 C4 Kafakumba Congo(Zaire)
86 A3 Kaffrine Senegal
19 L5 Kafireas, Akra pt Greece
28 C6 Kafr el Sheik Egypt
89 C5 Kafue Zambia
89 C5 Kafue r. Zambia
89 C5 Kafue National Park Zambia
41 E6 Kaga Japan
88 B3 Kaga Bandoro C.A.R.
21 G6 Kagal'nitskaya Rus. Fed.
31 G2 Kagan Uzbek.
69 F3 Kagawong Can.
6 R4 Kåge Sweden
29 J1 Kağızman Turkey
45 A3 Kagologolo Indon.
41 B9 Kagoshima Japan
30 C2 Kahak Iran
72 □1 Kahaluu U.S.A.
88 D4 Kahama Tanz.
72 □1 Kahana U.S.A.
21 D5 Kaharlyk Ukr.
45 D3 Kahayan r. Indon.
88 B4 Kahemba Congo(Zaire)
51 A6 Kaherekoau Mts mts N.Z.
13 K4 Kahla Ger.
Kahnu see Kahnūj
31 E5 Kahnūj Iran
68 B5 Kahoka U.S.A.
72 □2 Kahoolawe i. U.S.A.
28 F3 Kahraman Maraş Turkey
34 B3 Kahror Pak.
28 G3 Kahta Turkey
72 □1 Kahuku U.S.A.
72 □1 Kahuku Pt pt U.S.A.
72 □2 Kahului U.S.A.
51 D4 Kahurangi Point pt N.Z.
34 C2 Kahuta Pak.
88 C4 Kahuzi-Biega, Parc National du nat. park Congo(Zaire)
86 C4 Kaiama Nigeria
51 D5 Kaiapoi N.Z.
73 F3 Kaibab U.S.A.
63 D4 Kaibab Plat. plat. U.S.A.
37 F7 Kai Besar i. Indon.
73 G3 Kaibito U.S.A.
73 G3 Kaibito Plateau plat. U.S.A.
38 E3 Kaifeng Henan China
38 E3 Kaifeng Henan China
39 F4 Kaihua China
90 D4 Kaiingveld reg. S. Africa
38 C4 Kaijiang China
37 F7 Kai Kecil i. Indon.
37 F7 Kai, Kepulauan is Indon.
51 D5 Kaikoura N.Z.
51 D5 Kaikoura Peninsula N.Z.
39 □ Kai Kung Leng h. H.K. China
86 A4 Kailahun Sierra Leone
Kailas mt see Kangrinboqê Feng
35 G4 Kailashahar India
Kailas Range mts see Gangdisê Shan
39 C5 Kaili China
42 A2 Kailu China
72 □1 Kailua U.S.A.
72 □2 Kailua Kona U.S.A.
51 E2 Kaimai Range h. N.Z.
48 D2 Kaimana Indon.
51 E3 Kaimanawa Mountains N.Z.
35 H2 Kaimar China
34 E4 Kaimur Range h. India
7 S7 Käina Estonia
41 D8 Kainan Japan
41 D7 Kainan Japan
86 C3 Kainji Lake National Park Nigeria
86 C3 Kainji Reservoir Nigeria
51 E2 Kaipara Harbour in. N.Z.
73 G3 Kaiparowits Plateau plat. U.S.A.
39 D6 Kaiping China
59 J3 Kaipokok Bay in. Can.
34 D3 Kairana India
86 D1 Kairouan Tunisia
13 F5 Kaiserslautern Ger.
42 E2 Kaishantun China
51 D1 Kaitaia N.Z.
51 B7 Kaitangata N.Z.
51 E3 Kaitawa N.Z.
34 D3 Kaithal India
6 R3 Kaitum Sweden
48 C2 Kaiwatu Indon.
72 □2 Kaiwi Channel U.S.A.
38 C4 Kai Xian China

30 D4 Kavār Iran
33 A4 Kavaratti *i.* India
19 N3 Kavarna Bulg.
33 A3 Kāveri *r.* India
33 B4 Kāveri *r.* India
30 D4 Kavīr *des.* Iran
30 D3 Kavir *salt flat* Iran
30 D3 Kavir *salt flat* Iran
30 D3 Kavir, Dasht-e *des.* Iran
30 D3 Kavīr-e Hāj Ali Qoli *salt l.* Iran
31 E3 Kavir-i-Namak *salt flat* Iran
41 F7 Kawagoe Japan
41 F7 Kawaguchi Japan
72 □2 Kawaihae U.S.A.
51 E1 Kawakawa N.Z.
89 C4 Kawambwa Zambia
58 E5 Kawartha Lakes *l.* Can.
41 F7 Kawasaki Japan
51 E2 Kawau I. *i.* N.Z.
59 G2 Kawawachikamach Can.
51 F3 Kawerau N.Z.
51 E3 Kawhia N.Z.
51 E3 Kawhia Harbour *in.* N.Z.
72 D3 Kawich Range *mts* U.S.A.
44 A1 Kawkareik Myanmar
44 A1 Kawludo Myanmar
30 E6 Kawr, J. *mt* Oman
44 A3 Kawthaung Myanmar
86 B3 Kaya Burkina
28 F2 Kayadibi Turkey
25 M2 Kayak Rus. Fed.
45 E2 Kayan *r.* Indon.
88 C4 Kayanaza Burundi
33 B4 Kayankulam India
62 F3 Kaycee U.S.A.
89 C4 Kayembe-Mukulu Congo(Zaire)
73 G3 Kayenta U.S.A.
86 A3 Kayes Mali
86 A4 Kayima Sierra Leone
27 F2 Kaynar Kazak.
28 F2 Kaynar Turkey
28 F3 Kaypak Turkey
21 H5 Kaysatskoye Rus. Fed.
28 E2 Kayseri Turkey
45 B3 Kayuagung Indon.
24 K3 Kayyerkan Rus. Fed.
25 P2 Kazach'ye Rus. Fed.
Kazakh *see* Qazax
26 F1 Kazakskiy Melkosopochnik *reg.* Kazak.
23 E5 Kazakstan *country* Asia
20 J4 Kazan' Rus. Fed.
57 K2 Kazan *r.* Can.
28 D3 Kazancı Turkey
20 J4 Kazanka *r.* Rus. Fed.
19 L3 Kazanlŭk Bulg.
36 G4 Kazan-rettō *is* Japan
21 G5 Kazanskaya Rus. Fed.
21 H7 Kazbek *mt* Georgia/Rus. Fed.
19 M5 Kaz Dağı *mts* Turkey
30 C4 Kāzerūn Iran
20 J2 Kazhim Rus. Fed.
31 F5 Kazhmak *r.* Pak.
17 K6 Kazincbarcika Hungary
31 F5 Kazmīr Iran
21 H7 Kazret'i Georgia
21 J5 Kaztalovka Kazak.
40 G4 Kazuno Japan
24 H3 Kazymskiy Mys Rus. Fed.
19 L6 Kea *i.* Greece
11 E3 Keady U.K.
72 □2 Kealakekua Bay *b.* U.S.A.
29 M4 K-e-Alvand *mt* Iran
73 G4 Keams Canyon U.S.A.
64 D3 Kearney U.S.A.
73 G5 Kearny U.S.A.
28 G2 Keban Turkey
28 G2 Keban Barajı *resr* Turkey
86 A3 Kébémèr Senegal
28 F4 Kebīr *r.* Lebanon/Syria
87 E3 Kebkabiya Sudan
6 Q3 Kebnekaise *mt* Sweden
10 B2 Kebock Head *hd* U.K.
88 E3 K'ebrī Dehar Eth.
45 C4 Kebumen Indon.
56 D3 Kechika *r.* Can.
28 C3 Keçiborlu Turkey
17 J7 Kecskemét Hungary
29 H1 K'eda Georgia
7 S9 Kėdainiai Lith.
29 L4 K-e Dalakhāni *h.* Iraq
34 D3 Kedar Kanta *mt* India
34 D3 Kedarnath Peak *mt* India
59 G4 Kedgwick Can.
45 D4 Kediri Indon.
86 A3 Kédougou Senegal
56 D2 Keele *r.* Can.
56 C2 Keele Pk *summit* Can.
63 C4 Keeler U.S.A.
Keeling Is *terr. see* Cocos Is
43 A5 Keenapusan *i.* Phil.
73 G3 Keene U.S.A.
10 F4 Keen, Mount *mt* U.K.
50 H1 Keepit Reservoir Austr.
12 C3 Keerbergen Belgium
89 B6 Keetmanshoop Namibia
57 L6 Keewatin Can.
57 L5 Keewatin U.S.A.
19 J5 Kefallonia *i.* Greece
37 E7 Kefamenanu Indon.
6 B4 Keflavík Iceland
33 C5 Kegalla Sri Lanka
27 F2 Kegen Kazak.
59 G2 Keglo, Baie de *b.* Can.
21 H6 Kegul'ta Rus. Fed.
7 T7 Kehra Estonia
8 F4 Keighley U.K.
7 T7 Keila Estonia
90 D4 Keimoes S. Africa
6 U5 Keitele Fin.
6 T5 Keitele *l.* Fin.
50 C4 Keith Austr.
10 F3 Keith U.K.
56 E1 Keith Arm *b.* Can.
59 G5 Kejimkujik National Park Can.
72 □2 Kekaha U.S.A.
17 K7 Kékes *mt* Hungary
34 C4 Kekri India
27 F6 Kelai *i.* Maldives
38 D2 Kelan China
35 B2 Kelang Malaysia
44 B4 Kelantan *r.* Malaysia
12 E4 Kelberg Ger.
13 K6 Kelheim Ger.
18 D6 Kelibia Tunisia
31 G2 Kelif Turkm.
31 F2 Kelifskiy Uzboy *marsh* Turkm.
13 G4 Kelkheim (Taunus) Ger.
29 G1 Kelkit Turkey
28 F1 Kelkit *r.* Turkey
56 E2 Keller Lake *l.* Can.
70 B4 Kelleys I. *i.* U.S.A.
62 C2 Kellogg U.S.A.
6 V3 Kelloselkä Fin.
11 E4 Kells Rep. of Ireland
7 S9 Kelmė Lith.
12 E4 Kelmis Belgium
87 D4 Kelo Chad
56 F5 Kelowna Can.
56 D4 Kelsey Bay Can.
72 A2 Kelseyville U.S.A.
10 F5 Kelso U.K.
62 B2 Kelso *CA* U.S.A.
62 B2 Kelso *WA* U.S.A.
45 B2 Keluang Malaysia
57 J4 Kelvington Can.
20 E1 Kem' Rus. Fed.
20 E1 Kem' *r.* Rus. Fed.
29 G2 Kemah Turkey
28 G2 Kemaliye Turkey
19 M5 Kemalpaşa Turkey
56 D4 Kemano Can.
28 C3 Kemer *Antalya* Turkey
28 B3 Kemer *Muğla* Turkey
28 B3 Kemer Barajı *resr* Turkey
36 A1 Kemerovo Rus. Fed.
6 T4 Kemi Fin.
6 U3 Kemijärvi Fin.
6 U3 Kemijärvi *l.* Fin.
6 T3 Kemijoki *r.* Fin.
62 E3 Kemmerer U.S.A.
13 K5 Kemnath Ger.
10 F3 Kemnay U.K.
6 T4 Kempele Fin.
12 E3 Kempen Ger.
12 C3 Kempen *reg.* Belgium
65 D5 Kemp, L. *l.* U.S.A.
50 D4 Kemp Land *reg.* Ant.
92 B2 Kemp Pen. *pen.* Ant.
67 E7 Kemp's Bay Bahamas
16 E7 Kempten (Allgäu) Ger.
58 F4 Kempt, L. *l.* Can.
91 H3 Kempton Park S. Africa
69 K3 Kemptville Can.
45 D4 Kemujan *i.* Indon.
34 E4 Ken *r.* India
54 C3 Kenai U.S.A.
54 C4 Kenai Mts *mts* U.S.A.
31 F3 Kenar-e-Kapeh Afgh.
8 E3 Kendal U.K.
57 M2 Kendall, Cape *hd* Can.
68 E5 Kendallville U.S.A.
45 C4 Kendang, Gunung *volc.* Indon.
37 E7 Kendari Indon.
45 D3 Kendawangan Indon.
87 D3 Kendégué Chad
35 F5 Kendrāparha India
62 C2 Kendrick U.S.A.
73 G4 Kendrick Peak *summit* U.S.A.
50 G1 Kenebri Austr.
65 D6 Kenedy U.S.A.
86 A4 Kenema Sierra Leone
88 B4 Kenge Congo(Zaire)
37 B4 Kengtung Myanmar
90 D4 Kenhardt S. Africa
86 A3 Kéniéba Mali
86 B1 Kénitra Morocco
38 F2 Kenli China
11 B6 Kenmare Rep. of Ireland
64 C1 Kenmare U.S.A.
11 A6 Kenmare River *in.* Rep. of Ireland
12 E5 Kenn Ger.
63 G5 Kenna U.S.A.
71 J2 Kennebec *r.* U.S.A.
71 H3 Kennebunk U.S.A.
71 H3 Kennebunkport U.S.A.
65 F6 Kenner U.S.A.
9 F6 Kennet *r.* U.K.
65 F4 Kennett U.S.A.
62 C2 Kennewick U.S.A.
56 B2 Keno Can.
69 G1 Kenogami Lake Can.
69 G1 Kenogamissi Lake *l.* Can.
57 L5 Kenora Can.
68 D4 Kenosha U.S.A.
20 F2 Kenozero, Ozero *l.* Rus. Fed.
71 G4 Kent *CT* U.S.A.
65 B6 Kent *TX* U.S.A.
62 B2 Kent *WA* U.S.A.
8 E3 Kent *r.* U.K.
91 H6 Kentani S. Africa
68 D5 Kentland U.S.A.
70 B4 Kenton U.S.A.
70 A6 Kentucky *div.* U.S.A.
61 K4 Kentucky *r. KY* U.S.A.
67 B4 Kentucky Lake *l.* U.S.A.
59 H4 Kentville Can.
65 F6 Kentwood *LA* U.S.A.
68 E4 Kentwood *MI* U.S.A.
85 G5 Kenya *country* Africa
Kenya, Mount *mt see* Kirinyaga
68 A3 Kenyon U.S.A.
92 B2 Kenyon Pen. *pen.* Ant.
72 □2 Keokea U.S.A.
68 B5 Keokuk U.S.A.
44 C1 Keo Neua, Col de *pass* Laos/Vietnam
68 B5 Keosauqua U.S.A.
48 F4 Keppel Bay *b.* Austr.
44 □ Keppel Harbour *chan.* Sing.
28 B2 Kepsut Turkey
31 E4 Kerāh Iran
33 A4 Kerala *div.* India
50 D3 Kerang Austr.
86 C4 Kéran, Parc National de la *nat. park* Togo
7 T6 Kerava Fin.
15 G4 Kerba Alg.
21 F6 Kerch Ukr.
48 E2 Kerema P.N.G.
56 F5 Keremeos Can.
21 E7 Kerempe Burun *pt* Turkey
88 D2 Keren Eritrea
30 E2 Kergeli Turkm.
93 J7 Kerguélen *i.* Ind. Ocean
93 J7 Kerguelen Ridge *sea feature* Ind. Ocean
88 D4 Kericho Kenya
51 D1 Kerikeri N.Z.
7 V6 Kerimäki Fin.
45 B3 Kerinci, G. *volc.* Indon.
35 E2 Keriya Shankou *pass* China
12 E3 Kerken Ger.
31 G2 Kerki Turkm.
31 G2 Kerkichi Turkm.
19 K4 Kerkinitis, Limni *l.* Greece
19 H5 Kerkyra Greece
Kerkyra *i. see* Corfu
87 F3 Kerma Sudan
46 K7 Kermadec Is. *is* N.Z.
94 H8 Kermadec Tr. *sea feature* Pac. Oc.
30 E4 Kermān Iran
72 B3 Kerman U.S.A.
31 E4 Kermān Desert Iran
30 B3 Kermānshāh Iran
30 D4 Kermānshāhān Iran
65 C6 Kermit U.S.A.
63 C5 Kern *r.* U.S.A.
59 G2 Kernertut, Cap *pt* Can.
72 C4 Kernville U.S.A.
20 K2 Keros Rus. Fed.
19 L6 Keros *i.* Greece
86 B4 Kérouané Guinea
12 E4 Kerpen Ger.
92 B5 Kerr, C. *c.* Ant.
57 H4 Kerrobert Can.
65 D6 Kerrville U.S.A.
11 B5 Kerry Head *hd* Rep. of Ireland
44 B4 Kerteh Malaysia
7 M9 Kerteminde Denmark
28 D4 Kerynia Cyprus
20 H3 Kerzhenets *r.* Rus. Fed.
58 D3 Kesagami Lake *l.* Can.
7 V6 Kesälahti Fin.
21 C7 Keşan Turkey
28 G1 Keşap Turkey
40 G5 Kesennuma Japan
31 H2 Keshem Afgh.
31 G2 Keshendeh-ye Bala Afgh.
34 B5 Keshod India
29 M5 Keshvar Iran
28 D2 Keskin Turkey
20 E2 Keskozero Rus. Fed.
12 E3 Kessel Neth.
91 H4 Kestell S. Africa
6 W4 Kesten'ga Rus. Fed.
6 U4 Kestilä Fin.
69 H3 Keswick Can.
8 D3 Keswick U.K.
16 H7 Keszthely Hungary
24 K4 Ket' *r.* Rus. Fed.
86 C4 Keta Ghana
44 □ Ketam, P. *i.* Sing.
45 D3 Ketapang Indon.
56 C3 Ketchikan U.S.A.
12 D2 Ketelmeer *l.* Neth.
31 G5 Keti Bandar Pak.
9 G5 Kettering U.K.
70 A5 Kettering U.S.A.
56 F5 Kettle *r.* Can.
68 A2 Kettle *r.* U.S.A.
70 E4 Kettle Creek *r.* U.S.A.
72 C3 Kettleman City U.S.A.
62 C1 Kettle River Ra. *mts* U.S.A.
70 E3 Keuka Lake *l.* U.S.A.
7 T5 Keuruu Fin.
68 C5 Kewanee U.S.A.
68 D3 Kewaunee U.S.A.
68 C2 Keweenaw Bay *b.* U.S.A.
68 C2 Keweenaw Peninsula U.S.A.
68 D2 Keweenaw Pt *pt* U.S.A.
81 E3 Keweigek Guyana
58 F3 Keyano Can.
69 G3 Key Harbour Can.
67 D7 Key Largo U.S.A.
11 C3 Key, Lough *l.* Rep. of Ireland
9 E6 Keynsham U.K.
70 D5 Keyser U.S.A.
70 D5 Keysers Ridge U.S.A.
73 G6 Keystone Peak *summit* U.S.A.
70 D6 Keysville U.S.A.
51 A6 Key, The N.Z.
29 M4 Keytū Iran
67 D7 Key West *FL* U.S.A.
68 B4 Key West *IA* U.S.A.
71 H3 Kezar Falls U.S.A.
89 C6 Kezi Zimbabwe
17 K6 Kežmarok Slovakia
90 D2 Kgalagadi *div.* Botswana
91 G2 Kgatleng *div.* Botswana
90 D1 Kgomofatshe Pan *salt pan* Botswana
90 F2 Kgoro Pan *salt pan* Botswana
91 G3 Kgotsong S. Africa
36 F2 Khabarovsk Rus. Fed.
Khabis *see* Shahdāb
29 H4 Khabur *r.* Syria
29 J7 Khadd, W. al *watercourse* S. Arabia
30 B6 Khafs Daghrah S. Arabia
34 E4 Khaga India
35 G5 Khagrachari Bangl.
34 B3 Khairgarh Pak.
34 B4 Khairpur Pak.
31 G2 Khaja du Koh *h.* Afgh.
34 D4 Khajurāho India
89 C6 Khakhea Botswana
31 G3 Khakīr Afgh.
31 G4 Khak-rēz Afgh.
31 G4 Khakriz *reg.* Afgh.
31 G2 Khalach Turkm.
30 C4 Khalafabād Iran
30 C3 Khalajestan *reg.* Iran
34 D2 Khalatse Jammu and Kashmir
34 A3 Khalifat *mt* Pak.
31 E3 Khalilabad Iran
30 C2 Khalkhāl Iran
35 F6 Khallikot India
20 D4 Khalopyenichy Belarus
36 C1 Khamar-Daban, Khrebet *mts* Rus. Fed.
34 C5 Khambhat India
34 B5 Khambhat, Gulf of *g.* India
34 D5 Khamgaon India
44 C1 Khamkeut Laos
30 B5 Khamma *well* S. Arabia
33 C2 Khammam India
25 N3 Khamra Rus. Fed.
30 C3 Khamseh *reg.* Iran
31 H2 Khānābād Afgh.
29 J5 Khān al Baghdādī Iraq
29 K5 Khān al Maḥāwīl Iraq
29 K5 Khān al Mashāhidah Iraq
29 K5 Khān al Muşalla Iraq
33 A3 Khanapur India
30 B2 Khānaqāh Iran
29 K4 Khānaqīn Iraq
29 K2 Khanasur Pass Iran/Turkey
28 F6 Khān az Zabīb Jordan
34 C2 Khanbari Pass Jammu and Kashmir
50 G4 Khancoban Austr.
34 B2 Khand Pass Afgh./Pak.
34 D5 Khandwa India
25 P3 Khandyga Rus. Fed.
34 B3 Khanewal Pak.
44 D2 Khanh Dương Vietnam
34 D4 Khaniadhana India
30 D4 Khanīyak Iran
29 K5 Khān Jadwal Iraq
40 C2 Khanka, Lake *l.* China/Rus. Fed.
Khanka, Ozero *l. see* Khanka, Lake
34 C2 Khanki Weir *barrage* Pak.
34 D3 Khanna India
34 B3 Khanpur Pak.
29 K6 Khān Ruḥābah Iraq
28 F4 Khān Shaykhūn Syria
27 F2 Khantau Kazak.
24 L3 Khantayskoye, Ozero *l.* Rus. Fed.
24 H3 Khanty-Mansiysk Rus. Fed.
28 E6 Khān Yūnis Gaza
44 A3 Khao Chum Thong Thai.
34 D5 Khapa India
30 C3 Khar *r.* Iran
21 H6 Kharabali Rus. Fed.
35 F5 Kharagpur India
30 E2 Kharakī Iran
31 G4 Kharan Pak.
30 E5 Khārān *r.* Iran
30 D3 Kharānaq Iran
34 B2 Kharbin Pass Afgh.
34 C6 Khardi India
34 D2 Khardung La *pass* India
31 F3 Kharez Ilias Afgh.
29 L6 Kharfiyah Iraq
30 C4 Khārg Islands *is* Iran
34 C5 Khargon India
34 C4 Khari *r. Rajasthan* India
34 C4 Khari *r. Rajasthan* India
34 C2 Kharian Pak.
35 E5 Khariar India
30 C6 Kharit S. Arabia
21 F5 Kharkiv Ukr.
Khar'kov *see* Kharkiv
19 L4 Kharmanli Bulg.
20 G3 Kharovsk Rus. Fed.
35 E5 Kharsia India
87 F3 Khartoum Sudan
30 E2 Khasardag, Gora *mt* Turkm.
21 H7 Khasav'yurt Rus. Fed.
31 F4 Khash Afgh.
31 F4 Khāsh Iran
31 F4 Khash Desert Afgh.
30 C5 Khashm Bijrān *h.* S. Arabia
31 F4 Khash Rūd *r.* Afgh.
21 G7 Khashuri Georgia
35 G4 Khāsi Hills *h.* India
19 L4 Khaskovo Bulg.
25 M2 Khatanga Rus. Fed.
25 M2 Khatanga, Gulf of *b.* Rus. Fed.
28 D6 Khatmia Pass Egypt
25 T3 Khatyrka Rus. Fed.
30 C4 Khāvar Iran
34 B5 Khavda India
31 H3 Khawak Pass Afgh.
30 E5 Khawr Fakkan U.A.E.
44 A2 Khawsa Myanmar
91 F5 Khayamnandi S. Africa
90 C7 Khayelitsha S. Africa
29 J3 Khāzir *r.* Iraq
44 C1 Khê Bo Vietnam
33 A2 Khed India
34 C4 Khedbrahma India
31 E3 Khedrî Iran
34 E3 Khela India
15 H4 Khemis Miliana Alg.
86 C1 Khenchela Alg.
86 B1 Khenifra Morocco
30 D4 Kherāmeh Iran
34 D4 Kherli India
30 C4 Khersan *r.* Iran
21 E6 Kherson Ukr.
30 C4 Khesht Iran
25 L2 Kheta *r.* Rus. Fed.
30 D4 Kheyrābād Iran
30 D2 Khezerābād Iran
34 D4 Khilchipur India
28 F4 Khirbat Isrīyah Syria
29 J6 Khirr, Wādī al *watercourse* S. Arabia
34 D2 Khitai P. *pass* China/Jammu and Kashmir
30 B2 Khīyāv Iran
7 V6 Khiytola Rus. Fed.
21 C5 Khmel'nyts'kyy Ukr.
21 C5 Khmil'nyk Ukr.
30 B2 Khodā Āfarīn Iran
31 G2 Khodzhambass Turkm.
26 D2 Khodzheyli Uzbek.
90 D2 Khokhowe Pan *salt pan* Botswana
34 B4 Khokhropar Pak.
20 G1 Kholmogory Rus. Fed.
36 G2 Kholmsk Rus. Fed.
17 Q3 Kholm-Zhirkovskiy Rus. Fed.
29 M3 Khoman Iran
90 B1 Khomas *div.* Namibia
90 A1 Khomas Highland *reg.* Namibia
30 C3 Khomeyn Iran
29 M4 Khondāb Iran
21 G7 Khoni Georgia
30 D5 Khonj Iran
25 Q3 Khonuu Rus. Fed.
21 G5 Khoper *r.* Rus. Fed.
36 F2 Khor Rus. Fed.
36 F2 Khor *r.* Rus. Fed.
34 B4 Khora Pak.
35 F5 Khordha India
30 C5 Khor Duweihin *b.* S. Arabia/U.A.E.
36 C1 Khorinsk Rus. Fed.
89 B6 Khorixas Namibia
40 C2 Khorol Rus. Fed.
21 E5 Khorol Ukr.
29 L2 Khoroslū Dāgh *h.* Iran
30 C3 Khorramābād Iran
29 M3 Khorram Darreh Iran
30 C4 Khorramshahr Iran
31 H2 Khorugh Tajik.
31 E3 Khosf Iran
21 H6 Khosheutovo Rus. Fed.
30 C4 Khosravī Iran
30 C4 Khosrowabad Iran
29 K4 Khosrowvī Iran
30 D4 Khowrjān Iran
30 D3 Khowrnag, Kūh-e *mt* Iran
31 H3 Khowst Afgh.
36 E1 Khrebet Dzhagdy *mts* Rus. Fed.
35 H5 Khreum Myanmar
35 G4 Khri *r.* India
20 H2 Khristoforovo Rus. Fed.
25 Q2 Khroma *r.* Rus. Fed.
26 D1 Khromtau Kazak.
40 D2 Khrustalnyy Rus. Fed.
17 O6 Khrystynivka Ukr.
31 G5 Khude Hills *mts* Pak.
91 F1 Khudumelapye Botswana
30 B5 Khuff S. Arabia
31 F5 Khūh Lab, Ra's *pt* Iran
90 D3 Khuis Botswana
26 E3 Khŭjand Tajik.
44 C2 Khu Khan Thai.
31 G3 Khulm *r.* Afgh.
35 G5 Khulna Bangl.
29 J1 Khulo Georgia
91 G3 Khuma S. Africa
34 C2 Khunjerab Pass China/Jammu and Kashmir
30 C3 Khunsar Iran
35 F5 Khunti India
31 E3 Khūr Iran
34 D4 Khurai India
30 D5 Khūran *chan.* Iran
31 G3 Khurd, Koh-i- *mt* Afgh.
34 D3 Khurja India
31 F3 Khurmalik Afgh.
34 C2 Khushab Pak.
29 M3 Khūshāvar Iran
31 E4 Khushk Rud Iran
31 F3 Khuspas Afgh.
21 B5 Khust Ukr.
91 G3 Khutsong S. Africa
31 G5 Khuzdar Pak.
31 F3 Khvāf Iran
20 J4 Khvalynsk Rus. Fed.
30 D3 Khvor Iran
30 E3 Khvord Nārvan Iran
30 C4 Khvormūj Iran
29 L3 Khvosh Maqām Iran
30 B2 Khvoy Iran
20 E3 Khvoynaya Rus. Fed.
44 A2 Khwae Noi *r.* Thai.
31 F4 Khwaja Ali Afgh.
31 H2 Khwaja Muhammad Range *mts* Afgh.
34 B2 Khyber Pass Afgh./Pak.
50 H3 Kiama Austr.
43 C5 Kiamba Phil.
88 C4 Kiambi Congo(Zaire)
65 E5 Kiamichi *r.* U.S.A.
6 V4 Kiantajärvi *l.* Fin.
30 C3 Kīāseh Iran
34 D2 Kibar India
43 C5 Kibawe Phil.
88 D4 Kibaya Tanz.
89 D4 Kibiti Tanz.
88 C4 Kibombo Congo(Zaire)
88 D4 Kibondo Tanz.
19 J4 Kičevo Macedonia
20 H3 Kichmengskiy Gorodok Rus. Fed.
86 C3 Kidal Mali
9 E5 Kidderminster U.K.
88 D3 Kidepo Valley National Park Uganda
86 A3 Kidira Senegal
34 D2 Kidmang Jammu and Kashmir
51 F3 Kidnappers, Cape *c.* N.Z.
9 E4 Kidsgrove U.K.
16 E3 Kiel Ger.
68 C4 Kiel U.S.A.
17 K5 Kielce Pol.
8 E2 Kielder Water *resr* U.K.
16 E3 Kieler Bucht *b.* Ger.
89 C5 Kienge Congo(Zaire)
12 F3 Kierspe Ger.
21 D5 Kiev Ukr.
86 A3 Kiffa Maur.
19 K5 Kifisia Greece
29 K4 Kifrī Iraq
88 D4 Kigali Rwanda
29 H2 Kiğı Turkey
59 H2 Kiglapait Mts *mts* Can.
88 C4 Kigoma Tanz.
6 S3 Kihlanki Fin.
7 S5 Kihniö Fin.
6 T4 Kiiminki Fin.
41 D8 Kii-sanchi *mts* Japan
41 D8 Kii-suidō *chan.* Japan
19 J2 Kikinda Yugo.
31 F5 Kikki Pak.
20 H3 Kiknur Rus. Fed.
40 G4 Kikonai Japan
89 C4 Kikondja Congo(Zaire)
48 E2 Kikori P.N.G.
48 E2 Kikori *r.* P.N.G.
88 B4 Kikwit Congo(Zaire)
7 P6 Kilafors Sweden
33 B4 Kilakkarai India
34 D2 Kilar India
72 □2 Kilauea U.S.A.
72 □2 Kilauea Crater *crater* U.S.A.
10 C5 Kilbrannan Sound *chan.* U.K.
42 E3 Kilchu N. Korea
11 E4 Kilcoole Rep. of Ireland
11 D4 Kilcormac Rep. of Ireland
11 E4 Kildare Rep. of Ireland
6 X2 Kil'dinstroy Rus. Fed.
88 B4 Kilembe Congo(Zaire)
10 C5 Kilfinan U.K.
65 E5 Kilgore U.S.A.
8 E2 Kilham U.K.
88 D4 Kilifi Kenya
88 D4 Kilimanjaro *mt* Tanz.
49 F2 Kilinailau Is *is* P.N.G.
89 D4 Kilindoni Tanz.
7 T7 Kilingi-Nõmme Estonia
28 F3 Kilis Turkey
21 D6 Kiliya Ukr.
11 B5 Kilkee Rep. of Ireland
11 F3 Kilkeel U.K.
11 D5 Kilkenny Rep. of Ireland
9 C7 Kilkhampton U.K.
19 K4 Kilkis Greece
11 B3 Killala Rep. of Ireland
11 B3 Killala Bay *b.* Rep. of Ireland
11 C5 Killaloe Rep. of Ireland
69 J3 Killaloe Station Can.
57 G4 Killam Can.
69 G3 Killarney Can.
11 B5 Killarney Rep. of Ireland
69 G2 Killarney National Park Can.
11 B6 Killarney National Park Rep. of Ireland
11 B4 Killary Harbour *b.* Rep. of Ireland
65 D6 Killeen U.S.A.
11 D5 Killenaule Rep. of Ireland
11 C4 Killimor Rep. of Ireland
10 D4 Killin U.K.
11 F3 Killinchy U.K.
11 E5 Killinick Rep. of Ireland
59 H1 Killiniq Can.
59 H1 Killiniq Island *i.* Can.
11 B5 Killorglin Rep. of Ireland
11 E5 Killurin Rep. of Ireland
11 C3 Killybegs Rep. of Ireland
11 D2 Kilmacrenan Rep. of Ireland
11 B4 Kilmaine Rep. of Ireland
11 C5 Kilmallock Rep. of Ireland
10 B3 Kilmaluag U.K.
10 D5 Kilmarnock U.K.
10 C4 Kilmelford U.K.
20 J3 Kil'mez' Rus. Fed.
20 J3 Kil'mez' *r.* Rus. Fed.
11 C6 Kilmona Rep. of Ireland
50 E4 Kilmore Austr.
11 E5 Kilmore Quay Rep. of Ireland
88 D4 Kilosa Tanz.
6 R2 Kilpisjärvi Fin.
6 X2 Kilp"yavr Rus. Fed.
11 E3 Kilrea U.K.
11 B5 Kilrush Rep. of Ireland
10 D5 Kilsyth U.K.
33 A4 Kilttān *i.* India
11 C4 Kiltullagh Rep. of Ireland
89 C4 Kilwa Congo(Zaire)
89 D4 Kilwa Masoko Tanz.
10 D5 Kilwinning U.K.
89 D4 Kimambi Tanz.
88 B4 Kimba Congo
64 C3 Kimball U.S.A.
48 F2 Kimbe P.N.G.
56 F5 Kimberley Can.
90 F4 Kimberley S. Africa
48 C3 Kimberley Plateau *plat.* Austr.
51 E4 Kimbolton N.Z.
42 E3 Kimch'aek N. Korea
42 E5 Kimch'ŏn S. Korea
7 S6 Kimito Fin.
42 D6 Kimje S. Korea
19 L6 Kimolos *i.* Greece
20 F4 Kimovsk Rus. Fed.
88 B4 Kimpese Congo(Zaire)
41 F5 Kimpoku-san *mt* Japan
20 F3 Kimry Rus. Fed.
88 B4 Kimvula Congo(Zaire)
45 E1 Kinabalu, Gunung *mt* Malaysia
43 A5 Kinabatangan *r.* Malaysia
19 M6 Kinaros *i.* Greece
60 C1 Kinbasket Lake *l. B.C.* Can.
10 E2 Kinbrace U.K.
69 G3 Kincardine Can.
10 E4 Kincardine U.K.
50 D2 Kinchega National Park Austr.
56 D3 Kincolith Can.
89 C4 Kinda Congo(Zaire)
35 H5 Kindat Myanmar
65 E6 Kinder U.S.A.
9 F4 Kinder Scout *h.* U.K.
57 H4 Kindersley Can.
86 A3 Kindia Guinea
88 C4 Kindu Congo(Zaire)
20 G3 Kineshma Rus. Fed.
48 F4 Kingaroy Austr.
72 B3 King City U.S.A.
92 C1 King Edward Point *U.K. Base* Ant.
70 E3 King Ferry U.S.A.
71 H2 Kingfield U.S.A.

65 D5 **Kingfisher** U.S.A.
92 B1 **King George I.** *i.* Ant.
58 E2 **King George Islands** *is* Can.
56 D4 **King I.** *i.* Can.
20 D3 **Kingisepp** Rus. Fed.
48 E5 **King Island** *i.* Austr.
69 H1 **King Kirkland** Can.
92 D5 **King Leopold and Queen Astrid Coast** *coastal area* Ant.
48 C3 **King Leopold Ranges** *h.* Austr.
73 E4 **Kingman** *AZ* U.S.A.
65 D4 **Kingman** *KS* U.S.A.
71 J2 **Kingman** *ME* U.S.A.
56 D3 **King Mtn** *mt* Can.
92 A3 **King Pen.** *pen.* Ant.
11 D5 **Kings** *r.* Rep. of Ireland
72 C3 **Kings** *r.* U.S.A.
9 D7 **Kingsbridge** U.K.
72 C3 **Kingsburg** U.S.A.
71 J2 **Kingsbury** U.S.A.
72 C3 **Kings Canyon National Park** U.S.A.
50 A3 **Kingscote** Austr.
11 E4 **Kingscourt** Rep. of Ireland
92 B2 **King Sejong** *Korea Base* Ant.
68 C3 **Kingsford** U.S.A.
67 D6 **Kingsland** *GA* U.S.A.
68 E5 **Kingsland** *IN* U.S.A.
9 H5 **King's Lynn** U.K.
49 H2 **Kingsmill Group** *is* Kiribati
9 H6 **Kingsnorth** U.K.
48 C3 **King Sound** *b.* Austr.
62 E3 **Kings Peak** *summit* U.S.A.
70 B6 **Kingsport** U.S.A.
69 J3 **Kingston** Can.
75 J5 **Kingston** Jamaica
51 B6 **Kingston** N.Z.
68 B6 **Kingston** *IL* U.S.A.
71 F4 **Kingston** *NY* U.S.A.
73 E4 **Kingston Peak** *summit* U.S.A.
50 B4 **Kingston South East** Austr.
8 G4 **Kingston upon Hull** U.K.
75 M6 **Kingstown** St Vincent
65 D7 **Kingsville** U.S.A.
9 E6 **Kingswood** U.K.
9 D5 **Kington** U.K.
10 D3 **Kingussie** U.K.
55 J3 **King William I.** *i.* Can.
91 G6 **King William's Town** S. Africa
65 E6 **Kingwood** *TX* U.S.A.
70 D5 **Kingwood** *WV* U.S.A.
57 J4 **Kinistino** Can.
40 G5 **Kinka-san** *i.* Japan
51 B6 **Kinloch** N.Z.
10 E3 **Kinloss** U.K.
69 H3 **Kinmount** Can.
7 N8 **Kinna** Sweden
11 D4 **Kinnegad** Rep. of Ireland
33 C4 **Kinniyai** Sri Lanka
6 T5 **Kinnula** Fin.
57 J3 **Kinoosao** Can.
10 E4 **Kinross** U.K.
11 C6 **Kinsale** Rep. of Ireland
88 B4 **Kinshasa** Congo(Zaire)
64 D4 **Kinsley** U.S.A.
67 E5 **Kinston** U.S.A.
7 R9 **Kintai** Lith.
86 B4 **Kintampo** Ghana
10 F3 **Kintore** U.K.
10 C5 **Kintyre** *pen.* U.K.
10 C5 **Kintyre, Mull of** *hd* U.K.
56 F3 **Kinuso** Can.
87 F4 **Kinyeti** *mt* Sudan
13 H4 **Kinzig** *r.* Ger.
69 H2 **Kiosk** Can.
58 E4 **Kipawa, Lac** *l.* Can.
71 F6 **Kiptopeke** U.S.A.
89 C5 **Kipushi** Congo(Zaire)
49 G3 **Kirakira** Solomon Is
33 C2 **Kirandul** India
20 D4 **Kirawsk** Belarus
13 G2 **Kirchdorf** Ger.
13 G5 **Kirchheim-Bolanden** Ger.
36 C1 **Kirensk** Rus. Fed.
Kirghizia *see* **Kyrgyzstan**
47 L4 **Kiribati** *country* Pac. Oc.
29 H1 **Kırık** Turkey
28 F3 **Kırıkhan** Turkey
28 D2 **Kırıkkale** Turkey
20 F3 **Kirillov** Rus. Fed.
88 D3 **Kirinyaga** *mt* Kenya
20 E3 **Kirishi** Rus. Fed.
41 B9 **Kirishima-yama** *volc.* Japan
46 M3 **Kiritimati** *i.* Kiribati
28 A2 **Kırkağaç** Turkey
30 B2 **Kirk Bulāg D.** *mt* Iran
9 E4 **Kirkby** U.K.
9 F4 **Kirkby in Ashfield** U.K.
8 E3 **Kirkby Lonsdale** U.K.
8 E3 **Kirkby Stephen** U.K.
10 E4 **Kirkcaldy** U.K.
10 C6 **Kirkcolm** U.K.
11 F3 **Kirkcubbin** U.K.
10 D6 **Kirkcudbright** U.K.
7 N6 **Kirkenær** Norway
6 W2 **Kirkenes** Norway
69 H3 **Kirkfield** Can.
10 D5 **Kirkintilloch** U.K.
7 T6 **Kirkkonummi** Fin.
73 F4 **Kirkland** U.S.A.
73 F4 **Kirkland Junction** U.S.A.
69 G1 **Kirkland Lake** Can.
21 C7 **Kırklareli** Turkey
8 C3 **Kirk Michael** U.K.
8 E3 **Kirkoswald** U.K.
64 E3 **Kirksville** U.S.A.
29 K4 **Kirkūk** Iraq
10 F2 **Kirkwall** U.K.
91 F6 **Kirkwood** S. Africa
72 B2 **Kirkwood** *CA* U.S.A.
64 F4 **Kirkwood** *MO* U.S.A.
28 C1 **Kırmır** *r.* Turkey
12 F5 **Kirn** Ger.
20 E4 **Kirov** *Kaluzh. Obl.* Rus. Fed.
Kirov *see* **Vyatka**
Kirovabad *see* **Gäncä**
20 J3 **Kirovo-Chepetsk** Rus. Fed.
21 E5 **Kirovohrad** Ukr.
29 M2 **Kirovsk** Azer.
20 D3 **Kirovsk** *Leningrad.* Rus. Fed.
6 X3 **Kirovsk** *Murmansk.* Rus. Fed.
31 F2 **Kirovsk** Turkm.
20 J3 **Kirovskaya Oblast'** *div.* Rus. Fed.
40 C2 **Kirovskiy** Rus. Fed.
92 B4 **Kirpatrick, Mt** *mt* Ant.
30 E2 **Kirpili** Turkm.
10 E4 **Kirriemuir** U.K.
20 K3 **Kirs** Rus. Fed.
20 G4 **Kirsanov** Rus. Fed.
28 E2 **Kırşehir** Turkey
31 G5 **Kirthar Range** *mts* Pak.
13 H4 **Kirtorf** Ger.
6 R3 **Kiruna** Sweden
88 C4 **Kirundu** Congo(Zaire)
20 H4 **Kirya** Rus. Fed.
41 F6 **Kiryū** Japan
7 O8 **Kisa** Sweden
88 C3 **Kisangani** Congo(Zaire)
88 B4 **Kisantu** Congo(Zaire)
45 A2 **Kisaran** Indon.
36 A1 **Kiselevsk** Rus. Fed.
35 F4 **Kishanganj** India
34 B4 **Kishangarh** *Rajasthan* India
34 C4 **Kishangarh** *Rajasthan* India
34 C2 **Kishen Ganga** *r.* India/Pak.
41 B9 **Kishika-zaki** *pt* Japan
Kishinev *see* **Chişinău**
41 D7 **Kishiwada** Japan
35 G4 **Kishorganj** Bangl.
34 C2 **Kishtwar** Jammu and Kashmir
86 C4 **Kisi** Nigeria
88 D4 **Kisii** Kenya
57 K4 **Kiskittogisu L.** *l.* Can.
17 J7 **Kiskunfélegyháza** Hungary
17 J7 **Kiskunhalas** Hungary
21 G7 **Kislovodsk** Rus. Fed.
88 E4 **Kismaayo** Somalia
88 C4 **Kisoro** Uganda
41 E7 **Kiso-sanmyaku** *mts* Japan
86 A4 **Kissidougou** Guinea
67 D6 **Kissimmee** U.S.A.
67 D7 **Kissimmee, L.** *l.* U.S.A.
57 J3 **Kississing L.** *l.* Can.
Kistna *r. see* **Krishna**
88 D4 **Kisumu** Kenya
86 B3 **Kita** Mali
31 G2 **Kitab** Uzbek.
41 G6 **Kitaibaraki** Japan
40 G5 **Kitakami** Japan
40 G5 **Kitakami-gawa** *r.* Japan
41 F6 **Kitakata** Japan
41 B8 **Kita-Kyūshū** Japan
88 D3 **Kitale** Kenya
36 G2 **Kitami** Japan
63 G4 **Kit Carson** U.S.A.
69 G4 **Kitchener** Can.
6 W5 **Kitee** Fin.
88 D3 **Kitgum** Uganda
56 D4 **Kitimat** Can.
6 U3 **Kitinen** *r.* Fin.
88 B4 **Kitona** Congo(Zaire)
41 B8 **Kitsuki** Japan
70 D4 **Kittanning** U.S.A.
71 F4 **Kittatinny Mts** *h.* U.S.A.
71 H3 **Kittery** U.S.A.
6 T3 **Kittilä** Fin.
67 F4 **Kitty Hawk** U.S.A.
88 D4 **Kitunda** Tanz.
56 D3 **Kitwanga** Can.
89 C5 **Kitwe** Zambia
16 F7 **Kitzbüheler Alpen** *mts* Austria
13 J5 **Kitzingen** Ger.
13 L3 **Kitzscher** Ger.
6 U5 **Kiuruvesi** Fin.
6 T5 **Kivijärvi** Fin.
7 U7 **Kiviõli** Estonia
88 C4 **Kivu, Lake** *l.* Congo(Zaire)/Rwanda
40 C3 **Kiyevka** Rus. Fed.
19 N4 **Kıyıköy** Turkey
24 G4 **Kizel** Rus. Fed.
20 H2 **Kizema** Rus. Fed.
28 B3 **Kızılca D.** *mt* Turkey
28 D1 **Kızılcahamam** Turkey
28 G2 **Kızıl D.** *mt* Turkey
28 D1 **Kızılırmak** Turkey
28 D2 **Kızılırmak** *r.* Turkey
28 C3 **Kızılkaya** Turkey
28 D3 **Kızılören** Turkey
29 H3 **Kızıltepe** Turkey
21 H7 **Kizil"yurt** Rus. Fed.
21 H7 **Kizlyar** Rus. Fed.
31 D2 **Kizyl-Atrek** Turkm.
31 G2 **Kizylayak** Turkm.
6 U1 **Kjøllefjord** Norway
6 P2 **Kjøpsvik** Norway
16 G5 **Kladno** Czech Rep.
16 G7 **Klagenfurt** Austria
73 H4 **Klagetoh** U.S.A.
7 R9 **Klaipėda** Lith.
6 □ **Klaksvík** Faroe Is
62 B3 **Klamath** *r.* U.S.A.
62 B3 **Klamath Falls** U.S.A.
62 B3 **Klamath Mts** *mts* U.S.A.
7 N6 **Klarälven** *r.* Sweden
16 F6 **Klatovy** Czech Rep.
90 C5 **Klawer** S. Africa
56 C3 **Klawock** U.S.A.
12 E2 **Klazienaveen** Neth.
56 E4 **Kleena Kleene** Can.
90 D4 **Kleinbegin** S. Africa
90 C3 **Klein Karas** Namibia
90 D6 **Klein Roggeveldberg** *mts* S. Africa
90 B4 **Kleinsee** S. Africa
90 D6 **Klein Swartberg** *mts* S. Africa
56 D4 **Klemtu** Can.
91 G3 **Klerksdorp** S. Africa
20 E4 **Kletnya** Rus. Fed.
21 G5 **Kletskiy** Rus. Fed.
12 E3 **Kleve** Ger.
90 F6 **Klienpoort** S. Africa
20 D4 **Klimavichy** Belarus
21 E4 **Klimovo** Rus. Fed.
20 F4 **Klimovsk** Rus. Fed.
20 F3 **Klin** Rus. Fed.
56 D4 **Klinaklini** *r.* Can.
13 H5 **Klingenberg am Main** Ger.
13 L4 **Klingenthal** Ger.
13 L1 **Klink** Ger.
16 F5 **Klínovec** *mt* Czech Rep.
7 Q8 **Klintehamn** Sweden
21 J5 **Klintsovka** Rus. Fed.
20 E4 **Klintsy** Rus. Fed.
90 C5 **Kliprand** S. Africa
18 G2 **Ključ** Bos.-Herz.
16 H5 **Kłodzko** Pol.
12 E2 **Kloosterhaar** Neth.
16 H6 **Klosterneuburg** Austria
13 K2 **Klötze (Altmark)** Ger.
58 F1 **Klotz, Lac** *l.* Can.
56 A2 **Kluane Game Sanctuary** *res.* Can.
56 B2 **Kluane Lake** *l.* Can.
56 B2 **Kluane National Park** Can.
16 J5 **Kluczbork** Pol.
34 B4 **Klupro** Pak.
20 C4 **Klyetsk** Belarus
25 S4 **Klyuchevskaya Sopka** *volc.* Rus. Fed.
7 O6 **Knåda** Sweden
8 F3 **Knaresborough** U.K.
57 L3 **Knee Lake** *l.* Can.
13 J5 **Knetzgau** Ger.
68 B1 **Knife Lake** *l.* Can./U.S.A.
56 D4 **Knight In.** *in.* Can.
9 D5 **Knighton** U.K.
68 E6 **Knightstown** U.S.A.
18 G2 **Knin** Croatia
16 G7 **Knittelfeld** Austria
19 K3 **Knjaževac** Yugo.
11 C4 **Knock** Rep. of Ireland
11 B6 **Knockaboy** *h.* Rep. of Ireland
11 B5 **Knockacummer** *h.* Rep. of Ireland
11 C3 **Knockalongy** *h.* Rep. of Ireland
11 B5 **Knockalough** Rep. of Ireland
10 F3 **Knock Hill** *h.* U.K.
11 E2 **Knocklayd** *h.* U.K.
12 B3 **Knokke-Heist** Belgium
13 M1 **Knorrendorf** Ger.
9 F5 **Knowle** U.K.
92 B2 **Knowles, C.** *c.* Ant.
71 J1 **Knowles Corner** U.S.A.
71 G2 **Knowlton** Can.
68 D5 **Knox** U.S.A.
56 C4 **Knox, C.** *c.* Can.
92 C6 **Knox Coast** *coastal area* Ant.
72 A2 **Knoxville** *CA* U.S.A.
68 B5 **Knoxville** *IL* U.S.A.
67 D4 **Knoxville** *TN* U.S.A.
10 C3 **Knoydart** *reg.* U.K.
55 N1 **Knud Rasmussen Land** *reg.* Greenland
90 E7 **Knysna** S. Africa
41 B9 **Kobayashi** Japan
6 V2 **Kobbfoss** Norway
41 D7 **Kōbe** Japan
København *see* **Copenhagen**
86 B3 **Kobenni** Maur.
12 F4 **Koblenz** Ger.
20 J3 **Kobra** Rus. Fed.
37 F7 **Kobroör** *i.* Indon.
20 C4 **Kobryn** Belarus
21 G7 **K'obulet'i** Georgia
19 K4 **Kočani** Macedonia
28 B1 **Kocasu** *r.* Turkey
18 F2 **Kočevje** Slovenia
44 A3 **Ko Chan** *i.* Thai.
42 D6 **Koch'ang** S. Korea
42 D6 **Kŏch'ang** S. Korea
44 B2 **Ko Chang** *i.* Thai.
35 G4 **Koch Bihār** India
13 H5 **Kocher** *r.* Ger.
Kochi *see* **Cochin**
41 C8 **Kōchi** Japan
20 H4 **Kochkurovo** Rus. Fed.
21 H6 **Kochubey** Rus. Fed.
21 G6 **Kochubeyevskoye** Rus. Fed.
33 B4 **Kodaikanal** India
33 D2 **Kodala** India
54 C4 **Kodiak** U.S.A.
54 C4 **Kodiak Island** *i.* U.S.A.
91 G1 **Kodibeleng** Botswana
20 F2 **Kodino** Rus. Fed.
87 F4 **Kodok** Sudan
67 G7 **Kodori** *r.* Georgia
21 D5 **Kodyma** Ukr.
19 L4 **Kodzhaele** *mt* Bulg./Greece
90 D6 **Koedoesberg** *mts* S. Africa
90 D4 **Koegrabie** S. Africa
90 C5 **Koekenaap** S. Africa
35 E4 **Koel** *r.* India
12 D3 **Koersel** Belgium
89 B6 **Koës** Namibia
73 F5 **Kofa Mts** *mts* U.S.A.
90 F4 **Koffiefontein** S. Africa
86 B4 **Koforidua** Ghana
41 F7 **Kōfu** Japan
58 E2 **Kogaluc** *r.* Can.
58 E2 **Kogaluc, Baie de** *b.* Can.
59 H2 **Kogaluk** *r.* Can.
7 N9 **Køge** Denmark
31 G5 **Kohan** Pak.
34 B2 **Kohat** Pak.
7 T7 **Kohila** Estonia
35 H4 **Kohima** India
34 B3 **Kohlu** Pak.
31 F3 **Kohsan** Afgh.
7 U7 **Kohtla-Järve** Estonia
51 E2 **Kohukohunui** *h.* N.Z.
42 D6 **Kohŭng** S. Korea
41 F6 **Koide** Japan
56 A2 **Koidern** Can.
33 B3 **Koilkuntla** India
42 D3 **Koindong** N. Korea
29 K3 **Koi Sanjaq** Iraq
42 E6 **Kŏje do** *i.* S. Korea
41 F8 **Ko-jima** *i.* Japan
40 F4 **Ko-jima** *i.* Japan
44 A1 **Kok** *r.* Thai.
71 J2 **Kokadjo** U.S.A.
26 E3 **Kokand** Uzbek.
7 R7 **Kökar** Fin.
31 H2 **Kokcha** *r.* Afgh.
7 R6 **Kokemäenjoki** *r.* Fin.
90 C4 **Kokerboom** Namibia
17 O3 **Kokhanava** Belarus
20 G3 **Kokhma** Rus. Fed.
33 C4 **Kokkilai** Sri Lanka
6 S5 **Kokkola** Fin.
72 □1 **Koko Hd** *hd* U.S.A.
68 D5 **Kokomo** U.S.A.
90 E2 **Kokong** Botswana
91 G3 **Kokosi** S. Africa
27 G2 **Kokpekty** Kazak.
42 D4 **Koksan** N. Korea
20 H3 **Koksharka** Rus. Fed.
26 E1 **Kokshetau** Kazak.
59 G2 **Koksoak** *r.* Can.
91 H5 **Kokstad** S. Africa
44 B3 **Ko Kut** *i.* Thai.
6 X2 **Kola** Rus. Fed.
Kolab *r. see* **Sābari**
31 G5 **Kolachi** *r.* Pak.
34 C2 **Kolahoi** *mt* India
37 E7 **Kolaka** Indon.
44 A4 **Ko Lanta** Thai.
44 A4 **Ko Lanta** *i.* Thai.
24 E3 **Kola Peninsula** Rus. Fed.
33 B3 **Kolar** *Karnataka* India
34 E6 **Kolar** *Madhya Pradesh* India
34 D4 **Kolaras** India
33 B3 **Kolar Gold Fields** India
6 S3 **Kolari** Fin.
34 C4 **Kolayat** India
20 F3 **Kol'chugino** Rus. Fed.
86 A3 **Kolda** Senegal
7 L9 **Kolding** Denmark
88 C3 **Kole** *Haute-Zaïre* Congo(Zaire)
88 C4 **Kole** *Kasai-Oriental* Congo(Zaire)
15 H4 **Koléa** Alg.
6 R4 **Koler** Sweden
24 F3 **Kolguyev, O.** *i.* Rus. Fed.
35 F5 **Kolhan** *reg.* India
33 A2 **Kolhapur** India
44 A4 **Ko Libong** *i.* Thai.
7 S7 **Kõljala** Estonia
7 S8 **Kolkasrags** *pt* Latvia
Kolkata *see* **Calcutta**
31 H2 **Kolkhozobod** Tajik.
Kollam *see* **Quilon**
33 B3 **Kollegal** India
33 C2 **Kolleru L.** *l.* India
12 E1 **Kollum** Neth.
Köln *see* **Cologne**
16 G3 **Kołobrzeg** Pol.
20 H3 **Kologriv** Rus. Fed.
86 B3 **Kolokani** Mali
49 F2 **Kolombangara** *i.* Solomon Is
20 F4 **Kolomna** Rus. Fed.
21 C5 **Kolomyya** Ukr.
86 B3 **Kolondiéba** Mali
48 C2 **Kolonedale** Indon.
90 D3 **Kolonkwane** Botswana
24 K4 **Kolpashevo** Rus. Fed.
21 F4 **Kolpny** Rus. Fed.
Kol'skiy Poluostrov *pen. see* **Kola Peninsula**
32 B7 **Koluli** Eritrea
33 A2 **Kolvan** India
6 M4 **Kolvereid** Norway
6 T1 **Kolvik** Norway
31 G5 **Kolwa** *reg.* Pak.
89 C5 **Kolwezi** Congo(Zaire)
25 R3 **Kolyma** *r.* Rus. Fed.
25 R3 **Kolymskaya Nizmennost'** *lowland* Rus. Fed.
25 R3 **Kolymskiy, Khrebet** *mts* Rus. Fed.
20 H4 **Kolyshley** Rus. Fed.
19 K3 **Kom** *mt* Bulg.
40 G3 **Komaga-take** *volc.* Japan
90 B4 **Komaggas** S. Africa
90 B4 **Komaggas Mts** *mts* S. Africa
25 S4 **Komandorskiye Ostrova** *is* Rus. Fed.
16 J7 **Komárno** Slovakia
91 J2 **Komatipoort** S. Africa
41 E6 **Komatsu** Japan
41 D7 **Komatsushima** Japan
88 C4 **Kombe** Congo(Zaire)
86 B3 **Kombissiri** Burkina
45 B3 **Komering** *r.* Indon.
91 G6 **Komga** S. Africa
21 D6 **Kominternivs'ke** Ukr.
20 J2 **Komi, Respublika** *div.* Rus. Fed.
18 G3 **Komiža** Croatia
19 H1 **Komló** Hungary
31 F2 **Kommuna** Turkm.
88 B4 **Komono** Congo
41 F6 **Komoro** Japan
19 L4 **Komotini** Greece
90 D6 **Komsberg** *mts* S. Africa
26 E1 **Komsomolets** Kazak.
25 L1 **Komsomolets, O.** *i.* Rus. Fed.
20 G3 **Komsomol'sk** Rus. Fed.
31 F2 **Komsomol'sk** Turkm.
21 E5 **Komsomol's'k** Ukr.
21 H6 **Komsomol'skiy** *Kalmykiya* Rus. Fed.
20 H4 **Komsomol'skiy** *Mordov.* Rus. Fed.
36 F1 **Komsomol'sk-na-Amure** Rus. Fed.
24 H3 **Komsomol'skiy** Rus. Fed.
29 J1 **Kömürlü** Turkey
73 F6 **Kom Vo** U.S.A.
20 F3 **Konakovo** Rus. Fed.
35 F5 **Konar Res.** *resr* India
34 D4 **Konch** India
35 E6 **Kondagaon** India
69 J2 **Kondiaronk, Lac** *l.* Can.
88 D4 **Kondoa** Tanz.
20 E2 **Kondopoga** Rus. Fed.
20 E4 **Kondrovo** Rus. Fed.
55 P3 **Kong Christian IX Land** *reg.* Greenland
52 N2 **Kong Christian X Land** *reg.* Greenland
52 O2 **Kong Frederik VIII Land** *reg.* Greenland
55 O3 **Kong Frederik VI Kyst** *reg.* Greenland
92 C2 **Kong Håkon VII Hav** *sea* Ant.
42 D5 **Kongju** S. Korea
24 D2 **Kong Karl's Land** *is* Svalbard
45 E2 **Kongkemul** *mt* Indon.
88 C4 **Kongolo** Congo(Zaire)
55 Q2 **Kong Oscar Fjord** *in.* Greenland
86 B3 **Kongoussi** Burkina
7 L7 **Kongsberg** Norway
7 N6 **Kongsvinger** Norway
44 C2 **Kông, T.** *r.* Cambodia
88 D4 **Kongwa** Tanz.
55 Q2 **Kong Wilhelm Land** *reg.* Greenland
44 C2 **Kong, Xé** *r.* Laos
13 K4 **Königsee** Ger.
12 F4 **Königswinter** Ger.
16 J4 **Konin** Pol.
36 F1 **Konin** *r.* Rus. Fed.
18 G3 **Konjic** Bos.-Herz.
90 B3 **Konkiep** *watercourse* Namibia
86 B3 **Konna** Mali
13 K3 **Könnern** Ger.
6 U5 **Konnevesi** Fin.
20 G2 **Konosha** Rus. Fed.
41 F6 **Kōnosu** Japan
21 E5 **Konotop** Ukr.
44 D2 **Kon Plong** Vietnam
13 L5 **Konstantinovy Lázně** Czech Rep.
16 D7 **Konstanz** Ger.
86 C3 **Kontagora** Nigeria
6 V5 **Kontiolahti** Fin.
6 U4 **Konttila** Fin.
44 C2 **Kon Tum** Vietnam
44 D2 **Kontum, Plateau du** *plat.* Vietnam
28 D3 **Konya** Turkey
12 E5 **Konz** Ger.
72 □1 **Koolau Range** *mts* U.S.A.
50 E3 **Koondrook** Austr.
70 D5 **Koon Lake** *l.* U.S.A.
50 G3 **Koorawatha** Austr.
62 C2 **Kooskia** U.S.A.
56 F5 **Kootenay** *r.* Can./U.S.A.
56 F5 **Kootenay L.** *l.* Can.
56 F4 **Kootenay Nat. Park** Can.
90 D5 **Kootjieskolk** S. Africa
21 H6 **Kopanovka** Rus. Fed.
34 C6 **Kopargaon** India
6 E3 **Kópasker** Iceland
18 E2 **Koper** Slovenia
30 E2 **Kopet Dag, Khrebet** *mts* Turkm.
44 B3 **Ko Phangan** *i.* Thai.
44 A3 **Ko Phra Thong** *i.* Thai.
44 A4 **Ko Phuket** *i.* Thai.
7 P7 **Köping** Sweden
6 Q5 **Köpmanholmen** Sweden
91 F2 **Kopong** Botswana
33 B3 **Koppal** India
7 M6 **Koppang** Norway
7 O7 **Kopparberg** Sweden
91 G3 **Koppies** S. Africa
90 D3 **Koppieskraalpan** *salt pan* S. Africa
18 G1 **Koprivnica** Croatia
28 C3 **Köprü** *r.* Turkey
30 D4 **Kor** *watercourse* Iran
20 G4 **Korablino** Rus. Fed.
31 G5 **Korak** Pak.
58 E1 **Korak, Baie** *b.* Can.
33 B2 **Korangal** India
31 G5 **Korangi** Pak.
33 C2 **Koraput** India
Korat *see* **Nakhon Ratchasima**
35 E5 **Korba** India
18 D6 **Korba** Tunisia
13 G3 **Korbach** Ger.
44 B4 **Korbu, Gunung** *mt* Malaysia
19 J4 **Korçë** Albania
18 G3 **Korčula** Croatia
18 G3 **Korčula** *i.* Croatia
18 G3 **Korčulanski Kanal** *chan.* Croatia
29 M4 **Kord Khvord** Iran
30 D2 **Kord Küv** Iran
31 F5 **Kords** *reg.* Iran
30 D4 **Kord Sheykh** Iran
42 B4 **Korea Bay** *g.* China/N. Korea
23 M5 **Korea, North** *country* Asia
23 M6 **Korea, South** *country* Asia
41 A7 **Korea Strait** *str.* Japan/S. Korea
33 A2 **Koregaon** India
21 F6 **Korenovsk** Rus. Fed.
21 C5 **Korets'** Ukr.
28 B1 **Körfez** Turkey
92 B3 **Korff Ice Rise** *ice feature* Ant.
6 N3 **Korgen** Norway
86 B4 **Korhogo** Côte d'Ivoire
34 B5 **Kori Creek** *in.* India
19 K5 **Korinthiakos Kolpos** *chan.* Greece
19 K6 **Korinthos** Greece
16 H7 **Kőris-hegy** *mt* Hungary
19 J3 **Koritnik** *mt* Albania
41 G6 **Kōriyama** Japan
28 C3 **Korkuteli** Turkey
28 D4 **Kormakitis, Cape** *c.* Cyprus
16 H7 **Körmend** Hungary
86 B4 **Koro** Côte d'Ivoire
86 B3 **Koro** Mali
49 H3 **Koro** *i.* Fiji
21 F5 **Korocha** Rus. Fed.
28 D1 **Köroğlu Dağları** *mts* Turkey
28 D1 **Köroğlu Tepesi** *mt* Turkey
88 D4 **Korogwe** Tanz.
50 D5 **Koroit** Austr.
50 D4 **Korong Vale** Austr.
19 K4 **Koronia, L.** *l.* Greece
49 H3 **Koro Sea** *b.* Fiji
21 D5 **Korosten'** Ukr.
21 D5 **Korostyshiv** Ukr.
87 D3 **Koro Toro** Chad
7 T5 **Korpilahti** Fin.
7 R6 **Korpo** Fin.
36 G2 **Korsakov** Rus. Fed.
20 J3 **Korshik** Rus. Fed.
6 R5 **Korsnäs** Fin.
7 M9 **Korsør** Denmark
21 D5 **Korsun'-Shevchenkivs'kyy** Ukr.
17 K3 **Korsze** Pol.
6 S5 **Kortesjärvi** Fin.
20 J2 **Kortkeros** Rus. Fed.
12 B4 **Kortrijk** Belgium
20 G3 **Kortsovo** Rus. Fed.
50 E5 **Korumburra** Austr.
86 D4 **Korup, Parc National de** *nat. park* Cameroon
6 U3 **Korvala** Fin.
34 D4 **Korwai** India
36 H1 **Koryakskaya Sopka** *volc.* Rus. Fed.
25 S3 **Koryakskiy Khrebet** *mts* Rus. Fed.
20 H2 **Koryazhma** Rus. Fed.
42 E6 **Koryŏng** S. Korea
21 E5 **Koryukivka** Ukr.
19 M6 **Kos** *i.* Greece
44 B3 **Ko Samui** *i.* Thai.
42 D4 **Kosan** N. Korea
16 H4 **Kościan** Pol.
65 F5 **Kosciusko** U.S.A.
56 C3 **Kosciusko I.** *i.* U.S.A.
50 G4 **Kosciusko, Mt** *mt* Austr.
50 G4 **Kosciusko National Park** Austr.
29 G1 **Köse** Turkey
28 F1 **Köse Dağı** *mt* Turkey
33 B2 **Kosgi** India
27 G2 **Kosh-Agach** Rus. Fed.
41 A9 **Koshikijima-rettō** *is* Japan
31 F3 **Koshkak** Iran
31 F3 **Koshk-e-Kohneh** Afgh.
68 C4 **Koshkoning, Lake** *l.* U.S.A.
30 D1 **Koshoba** Turkm.
31 G1 **Koshrabad** Uzbek.
34 D4 **Kosi** India
34 D3 **Kosi** *r.* India
91 K3 **Kosi Bay** *b.* S. Africa
17 K6 **Košice** Slovakia
33 B3 **Kosigi** India
6 R3 **Koskullskule** Sweden
20 J2 **Koslan** Rus. Fed.
42 E4 **Kosŏng** N. Korea
42 E3 **Kosŏng-ni** N. Korea
19 J3 **Kosovo** *div.* Yugo.
19 J3 **Kosovska Mitrovica** Yugo.
46 H3 **Kosrae** *i.* Micronesia
13 K5 **Kösseine** *h.* Ger.
86 B4 **Kossou, Lac de** *l.* Côte d'Ivoire
19 K3 **Kostenets** Bulg.
91 G2 **Koster** S. Africa
87 F3 **Kosti** Sudan
19 K3 **Kostinbrod** Bulg.
24 K3 **Kostino** Rus. Fed.
20 D1 **Kostomuksha** Rus. Fed.
21 C5 **Kostopil'** Ukr.
20 G3 **Kostroma** Rus. Fed.
20 G3 **Kostroma** *r.* Rus. Fed.
20 G3 **Kostromskaya Oblast'** *div.* Rus. Fed.
16 G4 **Kostrzyn** Pol.
21 F5 **Kostyantynivka** Ukr.
16 H3 **Koszalin** Pol.
16 H7 **Kőszeg** Hungary
35 E5 **Kota** *Madhya Pradesh* India
34 C4 **Kota** *Rajasthan* India
45 B4 **Kotaagung** Indon.
34 C4 **Kota Barrage** *barrage* India
45 D3 **Kotabaru** Indon.
45 E3 **Kotabaru** Indon.
45 B1 **Kota Bharu** Malaysia
45 B3 **Kotabumi** Indon.
34 C4 **Kota Dam** *dam* India
45 E1 **Kota Kinabalu** Malaysia
44 A3 **Ko Tao** *i.* Thai.
33 C2 **Kotapārh** India
45 B5 **Kotapinang** Indon.
34 C4 **Kotari** *r.* India
45 B2 **Kota Tinggi** Malaysia
20 J3 **Kotel'nich** Rus. Fed.
21 G6 **Kotel'nikovo** Rus. Fed.
25 P2 **Kotel'nyy, O.** *i.* Rus. Fed.
34 D3 **Kotgarh** India
13 K3 **Köthen (Anhalt)** Ger.
34 E4 **Kothi** India
7 U6 **Kotka** Fin.
34 C3 **Kot Kapura** India
20 H2 **Kotlas** Rus. Fed.
34 C2 **Kotli** Pak.
54 B3 **Kotlik** *AK* U.S.A.
6 D5 **Kötlutangi** *pt* Iceland
7 V7 **Kotly** Rus. Fed.
18 G2 **Kotor Varoš** Bos.-Herz.
86 B4 **Kotouba** Côte d'Ivoire
21 H5 **Kotovo** Rus. Fed.
21 G4 **Kotovsk** Rus. Fed.
21 D6 **Kotovs'k** Ukr.
34 C4 **Kotra** India
34 B4 **Kotri** Pak.
34 E6 **Kotri** *r.* India
34 A5 **Kot Sarae** Pak.
33 C2 **Kottagudem** India
33 B4 **Kottarakara** India
33 B4 **Kottayam** India
33 B5 **Kotte** Sri Lanka
33 B3 **Kotturu** India
30 D2 **Koturdepe** Turkm.
25 M2 **Kotuy** *r.* Rus. Fed.
54 B3 **Kotzebue** U.S.A.
54 B3 **Kotzebue Sound** *b.* *AK* U.S.A.
13 L5 **Kötzting** Ger.
86 A3 **Koubia** Guinea
86 B3 **Koudougou** Burkina
90 E6 **Koueveldberg** *mts* S. Africa
87 D3 **Koufey** Niger
19 M7 **Koufonisi** *i.* Greece
90 E6 **Kougaberg** *mts* S. Africa

28 D4 Kouklia Cyprus
88 B4 Koulamoutou Gabon
86 B3 Koulikoro Mali
49 G4 Koumac New Caledonia
86 A3 Koundâra Guinea
86 B3 Koupéla Burkina
79 H2 Kourou Fr. Guiana
86 B3 Kouroussa Guinea
87 D3 Kousséri Cameroon
86 B3 Koutiala Mali
7 U6 Kouvola Fin.
6 W3 Kovdor Rus. Fed.
6 W3 Kovdozero, Oz. l. Rus. Fed.
21 C5 Kovel' Ukr.
20 G3 Kovernino Rus. Fed.
33 B4 Kovilpatti India
20 G3 Kovrov Rus. Fed.
20 G4 Kovylkino Rus. Fed.
20 F2 Kovzhskoye, Ozero l. Rus. Fed.
51 C5 Kowhitirangi N.Z.
39 □ Kowloon Peninsula H.K. China
39 □ Kowloon Pk h. H.K. China
42 D4 Kowŏn N. Korea
41 B7 Kōyama-misaki pt Japan
44 A3 Ko Yao Yai i. Thai.
28 B3 Köyceğiz Turkey
20 J2 Koygorodok Rus. Fed.
33 A2 Koyna Res. resr India
20 H1 Koynas Rus. Fed.
54 C3 Koyukuk r. U.S.A.
28 F1 Koyulhisar Turkey
20 F3 Koza Rus. Fed.
41 A7 Kō-zaki pt Japan
28 E3 Kozan Turkey
19 J4 Kozani Greece
18 G2 Kozara mts Bos.-Herz.
21 D5 Kozelets' Ukr.
20 E4 Kozel'sk Rus. Fed.
Kozhikode see Calicut
28 C1 Kozlu Turkey
20 H3 Koz'modem'yansk Rus. Fed.
19 K4 Kožuf mts Greece/Macedonia
41 F7 Kōzu-shima i. Japan
21 D5 Kozyatyn Ukr.
86 C4 Kpalimé Togo
44 A3 Krabi Thai.
44 A3 Kra Buri Thai.
44 C2 Krâcheh Cambodia
6 P4 Kraddsele Sweden
7 L7 Kragerø Norway
12 D2 Kraggenburg Neth.
19 J2 Kragujevac Yugo.
13 G5 Kraichgau reg. Ger.
44 A3 Kra, Isthmus of isth. Thai.
45 C4 Krakatau i. Indon.
44 C2 Krâkôr Cambodia
17 J5 Kraków Pol.
13 L1 Krakower See l. Ger.
44 B2 Krâlănh Cambodia
81 C1 Kralendijk Neth. Ant.
21 F5 Kramators'k Ukr.
6 P5 Kramfors Sweden
12 C3 Krammer est. Neth.
19 K6 Kranidi Greece
18 F1 Kranj Slovenia
44 □ Kranji Res. resr Sing.
91 J4 Kranskop S. Africa
20 H2 Krasavino Rus. Fed.
24 G2 Krasino Rus. Fed.
40 B3 Kraskino Rus. Fed.
7 U9 Krāslava Latvia
13 L4 Kraslice Czech Rep.
17 P4 Krasnapollye Belarus
20 D4 Krasnaya Gora Rus. Fed.
21 H5 Krasnoarmeysk Rus. Fed.
21 F6 Krasnoarmeyskaya Rus. Fed.
21 F5 Krasnoarmiys'k Ukr.
20 H2 Krasnoborsk Rus. Fed.
21 F6 Krasnodar Rus. Fed.
21 F6 Krasnodarskiy Kray div. Rus. Fed.
21 F5 Krasnodon Ukr.
20 D3 Krasnogorodskoye Rus. Fed.
21 G6 Krasnogvardeyskoye Rus. Fed.
21 E5 Krasnohrad Ukr.
21 E6 Krasnohvardiys'ke Ukr.
17 R2 Krasnomayskiy Rus. Fed.
21 E6 Krasnoperekops'k Ukr.
20 H2 Krasnorechenskiy Rus. Fed.
7 V6 Krasnosel'skoye Rus. Fed.
20 G4 Krasnoslobodsk Rus. Fed.
30 D2 Krasnovodskiy Zaliv b. Turkm.
30 D1 Krasnovodskoye Plato plat. Turkm.
36 B1 Krasnoyarsk Rus. Fed.
17 P3 Krasnyy Rus. Fed.
20 H3 Krasnyye Baki Rus. Fed.
21 H6 Krasnyye Barrikady Rus. Fed.
20 F3 Krasnyy Kholm Rus. Fed.
21 H5 Krasnyy Kut Rus. Fed.
20 D3 Krasnyy Luch Rus. Fed.
21 F5 Krasnyy Lyman Ukr.
21 J6 Krasnyy Yar Astrak. Rus. Fed.
21 H5 Krasnyy Yar Volgograd. Rus. Fed.
21 C5 Krasyliv Ukr.
21 H7 Kraynovka Rus. Fed.
12 E3 Krefeld Ger.
21 E5 Kremenchuk Ukr.
21 E5 Kremenchuts'ka Vodoskhovshche resr Ukr.
21 G5 Kremenskaya Rus. Fed.
16 G6 Křemešník h. Czech Rep.
62 F3 Kremmling U.S.A.
16 G6 Krems an der Donau Austria
25 U3 Kresta, Zaliv b. Rus. Fed.
20 E3 Kresttsy Rus. Fed.
7 R9 Kretinga Lith.
12 E4 Kreuzau Ger.
13 F4 Kreuztal Ger.
17 N3 Kreva Belarus
86 C4 Kribi Cameroon
91 H3 Kriel S. Africa
19 J5 Krikellos Greece
40 H2 Kril'on, Mys c. Rus. Fed.
27 F5 Krishna r. India
33 B3 Krishnagiri India
33 C3 Krishna, Mouths of the river mouth India
35 G5 Krishnanagar India
33 B3 Krishnaraja Sagara l. India
7 K7 Kristiansand Norway
7 O8 Kristianstad Sweden
6 K5 Kristiansund Norway
7 O7 Kristinehamn Sweden
7 R5 Kristinestad Fin.
Kriti i. see Crete
Krivoy Rog see Kryvyy Rih
18 G1 Križevci Croatia
18 F2 Krk i. Croatia
6 O5 Krokom Sweden
6 L5 Krokstadøra Norway
6 O3 Krokstranda Norway
21 E5 Krolevets' Ukr.
13 K4 Kronach Ger.
44 B3 Krŏng Kaôh Kŏng Cambodia
6 S5 Kronoby Fin.
55 P3 Kronprins Frederik Bjerge mt Greenland
44 A2 Kronwa Myanmar
91 G3 Kroonstad S. Africa
21 G6 Kropotkin Rus. Fed.
13 L3 Kropstädt Ger.
17 K6 Krosno Pol.
16 H5 Krotoszyn Pol.
91 J2 Kruger National Park S. Africa
17 O3 Kruhlaye Belarus
45 B4 Krui Indon.
90 F7 Kruisfontein S. Africa
19 H4 Krujë Albania
19 L4 Krumovgrad Bulg.
Krungkao see Ayutthaya
Krung Thep see Bangkok
17 O3 Krupki Belarus
19 J3 Kruševac Yugo.
13 L4 Krušné Hory mts Czech Rep.
56 B3 Kruzof I. i. U.S.A.
20 D4 Krychaw Belarus
21 F6 Krymsk Rus. Fed.
19 L6 Krytiko Pelagos sea Greece
21 E6 Kryvyy Rih Ukr.
86 B2 Ksabi Alg.
86 C1 Ksar el Boukhari Alg.
86 B1 Ksar el Kebir Morocco
21 F5 Kshenskiy Rus. Fed.
18 D7 Ksour Essaf Tunisia
20 H3 Kstovo Rus. Fed.
44 A4 Kuah Malaysia
44 B4 Kuala Kangsar Malaysia
44 B4 Kuala Kerai Malaysia
44 B5 Kuala Kubu Baharu Malaysia
45 B2 Kuala Lipis Malaysia
45 B2 Kuala Lumpur Malaysia
44 B4 Kuala Nerang Malaysia
44 B5 Kuala Pilah Malaysia
44 B5 Kuala Rompin Malaysia
45 D3 Kualasampit Indon.
44 A4 Kualasimpang Indon.
45 B1 Kuala Terengganu Malaysia
43 A5 Kuamut Malaysia
42 C3 Kuandian China
39 F6 Kuanshan Taiwan
45 B2 Kuantan Malaysia
21 G6 Kuban' r. Rus. Fed.
29 J5 Kubaysah Iraq
20 F3 Kubenskoye, Ozero l. Rus. Fed.
20 H4 Kubnya r. Rus. Fed.
19 M3 Kubrat Bulg.
34 C4 Kuchaman India
34 C4 Kuchera India
45 D2 Kuching Malaysia
41 A10 Kuchino-shima i. Japan
Kucing see Kuching
19 H4 Kuçovë Albania
33 A3 Kudal India
45 E1 Kudat Malaysia
33 B3 Kudligi India
33 A3 Kudremukh mt India
45 D4 Kudus Indon.
16 F7 Kufstein Austria
20 H3 Kugesi Rus. Fed.
54 E3 Kugmallit Bay b. Can.
31 F5 Kūhak Iran
35 E3 Kuhanbokano mt China
13 L1 Kuhbier Ger.
30 E4 Kūhbonān Iran
30 B3 Kūhdasht Iran
29 L2 Kūhhaye Sabalan mts Iran
29 M3 Kūhīn Iran
6 V4 Kuhmo Fin.
7 T6 Kuhmoinen Fin.
30 D3 Kūhpāyeh Iran
30 E5 Kūh, Ra's-al pt Iran
13 L3 Kühren Ger.
90 B2 Kuis Namibia
90 A1 Kuiseb Pass Namibia
89 B5 Kuito Angola
56 C3 Kuiu Island i. U.S.A.
6 T4 Kuivaniemi Fin.
30 B5 Kū', J. al h. S. Arabia
35 F5 Kujang India
42 C4 Kujang-Dong N. Korea
40 G4 Kuji Japan
41 B8 Kujū-san volc. Japan
69 F1 Kukatush Can.
19 J3 Kukës Albania
20 J3 Kukmor Rus. Fed.
44 B5 Kukup Malaysia
30 D5 Kūl r. Iran
28 B2 Kula Turkey
35 G3 Kula Kangri mt Bhutan
26 D2 Kulandy Kazak.
31 F5 Kulaneh reg. Pak.
31 G4 Kulao r. Pak.
25 P2 Kular Rus. Fed.
43 B5 Kulassein i. Phil.
35 H4 Kulaura Bangl.
7 R8 Kuldīga Latvia
90 D1 Kule Botswana
20 G4 Kulebaki Rus. Fed.
44 C2 Kulen Cambodia
20 H2 Kulikovo Rus. Fed.
44 B4 Kulim Malaysia
31 J2 Kuli Sarez l. Tajik.
34 D3 Kullu India
13 K4 Kulmbach Ger.
31 H2 Kŭlob Tajik.
29 H2 Kulp Turkey
34 D4 Kulpahar India
71 F4 Kulpsville U.S.A.
26 D2 Kul'sary Kazak.
13 H5 Külsheim Ger.
28 D2 Kulu Turkey
28 C3 Kulübe Tepe mt Turkey
24 J4 Kulunda Rus. Fed.
24 J4 Kulundinskoye, Ozero salt l. Rus. Fed.
30 D4 Külvand Iran
50 D3 Kulwin Austr.
42 D5 Kŭm r. S. Korea
21 H6 Kuma r. Rus. Fed.
41 F6 Kumagaya Japan
40 F3 Kumaishi Japan
45 D3 Kumai, Teluk b. Indon.
41 B8 Kumamoto Japan
41 E8 Kumano Japan
19 J3 Kumanovo Macedonia
86 B4 Kumasi Ghana
Kumayri see Gyumri
86 C4 Kumba Cameroon
33 B4 Kumbakonam India
28 C2 Kümbet Turkey
90 E1 Kumchuru Botswana
30 D3 Kumel well Iran
24 G4 Kumertau Rus. Fed.
42 E4 Kumgang-san mt N. Korea
42 E6 Kŭmho r. S. Korea
42 D4 Kumhwa S. Korea
42 E5 Kumi S. Korea
7 O7 Kumla Sweden
13 M2 Kummersdorf-Alexanderdorf Ger.
86 D3 Kumo Nigeria
42 D6 Kŭmō-do i. S. Korea
44 B1 Kumphawapi Thai.
90 C4 Kums Namibia
33 A3 Kumta India
21 H7 Kumukh Rus. Fed.
31 H3 Kunar r. Afgh.
36 G2 Kunashir, Ostrov i. Rus. Fed.
35 E2 Kunchuk Tso salt l. China
7 U7 Kunda Estonia
35 E4 Kunda India
33 A3 Kundāpura India
34 B2 Kundar r. Afgh./Pak.
31 H2 Kunduz Afgh.
31 H2 Kunduz r. Afgh.
7 M8 Kungälv Sweden
27 F2 Kungei Alatau mts Kazak./Kyrg.
56 C4 Kunghit I. i. Can.
7 N8 Kungsbacka Sweden
7 M7 Kungshamn Sweden
88 B3 Kungu Congo(Zaire)
34 D6 Kuni r. India
41 B8 Kunimi-dake mt Japan
35 F5 Kunjabar India
35 G4 Kunlui r. India/Nepal
27 F3 Kunlun Shan mts China
35 H2 Kunlun Shankou pass China
39 B5 Kunming China
34 D4 Kuno r. India
42 D6 Kunsan S. Korea
38 F4 Kunshan China
48 C3 Kununurra Austr.
34 D4 Kunwari r. India
20 D3 Kun'ya Rus. Fed.
42 A5 Kunyu Shan h. China
13 H5 Künzelsau Ger.
13 K3 Künzels-Berg h. Ger.
39 F4 Kuocang Shan mts China
7 T6 Kuohijärvi l. Fin.
6 V3 Kuolayarvi Rus. Fed.
6 U5 Kuopio Fin.
6 S5 Kuortane Fin.
18 F2 Kupa r. Croatia/Slovenia
37 E8 Kupang Indon.
7 T9 Kupiškis Lith.
56 C3 Kupreanof Island i. U.S.A.
21 F5 Kup"yans'k Ukr.
27 G2 Kuqa China
29 M2 Kür r. Azer.
29 K1 Kura r. Azer./Georgia
21 G7 Kura r. Georgia/Rus. Fed.
21 H7 Kurakh Rus. Fed.
41 C7 Kurashiki Japan
35 E5 Kurasia India
41 C7 Kurayoshi Japan
28 B1 Kurban Dağı mt Turkey
21 E5 Kurchatov Rus. Fed.
29 M1 Kürdämir Azer.
29 M2 Kür Dili pt Azer.
33 A2 Kurduvadi India
19 L4 Kŭrdzhali Bulg.
41 C7 Kure Japan
28 D1 Küre Turkey
94 H4 Kure Atoll atoll HI U.S.A.
7 S7 Kuressaare Estonia
24 H4 Kurgan Rus. Fed.
21 G6 Kurganinsk Rus. Fed.
31 H2 Kuri Afgh.
34 B4 Kuri India
Kuria Muria Islands is see Ḥalāniyāt, Juzur al
6 S5 Kurikka Fin.
40 G5 Kurikoma-yama volc. Japan
36 G2 Kuril Islands is Rus. Fed.
36 G2 Kuril'sk Japan
Kuril'skiye Ostrova is see Kuril Islands
94 F2 Kuril Trench sea feature Pac. Oc.
87 F3 Kurmuk Sudan
33 B3 Kurnool India
28 E6 Kurnub Israel
41 E6 Kurobe Japan
40 G4 Kuroishi Japan
41 G6 Kuroiso Japan
13 J4 Kurort Schmalkalden Ger.
41 A9 Kuro-shima i. Japan
20 F4 Kurovskoye Rus. Fed.
51 C6 Kurow N.Z.
34 B2 Kurram r. Afgh./Pak.
50 H2 Kurri Kurri Austr.
Kuršių Marios lag. see Courland Lagoon
21 F5 Kursk Rus. Fed.
21 H6 Kurskaya Rus. Fed.
21 F5 Kurskaya Oblast' div. Rus. Fed.
Kurskiy Zaliv lag. see Courland Lagoon
28 D1 Kurşunlu Turkey
29 H3 Kurtalan Turkey
35 G4 Kuru r. Bhutan
28 G2 Kuruçay Turkey
34 D3 Kurukshetra India
36 A2 Kuruktag mts China
90 E3 Kuruman S. Africa
90 D3 Kuruman watercourse S. Africa
41 B8 Kurume Japan
36 D1 Kurumkan Rus. Fed.
33 C5 Kurunegala Sri Lanka
87 F2 Kurūsh, Jebel reg. Sudan
19 M6 Kuşadası Turkey
19 M6 Kuşadası Körfezi b. Turkey
56 B2 Kusawa Lake l. Can.
12 F5 Kusel Ger.
28 A1 Kuş Gölü l. Turkey
21 F6 Kushchevskaya Rus. Fed.
41 B9 Kushikino Japan
41 D8 Kushimoto Japan
40 J3 Kushiro Japan
40 J3 Kushiro-Shitsugen National Park Japan
31 F3 Kushka r. Turkm.
29 M5 Kūshkak Iran
26 E1 Kushmurun Kazak.
33 B3 Kushtagi India
35 G5 Kushtia Bangl.
38 C2 Kushui r. China
54 C3 Kuskokwim r. U.S.A.
54 B4 Kuskokwim Bay b. AK U.S.A.
54 C3 Kuskokwim Mts U.S.A.
42 C4 Kusŏng N. Korea
40 J3 Kussharo-ko l. Japan
26 E1 Kustanay Kazak.
13 F1 Küstenkanal canal Ger.
30 C4 Kut Iran
29 M6 Kūt Abdollāh Iran
44 A5 Kutacane Indon.
28 B2 Kütahya Turkey
21 G7 K'ut'aisi Georgia
Kut-al-Imara see Al Kūt
21 H6 Kutan Rus. Fed.
40 G3 Kutchan Japan
29 M5 Kūt-e Gapu Iran
18 G2 Kutina Croatia
18 G2 Kutjevo Croatia
17 J4 Kutno Pol.
88 B4 Kutu Congo(Zaire)
35 G5 Kutubdia I. i. Bangl.
54 G2 Kuujjua r. Can.
59 G2 Kuujjuaq Can.
Kuujjuarapik see Poste-de-la-Baleine
30 D1 Kuuli-Mayak Turkm.
6 V4 Kuusamo Fin.
7 U6 Kuusankoski Fin.
89 B5 Kuvango Angola
20 E3 Kuvshinovo Rus. Fed.
29 L7 Kuwait Kuwait
23 D7 Kuwait country Asia
29 L7 Kuwait Jun b. Kuwait
41 E7 Kuwana Japan
20 G1 Kuya Rus. Fed.
24 J4 Kuybyshev Novosibirsk Rus. Fed.
Kuybyshev see Samara
20 J4 Kuybyshevskoye Vdkhr. resr Rus. Fed.
38 D2 Kuye r. China
27 G2 Kuytun China
19 N6 Kuyucak Turkey
7 V6 Kuznechnoye Rus. Fed.
20 H4 Kuznetsk Rus. Fed.
40 F1 Kuznetsovo Rus. Fed.
21 C5 Kuznetsovs'k Ukr.
6 R1 Kvænangen chan. Norway
6 Q2 Kvaløya i. Norway
6 S1 Kvalsund Norway
Kvareli see Qvareli
18 F2 Kvarnerić chan. Croatia
54 C4 Kvichak Bay b. U.S.A.
56 D3 Kwadacha Wilderness Prov. Park res. Can.
39 □ Kwai Tau Leng h. H.K. China
94 G5 Kwajalein i. Pac. Oc.
44 A5 Kwala Indon.
91 J4 KwaMashu S. Africa
91 H2 KwaMhlanga S. Africa
42 D5 Kwangch'ŏn S. Korea
42 D6 Kwangju S. Korea
88 B4 Kwango r. Congo(Zaire)
88 D4 Kwangwazi Tanz.
42 D6 Kwangyang S. Korea
91 F6 Kwanobuhle S. Africa
91 F6 KwaNojoli S. Africa
91 G6 Kwanonqubela S. Africa
90 F5 Kwanonzame S. Africa
91 G6 Kwatinidubu S. Africa
91 H3 KwaZamokhule S. Africa
90 F6 Kwazamukucinga S. Africa
90 F5 Kwazamuxolo S. Africa
91 H3 KwaZanele S. Africa
91 J4 Kwazulu-Natal div. S. Africa
89 C5 Kwekwe Zimbabwe
90 F1 Kweneng div. Botswana
88 B4 Kwenge r. Congo(Zaire)
91 G5 Kwezi-Naledi S. Africa
17 J4 Kwidzyn Pol.
54 B4 Kwigillingok AK U.S.A.
48 E2 Kwikila P.N.G.
88 B4 Kwilu r. Angola/Congo(Zaire)
37 F7 Kwoka mt Indon.
39 □ Kwun Tong H.K. China
87 D4 Kyabé Chad
50 E4 Kyabram Austr.
44 A1 Kya-in Seikkyi Myanmar
36 C1 Kyakhta Rus. Fed.
50 D3 Kyalite Austr.
48 D5 Kyancutta Austr.
20 F1 Kyanda Rus. Fed.
44 A1 Kyaukhnyat Myanmar
35 H6 Kyaukpyu Myanmar
35 H5 Kyauktaw Myanmar
7 S9 Kybartai Lith.
50 C4 Kybybolite Austr.
34 D2 Kyelang India
38 A2 Kyikug China
Kyiv see Kiev
Kyklades is see Cyclades
57 H4 Kyle Can.
10 C3 Kyle of Lochalsh U.K.
12 E5 Kyll r. Ger.
19 K6 Kyllini mt Greece
50 E4 Kyneton Austr.
88 D3 Kyoga, Lake l. Uganda
41 D7 Kyōga-misaki pt Japan
44 A1 Kyondo Myanmar
42 E6 Kyŏngju S. Korea
41 D7 Kyōto Japan
19 J6 Kyparissia Greece
19 J6 Kyparissiakos Kolpos b. Greece
24 H4 Kypshak, Ozero salt l. Kazak.
19 L5 Kyra Panagia i. Greece
23 G5 Kyrgyzstan country Asia
13 L2 Kyritz Ger.
6 L5 Kyrksæterøra Norway
24 G3 Kyrta Rus. Fed.
20 H1 Kyssa Rus. Fed.
25 P3 Kytalyktakh Rus. Fed.
19 K6 Kythira i. Greece
19 L6 Kythnos i. Greece
44 A2 Kyungyaung Myanmar
41 B8 Kyūshū i. Japan
94 D5 Kyushu - Palau Ridge sea feature Pac. Oc.
19 K3 Kyustendil Bulg.
50 F3 Kywong Austr.
21 D5 Kyyivs'ke Vdskh. resr Ukr.
6 T5 Kyyjärvi Fin.
36 B1 Kyzyl Rus. Fed.
26 E2 Kyzylkum Desert Uzbek.
27 H1 Kyzyl-Mazhalyk Rus. Fed.
26 E2 Kzyl-Orda Kazak.
26 F1 Kzyltu Kazak.

L

12 F4 Laacher See l. Ger.
7 T7 Laagri Estonia
6 U2 Laanila Fin.
83 B3 La Araucania div. Chile
88 E3 Laascaanood Somalia
88 E2 Laasgoray Somalia
81 E2 La Asunción Venez.
86 A2 Laâyoune Western Sahara
21 G6 Laba r. Rus. Fed.
65 C6 La Babia Mex.
80 D3 La Banda Arg.
62 E3 La Barge U.S.A.
49 H3 Labasa Fiji
14 C3 La Baule-Escoublac France
86 A3 Labé Guinea
58 F4 Labelle Can.
68 B5 La Belle U.S.A.
56 B2 Laberge, Lake l. Can.
45 A5 Labian, Tg pt Malaysia
56 E2 La Biche r. Can.
21 G6 Labinsk Rus. Fed.
45 E1 Labis Malaysia
43 B3 Labo Phil.
28 F4 Laboué Lebanon
14 D4 Labouheyre France
83 D2 Laboulaye Arg.
55 M3 Labrador Can.
59 G3 Labrador City Can.
55 N3 Labrador Sea Can./Greenland
78 F5 Lábrea Brazil
45 E1 Labuan Malaysia
45 C4 Labuhan Indon.
45 B2 Labuhanbilik Indon.
44 A5 Labuhanruku Indon.
43 A5 Labuk r. Malaysia
45 E1 Labuk, Telukan b. Malaysia
37 E7 Labuna Indon.
24 H3 Labytnangi Rus. Fed.
19 H4 Laç Albania
83 D1 La Calera Arg.
83 B2 La Calera Chile
14 F2 La Capelle France
83 B4 Lacar, L. l. Arg.
83 D2 La Carlota Arg.
15 E3 La Carolina Spain
19 M2 Lăcăuţi, Vârful mt Romania
71 J1 Lac-Baker Can.
26 F5 Laccadive Islands India
57 K4 Lac du Bonnet Can.
74 G5 La Ceiba Honduras
81 C2 La Ceiba Venez.
50 B4 Lacepede B. b. Austr.
71 E4 Laceyville U.S.A.
71 H1 Lac Frontière Can.
20 F2 Lacha, Ozero l. Rus. Fed.
13 J2 Lachendorf Ger.
69 F3 Lachine U.S.A.
50 E3 Lachlan r. Austr.
75 J7 La Chorrera Panama
58 F4 Lachute Can.
29 L2 Laçın Azer.
14 G5 La Ciotat France
70 D3 Lackawanna U.S.A.
57 G4 Lac La Biche Can.
56 E4 Lac La Hache Can.
56 F2 Lac La Martre Can.
57 H3 Lac La Ronge Provincial Park res. Can.
59 F4 Lac Mégantic Can.
71 G2 Lacolle Can.
63 E6 La Colorada Mex.
56 G4 Lacombe Can.
18 C5 Laconi Sardinia Italy
71 H3 Laconia U.S.A.
69 J1 La Corne Can.
68 B4 La Crescent U.S.A.
68 B4 La Crosse U.S.A.
81 A4 La Cruz Col.
64 E4 La Cygne U.S.A.
34 D2 Ladakh Range mts India
44 A4 Ladang i. Thai.
28 E1 Lâdik Turkey
90 D6 Ladismith S. Africa
31 F4 Lādīz Iran
34 C4 Ladnun India
81 B3 La Dorada Col.
Ladozhskoye Ozero l. see Lagoda, Lake
35 H4 Ladu mt India
20 E2 Ladva Rus. Fed.
20 E2 Ladva-Vetka Rus. Fed.
55 K2 Lady Ann Strait chan. Can.
10 E4 Ladybank U.K.
91 G4 Ladybrand S. Africa
69 G2 Lady Evelyn Lake l. Can.
91 G5 Lady Frere S. Africa
91 G5 Lady Grey S. Africa
56 E5 Ladysmith Can.
91 H4 Ladysmith S. Africa
68 B3 Ladysmith U.S.A.
48 E2 Lae P.N.G.
44 B2 Laem Ngop Thai.
44 B4 Laem Pho pt Thai.
7 K6 Lærdalsøyri Norway
78 F8 La Esmeralda Bol.
81 D4 La Esmeralda Venez.
7 M8 Læsø i. Denmark
42 B2 Lafa China
83 D1 La Falda Arg.
62 F4 Lafayette CO U.S.A.
68 D5 Lafayette IN U.S.A.
65 E6 Lafayette LA U.S.A.
67 C5 La Fayette U.S.A.
12 B5 La Fère France
12 B5 La-Ferté-Milon France
12 B6 La Ferté-sous-Jouarre France
30 C5 Laffān, Ra's pt Qatar
86 C4 Lafia Nigeria
14 D3 La Flèche France
70 A6 La Follette U.S.A.
69 H2 Laforce Can.
69 G2 Laforest Can.
59 F3 Laforge Can.
81 B2 La Fría Venez.
30 D5 Laft Iran
18 C6 La Galite i. Tunisia
21 H6 Lagan' Rus. Fed.
11 E3 Lagan r. U.K.
79 L6 Lagarto Brazil
13 G3 Lage Ger.
7 L7 Lågen r. Norway
10 C5 Lagg U.K.
10 D3 Laggan U.K.
10 D4 Laggan, Loch l. U.K.
86 C1 Laghouat Alg.
35 F2 Lagkor Co salt l. China
81 B2 La Gloria Col.
82 D2 Lagoa Santa Brazil
20 D2 Lagoda, Lake l. Rus. Fed.
29 L1 Lagodekhi Georgia
44 D5 Lagong i. Indon.
43 B3 Lagonoy Gulf b. Phil.
80 B7 Lago Posadas Arg.
83 B4 Lago Ranco Chile
86 C4 Lagos Nigeria
15 B4 Lagos Port.
74 D4 Lagos de Moreno Mex.
62 C2 La Grande U.S.A.
58 E3 La Grande r. Can.
58 F3 La Grande 4, Réservoir de resr Can.
58 E3 La Grande 2, Réservoir de resr Can.
58 E3 La Grande 3, Réservoir de resr Can.
48 C3 Lagrange Austr.
67 C5 La Grange GA U.S.A.
71 J2 La Grange ME U.S.A.
68 D5 La Grange MI U.S.A.
68 B5 La Grange MO U.S.A.
65 D6 La Grange TX U.S.A.
68 E5 Lagrange U.S.A.
81 E3 La Gran Sabana plat. Venez.
80 G3 Laguna Brazil
72 D5 Laguna Beach U.S.A.
83 B3 Laguna de Laja, Parque Nacional nat. park Chile
72 D5 Laguna Mts mts U.S.A.
78 C5 Lagunas Peru
80 A7 Laguna San Rafael, Parque Nacional nat. park Chile
81 C2 Lagunillas Venez.
45 E1 Lahad Datu Malaysia
43 A5 Lahad Datu, Telukan b. Malaysia
72 □2 Lahaina U.S.A.
29 M3 Lahargin Iran
45 B3 Lahat Indon.
44 A5 Lahewa Indon.
32 B7 Laḥij Yemen
30 C2 Lāhījān Iran
72 □1 Lahilahi Pt pt U.S.A.
13 F4 Lahn r. Ger.
12 F4 Lahnstein Ger.
7 N8 Laholm Sweden
72 C2 Lahontan Res. resr U.S.A.
34 C3 Lahore Pak.
81 E3 La Horqueta Venez.
34 B3 Lahri Pak.
7 T6 Lahti Fin.
87 D4 Laï Chad
38 F3 Lai'an China
39 C6 Laibin China
30 E4 Laidāru Iran
72 □1 Laie U.S.A.
72 □1 Laie Pt pt U.S.A.
39 C4 Laifeng China
14 E2 L'Aigle France
6 S5 Laihia Fin.
35 H4 Laimakuri India
90 D6 Laingsburg S. Africa
6 S3 Lainioälven r. Sweden
10 D2 Lairg U.K.
43 C5 Lais Phil.

7 R6 Laitila Fin.
18 D1 Laives Italy
38 E2 Laiwu China
38 F2 Laiyang China
38 E2 Laiyuan China
38 F2 Laizhou Wan b. China
83 B3 Laja r. Chile
83 B3 Laja, Lago de l. Chile
48 D3 Lajamanu Austr.
79 L5 Lajes Rio Grande do Norte Brazil
80 F3 Lajes Santa Catarina Brazil
63 G4 La Junta U.S.A.
62 E2 Lake U.S.A.
49 J3 Lakeba i. Fiji
28 D6 Lake Bardawīl Reserve res. Egypt
50 D4 Lake Bolac Austr.
50 F2 Lake Cargelligo Austr.
62 B1 Lake Chelan Nat. Recreation Area res. U.S.A.
67 D6 Lake City FL U.S.A.
68 E3 Lake City MI U.S.A.
68 A3 Lake City MN U.S.A.
67 E5 Lake City SC U.S.A.
8 D3 Lake District National Park U.K.
72 D5 Lake Elsinore U.S.A.
69 H3 Lakefield Can.
68 C4 Lake Geneva U.S.A.
55 M3 Lake Harbour Can.
73 E4 Lake Havasu City U.S.A.
72 C4 Lake Isabella U.S.A.
67 D6 Lakeland U.S.A.
68 C2 Lake Linden U.S.A.
56 F4 Lake Louise Can.
73 E4 Lake Mead National Recreation Area res. U.S.A.
71 J2 Lake Moxie U.S.A.
62 B2 Lake Oswego U.S.A.
51 B5 Lake Paringa N.Z.
71 G2 Lake Placid U.S.A.
72 A2 Lakeport U.S.A.
51 C6 Lake Pukaki N.Z.
58 D3 Lake River Can.
69 H3 Lake St Peter Can.
50 G4 Lakes Entrance Austr.
68 E2 Lake Superior National Park Can.
50 H3 Lake Tabourie Austr.
51 C6 Lake Tekapo N.Z.
58 E4 Lake Traverse Can.
62 B3 Lakeview U.S.A.
62 F4 Lakewood CO U.S.A.
71 F4 Lakewood NJ U.S.A.
70 C4 Lakewood OH U.S.A.
67 D7 Lake Worth U.S.A.
20 D2 Lakhdenpokh'ya Rus. Fed.
34 E4 Lakhimpur India
34 D5 Lakhnadon India
34 B5 Lakhpat India
19 K6 Lakonikos Kolpos b. Greece
86 B4 Lakota Côte d'Ivoire
6 U1 Laksefjorden chan. Norway
6 T1 Lakselv Norway
33 A4 Lakshadweep div. India
35 G5 Laksham Bangl.
33 B2 Lakshettipet India
35 G5 Lakshmikantapur India
43 B5 Lala Phil.
83 D2 La Laguna Arg.
83 B3 La Laja Chile
88 B3 Lalara Gabon
13 L1 Lalendorf Ger.
30 C3 Lālī Iran
83 B2 La Ligua Chile
42 D1 Lalin China
15 B1 Lalín Spain
42 C1 Lalin r. China
15 D4 La Línea de la Concepción Spain
34 D4 Lalitpur India
43 B2 Lal-Lo Phil.
57 H3 La Loche Can.
57 H3 La Loche, Lac l. Can.
12 C4 La Louvière Belgium
20 H2 Lal'sk Rus. Fed.
35 H5 Lama Bangl.
18 C4 La Maddalena Sardinia Italy
43 A5 Lamag Malaysia
44 A2 Lamaing Myanmar
La Manche str. see English Channel
64 C4 Lamar CO U.S.A.
65 E4 Lamar MO U.S.A.
30 D5 Lamard Iran
18 C5 La Marmora, Punta mt Sardinia Italy
83 D3 Lamarque Arg.
65 E6 La Marque U.S.A.
56 F2 La Martre, Lac l. Can.
88 B4 Lambaréné Gabon
78 C5 Lambayeque Peru
11 F4 Lambay Island i. Rep. of Ireland
92 D4 Lambert Gl. gl. Ant.
90 C6 Lambert's Bay S. Africa
34 C3 Lambi India
9 F6 Lambourn Downs h. U.K.
44 C2 Lam Chi r. Thai.
15 C2 Lamego Port.
59 H4 Lamèque, I. i. Can.
78 C6 La Merced Peru
50 C3 Lameroo Austr.
65 C5 Lamesa U.S.A.
72 D5 La Mesa U.S.A.
19 K5 Lamia Greece
63 E6 La Misa Mex.
72 D5 La Misión Mex.
43 B5 Lamitan Phil.
39 □ Lamma I. i. H.K. China
51 B6 Lammerlaw Ra. mts N.Z.
10 F5 Lammermuir Hills h. U.K.
7 O8 Lammhult Sweden
7 T6 Lammi Fin.
68 C5 La Moille U.S.A.
71 G2 Lamoille r. U.S.A.
68 B5 La Moine r. U.S.A.
43 B3 Lamon Bay b. Phil.
64 E3 Lamoni U.S.A.
62 F3 Lamont U.S.A.
65 B6 La Morita Mex.
69 H1 La Motte Can.
44 B1 Lam Pao Res. resr Thai.
65 D6 Lampasas U.S.A.
60 F6 Lampazos Mex.
18 E7 Lampedusa, Isola di i. Sicily Italy
9 C5 Lampeter U.K.
44 B2 Lam Plai Mat r. Thai.
20 F4 Lamskoye Rus. Fed.
39 □ Lam Tin H.K. China
88 E4 Lamu Kenya
35 H6 Lamu Myanmar
72 □2 Lanai i. U.S.A.
72 □2 Lanai City U.S.A.
43 C5 Lanao, Lake l. Phil.
69 J3 Lanark Can.
10 E5 Lanark U.K.
68 C4 Lanark U.S.A.
43 A5 Lanas Malaysia
44 A3 Lanbi Kyun i. Myanmar
Lancang Jiang r. see Mekong
71 F2 Lancaster Can.
8 E3 Lancaster U.K.
72 C4 Lancaster CA U.S.A.
68 A5 Lancaster MO U.S.A.
71 H2 Lancaster NH U.S.A.
70 B5 Lancaster OH U.S.A.
71 E4 Lancaster PA U.S.A.
67 D5 Lancaster SC U.S.A.
68 B4 Lancaster WI U.S.A.
8 E4 Lancaster Canal canal U.K.
55 K2 Lancaster Sound str. Can.
18 F3 Lanciano Italy
83 B3 Lanco Chile
38 F2 Lancun China
16 F6 Landau an der Isar Ger.
13 G5 Landau in der Pfalz Ger.
16 E7 Landeck Austria
62 E3 Lander U.S.A.
13 H2 Landesbergen Ger.
57 H4 Landis Can.
16 E6 Landsberg am Lech Ger.
9 B7 Land's End pt U.K.
16 F6 Landshut Ger.
7 N9 Landskrona Sweden
12 F5 Landstuhl Ger.
13 G1 Land Wursten reg. Ger.
11 D4 Lanesborough Rep. of Ireland
44 C3 La Nga r. Vietnam
35 E3 La'nga Co l. China
38 C3 Langao China
31 F3 Langar Iran
10 B2 Langavat, Loch l. U.K.
90 E4 Langberg mts S. Africa
64 D1 Langdon U.S.A.
90 C6 Langeberg mts S. Africa
7 M9 Langeland i. Denmark
7 T6 Längelmäki Fin.
7 T6 Längelmävesi l. Fin.
13 J3 Langelsheim Ger.
13 G1 Langen Ger.
13 H2 Langenhagen Ger.
13 F4 Langenhahn Ger.
13 F5 Langenlonsheim Ger.
16 C7 Langenthal Switz.
13 K2 Langenweddingen Ger.
12 F1 Langeoog Ger.
12 F1 Langeoog i. Ger.
7 L7 Langesund Norway
44 B5 Langgapayung Indon.
13 G4 Langgöns Ger.
57 H4 Langham Can.
6 C4 Langjökull ice cap Iceland
45 A2 Langka Indon.
45 A1 Langkawi i. Malaysia
44 A3 Lang Kha Toek, Khao mt Thai.
90 D4 Langklip S. Africa
43 A5 Langkon Malaysia
69 K1 Langlade Can.
68 C3 Langlade U.S.A.
14 F4 Langogne France
6 O2 Langøya i. Norway
35 F3 Langphu mt China
9 E6 Langport U.K.
39 F5 Langqi China
14 G3 Langres France
31 D1 Langru China
45 A2 Langsa Indon.
44 A4 Langsa, Teluk b. Indon.
6 P5 Långsele Sweden
38 C1 Langshan China
38 C1 Lang Shan mts China
39 C6 Lang Sơn Vietnam
8 G3 Langtoft U.K.
65 C6 Langtry U.S.A.
14 F5 Languedoc reg. France
6 R4 Långvattnet Sweden
13 H2 Langwedel Ger.
38 F4 Langxi China
38 C4 Langzhong China
69 H2 Laniel Can.
57 H4 Lanigan Can.
72 □1 Lanikai U.S.A.
83 B3 Lanín, Parque Nacional nat. park Arg.
83 B3 Lanín, Volcán volc. Arg.
38 E3 Lankao China
29 M2 Länkäran Azer.
14 C2 Lannion France
6 S3 Lansån Sweden
68 C2 L'Anse U.S.A.
68 B4 Lansing IA U.S.A.
68 E4 Lansing MI U.S.A.
56 C2 Lansing r. Can.
39 D6 Lantau I. i. H.K. China
39 □ Lantau Island i. H.K. China
39 □ Lantau Peak h. H.K. China
43 C4 Lanuza Bay b. Phil.
39 F4 Lanxi China
87 F4 Lanya Sudan
39 F6 Lan Yü i. Taiwan
86 A2 Lanzarote i. Canary Is
38 B2 Lanzhou China
42 B1 Lanzijing China
43 B2 Laoag Phil.
43 C3 Laoang Phil.
39 B6 Lao Cai Vietnam
38 F1 Laoha r. China
38 D3 Laohekou China
42 A4 Laohutun China
42 D3 Laoling China
42 D3 Lao Ling mts China
14 F2 Laon France
68 C3 Laona U.S.A.
23 K8 Laos country Asia
38 F2 Lao Shan mt China
42 E2 Laotougou China
42 C3 Laotuding Shan h. China
Laowohi pass see Khardung La
38 A1 Laoximiao China
42 E2 Laoye Ling mts China
82 C4 Lapa Brazil
43 B5 Lapac i. Phil.
75 J7 La Palma Panama
15 C4 La Palma del Condado Spain
83 F2 La Paloma Uru.
83 D3 La Pampa div. Arg.
72 B4 La Panza Range mts U.S.A.
81 E3 La Paragua Venez.
43 A5 Laparan i. Phil.
83 E1 La Paz Entre Ríos Arg.
83 C2 La Paz Mendoza Arg.
78 E7 La Paz Bol.
74 B4 La Paz Mex.
68 D5 Lapaz U.S.A.
74 E4 La Pedrera Col.
69 F4 Lapeer U.S.A.
40 G2 La Pérouse Strait str. Japan/Rus. Fed.
81 E3 La Piña r. Venez.
62 B3 La Pine U.S.A.
43 C3 Lapinig Phil.
43 C4 Lapinin i. Phil.
6 U5 Lapinlahti Fin.
28 D4 Lapithos Cyprus
65 F6 Laplace U.S.A.
64 C2 La Plant U.S.A.
83 F2 La Plata Arg.
81 B4 La Plata Col.
20 G1 Lapominka Rus. Fed.
68 D5 La Porte U.S.A.
68 A4 La Porte City U.S.A.
6 S5 Lappajärvi Fin.
6 S5 Lappajärvi l. Fin.
7 V6 Lappeenranta Fin.
13 L5 Lappersdorf Ger.
6 S2 Lappland reg. Europe
71 G2 La Prairie Can.
65 D6 La Pryor U.S.A.
19 M4 Lâpseki Turkey
25 N2 Laptev Sea sea Rus. Fed.
6 S5 Lapua Fin.
43 B4 Lapu-Lapu Phil.
80 C2 La Quiaca Arg.
18 E3 L'Aquila Italy
72 D5 La Quinta U.S.A.
30 D5 Lār Iran
86 B1 Larache Morocco
30 E5 Lārak i. Iran
62 F3 Laramie U.S.A.
62 F3 Laramie Mts mts U.S.A.
Laranda see Karaman
82 B4 Laranjeiras do Sul Brazil
82 B3 Laranjinha r. Brazil
37 E7 Larantuka Indon.
37 F7 Larat i. Indon.
15 H4 Larba Alg.
7 Q8 Lärbro Sweden
69 G2 Larchwood Can.
69 H1 Larder Lake Can.
15 E1 Laredo Spain
65 D7 Laredo U.S.A.
67 D7 Largo U.S.A.
10 D5 Largs U.K.
30 B2 Lārī Iran
18 D6 L'Ariana Tunisia
57 K5 Larimore U.S.A.
80 C3 La Rioja Arg.
83 C1 La Rioja div. Arg.
15 E1 La Rioja div. Spain
19 K5 Larisa Greece
30 E5 Laristan reg. Iran
34 B4 Larkana Pak.
16 C7 Larmont mt France/Switz.
28 D4 Larnaka Cyprus
11 F3 Larne U.K.
64 D4 Larned U.S.A.
10 C6 Larne Lough in U.K.
15 D1 La Robla Spain
12 D4 La Roche-en-Ardenne Belgium
14 D3 La Rochelle France
14 D3 La Roche-sur-Yon France
15 E3 La Roda Spain
75 L5 La Romana Dom. Rep.
57 H3 La Ronge Can.
65 C7 La Rosa Mex.
48 D3 Larrimah Austr.
92 B2 Larsen Ice Shelf ice feature Ant.
6 S5 Larsmo Fin.
7 M7 Larvik Norway
73 H2 La Sal Junction U.S.A.
71 G2 La Salle Can.
68 C5 La Salle U.S.A.
58 E4 La Sarre Can.
81 D2 Las Aves, Islas is Venez.
83 B2 Las Cabras Chile
59 J4 La Scie Can.
63 F5 Las Cruces U.S.A.
75 K5 La Selle mt Haiti
83 B1 La Serena Chile
65 C7 Las Esperanças Mex.
83 E3 Las Flores Arg.
31 F5 Lāshār r. Iran
57 H4 Lashburn Can.
83 C2 Las Heras Arg.
36 B4 Lashio Myanmar
31 G4 Lashkar Gāh Afgh.
83 B3 Las Lajas Arg.
81 D3 Las Lajitas Venez.
80 D2 Las Lomitas Arg.
15 C4 Las Marismas marsh Spain
80 C7 Las Martinetas Arg.
81 D2 Las Mercedes Venez.
65 B7 Las Nieves Mex.
72 D5 Las Palmas r. Mex.
86 A2 Las Palmas de Gran Canaria Canary Is
18 C2 La Spezia Italy
83 F2 Las Piedras Uru.
80 C6 Las Plumas Arg.
83 E2 Las Rosas Arg.
62 B3 Lassen Pk volc. U.S.A.
62 B3 Lassen Volcanic Nat. Park U.S.A.
92 B2 Lassiter Coast coastal area Ant.
75 H7 Las Tablas Panama
80 D3 Las Termas Arg.
57 H4 Last Mountain L. l. Can.
88 B4 Lastoursville Gabon
18 G3 Lastovo i. Croatia
81 D3 Las Trincheras Venez.
13 F2 Lastrup Ger.
63 F6 Las Varas Chihuahua Mex.
83 D1 Las Varillas Arg.
63 F5 Las Vegas NM U.S.A.
73 E3 Las Vegas NV U.S.A.
15 D3 Las Villuercas mt Spain
78 C4 Latacunga Ecuador
92 A2 Latady I. i. Ant.
81 B5 La Tagua Col.
28 E4 Latakia Syria
69 H2 Latchford Can.
35 F5 Latehar India
14 D4 La Teste France
12 F2 Lathen Ger.
10 E2 Latheron U.K.
18 E4 Latina Italy
83 D2 La Toma Arg.
81 D2 La Tortuga, Isla i. Venez.
70 D4 Latrobe U.S.A.
12 D2 Lattrop Neth.
69 H2 Latulipe Can.
58 F4 La Tuque Can.
33 B2 Latur India
5 F3 Latvia country Europe
80 C1 Lauca, Parque Nacional nat. park Chile
16 F5 Lauchhammer Ger.
10 F5 Lauder U.K.
13 H1 Lauenbrück Ger.
13 J1 Lauenburg (Elbe) Ger.
13 K5 Lauf an der Pegnitz Ger.
14 H3 Laufen Switz.
68 D2 Laughing Fish Pt pt U.S.A.
7 S7 Lauka Estonia
6 V1 Laukvik Norway
40 D2 Laulyu Rus. Fed.
44 A3 Laun Thai.
48 E6 Launceston Austr.
9 C7 Launceston U.K.
11 B5 Laune r. Rep. of Ireland
44 A2 Launglon Bok Is is Myanmar
83 B4 La Unión Chile
81 A4 La Unión Col.
74 G6 La Unión El Salvador
43 B3 Laur Phil.
50 B2 Laura S.A. Austr.
48 E3 Laura Austr.
81 D3 La Urbana Venez.
71 F5 Laurel DE U.S.A.
65 F6 Laurel MS U.S.A.
62 E2 Laurel MT U.S.A.
70 D4 Laurel Hill h. U.S.A.
70 A6 Laurel River Lake l. U.S.A.
10 F4 Laurencekirk U.K.
59 F4 Laurentides, Réserve faunique des res. Can.
18 F4 Lauria Italy
67 E5 Laurinburg U.S.A.
68 C2 Laurium U.S.A.
16 C7 Lausanne Switz.
45 E3 Laut i. Indon.
83 B3 Lautaro Chile
13 H4 Lautersbach (Hessen) Ger.
45 E3 Laut Kecil, Kepulauan is Indon.
49 H3 Lautoka Fiji
6 V5 Lauvuskylä Fin.
58 F4 Laval Can.
14 D2 Laval France
18 F1 Lavant r. Austria/Slovenia
80 B5 Lavapié, Pta pt Chile
30 C4 Lāvar Kabkān Iran
48 C4 Laverton Austr.
81 D2 La Victoria Venez.
69 G2 Lavigne Can.
62 E2 Lavina U.S.A.
82 D3 Lavras Brazil
83 G1 Lavras do Sul Brazil
91 J3 Lavumisa Swaziland
34 B2 Lawa Pak.
92 C6 Law Dome ice feature Ant.
44 B4 Lawit, Gunung mt Malaysia
29 J7 Lawqah waterhole S. Arabia
86 B3 Lawra Ghana
64 E4 Lawrence KS U.S.A.
71 H3 Lawrence MA U.S.A.
67 C5 Lawrenceburg U.S.A.
71 K2 Lawrence Station Can.
70 E6 Lawrenceville U.S.A.
65 D5 Lawton U.S.A.
26 B4 Lawz, J. al mt S. Arabia
7 O7 Laxå Sweden
90 E3 Laxey S. Africa
8 C3 Laxey U.K.
10 C2 Laxford, Loch in. U.K.
10 □ Laxo U.K.
50 D5 Layers Hill Austr.
29 K4 Laylān Iraq
94 H4 Laysan Island i. HI U.S.A.
72 A2 Laytonville U.S.A.
19 J2 Lazarevac Yugo.
92 D3 Lazarev Sea sea Ant.
21 F7 Lazarevskoye Rus. Fed.
63 D6 Lázaro Cárdenas Baja California Mex.
74 D5 Lázaro Cárdenas Michoacán Mex.
65 B7 Lázaro Cárdenas, Presa resr Mex.
83 F2 Lazcano Uru.
7 S9 Lazdijai Lith.
30 D5 Lāzeh Iran
25 P3 Lazo Rus. Fed.
40 C3 Lazo Rus. Fed.
44 B2 Leach Cambodia
68 E2 Leach I. i. Can.
64 C2 Lead U.S.A.
57 H4 Leader Can.
50 G2 Leadville Austr.
63 F4 Leadville U.S.A.
65 F6 Leaf r. U.S.A.
57 J3 Leaf Rapids Can.
65 D6 Leakey U.S.A.
69 F4 Leamington Can.
73 F2 Leamington U.S.A.
9 F5 Leamington Spa, Royal U.K.
39 E5 Le'an China
11 B5 Leane, Lough l. Rep. of Ireland
11 B6 Leap Rep. of Ireland
57 H4 Leask Can.
9 G6 Leatherhead U.K.
64 E4 Leavenworth KS U.S.A.
62 B2 Leavenworth WA U.S.A.
72 C2 Leavitt Peak summit U.S.A.
12 E5 Lebach Ger.
43 C5 Lebak Phil.
68 D5 Lebanon IN U.S.A.
64 D4 Lebanon KS U.S.A.
65 E4 Lebanon MO U.S.A.
71 G3 Lebanon NH U.S.A.
71 F4 Lebanon NJ U.S.A.
70 A5 Lebanon OH U.S.A.
62 B2 Lebanon OR U.S.A.
71 E4 Lebanon PA U.S.A.
67 C4 Lebanon TN U.S.A.
23 C6 Lebanon country Asia
12 C3 Lebbeke Belgium
20 F4 Lebedyan' Rus. Fed.
21 E5 Lebedyn Ukr.
14 E3 Le Blanc France
16 H3 Lębork Pol.
91 H2 Lebowakgomo S. Africa
15 C4 Lebrija Spain
16 H3 Łebsko, Jezioro lag. Pol.
83 B3 Lebu Chile
12 B4 Le Cateau-Cambrésis France
12 B4 Le Catelet France
19 H4 Lecce Italy
18 C2 Lecco Italy
16 E7 Lech r. Austria/Ger.
19 J6 Lechaina Greece
39 D5 Lechang China
12 C5 Le Chesne France
16 E7 Lechtaler Alpen mts Austria
16 D3 Leck Ger.
14 G3 Le Creusot France
14 E5 Lectoure France
44 B5 Ledang, Gunung mt Malaysia
9 E5 Ledbury U.K.
15 D2 Ledesma Spain
10 D2 Ledmore U.K.
20 E1 Ledmozero Rus. Fed.
39 C7 Ledong China
38 B2 Ledu China
56 G4 Leduc Can.
71 G3 Lee U.S.A.
64 E2 Leech L. l. U.S.A.
8 F4 Leeds U.K.
71 H2 Leeds Junction U.S.A.
9 B7 Leedstown U.K.
12 E1 Leek Neth.
9 E4 Leek U.K.
12 D3 Leende Neth.
70 D4 Leeper U.S.A.
12 F1 Leer (Ostfriesland) Ger.
67 D6 Leesburg FL U.S.A.
70 E5 Leesburg VA U.S.A.
13 H2 Leese Ger.
65 E6 Leesville U.S.A.
70 C4 Leesville Lake l. U.S.A.
50 F3 Leeton Austr.
90 D6 Leeu-Gamka S. Africa
12 D1 Leeuwarden Neth.
48 B5 Leeuwin, C. c. Austr.
72 C3 Lee Vining U.S.A.
75 M5 Leeward Islands is Caribbean Sea
28 D4 Lefka Cyprus
19 J5 Lefkada Greece
19 J5 Lefkada i. Greece
28 D4 Lefkara Cyprus
19 J5 Lefkimmi Greece
Lefkosia see Nicosia
43 B3 Legaspi Phil.
12 F2 Legden Ger.
72 A2 Leggett U.S.A.
18 D2 Legnago Italy
16 H5 Legnica Pol.
34 D2 Leh Jammu and Kashmir
14 E2 Le Havre France
71 F4 Lehighton U.S.A.
6 V5 Lehmo Fin.
13 L2 Lehnin Ger.
13 J2 Lehre Ger.
13 H2 Lehrte Ger.
6 S5 Lehtimäki Fin.
90 D1 Lehututu Botswana
34 B3 Leiah Pak.
16 G7 Leibnitz Austria
9 F5 Leicester U.K.
48 D3 Leichhardt r. Austr.
12 C2 Leiden Neth.
51 E2 Leigh N.Z.
8 E4 Leigh U.K.
9 G6 Leighton Buzzard U.K.
13 G5 Leimen Ger.
13 H2 Leine r. Ger.
13 J3 Leinefelde Ger.
11 E5 Leinster, Mount h. Rep. of Ireland
19 M6 Leipsoi i. Greece
13 L3 Leipzig Ger.
6 O3 Leiranger Norway
15 B3 Leiria Port.
39 C5 Leishan China
39 D5 Lei Shui r. China
13 L3 Leisnig Ger.
66 C4 Leitchfield U.S.A.
81 B4 Leiva, Co mt Col.
11 E4 Leixlip Rep. of Ireland
39 D5 Leiyang China
39 C6 Leizhou Bandao pen. China
39 D6 Leizhou Wan b. China
6 M4 Leka Norway
88 B4 Lékana Congo
18 C6 Le Kef Tunisia
90 B4 Lekkersing S. Africa
88 B4 Lékoni Gabon
7 O6 Leksand Sweden
6 W5 Leksozero, Oz. l. Rus. Fed.
68 E3 Leland MI U.S.A.
65 F5 Leland MS U.S.A.
86 A3 Lélouma Guinea
12 D2 Lelystad Neth.
80 C9 Le Maire, Estrecho de chan. Arg.
14 H3 Léman, Lac l. France/Switz.
14 E2 Le Mans France
64 D3 Le Mars U.S.A.
12 F5 Lemberg France
13 G2 Lembruch Ger.
82 C3 Leme Brazil
12 E2 Lemele Neth.
43 B3 Lemery Phil.
Lemesos see Limassol
13 G2 Lemgo Ger.
7 U6 Lemi Fin.
55 M3 Lemieux Islands is Can.
6 T2 Lemmenjoen Kansallispuisto nat. park Fin.
12 D2 Lemmer Neth.
64 C2 Lemmon U.S.A.
73 G5 Lemmon, Mt mt U.S.A.
72 C3 Lemoore U.S.A.
35 H5 Lemro r. Myanmar
44 A3 Lem Tom Chob pt Thai.
18 G4 Le Murge reg. Italy
7 L8 Lemvig Denmark
68 C4 Lena U.S.A.
36 C1 Lena r. Rus. Fed.
35 E2 Lenchung Tso salt l. China
79 K4 Lençóis Maranhenses, Parque Nacional dos nat. park Brazil
31 E4 Lengbarūt Iran
13 F2 Lengerich Ger.
38 A2 Lenglong Ling mts China
39 D5 Lengshuijiang China
39 D5 Lengshuitan China
83 B1 Lengua de Vaca, Pta hd Chile
9 H6 Lenham U.K.
7 O8 Lenhovda Sweden
31 H2 Lenin Tajik.
21 H7 Lenina, Kanal canal Rus. Fed.
Leningrad see St Petersburg
21 F6 Leningradskaya Rus. Fed.
20 E3 Leningradskaya Oblast' div. Rus. Fed.
25 T3 Leningradskiy Rus. Fed.
40 D2 Lenino Rus. Fed.
26 E2 Leninsk Kazak.
21 H5 Leninsk Rus. Fed.
20 F4 Leninskiy Rus. Fed.
36 A1 Leninsk-Kuznetskiy Rus. Fed.
20 H3 Leninskoye Rus. Fed.
13 F3 Lenne r. Ger.
67 D5 Lenoir U.S.A.
71 G3 Lenox U.S.A.
14 F1 Lens France
25 N3 Lensk Rus. Fed.
21 G7 Lentekhi Georgia
16 H7 Lenti Hungary
18 F6 Lentini Sicily Italy
13 K1 Lenzen Ger.
86 B3 Léo Burkina
16 G7 Leoben Austria
9 E5 Leominster U.K.
71 H3 Leominster U.S.A.
74 D4 León Mex.
74 G6 León Nic.
15 D1 León Spain
81 A3 León r. Col.
89 B6 Leonardville Namibia
28 E4 Leonarisson Cyprus
50 E5 Leongatha Austr.
48 C4 Leonora Austr.
82 D3 Leopoldina Brazil
57 H4 Leoville Can.
91 G1 Lephalala r. S. Africa
89 C6 Lephepe Botswana
91 F5 Lephoi S. Africa
39 E4 Leping China
14 G4 Le Pont-de-Claix France
6 U5 Leppävirta Fin.
14 F4 Le-Puy-en-Velay France
12 B4 Le Quesnoy France
91 G1 Lerala Botswana
91 G4 Leratswana S. Africa
87 D4 Léré Chad
81 C5 Lerida Col.
Lérida see Lleida
29 M2 Lerik Azer.
15 E1 Lerma Spain
21 G6 Lermontov Rus. Fed.
40 D1 Lermontovka Rus. Fed.
19 M6 Leros i. Greece
68 C5 Le Roy U.S.A.
7 N8 Lerum Sweden
10 □ Lerwick U.K.
19 L5 Lesbos i. Greece
75 K5 Les Cayes Haiti
59 G4 Les Escoumins Can.
71 J1 Les Étroits Can.
15 G1 Le Seu d'Urgell Spain
39 B4 Leshan China
19 J3 Leskovac Yugo.
10 E4 Leslie U.K.
14 B2 Lesneven France
20 K3 Lesnoy Rus. Fed.
40 D1 Lesopil'noye Rus. Fed.
24 L4 Lesosibirsk Rus. Fed.
85 F8 Lesotho country Africa
40 C2 Lesozavodsk Rus. Fed.
14 D3 Les Sables-d'Olonne France
12 D4 Lesse r. Belgium
75 L6 Lesser Antilles is Caribbean Sea
Lesser Caucasus mts see Malyy Kavkaz
56 G3 Lesser Slave Lake l. Can.
56 G3 Lesser Slave Lake Provincial Park res. Can.

12 B4 Lessines Belgium
6 T5 Lestijärvi Fin.
6 T5 Lestijärvi *l.* Fin.
Lesvos *i. see* Lesbos
16 H5 Leszno Pol.
91 J1 Letaba S. Africa
9 G6 Letchworth U.K.
34 D4 Leteri India
35 H5 Letha Range *mts* Myanmar
56 G5 Lethbridge Can.
78 G3 Lethem Guyana
78 E4 Leticia Col.
37 E7 Leti, Kepulauan *is* Indon.
38 F2 Leting China
91 F2 Letlhakeng Botswana
9 J7 Le Touquet-Paris-Plage France
14 E1 Le Tréport France
91 J1 Letsitele S. Africa
44 A3 Letsok-aw Kyun *i.* Myanmar
91 F3 Letsopa S. Africa
11 D3 Letterkenny Rep. of Ireland
45 C2 Letung Indon.
13 K2 Letzlingen Ger.
10 F4 Leuchars U.K.
20 G1 Leunovo Rus. Fed.
73 G4 Leupp Corner U.S.A.
12 D2 Leusden Neth.
45 A2 Leuser, G. *mt* Indon.
13 J5 Leutershausen Ger.
12 C4 Leuven Belgium
19 K5 Levadeia Greece
73 G2 Levan U.S.A.
6 M5 Levanger Norway
18 C2 Levanto Italy
18 E5 Levanzo, Isola di *i. Sicily* Italy
21 H7 Levashi Rus. Fed.
65 C5 Levelland U.S.A.
8 G4 Leven *Eng.* U.K.
10 F4 Leven *Scot.* U.K.
10 C4 Leven, Loch *in.* U.K.
10 E4 Leven, Loch *l.* U.K.
48 C3 Lévêque, C. *c.* Austr.
68 E3 Levering U.S.A.
12 E3 Leverkusen Ger.
17 J6 Levice Slovakia
51 E4 Levin N.Z.
59 F4 Lévis Can.
19 M6 Levitha *i.* Greece
71 G4 Levittown *NY* U.S.A.
71 F4 Levittown *PA* U.S.A.
19 L3 Levski Bulg.
9 H7 Lewes U.K.
71 F5 Lewes U.S.A.
10 B2 Lewis *i.* U.K.
70 E4 Lewisburg *PA* U.S.A.
70 C6 Lewisburg *WV* U.S.A.
51 D5 Lewis Pass N.Z.
62 D1 Lewis Range *mts* U.S.A.
67 C5 Lewis Smith, L. *l.* U.S.A.
73 G6 Lewis Springs U.S.A.
62 C2 Lewiston *ID* U.S.A.
71 H2 Lewiston *ME* U.S.A.
68 B4 Lewiston *MN* U.S.A.
68 B5 Lewistown *IL* U.S.A.
62 E2 Lewistown *MT* U.S.A.
70 E4 Lewistown *PA* U.S.A.
65 E5 Lewisville U.S.A.
65 D5 Lewisville, Lake *l.* U.S.A.
68 C5 Lexington *IL* U.S.A.
66 C4 Lexington *KY* U.S.A.
64 E4 Lexington *MO* U.S.A.
67 D5 Lexington *NC* U.S.A.
64 D3 Lexington *NE* U.S.A.
67 B5 Lexington *TN* U.S.A.
70 D6 Lexington *VA* U.S.A.
70 E5 Lexington Park U.S.A.
91 J1 Leydsdorp S. Africa
39 C5 Leye China
29 L3 Leyla D. *h.* Iran
43 C4 Leyte *i.* Phil.
43 C4 Leyte Gulf *g.* Phil.
19 H4 Lezhë Albania
39 B4 Lezhi China
21 E5 L'gov Rus. Fed.
35 H3 Lhari China
35 G3 Lhasa China
35 G3 Lhasa He *r.* China
35 F3 Lhazê China
35 F3 Lhazhong China
45 A1 Lhokseumawe Indon.
44 A4 Lhoksukon Indon.
35 H3 Lhorong China
35 H3 Lhünzê China
35 G3 Lhünzhub China
39 E5 Liancheng China
12 A5 Liancourt France
Liancourt Rocks *i. see* Tok-tō
43 C4 Lianga Phil.
43 C4 Lianga Bay *b.* Phil.
39 E4 Liangaz Hu *l.* China
38 D1 Liangcheng China
38 C3 Liangdang China
38 B3 Langhekou China
39 C4 Liangping China
39 B5 Liangwang Shan *mts* China
38 C2 Liangzhen China
39 D5 Lianhua China
39 E6 Lianhua Shan *mts* China
39 F5 Lianjiang *Fujian* China
39 D6 Lianjiang *Guangdong* China
39 D5 Liannan China
39 E5 Lianping China
39 D5 Lianshan China
38 F3 Lianshui China
44 B2 Liant, C. *pt* Thai.
39 D5 Lian Xian China
39 D5 Lianyuan China
38 F3 Lianyungang *Jiangsu* China
38 F3 Lianyungang *Jiangsu* China
42 F1 Lianzhushan China
42 B2 Liao *r.* China
38 E2 Liaocheng China
42 B3 Liaodong Bandao *pen.* China
42 A3 Liaodong Wan *b.* China
42 B3 Liaohe Kou *river mouth* China
42 B3 Liaoning *div.* China
42 B3 Liaoyang China
42 C2 Liaoyuan China
42 B3 Liaozhong China
19 H5 Liapades Greece
34 B2 Liaqatabad Pak.
56 E2 Liard *r.* Can.
56 D3 Liard River Can.
31 G5 Liari Pak.
10 C3 Liathach *mt* U.K.
28 F4 Liban, Jebel *mts* Lebanon
81 B3 Líbano Col.
62 D1 Libby U.S.A.
88 B3 Libenge Congo(Zaire)
65 C4 Liberal U.S.A.
16 G5 Liberec Czech Rep.
75 G6 Liberia Costa Rica
85 C5 Liberia *country* Africa
81 C2 Libertad Venez.
81 C2 Libertad Venez.
68 B6 Liberty *IL* U.S.A.
71 J2 Liberty *ME* U.S.A.
64 E4 Liberty *MO* U.S.A.
71 F4 Liberty *NY* U.S.A.
65 E6 Liberty *TX* U.S.A.
12 D5 Libin Belgium
43 B3 Libmanan Phil.
39 C5 Libo China
91 H5 Libode S. Africa
14 D4 Libourne France
88 A3 Libreville Gabon
43 C5 Libuganon *r.* Phil.
85 E3 Libya *country* Africa
84 E3 Libyan Desert Egypt/Libya
87 E1 Libyan Plateau *plat.* Egypt
83 B2 Licantén Chile
18 E6 Licata *Sicily* Italy
29 H2 Lice Turkey
13 G4 Lich Ger.
9 F5 Lichfield U.K.
89 D5 Lichinga Moz.
13 K4 Lichte Ger.
13 G3 Lichtenau Ger.
91 G3 Lichtenburg S. Africa
13 K4 Lichtenfels Ger.
12 E3 Lichtenvoorde Neth.
39 C4 Lichuan *Hubei* China
39 E5 Lichuan *Jiangxi* China
70 B5 Licking *r.* U.S.A.
20 C4 Lida Belarus
72 D3 Lida U.S.A.
90 C2 Lidfontein Namibia
7 N7 Lidköping Sweden
6 O4 Lidsjöberg Sweden
13 H2 Liebenau Ger.
13 J2 Liebenburg Ger.
13 M2 Liebenwalde Ger.
48 D4 Liebig, Mt *mt* Austr.
5 D4 Liechtenstein *country* Europe
12 D4 Liège Belgium
6 W5 Lieksa Fin.
17 M2 Lielupe *r.* Latvia
7 T8 Lielvārde Latvia
6 P5 Lien Sweden
88 C3 Lienart Congo(Zaire)
16 F7 Lienz Austria
7 R8 Liepāja Latvia
12 C3 Lier Belgium
7 J7 Liervik Norway
12 D3 Lieshout Neth.
12 A4 Liévin France
69 K2 Lièvre *r.* Can.
16 G7 Liezen Austria
11 E4 Liffey *r.* Rep. of Ireland
11 D3 Lifford Rep. of Ireland
83 C4 Lifi Mahuida *mt* Arg.
49 G4 Lifou *i.* New Caledonia
43 B3 Ligao Phil.
7 T8 Līgatne Latvia
89 D5 Ligonha *r.* Moz.
68 E5 Ligonier U.S.A.
Ligure, Mar *sea see* Ligurian Sea
14 J5 Ligurian Sea *sea* France/Italy
48 F2 Lihir Group *is* P.N.G.
72 □2 Lihue U.S.A.
39 D5 Li Jiang *r.* China
38 F2 Lijin China
89 C5 Likasi Congo(Zaire)
56 E4 Likely Can.
20 E3 Likhoslavl' Rus. Fed.
45 C2 Liku Indon.
20 G3 Likurga Rus. Fed.
18 C3 L'Île-Rousse *Corsica* France
13 G1 Lilienthal Ger.
39 D5 Liling China
34 C2 Lilla Pak.
7 N7 Lilla Edet Sweden
12 C3 Lille Belgium
14 F1 Lille France
7 L9 Lille Bælt *chan.* Denmark
7 M6 Lillehammer Norway
12 A4 Lillers France
7 L7 Lillesand Norway
7 M7 Lillestrom Norway
68 E4 Lilley U.S.A.
6 O5 Lillholmsjö Sweden
56 E4 Lillooet Can.
56 E4 Lillooet *r.* Can.
35 H4 Lilong India
89 D5 Lilongwe Malawi
43 B4 Liloy Phil.
50 B2 Lilydale Austr.
78 C6 Lima Peru
62 D2 Lima *MT* U.S.A.
70 A4 Lima *OH* U.S.A.
30 E5 Līmah Oman
21 H6 Liman Rus. Fed.
83 B1 Limarí *r.* Chile
35 E2 Lima Ringma Tso *salt l.* China
28 D4 Limassol Cyprus
11 E2 Limavady U.K.
83 C3 Limay *r.* Arg.
83 C3 Limay Mahuida Arg.
7 T8 Limbaži Latvia
86 C4 Limbe Cameroon
45 E3 Limbungan Indon.
13 G4 Limburg an der Lahn Ger.
44 □ Lim Chu Kang Sing.
44 □ Lim Chu Kang *h.* Sing.
90 E4 Lime Acres S. Africa
82 C3 Limeira Brazil
11 C5 Limerick Rep. of Ireland
68 A4 Lime Springs U.S.A.
71 K1 Limestone U.S.A.
6 N4 Limingen Norway
6 N4 Limingen *l.* Norway
71 H3 Limington U.S.A.
6 T4 Liminka Fin.
19 L5 Limnos *i.* Greece
71 F2 Limoges Can.
14 E4 Limoges France
75 H6 Limón Costa Rica
63 G4 Limon U.S.A.
28 E3 Limonlu Turkey
14 E4 Limousin *reg.* France
14 F5 Limoux France
91 K1 Limpopo *r.* Africa
30 A4 Līnah S. Arabia
6 W2 Linakhamari Rus. Fed.
39 F4 Lin'an China
43 A4 Linapacan *i.* Phil.
43 A4 Linapacan Strait *chan.* Phil.
83 B2 Linares Chile
74 E4 Linares Mex.
15 E3 Linares Spain
36 C4 Lincang China
38 E2 Lincheng China
39 E5 Linchuan China
83 E2 Lincoln Arg.
9 G4 Lincoln U.K.
72 B2 Lincoln *CA* U.S.A.
68 C5 Lincoln *IL* U.S.A.
71 J2 Lincoln *ME* U.S.A.
69 F3 Lincoln *MI* U.S.A.
64 D3 Lincoln *NE* U.S.A.
71 H2 Lincoln *NH* U.S.A.
62 A2 Lincoln City U.S.A.
69 F4 Lincoln Park U.S.A.
9 G4 Lincolnshire Wolds *reg.* U.K.
71 J2 Lincolnville U.S.A.
82 E1 Linda, Sa *h.* Brazil
13 L2 Lindau Ger.
16 D7 Lindau (Bodensee) Ger.
13 G4 Linden Ger.
79 G2 Linden Guyana
67 C5 Linden *AL* U.S.A.
67 C5 Linden *TN* U.S.A.
68 A2 Linden Grove U.S.A.
55 O3 Lindenow Fjord *in.* Greenland
13 F2 Lindern (Oldenburg) Ger.
7 K7 Lindesnes *c.* Norway
89 D4 Lindi Tanz.
88 C3 Lindi *r.* Congo(Zaire)
Lindisfarne *i. see* Holy Island
91 G3 Lindley S. Africa
19 N6 Lindos, Akra *pt* Greece
71 K1 Lindsay *N.B.* Can.
69 H3 Lindsay *Ont.* Can.
72 C3 Lindsay U.S.A.
46 L3 Line Islands *is* Pac. Oc.
38 D2 Linfen China
33 A3 Linganamakki Reservoir India
43 B2 Lingayen Phil.
43 B2 Lingayen Gulf *b.* Phil.
38 D3 Lingbao China
38 E3 Lingbi China
39 D5 Lingchuan *Guangxi* China
38 D3 Lingchuan *Shanxi* China
91 G6 Lingelethu S. Africa
91 F6 Lingelihle S. Africa
12 F2 Lingen (Ems) Ger.
45 B3 Lingga, Kepulauan *is* Indon.
43 C5 Lingig Phil.
62 F3 Lingle U.S.A.
88 C3 Lingomo Congo(Zaire)
38 E2 Lingqiu China
39 C6 Lingshan China
39 C7 Lingshui China
33 B2 Lingsugur India
38 C3 Lingtai China
39 C7 Lingtou China
86 A3 Linguère Senegal
39 D5 Lingui China
38 C2 Lingwu China
39 D5 Ling Xian China
38 F1 Lingyuan China
39 C5 Lingyun China
34 D2 Lingzi Thang Plains *l.* China/Jammu and Kashmir
39 F4 Linhai China
82 E2 Linhares Brazil
44 C1 Linh Cam Vietnam
38 C1 Linhe China
71 H1 Linière Can.
42 D3 Linjiang China
7 O7 Linköping Sweden
42 F1 Linkou China
39 D4 Linli China
10 E5 Linlithgow U.K.
38 D2 Linlü Shan *mt* China
10 C4 Linnhe, Loch *in.* U.K.
12 E4 Linnich Ger.
72 A1 Linn, Mt *mt* U.S.A.
38 E2 Linqing China
38 F2 Linqu China
38 E3 Linquan China
38 D3 Linru China
82 C3 Lins Brazil
38 F3 Linshu China
39 C4 Linshui China
38 B3 Lintan China
38 B3 Lintao China
64 C2 Linton U.S.A.
38 C3 Lintong China
38 F1 Linxi China
38 B3 Linxia China
38 D2 Lin Xian China
39 D4 Linxiang China
38 F3 Linyi *Shandong* China
38 E2 Linyi *Shandong* China
38 D3 Linyi *Shanxi* China
38 E3 Linying China
16 G6 Linz Austria
38 A2 Linze China
14 F5 Lion, Golfe du *g.* France
69 G3 Lion's Head Can.
71 F4 Lionville U.S.A.
88 B3 Liouesso Congo
43 B3 Lipa Phil.
18 F5 Lipari Italy
18 F5 Lipari, Isola *i.* Italy
18 F5 Lipari, Isole *is* Italy
21 F4 Lipetsk Rus. Fed.
21 F4 Lipetskaya Oblast' *div.* Rus. Fed.
20 F2 Lipin Bor Rus. Fed.
39 C5 Liping China
19 J1 Lipova Romania
40 B2 Lipovtsy Rus. Fed.
12 E3 Lippe *r.* Ger.
13 G3 Lippstadt Ger.
34 E3 Lipti Lekh *pass* Nepal
50 E5 Liptrap, C. *hd* Austr.
39 D5 Lipu China
88 D3 Lira Uganda
88 B4 Liranga Congo
43 C6 Lirung Indon.
88 C3 Lisala Congo(Zaire)
11 D3 Lisbellaw U.K.
Lisboa *see* Lisbon
15 B3 Lisbon Port.
68 C5 Lisbon *IL* U.S.A.
71 H2 Lisbon *ME* U.S.A.
64 D2 Lisbon *ND* U.S.A.
71 H2 Lisbon *NH* U.S.A.
70 C4 Lisbon *OH* U.S.A.
11 E3 Lisburn U.K.
11 B5 Liscannor Bay *b.* Rep. of Ireland
11 B4 Lisdoonvarna Rep. of Ireland
39 F5 Li-shan Taiwan
38 D2 Lishi China
42 C2 Lishu China
38 F4 Lishui *Jiangsu* China
39 F4 Lishui *Zhejiang* China
39 D4 Li Shui *r.* China
14 E2 Lisieux France
9 C7 Liskeard U.K.
21 F5 Liski Rus. Fed.
12 A5 L'Isle-Adam France
14 G5 L'Isle-sur-la-Sorgue France
11 D5 Lismore Rep. of Ireland
10 C4 Lismore *i.* U.K.
11 D3 Lisnarrick U.K.
11 D3 Lisnaskea U.K.
69 G4 Listowel Can.
11 B5 Listowel Rep. of Ireland
6 O5 Lit Sweden
39 C6 Litang *Guangxi* China
36 C3 Litang *Sichuan* China
79 H3 Litani *r.* Fr. Guiana/Suriname
28 E5 Līṭānī *r.* Lebanon
72 B1 Litchfield *CA* U.S.A.
66 B4 Litchfield *IL* U.S.A.
61 H2 Litchfield *MN* U.S.A.
14 D4 Lit-et-Mixe France
50 H2 Lithgow Austr.
5 F3 Lithuania *country* Europe
71 E4 Lititz U.S.A.
16 G5 Litoměřice Czech Rep.
67 E7 Little Abaco *i.* Bahamas
67 E7 Little Bahama Bank *sand bank* Bahamas
51 E2 Little Barrier *i.* N.Z.
68 D3 Little Bay de Noc *b.* U.S.A.
62 E2 Little Belt Mts *mts* U.S.A.
75 H5 Little Cayman *i.* Cayman Is
73 H4 Little Colorado *r.* U.S.A.
73 F3 Little Creek Peak *summit* U.S.A.
69 G3 Little Current Can.
58 C3 Little Current *r.* Can.
9 D7 Little Dart *r.* U.K.
50 C4 Little Desert Nat. Park Austr.
71 F5 Little Egg Harbor *in.* U.S.A.
67 F7 Little Exuma *i.* Bahamas
64 E2 Little Falls *MN* U.S.A.
71 F3 Little Falls *NY* U.S.A.
73 F3 Littlefield *AZ* U.S.A.
65 C5 Littlefield *TX* U.S.A.
64 E1 Little Fork U.S.A.
68 A1 Little Fork *r.* U.S.A.
35 F4 Little Gandak *r.* India
57 K4 Little Grand Rapids Can.
9 G7 Littlehampton U.K.
70 C5 Little Kanawha *r.* U.S.A.
90 C3 Little Karas Berg *plat.* Namibia
90 D6 Little Karoo *plat.* S. Africa
68 D2 Little Lake U.S.A.
59 H3 Little Mecatina *r.* Can.
70 A5 Little Miami *r.* U.S.A.
10 B3 Little Minch *str.* U.K.
64 C2 Little Missouri *r.* U.S.A.
9 H5 Little Ouse *r.* U.K.
68 D1 Little Pic *r.* Can.
34 B5 Little Rann *marsh* India
65 E5 Little Rock U.S.A.
68 D4 Little Sable Pt *pt* U.S.A.
67 F7 Little San Salvador *i.* Bahamas
56 F4 Little Smoky *r.* Can.
63 F4 Littleton *CO* U.S.A.
71 H2 Littleton *NH* U.S.A.
70 C5 Littleton *WV* U.S.A.
68 E3 Little Traverse Bay *b.* U.S.A.
29 J4 Little Zab *r.* Iraq
89 D5 Litunde Moz.
56 B3 Lituya Bay *b.* U.S.A.
42 B2 Liu *r.* China
38 C3 Liuba China
39 F6 Liuchiu Yü *i.* Taiwan
39 C5 Liuchong He *r.* China
42 B5 Liugong Dao *i.* China
38 F1 Liugu *r.* China
42 C2 Liuhe China
39 D4 Liujiachang China
39 C5 Liujiang China
38 B3 Liujiaxia Sk. *resr* China
38 C3 Liupan Shan *mts* China
39 B5 Liupanshui China
39 D4 Liuyang China
39 C5 Liuzhou China
40 C3 Livadiya Rus. Fed.
7 U8 Līvāni Latvia
72 B2 Live Oak *CA* U.S.A.
67 D6 Live Oak *FL* U.S.A.
48 C3 Liveringa Austr.
72 B3 Livermore U.S.A.
71 H2 Livermore Falls U.S.A.
65 B6 Livermore, Mt *mt* U.S.A.
50 H2 Liverpool Austr.
59 H5 Liverpool Can.
9 E4 Liverpool U.K.
9 D4 Liverpool Bay U.K.
54 E3 Liverpool Bay *b. N.W.T.* Can.
55 L2 Liverpool, C. *c.* Can.
50 H1 Liverpool Plains Austr.
50 H1 Liverpool Ra. *mts* Austr.
10 E5 Livingston U.K.
72 B3 Livingston *CA* U.S.A.
62 E2 Livingston *MT* U.S.A.
67 C4 Livingston *TN* U.S.A.
65 E6 Livingston *TX* U.S.A.
89 C5 Livingstone Zambia
92 B2 Livingston I. *i.* Ant.
65 E6 Livingston, L. *l.* U.S.A.
18 G3 Livno Bos.-Herz.
21 F4 Livny Rus. Fed.
6 U4 Livojoki *r.* Fin.
69 F4 Livonia U.S.A.
18 D3 Livorno Italy
82 E1 Livramento do Brumado Brazil
30 E5 Liwā Oman
89 D4 Liwale Tanz.
38 B3 Li Xian *Gansu* China
39 D4 Li Xian *Hunan* China
38 B4 Li Xian *Sichuan* China
38 E3 Lixin China
38 F4 Liyang China
9 B8 Lizard U.K.
9 B8 Lizard Point *pt* U.K.
12 B5 Lizy-sur-Ourcq France
18 F1 Ljubljana Slovenia
7 Q8 Ljugarn Sweden
7 P5 Ljungan *r.* Sweden
7 P5 Ljungaverk Sweden
7 N8 Ljungby Sweden
7 P6 Ljusdal Sweden
7 O6 Ljusnan *r.* Sweden
7 P6 Ljusne Sweden
80 B5 Llaima, Volcán *volc.* Chile
9 C5 Llanbadarn Fawr U.K.
9 D5 Llanbister U.K.
9 D6 Llandeilo U.K.
9 C6 Llandissilio U.K.
9 D6 Llandovery U.K.
9 D5 Llandrindod Wells U.K.
9 D4 Llandudno U.K.
9 C5 Llandysul U.K.
9 C6 Llanegwad U.K.
9 C6 Llanelli U.K.
9 C4 Llanerchymedd U.K.
9 D5 Llanfair Caereinion U.K.
9 C4 Llangefni U.K.
9 D5 Llangollen U.K.
9 D5 Llangurig U.K.
9 C4 Llanllyfni U.K.
9 C5 Llannor U.K.
65 D6 Llano U.S.A.
65 D6 Llano *r.* U.S.A.
65 C5 Llano Estacado *plain* U.S.A.
81 C3 Llanos *reg.* Col./Venez.
83 B4 Llanquihue, L. *l.* Chile
9 C5 Llanrhystud U.K.
9 D6 Llantrisant U.K.
9 D5 Llanuwchllyn U.K.
9 D5 Llanwnog U.K.
9 D4 Llay U.K.
15 G2 Lleida Spain
15 C3 Llerena Spain
15 F3 Lliria Spain
15 E1 Llodio Spain
54 F4 Lloyd George, Mt Can.
57 H3 Lloyd Lake *l.* Can.
57 G4 Lloydminster Can.
15 H3 Llucmajor Spain
80 C2 Llullaillaco, Vol. *volc.* Chile
39 B6 Lô *r.* China/Vietnam
73 G2 Loa U.S.A.
80 C2 Loa *r.* Chile
20 J3 Loban' *r.* Rus. Fed.
15 D4 Lobatejo *mt* Spain
89 C6 Lobatse Botswana
13 K3 Löbejün Ger.
13 L3 Löbenberg *h.* Ger.
83 E3 Loberia Arg.
89 B5 Lobito Angola
83 E2 Lobos Arg.
13 L2 Loburg Ger.
10 D4 Lochaber *reg.* U.K.
10 C4 Lochaline U.K.
69 E1 Lochalsh Can.
10 A3 Lochboisdale U.K.
10 C3 Lochcarron U.K.
8 C1 Lochearnhead U.K.
12 E2 Lochem Neth.
14 E3 Loches France
10 E4 Lochgelly U.K.
10 C4 Lochgilphead U.K.
10 C2 Lochinver U.K.
10 A3 Lochmaddy U.K.
10 E4 Lochnagar *mt* U.K.
70 E5 Loch Raven Reservoir U.S.A.
10 D4 Lochy, Loch *l.* U.K.
10 E5 Lockerbie U.K.
50 F3 Lockhart Austr.
65 D6 Lockhart U.S.A.
70 E4 Lock Haven U.S.A.
70 D3 Lockport U.S.A.
44 C3 Lôc Ninh Vietnam
70 B5 Locust Grove U.S.A.
28 E6 Lod Israel
50 D3 Loddon *r.* Austr.
14 F5 Lodève France
20 E2 Lodeynoye Pole Rus. Fed.
62 F2 Lodge Grass U.S.A.
34 B3 Lodhran Pak.
18 C2 Lodi Italy
72 B2 Lodi *CA* U.S.A.
70 B4 Lodi *OH* U.S.A.
6 O2 Lødingen Norway
88 D3 Lodwar Kenya
17 J5 Łódź Pol.
31 H3 Loe Dakka Afgh.
90 C5 Loeriesfontein S. Africa
6 N2 Lofoten *is* Norway
21 G5 Log Rus. Fed.
63 G5 Logan *NM* U.S.A.
70 B5 Logan *OH* U.S.A.
62 E3 Logan *UT* U.S.A.
70 C6 Logan *WV* U.S.A.
56 D2 Logan Mountains Can.
56 A2 Logan, Mt *mt* Can.
54 D3 Logan, Mt *mt* Can.
68 D5 Logansport U.S.A.
18 F2 Logatec Slovenia
15 E1 Logroño Spain
35 H4 Logtak L. *l.* India
90 E4 Lohatlha S. Africa
13 H3 Lohfelden Ger.
6 T3 Lohiniva Fin.
7 S6 Lohjanjärvi *l.* Fin.
13 G2 Löhne Ger.
13 G2 Lohne (Oldenburg) Ger.
6 S4 Lohtaja Fin.
44 A1 Loikaw Myanmar
44 A1 Loi Lan *mt* Myanmar/Thai.
7 S6 Loimaa Fin.
14 E3 Loire *r.* France
78 C4 Loja Ecuador
15 D4 Loja Spain
45 E1 Lokan *r.* Malaysia
6 U3 Lokan tekojärvi *l.* Fin.
12 C3 Lokeren Belgium
90 D2 Lokgwabe Botswana
88 D3 Lokichar Kenya
88 D3 Lokichokio Kenya
7 L8 Løkken Denmark
6 L5 Løkken Norway
17 P2 Loknya Rus. Fed.
86 C4 Lokoja Nigeria
86 C4 Lokossa Benin
21 E4 Lokot' Rus. Fed.
7 T7 Loksa Estonia
55 M3 Loks Land *i.* Can.
86 B4 Lola Guinea
72 B2 Lola, Mt *mt* U.S.A.
7 M9 Lolland *i.* Denmark
89 D4 Lollondo Tanz.
62 D2 Lolo U.S.A.
90 E3 Lolwane S. Africa
19 K3 Lom Bulg.
7 L6 Lom Norway
88 C4 Lomami *r.* Congo(Zaire)
83 D3 Loma Negra, Planicie de la *plain* Arg.
31 G3 Lomar Pass Afgh.
83 E2 Lomas de Zamora Arg.
45 E4 Lombok *i.* Indon.
45 E4 Lombok, Selat *chan.* Indon.
86 C4 Lomé Togo
88 C4 Lomela Congo(Zaire)
88 C4 Lomela *r.* Congo(Zaire)
12 A4 Lomme France
12 D3 Lommel Belgium
10 D4 Lomond, Loch *l.* U.K.
20 G1 Lomovoye Rus. Fed.
37 D7 Lompobattang, Gunung *mt* Indon.
72 B4 Lompoc U.S.A.
17 L4 Łomża Pol.
34 D6 Lonar India
83 B3 Loncoche Chile
83 B3 Loncopue Arg.
69 G4 London Can.
9 G6 London U.K.
70 A6 London *KY* U.S.A.
70 B5 London *OH* U.S.A.
11 D3 Londonderry U.K.
71 G3 Londonderry U.S.A.
48 C3 Londonderry, C. *c.* Austr.
80 B9 Londonderry, I. *i.* Chile
82 B3 Londrina Brazil
72 C3 Lone Pine U.S.A.
39 C6 Long'an China
25 T2 Longa, Proliv *chan.* Rus. Fed.
9 E6 Long Ashton U.K.
83 B3 Longavi, Nev. de *mt* Chile
67 E5 Long Bay *b.* U.S.A.
51 C6 Longbeach N.Z.
72 C5 Long Beach *CA* U.S.A.
71 G4 Long Beach *NY* U.S.A.
71 F4 Long Branch U.S.A.
68 A6 Long Branch Lake *l.* U.S.A.
39 B4 Longchang China
39 E5 Longchuan China
9 F5 Long Eaton U.K.
42 D1 Longfenshan Sk. *resr* China
11 D4 Longford Rep. of Ireland
39 E5 Longhai China
39 □ Long Harbour *in. H.K.* China
8 F2 Longhoughton U.K.
45 E3 Longiram Indon.
75 J4 Long Island *i.* Bahamas
58 E3 Long Island *i.* Can.
48 E2 Long Island *i.* P.N.G.
71 G4 Long Island *i.* U.S.A.
71 G4 Long Island Sound *chan.* U.S.A.
39 C5 Long Jiang *r.* China
35 H3 Longju China
38 F2 Longkou Wan *b.* China
58 C4 Longlac Can.
71 F3 Long Lake *NY* U.S.A.
58 C4 Long Lake *l.* Can.
71 J1 Long Lake *l. ME* U.S.A.
68 E3 Long Lake *l. MI* U.S.A.
69 F3 Long Lake *l. MI* U.S.A.
64 C2 Long Lake *l. ND* U.S.A.
71 F2 Long Lake *l. NY* U.S.A.
39 C5 Longli China
39 B5 Longlin China
10 D4 Long, Loch *in.* U.K.
9 H5 Long Melford U.K.
39 E6 Longmen China
38 B3 Longmen Shan *mts* China
62 F3 Longmont U.S.A.
39 F5 Longnan China
69 G4 Long Point *pt* Can.
51 B7 Long Point *pt* N.Z.
69 G4 Long Point Bay *b.* Can.
8 E3 Long Preston U.K.
39 F4 Longquan China

M

88 B4 Madingou Congo
78 E6 Madini r. Bol.
89 E5 Madirovalo Madag.
66 C4 Madison IN U.S.A.
71 J2 Madison ME U.S.A.
64 D2 Madison MN U.S.A.
64 D3 Madison NE U.S.A.
64 D2 Madison SD U.S.A.
70 C5 Madison WV U.S.A.
68 C4 Madison WV U.S.A.
60 D2 Madison r. MT U.S.A.
66 C4 Madisonville KY U.S.A.
65 E6 Madisonville TX U.S.A.
45 D4 Madiun Indon.
69 J3 Madoc Can.
88 D3 Mado Gashi Kenya
36 B3 Madoi China
7 U8 Madona Latvia
34 B4 Madpura India
19 M5 Madra Dağı mts Turkey
Madras see Chennai
62 B2 Madras U.S.A.
78 D6 Madre de Dios r. Peru
80 A8 Madre de Dios, I. i. Chile
74 D5 Madre del Sur, Sierra mts Mex.
74 E4 Madre, Laguna lag. Mex.
65 D7 Madre, Laguna lag. U.S.A.
74 C3 Madre Occidental, Sierra mts Mex.
74 D3 Madre Oriental, Sierra mts Mex.
43 B2 Madre, Sierra mt Phil.
43 C4 Madrid Phil.
15 E2 Madrid Spain
43 B4 Madridejos Phil.
15 E3 Madridejos Spain
33 C2 Madugula India
45 D4 Madura i. Indon.
33 B4 Madurai India
45 D4 Madura, Selat chan. Indon.
35 E4 Madwas India
34 C2 Madyan Pak.
21 H7 Madzhalis Rus. Fed.
41 F6 Maebashi Japan
44 A1 Mae Hong Son Thai.
44 B2 Mae Khlong r. Thai.
44 A1 Mae Lao r. Thai.
44 A1 Mae Li r. Thai.
44 B1 Mae Nam Ing r. Thai.
44 C2 Mae Nam Mun r. Thai.
44 B2 Mae Nam Nan r. Thai.
44 B2 Mae Nam Pa Sak r. Thai.
44 B2 Mae Nam Ping r. Thai.
44 A1 Mae Nam Wang r. Thai.
44 B2 Mae Nam Yom r. Thai.
75 J5 Maestra, Sierra mts Cuba
89 E5 Maevatanana Madag.
49 G3 Maéwo i. Vanuatu
44 A1 Mae Yuam r. Myanmar/Thai.
57 J4 Mafeking Can.
91 G4 Mafeteng Lesotho
50 F4 Maffra Austr.
89 D4 Mafia I. i. Tanz.
91 F2 Mafikeng S. Africa
89 D4 Mafinga Tanz.
82 C4 Mafra Brazil
28 F5 Mafraq Jordan
91 J5 Magabeni S. Africa
25 R4 Magadan Rus. Fed.
88 D4 Magadi Kenya
91 K1 Magaiza Moz.
43 B3 Magallanes Phil.
80 B8 Magallanes, Estrecho de chan. Chile
81 B2 Magangue Col.
28 D3 Mağara Turkey
Magas see Zābolī
43 B2 Magat r. Phil.
83 F2 Magdalena Arg.
78 F6 Magdalena Bol.
74 B2 Magdalena Mex.
63 F5 Magdalena U.S.A.
81 B3 Magdalena r. Col.
60 D7 Magdalena, Bahía b. Mex.
80 B6 Magdalena, Isla i. Chile
43 A5 Magdaleno, Mt mt Malaysia
13 K2 Magdeburg Ger.
94 F4 Magellan Seamounts sea feature Pac. Oc.
6 T1 Magerøya i. Norway
41 B9 Mage-shima i. Japan
18 C2 Maggiorasca, Monte mt Italy
18 C2 Maggiore, Lago l. Italy
86 A3 Maghama Maur.
11 E3 Maghera U.K.
11 E3 Magherafelt U.K.
8 E4 Maghull U.K.
62 D3 Magna U.S.A.
18 F6 Magna Grande mt Sicily Italy
92 D4 Magnet Bay b. Ant.
48 E3 Magnetic I. i. Austr.
6 X2 Magnetity Rus. Fed.
24 G4 Magnitogorsk Rus. Fed.
65 E5 Magnolia U.S.A.
59 F4 Magog Can.
59 H3 Magpie Can.
68 E1 Magpie r. Can.
59 H3 Magpie L. l. Can.
68 E1 Magpie Lake l. Can.
56 G5 Magrath Can.
72 D3 Magruder Mt mt U.S.A.
86 A3 Magṭa' Laḥjar Maur.
88 D4 Magu Tanz.
39 B6 Maguan China
79 J4 Maguarinho, Cabo pt Brazil
91 K2 Magude Moz.
71 K2 Magundy Can.
57 K2 Maguse Lake l. Can.
35 H5 Magwe Myanmar
35 H5 Magyichaung Myanmar
30 B2 Mahābād Iran
33 A2 Mahabaleshwar India
Mahabalipuram see Māmallapuram
35 F4 Mahabharat Range mts Nepal
89 E6 Mahabo Madag.
33 A2 Mahad India
34 D5 Mahadeo Hills h. India
88 D3 Mahagi Congo(Zaire)
34 C3 Mahajan India
89 E5 Mahajanga Madag.
45 D2 Mahakam r. Indon.
89 C6 Mahalapye Botswana
89 E5 Mahalevona Madag.
30 C3 Mahallāt Iran
34 D3 Maham India
45 D4 Mahameru, Gunung volc. Indon.
30 E4 Mahān Iran
35 F5 Mahanadi r. India
89 E5 Mahanoro Madag.
34 C6 Maharashtra div. India
35 E5 Mahasamund India
44 B1 Maha Sarakham Thai.
89 E6 Mahatalaky Madag.
89 E5 Mahavanona Madag.
89 E5 Mahavavy r. Madag.
33 C5 Mahaweli Ganga r. Sri Lanka
44 C1 Mahaxai Laos
33 C2 Mahbubabad India
33 B2 Mahbubnagar India
30 D5 Maḥḍah Oman
79 G2 Mahdia Guyana
18 D7 Mahdia Tunisia
93 H4 Mahé i. Seychelles
33 D2 Mahendragiri mt India
34 C5 Mahesāna India
34 C5 Maheshwar India
34 C5 Mahi r. India
31 E4 Māhī watercourse Iran
51 F3 Mahia Peninsula N.Z.
20 D4 Mahilyow Belarus
33 C5 Mahiyangana Sri Lanka
91 J4 Mahlabatini S. Africa
13 K2 Mahlsdorf Ger.
31 H3 Maḥmūd-e 'Erāqī Afgh.
29 M4 Mahniān Iran
64 D2 Mahnomen U.S.A.
34 D4 Mahoba India
15 J3 Mahón Spain
70 D4 Mahoning Creek Lake l. U.S.A.
35 H5 Mahudaung Hgts mts Myanmar
34 B5 Mahuva India
19 M4 Mahya Dağı mt Turkey
30 C3 Mahyār Iran
35 H4 Maibang India
81 B2 Maicao Col.
58 E4 Maicasagi, Lac l. Can.
39 C6 Maichen China
9 G6 Maidenhead U.K.
57 H4 Maidstone Can.
9 H6 Maidstone U.K.
87 D3 Maiduguri Nigeria
81 D3 Maigualida, Sierra mts Venez.
11 C5 Maigue r. Rep. of Ireland
34 E4 Maihar India
33 C3 Maiji Shan mt China
34 E5 Maikala Range h. India
88 C4 Maiko, Parc National de la nat. park Congo(Zaire)
34 E3 Mailani India
13 H5 Main r. Ger.
11 E3 Main r. U.K.
59 J3 Main Brook Can.
69 F3 Main Channel Can.
88 B4 Mai-Ndombe, Lac l. Congo(Zaire)
13 K5 Main-Donau-Kanal canal Ger.
69 J4 Main Duck I. i. Can.
71 J2 Maine div. U.S.A.
86 D3 Maïné-Soroa Niger
42 A2 Maingy I. i. Myanmar
13 H5 Mainhardt Ger.
43 C4 Mainit Phil.
43 C4 Mainit, Lake l. Phil.
10 E1 Mainland i. Orkney U.K.
10 □ Mainland i. Shetland U.K.
13 K4 Mainleus Ger.
35 E5 Mainpat reg. India
34 D4 Mainpuri India
89 E5 Maintirano Madag.
13 G4 Mainz Ger.
86 □ Maio i. Cape Verde
83 C2 Maipó, Vol. volc. Chile
83 F3 Maipú Buenos Aires Arg.
83 C2 Maipú Mendoza Arg.
81 D2 Maiquetía Venez.
35 G5 Maiskhal I. i. Bangl.
89 C6 Maitengwe Botswana
50 H2 Maitland N.S.W. Austr.
50 A3 Maitland S.A. Austr.
92 D3 Maitri India Base Ant.
35 G3 Maizhokunggar China
75 H6 Maíz, Islas del is Nic.
41 D7 Maizuru Japan
19 H3 Maja Jezercë mt Albania
33 B2 Mājalgaon India
81 E4 Majari r. Brazil
45 E3 Majene Indon.
30 C6 Majhūd well S. Arabia
88 D3 Majī Eth.
38 E2 Majia r. China
39 D6 Majiang China
Majorca i. see Mallorca
35 H4 Majuli I. i. India
94 G5 Majuro i. Pac. Oc.
91 G4 Majwemasweu S. Africa
88 B4 Makabana Congo
72 □1 Makaha U.S.A.
30 C2 Makale Indon.
35 F4 Makalu, Mt mt China
88 C4 Makamba Burundi
27 G2 Makanchi Kazak.
72 □1 Makapuu Hd hd U.S.A.
20 J2 Makar-Ib Rus. Fed.
18 G3 Makarska Croatia
26 D2 Makat Kazak.
91 K3 Makatini Flats lowland S. Africa
86 A4 Makeni Sierra Leone
89 C6 Makgadikgadi salt pan Botswana
21 H7 Makhachkala Rus. Fed.
28 G4 Makhfar al Ḥammām Syria
29 J4 Makhmūr Iraq
88 D4 Makindu Kenya
26 F1 Makinsk Kazak.
21 F5 Makiyivka Ukr.
Makkah see Mecca
59 J2 Makkovik Can.
59 J2 Makkovik, Cape c. Can.
12 D1 Makkum Neth.
19 J1 Makó Hungary
88 B3 Makokou Gabon
89 D4 Makongolosi Tanz.
90 E2 Makopong Botswana
88 B4 Makotipoko Congo
31 F5 Makran reg. Iran/Pak.
34 C4 Makrana India
Makran Coast Range mts see Talar-i-Band
35 E6 Makri India
19 L6 Makronisi i. Greece
20 E3 Maksatikha Rus. Fed.
40 E1 Maksimovka Rus. Fed.
31 F4 Maksotag Iran
30 B2 Mākū Iran
35 H4 Makum India
89 D4 Makumbako Tanz.
89 D5 Makunguwiro Tanz.
41 B9 Makurazaki Japan
86 C4 Makurdi Nigeria
30 D4 Makūyeh Iran
91 F3 Makwassie S. Africa
6 Q4 Malå Sweden
43 C5 Malabang Phil.
33 A3 Malabar Coast coastal area India
86 C4 Malabo Equatorial Guinea
43 A4 Malabuñgan Phil.
45 A2 Malacca, Strait of str. Indon./Malaysia
62 D3 Malad City U.S.A.
20 C4 Maladzyechna Belarus
15 D4 Málaga Spain
71 F5 Malaga NJ U.S.A.
63 F5 Malaga NM U.S.A.
49 G2 Malaita i. Solomon Is
87 F4 Malakal Sudan
33 C2 Malakanagiri India
49 G3 Malakula i. Vanuatu
34 C2 Malakwal Pak.
37 E7 Malamala Indon.
45 D4 Malang Indon.
89 B4 Malanje Angola
31 G5 Malan, Ras pt Pak.
83 C1 Malanzán, Sa de mts Arg.
33 B4 Malappuram India
75 H7 Mala, Pta pt Panama
7 P7 Mälaren l. Sweden
83 C2 Malargüe Arg.
69 H1 Malartic Can.
69 H1 Malartic, Lac l. Can.
56 A3 Malaspina Glacier gl. U.S.A.
28 G2 Malatya Turkey
34 C3 Malaut India
29 L5 Malāvi Iran
43 A5 Malawali i. Malaysia
85 G7 Malawi country Africa
Malawi, Lake l. see Nyasa, Lake
44 B5 Malaya reg. Malaysia
20 E3 Malaya Vishera Rus. Fed.
43 C4 Malaybalay Phil.
30 C3 Malāyer Iran
23 K9 Malaysia country Asia
29 J2 Malazgirt Turkey
17 J3 Malbork Pol.
12 E5 Malborn Ger.
13 L1 Malchin Ger.
13 L1 Malchiner See l. Ger.
35 G4 Māldah India
12 B3 Maldegem Belgium
65 F4 Malden U.S.A.
46 M4 Malden Island i. Kiribati
93 J4 Maldive Ridge sea feature Ind. Ocean
23 G9 Maldives country Ind. Ocean
9 H6 Maldon U.K.
83 F2 Maldonado Uru.
19 K6 Maleas, Akra i. Greece
27 F6 Male Atoll Maldives
91 F4 Malebogo S. Africa
34 C5 Malegaon India
33 B2 Malegaon India
16 H6 Malé Karpaty h. Slovakia
29 L3 Malek Kandī Iran
88 B4 Malele Congo(Zaire)
89 D5 Malema Moz.
34 C3 Maler Kōtla India
31 G3 Mālestān Afgh.
21 H7 Malgobek Rus. Fed.
6 P4 Malgomaj l. Sweden
30 B5 Malham S. Arabia
62 C3 Malheur L. l. U.S.A.
88 C4 Mali Congo(Zaire)
86 A3 Mali Guinea
85 C4 Mali country Africa
38 C3 Malian r. China
34 E4 Malihabad India
31 F4 Malik Naro mt Pak.
44 A2 Mali Kyun i. Myanmar
37 E7 Malili Indon.
45 C4 Malimping Indon.
88 E4 Malindi Kenya
11 D2 Malin Head hd Rep. of Ireland
11 C3 Malin More Rep. of Ireland
40 D2 Malinovka r. Rus. Fed.
39 B6 Malipo China
18 F2 Mali Raginac mt Croatia
43 C5 Malita Phil.
44 A3 Maliwun Myanmar
34 B5 Maliya India
29 L5 Malkaili Iran
34 D5 Malkapur India
21 C7 Malkara Turkey
17 N4 Mal'kavichy Belarus
19 M4 Malko Tŭrnovo Bulg.
50 G4 Mallacoota Austr.
50 G4 Mallacoota Inlet Austr.
10 C4 Mallaig U.K.
50 B3 Mallala Austr.
50 D3 Mallee Cliffs Nat. Park Austr.
57 K2 Mallery Lake l. Can.
15 H3 Mallorca i. Spain
11 C5 Mallow Rep. of Ireland
9 D5 Mallwyd U.K.
6 M4 Malm Norway
6 R3 Malmberget Sweden
12 E4 Malmédy Belgium
12 E4 Malmesbury S. Africa
9 E6 Malmesbury U.K.
7 N9 Malmö Sweden
20 J3 Malmyzh Rus. Fed.
49 G3 Malo i. Vanuatu
43 B3 Malolos Phil.
71 F2 Malone U.S.A.
39 B5 Malong China
89 C5 Malonga Congo(Zaire)
20 F2 Maloshuyka Rus. Fed.
7 J6 Måløy Norway
20 F4 Maloyaroslavets Rus. Fed.
78 B3 Malpelo, Isla de i. Col.
33 A3 Malprabha r. India
7 U8 Malta Latvia
62 F1 Malta U.S.A.
5 E5 Malta country Europe
18 F6 Malta Channel Italy/Malta
89 B6 Maltahöhe Namibia
9 F4 Maltby U.K.
9 H4 Maltby le Marsh U.K.
8 G3 Malton U.K.
37 E7 Maluku is Indon.
7 N6 Malung Sweden
91 H4 Maluti Mountains Lesotho
49 G2 Malu'u Solomon Is
33 A2 Malvan India
65 E5 Malvern U.S.A.
Malvinas, Islas terr. see Falkland Islands
21 D5 Malyn Ukr.
25 S3 Malyy Anyuy r. Rus. Fed.
30 D2 Malyy Balkhan, Khrebet h. Turkm.
21 H6 Malyye Derbety Rus. Fed.
21 G7 Malyy Kavkaz mts Asia
25 Q2 Malyy Lyakhovskiy, Ostrov i. Rus. Fed.
21 J5 Malyy Uzen' r. Kazak./Rus. Fed.
25 Q3 Mama r. Rus. Fed.
91 H3 Mamafubedu S. Africa
33 C3 Māmallapuram India
43 A5 Mambahenauhan i. Phil.
43 C4 Mambajao Phil.
88 C3 Mambasa Congo(Zaire)
88 B3 Mambéré r. C.A.R.
43 B3 Mamburao Phil.
91 H2 Mamelodi S. Africa
86 C4 Mamfé Cameroon
73 G5 Mammoth U.S.A.
66 C4 Mammoth Cave Nat. Park U.S.A.
72 C3 Mammoth Lakes U.S.A.
78 E6 Mamoré r. Bol./Brazil
86 A3 Mamou Guinea
89 E5 Mampikony Madag.
86 B4 Mampong Ghana
83 B3 Mamuil Malal, P. pass Arg./Chile
45 E3 Mamuju Indon.
90 D1 Mamuno Botswana
86 B4 Man Côte d'Ivoire
81 B3 Manacacias r. Col.
78 F4 Manacapuru Brazil
15 H3 Manacor Spain
37 E6 Manadao Indon.
74 G6 Managua Nic.
74 G6 Managua, L. de l. Nic.
89 E6 Manakara Madag.
51 D5 Manakau mt N.Z.
48 E2 Manam I. i. P.N.G.
72 □1 Manana i. U.S.A.
89 E6 Mananara r. Madag.
89 E5 Mananara Avaratra Madag.
89 E5 Mananara, Parc National de nat. park Madag.
50 D3 Manangatang Austr.
89 E6 Mananjary Madag.
33 B4 Mānantavādi India
81 D2 Manapire r. Venez.
51 A6 Manapouri, L. l. N.Z.
89 E5 Manarantsandry Madag.
35 G4 Manas r. Bhutan
34 D3 Mana Shankou pass India
36 A2 Manas Hu l. China
35 F3 Manaslu mt Nepal
70 E5 Manassas U.S.A.
37 E7 Manatuto Indon.
78 F4 Manaus Brazil
28 C3 Manavgat Turkey
51 E4 Manawatu r. N.Z.
43 C5 Manay Phil.
28 F3 Manbij Syria
9 H4 Manby U.K.
68 E3 Mancelona U.S.A.
9 E4 Manchester U.K.
72 A2 Manchester CA U.S.A.
71 G4 Manchester CT U.S.A.
68 B4 Manchester IA U.S.A.
70 B6 Manchester KY U.S.A.
69 E4 Manchester MI U.S.A.
71 H3 Manchester NH U.S.A.
70 B5 Manchester OH U.S.A.
67 C5 Manchester TN U.S.A.
71 G3 Manchester VT U.S.A.
34 A4 Manchhar L. l. Pak.
28 F2 Mancılık Turkey
73 H3 Mancos U.S.A.
73 H3 Mancos r. U.S.A.
31 F5 Mand Pak.
30 D4 Mand r. Iran
89 E6 Mandabe Madag.
45 B2 Mandah Indon.
44 □ Mandai Sing.
31 F3 Mandal Afgh.
34 C4 Mandal India
7 K7 Mandal Norway
37 G7 Mandala, Pk mt Indon.
37 B4 Mandalay Myanmar
36 C2 Mandalgovĭ Mongolia
29 K5 Mandalī Iraq
38 D1 Mandalt Sum China
64 C2 Mandan U.S.A.
43 B3 Mandaon Phil.
87 D4 Manda, Parc National de nat. park Chad
87 D3 Mandara Mountains Cameroon/Nigeria
18 C5 Mandas Sardinia Italy
88 E3 Mandera Kenya
73 F2 Manderfield U.S.A.
12 E4 Manderscheid Ger.
75 J5 Mandeville Jamaica
51 B6 Mandeville N.Z.
34 B4 Mandha India
86 B3 Mandiana Guinea
34 C3 Mandi Burewala Pak.
89 D5 Mandié Moz.
89 D5 Mandimba Moz.
91 J4 Mandini S. Africa
35 F5 Mandira Dam dam India
34 E5 Mandla India
89 E5 Mandritsara Madag.
34 C4 Mandsaur India
43 A6 Mandul i. Indon.
48 B5 Mandurah Austr.
18 G4 Manduria Italy
34 B5 Mandvi Gujarat India
34 C5 Mandvi Gujarat India
33 B3 Mandya India
33 B2 Maner r. India
18 D2 Manerbio Italy
17 M5 Manevychi Ukr.
18 F4 Manfredonia Italy
18 G4 Manfredonia, Golfo di g. Italy
82 D1 Manga Brazil
86 B3 Manga Burkina
88 B4 Mangai Congo(Zaire)
46 M6 Mangaia i. Cook Is Pac. Oc.
51 E3 Mangakino N.Z.
33 C2 Mangalagiri India
35 H4 Mangaldai India
19 N3 Mangalia Romania
33 A3 Mangalore India
33 A2 Mangalvedha India
35 G4 Mangan India
33 C2 Mangapet India
43 C6 Mangarang Indon.
91 G4 Mangaung S. Africa
51 E3 Mangaweka N.Z.
35 G4 Mangde r. Bhutan
11 B6 Mangerton Mt h. Rep. of Ireland
45 C3 Manggar Indon.
36 B3 Mangnai China
89 D5 Mangochi Malawi
37 E7 Mangole i. Indon.
9 E6 Mangotsfield U.K.
34 B5 Māngral India
67 E7 Mangrove Cay Bahamas
15 C2 Mangualde Port.
31 G4 Manguchar Pak.
83 G2 Mangueira, L. l. Brazil
82 B4 Mangueirinha Brazil
87 D2 Manguéni, Plateau de plat. Niger
36 E1 Mangui China
43 C5 Mangupung i. Indon.
26 D2 Mangyshlak Kazak.
64 D4 Manhattan KS U.S.A.
72 D2 Manhattan NV U.S.A.
89 D6 Manhica Moz.
91 K3 Manhoca Moz.
82 D3 Manhuaçu Brazil
82 E2 Manhuaçu r. Brazil
81 B3 Mani Col.
89 E5 Mania r. Madag.
18 E1 Maniago Italy
78 F5 Manicoré Brazil
59 G3 Manicouagan Can.
59 G3 Manicouagan r. Can.
59 G3 Manicouagan, Réservoir resr Can.
30 C5 Manīfah S. Arabia
46 L5 Manihiki i. Cook Is Pac. Oc.
Manikgarh see Rajura
34 E4 Manikpur India
43 B3 Manila Phil.
62 E3 Manila U.S.A.
50 G2 Manildra Austr.
50 H1 Manilla Austr.
Manipur see Imphal
35 H4 Manipur div. India
19 M5 Manisa Turkey
29 L5 Manisht Kūh mt Iran
8 C3 Man, Isle of terr. Europe
68 D3 Manistee U.S.A.
68 E3 Manistee r. U.S.A.
68 D3 Manistique U.S.A.
68 E2 Manistique Lake l. U.S.A.
58 B2 Manitoba div. Can.
57 K4 Manitoba, Lake l. Can.
57 H4 Manito L. l. Can.
57 K5 Manitou Can.
70 E3 Manitou Beach U.S.A.
58 B3 Manitou Falls Can.
68 D2 Manitou Island i. U.S.A.
66 C2 Manitou Islands is U.S.A.
69 G3 Manitou, Lake l. Can.
69 F3 Manitoulin I. i. Can.
69 G3 Manitowaning Can.
58 D4 Manitowik Lake l. Can.
68 D3 Manitowoc U.S.A.
69 K2 Maniwaki Can.
81 B3 Manizales Col.
89 E6 Manja Madag.
91 K2 Manjacaze Moz.
33 B4 Manjeri India
42 D3 Man Jiang r. China
29 M3 Manjil Iran
33 B2 Manjra r. India
64 E2 Mankato U.S.A.
91 J3 Mankayane Swaziland
86 B4 Mankono Côte d'Ivoire
33 C4 Mankulam Sri Lanka
50 H2 Manly Austr.
34 C5 Manmad India
45 B3 Manna Indon.
50 B2 Mannahill Austr.
33 B4 Mannar Sri Lanka
27 F6 Mannar, Gulf of India/Sri Lanka
33 B4 Mannar, Gulf of g. India/Sri Lanka
33 B3 Manneru r. India
13 G5 Mannheim Ger.
11 A4 Mannin Bay b. Rep. of Ireland
56 F3 Manning Can.
67 D5 Manning U.S.A.
9 J6 Manningtree U.K.
18 C4 Mannu, Capo pt Sardinia Italy
50 B3 Mannum Austr.
37 F7 Manokwari Indon.
88 C4 Manono Congo(Zaire)
44 A3 Manoron Myanmar
14 G5 Manosque France
55 L4 Manouane Lake l. Can.
42 D3 Manp'o N. Korea
49 J2 Manra i. Kiribati
15 G2 Manresa Spain
34 C3 Mānsa India
89 C5 Mansa Zambia
86 A3 Mansa Konko The Gambia
34 C2 Mansehra Pak.
55 L3 Mansel Island i. Can.
50 F4 Mansfield Austr.
9 F4 Mansfield U.K.
65 E5 Mansfield LA U.S.A.
70 B4 Mansfield OH U.S.A.
70 E4 Mansfield PA U.S.A.
79 H6 Manso r. Brazil
56 E3 Manson Creek Can.
29 M6 Manṣūrī Iran
28 E3 Mansurlu Turkey
78 B4 Manta Ecuador
78 B4 Manta, B. de b. Ecuador
43 A4 Mantalingajan, Mount mt Phil.
42 E3 Mantapsan mt N. Korea
72 B3 Manteca U.S.A.
81 C3 Mantecal Venez.
13 L5 Mantel Ger.
67 F5 Manteo U.S.A.
14 E2 Mantes-la-Jolie France
33 B2 Manthani India
73 G2 Manti U.S.A.
82 D3 Mantiqueira, Serra da mts Brazil
68 E3 Manton U.S.A.
18 D2 Mantova Italy
7 T6 Mäntsälä Fin.
7 T5 Mänttä Fin.
Mantua see Mantova
20 H3 Manturovo Rus. Fed.
7 U6 Mäntyharju Fin.
6 U3 Mäntyjärvi Fin.
46 L5 Manua Islands is Pac. Oc.
73 H4 Manuelito U.S.A.
83 F2 Manuel J. Cobo Arg.
82 E1 Manuel Vitorino Brazil
79 H5 Manuelzinho Brazil
37 E7 Manui i. Indon.
31 E5 Manūjān Iran
43 B4 Manukan Phil.
51 E2 Manukau N.Z.
51 E2 Manukau Harbour in. N.Z.
43 A5 Manuk Manka i. Phil.
50 B2 Manunda r. Austr.
78 D6 Manu, Parque Nacional nat. park Peru
48 E2 Manus I. i. P.N.G.
33 B3 Manvi India
91 F2 Manyana Botswana
21 G6 Manych-Gudilo, Ozero l. Rus. Fed.
73 H3 Many Farms U.S.A.
88 D4 Manyoni Tanz.
28 D6 Manzala, Bahra el l. Egypt
15 E3 Manzanares Spain
75 J4 Manzanillo Cuba
74 D5 Manzanillo Mex.
30 C3 Manzariyeh Iran
36 D2 Manzhouli China
91 J3 Manzini Swaziland
87 D3 Mao Chad
Maó see Mahón
38 D4 Maocifan China
38 C2 Maojiachuan China
91 G3 Maokeng S. Africa
37 F7 Maoke, Pegunungan mts Indon.
42 B3 Maokui Shan h. China
42 B2 Maolin China
38 B2 Maomao Shan mt China
39 D6 Maoming China
39 □ Ma On Shan h. H.K. China
89 D6 Mapai Moz.
34 E3 Mapam Yumco l. China
91 F5 Maphodi S. Africa
65 C7 Mapimí Mex.
43 A5 Mapin i. Phil.
89 D6 Mapinhane Moz.
81 D3 Mapire Venez.
68 E4 Maple r. U.S.A.
57 H5 Maple Creek Can.
91 G4 Mapoteng Lesotho
79 G4 Mapuera r. Brazil
91 K2 Mapulanguene Moz.
89 D6 Maputo Moz.
91 K2 Maputo div. Moz.
91 K3 Maputo r. Moz.
91 G4 Maputsoe Lesotho
29 H6 Maqar an Na'am well Iraq
38 B3 Maqu China
35 E3 Maquan He r. China
88 B4 Maquela do Zombo Angola
83 C4 Maquinchao Arg.
83 C4 Maquinchao r. Arg.
68 B4 Maquoketa U.S.A.
68 B4 Maquoketa r. U.S.A.
31 G5 Mar r. Pak.
35 E5 Māra India
91 H1 Mara S. Africa
81 C2 Mara Venez.
57 H1 Mara r. Can.
78 E4 Maraã Brazil
79 J5 Maraba Brazil
81 C2 Maracaibo Venez.
81 C2 Maracaibo, Lago de l. Venez.
79 H3 Maracá, Ilha de i. Brazil
82 A3 Maracaju Brazil

82 A3 Maracajú, Serra de h. Brazil
82 E1 Maracás, Chapada de reg. Brazil
81 D2 Maracay Venez.
87 D2 Marādah Libya
86 C3 Maradi Niger
30 B2 Marāgheh Iran
82 E1 Maragogipe Brazil
43 B3 Maragondon Phil.
81 D4 Marahuaca, Co mt Venez.
79 J4 Marajó, Baía de est. Brazil
79 J3 Marajó, Ilha de i. Brazil
33 B3 Marakkanam India
88 D3 Maralal Kenya
34 C2 Marala Weir barrage Pak.
29 J1 Maralik Armenia
48 D5 Maralinga Austr.
49 G2 Maramasike i. Solomon Is
43 C5 Marampit i. Indon.
31 G4 Maran mt Pak.
29 K4 Marāna Iraq
73 G5 Marana U.S.A.
30 B2 Marand Iran
44 B4 Marang Malaysia
44 A3 Marang Myanmar
82 C1 Maranhão r. Brazil
78 D4 Marañón r. Peru
91 L2 Marão Moz.
15 C2 Marão mt Port.
81 D4 Marari r. Brazil
51 A6 Mararoa r. N.Z.
68 D1 Marathon Can.
67 D7 Marathon FL U.S.A.
65 C6 Marathon TX U.S.A.
82 E1 Maraú Brazil
45 D3 Marau Indon.
81 D4 Marauiá r. Brazil
43 C4 Marawi Phil.
29 M1 Märäzä Azer.
15 D4 Marbella Spain
48 B4 Marble Bar Austr.
73 G3 Marble Canyon U.S.A.
73 G3 Marble Canyon gorge U.S.A.
91 H2 Marble Hall S. Africa
71 H3 Marblehead U.S.A.
57 L2 Marble I. i. Can.
91 J5 Marburg S. Africa
13 G4 Marburg an der Lahn Ger.
70 E5 Marburg, Lake l. U.S.A.
16 H7 Marcali Hungary
9 H5 March U.K.
50 B2 Marchant Hill h. Austr.
12 D4 Marche-en-Famenne Belgium
15 D4 Marchena Spain
78 □ Marchena, Isla i. Galapagos Is Ecuador
83 D1 Mar Chiquita, L. l. Arg.
16 G6 Marchtrenk Austria
67 D7 Marco U.S.A.
12 B4 Marcoing France
58 E2 Marcopeet Islands is Can.
83 D2 Marcos Juárez Arg.
71 G2 Marcy, Mt mt U.S.A.
34 C2 Mardan Pak.
83 F3 Mar del Plata Arg.
29 H3 Mardın Turkey
49 G4 Maré i. New Caledonia
10 C3 Maree, Loch l. U.K.
68 A5 Marengo IA U.S.A.
68 C4 Marengo IL U.S.A.
18 E6 Marettimo, Isola i. Sicily Italy
20 E3 Marevo Rus. Fed.
65 B6 Marfa U.S.A.
35 F2 Margai Caka salt l. China
48 B5 Margaret River Austr.
81 E2 Margarita, Isla de i. Venez.
40 D3 Margaritovo Rus. Fed.
91 J5 Margate S. Africa
9 J6 Margate U.K.
31 F4 Margo, Dasht-i des. Afgh.
43 B5 Margosatubig Phil.
12 D4 Margraten Neth.
68 E3 Margrethe, Lake l. U.S.A.
56 E4 Marguerite Can.
92 B2 Marguerite Bay b. Ant.
35 G3 Margyang China
29 L5 Marhaj Khalīl Iraq
29 J3 Marhan D. h. Iraq
21 E6 Marhanets' Ukr.
80 C2 María Elena Chile
48 D3 Maria I. i. Austr.
83 E3 María Ignacia Arg.
46 M6 Maria, Îles i. Fr. Polynesia Pac. Oc.
95 J7 Maria, Îles is Pac. Oc.
94 E4 Marianas Ridge sea feature Pac. Oc.
94 E5 Marianas Tr. sea feature Pac. Oc.
35 H4 Mariani India
56 F2 Marian Lake l. Can.
65 F5 Marianna AR U.S.A.
67 C6 Marianna FL U.S.A.
16 F6 Mariánské Lázně Czech Rep.
74 C4 Marías, Islas is Mex.
75 H7 Mariato, Pta pt Panama
51 D1 Maria van Diemen, Cape c. N.Z.
18 F1 Maribor Slovenia
73 F5 Maricopa AZ U.S.A.
72 C4 Maricopa CA U.S.A.
73 F5 Maricopa Mts mts U.S.A.
87 E4 Maridi watercourse Sudan
92 A4 Marie Byrd Land reg. Ant.
75 M5 Marie Galante i. Guadeloupe
7 Q6 Mariehamn Fin.
82 B1 Mariembero r. Brazil
13 M4 Marienberg Ger.
12 F1 Marienhafe Ger.
89 B6 Mariental Namibia
7 N7 Mariestad Sweden
67 C5 Marietta GA U.S.A.
70 C5 Marietta OH U.S.A.
14 G5 Marignane France
36 G1 Marii, Mys pt Rus. Fed.
36 A1 Mariinsk Rus. Fed.
7 S9 Marijampolė Lith.
82 C3 Marília Brazil
65 C7 Marin Mex.
15 B1 Marín Spain
18 G5 Marina di Gioiosa Ionica Italy
20 D4 Mar"ina Horka Belarus
43 B3 Marinduque i. Phil.
68 D3 Marinette U.S.A.
82 B3 Maringá Brazil
15 B3 Marinha Grande Port.
66 B4 Marion IL U.S.A.
68 E5 Marion IN U.S.A.
71 K2 Marion ME U.S.A.
70 B4 Marion OH U.S.A.
67 E5 Marion SC U.S.A.
70 C6 Marion VA U.S.A.
67 D5 Marion, L. l. U.S.A.
81 D3 Maripa Venez.
72 C3 Mariposa U.S.A.
80 D2 Mariscal Estigarribia Para.
14 H4 Maritime Alps mts France/Italy
19 L3 Maritsa r. Bulg.
20 J3 Mari-Turek Rus. Fed.
21 F6 Mariupol' Ukr.
30 B3 Marīvān Iran
20 J3 Mariy El, Respublika div. Rus. Fed.
88 E3 Marka Somalia
29 K2 Märkän Iran
33 B3 Markapur India
7 N8 Markaryd Sweden
69 G3 Markdale Can.
91 H1 Marken S. Africa
12 D2 Markermeer l. Neth.
9 G5 Market Deeping U.K.
9 E5 Market Drayton U.K.
9 G5 Market Harborough U.K.
11 E3 Markethill U.K.
8 G4 Market Weighton U.K.
25 N3 Markha r. Rus. Fed.
69 H4 Markham Can.
92 B4 Markham, Mt mt Ant.
21 F5 Markivka Ukr.
13 L3 Markkleeberg Ger.
13 H2 Marklohe Ger.
25 T3 Markovo Rus. Fed.
13 L3 Markranstädt Ger.
21 H5 Marks Rus. Fed.
13 H5 Marktheidenfeld Ger.
16 E7 Marktoberdorf Ger.
13 L4 Marktredwitz Ger.
68 B6 Mark Twain Lake l. U.S.A.
12 F3 Marl Ger.
71 H3 Marlborough U.S.A.
9 F6 Marlborough Downs h. U.K.
12 B5 Marle France
65 D6 Marlin U.S.A.
70 C5 Marlinton U.S.A.
50 G4 Marlo Austr.
14 E4 Marmande France
Marmara Denizi g. see Marmara, Sea of
28 B2 Marmara Gölü l. Turkey
28 B1 Marmara, Sea of g. Turkey
28 B3 Marmaris Turkey
64 C2 Marmarth U.S.A.
70 C5 Marmet U.S.A.
58 B4 Marmion L. l. Can.
18 D1 Marmolada mt Italy
14 F2 Marne-la-Vallée France
29 K1 Marneuli Georgia
13 K1 Marnitz Ger.
50 D4 Marnoo Austr.
89 E5 Maroantsetra Madag.
13 J4 Maroldsweisach Ger.
89 E5 Maromokotro mt Madag.
89 D5 Marondera Zimbabwe
79 H2 Maroni r. Fr. Guiana
46 N6 Marotiri is Fr. Polynesia Pac. Oc.
87 D3 Maroua Cameroon
89 E5 Marovoay Madag.
29 H4 Marqādah Syria
38 A3 Mar Qu r. China
91 G4 Marquard S. Africa
67 D7 Marquesas Keys is U.S.A.
68 D2 Marquette U.S.A.
12 B4 Marquion France
46 O4 Marquises, Îles is Fr. Polynesia Pac. Oc.
50 D1 Marra Austr.
91 K2 Marracuene Moz.
86 B1 Marrakech Morocco
Marrakesh see Marrakech
91 L2 Marrangua, Lagoa l. Moz.
87 E3 Marra Plateau plat. Sudan
50 F3 Marrar Austr.
65 F6 Marrero U.S.A.
89 D5 Marromeu Moz.
89 D5 Marrupa Moz.
87 F2 Marsa Alam Egypt
87 D1 Marsa al Burayqah Libya
88 D3 Marsabit Kenya
18 E6 Marsala Sicily Italy
87 E1 Marsa Matrûh Egypt
13 G3 Marsberg Ger.
18 E3 Marsciano Italy
50 F2 Marsden Austr.
12 C2 Marsdiep chan. Neth.
14 G5 Marseille France
68 C5 Marseilles U.S.A.
82 D3 Mar, Serra do mts Brazil
6 O4 Marsfjället mt Sweden
57 H4 Marshall Can.
65 E5 Marshall AR U.S.A.
66 C4 Marshall IL U.S.A.
68 E4 Marshall MI U.S.A.
64 E2 Marshall MN U.S.A.
64 E4 Marshall MO U.S.A.
65 E5 Marshall TX U.S.A.
47 H2 Marshall Islands country Pac. Oc.
64 E3 Marshalltown U.S.A.
68 B3 Marshfield U.S.A.
67 F7 Marsh Harbour Bahamas
71 K1 Mars Hill U.S.A.
65 F6 Marsh Island i. U.S.A.
56 C2 Marsh Lake l. Can.
29 M3 Marshūn Iran
62 C3 Marsing U.S.A.
7 P7 Märsta Sweden
35 F4 Marsyangdi r. Nepal
44 A1 Martaban Myanmar
37 B5 Martaban, Gulf of Myanmar
45 D3 Martapura Kalimantan Indon.
45 B3 Martapura Sumatera Indon.
69 H2 Marten River Can.
57 H4 Martensville Can.
71 H4 Martha's Vineyard i. U.S.A.
16 C7 Martigny Switz.
17 J6 Martin Slovakia
64 C3 Martin SD U.S.A.
67 B4 Martin TN U.S.A.
65 B7 Martínez, E. Mex.
73 E5 Martinez Lake U.S.A.
53 K8 Martinique terr. Caribbean Sea
67 C5 Martin, L. l. U.S.A.
92 A3 Martin Pen. pen. Ant.
70 D4 Martinsburg PA U.S.A.
70 E5 Martinsburg WV U.S.A.
70 C4 Martins Ferry U.S.A.
70 D6 Martinsville U.S.A.
96 H7 Martin Vas, Is is Atl. Ocean
51 E4 Marton N.Z.
15 G2 Martorell Spain
15 E4 Martos Spain
26 D1 Martuk Kazak.
29 K1 Martuni Armenia
31 F3 Maruchak Afgh.
41 C7 Marugame Japan
51 D5 Maruia r. N.Z.
79 L6 Maruim Brazil
21 G7 Marukhis Ugheltekhili pass Georgia/Rus. Fed.
50 G3 Marulan Austr.
30 D4 Marvast Iran
14 F4 Marvejols France
73 G2 Marvine, Mt mt U.S.A.
57 G4 Marwayne Can.
31 F2 Mary Turkm.
50 D4 Maryborough Vic. Austr.
49 F4 Maryborough Austr.
90 E4 Marydale S. Africa
20 J4 Mar'yevka Rus. Fed.
57 H2 Mary Frances Lake l. Can.
71 E5 Maryland div. U.S.A.
8 D3 Maryport U.K.
59 J3 Mary's Harbour Can.
59 K4 Marystown Can.
73 F2 Marysvale U.S.A.
59 G4 Marysville Can.
72 B2 Marysville CA U.S.A.
64 D4 Marysville KS U.S.A.
70 B4 Marysville OH U.S.A.
67 C5 Maryville U.S.A.
64 E3 Maryville U.S.A.
13 L2 Marzahna Ger.
30 D4 Masāhūn, Kūh-e mt Iran
88 D4 Masaka Uganda
91 G5 Masakhane S. Africa
29 M2 Masallı Azer.
48 C2 Masamba Indon.
42 E6 Masan S. Korea
71 J1 Masardis U.S.A.
89 D5 Masasi Tanz.
78 F7 Masavi Bol.
43 B3 Masbate Phil.
43 B4 Masbate i. Phil.
86 C1 Mascara Alg.
93 H4 Mascarene Basin sea feature Ind. Ocean
93 J4 Mascarene Ridge sea feature Ind. Ocean
71 G2 Mascouche Can.
91 G4 Maseru Lesotho
91 H4 Mashai Lesotho
39 C6 Mashan China
34 D2 Masherbrum mt Pak.
31 E2 Mashhad Iran
34 C4 Mashi r. India
29 L2 Mashīrān Iran
30 E4 Mashīz Iran
31 F5 Mashket r. Pak.
31 F4 Mashki Chah Pak.
31 F5 Māshkīd r. Iran
6 S2 Masi Norway
91 G5 Masibambane S. Africa
91 G4 Masilo S. Africa
88 D3 Masindi Uganda
43 A3 Masinloc Phil.
90 E5 Masinyusane S. Africa
32 E5 Maṣīrah i. Oman
32 E6 Maṣīrah, Gulf of b. Oman
29 K1 Masis Armenia
30 C4 Masjed Soleymān Iran
28 G3 Maskanah Syria
11 B4 Mask, Lough l. Rep. of Ireland
31 E5 Maskūtān Iran
31 G4 Maslti Pak.
89 F5 Masoala, Tanjona c. Madag.
68 E4 Mason MI U.S.A.
72 C2 Mason NV U.S.A.
65 D6 Mason TX U.S.A.
51 A7 Mason Bay b. N.Z.
68 E3 Mason City IA U.S.A.
68 C5 Mason City IL U.S.A.
70 D5 Masontown U.S.A.
Masqaṭ see Muscat
18 D2 Massa Italy
71 G3 Massachusetts div. U.S.A.
71 H3 Massachusetts Bay b. U.S.A.
73 H1 Massadona U.S.A.
18 G4 Massafra Italy
87 D3 Massakory Chad
18 D3 Massa Marittimo Italy
89 D6 Massangena Moz.
89 B4 Massango Angola
88 D2 Massawa Eritrea
71 F2 Massawippi, Lac l. Can.
71 F2 Massena U.S.A.
56 C4 Masset Can.
69 F2 Massey Can.
14 F4 Massif Central mts France
70 C4 Massillon U.S.A.
86 B3 Massina Mali
89 D6 Massinga Moz.
89 D6 Massingir Moz.
91 K1 Massingir, Barragem de resr Moz.
91 K2 Massintonto r. Moz./S. Africa
92 D3 Massivet mts Ant.
69 K3 Masson Can.
92 D5 Masson I. i. Ant.
29 M1 Maştağa Azer.
31 H2 Mastchoh Tajik.
51 E4 Masterton N.Z.
19 M5 Mastícho, Akra pt Greece
67 E7 Mastic Point Bahamas
34 C1 Mastuj Pak.
31 G4 Mastung Pak.
20 C4 Masty Belarus
41 B7 Masuda Japan
29 M3 Masuleh Iran
Masulipatam see Machilipatnam
89 D6 Masvingo Zimbabwe
28 F4 Maşyāf Syria
69 G2 Matachewan Can.
63 F6 Matachic Mex.
81 D4 Matacuni r. Venez.
88 B4 Matadi Congo(Zaire)
75 G6 Matagalpa Nic.
58 E4 Matagami Can.
58 E4 Matagami, Lac l. Can.
65 D6 Matagorda I. i. U.S.A.
44 C5 Matak i. Indon.
51 F2 Matakana Island i. N.Z.
89 B5 Matala Angola
33 C5 Matale Sri Lanka
86 A3 Matam Senegal
65 C7 Matamoros Coahuila Mex.
65 D7 Matamoros Tamaulipas Mex.
43 B5 Matanal Point pt Phil.
89 D4 Matandu r. Tanz.
59 G4 Matane Can.
34 B2 Matanui Pak.
75 H4 Matanzas Cuba
Matapan, Cape pt see Tainaro, Akra
59 G4 Matapédia r. Can.
83 B2 Mataquito r. Chile
33 C5 Matara Sri Lanka
45 E4 Mataram Indon.
78 D7 Matarani Peru
48 D3 Mataranka Austr.
15 H2 Mataró Spain
91 H5 Matatiele S. Africa
51 B7 Mataura N.Z.
51 B7 Mataura r. N.Z.
81 C3 Mataveni r. Col.
51 F3 Matawai N.Z.
78 F6 Mategua Bol.
74 D4 Matehuala Mex.
89 D5 Matemanga Tanz.
18 G4 Matera Italy
18 C6 Mateur Tunisia
58 D4 Matheson Can.
65 D6 Mathis U.S.A.
50 E3 Mathoura Austr.
34 D4 Mathura India
43 C5 Mati Phil.
35 G4 Matiali India
39 D5 Matianxu China
34 B4 Matiari Pak.
74 E5 Matías Romero Mex.
59 G3 Matimekosh Can.
69 F2 Matinenda Lake l. Can.
71 J3 Matinicus I. i. U.S.A.
35 G5 Matla r. India
91 G2 Matlabas S. Africa
91 G2 Matlabas r. S. Africa
34 B4 Matli Pak.
9 F4 Matlock U.K.
81 D3 Mato r. Venez.
81 D3 Mato, Co mt Venez.
78 G7 Mato Grosso Brazil
82 A1 Mato Grosso div. Brazil
82 A3 Mato Grosso do Sul div. Brazil
82 A1 Mato Grosso, Planalto do plat. Brazil
91 K2 Matola Moz.
15 B2 Matosinhos Port.
32 E5 Maṭraḥ Oman
90 C6 Matroosberg mt S. Africa
41 C7 Matsue Japan
40 G4 Matsumae Japan
41 E6 Matsumoto Japan
41 E7 Matsusaka Japan
39 F5 Matsu Tao i. Taiwan
41 C8 Matsuyama Japan
58 D4 Mattagami r. Can.
69 H2 Mattawa Can.
71 J2 Mattawamkeag U.S.A.
62 D3 Matterhorn mt U.S.A.
81 E3 Matthews Ridge Guyana
75 K4 Matthew Town Bahamas
30 D6 Maṭṭī, Sabkhat salt pan S. Arabia
66 B4 Mattoon U.S.A.
Matturai see Matara
33 C5 Matugama Sri Lanka
49 H3 Matuku i. Fiji
Matun see Khowst
81 E2 Maturín Venez.
43 C5 Matutuang i. Indon.
91 G4 Matwabeng S. Africa
34 E4 Mau Uttar Pradesh India
35 E4 Mau Uttar Pradesh India
35 E4 Mau Aimma India
12 B4 Maubeuge France
14 E5 Maubourguet France
10 D5 Mauchline U.K.
92 C3 Maudheimvidda mts Ant.
93 E7 Maud Seamount depth Ind. Ocean
79 G4 Maués Brazil
35 E4 Mauganj India
72 □2 Maui i. U.S.A.
95 J7 Mauke i. Pac. Oc.
13 G6 Maulbronn Ger.
83 B2 Maule div. Chile
83 B2 Maule r. Chile
83 B4 Maullín Chile
11 B3 Maumakeogh h. Rep. of Ireland
70 B4 Maumee U.S.A.
70 B4 Maumee r. U.S.A.
69 F5 Maumee Bay b. U.S.A.
11 B4 Maumturk Mts h. Rep. of Ireland
89 C5 Maun Botswana
72 □2 Mauna Kea volc. U.S.A.
72 □2 Mauna Loa volc. U.S.A.
72 □1 Maunalua B. b. U.S.A.
91 G1 Maunatlala Botswana
51 E2 Maungaturoto N.Z.
35 H5 Maungdaw Myanmar
44 A2 Maungmagan Is is Myanmar
54 F3 Maunoir, Lac l. Can.
48 D4 Maurice, L. salt flat Austr.
12 D3 Maurik Neth.
85 B4 Mauritania country Africa
3 □ Mauritius country Indian Ocean
68 B4 Mauston U.S.A.
81 D4 Mavaca r. Venez.
89 C5 Mavinga Angola
91 G5 Mavuya S. Africa
34 D3 Mawana India
88 B4 Mawanga Congo(Zaire)
39 D4 Ma Wang Dui China
44 A3 Mawdaung Pass Myanmar/Thai.
51 G3 Mawhai Pt pt N.Z.
92 D4 Mawson Austr. Base Ant.
92 D5 Mawson Coast coastal area Ant.
92 D4 Mawson Escarpment esc. Ant.
92 B6 Mawson Pen. pen. Ant.
44 A3 Maw Taung mt Myanmar
64 C2 Max U.S.A.
18 C5 Maxia, Punta mt Sardinia Italy
68 D5 Maxinkuckee, Lake l. U.S.A.
6 S5 Maxmo Fin.
69 F2 Maxton U.S.A.
72 A2 Maxwell U.S.A.
45 C3 Maya i. Indon.
36 F1 Maya r. Rus. Fed.
75 K4 Mayaguana i. Bahamas
75 L5 Mayagüez Puerto Rico
86 C3 Mayahi Niger
31 H2 Mayakovskogo mt Tajik.
88 B4 Mayama Congo
30 D2 Mayamey Iran
74 G5 Maya Mountains Belize/Guatemala
38 B3 Mayan China
39 C5 Mayang China
40 F5 Maya-san mt Japan
10 D5 Maybole U.K.
29 K4 Maydān Iraq
31 H3 Maydā Shahr Afgh.
12 F4 Mayen Ger.
14 D2 Mayenne France
14 D2 Mayenne r. France
73 F4 Mayer U.S.A.
56 F4 Mayerthorpe Can.
51 C5 Mayfield N.Z.
66 B4 Mayfield U.S.A.
63 F5 Mayhill U.S.A.
42 E1 Mayi r. China
10 F4 May, Isle of i. U.K.
21 G6 Maykop Rus. Fed.
36 B4 Maymyo Myanmar
36 B1 Mayna Rus. Fed.
33 A2 Mayni India
69 J3 Maynooth Can.
83 E2 Mayo, 25 de Buenos Aires Arg.
83 C3 Mayo, 25 de La Pampa Arg.
56 B2 Mayo Can.
43 C5 Mayo Bay b. Phil.
88 B4 Mayoko Congo
56 B2 Mayo Lake l. Can.
43 B3 Mayon volc. Phil.
83 D3 Mayor Buratovich Arg.
51 F2 Mayor I. i. N.Z.
80 D1 Mayor Pablo Lagerenza Para.
89 E5 Mayotte terr. Africa
43 B2 Mayraira Point pt Phil.
36 E1 Mayskiy Rus. Fed.
70 B5 Maysville U.S.A.
88 B4 Mayumba Gabon
35 E3 Mayum La pass China
33 B4 Mayuram India
69 F4 Mayville MI U.S.A.
64 D2 Mayville ND U.S.A.
70 D3 Mayville NY U.S.A.
68 C4 Mayville WV U.S.A.
64 C3 Maywood U.S.A.
83 D3 Maza Arg.
20 F3 Maza Rus. Fed.
89 C5 Mazabuka Zambia
79 H4 Mazagão Brazil
14 F5 Mazamet France
34 D1 Mazar China
18 E6 Mazara del Vallo Sicily Italy
31 G2 Mazār-e Sharīf Afgh.
31 G3 Mazar, Koh-i- mt Afgh.
81 E3 Mazaruni r. Guyana
74 F6 Mazatenango Guatemala
74 C4 Mazatlán Mex.
73 G4 Mazatzal Peak summit U.S.A.
30 C3 Mazdaj Iran
7 S8 Mažeikiai Lith.
29 G2 Mazgirt Turkey
7 S8 Mazirbe Latvia
88 D4 Mazomora Tanz.
29 M3 Mazr'eh Iran
29 M5 Māzū Iran
89 C6 Mazunga Zimbabwe
21 D4 Mazyr Belarus
91 J3 Mbabane Swaziland
86 B4 Mbahiakro Côte d'Ivoire
88 B3 Mbaïki C.A.R.
89 D4 Mbala Zambia
88 D3 Mbale Uganda
86 D4 Mbalmayo Cameroon
88 B4 Mbandaka Congo(Zaire)
86 C4 Mbanga Cameroon
88 B4 M'banza Congo Angola
88 D4 Mbarara Uganda
88 C3 Mbari r. C.A.R.
91 K3 Mbaswana S. Africa
86 D4 Mbengwi Cameroon
89 D4 Mbeya Tanz.
89 D5 Mbinga Tanz.
89 D6 Mbizi Zimbabwe
88 B3 Mbomo Congo
86 D4 Mbouda Cameroon
86 A3 Mbour Senegal
86 A3 Mbout Maur.
89 D4 Mbozi Tanz.
88 C4 Mbuji-Mayi Congo(Zaire)
88 D4 Mbulu Tanz.
88 D4 Mbuyuni Tanz.
89 D4 Mchinga Tanz.
91 G6 Mdantsane S. Africa
18 B6 M'Daourouch Alg.
65 C4 Meade U.S.A.
73 E3 Mead, Lake l. U.S.A.
57 H4 Meadow Lake Can.
57 H4 Meadow Lake Provincial Park res. Can.
73 E3 Meadow Valley Wash r. U.S.A.
70 C4 Meadville U.S.A.
69 G3 Meaford Can.
40 J3 Meaken-dake volc. Japan
10 A2 Mealasta Island i. U.K.
15 B2 Mealhada Port.
10 D4 Meall a'Bhuiridh mt U.K.
59 J3 Mealy Mountains Can.
31 F2 Meana Turkm.
56 F3 Meander River Can.
43 C5 Meares i. Indon.
14 F2 Meaux France
88 B4 Mebridege r. Angola
32 A5 Mecca S. Arabia
71 H2 Mechanic Falls U.S.A.
70 B4 Mechanicsburg U.S.A.
68 B5 Mechanicsville U.S.A.
12 C3 Mechelen Belgium
12 D4 Mechelen Neth.
86 B1 Mecheria Alg.
12 E4 Mechernich Ger.
28 E1 Mecitözü Turkey
12 F4 Meckenheim Ger.
16 E3 Mecklenburger Bucht b. Ger.
13 K1 Mecklenburgische Seenplatte reg. Ger.
13 L1 Mecklenburg-Vorpommern div. Ger.
89 D5 Mecula Moz.
15 C2 Meda Port.
33 B2 Medak India
45 A2 Medan Indon.
83 D3 Médanos Arg.
80 C7 Medanosa, Pta pt Arg.
33 C4 Medawachchiya Sri Lanka
33 B2 Medchal India
71 K2 Meddybemps L. l. U.S.A.
15 H4 Médéa Alg.
13 G3 Medebach Ger.
81 B3 Medellín Col.
9 F4 Meden r. U.K.
86 D1 Medenine Tunisia
86 A3 Mederdra Maur.
62 B3 Medford OR U.S.A.
68 B3 Medford WV U.S.A.
71 F5 Medford Farms U.S.A.
19 N2 Medgidia Romania
29 L4 Medhīkhan Iran
68 B5 Media U.S.A.
83 C2 Media Luna Arg.
17 M7 Mediaş Romania
62 C2 Medical Lake U.S.A.
62 F3 Medicine Bow U.S.A.
62 F3 Medicine Bow Mts mts U.S.A.
62 F3 Medicine Bow Peak summit U.S.A.
57 G4 Medicine Hat Can.
65 D4 Medicine Lodge U.S.A.
82 E2 Medina Brazil
32 A5 Medina S. Arabia
70 D3 Medina NY U.S.A.
70 C4 Medina OH U.S.A.
15 E2 Medinaceli Spain
15 D2 Medina del Campo Spain
15 D2 Medina de Rioseco Spain
35 F5 Medinīpur India
4 C5 Mediterranean Sea sea Africa/Europe
18 B6 Medjerda, Monts de la mts Alg.
24 G4 Mednogorsk Rus. Fed.
14 D4 Médoc reg. France
20 H3 Medvedevo Rus. Fed.
21 H5 Medveditsa r. Rus. Fed.
18 F2 Medvednica mts Croatia
25 S2 Medvezh'i, O-va is Rus. Fed.
36 F2 Medvezh'ya, Gora mt China/Rus. Fed.
20 E2 Medvezh'yegorsk Rus. Fed.
9 H6 Medway r. U.K.
48 B4 Meekatharra Austr.
73 H1 Meeker U.S.A.
72 B2 Meeks Bay U.S.A.
59 J4 Meelpaeg Res. resr Can.
13 L4 Meerane Ger.
12 E3 Meerlo Neth.
34 D3 Meerut India
62 E2 Meeteetse U.S.A.
88 D3 Mēga Eth.
45 B3 Mega i. Indon.
35 G4 Meghalaya div. India
35 F5 Meghāsani mt India
35 G5 Meghna r. Bangl.
29 L2 Meghri Armenia
28 B3 Megisti i. Greece
6 U1 Mehamn Norway
31 G5 Mehar Pak.
48 B4 Meharry, Mt mt Austr.
34 D5 Mehekar India
35 G5 Meherpur Bangl.
70 E6 Meherrin r. U.S.A.
46 N5 Méhétia i. Pac. Oc.
29 L2 Mehrābān Iran
29 L5 Mehrān Iraq

30 D5 Mehrān *watercourse* Iran
12 E4 Mehren Ger.
30 D4 Mehriz Iran
31 H3 Mehtar Lām Afgh.
82 C2 Meia Ponte *r.* Brazil
87 D4 Meiganga Cameroon
39 B4 Meigu China
39 E5 Mei Jiang *r.* China
12 D3 Meijnweg, Nationaal Park De *nat. park* Neth.
10 D5 Meikle Millyea *h.* U.K.
37 B4 Meiktila Myanmar
13 J2 Meine Ger.
13 J2 Meinersen Ger.
13 J4 Meiningen Ger.
90 E6 Meiringspoort *pass* S. Africa
39 B4 Meishan China
16 F5 Meißen Ger.
39 C5 Meitan China
38 C3 Mei Xian China
39 E5 Meizhou China
34 D4 Mej *r.* India
80 C3 Mejicana *mt* Arg.
80 B2 Mejillones Chile
88 D2 Mek'elē Eth.
86 A3 Mékhé Senegal
34 B3 Mekhtar Pak.
18 C7 Meknassy Tunisia
86 B1 Meknès Morocco
44 C2 Mekong *r.* Asia
36 B3 Mekong *r.* China
44 C3 Mekong, Mouths of the *est.* Vietnam
45 B2 Melaka Malaysia
94 G6 Melanesia *is* Pac. Oc.
43 A5 Melaut *r.* Malaysia
45 D3 Melawi *r.* Indon.
50 E4 Melbourne Austr.
67 D6 Melbourne U.S.A.
10 □ Melby U.K.
16 D3 Meldorf Ger.
69 F3 Meldrum Bay Can.
28 E2 Melendiz Dağı *mt* Turkey
20 G4 Melenki Rus. Fed.
59 F2 Mélèzes, Rivière aux *r.* Can.
87 D3 Mélfi Chad
18 F4 Melfi Italy
57 J4 Melfort Can.
6 M5 Melhus Norway
15 C1 Melide Spain
86 B1 Melilla Spain
83 E2 Melincué Arg.
45 E3 Melintang, Danau *l.* Indon.
83 B2 Melipilla Chile
12 B3 Meliskerke Neth.
57 J5 Melita Can.
21 E6 Melitopol' Ukr.
16 G6 Melk Austria
91 H1 Melkrivier S. Africa
9 E6 Melksham U.K.
6 T3 Mellakoski Fin.
6 Q5 Mellansel Sweden
13 G2 Melle Ger.
68 B2 Mellen U.S.A.
7 N7 Mellerud Sweden
13 J4 Mellrichstadt Ger.
13 G1 Mellum *i.* Ger.
91 J4 Melmoth S. Africa
83 F2 Melo Uru.
50 B2 Melrose Austr.
10 F5 Melrose U.K.
13 H3 Melsungen Ger.
43 A5 Melta, Mt *mt* Malaysia
9 G5 Melton Mowbray U.K.
14 F2 Melun France
57 J4 Melville Can.
55 M2 Melville Bugt *b.* Greenland
48 E3 Melville, C. *c.* Austr.
43 A5 Melville, C. *c.* Phil.
48 D3 Melville Island *i.* Austr.
54 G2 Melville Island *i.* N.W.T. Can.
59 J3 Melville, Lake *l.* Can.
55 K3 Melville Peninsula Can.
11 C3 Melvin, Lough *l.* Rep. of Ireland/U.K.
25 T3 Melyuveyem Rus. Fed.
35 E2 Mêmar Co *salt l.* China
37 F7 Memberamo *r.* Indon.
91 H3 Memel S. Africa
13 J5 Memmelsdorf Ger.
16 E7 Memmingen Ger.
12 C5 Mémorial Américain *h.* France
45 C2 Mempawah Indon.
28 C7 Memphis Egypt
68 A5 Memphis *MO* U.S.A.
67 B5 Memphis *TN* U.S.A.
65 C5 Memphis *TX* U.S.A.
71 G2 Memphrémagog, Lac *l.* Can.
40 H3 Memuro-dake *mt* Japan
21 E5 Mena Ukr.
65 E5 Mena U.S.A.
86 C3 Ménaka Mali
Mènam Khong *r. see* Mekong
65 D6 Menard U.S.A.
68 C3 Menasha U.S.A.
45 D3 Mendawai *r.* Indon.
14 F4 Mende France
29 M3 Mendejīn Iran
54 B4 Mendenhall, C. *pt* U.S.A.
56 C3 Mendenhall Glacier *gl.* U.S.A.
88 D3 Mendī Eth.
48 E2 Mendi P.N.G.
9 E6 Mendip Hills *h.* U.K.
72 A2 Mendocino U.S.A.
62 A3 Mendocino, C. *c.* U.S.A.
95 K3 Mendocino Seascarp *sea feature* Pac. Oc.
68 E4 Mendon U.S.A.
50 G1 Mendooran Austr.
72 B3 Mendota *CA* U.S.A.
68 C5 Mendota *IL* U.S.A.
68 C4 Mendota, Lake *l.* U.S.A.
83 C2 Mendoza Arg.
83 C2 Mendoza *div.* Arg.
83 C2 Mendoza *r.* Arg.
81 C2 Mene de Mauroa Venez.
81 C2 Mene Grande Venez.
19 M5 Menemen Turkey
38 E3 Mengcheng China
28 D1 Mengen Turkey
45 C3 Menggala Indon.
39 D5 Mengshan China
38 F3 Meng Shan *mts* China
38 E3 Mengyin China
39 B6 Mengzi China
59 G3 Menihek Can.
59 G3 Menihek Lakes *l.* Can.
50 D2 Menindee Austr.
50 D2 Menindee Lake *l.* Austr.
50 B3 Meningie Austr.
29 M4 Menjān Iran
25 O3 Menkere Rus. Fed.
14 F2 Mennecy France
68 D3 Menominee U.S.A.
68 D3 Menominee *r.* U.S.A.
68 C4 Menomonee Falls U.S.A.
68 B3 Menomonie U.S.A.
89 B5 Menongue Angola
15 J2 Menorca *i.* Spain
43 A6 Mensalong Indon.
45 A3 Mentawai, Kepulauan *is* Indon.
44 B5 Mentekab Malaysia
13 J3 Menteroda Ger.
73 H4 Mentmore U.S.A.
45 C3 Mentok Indon.
14 H5 Menton France
70 C4 Mentor U.S.A.
86 C1 Menzel Bourguiba Tunisia
18 D6 Menzel Temime Tunisia
48 C4 Menzies Austr.
92 D4 Menzies, Mt *mt* Ant.
12 E2 Meppel Neth.
12 F2 Meppen Ger.
91 K1 Mepuze Moz.
91 G4 Meqheleng S. Africa
20 G3 Mera *r.* Rus. Fed.
45 C4 Merak Indon.
6 M5 Meråker Norway
64 F4 Meramec *r.* U.S.A.
18 D1 Merano Italy
33 B4 Merath India
81 E3 Merari, Sa. *mt* Brazil
90 F1 Meratswe *r.* Botswana
45 E3 Meratus, Pegunungan *mts* Indon.
37 G7 Merauke Indon.
50 D3 Merbein Austr.
72 B3 Merced U.S.A.
83 B1 Mercedario, Cerro *mt* Arg.
83 E2 Mercedes *Buenos Aires* Arg.
80 E3 Mercedes *Corrientes* Arg.
83 D2 Mercedes *San Luis* Arg.
83 E2 Mercedes Uru.
73 A4 Mercer *OH* U.S.A.
68 B2 Mercer *WV* U.S.A.
57 F4 Mercoal Can.
51 E2 Mercury Islands *is* N.Z.
55 M3 Mercy, C. *hd* Can.
12 B4 Mere Belgium
9 E6 Mere U.K.
71 H3 Meredith U.S.A.
65 C5 Meredith, Lake *l.* U.S.A.
65 C5 Meredith Nat. Recreation Area, Lake *res.* U.S.A.
68 B6 Meredosia U.S.A.
21 F5 Merefa Ukr.
87 E3 Merga Oasis *oasis* Sudan
44 A2 Mergui Myanmar
44 A3 Mergui Archipelago *is* Myanmar
50 C3 Meribah Austr.
19 M4 Meriç *r.* Greece/Turkey
74 G4 Mérida Mex.
15 C3 Mérida Spain
81 C2 Mérida Venez.
81 C2 Mérida, Cordillera de *mts* Venez.
71 G4 Meriden U.S.A.
72 B2 Meridian *CA* U.S.A.
65 F5 Meridian *MS* U.S.A.
14 D4 Mérignac France
6 T4 Merijärvi Fin.
7 R6 Merikarvia Fin.
50 G4 Merimbula Austr.
50 C3 Meringur Austr.
50 C4 Merino Austr.
65 C5 Merkel U.S.A.
44 □ Merlimau, P. *i.* Sing.
87 F3 Merowe Sudan
48 B5 Merredin Austr.
10 D5 Merrick *h.* U.K.
71 K3 Merrickville Can.
69 K3 Merrill U.S.A.
68 D5 Merrillville U.S.A.
68 C3 Merriman U.S.A.
56 E4 Merritt Can.
67 D6 Merritt Island U.S.A.
50 H2 Merriwa Austr.
50 G1 Merrygoen Austr.
88 E2 Mersa Fatma Eritrea
12 E5 Mersch Lux.
13 K3 Merseburg (Saale) Ger.
9 E4 Mersey *est.* U.K.
Mersin *see* İçel
45 B2 Mersing Malagsia
7 S8 Mērsrags Latvia
34 C4 Merta India
9 D6 Merthyr Tydfil U.K.
88 D3 Merti Kenya
15 C4 Mértola Port.
92 B6 Mertz Gl. *gl.* Ant.
88 D4 Meru *volc.* Tanz.
31 F4 Merui Pak.
Merv *see* Mary
90 D6 Merweville S. Africa
28 E1 Merzifon Turkey
12 E5 Merzig Ger.
82 B2 Merz Pen. *pen.* Ant.
73 G5 Mesa U.S.A.
42 A2 Mesabi Range *h.* U.S.A.
18 G4 Mesagne Italy
19 L7 Mesara, Ormos *b.* Greece
73 H3 Mesa Verde Nat. Park U.S.A.
81 B4 Mesay *r.* Col.
13 G3 Meschede Ger.
6 P4 Meselefors Sweden
58 F3 Mesgouez L. *l.* Can.
20 J2 Meshchura Rus. Fed.
Meshed *see* Mashhad
31 E2 Meshkān Iran
21 G5 Meshkovskaya Rus. Fed.
68 E3 Mesick U.S.A.
19 K4 Mesimeri Greece
19 J5 Mesolongi Greece
29 J4 Mesopotamia *reg.* Iraq
73 E3 Mesquite *NV* U.S.A.
65 D5 Mesquite *TX* U.S.A.
73 E4 Mesquite Lake *l.* U.S.A.
89 D5 Messalo *r.* Moz.
18 F5 Messina *Sicily* Italy
91 J1 Messina S. Africa
18 F5 Messina, Stretta di *str.* Italy
69 J2 Messines Can.
19 K6 Messini Greece
19 K6 Messiniakos Kolpos *b.* Greece
55 Q2 Mesters Vig Greenland
13 K1 Mestlin Ger.
19 L5 Meston, Akra *pt* Greece
18 E2 Mestre Italy
28 F1 Mesudiye Turkey
81 C3 Meta *r.* Col./Venez.
69 G2 Metagama Can.
55 L3 Meta Incognita Pen. Can.
65 F6 Metairie U.S.A.
68 C5 Metamora U.S.A.
80 C3 Metán Arg.
96 H9 Meteor Depth *depth* Atl. Ocean
19 J6 Methoni Greece
71 H3 Methuen U.S.A.
10 E4 Methven U.K.
18 G3 Metković Croatia
56 C3 Metlakatla U.S.A.
89 D5 Metoro Moz.
45 C4 Metro Indon.
66 B4 Metropolis U.S.A.
12 C4 Mettet Belgium
13 F2 Mettingen Ger.
72 C4 Mettler U.S.A.
33 B4 Mettur India
88 D3 Metu Eth.
14 H2 Metz France
12 D4 Meuse *r.* Belgium/France
13 L3 Meuselwitz Ger.
9 C7 Mevagissey U.K.
38 B3 Mêwa China
65 D6 Mexia U.S.A.
74 A2 Mexicali Mex.
73 H3 Mexican Hat U.S.A.
63 F6 Mexicanos, L. de los *l.* Mex.
73 H3 Mexican Water U.S.A.
74 E5 México Mex.
71 H2 Mexico *ME* U.S.A.
64 F4 Mexico *MO* U.S.A.
71 E3 Mexico *NY* U.S.A.
53 F7 Mexico *country* Central America
52 G7 Mexico, Gulf of Mex./U.S.A.
30 D3 Meybod Iran
13 L1 Meyenburg Ger.
31 G3 Meymaneh Afgh.
30 C3 Meymeh Iran
30 B3 Meymeh *r.* Iran
19 K3 Mezdra Bulg.
24 F3 Mezen' Rus. Fed.
14 G4 Mézenc, Mont *mt* France
36 A1 Mezhdurechensk Rus. Fed.
20 J2 Mezhdurechensk Rus. Fed.
24 G2 Mezhdusharskiy, O. *i.* Rus. Fed.
17 K7 Mezőtúr Hungary
74 D4 Mezquital *r.* Mex.
7 U8 Mežvidi Latvia
89 D5 Mfuwe Zambia
33 A2 Mhasvad India
91 J3 Mhlume Swaziland
34 C5 Mhow India
35 H5 Mi *r.* Myanmar
74 E5 Miahuatlán Mex.
15 D3 Miajadas Spain
73 G5 Miami *AZ* U.S.A.
67 D7 Miami *FL* U.S.A.
65 E4 Miami *OK* U.S.A.
67 D7 Miami Beach U.S.A.
30 C4 Mīān Āb Iran
31 F5 Mianaz Pak.
30 D3 Mīāndarreh Iran
30 B2 Miandowāb Iran
89 E5 Miandrivazo Madag.
30 B2 Mīāneh Iran
43 C5 Miangas *i.* Phil.
31 F5 Miani Hor *b.* Pak.
31 G3 Mianjoi Afgh.
39 B4 Mianning China
34 B2 Mianwali Pak.
38 C3 Mian Xian China
39 D4 Mianyang *Hubei* China
38 B4 Mianyang *Sichuan* China
38 B4 Mianzhu China
38 F2 Miao Dao *i.* China
38 F2 Miaodao Qundao *is* China
39 F5 Miaoli Taiwan
89 E5 Miarinarivo Madag.
24 H4 Miass Rus. Fed.
73 G5 Mica Mt *mt* U.S.A.
38 C3 Micang Shan *mts* China
17 K6 Michalovce Slovakia
57 H3 Michel Can.
13 K4 Michelau in Oberfranken Ger.
13 H5 Michelstadt Ger.
13 M2 Michendorf Ger.
68 C2 Michigamme Lake *l.* U.S.A.
68 C2 Michigamme Reservoir U.S.A.
68 D2 Michigan *div.* U.S.A.
68 D5 Michigan City U.S.A.
68 D4 Michigan, Lake *l.* U.S.A.
68 E2 Michipicoten Bay *b.* Can.
68 E2 Michipicoten I. *i.* Can.
68 E1 Michipicoten River Can.
19 M3 Michurin Bulg.
20 G4 Michurinsk Rus. Fed.
75 H6 Mico *r.* Nic.
94 E5 Micronesia *is* Pac. Oc.
47 G3 Micronesia, Federated States of *country* Pac. Oc.
45 C2 Midai *i.* Indon.
96 F4 Mid-Atlantic Ridge *sea feature* Atl. Ocean
90 C6 Middelberg Pass S. Africa
12 B3 Middelburg Neth.
90 F5 Middelburg *Eastern Cape* S. Africa
91 H2 Middelburg *Mpumalanga* S. Africa
7 L9 Middelfart Denmark
12 C3 Middelharnis Neth.
90 D5 Middelpos S. Africa
91 G2 Middelwit S. Africa
62 C3 Middle Alkali Lake *l.* U.S.A.
95 N5 Middle America Trench *sea feature* Pac. Oc.
71 H4 Middleboro U.S.A.
70 E4 Middleburg U.S.A.
71 F3 Middleburgh U.S.A.
71 G2 Middlebury U.S.A.
51 C6 Middlemarch N.Z.
70 B6 Middlesboro U.S.A.
8 F3 Middlesbrough U.K.
72 A2 Middletown *CA* U.S.A.
71 G4 Middletown *CT* U.S.A.
71 F5 Middletown *DE* U.S.A.
71 F4 Middletown *NY* U.S.A.
70 A5 Middletown *OH* U.S.A.
68 E4 Middleville U.S.A.
9 G7 Midhurst U.K.
93 K4 Mid-Indian Basin *sea feature* Ind. Ocean
93 K6 Mid-Indian Ridge *sea feature* Ind. Ocean
69 H3 Midland Can.
69 E4 Midland *MI* U.S.A.
65 C5 Midland *TX* U.S.A.
11 C6 Midleton Rep. of Ireland
94 F4 Mid-Pacific Mountains *sea feature* Pac. Oc.
6 □ Miðvágur Faroe Is
Midway *see* Thamarīt
94 H4 Midway Islands *is* Pac. Oc.
62 F3 Midwest U.S.A.
65 D5 Midwest City U.S.A.
12 D2 Midwoud Neth.
29 H3 Midyat Turkey
10 □ Mid Yell U.K.
19 K3 Midzhur *mt* Bulg./Yugo.
7 U6 Miehikkälä Fin.
6 T3 Miekojärvi *l.* Fin.
17 K5 Mielec Pol.
89 D4 Miembwe Tanz.
6 U2 Mieraslompolo Fin.
17 M7 Miercurea-Ciuc Romania
15 D1 Mieres Spain
88 E3 Mī'ēso Eth.
13 K2 Mieste Ger.
70 E4 Mifflinburg U.S.A.
70 E4 Mifflintown U.S.A.
38 C3 Migang Shan *mt* China
91 F3 Migdol S. Africa
31 E4 Mīghān Iran
35 H3 Miging India
28 C2 Mihalıççık Turkey
41 C7 Mihara Japan
41 F7 Mihara-yama *volc.* Japan
15 F2 Mijares *r.* Spain
12 C2 Mijdrecht Neth.
69 F3 Mikado U.S.A.
17 N4 Mikashevichy Belarus
20 F4 Mikhaylov Rus. Fed.
92 D5 Mikhaylov I. *i.* Ant.
40 C3 Mikhaylovka *Primorskiy Kray* Rus. Fed.
21 G5 Mikhaylovka *Volgograd.* Rus. Fed.
24 J4 Mikhaylovskiy Rus. Fed.
35 H4 Mikīr Hills *mts* India
7 U6 Mikkeli Fin.
7 U6 Mikkelin mlk Fin.
56 G3 Mikkwa *r.* Can.
88 D4 Mikumi Tanz.
20 J2 Mikun' Rus. Fed.
41 F6 Mikuni-sammyaku *mts* Japan
41 F8 Mikura-jima *i.* Japan
64 E2 Milaca U.S.A.
33 A5 Miladhunmadulu Atoll *atoll* Maldives
18 C2 Milan Italy
67 B5 Milan U.S.A.
50 B3 Milang Austr.
89 D5 Milange Moz.
Milano *see* Milan
28 A3 Milas Turkey
18 F5 Milazzo *Sicily* Italy
64 D2 Milbank U.S.A.
9 H5 Mildenhall U.K.
50 D3 Mildura Austr.
39 B5 Mile China
62 F2 Miles City U.S.A.
11 C5 Milestone Rep. of Ireland
18 F4 Miletto, Monte *mt* Italy
11 D2 Milford Rep. of Ireland
72 B1 Milford *CA* U.S.A.
71 G4 Milford *CT* U.S.A.
71 F5 Milford *DE* U.S.A.
68 D5 Milford *IL* U.S.A.
71 H3 Milford *MA* U.S.A.
71 J2 Milford *ME* U.S.A.
71 H3 Milford *NH* U.S.A.
71 F3 Milford *NY* U.S.A.
73 F2 Milford *UT* U.S.A.
9 B6 Milford Haven U.K.
51 A6 Milford Sound N.Z.
51 A6 Milford Sound *in.* N.Z.
15 H4 Miliana Alg.
54 G5 Milk *r. Alta.* Can.
62 F1 Milk *r.* Can./U.S.A.
25 R4 Mil'kovo Rus. Fed.
15 F2 Millárs *r.* Spain
14 F4 Millau France
72 B1 Mill Creek *r.* U.S.A.
67 D5 Milledgeville *GA* U.S.A.
68 C5 Milledgeville *IL* U.S.A.
64 E2 Mille Lacs *L. l.* U.S.A.
58 B4 Mille Lacs, Lac des *l.* Can.
64 D2 Miller U.S.A.
68 B3 Miller Dam Flowage *resr* U.S.A.
69 G3 Miller Lake Can.
21 G5 Millerovo Rus. Fed.
73 G6 Miller Peak *summit* U.S.A.
70 C4 Millersburg *OH* U.S.A.
70 E4 Millersburg *PA* U.S.A.
70 E6 Millers Tavern U.S.A.
72 C3 Millerton Lake *l.* U.S.A.
10 C5 Milleur Point *pt* U.K.
92 C6 Mill I. *i.* Ant.
50 C4 Millicent Austr.
69 F4 Millington *MI* U.S.A.
67 B5 Millington *TN* U.S.A.
71 J2 Millinocket U.S.A.
8 D3 Millom U.K.
10 D5 Millport U.K.
71 F5 Millsboro U.S.A.
56 F2 Mills Lake *l.* Can.
70 C5 Millstone U.S.A.
59 G4 Milltown Can.
11 B5 Milltown Malbay Rep. of Ireland
71 K1 Millville Can.
71 F5 Millville U.S.A.
71 J2 Milo U.S.A.
40 D3 Milogradovo Rus. Fed.
19 L6 Milos *i.* Greece
20 F4 Miloslavskoye Rus. Fed.
70 E4 Milroy U.S.A.
69 H4 Milton Can.
51 B7 Milton N.Z.
67 C6 Milton *FL* U.S.A.
68 A5 Milton *IA* U.S.A.
70 E4 Milton *PA* U.S.A.
71 G2 Milton *VT* U.S.A.
62 C2 Milton-Freewater U.S.A.
9 G5 Milton Keynes U.K.
70 C4 Milton, Lake *l.* U.S.A.
39 D4 Miluo China
68 D4 Milwaukee U.S.A.
21 G5 Milyutinskaya Rus. Fed.
14 D4 Mimizan France
88 B4 Mimongo Gabon
65 C7 Mina Mex.
72 C2 Mina U.S.A.
30 E5 Mīnāb Iran
37 E6 Minahassa, Semenanjung *pen.* Indon.
30 D5 Mina Jebel Ali U.A.E.
57 L4 Minaki Can.
41 B8 Minamata Japan
41 E7 Minami Alps National Park Japan
45 B2 Minas Indon.
83 F2 Minas Uru.
29 M7 Mīnā Sa'ūd Kuwait
59 H4 Minas Basin *b.* Can.
83 F1 Minas de Corrales Uru.
82 D2 Minas Gerais *div.* Brazil
82 D2 Minas Novas Brazil
74 F5 Minatitlán Mex.
35 H5 Minbu Myanmar
35 H5 Minbya Myanmar
80 B6 Minchinmávida *volc.* Chile
10 C2 Minch, The *str.* U.K.
18 D2 Mincio *r.* Italy
29 L2 Mincivan Azer.
43 C5 Mindanao *i.* Phil.
50 C3 Mindarie Austr.
86 □ Mindelo Cape Verde
69 H3 Minden Can.
13 G2 Minden Ger.
65 E5 Minden *LA* U.S.A.
72 C2 Minden *NV* U.S.A.
35 H6 Mindon Myanmar
50 D2 Mindona L. *l.* Austr.
43 B3 Mindoro *i.* Phil.
43 A3 Mindoro Strait *str.* Phil.
88 B4 Mindouli Congo
9 D6 Minehead U.K.
11 D6 Mine Head *hd* Rep. of Ireland
82 B2 Mineiros Brazil
65 E5 Mineola U.S.A.
72 B1 Mineral U.S.A.
72 C3 Mineral King U.S.A.
21 G6 Mineral'nyye Vody Rus. Fed.
68 B4 Mineral Point U.S.A.
65 D5 Mineral Wells U.S.A.
73 F2 Minersville U.S.A.
18 G4 Minervino Murge Italy
35 F1 Minfeng China
89 C5 Minga Congo(Zaire)
29 L1 Mingäçevir Azer.
29 L1 Mingäçevir Su Anbarı *resr* Azer.
59 H3 Mingan Can.
50 C2 Mingary Austr.
38 E3 Minggang China
15 F3 Minglanilla Spain
89 D5 Mingoyo Tanz.
39 B4 Ming-shan China
36 E2 Mingshui China
10 A4 Mingulay *i.* U.K.
39 E5 Mingxi China
38 B2 Minhe China
39 F5 Minhou China
33 A4 Minicoy *i.* India
48 B4 Minilya Austr.
59 H3 Minipi Lake *l.* Can.
57 J4 Minitonas Can.
39 F5 Min Jiang *r. Fujian* China
38 B4 Min Jiang *r. Sichuan* China
38 A2 Minle China
86 C4 Minna Nigeria
7 O5 Minne Sweden
64 E2 Minneapolis U.S.A.
57 K4 Minnedosa Can.
68 A2 Minnesota *div.* U.S.A.
61 G2 Minnesota *r. MN* U.S.A.
58 B4 Minnitaki L. *l.* Can.
15 B2 Miño *r.* Port./Spain
68 C3 Minocqua U.S.A.
68 B2 Minong U.S.A.
68 C5 Minonk U.S.A.
Minorca *i. see* Menorca
64 C1 Minot U.S.A.
38 B2 Minqin China
39 F5 Minqing China
38 B3 Min Shan *mts* China
35 H4 Minsin Myanmar
20 C4 Minsk Belarus
17 K4 Mińsk Mazowiecki Pol.
9 E5 Minsterley U.K.
34 C1 Mintaka Pass China/Jammu and Kashmir
59 G4 Minto Can.
54 G2 Minto Inlet *in.* Can.
58 F2 Minto, Lac *l.* Can.
63 F4 Minturn U.S.A.
28 C6 Minûf Egypt
36 B1 Minusinsk Rus. Fed.
35 J3 Minutang India
38 B3 Min Xian China
50 D4 Minyip Austr.
69 E3 Mio U.S.A.
58 E4 Miquelon Can.
59 J4 Miquelon *i.* N. America
81 A4 Mira *r.* Col.
31 F4 Mirabad Afgh.
71 F2 Mirabel Can.
82 D2 Mirabela Brazil
79 J5 Miracema do Norte Brazil
79 J5 Mirador, Parque Nacional de *nat. park* Brazil
81 B4 Miraflores Col.
82 D2 Miralta Brazil
83 F3 Miramar Arg.
14 G5 Miramas France
59 G4 Miramichi *r.* Can.
19 L7 Mirampelou, Kolpos *b.* Greece
34 B2 Miram Shah Pak.
82 A3 Miranda Brazil
72 A1 Miranda U.S.A.
82 A3 Miranda *r.* Brazil
15 E1 Miranda de Ebro Spain
15 C2 Mirandela Port.
18 D2 Mirandola Italy
82 B3 Mirandópolis Brazil
29 H5 Mirā', Wādī al *watercourse* Iraq/S. Arabia
32 D6 Mirbāṭ Oman
14 E5 Mirepoix France
45 D2 Miri Malaysia
31 F4 Miri *mt* Pak.
33 B2 Mirialguda India
83 G2 Mirim, Lagoa *l.* Brazil
31 F4 Mīrjāveh Iran
20 G2 Mirnyy Rus. Fed.
25 N3 Mirnyy Rus. Fed.
92 D5 Mirnyy *Rus. Fed. Base* Ant.
57 J3 Mirond L. *l.* Can.
13 L1 Mirow Ger.
34 C2 Mirpur Pak.
34 B4 Mirpur Batoro Pak.
34 B4 Mirpur Khas Pak.
34 A4 Mirpur Sakro Pak.
56 G4 Mirror Can.
39 □ Mirs Bay *b. H.K.* China
31 E5 Mīr Shahdād Iran
19 K6 Mirtoö Pelagos *sea* Greece
42 E6 Miryang S. Korea
31 F2 Mirzachirla Turkm.
35 E4 Mirzapur India
41 C8 Misaki Japan
40 G4 Misawa Japan
59 H4 Miscou I. *i.* Can.
34 C1 Misgar Pak.
40 B2 Mishan China
30 C5 Mishāsh al Hādī *well* S. Arabia
68 D5 Mishawaka U.S.A.
68 E1 Mishibishu Lake *l.* Can.
41 B7 Mi-shima *i.* Japan
35 H3 Mishmi Hills *mts* India
63 F3 Misima I. *i.* P.N.G.
75 H6 Miskitos, Cayos *atolls* Nic.
17 K6 Miskolc Hungary
37 F7 Misoöl *i.* Indon.
82 B3 Misquah Hills *h.* U.S.A.
87 D1 Miṣrātah Libya
34 E4 Misrikh India
69 E1 Missanabie Can.
58 D3 Missinaibi *r.* Can.
69 F1 Missinaibi Lake *l.* Can.
57 J3 Missinipe Can.
56 E5 Mission Can.
64 C3 Mission *SD* U.S.A.
58 D3 Missisa L. *l.* Can.
69 F2 Mississagi *r.* Can.
69 H4 Mississauga Can.
68 E5 Mississinewa Lake *l.* U.S.A.
65 F5 Mississippi *div.* U.S.A.
69 J3 Mississippi *r.* Can.
65 F6 Mississippi *r.* U.S.A.
65 F6 Mississippi Delta *delta* U.S.A.
62 D2 Missoula U.S.A.
68 A6 Missouri *div.* U.S.A.
64 C2 Missouri *r.* U.S.A.
64 E3 Missouri Valley U.S.A.
55 L4 Mistassibi *r.* Can.
59 F4 Mistassini Can.
59 F4 Mistassini *r.* Can.
58 F3 Mistassini, L. *l.* Can.
59 H2 Mistastin Lake *l.* Can.
16 H6 Mistelbach Austria
56 C3 Misty Fjords National Monument *res.* U.S.A.
48 E4 Mitchell Austr.
69 G4 Mitchell Can.
64 D3 Mitchell U.S.A.
48 E3 Mitchell *r. Qld.* Austr.
50 F4 Mitchell *r. Vic.* Austr.
68 E3 Mitchell, Lake *l.* U.S.A.
67 D5 Mitchell, Mt *mt* U.S.A.
11 C5 Mitchelstown Rep. of Ireland
28 C6 Mit Ghamr Egypt
34 B3 Mithankot Pak.
34 B4 Mithi Pak.
34 B4 Mithrani Canal *canal* Pak.
19 M5 Mithymna Greece
56 C3 Mitkof I. *i.* U.S.A.
41 G6 Mito Japan
89 D4 Mitole Tanz.
51 E4 Mitre *mt* N.Z.
49 H3 Mitre Island *i.* Solomon Is
50 H3 Mittagong Austr.
50 F4 Mitta Mitta Austr.
13 G2 Mittellandkanal *canal* Ger.

13 L5 Mitterteich Ger.
13 L4 Mittweida Ger.
81 C4 Mitú Col.
81 C4 Mituas Col.
89 C5 Mitumba, Chaîne des mts Congo(Zaire)
88 C4 Mitumba, Monts mts Congo(Zaire)
88 B3 Mitzic Gabon
41 F7 Miura Japan
29 G4 Miyah, Wādī el watercourse Syria
41 F7 Miyake-jima i. Japan
40 G5 Miyako Japan
41 B9 Miyakonojō Japan
38 B4 Miyaluo China
34 B5 Miyāni India
41 B9 Miyazaki Japan
41 D7 Miyazu Japan
39 B5 Miyi China
41 C7 Miyoshi Japan
38 E1 Miyun China
38 E1 Miyun Sk. resr China
31 G3 Mīzāni Afgh.
88 D3 Mīzan Teferī Eth.
87 D1 Mizdah Libya
11 B6 Mizen Head hd Rep. of Ireland
21 B5 Mizhhir''ya Ukr.
38 D2 Mizhi China
35 H5 Mizoram div. India
40 G5 Mizusawa Japan
7 O7 Mjölby Sweden
88 D4 Mkata Tanz.
88 D4 Mkomazi Tanz.
89 C5 Mkushi Zambia
16 G5 Mladá Boleslav Czech Rep.
19 J2 Mladenovac Yugo.
17 K4 Mława Pol.
18 G3 Mljet i. Croatia
91 G5 Mlungisi S. Africa
17 M5 Mlyniv Ukr.
91 F2 Mmabatho S. Africa
91 G1 Mmamabula Botswana
91 F2 Mmathethe Botswana
7 J6 Mo Norway
73 H2 Moab U.S.A.
48 E3 Moa I. i. Austr.
49 H3 Moala i. Fiji
30 D3 Mo'alla Iran
91 K2 Moamba Moz.
73 E3 Moapa U.S.A.
11 D4 Moate Rep. of Ireland
88 C4 Moba Congo(Zaire)
41 G7 Mobara Japan
30 C3 Mobārakeh Iran
88 C3 Mobayi-Mbongo Congo(Zaire)
64 E4 Moberly U.S.A.
67 B6 Mobile AL U.S.A.
73 F5 Mobile AZ U.S.A.
67 B6 Mobile Bay b. U.S.A.
64 C2 Mobridge U.S.A.
Mobutu, Lake l. see Albert, Lake
79 J4 Mocajuba Brazil
89 E5 Moçambique Moz.
81 D2 Mocapra r. Venez.
39 B6 Môc Châu Vietnam
81 D2 Mochirma, Parque Nacional nat. park Venez.
89 C6 Mochudi Botswana
89 E5 Mocimboa da Praia Moz.
13 K2 Möckern Ger.
13 H5 Möckmühl Ger.
6 R4 Mockträsk Sweden
81 A4 Mocoa Col.
82 C3 Mococa Brazil
89 D5 Mocuba Moz.
14 H4 Modane France
34 C5 Modasa India
90 F4 Modder r. S. Africa
18 D2 Modena Italy
73 F3 Modena U.S.A.
72 B3 Modesto U.S.A.
50 F5 Moe Austr.
9 D5 Moel Sych h. U.K.
7 M6 Moely Norway
6 Q2 Moen Norway
73 G3 Moenkopi U.S.A.
51 C6 Moeraki Pt pt N.Z.
12 E3 Moers Ger.
10 E5 Moffat U.K.
34 C3 Moga India
Mogadishu see Muqdisho
70 C4 Mogadore Reservoir U.S.A.
91 H1 Mogalakwena r. S. Africa
91 H2 Moganyaka S. Africa
13 L2 Mögelin Ger.
31 G2 Moghiyon Tajik.
82 C3 Mogi-Mirim Brazil
36 D1 Mogocha Rus. Fed.
18 C6 Mogod mts Tunisia
91 F2 Mogoditshane Botswana
36 B4 Mogok Myanmar
73 H5 Mogollon Baldy mt U.S.A.
73 H5 Mogollon Mts mts U.S.A.
73 G4 Mogollon Rim plat. U.S.A.
91 G2 Mogwase S. Africa
19 H2 Mohács Hungary
51 F3 Mohaka r. N.Z.
91 G5 Mohale's Hoek Lesotho
57 J5 Mohall U.S.A.
31 E3 Mohammad Iran
Moḥammadābād see Darreh Gaz
15 G5 Mohammadia Alg.
34 E3 Mohan r. India/Nepal
73 E4 Mohave, L. l. U.S.A.
73 F5 Mohawk U.S.A.
71 F3 Mohawk r. U.S.A.
73 F5 Mohawk Mts mts U.S.A.
89 E5 Moheli i. Comoros
11 D4 Mohill Rep. of Ireland
13 G3 Möhne r. Ger.
73 F4 Mohon Peak summit U.S.A.
89 D4 Mohoro Tanz.
65 C7 Mohovano Ranch Mex.
29 M5 Moh Reza Shah Pahlavi resr Iran
21 C5 Mohyliv Podil's'kyy Ukr.
7 K7 Moi Norway
91 G1 Moijabana Botswana
91 K2 Moine Moz.
17 N7 Moinești Romania
71 F2 Moira U.S.A.
6 O3 Mo i Rana Norway
35 H4 Moirang India
7 T7 Mõisaküla Estonia
83 E1 Moisés Ville Arg.
59 G3 Moisie Can.
59 G3 Moisie r. Can.
14 E4 Moissac France
72 C4 Mojave U.S.A.
72 D4 Mojave r. U.S.A.
72 D4 Mojave Desert U.S.A.
82 C3 Moji das Cruzes Brazil
82 C3 Moji-Guaçu r. Brazil
41 B8 Mojikō Japan
35 F4 Mokāma India
72 □1 Mokapu Pen. pen. U.S.A.
51 E3 Mokau N.Z.
51 E3 Mokau r. N.Z.
72 B2 Mokelumne r. U.S.A.
91 H4 Mokhoabong Pass Lesotho
91 H4 Mokhotlong Lesotho
18 D7 Moknine Tunisia
51 E1 Mokohinau Is is N.Z.
87 D3 Mokolo Cameroon
91 G2 Mokolo r. S. Africa
42 D6 Mokp'o S. Korea
20 G4 Moksha r. Rus. Fed.
20 H4 Mokshan Rus. Fed.
72 □1 Mokuauia I. i. U.S.A.
72 □1 Mokulua Is is U.S.A.
15 F3 Molatón mt Spain
Moldavia country see Moldova
6 K5 Molde Norway
6 O3 Moldjord Norway
5 F4 Moldova country Europe
19 L2 Moldoveanu, Vârful mt Romania
9 D7 Mole r. U.K.
86 B4 Mole National Park Ghana
89 C6 Molepolole Botswana
7 T9 Molėtai Lith.
18 G4 Molfetta Italy
42 C2 Molihong Shan h. China
15 F2 Molina de Aragón Spain
68 B5 Moline U.S.A.
7 N7 Molkom Sweden
29 M4 Mollā Bodāgh Iran
35 H4 Mol Len mt India
13 M1 Möllenbeck Ger.
78 D7 Mollendo Peru
13 J1 Mölln Ger.
7 N8 Mölnlycke Sweden
20 F3 Molochnoye Rus. Fed.
6 X2 Molochnyy Rus. Fed.
92 D4 Molodezhnaya Rus. Fed. Base Ant.
20 E3 Molodoy Tud Rus. Fed.
72 □2 Molokai i. U.S.A.
95 K4 Molokai Fracture Zone sea feature Pac. Oc.
20 J3 Moloma r. Rus. Fed.
50 G2 Molong Austr.
90 F2 Molopo watercourse Botswana/S. Africa
87 D4 Moloundou Cameroon
57 K4 Molson L. l. Can.
Moluccas is see Maluku
37 E7 Molucca Sea g. Indon.
89 D5 Moma Moz.
50 D1 Momba Austr.
88 D4 Mombasa Kenya
35 H4 Mombi New India
82 B2 Mombuca, Serra da h. Brazil
21 C7 Momchilgrad Bulg.
68 D5 Momence U.S.A.
81 B2 Mompós Col.
7 N9 Møn i. Denmark
73 G2 Mona U.S.A.
10 A3 Monach Islands is U.K.
10 A3 Monach, Sound of chan. U.K.
5 D4 Monaco country Europe
10 D3 Monadhliath Mountains U.K.
11 E3 Monaghan Rep. of Ireland
65 C6 Monahans U.S.A.
75 L5 Mona, I. i. Puerto Rico
75 L5 Mona Passage chan. Dom. Rep./Puerto Rico
89 E5 Monapo Moz.
56 D4 Monarch Mt. mt Can.
63 F4 Monarch Pass U.S.A.
10 C3 Monar, Loch l. U.K.
56 F4 Monashee Mts mts Can.
18 D7 Monastir Tunisia
17 P3 Monastyrshchina Rus. Fed.
21 D5 Monastyryshche Ukr.
40 H2 Monbetsu Japan
40 H3 Monbetsu Japan
18 B2 Moncalieri Italy
15 F2 Moncayo mt Spain
6 X3 Monchegorsk Rus. Fed.
12 E3 Mönchengladbach Ger.
15 B4 Monchique Port.
67 E5 Moncks Corner U.S.A.
74 D3 Monclova Mex.
59 H4 Moncton Can.
15 C2 Mondego r. Port.
91 J3 Mondlo S. Africa
18 B2 Mondovì Italy
68 B3 Mondovi U.S.A.
18 E4 Mondragone Italy
19 K6 Monemvasia Greece
40 G1 Moneron, Ostrov i. Rus. Fed.
70 D4 Monessen U.S.A.
69 K1 Monet Can.
11 D5 Moneygall Rep. of Ireland
11 E3 Moneymore U.K.
18 E2 Monfalcone Italy
15 C1 Monforte Spain
88 C3 Monga Congo(Zaire)
39 C6 Móng Cai Vietnam
42 C4 Monggŭmp'o-ri N. Korea
44 A1 Mong Mau Myanmar
23 J5 Mongolia country Asia
34 C2 Mongora Pak.
89 C5 Mongu Zambia
71 J3 Monhegan I. i. U.S.A.
10 E5 Moniaive U.K.
72 D2 Monitor Mt mt U.S.A.
72 D2 Monitor Range mts U.S.A.
11 C4 Monivea Rep. of Ireland
69 G4 Monkton Can.
35 F3 Mon La pass China
9 E6 Monmouth U.K.
68 B5 Monmouth IL U.S.A.
71 H2 Monmouth ME U.S.A.
56 E4 Monmouth Mt. mt Can.
9 E6 Monnow r. U.K.
86 C3 Mono r. Togo
72 C3 Mono Lake l. U.S.A.
71 H4 Monomoy Pt pt U.S.A.
68 D5 Monon U.S.A.
68 B4 Monona U.S.A.
18 G4 Monopoli Italy
70 C5 Monongahela r. U.S.A.
15 F2 Monreal del Campo Spain
18 E5 Monreale Sicily Italy
65 E5 Monroe LA U.S.A.
69 F5 Monroe MI U.S.A.
67 D5 Monroe NC U.S.A.
71 F4 Monroe NY U.S.A.
73 F2 Monroe UT U.S.A.
68 C4 Monroe WI U.S.A.
68 B6 Monroe City U.S.A.
67 C6 Monroeville U.S.A.
86 A4 Monrovia Liberia
12 B4 Mons Belgium
12 E4 Monschau Ger.
18 D2 Monselice Italy
13 F4 Montabaur Ger.
89 E5 Montagne d'Ambre, Parc National de la nat. park Madag.
90 D6 Montagu S. Africa
68 D4 Montague U.S.A.
92 C1 Montagu I. i. Atl. Ocean
18 F5 Montalto mt Italy
18 G5 Montalto Uffugo Italy
19 K3 Montana Bulg.
62 E2 Montana div. U.S.A.
14 F3 Montargis France
14 E4 Montauban France
71 G4 Montauk U.S.A.
71 H4 Montauk Pt pt U.S.A.
14 G3 Montbard France
15 G2 Montblanc Spain
14 G4 Montbrison France
14 G3 Montceau-les-Mines France
12 C5 Montcornet France
14 D5 Mont-de-Marsan France
14 F2 Montdidier France
79 H4 Monte Alegre Brazil
82 C2 Monte Alegre de Goiás Brazil
82 D1 Monte Azul Brazil
58 E4 Montebello Can.
18 F6 Montebello Ionico Italy
18 E2 Montebelluna Italy
83 D2 Monte Buey Arg.
14 H5 Monte Carlo Monaco
83 F1 Monte Caseros Arg.
91 G1 Monte Christo S. Africa
83 C2 Monte Comán Arg.
75 K5 Monte Cristi Dom. Rep.
18 D3 Montecristo, Isola di i. Italy
75 J5 Montego Bay Jamaica
14 G4 Montélimar France
83 E2 Monte Lindo r. Para.
18 F4 Montella Italy
68 C4 Montello U.S.A.
74 E3 Montemorelos Mex.
15 B3 Montemor-o-Novo Port.
19 H3 Montenegro div. Yugo.
89 D5 Montepuez Moz.
18 D3 Montepulciano Italy
14 F2 Montereau-faut-Yonne France
72 B3 Monterey CA U.S.A.
70 D5 Monterey VA U.S.A.
72 B3 Monterey Bay b. U.S.A.
81 B2 Montería Col.
78 F7 Montero Bol.
65 C7 Monterrey Mex.
18 F4 Montesano sulla Marcellana Italy
79 L6 Monte Santo Brazil
82 D2 Montes Claros Brazil
18 F3 Montesilvano Italy
18 D3 Montevarchi Italy
83 F2 Montevideo Uru.
64 E2 Montevideo U.S.A.
63 F4 Monte Vista U.S.A.
68 A5 Montezuma U.S.A.
73 G4 Montezuma Castle National Monument res. U.S.A.
73 H3 Montezuma Creek U.S.A.
72 D3 Montezuma Peak summit U.S.A.
12 D3 Montfort Neth.
9 D5 Montgomery U.K.
67 C5 Montgomery U.S.A.
16 C7 Monthey Switz.
65 F5 Monticello AR U.S.A.
67 D6 Monticello FL U.S.A.
68 B4 Monticello IA U.S.A.
68 D5 Monticello IN U.S.A.
71 K1 Monticello ME U.S.A.
68 B5 Monticello MO U.S.A.
71 F4 Monticello NY U.S.A.
73 H3 Monticello UT U.S.A.
68 C4 Monticello WI U.S.A.
83 E1 Montiel, Cuchilla de h. Arg.
14 E4 Montignac France
12 C4 Montignies-le-Tilleul Belgium
12 E5 Montigny-lès-Metz France
15 D4 Montilla Spain
59 G4 Mont Joli Can.
69 K2 Mont-Laurier Can.
59 G4 Mont Louis Can.
14 F3 Montluçon France
59 F4 Montmagny Can.
12 D5 Montmédy France
12 B6 Montmirail France
68 D5 Montmorenci U.S.A.
59 F4 Montmorency Can.
14 E3 Montmorillon France
12 B6 Montmort-Lucy France
48 F4 Monto Austr.
62 E3 Montpelier ID U.S.A.
68 E5 Montpelier IN U.S.A.
70 A4 Montpelier OH U.S.A.
71 G2 Montpelier VT U.S.A.
14 F5 Montpellier France
58 F4 Montréal Can.
69 G2 Montreal r. Can.
69 F2 Montreal r. Can.
68 E2 Montreal I. i. Can.
57 H4 Montreal L. l. Can.
57 H4 Montreal Lake Can.
71 F2 Montréal-Mirabel Can.
68 E2 Montreal River Can.
16 C7 Montreux Switz.
10 F4 Montrose U.K.
63 F4 Montrose CO U.S.A.
69 F4 Montrose MI U.S.A.
71 F4 Montrose PA U.S.A.
90 D3 Montrose well S. Africa
53 K8 Montserrat terr. Caribbean Sea
59 G4 Monts, Pte des pt Can.
73 G3 Monument Valley reg. U.S.A.
36 B4 Monywa Myanmar
18 C2 Monza Italy
89 C5 Monze Zambia
15 G2 Monzón Spain
91 J4 Mooi r. S. Africa
90 B3 Mooifontein Namibia
91 J4 Mooirivier S. Africa
91 G1 Mookane Botswana
50 H1 Moonbi Ra. mts Austr.
50 A3 Moonta Austr.
62 F2 Moorcroft U.S.A.
70 D5 Moorefield U.S.A.
48 B4 Moore, Lake salt flat Austr.
67 E7 Moores I. i. Bahamas
71 K2 Moores Mills Can.
10 E5 Moorfoot Hills h. U.K.
64 D2 Moorhead U.S.A.
50 D2 Moornanyah Lake Austr.
50 C3 Moorook Austr.
50 E4 Mooroopna Austr.
90 C6 Moorreesburg S. Africa
58 D3 Moose r. Can.
58 D3 Moose Factory Can.
71 J2 Moosehead Lake l. U.S.A.
57 H4 Moose Jaw Can.
68 A2 Moose Lake U.S.A.
57 J4 Moose Lake l. Can.
71 H2 Mooselookmeguntic Lake l. U.S.A.
58 D3 Moose River Can.
57 J4 Moosomin Can.
58 D3 Moosonee Can.
50 D1 Mootwingee Austr.
91 H1 Mopane S. Africa
86 B3 Mopti Mali
31 G3 Moqor Afgh.
78 D7 Moquegua Peru
87 D3 Mora Cameroon
15 E3 Mora Spain
7 O6 Mora Sweden
83 B2 Mora, Cerro mt Arg./Chile
34 A3 Morad r. Pak.
34 D3 Moradabad India
89 E5 Morafenobe Madag.
33 B2 Moram India
89 E5 Moramanga Madag.
68 E3 Moran MI U.S.A.
62 E3 Moran WY U.S.A.
10 C4 Morar, Loch l. U.K.
33 B5 Moratuwa Sri Lanka
16 H6 Morava r. Austria/Slovakia
30 D2 Moraveh Tappeh Iran
71 E3 Moravia U.S.A.
10 E3 Moray Firth est. U.K.
12 F5 Morbach Ger.
18 C1 Morbegno Italy
34 B5 Morbi India
14 D4 Morcenx France
36 E1 Mordaga China
29 K3 Mor Dağı mt Turkey
57 K5 Morden Can.
50 E5 Mordialloc Austr.
20 H4 Mordoviya, Respublika div. Rus. Fed.
21 G4 Mordovo Rus. Fed.
64 C2 Moreau r. U.S.A.
8 E3 Morecambe U.K.
8 D3 Morecambe Bay b. U.K.
48 E4 Moree Austr.
48 E2 Morehead P.N.G.
70 B5 Morehead U.S.A.
67 E5 Morehead City U.S.A.
34 D4 Morel r. India
More Laptevykh sea see Laptev Sea
74 D5 Morelia Mex.
15 F2 Morella Spain
10 D2 More, Loch l. U.K.
34 D4 Morena India
15 D3 Morena, Sierra mts Spain
73 H5 Morenci AZ U.S.A.
69 E5 Morenci MI U.S.A.
19 L2 Moreni Romania
83 E2 Moreno Arg.
63 E6 Moreno Mex.
72 D5 Moreno Valley U.S.A.
56 C4 Moresby Island i. Can.
90 F1 Moreswe Pan salt pan Botswana
9 F6 Moreton-in-Marsh U.K.
12 A5 Moreuil France
28 D4 Morfou Cyprus
28 D4 Morfou Bay b. Cyprus
50 B3 Morgan Austr.
65 F6 Morgan City U.S.A.
72 B3 Morgan Hill U.S.A.
72 C3 Morgan, Mt mt U.S.A.
71 F4 Morgantown PA U.S.A.
70 D5 Morgantown WV U.S.A.
91 H3 Morgenzon S. Africa
16 C7 Morges Switz.
35 F4 Morhar r. India
40 G3 Mori Japan
73 E2 Moriah, Mt mt U.S.A.
63 F5 Moriarty U.S.A.
81 C4 Morichal Col.
81 E2 Morichal Largo r. Venez.
91 G4 Morija Lesotho
13 H3 Moringen Ger.
20 D3 Morino Rus. Fed.
40 G5 Morioka Japan
50 H2 Morisset Austr.
40 G5 Moriyoshi-zan volc. Japan
6 S3 Morjärv Sweden
31 F4 Morjen r. Pak.
20 J3 Morki Rus. Fed.
14 C2 Morlaix France
8 F4 Morley U.K.
73 G4 Mormon Lake l. U.S.A.
48 D3 Mornington I. i. Austr.
80 A7 Mornington, I. i. Chile
34 A4 Moro Pak.
48 E2 Morobe P.N.G.
68 D5 Morocco U.S.A.
85 C2 Morocco country Africa
88 D4 Morogoro Tanz.
43 B5 Moro Gulf g. Phil.
91 G4 Morojaneng S. Africa
90 E3 Morokweng S. Africa
89 E6 Morombe Madag.
75 J4 Morón Cuba
36 C2 Mörön Mongolia
89 E6 Morondava Madag.
15 D4 Morón de la Frontera Spain
89 E5 Moroni Comoros
37 E6 Morotai i. Indon.
88 D3 Moroto Uganda
21 G5 Morozovsk Rus. Fed.
69 G4 Morpeth Can.
8 F2 Morpeth U.K.
82 C2 Morrinhos Brazil
57 K5 Morris Can.
68 C5 Morris IL U.S.A.
64 E2 Morris MN U.S.A.
71 F2 Morrisburg Can.
68 C5 Morrison U.S.A.
73 F5 Morristown AZ U.S.A.
71 F4 Morristown NJ U.S.A.
71 F2 Morristown NY U.S.A.
67 D4 Morristown TN U.S.A.
71 F4 Morrisville PA U.S.A.
71 G2 Morrisville VT U.S.A.
72 B4 Morro Bay U.S.A.
81 C2 Morrocoy, Parque Nacional nat. park Venez.
79 H4 Morro Grande h. Brazil
80 B3 Morro, Pta pt Chile
81 B2 Morrosquillo, Golfo de b. Col.
13 H3 Morschen Ger.
68 D5 Morse Reservoir U.S.A.
20 G4 Morshansk Rus. Fed.
20 E2 Morskaya Masel'ga Rus. Fed.
18 C7 Morsott Alg.
14 E2 Mortagne-au-Perche France
14 D3 Mortagne-sur-Sèvre France
9 C6 Mortehoe U.K.
83 E1 Morteros Arg.
Mortes r. see Manso
50 D5 Mortlake Austr.
Mortlock Is is see Tauu
9 G5 Morton U.K.
68 C5 Morton IL U.S.A.
62 B2 Morton WA U.S.A.
50 H3 Morton Nat. Park Austr.
50 F3 Morundah Austr.
91 G1 Morupule Botswana
50 H3 Moruya Austr.
10 C4 Morvern reg. U.K.
Morvi see Morbi
50 F5 Morwell Austr.
13 H5 Mosbach Ger.
9 F4 Mosborough U.K.
20 F4 Moscow Rus. Fed.
62 C2 Moscow U.S.A.
92 C6 Moscow Univ. Ice Shelf ice feature Ant.
92 B6 Mose, C. c. Ant.
12 F4 Mosel r. Ger.
90 E2 Moselebe watercourse Botswana
14 H2 Moselle r. France
13 K2 Möser Ger.
62 C2 Moses Lake U.S.A.
72 D1 Moses, Mt mt U.S.A.
51 C6 Mosgiel N.Z.
90 E3 Moshaweng watercourse S. Africa
88 D4 Moshi Tanz.
68 C3 Mosinee U.S.A.
6 N4 Mosjøen Norway
6 N3 Moskenesøy i. Norway
20 F4 Moskovskaya Oblast' div. Rus. Fed.
Moskva see Moscow
16 H7 Mosonmagyaróvár Hungary
81 A4 Mosquera Col.
63 F5 Mosquero U.S.A.
75 H5 Mosquitia reg. Honduras
82 E1 Mosquito r. Brazil
70 C4 Mosquito Creek Lake l. U.S.A.
75 H7 Mosquitos, Golfo de los b. Panama
57 J2 Mosquito Lake l. Can.
7 M7 Moss Norway
10 F3 Mossat U.K.
51 B6 Mossburn N.Z.
90 E7 Mossel Bay S. Africa
90 E7 Mossel Bay b. S. Africa
88 B4 Mossendjo Congo
50 E2 Mossgiel Austr.
48 E3 Mossman Austr.
79 L5 Mossoró Brazil
50 H3 Moss Vale Austr.
16 F5 Most Czech Rep.
30 D3 Moṣṭafaabad Iran
86 C1 Mostaganem Alg.
18 G3 Mostar Bos.-Herz.
80 F4 Mostardas Brazil
57 G3 Mostoos Hills h. Can.
21 G6 Mostovskoy Rus. Fed.
45 E2 Mostyn Malaysia
29 J3 Mosul Iraq
7 L7 Møsvatnet l. Norway
7 O7 Motala Sweden
81 C2 Motatán r. Venez.
91 K2 Motaze Moz.
91 H2 Motetema S. Africa
34 D4 Moth India
10 E5 Motherwell U.K.
35 F4 Motihari India
15 F3 Motilla del Palancar Spain
51 F2 Motiti I. i. N.Z.
42 B3 Motlan Ling h. China
90 E2 Motokwe Botswana
15 E4 Motril Spain
19 K2 Motru Romania
74 G4 Motul Mex.
46 M5 Motu One i. Pac. Oc.
39 A5 Mouding China
86 A3 Moudjéria Maur.
19 L5 Moudros Greece
7 S6 Mouhijärvi Fin.
88 B4 Mouila Gabon
50 E3 Moulamein Austr.
50 E3 Moulamein r. Austr.
88 B4 Moulèngui Binza Gabon
14 F3 Moulins France
44 A1 Moulmein Myanmar
67 D6 Moultrie U.S.A.
61 L5 Moultrie, Lake l. SC U.S.A.
66 B4 Mound City IL U.S.A.
64 E3 Mound City MO U.S.A.
87 D4 Moundou Chad
70 C5 Moundsville U.S.A.
34 C4 Mount Abu India
67 C5 Mountain Brook U.S.A.
70 C6 Mountain City U.S.A.
65 E4 Mountain Grove U.S.A.
65 E4 Mountain Home AR U.S.A.
62 D3 Mountain Home ID U.S.A.
91 F6 Mountain Zebra National Park S. Africa
70 C6 Mount Airy U.S.A.
51 B6 Mount Aspiring National Park N.Z.
91 H5 Mount Ayliff S. Africa
64 E3 Mount Ayr U.S.A.
50 B3 Mount Barker Austr.
50 F4 Mount Beauty Austr.
11 C4 Mount Bellew Rep. of Ireland
50 F4 Mt Bogong Nat.Park Austr.
50 F4 Mount Buffalo National Park Austr.
71 K1 Mount Carleton Provincial Park res. Can.
73 F3 Mount Carmel Junction U.S.A.
68 C4 Mount Carroll U.S.A.
51 C5 Mount Cook N.Z.
51 C5 Mount Cook National Park N.Z.
89 D5 Mount Darwin Zimbabwe
71 J2 Mount Desert Island i. U.S.A.
91 H5 Mount Fletcher S. Africa
69 G4 Mount Forest Can.
91 H5 Mount Frere S. Africa
50 C4 Mount Gambier Austr.
70 B4 Mount Gilead U.S.A.
48 E2 Mount Hagen P.N.G.
50 E2 Mount Hope N.S.W. Austr.
70 C6 Mount Hope U.S.A.
48 D4 Mount Isa Austr.
71 G4 Mount Kisco U.S.A.
50 B3 Mount Lofty Range mts Austr.
69 G2 Mount MacDonald Can.
48 B4 Mount Magnet Austr.
50 D2 Mount Manara Austr.
72 B1 Mount Meadows Reservoir U.S.A.
11 D4 Mountmellick Rep. of Ireland
91 G5 Mount Moorosi Lesotho
50 D1 Mount Murchison Austr.
68 B5 Mount Pleasant IA U.S.A.
68 E4 Mount Pleasant MI U.S.A.
66 C3 Mount Pleasant MI U.S.A.
70 D4 Mount Pleasant PA U.S.A.
67 E5 Mount Pleasant SC U.S.A.
65 E5 Mount Pleasant TX U.S.A.
73 G2 Mount Pleasant UT U.S.A.
68 C5 Mount Pulaski U.S.A.
62 B2 Mount Rainier Nat. Park U.S.A.
56 F4 Mount Robson Prov. Park res. Can.
70 C6 Mount Rogers National Recreation Area res. U.S.A.
9 B7 Mount's Bay b. U.K.
9 F5 Mountsorrel U.K.
68 B6 Mount Sterling IL U.S.A.
70 B5 Mount Sterling KY U.S.A.
70 D5 Mount Storm U.S.A.
70 E4 Mount Union U.S.A.
67 B6 Mount Vernon AL U.S.A.
68 A5 Mount Vernon IA U.S.A.
66 B4 Mount Vernon IL U.S.A.
70 A6 Mount Vernon KY U.S.A.
70 B4 Mount Vernon OH U.S.A.
62 B1 Mount Vernon WA U.S.A.
92 C3 Mt. Victor mt Ant.
48 E4 Moura Austr.
78 F4 Moura Brazil
87 E3 Mourdi, Dépression du depression Chad
11 D3 Mourne r. U.K.
11 E3 Mourne Mountains h. U.K.
12 B4 Mouscron Belgium
87 D3 Moussoro Chad
37 E6 Moutong Indon.
12 A5 Mouy France
86 C2 Mouydir, Mts de plat. Alg.
12 D5 Mouzon France
11 C4 Moy r. Rep. of Ireland
88 D3 Moyale Eth.
86 A4 Moyamba Sierra Leone
33 B4 Moyar r. India
86 B1 Moyen Atlas mts Morocco

N

71 H4 **Nantucket** U.S.A.
71 H4 **Nantucket I.** *i.* U.S.A.
71 H4 **Nantucket Sound** *g.* U.S.A.
9 E4 **Nantwich** U.K.
49 H2 **Nanumanga** *i.* Tuvalu
49 H2 **Nanumea** *i.* Tuvalu
82 E2 **Nanuque** Brazil
43 C5 **Nanusa, Kepulauan** *is* Indon.
39 B4 **Nanxi** China
39 D4 **Nan Xian** China
39 E5 **Nanxiong** China
38 D3 **Nanyang** China
42 C3 **Nanzamu** China
38 D4 **Nanzhang** China
38 D3 **Nanzhao** China
15 G3 **Nao, Cabo de la** *hd* Spain
59 F3 **Naococane, Lac** *l.* Can.
35 G4 **Naogaon** Bangl.
34 B4 **Naokot** Pak.
40 C1 **Naoli** *r.* China
31 F3 **Naomid, Dasht-e** *des.* Afgh./Iran
34 C2 **Naoshera** Jammu and Kashmir
39 D6 **Naozhou Dao** *i.* China
72 A2 **Napa** U.S.A.
71 K1 **Napadogan** Can.
69 J3 **Napanee** Can.
34 C4 **Napasar** India
55 N3 **Napasoq** Greenland
68 C5 **Naperville** U.S.A.
51 F3 **Napier** N.Z.
92 D4 **Napier Mts** *mts* Ant.
71 G2 **Napierville** Can.
18 F4 **Naples** Italy
67 D7 **Naples** *FL* U.S.A.
71 H3 **Naples** *ME* U.S.A.
39 B6 **Napo** China
78 D4 **Napo** *r.* Ecuador/Peru
70 A4 **Napoleon** U.S.A.
Napoli *see* **Naples**
83 D3 **Naposta** Arg.
83 D3 **Naposta** *r.* Arg.
68 E5 **Nappanee** U.S.A.
29 K3 **Naqadeh** Iran
28 E6 **Naqb Ashtar** Jordan
29 M4 **Naqqash** Iran
41 D7 **Nara** Japan
86 B3 **Nara** Mali
17 N3 **Narach** Belarus
50 C4 **Naracoorte** Austr.
50 F2 **Naradhan** Austr.
34 C4 **Naraina** India
34 E6 **Narainpur** India
33 D2 **Narasannapeta** India
33 C2 **Narasapatnam, Pt** *pt* India
33 C2 **Narasapur** India
33 C2 **Narasaraopet** India
35 F5 **Narasinghapur** India
44 B4 **Narathiwat** Thai.
33 A2 **Narayangaon** India
Narbada *r. see* **Narmada**
9 C6 **Narberth** U.K.
14 F5 **Narbonne** France
15 C1 **Narcea** *r.* Spain
30 D2 **Nardin** Iran
19 H4 **Nardò** Italy
83 E1 **Nare** Arg.
34 B3 **Narechi** *r.* Pak.
55 M1 **Nares Strait** *str.* Can./Greenland
17 K4 **Narew** *r.* Pol.
42 D2 **Narhong** China
34 A3 **Nari** *r.* Pak.
89 B6 **Narib** Namibia
90 B5 **Nariep** S. Africa
21 H6 **Narimanov** Rus. Fed.
31 H2 **Narin** Afgh.
31 H3 **Narin** *reg.* Afgh.
28 G3 **Narince** Turkey
35 H1 **Narin Gol** *watercourse* China
41 G7 **Narita** Japan
34 C5 **Narmada** *r.* India
29 H1 **Narman** Turkey
34 D3 **Narnaul** India
18 E3 **Narni** Italy
17 O5 **Narodychi** Ukr.
20 F4 **Naro-Fominsk** Rus. Fed.
50 H4 **Narooma** Austr.
20 G4 **Narovchat** Rus. Fed.
21 D5 **Narowlya** Belarus
7 R5 **Närpes** Fin.
48 E5 **Narrabri** Austr.
71 H4 **Narragansett Bay** *b.* U.S.A.
50 F3 **Narrandera** Austr.
50 G2 **Narromine** Austr.
57 J4 **Narrow Hills Provincial Park** *res.* Can.
70 C6 **Narrows** U.S.A.
71 F4 **Narrowsburg** U.S.A.
34 D5 **Narsimhapur** India
35 G5 **Narsingdi** Bangl.
34 D5 **Narsinghgarh** India
33 C2 **Narsipatnam** India
38 E1 **Nart** China
41 D7 **Naruto** Japan
7 V7 **Narva** Estonia
7 U7 **Narva Bay** *b.* Estonia/Rus. Fed.
43 B2 **Narvacan** Phil.
6 P2 **Narvik** Norway
7 V7 **Narvskoye Vdkhr.** *resr* Estonia/Rus. Fed.
34 D3 **Narwana** India
34 D4 **Narwar** India
24 G3 **Nar'yan-Mar** Rus. Fed.
27 F2 **Naryn** Kyrg.
6 P5 **Näsåker** Sweden
73 H3 **Naschitti** U.S.A.
51 C6 **Naseby** N.Z.
68 A4 **Nashua** *IA* U.S.A.
71 H3 **Nashua** *NH* U.S.A.
67 C4 **Nashville** U.S.A.
28 F5 **Nasib** Syria
7 S6 **Näsijärvi** *l.* Fin.
34 C5 **Nasik** India
87 F4 **Nasir** Sudan
Nasirabad *see* **Mymensingh**
34 B3 **Nasirabad** Pak.
89 C5 **Nasondoye** Congo(Zaire)
28 C6 **Nasr** Egypt
30 C3 **Naşrābād** Iran
31 E3 **Naşrābād** Iran
Nasratabad *see* **Zābol**
29 L5 **Nasrīān-e-Pā'īn** Iran
56 D3 **Nass** *r.* Can.
67 E7 **Nassau** Bahamas
46 L5 **Nassau** *i. Cook Is* Pac. Oc.
87 F2 **Nasser, Lake** *resr* Egypt
7 O8 **Nässjö** Sweden
58 E2 **Nastapoca** *r.* Can.
58 E2 **Nastapoka Islands** *is* Can.
41 F6 **Nasu-dake** *volc.* Japan
43 B3 **Nasugbu** Phil.
17 P2 **Nasva** Rus. Fed.
89 C6 **Nata** Botswana
88 D4 **Nata** Tanz.
81 B4 **Natagaima** Col.
79 L5 **Natal** Brazil
Natal *div. see* **Kwazulu-Natal**
93 G6 **Natal Basin** *sea feature* Ind. Ocean
30 C3 **Naţanz** Iran
59 H3 **Natashquan** Can.
59 H3 **Natashquan** *r.* Can.
65 F6 **Natchez** U.S.A.
65 E6 **Natchitoches** U.S.A.
50 E4 **Nathalia** Austr.
34 C4 **Nathdwara** India
50 C4 **Natimuk** Austr.
72 D5 **National City** U.S.A.
15 H2 **Nati, Pta** *pt* Spain
86 C3 **Natitingou** Benin
79 J6 **Natividade** Brazil
40 G5 **Natori** Japan
88 D4 **Natron, Lake** *salt l.* Tanz.
44 A1 **Nattaung** *mt* Myanmar
45 C2 **Natuna Besar** *i.* Indon.
45 C2 **Natuna, Kepulauan** *is* Indon.
71 F2 **Natural Bridge** U.S.A.
73 G3 **Natural Bridges National Monument** *res.* U.S.A.
93 M6 **Naturaliste Plateau** *sea feature* Ind. Ocean
73 H2 **Naturita** U.S.A.
68 E2 **Naubinway** U.S.A.
89 B6 **Nauchas** Namibia
13 L2 **Nauen** Ger.
71 G4 **Naugatuck** U.S.A.
43 B3 **Naujan** Phil.
43 B3 **Naujan, L.** *l.* Phil.
7 S8 **Naujoji Akmenė** Lith.
34 C4 **Naukh** India
13 H3 **Naumburg (Hessen)** Ger.
13 K3 **Naumburg (Saale)** Ger.
44 A1 **Naungpale** Myanmar
28 E6 **Na'ūr** Jordan
31 G4 **Nauroz Kalat** Pak.
47 H4 **Nauru** *country* Pac. Oc.
34 B4 **Naushara** Pak.
7 J6 **Naustdal** Norway
78 D4 **Nauta** Peru
90 C3 **Naute Dam** *dam* Namibia
74 E4 **Nautla** Mex.
31 G3 **Nauzad** Afgh.
35 G5 **Navadwīp** India
20 C4 **Navahrudak** Belarus
73 H4 **Navajo** U.S.A.
63 F4 **Navajo Lake** *l.* U.S.A.
73 G3 **Navajo Mt** *mt* U.S.A.
43 C4 **Naval** Phil.
15 D3 **Navalmoral de la Mata** Spain
15 D3 **Navalvillar de Pela** Spain
11 E4 **Navan** Rep. of Ireland
20 D4 **Navapolatsk** Belarus
25 T3 **Navarin, Mys** *c.* Rus. Fed.
80 C9 **Navarino, I.** *i.* Chile
15 F1 **Navarra** *div.* Spain
50 D4 **Navarre** Austr.
72 A2 **Navarro** U.S.A.
20 G4 **Navashino** Rus. Fed.
65 D6 **Navasota** U.S.A.
6 O5 **Näverede** Sweden
10 D2 **Naver, Loch** *l.* U.K.
83 B2 **Navidad** Chile
79 H3 **Navio, Serra do** Brazil
20 E4 **Navlya** Rus. Fed.
19 N2 **Năvodari** Romania
31 G1 **Navoi** Uzbek.
74 C3 **Navojoa** Mex.
20 G3 **Navoloki** Rus. Fed.
34 C5 **Navsari** India
34 C4 **Nawa** India
28 F5 **Nawá** Syria
35 G4 **Nawabganj** Bangl.
34 B4 **Nawabshah** Pak.
35 F4 **Nawada** India
31 G3 **Nāwah** Afgh.
34 C4 **Nawalgarh** India
29 K2 **Naxçıvan** Azer.
39 B4 **Naxi** China
19 L6 **Naxos** Greece
19 L6 **Naxos** *i.* Greece
81 A4 **Naya** Col.
35 F5 **Nayagarh** India
30 D5 **Nāy Band** Iran
40 H2 **Nayoro** Japan
33 B3 **Nāyudupeta** India
82 E1 **Nazaré** Brazil
33 B4 **Nazareth** India
28 E5 **Nazareth** Israel
65 B7 **Nazas** Mex.
74 D3 **Nazas** *r.* Mex.
78 D6 **Nazca** Peru
Nazca Ridge *sea feature see* **South-West Peru Ridge**
29 M5 **Nazian** Iran
29 K2 **Nāzīk** Iran
29 J2 **Nazik Gölü** *l.* Turkey
31 F4 **Nāzīl** Iran
28 B3 **Nazilli** Turkey
28 G5 **Nazimabad** Pak.
29 G2 **Nazımiye** Turkey
35 H4 **Nazira** India
56 E4 **Nazko** Can.
56 E4 **Nazko** *r.* Can.
29 K3 **Nāzlū** *r.* Iran
21 H7 **Nazran'** Rus. Fed.
88 D3 **Nazrēt** Eth.
32 E5 **Nazwá** Oman
89 C4 **Nchelenge** Zambia
89 C6 **Ncojane** Botswana
88 B4 **N'dalatando** Angola
88 C3 **Ndélé** C.A.R.
88 B4 **Ndendé** Gabon
49 G3 **Ndeni** *i.* Solomon Is
87 D3 **Ndjamena** Chad
89 C5 **Ndola** Zambia
91 J4 **Ndwedwe** S. Africa
11 E3 **Neagh, Lough** *l.* U.K.
62 A1 **Neah Bay** U.S.A.
48 D4 **Neale, L.** *salt flat* Austr.
19 K5 **Nea Liosia** Greece
19 K6 **Neapoli** Greece
9 D6 **Neath** U.K.
9 D6 **Neath** *r.* U.K.
30 D2 **Nebitdag** Turkm.
20 E3 **Nebolchi** Rus. Fed.
73 G2 **Nebo, Mount** *mt* U.S.A.
64 C3 **Nebraska** *div.* U.S.A.
64 E3 **Nebraska City** U.S.A.
18 F6 **Nebrodi, Monti** *mts Sicily* Italy
65 E6 **Neches** *r.* U.S.A.
81 B3 **Nechí** *r.* Col.
88 D3 **Nechisar National Park** Eth.
13 G5 **Neckar** *r.* Ger.
13 H5 **Neckarsulm** Ger.
94 H4 **Necker I.** *HI* U.S.A.
83 E3 **Necochea** Arg.
13 M1 **Neddemin** Ger.
58 F2 **Neddouc, Lac** *l.* Can.
6 R2 **Nedre Soppero** Sweden
73 E4 **Needles** U.S.A.
9 F7 **Needles, The** *stack* U.K.
68 C3 **Neenah** U.S.A.
57 K4 **Neepawa** Can.
55 K2 **Neergaard Lake** *l.* Can.
12 D3 **Neerijnen** Neth.
12 D3 **Neerpelt** Belgium
29 M2 **Neftçala** Azer.
24 G4 **Neftekamsk** Rus. Fed.
21 H6 **Neftekumsk** Rus. Fed.
24 J3 **Nefteyugansk** Rus. Fed.
9 C5 **Nefyn** U.K.
18 C6 **Nefza** Tunisia
88 B4 **Negage** Angola
88 D3 **Negēlē** Eth.
82 A3 **Negla** *r.* Para.
89 D5 **Negomane** Moz.
33 B5 **Negombo** Sri Lanka
19 K4 **Negotino** Macedonia
78 C5 **Negra, Cordillera** *mts* Peru
78 B5 **Negra, Pta** *pt* Peru
18 B7 **Négrine** Alg.
78 B4 **Negritos** Peru
83 D4 **Negro** *r.* Arg.
82 A2 **Negro** *r. Mato Grosso do Sul* Brazil
78 F4 **Negro** *r.* S. America
83 F2 **Negro** *r.* Uru.
43 B4 **Negros** *i.* Phil.
19 N3 **Negru Vodă** Romania
29 M4 **Nehavand** Iran
31 F4 **Nehbandān** Iran
36 E2 **Nehe** China
39 B4 **Neijiang** China
57 H4 **Neilburg** Can.
42 A2 **Nei Monggol Zizhiqu** *div.* China
13 K3 **Neinstedt** Ger.
16 G5 **Neiße** *r.* Ger./Pol.
81 B4 **Neiva** Col.
38 D3 **Neixiang** China
57 K3 **Nejanilini Lake** *l.* Can.
30 D2 **Neka** Iran
30 B3 **Nek'emtē** Eth.
40 E2 **Nekrasovka** Rus. Fed.
7 O9 **Neksø** Denmark
20 E3 **Nelidovo** Rus. Fed.
64 D3 **Neligh** U.S.A.
36 F1 **Nel'kan** Rus. Fed.
25 Q3 **Nel'kan** Rus. Fed.
33 B3 **Nellore** India
56 F5 **Nelson** Can.
51 D4 **Nelson** N.Z.
8 E4 **Nelson** U.K.
73 E4 **Nelson** U.S.A.
55 J4 **Nelson** *r. Man.* Can.
57 L3 **Nelson** *r.* Can.
50 J2 **Nelson Bay** Austr.
50 C5 **Nelson, C.** *c.* Austr.
80 B8 **Nelson, Estrecho** *chan.* Chile
56 E3 **Nelson Forks** Can.
57 K3 **Nelson House** Can.
91 J2 **Nelspruit** S. Africa
86 B3 **Néma** Maur.
20 J3 **Nema** Rus. Fed.
68 A2 **Nemadji** *r.* U.S.A.
20 B4 **Neman** Rus. Fed.
28 F5 **Nemara** Syria
20 G3 **Nemda** *r.* Rus. Fed.
20 K2 **Nemed** Rus. Fed.
69 F2 **Nemegos** Can.
6 W2 **Nemetskiy, Mys** *c.* Rus. Fed.
14 F2 **Nemours** France
29 J2 **Nemrut Dağı** *h.* Turkey
40 J3 **Nemuro** Japan
40 J3 **Nemuro-kaikyō** *chan.* Japan
21 D5 **Nemyriv** Ukr.
11 C5 **Nenagh** Rep. of Ireland
9 H5 **Nene** *r.* U.K.
36 E2 **Nenjiang** China
12 E5 **Nennig** Ger.
20 F1 **Nenoksa** Rus. Fed.
65 E4 **Neosho** U.S.A.
64 E4 **Neosho** *r.* U.S.A.
23 H7 **Nepal** *country* Asia
69 K3 **Nepean** Can.
73 G2 **Nephi** U.S.A.
11 B3 **Nephin** *h.* Rep. of Ireland
11 B3 **Nephin Beg Range** *h.* Rep. of Ireland
88 C3 **Nepoko** *r.* Congo(Zaire)
71 F4 **Neptune** U.S.A.
14 E4 **Nérac** France
36 D1 **Nerchinsk** Rus. Fed.
20 G3 **Nerekhta** Rus. Fed.
18 G3 **Neretva** *r.* Bos.-Herz./Croatia
89 C5 **Neriquinha** Angola
7 T9 **Neris** *r.* Lith.
20 F3 **Nerl'** *r.* Rus. Fed.
82 C2 **Nerópolis** Brazil
25 O4 **Neryungri** Rus. Fed.
12 D1 **Nes** Neth.
7 L6 **Nes** Norway
7 L6 **Nesbyen** Norway
6 G4 **Neskaupstaður** Iceland
12 A5 **Nesle** France
6 N3 **Nesna** Norway
64 D4 **Ness City** U.S.A.
13 J4 **Nesse** *r.* Ger.
56 C3 **Nesselrode, Mt** *mt* Can./U.S.A.
10 D3 **Ness, Loch** *l.* U.K.
19 L4 **Nestos** *r.* Greece
28 E5 **Netanya** Israel
5 D3 **Netherlands** *country* Europe
53 K8 **Netherlands Antilles** *terr.* Caribbean Sea
13 G4 **Netphen** Ger.
35 G4 **Netrakona** Bangl.
34 C5 **Netrang** India
55 L3 **Nettilling Lake** *l.* Can.
68 A1 **Nett Lake** U.S.A.
68 A1 **Nett Lake** *l.* U.S.A.
74 F5 **Netzahualcóyotl, Presa** *resr* Mex.
13 M1 **Neubrandenburg** Ger.
16 C7 **Neuchâtel** Switz.
16 C7 **Neuchâtel, Lac de** *l.* Switz.
13 J5 **Neuendettelsau** Ger.
12 E2 **Neuenhaus** Ger.
13 H1 **Neuenkirchen** Ger.
13 G2 **Neuenkirchen (Oldenburg)** Ger.
12 D5 **Neufchâteau** Belgium
14 G2 **Neufchâteau** France
14 E2 **Neufchâtel-en-Bray** France
13 F1 **Neuharlingersiel** Ger.
13 H1 **Neuhaus (Oste)** Ger.
13 H4 **Neuhof** Ger.
13 K1 **Neu Kaliß** Ger.
13 H4 **Neukirchen** *Hessen* Ger.
13 L4 **Neukirchen** *Sachsen* Ger.
57 K2 **Neultin Lake** *l.* Can.
13 K5 **Neumarkt in der Oberpfalz** Ger.
92 C2 **Neumayer** *Ger. Base* Ant.
16 D3 **Neumünster** Ger.
13 L5 **Neunburg vorm Wald** Ger.
16 H7 **Neunkirchen** Austria
12 F5 **Neunkirchen** Ger.
83 C3 **Neuquén** Arg.
83 C3 **Neuquén** *div.* Arg.
83 C3 **Neuquén** *r.* Arg.
13 L2 **Neuruppin** Ger.
67 E5 **Neuse** *r.* U.S.A.
16 H7 **Neusiedler See** *l.* Austria/Hungary
12 E3 **Neuss** Ger.
13 H2 **Neustadt am Rübenberge** Ger.
13 J5 **Neustadt an der Aisch** Ger.
13 L5 **Neustadt an der Waldnaab** Ger.
13 G5 **Neustadt an der Weinstraße** Ger.
13 K4 **Neustadt bei Coburg** Ger.
13 K1 **Neustadt-Glewe** Ger.
12 F4 **Neustadt (Wied)** Ger.
13 M1 **Neustrelitz** Ger.
13 L6 **Neutraubling** Ger.
12 F4 **Neuwied** Ger.
13 H1 **Neu Wulmstorf** Ger.
65 E4 **Nevada** *MO* U.S.A.
72 D2 **Nevada** *div.* U.S.A.
15 E4 **Nevada, Sierra** *mts* Spain
83 C2 **Nevado, Cerro** *mt* Arg.
74 D5 **Nevado de Colima** *volc.* Mex.
83 C3 **Nevado, Sierra del** *mts* Arg.
20 D3 **Nevel'** Rus. Fed.
14 F3 **Nevers** France
50 F1 **Nevertire** Austr.
19 H3 **Nevesinje** Bos.-Herz.
21 G6 **Nevinnomyssk** Rus. Fed.
10 C3 **Nevis, Loch** *in.* U.K.
28 E2 **Nevşehir** Turkey
40 C2 **Nevskoye** Rus. Fed.
73 E5 **New** *r. CA* U.S.A.
70 C6 **New** *r. WV* U.S.A.
66 C4 **New Albany** *IN* U.S.A.
65 F5 **New Albany** *MS* U.S.A.
71 E4 **New Albany** *PA* U.S.A.
79 G2 **New Amsterdam** Guyana
71 F5 **Newark** *DE* U.S.A.
71 F5 **Newark** *MD* U.S.A.
71 F4 **Newark** *NJ* U.S.A.
70 E3 **Newark** *NY* U.S.A.
70 B4 **Newark** *OH* U.S.A.
73 E2 **Newark Lake** *l.* U.S.A.
9 G4 **Newark-on-Trent** U.K.
71 E3 **Newark Valley** U.S.A.
71 H4 **New Bedford** U.S.A.
62 B2 **Newberg** U.S.A.
71 F3 **New Berlin** U.S.A.
67 E5 **New Bern** U.S.A.
68 E2 **Newberry** *MI* U.S.A.
67 D5 **Newberry** *SC* U.S.A.
72 D4 **Newberry Springs** U.S.A.
8 F2 **Newbiggin-by-the-Sea** U.K.
69 J3 **Newboro** Can.
71 G3 **New Boston** *MA* U.S.A.
70 B5 **New Boston** *OH* U.S.A.
65 D6 **New Braunfels** U.S.A.
11 E4 **Newbridge** Rep. of Ireland
71 G4 **New Britain** U.S.A.
48 E2 **New Britain** *i.* P.N.G.
71 F4 **New Brunswick** U.S.A.
59 G4 **New Brunswick** *div.* Can.
68 D5 **New Buffalo** U.S.A.
10 F3 **Newburgh** U.K.
71 F4 **Newburgh** U.S.A.
9 F6 **Newbury** U.K.
71 H3 **Newburyport** U.S.A.
8 E3 **Newby Bridge** U.K.
47 G6 **New Caledonia** *is* Pac. Oc.
59 G4 **New Carlisle** Can.
50 H2 **Newcastle** Austr.
59 G4 **Newcastle** *N.B.* Can.
69 H4 **Newcastle** *Ont.* Can.
11 E4 **Newcastle** Rep. of Ireland
91 H3 **Newcastle** S. Africa
11 F3 **Newcastle** *N. Ireland* U.K.
72 B2 **Newcastle** *CA* U.S.A.
68 E6 **New Castle** *IN* U.S.A.
70 B4 **Newcastle** *OH* U.S.A.
70 C4 **New Castle** *PA* U.S.A.
73 F3 **Newcastle** *UT* U.S.A.
70 C6 **New Castle** *VA* U.S.A.
62 F3 **Newcastle** *WY* U.S.A.
9 C5 **Newcastle Emlyn** U.K.
9 E4 **Newcastle-under-Lyme** U.K.
8 F3 **Newcastle upon Tyne** U.K.
11 B5 **Newcastle West** Rep. of Ireland
71 F6 **New Church** U.S.A.
73 H3 **Newcomb** U.S.A.
10 D5 **New Cumnock** U.K.
10 F3 **New Deer** U.K.
34 D3 **New Delhi** India
71 K1 **New Denmark** Can.
72 B3 **New Don Pedro Reservoir** U.S.A.
50 H1 **New England Range** *mts* Austr.
9 E6 **Newent** U.K.
59 J4 **Newfoundland** *div.* Can.
55 N5 **Newfoundland** *i.* Can.
96 G2 **Newfoundland Basin** *sea feature* Atl. Ocean
10 D5 **New Galloway** U.K.
49 F2 **New Georgia** *i.* Solomon Is
49 F2 **New Georgia Islands** *is* Solomon Is
59 H4 **New Glasgow** Can.
37 G7 **New Guinea** *i.* Asia
70 B4 **New Hampshire** *OH* U.S.A.
71 G3 **New Hampshire** *div.* U.S.A.
68 A4 **New Hampton** U.S.A.
91 J4 **New Hanover** S. Africa
48 F2 **New Hanover** *i.* P.N.G.
71 G4 **New Haven** U.S.A.
56 D3 **New Hazelton** Can.
72 B2 **New Hogan Reservoir** U.S.A.
68 C4 **New Holstein** U.S.A.
65 F6 **New Iberia** U.S.A.
91 J2 **Newington** S. Africa
11 D5 **Newinn** Rep. of Ireland
48 F2 **New Ireland** *i.* P.N.G.
71 F5 **New Jersey** *div.* U.S.A.
70 E6 **New Kent** U.S.A.
70 B5 **New Lexington** U.S.A.
68 B4 **New Lisbon** U.S.A.
69 H2 **New Liskeard** Can.
71 G4 **New London** *CT* U.S.A.
68 B5 **New London** *IA* U.S.A.
68 B6 **New London** *MO* U.S.A.
68 C3 **New London** *WV* U.S.A.
48 B4 **Newman** Austr.
68 D6 **Newman** U.S.A.
69 H3 **Newmarket** Can.
11 B5 **Newmarket** Rep. of Ireland
9 H5 **Newmarket** U.K.
70 D5 **New Market** U.S.A.
11 C5 **Newmarket on-Fergus** Rep. of Ireland
70 C5 **New Martinsville** U.S.A.
62 C2 **New Meadows** U.S.A.
72 B3 **New Melanes L.** *l.* U.S.A.
63 F5 **New Mexico** *div.* U.S.A.
67 C5 **Newnan** U.S.A.
65 F6 **New Orleans** U.S.A.
71 F4 **New Paltz** U.S.A.
70 C4 **New Philadelphia** U.S.A.
10 F3 **New Pitsligo** U.K.
51 E3 **New Plymouth** N.Z.
11 B4 **Newport** *Mayo* Rep. of Ireland
11 C5 **Newport** *Tipperary* Rep. of Ireland
9 F7 **Newport** *Eng.* U.K.
9 E5 **Newport** *Eng.* U.K.
9 D6 **Newport** *Wales* U.K.
65 F5 **Newport** *AR* U.S.A.
70 A5 **Newport** *KY* U.S.A.
71 J2 **Newport** *ME* U.S.A.
69 F5 **Newport** *MI* U.S.A.
71 G3 **Newport** *NH* U.S.A.
62 A2 **Newport** *OR* U.S.A.
71 H4 **Newport** *RI* U.S.A.
71 G2 **Newport** *VT* U.S.A.
62 C1 **Newport** *WA* U.S.A.
72 D5 **Newport Beach** U.S.A.
70 E6 **Newport News** U.S.A.
9 G5 **Newport Pagnell** U.K.
67 E7 **New Providence** *i.* Bahamas
9 B7 **Newquay** U.K.
59 G4 **New Richmond** Can.
68 A3 **New Richmond** U.S.A.
73 F5 **New River** U.S.A.
65 F6 **New Roads** U.S.A.
9 H7 **New Romney** U.K.
11 E5 **New Ross** Rep. of Ireland
11 E3 **Newry** U.K.
10 E4 **New Scone** U.K.
68 A5 **New Sharon** U.S.A.
New Siberian Islands *is see* **Novosibirskiye Ostrova**
67 D6 **New Smyrna Beach** U.S.A.
50 D2 **New South Wales** *div.* Austr.
39 □ **New Territories** *reg. H.K.* China
8 E4 **Newton** U.K.
64 E3 **Newton** *IA* U.S.A.
64 D4 **Newton** *KS* U.S.A.
71 H3 **Newton** *MA* U.S.A.
65 F5 **Newton** *MS* U.S.A.
71 F4 **Newton** *NJ* U.S.A.
9 D7 **Newton Abbot** U.K.
10 F3 **Newtonhill** U.K.
10 D5 **Newton Mearns** U.K.
10 D6 **Newton Stewart** U.K.
11 C5 **Newtown** Rep. of Ireland
9 E5 **Newtown** *Eng.* U.K.
9 D5 **Newtown** *Wales* U.K.
64 C1 **New Town** U.S.A.
11 F3 **Newtownabbey** U.K.
11 F3 **Newtownards** U.K.
11 D3 **Newtownbutler** U.K.
11 E4 **Newtownmountkennedy** Rep. of Ireland
10 F5 **Newtown St Boswells** U.K.
11 D3 **Newtownstewart** U.K.
64 E2 **New Ulm** U.S.A.
72 A2 **Newville** U.S.A.
56 E5 **New Westminster** Can.
71 G4 **New York** U.S.A.
71 E3 **New York** *div.* U.S.A.
71 G4 **New York-John F. Kennedy** *airport* U.S.A.
71 F4 **New York-Newark** *airport* U.S.A.
47 J8 **New Zealand** *country* Oceania
94 G9 **New Zealand Plateau** *sea feature* Pac. Oc.
20 G3 **Neya** Rus. Fed.
30 D4 **Neyrīz** Iran
31 E2 **Neyshābūr** Iran
33 B4 **Neyyattinkara** India
45 D2 **Ngabang** Indon.
88 B4 **Ngabé** Congo
44 A2 **Nga Chong, Khao** *mt* Myanmar/Thai.
43 C6 **Ngalipaëng** Indon.
89 C6 **Ngami, Lake** *l.* Botswana
35 F3 **Ngamring** China
35 E3 **Ngangla Ringco** *salt l.* China
34 E2 **Nganglong Kangri** *mt* China
34 E2 **Nganglong Kangri** *mts Xizang* China
35 F3 **Ngangzê Co** *salt l.* China
44 A1 **Ngao** Thai.
87 D4 **Ngaoundéré** Cameroon
51 E2 **Ngaruawahia** N.Z.
51 F3 **Ngaruroro** *r.* N.Z.
51 E3 **Ngauruhoe, Mt** *volc.* N.Z.
44 B1 **Ngiap** *r.* Laos
88 B4 **Ngo** Congo
44 C2 **Ngoc Linh** *mt* Vietnam
35 F3 **Ngoin, Co** *salt l.* China
86 D4 **Ngol Bembo** Nigeria
35 H2 **Ngom Qu** *r.* China
35 F2 **Ngoqumaima** China
36 B3 **Ngoring Hu** *l.* China
87 D3 **Ngourti** Niger
87 D3 **Nguigmi** Niger
37 F6 **Ngulu** *i.* Micronesia
86 D3 **Nguru** Nigeria
39 B6 **Nguyên Binh** Vietnam
90 E2 **Ngwaketse** *div.* Botswana
91 G3 **Ngwathe** S. Africa
91 J3 **Ngwavuma** *r.* Swaziland
91 J4 **Ngwelezana** S. Africa
89 D5 **Nhamalabué** Moz.
44 D2 **Nha Trang** Vietnam
50 C4 **Nhill** Austr.
91 J3 **Nhlangano** Swaziland
39 B6 **Nho Quan** Vietnam
48 D3 **Nhulunbuy** Austr.
57 J4 **Niacam** Can.
86 B3 **Niafounké** Mali
68 D3 **Niagara** U.S.A.
69 H4 **Niagara Falls** Can.
70 D3 **Niagara Falls** U.S.A.
69 H4 **Niagara River** *r.* Can./U.S.A.
86 C3 **Niamey** Niger
43 C5 **Niampak** Indon.
89 D4 **Niangandu** Tanz.
88 C3 **Niangara** Congo(Zaire)
45 A2 **Nias** *i.* Indon.
Niassa, Lago *l. see* **Nyasa, Lake**
7 R8 **Nīca** Latvia
53 H8 **Nicaragua** *country* Central America
75 G6 **Nicaragua, Lago de** *l.* Nic.
18 G5 **Nicastro** Italy
14 H5 **Nice** France
59 F3 **Nichicun, Lac** *l.* Can.
35 E4 **Nichlaul** India
67 E7 **Nicholl's Town** Bahamas
69 F2 **Nicholson** Can.
27 H6 **Nicobar Islands** *is* Andaman and Nicobar Is
28 D4 **Nicosia** Cyprus
75 H7 **Nicoya, G. de** *b.* Costa Rica
75 G7 **Nicoya, Pen. de** *pen.* Costa Rica
71 K1 **Nictau** Can.
7 R9 **Nida** Lith.
8 F4 **Nidd** *r.* U.K.
13 H4 **Nidda** Ger.
13 H4 **Nidder** *r.* Ger.
17 K4 **Nidzica** Pol.
16 D3 **Niebüll** Ger.
12 E5 **Niederanven** Lux.
13 H4 **Niederaula** Ger.
16 F7 **Niedere Tauern** *mts* Austria
13 G2 **Niedersachsen** *div.* Ger.
12 E1 **Niedersächsisches Wattenmeer, Nationalpark** *nat. park* Ger.
86 D4 **Niefang** Equatorial Guinea
86 B3 **Niellé** Côte d'Ivoire
13 H2 **Nienburg (Weser)** Ger.
12 E3 **Niers** *r.* Ger.
13 G5 **Nierstein** Ger.
79 G2 **Nieuw Amsterdam** Suriname
12 C2 **Nieuwe-Niedorp** Neth.
12 E1 **Nieuwe Pekela** Neth.
12 C3 **Nieuwerkerk aan de IJssel** Neth.
79 G2 **Nieuw Nickerie** Suriname
12 E1 **Nieuwolda** Neth.
90 C5 **Nieuwoudtville** S. Africa
12 A3 **Nieuwpoort** Belgium
12 C3 **Nieuw-Vossemeer** Neth.
28 E3 **Niğde** Turkey
85 D4 **Niger** *country* Africa
86 C4 **Niger** *r.* Africa
85 D5 **Nigeria** *country* Africa

86 C4 Niger, Mouths of the *est.* Nigeria
69 G1 Nighthawk Lake *l.* Can.
19 K4 Nigrita Greece
41 G6 Nihonmatsu Japan
41 F6 Niigata Japan
41 C8 Niihama Japan
72 □2 Niihau *i.* U.S.A.
41 F7 Nii-jima *i.* Japan
40 H3 Niikappu Japan
41 C7 Niimi Japan
41 F6 Niitsu Japan
12 D2 Nijkerk Neth.
12 D3 Nijmegen Neth.
12 E2 Nijverdal Neth.
6 W2 Nikel' Rus. Fed.
86 C4 Nikki Benin
41 F6 Nikkō Nat. Park Japan
20 H4 Nikolayevka Rus. Fed.
21 H5 Nikolayevsk Rus. Fed.
20 H4 Nikol'sk *Penzen.* Rus. Fed.
20 H3 Nikol'sk *Vologod.* Rus. Fed.
25 S4 Nikol'skoye Rus. Fed.
21 E6 Nikopol' Ukr.
29 M3 Nik Pey Iran
28 F1 Niksar Turkey
31 F5 Nikshahr Iran
19 H3 Nikšić Yugo.
49 J2 Nikumaroro *i.* Kiribati
49 H2 Nikunau *i.* Kiribati
34 C2 Nila Pak.
35 F5 Nilagiri India
73 E5 Niland U.S.A.
34 D3 Nilang India
33 B2 Nilanga India
88 D2 Nile *r.* Africa
68 D5 Niles U.S.A.
33 A3 Nileswaram India
33 B4 Nilgiri Hills *mts* India
6 V5 Nilsiä Fin.
34 C4 Nimach India
14 G5 Nîmes France
50 G4 Nimmitabel Austr.
92 B4 Nimrod Glacier *gl.* Ant.
87 F4 Nimule Sudan
33 A4 Nine Degree Chan. India
50 D1 Nine Mile Lake Austr.
72 D2 Ninemile Peak *summit* U.S.A.
39 □ Ninepin Group *is* H.K. China
93 K5 Ninety-East Ridge *sea feature* Ind. Ocean
50 F5 Ninety Mile Beach *beach* Austr.
51 D1 Ninety Mile Beach *beach* N.Z.
29 J3 Nineveh Iraq
71 F3 Nineveh U.S.A.
42 E1 Ning'an China
39 F4 Ningbo China
38 F1 Ningcheng China
39 F5 Ningde China
39 E5 Ningdu China
39 D5 Ninggang China
39 F4 Ningguo China
39 F4 Ninghai China
38 E2 Ninghe China
39 E5 Ninghua China
36 B3 Ningjing Shan *mts* China
38 E3 Ningling China
39 C6 Ningming China
39 B5 Ningnan China
38 C3 Ningqiang China
38 C3 Ningshan China
38 D2 Ningwu China
38 B2 Ningxia *div.* China
38 C3 Ning Xian China
39 D4 Ningxiang China
38 E3 Ningyang China
39 D5 Ningyuan China
39 C6 Ninh Binh Vietnam
44 D2 Ninh Hoa Vietnam
92 B6 Ninnis Gl. *gl.* Ant.
40 G4 Ninohe Japan
82 A3 Nioaque Brazil
64 C3 Niobrara *r.* U.S.A.
35 H4 Nioko India
86 A3 Niokolo Koba, Parc National du *nat. park* Senegal
86 B3 Niono Mali
86 B3 Nioro Mali
14 D3 Niort France
33 A2 Nipani India
57 J4 Nipawin Can.
58 C4 Nipigon Can.
68 C1 Nipigon Bay *b.* Can.
58 C4 Nipigon, Lake *l.* Can.
59 H3 Nipishish Lake *l.* Can.
69 H2 Nipissing Can.
69 G2 Nipissing, L. *l.* Can.
72 B4 Nipomo U.S.A.
29 K5 Nippur Iraq
73 E4 Nipton U.S.A.
82 C1 Niquelândia Brazil
30 B2 Nīr Iran
33 A2 Nira *r.* India
33 B2 Nirmal India
33 B2 Nirmal Range *h.* India
19 J3 Niš Yugo.
15 C3 Nisa Port.
30 B5 Nisah, W. *watercourse* S. Arabia
18 F6 Niscemi *Sicily* Italy
Nīshāpūr *see* Neyshābūr
41 B9 Nishino-'omote Japan
41 C6 Nishino-shima *i.* Japan
41 A8 Nishi-Sonogi-hantō *pen.* Japan
41 D7 Nishiwaki Japan
56 B2 Nisling *r.* Can.
12 C3 Nispen Neth.
7 N8 Nissan *r.* Sweden
17 O7 Nistrului Inferior, Câmpia *lowland* Moldova
56 C2 Nisutlin *r.* Can.
19 M6 Nisyros *i.* Greece
30 C5 Niṭā S. Arabia
59 F3 Nitchequon Can.
82 D3 Niterói Brazil
10 E5 Nith *r.* U.K.
10 E5 Nithsdale *v.* U.K.
34 D3 Niti Pass China
16 J6 Nitra Slovakia
70 C5 Nitro U.S.A.
49 J3 Niuatoputopu *i.* Tonga
47 L5 Niue *terr.* Pac. Oc.
49 H3 Niulakita *i.* Tuvalu
39 B5 Niulan Jiang *r.* China
49 H2 Niutao *i.* Tuvalu
42 B3 Niuzhuang China
6 T5 Nivala Fin.
12 C4 Nivelles Belgium
20 K2 Nivshera Rus. Fed.
34 C4 Niwāi India
72 C2 Nixon U.S.A.
35 E1 Niya He *r.* China
29 M1 Niyazoba Azer.
33 B2 Nizamabad India
33 B2 Nizam Sagar *l.* India
20 H3 Nizhegorodskaya Oblast' *div.* Rus. Fed.
25 S3 Nizhnekolymsk Rus. Fed.
36 B1 Nizhneudinsk Rus. Fed.
24 J3 Nizhnevartovsk Rus. Fed.
25 P2 Nizhneyansk Rus. Fed.
20 G4 Nizhniy Lomov Rus. Fed.
20 G3 Nizhniy Novgorod Rus. Fed.
20 K2 Nizhniy Odes Rus. Fed.
20 H3 Nizhniy Yenangsk Rus. Fed.
21 D5 Nizhyn Ukr.
17 K4 Nizina *reg.* Pol.
28 F3 Nizip Turkey
40 D3 Nizmennyy, Mys *pt* Rus. Fed.
6 R2 Njallavarri *mt* Norway
6 Q3 Njavve Sweden
Njazidja *i. see* Grande Comore
89 D4 Njinjo Tanz.
89 D4 Njombe Tanz.
7 P5 Njurundabommen Sweden
86 D4 Nkambe Cameroon
91 J4 Nkandla S. Africa
86 B4 Nkawkaw Ghana
89 C5 Nkayi Zimbabwe
89 D5 Nkhata Bay Malawi
89 D5 Nkhotakota Malawi
86 D4 Nkongsamba Cameroon
91 G5 Nkululeko S. Africa
89 B5 Nkurenkuru Namibia
91 G6 Nkwenkwezi S. Africa
35 J4 Noa Dihing *r.* India
35 G5 Noakhali Bangl.
35 F5 Noamundi India
11 E4 Nobber Rep. of Ireland
41 B8 Nobeoka Japan
40 G3 Noboribetsu Japan
82 A1 Nobres Brazil
69 G2 Noelville Can.
74 B2 Nogales Mex.
60 D5 Nogales *AZ* U.S.A.
41 B8 Nōgata Japan
14 E2 Nogent-le-Rotrou France
12 A5 Nogent-sur-Oise France
20 F4 Noginsk Rus. Fed.
41 E7 Nōgōhaku-san *mt* Japan
83 E2 Nogoyá Arg.
83 E2 Nogoya *r.* Arg.
43 E5 Nogwak-san *mt* S. Korea
34 C3 Nohar India
40 G4 Noheji Japan
12 F5 Nohfelden Ger.
14 C3 Noirmoutier-en-l'Île France
14 C3 Noirmoutier, Île de *i.* France
12 E5 Noisseville France
41 F7 Nojima-zaki *c.* Japan
34 C4 Nokha India
31 F4 Nok Kundi Pak.
57 J3 Nokomis Lake *l.* Can.
88 B3 Nola C.A.R.
20 J3 Nolinsk Rus. Fed.
71 H4 No Mans Land *i.* U.S.A.
54 B3 Nome *AK* U.S.A.
38 B1 Nomgon Mongolia
35 J1 Nomhon China
42 G3 Nomoi Islands *is* Micronesia
91 G5 Nomonde S. Africa
41 A8 Nomo-zaki *pt* Japan
20 G3 Nomzha Rus. Fed.
57 H2 Nonacho Lake *l.* Can.
91 J4 Nondweni S. Africa
42 C1 Nong'an China
44 C1 Nông Hèt Laos
44 B2 Nong Hong Thai.
44 B1 Nong Khai Thai.
91 J3 Nongoma S. Africa
12 E5 Nonnweiler Ger.
49 H2 Nonouti *i.* Kiribati
42 D5 Nonsan S. Korea
44 B2 Nonthaburi Thai.
91 F5 Nonzwakazi S. Africa
12 B3 Noordbeveland *i.* Neth.
12 E1 Noordbroek-Uiterburen Neth.
12 C2 Noorderhaaks *i.* Neth.
12 D2 Noordoost Polder *reclaimed land* Neth.
12 C2 Noordwijk-Binnen Neth.
56 D5 Nootka I. *i.* Can.
31 H2 Norak Tajik.
43 C5 Norala Phil.
69 H1 Noranda Can.
7 O6 Norberg Sweden
24 D2 Nordaustlandet *i.* Svalbard
12 F1 Norden Ger.
24 L2 Nordenshel'da, Arkhipelag *is* Rus. Fed.
12 F1 Norderland *reg.* Ger.
12 F1 Norderney Ger.
12 F1 Norderney *i.* Ger.
13 J1 Norderstedt Ger.
7 J6 Nordfjordeid Norway
6 O3 Nordfold Norway
Nordfriesische Inseln *is see* North Frisian Islands
13 J3 Nordhausen Ger.
13 G1 Nordholz Ger.
12 F2 Nordhorn Ger.
6 T1 Nordkapp *c.* Norway
6 Q2 Nordkjosbotn Norway
6 N4 Nordli Norway
16 E6 Nördlingen Ger.
6 Q5 Nordmaling Sweden
16 D3 Nord-Ostsee-Kanal *canal* Ger.
13 F5 Nordpfälzer Bergland *reg.* Ger.
55 N3 Nordre Strømfjord *in.* Greenland
12 F3 Nordrhein-Westfalen *div.* Ger.
11 D5 Nore *r.* Rep. of Ireland
14 F5 Nore, Pic de *mt* France
64 D3 Norfolk *NE* U.S.A.
71 F2 Norfolk *NY* U.S.A.
71 E6 Norfolk *VA* U.S.A.
49 G4 Norfolk Island *terr.* Pac. Oc.
94 G7 Norfolk Island Ridge *sea feature* Pac. Oc.
94 F7 Norfolk Island Trough *sea feature* Pac. Oc.
65 E4 Norfork L. *l.* U.S.A.
12 E1 Norg Neth.
7 K6 Norheimsund Norway
41 E6 Norikura-dake *volc.* Japan
24 K3 Noril'sk Rus. Fed.
29 K1 Nor Kharberd Armenia
69 H3 Norland Can.
68 C5 Normal U.S.A.
65 D5 Norman U.S.A.
48 F2 Normanby I. *i.* P.N.G.
Normandes, Îles *terr. see* Channel Islands
14 D2 Normandie *reg.* France
67 D5 Norman, L. *l.* U.S.A.
48 E3 Normanton Austr.
50 B3 Normanville Austr.
56 D1 Norman Wells Can.
83 B4 Ñorquinco Arg.
6 R5 Norra Kvarken *str.* Fin./Sweden
6 O4 Norra Storfjället *mts* Sweden
12 A4 Norrent-Fontes France
70 B6 Norris Lake *l.* U.S.A.
71 F4 Norristown U.S.A.
7 P7 Norrköping Sweden
7 Q7 Norrtälje Sweden
48 C5 Norseman Austr.
6 Q4 Norsjö Sweden
49 G3 Norsup Vanuatu
13 H3 Nörten-Hardenberg Ger.
83 F3 Norte, Pta *pt Buenos Aires* Arg.
80 D6 Norte, Pta *pt Chubut* Arg.
32 C6 North *div.* Yemen
71 G3 North Adams U.S.A.
8 F3 Northallerton U.K.
96 E4 North American Basin *sea feature* Atl. Ocean
48 B4 Northampton Austr.
9 G5 Northampton U.K.
71 G3 Northampton U.S.A.
70 E5 North Anna *r.* U.S.A.
71 J2 North Anson U.S.A.
56 G2 North Arm *b.* Can.
67 D5 North Augusta U.S.A.
59 H2 North Aulatsivik Island *i.* Can.
57 H4 North Battleford Can.
69 H2 North Bay Can.
58 E2 North Belcher Islands *is* Can.
62 A3 North Bend U.S.A.
10 F4 North Berwick U.K.
71 H3 North Berwick U.S.A.
68 A3 North Branch U.S.A.
92 A5 North, C. *c.* Ant.
59 H4 North, C. *c.* Can.
North Cape *c. see* Nordkapp
51 D1 North Cape *c.* N.Z.
59 H4 North Cape *pt P.E.I.* Can.
58 B3 North Caribou Lake *l.* Can.
67 D5 North Carolina *div.* U.S.A.
62 B1 North Cascades Nat. Park U.S.A.
69 F2 North Channel Can.
11 E2 North Channel *str. N. Ireland/Scot.* U.K.
71 H2 North Conway U.S.A.
64 C2 North Dakota *div.* U.S.A.
9 H6 North Downs *h.* U.K.
70 D3 North East U.S.A.
96 H2 North-Eastern Atlantic Basin *sea feature* Atl. Ocean
67 E7 Northeast Providence Chan. *chan.* Bahamas
13 H3 Northeim Ger.
67 F7 North End Pt *pt* Bahamas
34 C1 Northern Areas *div.* Pak.
90 D4 Northern Cape *div.* S. Africa
57 K3 Northern Indian Lake *l.* Can.
11 E3 Northern Ireland *div.* U.K.
58 B4 Northern Light L. *l.* Can.
47 F2 Northern Mariana Islands *terr.* Pac. Oc.
91 H1 Northern Province *div.* S. Africa
48 D3 Northern Territory *div.* Austr.
10 F4 North Esk *r.* U.K.
71 G3 Northfield *MA* U.S.A.
64 E2 Northfield *MN* U.S.A.
71 G2 Northfield *VT* U.S.A.
9 J6 North Foreland *c.* U.K.
72 C3 North Fork U.S.A.
72 B2 North Fork American *r.* U.S.A.
72 B2 North Fork Feather *r.* U.S.A.
68 E3 North Fox I. *i.* U.S.A.
58 D3 North French *r.* Can.
16 C3 North Frisian Islands *is* Ger.
8 G3 North Grimston U.K.
71 K2 North Head Can.
51 E2 North Head *hd* N.Z.
57 K2 North Henik Lake *l.* Can.
71 G3 North Hudson U.S.A.
51 E3 North Island *i.* N.Z.
43 B1 North Island *i.* Phil.
43 B4 North Islet *rf* Phil.
73 G4 North Jadito Canyon U.S.A.
68 D5 North Judson U.S.A.
57 K3 North Knife *r.* Can.
35 E4 North Koel *r.* India
35 H4 North Lakhimpur India
73 E3 North Las Vegas U.S.A.
65 E5 North Little Rock U.S.A.
89 D5 North Luangwa National Park Zambia
68 E5 North Manchester U.S.A.
68 D3 North Manitou I. *i.* U.S.A.
56 D2 North Nahanni *r.* Can.
57 L5 Northome U.S.A.
72 C3 North Palisade *summit* U.S.A.
64 C3 North Platte U.S.A.
64 C3 North Platte *r.* U.S.A.
39 □ North Point *H.K.* China
66 D2 North Point *pt* U.S.A.
68 E3 Northport U.S.A.
73 F3 North Rim U.S.A.
10 F1 North Ronaldsay *i.* U.K.
10 F1 North Ronaldsay Firth *chan.* U.K.
72 B2 North San Juan U.S.A.
57 G4 North Saskatchewan *r.* Can.
4 D3 North Sea *sea* Europe
57 J3 North Seal *r.* Can.
8 F2 North Shields U.K.
72 D2 North Shoshone Peak *summit* U.S.A.
54 D3 North Slope *plain* U.S.A.
9 H4 North Somercotes U.K.
71 H2 North Stratford U.S.A.
8 F2 North Sunderland U.K.
51 E3 North Taranaki Bight *b.* N.Z.
56 F4 North Thompson *r.* Can.
10 A3 Northton U.K.
70 D3 North Tonawanda U.S.A.
35 F4 North Tons *r.* India
51 A7 North Trap *rf* N.Z.
71 G2 North Troy U.S.A.
58 D3 North Twin I. *i.* Can.
8 E2 North Tyne *r.* U.K.
10 A3 North Uist *i.* U.K.
8 E2 Northumberland National Park U.K.
59 H4 Northumberland Strait *chan.* Can.
56 E5 North Vancouver Can.
71 F3 Northville U.S.A.
9 J5 North Walsham U.K.
90 F3 North West *div.* S. Africa
48 B4 North West C. *c.* Austr.
34 C2 North West Frontier *div.* Pak.
67 E7 Northwest Providence Chan. *chan.* Bahamas
59 J3 North West River Can.
57 G2 Northwest Territories *div.* Can.
9 E4 Northwich U.K.
71 F5 North Wildwood U.S.A.
71 H2 North Woodstock U.S.A.
8 G3 North York Moors *reg.* U.K.
8 G3 North York Moors National Park U.K.
59 G4 Norton Can.
8 G3 Norton U.K.
64 D4 Norton *KS* U.S.A.
70 B6 Norton *VA* U.S.A.
71 H2 Norton *VT* U.S.A.
89 D5 Norton Zimbabwe
54 B3 Norton Sound *b. AK* U.S.A.
92 C2 Norvegia, K. *c.* Ant.
71 G4 Norwalk *CT* U.S.A.
70 B4 Norwalk *OH* U.S.A.
71 H2 Norway U.S.A.
5 D2 Norway *country* Europe
69 J3 Norway Bay Can.
57 K4 Norway House Can.
96 J1 Norwegian Basin *sea feature* Atl. Ocean
55 J2 Norwegian Bay *b.* Can.
4 C2 Norwegian Sea *sea* Atl. Ocean
69 G4 Norwich Can.
9 J5 Norwich U.K.
71 G4 Norwich *CT* U.S.A.
71 F3 Norwich *NY* U.S.A.
71 H3 Norwood *MA* U.S.A.
71 F2 Norwood *NY* U.S.A.
70 A5 Norwood *OH* U.S.A.
80 C2 Nos de Cachi *mt* Arg.
57 H1 Nose Lake *l.* Can.
19 M3 Nos Emine *pt* Bulg.
19 M3 Nos Galata *pt* Bulg.
40 G2 Noshappu-misaki *hd* Japan
40 G4 Noshiro Japan
21 D5 Nosivka Ukr.
19 N3 Nos Kaliakra *pt* Bulg.
20 H3 Noskovo Rus. Fed.
90 D2 Nosop *r.* Botswana/S. Africa
24 G3 Nosovaya Rus. Fed.
31 E4 Noṣratābād Iran
82 A1 Nossa Senhora do Livramento Brazil
7 N7 Nossebro Sweden
19 N3 Nos Shabla *pt* Bulg.
10 □ Noss, Isle of *i.* U.K.
90 C2 Nossob *r.* Namibia
89 E5 Nosy Be *i.* Madag.
89 F5 Nosy Boraha *i.* Madag.
89 E6 Nosy Varika Madag.
73 F2 Notch Peak *summit* U.S.A.
16 H4 Noteć *r.* Pol.
7 L7 Notodden Norway
18 F6 Noto, Golfo di *g. Sicily* Italy
41 E6 Noto-hantō *pen.* Japan
59 K4 Notre Dame Bay *b.* Can.
69 K3 Notre-Dame-de-la-Salette Can.
71 H2 Notre-Dame-des-Bois Can.
69 K2 Notre-Dame-du-Laus Can.
69 H2 Notre-Dame-du-Nord Can.
59 G4 Notre Dame, Monts *mts* Can.
69 G3 Nottawasaga Bay *b.* Can.
58 E3 Nottaway *r.* Can.
9 F5 Nottingham U.K.
70 E6 Nottoway *r.* U.S.A.
12 F3 Nottuln Ger.
57 H5 Notukeu Cr. *r.* Can.
86 A2 Nouâdhibou Maur.
86 A3 Nouakchott Maur.
86 A3 Nouâmghâr Maur.
44 C2 Nouei Vietnam
49 G4 Nouméa New Caledonia
86 B3 Nouna Burkina
90 F5 Noupoort S. Africa
6 V3 Nousu Fin.
Nouveau-Comptoir *see* Wemindji
Nouvelle Calédonie *is see* New Caledonia
82 C1 Nova América Brazil
82 B3 Nova Esperança Brazil
82 D3 Nova Friburgo Brazil
18 G2 Nova Gradiška Croatia
82 C3 Nova Granada Brazil
82 D3 Nova Iguaçu Brazil
21 E6 Nova Kakhovka Ukr.
82 D2 Nova Lima Brazil
20 D4 Novalukoml' Belarus
21 D6 Nova Odesa Ukr.
18 C2 Novara Italy
82 C1 Nova Roma Brazil
59 H5 Nova Scotia *div.* Can.
72 A2 Novato U.S.A.
82 E2 Nova Venécia Brazil
82 B1 Nova Xavantino Brazil
25 R2 Novaya Sibir', Ostrov *i.* Rus. Fed.
24 G2 Novaya Zemlya *is* Rus. Fed.
19 M3 Nova Zagora Bulg.
15 F3 Novelda Spain
16 J7 Nové Zámky Slovakia
20 D3 Novgorod Rus. Fed.
20 E3 Novgorodskaya Oblast' *div.* Rus. Fed.
21 E5 Novhorod-Sivers'kyy Ukr.
19 K3 Novi Iskŭr Bulg.
18 C2 Novi Ligure Italy
19 M3 Novi Pazar Bulg.
19 J3 Novi Pazar Yugo.
19 H2 Novi Sad Yugo.
21 G6 Novoaleksandrovsk Rus. Fed.
21 G5 Novoanninskiy Rus. Fed.
78 F5 Novo Aripuanã Brazil
21 F6 Novoazovs'k Ukr.
31 H2 Novobod Tajik.
20 H3 Novocheboksarsk Rus. Fed.
21 G6 Novocherkassk Rus. Fed.
20 G1 Novodvinsk Rus. Fed.
80 F3 Novo Hamburgo Brazil
82 C3 Novo Horizonte Brazil
16 G6 Novohradské Hory *mts* Czech Rep.
21 C5 Novohrad-Volyns'kyy Ukr.
26 E2 Novokazalinsk Kazak.
21 G6 Novokubansk Rus. Fed.
36 A1 Novokuznetsk Rus. Fed.
92 D3 Novolazarevskaya *Rus. Fed. Base* Ant.
25 M2 Novoletov'ye Rus. Fed.
18 F2 Novo Mesto Slovenia
20 F4 Novomichurinsk Rus. Fed.
21 F6 Novomikhaylovskiy Rus. Fed.
20 F4 Novomoskovsk Rus. Fed.
21 E5 Novomoskovs'k Ukr.
21 D5 Novomyrhorod Ukr.
21 G5 Novonikolayevskiy Rus. Fed.
21 E6 Novooleksiyivka Ukr.
40 D2 Novopokrovka Rus. Fed.
21 G6 Novopokrovskaya Rus. Fed.
21 J5 Novorepnoye Rus. Fed.
21 F6 Novorossiysk Rus. Fed.
25 M2 Novorybnoye Rus. Fed.
17 O2 Novorzhev Rus. Fed.
21 E6 Novoselivs'ke Ukr.
17 O1 Novosel'ye Rus. Fed.
21 F6 Novoshakhtinsk Rus. Fed.
40 C2 Novoshakhtinskiy Rus. Fed.
24 K4 Novosibirsk Rus. Fed.
25 Q2 Novosibirskiye Ostrova *is* Rus. Fed.
20 D3 Novosokol'niki Rus. Fed.
20 H4 Novospasskoye Rus. Fed.
21 E6 Novotroyits'ke Ukr.
21 D5 Novoukrayinka Ukr.
21 J5 Novouzensk Rus. Fed.
21 C5 Novovolyns'k Ukr.
21 F5 Novovoronezh Rus. Fed.
21 D4 Novozybkov Rus. Fed.
16 H6 Nový Jičín Czech Rep.
25 M2 Novyy Rus. Fed.
21 F5 Novyy Oskol Rus. Fed.
24 J3 Novyy Port Rus. Fed.
20 J3 Novyy Tor'yal Rus. Fed.
24 J3 Novyy Urengoy Rus. Fed.
36 F1 Novyy Urgal Rus. Fed.
26 D2 Novyy Uzen' Kazak.
30 D4 Now Iran
65 E4 Nowata U.S.A.
30 C3 Nowbarān Iran
31 E3 Now Deh Iran
29 M3 Nowdī Iran
Nowgong *see* Nagaon
34 D4 Nowgong *Madhya Pradesh* India
57 J2 Nowleye Lake *l.* Can.
16 G4 Nowogard Pol.
50 H3 Nowra Austr.
30 C2 Now Shahr Iran
30 C2 Nowshahr Iran
34 C2 Nowshera Pak.
17 K6 Nowy Sącz Pol.
17 K6 Nowy Targ Pol.
71 E4 Noxen U.S.A.
24 J3 Noyabr'sk *r.* Rus. Fed.
56 C3 Noyes I. *i.* U.S.A.
14 F2 Noyon France
44 C1 Noy, Xé *r.* Laos
44 C1 Noy, Xé *r.* Laos
91 F5 Nozizwe S. Africa
91 G6 Nqamakwe S. Africa
91 J4 Nqutu S. Africa
89 D5 Nsanje Malawi
88 B4 Ntandembele Congo(Zaire)
91 G3 Ntha S. Africa
88 D4 Ntungamo Uganda
87 F3 Nuba Mountains Sudan
29 K1 Nubarashen Armenia
87 F2 Nubian Desert Sudan
83 B3 Nuble *r.* Chile
38 D1 Nüden Mongolia
78 D7 Nudo Coropuna *mt* Peru
65 D6 Nueces *r.* U.S.A.
83 F2 Nueva Helvecia Uru.
83 B3 Nueva Imperial Chile
81 A4 Nueva Loja Ecuador
80 B6 Nueva Lubecka Arg.
74 D3 Nueva Rosita Mex.
75 J4 Nuevitas Cuba
74 C2 Nuevo Casas Grandes Mex.
83 D4 Nuevo, Golfo *g.* Arg.
74 E3 Nuevo Laredo Mex.
65 C7 Nuevo León *div.* Mex.
88 E3 Nugaal *watercourse* Somalia
51 B7 Nugget Pt *pt* N.Z.
49 F2 Nuguria Is *is* P.N.G.
51 F3 Nuhaka N.Z.
49 H2 Nui *i.* Tuvalu
44 C2 Nui Ti On *mt* Vietnam
36 B3 Nu Jiang *r.* China
49 J4 Nuku'alofa Tonga
49 H2 Nukufetau *i.* Tuvalu
46 O4 Nuku Hiva *i.* Pac. Oc.
49 H2 Nukulaelae *i.* Tuvalu
49 F2 Nukumanu Is *is* P.N.G.
49 J2 Nukunono *i.* Pac. Oc.
26 D2 Nukus Uzbek.
48 C4 Nullagine Austr.
48 C5 Nullarbor Plain *plain* Austr.
38 F1 Nulu'erhu Shan *mts* China
86 D4 Numan Nigeria
41 F6 Numata Japan
41 F7 Numazu Japan
7 L6 Numedal *v.* Norway
37 F7 Numfor *i.* Indon.
50 E4 Numurkah Austr.
59 H2 Nunaksaluk Island *i.* Can.
55 O3 Nunarsuit *i.* Greenland
54 G3 Nunavut *div.* Canada
70 E3 Nunda U.S.A.
50 H1 Nundle Austr.
9 F5 Nuneaton U.K.
58 B3 Nungesser L. *l.* Can.
54 B4 Nunivak I. *i. AK* U.S.A.
34 D2 Nunkun *mt* India
25 U3 Nunligran Rus. Fed.
15 C2 Nuñomoral Spain
12 D2 Nunspeet Neth.
18 C4 Nuoro *Sardinia* Italy
49 G3 Nupani *i.* Solomon Is
32 B4 Nuqrah S. Arabia
81 A3 Nuquí Col.
34 E1 Nur China
30 D2 Nur *r.* Iran
30 C4 Nurābād Iran
Nuremberg *see* Nürnberg
29 J2 Nurettin Turkey
31 G4 Nur Gamma Pak.
50 B3 Nuriootpa Austr.
31 H3 Nuristan *reg.* Afgh.
20 J4 Nurlaty Rus. Fed.
6 V5 Nurmes Fin.
6 S5 Nurmo Fin.
13 K5 Nürnberg Ger.
50 F1 Nurri, Mt *h.* Austr.
35 H1 Nur Turu China
29 H3 Nusaybin Turkey
31 G4 Nushki Pak.
59 H2 Nutak Can.
73 H5 Nutrioso U.S.A.
34 B3 Nuttal Pak.
6 U3 Nuupas Fin.
55 N2 Nuussuaq Greenland
55 N2 Nuussuaq *pen.* Greenland
33 C5 Nuwara Eliya Sri Lanka
90 C5 Nuwerus S. Africa
90 D6 Nuweveldberg *mts* S. Africa
29 K4 Nuzi Iraq
91 J1 Nwanedi National Park S. Africa
24 H3 Nyagan' Rus. Fed.
50 D3 Nyah West Austr.
35 G3 Nyainqêntanglha Feng *mt* China
35 G3 Nyainqêntanglha Shan *mts* China
35 H2 Nyainrong China
6 Q5 Nyaker Sweden
87 E3 Nyala Sudan
35 F3 Nyalam China
89 C5 Nyamandhiovu Zimbabwe
20 G2 Nyandoma Rus. Fed.
20 F2 Nyandomskiy Vozvyshennost' *reg.* Rus. Fed.
89 D5 Nyanga Zimbabwe
88 B4 Nyanga *r.* Gabon
35 H3 Nyang Qu *r. Xizang* China
35 G3 Nyang Qu *r. Xizang* China
89 D5 Nyasa, Lake *l.* Africa
20 C4 Nyasvizh Belarus
7 M9 Nyborg Denmark
6 V1 Nyborg Norway
7 O8 Nybro Sweden
55 N1 Nyeboe Land *reg.* Greenland
35 G3 Nyêmo China
88 D4 Nyeri Kenya
35 F3 Nyima China
36 B4 Nyingchi China
17 K7 Nyíregyháza Hungary
6 S5 Nykarleby Fin.
7 M9 Nykøbing Denmark
7 M9 Nykøbing Sjælland Denmark
7 P7 Nyköping Sweden
6 P5 Nyland Sweden
91 H2 Nylstroom S. Africa
50 F2 Nymagee Austr.
7 P7 Nynäshamn Sweden
50 F1 Nyngan Austr.
17 L4 Nyoman *r.* Belarus/Lith.
16 C7 Nyon Switz.
42 E5 Nyongwol S. Korea

35 F3 Nyonni Ri *mt* China
14 G4 Nyons France
24 G3 Nyrob Rus. Fed.
16 H5 Nysa Pol.
Nysa Łużycka *r.* *see* Neiß
20 J2 Nyuchpas Rus. Fed.
40 F5 Nyūdō-zaki *pt* Japan
88 C4 Nyunzu Congo(Zaire)
25 N3 Nyurba Rus. Fed.
20 J2 Nyuvchim Rus. Fed.
21 E6 Nyzhn'ohirs'kyy Ukr.
88 D4 Nzega Tanz.
86 B4 Nzérékoré Guinea
88 B4 N'zeto Angola
91 J1 Nzhelele Dam *dam* S. Africa
Nzwani *i.* *see* Anjouan

O

64 C2 Oahe, Lake *l.* U.S.A.
72 □1 Oahu *i.* U.S.A.
50 C2 Oakbank Austr.
73 F2 Oak City U.S.A.
65 E6 Oakdale U.S.A.
64 D2 Oakes U.S.A.
9 G5 Oakham U.K.
62 B1 Oak Harbor U.S.A.
70 C6 Oak Hill U.S.A.
72 C3 Oakhurst U.S.A.
68 B2 Oak I. *i.* U.S.A.
72 A3 Oakland *CA* U.S.A.
70 D5 Oakland *MD* U.S.A.
64 D3 Oakland *NE* U.S.A.
62 B3 Oakland *OR* U.S.A.
72 A3 Oakland *airport* *CA* U.S.A.
50 F3 Oaklands Austr.
68 D5 Oak Lawn U.S.A.
64 C4 Oakley U.S.A.
48 C4 Oakover *r.* Austr.
62 B3 Oakridge U.S.A.
67 C4 Oak Ridge U.S.A.
50 C2 Oakvale Austr.
69 H4 Oakville Can.
51 C6 Oamaru N.Z.
10 B5 Oa, Mull of *hd* U.K.
51 D5 Oaro N.Z.
43 B3 Oas Phil.
62 D3 Oasis U.S.A.
92 B5 Oates Land *reg.* Ant.
73 E4 Oatman U.S.A.
74 E5 Oaxaca Mex.
24 H3 Ob' *r.* Rus. Fed.
86 D4 Obala Cameroon
41 D7 Obama Japan
10 C4 Oban U.K.
40 G5 Obanazawa Japan
15 C1 O Barco Spain
58 F4 Obatogama L. *l.* Can.
56 F4 Obed Can.
51 B6 Obelisk *mt* N.Z.
13 H4 Oberaula Ger.
13 J3 Oberdorla Ger.
13 J3 Oberharz *nat. park* Ger.
12 E3 Oberhausen Ger.
64 C4 Oberlin *KS* U.S.A.
70 B4 Oberlin *OH* U.S.A.
13 F5 Obermoschel Ger.
50 G2 Oberon Austr.
13 L5 Oberpfälzer Wald *mts* Ger.
13 H4 Obersinn Ger.
13 H4 Oberthulba Ger.
13 G4 Obertshausen Ger.
13 H3 Oberwälder Land *reg.* Ger.
37 E7 Obi *i.* Indon.
79 G4 Óbidos Brazil
31 H2 Obigarm Tajik.
40 H3 Obihiro Japan
21 H6 Obil'noye Rus. Fed.
81 C2 Obispos Venez.
36 F2 Obluch'ye Rus. Fed.
20 F4 Obninsk Rus. Fed.
88 C3 Obo C.A.R.
38 A2 Obo China
88 E2 Obock Djibouti
88 C4 Obokote Congo(Zaire)
42 E3 Obŏk-tong N. Korea
88 B4 Obouya Congo
21 F5 Oboyan' Rus. Fed.
20 G2 Obozerskiy Rus. Fed.
35 E4 Obra India
35 E4 Obra Dam *dam* India
60 E6 Obregón, Presa *resr* Mex.
19 J2 Obrenovac Yugo.
28 D2 Obruk Turkey
24 J2 Obskaya Guba *chan.* Rus. Fed.
86 B4 Obuasi Ghana
21 D5 Obukhiv Ukr.
20 J2 Ob''yachevo Rus. Fed.
67 D6 Ocala U.S.A.
81 D4 Ocamo *r.* Venez.
81 B2 Ocaña Col.
15 E3 Ocaña Spain
78 E7 Occidental, Cordillera *mts* Chile
81 A4 Occidental, Cordillera *mts* Col.
78 C6 Occidental, Cordillera *mts* Peru
56 B3 Ocean Cape *pt* U.S.A.
71 F5 Ocean City *MD* U.S.A.
71 F5 Ocean City *NJ* U.S.A.
56 D4 Ocean Falls Can.
96 G3 Oceanographer Fracture *sea feature* Atl. Ocean
72 D5 Oceanside U.S.A.
65 F6 Ocean Springs U.S.A.
21 D6 Ochakiv Ukr.
21 G7 Och'amch'ire Georgia
10 E4 Ochil Hills *h.* U.K.
34 C1 Ochili Pass Afgh.
13 J5 Ochsenfurt Ger.
12 F2 Ochtrup Ger.
7 P6 Ockelbo Sweden
17 M7 Ocolașul Mare, Vârful *mt* Romania
61 K5 Oconee *r.* *GA* U.S.A.
68 C4 Oconomowoc U.S.A.
68 D3 Oconto U.S.A.
72 D5 Ocotillo Wells U.S.A.
86 B4 Oda Ghana
41 C7 Ōda Japan
6 E4 Ódáðahraun *lava* Iceland
42 E3 Ŏdaejin N. Korea
40 G4 Ōdate Japan
41 F7 Odawara Japan
7 K6 Odda Norway
57 K3 Odei *r.* Can.
68 C5 Odell U.S.A.
15 B4 Odemira Port.
28 A2 Ödemiş Turkey
91 G3 Odendaalsrus S. Africa
7 M9 Odense Denmark
13 G5 Odenwald *reg.* Ger.
13 J3 Oder *r.* Ger./Pol.
16 G3 Oderbucht *b.* Ger.
21 D6 Odesa Ukr.
7 O7 Ödeshog Sweden
65 C6 Odessa U.S.A.
15 C4 Odiel *r.* Spain
86 B4 Odienné Côte d'Ivoire
20 F4 Odintsovo Rus. Fed.
44 C3 Ŏdŏngk Cambodia
16 J6 Odra *r.* Ger./Pol.
79 K5 Oeiras Brazil
64 C3 Oelrichs U.S.A.
13 L4 Oelsnitz Ger.
68 B4 Oelwein U.S.A.
12 D1 Oenkerk Neth.
46 O6 Oeno *i.* *Pitcairn Is* Pac. Oc.
29 H1 Of Turkey
18 G4 Ofanto *r.* Italy
13 G4 Offenbach am Main Ger.
12 F6 Offenburg Ger.
19 M6 Ofidoussa *i.* Greece
40 G5 Ōfunato Japan
40 F5 Oga Japan
88 E3 Ogadēn *reg.* Eth.
40 F5 Oga-hantō *pen.* Japan
41 E7 Ōgaki Japan
64 C3 Ogallala U.S.A.
23 G4 Ogasawara-shotō *is* Japan
69 H2 Ogascanane, Lac *l.* Can.
86 C4 Ogbomoso Nigeria
64 E3 Ogden *IA* U.S.A.
62 E3 Ogden *UT* U.S.A.
56 C3 Ogden, Mt *mt* Can.
71 F2 Ogdensburg U.S.A.
54 E3 Ogilvie *r.* Can.
54 E3 Ogilvie Mts *mts* Can.
30 D2 Oglanly Turkm.
67 C5 Oglethorpe, Mt *mt* U.S.A.
18 D1 Oglio *r.* Italy
86 C4 Ogoja Nigeria
58 C3 Ogoki *r.* Can.
58 C3 Ogoki Res. *resr* Can.
19 K3 Ogosta *r.* Bulg.
7 T8 Ogre Latvia
18 F2 Ogulin Croatia
30 D2 Ogurchinskiy, Ostrov *i.* Turkm.
29 L1 Oğuz Azer.
51 A6 Ohai N.Z.
51 E3 Ohakune N.Z.
40 G4 Ōhata Japan
51 B6 Ohau, L. *l.* N.Z.
83 B2 O'Higgins *div.* Chile
80 B7 O'Higgins, L. *l.* Chile
70 B4 Ohio *div.* U.S.A.
66 C4 Ohio *r.* U.S.A.
13 G4 Ohm *r.* Ger.
13 J4 Ohrdruf Ger.
13 L4 Ohře *r.* Czech Rep.
13 K2 Ohre *r.* Ger.
19 J4 Ohrid Macedonia
19 J4 Ohrid, Lake *l.* Albania/Macedonia
91 J2 Ohrigstad S. Africa
13 H5 Öhringen Ger.
51 E3 Ohura N.Z.
79 H3 Oiapoque Brazil
10 D3 Oich, Loch *l.* U.K.
35 H3 Oiga China
12 A4 Oignies France
64 D4 Oil City U.S.A.
72 C4 Oildale U.S.A.
14 F2 Oise *r.* France
12 B5 Oise à l'Aisne, Canal de l' *canal* France
41 B8 Ōita Japan
19 K5 Oiti *mt* Greece
72 C4 Ojai U.S.A.
83 D2 Ojeda Arg.
68 B3 Ojibwa U.S.A.
60 D3 Ojinaga Mex.
41 F6 Ojiya Japan
80 C3 Ojos del Salado *mt* Arg.
20 G4 Oka *r.* Rus. Fed.
89 B6 Okahandja Namibia
51 E3 Okahukura N.Z.
89 B6 Okakarara Namibia
59 H2 Okak Islands *is* Can.
56 F5 Okanagan Falls Can.
56 F4 Okanagan Lake *l.* Can.
56 F5 Okanogan U.S.A.
62 C1 Okanogan *r.* Can./U.S.A.
62 B1 Okanogan Range *mts* U.S.A.
88 C3 Okapi, Parc National de la *nat. park* Congo(Zaire)
34 C3 Okara Pak.
30 D2 Okarem Turkm.
89 B5 Okaukuejo Namibia
89 C5 Okavango *r.* Botswana/Namibia
89 C5 Okavango Delta *swamp* Botswana
41 F6 Okaya Japan
41 C7 Okayama Japan
41 E7 Okazaki Japan
67 D7 Okeechobee U.S.A.
67 D7 Okeechobee, L. *l.* U.S.A.
67 D6 Okefenokee Swamp *swamp* U.S.A.
9 C7 Okehampton U.K.
86 C4 Okene Nigeria
13 J2 Oker *r.* Ger.
34 B5 Okha India
36 G1 Okha Rus. Fed.
35 F4 Okhaldhunga Nepal
34 B5 Okha Rann *marsh* India
25 Q3 Okhotka *r.* Rus. Fed.
25 Q4 Okhotsk Rus. Fed.
36 G2 Okhotsk, Sea of *g.* Rus. Fed.
21 E5 Okhtyrka Ukr.
36 E4 Okinawa *i.* Japan
41 B7 Okino-shima *i.* Japan
41 C6 Oki-shōtō *is* Japan
65 D5 Oklahoma *div.* U.S.A.
65 D5 Oklahoma City U.S.A.
65 D5 Okmulgee U.S.A.
88 B4 Okondja Gabon
56 G4 Okotoks Can.
20 E4 Okovskiy Les *forest* Rus. Fed.
88 B4 Okoyo Congo
6 S1 Øksfjord Norway
20 F2 Oksovskiy Rus. Fed.
31 H2 Oktyabr' Tajik.
26 D2 Oktyabr'sk Kazak.
20 J4 Oktyabr'sk Rus. Fed.
20 G2 Oktyabr'skiy *Archangel.* Rus. Fed.
21 G6 Oktyabr'skiy *Volgograd.* Rus. Fed.
36 H1 Oktyabr'skiy Rus. Fed.
24 G4 Oktyabr'skiy Rus. Fed.
31 G2 Oktyabr'skiy Uzbek.
24 H3 Oktyabr'skoye Rus. Fed.
25 L2 Oktyabr'skoy Revolyutsii, Ostrov *i.* Rus. Fed.
20 E3 Okulovka Rus. Fed.
40 F3 Okushiri-tō *i.* Japan
90 E1 Okwa *watercourse* Botswana
6 B4 Ólafsvík Iceland
72 C3 Olancha U.S.A.
72 C3 Olancha Peak *summit* U.S.A.
7 P8 Öland *i.* Sweden
6 W3 Olanga Rus. Fed.
50 C2 Olary Austr.
50 C2 Olary *r.* Austr.
64 E4 Olathe U.S.A.
83 E3 Olavarría Arg.
16 H5 Oława Pol.
73 G5 Olberg U.S.A.
18 C4 Olbia *Sardinia* Italy
70 D3 Olcott U.S.A.
33 C2 Old Bastar India
11 D4 Oldcastle Rep. of Ireland
54 E3 Old Crow Can.
12 D1 Oldeboorn Neth.
13 G1 Oldenburg Ger.
16 E3 Oldenburg in Holstein Ger.
12 E2 Oldenzaal Neth.
6 R2 Olderdalen Norway
71 F3 Old Forge *NY* U.S.A.
71 F4 Old Forge *PA* U.S.A.
8 E4 Oldham U.K.
11 C6 Old Head of Kinsale *hd* Rep. of Ireland
56 G4 Oldman *r.* Can.
10 F3 Oldmeldrum U.K.
71 H3 Old Orchard Beach U.S.A.
59 K4 Old Perlican Can.
56 G4 Olds Can.
71 J2 Old Town U.S.A.
57 H4 Old Wives L. *l.* Can.
73 E4 Old Woman Mts *mts* U.S.A.
70 D3 Olean U.S.A.
17 L3 Olecko Pol.
25 O4 Olekma *r.* Rus. Fed.
25 O3 Olekminsk Rus. Fed.
21 E5 Oleksandriya Ukr.
20 H1 Olema Rus. Fed.
7 J7 Ølen Norway
6 X2 Olenegorsk Rus. Fed.
25 N3 Olenek Rus. Fed.
25 O2 Olenek *r.* Rus. Fed.
25 O2 Olenek B. *b.* Rus. Fed.
20 E3 Olenino Rus. Fed.
21 C5 Olevs'k Ukr.
40 D3 Ol'ga Rus. Fed.
15 C4 Olhão Port.
91 J2 Olifants S. Africa
90 C5 Olifants *r.* S. Africa
90 C2 Olifants *watercourse* Namibia
90 E3 Olifantshoek S. Africa
90 C6 Olifantsrivierberg *mts* S. Africa
83 F2 Olimar Grande *r.* Uru.
82 C3 Olímpia Brazil
79 M5 Olinda Brazil
89 D5 Olinga Moz.
91 G2 Oliphants Drift Botswana
83 D2 Oliva Arg.
15 F3 Oliva Spain
80 C3 Oliva, Cordillera de *mts* Arg./Chile
83 C1 Olivares, Co del *mt* Chile
70 B5 Olive Hill U.S.A.
82 D3 Oliveira Brazil
15 C3 Olivenza Spain
64 E2 Olivia U.S.A.
20 G4 Ol'khi Rus. Fed.
80 C2 Ollagüe Chile
83 B1 Ollita, Cordillera de *mts* Arg./Chile
83 B1 Ollitas *mt* Arg.
78 C5 Olmos Peru
71 G3 Olmstedville U.S.A.
9 G5 Olney U.K.
66 C4 Olney U.S.A.
7 O8 Olofström Sweden
16 H6 Olomouc Czech Rep.
20 E2 Olonets Rus. Fed.
43 B3 Olongapo Phil.
14 D5 Oloron-Ste-Marie France
15 H1 Olot Spain
36 D1 Olovyannaya Rus. Fed.
34 C5 Olpad India
13 F3 Olpe Ger.
17 K4 Olsztyn Pol.
16 C7 Olten Switz.
19 M2 Oltenița Romania
29 H1 Oltu Turkey
43 B5 Olutanga *i.* Phil.
62 B2 Olympia U.S.A.
62 B2 Olympic Nat. Park *WA* U.S.A.
62 A2 Olympic Nat. Park *WA* U.S.A.
Olympus *mt* *see* Troödos, Mount
19 K4 Olympus *mt* Greece
62 B2 Olympus, Mt *mt* U.S.A.
25 S3 Olyutorskiy Rus. Fed.
25 T4 Olyutorskiy, Mys *c.* Rus. Fed.
25 S4 Olyutorskiy Zaliv *b.* Rus. Fed.
35 E2 Oma China
40 G4 Ōma Japan
41 E6 Ōmachi Japan
41 F7 Omae-zaki *pt* Japan
11 D3 Omagh U.K.
64 E3 Omaha U.S.A.
90 C1 Omaheke *div.* Namibia
62 C1 Omak U.S.A.
23 E8 Oman *country* Asia
31 E5 Oman, Gulf of *g.* Asia
51 B6 Omarama N.Z.
89 B6 Omaruru Namibia
89 B5 Omatako *watercourse* Namibia
78 D7 Omate Peru
90 E2 Omaweneno Botswana
40 G4 Ōma-zaki *c.* Japan
88 A4 Omboué Gabon
18 D3 Ombrone *r.* Italy
35 F3 Ombu China
35 E5 Omdraaisvlei S. Africa
87 F3 Omdurman Sudan
18 C2 Omegna Italy
50 F4 Omeo Austr.
88 D2 Om Häjer Eritrea
30 C4 Omīdiyeh Iran
56 D3 Omineca Mountains Can.
90 C1 Omitara Namibia
41 F7 Ōmiya Japan
56 C3 Ommaney, Cape *hd* U.S.A.
12 E2 Ommen Neth.
38 B1 Ömnögovĭ *div.* Mongolia
25 R3 Omolon *r.* Rus. Fed.
88 D3 Omo National Park Eth.
40 G5 Omono-gawa *r.* Japan
24 J4 Omsk Rus. Fed.
25 R3 Omsukchan Rus. Fed.
40 H2 Ōmū Japan
41 A8 Ōmura Japan
19 L2 Omu, Vârful *mt* Romania
68 B4 Onalaska U.S.A.
71 F6 Onancock U.S.A.
58 D4 Onaping Lake *l.* Can.
69 E3 Onaway U.S.A.
44 A2 Onbingwin Myanmar
83 D1 Oncativo Arg.
8 C3 Onchan U.K.
89 B5 Oncócua Angola
89 B5 Ondangwa Namibia
90 B1 Ondekaremba Namibia
90 D5 Onderstedorings S. Africa
89 B5 Ondjiva Angola
86 C4 Ondo Nigeria
36 D2 Öndörhaan Mongolia
42 A1 Ondor Had China
38 B1 Ondor Mod China
38 D1 Ondor Sum China
20 E2 Ondozero Rus. Fed.
90 D1 One Botswana
20 F2 Onega Rus. Fed.
20 F2 Onega *r.* Rus. Fed.
20 E2 Onega, Lake *l.* Rus. Fed.
56 E4 100 Mile House Can.
71 F3 Oneida U.S.A.
71 F3 Oneida Lake *l.* U.S.A.
64 D3 O'Neill U.S.A.
36 H2 Onekotan, O. *i.* Rus. Fed.
71 F3 Oneonta U.S.A.
51 E2 Oneroa N.Z.
17 N7 Onești Romania
20 E1 Onezhskaya Guba *g.* Rus. Fed.
Onezhskoye Ozero *l.* *see* Onega, Lake
35 E5 Ong *r.* India
88 B4 Onga Gabon
51 F3 Ongaonga N.Z.
90 E4 Ongers *watercourse* S. Africa
42 C5 Ongjin N. Korea
38 F1 Ongniud Qi China
33 C3 Ongole India
21 G7 Oni Georgia
89 E6 Onilahy *r.* Madag.
86 C4 Onitsha Nigeria
90 B1 Onjati Mountain *mt* Namibia
41 E7 Ōno Japan
49 J4 Ono-i-Lau *i.* Fiji
41 C7 Onomichi Japan
49 H2 Onotoa *i.* Kiribati
56 G4 Onoway Can.
90 C4 Onseepkans S. Africa
48 B4 Onslow Austr.
67 E5 Onslow Bay *b.* U.S.A.
42 F2 Onsong N. Korea
12 F1 Onstwedde Neth.
41 E7 Ontake-san *volc.* Japan
62 C2 Ontario U.S.A.
58 B3 Ontario *div.* Can.
69 H4 Ontario, Lake *l.* Can./U.S.A.
68 C2 Ontonagon U.S.A.
49 F2 Ontong Java Atoll *atoll* Solomon Is
48 D4 Oodnadatta Austr.
65 E4 Oologah L. *resr* U.S.A.
12 B3 Oostburg Neth.
Oostende *see* Ostend
12 D2 Oostendorp Neth.
12 C3 Oosterhout Neth.
12 B3 Oosterschelde *est.* Neth.
12 E2 Oosterwolde Neth.
12 A4 Oostvleteren Belgium
12 D1 Oost-Vlieland Neth.
56 D4 Ootsa Lake Can.
56 D4 Ootsa Lake *l.* Can.
70 E5 Opal U.S.A.
88 C4 Opala Congo(Zaire)
20 J3 Oparino Rus. Fed.
58 B3 Opasquia Can.
58 B3 Opasquia Provincial Park *res.* Can.
58 F3 Opataca L. *l.* Can.
16 H6 Opava Czech Rep.
67 C5 Opelika U.S.A.
65 E6 Opelousas U.S.A.
62 F1 Opheim U.S.A.
69 F2 Ophir Can.
45 B2 Ophir, Gunung *volc.* Indon.
51 C6 Opihi *r.* N.Z.
58 E3 Opinaca *r.* Can.
58 E3 Opinaca, Réservoir *resr* Can.
58 D3 Opinnagau *r.* Can.
29 K5 Opis Iraq
59 G3 Opiscotéo L. *l.* Can.
12 C2 Opmeer Neth.
20 D3 Opochka Rus. Fed.
16 H5 Opole Pol.
15 B2 Oporto Port.
51 F3 Opotiki N.Z.
67 C6 Opp U.S.A.
6 L5 Oppdal Norway
51 D3 Opunake N.Z.
89 B5 Opuwo Namibia
68 B5 Oquawka U.S.A.
71 H2 Oquossoc U.S.A.
73 G5 Oracle U.S.A.
73 G5 Oracle Junction U.S.A.
17 K7 Oradea Romania
6 E4 Öræfajökull *gl.* Iceland
19 J3 Orahovac Yugo.
34 D4 Orai India
86 B1 Oran Alg.
80 D2 Orán Arg.
44 C2 O Rang Cambodia
42 E3 Orang N. Korea
50 G2 Orange Austr.
14 G4 Orange France
71 G3 Orange *MA* U.S.A.
65 E6 Orange *TX* U.S.A.
70 D5 Orange *VA* U.S.A.
89 B6 Orange *r.* Namibia/S. Africa
67 D5 Orangeburg U.S.A.
79 H3 Orange, Cabo *c.* Brazil
Orange Free State *div.* *see* Free State
69 G3 Orangeville Can.
73 G2 Orangeville U.S.A.
74 G5 Orange Walk Belize
43 B3 Orani Phil.
13 M2 Oranienburg Ger.
89 B6 Oranjemund Namibia
81 C1 Oranjestad Aruba
11 C4 Oranmore Rep. of Ireland
89 C6 Orapa Botswana
43 C3 Oras Phil.
19 K2 Orăștie Romania
6 S5 Oravais Fin.
19 J2 Oravita Romania
34 E2 Orba Co *l.* China
18 D3 Orbetello Italy
15 D1 Orbigo *r.* Spain
50 G4 Orbost Austr.
92 B1 Orcadas *Arg. Base* Ant.
73 H2 Orchard Mesa U.S.A.
81 D2 Orchila, Isla *i.* Venez.
72 B4 Orcutt U.S.A.
48 C3 Ord *r.* Austr.
63 D4 Orderville U.S.A.
15 B1 Ordes Spain
48 C3 Ord, Mt *h.* Austr.
72 D4 Ord Mt *mt* U.S.A.
28 F1 Ordu Turkey
29 L2 Ordubad Azer.
63 G4 Ordway U.S.A.
Ordzhonikidze *see* Vladikavkaz
21 E6 Ordzhonikidze Ukr.
72 C1 Oreana U.S.A.
7 O7 Örebro Sweden
68 C4 Oregon *IL* U.S.A.
70 B4 Oregon *OH* U.S.A.
68 C4 Oregon *WV* U.S.A.
62 B3 Oregon *div.* U.S.A.
62 B2 Oregon City U.S.A.
20 F4 Orekhovo-Zuyevo Rus. Fed.
20 F4 Orel Rus. Fed.
36 F1 Orel', Ozero *l.* Rus. Fed.
73 G1 Orem U.S.A.
19 M6 Ören Turkey
28 A2 Ören Turkey
24 G4 Orenburg Rus. Fed.
83 E3 Orense Arg.
51 A7 Orepuki N.Z.
7 N9 Øresund *str.* Denmark
51 B7 Oreti *r.* N.Z.
51 E2 Orewa N.Z.
12 D4 Oreye Belgium
19 K4 Orfanou, Kolpos *b.* Greece
9 J5 Orford U.K.
9 J5 Orford Ness *spit* U.K.
73 F5 Organ Pipe Cactus National Monument *res.* U.S.A.
31 H3 Orgūn Afgh.
28 B2 Orhaneli Turkey
21 D7 Orhangazi Turkey
20 J3 Orichi Rus. Fed.
71 K2 Orient U.S.A.
78 E7 Oriental, Cordillera *mts* Bol.
81 B3 Oriental, Cordillera *mts* Col.
78 D6 Oriental, Cordillera *mts* Peru
83 E3 Oriente Arg.
15 F3 Orihuela Spain
21 E6 Orikhiv Ukr.
69 H3 Orillia Can.
7 T6 Orimattila Fin.
81 E2 Orinoco *r.* Col./Venez.
81 E2 Orinoco Delta *delta* Venez.
35 F5 Orissa *div.* India
7 S7 Orissaare Estonia
18 C5 Oristano *Sardinia* Italy
7 T6 Orivesi Fin.
6 V5 Orivesi *l.* Fin.
79 G4 Oriximiná Brazil
74 E5 Orizaba Mex.
6 L5 Orkanger Norway
7 N8 Örkelljunga Sweden
6 L5 Orkla *r.* Norway
91 G3 Orkney S. Africa
10 E1 Orkney Islands *is* U.K.
65 C6 Orla U.S.A.
72 A2 Orland U.S.A.
82 C3 Orlândia Brazil
67 D6 Orlando U.S.A.
14 E3 Orléans France
71 J4 Orleans *MA* U.S.A.
71 G2 Orleans *VT* U.S.A.
20 J3 Orlov Rus. Fed.
20 F4 Orlovskaya Oblast' *div.* Rus. Fed.
21 G6 Orlovskiy Rus. Fed.
31 G5 Ormara Pak.
31 G5 Ormara, Ras *hd* Pak.
43 C4 Ormoc Phil.
67 D6 Ormond Beach U.S.A.
8 E4 Ormskirk U.K.
71 G2 Ormstown Can.
14 D2 Orne *r.* France
6 N3 Ørnes Norway
6 Q5 Örnsköldsvik Sweden
42 D4 Oro N. Korea
81 C3 Orocué Col.
86 B3 Orodara Burkina
62 C2 Orofino U.S.A.
63 F5 Orogrande U.S.A.
59 G4 Oromocto Can.
28 E6 Oron Israel
49 J2 Orona *i.* Kiribati
71 J2 Orono U.S.A.
10 B4 Oronsay *i.* U.K.
Orontes *r.* *see* 'Āṣī, Nahr al
36 E1 Oroqen Zizhiqi China
43 B4 Oroquieta Phil.
79 L5 Orós, Açude *resr* Brazil
18 C4 Orosei *Sardinia* Italy
18 C4 Orosei, Golfo di *b.* *Sardinia* Italy
17 K7 Orosháza Hungary
73 G5 Oro Valley U.S.A.
72 B2 Oroville *CA* U.S.A.
62 C1 Oroville *WA* U.S.A.
72 B2 Oroville, Lake *l.* U.S.A.
50 B2 Orroroo Austr.
7 O6 Orsa Sweden
20 D4 Orsha Belarus
24 G4 Orsk Rus. Fed.
7 K5 Ørsta Norway
15 C1 Ortegal, Cabo *c.* Spain
14 D5 Orthez France
15 C1 Ortigueira Spain
81 D2 Ortíz Venez.
18 D1 Ortles *mt* Italy
8 E3 Orton U.K.
18 F3 Ortona Italy
64 D2 Ortonville U.S.A.
25 O3 Orulgan, Khrebet *mts* Rus. Fed.
90 B1 Orumbo Namibia
30 B2 Orūmīyeh Iran
30 B2 Orūmīyeh, Daryācheh-ye *salt l.* Iran
78 E7 Oruro Bol.
12 D5 Orval, Abbaye d' Belgium
18 E3 Orvieto Italy
92 B3 Orville Coast *coastal area* Ant.
70 C4 Orwell *OH* U.S.A.
71 G3 Orwell *VT* U.S.A.
7 M5 Os Norway
68 A4 Osage U.S.A.
64 E4 Osage *r.* U.S.A.
41 D7 Ōsaka Japan
75 H7 Osa, Pen. de *pen.* Costa Rica
7 N8 Osby Sweden
65 F5 Osceola *AR* U.S.A.
64 E3 Osceola *IA* U.S.A.
13 M3 Oschatz Ger.
13 K2 Oschersleben (Bode) Ger.
18 C4 Oschiri *Sardinia* Italy
69 F3 Oscoda U.S.A.
20 F4 Osetr *r.* Rus. Fed.
41 A8 Ōse-zaki *pt* Japan
69 K3 Osgoode Can.
27 F2 Osh Kyrg.
89 B5 Oshakati Namibia
40 G3 Oshamanbe Japan
69 H4 Oshawa Can.
40 G5 Oshika-hantō *pen.* Japan
40 F4 Ō-shima *i.* Japan
41 F7 Ō-shima *i.* Japan
64 C3 Oshkosh *NE* U.S.A.
68 C3 Oshkosh *WV* U.S.A.
30 B2 Oshnovīyeh Iran
86 C4 Oshogbo Nigeria
29 M5 Oshtorān Kūh *mt* Iran
29 M5 Oshtorīnān Iran
88 B4 Oshwe Congo(Zaire)
19 H2 Osijek Croatia
18 E3 Osimo Italy
34 C4 Osiyān India
91 J3 Osizweni S. Africa
18 G2 Osječenica *mt* Bos.-Herz.
6 O5 Ösjön *l.* Sweden
64 E3 Oskaloosa U.S.A.
7 P8 Oskarshamn Sweden
69 K1 Oskélanéo Can.
21 F5 Oskol *r.* Rus. Fed.
7 M7 Oslo Norway
43 B4 Oslob Phil.
7 M7 Oslofjorden *chan.* Norway
33 B2 Osmānābād India
28 E1 Osmancık Turkey
28 B1 Osmaneli Turkey
28 F3 Osmaniye Turkey
7 V7 Os'mino Rus. Fed.
13 G2 Osnabrück Ger.
19 K3 Osogovske Planine *mts* Bulg./Macedonia
83 B4 Osorno Chile
15 D1 Osorno Spain
83 B4 Osorno, Vol. *volc.* Chile
56 F5 Osoyoos Can.
7 J6 Osøyri Norway
48 E3 Osprey Reef *rf* Coral Sea Is Terr.
12 D3 Oss Neth.
48 E6 Ossa, Mt *mt* Austr.

68 B3 **Osseo** U.S.A.
69 F3 **Ossineke** U.S.A.
71 H3 **Ossipee Lake** *l.* U.S.A.
13 K3 **Oßmannstedt** Ger.
59 H3 **Ossokmanuan Lake** *l.* Can.
20 E3 **Ostashkov** Rus. Fed.
13 F2 **Ostbevern** Ger.
13 H1 **Oste** *r.* Ger.
12 A3 **Ostend** Belgium
17 P5 **Oster** Ukr.
13 K2 **Osterburg (Altmark)** Ger.
7 O8 **Österbymo** Sweden
7 N6 **Österdalälven** *l.* Sweden
7 M5 **Østerdalen** *v.* Norway
13 K3 **Osterfeld** Ger.
13 G1 **Osterholz-Scharmbeck** Ger.
13 J3 **Osterode am Harz** Ger.
6 O5 **Östersund** Sweden
13 J3 **Osterwieck** Ger.
Ostfriesische Inseln *is see* **East Frisian Islands**
12 F1 **Ostfriesland** *reg.* Ger.
7 Q6 **Östhammar** Sweden
16 J6 **Ostrava** Czech Rep.
17 J4 **Ostróda** Pol.
21 F5 **Ostrogozhsk** Rus. Fed.
13 L4 **Ostrov** Czech Rep.
20 D3 **Ostrov** Rus. Fed.
17 K5 **Ostrowiec Świętokrzyski** Pol.
17 K4 **Ostrów Mazowiecka** Pol.
16 H5 **Ostrów Wielkopolski** Pol.
19 L3 **Osŭm** *r.* Bulg.
41 B9 **Ōsumi-Kaikyō** *chan.* Japan
41 B9 **Ōsumi-shotō** *is* Japan
15 D4 **Osuna** Spain
71 F2 **Oswegatchie** U.S.A.
68 C5 **Oswego** *IL* U.S.A.
70 E3 **Oswego** *NY* U.S.A.
71 E3 **Oswego** *r.* U.S.A.
9 D5 **Oswestry** U.K.
41 F6 **Ōta** Japan
51 C6 **Otago Peninsula** N.Z.
51 E4 **Otaki** N.Z.
6 U4 **Otanmäki** Fin.
81 B4 **Otare, Co** *h.* Col.
40 G3 **Otaru** Japan
51 B7 **Otatara** N.Z.
78 C3 **Otavalo** Ecuador
89 B5 **Otavi** Namibia
41 G6 **Ōtawara** Japan
51 C6 **Otematata** N.Z.
7 U7 **Otepää** Estonia
62 C2 **Othello** U.S.A.
51 C5 **Otira** N.Z.
71 E3 **Otisco Lake** *l.* U.S.A.
59 F3 **Otish, Monts** *mts* Can.
89 B6 **Otjiwarongo** Namibia
8 F4 **Otley** U.K.
38 C2 **Otog Qi** China
40 H2 **Otoineppu** Japan
51 E3 **Otorohanga** N.Z.
58 C3 **Otoskwin** *r.* Can.
19 H4 **Otranto** Italy
19 H4 **Otranto, Strait of** *str.* Albania/Italy
25 T3 **Otrozhnyy** Rus. Fed.
68 E4 **Otsego** U.S.A.
68 E3 **Otsego Lake** *l. MI* U.S.A.
71 F3 **Otsego Lake** *l. NY* U.S.A.
71 F3 **Otselic** U.S.A.
41 D7 **Ōtsu** Japan
7 L6 **Otta** Norway
69 K3 **Ottawa** Can.
68 C5 **Ottawa** *IL* U.S.A.
64 E4 **Ottawa** *KS* U.S.A.
70 A4 **Ottawa** *OH* U.S.A.
69 H2 **Ottawa** *r.* Can.
58 D2 **Ottawa Islands** *is* Can.
8 E2 **Otterburn** U.K.
73 G2 **Otter Creek Reservoir** U.S.A.
68 D1 **Otter I.** *i.* Can.
58 D3 **Otter Rapids** Can.
13 H1 **Ottersberg** Ger.
9 C7 **Ottery** *r.* U.K.
12 C4 **Ottignies** Belgium
55 K1 **Otto Fjord** *in.* Can.
68 A5 **Ottumwa** U.S.A.
12 F5 **Ottweiler** Ger.
86 C4 **Otukpo** Nigeria
80 D3 **Otumpa** Arg.
78 C5 **Otuzco** Peru
50 D5 **Otway, C.** *c.* Austr.
65 E5 **Ouachita** *r.* U.S.A.
65 E5 **Ouachita, L.** *l.* U.S.A.
65 E5 **Ouachita Mts** *mts* U.S.A.
88 C3 **Ouadda** C.A.R.
87 E3 **Ouaddaï** *reg.* Chad
86 B3 **Ouagadougou** Burkina
86 B3 **Ouahigouya** Burkina
86 B3 **Oualâta** Maur.
88 C3 **Ouanda-Djailé** C.A.R.
86 B2 **Ouarâne** *reg.* Maur.
86 C1 **Ouargla** Alg.
86 B1 **Ouarzazate** Morocco
90 F6 **Oubergpas** *pass* S. Africa
12 B4 **Oudenaarde** Belgium
12 F1 **Oude Pekela** Neth.
90 E6 **Oudtshoorn** S. Africa
12 C3 **Oud-Turnhout** Belgium
15 F5 **Oued Tlélat** Alg.
86 B1 **Oued Zem** Morocco
18 B6 **Oued Zénati** Alg.
14 B2 **Ouessant, Île d'** *i.* France
88 B3 **Ouésso** Congo
86 C4 **Ouidah** Benin
86 B1 **Oujda** Morocco
6 T4 **Oulainen** Fin.
15 G4 **Ouled Farès** Alg.
6 T4 **Oulu** Fin.
6 U4 **Oulujärvi** *l.* Fin.
6 U4 **Oulujoki** *r.* Fin.
6 T4 **Oulunsalo** Fin.
14 H4 **Oulx** Italy
87 E3 **Oum-Chalouba** Chad
86 B4 **Oumé** Côte d'Ivoire
87 D3 **Oum-Hadjer** Chad
6 T3 **Ounasjoki** *r.* Fin.
9 G5 **Oundle** U.K.
87 E3 **Ounianga Kébir** Chad
12 D4 **Oupeye** Belgium
12 E5 **Our** *r.* Lux.
63 F4 **Ouray** *CO* U.S.A.
73 H1 **Ouray** *UT* U.S.A.
15 C1 **Ourense** Spain
79 K5 **Ouricurí** Brazil
82 C3 **Ourinhos** Brazil
82 C1 **Ouro** *r.* Brazil
82 D3 **Ouro Preto** Brazil
12 D4 **Ourthe** *r.* Belgium
12 E5 **Our, Vallée de l'** *v.* Ger./Lux.
8 G4 **Ouse** *r. Eng.* U.K.
9 H7 **Ouse** *r. Eng.* U.K.
59 G3 **Outardes** *r.* Can.
90 E6 **Outeniekpas** *pass* S. Africa
10 A2 **Outer Hebrides** *is* U.K.
68 B2 **Outer I.** *i.* U.S.A.
72 C5 **Outer Santa Barbara Channel** U.S.A.
89 B6 **Outjo** Namibia
54 H4 **Outlook** Can.
6 V5 **Outokumpu** Fin.
10 □ **Out Skerries** *is* U.K.
49 G4 **Ouvéa** *i.* New Caledonia
39 D5 **Ouyang Hai Sk.** *resr* China
50 D3 **Ouyen** Austr.
9 G5 **Ouzel** *r.* U.K.
18 C4 **Ovace, Pte d'** *mt Corsica* France
29 G2 **Ovacık** Turkey
18 C2 **Ovada** Italy
49 H3 **Ovalau** *i.* Fiji
83 B1 **Ovalle** Chile
15 B2 **Ovar** Port.
83 D2 **Oveja** *mt* Arg.
50 F4 **Ovens** *r.* Austr.
12 F4 **Overath** Ger.
6 S3 **Överkalix** Sweden
73 E3 **Overton** U.S.A.
6 S3 **Övertorneå** Sweden
7 P8 **Överum** Sweden
12 C2 **Overveen** Neth.
68 E4 **Ovid** U.S.A.
15 D1 **Oviedo** Spain
6 T2 **Øvre Anarjåkka Nasjonalpark** *nat. park* Norway
6 Q2 **Øvre Dividal Nasjonalpark** *nat. park* Norway
7 M6 **Øvre Rendal** Norway
21 D5 **Ovruch** Ukr.
51 B7 **Owaka** N.Z.
88 B4 **Owando** Congo
41 E7 **Owase** Japan
64 E2 **Owatonna** U.S.A.
31 F3 **Owbeh** Afgh.
71 E3 **Owego** U.S.A.
93 H3 **Owen Fracture** *sea feature* Ind. Ocean
11 B3 **Owenmore** *r.* Rep. of Ireland
51 D4 **Owen River** N.Z.
72 C3 **Owens** *r.* U.S.A.
66 C4 **Owensboro** U.S.A.
72 D3 **Owens Lake** *l.* U.S.A.
69 G3 **Owen Sound** Can.
69 G3 **Owen Sound** *in.* Can.
48 E2 **Owen Stanley Range** *mts* P.N.G.
86 C4 **Owerri** Nigeria
56 D4 **Owikeno L.** *l.* Can.
70 B5 **Owingsville** U.S.A.
71 J2 **Owls Head** U.S.A.
86 C4 **Owo** Nigeria
69 E4 **Owosso** U.S.A.
29 L4 **Owrāmān, Kūh-e** *mts* Iran/Iraq
62 C3 **Owyhee** U.S.A.
62 C3 **Owyhee** *r.* U.S.A.
62 C3 **Owyhee Mts** *mts* U.S.A.
78 C6 **Oxapampa** Peru
6 E3 **Öxarfjörður** *b.* Iceland
57 J5 **Oxbow** Can.
71 J1 **Oxbow** U.S.A.
7 P7 **Oxelösund** Sweden
51 D5 **Oxford** N.Z.
9 F6 **Oxford** U.K.
69 F4 **Oxford** *MI* U.S.A.
65 F5 **Oxford** *MS* U.S.A.
71 F3 **Oxford** *NY* U.S.A.
71 F5 **Oxford** *PA* U.S.A.
57 K4 **Oxford House** Can.
57 K4 **Oxford L.** *l.* Can.
50 E3 **Oxley** Austr.
50 H1 **Oxleys Pk** *mt* Austr.
72 C4 **Oxnard** U.S.A.
69 H3 **Oxtongue Lake** Can.
6 N3 **Øya** Norway
41 F6 **Oyama** Japan
79 H3 **Oyapock** *r.* Brazil/Fr. Guiana
88 B3 **Oyem** Gabon
10 D3 **Oykel** *r.* U.K.
86 C4 **Oyo** Nigeria
14 G3 **Oyonnax** France
35 H5 **Oyster I.** *i.* Myanmar
13 H1 **Oyten** Ger.
30 A2 **Özalp** Turkey
43 B4 **Ozamiz** Phil.
67 C6 **Ozark** *AL* U.S.A.
68 E2 **Ozark** *MI* U.S.A.
65 E4 **Ozark Plateau** *plat.* U.S.A.
64 E4 **Ozarks, Lake of the** *l.* U.S.A.
30 E3 **Ozbagū** Iran
21 G7 **Ozerget'i** Georgia
36 H1 **Ozernovskiy** Rus. Fed.
20 E4 **Ozernyy** Rus. Fed.
17 L3 **Ozersk** Rus. Fed.
20 F4 **Ozery** Rus. Fed.
25 Q3 **Ozhogino** Rus. Fed.
18 C4 **Ozieri** *Sardinia* Italy
65 C6 **Ozona** U.S.A.
41 B7 **Ozuki** Japan

P

55 O3 **Paamiut** Greenland
44 A1 **Pa-an** Myanmar
90 C6 **Paarl** S. Africa
90 D4 **Paballelo** S. Africa
42 E3 **Pabal-ri** N. Korea
10 A3 **Pabbay** *i. Scot.* U.K.
10 A4 **Pabbay** *i. Scot.* U.K.
17 J5 **Pabianice** Pol.
35 G4 **Pabna** Bangl.
7 T9 **Pabradė** Lith.
31 G5 **Pab Range** *mts* Pak.
78 F6 **Pacaás Novos, Parque Nacional** *nat. park* Brazil
81 E4 **Pacaraima, Serra** *mts* Brazil
78 C5 **Pacasmayo** Peru
63 E6 **Pacheco** *Chihuahua* Mex.
20 H2 **Pachikha** Rus. Fed.
18 F6 **Pachino** *Sicily* Italy
33 B1 **Pachmarhi** India
34 D5 **Pachore** India
74 E4 **Pachuca** Mex.
72 B2 **Pacific** U.S.A.
95 L9 **Pacific-Antarctic Ridge** *sea feature* Pac. Oc.
41 F8 **Pacific Ocean** *ocean*
43 C4 **Pacijan** *i.* Phil.
45 D4 **Pacitan** Indon.
79 H4 **Pacoval** Brazil
82 D2 **Pacuí** *r.* Brazil
16 H5 **Paczków** Pol.
43 C5 **Padada** Phil.
81 D4 **Padamo** *r.* Venez.
45 B3 **Padang** Indon.
45 B3 **Padangpanjang** Indon.
45 A2 **Padangsidimpuan** Indon.
45 C3 **Padangtikar** *i.* Indon.
20 E2 **Padany** Rus. Fed.
29 M5 **Padatha, Kūh-e** *mt* Iran
81 D4 **Padauiri** *r.* Brazil
78 F8 **Padcaya** Bol.
56 F3 **Paddle Prairie** Can.
70 C5 **Paden City** U.S.A.
13 G3 **Paderborn** Ger.
19 K2 **Padeşu, Vârful** *mt* Romania
78 F7 **Padilla** Bol.
6 P3 **Padjelanta Nationalpark** *nat. park* Sweden
35 G5 **Padma** *r.* Bangl.
Padova *see* **Padua**
65 D7 **Padre Island** *i.* U.S.A.
18 C3 **Padro, Monte** *mt Corsica* France
9 C7 **Padstow** U.K.
17 N3 **Padsvillye** Belarus
50 C4 **Padthaway** Austr.
33 C2 **Pādua** India
18 D2 **Padua** Italy
66 B4 **Paducah** *KY* U.S.A.
65 C5 **Paducah** *TX* U.S.A.
34 D2 **Padum** Jammu and Kashmir
42 E3 **Paegam** N. Korea
42 C5 **Paengnyŏng-do** *i.* N. Korea
51 E2 **Paeroa** N.Z.
43 B3 **Paete** Phil.
28 D4 **Pafos** Cyprus
91 J1 **Pafúri** Moz.
18 F2 **Pag** Croatia
18 F2 **Pag** *i.* Croatia
43 B5 **Pagadian** Phil.
45 B3 **Pagai Selatan** *i.* Indon.
45 B3 **Pagai Utara** *i.* Indon.
37 G5 **Pagan** *i.* N. Mariana Is
45 E3 **Pagatan** Indon.
73 G3 **Page** U.S.A.
7 R9 **Pagėgiai** Lith.
80 □ **Paget, Mt** *mt* Atl. Ocean
63 F4 **Pagosa Springs** U.S.A.
35 G4 **Pagri** China
58 C3 **Pagwa River** Can.
72 □2 **Pahala** U.S.A.
34 B2 **Paharpur** Pak.
51 A7 **Pahia Pt** *pt* N.Z.
72 □2 **Pahoa** U.S.A.
67 D7 **Pahokee** U.S.A.
31 F3 **Pahra Kariz** Afgh.
73 E3 **Pahranagat Range** *mts* U.S.A.
34 D4 **Pahuj** *r.* India
72 D3 **Pahute Mesa** *plat.* U.S.A.
44 A1 **Pai** Thai.
7 T7 **Paide** Estonia
9 D7 **Paignton** U.K.
7 T6 **Päijänne** *l.* Fin.
35 F3 **Paĭku Co** *l.* China
44 B2 **Pailin** Cambodia
83 B4 **Pailluco** Chile
72 □2 **Pailolo Chan.** *chan.* U.S.A.
7 S6 **Paimio** Fin.
83 B2 **Paine** Chile
70 C4 **Painesville** U.S.A.
73 G3 **Painted Desert** U.S.A.
73 F5 **Painted Rock Reservoir** U.S.A.
57 K3 **Paint Lake Provincial Recr. Park** *res.* Can.
70 B6 **Paintsville** U.S.A.
69 G3 **Paisley** Can.
10 D5 **Paisley** U.K.
78 B5 **Paita** Peru
43 A5 **Paitan, Teluk** *b.* Malaysia
39 D4 **Paizhou** China
6 S3 **Pajala** Sweden
79 L5 **Pajeú** *r.* Brazil
44 B4 **Paka** Malaysia
78 F2 **Pakaraima Mountains** Guyana
42 C4 **Pakch'ŏn** N. Korea
69 G3 **Pakesley** Can.
25 S3 **Pakhacha** Rus. Fed.
23 F7 **Pakistan** *country* Asia
Paknampho *see* **Muang Nakhon Sawan**
51 D1 **Pakotai** N.Z.
34 C3 **Pakpattan** Pak.
44 B4 **Pak Phayun** Thai.
7 S9 **Pakruojis** Lith.
17 J7 **Paks** Hungary
31 H3 **Paktīkā** *reg.* Afgh.
44 C2 **Pakxé** Laos
87 D4 **Pala** Chad
44 A2 **Pala** Myanmar
45 C4 **Palabuhanratu** Indon.
45 C4 **Palabuhanratu, Teluk** *b.* Indon.
18 G3 **Palagruža** *i.* Croatia
19 K7 **Palaiochora** Greece
14 F2 **Palaiseau** France
Palakkat *see* **Palghat**
33 D1 **Pāla Laharha** India
90 E1 **Palamakoloi** Botswana
15 H2 **Palamós** Spain
34 C4 **Palana** India
25 R4 **Palana** Rus. Fed.
43 B2 **Palanan** Phil.
43 B2 **Palanan Point** *pt* Phil.
31 F4 **Palangān, Kūh-e** *mts* Iran
45 D3 **Palangkaraya** Indon.
33 B4 **Palani** India
34 C4 **Palanpur** India
31 G5 **Palantak** Pak.
43 C3 **Palapag** Phil.
89 C6 **Palapye** Botswana
33 B3 **Palar** *r.* India
35 G4 **Palasbari** India
25 R3 **Palatka** Rus. Fed.
23 N9 **Palau** *country* Pac. Oc.
43 B2 **Palaui** *i.* Phil.
43 A3 **Palauig** Phil.
44 A2 **Palauk** Myanmar
94 E5 **Palau Tr.** *sea feature* Pac. Oc.
44 A2 **Palaw** Myanmar
43 A4 **Palawan** *i.* Phil.
43 B3 **Palayan** Phil.
7 T7 **Paldiski** Estonia
35 H5 **Pale** Myanmar
12 D2 **Paleis Het Loo** Neth.
45 B3 **Palembang** Indon.
80 B6 **Palena** Chile
15 D1 **Palencia** Spain
74 F5 **Palenque** Mex.
18 E5 **Palermo** *Sicily* Italy
65 E6 **Palestine** U.S.A.
35 H5 **Paletwa** Myanmar
33 B4 **Palghat** India
34 C4 **Pali** India
47 G3 **Palikir** Micronesia
43 C5 **Palimbang** Phil.
18 F4 **Palinuro, Capo** *c.* Italy
73 H2 **Palisade** U.S.A.
12 D5 **Paliseul** Belgium
34 B5 **Palitana** India
7 S7 **Palivere** Estonia
33 B4 **Palk Bay** *b.* Sri Lanka
20 D3 **Palkino** Rus. Fed.
33 C2 **Pālkohda** India
33 B3 **Palkonda Range** *mts* India
33 B4 **Palk Strait** *str.* India/Sri Lanka
11 C5 **Pallas Green** Rep. of Ireland
6 S2 **Pallas-ja Ounastunturin Kansallispuisto** *nat. park* Fin.
21 H5 **Pallasovka** Rus. Fed.
33 C3 **Pallavaram** India
33 B2 **Palleru** *r.* India
51 E4 **Palliser Bay** *b.* N.Z.
51 E4 **Palliser, Cape** *c.* N.Z.
34 C3 **Pallu** India
15 D4 **Palma del Río** Spain
15 H3 **Palma de Mallorca** Spain
86 A2 **Palma, La** *i.* Canary Is
81 B2 **Palmar** *r.* Venez.
81 C3 **Palmarito** Venez.
86 B4 **Palmas, Cape** *c.* Liberia
82 D1 **Palmas de Monte Alto** Brazil
67 D7 **Palm Bay** U.S.A.
67 D7 **Palm Beach** U.S.A.
72 C4 **Palmdale** U.S.A.
82 B4 **Palmeira** Brazil
79 L5 **Palmeira dos Índios** Brazil
79 K5 **Palmeirais** Brazil
54 D3 **Palmer** *AK* U.S.A.
92 B2 **Palmer** *U.S.A. Base* Ant.
92 B2 **Palmer Land** *reg.* Ant.
51 C6 **Palmerston** N.Z.
46 L5 **Palmerston Island** *i. Cook Is* Pac. Oc.
51 E4 **Palmerston North** N.Z.
71 F4 **Palmerton** U.S.A.
67 E7 **Palmetto Pt** *pt* Bahamas
18 F5 **Palmi** Italy
81 A4 **Palmira** Col.
72 D5 **Palm Springs** U.S.A.
Palmyra *see* **Tadmur**
68 B6 **Palmyra** *MO* U.S.A.
70 E3 **Palmyra** *NY* U.S.A.
68 C4 **Palmyra** *WV* U.S.A.
46 L3 **Palmyra I.** *i.* Pac. Oc.
35 F5 **Palmyras Point** *pt* India
72 A3 **Palo Alto** U.S.A.
81 A3 **Palo de las Letras** Col.
87 F3 **Paloich** Sudan
6 S2 **Palojärvi** Fin.
6 U2 **Palomaa** Fin.
72 D5 **Palomar Mt** *mt* U.S.A.
73 G6 **Palominas** U.S.A.
33 C2 **Paloncha** India
37 E7 **Palopo** Indon.
15 F4 **Palos, Cabo de** *c.* Spain
73 F5 **Palo Verde** *AZ* U.S.A.
73 E5 **Palo Verde** *CA* U.S.A.
6 U4 **Paltamo** Fin.
37 D7 **Palu** Indon.
29 G2 **Palu** Turkey
43 B3 **Paluan** Phil.
31 G2 **Pal'vart** Turkm.
33 D3 **Palwal** India
25 T3 **Palyavaam** *r.* Rus. Fed.
33 B4 **Pamban Channel** India
50 G4 **Pambula** Austr.
45 C4 **Pameungpeuk** Indon.
33 B3 **Pamidi** India
14 E5 **Pamiers** France
27 F3 **Pamir** *mts* Asia
67 E5 **Pamlico Sound** *chan.* U.S.A.
65 C5 **Pampa** U.S.A.
83 C2 **Pampa de la Salinas** *salt pan* Arg.
78 F7 **Pampa Grande** Bol.
83 D2 **Pampas** *reg.* Arg.
81 B3 **Pamplona** Col.
43 B4 **Pamplona** Phil.
15 F1 **Pamplona** Spain
13 K1 **Pampow** Ger.
28 C1 **Pamukova** Turkey
70 E6 **Pamunkey** *r.* U.S.A.
34 D2 **Pamzal** Jammu and Kashmir
66 B4 **Pana** U.S.A.
43 C5 **Panabo** Phil.
73 E3 **Panaca** U.S.A.
43 A4 **Panagtaran Point** *pt* Phil.
45 C4 **Panaitan** *i.* Indon.
33 A3 **Panaji** India
75 J7 **Panamá** Panama
53 H9 **Panama** *country* S. America
75 J7 **Panama Canal** *canal* Panama
67 C6 **Panama City** U.S.A.
75 J7 **Panamá, Golfo de** *b.* Panama
72 D3 **Panamint Range** *mts* U.S.A.
72 D3 **Panamint Springs** U.S.A.
72 D3 **Panamint Valley** U.S.A.
43 C4 **Panaon** *i.* Phil.
35 G4 **Panar** *r.* India
18 F5 **Panarea, Isola** *i.* Italy
45 C2 **Panarik** Indon.
43 B4 **Panay** *i.* Phil.
43 C3 **Panay** *i.* Phil.
43 B4 **Panay Gulf** *b.* Phil.
73 E2 **Pancake Range** *mts* U.S.A.
19 J2 **Pančevo** Yugo.
43 B4 **Pandan** Phil.
43 C3 **Pandan** Phil.
43 B4 **Pandan B.** *b.* Phil.
44 □ **Pandan Res.** *resr* Sing.
34 E5 **Pandaria** India
82 D1 **Pandeiros** *r.* Brazil
33 A2 **Pandharpur** India
34 D5 **Pandhurna** India
83 F2 **Pando** Uru.
9 E6 **Pandy** U.K.
7 T9 **Panevėžys** Lith.
34 C2 **Pangi Range** *mts* Pak.
45 D3 **Pangkalanbuun** Indon.
45 A2 **Pangkalansusu** Indon.
45 C3 **Pangkalpinang** Indon.
37 E7 **Pangkalsiang, Tanjung** *pt* Indon.
43 B4 **Panglao** *i.* Phil.
55 M3 **Pangnirtung** Can.
24 J3 **Pangody** Rus. Fed.
34 D2 **Pangong Tso** *l.* India
83 B3 **Panguipulli** Chile
83 B3 **Panguipulli, L.** *l.* Chile
73 F3 **Panguitch** U.S.A.
44 A5 **Pangururan** Indon.
43 B5 **Pangutaran** *i.* Phil.
43 B5 **Pangutaran Group** *is* Phil.
65 C5 **Panhandle** U.S.A.
88 C4 **Pania-Mwanga** Congo(Zaire)
34 B5 **Pānikoita** *i.* India
21 G5 **Panino** Rus. Fed.
34 D3 **Panipat** India
43 A4 **Panitan** Phil.
31 H2 **Panj** Tajik.
31 G3 **Panjāb** Afgh.
31 G2 **Panjakent** Tajik.
44 D5 **Panjang** *i.* Indon.
29 L5 **Panjbarār** Iran
31 G5 **Panjgur** Pak.
34 C5 **Panjhra** *r.* India
Panjim *see* **Panaji**
34 B2 **Panjkora** *r.* Pak.
34 B3 **Panjnad** *r.* Pak.
6 W5 **Pankakoski** Fin.
86 C4 **Pankshin** Nigeria
42 F2 **Pan Ling** *mts* China
34 D4 **Panna** *reg.* India
48 B4 **Pannawonica** Austr.
82 B3 **Panorama** Brazil
33 B4 **Panruti** India
42 B3 **Panshan** China
42 D2 **Panshi** China
82 A2 **Pantanal de São Lourenço** *marsh* Brazil
82 A2 **Pantanal do Taquarí** *marsh* Brazil
79 G7 **Pantanal Matogrossense, Parque Nacional do** *nat. park* Brazil
18 D6 **Pantelleria** *Sicily* Italy
18 E6 **Pantelleria, Isola di** *i. Sicily* Italy
43 C5 **Pantukan** Phil.
74 E4 **Pánuco** Mex.
33 A2 **Panvel** India
39 B5 **Pan Xian** China
39 D6 **Panyu** China
88 B4 **Panzi** Congo(Zaire)
81 E3 **Pao** *r.* Venez.
18 G5 **Paola** Italy
66 C4 **Paoli** U.S.A.
88 B3 **Paoua** C.A.R.
16 H7 **Pápa** Hungary
51 E2 **Papakura** N.Z.
18 F4 **Papa, Monte del** *mt* Italy
74 E4 **Papantla** Mex.
33 C2 **Pāparhāhandi** India
51 C5 **Paparoa Range** *mts* N.Z.
10 □ **Papa Stour** *i.* U.K.
51 E2 **Papatoetoe** N.Z.
51 B7 **Papatowai** N.Z.
10 F1 **Papa Westray** *i.* U.K.
12 F1 **Papenburg** Ger.
60 E6 **Papigochic** *r.* Mex.
69 K2 **Papineau-Labelle, Réserve faunique de** *res.* Can.
73 E3 **Papoose L.** *l.* U.S.A.
13 J6 **Pappenheim** Ger.
10 B5 **Paps of Jura** *h.* U.K.
11 B5 **Paps, The** *h.* Rep. of Ireland
48 E2 **Papua, Gulf of** *g.* P.N.G.
47 F4 **Papua New Guinea** *country* Oceania
9 C7 **Par** U.K.
79 J4 **Pará** *r.* Brazil
82 D2 **Pará** *r.* Brazil
20 G4 **Para** *r.* Rus. Fed.
48 B4 **Paraburdoo** Austr.
43 B3 **Paracale** Phil.
82 C2 **Paracatu** *Minas Gerais* Brazil
82 D2 **Paracatu** *r.* Brazil
50 B1 **Parachilna** Austr.
19 J3 **Paraćin** Yugo.
82 D2 **Pará de Minas** Brazil
69 J1 **Paradis** Can.
72 B2 **Paradise** *CA* U.S.A.
68 E2 **Paradise** *MI* U.S.A.
57 H4 **Paradise Hill** Can.
72 D2 **Paradise Peak** *summit* U.S.A.
59 J3 **Paradise River** Can.
65 F4 **Paragould** U.S.A.
78 F6 **Paragua** *r.* Bol.
81 E3 **Paragua** *r.* Venez.
79 G7 **Paraguai** *r.* Brazil
81 C2 **Paraguáipoa** Venez.
81 C1 **Paraguaná, Pen. de** *pen.* Venez.
77 E5 **Paraguay** *country* S. America
80 E3 **Paraguay** *r.* Arg./Para.
79 L5 **Paraíba** *r.* Brazil
82 D3 **Paraíba do Sul** *r.* Brazil
86 C4 **Parakou** Benin
33 D2 **Paralākhemundi** India
34 E6 **Paralkot** India
33 B4 **Paramakkudi** India
79 G2 **Paramaribo** Suriname
81 B3 **Paramillo** *mt* Col.
81 A3 **Paramillo, Parque Nacional** *nat. park* Col.
82 D1 **Paramirim** Brazil
81 A3 **Paramo Frontino** *mt* Col.
71 F4 **Paramus** U.S.A.
36 H1 **Paramushir, O.** *i.* Rus. Fed.
83 E1 **Paraná** Arg.
79 J6 **Paranã** Brazil
82 B4 **Paraná** *div.* Brazil
82 C1 **Paranã** *r.* Brazil
82 E2 **Paraná** *r.* S. America
82 C4 **Paranaguá** Brazil
82 B2 **Paranaíba** Brazil
82 B2 **Paranaíba** *r.* Brazil
83 E2 **Paraná Ibicuy** *r.* Arg.
82 B3 **Paranapanema** *r.* Brazil
82 C4 **Paranapiacaba, Serra** *mts* Brazil
82 C1 **Paranã, Sa do** *h.* Brazil
82 B3 **Paranavaí** Brazil
43 B5 **Parang** Phil.
33 B4 **Parangipettai** India
19 K2 **Parângul Mare, Vârful** *mt* Romania
34 C5 **Parantij** India
82 D2 **Paraopeba** *r.* Brazil
29 K4 **Pārapāra** Iraq
51 E4 **Paraparaumu** N.Z.
81 D3 **Paraque, Co** *mt* Venez.
65 D7 **Paras** Mex.
34 D5 **Paratwada** India
82 A1 **Paraúna** Brazil
14 G3 **Paray-le-Monial** France
34 D4 **Parbati** *r.* India
33 B2 **Parbhani** India
13 K1 **Parchim** Ger.
68 C4 **Pardeeville** U.S.A.
35 G2 **Parding** China
82 E1 **Pardo** *r. Bahia/Minas Gerais* Brazil
82 B3 **Pardo** *r. Mato Grosso do Sul* Brazil
82 D1 **Pardo** *r. Minas Gerais* Brazil
82 C3 **Pardo** *r. São Paulo* Brazil
16 G5 **Pardubice** Czech Rep.
34 D2 **Pare Chu** *r.* China
35 G4 **Pare Chu** *r.* India
78 F6 **Parecis, Serra dos** *h.* Brazil
65 C7 **Paredón** Mex.
30 D3 **Pareh** Iran
51 D1 **Parengarenga Harbour** *in.* N.Z.
58 E4 **Parent, Lac** *l.* Can.
51 C6 **Pareora** N.Z.
45 E3 **Parepare** Indon.
83 D2 **Parera** Arg.
20 G3 **Parfen'yevo** Rus. Fed.
17 P2 **Parfino** Rus. Fed.
19 J5 **Parga** Greece
7 S6 **Pargas** Fin.
81 D2 **Pariaguán** Venez.
81 E2 **Paria, Gulf of** *g.* Trinidad/Venez.
81 E2 **Paria, Península de** *pen.* Venez.
73 F3 **Paria Plateau** *plat.* U.S.A.
7 V6 **Parikkala** Fin.
Parima *r. see* **Uatatás**
81 D4 **Parima, Serra** *mts* Brazil
81 D4 **Parima-Tapirapecó, Parque Nacional** *nat. park* Venez.
78 B4 **Pariñas, Pta** *pt* Peru
50 C3 **Paringa** Austr.
79 G4 **Parintins** Brazil
69 G4 **Paris** Can.
14 F2 **Paris** France
70 A5 **Paris** *KY* U.S.A.
67 B4 **Paris** *TN* U.S.A.
65 E5 **Paris** *TX* U.S.A.
68 E2 **Parisienne, Île** *i.* Can.
30 D4 **Pārīz** Iran
11 D3 **Park** U.K.
31 E5 **Parkā Bandar** Iran
33 B2 **Parkal** India
7 S5 **Parkano** Fin.
73 F4 **Parke Lake** *l.* Can.
73 E4 **Parker** U.S.A.
73 E4 **Parker Dam** *dam* U.S.A.
57 K2 **Parker Lake** *l.* Can.
39 □ **Parker, Mt** *h. H.K.* China
68 A4 **Parkersburg** *IA* U.S.A.
70 C5 **Parkersburg** *WV* U.S.A.
50 G2 **Parkes** Austr.
68 B3 **Park Falls** U.S.A.
68 D5 **Park Forest** U.S.A.
69 F2 **Parkinson** Can.
64 E2 **Park Rapids** U.S.A.
56 E5 **Parksville** Can.
71 F4 **Parksville** U.S.A.
33 D2 **Parla Kimedi** India
33 B2 **Parli Vaijnath** India
18 D2 **Parma** Italy
62 C3 **Parma** *ID* U.S.A.
70 C4 **Parma** *OH* U.S.A.
81 D3 **Parmana** Venez.
79 K4 **Parnaíba** Brazil
79 K4 **Parnaíba** *r.* Brazil
19 K5 **Parnassos** *mt* Greece

51 D5 Parnassus N.Z.
68 A5 Parnell U.S.A.
19 K6 Parnon mts Greece
7 T7 Pärnu Estonia
7 T7 Pärnu-Jaagupi Estonia
31 F3 Paropamisus mts Afgh.
19 L6 Paros Greece
19 L6 Paros i. Greece
73 F3 Parowan U.S.A.
83 B3 Parral Chile
71 F6 Parramore I. i. U.S.A.
65 C7 Parras Mex.
83 F3 Parravicini Arg.
9 E6 Parrett r. U.K.
59 H4 Parrsboro Can.
54 F2 Parry, Cape pt Can.
54 G2 Parry Islands is Can.
55 L2 Parry, Kap c. Greenland
69 G3 Parry Sound Can.
65 E4 Parsons KS U.S.A.
70 D5 Parsons WV U.S.A.
13 H4 Partenstein Ger.
14 D3 Parthenay France
40 C3 Partizansk Rus. Fed.
9 H4 Partney U.K.
11 B4 Partry Rep. of Ireland
11 B4 Partry Mts h. Rep. of Ireland
79 H4 Paru r. Brazil
81 D3 Parucito r. Venez.
33 C2 Parvatipuram India
34 C4 Parvatsar India
34 D4 Parwan r. India
35 E3 Paryang China
91 G3 Parys S. Africa
72 C4 Pasadena CA U.S.A.
65 E6 Pasadena TX U.S.A.
78 B4 Pasado, C. pt Ecuador
30 D4 Pasargadae Iran
45 B3 Pasarseblat Indon.
44 A1 Pasawng Myanmar
65 F6 Pascagoula U.S.A.
69 J1 Pascalis Can.
17 N7 Paşcani Romania
62 C2 Pasco U.S.A.
82 E2 Pascoal, Monte h. Brazil
43 B3 Pascual Phil.
Pas de Calais str. see Dover, Strait of
16 G4 Pasewalk Ger.
57 H3 Pasfield Lake l. Can.
20 E2 Pasha Rus. Fed.
43 B3 Pasig Phil.
29 H2 Pasinler Turkey
44 □ Pasir Gudang Malaysia
44 □ Pasir Panjang Sing.
45 B1 Pasir Putih Malaysia
72 A2 Paskenta U.S.A.
31 F5 Paskūh Iran
31 F5 Pasni Pak.
81 B4 Paso de las Cruces mt Col.
83 F2 Paso de los Toros Uru.
80 B7 Paso Río Mayo Arg.
72 B4 Paso Robles U.S.A.
57 J4 Pasquia Hills h. Can.
30 D4 Pasrūdak Iran
71 J2 Passadumkeag U.S.A.
68 C1 Passage I. i. U.S.A.
16 F6 Passau Ger.
43 B4 Passi Phil.
80 F3 Passo Fundo Brazil
82 C3 Passos Brazil
20 C4 Pastavy Belarus
78 C4 Pastaza r. Peru
57 J4 Pas, The Can.
81 A4 Pasto Col.
73 H3 Pastora Peak summit U.S.A.
43 B2 Pasuquin Phil.
45 D4 Pasuruan Indon.
7 T8 Pasvalys Lith.
43 B5 Pata i. Phil.
73 G6 Patagonia U.S.A.
76 C8 Patagonia reg. Arg.
35 G4 Patakata India
31 F4 Patambar Iran
34 C5 Patan Gujarat India
34 D5 Patan Madhya Pradesh India
Patan see Somnath
35 F4 Patan Nepal
50 D3 Patchewollock Austr.
51 E3 Patea N.Z.
51 E3 Patea r. N.Z.
8 F3 Pateley Bridge U.K.
35 G5 Patenga Point pt Bangl.
90 F6 Patensie S. Africa
18 F6 Paternò Sicily Italy
50 H2 Paterson Austr.
71 F4 Paterson U.S.A.
34 C2 Pathankot India
62 F3 Pathfinder Res. resr U.S.A.
44 A3 Pathiu Thai.
33 B2 Pathri India
44 B2 Pathum Thani Thai.
45 D4 Pati Indon.
81 A4 Patía r. Col.
34 D3 Patiala India
19 M6 Patmos i. Greece
35 F4 Patna India
35 E5 Patnagarh India
43 B3 Patnanongan i. Phil.
29 J2 Patnos Turkey
34 E3 Paton India
19 H4 Patos Albania
79 L5 Patos Brazil
82 C2 Patos de Minas Brazil
80 F4 Patos, Lagoa dos l. Brazil
83 C1 Patquía Arg.
19 J5 Patra Greece
6 B4 Patreksfjörður Iceland
82 C2 Patrocínio Brazil
6 V2 Patsoyoki r. Europe
44 B4 Pattani Thai.
44 B4 Pattani r. Thai.
44 B2 Pattaya Thai.
71 J2 Patten U.S.A.
13 H2 Pattensen Ger.
72 B3 Patterson U.S.A.
70 D5 Patterson r. U.S.A.
56 C2 Patterson, Mt mt Can.
72 C3 Patterson Mt mt U.S.A.
68 E3 Patterson, Pt pt U.S.A.
6 T4 Pattijoki Fin.
6 R2 Pättikkä Fin.
33 B3 Pattikonda India
56 D3 Pattullo, Mt mt Can.
35 G5 Patuakhali Bangl.
57 H3 Patuanak Can.
70 E5 Patuxent r. U.S.A.
92 B3 Patuxent Ra. mts Ant.
74 D5 Pátzcuaro Mex.
14 D5 Pau France
14 D4 Pauillac France
35 H5 Pauktaw Myanmar
73 F4 Paulden U.S.A.
70 A4 Paulding U.S.A.
59 H2 Paul Island i. Can.
79 K5 Paulistana Brazil
79 L5 Paulo Afonso Brazil
91 J3 Paulpietersburg S. Africa
91 G4 Paul Roux S. Africa
71 F2 Paul Smiths U.S.A.
65 D5 Pauls Valley U.S.A.
81 C3 Pauto r. Col.
82 E2 Pavão Brazil
30 B3 Pāveh Iran
18 C2 Pavia Italy
7 R8 Pāvilosta Latvia
20 H3 Pavino Rus. Fed.
19 L3 Pavlikeni Bulg.
27 F1 Pavlodar Kazak.
21 E5 Pavlohrad Ukr.
20 H4 Pavlovka Rus. Fed.
20 G4 Pavlovo Rus. Fed.
21 G5 Pavlovsk Rus. Fed.
21 F6 Pavlovskaya Rus. Fed.
81 B4 Pavon Col.
34 E3 Pawayan India
68 E4 Paw Paw U.S.A.
71 H4 Pawtucket U.S.A.
44 A2 Pawut Myanmar
68 C5 Paxton U.S.A.
45 B3 Payakumbuh Indon.
44 □ Paya Lebar Sing.
81 B4 Paya, Parque Nacional la nat. park Col.
62 C2 Payette U.S.A.
24 H3 Pay-Khoy, Khrebet h. Rus. Fed.
58 F2 Payne, Lac l. Can.
72 B1 Paynes Creek U.S.A.
83 E2 Paysandú Uru.
73 G4 Payson AZ U.S.A.
73 G1 Payson UT U.S.A.
83 C3 Payún, Cerro volc. Arg.
28 D1 Pazar Turkey
29 H1 Pazar Turkey
28 F3 Pazarcık Turkey
19 L3 Pazardzhik Bulg.
81 C3 Paz de Ariporo Col.
81 B3 Paz de Rio Col.
18 E2 Pazin Croatia
56 G3 Peace r. Can.
54 G4 Peace r. U.S.A.
56 F3 Peace River Can.
73 F4 Peach Springs U.S.A.
9 F4 Peak District National Park U.K.
59 G4 Peaked Mt. h. U.S.A.
43 A4 Peaked Point pt Phil.
50 G2 Peak Hill Austr.
73 H2 Peale, Mt mt U.S.A.
73 H6 Pearce U.S.A.
68 C1 Pearl Can.
65 F6 Pearl r. U.S.A.
72 □1 Pearl City U.S.A.
72 □1 Pearl Harbor in. U.S.A.
65 D6 Pearsall U.S.A.
67 D6 Pearson U.S.A.
55 H2 Peary Channel Can.
58 C2 Peawanuck Can.
89 D5 Pebane Moz.
19 J3 Peć Yugo.
82 D2 Peçanha Brazil
6 W2 Pechenga Rus. Fed.
24 G3 Pechora Rus. Fed.
20 C3 Pechory Rus. Fed.
69 F4 Peck U.S.A.
65 C6 Pecos U.S.A.
65 C6 Pecos r. U.S.A.
19 H1 Pécs Hungary
91 G6 Peddie S. Africa
6 S5 Pedersöre Fin.
35 E3 Pêdo La pass China
82 E1 Pedra Azul Brazil
81 C3 Pedraza La Vieja Venez.
81 C2 Pedregal Venez.
82 C3 Pedregulho Brazil
79 K4 Pedreiras Brazil
79 J5 Pedro Afonso Brazil
81 C4 Pedro Chico Col.
80 C2 Pedro de Valdivia Chile
82 A2 Pedro Gomes Brazil
81 D4 Pedro II, Ilha i. Brazil
80 E2 Pedro Juan Caballero Para.
79 K4 Pedroll Brazil
83 G1 Pedro Osório Brazil
33 C4 Pedro, Pt pt Sri Lanka
10 E5 Peebles U.K.
67 E5 Pee Dee r. U.S.A.
71 G4 Peekskill U.S.A.
8 C3 Peel U.K.
50 H1 Peel r. Austr.
54 E3 Peel r. N.W.T. Can.
12 D3 Peer Belgium
56 F4 Peers Can.
51 D5 Pegasus Bay b. N.Z.
13 K5 Pegnitz Ger.
13 K5 Pegnitz r. Ger.
37 B5 Pegu Myanmar
20 J2 Pegysh Rus. Fed.
83 E2 Pehuajó Arg.
39 F6 Peikang Taiwan
13 J2 Peine Ger.
Peipsi Järve l. see Peipus, Lake
7 U7 Peipus, Lake l. Estonia/Rus. Fed.
19 K6 Peiraias Greece
13 K3 Peißen Ger.
38 E3 Peitun China
79 J6 Peixe Brazil
82 B1 Peixe r. Goiás Brazil
82 B3 Peixe r. São Paulo Brazil
38 E3 Pei Xian Jiangsu China
38 F3 Pei Xian Jiangsu China
82 A2 Peixo de Couro r. Brazil
91 G4 Peka Lesotho
45 C4 Pekalongan Indon.
44 B5 Pekan Malaysia
45 B2 Pekanbaru Indon.
68 C5 Pekin U.S.A.
44 B5 Pelabuhan Kelang Malaysia
69 F5 Pelee I. i. Can.
69 F5 Pelee Pt pt Can.
37 E7 Peleng i. Indon.
20 J2 Peles Rus. Fed.
68 A1 Pelican Lake l. MN U.S.A.
68 C3 Pelican Lake l. WI U.S.A.
57 J3 Pelican Narrows Can.
6 U3 Pelkosenniemi Fin.
90 C4 Pella S. Africa
57 H1 Pellat Lake l. Can.
48 E2 Pelleluhu Is is P.N.G.
68 C4 Pell Lake U.S.A.
6 S3 Pello Fin.
56 B2 Pelly r. Can.
55 K3 Pelly Bay Can.
56 B2 Pelly Crossing Can.
57 J1 Pelly Lake l. Can.
56 C2 Pelly Mountains Can.
83 G1 Pelotas Brazil
80 F3 Pelotas, R. das r. Brazil
28 D6 Pelusium Egypt
14 H4 Pelvoux, Massif du mts France
71 J2 Pemadumcook Lake l. U.S.A.
45 C4 Pemalang Indon.
45 C2 Pemangkat Indon.
45 A2 Pematangsiantar Indon.
89 E5 Pemba Moz.
89 C5 Pemba Zambia
88 D4 Pemba I. i. Tanz.
64 D1 Pembina U.S.A.
56 F4 Pembina r. Can.
69 J3 Pembroke Can.
9 C6 Pembroke U.K.
71 K2 Pembroke U.S.A.
9 B6 Pembrokeshire Coast National Park U.K.
33 A2 Pen India
35 H5 Pen r. Myanmar
15 D1 Peña Cerredo mt Spain
15 E2 Peñalara mt Spain
74 E4 Peña Nevada, Cerro mt Mex.
82 B3 Penápolis Brazil
15 D1 Peña Prieta mt Spain
15 D2 Peñaranda de Bracamonte Spain
50 D3 Penarie Austr.
15 F2 Peñarroya mt Spain
15 D3 Peñarroya-Pueblonuevo Spain
9 D6 Penarth U.K.
15 D1 Peñas, Cabo de c. Spain
74 B2 Peñasco, Pto Mex.
80 A7 Penas, Golfo de b. Chile
81 E2 Peñas, Pta pt Venez.
15 D1 Peña Ubiña mt Spain
34 D5 Pench r. India
92 D5 Penck, C. c. Ant.
86 C3 Pendjari, Parc National de la nat. park Benin
8 E4 Pendle Hill h. U.K.
62 C2 Pendleton U.S.A.
56 D4 Pendleton Bay Can.
62 C1 Pend Oreille r. U.S.A.
62 C2 Pend Oreille L. l. U.S.A.
35 E5 Pendra India
69 H3 Penetanguishene Can.
38 C4 Peng'an China
33 B2 Penganga r. India
34 D6 Penganga r. India
39 □ Peng Chau i. H.K. China
39 G5 P'eng-chia Hsü i. Taiwan
88 C4 Penge Congo(Zaire)
91 J2 Penge S. Africa
39 F6 P'eng-hu Lieh-tao is Taiwan
39 F6 Peng-hu Tao i. Taiwan
44 □ Peng Kang h. Sing.
38 F2 Penglai China
39 B4 Pengshan China
39 C4 Pengshui China
39 B4 Pengxi China
39 E4 Pengze China
91 G5 Penhoek Pass S. Africa
15 B3 Peniche Port.
10 E5 Penicuik U.K.
13 L4 Penig Ger.
20 E2 Peninga Rus. Fed.
45 B2 Peninsular Malaysia pen. Malaysia
29 K4 Penjwin Iraq
18 E3 Penne Italy
92 A5 Pennell Coast coastal area Ant.
33 B3 Penner r. India
50 A3 Penneshaw Austr.
8 E3 Pennines h. U.K.
91 J5 Pennington S. Africa
71 F5 Pennsville U.S.A.
70 D4 Pennsylvania div. U.S.A.
70 E3 Penn Yan U.S.A.
55 M3 Penny Icecap ice cap Can.
57 H2 Pennylan Lake l. Can.
92 B4 Penny Pt pt Ant.
71 J2 Penobscot r. U.S.A.
71 J2 Penobscot Bay b. U.S.A.
50 C4 Penola Austr.
48 D5 Penong Austr.
8 E3 Penrith U.K.
67 C6 Pensacola U.S.A.
92 B3 Pensacola Mts mts Ant.
29 M2 Pensär Azer.
50 D4 Penshurst Austr.
49 G3 Pentecost I. i. Vanuatu
56 F5 Penticton Can.
9 B7 Pentire Point pt U.K.
10 E2 Pentland Firth chan. U.K.
10 E5 Pentland Hills h. U.K.
68 D4 Pentwater U.S.A.
33 B3 Penukonda India
9 D5 Penygadair h. U.K.
8 E3 Pen-y-Ghent h. U.K.
20 H4 Penza Rus. Fed.
9 B7 Penzance U.K.
20 H4 Penzenskaya Oblast' div. Rus. Fed.
25 S3 Penzhino Rus. Fed.
25 S3 Penzhinskaya Guba b. Rus. Fed.
73 F5 Peoria AZ U.S.A.
68 C5 Peoria IL U.S.A.
44 B4 Perai Malaysia
44 A4 Perak i. Malaysia
44 B4 Perak r. Malaysia
15 F2 Perales del Alfambra Spain
33 B4 Perambalur India
Perämeri g. see Bottenviken
59 H4 Percé Can.
71 H2 Percy U.S.A.
48 F4 Percy Is is Austr.
69 J3 Percy Reach l. Can.
15 G1 Perdido, Monte mt Spain
24 H3 Peregrebnoye Rus. Fed.
81 B3 Pereira Col.
82 B3 Pereira Barreto Brazil
20 D3 Perekhoda r. Rus. Fed.
21 G5 Perelazovskiy Rus. Fed.
68 D4 Pere Marquette r. U.S.A.
92 C6 Peremennyy, C. c. Ant.
17 M6 Peremyshlyany Ukr.
20 F3 Pereslavl'-Zalesskiy Rus. Fed.
20 H4 Perevoz Rus. Fed.
21 D5 Pereyaslav-Khmel'nyts'kyy Ukr.
83 E2 Pergamino Arg.
44 B4 Perhentian Besar i. Malaysia
6 T5 Perho Fin.
59 F3 Péribonca, Lac l. Can.
80 C2 Perico Arg.
14 E4 Périgueux France
81 B2 Perijá, Parque Nacional nat. park Venez.
81 B2 Perija, Sierra de mts Venez.
80 B7 Perito Moreno Arg.
68 D3 Perkins U.S.A.
75 H6 Perlas, Pta de pt Nic.
13 K1 Perleberg Ger.
24 G4 Perm' Rus. Fed.
20 H3 Permas Rus. Fed.
19 K3 Pernik Bulg.
12 F5 Péronne France
14 F5 Perpignan France
9 B7 Perranporth U.K.
72 D5 Perris U.S.A.
14 C2 Perros-Guirec France
67 D6 Perry FL U.S.A.
67 D5 Perry GA U.S.A.
64 E3 Perry IA U.S.A.
65 D4 Perry OK U.S.A.
70 B4 Perrysburg U.S.A.
65 C4 Perryton U.S.A.
65 F4 Perryville U.S.A.
9 E5 Pershore U.K.
Persia country see Iran
29 G2 Pertek Turkey
48 B5 Perth Austr.
69 J3 Perth Can.
10 E4 Perth U.K.
71 F4 Perth Amboy U.S.A.
71 K1 Perth-Andover Can.
20 F1 Pertominsk Rus. Fed.
14 G5 Pertuis France
7 U6 Pertunmaa Fin.
18 C4 Pertusato, Capo pt Corsica France
68 C5 Peru U.S.A.
77 C4 Peru country S. America
95 N7 Peru Basin sea feature Pac. Oc.
95 P7 Peru-Chile Trench sea feature Pac. Oc.
18 E3 Perugia Italy
82 C4 Peruíbe Brazil
12 B4 Péruwelz Belgium
20 G4 Pervomaysk Rus. Fed.
21 D5 Pervomays'k Ukr.
20 K2 Pervomayskaya Rus. Fed.
21 E6 Pervomays'ke Ukr.
20 G4 Pervomayskiy Rus. Fed.
21 F5 Pervomays'kyy Ukr.
18 E3 Pesaro Italy
72 A3 Pescadero U.S.A.
73 H4 Pescado U.S.A.
18 F3 Pescara Italy
18 F3 Pescara r. Italy
21 G6 Peschanokopskoye Rus. Fed.
44 □ Pesek, P. i. Sing.
34 B2 Peshawar Pak.
19 J4 Peshkopi Albania
19 L3 Peshtera Bulg.
68 D3 Peshtigo U.S.A.
68 C3 Peshtigo r. U.S.A.
31 F2 Peski Turkm.
18 F1 Pesnica Slovenia
14 D4 Pessac France
13 L2 Pessin Ger.
20 E3 Pestovo Rus. Fed.
20 G4 Pet r. Rus. Fed.
28 E5 Petah Tiqwa Israel
19 L5 Petalioi i. Greece
72 A2 Petaluma U.S.A.
12 D5 Pétange Lux.
45 E3 Petangis Indon.
81 D2 Petare Venez.
74 D5 Petatlán Mex.
89 D5 Petauke Zambia
69 J3 Petawawa Can.
68 C3 Petenwell Lake l. U.S.A.
50 B2 Peterborough S.A. Austr.
50 D5 Peterborough Vic. Austr.
69 H3 Peterborough Can.
9 G5 Peterborough U.K.
10 F3 Peterculter U.K.
10 G3 Peterhead U.K.
92 A3 Peter I Øy i. Ant.
57 L2 Peter Lake l. Can.
8 F3 Peterlee U.K.
48 C4 Petermann Ranges mts Austr.
83 B2 Peteroa, Vol. volc. Chile
57 H3 Peter Pond L. l. Can.
13 H4 Petersberg Ger.
56 C3 Petersburg AK U.S.A.
68 C6 Petersburg IL U.S.A.
70 E6 Petersburg VA U.S.A.
70 D5 Petersburg WV U.S.A.
9 G6 Petersfield U.K.
13 G2 Petershagen Ger.
59 F2 Peters, Lac l. Can.
18 G5 Petilia Policastro Italy
58 E2 Petite Rivière de la Baleine r. Can.
59 G3 Petit Lac Manicouagan l. Can.
71 K2 Petit Manan Pt pt U.S.A.
59 J3 Petit Mécatina r. Can.
56 E3 Petitot r. Can.
74 G4 Peto Mex.
68 E3 Petoskey U.S.A.
28 E6 Petra Jordan
36 F2 Petra Velikogo, Zaliv b. Rus. Fed.
69 J4 Petre, Pt pt Can.
19 K4 Petrich Bulg.
73 H4 Petrified Forest Nat. Park U.S.A.
18 G2 Petrinja Croatia
19 K3 Petrokhanski Prokhod pass Bulg.
69 F4 Petrolia Can.
79 K5 Petrolina Brazil
21 G5 Petropavlovka Rus. Fed.
24 H4 Petropavlovsk Kazak.
36 H1 Petropavlovsk-Kamchatskiy Rus. Fed.
19 K2 Petroşani Romania
21 H4 Petrovsk Rus. Fed.
36 C1 Petrovsk-Zabaykal'skiy Rus. Fed.
21 H5 Petrov Val Rus. Fed.
20 E2 Petrozavodsk Rus. Fed.
91 F4 Petrusburg S. Africa
91 H3 Petrus Steyn S. Africa
90 F5 Petrusville S. Africa
12 C2 Petten Neth.
11 D3 Pettigo U.K.
24 H4 Petukhovo Rus. Fed.
44 A4 Peureula Indon.
25 T3 Pevek Rus. Fed.
16 H6 Pezinok Slovakia
13 F5 Pfälzer Wald forest Ger.
13 G6 Pforzheim Ger.
16 D7 Pfullendorf Ger.
13 G5 Pfungstadt Ger.
34 C3 Phagwara India
91 G4 Phahameng Free State S. Africa
91 H2 Phahameng Northern Province S. Africa
91 J1 Phalaborwa S. Africa
34 C4 Phalodi India
34 B4 Phalsund India
33 A2 Phaltan India
44 A3 Phangnga Thai.
44 D3 Phan Rang Vietnam
44 D3 Phan Ri Vietnam
44 D3 Phan Thiêt Vietnam
65 D7 Pharr U.S.A.
39 C6 Phat Diêm Vietnam
44 B4 Phatthalung Thai.
35 H4 Phek India
57 J3 Phelps Lake l. Can.
44 B1 Phen Thai.
67 C5 Phenix City U.S.A.
44 A2 Phet Buri Thai.
44 C2 Phiafai Laos
65 F5 Philadelphia MS U.S.A.
71 F2 Philadelphia NY U.S.A.
71 F5 Philadelphia PA U.S.A.
71 F4 Philadelphia airport PA U.S.A.
64 C2 Philip U.S.A.
12 C4 Philippeville Belgium
70 C5 Philippi U.S.A.
12 B3 Philippine Neth.
23 M8 Philippines country Asia
43 C2 Philippine Sea sea Phil.
94 D5 Philippine Trench sea feature Pac. Oc.
91 F5 Philippolis S. Africa
13 G5 Philippsburg Ger.
70 D4 Philipsburg U.S.A.
12 C3 Philipsdam barrage Neth.
54 D3 Philip Smith Mts U.S.A.
90 F5 Philipstown S. Africa
50 E5 Phillip I. i. Austr.
71 H2 Phillips ME U.S.A.
68 B3 Phillips WV U.S.A.
64 D4 Phillipsburg KS U.S.A.
71 F4 Phillipsburg NJ U.S.A.
55 J1 Phillips Inlet in. Can.
70 D4 Phillipston U.S.A.
71 G3 Philmont U.S.A.
57 G3 Philomena Can.
70 C6 Philpott Reservoir U.S.A.
44 B2 Phimae Thai.
44 C2 Phimun Mangsahan Thai.
91 G3 Phiritona S. Africa
Phnom Penh see Phnum Penh
44 C2 Phnum Aôral mt Cambodia
44 C3 Phnum Penh Cambodia
73 F5 Phoenix U.S.A.
49 J2 Phoenix Islands is Pac. Oc.
91 G3 Phomolong S. Africa
37 C4 Phôngsali Laos
39 B6 Phong Thô Vietnam
44 B1 Phon Phisai Thai.
44 B1 Phou Bia mt Laos
44 C1 Phou Cô Pi mt Laos/Vietnam
39 B6 Phou Sam Sao mts Laos/Vietnam
44 A1 Phrao Thai.
44 B2 Phra Phutthabat Thai.
39 B6 Phuc Yên Vietnam
44 D2 Phu Hôi Vietnam
44 A4 Phuket Thai.
34 C4 Phulera India
35 G5 Phultala Bangl.
39 B6 Phu Ly Vietnam
44 B2 Phumĭ Bânhchok Kon Cambodia
44 C3 Phumĭ Chhuk Cambodia
44 C2 Phumĭ Kâmpóng Trâlach Cambodia
44 B3 Phumĭ Kaôh Kŏng Cambodia
44 B2 Phumĭ Kiliĕk Cambodia
44 C2 Phumĭ Mlu Prey Cambodia
44 B2 Phumĭ Moŭng Cambodia
44 B2 Phumĭ Prâmaôy Cambodia
44 B2 Phumĭ Sâmraông Cambodia
44 C2 Phumĭ Toêng Cambodia
44 D2 Phu My Vietnam
44 D2 Phu Nhơn Vietnam
44 C3 Phước Long Vietnam
44 C3 Phu Quôc Vietnam
91 H4 Phuthaditjhaba S. Africa
39 B6 Phư Tho Vietnam
44 B1 Phu Wiang Thai.
79 J5 Piaca Brazil
18 C2 Piacenza Italy
38 D2 Pianguan China
18 D3 Pianosa, Isola i. Italy
17 N7 Piatra Neamţ Romania
79 K5 Piauí r. Brazil
18 E1 Piave r. Italy
87 F4 Pibor r. Sudan
87 F4 Pibor Post Sudan
68 D1 Pic r. Can.
73 F4 Pica U.S.A.
73 G5 Picacho AZ U.S.A.
73 E5 Picacho CA U.S.A.
14 F2 Picardie reg. France
67 B6 Picayune U.S.A.
80 D2 Pichanal Arg.
83 C2 Pichi Ciego Arg.
83 B2 Pichilemu Chile
60 D7 Pichilingue Mex.
83 D3 Pichi Mahuida Arg.
34 D4 Pichor India
68 D1 Pic, I. i. Can.
8 G3 Pickering U.K.
8 G3 Pickering, Vale of v. U.K.
68 E2 Pickford U.S.A.
58 B3 Pickle Lake Can.
81 C2 Pico Bolívar mt Venez.
81 D4 Pico da Neblina mt Brazil
81 D4 Pico da Neblina, Parque Nacional do nat. park Brazil
75 K5 Pico Duarte mt Dom. Rep.
81 E4 Pico Redondo summit Brazil
81 E4 Pico Rondon summit Brazil
79 K5 Picos Brazil
80 C7 Pico Truncado Arg.
68 D1 Pic River Can.
50 H3 Picton Austr.
69 J4 Picton Can.
59 H4 Pictou Can.
68 D2 Pictured Rocks National Lakeshore res. U.S.A.
83 C3 Picún Leufú r. Arg.
31 F5 Pidarak Pak.
33 C5 Pidurutalagala mt Sri Lanka
81 B3 Piedecuesta Col.
83 C1 Pie de Palo, Sa mts Arg.
67 C5 Piedmont U.S.A.
70 C4 Piedmont Lake l. U.S.A.
74 D3 Piedras Negras Coahuila Mex.
83 F2 Piedras, Punta pt Arg.
78 D6 Piedras, Río de las r. Peru
68 C1 Pie Island i. Can.
6 U5 Pieksämäki Fin.
6 U5 Pielavesi Fin.
6 V5 Pielinen l. Fin.
91 H2 Pienaarsrivier S. Africa
68 E5 Pierceton U.S.A.
72 A2 Piercy U.S.A.
19 K4 Pieria mts Greece
10 F1 Pierowall U.K.
64 C2 Pierre U.S.A.
14 G4 Pierrelatte France
91 J4 Pietermaritzburg S. Africa
91 H1 Pietersburg S. Africa
18 G5 Pietra Spada, Passo di Italy
91 J3 Piet Retief S. Africa
17 M7 Pietrosa mt Romania
69 F4 Pigeon U.S.A.
69 F5 Pigeon Bay b. Can.
70 D6 Pigg r. U.S.A.
65 F4 Piggott U.S.A.
91 J2 Pigg's Peak Swaziland
83 D3 Pigüé Arg.
34 E4 Pihani India
38 E3 Pi He r. China
7 V6 Pihlajavesi l. Fin.
7 R6 Pihlava Fin.
6 T5 Pihtipudas Fin.
6 T4 Piippola Fin.
6 V4 Piispajärvi Fin.
74 F5 Pijijiapan Mex.
20 E3 Pikalevo Rus. Fed.
70 D3 Pike U.S.A.
69 G3 Pike Bay Can.
46 F3 Pikelot i. Micronesia
90 C6 Piketberg S. Africa
70 B6 Pikeville U.S.A.
42 B4 Pikou China
83 E3 Pila Arg.
16 H4 Piła Pol.
91 G2 Pilanesberg National Park S. Africa
83 E2 Pilar Arg.
80 E3 Pilar Para.
43 B5 Pilas i. Phil.
83 B4 Pilcaniyeu Arg.
80 E2 Pilcomayo r. Bol./Para.
43 B3 Pili Phil.
34 D3 Pilibhit India
39 □ Pillar Pt pt H.K. China
83 E2 Pillo, Isla del i. Arg.
82 C2 Pilões, Serra dos mts Brazil
72 D2 Pilot Peak summit U.S.A.
50 G4 Pilot, The mt Austr.
65 F6 Pilottown U.S.A.
7 R8 Piltene Latvia
78 F6 Pimenta Bueno Brazil
34 C5 Pimpalner India
34 D2 Pin r. India
73 F6 Pinacate, Cerro del summit Mex.

13 K4 Pößneck Ger.
65 C5 Post U.S.A.
58 E2 Poste-de-la-Baleine Can.
90 E4 Postmasburg S. Africa
59 J3 Postville Can.
68 B4 Postville U.S.A.
18 G3 Posušje Bos.-Herz.
40 B3 Pos'yet Rus. Fed.
91 G3 Potchefstroom S. Africa
65 E5 Poteau U.S.A.
79 L5 Potengi r. Brazil
18 F4 Potenza Italy
51 A7 Poteriteri, L. l. N.Z.
90 F5 Potfontein S. Africa
91 H2 Potgietersrus S. Africa
65 D6 Poth U.S.A.
58 F2 Potherie, Lac La l. Can.
21 G7 P'ot'i Georgia
79 K5 Poti r. Brazil
33 C2 Potikal India
86 D3 Potiskum Nigeria
62 D2 Pot Mt. mt U.S.A.
70 E5 Potomac r. U.S.A.
70 D5 Potomac South Branch r. U.S.A.
78 E7 Potosí Bol.
64 F4 Potosi U.S.A.
73 E4 Potosi Mt mt U.S.A.
43 B4 Pototan Phil.
13 M2 Potsdam Ger.
71 F2 Potsdam U.S.A.
9 E6 Potterne U.K.
9 G6 Potters Bar U.K.
71 F4 Pottstown U.S.A.
71 E4 Pottsville U.S.A.
33 C5 Pottuvil Sri Lanka
56 E3 Pouce Coupe Can.
59 K4 Pouch Cove Can.
71 G4 Poughkeepsie U.S.A.
71 G3 Poultney U.S.A.
8 E4 Poulton-le-Fylde U.K.
44 B1 Pou San mt Laos
82 D3 Pouso Alegre Brazil
44 B2 Poŭthĭsăt Cambodia
17 J6 Považská Bystrica Slovakia
20 E2 Povenets Rus. Fed.
51 F3 Poverty Bay b. N.Z.
19 H2 Povlen mt Yugo.
21 B2 Póvoa de Varzim Port.
21 G5 Povorino Rus. Fed.
40 C3 Povorotnyy, Mys hd Rus. Fed.
72 D5 Poway U.S.A.
62 F2 Powder r. U.S.A.
62 F3 Powder River U.S.A.
62 E2 Powell U.S.A.
70 B6 Powell r. U.S.A.
73 G3 Powell, Lake resr U.S.A.
72 C2 Powell Mt mt U.S.A.
67 E7 Powell Pt pt Bahamas
56 E5 Powell River Can.
68 D3 Powers U.S.A.
70 E6 Powhatan U.S.A.
82 A1 Poxoréu Brazil
39 E4 Poyang Hu l. China
44 □ Poyan Res. resr Sing.
68 C3 Poygan, Lake l. U.S.A.
28 E3 Pozantı Turkey
19 J2 Požarevac Yugo.
74 E4 Poza Rica Mex.
18 G2 Požega Croatia
19 J3 Požega Yugo.
40 D1 Pozharskoye Rus. Fed.
16 H4 Poznań Pol.
15 D3 Pozoblanco Spain
18 F4 Pozzuoli Italy
45 B3 Prabumulih Indon.
16 G6 Prachatice Czech Rep.
35 F6 Prachi r. India
44 B2 Prachin Buri Thai.
44 A3 Prachuap Khiri Khan Thai.
14 F5 Prades France
82 E2 Prado Brazil
16 G5 Prague Czech Rep.
Praha see Prague
86 □ Praia Cape Verde
91 K2 Praia do Bilene Moz.
82 A1 Praia Rica Brazil
68 E5 Prairie Creek Reservoir U.S.A.
65 C5 Prairie Dog Town Fork r. U.S.A.
68 B4 Prairie du Chien U.S.A.
44 B2 Prakhon Chai Thai.
44 B2 Pran r. Thai.
33 B2 Pranhita r. India
45 A2 Prapat Indon.
19 M7 Prasonisi, Akra pt Greece
82 C2 Prata Brazil
82 C2 Prata r. Brazil
18 D3 Prato Italy
65 D4 Pratt U.S.A.
65 G5 Prattville U.S.A.
33 A2 Pravara r. India
17 K3 Pravdinsk Rus. Fed.
45 E4 Praya Indon.
44 C2 Preăh Vihear Cambodia
17 Q3 Prechistoye Rus. Fed.
57 J4 Preeceville Can.
20 B4 Pregolya r. Rus. Fed.
7 U8 Preiļi Latvia
69 H1 Preissac, Lac l. Can.
44 C3 Prêk Tnaôt l. Cambodia
50 G1 Premer Austr.
14 F3 Prémery France
13 L2 Premnitz Ger.
68 B3 Prentice U.S.A.
16 F4 Prenzlau Ger.
40 C3 Preobrazheniye Rus. Fed.
16 H6 Přerov Czech Rep.
71 F2 Prescott Can.
73 F4 Prescott U.S.A.
73 F4 Prescott Valley U.S.A.
19 J3 Preševo Yugo.
64 C3 Presho U.S.A.
80 D3 Presidencia Roque Sáenz Peña Arg.
79 K5 Presidente Dutra Brazil
82 B3 Presidente Epitácio Brazil
78 F6 Presidente Hermes Brazil
82 B3 Presidente Prudente Brazil
82 B3 Presidente Venceslau Brazil
65 B6 Presidio U.S.A.
19 M3 Preslav Bulg.
17 K6 Prešov Slovakia
19 J4 Prespa, Lake l. Europe
71 K1 Presque Isle U.S.A.
68 D2 Presque Isle Pt pt U.S.A.
9 D5 Presteigne U.K.
8 E4 Preston U.K.
62 E3 Preston ID U.S.A.
68 A4 Preston MN U.S.A.
65 E4 Preston MO U.S.A.
73 E2 Preston NV U.S.A.
10 F5 Prestonpans U.K.
70 B6 Prestonsburg U.S.A.
10 D5 Prestwick U.K.
82 E1 Preto r. Bahia Brazil
82 C2 Preto r. Minas Gerais Brazil
91 H2 Pretoria S. Africa
70 E5 Prettyboy Lake l. U.S.A.
13 L3 Pretzsch Ger.
19 J5 Preveza Greece
44 C3 Prey Vêng Cambodia
25 V4 Pribilof Islands is U.S.A.
19 H3 Priboj Yugo.
59 G4 Price Can.
73 G2 Price U.S.A.
56 D4 Price I. i. Can.
67 B6 Prichard U.S.A.
7 R8 Priekule Latvia
7 T8 Priekuļi Latvia
7 S9 Prienai Lith.
90 E4 Prieska S. Africa
62 C1 Priest L. l. U.S.A.
62 C1 Priest River U.S.A.
17 J6 Prievidza Slovakia
13 L1 Prignitz reg. Ger.
18 G2 Prijedor Bos.-Herz.
19 H3 Prijepolje Yugo.
24 F5 Prikaspiyskaya Nizmennost' lowland Kazak./Rus. Fed.
19 J4 Prilep Macedonia
13 L5 Přimda Czech Rep.
83 D1 Primero r. Arg.
7 V6 Primorsk Rus. Fed.
40 C2 Primorskiy Kray div. Rus. Fed.
21 F6 Primorsko-Akhtarsk Rus. Fed.
57 H4 Primrose Lake l. Can.
57 H4 Prince Albert Can.
90 E6 Prince Albert S. Africa
92 B5 Prince Albert Mts mts Ant.
57 H4 Prince Albert National Park Can.
54 G2 Prince Albert Peninsula Can.
90 D6 Prince Albert Road S. Africa
54 G2 Prince Albert Sound chan. Can.
54 F2 Prince Alfred, C. c. Can.
55 L3 Prince Charles I. Can.
92 D4 Prince Charles Mts mts Ant.
59 H4 Prince Edward Island div. Can.
93 G7 Prince Edward Islands is Ind. Ocean
69 J4 Prince Edward Pt pt Can.
70 E5 Prince Frederick U.S.A.
56 E4 Prince George Can.
54 B3 Prince of Wales, Cape c. U.S.A.
55 J2 Prince of Wales I. N.W.T. Can.
48 E3 Prince of Wales I. i. Austr.
56 C3 Prince of Wales Island i. U.S.A.
54 G2 Prince of Wales Strait chan. Can.
54 F2 Prince Patrick I. i. Can.
55 J2 Prince Regent Inlet chan. Can.
56 C4 Prince Rupert Can.
57 K2 Princess Mary Lake l. Can.
71 F5 Princess Anne U.S.A.
92 D3 Princess Astrid Coast coastal area Ant.
48 E3 Princess Charlotte Bay b. Austr.
92 D5 Princess Elizabeth Land reg. Ant.
92 D3 Princess Ragnhild Coast coastal area Ant.
56 D4 Princess Royal I. i. Can.
56 E5 Princeton Can.
72 A2 Princeton CA U.S.A.
68 C5 Princeton IL U.S.A.
66 C4 Princeton IN U.S.A.
66 C4 Princeton KY U.S.A.
71 K2 Princeton ME U.S.A.
64 E3 Princeton MO U.S.A.
71 F4 Princeton NJ U.S.A.
70 C6 Princeton WV U.S.A.
68 C4 Princeton WV U.S.A.
71 K2 Prince William Can.
54 D3 Prince William Sound b. U.S.A.
86 C4 Príncipe i. Sao Tome and Principe
62 B2 Prineville U.S.A.
24 C2 Prins Karls Forland i. Svalbard
75 H6 Prinzapolca Nic.
20 D2 Priozersk Rus. Fed.
Pripet r. see Prypʺyat
6 W2 Prirechnyy Rus. Fed.
19 J3 Priština Yugo.
13 K1 Pritzier Ger.
13 L1 Pritzwalk Ger.
14 G4 Privas France
18 F2 Privlaka Croatia
20 G3 Privolzhsk Rus. Fed.
20 H4 Privolzhskaya Vozvyshennost' reg. Rus. Fed.
21 G6 Priyutnoye Rus. Fed.
19 J3 Prizren Yugo.
45 D4 Probolinggo Indon.
13 K4 Probstzella Ger.
9 C7 Probus U.K.
68 A2 Proctor MN U.S.A.
71 G3 Proctor VT U.S.A.
79 G3 Professor van Blommestein Meer resr Suriname
74 G5 Progreso Honduras
65 C7 Progreso Coahuila Mex.
74 G4 Progreso Yucatán Mex.
21 H7 Prokhladnyy Rus. Fed.
24 K4 Prokop'yevsk Rus. Fed.
19 J3 Prokuplje Yugo.
20 D3 Proletariy Rus. Fed.
21 G6 Proletarsk Rus. Fed.
82 A2 Promissão Brazil
54 F4 Prophet r. Can.
56 E3 Prophet River Can.
68 C5 Prophetstown U.S.A.
48 E4 Proserpine Austr.
71 F3 Prospect U.S.A.
43 C4 Prosperidad Phil.
90 D7 Protem S. Africa
68 A4 Protivin U.S.A.
19 M3 Provadiya Bulg.
Prøven see Kangersuatsiaq
14 H5 Provence reg. France
71 H4 Providence U.S.A.
69 F3 Providence Bay Can.
51 A7 Providence, Cape c. N.Z.
65 F5 Providence, Lake U.S.A.
78 B1 Providencia, Isla de i. Col.
54 A3 Provideniya Rus. Fed.
71 H3 Provincetown U.S.A.
73 G1 Provo U.S.A.
57 G4 Provost Can.
82 B4 Prudentópolis Brazil
54 D2 Prudhoe Bay U.S.A.
12 E4 Prüm Ger.
12 E4 Prüm r. Ger.
18 C3 Prunelli-di-Fiumorbo Corsica France
17 K4 Pruszków Pol.
21 D6 Prut r. Moldova/Romania
92 D5 Prydz Bay b. Ant.
21 E5 Pryluky Ukr.
21 F6 Prymors'k Ukr.
61 G4 Pryor OK U.S.A.
17 M5 Prypʺyat r. Ukr.
17 N4 Prypyats' r. Belarus
17 L6 Przemyśl Pol.
19 L5 Psara i. Greece
21 G6 Psebay Rus. Fed.
21 F6 Pshish r. Rus. Fed.
20 D3 Pskov Rus. Fed.
7 U7 Pskov, Lake l. Estonia/Rus. Fed.
20 D3 Pskovskaya Oblast' div. Rus. Fed.
19 J4 Ptolemaïda Greece
18 F1 Ptuj Slovenia
38 C3 Pu r. China
83 D3 Puán Arg.
39 B5 Pu'an China
42 D6 Puan S. Korea
39 C6 Pubei China
78 D5 Pucallpa Peru
39 F5 Pucheng Fujian China
38 C3 Pucheng Shaanxi China
20 G3 Puchezh Rus. Fed.
42 D5 Puch'ŏn S. Korea
43 B4 Pucio Pt pt Phil.
16 J3 Puck Pol.
68 C4 Puckaway Lake l. U.S.A.
83 B3 Pucón Chile
Pudai watercourse see Dor
30 D3 Pūdanū Iran
6 U4 Pudasjärvi Fin.
90 F3 Pudimoe S. Africa
20 F2 Pudozh Rus. Fed.
8 F4 Pudsey U.K.
Puduchcheri see Pondicherry
33 B4 Pudukkottai India
74 E5 Puebla Mex.
15 C1 Puebla de Sanabria Spain
63 F4 Pueblo U.S.A.
82 C2 Pueblo Nuevo Venez.
83 D3 Puelches Arg.
83 C3 Puelén Arg.
83 B2 Puente Alto Chile
15 D4 Puente-Genil Spain
81 C2 Puente Torres Venez.
78 F6 Puerto Alegre Bol.
74 E5 Puerto Angel Mex.
75 H7 Puerto Armuelles Panama
81 A4 Puerto Asís Col.
81 D3 Puerto Ayacucho Venez.
74 G5 Puerto Barrios Guatemala
81 B3 Puerto Berrío Col.
81 C2 Puerto Cabello Venez.
75 H6 Puerto Cabezas Nic.
81 D3 Puerto Carreño Col.
80 E2 Puerto Casado Para.
80 B6 Puerto Cisnes Chile
80 C8 Puerto Coig Arg.
75 H7 Puerto Cortés Costa Rica
81 C2 Puerto Cumarebo Venez.
74 E5 Puerto Escondido Mex.
81 C1 Puerto Estrella Col.
78 F6 Puerto Frey Bol.
80 E2 Puerto Guarani Para.
78 E6 Puerto Heath Bol.
81 D4 Puerto Inírida Col.
79 G7 Puerto Isabel Bol.
81 D2 Puerto La Cruz Venez.
78 D4 Puerto Leguízamo Col.
15 D3 Puertollano Spain
83 D4 Puerto Lobos Arg.
81 B3 Puerto Lopéz Col.
83 D4 Puerto Madryn Arg.
78 E6 Puerto Maldonado Peru
78 B4 Puerto Máncora Peru
82 A4 Puerto Mendes Para.
81 D3 Puerto Miranda Venez.
83 B4 Puerto Montt Chile
80 B8 Puerto Natáles Chile
81 C3 Puerto Nuevo Col.
81 A2 Puerto Obaldia Panama
81 E2 Puerto Ordaz Venez.
81 D3 Puerto Páez Venez.
80 E2 Puerto Pinasco Para.
83 D4 Puerto Pirámides Arg.
75 K5 Puerto Plata Dom. Rep.
78 D5 Puerto Portillo Peru
43 A4 Puerto Princesa Phil.
81 A2 Puerto Rey Col.
53 K8 Puerto Rico terr. Caribbean Sea
92 E4 Puerto Rico Trench sea feature Atl. Ocean
80 E2 Puerto Sastre Para.
81 A4 Puerto Tejado Col.
74 C4 Puerto Vallarta Mex.
83 B4 Puerto Varas Chile
21 J4 Pugachev Rus. Fed.
34 C3 Pugal India
39 B5 Puge China
30 D5 Pūhāl-e Khamīr, Kūh-e mts Iran
15 H3 Puig Major mt Spain
15 H1 Puigmal mt France/Spain
39 □ Pui O Wan b. H.K. China
39 F4 Pujiang China
42 D3 Pujŏn Reservoir N. Korea
42 E3 Pujonryong Sanmaek mts N. Korea
51 C6 Pukaki, Lake l. N.Z.
47 O5 Pukapuka atoll Fr. Polynesia Pac. Oc.
68 E1 Pukaskwa r. Can.
68 E1 Pukaskwa National Park Can.
57 J3 Pukatawagan Can.
42 C3 Pukchin N. Korea
42 E3 Pukch'ŏng N. Korea
51 E2 Pukekohe N.Z.
51 D5 Puketeraki Ra. mts N.Z.
51 F4 Puketoi Range h. N.Z.
51 C6 Pukeuri Junction N.Z.
17 P3 Pukhnovo Rus. Fed.
20 G2 Puksoozero Rus. Fed.
42 D3 Puksubaek-san mt N. Korea
18 E2 Pula Croatia
78 E8 Pulacayo Bol.
42 A4 Pulandian Wan b. China
43 C5 Pulangi r. Phil.
71 E3 Pulaski NY U.S.A.
67 C5 Pulaski TN U.S.A.
70 C6 Pulaski VA U.S.A.
68 C3 Pulaski WV U.S.A.
17 K5 Puławy Pol.
12 E3 Pulheim Ger.
33 C3 Pulicat L. b. India
33 B3 Pulivendla India
33 B4 Puliyangudi India
6 T4 Pulkkila Fin.
62 C2 Pullman U.S.A.
6 X2 Pulozero Rus. Fed.
34 E1 Pulu China
29 G2 Pülümür Turkey
43 C5 Pulutan Indon.
35 G3 Puma Yumco l. China
78 B4 Puná, Isla i. Ecuador
35 G4 Punakha Bhutan
34 C2 Punch Jammu and Kashmir
56 E4 Punchaw Can.
35 G3 Püncogling China
91 J1 Punda Maria S. Africa
34 D3 Pundri India
33 A2 Pune India
44 □ Punggol Sing.
42 E3 P'ungsan N. Korea
89 D5 Púnguè r. Moz.
88 C4 Punia Congo(Zaire)
83 B1 Punitaqui Chile
34 C3 Punjab div. India
34 B3 Punjab div. Pak.
34 D2 Punmah Gl. gl. China/Jammu and Kashmir
35 F4 Punpun r. India
83 D3 Punta Alta Arg.
80 B8 Punta Arenas Chile
18 C4 Punta Balestrieri mt Italy
75 L5 Punta, Cerro de mt Puerto Rico
83 D4 Punta Delgada Arg.
74 G5 Punta Gorda Belize
67 D7 Punta Gorda U.S.A.
83 D4 Punta Norte Arg.
75 H6 Puntarenas Costa Rica
81 C2 Punto Fijo Venez.
70 D4 Punxsutawney U.S.A.
6 U4 Puokio Fin.
6 U4 Puolanka Fin.
39 D4 Puqi China
30 E5 Pūr Iran
24 J3 Pur r. Rus. Fed.
81 A4 Puracé, Parque Nacional nat. park Col.
81 A4 Purace, Volcán de volc. Col.
65 D5 Purcell U.S.A.
56 F4 Purcell Mts mts Can.
83 B3 Purén Chile
63 G4 Purgatoire r. U.S.A.
35 F6 Puri India
12 C2 Purmerend Neth.
33 B2 Purna India
34 D5 Purna r. Maharashtra India
34 D6 Purna r. Maharashtra India
33 B1 Purna r. India
34 G4 Purnabhaba r. India
35 F4 Pūrnia India
83 B4 Purranque Chile
35 F5 Puruliya India
78 F4 Purus r. Brazil
7 V6 Puruvesi l. Fin.
45 C4 Purwakarta Indon.
45 D4 Purwodadi Indon.
45 C4 Purwokerto Indon.
42 E2 Puryŏng N. Korea
34 D6 Pus r. India
34 D6 Pusad India
42 E6 Pusan S. Korea
71 J2 Pushaw Lake l. U.S.A.
20 H2 Pushemskiy Rus. Fed.
34 C4 Pushkar India
20 D3 Pushkin Rus. Fed.
21 H5 Pushkino Rus. Fed.
20 D3 Pushkinskiye Gory Rus. Fed.
31 F4 Pusht-i-Rud reg. Afgh.
17 O2 Pustoshka Rus. Fed.
17 L4 Puszcza Augustowska forest Pol.
16 G4 Puszcza Natecka forest Pol.
36 B4 Putao Myanmar
39 F5 Putian China
45 D3 Puting, Tanjung pt Indon.
31 G4 Putla Khan Afgh.
13 L1 Putlitz Ger.
19 M2 Putna r. Romania
71 H4 Putnam U.S.A.
71 G3 Putney U.S.A.
35 H3 Putrang La pass China
90 D4 Putsonderwater S. Africa
33 B4 Puttalam Sri Lanka
33 B4 Puttalam Lagoon lag. Sri Lanka
12 E5 Puttelange-aux-Lacs France
12 D2 Putten Neth.
12 C3 Puttershoek Neth.
16 E3 Puttgarden Ger.
78 D4 Putumayo r. Col.
28 G2 Pütürge Turkey
45 D2 Putusibau Indon.
20 G4 Putyatino Rus. Fed.
21 E5 Putyvl' Ukr.
7 V6 Puumala Fin.
72 □2 Puuwai U.S.A.
58 E1 Puvurnituq Can.
62 B2 Puyallup U.S.A.
38 E3 Puyang China
83 B4 Puyehue Chile
83 B4 Puyehue, Parque Nacional nat. park Chile
14 F5 Puylaurens France
51 A7 Puysegur Pt pt N.Z.
89 C4 Pweto Congo(Zaire)
9 C5 Pwllheli U.K.
20 E2 Pyal'ma Rus. Fed.
20 H4 P'yana r. Rus. Fed.
34 B1 Pyandzh r. Afgh./Tajik.
6 W3 Pyaozero, Ozero l. Rus. Fed.
6 W4 Pyaozerskiy Rus. Fed.
24 K2 Pyasina r. Rus. Fed.
21 G6 Pyatigorsk Rus. Fed.
21 E5 P"yatykhatky Ukr.
37 B5 Pyè Myanmar
51 B7 Pye, Mt h. N.Z.
21 D4 Pyetrykaw Belarus
6 T4 Pyhäjoki Fin.
6 T4 Pyhäjoki r. Fin.
6 U4 Pyhäntä Fin.
6 T5 Pyhäsalmi Fin.
6 V5 Pyhäselkä l. Fin.
35 H5 Pyingaing Myanmar
9 D6 Pyle U.K.
24 K3 Pyl'karamo Rus. Fed.
19 J6 Pylos Greece
70 C4 Pymatuning Reservoir U.S.A.
42 C5 Pyŏksŏng N. Korea
42 C3 Pyŏktong N. Korea
42 D4 P'yŏnggang N. Korea
42 E5 P'yŏnghae S. Korea
42 C4 P'yŏngsong N. Korea
42 D5 P'yŏngt'aek S. Korea
42 C4 P'yŏngyang N. Korea
50 E4 Pyramid Hill Austr.
72 C1 Pyramid Lake l. U.S.A.
68 E3 Pyramid Pt pt U.S.A.
72 C2 Pyramid Range mts U.S.A.
Pyrénées mts see Pyrenees
4 C4 Pyrenees mts France/Spain
19 J6 Pyrgos Greece
21 E5 Pyryatyn Ukr.
16 G4 Pyrzyce Pol.
20 H3 Pyshchug Rus. Fed.
17 N2 Pytalovo Rus. Fed.
19 K5 Pyxaria mt Greece

Q

55 M2 Qaanaaq Greenland
30 D6 Qābil Oman
29 J6 Qabr Bandar Iraq
91 H5 Qacha's Nek Lesotho
29 K4 Qādir Karam Iraq
29 J4 Qadissiya Dam dam Iraq
38 C1 Qagan Ders China
38 D1 Qagan Nur China
38 C2 Qagan Nur China
42 C1 Qagan Nur l. Jilin China
38 E1 Qagan Nur l. Nei Monggol China
38 E1 Qagan Nur resr China
38 D1 Qagan Teg China
38 E1 Qagan Us China
35 H3 Qagbasêrag China
35 E2 Qagcaka China
55 O3 Qagssimiut Greenland
38 D1 Qahar Youyi Qianqi China
38 D1 Qahar Youyi Zhongqi China
36 B3 Qaidam Pendi basin China
31 G3 Qaisar Afgh.
31 G3 Qaisar, Koh-i- mt Afgh.
29 K3 Qalā Diza Iraq
31 H2 Qal'aikhum Tajik.
31 G3 Qala Shinia Takht Afgh.
31 G3 Qalāt Afgh.
30 D4 Qalat Iran
29 H4 Qal'at as Sālihīyah Syria
28 E6 Qal'at el Hasal Jordan
29 L6 Qal'at Sālih Iraq
29 L6 Qal'at Sukkar Iraq
31 F3 Qala Vali Afgh.
30 B2 Qal'eh D. mt Iran
31 F3 Qal 'eh-ye Now Afgh.
31 G4 Qal 'eh-ye Bost Afgh.
29 M5 Qal'eh-ye-Now Iran
29 K7 Qalīb Bāqūr well Iraq
28 C6 Qalyūb Egypt
91 G5 Qamata S. Africa
34 B4 Qambar Pak.
34 B3 Qamruddin Karez Pak.
30 C3 Qamşar Iran
30 B2 Qandaranbashi mt Iran
38 E1 Qangdin Sum China
29 M2 Qaraçala Azer.
29 J4 Qarachōq, J. mts Iraq
29 K4 Qara D. r. Iraq
29 H7 Qārah S. Arabia
31 H3 Qarah Bāgh Afgh.
30 A5 Qa'rah, J. al h. S. Arabia
29 L3 Qaranqu r. Iran
88 E3 Qardho Somalia
29 L3 Qar'eh Aqāj Iran
29 L2 Qareh D. mts Iran
29 L3 Qareh Dāsh, Kūh-e mt Iran
30 B2 Qareh Sū r. Iran
29 L3 Qareh Urgān, Kūh-e mt Iran
35 H1 Qarhan China
31 G2 Qarqīn Afgh.
29 K6 Qaryat al Gharab Iraq
30 B5 Qaryat al Ulyā S. Arabia
30 E3 Qasamī Iran
31 F3 Qasa Murg mts Afgh.
30 C4 Qash Qai reg. Iran
55 N3 Qasigiannguit Greenland
29 J5 Qasr al Khubbāz Iraq
30 C4 Qaşr aş Şabīyah Kuwait
28 F6 Qasr el Azraq Jordan
31 F5 Qaşr-e-Qand Iran
30 B3 Qasr-e-Shirin Iran
29 L6 Qaşr Shaqrah Iraq
28 F5 Qaţanā Syria
23 E7 Qatar country Asia
28 F6 Qatrāna Jordan
28 C7 Qaṭrâni, Gebel esc. Egypt
87 E2 Qattâra Depression depression Egypt
29 L1 Qax Azer.
31 E3 Qāyen Iran
35 H3 Qayü China
29 J4 Qayyarah Iraq
29 L2 Qazangöldağ mt Azer.
29 K1 Qazax Azer.
34 B4 Qazi Ahmad Pak.
29 M1 Qazımämmäd Azer.
30 C2 Qazvīn Iran
38 A1 Qeh China
87 F2 Qena Egypt
55 N3 Qeqertarsuatsiaat Greenland
55 N3 Qeqertarsuatsiaq i. Greenland
55 N3 Qeqertarsuup Tunua b. Greenland
30 B3 Qeshlag r. Iran
29 L4 Qeshlaq Iran
30 E5 Qeshm Iran
30 C2 Qeydār Iran
30 D5 Qeys i. Iran
30 C2 Qezel Owzan r. Iran
28 E6 Qeẓi'ot Israel
38 C3 Qian r. China
42 C1 Qian'an China
38 F2 Qian'an China
39 C5 Qiancheng China
38 F3 Qiang r. China
42 C1 Qian Gorlos China
39 D4 Qianjiang Hubei China
39 C4 Qianjiang Sichuan China
42 E1 Qianjin China
38 A4 Qianning China
42 B1 Qianqihao China
42 B3 Qian Shan mts China
39 C5 Qianxi China
38 C3 Qian Xian China
39 D5 Qianyang Hunan China
38 C3 Qianyang Shaanxi China
39 F4 Qianyang Zhejiang China
38 D2 Qiaocun China
39 B5 Qiaojia China
29 K2 Qīās Iran
30 B5 Qibā' S. Arabia
91 G4 Qibing S. Africa
39 D5 Qidong Hunan China
38 F4 Qidong Jiangsu China
35 H2 Qidukou China
27 G3 Qiemo China
38 E2 Qihe China
39 C4 Qijiang China
24 L5 Qijiaojing China
31 G4 Qila Abdullah Pak.
31 F5 Qila Ladgasht Pak.
38 E1 Qilaotu Shan mts China
31 F4 Qila Safed Pak.
34 B3 Qila Saifullah Pak.
36 B3 Qilian Shan mts China
55 P3 Qillak i. Greenland
35 G1 Qimantag mts China
39 E4 Qimen China
38 D3 Qin r. China
38 B3 Qin'an China
42 C2 Qing r. China
42 B3 Qingchengzi China
38 F2 Qingdao China
38 A2 Qinghai div. China
38 A2 Qinghai Hu salt l. China
36 B3 Qinghai Nanshan mts China
40 A1 Qinghe China
42 C3 Qinghecheng China
38 D2 Qingjian China
38 F3 Qingjiang Jiangsu China
39 E4 Qingjiang Jiangxi China
39 D4 Qing Jiang r. China
39 E5 Qingliu China
39 B5 Qinglong Guizhou China
38 F1 Qinglong Hebei China
38 F2 Qinglong r. China
39 C6 Qingping China
38 F4 Qingpu China
38 C3 Qingshui China
38 D2 Qingshuihe China
38 D2 Qingtian China
38 E2 Qing Xian China
38 D2 Qingxu China
39 E4 Qingyang Anhui China
38 C2 Qingyang Gansu China
39 D6 Qingyuan Guangdong China
39 F5 Qingyuan Zhejiang China
42 C2 Qingyuan China
39 C5 Qingzhen China
38 F2 Qinhuangdao China
38 C3 Qin Ling mts China
38 C2 Qintongxia China
38 D2 Qin Xian China
38 D3 Qinyang China
38 D2 Qinyuan China
39 C6 Qinzhou China
39 C6 Qinzhou Wan b. China
39 D7 Qionghai China
39 B4 Qionglai China
38 B4 Qionglai Shan mts China

40 H3 Rubeshibe Japan
10 C2 Rubha Coigeach pt U.K.
10 B3 Rubha Hunish pt U.K.
10 C3 Rubha Reidh pt U.K.
72 B2 Rubicon r. U.S.A.
21 F5 Rubizhne Ukr.
24 K4 Rubtsovsk Rus. Fed.
54 C3 Ruby U.S.A.
73 E1 Ruby Lake l. U.S.A.
73 E1 Ruby Mountains U.S.A.
39 D5 Rucheng China
70 D5 Ruckersville U.S.A.
30 E5 Rudan Iran
35 E4 Rudauli India
31 F4 Rudbar Afgh.
29 M3 Rūdbār Iran
30 E2 Rūd-e Kāl-Shūr r. Iran
31 E4 Rūd-i-Shur watercourse Iran
7 M9 Rudkøbing Denmark
36 F2 Rudnaya Pristan' Rus. Fed.
20 K3 Rudnichnyy Rus. Fed.
20 D4 Rudnya Rus. Fed.
26 E1 Rudnyy Kazak.
40 D2 Rudnyy Rus. Fed.
24 G1 Rudolfa, O. i. Rus. Fed.
13 K4 Rudolstadt Ger.
38 F3 Rudong China
30 C2 Rūdsar Iran
68 E2 Rudyard U.S.A.
89 D4 Rufiji r. Tanz.
83 D2 Rufino Arg.
86 A3 Rufisque Senegal
89 C5 Rufunsa Zambia
38 F3 Rugao China
9 F5 Rugby U.K.
64 C1 Rugby U.S.A.
9 F5 Rugeley U.K.
16 F3 Rügen i. Ger.
70 B4 Ruggles U.S.A.
13 J5 Rügland Ger.
30 B5 Ruḩayyat al Ḩamr'ā' waterhole S. Arabia
88 C4 Ruhengeri Rwanda
7 S8 Ruhnu i. Estonia
12 E4 Ruhr r. Ger.
39 F5 Rui'an China
73 F5 Ruidoso U.S.A.
39 E5 Ruijin China
57 N2 Ruin Point pt Can.
89 D4 Ruipa Tanz.
81 B3 Ruiz, Nevado del volc. Col.
7 T8 Rūjiena Latvia
30 C5 Rukbah well S. Arabia
35 E3 Rukumkot Nepal
88 D4 Rukwa, Lake l. Tanz.
30 E5 Rūl Ḑadnah U.A.E.
31 E3 Rūm Iran
10 B4 Rum i. Scot. U.K.
19 H2 Ruma Yugo.
30 B5 Rumāh S. Arabia
87 E4 Rumbek Sudan
67 F7 Rum Cay i. Bahamas
71 H2 Rumford U.S.A.
14 G4 Rumilly France
48 D3 Rum Jungle Austr.
40 G3 Rumoi Japan
38 E3 Runan China
51 C5 Runanga N.Z.
51 F2 Runaway, Cape c. N.Z.
9 E4 Runcorn U.K.
89 B5 Rundu Namibia
6 Q5 Rundvik Sweden
38 E3 Runheji China
38 A3 Ru'nying China
7 V6 Ruokolahti Fin.
36 A3 Ruoqiang China
35 H4 Rupa India
83 B4 Rupanco, L. l. Chile
50 D4 Rupanyup Austr.
45 B2 Rupat i. Indon.
62 D3 Rupert U.S.A.
58 E3 Rupert r. Can.
58 E3 Rupert Bay b. Can.
92 A4 Ruppert Coast coastal area Ant.
46 M6 Rurutu i. Fr. Polynesia Pac. Oc.
89 D5 Rusape Zimbabwe
19 L3 Ruse Bulg.
42 A5 Rushan China
9 G5 Rushden U.K.
68 B4 Rushford U.S.A.
68 C4 Rush Lake l. U.S.A.
35 H3 Rushon India
31 H2 Rushon Tajik.
68 B5 Rushville IL U.S.A.
64 C3 Rushville NE U.S.A.
50 E4 Rushworth Austr.
65 E6 Rusk U.S.A.
67 D7 Ruskin U.S.A.
57 J4 Russell Man. Can.
71 F2 Russell Ont. Can.
51 E1 Russell N.Z.
64 D4 Russell U.S.A.
56 F2 Russel Lake l. Can.
55 J2 Russell I. i. Can.
49 F2 Russell Is is Solomon Is
67 C4 Russellville AL U.S.A.
65 E5 Russellville AR U.S.A.
66 C4 Russellville KY U.S.A.
13 G4 Rüsselsheim Ger.
23 E3 Russian Federation country Asia/Europe
40 C3 Russkiy, Ostrov i. Rus. Fed.
29 K1 Rust'avi Georgia
91 G2 Rustenburg S. Africa
65 E5 Ruston U.S.A.
37 E7 Ruteng Indon.
73 E2 Ruth U.S.A.
13 G3 Rüthen Ger.
69 H2 Rutherglen Can.
9 D4 Ruthin U.K.
20 H3 Rutka r. Rus. Fed.
71 G3 Rutland U.S.A.
9 G5 Rutland Water resr U.K.
57 G2 Rutledge Lake l. Can.
34 D2 Rutog China
69 G2 Rutter Can.
6 T4 Ruukki Fin.
30 E5 Rū'us al Jibāl pen. Oman
89 D5 Ruvuma r. Moz./Tanz.
28 F5 Ruwayshid, Wādī watercourse Jordan
30 D5 Ruweis U.A.E.
39 D5 Ruyuan China
26 E1 Ruzayevka Kazak.
20 H4 Ruzayevka Rus. Fed.
17 J6 Ružomberok Slovakia
85 F6 Rwanda country Africa
30 D2 Ryābād Iran
20 H2 Ryadovo Rus. Fed.
10 C5 Ryan, Loch b. U.K.
20 F4 Ryazan' Rus. Fed.
20 G4 Ryazanskaya Oblast' div. Rus. Fed.
20 G4 Ryazhsk Rus. Fed.
24 E2 Rybachiy, Poluostrov pen. Rus. Fed.
20 F3 Rybinsk Rus. Fed.
20 F3 Rybinskoye Vdkhr. resr Rus. Fed.
20 J4 Rybnaya Sloboda Rus. Fed.
17 J5 Rybnik Pol.
20 F4 Rybnoye Rus. Fed.
56 F3 Rycroft Can.
7 O8 Ryd Sweden
92 B3 Rydberg Pen. pen. Ant.
9 F7 Ryde U.K.
9 H7 Rye U.K.
8 G3 Rye r. U.K.
21 E5 Ryl'sk Rus. Fed.
50 G2 Rylstone Austr.
42 D5 Ryoju S. Korea
41 F5 Ryōtsu Japan
17 L5 Rzeszów Pol.
21 G4 Rzhaksa Rus. Fed.
20 E3 Rzhev Rus. Fed.

S

30 E3 Sa'ābād Iran
30 D4 Sa'ādatābād Iran
30 D4 Sa'ādatābād Iran
13 K6 Saal an der Donau Ger.
13 K3 Saale r. Ger.
13 K4 Saalfeld Ger.
12 E5 Saar r. Ger.
12 E5 Saarbrücken Ger.
7 S7 Saaremaa i. Estonia
6 T3 Saarenkylä Fin.
12 E5 Saargau reg. Ger.
6 T5 Saarijärvi Fin.
6 U3 Saari-Kämä Fin.
6 R2 Saarikoski Fin.
12 E5 Saarland div. Ger.
12 E5 Saarlouis Ger.
29 M2 Saatlı Azer.
83 D3 Saavedra Arg.
28 F5 Şab' Ābār Syria
19 H2 Šabac Yugo.
15 H2 Sabadell Spain
41 E7 Sabae Japan
45 E1 Sabah div. Malaysia
44 B5 Sabak Malaysia
45 E4 Sabalana, Kep. is Indon.
34 D4 Sabalgarh India
75 H4 Sabana, Arch. de is Cuba
81 B2 Sabanalarga Col.
28 D1 Şabanözü Turkey
82 D2 Sabará Brazil
33 C2 Sābari r. India
34 C5 Sabarmati r. India
18 E4 Sabaudia Italy
31 E3 Sabeh Iran
90 E5 Sabelo S. Africa
87 D2 Sabhā Libya
30 B6 Şabḩā' S. Arabia
34 D3 Sabi r. India
91 K2 Sabie Moz.
91 J2 Sabie S. Africa
91 K2 Sabie r. Moz./S. Africa
74 D3 Sabinas Mex.
74 D3 Sabinas Hidalgo Mex.
65 E6 Sabine L. l. U.S.A.
29 M1 Sabirabad Azer.
43 B3 Sablayan Phil.
67 D7 Sable, Cape c. U.S.A.
49 F3 Sable, Île de i. New Caledonia
55 N5 Sable Island i. N.S. Can.
69 F2 Sables, River aux r. Can.
92 C6 Sabrina Coast coastal area Ant.
43 B1 Sabtang i. Phil.
15 C2 Sabugal Port.
68 B4 Sabula U.S.A.
32 B6 Şabyā S. Arabia
Sabzawar see Shīndand
31 E2 Sabzevār Iran
19 N2 Sacalinul Mare, Insula i. Romania
19 L2 Săcele Romania
89 B5 Sachanga Angola
58 B3 Sachigo r. Can.
58 B3 Sachigo L. l. Can.
34 C5 Sachin India
42 E6 Sach'ŏn S. Korea
34 D2 Sach Pass India
13 L3 Sachsen div. Ger.
13 K3 Sachsen-Anhalt div. Ger.
13 H6 Sachsenheim Ger.
54 F2 Sachs Harbour Can.
71 E3 Sackets Harbor U.S.A.
13 G4 Sackpfeife h. Ger.
59 H4 Sackville Can.
71 H3 Saco ME U.S.A.
62 F1 Saco MT U.S.A.
43 B5 Sacol i. Phil.
72 B2 Sacramento U.S.A.
72 B2 Sacramento airport CA U.S.A.
72 B2 Sacramento r. U.S.A.
63 F5 Sacramento Mts mts U.S.A.
62 B3 Sacramento Valley v. U.S.A.
91 G6 Sada S. Africa
15 F1 Sádaba Spain
30 C4 Sa'dabad Iran
28 F4 Şadad Syria
44 B4 Sadao Thai.
91 J2 Saddleback pass S. Africa
44 C3 Sa Đec Vietnam
35 H3 Sadêng China
31 E5 Sadīj watercourse Iran
34 B3 Sadiqabad Pak.
34 C1 Sad Istragh mt Afgh./Pak.
29 L5 Sa'dīyah, Hawr as l. Iraq
30 D5 Sa'diyyat i. U.A.E.
30 E2 Sad-Kharv Iran
15 B3 Sado r. Port.
41 F6 Sadoga-shima i. Japan
36 F3 Sado-Shima i. Japan
15 H3 Sa Dragonera i. Spain
7 M8 Sæby Denmark
Safad see Zefat
29 L6 Safayal Maqūf well Iraq
31 H2 Safed Khirs mts Afgh.
31 G3 Safed Koh mts Afgh.
7 N7 Säffle Sweden
73 H5 Safford U.S.A.
9 H5 Saffron Walden U.K.
28 E6 Safi Jordan
86 B1 Safi Morocco
30 C2 Safīd r. Iran
30 D3 Safid Ab Iran
31 F4 Safidabeh Iran
29 M5 Safid Dasht Iran
28 F4 Şāfītā Syria
6 X2 Safonovo Murmansk. Rus. Fed.
20 E4 Safonovo Smolensk. Rus. Fed.
24 F3 Safonovo Rus. Fed.
30 A5 Safrā' al Asyāḩ esc. S. Arabia
28 D1 Safranbolu Turkey
29 L6 Safwān Iraq
35 F3 Saga China
41 B8 Saga Japan
41 F7 Sagamihara Japan
41 F7 Sagami-nada g. Japan
41 F7 Sagami-wan b. Japan
81 B3 Sagamoso r. Col.
44 A2 Saganthit Kyun i. Myanmar
33 B2 Sagar Karnataka India
33 A3 Sagar Karnataka India
34 D5 Sagar Madhya Pradesh India
21 H7 Sagarejo Georgia
35 G5 Sagar I. i. India
25 O2 Sagastyr Rus. Fed.
30 D3 Saghand Iran
31 F3 Saghar Afgh.
33 B3 Sagileru r. India
69 F4 Saginaw U.S.A.
69 F4 Saginaw Bay b. U.S.A.
59 H2 Saglek Bay b. Can.
18 C3 Sagone, Golfe de b. Corsica France
15 B4 Sagres Port.
35 H5 Sagu Myanmar
63 F4 Saguache U.S.A.
75 H4 Sagua la Grande Cuba
73 G5 Saguaro National Monument res. U.S.A.
59 F4 Saguenay r. Can.
15 F3 Sagunto-Sagunt Spain
34 C5 Sagwara India
81 B2 Sahagún Col.
15 D1 Sahagún Spain
29 L3 Sahand, Kūh-e mt Iran
84 B3 Sahara des. Africa
Saharan Atlas mts see Atlas Saharien
34 D3 Saharanpur India
35 F4 Saharsa India
34 D3 Sahaswan India
30 C6 Sahba', W. as watercourse S. Arabia
34 C3 Sahiwal Pak.
31 E3 Sahlābād Iran
29 L4 Şahneh Iran
29 K6 Şaḩrā al Ḩijārah reg. Iraq
73 G6 Sahuarita U.S.A.
44 D2 Sa Huynh Vietnam
Sahyadri mts see Western Ghats
34 C5 Sahyadriparvat Range h. India
34 E4 Sai r. India
44 B4 Sai Buri Thai.
44 B4 Sai Buri r. Thai.
Saïda see Sidon
30 D4 Sa'īdābād Iran
44 B2 Sai Dao Tai, Khao mt Thai.
31 F5 Sa'īdī Iran
35 G4 Saidpur Bangl.
34 C2 Saidu Pak.
41 C6 Saigō Japan
Saigon see Hô Chi Minh
35 H5 Saiha India
38 A1 Saihan Toroi China
41 C8 Saijō Japan
41 B8 Saiki Japan
39 □ Sai Kung H.K. China
7 V6 Saimaa l. Fin.
28 F2 Saimbeyli Turkey
30 D4 Sā'īn Iran
31 F4 Saindak Pak.
30 B2 Sa'īndezh Iran
10 F5 St Abb's Head hd U.K.
9 B7 St Agnes U.K.
9 A8 St Agnes i. U.K.
59 J4 St Alban's Can.
9 G6 St Albans U.K.
71 G2 St Albans VT U.S.A.
70 C5 St Albans WV U.S.A.
9 E7 St Alban's Head hd U.K.
56 G4 St Albert Can.
12 B4 St-Amand-les-Eaux France
14 F3 St-Amand-Montrond France
14 G3 St-Amour France
71 K2 St Andrews Can.
10 F4 St Andrews U.K.
75 J5 St Ann's Bay Jamaica
11 F6 St Ann's Head hd U.K.
59 J3 St Anthony Can.
62 E3 St Anthony U.S.A.
50 D4 St Arnaud Austr.
51 D5 St Arnaud Range mts N.Z.
59 J3 St-Augustin Can.
12 F4 St Augustin Ger.
67 D6 St Augustine U.S.A.
9 C7 St Austell U.K.
14 E3 St-Avertin France
12 E5 St-Avold France
75 M5 St Barthélémy i. Guadeloupe
8 D3 St Bees U.K.
8 D3 St Bees Head hd U.K.
9 B6 St Bride's Bay b. U.K.
14 C2 St-Brieuc France
73 G5 St Carlos Lake l. U.S.A.
69 H4 St Catharines Can.
67 D6 St Catherines I. i. U.S.A.
9 F7 St Catherine's Point pt U.K.
14 E4 St-Céré France
71 G2 St-Césaire Can.
14 G4 St-Chamond France
62 E3 St Charles ID U.S.A.
70 E5 St Charles MD U.S.A.
68 A4 St Charles MN U.S.A.
64 F4 St Charles MO U.S.A.
69 F4 St Clair U.S.A.
69 F4 St Clair Shores U.S.A.
14 G3 St-Claude France
9 C6 St Clears U.K.
64 E2 St Cloud U.S.A.
75 M5 St Croix i. Virgin Is
59 G4 St Croix r. Can.
68 A2 St Croix r. U.S.A.
68 A3 St Croix Falls U.S.A.
73 G6 St David U.S.A.
11 F6 St David's U.K.
9 B6 St David's Head hd U.K.
12 A6 St-Denis France
14 H2 St-Dié France
14 G2 St-Dizier France
57 K5 Ste Anne Can.
59 F4 Ste-Anne-de-Beaupré Can.
71 J1 Sainte-Anne-de-Madawaska Can.
69 K2 Sainte-Anne-du-Lac Can.
59 G3 Ste Anne, L. l. Can.
71 H1 Ste-Camille-de-Lellis Can.
14 G4 St-Égrève France
71 H1 Sainte-Justine Can.
71 J1 St-Éleuthère Can.
56 B2 St Elias Mountains Can.
59 G3 Ste Marguerite r. Can.
14 H5 Ste-Maxime France
14 D4 Saintes France
71 G2 Ste-Thérèse Can.
14 G4 St-Étienne France
71 F2 St Eugene Can.
71 G2 St-Eustache Can.
75 M5 St Eustatius i. Neth. Ant.
59 F4 St-Félicien Can.
11 F3 Saintfield U.K.
18 C3 St-Florent Corsica France
14 F3 St-Florent-sur-Cher France
88 C3 St. Floris, Parc National nat. park C.A.R.
64 C4 St Francis KS U.S.A.
71 J1 St Francis ME U.S.A.
71 J1 St-Francis r. Can./U.S.A.
65 F4 St Francis r. U.S.A.
59 K4 St Francis, C. c. Can.
71 J1 St Froid Lake l. U.S.A.
16 D7 St Gallen Switz.
14 E5 St-Gaudens France
71 H2 St-Gédéon Can.
48 E4 St George Austr.
71 K2 St George Can.
67 D5 St George SC U.S.A.
73 F3 St George UT U.S.A.
49 F2 St George, C. pt P.N.G.
67 C6 St George I. i. U.S.A.
62 A3 St George, Pt pt U.S.A.
59 F4 St Georges Can.
75 M6 St George's Grenada
59 J4 St George's B. b. Can.
48 F2 St George's Channel P.N.G.
9 A6 St George's Channel Rep. of Ireland/U.K.
9 C6 St Govan's Head hd U.K.
68 E3 St Helen U.S.A.
72 A2 St Helena U.S.A.
85 C7 St Helena terr. Atl. Ocean
90 C6 St Helena Bay S. Africa
90 C6 St Helena Bay b. S. Africa
96 J7 St Helena Fracture sea feature Atl. Ocean
9 E4 St Helens U.K.
62 B2 St Helens U.S.A.
62 B2 St Helens, Mt volc. U.S.A.
14 C2 St Helier Channel Is U.K.
12 D4 St-Hubert Belgium
58 F4 St-Hyacinthe Can.
68 E3 St Ignace U.S.A.
68 C1 St Ignace I. i. Can.
9 C6 St Ishmael U.K.
9 B7 St Ives Eng. U.K.
9 G5 St Ives Eng. U.K.
71 J1 St-Jacques Can.
68 E3 St James U.S.A.
56 C4 St James, Cape pt Can.
14 D4 St-Jean-d'Angély France
14 C3 St-Jean-de-Monts France
59 F4 St-Jean, Lac l. Can.
58 F4 St-Jean-sur-Richelieu Can.
58 F4 St-Jérôme Can.
62 C2 St Joe r. U.S.A.
59 G4 St John Can.
73 F1 St John U.S.A.
75 M5 St John i. Virgin Is
71 K2 St John r. Can./U.S.A.
75 M5 St John's Antigua
59 K4 St John's Can.
73 H4 St Johns AZ U.S.A.
68 E4 St Johns MI U.S.A.
67 D6 St Johns r. U.S.A.
71 H2 St Johnsbury U.S.A.
8 E3 St John's Chapel U.K.
59 F4 St Joseph Can.
68 D4 St Joseph MI U.S.A.
64 E4 St Joseph MO U.S.A.
68 E5 St Joseph r. U.S.A.
69 F2 St Joseph I. i. Can.
65 D7 St Joseph I. i. U.S.A.
58 B3 St Joseph, Lac l. Can.
58 F4 St Jovité Can.
14 E4 St-Junien France
9 B7 St Just U.K.
12 A5 St-Just-en-Chaussée France
9 B7 St Keverne U.K.
53 K8 St Kitts-Nevis country Caribbean Sea
12 B3 St-Laureins Belgium
79 H2 St Laurent Fr. Guiana
St-Laurent, Golfe du g. see St Lawrence, Gulf of
59 K4 St Laurent Nfld Can.
59 G4 St Lawrence in. Que. Can.
59 H4 St Lawrence, Gulf of g. Can./U.S.A.
54 B3 St Lawrence I. i. AK U.S.A.
69 K3 St Lawrence Islands National Park Can.
71 F2 St Lawrence Seaway chan. Can./U.S.A.
59 G4 St-Léonard Can.
59 J3 St Lewis Can.
59 J3 Saint Lewis r. Can.
14 D2 St-Lô France
86 A3 St Louis Senegal
68 E4 St Louis MI U.S.A.
64 F4 St Louis MO U.S.A.
68 A2 St Louis r. U.S.A.
53 K8 St Lucia country Caribbean Sea
91 K4 St Lucia Estuary S. Africa
91 K3 St Lucia, Lake l. S. Africa
75 M5 St Maarten i. Neth. Ant.
10 □ St Magnus Bay b. U.K.
14 D3 St-Maixent-l'École France
14 C2 St-Malo France
14 C2 St-Malo, Golfe de g. France
91 G6 St Marks S. Africa
75 M5 Saint Martin i. Guadeloupe
90 B6 St Martin, Cape hd S. Africa
68 D3 St Martin I. i. U.S.A.
57 K4 St Martin, L. l. Can.
9 A8 St Martin's i. U.K.
35 H5 St Martin's I. i. Bangl.
50 B1 St Mary Pk mt Austr.
69 G4 St Mary's Can.
10 F2 St Mary's U.K.
70 A4 St Marys OH U.S.A.
70 D4 St Marys PA U.S.A.
70 C5 Saint Marys U.S.A.
9 A8 St Mary's i. U.K.
70 A4 St Marys r. U.S.A.
59 K4 St Mary's, C. hd Can.
54 A3 St Matthew I. i. AK U.S.A.
48 E2 St Matthias Group is P.N.G.
58 F4 St Maurice r. Can.
9 B7 St Mawes U.K.
14 D4 St-Médard-en-Jalles France
59 J3 St Michaels Bay b. Can.
16 D7 St Moritz Switz.
14 C3 St-Nazaire France
9 G5 St Neots U.K.
14 H2 St-Nicolas-de-Port France
12 C3 St-Niklaas Belgium
14 F1 St-Omer France
71 J1 St-Pamphile Can.
59 G4 St Pascal Can.
57 G4 St Paul Can.
68 A3 St Paul MN U.S.A.
64 D3 St Paul NE U.S.A.
68 B5 St Paul VA U.S.A.
93 K6 St Paul, Île i. Ind. Ocean
61 H3 St Peter MN U.S.A.
14 C2 St Peter Port Channel Is U.K.
20 D3 St Petersburg Rus. Fed.
67 D7 St Petersburg U.S.A.
59 J4 St-Pierre St Pierre and Miquelon N. America
14 G5 St-Pierre mt France
55 N5 St Pierre and Miquelon terr. N. America
14 D4 St-Pierre-d'Oléron France
58 F4 St Pierre, Lac l. Can.
14 F3 St-Pierre-le-Moûtier France
12 A4 St-Pol-sur-Ternoise France
16 G6 St Pölten Austria
14 F3 St-Pourçain-sur-Sioule France
71 H1 Saint-Prosper Can.
14 F2 St-Quentin France
14 H5 St-Raphaël France
71 F2 St Regis r. U.S.A.
71 F2 St Regis Falls U.S.A.
71 G2 St-Rémi Can.
71 H2 St-Sébastien Can.
59 G4 St Siméon Can.
67 D6 St Simons I. i. U.S.A.
71 K2 St Stephen Can.
67 E5 St Stephen U.S.A.
71 H2 St-Théophile Can.
57 L4 St Theresa Point Can.
69 G4 St Thomas Can.
14 H5 St-Tropez France
12 D4 St-Truiden Belgium
57 K5 St Vincent U.S.A.
53 K8 St Vincent and the Grenadines country Caribbean Sea
St Vincent, Cape c. see São Vicente, Cabo de
50 A3 St. Vincent, Gulf Austr.
12 E4 St-Vith Belgium
57 H4 St Walburg Can.
12 F5 St Wendel Ger.
69 G4 St Williams Can.
14 E4 St-Yrieix-la-Perche France
34 E3 Saipal mt Nepal
37 G5 Saipan i. N. Mariana Is
35 H5 Saitlai Myanmar
6 T3 Saittanulkki h. Fin.
39 □ Sai Wan H.K. China
78 E7 Sajama, Nevado mt Bol.
30 B5 Sājir S. Arabia
90 D5 Sak watercourse S. Africa
41 D7 Sakai Japan
41 C6 Sakaide Japan
41 C7 Sakaiminato Japan
32 B3 Sakākah S. Arabia
31 G5 Saka Kalat Pak.
64 C2 Sakakawea, Lake l. U.S.A.
58 E3 Sakami Can.
58 F3 Sakami r. Can.
58 E3 Sakami, Lac l. Can.
19 M4 Sakar mts Bulg.
28 C1 Sakarya Turkey
28 C1 Sakarya r. Turkey
40 F5 Sakata Japan
42 C3 Sakchu N. Korea
44 B2 Sa Keo r. Thai.
86 C4 Sakété Benin
36 G2 Sakhalin i. Rus. Fed.
36 G1 Sakhalinskiy Zaliv b. Rus. Fed.
34 C3 Sakhi India
91 H3 Sakhile S. Africa
30 C2 Sakht-Sar Iran
29 L1 Şäki Azer.
7 S9 Šakiai Lith.
34 A3 Sakir mt Pak.
36 E4 Sakishima-guntō is Japan
34 B4 Sakrand Pak.
44 □ Sakra, P. i. Sing.
90 D5 Sakrivier S. Africa
41 B9 Sakura-jima volc. Japan
21 E6 Saky Ukr.
7 S6 Säkylä Fin.
86 □ Sal i. Cape Verde
21 G6 Sal r. Rus. Fed.
7 S8 Sala Latvia
7 P7 Sala Sweden
58 F4 Salaberry-de-Valleyfield Can.
7 T8 Salacgrīva Latvia
18 F4 Sala Consilina Italy
73 E5 Salada, Laguna salt l. Mex.
83 E2 Saladillo Buenos Aires Arg.
83 D2 Saladillo r. Córdoba Arg.
83 E2 Salado r. Buenos Aires Arg.
83 C2 Salado r. Mendoza/San Luis Arg.
83 D4 Salado r. Río Negro Arg.
83 E1 Salado r. Santa Fé Arg.
74 E3 Salado r. Mex.
80 B3 Salado, Quebrada de r. Chile
86 B4 Salaga Ghana
90 F1 Salajwe Botswana
87 D3 Salal Chad
32 D6 Şalālah Oman
83 B1 Salamanca Chile
74 D4 Salamanca Mex.
15 D2 Salamanca Spain
70 D3 Salamanca U.S.A.
91 K3 Salamanga Moz.
30 B3 Salamatabad Iran
81 B3 Salamina Col.
28 F4 Salamīyah Syria
68 E5 Salamonie r. U.S.A.
68 E5 Salamonie Lake l. U.S.A.
35 F5 Salandi r. India
7 R8 Salantai Lith.
80 C2 Salar de Arizaro salt flat Arg.
80 C2 Salar de Atacama salt flat Chile
15 C1 Salas Spain
7 T8 Salaspils Latvia
37 F7 Salawati i. Indon.
34 B5 Salaya India
37 E7 Salayar i. Indon.
95 N7 Sala y Gómez, Isla i. Chile
83 D3 Salazar Arg.
7 T9 Šalčininkai Lith.
9 D7 Salcombe U.K.
15 D1 Saldaña Spain
81 B4 Saldaña r. Col.
90 B6 Saldanha S. Africa
90 B6 Saldanha Bay b. S. Africa
83 E3 Saldungaray Arg.
7 S8 Saldus Latvia
50 F5 Sale Austr.
29 L5 Şālehābād Iran
30 C3 Şālehābād Iran
24 H3 Salekhard Rus. Fed.
33 B4 Salem India
71 H3 Salem MA U.S.A.
65 F4 Salem MO U.S.A.
66 F4 Salem NJ U.S.A.
71 G3 Salem NY U.S.A.
70 C4 Salem OH U.S.A.
62 B2 Salem OR U.S.A.
66 D4 Salem VA U.S.A.
10 C4 Salen U.K.
10 C4 Salen U.K.
18 F4 Salerno Italy
18 F4 Salerno, Golfo di g. Italy
9 E4 Salford U.K.
79 L5 Salgado r. Brazil
17 J6 Salgótarján Hungary
79 L5 Salgueiro Brazil
31 F4 Salian Afgh.
43 C6 Salibabu i. Indon.
60 E4 Salida CO U.S.A.
14 D5 Salies-de-Béarn France
28 B2 Salihli Turkey
20 C4 Salihorsk Belarus
89 D5 Salima Malawi
89 D5 Salimo Moz.
64 D4 Salina KS U.S.A.
73 G2 Salina UT U.S.A.
74 E5 Salina Cruz Mex.
83 D4 Salina Gualicho salt flat Arg.
18 F5 Salina, Isola i. Italy
83 C2 Salina Llancanelo salt flat Arg.
82 D2 Salinas Brazil
78 B4 Salinas Ecuador
72 B3 Salinas CA U.S.A.
72 B3 Salinas r. CA U.S.A.
80 C4 Salinas Grandes salt flat Arg.
63 F5 Salinas Peak summit U.S.A.
65 E5 Saline r. AR U.S.A.
64 C4 Saline r. KS U.S.A.
15 H3 Salines, Cap de ses pt Spain
72 D3 Saline Valley v. U.S.A.
79 J4 Salinópolis Brazil

78 C6 **Salinosó Lachay, Pta** *pt* Peru
9 F6 **Salisbury** U.K.
71 F5 **Salisbury** *MD* U.S.A.
67 D5 **Salisbury** *NC* U.S.A.
9 E6 **Salisbury Plain** *plain* U.K.
79 K6 **Salitre** *r.* Brazil
28 F5 **Şalkhad** Syria
35 F5 **Salki** *r.* India
6 V3 **Salla** Fin.
83 D3 **Salliqueló** Arg.
65 E5 **Sallisaw** U.S.A.
55 L3 **Salluit** Can.
35 E3 **Sallyana** Nepal
30 B2 **Salmās** Iran
20 D2 **Salmi** Rus. Fed.
56 F5 **Salmo** Can.
62 D2 **Salmon** U.S.A.
62 D2 **Salmon** *r.* U.S.A.
56 F4 **Salmon Arm** Can.
71 F3 **Salmon Reservoir** U.S.A.
62 D2 **Salmon River Mountains** U.S.A.
12 E5 **Salmtal** Ger.
7 S6 **Salo** Fin.
35 E4 **Salon** India
14 G5 **Salon-de-Provence** France
88 C4 **Salonga Nord, Parc National de la** *nat. park* Congo(Zaire)
88 C4 **Salonga Sud, Parc National de la** *nat. park* Congo(Zaire)
17 K7 **Salonta** Romania
83 D1 **Salsacate** Arg.
21 G6 **Sal'sk** Rus. Fed.
18 C2 **Salsomaggiore Terme** Italy
28 E5 **Salt** Jordan
73 G5 **Salt** *r. AZ* U.S.A.
68 B6 **Salt** *r. MO* U.S.A.
90 E5 **Salt** *watercourse* S. Africa
80 C2 **Salta** Arg.
9 C7 **Saltash** U.K.
10 D5 **Saltcoats** U.K.
70 B5 **Salt Creek** *r.* U.S.A.
11 E5 **Saltee Islands** *is* Rep. of Ireland
6 O3 **Saltfjellet Svartisen Nasjonalpark** *nat. park* Norway
65 B6 **Salt Flat** U.S.A.
70 C4 **Salt Fork Lake** *l.* U.S.A.
65 C7 **Saltillo** Mex.
62 E3 **Salt Lake City** U.S.A.
83 E2 **Salto** Arg.
82 C3 **Salto** Brazil
83 F1 **Salto** Uru.
82 E2 **Salto da Divisa** Brazil
80 E4 **Salto Grande, Embalse de** *resr* Uru.
73 E5 **Salton Sea** *salt l.* U.S.A.
34 C2 **Salt Ra.** *h.* Pak.
57 G2 **Salt River** Can.
70 B5 **Salt Rock** U.S.A.
67 D5 **Saluda** *SC* U.S.A.
70 E6 **Saluda** *VA* U.S.A.
34 C4 **Salumbar** India
33 C2 **Salur** India
18 B2 **Saluzzo** Italy
83 D1 **Salvador** Arg.
82 E1 **Salvador** Brazil
65 F6 **Salvador, L.** *l.* U.S.A.
73 G2 **Salvation Creek** *r.* U.S.A.
30 C5 **Salwah** Qatar
37 B5 **Salween** *r.* Myanmar
29 M2 **Salyan** Azer.
70 B6 **Salyersville** U.S.A.
90 B2 **Salzbrunn** Namibia
16 F7 **Salzburg** Austria
13 J2 **Salzgitter** Ger.
13 J1 **Salzhausen** Ger.
13 G3 **Salzkotten** Ger.
13 K3 **Salzmünde** Ger.
13 K2 **Salzwedel** Ger.
34 B4 **Sam** India
30 B4 **Samāh** *well* S. Arabia
30 B3 **Samaida** Iran
43 C5 **Samal** *i.* Phil.
43 B5 **Samales Group** *is* Phil.
33 C2 **Samalkot** India
28 E3 **Samandağı** Turkey
40 H3 **Samani** Japan
28 C6 **Samannûd** Egypt
43 C4 **Samar** *i.* Phil.
24 G4 **Samara** Rus. Fed.
81 D3 **Samariapo** Venez.
45 E3 **Samarinda** Indon.
40 D2 **Samarka** Rus. Fed.
31 G2 **Samarkand** Uzbek.
31 H2 **Samarkand, Pik** *mt* Tajik.
29 J4 **Sāmarrā'** Iraq
43 C4 **Samar Sea** *g.* Phil.
20 J4 **Samarskaya Oblast'** *div.* Rus. Fed.
29 M1 **Şamaxı** Azer.
88 C4 **Samba** Congo(Zaire)
45 E2 **Sambaliung** *mts* Indon.
35 F5 **Sambalpur** India
45 D3 **Sambar, Tanjung** *pt* Indon.
45 C2 **Sambas** Indon.
89 F5 **Sambava** Madag.
35 G4 **Sambha** India
34 D3 **Sambhal** India
34 C4 **Sambhar L.** *l.* India
21 B5 **Sambir** Ukr.
79 K5 **Sambito** *r.* Brazil
83 F2 **Samborombón, Bahía** *b.* Arg.
12 B4 **Sambre** *r.* Belgium/France
81 A3 **Sambú** *r.* Panama
42 E5 **Samch'ŏk** S. Korea
42 E6 **Samch'ŏnp'o** S. Korea
29 K3 **Samdi Dag** *mt* Turkey
88 D4 **Same** Tanz.
Samirum *see* **Yazd-e Khväst**
42 E3 **Samjiyŏn** N. Korea
29 L1 **Şämkir** Azer.
30 D3 **Şamnan va Damghan** *reg.* Iran
47 K5 **Samoa** *country* Pac. Oc.
18 F2 **Samobor** Croatia
20 G2 **Samoded** Rus. Fed.
19 K3 **Samokov** Bulg.
16 H6 **Šamorín** Slovakia
19 M6 **Samos** *i.* Greece
45 A2 **Samosir** *i.* Indon.
19 L4 **Samothraki** Greece
19 L4 **Samothraki** *i.* Greece
43 B3 **Sampaloc Point** *pt* Phil.
45 D3 **Sampit** Indon.
45 D3 **Sampit, Teluk** *b.* Indon.
89 C4 **Sampwe** Congo(Zaire)
42 E6 **Samrangjin** S. Korea
65 E6 **Sam Rayburn Res.** *resr* U.S.A.
35 E3 **Samsang** China
44 C1 **Sâm Sơn** Vietnam
28 F1 **Samsun** Turkey
21 G7 **Samtredia** Georgia
21 J7 **Samur** *r.* Azer./Rus. Fed.
44 B2 **Samut Sakhon** Thai.
44 B2 **Samut Songkhram** Thai.
35 G3 **Samyai** China
86 B3 **San** Mali
32 B6 **Şan'ā** Yemen
92 C3 **Sanae** *S. Africa Base* Ant.
87 D4 **Sanaga** *r.* Cameroon
81 A4 **San Agustín** Col.
43 C5 **San Agustin, Cape** *c.* Phil.
30 B6 **Sanām** S. Arabia
30 B3 **Sanandaj** Iran
72 B2 **San Andreas** U.S.A.
43 C3 **San Andres** Phil.
78 B1 **San Andrés, Isla de** *i.* Col.
63 F5 **San Andres Mts** *mts* U.S.A.
74 E5 **San Andrés Tuxtla** Mex.
65 C6 **San Angelo** U.S.A.
83 B2 **San Antonio** Chile
43 B3 **San Antonio** Phil.
65 D6 **San Antonio** U.S.A.
15 G3 **San Antonio Abad** Spain
75 H4 **San Antonio, C.** *pt* Cuba
83 F3 **San Antonio, Cabo** *pt* Arg.
80 C2 **San Antonio de los Cobres** Arg.
81 D2 **San Antonio de Tamanaco** Venez.
72 D4 **San Antonio, Mt** *mt* U.S.A.
83 D4 **San Antonio Oeste** Arg.
72 B4 **San Antonio Reservoir** U.S.A.
72 B3 **San Ardo** U.S.A.
83 E3 **San Augustín** Arg.
83 C1 **San Augustín de Valle Fértil** Arg.
34 D5 **Sanawad** India
18 E3 **San Benedetto del Tronto** Italy
74 B5 **San Benedicto, I.** *i.* Mex.
65 D7 **San Benito** U.S.A.
72 B3 **San Benito** *r.* U.S.A.
72 B3 **San Benito Mt** *mt* U.S.A.
72 D4 **San Bernardino** U.S.A.
63 C5 **San Bernardino Mts** *mts* U.S.A.
83 B2 **San Bernardo** Chile
65 B7 **San Bernardo** Mex.
41 C7 **Sanbe-san** *volc.* Japan
67 C6 **San Blas, C.** *c.* U.S.A.
78 E6 **San Borja** Bol.
71 H3 **Sanbornville** U.S.A.
60 F6 **San Buenaventura** Mex.
83 C2 **San Carlos** Arg.
83 B3 **San Carlos** Chile
65 C6 **San Carlos** *Coahuila* Mex.
43 B3 **San Carlos** *Luzon* Phil.
43 B4 **San Carlos** *Negros* Phil.
83 F2 **San Carlos** Uru.
73 G5 **San Carlos** U.S.A.
81 D4 **San Carlos** *Amazonas* Venez.
81 C2 **San Carlos** *Cojedes* Venez.
83 E1 **San Carlos Centro** Arg.
83 B4 **San Carlos de Bariloche** Arg.
83 E3 **San Carlos de Bolívar** Arg.
81 C2 **San Carlos del Zulia** Venez.
63 D6 **San Carlos, Mesa de** *h.* Mex.
38 C2 **Sancha** *Gansu* China
38 D2 **Sancha** *Shanxi* China
42 D1 **Sanchahe** China
39 C5 **Sancha He** *r.* China
39 B6 **San Chien Pau** *mt* Laos
34 B4 **Sanchor** India
38 D2 **Sanchuan** *r.* China
20 H3 **Sanchursk** Rus. Fed.
83 B2 **San Clemente** Chile
72 D5 **San Clemente** U.S.A.
72 C5 **San Clemente I.** *i.* U.S.A.
14 F3 **Sancoins** France
83 E1 **San Cristóbal** Arg.
81 B3 **San Cristóbal** Venez.
49 G3 **San Cristobal** *i.* Solomon Is
74 F5 **San Cristóbal de las Casas** Mex.
78 □ **San Cristóbal, Isla** *i.* *Galapagos Is* Ecuador
73 F5 **San Cristobal Wash** *r.* U.S.A.
75 J4 **Sancti Spíritus** Cuba
91 H1 **Sand** *r.* S. Africa
40 D3 **Sandagou** Rus. Fed.
10 C5 **Sanda Island** *i.* U.K.
45 E1 **Sandakan** Malaysia
7 K6 **Sandane** Norway
19 K4 **Sandanski** Bulg.
13 L2 **Sandau** Ger.
10 F1 **Sanday** *i.* U.K.
10 F1 **Sanday Sound** *chan.* U.K.
9 E4 **Sandbach** U.K.
7 M7 **Sandefjord** Norway
92 D4 **Sandercock Nunataks** *nunatak* Ant.
73 H4 **Sanders** U.S.A.
13 K3 **Sandersleben** Ger.
65 C6 **Sanderson** U.S.A.
10 D6 **Sandhead** U.K.
68 B2 **Sand I.** *i.* U.S.A.
78 E6 **Sandia** Peru
72 D5 **San Diego** U.S.A.
80 C8 **San Diego, C.** *c.* Arg.
28 C2 **Sandıklı** Turkey
34 E4 **Sandila** India
68 E2 **Sand Lake** Can.
7 J7 **Sandnes** Norway
6 N3 **Sandnessjøen** Norway
89 C4 **Sandoa** Congo(Zaire)
17 K5 **Sandomierz** Pol.
81 A4 **Sandoná** Col.
18 E2 **San Donà di Piave** Italy
37 B5 **Sandoway** Myanmar
9 F7 **Sandown** U.K.
90 C7 **Sandown Bay** *b.* S. Africa
6 □ **Sandoy** *i.* Faroe Is
62 C1 **Sandpoint** U.S.A.
10 A4 **Sandray** *i.* U.K.
17 N7 **Şandrul Mare, Vârful** *mt* Romania
7 O6 **Sandsjö** Sweden
56 C4 **Sandspit** Can.
65 D4 **Sand Springs** U.S.A.
72 C2 **Sand Springs Salt Flat** *salt flat* U.S.A.
68 A2 **Sandstone** U.S.A.
73 F5 **Sand Tank Mts** *mts* U.S.A.
39 C5 **Sandu** *Guizhou* China
39 D5 **Sandu** *Hunan* China
69 F4 **Sandusky** *MI* U.S.A.
70 B4 **Sandusky** *OH* U.S.A.
70 B4 **Sandusky Bay** *b.* U.S.A.
90 C5 **Sandveld** *mts* S. Africa
90 B3 **Sandverhaar** Namibia
7 M7 **Sandvika** Norway
6 N5 **Sandvika** Sweden
7 P6 **Sandviken** Sweden
59 J3 **Sandwich Bay** *b.* Can.
10 □ **Sandwick** U.K.
35 G5 **Sandwip Ch.** *chan.* Bangl.
71 H2 **Sandy** *r.* U.S.A.
57 J3 **Sandy Bay** Can.
49 F4 **Sandy Cape** *c.* Austr.
70 B5 **Sandy Hook** U.S.A.
71 F4 **Sandy Hook** *pt* U.S.A.
31 F2 **Sandykachi** Turkm.
58 B3 **Sandy L.** *l.* Can.
58 B3 **Sandy Lake** Can.
71 E3 **Sandy Pond** U.S.A.
82 A4 **San Estanislao** Para.
43 B2 **San Fabian** Phil.
83 B2 **San Felipe** Chile
74 B2 **San Felipe** *Baja California Norte* Mex.
81 C2 **San Felipe** Venez.
83 E2 **San Fernando** Arg.
83 B2 **San Fernando** Chile
74 E4 **San Fernando** Mex.
43 B2 **San Fernando** *Luzon* Phil.
43 B3 **San Fernando** *Luzon* Phil.
15 C4 **San Fernando** Spain
81 E2 **San Fernando** Trinidad and Tobago
72 C4 **San Fernando** U.S.A.
81 D3 **San Fernando de Apure** Venez.
81 D3 **San Fernando de Atabapo** Venez.
72 D5 **San Filipe Creek** *r.* U.S.A.
67 D6 **Sanford** *FL* U.S.A.
71 H3 **Sanford** *ME* U.S.A.
67 E5 **Sanford** *NC* U.S.A.
68 E4 **Sanford Lake** *l.* U.S.A.
83 D1 **San Francisco** Arg.
72 A3 **San Francisco** *CA* U.S.A.
72 A3 **San Francisco** *airport CA* U.S.A.
73 H5 **San Francisco** *r. NM* U.S.A.
72 A3 **San Francisco Bay** *in.* U.S.A.
75 K5 **San Francisco de Macorís** Dom. Rep.
80 C7 **San Francisco de Paula, C.** *pt* Arg.
15 G3 **San Francisco Javier** Spain
80 C3 **San Francisco, Paso de** *pass* Arg.
81 A4 **San Gabriel** Ecuador
72 C4 **San Gabriel Mts** *mts* U.S.A.
78 C4 **Sangai, Parque Nacional** *nat. park* Ecuador
34 C6 **Sangamner** India
68 C6 **Sangamon** *r.* U.S.A.
31 G3 **Sangan** Afgh.
31 F4 **Sangān** Iran
31 G3 **Sangan, Koh-i-** *mt* Afgh.
25 O3 **Sangar** Rus. Fed.
34 B3 **Sangar** *r.* Pak.
33 B2 **Sangāreddi** India
18 C5 **San Gavino Monreale** *Sardinia* Italy
31 E3 **Sang Bast** Iran
43 B5 **Sangboy Islands** *is* Phil.
45 E2 **Sangeang** *i.* Indon.
38 B1 **Sangejing** China
72 C3 **Sanger** U.S.A.
13 K3 **Sangerhausen** Ger.
38 E1 **Sanggan** *r.* China
38 B3 **Sanggarmai** China
45 D2 **Sanggau** Indon.
42 B5 **Sanggou Wan** *b.* China
88 B3 **Sangha** *r.* Congo
34 B4 **Sanghar** Pak.
81 B3 **San Gil** Col.
18 G5 **San Giovanni in Fiore** Italy
18 F4 **San Giovanni Rotondo** Italy
43 C6 **Sangir** *i.* Indon.
37 E6 **Sangir, Kepulauan** *is* Indon.
45 E2 **Sangkulirang** Indon.
33 A2 **Sangli** India
31 H2 **Sanglich** Afgh.
86 D4 **Sangmélima** Cameroon
34 D3 **Sangnam** India
35 H3 **Sangngagqoling** China
42 E3 **Sang-ni** N. Korea
89 D6 **Sango** Zimbabwe
33 A2 **Sāngole** India
72 D4 **San Gorgonio Mt** *mt* U.S.A.
16 D7 **San Gottardo, Passo del** Switz.
63 F4 **Sangre de Cristo Range** *mts* U.S.A.
81 E2 **Sangre Grande** Trinidad and Tobago
34 C3 **Sangrur** India
35 F3 **Sangsang** China
56 G4 **Sangudo** Can.
79 G6 **Sangue** *r.* Brazil
91 K1 **Sangutane** *r.* Moz.
31 H2 **Sangvor** Tajik.
39 D4 **Sangzhi** China
74 B3 **San Hipólito, Pta** *pt* Mex.
28 C7 **Sanhûr** Egypt
78 E6 **San Ignacio** *Beni* Bol.
78 F7 **San Ignacio** *Santa Cruz* Bol.
58 E2 **Sanikiluaq** Can.
43 B2 **San Ildefonso, Cape** *c.* Phil.
43 B2 **San Ildefonso Peninsula** Phil.
43 C4 **San Isidro** Phil.
43 B3 **San Jacinto** Phil.
72 D5 **San Jacinto** U.S.A.
72 D5 **San Jacinto Peak** *summit* U.S.A.
35 F5 **Sanjai, R** *r.* India
83 E1 **San Javier** Arg.
83 B2 **San Javier de Loncomilla** Chile
34 B3 **Sanjawi** Pak.
89 D4 **Sanje** Tanz.
81 A3 **San Jerónimo, Serranía de** *mts* Col.
39 C5 **Sanjiang** China
42 B2 **Sanjiangkou** China
42 B2 **Sanjiazi** China
41 F6 **Sanjō** Japan
72 B3 **San Joaquin** *CA* U.S.A.
72 B3 **San Joaquin** *r. CA* U.S.A.
72 B3 **San Joaquin Valley** *v.* U.S.A.
83 E1 **San Jorge** Arg.
81 B2 **San Jorge** *r.* Col.
80 C7 **San Jorge, Golfo de** *g.* Arg.
75 H7 **San José** Costa Rica
43 B3 **San Jose** Phil.
43 B3 **San Jose** Phil.
72 B3 **San Jose** U.S.A.
74 B4 **San José** *i.* Mex.
81 E2 **San José de Amacuro** Venez.
43 B4 **San Jose de Buenavista** Phil.
78 F7 **San José de Chiquitos** Bol.
83 E1 **San José de Feliciano** Arg.
81 D2 **San José de Guanipa** Venez.
83 C1 **San Jose de Jáchal** Arg.
83 D1 **San José de la Dormida** Arg.
83 B3 **San José de la Mariquina** Chile
74 C4 **San José del Cabo** Mex.
81 B4 **San José del Guaviare** Col.
83 F2 **San José de Mayo** Uru.
81 C3 **San José de Ocuné** Col.
83 D4 **San José, Golfo** *g.* Arg.
83 C2 **San José, Vol.** *volc.* Chile
42 E5 **Sanju** S. Korea
83 C1 **San Juan** Arg.
65 C7 **San Juan** Mex.
43 C4 **San Juan** Phil.
75 L5 **San Juan** Puerto Rico
81 D3 **San Juan** Venez.
83 C1 **San Juan** *div.* Arg.
81 A3 **San Juan** *r.* Col.
75 H6 **San Juan** *r.* Costa Rica/Nic.
72 B4 **San Juan** *r. CA* U.S.A.
73 H3 **San Juan** *r. UT* U.S.A.
80 E3 **San Juan Bautista** Para.
15 G3 **San Juan Bautista** Spain
74 E5 **San Juan Bautista Tuxtepec** Mex.
83 B4 **San Juan dela Costa** Chile
81 C2 **San Juan de los Cayos** Venez.
81 D2 **San Juan de los Morros** Venez.
73 F4 **San Juan Mts** *mts* U.S.A.
34 D1 **Sanju He** *watercourse* China
80 C7 **San Julián** Arg.
83 E1 **San Justo** Arg.
33 A2 **Sankeshwar** India
35 F5 **Sankh** *r.* India
Sankt-Peterburg *see* **St Petersburg**
28 G3 **Şanlıurfa** Turkey
83 E2 **San Lorenzo** Arg.
78 F8 **San Lorenzo** Bol.
78 C3 **San Lorenzo** Ecuador
63 F6 **San Lorenzo** Mex.
15 E1 **San Lorenzo** *mt* Spain
80 B7 **San Lorenzo, Cerro** *mt* Arg./Chile
78 C6 **San Lorenzo, I.** *i.* Peru
15 C4 **Sanlúcar de Barrameda** Spain
74 C4 **San Lucas** Mex.
83 C2 **San Luis** Arg.
73 E5 **San Luis** *AZ* U.S.A.
73 G5 **San Luis** *AZ* U.S.A.
83 C2 **San Luis** *div.* Arg.
78 F6 **San Luis, Lago de** *l.* Bol.
72 B4 **San Luis Obispo** U.S.A.
72 B4 **San Luis Obispo Bay** *b.* U.S.A.
74 D4 **San Luis Potosí** Mex.
72 B3 **San Luis Reservoir** U.S.A.
74 B2 **San Luis Río Colorado** Mex.
83 C2 **San Luis, Sa de** *mts* Arg.
18 E6 **San Marco, Capo** *c.* *Sicily* Italy
65 D6 **San Marcos** U.S.A.
18 E3 **San Marino** San Marino
5 E4 **San Marino** *country* Europe
80 C3 **San Martín** *Catamarca* Arg.
83 C2 **San Martín** *Mendoza* Arg.
81 B4 **San Martín** Col.
78 F6 **San Martín** *r.* Bol.
83 B4 **San Martín de los Andes** Arg.
80 B7 **San Martín, L.** *l.* Arg./Chile
72 A3 **San Mateo** U.S.A.
83 D4 **San Matías, Golfo** *g.* Arg.
81 E3 **San Mauricio** Venez.
39 F4 **Sanmen** China
39 F4 **Sanmen Wan** *b.* China
38 D3 **Sanmenxia** China
74 G6 **San Miguel** El Salvador
73 G6 **San Miguel** *AZ* U.S.A.
72 B4 **San Miguel** *CA* U.S.A.
78 F6 **San Miguel** *r.* Bol.
81 B4 **San Miguel** *r.* Col.
73 H2 **San Miguel** *r.* U.S.A.
43 B3 **San Miguel Bay** *b.* Phil.
83 E2 **San Miguel del Monte** Arg.
80 C3 **San Miguel de Tucumán** Arg.
72 B4 **San Miguel I.** *i.* U.S.A.
43 A5 **San Miguel Islands** *is* Phil.
39 E5 **Sanming** China
43 B3 **San Narciso** Phil.
18 F4 **Sannicandro Garganico** Italy
83 E2 **San Nicolás de los Arroyos** Arg.
72 C5 **San Nicolas I.** *i.* U.S.A.
91 F3 **Sannieshof** S. Africa
86 B4 **Sanniquellie** Liberia
17 L6 **Sanok** Pol.
43 B3 **San Pablo** Phil.
83 E2 **San Pedro** *Buenos Aires* Arg.
80 D2 **San Pedro** *Jujuy* Arg.
78 F7 **San Pedro** Bol.
86 B4 **San-Pédro** Côte d'Ivoire
80 E2 **San Pedro** Para.
43 B3 **San Pedro** Phil.
73 G5 **San Pedro** *r.* U.S.A.
72 C5 **San Pedro Channel** U.S.A.
81 C3 **San Pedro de Arimena** Col.
81 E3 **San Pedro de las Bocas** Venez.
65 C7 **San Pedro de las Colonias** Mex.
15 C3 **San Pedro, Sierra de** *mts* Spain
74 G5 **San Pedro Sula** Honduras
18 C5 **San Pietro, Isola di** *i.* *Sardinia* Italy
10 E5 **Sanquhar** U.K.
78 C3 **Sanquianga, Parque Nacional** *nat. park* Col.
74 A2 **San Quintín** Mex.
83 C2 **San Rafael** Arg.
72 A3 **San Rafael** U.S.A.
81 C2 **San Rafael** Venez.
73 G2 **San Rafael** *r.* U.S.A.
73 G2 **San Rafael Knob** *summit* U.S.A.
72 C4 **San Rafael Mts** *mts* U.S.A.
78 F6 **San Ramón** Bol.
18 B3 **San Remo** Italy
81 C1 **San Román, C.** *pt* Venez.
15 B1 **San Roque** Spain
65 D6 **San Saba** U.S.A.
83 E1 **San Salvador** Arg.
74 G6 **San Salvador** El Salvador
75 K4 **San Salvador** *i.* Bahamas
80 C2 **San Salvador de Jujuy** Arg.
78 □ **San Salvador, Isla** *i.* *Galapagos Is* Ecuador
34 D5 **Sansar** India
15 F1 **San Sebastián** Spain
15 E2 **San Sebastián de los Reyes** Spain
18 E3 **Sansepolcro** Italy
18 F4 **San Severo** Italy
39 F5 **Sansha** China
39 D6 **Sanshui** China
18 G2 **Sanski Most** Bos.-Herz.
39 C5 **Sansui** China
44 C2 **San, T.** *r.* Cambodia
78 E7 **Santa Ana** Bol.
74 G6 **Santa Ana** El Salvador
72 D5 **Santa Ana** U.S.A.
49 G3 **Santa Ana** *i.* Solomon Is
65 D6 **Santa Anna** U.S.A.
81 B3 **Sta Bárbara** Col.
74 C3 **Santa Bárbara** Mex.
72 C4 **Santa Barbara** U.S.A.
72 B4 **Santa Barbara Channel** U.S.A.
72 C5 **Santa Barbara I.** *i.* U.S.A.
80 C3 **Sta Catalina** Chile
15 B1 **Santa Catalina de Armada** Spain
72 D5 **Santa Catalina, Gulf of** *b.* U.S.A.
72 C5 **Santa Catalina I.** *i.* U.S.A.
65 C7 **Sta Catarina** Mex.
78 E4 **Santa Clara** Col.
75 J4 **Santa Clara** Cuba
72 B3 **Santa Clara** *CA* U.S.A.
73 F3 **Santa Clara** *UT* U.S.A.
83 F2 **Santa Clara de Olimar** Uru.
72 C4 **Santa Clarita** U.S.A.
18 F6 **Sta Croce, Capo** *c.* *Sicily* Italy
78 F7 **Santa Cruz** Bol.
83 B2 **Sta Cruz** Chile
43 B2 **Santa Cruz** *Luzon* Phil.
43 B3 **Santa Cruz** *Luzon* Phil.
43 B3 **Sta Cruz** Phil.
72 A3 **Santa Cruz** U.S.A.
80 C8 **Santa Cruz** *r.* Arg.
63 E5 **Santa Cruz** *r.* U.S.A.
82 E2 **Santa Cruz Cabrália** Brazil
15 F3 **Santa Cruz de Moya** Spain
86 A2 **Santa Cruz de Tenerife** Canary Is
80 F3 **Santa Cruz do Sul** Brazil
72 C4 **Santa Cruz I.** *i.* U.S.A.
78 □ **Santa Cruz, Isla** *i.* *Galapagos Is* Ecuador
49 G3 **Santa Cruz Islands** *is* Solomon Is
80 C8 **Santa Cruz, Pto** Arg.
83 E1 **Sta Elena** Arg.
78 B4 **Sta Elena, B. de** *b.* Ecuador
74 G6 **Sta Elena, C.** *hd* Costa Rica
18 G5 **Sta Eufemia, Golfo di** *g.* Italy
81 E1 **Santa Fé** Arg.
63 F5 **Santa Fe** U.S.A.
83 E1 **Santa Fé** *div.* Arg.
82 B2 **Santa Helena de Goiás** Brazil
38 B4 **Santai** China
80 B8 **Santa Inés, Isla** *i.* Chile
83 C3 **Santa Isabel** Arg.
49 F2 **Santa Isabel** *i.* Solomon Is
83 F2 **Sta Lucia** *r.* Uru.
63 B4 **Santa Lucia Range** *mts* U.S.A.
82 A2 **Santa Luisa, Serra de** *h.* Brazil
86 □ **Santa Luzia** *i.* Cape Verde
74 B4 **Sta Margarita** *i.* Mex.
80 C3 **Sta María** Arg.
79 G4 **Santa Maria** *Amazonas* Brazil
80 F3 **Santa Maria** *Rio Grande do Sul* Brazil
86 □ **Santa Maria** Cape Verde
65 B7 **Sta María** Mex.
78 D4 **Santa María** Peru
72 B4 **Santa Maria** U.S.A.
83 F1 **Santa Maria** *r.* Brazil
63 F6 **Sta María** *r.* Mex.
74 C2 **Sta María** *r.* Mex.
15 C4 **Santa Maria, Cabo de** *c.* Port.
91 K3 **Santa Maria, Cabo de** *pt* Moz.
79 J5 **Santa Maria das Barreiras** Brazil
82 D1 **Santa Maria da Vitória** Brazil
81 D2 **Sta María de Ipire** Venez.
19 H5 **Sta Maria di Leuca, Capo** *c.* Italy
83 B3 **Santa María, I.** *i.* Chile
49 G3 **Santa María I.** *i.* Vanuatu
78 □ **Santa María, Isla** *i.* *Galapagos Is* Ecuador
60 E5 **Sta María, L. de** *l.* Mex.
67 F7 **Sta Marie, Cape** *c.* Bahamas
81 B2 **Santa Marta** Col.
81 B2 **Santa Marta, Sierra Nevada de** *mts* Col.
72 C4 **Santa Monica** U.S.A.
72 C5 **Santa Monica Bay** *b.* U.S.A.
79 K6 **Santana** Brazil
82 B2 **Santana** *r.* Brazil
83 G1 **Santana da Boa Vista** Brazil
83 F1 **Santana do Livramento** Brazil
81 A4 **Santander** Col.
15 E1 **Santander** Spain
73 G5 **Santan Mt** *mt* U.S.A.
18 C5 **Sant'Antioco** *Sardinia* Italy
18 C5 **Sant'Antioco, Isola di** *i.* *Sardinia* Italy
72 C4 **Santa Paula** U.S.A.
79 K4 **Santa Quitéria** Brazil
79 H4 **Santarém** Brazil
15 B3 **Santarém** Port.
81 C2 **Sta Rita** Venez.
82 B2 **Sta Rita do Araguaia** Brazil
72 B3 **Santa Rita Park** U.S.A.
83 D3 **Santa Rosa** *La Pampa* Arg.
83 C4 **Santa Rosa** *Rio Negro* Arg.
78 D5 **Santa Rosa** *Acre* Brazil
80 F3 **Sta Rosa** Brazil
72 A2 **Santa Rosa** *CA* U.S.A.
63 F5 **Santa Rosa** *NM* U.S.A.
74 G6 **Santa Rosa de Copán** Honduras
83 D1 **Sta Rosa del Río Primero** Arg.
72 B5 **Santa Rosa I.** *i.* U.S.A.
74 B3 **Sta Rosalía** Mex.
62 C3 **Sta Rosa Ra.** *mts* U.S.A.
73 G5 **Santa Rosa Wash** *r.* U.S.A.
83 G2 **Sta Vitória do Palmar** Brazil
72 D5 **Santee** U.S.A.
67 E5 **Santee** *r.* U.S.A.
80 F3 **Santiago** Brazil
83 B2 **Santiago** Chile
75 K5 **Santiago** Dom. Rep.
75 H7 **Santiago** Panama
43 B2 **Santiago** Phil.
83 B2 **Santiago** *div.* Chile
15 B1 **Santiago de Compostela** Spain
75 J4 **Santiago de Cuba** Cuba
83 F2 **Santiago Vazquez** Uru.
15 G2 **Sant Jordi, Golf de** *g.* Spain
82 E1 **Santo Amaro** Brazil
82 E3 **Santo Amaro de Campos** Brazil
82 C4 **Sto Amaro, I. de** *i.* Brazil
82 C3 **Santo Anastácio** Brazil
80 F3 **Santo Angelo** Brazil
86 □ **Santo Antão** *i.* Cape Verde
82 D2 **Sto Antônio** *r.* Brazil
82 E1 **Sto Antônio, Cabo** *c.* Brazil
82 B3 **Santo Antônio da Platina** Brazil
82 E1 **Sto Antônio de Jesus** Brazil
82 A1 **Sto Antônio de Leverger** Brazil
78 E4 **Santo Antônio do Içá** Brazil
82 D3 **Santo Antônio do Monte** Brazil
79 G7 **Santo Corazón** Bol.
75 L5 **Santo Domingo** Dom. Rep.
81 C2 **Sto Domingo** *r.* Venez.
60 E4 **Santo Domingo Pueblo** *NM* U.S.A.
15 E1 **Santoña** Spain
42 D2 **Santong** *r.* China
82 D1 **Sto Onofre** *r.* Brazil
19 L6 **Santorini** *i.* Greece
82 C3 **Santos** Brazil
82 D3 **Santos Dumont** Brazil
78 D6 **Santos Tomás** Peru
80 E3 **Santo Tomé** Arg.
73 F3 **Sanup Plateau** *plat.* U.S.A.
80 B7 **San Valentín, Cerro** *mt* Chile
74 G6 **San Vicente** El Salvador
43 B2 **San Vicente** Phil.
78 C6 **San Vicente de Cañete** Peru
81 B4 **San Vicente del Caguán** Col.
18 D3 **San Vincenzo** Italy

56 E3 Sikanni Chief Can.
56 E3 Sikanni Chief r. Can.
34 C4 Sikar India
31 H3 Sikaram mt Afgh.
86 B3 Sikasso Mali
65 F4 Sikeston U.S.A.
36 F2 Sikhote-Alin' mts Rus. Fed.
19 L6 Sikinos i. Greece
35 G4 Sikkim div. India
6 P4 Siksjö Sweden
45 E1 Sikuati Malaysia
15 C1 Sil r. Spain
43 C4 Silago Phil.
7 S9 Šilalė Lith.
74 D4 Silao Mex.
43 B4 Silay Phil.
13 H1 Silberberg h. Ger.
35 H4 Silchar India
28 B1 Şile Turkey
33 C2 Sileru r. India
34 E3 Silgarhi Nepal
18 C6 Siliana Tunisia
28 D3 Silifke Turkey
35 G3 Siling Co salt l. China
Silistat see Bozkır
19 M2 Silistra Bulg.
28 B1 Silivri Turkey
7 O6 Siljan l. Sweden
7 L8 Silkeborg Denmark
7 U7 Sillamäe Estonia
34 C5 Sillod India
91 J3 Silobela S. Africa
35 G3 Silong China
65 E6 Silsbee U.S.A.
6 U3 Siltaharju Fin.
31 F5 Sīlūp r. Iran
7 R9 Šilutė Lith.
29 H2 Silvan Turkey
34 C5 Silvassa India
68 B2 Silver Bay U.S.A.
63 E5 Silver City U.S.A.
68 C1 Silver Islet Can.
62 B3 Silver Lake U.S.A.
72 D4 Silver Lake l. CA U.S.A.
68 D2 Silver Lake l. MI U.S.A.
11 C5 Silvermine Mts h. Rep. of Ireland
72 D3 Silver Peak Range mts U.S.A.
70 E5 Silver Spring U.S.A.
72 C2 Silver Springs U.S.A.
50 C1 Silverton Austr.
9 D7 Silverton U.K.
69 F3 Silver Water Can.
45 D2 Simanggang Malaysia
43 B3 Simara i. Phil.
69 H2 Simard, Lac l. Can.
29 L5 Sīmareh r. Iran
35 F4 Simaria India
28 B2 Simav Turkey
28 B2 Simav Dağları mts Turkey
88 C3 Simba Congo(Zaire)
Simbirsk see Ul'yanovsk
Simbor i. see Pānikoita
69 G4 Simcoe Can.
69 H3 Simcoe, Lake l. Can.
35 F5 Simdega India
88 D2 Simēn Mountains Eth.
45 A2 Simeulue i. Indon.
21 E6 Simferopol' Ukr.
35 E3 Simikot Nepal
81 B3 Simití Col.
72 C4 Simi Valley U.S.A.
63 F4 Simla U.S.A.
17 L7 Şimleu Silvaniei Romania
12 E4 Simmerath Ger.
12 F5 Simmern (Hunsrück) Ger.
72 C4 Simmler U.S.A.
73 F4 Simmons U.S.A.
67 F7 Simms Bahamas
6 U3 Simojärvi l. Fin.
56 F4 Simonette r. Can.
57 J4 Simonhouse Can.
16 D7 Simplon Pass Switz.
48 D4 Simpson Desert Austr.
68 D1 Simpson I. i. Can.
72 D2 Simpson Park Mts mts U.S.A.
7 O9 Simrishamn Sweden
43 A5 Simunul i. Phil.
36 H2 Simushir, O. i. Rus. Fed.
33 A2 Sina r. India
45 A2 Sinabang Indon.
44 A5 Sinabung volc. Indon.
87 F2 Sinai reg. Egypt
12 C5 Sinai, Mont h. France
60 E6 Sinaloa div. Mex.
18 D3 Sinalunga Italy
39 C5 Sinan China
42 C4 Sinanju N. Korea
35 H5 Sinbyugyun Myanmar
28 F2 Sincan Turkey
81 B2 Sincé Col.
81 B2 Sincelejo Col.
67 D5 Sinclair, L. l. U.S.A.
56 E4 Sinclair Mills Can.
90 B2 Sinclair Mine Namibia
10 E2 Sinclair's Bay b. U.K.
34 D4 Sind r. India
43 B4 Sindañgan Phil.
45 C4 Sindangbarang Indon.
34 B4 Sindari India
16 D6 Sindelfingen Ger.
33 B2 Sindgi India
34 B4 Sindh div. Pak.
33 B3 Sindhnur India
28 B2 Sındırgı Turkey
34 D6 Sindkhed India
34 C5 Sindkheda India
42 C4 Sin-do i. China
20 J2 Sindor Rus. Fed.
35 F5 Sindri India
34 B3 Sind Sagar Doab lowland Pak.
20 J3 Sinegor'ye Rus. Fed.
19 M4 Sinekçi Turkey
15 B4 Sines Port.
15 B4 Sines, Cabo de pt Port.
6 T3 Sinettä Fin.
86 B4 Sinfra Côte d'Ivoire
87 F3 Singa Sudan
34 E3 Singahi India
42 D3 Sin'galp'a China
34 D2 Singa Pass India
44 B5 Singapore Sing.
23 K9 Singapore country Asia
44 B5 Singapore, Strait of chan. Indon./Sing.
45 E4 Singaraja Indon.
44 B2 Sing Buri Thai.
69 G3 Singhampton Can.
88 D4 Singida Tanz.
48 C2 Singkang Indon.
45 C2 Singkawang Indon.
44 A5 Singkil Indon.
50 H2 Singleton Austr.
Singora see Songkhla
42 D4 Sin'gye N. Korea
42 D3 Sinhŭng N. Korea
18 C4 Siniscola Sardinia Italy
18 G3 Sinj Croatia
48 C2 Sinjai Indon.
29 H3 Sinjār Iraq
29 H3 Sinjār, Jabal mt Iraq
29 K3 Sinji Iran
87 F3 Sinkat Sudan
Sinkiang Uighur Aut. Region div. see Xinjiang Uygur Zizhiqu
42 C4 Sinmi i. N. Korea
13 G4 Sinn Ger.
79 H2 Sinnamary Fr. Guiana
Sinneh see Sanandaj
19 N2 Sinoie, Lacul lag. Romania
21 E7 Sinop Turkey
33 D3 Sinpa N. Korea
42 E3 Sinp'o N. Korea
42 E3 Sinp'ung-dong N. Korea
42 D4 Sinp'yŏng N. Korea
42 D4 Sinsang N. Korea
13 G5 Sinsheim Ger.
45 D2 Sintang Indon.
65 D6 Sinton U.S.A.
81 A2 Sinú r. Col.
42 C3 Sinŭiju N. Korea
12 F4 Sinzig Ger.
43 B5 Siocon Phil.
16 J7 Siófok Hungary
16 C7 Sion Switz.
11 D3 Sion Mills U.K.
64 D3 Sioux Center U.S.A.
64 D3 Sioux City U.S.A.
64 D3 Sioux Falls U.S.A.
58 B3 Sioux Lookout Can.
43 B4 Sipalay Phil.
42 C2 Siping China
57 K3 Sipiwesk Can.
57 K3 Sipiwesk L. l. Can.
92 B4 Siple Coast coastal area Ant.
92 A4 Siple, Mt mt Ant.
34 C5 Sipra r. India
67 C5 Sipsey r. U.S.A.
45 A3 Sipura i. Indon.
75 H6 Siquia r. Nic.
43 B4 Siquijor Phil.
43 B4 Siquijor i. Phil.
34 B5 Sir r. Pak.
33 B3 Sira India
7 K7 Sira r. Norway
30 D5 Şīr Abū Nu'āyr i. U.A.E.
Siracusa see Syracuse
56 E4 Sir Alexander, Mt mt Can.
29 G1 Şiran Turkey
31 G5 Siranda Lake l. Pak.
30 D5 Şīr Banī Yās i. U.A.E.
29 M3 Sīrdān Iran
48 D3 Sir Edward Pellew Group is Austr.
68 A3 Siren U.S.A.
31 F5 Sīrgān Iran
44 B1 Siri Kit Dam dam Thai.
30 D4 Sīrīz Iran
56 D2 Sir James McBrien, Mt mt Can.
Sirjan see Sa'īdābād
30 D4 Sīrjan salt flat Iran
30 E5 Sirk Iran
34 E4 Sirmour India
29 J3 Şırnak Turkey
33 C2 Sironcha India
34 D4 Sironj India
33 B2 Sirpur India
72 C4 Sirretta Peak summit U.S.A.
30 D5 Sirrī, Jazīreh-ye i. Iran
34 C3 Sirsa Haryana India
35 E4 Sirsa Uttar Pradesh India
56 F4 Sir Sanford, Mt mt Can.
33 A3 Sirsi Karnataka India
34 D3 Sirsi India
33 B2 Sirsilla India
87 D1 Sirte Libya
87 D1 Sirte, Gulf of g. Libya
33 A2 Sirur India
29 J2 Şirvan Turkey
7 T9 Širvintos Lith.
29 K4 Sīrwān r. Iraq
56 F4 Sir Wilfred Laurier, Mt mt Can.
18 G2 Sisak Croatia
44 C2 Sisaket Thai.
30 C4 Sīsakht Iran
90 E3 Sishen S. Africa
29 L2 Sisian Armenia
68 C2 Siskiwit Bay b. U.S.A.
44 B2 Sisŏphŏn Cambodia
72 B4 Sisquoc r. U.S.A.
64 D2 Sisseton U.S.A.
71 K1 Sisson Branch Reservoir Can.
31 F4 Sistan reg. Iran
31 F4 Sīstan, Daryācheh-ye marsh Afgh.
34 C5 Sitamau India
43 A5 Sitangkai Phil.
34 E4 Sitapur India
19 M7 Siteia Greece
91 J3 Siteki Swaziland
19 K4 Sithonia pen. Greece
82 C1 Sítio da Abadia Brazil
82 D1 Sítio do Mato Brazil
56 B3 Sitka U.S.A.
34 B3 Sitpur Pak.
12 D4 Sittard Neth.
35 H4 Sittaung Myanmar
13 H1 Sittensen Ger.
9 H6 Sittingbourne U.K.
35 H5 Sittwe Myanmar
39 □ Siu A Chau i. H.K. China
35 F5 Siuri India
33 B4 Sivaganga India
33 B4 Sivakasi India
30 D4 Sivand Iran
28 F2 Sivas Turkey
28 B2 Sivaslı Turkey
29 G3 Siverek Turkey
29 G2 Sivrice Turkey
28 C2 Sivrihisar Turkey
91 H3 Sivukile S. Africa
87 E2 Siwa Egypt
34 D3 Siwalik Range mts India/Nepal
35 F4 Siwan India
34 C4 Siwana India
14 G5 Six-Fours-les-Plages France
38 E3 Si Xian China
68 E4 Six Lakes U.S.A.
11 D3 Sixmilecross U.K.
91 H2 Siyabuswa S. Africa
38 F3 Siyang China
29 M1 Siyäzän Azer.
38 C1 Siyitang China
30 D3 Sīyunī Iran
38 D1 Siziwang Qi China
Sjælland i. see Zealand
19 J3 Sjenica Yugo.
7 N9 Sjöbo Sweden
6 P2 Sjøvegan Norway
81 E2 S. Juan r. Venez.
21 E6 Skadovs'k Ukr.
6 E4 Skaftafell National Park Iceland
6 E5 Skaftárós est. Iceland
6 D3 Skagafjörður in. Iceland
7 M8 Skagen Denmark
7 L8 Skagerrak str. Denmark/Norway
62 B1 Skagit r. Can./U.S.A.
56 B3 Skagway U.S.A.
6 T1 Skaidi Norway
6 P2 Skaland Norway
6 O4 Skalmodal Sweden
7 L8 Skanderborg Denmark
71 E3 Skaneateles Lake l. U.S.A.
68 C2 Skanee U.S.A.
19 L5 Skantzoura i. Greece
7 N7 Skara Sweden
7 R7 Skargadshavets Nationalpark nat. park Fin.
7 M6 Skarnes Norway
17 K5 Skarżysko-Kamienna Pol.
6 R3 Skaulo Sweden
17 J6 Skawina Pol.
56 D3 Skeena r. Can.
56 D3 Skeena Mountains Can.
9 H4 Skegness U.K.
6 R4 Skellefteå Sweden
6 Q4 Skellefteälven r. Sweden
6 R4 Skelleftehamn Sweden
11 A6 Skellig Rocks is Rep. of Ireland
8 E4 Skelmersdale U.K.
11 E4 Skerries Rep. of Ireland
7 M7 Ski Norway
19 K5 Skiathos i. Greece
11 B6 Skibbereen Rep. of Ireland
6 R2 Skibotn Norway
8 D3 Skiddaw mt U.K.
7 L7 Skien Norway
17 K5 Skierniewice Pol.
86 C1 Skikda Alg.
8 G4 Skipsea U.K.
50 D4 Skipton Austr.
8 E4 Skipton U.K.
7 L8 Skive Denmark
6 E4 Skjálfandafljót r. Iceland
7 L9 Skjern Denmark
7 K6 Skjolden Norway
6 K5 Skodje Norway
6 T2 Skoganvarre Norway
11 F6 Skokholm Island i. U.K.
68 D4 Skokie U.S.A.
9 B6 Skomer Island i. U.K.
19 K5 Skopelos i. Greece
20 F4 Skopin Rus. Fed.
19 J4 Skopje Macedonia
21 F5 Skorodnoye Rus. Fed.
7 N7 Skövde Sweden
71 J2 Skowhegan U.S.A.
7 S8 Skrunda Latvia
56 B2 Skukum, Mt mt Can.
91 J2 Skukuza S. Africa
72 D3 Skull Peak summit U.S.A.
68 B5 Skunk r. U.S.A.
7 R8 Skuodas Lith.
7 N9 Skurup Sweden
7 P6 Skutskär Sweden
21 D5 Skvyra Ukr.
10 B3 Skye i. U.K.
19 L5 Skyros Greece
19 L5 Skyros i. Greece
92 B3 Skytrain Ice Rise ice feature Ant.
7 M9 Slagelse Denmark
6 Q4 Slagnäs Sweden
45 C4 Slamet, Gunung volc. Indon.
11 E4 Slane Rep. of Ireland
11 E5 Slaney r. Rep. of Ireland
20 D3 Slantsy Rus. Fed.
21 G5 Slashchevskaya Rus. Fed.
68 D1 Slate Is is Can.
18 G2 Slatina Croatia
19 L2 Slatina Romania
57 G2 Slave r. Can.
86 C4 Slave Coast coastal area Africa
56 G3 Slave Lake Can.
27 F1 Slavgorod Rus. Fed.
17 O2 Slavkovichi Rus. Fed.
19 H2 Slavonija reg. Croatia
19 H2 Slavonski Brod Croatia
21 C5 Slavuta Ukr.
21 D5 Slavutych Ukr.
40 B3 Slavyanka Rus. Fed.
21 F6 Slavyansk-na-Kubani Rus. Fed.
20 D4 Slawharad Belarus
16 H3 Sławno Pol.
9 G4 Sleaford U.K.
11 A5 Slea Head hd Rep. of Ireland
10 C3 Sleat pen. U.K.
10 C3 Sleat, Sound of chan. U.K.
58 E2 Sleeper Islands is Can.
68 D3 Sleeping Bear Dunes National Seashore res. U.S.A.
68 D3 Sleeping Bear Pt pt U.S.A.
21 H7 Sleptsovskaya Rus. Fed.
92 C3 Slessor Glacier gl. Ant.
65 F6 Slidell U.S.A.
11 A5 Slievanea h. Rep. of Ireland
11 D3 Slieve Anierin h. Rep. of Ireland
11 D5 Slieveardagh Hills h. Rep. of Ireland
11 C4 Slieve Aughty Mts h. Rep. of Ireland
11 D3 Slieve Beagh h. Rep. of Ireland/U.K.
11 C5 Slieve Bernagh h. Rep. of Ireland
11 D4 Slieve Bloom Mts h. Rep. of Ireland
11 B5 Slievecallan h. Rep. of Ireland
11 B3 Slieve Car h. Rep. of Ireland
11 F3 Slieve Donard h. U.K.
11 B4 Slieve Elva h. Rep. of Ireland
11 C3 Slieve Gamph h. Rep. of Ireland
11 C3 Slieve League h. Rep. of Ireland
11 B5 Slieve Mish Mts h. Rep. of Ireland
11 B5 Slieve Miskish Mts h. Rep. of Ireland
11 A3 Slieve More h. Rep. of Ireland
11 D4 Slieve na Calliagh h. Rep. of Ireland
11 D5 Slievenamon h. Rep. of Ireland
11 D2 Slieve Snaght mt Rep. of Ireland
10 B3 Sligachan U.K.
11 C3 Sligo Rep. of Ireland
11 C3 Sligo Bay b. Rep. of Ireland
7 Q8 Slite Sweden
19 M3 Sliven Bulg.
20 H2 Sloboda Rus. Fed.
20 J2 Slobodchikovo Rus. Fed.
19 M2 Slobozia Romania
56 F5 Slocan Can.
12 E1 Slochteren Neth.
20 C4 Slonim Belarus
12 C2 Slootdorp Neth.
12 D2 Sloten Neth.
12 D2 Slotermeer l. Neth.
49 F2 Slot, The chan. Solomon Is
9 G6 Slough U.K.
5 E4 Slovakia country Europe
5 E4 Slovenia country Europe
18 F1 Slovenj Gradec Slovenia
21 F5 Slov"yans'k Ukr.
16 H3 Słupsk Pol.
6 P4 Slussfors Sweden
20 C4 Slutsk Belarus
11 A4 Slyne Head hd Rep. of Ireland
25 M4 Slyudyanka Rus. Fed.
71 J3 Small Pt pt U.S.A.
59 H3 Smallwood Reservoir Can.
20 D4 Smalyavichy Belarus
17 N3 Smarhon' Belarus
90 E5 Smartt Syndicate Dam resr S. Africa
57 J4 Smeaton Can.
19 J2 Smederevo Yugo.
19 J2 Smederevska Palanka Yugo.
70 D4 Smethport U.S.A.
21 D5 Smila Ukr.
12 E2 Smilde Neth.
7 T8 Smiltene Latvia
56 G3 Smith Can.
72 C2 Smith U.S.A.
70 C6 Smith r. U.S.A.
54 C2 Smith Bay b. U.S.A.
56 D4 Smithers Can.
91 G5 Smithfield S. Africa
67 E5 Smithfield NC U.S.A.
62 E3 Smithfield UT U.S.A.
92 A3 Smith Glacier gl. Ant.
92 B2 Smith I. i. S. Shetland Is Ant.
71 E5 Smith I. i. MD U.S.A.
71 F6 Smith I. i. VA U.S.A.
70 D6 Smith Mountain Lake l. U.S.A.
56 D3 Smith River Can.
69 J3 Smiths Falls Can.
55 L2 Smith Sound str. Can./Greenland
72 C1 Smoke Creek Desert U.S.A.
56 F4 Smoky r. Can.
64 C4 Smoky r. U.S.A.
58 D3 Smoky Falls Can.
64 D4 Smoky Hills h. U.S.A.
56 G4 Smoky Lake Can.
6 K5 Smøla i. Norway
20 E4 Smolensk Rus. Fed.
20 E4 Smolenskaya Oblast' div. Rus. Fed.
19 L4 Smolyan Bulg.
40 C3 Smolyoninovo Rus. Fed.
58 D4 Smooth Rock Falls Can.
58 C3 Smoothrock L. l. Can.
57 H4 Smoothstone Lake l. Can.
6 T1 Smørfjord Norway
92 B3 Smyley I. i. Ant.
71 F5 Smyrna DE U.S.A.
67 C5 Smyrna GA U.S.A.
70 C4 Smyrna OH U.S.A.
71 J1 Smyrna Mills U.S.A.
8 C3 Snaefell h. U.K.
6 F4 Snæfell mt Iceland
56 A2 Snag Can.
62 D3 Snake r. U.S.A.
73 E2 Snake Range mts U.S.A.
62 D3 Snake River Plain plain U.S.A.
67 E7 Snap Pt pt Bahamas
56 G2 Snare Lake Can.
49 G6 Snares Is is N.Z.
6 N4 Snasa Norway
12 D1 Sneek Neth.
11 B6 Sneem Rep. of Ireland
90 F6 Sneeuberg mts S. Africa
59 H3 Snegamook Lake l. Can.
9 H5 Snettisham U.K.
24 K3 Snezhnogorsk Rus. Fed.
18 F2 Snežnik mt Slovenia
17 K4 Śniardwy, Jezioro l. Pol.
21 E6 Snihurivka Ukr.
10 B3 Snizort, Loch b. U.K.
62 B2 Snohomish U.S.A.
62 B2 Snoqualmie Pass U.S.A.
6 N3 Snøtinden mt Norway
57 J2 Snowbird Lake l. Can.
9 C4 Snowdon mt U.K.
9 D5 Snowdonia National Park U.K.
73 G4 Snowflake U.S.A.
71 F5 Snow Hill MD U.S.A.
67 E5 Snow Hill NC U.S.A.
57 J4 Snow Lake Can.
50 B2 Snowtown Austr.
62 D3 Snowville U.S.A.
50 G4 Snowy r. Austr.
50 G4 Snowy Mts mts Austr.
59 J3 Snug Harbour Nfld Can.
69 G3 Snug Harbour Ont. Can.
44 C2 Snuŏl Cambodia
65 D5 Snyder OK U.S.A.
65 C5 Snyder TX U.S.A.
89 E5 Soalala Madag.
89 E5 Soanierana-Ivongo Madag.
42 D6 Soan kundo i. S. Korea
81 B3 Soata Col.
10 B3 Soay i. U.K.
42 D6 Sobaek Sanmaek mts S. Korea
87 F4 Sobat r. Sudan
13 F5 Sobernheim Ger.
37 G7 Sobger r. Indon.
41 B8 Sobo-san mt Japan
79 K6 Sobradinho, Barragem de resr Brazil
79 K4 Sobral Brazil
So-chaoson-man g. see Korea Bay
21 F7 Sochi Rus. Fed.
42 D5 Sŏch'on S. Korea
46 M5 Société, Arch. de la arch. Pac. Oc.
82 C3 Socorro Brazil
81 B3 Socorro Col.
63 F5 Socorro U.S.A.
74 B5 Socorro, I. i. Mex.
32 D7 Socotra i. Yemen
44 C3 Soc Trăng Vietnam
15 E3 Socuéllamos Spain
72 D4 Soda Lake l. U.S.A.
6 U3 Sodankylä Fin.
34 D2 Soda Plains plain China/Jammu and Kashmir
62 E3 Soda Springs U.S.A.
7 P6 Söderhamn Sweden
7 P7 Söderköping Sweden
7 P7 Södertälje Sweden
87 E3 Sodiri Sudan
88 D3 Sodo Eth.
7 Q6 Södra Kvarken str. Fin./Sweden
91 H1 Soekmekaar S. Africa
12 D3 Soerendonk Neth.
13 G3 Soest Ger.
12 D2 Soest Neth.
50 G2 Sofala Austr.
19 K3 Sofia Bulg.
Sofiya see Sofia
6 W4 Sofporog Rus. Fed.
41 G10 Sōfu-gan i. Japan
81 B3 Sogamoso Col.
29 G1 Soğanlı Dağları mts Turkey
12 F2 Sögel Ger.
7 K7 Søgne Norway
7 J6 Sognefjorden in. Norway
43 C4 Sogod Phil.
38 A1 Sogo Nur l. China
20 H2 Sogra Rus. Fed.
38 A3 Sogruma China
28 C1 Söğüt Turkey
42 D7 Sŏgwip'o S. Korea
35 H3 Sog Xian China
87 F2 Sohâg Egypt
34 D5 Sohagpur India
9 H5 Soham U.K.
34 B2 Sohan r. Pak.
49 F2 Sohano P.N.G.
35 E5 Sohela India
34 D3 Sohna India
42 E3 Sŏho-ri N. Korea
42 C6 Sohŭksan i. S. Korea
12 C4 Soignes, Forêt de forest Belgium
12 C4 Soignies Belgium
6 T5 Soini Fin.
14 F2 Soissons France
34 C4 Sojat India
43 B4 Sojoton Point pt Phil.
21 C5 Sokal' Ukr.
42 E4 Sokch'o S. Korea
19 M6 Söke Turkey
21 G7 Sokhumi Georgia
86 C4 Sokodé Togo
39 □ Soko Islands is H.K. China
20 G3 Sokol Rus. Fed.
17 L4 Sokółka Pol.
86 B3 Sokolo Mali
13 L4 Sokolov Czech Rep.
31 C3 Sokolovka Rus. Fed.
17 L4 Sokołów Podlaski Pol.
86 C3 Sokoto Nigeria
86 C3 Sokoto r. Nigeria
21 C5 Sokyryany Ukr.
34 D3 Solan India
51 A7 Solander I. i. N.Z.
33 A2 Solāpur India
81 B2 Soledad Col.
72 B3 Soledad U.S.A.
81 E2 Soledad Venez.
21 G6 Solenoye Rus. Fed.
9 F7 Solent, The str. U.K.
6 N3 Solfjellsjøen Norway
29 H2 Solhan Turkey
20 G3 Soligalich Rus. Fed.
9 F5 Solihull U.K.
24 G4 Solikamsk Rus. Fed.
24 G4 Sol'-Iletsk Rus. Fed.
12 F3 Solingen Ger.
90 A1 Solitaire Namibia
29 M1 Şollar Azer.
6 P5 Sollefteå Sweden
13 L3 Söllichau Ger.
13 H3 Solling h. Ger.
13 J3 Sollstedt Ger.
13 G4 Solms Ger.
20 F3 Solnechnogorsk Rus. Fed.
45 B3 Solok Indon.
47 H4 Solomon Islands country Pac. Oc.
48 F2 Solomon Sea sea P.N.G./Solomon Is
68 B2 Solon Springs U.S.A.
37 E7 Solor, Kepulauan is Indon.
16 C7 Solothurn Switz.
20 E1 Solovetskiye Ostrova is Rus. Fed.
20 H3 Solovetskoye Rus. Fed.
18 G3 Šolta i. Croatia
31 E2 Soltānābād Iran
31 E3 Solţānābād Iran
30 C4 Solţānābād Iran
13 H2 Soltau Ger.
20 D3 Sol'tsy Rus. Fed.
71 E3 Solvay U.S.A.
7 O8 Sölvesborg Sweden
10 E6 Solway Firth est. U.K.
89 C5 Solwezi Zambia
41 G6 Sōma Japan
28 A2 Soma Turkey
12 B4 Somain France
85 H5 Somalia country Africa
93 H3 Somali Basin sea feature Ind. Ocean
89 C4 Sombo Angola
19 H2 Sombor Yugo.
34 C4 Somdari India
71 J2 Somerest Junction U.S.A.
7 S6 Somero Fin.
66 C4 Somerset KY U.S.A.
68 E4 Somerset MI U.S.A.
70 D5 Somerset PA U.S.A.
91 F6 Somerset East S. Africa
55 J2 Somerset Island i. Can.
71 G3 Somerset Reservoir U.S.A.
90 C7 Somerset West S. Africa
71 H3 Somersworth U.S.A.
65 D6 Somerville Res. resr U.S.A.
7 O7 Sommen l. Sweden
13 K3 Sömmerda Ger.
59 G3 Sommet, Lac du l. Can.
34 B5 Somnath India
68 C5 Somonauk U.S.A.
83 C4 Somuncurá, Mesa Volcánica de plat. Arg.
35 F4 Son r. India
35 F5 Sonamukhi India
35 G5 Sonamura India
35 E5 Sonapur India
34 D4 Sonar r. India
35 H4 Sonari India
42 C4 Sŏnch'ŏn N. Korea
20 E2 Sondaly Rus. Fed.
7 L9 Sønderborg Denmark
13 J3 Sondershausen Ger.
55 N3 Søndre Strømfjord in. Greenland
18 C1 Sondrio Italy
33 B2 Sonepet India
34 B5 Songad India
38 E4 Songbu China
44 D2 Sông Cau Vietnam
44 C1 Song Con r. Vietnam
39 B6 Sông Đa r. Vietnam
44 D2 Sông Đa Răng r. Vietnam
89 D5 Songea Tanz.
42 D3 Songgan N. Korea
44 C3 Song Hậu Giang r. Vietnam
42 D2 Songhua Hu resr China
42 C1 Songhua Jiang China
40 B1 Songhua Jiang r. China
38 F4 Songjiang China
42 D2 Songjianghe China
39 C4 Songkan China
44 B4 Songkhla Thai.
39 C6 Sông Ky Cung r. Vietnam
36 E2 Songling China
38 F1 Song Ling mts China
39 B6 Sông Ma r. Laos/Vietnam
42 D5 Sŏngnam S. Korea
44 C1 Sông Ngan Sau r. Vietnam
42 C4 Songnim N. Korea
88 B4 Songo Angola
89 D5 Songo Moz.
38 B3 Songpan China
44 C3 Song Saigon r. Vietnam
35 G4 Songsak India
42 D7 Sŏngsan S. Korea
38 D3 Song Shan mt China
42 D3 Songshuzhen China
39 C4 Songtao China
39 F5 Songxi China
38 D3 Song Xian China
39 D4 Songzi China
44 D2 Sơn Ha Vietnam
38 D1 Sonid Youqi China
38 D1 Sonid Zuoqi China
34 D3 Sonīpat India
6 U5 Sonkajärvi Fin.
39 B6 Sơn La Vietnam
31 G5 Sonmiani Pak.
31 G5 Sonmiani Bay b. Pak.
13 K4 Sonneberg Ger.
82 D2 Sono r. Minas Gerais Brazil
79 J6 Sono r. Tocantins Brazil

73 G6 Sonoita U.S.A.
73 F6 Sonoita r. Mex.
72 B3 Sonora CA U.S.A.
65 C6 Sonora TX U.S.A.
60 D6 Sonora div. Mex.
74 B3 Sonora r. Mex.
73 F6 Sonoyta Mex.
30 B3 Sonqor Iran
81 B3 Sonsón Col.
74 G6 Sonsonate El Salvador
39 B6 Sơn Tây Vietnam
91 H5 Sonwabile S. Africa
83 F1 Sopas r. Uru.
25 S4 Sopka Shiveluch mt Rus. Fed.
87 E4 Sopo watercourse Sudan
19 L3 Sopot Bulg.
17 J3 Sopot Pol.
16 H7 Sopron Hungary
18 E4 Sora Italy
35 F6 Sorada India
7 P5 Soråker Sweden
42 E4 Sŏraksan mt S. Korea
58 F4 Sorel Can.
48 E6 Sorell Austr.
28 E2 Sorgun Turkey
15 E2 Soria Spain
24 C2 Sørkappøya i. Svalbard
30 D3 Sorkheh Iran
30 D3 Sorkh, Kūh-e mts Iran
6 N4 Sørli Norway
35 F5 Soro India
21 D5 Soroca Moldova
82 C3 Sorocaba Brazil
24 G4 Sorochinsk Rus. Fed.
37 G6 Sorol i. Micronesia
37 F7 Sorong Indon.
88 D3 Soroti Uganda
6 S1 Sørøya i. Norway
15 B3 Sorraia r. Port.
6 Q2 Sorreisa Norway
50 E5 Sorrento Austr.
89 B6 Sorris Sorris Namibia
92 D3 Sør-Rondane mts Ant.
6 P4 Sorsele Sweden
43 C3 Sorsogon Phil.
20 D2 Sortavala Rus. Fed.
6 O2 Sortland Norway
20 J2 Sortopolovskaya Rus. Fed.
20 J3 Sorvizhi Rus. Fed.
42 D5 Sŏsan S. Korea
91 H2 Soshanguve S. Africa
21 F4 Sosna r. Rus. Fed.
83 C2 Sosneado mt Arg.
20 K2 Sosnogorsk Rus. Fed.
20 H2 Sosnovka Archangel. Rus. Fed.
20 G4 Sosnovka Tambov. Rus. Fed.
24 F3 Sosnovka Rus. Fed.
6 X4 Sosnovyy Rus. Fed.
7 V7 Sosnovyy Bor Rus. Fed.
17 J5 Sosnowiec Pol.
21 F6 Sosyka r. Rus. Fed.
81 A4 Sotara, Volcán volc. Col.
6 V4 Sotkamo Fin.
83 D1 Soto Arg.
74 E4 Soto la Marina Mex.
88 B3 Souanké Congo
86 B4 Soubré Côte d'Ivoire
71 F4 Souderton U.S.A.
19 M4 Soufli Greece
14 E4 Souillac France
12 D5 Souilly France
86 C1 Souk Ahras Alg.
Sŏul see Seoul
14 D5 Soulom France
Soûr see Tyre
15 H4 Sour el Ghozlane Alg.
57 J5 Souris Man. Can.
59 H4 Souris P.E.I. Can.
57 J5 Souris r. Can./U.S.A.
79 L5 Sousa Brazil
86 D1 Sousse Tunisia
14 D5 Soustons France
32 C7 South div. Yemen
85 F9 South Africa, Republic of country Africa
69 G3 Southampton Can.
9 F7 Southampton U.K.
71 G4 Southampton U.S.A.
55 K3 Southampton I. Can.
57 M2 Southampton Island i. Can.
70 E6 South Anna r. U.S.A.
9 F4 South Anston U.K.
59 H2 South Aulatsivik Island i. Can.
48 D5 South Australia div. Austr.
93 N6 South Australian Basin sea feature Ind. Ocean
65 F5 Southaven U.S.A.
63 F5 South Baldy mt U.S.A.
8 F3 South Bank U.K.
70 B4 South Bass I. i. U.S.A.
57 N2 South Bay b. Can.
69 F3 South Baymouth Can.
68 D5 South Bend IN U.S.A.
62 B2 South Bend WA U.S.A.
67 E7 South Bight chan. Bahamas
70 D6 South Boston U.S.A.
51 D5 Southbridge N.Z.
71 G3 Southbridge U.S.A.
South Cape c. see Ka Lae
67 D5 South Carolina div. U.S.A.
71 J2 South China U.S.A.
45 C1 South China Sea sea Pac. Oc.
64 C2 South Dakota div. U.S.A.
71 G3 South Deerfield U.S.A.
9 G7 South Downs h. U.K.
91 F2 South East div. Botswana
50 F5 South East Cape Vic. Austr.
48 E6 South East Cape c. Austr.
95 N10 South-East Pacific Basin sea feature Pac. Oc.
57 J3 Southend Can.
10 C5 Southend U.K.
9 H6 Southend-on-Sea U.K.
68 A5 South English U.S.A.
51 C5 Southern Alps mts N.Z.
48 B5 Southern Cross Austr.
57 K3 Southern Indian Lake l. Can.
87 E4 Southern National Park Sudan
47 C7 Southern Ocean ocean
67 E5 Southern Pines U.S.A.
92 C1 Southern Thule I. i. Atl. Ocean
10 D5 Southern Uplands reg. U.K.
10 F4 South Esk r. U.K.
68 B6 South Fabius r. U.S.A.
94 G7 South Fiji Basin sea feature Pac. Oc.
63 F4 South Fork U.S.A.
72 A2 South Fork Eel r. U.S.A.
72 C4 South Fork Kern r. U.S.A.
70 D5 South Fork South Branch r. U.S.A.
68 E3 South Fox I. i. U.S.A.
92 C5 South Geomagnetic Pole Ant.
10 A3 South Harris i. U.K.
35 G5 South Hatia I. i. Bangl.
68 D4 South Haven U.S.A.
57 K2 South Henik Lake l. Can.
71 G2 South Hero U.S.A.
70 D6 South Hill U.S.A.
94 E4 South Honshu Ridge sea feature Pac. Oc.
57 K3 South Indian Lake Can.
71 G4 Southington U.S.A.
51 C6 South Island i. N.Z.
43 A4 South Islet rf Phil.
35 F5 South Koel r. India
72 B2 South Lake Tahoe U.S.A.
89 D5 South Luangwa National Park Zambia
92 B6 South Magnetic Pole Ant.
68 D3 South Manitou I. i. U.S.A.
67 D7 South Miami U.S.A.
9 H6 Southminster U.K.
57 J4 South Moose L. l. Can.
70 E5 South Mts h. U.S.A.
56 D2 South Nahanni r. Can.
10 □ South Nesting Bay b. U.K.
96 G10 South Orkney Is is Atl. Ocean
71 H2 South Paris U.S.A.
62 G3 South Platte r. U.S.A.
92 B4 South Pole Ant.
69 G1 South Porcupine Can.
8 D4 Southport U.K.
71 H3 South Portland U.S.A.
69 H3 South River Can.
10 F2 South Ronaldsay i. U.K.
71 G3 South Royalton U.S.A.
91 J5 South Sand Bluff pt S. Africa
96 H9 South Sandwich Islands is Atl. Ocean
96 H9 South Sandwich Trench sea feature Atl. Ocean
57 H4 South Saskatchewan r. Can.
57 K3 South Seal r. Can.
96 F9 South Shetland Is is Ant.
8 F3 South Shields U.K.
8 G4 South Skirlaugh U.K.
68 A5 South Skunk r. U.S.A.
51 E3 South Taranaki Bight b. N.Z.
73 G2 South Tent summit U.S.A.
35 E4 South Tons r. India
13 E3 South Twin I. i. Can.
8 E3 South Tyne r. U.K.
10 A3 South Uist i. U.K.
51 A7 South West Cape c. N.Z.
93 H6 South-West Indian Ridge sea feature Ind. Ocean
95 J8 South-West Pacific Basin sea feature Pa. Oc.
95 O7 South-West Peru Ridge sea feature Pac. Oc.
68 E5 South Whitley U.S.A.
71 H3 South Windham U.S.A.
9 J5 Southwold U.K.
91 H1 Soutpansberg mts S. Africa
18 G5 Soverato Italy
20 B4 Sovetsk Kaliningrad. Rus. Fed.
20 J3 Sovetsk Kirovsk. Rus. Fed.
36 G2 Sovetskaya Gavan' Rus. Fed.
20 D2 Sovetskiy Leningrad. Rus. Fed.
20 J3 Sovetskiy Mariy El. Rus. Fed.
24 H3 Sovetskiy Rus. Fed.
91 G3 Soweto S. Africa
30 E4 Sowghān Iran
40 G2 Sōya-misaki c. Japan
42 D4 Soyang-ho l. S. Korea
17 P4 Sozh r. Belarus
19 M3 Sozopol Bulg.
12 D4 Spa Belgium
92 B3 Spaatz I. i. Ant.
5 C4 Spain country Europe
9 G5 Spalding U.K.
9 D6 Span Head h. U.K.
69 F2 Spanish Can.
69 G2 Spanish r. Can.
73 G1 Spanish Fork U.S.A.
75 J5 Spanish Town Jamaica
72 C2 Sparks U.S.A.
70 C6 Sparta NC U.S.A.
68 B4 Sparta WV U.S.A.
67 D5 Spartanburg U.S.A.
19 K6 Sparti Greece
18 G6 Spartivento, Capo c. Italy
56 G5 Sparwood Can.
20 E4 Spas-Demensk Rus. Fed.
20 E2 Spasskaya Guba Rus. Fed.
36 F2 Spassk-Dal'niy Rus. Fed.
19 K7 Spatha, Akra pt Greece
56 D3 Spatsizi Plateau Wilderness Provincial Park res. Can.
64 C2 Spearfish U.S.A.
65 C4 Spearman U.S.A.
71 F3 Speculator U.S.A.
64 E3 Spencer IA U.S.A.
62 D2 Spencer ID U.S.A.
70 C5 Spencer WV U.S.A.
56 B3 Spencer, Cape c. U.S.A.
48 D5 Spencer Gulf est. Austr.
56 E4 Spences Bridge Can.
8 F3 Spennymoor U.K.
11 D3 Sperrin Mountains h. U.K.
70 D5 Sperryville U.S.A.
13 H5 Spessart reg. Ger.
19 K6 Spetses i. Greece
10 E3 Spey r. U.K.
13 G5 Speyer Ger.
31 G4 Spezand Pak.
13 F1 Spiekeroog i. Ger.
16 C7 Spiez Switz.
12 E1 Spijk Neth.
12 C3 Spijkenisse Neth.
18 E1 Spilimbergo Italy
9 H4 Spilsby U.K.
31 G4 Spīn Būldak Afgh.
34 B3 Spintangi Pak.
56 F3 Spirit River Can.
68 C3 Spirit River Flowage resr U.S.A.
57 H4 Spiritwood Can.
31 G3 Spirsang Pass Afgh.
17 K6 Spišská Nová Ves Slovakia
29 K1 Spitak Armenia
34 D3 Spiti r. India
24 C2 Spitsbergen i. Svalbard
16 F7 Spittal an der Drau Austria
18 G3 Split Croatia
57 K3 Split Lake Can.
57 K3 Split Lake l. Can.
62 C2 Spokane U.S.A.
18 E3 Spoleto Italy
42 C2 Spong Cambodia
68 B3 Spooner U.S.A.
13 K1 Spornitz Ger.
62 F2 Spotted Horse U.S.A.
59 J3 Spotted Island Can.
69 F2 Spragge Can.
56 E4 Spranger, Mt mt Can.
62 C2 Spray U.S.A.
16 G5 Spree r. Ger.
12 D4 Sprimont Belgium
69 F3 Spring Bay Can.
90 B4 Springbok S. Africa
59 J4 Springdale Can.
65 E4 Springdale U.S.A.
13 H2 Springe Ger.
63 F4 Springer U.S.A.
73 H4 Springerville U.S.A.
65 C4 Springfield CO U.S.A.
68 C6 Springfield IL U.S.A.
71 G3 Springfield MA U.S.A.
71 J2 Springfield ME U.S.A.
64 E2 Springfield MN U.S.A.
65 E4 Springfield MO U.S.A.
70 B5 Springfield OH U.S.A.
65 C4 Springfield OR U.S.A.
71 G3 Springfield VT U.S.A.
70 D5 Springfield WV U.S.A.
68 C6 Springfield, Lake l. U.S.A.
91 F5 Springfontein S. Africa
68 B4 Spring Green U.S.A.
68 B4 Spring Grove U.S.A.
59 H4 Springhill Can.
67 D6 Spring Hill U.S.A.
68 D4 Spring Lake U.S.A.
73 E3 Spring Mountains U.S.A.
51 D5 Springs Junction N.Z.
68 A4 Spring Valley U.S.A.
70 D3 Springville NY U.S.A.
73 G1 Springville UT U.S.A.
9 J5 Sprowston U.K.
56 G4 Spruce Grove Can.
70 D5 Spruce Knob-Seneca Rocks National Recreation Area res. U.S.A.
62 D3 Spruce Mt. mt U.S.A.
8 H4 Spurn Head c. U.K.
56 E5 Spuzzum Can.
56 E5 Squamish Can.
71 H3 Squam Lake l. U.S.A.
71 J1 Squapan Lake l. U.S.A.
71 J1 Square Lake l. U.S.A.
18 G5 Squillace, Golfo di g. Italy
74 A2 S. Quintín, C. pt Mex.
Srbija div. see Serbia
44 B3 Srê Âmbĕl Cambodia
25 R4 Sredinnyy Khrebet mts Rus. Fed.
19 K3 Sredna Gora mts Bulg.
25 R3 Srednekolymsk Rus. Fed.
24 E4 Sredne-Russkaya Vozvyshennost' reg. Rus. Fed.
25 M3 Sredne-Sibirskoye Ploskogor'ye plat. Rus. Fed.
6 W4 Sredneye Kuyto, Oz. l. Rus. Fed.
19 L3 Srednogorie Bulg.
44 C2 Srêpok, T. r. Cambodia
36 D1 Sretensk Rus. Fed.
33 C3 Sriharikota I. i. India
33 D2 Srikakulam India
33 B2 Sri Kālahasti India
34 D3 Sri Kanta mt India
23 H9 Sri Lanka country Asia
34 D3 Srinagar India
34 C2 Srinagar Jammu and Kashmir
33 B4 Srirangam India
44 B1 Sri Thep Thai.
33 B4 Srivaikuntam India
33 A2 Srivardhan India
33 B4 Srivilliputtur India
33 C2 Srungavarapukota India
13 H1 Stade Ger.
12 B4 Staden Belgium
12 E2 Stadskanaal Neth.
13 H4 Stadtallendorf Ger.
13 H2 Stadthagen Ger.
13 K4 Stadtilm Ger.
13 E3 Stadtlohn Ger.
13 H3 Stadtoldendorf Ger.
13 K4 Stadtroda Ger.
10 B4 Staffa i. U.K.
13 K4 Staffelberg h. Ger.
13 J4 Staffelstein Ger.
9 E5 Stafford U.K.
70 E5 Stafford U.S.A.
7 T8 Staicele Latvia
9 G6 Staines U.K.
21 F5 Stakhanov Ukr.
9 E7 Stalbridge U.K.
9 J5 Stalham U.K.
Stalingrad see Volgograd
56 E3 Stalin, Mt mt Can.
17 L5 Stalowa Wola Pol.
19 L3 Stamboliyski Bulg.
9 G5 Stamford U.K.
71 G4 Stamford CT U.S.A.
71 F3 Stamford NY U.S.A.
Stampalia i. see Astypalaia
89 B6 Stampriet Namibia
6 N2 Stamsund Norway
64 E3 Stanberry U.S.A.
12 C3 Standdaarbuiten Neth.
91 H3 Standerton S. Africa
69 F4 Standish U.S.A.
66 C4 Stanford U.S.A.
91 J4 Stanger S. Africa
67 E7 Staniard Ck Bahamas
19 K3 Stanke Dimitrov Bulg.
13 M5 Staňkov Czech Rep.
71 K1 Stanley Can.
39 □ Stanley H.K. China
80 E8 Stanley Falkland Is
8 F3 Stanley U.K.
62 D2 Stanley ID U.S.A.
64 C1 Stanley ND U.S.A.
68 B3 Stanley WV U.S.A.
88 C3 Stanley, Mount mt Congo(Zaire)/Uganda
33 B4 Stanley Reservoir India
8 F2 Stannington U.K.
25 R3 Stanovaya Rus. Fed.
36 D1 Stanovoye Nagor'ye mts Rus. Fed.
36 E1 Stanovoy Khrebet mts Rus. Fed.
9 H5 Stanton U.K.
70 B6 Stanton KY U.S.A.
68 E4 Stanton MI U.S.A.
64 C3 Stapleton U.S.A.
17 K5 Starachowice Pol.
Stara Planina mts see Balkan Mountains
20 H4 Staraya Kulatka Rus. Fed.
21 H5 Staraya Poltavka Rus. Fed.
20 D3 Staraya Russa Rus. Fed.
17 P2 Staraya Toropa Rus. Fed.
20 J4 Staraya Tumba Rus. Fed.
19 L3 Stara Zagora Bulg.
46 M4 Starbuck Island i. Kiribati
16 G4 Stargard Szczeciński Pol.
20 E3 Staritsa Rus. Fed.
67 D6 Starke U.S.A.
65 F5 Starkville U.S.A.
16 E7 Starnberger See l. Ger.
21 F5 Starobil's'k Ukr.
17 Q4 Starodub Rus. Fed.
17 J4 Starogard Gdański Pol.
21 C5 Starokostyantyniv Ukr.
21 F6 Starominskaya Rus. Fed.
21 F6 Staroshcherbinovskaya Rus. Fed.
72 C1 Star Peak mt U.S.A.
9 D7 Start Point pt U.K.
17 O4 Staryya Darohi Belarus
21 F5 Staryy Oskol Rus. Fed.
13 K3 Staßfurt Ger.
70 E4 State College U.S.A.
67 D5 Statesboro U.S.A.
67 D5 Statesville U.S.A.
13 M3 Stauchitz Ger.
13 G4 Staufenberg Ger.
70 D5 Staunton U.S.A.
7 J7 Stavanger Norway
9 F4 Staveley U.K.
21 G6 Stavropol' Rus. Fed.
21 G6 Stavropol'skaya Vozvyshennost' reg. Rus. Fed.
21 G6 Stavropol'skiy Kray div. Rus. Fed.
50 D4 Stawell Austr.
91 H4 Steadville S. Africa
72 C2 Steamboat U.S.A.
62 F3 Steamboat Springs U.S.A.
92 B2 Steele I. i. Ant.
70 E4 Steelton U.S.A.
12 E2 Steenderen Neth.
91 J2 Steenkampsberge mts S. Africa
56 F3 Steen River Can.
62 C3 Steens Mt. mt U.S.A.
55 N2 Steenstrup Gletscher gl. Greenland
12 A4 Steenvoorde France
12 E2 Steenwijk Neth.
92 D4 Stefansson Bay b. Ant.
54 H2 Stefansson I. i. Can.
13 J5 Steigerwald forest Ger.
13 E5 Stein Ger.
13 K4 Steinach Ger.
57 K5 Steinbach Can.
13 G2 Steinfeld (Oldenburg) Ger.
12 F2 Steinfurt Ger.
89 B6 Steinhausen Namibia
13 H3 Steinheim Ger.
13 H2 Steinhuder Meer l. Ger.
6 M4 Steinkjer Norway
90 B4 Steinkopf S. Africa
73 H5 Steins U.S.A.
6 M4 Steinsdalen Norway
90 B3 Stella S. Africa
90 C6 Stellenbosch S. Africa
18 C3 Stello, Monte mt Corsica France
12 D5 Stenay France
13 K2 Stendal Ger.
39 □ Stenhouse, Mt h. H.K. China
10 E4 Stenhousemuir U.K.
7 M7 Stenungsund Sweden
Stepanakert see Xankändi
21 H7 Step'anavan Armenia
57 K5 Stephen U.S.A.
50 C2 Stephens r. Austr.
51 D4 Stephens, Cape c. N.Z.
50 C1 Stephens Creek Austr.
68 D3 Stephenson U.S.A.
56 C3 Stephens Passage chan. U.S.A.
59 J4 Stephenville Can.
65 D5 Stephenville U.S.A.
21 H5 Stepnoye Rus. Fed.
91 H4 Sterkfontein Dam resr S. Africa
91 G5 Sterkstroom S. Africa
90 D5 Sterling S. Africa
62 G3 Sterling CO U.S.A.
68 C5 Sterling IL U.S.A.
64 C2 Sterling ND U.S.A.
73 G2 Sterling UT U.S.A.
65 C6 Sterling City U.S.A.
69 F4 Sterling Hgts U.S.A.
26 D1 Sterlitamak Rus. Fed.
13 K1 Sternberg Ger.
56 G4 Stettler Can.
68 D2 Steuben U.S.A.
70 C4 Steubenville U.S.A.
9 G6 Stevenage U.K.
57 K4 Stevenson L. l. Can.
68 C3 Stevens Point U.S.A.
54 D3 Stevens Village U.S.A.
56 D3 Stewart Can.
56 B2 Stewart r. Can.
56 B2 Stewart Crossing Can.
51 A7 Stewart Island i. N.Z.
49 G2 Stewart Islands is Solomon Is
55 K3 Stewart Lake l. Can.
10 D5 Stewarton U.K.
68 A4 Stewartville U.S.A.
91 F5 Steynsburg S. Africa
16 G6 Steyr Austria
90 F6 Steytlerville S. Africa
12 D1 Stiens Neth.
56 C3 Stikine r. Can./U.S.A.
56 C3 Stikine Ranges mts Can.
90 D7 Stilbaai S. Africa
68 A3 Stillwater MN U.S.A.
72 C2 Stillwater NV U.S.A.
65 D4 Stillwater OK U.S.A.
63 C4 Stillwater Ra. mts U.S.A.
9 G5 Stilton U.K.
19 K4 Štip Macedonia
50 B3 Stirling Austr.
10 E4 Stirling U.K.
72 B2 Stirling City U.S.A.
50 A2 Stirling North Austr.
6 M5 Stjørdalshalsen Norway
16 H6 Stockerau Austria
13 K4 Stockheim Ger.
7 Q7 Stockholm Sweden
71 J1 Stockholm U.S.A.
9 E4 Stockport U.K.
72 B3 Stockton CA U.S.A.
64 D4 Stockton KS U.S.A.
73 F1 Stockton UT U.S.A.
68 B2 Stockton I. i. U.S.A.
65 E4 Stockton L. l. U.S.A.
8 F3 Stockton-on-Tees U.K.
71 J2 Stockton Springs U.S.A.
7 P5 Stöde Sweden
44 B2 Stœng Sângke r. Cambodia
44 C2 Stœng Sên r. Cambodia
44 C2 Stœng Trêng Cambodia
10 C2 Stoer, Point of pt U.K.
9 E4 Stoke-on-Trent U.K.
8 F3 Stokesley U.K.
6 C5 Stokkseyri Iceland
6 N3 Stokkvågen Norway
6 O2 Stokmarknes Norway
18 G3 Stolac Bos.-Herz.
12 E4 Stolberg (Rheinland) Ger.
21 C5 Stolin Belarus
13 L4 Stollberg Ger.
13 H2 Stolzenau Ger.
9 E5 Stone U.K.
69 J2 Stonecliffe Can.
71 F5 Stone Harbor U.S.A.
10 F4 Stonehaven U.K.
56 E3 Stone Mountain Prov. Park res. Can.
73 H3 Stoner U.S.A.
71 F4 Stone Ridge U.S.A.
57 K4 Stonewall Can.
70 C5 Stonewall Jackson Lake l. U.S.A.
69 F4 Stoney Point Can.
71 J2 Stonington U.S.A.
72 A2 Stonyford U.S.A.
71 E3 Stony Pt pt U.S.A.
57 H3 Stony Rapids Can.
6 Q3 Stora Inlevatten l. Sweden
6 P3 Stora Sjöfallets Nationalpark nat. park Sweden
6 Q4 Storavan l. Sweden
7 M9 Store Bælt chan. Denmark
6 M5 Støren Norway
6 O3 Storforshei Norway
6 O3 Storjord Norway
54 H2 Storkerson Peninsula Can.
91 G5 Stormberg S. Africa
91 G5 Stormberg mts S. Africa
64 E3 Storm Lake U.S.A.
7 K6 Stornosa mt Norway
10 B2 Stornoway U.K.
20 K2 Storozhevsk Rus. Fed.
21 C5 Storozhynets' Ukr.
71 G4 Storrs U.S.A.
10 B3 Storr, The h. U.K.
6 P4 Storseleby Sweden
6 O5 Storsjön l. Sweden
7 L5 Storskrymten mt Norway
6 R2 Storslett Norway
12 D1 Stortemelk chan. Neth.
6 P4 Storuman Sweden
6 P4 Storuman l. Sweden
7 P6 Storvik Sweden
7 M8 Storvorde Denmark
7 P7 Storvreta Sweden
9 G5 Stotfold U.K.
68 C4 Stoughton U.S.A.
9 E7 Stour r. Eng. U.K.
9 J6 Stour r. Eng. U.K.
9 H6 Stour r. Eng. U.K.
9 F5 Stour r. Eng. U.K.
9 E5 Stourbridge U.K.
9 E5 Stourport-on-Severn U.K.
57 L4 Stout L. l. Can.
20 C4 Stowbtsy Belarus
71 F4 Stowe U.S.A.
9 H5 Stowmarket U.K.
11 D3 Strabane U.K.
11 D4 Stradbally Rep. of Ireland
9 J5 Stradbroke U.K.
18 C2 Stradella Italy
73 G3 Straight Cliffs cliff U.S.A.
16 F6 Strakonice Czech Rep.
16 F3 Stralsund Ger.
90 C7 Strand S. Africa
6 K5 Stranda Norway
67 E7 Strangers Cay i. Bahamas
11 F3 Strangford U.K.
11 F3 Strangford Lough l. U.K.
10 C6 Stranraer U.K.
14 H2 Strasbourg France
70 D5 Strasburg U.S.A.
50 F4 Stratford Austr.
69 G4 Stratford Can.
51 E3 Stratford N.Z.
65 C4 Stratford TX U.S.A.
68 B3 Stratford WV U.S.A.
9 F5 Stratford-upon-Avon U.K.
50 B3 Strathalbyn Austr.
10 D5 Strathaven U.K.
10 G3 Strathbeg, Loch of l. U.K.
10 D3 Strathcarron v. U.K.
56 D5 Strathcona Prov. Park res. Can.
10 D3 Strathconon v. U.K.
10 D3 Strath Dearn v. U.K.
10 D2 Strath Fleet v. U.K.
56 G4 Strathmore Can.
56 E4 Strathnaver Can.
10 D2 Strathnaver v. U.K.
10 E2 Strath of Kildonan v. U.K.
69 G4 Strathroy Can.
10 E3 Strathspey v. U.K.
10 E2 Strathy U.K.
10 D2 Strathy Point pt U.K.
9 C7 Stratton U.K.
71 H2 Stratton U.S.A.
13 L6 Straubing Ger.
6 B3 Straumnes pt Iceland
68 B4 Strawberry Point U.S.A.
73 G1 Strawberry Reservoir U.S.A.
48 D5 Streaky Bay Austr.
48 D5 Streaky Bay b. Austr.
68 C5 Streator U.S.A.
9 E6 Street U.K.
19 K2 Strehaia Romania
13 M3 Strehla Ger.
25 R3 Strelka Rus. Fed.
7 T8 Strenči Latvia
13 L5 Stříbro Czech Rep.
10 F3 Strichen U.K.
19 K4 Strimonas r. Greece
83 D4 Stroeder Arg.
11 C4 Strokestown Rep. of Ireland
10 E2 Stroma, Island of i. U.K.
18 F5 Stromboli, Isola i. Italy
10 E2 Stromness U.K.
64 D3 Stromsburg U.S.A.
7 M7 Strömstad Sweden
6 O5 Strömsund Sweden
70 C4 Strongsville U.S.A.
10 F1 Stronsay i. U.K.
50 H2 Stroud Austr.
9 E6 Stroud U.K.
50 H2 Stroud Road Austr.
71 F4 Stroudsburg U.S.A.
7 L8 Struer Denmark
19 J4 Struga Macedonia
20 D3 Strugi-Krasnyye Rus. Fed.
90 D7 Struis Bay S. Africa
13 J5 Strullendorf Ger.
19 K4 Struma r. Bulg.
9 B5 Strumble Head hd U.K.
19 K4 Strumica Macedonia
19 L3 Stryama r. Bulg.
90 E4 Strydenburg S. Africa
7 K6 Stryn Norway
21 B5 Stryy Ukr.
67 D7 Stuart FL U.S.A.
70 C6 Stuart VA U.S.A.
56 E4 Stuart Lake l. Can.
70 D5 Stuarts Draft U.S.A.
50 G2 Stuart Town Austr.
51 C6 Studholme Junction N.Z.
6 Q5 Studsviken Sweden
65 C6 Study Butte U.S.A.
57 L4 Stull L. l. Can.
44 C2 Stung Chinit r. Cambodia
20 F4 Stupino Rus. Fed.
92 A6 Sturge I. i. Ant.
68 D2 Sturgeon r. U.S.A.
68 D3 Sturgeon Bay WV U.S.A.
57 K4 Sturgeon Bay b. Can.
68 E3 Sturgeon Bay b. U.S.A.
68 D3 Sturgeon Bay Canal chan. U.S.A.
69 H2 Sturgeon Falls Can.
58 B3 Sturgeon L. l. Can.
66 C4 Sturgis KY U.S.A.
68 E5 Sturgis MI U.S.A.
64 C2 Sturgis SD U.S.A.
48 C3 Sturt Creek r. Austr.
48 E4 Sturt Desert Austr.
91 G6 Stutterheim S. Africa
16 D6 Stuttgart Ger.
65 F5 Stuttgart U.S.A.
6 B4 Stykkishólmur Iceland
17 M5 Styr r. Ukr.
82 D2 Suaçuí Grande r. Brazil
87 F3 Suakin Sudan
39 F5 Su'ao Taiwan
63 E6 Suaqui Gde Mex.
81 B3 Suárez r. Col.
17 M3 Subačius Lith.
35 H4 Subansiri r. India
35 F5 Subarnarekha r. India
29 G6 Şubayḩah S. Arabia
45 C2 Subi Besar i. Indon.
19 H1 Subotica Yugo.
17 N7 Suceava Romania
40 C3 Suchan r. Rus. Fed.
11 C4 Suck r. Rep. of Ireland
13 K1 Suckow Ger.
78 E7 Sucre Bol.
81 B2 Sucre Col.
81 C3 Sucuaro Col.
82 B2 Sucuriú r. Brazil
21 E6 Sudak Ukr.

85 F4 Sudan country Africa
20 G3 Suday Rus. Fed.
29 K6 Sudayr watercourse Iraq
69 G2 Sudbury Can.
9 H5 Sudbury U.K.
87 E4 Sudd swamp Sudan
13 K1 Sude r. Ger.
16 H5 Sudety mts Czech Rep./Pol.
71 F5 Sudlersville U.S.A.
20 G4 Sudogda Rus. Fed.
28 D7 Sudr Egypt
6 □ Suðuroy i. Faroe Is
87 E4 Sue watercourse Sudan
15 F3 Sueca Spain
87 F2 Suez Egypt
87 F1 Suez Canal canal Egypt
87 F2 Suez, Gulf of g. Egypt
70 E6 Suffolk U.S.A.
30 B2 Sūfiān Iran
68 C4 Sugar r. U.S.A.
71 H2 Sugarloaf Mt. mt U.S.A.
43 C4 Sugbuhan Point pt Phil.
45 E1 Sugut r. Malaysia
43 A5 Sugut, Tg pt Malaysia
38 B2 Suhait China
32 E5 Şuḩār Oman
36 C1 Sühbaatar Mongolia
13 J4 Suhl Ger.
13 J2 Suhlendorf Ger.
28 C2 Şuhut Turkey
34 B3 Sui Pak.
40 B1 Suibin China
39 F4 Suichang China
39 E5 Suichuan China
38 D2 Suide China
42 F1 Suifenhe China
34 B4 Suigam India
36 E2 Suihua China
39 B4 Suijiang China
39 D5 Suining Hunan China
39 E3 Suining Jiangsu China
38 B4 Suining Sichuan China
38 E3 Suiping China
12 C5 Suippes France
11 D5 Suir r. Rep. of Ireland
38 E3 Suixi China
38 E3 Sui Xian China
39 C5 Suiyang China
38 F1 Suizhong China
38 D4 Suizhou China
38 C1 Suj China
34 C4 Sujangarh India
34 D3 Sujanpur India
34 B4 Sujawal Pak.
45 C4 Sukabumi Indon.
45 C3 Sukadana Indon.
41 G6 Sukagawa Japan
43 A5 Sukau Malaysia
42 C4 Sukchŏn N. Korea
40 C1 Sukhanovka Rus. Fed.
20 E4 Sukhinichi Rus. Fed.
20 H2 Sukhona r. Rus. Fed.
44 A1 Sukhothai Thai.
20 E2 Sukkozero Rus. Fed.
34 B4 Sukkur Pak.
33 C2 Sukma India
34 C4 Sukri r. India
73 F3 Sukromny Rus. Fed.
41 C8 Sukumo Japan
7 J6 Sula i. Norway
34 B3 Sulaiman Ranges mts Pak.
21 H7 Sulak r. Rus. Fed.
37 E7 Sula, Kepulauan is Indon.
30 C4 Sülär Iran
10 B1 Sula Sgeir i. U.K.
45 E3 Sulawesi i. Indon.
29 K4 Sulaymān Beg Iraq
30 C2 Suledeh Iran
10 D1 Sule Skerry i. U.K.
10 D1 Sule Stack i. U.K.
28 F3 Süleymanlı Turkey
86 A4 Sulima Sierra Leone
13 G2 Sulingen Ger.
6 P3 Sulitjelma Norway
7 V6 Sulkava Fin.
78 B4 Sullana Peru
64 F4 Sullivan U.S.A.
57 G4 Sullivan L. l. Can.
71 J1 Sully Can.
18 E3 Sulmona Italy
65 E6 Sulphur U.S.A.
65 E5 Sulphur Springs U.S.A.
56 F2 Sultan Can.
Sultanabad see Arāk
28 C2 Sultan Dağları mts Turkey
28 D2 Sultanhanı Turkey
31 F4 Sultan, Koh-i- mts Pak.
35 E4 Sultanpur India
43 B5 Sulu Archipelago is Phil.
31 H2 Sülüktü Kyrg.
28 F2 Sulusaray Turkey
43 A4 Sulu Sea sea Phil.
13 K5 Sulzbach-Rosenberg Ger.
92 A4 Sulzberger Bay b. Ant.
31 E6 Sumāil Oman
80 D3 Sumampa Arg.
81 B4 Sumapaz, Parque Nacional nat. park Col.
29 K5 Sūmar Iran
45 B3 Sumatera i. Indon.
Sumatra i. see Sumatera
16 F6 Šumava mts Czech Rep.
37 E7 Sumba i. Indon.
30 D2 Sumbar r. Turkm.
37 D7 Sumba, Selat chan. Indon.
45 E4 Sumbawa i. Indon.
45 E4 Sumbawabesar Indon.
89 D4 Sumbawanga Tanz.
89 B5 Sumbe Angola
10 □ Sumburgh U.K.
10 □ Sumburgh Head hd U.K.
34 D2 Sumdo China/Jammu and Kashmir
29 M3 Sume'eh Sarā Iran
45 D4 Sumenep Indon.
Sumgait see Sumqayıt
41 F9 Sumisu-jima i. Japan
29 J3 Summēl Iraq
58 C3 Summer Beaver Can.
59 K4 Summerford Can.
68 D3 Summer I. i. U.S.A.
10 C2 Summer Isles is U.K.
59 H4 Summerside Can.
70 C5 Summersville U.S.A.
70 C5 Summersville Lake l. U.S.A.
56 E4 Summit Lake Can.
68 E5 Summit Lake l. U.S.A.
72 D2 Summit Mt mt U.S.A.
34 D2 Sumnal China/India
51 D5 Sumner N.Z.
68 A4 Sumner U.S.A.
51 D5 Sumner, L. l. N.Z.
56 C3 Sumner Strait chan. U.S.A.
41 F6 Sumon-dake mt Japan
41 D7 Sumoto Japan
16 H6 Šumperk Czech Rep.
29 M1 Sumqayıt Azer.
29 M1 Sumqayıt r. Azer.
34 B4 Sumrahu Pak.
67 D5 Sumter U.S.A.
21 E5 Sumy Ukr.
62 D2 Sun r. U.S.A.
20 J3 Suna Rus. Fed.
40 G3 Sunagawa Japan
35 G4 Sunamganj Bangl.
42 C4 Sunan N. Korea
10 C4 Sunart, Loch in. U.K.
30 D6 Şunaynah Oman
29 K4 Sunbula Kuh mts Iran
62 E1 Sunburst U.S.A.
50 E4 Sunbury Austr.
70 B4 Sunbury OH U.S.A.
70 E4 Sunbury PA U.S.A.
83 E1 Sunchales Arg.
42 C4 Sunch'ŏn N. Korea
42 D6 Sunch'ŏn S. Korea
91 G2 Sun City S. Africa
71 H3 Suncook U.S.A.
62 F2 Sundance U.S.A.
35 F5 Sundargarh India
34 D3 Sundarnagar India
45 C4 Sunda, Selat chan. Indon.
93 M4 Sunda Trench sea feature Ind. Ocean
8 F3 Sunderland U.K.
13 G3 Sundern (Sauerland) Ger.
28 C2 Sündiken Dağları mts Turkey
69 H3 Sundridge Can.
7 P5 Sundsvall Sweden
31 F2 Sundukli, Peski des. Turkm.
91 J4 Sundumbili S. Africa
34 D4 Sunel India
44 B5 Sungaikabung Indon.
45 C3 Sungailiat Indon.
45 B2 Sungai Pahang r. Malaysia
45 B3 Sungaipenuh Indon.
45 B1 Sungei Petani Malaysia
44 □ Sungei Seletar Res. resr Sing.
28 E1 Sungurlu Turkey
35 F4 Sun Kosi r. Nepal
7 K6 Sunndal Norway
6 L5 Sunndalsøra Norway
7 N7 Sunne Sweden
62 C2 Sunnyside U.S.A.
72 A3 Sunnyvale U.S.A.
68 C4 Sun Prairie U.S.A.
73 □1 Sunset Beach U.S.A.
73 G4 Sunset Crater National Monument res. U.S.A.
25 N3 Suntar Rus. Fed.
31 F5 Suntsar Pak.
62 D3 Sun Valley U.S.A.
42 C5 Sunwi Do i. N. Korea
86 B4 Sunyani Ghana
6 U3 Suolijärvet l. Fin.
68 C1 Suomi Can.
6 V4 Suomussalmi Fin.
41 B8 Suō-nada b. Japan
6 U5 Suonenjoki Fin.
44 C3 Suŏng Cambodia
39 B7 Suong r. Laos
20 E2 Suoyarvi Rus. Fed.
33 A3 Supa India
73 F3 Supai U.S.A.
81 E3 Supamo r. Venez.
35 F4 Supaul India
73 G5 Superior AZ U.S.A.
64 D3 Superior NE U.S.A.
68 A2 Superior WV U.S.A.
68 C2 Superior, Lake l. Can./U.S.A.
44 B2 Suphan Buri Thai.
29 J2 Süphan Dağı mt Turkey
20 E4 Suponevo Rus. Fed.
92 B3 Support Force Glacier gl. Ant.
42 C3 Supung N. Korea
29 L6 Sūq ash Shuyūkh Iraq
38 F3 Suqian China
Suquṭrā i. see Socotra
32 E5 Şūr Oman
20 H4 Sura Rus. Fed.
20 H4 Sura r. Rus. Fed.
29 M1 Şuraabad Azer.
31 G4 Surab Pak.
45 D4 Surabaya Indon.
31 E5 Sūrak Iran
45 D4 Surakarta Indon.
34 C5 Surat India
34 C3 Suratgarh India
44 A3 Surat Thani Thai.
20 E4 Surazh Rus. Fed.
29 K4 Sūrdāsh Iraq
19 K3 Surdulica Yugo.
12 E5 Sûre r. Lux.
34 B5 Surendranagar India
72 B4 Surf U.S.A.
24 J3 Surgut Rus. Fed.
33 B2 Suriapet India
43 C4 Surigao Phil.
43 C4 Surigao Str. chan. Phil.
44 B2 Surin Thai.
77 E2 Suriname country S. America
31 H3 Surkhab r. Afgh.
31 G2 Surkhandar'ya r. Uzbek.
35 E3 Surkhet Nepal
31 H2 Surkhob r. Tajik.
30 D4 Surmāq Iran
29 H1 Sürmene Turkey
21 G5 Surovikino Rus. Fed.
72 B3 Sur, Pt pt U.S.A.
83 F3 Sur, Pta pt Arg.
70 E6 Surry U.S.A.
20 H4 Sursk Rus. Fed.
Surt see Sirte
Surt, Khalīj g. see Sirte, Gulf of
6 C5 Surtsey i. Iceland
28 G3 Sürüç Turkey
41 F7 Suruga-wan b. Japan
45 B3 Surulangun Indon.
43 C5 Surup Phil.
12 F2 Surwold Ger.
30 B2 Şuşa Azer.
41 B7 Ṡusa Japan
41 C8 Susaki Japan
30 C4 Sūsangerd Iran
20 G3 Susanino Rus. Fed.
72 B1 Susanville U.S.A.
28 G1 Suşehri Turkey
44 A4 Suso Thai.
39 E4 Susong China
71 E4 Susquehanna r. U.S.A.
59 G4 Sussex Can.
71 F4 Sussex U.S.A.
43 A5 Susul Malaysia
25 Q3 Susuman Rus. Fed.
28 B2 Susurluk Turkey
34 D2 Sutak Jammu and Kashmir
72 C2 Sutcliffe U.S.A.
90 D6 Sutherland S. Africa
64 C3 Sutherland U.S.A.
34 C3 Sutlej r. Pak.
72 B2 Sutter Creek U.S.A.
9 G5 Sutterton U.K.
71 G2 Sutton Can.
9 H5 Sutton U.K.
70 C5 Sutton U.S.A.
58 D3 Sutton r. Can.
9 F5 Sutton Coldfield U.K.
9 F4 Sutton in Ashfield U.K.
58 D3 Sutton L. l. Can.
70 C5 Sutton Lake l. U.S.A.
40 G3 Suttsu Japan
40 D1 Sutungu Rus. Fed.
49 H3 Suva Fiji
20 F4 Suvorov Rus. Fed.
46 L5 Suvorov I. i. Cook Is Pac. Oc.
41 F6 Suwa Japan
17 L3 Suwałki Pol.
44 B2 Suwannaphum Thai.
67 D6 Suwannee r. U.S.A.
29 K5 Suwayqīyah, Hawr as l. Iraq
29 H6 Suwayr well S. Arabia
42 D5 Suwŏn S. Korea
41 F6 Suzaka Japan
20 G3 Suzdal' Rus. Fed.
38 E3 Suzhou Anhui China
38 F4 Suzhou Jiangsu China
42 C3 Suzi r. China
41 E6 Suzu Japan
41 E7 Suzuka Japan
41 E6 Suzu-misaki pt Japan
6 U1 Sværholthalvøya pen. Norway
96 K1 Svalbard terr. Arctic Ocean
55 N2 Svartenhuk Halvø pen. Greenland
21 F5 Svatove Ukr.
44 C3 Svay Riĕng Cambodia
7 O5 Sveg Sweden
7 U8 Sveķi Latvia
7 J6 Svelgen Norway
6 L5 Svellingen Norway
7 T9 Švenčionėliai Lith.
7 U9 Švenčionys Lith.
7 M9 Svendborg Denmark
6 Q2 Svensby Norway
6 O5 Svenstavik Sweden
Sverdlovsk see Yekaterinburg
21 F5 Sverdlovs'k Ukr.
55 J1 Sverdrup Channel Can.
19 J4 Sveti Nikole Macedonia
36 F2 Svetlaya Rus. Fed.
24 K3 Svetlogorsk Rus. Fed.
20 B4 Svetlogorsk Rus. Fed.
21 G6 Svetlograd Rus. Fed.
20 B4 Svetlyy Rus. Fed.
21 H5 Svetlyy Yar Rus. Fed.
20 D2 Svetogorsk Rus. Fed.
6 E4 Sviahnúkar volc. Iceland
19 M4 Svilengrad Bulg.
19 K2 Svinecea Mare, Vârful mt Romania
20 C4 Svir Belarus
20 E2 Svir' r. Rus. Fed.
19 L3 Svishtov Bulg.
16 H6 Svitava r. Czech Rep.
16 H6 Svitavy Czech Rep.
21 E5 Svitlovods'k Ukr.
20 J4 Sviyaga r. Rus. Fed.
36 E1 Svobodnyy Rus. Fed.
6 O2 Svolvær Norway
19 K3 Svrljiške Planine mts Yugo.
21 D4 Svyetlahorsk Belarus
9 F5 Swadlincote U.K.
9 H5 Swaffham U.K.
48 F4 Swain Reefs rf Austr.
67 D5 Swainsboro U.S.A.
46 K5 Swains Island i. Pac. Oc.
89 B6 Swakopmund Namibia
8 F3 Swale r. U.K.
49 G3 Swallow Is is Solomon Is
57 J4 Swan r. Can.
9 F7 Swanage U.K.
50 D3 Swan Hill Austr.
56 F4 Swan Hills Can.
75 H5 Swan Islands is Honduras
57 J4 Swan L. l. Can.
9 H6 Swanley U.K.
50 B3 Swan Reach Austr.
57 J4 Swan River Can.
50 H2 Swansea N.S.W. Austr.
9 D6 Swansea U.K.
9 D6 Swansea Bay b. U.K.
71 J2 Swans I. i. U.S.A.
71 G2 Swanton U.S.A.
91 G2 Swartruggens S. Africa
73 F2 Swasey Peak summit U.S.A.
69 G1 Swastika Can.
34 B2 Swat r. Pak.
Swatow see Shantou
85 G8 Swaziland country Africa
5 E3 Sweden country Europe
62 B2 Sweet Home U.S.A.
67 C5 Sweetwater TN U.S.A.
65 C5 Sweetwater TX U.S.A.
62 E3 Sweetwater r. U.S.A.
90 D7 Swellendam S. Africa
16 H5 Świdnica Pol.
16 G4 Świdwin Pol.
16 G4 Świebodzin Pol.
17 J4 Świecie Pol.
71 H2 Swift r. U.S.A.
57 H4 Swift Current Can.
57 H5 Swiftcurrent Cr. r. Can.
56 C2 Swift River Can.
11 D2 Swilly, Lough in. Rep. of Ireland
9 F6 Swindon U.K.
11 C4 Swinford Rep. of Ireland
16 G4 Świnoujście Pol.
10 F5 Swinton U.K.
5 D4 Switzerland country Europe
11 E4 Swords Rep. of Ireland
40 D1 Syain Rus. Fed.
20 E2 Syamozero, Oz. l. Rus. Fed.
20 G2 Syamzha Rus. Fed.
17 O3 Syanno Belarus
20 E2 Syas'troy Rus. Fed.
20 H3 Syava Rus. Fed.
68 C5 Sycamore U.S.A.
50 H2 Sydney Austr.
59 H4 Sydney Can.
57 L4 Sydney L. l. Can.
59 H4 Sydney Mines Can.
21 F5 Syeverodonets'k Ukr.
13 G2 Syke Ger.
20 J2 Syktyvkar Rus. Fed.
67 C5 Sylacauga U.S.A.
6 N5 Sylarna mt Norway/Sweden
35 G4 Sylhet Bangl.
20 G2 Syloga Rus. Fed.
16 D3 Sylt i. Ger.
67 D5 Sylvania GA U.S.A.
70 B4 Sylvania OH U.S.A.
56 G4 Sylvan Lake Can.
67 D6 Sylvester U.S.A.
56 E3 Sylvia, Mt mt Can.
19 M6 Symi i. Greece
21 E5 Synel'nykove Ukr.
92 D4 Syowa Japan Base Ant.
18 F6 Syracuse Sicily Italy
64 C4 Syracuse KS U.S.A.
71 E3 Syracuse NY U.S.A.
71 E3 Syracuse airport NY U.S.A.
26 E2 Syrdar'ya r. Kazak.
23 C6 Syria country Asia
32 A3 Syrian Desert Asia
19 M6 Syrna i. Greece
19 L6 Syros i. Greece
7 T6 Sysmä Fin.
20 J2 Sysola r. Rus. Fed.
20 J4 Syzran' Rus. Fed.
16 G4 Szczecin Pol.
16 H4 Szczecinek Pol.
17 K4 Szczytno Pol.
17 K7 Szeged Hungary
17 J7 Székesfehérvár Hungary
17 J7 Szekszárd Hungary
17 K7 Szentes Hungary
16 H7 Szentgotthárd Hungary
18 G1 Szigetvár Hungary
17 K7 Szolnok Hungary
16 H7 Szombathely Hungary

T

43 B3 Taal, L. l. Phil.
43 B3 Tabaco Phil.
91 H5 Tabankulu S. Africa
28 G4 Ţabaqah Syria
48 F2 Tabar Is is P.N.G.
28 E4 Tabarja Lebanon
18 C6 Tabarka Tunisia
30 E3 Ţabas Iran
31 E4 Tabāsin Iran
30 C4 Tābask, Kūh-e mt Iran
59 J3 Tabatière Can.
78 E4 Tabatinga Col.
43 B2 Tabayoo, Mt mt Phil.
50 E3 Tabbita Austr.
86 B2 Tabelbala Alg.
57 G5 Taber Can.
35 F3 Tabia Tsaka salt l. China
49 H2 Tabiteuea i. Kiribati
7 U7 Tabivere Estonia
43 B3 Tablas i. Phil.
43 B3 Tablas Strait chan. Phil.
51 F3 Table Cape c. N.Z.
90 C6 Table Mountain mt S. Africa
65 E4 Table Rock Res. resr U.S.A.
82 A2 Tabocó r. Brazil
16 G6 Tábor Czech Rep.
88 D4 Tabora Tanz.
86 B4 Tabou Côte d'Ivoire
30 B2 Tabrīz Iran
46 M3 Tabuaeran i. Kiribati
32 A4 Tabūk S. Arabia
49 G3 Tabwémasana mt Vanuatu
7 Q7 Täby Sweden
81 A2 Tacarcuna, Cerro mt Panama
27 G2 Tacheng China
16 F6 Tachov Czech Rep.
43 C4 Tacloban Phil.
78 D7 Tacna Peru
62 B2 Tacoma U.S.A.
83 F1 Tacuarembó Uru.
83 G2 Tacuarí r. Uru.
81 E4 Tacutu r. Brazil
8 F4 Tadcaster U.K.
86 C2 Tademaït, Plateau du plat. Alg.
49 G4 Tadine New Caledonia
88 E2 Tadjoura Djibouti
28 G4 Tadmur Syria
57 K3 Tadoule Lake l. Can.
59 G4 Tadoussac Can.
42 D4 T'aebaek Sanmaek mts N. Korea/S. Korea
42 D5 Taech'ŏn S. Korea
42 C5 Taech'ŏngdo i. N. Korea
42 C4 Taedasa-do N. Korea
42 D4 Taedong r. N. Korea
42 C5 Taedong man b. N. Korea
42 E6 Taegu S. Korea
42 C6 Taehŭksan-kundo i. S. Korea
42 D5 Taejŏn S. Korea
42 D7 Taejŏng S. Korea
42 E5 T'aepaek S. Korea
9 C6 Taf r. U.K.
49 J3 Tafahi i. Tonga
15 F1 Tafalla Spain
30 D4 Tafīhān Iran
28 E6 Tafila Jordan
86 B4 Tafiré Côte d'Ivoire
80 C3 Tafí Viejo Arg.
30 C3 Tafresh Iran
30 D4 Taft Iran
72 C4 Taft U.S.A.
31 F4 Taftān, Kūh-e mt Iran
21 F6 Taganrog Rus. Fed.
21 F6 Taganrog, Gulf of b. Rus. Fed./Ukr.
43 C3 Tagapula i. Phil.
43 B3 Tagaytay City Phil.
43 B4 Tagbilaran Phil.
35 E2 Tagchagpu Ri mt China
11 E5 Taghmon Rep. of Ireland
56 C2 Tagish Can.
18 E1 Tagliamento r. Italy
15 J4 Tagma, Col de pass Alg.
43 C4 Tagoloan r. Phil.
43 B4 Tagolo Point pt Phil.
49 F3 Tagula I. i. P.N.G.
43 C5 Tagum Phil.
15 B3 Tagus r. Port./Spain
56 F4 Tahaetkun Mt. mt Can.
44 B4 Tahan, Gunung mt Malaysia
86 C2 Tahat, Mt mt Alg.
36 E1 Tahe China
51 D1 Taheke N.Z.
46 N5 Tahiti i. Pac. Oc.
31 F4 Tahlab r. Iran/Pak.
31 F4 Tahlab, Dasht-i plain Pak.
65 E5 Tahlequah U.S.A.
72 B2 Tahoe City U.S.A.
54 H3 Tahoe Lake l. Can.
72 B2 Tahoe, Lake l. U.S.A.
65 C5 Tahoka U.S.A.
86 C3 Tahoua Niger
56 D4 Tahtsa Pk summit Can.
43 C6 Tahuna Indon.
39 □ Tai a Chau i. H.K. China
42 B3 Tai'an Liaoning China
38 E2 Tai'an Shandong China
38 C3 Taibai Shan mt China
38 E1 Taibus Qi China
39 F5 T'ai-chung Taiwan
51 C6 Taieri r. N.Z.
38 D2 Taigu China
38 D2 Taihang Shan mts China
51 E3 Taihape N.Z.
38 E3 Taihe Anhui China
39 E5 Taihe Jiangxi China
39 E4 Taihu China
36 E3 Tai Hu l. China
39 C5 Taijiang China
38 E3 Taikang China
39 □ Tai Lam Chung Res. resr H.K. China
50 B3 Tailem Bend Austr.
39 □ Tai Long Bay b. H.K. China
39 F5 T'ai-lu-ko Taiwan
31 F3 Taimani reg. Afgh.
39 □ Tai Mo Shan h. H.K. China
39 F6 T'ai-nan Taiwan
39 F6 T'ainan Taiwan
19 K6 Tainaro, Akra pt Greece
39 E5 Taining China
39 □ Tai O H.K. China
82 D1 Taiobeiras Brazil
86 B4 Taï, Parc National de nat. park Côte d'Ivoire
39 F5 T'ai-pei Taiwan
39 F4 Taiping Anhui China
39 D6 Taiping Guangxi China
45 B2 Taiping Malaysia
38 A2 Taipingbao China
42 B1 Taipingchuan China
39 □ Tai Po H.K. China
40 H3 Taisetsu-zan National Park Japan
41 C7 Taisha Japan
39 D6 Taishan China
39 F5 Taishun China
12 C5 Taissy France
51 D5 Taitanu N.Z.
80 B7 Taitao, Peninsula de pen. Chile
39 F6 T'ai-tung Taiwan
6 V4 Taivalkoski Fin.
6 T2 Taivaskero h. Fin.
23 M7 Taiwan country Asia
39 F6 Taiwan Shan mts Taiwan
39 F5 Taiwan Strait str. China/Taiwan
38 F3 Tai Xian China
38 F3 Taixing China
38 D2 Taiyuan China
38 D2 Taiyue Shan mts China
38 F3 Taizhou China
39 F4 Taizhou Wan b. China
42 C3 Taizi r. China
32 B7 Ta'izz Yemen
34 B4 Tajal Pak.
74 F5 Tajamulco, Volcano de volc. Guatemala
18 C7 Tajerouine Tunisia
23 G6 Tajikistan country Asia
Tajo r. see Tagus
44 A1 Tak Thai.
30 B2 Takāb Iran
41 C7 Takahashi Japan
51 D4 Takaka N.Z.
34 D5 Takal India
41 D7 Takamatsu Japan
34 D4 Takanpur India
41 E6 Takaoka Japan
51 F4 Takapau N.Z.
51 E2 Takapuna N.Z.
41 F6 Takasaki Japan
90 F2 Takatokwane Botswana
90 D1 Takatshwaane Botswana
41 C8 Takatsuki-yama mt Japan
41 E6 Takayama Japan
44 B4 Tak Bai Thai.
41 E7 Takefu Japan
41 B8 Takeo Japan
Take-shima i. see Tok-tō
41 B9 Take-shima i. Japan
30 C2 Takestān Iran
41 B8 Taketa Japan
44 C3 Takêv Cambodia
29 K7 Takhādīd well Iraq
32 E1 Takhiatash Uzbek.
44 C3 Ta Khmau Cambodia
31 F3 Takhta-Bazar Turkm.
29 M5 Takht Apān, Kūh-e mt Iran
31 G4 Takhta Pul Post Afgh.
34 B3 Takht-i-Sulaiman mt Pak.
30 C2 Takht-i-Suleiman mt Iran
57 G1 Takijuq Lake l. Can.
40 G3 Takikawa Japan
40 H2 Takinoue Japan
51 A6 Takitimu Mts mts N.Z.
56 D3 Takla Lake l. Can.
56 D3 Takla Landing Can.
Taklimakan Desert see Taklimakan Shamo
22 F6 Taklimakan Shamo des. China
31 H2 Takob Tajik.
35 H3 Takpa Shiri mt China
56 C3 Taku r. Can.
86 C4 Takum Nigeria
83 F2 Tala Uru.
20 D4 Talachyn Belarus
33 B4 Talaimannar Sri Lanka
34 C5 Talaja India
35 H4 Talap India
78 B4 Talara Peru
31 F5 Talar-i-Band mts Pak.
37 E6 Talaud, Kepulauan is Indon.
15 D3 Talavera de la Reina Spain
25 R3 Talaya Rus. Fed.
43 C5 Talayan Phil.
55 L2 Talbot Inlet b. Can.
50 G2 Talbragar r. Austr.
83 B2 Talca Chile
83 B3 Talcahuano Chile
35 F5 Talcher India
27 F2 Taldykorgan Kazak.
29 M5 Taleh Zang Iran
30 C2 Tālesh Iran
9 D6 Talgarth U.K.
37 E7 Taliabu i. Indon.
43 C4 Talibon Phil.
33 B2 Talikota India
31 G2 Talimardzhan Uzbek.
29 J1 T'alin Armenia
33 A3 Taliparamba India
43 B4 Talisay Phil.
43 C4 Talisayan Phil.
29 M2 Talış Dağları mts Azer./Iran
20 H3 Talitsa Rus. Fed.
45 E4 Taliwang Indon.
67 C5 Talladega U.S.A.
29 J3 Tall 'Afar Iraq
67 C6 Tallahassee U.S.A.
50 F4 Tallangatta Austr.
67 C5 Tallassee U.S.A.
28 F6 Tall as Suwaysh h. Jordan
29 H3 Tall Baydar Syria
29 H4 Tall Fadghāmī Syria
7 T7 Tallinn Estonia
28 F4 Tall Kalakh Syria
29 J3 Tall Kayf Iraq
11 C5 Tallow Rep. of Ireland
65 F5 Tallulah U.S.A.
29 J3 Tall 'Uwaynāt Iraq
14 D3 Talmont-St-Hilaire France
21 D5 Tal'ne Ukr.
87 F3 Talodi Sudan
59 G2 Talon, Lac l. Can.
31 H2 Tāloqān Afgh.
21 G5 Talovaya Rus. Fed.
55 J3 Taloyoak Can.
34 C2 Tal Pass Pak.
7 S8 Talsi Latvia
80 B3 Taltal Chile
57 G2 Taltson r. Can.
30 B3 Talvar r. Iran
6 S1 Talvik Norway
21 G5 Taly Rus. Fed.
50 D2 Talyawalka r. Austr.
68 A4 Tama U.S.A.
81 B2 Tamalameque Col.
86 B4 Tamale Ghana
49 H2 Tamana i. Kiribati
81 A3 Tamana mt Col.
41 C7 Tamano Japan
86 C2 Tamanrasset Alg.
35 H4 Tamanthi Myanmar
81 B3 Tama, Parque Nacional el nat. park Venez.
71 F4 Tamaqua U.S.A.
9 C7 Tamar r. U.K.
91 G1 Tamasane Botswana
65 D7 Tamaulipas div. Mex.
74 E4 Tamazunchale Mex.
88 D3 Tambach Kenya
86 A3 Tambacounda Senegal
35 F4 Tamba Kosi r. Nepal
43 A5 Tambisan Malaysia
50 F4 Tambo r. Austr.
45 E4 Tambora, Gunung volc. Indon.
50 F4 Tamboritha mt Austr.
20 G4 Tambov Rus. Fed.
20 G4 Tambovskaya Oblast' div. Rus. Fed.
15 B1 Tambre r. Spain
43 A5 Tambunan, Bukit h. Malaysia
87 E4 Tambura Sudan
43 A5 Tambuyukon, Gunung mt Malaysia
86 A3 Tâmchekket Maur.

81 C3 **Tame** Col.
15 C2 **Tâmega** *r.* Port.
35 H4 **Tamenglong** India
18 B7 **Tamerza** Tunisia
74 E4 **Tamiahua, Lag. de** *lag.* Mex.
44 A4 **Tamiang, Ujung** *pt* Indon.
33 B4 **Tamil Nadu** *div.* India
20 F1 **Tamitsa** Rus. Fed.
28 C7 **Tâmîya** Egypt
44 D2 **Tam Ky** Vietnam
67 D7 **Tampa** U.S.A.
67 D7 **Tampa Bay** *b.* U.S.A.
31 E5 **Tamp-e Gīrān** Iran
7 S6 **Tampere** Fin.
74 E4 **Tampico** Mex.
44 □ **Tampines** Sing.
36 D2 **Tamsagbulag** Mongolia
38 B1 **Tamsag Muchang** China
16 F7 **Tamsweg** Austria
35 H4 **Tamu** Myanmar
35 F4 **Tamur** *r.* Nepal
50 H1 **Tamworth** Austr.
9 F5 **Tamworth** U.K.
88 D4 **Tana** *r.* Kenya
41 D8 **Tanabe** Japan
6 V1 **Tana Bru** Norway
6 V1 **Tanafjorden** *chan.* Norway
T'ana Hāyk' *l. see* **Tana, Lake**
45 E3 **Tanahgrogot** Indon.
37 E7 **Tanahjampea** *i.* Indon.
45 A3 **Tanahmasa** *i.* Indon.
43 A6 **Tanahmerah** Indon.
44 B4 **Tanah Merah** Malaysia
45 C4 **Tanah, Tanjung** *pt* Indon.
88 D2 **Tana, Lake** *l.* Eth.
48 D3 **Tanami Desert** Austr.
44 C3 **Tân An** Vietnam
54 C3 **Tanana** U.S.A.
18 C2 **Tanaro** *r.* Italy
43 C4 **Tanauan** Phil.
38 F3 **Tancheng** China
42 E3 **Tanch'ŏn** N. Korea
86 B4 **Tanda** Côte d'Ivoire
35 E4 **Tanda** India
43 C4 **Tandag** Phil.
19 M2 **Țăndărei** Romania
43 A5 **Tandek** Malaysia
34 D2 **Tandi** India
83 E3 **Tandil** Arg.
83 E3 **Tandil, Sa del** *h.* Arg.
34 B4 **Tando Adam** Pak.
34 B4 **Tando Bago** Pak.
50 D2 **Tandou L.** *l.* Austr.
11 E3 **Tandragee** U.K.
33 B2 **Tandur** India
51 F3 **Taneatua** N.Z.
41 B9 **Tanega-shima** *i.* Japan
44 A1 **Tanen Taunggyi** *mts* Thai.
70 E5 **Taneytown** U.S.A.
86 B2 **Tanezrouft** *reg.* Alg./Mali
88 D4 **Tanga** Tanz.
51 E2 **Tangaehe** N.Z.
35 G4 **Tangail** Bangl.
49 F2 **Tanga Is** *is* P.N.G.
33 C5 **Tangalla** Sri Lanka
88 C4 **Tanganyika, Lake** *l.* Africa
30 D2 **Tangar** Iran
33 B4 **Tangasseri** India
39 B5 **Tangdan** China
92 D4 **Tange Prom.** *hd* Ant.
Tanger *see* **Tangier**
45 C4 **Tangerang** Indon.
13 K2 **Tangerhütte** Ger.
13 K2 **Tangermünde** Ger.
38 B3 **Tanggor** China
35 G2 **Tanggula Shan** *mts* China
35 G2 **Tanggula Shankou** *pass* China
38 D3 **Tanghe** China
34 B2 **Tangi** Pak.
86 B1 **Tangier** Morocco
71 E6 **Tangier I.** *i.* U.S.A.
42 D5 **Tangjin** S. Korea
35 G4 **Tangla** India
44 □ **Tanglin** Sing.
35 H3 **Tangmai** China
35 F3 **Tangra Yumco** *salt l.* China
38 F2 **Tangshan** China
43 B4 **Tangub** Phil.
86 C3 **Tanguieta** Benin
40 A1 **Tangwang** *r.* China
39 C4 **Tangyan He** *r.* China
38 E3 **Tangyin** China
40 A1 **Tangyuan** China
6 U3 **Tanhua** Fin.
44 C3 **Tani** Cambodia
35 H3 **Taniantaweng Shan** *mts* China
37 F7 **Tanimbar, Kepulauan** *is* Indon.
43 B4 **Tanjay** Phil.
Tanjore *see* **Thanjavur**
44 A5 **Tanjungbalai** Indon.
45 C4 **Tanjungkarang Telukbetung** Indon.
45 C3 **Tanjungpandan** Indon.
45 B2 **Tanjungpinang** Indon.
44 A5 **Tanjungpura** Indon.
45 E2 **Tanjungredeb** Indon.
45 E2 **Tanjungselor** Indon.
34 B2 **Tank** Pak.
34 D2 **Tankse** Jammu and Kashmir
35 F4 **Tankuhi** India
49 G3 **Tanna** *i.* Vanuatu
10 F4 **Tannadice** U.K.
7 N5 **Tannäs** Sweden
36 B1 **Tannu Ola, Khrebet** *mts* Rus. Fed.
43 B4 **Tañon Strait** *chan.* Phil.
34 B4 **Tanot** India
86 C3 **Tanout** Niger
35 E4 **Tansen** Nepal
39 F5 **Tan-shui** Taiwan
87 F1 **Tanta** Egypt
86 A2 **Tan-Tan** Morocco
50 C4 **Tantanoola** Austr.
74 E4 **Tantoyuca** Mex.
33 C2 **Tanuku** India
7 M7 **Tanumshede** Sweden
50 B3 **Tanunda** Austr.
42 E5 **Tanyang** S. Korea
85 G6 **Tanzania** *country* Africa
42 B1 **Tao'an** China
42 B1 **Tao'er** *r.* China
38 B3 **Tao He** *r.* China
39 D4 **Taojiang** China
38 C2 **Taole** China
94 G5 **Taongi** *i.* Pac. Oc.
44 □ **Tao Payoh** Sing.
18 F6 **Taormina** *Sicily* Italy
63 F4 **Taos** U.S.A.
86 B2 **Taoudenni** Mali
86 B1 **Taourirt** Morocco
39 E5 **Taoxi** China
39 D4 **Taoyuan** China
39 F5 **T'ao-yuan** Taiwan
7 T7 **Tapa** Estonia
43 B5 **Tapaan Passage** *chan.* Phil.
74 F6 **Tapachula** Mex.
79 G4 **Tapajós** *r.* Brazil
45 A2 **Tapaktuan** Indon.
83 E3 **Tapalqué** Arg.
44 A5 **Tapanuli, Teluk** *b.* Indon.
78 F5 **Tapauá** Brazil
78 E5 **Tapauá** *r.* Brazil
86 B4 **Tapeta** Liberia
34 C5 **Tāpi** *r.* India
43 B5 **Tapiantana** *i.* Phil.
68 C2 **Tapiola** U.S.A.
44 B4 **Tapis** *mt* Malaysia
35 F4 **Taplejung** Nepal
39 □ **Tap Mun Chau** *i. H.K.* China
70 E6 **Tappahannock** U.S.A.
70 C4 **Tappan Lake** *l.* U.S.A.
30 C3 **Tappeh, Kūh-e** *h.* Iran
51 D4 **Tapuaenuku** *mt* N.Z.
43 B5 **Tapul** Phil.
43 B5 **Tapul Group** *is* Phil.
81 D5 **Tapurucuara** Brazil
29 L4 **Tāq-e Bostan** *mt* Iraq
29 K4 **Ţaqţaq** Iraq
82 B1 **Taquaral, Serra do** *h.* Brazil
82 B2 **Taquari** Brazil
79 G7 **Taquari** *r.* Brazil
82 A2 **Taquari, Serra do** *h.* Brazil
82 C3 **Taquaritinga** Brazil
82 B3 **Taquaruçu** *r.* Brazil
11 D5 **Tar** *r.* Rep. of Ireland
86 D4 **Taraba** *r.* Nigeria
78 E7 **Tarabuco** Bol.
Ţarābulus *see* **Tripoli**
81 C4 **Taracua** Brazil
11 E4 **Tara, Hill of** *h.* Rep. of Ireland
34 B4 **Tar Ahmad Rind** Pak.
34 E4 **Tarahuwan** India
35 G4 **Tarai** *reg.* India
45 E2 **Tarakan** Indon.
43 A6 **Tarakan** *i.* Indon.
28 C1 **Taraklı** Turkey
50 G3 **Taralga** Austr.
50 G2 **Tarana** Austr.
34 D5 **Tarana** India
34 C3 **Tārānagar** India
Taranaki, Mt *volc. see* **Egmont, Mt**
15 E2 **Tarancón** Spain
17 J3 **Taran, Mys** *pt* Rus. Fed.
10 A3 **Taransay** *i.* U.K.
18 G4 **Taranto** Italy
18 G4 **Taranto, Golfo di** *g.* Italy
78 C5 **Tarapoto** Peru
51 E4 **Tararua Range** *mts* N.Z.
17 P6 **Tarashcha** Ukr.
78 D5 **Tarauacá** Brazil
78 E5 **Tarauacá** *r.* Brazil
46 J3 **Tarawa** *i.* Kiribati
51 F3 **Tarawera** N.Z.
51 F3 **Tarawera, Mt** *mt* N.Z.
15 F2 **Tarazona** Spain
15 F3 **Tarazona de la Mancha** Spain
27 G2 **Tarbagatay, Khrebet** *mts* Kazak.
10 E3 **Tarbat Ness** *pt* U.K.
34 C2 **Tarbela Dam** *dam* Pak.
11 B5 **Tarbert** Rep. of Ireland
10 B3 **Tarbert** *Scot.* U.K.
10 C5 **Tarbert** *Scot.* U.K.
14 E5 **Tarbes** France
67 E5 **Tarboro** U.S.A.
50 F3 **Tarcutta** Austr.
36 F2 **Tardoki-Yani, Gora** *mt* Rus. Fed.
49 F5 **Taree** Austr.
24 L2 **Tareya** Rus. Fed.
62 E2 **Targhee Pass** U.S.A.
19 L2 **Târgoviște** Romania
19 K2 **Târgu Jiu** Romania
17 M7 **Târgu Mureș** Romania
17 N7 **Târgu Neamț** Romania
17 N7 **Târgu Secuiesc** Romania
30 B3 **Tarhān** Iran
38 C2 **Tarian Gol** China
30 D5 **Tarif** U.A.E.
15 D4 **Tarifa** Spain
15 D4 **Tarifa o Marroqui, Pta de** *pt* Spain
78 F8 **Tarija** Bol.
37 F7 **Tariku** *r.* Indon.
32 C6 **Tarīm** Yemen
Tarim Basin *basin see* **Tarim Pendi**
27 G3 **Tarim Pendi** *basin* China
31 G3 **Tarīn Kowt** Afgh.
37 F7 **Taritatu** *r.* Indon.
29 K4 **Tarjīl** Iraq
91 F6 **Tarka** *r.* S. Africa
91 G6 **Tarkastad** S. Africa
64 E3 **Tarkio** U.S.A.
24 J3 **Tarko-Sale** Rus. Fed.
86 B4 **Tarkwa** Ghana
43 B3 **Tarlac** Phil.
13 H1 **Tarmstedt** Ger.
14 F4 **Tarn** *r.* France
6 O4 **Tärnaby** Sweden
31 G3 **Tarnak** *r.* Afgh.
17 M7 **Târnăveni** Romania
17 K5 **Tarnobrzeg** Pol.
20 G2 **Tarnogskiy Gorodok** Rus. Fed.
17 K5 **Tarnów** Pol.
35 E3 **Tarok Tso** *salt l.* China
30 D4 **Ţārom** Iran
86 B1 **Taroudannt** Morocco
50 C4 **Tarpenna** Austr.
67 E7 **Tarpum Bay** Bahamas
30 C3 **Tarq** Iran
18 D3 **Tarquinia** Italy
15 G2 **Tarragona** Spain
6 Q3 **Tårrajaur** Sweden
50 F2 **Tarran Hills** *h.* Austr.
51 B6 **Tarras** N.Z.
15 G2 **Tàrrega** Spain
28 E3 **Tarsus** Turkey
80 D2 **Tartagal** Arg.
29 L1 **Tärtär** Azer.
29 L1 **Tärtär** *r.* Azer.
14 D5 **Tartas** France
7 U7 **Tartu** Estonia
28 E4 **Ţarţūs** Syria
82 E2 **Tarumirim** Brazil
21 H6 **Tarumovka** Rus. Fed.
44 A5 **Tarutung** Indon.
18 E1 **Tarvisio** Italy
30 E4 **Tarz** Iran
58 E4 **Taschereau** Can.
33 A2 **Tasgaon** India
42 A3 **Tashan** China
35 G4 **Tashigang** Bhutan
Tashio Chho *see* **Thimphu**
29 K1 **Tashir** Armenia
30 D4 **Tashk** Iran
30 D4 **Tashk, Daryācheh-ye** *l.* Iran
26 E2 **Tashkent** Uzbek.
31 F2 **Tashkepri** Turkm.
58 F2 **Tasiat, Lac** *l.* Can.
55 P3 **Tasiilaq** Greenland
45 C4 **Tasikmalaya** Indon.
59 G2 **Tasiujaq** Can.
32 G2 **Taskesken** Kazak.
28 E1 **Taşköprü** Turkey
29 J2 **Taşlıçay** Turkey
94 F8 **Tasman Basin** *sea feature* Pac. Oc.
51 D4 **Tasman Bay** *b.* N.Z.
48 E6 **Tasmania** *div.* Austr.
51 D4 **Tasman Mountains** N.Z.
94 E9 **Tasman Plateau** *sea feature* Pac. Oc.
49 F5 **Tasman Sea** *sea* Pac. Oc.
28 F1 **Taşova** Turkey
72 B3 **Tassajara Hot Springs** U.S.A.
59 F2 **Tassialujjuaq, Lac** *l.* Can.
86 C2 **Tassili du Hoggar** *plat.* Alg.
86 C2 **Tassili n'Ajjer** *plat.* Alg.
29 K2 **Tasūj** Iran
25 N3 **Tas-Yuryakh** Rus. Fed.
17 J7 **Tatabánya** Hungary
21 D6 **Tatarbunary** Ukr.
24 J4 **Tatarsk** Rus. Fed.
36 G1 **Tatarskiy Proliv** *str.* Rus. Fed.
20 J4 **Tatarstan, Respublika** *div.* Rus. Fed.
30 B2 **Tatavi** *r.* Iran
41 F7 **Tateyama** Japan
41 E6 **Tate-yama** *volc.* Japan
56 F2 **Tathlina Lake** *l.* Can.
32 B5 **Tathlīth, W.** *watercourse* S. Arabia
50 G4 **Tathra** Austr.
57 K2 **Tatinnai Lake** *l.* Can.
21 H5 **Tatishchevo** Rus. Fed.
62 A1 **Tatla Lake** Can.
56 D3 **Tatlatui Prov. Park** *res.* Can.
37 E7 **Tat Mailau, G.** *mt* Indon.
50 F4 **Tatong** Austr.
17 J6 **Tatry** *reg.* Pol.
56 B3 **Tatshenshini** *r.* Can.
21 G5 **Tatsinskiy** Rus. Fed.
41 D7 **Tatsuno** Japan
34 A4 **Tatta** Pak.
82 C3 **Tatuí** Brazil
56 E4 **Tatuk Mtn** *mt* Can.
65 C5 **Tatum** U.S.A.
50 E4 **Tatura** Austr.
29 J2 **Tatvan** Turkey
7 J7 **Tau** Norway
79 K5 **Taua** Brazil
82 D3 **Taubaté** Brazil
13 H5 **Tauber** *r.* Ger.
13 H5 **Tauberbischofsheim** Ger.
13 L3 **Taucha** Ger.
13 H4 **Taufstein** *h.* Ger.
90 F3 **Taung** S. Africa
37 B4 **Taung-gyi** Myanmar
44 A2 **Taungnyo Range** *mts* Myanmar
9 D6 **Taunton** U.K.
71 H4 **Taunton** U.S.A.
13 F4 **Taunus** *h.* Ger.
51 F3 **Taupo** N.Z.
51 E3 **Taupo, Lake** *l.* N.Z.
7 S9 **Tauragė** Lith.
51 F2 **Tauranga** N.Z.
18 G5 **Taurianova** Italy
51 D1 **Tauroa Pt** *pt* N.Z.
49 F2 **Tauu** *is* P.N.G.
28 B3 **Tavas** Turkey
9 J5 **Taverham** U.K.
15 C4 **Tavira** Port.
9 C7 **Tavistock** U.K.
44 A2 **Tavoy** Myanmar
44 A2 **Tavoy Pt** *pt* Myanmar
40 B3 **Tavrichanka** Rus. Fed.
28 B2 **Tavşanlı** Turkey
9 C6 **Taw** *r.* U.K.
69 F3 **Tawas Bay** *b.* U.S.A.
69 F3 **Tawas City** U.S.A.
45 E2 **Tawau** Malaysia
9 D6 **Tawe** *r.* U.K.
34 C2 **Tawi** *r.* India
43 A5 **Tawitawi** *i.* Phil.
39 F6 **T'a-wu** Taiwan
74 E5 **Taxco** Mex.
27 F3 **Taxkorgan** China
56 C2 **Tay** *r.* Can.
10 E4 **Tay** *r.* U.K.
43 B3 **Tayabas Bay** *b.* Phil.
6 X2 **Taybola** Rus. Fed.
10 E4 **Tay, Firth of** *est.* U.K.
10 C5 **Tayinloan** U.K.
10 D4 **Tay, Loch** *l.* U.K.
56 E3 **Taylor** Can.
73 G4 **Taylor** *AZ* U.S.A.
69 F4 **Taylor** *MI* U.S.A.
68 B6 **Taylor** *MO* U.S.A.
64 D3 **Taylor** *NE* U.S.A.
65 D6 **Taylor** *TX* U.S.A.
71 E5 **Taylors Island** U.S.A.
66 B4 **Taylorville** U.S.A.
32 A4 **Taymā'** S. Arabia
25 L3 **Taymura** *r.* Rus. Fed.
25 M2 **Taymyr, Ozero** *l.* Rus. Fed.
25 L2 **Taymyr, Poluostrov** *pen.* Rus. Fed.
44 C3 **Tây Ninh** Vietnam
43 B3 **Taytay** Phil.
43 A4 **Taytay** Phil.
43 A4 **Taytay Bay** *b.* Phil.
31 F3 **Tayyebād** Iran
25 K2 **Taz** *r.* Rus. Fed.
86 B1 **Taza** Morocco
29 K4 **Tāza Khurmātū** Iraq
29 L2 **Tazeh Kand** Azer.
70 B6 **Tazewell** *TN* U.S.A.
70 C6 **Tazewell** *VA* U.S.A.
57 H2 **Tazin** *r.* Can.
57 H3 **Tazin Lake** *l.* Can.
87 E2 **Tāzirbū** Libya
15 J4 **Tazmalt** Alg.
24 J3 **Tazovskaya Guba** *chan.* Rus. Fed.
29 J1 **Tba Khozap'ini** *l.* Georgia
29 K1 **T'bilisi** Georgia
21 G6 **Tbilisskaya** Rus. Fed.
88 B4 **Tchibanga** Gabon
87 D2 **Tchigaï, Plateau du** *plat.* Niger
87 D4 **Tcholliré** Cameroon
17 J3 **Tczew** Pol.
51 A6 **Te Anau** N.Z.
51 A6 **Te Anau, L.** *l.* N.Z.
74 F5 **Teapa** Mex.
51 G2 **Te Araroa** N.Z.
51 E2 **Te Aroha** N.Z.
51 E3 **Te Awamutu** N.Z.
8 E3 **Tebay** U.K.
57 K2 **Tebesjuak Lake** *l.* Can.
86 C1 **Tébessa** Alg.
18 B7 **Tébessa, Monts de** *mts* Alg.
80 E3 **Tebicuary** *r.* Para.
45 A2 **Tebingtinggi** Indon.
45 B3 **Tebingtinggi** Indon.
18 C6 **Tébourba** Tunisia
18 C6 **Téboursouk** Tunisia
21 H7 **Tebulos Mt'a** *mt* Georgia/Rus. Fed.
86 B4 **Techiman** Ghana
80 B6 **Tecka** Arg.
12 F2 **Tecklenburger Land** *reg.* Ger.
74 D5 **Tecomán** Mex.
72 D4 **Tecopa** U.S.A.
17 N7 **Tecuci** Romania
69 F5 **Tecumseh** U.S.A.
31 F2 **Tedzhen** Turkm.
31 F2 **Tedzhen** *r.* Turkm.
31 F2 **Tedzhenstroy** Turkm.
73 H3 **Teec Nos Pos** U.S.A.
27 H1 **Teeli** Rus. Fed.
8 F3 **Tees** *r.* U.K.
8 E3 **Teesdale** *reg.* U.K.
43 A4 **Teeth, The** *mt* Phil.
78 E4 **Tefé** *r.* Brazil
28 B3 **Tefenni** Turkey
45 C4 **Tegal** Indon.
13 M2 **Tegel** *airport* Ger.
9 D5 **Tegid, Llyn** *l.* U.K.
74 G6 **Tegucigalpa** Honduras
86 C3 **Teguidda-n-Tessoumt** Niger
72 C4 **Tehachapi** U.S.A.
63 C5 **Tehachapi Mts** *mts* U.S.A.
72 C4 **Tehachapi Pass** U.S.A.
57 K2 **Tehek Lake** *l.* Can.
Teheran *see* **Tehrān**
86 B4 **Téhini** Côte d'Ivoire
30 C3 **Tehrān** Iran
34 D3 **Tehri** *Uttar Pradesh* India
Tehri *see* **Tikamgarh**
74 E5 **Tehuantepec, Golfo de** *g.* Mex.
74 F5 **Tehuantepec, Istmo de** *isth.* Mex.
95 N5 **Tehuantepec Ridge** *sea feature* Pac. Oc.
9 C5 **Teifi** *r.* U.K.
9 D7 **Teign** *r.* U.K.
9 D7 **Teignmouth** U.K.
Tejo *r. see* **Tagus**
72 C4 **Tejon Pass** U.S.A.
51 D1 **Te Kao** N.Z.
51 C5 **Tekapo, L.** *l.* N.Z.
35 F4 **Tekari** India
74 G4 **Tekax** Mex.
88 D2 **Tekezē Wenz** *r.* Eritrea/Eth.
34 E1 **Tekiliktag** *mt* China
28 A1 **Tekirdağ** Turkey
33 D2 **Tekkali** India
29 H2 **Tekman** Turkey
35 H5 **Teknaf** Bangl.
68 E4 **Tekonsha** U.S.A.
51 E3 **Te Kuiti** N.Z.
35 E5 **Tel** *r.* India
21 H7 **T'elavi** Georgia
28 E5 **Tel Aviv-Yafo** Israel
16 G6 **Telč** Czech Rep.
74 G4 **Telchac Puerto** Mex.
56 C3 **Telegraph Creek** Can.
14 G3 **Télégraphe, Le** *h.* France
82 B4 **Telêmaco Borba** Brazil
83 D3 **Telén** Arg.
45 E2 **Telen** *r.* Indon.
19 L2 **Teleorman** *r.* Romania
72 D3 **Telescope Peak** *summit* U.S.A.
79 G5 **Teles Pires** *r.* Brazil
9 E5 **Telford** U.K.
13 F3 **Telgte** Ger.
86 A3 **Télimélé** Guinea
29 J3 **Tel Kotchek** Syria
56 D4 **Telkwa** Can.
54 B3 **Teller** *AK* U.S.A.
33 A4 **Tellicherry** India
12 D4 **Tellin** Belgium
29 L6 **Telloh** Iraq
44 □ **Telok Blangah** Sing.
83 C4 **Telsen** Arg.
7 S9 **Telšiai** Lith.
13 M2 **Teltow** Ger.
45 B2 **Teluk Anson** Malaysia
45 A2 **Telukdalam** Indon.
69 H2 **Temagami** Can.
69 G2 **Temagami Lake** *l.* Can.
45 D4 **Temanggung** Indon.
91 H2 **Temba** S. Africa
45 C2 **Tembelan, Kepulauan** *is* Indon.
25 L3 **Tembenchi** *r.* Rus. Fed.
45 B3 **Tembilahan** Indon.
91 H3 **Tembisa** S. Africa
88 B4 **Tembo Aluma** Angola
9 E5 **Teme** *r.* U.K.
72 D5 **Temecula** U.S.A.
28 D2 **Temelli** Turkey
45 B2 **Temerloh** Malaysia
29 M5 **Temīleh** Iran
27 F1 **Temirtau** Kazak.
69 H2 **Temiscaming** Can.
69 H2 **Témiscamingue, Lac** *l.* Can.
59 G4 **Témiscouata, L.** *l.* Can.
6 T4 **Temmes** Fin.
20 G4 **Temnikov** Rus. Fed.
50 F3 **Temora** Austr.
73 G5 **Tempe** U.S.A.
13 M2 **Tempelhof** *airport* Ger.
18 C4 **Tempio Pausania** *Sardinia* Italy
68 E3 **Temple** *MI* U.S.A.
65 D6 **Temple** *TX* U.S.A.
9 C5 **Temple Bar** U.K.
11 D5 **Templemore** Rep. of Ireland
43 A4 **Templer Bank** *sand bank* Phil.
8 E3 **Temple Sowerby** U.K.
13 M1 **Templin** Ger.
21 F6 **Temryuk** Rus. Fed.
83 B3 **Temuco** Chile
51 C6 **Temuka** N.Z.
78 C4 **Tena** Ecuador
72 D1 **Tenabo, Mt** *mt* U.S.A.
33 C2 **Tenali** India
44 A2 **Tenasserim** Myanmar
44 A2 **Tenasserim** *r.* Myanmar
9 E5 **Tenbury Wells** U.K.
9 C6 **Tenby** U.K.
69 F2 **Tenby Bay** Can.
88 E2 **Tendaho** Eth.
14 H4 **Tende** France
27 H6 **Ten Degree Chan.** Andaman and Nicobar Is
40 G5 **Tendō** Japan
29 J2 **Tendürük Dağı** *mt* Turkey
86 B3 **Ténenkou** Mali
86 D3 **Ténéré** *reg.* Niger
86 D2 **Ténéré du Tafassâsset** *des.* Niger
86 A2 **Tenerife** *i.* Canary Is
15 G4 **Ténès** Alg.
45 E4 **Tengah, Kepulauan** *is* Indon.
44 □ **Tengeh Res.** *resr* Sing.
38 B2 **Tengger Shamo** *des.* China
44 B4 **Tenggul** *i.* Malaysia
26 E1 **Tengiz, Oz.** *l.* Kazak.
39 C7 **Tengqiao** China
86 B3 **Tengréla** Côte d'Ivoire
39 D6 **Teng Xian** *Guangxi* China
38 E3 **Teng Xian** *Shandong* China
92 B2 **Teniente Jubany** *Arg. Base* Ant.
92 B2 **Teniente Rodolfo Marsh** *Chile Base* Ant.
89 C5 **Tenke** Congo(Zaire)
25 Q2 **Tenkeli** Rus. Fed.
86 B3 **Tenkodogo** Burkina
48 D3 **Tennant Creek** Austr.
70 B6 **Tennessee** *div.* U.S.A.
67 C5 **Tennessee** *r.* U.S.A.
63 F4 **Tennessee Pass** U.S.A.
6 P2 **Tennevoll** Norway
83 B2 **Teno** *r.* Chile
6 U2 **Tenojoki** *r.* Fin./Norway
74 F5 **Tenosique** Mex.
62 F2 **Ten Sleep** U.S.A.
48 C2 **Tenteno** Indon.
9 H6 **Tenterden** U.K.
67 D7 **Ten Thousand Islands** *is* U.S.A.
15 C3 **Tentudia** *mt* Spain
82 B3 **Teodoro Sampaio** Brazil
82 E2 **Teófilo Otôni** Brazil
63 E6 **Tepachi** Mex.
51 D1 **Te Paki** N.Z.
74 D4 **Tepatitlán** Mex.
29 H3 **Tepe** Turkey
29 J3 **Tepe Gawra** Iraq
74 C3 **Tepehuanes** Mex.
19 J4 **Tepelenë** Albania
13 L5 **Tepelská Vrchovina** *reg.* Czech Rep.
81 E4 **Tepequem, Serra** *mts* Brazil
74 D4 **Tepic** Mex.
51 C5 **Te Pirita** N.Z.
16 F5 **Teplice** Czech Rep.
20 K2 **Teplogorka** Rus. Fed.
21 F5 **Teploye** Rus. Fed.
51 F2 **Te Puke** N.Z.
15 H1 **Ter** *r.* Spain
46 L3 **Teraina** *i.* Kiribati
34 D2 **Teram Kangri** *mt* China/Jammu and Kashmir
18 E3 **Teramo** Italy
50 D5 **Terang** Austr.
12 F2 **Ter Apel** Neth.
34 B3 **Teratani** *r.* Pak.
21 F4 **Terbuny** Rus. Fed.
29 H2 **Tercan** Turkey
17 M6 **Terebovlya** Ukr.
21 H7 **Terek** Rus. Fed.
21 H7 **Terek** *r.* Rus. Fed.
20 J4 **Teren'ga** Rus. Fed.
82 A3 **Terenos** Brazil
81 C2 **Terepaima, Parque Nacional** *nat. park* Venez.
20 H4 **Tereshka** *r.* Rus. Fed.
79 K5 **Teresina** Brazil
82 D3 **Teresópolis** Brazil
12 B5 **Tergnier** France
28 F1 **Terme** Turkey
31 G2 **Termez** Uzbek.
18 E6 **Termini Imerese** *Sicily* Italy
74 F5 **Términos, Lag. de** *lag.* Mex.
18 F4 **Termoli** Italy
9 E5 **Tern** *r.* U.K.
37 E6 **Ternate** Indon.
12 B3 **Terneuzen** Neth.
40 E2 **Terney** Rus. Fed.
18 E3 **Terni** Italy
21 C5 **Ternopil'** Ukr.
50 B2 **Terowie** Austr.
36 G2 **Terpeniya, Mys** *c.* Rus. Fed.
36 G2 **Terpeniya, Zaliv** *g.* Rus. Fed.
56 D4 **Terrace** Can.
68 D1 **Terrace Bay** Can.
90 E2 **Terra Firma** S. Africa
6 N4 **Terråk** Norway
18 C5 **Terralba** *Sardinia* Italy
59 K4 **Terra Nova Nat. Pk** *nat. park* Can.
92 B6 **Terre Adélie** *reg.* Ant.
65 F6 **Terre Bonne Bay** *b.* U.S.A.
66 C4 **Terre Haute** U.S.A.
59 K4 **Terrenceville** Can.
62 F2 **Terry** U.S.A.
21 G5 **Tersa** *r.* Rus. Fed.
12 D1 **Terschelling** *i.* Neth.
18 C5 **Tertenia** *Sardinia* Italy
15 F2 **Teruel** Spain
44 A4 **Terutao** *i.* Thai.
6 T3 **Tervola** Fin.
18 G2 **Tešanj** Bos.-Herz.
88 D2 **Teseney** Eritrea
20 G4 **Tesha** *r.* Rus. Fed.
54 C2 **Teshekpuk Lake** *l.* U.S.A.
40 J3 **Teshikaga** Japan
40 G2 **Teshio** Japan
40 H3 **Teshio-dake** *mt* Japan
40 G2 **Teshio-gawa** *r.* Japan
56 C2 **Teslin** Can.
56 C2 **Teslin** *r.* Can.
56 C2 **Teslin Lake** *l.* Can.
82 B1 **Tesouras** *r.* Brazil
82 B2 **Tesouro** Brazil
86 C3 **Tessaoua** Niger
9 F6 **Test** *r.* U.K.
18 C6 **Testour** Tunisia
80 B2 **Tetas, Pta** *pt* Chile
89 D5 **Tete** Moz.
51 F3 **Te Teko** N.Z.
17 P5 **Teteriv** *r.* Ukr.
13 L1 **Teterow** Ger.
17 O6 **Tetiyiv** Ukr.
8 G4 **Tetney** U.K.
62 E2 **Teton** *r.* U.S.A.
62 E3 **Teton Ra.** *mts* U.S.A.
86 B1 **Tétouan** Morocco
19 J3 **Tetovo** Macedonia
34 B5 **Tetpur** India
20 J4 **Tetyushi** Rus. Fed.
80 D2 **Teuco** *r.* Arg.
90 B1 **Teufelsbach** Namibia
13 G1 **Teufels Moor** *reg.* Ger.
40 G2 **Teuri-tō** *i.* Japan
13 G2 **Teutoburger Wald** *h.* Ger.
7 R5 **Teuva** Fin.
Tevere *r. see* **Tiber**
Teverya *see* **Tiberias**
10 F5 **Teviot** *r.* U.K.
10 F5 **Teviotdale** *v.* U.K.
51 A7 **Te Waewae Bay** *b.* N.Z.
91 G1 **Tewane** Botswana
49 F4 **Tewantin** Austr.
51 E4 **Te Wharau** N.Z.
9 E6 **Tewkesbury** U.K.
38 B3 **Têwo** China
56 E5 **Texada I.** *i.* Can.
65 E5 **Texarkana** U.S.A.
65 D6 **Texas** *div.* U.S.A.
65 E6 **Texas City** U.S.A.
12 C1 **Texel** *i.* Neth.
65 C4 **Texhoma** U.S.A.
65 D5 **Texoma, Lake** *l.* U.S.A.
91 G4 **Teyateyaneng** Lesotho
20 G3 **Teykovo** Rus. Fed.
31 G3 **Teyvareh** Afgh.
20 G3 **Teza** *r.* Rus. Fed.
35 H4 **Tezpur** India
35 J4 **Tezu** India
57 K2 **Tha-anne** *r.* Can.
91 H4 **Thabana-Ntlenyana** *mt* Lesotho
91 G4 **Thaba Nchu** S. Africa
91 G4 **Thaba Putsoa** *mt* Lesotho
91 H4 **Thaba-Tseka** Lesotho
91 G2 **Thabazimbi** S. Africa
44 B1 **Tha Bo** Laos
91 G3 **Thabong** S. Africa
30 B5 **Thādiq** S. Arabia
44 A2 **Thagyettaw** Myanmar
39 C6 **Thai Binh** Vietnam
34 B3 **Thai Desert** Pak.
23 K8 **Thailand** *country* Asia
44 B3 **Thailand, Gulf of** *g.* Asia
39 B6 **Thai Nguyên** Vietnam
30 B5 **Thaj** S. Arabia
35 E5 **Thakurtola** India
13 J4 **Thal** Ger.
34 B2 **Thal** Pak.
18 C7 **Thala** Tunisia
44 A3 **Thalang** Thai.
Thalassery *see* **Tellicherry**
13 K3 **Thale (Harz)** Ger.
44 B4 **Thale Luang** *lag.* Thai.
44 B1 **Tha Li** Thai.
31 G4 **Thalo** Pak.
91 G1 **Thamaga** Botswana
32 D6 **Thamarīt** Oman
32 C7 **Thamar, J.** *mt* Yemen
9 G5 **Thame** *r.* U.K.
51 E2 **Thames** N.Z.
9 H6 **Thames** *est. Eng.* U.K.
9 G6 **Thames** *r. Eng.* U.K.
69 G4 **Thamesville** Can.
44 A2 **Thanbyuzayat** Myanmar

34 C5 Thandla India
34 B5 Thangadh India
44 D2 Thăng Binh Vietnam
44 C1 Thanh Hoa Vietnam
33 B4 Thanjavur India
44 B1 Tha Pla Thai.
44 A3 Thap Put Thai.
44 A3 Thap Sakae Thai.
34 B4 Tharad India
34 B4 Thar Desert India/Pak.
19 L4 Thasos i. Greece
73 H5 Thatcher U.S.A.
39 C6 Thât Khê Vietnam
37 B5 Thaton Myanmar
35 H4 Thaungdut Myanmar
44 A1 Thaungyin r. Myanmar/Thai.
37 B5 Thayetmyo Myanmar
73 F5 Theba U.S.A.
64 C3 Thedford U.S.A.
12 C2 The Hague Neth.
44 A3 Theinkun Myanmar
57 H2 Thekulthili Lake l. Can.
57 J2 Thelon r. Can.
57 J2 Thelon Game Sanctuary res. Can.
13 J4 Themar Ger.
90 F6 Thembalesizwe S. Africa
91 H3 Thembalihle S. Africa
15 H4 Thenia Alg.
15 H5 Theniet El Had Alg.
78 F5 Theodore Roosevelt r. Brazil
73 G5 Theodore Roosevelt Lake l. U.S.A.
64 C2 Theodore Roosevelt Nat. Park U.S.A.
12 A5 Thérain r. France
71 F2 Theresa U.S.A.
19 K4 Thermaïkos Kolpos g. Greece
72 B2 Thermalito U.S.A.
62 E3 Thermopolis U.S.A.
12 A4 Thérouanne France
54 F2 Thesiger Bay b. Can.
69 F2 Thessalon Can.
19 K4 Thessaloniki Greece
9 H5 Thet r. U.K.
9 H5 Thetford U.K.
59 F4 Thetford Mines Can.
44 C1 Theun r. Laos
91 G4 Theunissen S. Africa
65 F6 Thibodaux U.S.A.
57 K3 Thicket Portage Can.
64 D1 Thief River Falls U.S.A.
92 B4 Thiel Mts mts Ant.
14 F4 Thiers France
86 A3 Thiès Senegal
88 D4 Thika Kenya
33 A5 Thiladhunmathee Atoll atoll Maldives
35 G4 Thimphu Bhutan
14 H2 Thionville France
Thira i. see Santorini
19 L6 Thirasia i. Greece
8 F3 Thirsk U.K.
Thiruvananthapuram see Trivandrum
7 L8 Thisted Denmark
19 K5 Thiva Greece
57 K2 Thlewiaza r. Can.
57 H2 Thoa r. Can.
91 J1 Thohoyandou S. Africa
12 C3 Tholen Neth.
12 F5 Tholey Ger.
70 D5 Thomas U.S.A.
67 C5 Thomaston GA U.S.A.
71 J2 Thomaston ME U.S.A.
71 K2 Thomaston Corner Can.
11 D5 Thomastown Rep. of Ireland
67 D6 Thomasville U.S.A.
12 E4 Thommen Belgium
57 K3 Thompson Man. Can.
68 D3 Thompson MI U.S.A.
71 F4 Thompson PA U.S.A.
56 E4 Thompson r. Can.
64 E3 Thompson r. U.S.A.
62 D2 Thompson Falls U.S.A.
65 D5 Thomson U.S.A.
44 C1 Thôn Cư Lai Vietnam
16 C7 Thonon-les-Bains France
44 D3 Thôn Sơn Hai Vietnam
63 E5 Thoreau U.S.A.
12 D3 Thorn Neth.
8 F3 Thornaby-on-Tees U.K.
68 E4 Thornapple r. U.S.A.
9 E6 Thornbury U.K.
69 H2 Thorne Can.
8 G4 Thorne U.K.
72 C2 Thorne U.S.A.
56 C3 Thorne Bay U.S.A.
68 D5 Thorntown U.S.A.
68 B3 Thorp U.S.A.
92 D3 Thorshavnheiane mts Ant.
91 G4 Thota-ea-Moli Lesotho
14 D3 Thouars France
71 E2 Thousand Islands is Can.
73 G2 Thousand Lake Mt mt U.S.A.
72 C4 Thousand Oaks U.S.A.
19 L4 Thrakiko Pelagos sea Greece
62 E2 Three Forks U.S.A.
56 G4 Three Hills Can.
51 D1 Three Kings Is is N.Z.
68 C3 Three Lakes U.S.A.
68 D5 Three Oaks U.S.A.
44 A2 Three Pagodas Pass Myanmar/Thai.
86 B4 Three Points, Cape c. Ghana
68 E5 Three Rivers MI U.S.A.
65 D6 Three Rivers TX U.S.A.
62 B2 Three Sisters mt U.S.A.
Thrissur see Trichur
65 D5 Throckmorton U.S.A.
57 G2 Thubun Lakes l. Can.
44 C3 Thu Dâu Môt Vietnam
12 C4 Thuin Belgium
Thule see Qaanaaq
89 C6 Thuli Zimbabwe
16 C7 Thun Switz.
68 C1 Thunder Bay Can.
68 C1 Thunder Bay b. Can.
69 F3 Thunder Bay b. U.S.A.
13 H5 Thüngen Ger.
44 A3 Thung Song Thai.
44 A4 Thung Wa Thai.
13 J4 Thüringen div. Ger.
13 K3 Thüringer Becken reg. Ger.
13 J4 Thüringer Wald mts Ger.
11 D5 Thurles Rep. of Ireland
70 E5 Thurmont U.S.A.
16 F7 Thurn, Paß pass Austria
71 F2 Thurso Can.
10 E2 Thurso U.K.
10 E2 Thurso r. Scot. U.K.
92 A3 Thurston I. i. Ant.
13 H2 Thüster Berg h. Ger.
8 E3 Thwaite U.K.
92 A3 Thwaites Gl. gl. Ant.
7 L8 Thyborøn Denmark
38 A1 Tiancang China
38 F3 Tianchang China
39 C6 Tiandeng China
39 C6 Tiandong China
39 C5 Tian'e China
79 K4 Tianguá Brazil
38 E2 Tianjin China
38 E2 Tianjin div. China
36 B3 Tianjun China
39 C5 Tianlin China
39 D4 Tianmen China
39 F4 Tianmu Shan mts China
42 E2 Tianqiaoling China
39 B4 Tianquan China
42 C3 Tianshifu China
38 B3 Tianshui China
34 D2 Tianshuihai China/Jammu and Kashmir
39 F4 Tiantai China
38 E1 Tiantaiyong China
39 C6 Tianyang China
38 B2 Tianzhu Gansu China
39 C5 Tianzhu Guizhou China
86 C1 Tiaret Alg.
86 B4 Tiassalé Côte d'Ivoire
82 B4 Tibagi r. Brazil
29 J5 Tibal, Wādī watercourse Iraq
87 D4 Tibati Cameroon
18 E3 Tiber r. Italy
28 E5 Tiberias Israel
Tiberias, Lake l. see Galilee, Sea of
62 E1 Tiber Res. resr U.S.A.
87 D2 Tibesti mts Chad
Tibet Aut. Region div. see Xizang Zizhiqu
Tibet, Plateau of plat. see Xizang Gaoyuan
48 E4 Tibooburra Austr.
35 E3 Tibrikot Nepal
35 E3 Tibrikot Nepal
7 O7 Tibro Sweden
74 B3 Tiburón i. Mex.
43 B3 Ticao i. Phil.
9 H6 Ticehurst U.K.
69 J3 Tichborne Can.
86 B3 Tichît Maur.
86 A2 Tichla Western Sahara
16 D7 Ticino r. Switz.
71 G3 Ticonderoga U.S.A.
74 G4 Ticul Mex.
7 N7 Tidaholm Sweden
35 H5 Tiddim Myanmar
86 C2 Tidikelt, Plaine du plain Alg.
86 A3 Tidjikja Maur.
12 D3 Tiel Neth.
40 A1 Tieli China
42 B2 Tieling China
34 D2 Tielongtan China/Jammu and Kashmir
12 B4 Tielt Belgium
86 B4 Tiémé Côte d'Ivoire
12 C4 Tienen Belgium
22 E5 Tien Shan mts China/Kyrg.
Tientsin see Tianjin
7 P6 Tierp Sweden
63 F4 Tierra Amarilla U.S.A.
74 E5 Tierra Blanca Mex.
80 C8 Tierra del Fuego, Isla Grande de i. Arg./Chile
15 D2 Tiétar r. Spain
15 D2 Tiétar, Valle de v. Spain
82 C3 Tietê Brazil
82 B3 Tietê r. Brazil
70 B4 Tiffin U.S.A.
Tiflis see T'bilisi
67 D6 Tifton U.S.A.
19 L3 Tigheciului, Dealurile h. Moldova
21 D6 Tighina Moldova
35 F5 Tigiria India
87 D4 Tignère Cameroon
59 H4 Tignish Can.
78 C4 Tigre r. Ecuador/Peru
81 E2 Tigre r. Venez.
29 L5 Tigris r. Iraq/Turkey
32 B6 Tihāmah reg. S. Arabia
28 D7 Tīh, Gebel el plat. Egypt
74 A2 Tijuana Mex.
82 C2 Tijuco r. Brazil
34 D4 Tikamgarh India
21 G6 Tikhoretsk Rus. Fed.
20 E3 Tikhvin Rus. Fed.
20 E3 Tikhvinskaya Gryada ridge Rus. Fed.
51 F3 Tikokino N.Z.
49 G3 Tikopia i. Solomon Is
29 J4 Tikrīt Iraq
6 W3 Tiksheozero, Oz. l. Rus. Fed.
25 O2 Tiksi Rus. Fed.
35 E3 Tila r. Nepal
35 F4 Tilaiya Reservoir India
30 D2 Tilavar Iran
12 D3 Tilburg Neth.
9 H6 Tilbury U.K.
80 C2 Tilcara Arg.
35 H5 Tilin Myanmar
86 C3 Tillabéri Niger
62 B2 Tillamook U.S.A.
10 E4 Tillicoultry U.K.
69 G4 Tillsonburg Can.
10 F3 Tillyfourie U.K.
19 M6 Tilos i. Greece
50 E1 Tilpa Austr.
21 F5 Tim Rus. Fed.
20 K1 Timanskiy Kryazh ridge Rus. Fed.
29 J2 Timar Turkey
51 C6 Timaru N.Z.
21 F6 Timashevsk Rus. Fed.
86 B3 Timbedgha Maur.
48 D3 Timber Creek Austr.
72 D3 Timber Mt mt U.S.A.
70 D5 Timberville U.S.A.
50 D5 Timboon Austr.
86 B3 Timétrine reg. Mali
86 C2 Timimoun Alg.
19 J2 Timișoara Romania
69 G1 Timmins Can.
20 F3 Timokhino Rus. Fed.
79 K5 Timon Brazil
37 E7 Timor i. Indon.
48 C3 Timor Sea sea Austr./Indon.
20 H3 Timoshino Rus. Fed.
83 D2 Timote Arg.
7 P5 Timrå Sweden
67 C5 Tims Ford L. l. U.S.A.
34 D5 Timurni Muafi India
81 C2 Tinaco Venez.
33 B3 Tindivanam India
86 B2 Tindouf Alg.
44 C5 Tinggi i. Malaysia
39 E5 Ting Jiang r. China
35 F3 Tingri China
7 O8 Tingsryd Sweden
83 B2 Tinguiririca, Vol. volc. Chile
6 L5 Tingvoll Norway
10 E1 Tingwall U.K.
82 E1 Tinharé, Ilha de i. Brazil
44 C1 Tinh Gia Vietnam
37 G5 Tinian i. N. Mariana Is
80 C3 Tinogasta Arg.
19 L6 Tinos i. Greece
12 B5 Tinqueux France
86 C2 Tinrhert, Plateau du plat. Alg.
35 H4 Tinsukia India
9 C7 Tintagel U.K.
50 C3 Tintinara Austr.
10 E5 Tinto h. U.K.
70 E4 Tioga r. U.S.A.
45 B2 Tioman i. Malaysia
69 F1 Tionaga Can.
70 D4 Tionesta Lake l. U.S.A.
71 E3 Tioughnioga r. U.S.A.
15 H4 Tipasa Alg.
68 D5 Tippecanoe r. U.S.A.
68 E5 Tippecanoe Lake l. U.S.A.
11 C5 Tipperary Rep. of Ireland
35 F4 Tiptala Bhanjyang pass Nepal
68 B5 Tipton IA U.S.A.
68 D5 Tipton IN U.S.A.
73 E4 Tipton, Mt mt U.S.A.
68 E1 Tip Top Hill h. Can.
9 H6 Tiptree U.K.
81 C4 Tiquié r. Brazil
79 J4 Tiracambu, Serra do h. Brazil
19 H4 Tirana Albania
Tiranë see Tirana
18 D1 Tirano Italy
21 D6 Tiraspol Moldova
90 B3 Tiraz Mts mts Namibia
28 A2 Tire Turkey
10 B4 Tiree i. U.K.
34 B1 Tirich Mir mt Pak.
33 B2 Tirna r. India
33 A3 Tirthahalli India
35 F5 Tirtol India
33 B4 Tiruchchendur India
33 B4 Tiruchchirāppalli India
33 B4 Tiruchengodu India
33 B4 Tirunelveli India
33 B3 Tirupati India
33 B3 Tiruppattur India
33 B4 Tiruppur India
33 B4 Tirutturaippundi India
33 B3 Tiruvannamalai India
33 B4 Tisaiyanvilai India
57 J4 Tisdale Can.
33 C5 Tissamaharama Sri Lanka
15 G5 Tissemsilt Alg.
35 G4 Tista r. India
92 B4 Titan Dome ice feature Ant.
25 O2 Tit-Ary Rus. Fed.
78 E7 Titicaca, Lago l. Bol./Peru
35 E5 Titlagarh India
18 G2 Titov Drvar Bos.-Herz.
69 E4 Tittabawassee r. U.S.A.
19 L2 Titu Romania
67 D6 Titusville FL U.S.A.
70 D4 Titusville PA U.S.A.
69 G3 Tiverton Can.
9 D7 Tiverton U.K.
18 E4 Tivoli Italy
15 H4 Tizi El Arba h. Alg.
74 G4 Tizimín Mex.
15 J4 Tizi Ouzou Alg.
81 D2 Tiznados r. Venez.
86 B2 Tiznit Morocco
65 C7 Tizoc Mex.
91 J2 Tjaneni Swaziland
6 Q4 Tjappsåive Sweden
12 D2 Tjeukemeer l. Neth.
7 K7 Tjorhom Norway
65 C7 Tlahualilo Mex.
74 E5 Tlaxcala Mex.
86 B1 Tlemcen Alg.
90 E4 Tlhakalatlou S. Africa
91 H4 Tlholong S. Africa
91 F2 Tlokweng Botswana
56 D3 Toad River Can.
89 E5 Toamasina Madag.
83 D3 Toay Arg.
41 E7 Toba Japan
44 A5 Toba, Danau l. Indon.
78 F1 Tobago i. Trinidad and Tobago
34 A3 Toba & Kakar Ranges mts Pak.
37 E6 Tobelo Indon.
69 G3 Tobermory Can.
10 B4 Tobermory U.K.
57 J4 Tobin L. l. Can.
72 D1 Tobin, Mt mt U.S.A.
71 K1 Tobique r. Can.
40 F5 Tobi-shima i. Japan
45 C3 Toboali Indon.
24 H4 Tobol r. Kazak./Rus. Fed.
44 D2 Tô Bong Vietnam
79 J5 Tocantinópolis Brazil
79 J4 Tocantins r. Brazil
82 C1 Tocantinzinha r. Brazil
67 D5 Toccoa U.S.A.
34 B2 Tochi r. Pak.
7 M7 Töcksfors Sweden
80 B2 Tocopilla Chile
50 E3 Tocumwal Austr.
81 C2 Tocuyo r. Venez.
18 E3 Todi Italy
16 D7 Todi mt Switz.
40 H5 Todoga-saki pt Japan
40 G4 Todohokke Japan
78 E7 Todos Santos Bol.
72 D6 Todos Santos, Bahía de b. Mex.
56 G4 Tofield Can.
56 D5 Tofino Can.
10 Toft U.K.
68 B2 Tofte U.S.A.
49 J3 Tofua i. Tonga
37 E7 Togian, Kepulauan is Indon.
68 A2 Togo U.S.A.
85 D5 Togo country Africa
38 D1 Togtoh China
73 H4 Tohatchi U.S.A.
6 T5 Toholampi Fin.
38 B1 Tohom China
7 S6 Toijala Fin.
41 B9 Toi-misaki pt Japan
7 U5 Toivakka Fin.
72 D2 Toiyabe Range mts U.S.A.
31 H2 Tojikobod Tajik.
54 D3 Tok U.S.A.
41 F6 Tōkamachi Japan
51 B7 Tokanui N.Z.
87 F3 Tokar Sudan
36 E4 Tokara-rettō is Japan
28 F1 Tokat Turkey
42 D5 Tŏkchoktŏ i. S. Korea
42 D4 Tŏkch'ŏn N. Korea
47 K4 Tokelau terr. Pac. Oc.
27 F2 Tokmak Kyrg.
21 E6 Tokmak Ukr.
51 G3 Tokomaru Bay N.Z.
51 E3 Tokoroa N.Z.
91 H3 Tokoza S. Africa
24 K5 Toksun China
41 B6 Tok-tō i. Japan
41 D7 Tokushima Japan
41 B7 Tokuyama Japan
41 F7 Tōkyō Japan
41 F7 Tōkyō-wan b. Japan
31 G3 Tokzār Afgh.
51 G3 Tolaga Bay N.Z.
89 E6 Tōlañaro Madag.
82 B4 Toledo Brazil
15 D3 Toledo Spain
68 A5 Toledo IA U.S.A.
70 B4 Toledo OH U.S.A.
65 E6 Toledo Bend Reservoir U.S.A.
15 D3 Toledo, Montes de mts Spain
83 B3 Tolhuaca, Parque Nacional nat. park Chile
89 E6 Toliara Madag.
81 B3 Tolima, Nev. del volc. Col.
37 E6 Tolitoli Indon.
24 K3 Tol'ka Rus. Fed.
13 M1 Tollensesee l. Ger.
20 D3 Tolmachevo Rus. Fed.
18 E1 Tolmezzo Italy
39 Tolo Channel H.K. China
39 Tolo Harbour b. H.K. China
15 E1 Tolosa Spain
42 D6 Tolsan-do i. S. Korea
69 F3 Tolsmaville Can.
10 B2 Tolsta Head hd U.K.
81 B2 Tolú Col.
74 E5 Toluca Mex.
60 B4 Tolumne r. CA U.S.A.
6 W3 Tolvand, Oz. l. Rus. Fed.
20 J4 Tol'yatti Rus. Fed.
68 B4 Tomah U.S.A.
68 C3 Tomahawk U.S.A.
40 G3 Tomakomai Japan
40 G2 Tomamae Japan
49 H3 Tomanivi mt Fiji
81 E5 Tomar Brazil
15 B3 Tomar Port.
28 E2 Tomarza Turkey
83 F1 Tomás Gomensoro Uru.
17 L5 Tomaszów Lubelski Pol.
17 K5 Tomaszów Mazowiecki Pol.
10 E3 Tomatin U.K.
67 B6 Tombigbee r. U.S.A.
88 B4 Tomboco Angola
82 D3 Tombos Brazil
86 B3 Tombouctou Mali
73 G6 Tombstone U.S.A.
89 B5 Tombua Angola
91 H1 Tom Burke S. Africa
83 B3 Tomé Chile
91 L1 Tome Moz.
7 N9 Tomelilla Sweden
15 E3 Tomelloso Spain
69 H2 Tomiko Can.
50 G2 Tomingley Austr.
86 B3 Tominian Mali
37 E7 Tomini, Teluk g. Indon.
10 E3 Tomintoul U.K.
18 G3 Tomislavgrad Bos.-Herz.
6 O3 Tømmerneset Norway
25 O4 Tommot Rus. Fed.
81 D4 Tomo Col.
81 C3 Tomo r. Col.
38 D1 Tomortei China
25 P3 Tompo Rus. Fed.
48 B4 Tom Price Austr.
36 A1 Tomsk Rus. Fed.
7 O8 Tomtabacken h. Sweden
25 Q3 Tomtor Rus. Fed.
40 H3 Tomuraushi-yama mt Japan
21 G6 Tomuzlovka r. Rus. Fed.
74 F5 Tonalá Mex.
73 G3 Tonalea U.S.A.
78 E4 Tonantins Brazil
62 C1 Tonasket U.S.A.
9 H6 Tonbridge U.K.
37 E6 Tondano Indon.
7 L9 Tønder Denmark
9 E6 Tone r. U.K.
47 K5 Tonga country Pac. Oc.
91 J4 Tongaat S. Africa
50 E4 Tongala Austr.
39 F5 Tong'an China
46 M4 Tongareva i. Cook Is Kiribati
51 E3 Tongariro National Park N.Z.
49 J4 Tongatapu Group is Tonga
94 H7 Tonga Tr. sea feature Pac. Oc.
38 D3 Tongbai China
38 D3 Tongbai Shan mts China
38 E4 Tongcheng Anhui China
39 D4 Tongcheng Hubei China
42 D4 T'ongch'ŏn N. Korea
38 C3 Tongchuan China
39 C5 Tongdao China
38 A3 Tongde China
42 D5 Tongduch'ŏn S. Korea
12 D4 Tongeren Belgium
39 E4 Tonggu China
39 D7 Tonggu Jiao pt China
42 E5 Tonghae S. Korea
39 B5 Tonghai China
40 A2 Tonghe China
42 C3 Tonghua Jilin China
42 C3 Tonghua Jilin China
38 C4 Tongjiang China
42 B2 Tongjiangkou China
42 D4 Tongjosŏn Man b. N. Korea
39 C6 Tongking, Gulf of g. China/Vietnam
39 C4 Tongliang China
42 B2 Tongliao China
38 E4 Tongling China
39 F4 Tonglu China
42 E6 Tongnae S. Korea
39 B4 Tongnan China
43 B5 Tongquil i. Phil.
39 C5 Tongren Guizhou China
38 A3 Tongren Qinghai China
35 G4 Tongsa r. Bhutan
39 E4 Tongshan China
35 H2 Tongtian He r. China
10 D2 Tongue U.K.
62 F2 Tongue r. U.S.A.
67 E7 Tongue of the Ocean chan. Bahamas
38 B3 Tongwei China
38 E2 Tong Xian China
38 B2 Tongxin China
38 E4 Tongyanghe China
42 B1 Tongyu China
42 B3 Tongyuanpu China
39 C4 Tongzi China
68 C5 Tonica U.S.A.
34 C4 Tonk India
30 C2 Tonkābon Iran
39 B6 Tonkin reg. Vietnam
20 H3 Tonkino Rus. Fed.
44 C3 Tônle Basăk r. Cambodia
44 C2 Tônle Repou r. Laos
44 B2 Tônlé Sab l. Cambodia
40 G5 Tōno Japan
72 D2 Tonopah U.S.A.
81 E2 Tonoro r. Venez.
7 M7 Tønsberg Norway
7 K7 Tonstad Norway
73 G5 Tonto National Monument res. U.S.A.
35 H5 Tonzang Myanmar
62 D3 Tooele U.S.A.
50 D3 Toolebuc Austr.
50 G3 Tooma r. Austr.
50 F5 Toora Austr.
50 G1 Tooraweenah Austr.
90 F6 Toorberg mt S. Africa
48 F4 Toowoomba Austr.
73 G6 Topawa U.S.A.
72 C2 Topaz U.S.A.
64 E4 Topeka U.S.A.
56 D4 Topley Landing Can.
13 L2 Töplitz Ger.
83 B2 Topocalma, Pta pt Chile
72 E4 Topock U.S.A.
16 J6 Topoľčany Slovakia
74 C3 Topolobampo Mex.
19 M3 Topolovgrad Bulg.
6 W4 Topozero, Oz. l. Rus. Fed.
62 B2 Toppenish U.S.A.
71 K2 Topsfield U.S.A.
73 F3 Toquerville U.S.A.
88 D3 Tor Eth.
19 M5 Torbalı Turkey
31 E3 Torbat-e-Heydarīyeh Iran
31 F3 Torbat-e Jām Iran
20 G4 Torbeyevo Rus. Fed.
68 E3 Torch Lake l. U.S.A.
15 D2 Tordesillas Spain
6 S4 Töre Sweden
15 H1 Torelló Spain
12 D2 Torenberg h. Neth.
13 L3 Torgau Ger.
21 H5 Torgun r. Rus. Fed.
12 B3 Torhout Belgium
Torino see Turin
41 G9 Tori-shima i. Japan
87 F4 Torit Sudan
82 B2 Torixoreu Brazil
29 L3 Torkamān Iran
20 G3 Tor'kovskoye Vdkhr. resr Rus. Fed.
15 D2 Tormes r. Spain
6 S3 Torneälven r. Fin./Sweden
6 Q2 Torneträsk Sweden
6 Q2 Torneträsk l. Sweden
59 H2 Torngat Mountains Can.
6 T4 Tornio Fin.
83 D3 Tornquist Arg.
15 D2 Toro Spain
36 F1 Torom r. Rus. Fed.
50 H2 Toronto Austr.
69 H4 Toronto Can.
20 D3 Toropets Rus. Fed.
72 D5 Toro Pk summit U.S.A.
88 D3 Tororo Uganda
28 D3 Toros Dağları mts Turkey
10 F3 Torphins U.K.
9 D7 Torquay U.K.
72 C5 Torrance U.S.A.
15 B3 Torrão Port.
15 C2 Torre mt Port.
15 G2 Torreblanca Spain
18 F4 Torre del Greco Italy
15 D1 Torrelavega Spain
15 D4 Torremolinos Spain
50 A1 Torrens, Lake Austr.
15 F3 Torrent Spain
65 C7 Torreón Mex.
49 G3 Torres Islands is Vanuatu
15 B3 Torres Novas Port.
48 E2 Torres Strait str. Austr.
15 B3 Torres Vedras Port.
15 G3 Torreta, Sa h. Spain
15 F4 Torrevieja Spain
73 G2 Torrey U.S.A.
9 C7 Torridge r. U.K.
10 C3 Torridon, Loch in. U.K.
15 D3 Torrijos Spain
71 G4 Torrington CT U.S.A.
62 F3 Torrington WY U.S.A.
15 H1 Torroella de Montgrí Spain
7 N6 Torsby Sweden
6 Tórshavn Faroe Is
83 C1 Tórtolas, Cerro Las mt Chile
18 C5 Tortoli Sardinia Italy
18 C2 Tortona Italy
15 G2 Tortosa Spain
19 H1 Tortum Turkey
30 D3 Ţorūd Iran
29 G1 Torul Turkey
17 J4 Toruń Pol.
11 C2 Tory Island i. Rep. of Ireland
11 C2 Tory Sound chan. Rep. of Ireland
20 E3 Torzhok Rus. Fed.
41 C8 Tosa Japan
41 C8 Tosashimizu Japan
6 N4 Tosbotn Norway
90 E2 Tosca S. Africa
18 C3 Toscano, Arcipelago is Italy
40 G4 Tōshima-yama mt Japan
20 D3 Tosno Rus. Fed.
80 D3 Tostado Arg.
13 H1 Tostedt Ger.
41 B8 Tosu Japan
28 E1 Tosya Turkey
20 G3 Tot'ma Rus. Fed.
92 C6 Totten Glacier gl. Ant.
9 F7 Totton U.K.
41 D7 Tottori Japan
86 B4 Touba Côte d'Ivoire
86 A3 Touba Senegal
86 B1 Toubkal, Jbel mt Morocco
38 B2 Toudaohu China
86 B3 Tougan Burkina
86 C1 Touggourt Alg.
86 A3 Tougué Guinea
14 G2 Toul France
14 G5 Toulon France
14 E5 Toulouse France
86 B4 Toumodi Côte d'Ivoire
37 B5 Toungoo Myanmar
39 D5 Toupai China
44 B1 Tourakom Laos
12 B4 Tourcoing France
12 B4 Tournai Belgium
14 G4 Tournon-sur-Rhône France
14 G3 Tournus France
79 L5 Touros Brazil
14 E3 Tours France
90 D6 Touwsrivier S. Africa
13 L4 Toužim Czech Rep.
81 C2 Tovar Venez.
9 F5 Tove r. U.K.
29 K1 Tovuz Azer.
40 G4 Towada Japan
40 G5 Towada-Hachimantai National Park Japan
40 G4 Towada-ko l. Japan
51 E1 Towai N.Z.
71 E4 Towanda U.S.A.
73 H3 Towaoc U.S.A.
9 G5 Towcester U.K.
11 C6 Tower Rep. of Ireland
68 A2 Tower U.S.A.
57 J5 Towner U.S.A.
72 D3 Townes Pass U.S.A.
62 E2 Townsend U.S.A.
50 G4 Townsend, Mt mt Austr.
48 E3 Townsville Austr.
37 E7 Towori, Teluk b. Indon.
70 E5 Towson U.S.A.
40 G3 Tōya-ko l. Japan
41 E6 Toyama Japan
41 E6 Toyama-wan b. Japan
41 E7 Toyohashi Japan
41 E7 Toyokawa Japan
41 D7 Toyonaka Japan
41 D7 Toyooka Japan
41 E7 Toyota Japan
86 C1 Tozeur Tunisia
21 G7 Tqibuli Georgia
21 G7 Tqvarch'eli Georgia
13 F5 Traben Ger.
28 E4 Trâblous Lebanon
19 K4 Trabotivište Macedonia
29 G1 Trabzon Turkey
71 K2 Tracy Can.
72 B3 Tracy CA U.S.A.
64 E2 Tracy MN U.S.A.
68 A4 Traer U.S.A.
15 C4 Trafalgar, Cabo pt Spain
83 B3 Traiguén Chile
56 F5 Trail Can.
7 T9 Trakai Lith.
20 J2 Trakt Rus. Fed.
11 B5 Tralee Rep. of Ireland
11 B5 Tralee Bay b. Rep. of Ireland

81 E3 Tramán Tepui mt Venez.
11 D5 Tramore Rep. of Ireland
7 O7 Tranås Sweden
80 C3 Trancas Arg.
7 N8 Tranemo Sweden
10 F5 Tranent U.K.
44 A4 Trang Thai.
37 F7 Trangan i. Indon.
50 F2 Trangie Austr.
83 F1 Tranqueras Uru.
92 B5 Transantarctic Mountains Ant.
57 K5 Transcona Can.
19 K2 Transylvanian Alps mts Romania
18 E5 Trapani Sicily Italy
50 F5 Traralgon Austr.
18 E3 Trasimeno, Lago l. Italy
15 E3 Trasvase, Canal de canal Spain
44 B2 Trat Thai.
16 F7 Traunsee l. Austria
16 F7 Traunstein Ger.
50 D2 Travellers L. l. Austr.
92 C1 Traversay Is is Atl. Ocean
68 E3 Traverse City U.S.A.
51 D5 Travers, Mt mt N.Z.
44 C3 Tra Vinh Vietnam
65 D6 Travis, L. l. U.S.A.
18 G2 Travnik Bos.-Herz.
18 F1 Trbovlje Slovenia
49 F2 Treasury Is is Solomon Is
13 M2 Trebbin Ger.
16 G6 Třebíč Czech Rep.
19 H3 Trebinje Bos.-Herz.
17 K6 Trebišov Slovakia
18 F2 Trebnje Slovenia
13 G5 Trebur Ger.
13 J3 Treffurt Ger.
68 B3 Trego U.S.A.
10 D4 Treig, Loch l. U.K.
83 F2 Treinta-y-Tres Uru.
80 C6 Trelew Arg.
7 N9 Trelleborg Sweden
12 C4 Trélon France
9 C5 Tremadoc Bay b. U.K.
58 F4 Tremblant, Mt h. Can.
18 F3 Tremiti, Isole is Italy
62 D3 Tremonton U.S.A.
15 G1 Tremp Spain
68 B3 Trempealeau r. U.S.A.
9 B7 Trenance U.K.
16 J6 Trenčín Slovakia
13 H3 Trendelburg Ger.
83 D2 Trenque Lauquén Arg.
8 G4 Trent r. U.K.
18 D1 Trento Italy
69 J3 Trenton Can.
64 E3 Trenton MO U.S.A.
71 F4 Trenton NJ U.S.A.
59 K4 Trepassey Can.
83 E3 Tres Arroyos Arg.
9 A8 Tresco i. U.K.
82 D3 Três Corações Brazil
81 B4 Tres Esquinas Col.
10 B4 Treshnish Isles is U.K.
82 B3 Três Lagoas Brazil
80 B7 Tres Lagos Arg.
83 D3 Tres Lomas Arg.
82 D2 Três Marias, Represa resr Brazil
83 B4 Tres Picos mt Arg.
83 E3 Tres Picos, Cerro mt Arg.
63 F4 Tres Piedras U.S.A.
82 D3 Três Pontas Brazil
80 C7 Tres Puntas, C. pt Arg.
82 D3 Três Rios Brazil
7 M6 Tretten Norway
13 J6 Treuchtlingen Ger.
13 L2 Treuenbrietzen Ger.
7 L7 Treungen Norway
18 C2 Treviglio Italy
18 E2 Treviso Italy
9 B7 Trevose Head hd U.K.
19 M6 Tria Nisia i. Greece
19 N6 Trianta Greece
34 B2 Tribal Areas div. Pak.
19 H5 Tricase Italy
33 B4 Trichur India
12 A5 Tricot France
50 E2 Trida Austr.
12 E5 Trier Ger.
18 E2 Trieste Italy
18 E1 Triglav mt Slovenia
19 J5 Trikala Greece
28 D4 Trikomon Cyprus
37 F7 Trikora, Pk mt Indon.
11 E4 Trim Rep. of Ireland
33 C4 Trincomalee Sri Lanka
82 C2 Trindade Brazil
96 G7 Trindade, Ilha da i. Atl. Ocean
78 F6 Trinidad Bol.
81 C3 Trinidad Col.
75 J4 Trinidad Cuba
83 F2 Trinidad Uru.
63 F4 Trinidad U.S.A.
78 F1 Trinidad i. Trinidad and Tobago
53 K8 Trinidad and Tobago country Caribbean Sea
59 K4 Trinity Bay b. Can.
54 C4 Trinity Islands is U.S.A.
72 C1 Trinity Range mts U.S.A.
67 C5 Trion U.S.A.
13 K1 Tripkau Ger.
19 K6 Tripoli Greece
Tripoli see Trâblous
87 D1 Tripoli Libya
33 B4 Tripunittura India
35 G5 Tripura div. India
96 J8 Tristan da Cunha i. Atlantic Ocean
34 D3 Trisul mt India
35 F4 Trisul Dam dam Nepal
13 J1 Trittau Ger.
12 F5 Trittenheim Ger.
33 B4 Trivandrum India
18 F4 Trivento Italy
16 H6 Trnava Slovakia
48 F2 Trobriand Islands is P.N.G.
6 N4 Trofors Norway
18 G3 Trogir Croatia
18 F4 Troia Italy
12 F4 Troisdorf Ger.
12 D4 Trois-Ponts Belgium
59 F4 Trois-Rivières Can.
21 H6 Troitskoye Rus. Fed.
7 N7 Trollhättan Sweden
79 G3 Trombetas r. Brazil
93 H5 Tromelin, Île i. Ind. Ocean
83 B3 Tromen, Volcán volc. Arg.
91 F5 Trompsburg S. Africa
6 Q2 Tromsø Norway
72 D4 Trona U.S.A.
83 B4 Tronador, Monte mt Arg.
6 M5 Trondheim Norway
6 M5 Trondheimsfjorden chan. Norway
28 D4 Troodos Cyprus
28 D4 Troödos, Mount mt Cyprus
10 D5 Troon U.K.
82 D1 Tropeiros, Serra dos h. Brazil
73 F3 Tropic U.S.A.
10 D4 Trossachs, The reg. U.K.
11 E2 Trostan h. U.K.
10 F3 Troup Head hd U.K.
56 E2 Trout r. Can.
69 H3 Trout Creek Can.
73 F2 Trout Creek U.S.A.
58 B3 Trout L. l. Can.
56 F2 Trout Lake Alta. Can.
56 E2 Trout Lake N.W.T. Can.
68 E2 Trout Lake U.S.A.
56 E2 Trout Lake l. Can.
68 C2 Trout Lake l. U.S.A.
62 E2 Trout Peak summit U.S.A.
70 E4 Trout Run U.S.A.
9 E6 Trowbridge U.K.
67 C6 Troy AL U.S.A.
62 D2 Troy MT U.S.A.
71 G3 Troy NH U.S.A.
71 G3 Troy NY U.S.A.
70 A4 Troy OH U.S.A.
70 E4 Troy PA U.S.A.
19 L3 Troyan Bulg.
14 G2 Troyes France
72 D4 Troy Lake l. U.S.A.
73 E2 Troy Peak summit U.S.A.
19 J3 Trstenik Yugo.
21 E4 Trubchevsk Rus. Fed.
15 C1 Truchas Spain
20 E3 Trud Rus. Fed.
40 C3 Trudovoye Rus. Fed.
75 G5 Trujillo Honduras
78 C5 Trujillo Peru
15 D3 Trujillo Spain
81 C2 Trujillo Venez.
12 F5 Trulben Ger.
71 G4 Trumbull U.S.A.
73 F3 Trumbull, Mt mt U.S.A.
45 A2 Trumon Indon.
50 F2 Trundle Austr.
44 C2 Trung Hiệp Vietnam
39 C6 Trung Khanh China
59 H4 Truro Can.
9 B7 Truro U.K.
11 C3 Truskmore h. Rep. of Ireland
56 E3 Trutch Can.
63 F5 Truth or Consequences U.S.A.
16 G5 Trutnov Czech Rep.
19 L7 Trypiti, Akra pt Greece
7 N6 Trysil Norway
16 G3 Trzebiatów Pol.
36 A2 Tsagaannuur Mongolia
21 H6 Tsagan Aman Rus. Fed.
21 H6 Tsagan-Nur Rus. Fed.
21 G7 Ts'ageri Georgia
29 K1 Tsalka Georgia
89 E5 Tsaratanana, Massif du mts Madag.
90 B2 Tsaris Mts mts Namibia
21 H5 Tsatsa Rus. Fed.
90 A3 Tsaukaib Namibia
88 D4 Tsavo National Park Kenya
21 G6 Tselina Rus. Fed.
89 B6 Tses Namibia
89 C6 Tsetseng Botswana
36 C2 Tsetserleg Mongolia
89 C6 Tshabong Botswana
89 C6 Tshane Botswana
21 F6 Tshchikskoye Vdkhr. resr Rus. Fed.
88 B4 Tshela Congo(Zaire)
88 C4 Tshibala Congo(Zaire)
88 C4 Tshikapa Congo(Zaire)
88 C4 Tshikapa r. Congo(Zaire)
91 G3 Tshing S. Africa
91 J1 Tshipise S. Africa
89 C4 Tshitanzu Congo(Zaire)
88 C4 Tshofa Congo(Zaire)
91 J2 Tshokwane S. Africa
88 C4 Tshuapa r. Congo(Zaire)
21 G6 Tsimlyansk Rus. Fed.
21 G6 Tsimlyanskoye Vdkhr. resr Rus. Fed.
90 E3 Tsineng S. Africa
Tsingtao see Qingdao
39 □ Tsing Yi i. H.K. China
89 E6 Tsiombe Madag.
89 E5 Tsiroanomandidy Madag.
90 E6 Tsitsikamma Forest and Coastal National Park S. Africa
56 D4 Tsitsutl Pk summit Can.
20 H4 Tsivil'sk Rus. Fed.
21 G7 Ts'khinvali Georgia
20 G4 Tsna r. Rus. Fed.
34 D2 Tsokr Chumo l. India
91 H5 Tsolo S. Africa
91 G6 Tsomo S. Africa
34 D2 Tso Morari L. l. India
21 G7 Tsqaltubo Georgia
41 E7 Tsu Japan
41 G6 Tsuchiura Japan
39 □ Tsuen Wan H.K. China
40 G4 Tsugarū-Kaikyō str. Japan
89 B5 Tsumeb Namibia
89 B6 Tsumis Park Namibia
89 C5 Tsumkwe Namibia
35 G4 Tsunthang India
41 E7 Tsuruga Japan
41 D8 Tsurugi-san mt Japan
40 F5 Tsuruoka Japan
41 A7 Tsushima i. Japan
Tsushima-kaikyō str. see Korea Strait
41 D7 Tsuyama Japan
90 D1 Tswaane Botswana
91 F4 Tswaraganang S. Africa
91 F3 Tswelelang S. Africa
17 M4 Tsyelyakhany Belarus
6 X2 Tsyp-Navolok Rus. Fed.
21 E6 Tsyurupyns'k Ukr.
37 F7 Tual Indon.
11 C4 Tuam Rep. of Ireland
51 D4 Tuamarina N.Z.
46 N5 Tuamotu, Archipel des arch. Pac. Oc.
39 B6 Tuân Giao Vietnam
44 A5 Tuangku i. Indon.
21 F6 Tuapse Rus. Fed.
44 □ Tuas Sing.
51 A7 Tuatapere N.Z.
73 G3 Tuba City U.S.A.
45 D4 Tuban Indon.
80 G3 Tubarão Brazil
43 A4 Tubbataha Reefs rf Phil.
11 C3 Tubbercurry Rep. of Ireland
16 D6 Tübingen Ger.
86 A4 Tubmanburg Liberia
43 B4 Tubod Phil.
87 E1 Tubruq Libya
46 N6 Tubuai i. Fr. Polynesia Pac. Oc.
Tubuai Islands is see Australes, Îles
79 L6 Tucano Brazil
83 B3 Tucapel, Pta pt Chile
79 G7 Tucavaca Bol.
13 L1 Tüchen Ger.
13 L2 Tuchheim Ger.
56 D2 Tuchitua Can.
71 F5 Tuckerton U.S.A.
73 G5 Tucson U.S.A.
73 G5 Tucson Mts mts U.S.A.
81 B2 Tucuco r. Venez.
63 G5 Tucumcari U.S.A.
81 E2 Tucupita Venez.
79 J4 Tucuruí Brazil
79 J4 Tucuruí, Represa resr Brazil
29 M5 Tū Dār Iran
15 F1 Tudela Spain
15 C2 Tuela r. Port.
39 □ Tuen Mun H.K. China
35 H4 Tuensang India
30 C5 Ţufayḩ S. Arabia
91 J4 Tugela r. S. Africa
43 C4 Tugnug Point pt Phil.
43 B2 Tuguegarao Phil.
25 P4 Tugur Rus. Fed.
38 F2 Tuhai r. China
44 A5 Tuhemberua Indon.
15 B1 Tui Spain
81 A2 Tuira r. Panama
37 E7 Tukangbesi, Kepulauan is Indon.
58 E2 Tukarak Island i. Can.
51 F3 Tukituki r. N.Z.
54 E3 Tuktoyaktuk Can.
7 S8 Tukums Latvia
20 F4 Tula Rus. Fed.
35 H1 Tulagt Ar Gol r. China
74 E4 Tulancingo Mex.
72 C3 Tulare U.S.A.
72 C4 Tulare Lake Bed l. U.S.A.
63 F5 Tularosa U.S.A.
33 C2 Tulasi mt India
90 C6 Tulbagh S. Africa
78 C3 Tulcán Ecuador
19 N2 Tulcea Romania
21 D5 Tul'chyn Ukr.
72 C3 Tule r. U.S.A.
30 D3 Tuleh Iran
35 G4 Tule-la Pass Bhutan
57 J2 Tulemalu Lake l. Can.
65 C5 Tulia U.S.A.
28 E5 Tulkarm West Bank
11 C5 Tulla Rep. of Ireland
67 C5 Tullahoma U.S.A.
50 F2 Tullamore Austr.
11 D4 Tullamore Rep. of Ireland
14 E4 Tulle France
6 O5 Tulleråsen Sweden
50 F2 Tullibigeal Austr.
65 E6 Tullos U.S.A.
11 E5 Tullow Rep. of Ireland
48 E3 Tully Austr.
11 D3 Tully U.K.
71 E3 Tully U.S.A.
20 D2 Tulos Rus. Fed.
65 D4 Tulsa U.S.A.
20 F4 Tul'skaya Oblast' div. Rus. Fed.
81 A3 Tuluá Col.
83 B3 Tuluksak AK U.S.A.
83 C1 Tulum, Valle de v. Arg.
36 C1 Tulun Rus. Fed.
45 D4 Tulungagung Indon.
35 H4 Tulung La pass China
43 A4 Tuluran i. Phil.
81 A4 Tumaco Col.
91 G3 Tumahole S. Africa
21 J6 Tumak Rus. Fed.
7 P7 Tumba Sweden
88 B4 Tumba, Lac l. Congo(Zaire)
45 D3 Tumbangsamba Indon.
43 C5 Tumbao Phil.
78 B4 Tumbes Peru
56 E3 Tumbler Ridge Can.
38 D1 Tumd Youqi China
38 D1 Tumd Zuoqi China
42 E2 Tumen China
42 E2 Tumen Jiang r. China/N. Korea
38 B2 Tumenzi China
78 F2 Tumereng Guyana
43 A5 Tumindao i. Phil.
33 B3 Tumkur India
35 G3 Tum La pass China
10 E4 Tummel, Loch l. U.K.
36 G2 Tumnin r. Rus. Fed.
31 F5 Tump Pak.
44 B4 Tumpat Malaysia
86 B3 Tumu Ghana
79 G3 Tumucumaque, Serra h. Brazil
50 G3 Tumut Austr.
30 D5 Tunb al Kubrā i. Iran
9 H6 Tunbridge Wells, Royal U.K.
29 G2 Tunceli Turkey
39 D7 Tunchang China
34 D4 Tundla India
89 D5 Tunduru Tanz.
19 M3 Tundzha r. Bulg.
33 B3 Tungabhadra r. India
33 A3 Tungabhadra Reservoir India
35 H3 Tunga Pass China/India
43 B5 Tungawan Phil.
39 □ Tung Chung Wan b. H.K. China
6 D4 Tungnaá r. Iceland
56 D2 Tungsten Can.
20 E1 Tunguda Rus. Fed.
36 C1 Tunguska, Nizhnyaya r. Rus. Fed.
39 □ Tung Wan b. H.K. China
33 C2 Tuni India
86 D1 Tunis Tunisia
18 D6 Tunis, Golfe de g. Tunisia
85 D2 Tunisia country Africa
53 G3 Tuniut r. Austr.
81 B3 Tunja Col.
38 D2 Tunliu China
6 N4 Tunnsjøen l. Norway
9 J5 Tunstall U.K.
6 V3 Tuntsa Fin.
6 W3 Tuntsayoki r. Fin./Rus. Fed.
59 H2 Tunungayualok Island i. Can.
83 C2 Tunuyán Arg.
83 C2 Tunuyán r. Arg.
38 E3 Tuo He r. China
38 F2 Tuoji Dao i. China
44 C3 Tuŏl Khpos Cambodia
72 B3 Tuolumne U.S.A.
72 C3 Tuolumne Meadows U.S.A.
39 B5 Tuoniang Jiang r. China
35 H2 Tuotuo He r. China
35 H2 Tuotuoyan China
82 B3 Tupã Brazil
82 C2 Tupaciguara Brazil
29 L3 Tūp Āghāj Iran
80 F3 Tupanciretã Brazil
53 C3 Tuparro r. Col.
65 F5 Tupelo U.S.A.
78 E8 Tupiza Bol.
71 F2 Tupper Lake U.S.A.
71 F2 Tupper Lake l. U.S.A.
83 C2 Tupungato Arg.
83 C2 Tupungato, Cerro mt Arg./Chile
29 K7 Tuqayyid well Iraq
42 A1 Tuquan China
81 A4 Túquerres Col.
39 C7 Tuqu Wan b. China
35 G4 Tura India
25 M3 Tura Rus. Fed.
32 B5 Turabah S. Arabia
81 D3 Turagua, Serranía mt Venez.
51 E4 Turakina N.Z.
30 E3 Turan Iran
36 F1 Turana, Khrebet mts Rus. Fed.
51 E3 Turangi N.Z.
30 E2 Turan Lowland lowland Asia
28 G6 Turayf S. Arabia
30 C5 Turayf well S. Arabia
7 T7 Turba Estonia
81 B2 Turbaco Col.
31 F5 Turbat Pak.
81 A2 Turbo Col.
17 L7 Turda Romania
30 C3 Tūreh Iran
Turfan see Turpan
26 E2 Turgay Kazak.
19 M3 Tŭrgovishte Bulg.
28 C2 Turgut Turkey
28 A2 Turgutlu Turkey
28 F1 Turhal Turkey
7 T7 Türi Estonia
15 F3 Turia r. Spain
81 D2 Turiamo Venez.
18 B2 Turin Italy
40 B2 Turiy Rog Rus. Fed.
21 C5 Turiys'k Ukr.
88 D3 Turkana, Lake salt l. Eth./Kenya
19 M4 Türkeli Adası i. Turkey
26 F2 Turkestan Kazak.
31 G2 Turkestan Range mts Asia
23 C6 Turkey country Asia
68 B4 Turkey r. U.S.A.
21 G5 Turki Rus. Fed.
24 G6 Turkmenbashi Turkm.
28 C2 Türkmen Dağı mt Turkey
23 E5 Turkmenistan country Asia
31 F2 Turkmen-Kala Turkm.
30 D2 Turkmenskiy Zaliv b. Turkm.
28 F3 Türkoğlu Turkey
53 J7 Turks and Caicos Islands terr. Caribbean Sea
75 K4 Turks Islands is Turks and Caicos Is
7 S6 Turku Fin.
88 D3 Turkwel watercourse Kenya
72 B3 Turlock U.S.A.
72 B3 Turlock L. l. U.S.A.
51 F4 Turnagain, Cape c. N.Z.
10 D5 Turnberry U.K.
73 G5 Turnbull, Mt mt U.S.A.
74 G5 Turneffe Is is Belize
73 F3 Turner U.S.A.
12 C3 Turnhout Belgium
57 H3 Turnor Lake l. Can.
19 L3 Turnu Măgurele Romania
50 G2 Turon r. Austr.
20 G3 Turovets Rus. Fed.
36 A2 Turpan China
36 A2 Turpan Pendi China
75 J4 Turquino mt Cuba
10 F3 Turriff U.K.
29 K5 Tursāq Iraq
32 F1 Turtkul' Uzbek.
68 B2 Turtle Flambeau Flowage resr U.S.A.
57 H4 Turtleford Can.
68 A3 Turtle Lake U.S.A.
27 F2 Turugart Pass China/Kyrg.
82 B2 Turvo r. Goiás Brazil
82 C3 Turvo r. São Paulo Brazil
73 F4 Tusayan U.S.A.
67 C5 Tuscaloosa U.S.A.
70 C4 Tuscarawas r. U.S.A.
70 E4 Tuscarora Mts h. U.S.A.
68 C6 Tuscola IL U.S.A.
65 D5 Tuscola TX U.S.A.
30 E3 Tusharīk Iran
67 C5 Tuskegee U.S.A.
70 D4 Tussey Mts h. U.S.A.
31 E4 Tūtak Iran
29 J2 Tutak Turkey
20 F3 Tutayev Rus. Fed.
33 B4 Tuticorin India
64 D4 Tuttle Creek Res. resr U.S.A.
16 D7 Tuttlingen Ger.
55 Q2 Tuttut Nunaat reg. Greenland
49 J3 Tutuila i. Pac. Oc.
89 C6 Tutume Botswana
42 D3 Tuun, Mt mt N. Korea
6 W5 Tuupovaara Fin.
6 V5 Tuusniemi Fin.
47 J4 Tuvalu country Pac. Oc.
30 B5 Tuwayq, Jabal h. S. Arabia
74 E4 Tuxpan Veracruz Mex.
74 F5 Tuxtla Gutiérrez Mex.
81 D2 Tuy r. Venez.
44 C2 Tuy Đức Vietnam
39 B6 Tuyên Quang Vietnam
44 D2 Tuy Hoa Vietnam
30 C3 Tūysarkān Iran
28 D2 Tuz Gölü salt l. Turkey
73 F4 Tuzigoot National Monument res. U.S.A.
29 K4 Tuz Khurmātū Iraq
19 H2 Tuzla Bos.-Herz.
29 H2 Tuzlu r. Turkey
Tuz, Lake salt l. see Tuz Gölü
21 F6 Tuzlov r. Rus. Fed.
7 L7 Tvedestrand Norway
20 E3 Tver' Rus. Fed.
20 E3 Tverskaya Oblast' div. Rus. Fed.
69 J3 Tweed Can.
10 F5 Tweed r. Eng./Scot. U.K.
56 D4 Tweedsmuir Prov. Park res. Can.
90 C6 Tweefontein S. Africa
90 C2 Twee Rivier Namibia
12 E2 Twente reg. Neth.
72 D4 Twentynine Palms U.S.A.
59 K4 Twillingate Can.
62 D2 Twin Bridges U.S.A.
65 C6 Twin Buttes Res. resr U.S.A.
59 H3 Twin Falls Can.
62 D3 Twin Falls U.S.A.
56 F3 Twin Lakes Can.
71 H2 Twin Mountain U.S.A.
70 C6 Twin Oaks U.S.A.
72 B2 Twin Peak summit U.S.A.
13 G2 Twistringen Ger.
50 G4 Twofold B. b. Austr.
73 G4 Two Guns U.S.A.
68 B2 Two Harbors U.S.A.
57 G4 Two Hills Can.
62 D1 Two Medicine r. U.S.A.
68 D3 Two Rivers U.S.A.
35 H5 Tyao r. India/Myanmar
6 M5 Tydal Norway
70 D5 Tygart Lake l. U.S.A.
70 D5 Tygart Valley v. U.S.A.
36 E1 Tygda Rus. Fed.
65 E5 Tyler U.S.A.
65 F6 Tylertown U.S.A.
36 E1 Tynda Rus. Fed.
56 A2 Tyndall Gl. gl. U.S.A.
10 F4 Tyne r. U.K.
8 F2 Tynemouth U.K.
7 M5 Tynset Norway
28 E5 Tyre Lebanon
57 H2 Tyrell Lake l. Can.
6 T4 Tyrnävä Fin.
19 K5 Tyrnavos Greece
70 D4 Tyrone U.S.A.
50 D3 Tyrrell r. Austr.
50 D3 Tyrrell, L. l. Austr.
18 D4 Tyrrhenian Sea sea France/Italy
25 Q3 Tyubelyakh Rus. Fed.
24 J4 Tyukalinsk Rus. Fed.
94 D4 Tyukyu Trench sea feature Pac. Oc.
24 H4 Tyumen' Rus. Fed.
25 N3 Tyung r. Rus. Fed.
9 C6 Tywi r. U.K.
9 C5 Tywyn U.K.
91 J1 Tzaneen S. Africa

U

89 C5 Uamanda Angola
81 E4 Uatatás r. Brazil
79 L5 Uauá Brazil
81 D5 Uaupés Brazil
81 C4 Uaupés r. Brazil
30 B4 U'aywij well S. Arabia
29 J7 U'aywij, W. watercourse S. Arabia
82 D3 Ubá Brazil
82 D2 Ubaí Brazil
82 E1 Ubaitaba Brazil
88 B3 Ubangi r. C.A.R./Congo(Zaire)
81 B3 Ubate Col.
29 J5 Ubayyid, Wādī al watercourse Iraq/S. Arabia
41 B8 Ube Japan
15 E3 Úbeda Spain
82 C2 Uberaba Brazil
79 G7 Uberaba, Lagoa l. Bol./Brazil
82 C2 Uberlândia Brazil
44 □ Ubin, Pulau i. Sing.
44 B1 Ubolratna Res. resr Thai.
91 K3 Ubombo S. Africa
44 C2 Ubon Ratchathani Thai.
13 G5 Ubstadt-Weiher Ger.
88 C4 Ubundu Congo(Zaire)
29 L1 Ucar Azer.
78 D5 Ucayali r. Peru
34 B3 Uch Pak.
31 F2 Uch-Adzhi Turkm.
30 C2 Ūchān Iran
27 G2 Ucharal Kazak.
40 G3 Uchiura-wan b. Japan
13 G2 Uchte Ger.
13 K2 Uchte r. Ger.
36 F1 Uchur r. Rus. Fed.
9 H7 Uckfield U.K.
56 D5 Ucluelet Can.
73 H3 Ucolo U.S.A.
62 F2 Ucross U.S.A.
25 P4 Uda r. Rus. Fed.
21 H6 Udachnoye Rus. Fed.
25 N3 Udachnyy Rus. Fed.
33 B4 Udagamandalam India
34 C4 Udaipur Rajasthan India
35 G5 Udaipur Tripura India
35 E5 Udanti r. India/Myanmar
33 B3 Udayagiri India
7 M7 Uddevalla Sweden
10 D5 Uddingston U.K.
6 P4 Uddjaure l. Sweden
12 D3 Uden Neth.
33 B2 Udgir India
20 H2 Udimskiy Rus. Fed.
18 E1 Udine Italy
59 J2 Udjuktok Bay b. Can.
20 E3 Udomlya Rus. Fed.
44 B1 Udon Thani Thai.
36 F1 Udskaya Guba b. Rus. Fed.
33 B4 Udumalaippetai India
33 A3 Udupi India
36 F1 Udyl', Ozero l. Rus. Fed.
16 G4 Ueckermünde Ger.
41 F6 Ueda Japan
48 C2 Uekuli Indon.
88 C3 Uele r. Congo(Zaire)
54 B3 Uelen Rus. Fed.
13 J2 Uelzen Ger.
88 C3 Uere r. Congo(Zaire)
13 H1 Uetersen Ger.
13 H5 Uettingen Ger.
13 J2 Uetze Ger.
24 G4 Ufa Rus. Fed.
13 J5 Uffenheim Ger.
89 B6 Ugab watercourse Namibia
88 D4 Ugalla r. Tanz.
85 G5 Uganda country Africa
91 H5 Ugie S. Africa
36 G2 Uglegorsk Rus. Fed.
40 C3 Uglekamensk Rus. Fed.
20 F3 Uglich Rus. Fed.
18 F2 Ugljan i. Croatia
20 E3 Uglovka Rus. Fed.
40 C3 Uglovoye Rus. Fed.
25 Q3 Ugol'naya Zyryanka Rus. Fed.
25 T3 Ugol'nyye Kopi Rus. Fed.
20 E4 Ugra Rus. Fed.
16 H6 Uherské Hradiště Czech Rep.
70 C4 Uhrichsville U.S.A.
10 B3 Uig U.K.
88 B4 Uíge Angola
42 D5 Ŭijŏngbu S. Korea
42 C3 Ŭiju N. Korea
6 W5 Uimaharju Fin.
73 F3 Uinkaret Plateau plat. U.S.A.
62 E3 Uinta Mts mts UT U.S.A.
89 B6 Uis Mine Namibia
11 D4 Uisneach h. Rep. of Ireland
42 E5 Ŭisŏng S. Korea
91 F6 Uitenhage S. Africa
12 C2 Uithoorn Neth.
12 E1 Uithuizen Neth.
59 H2 Uivak, Cape hd Can.
41 D7 Uji Japan
41 A9 Uji-guntō is Japan
34 C5 Ujjain India
45 E4 Ujung Pandang Indon.
29 J5 Ukhaydir Iraq
35 H4 Ukhrul India
20 K2 Ukhta Rus. Fed.
20 K2 Ukhta r. Rus. Fed.
72 A2 Ukiah CA U.S.A.
62 C2 Ukiah OR U.S.A.
55 N2 Ukkusissat Greenland
7 T9 Ukmergė Lith.
5 F4 Ukraine country Europe
20 J2 Uktym Rus. Fed.
41 A8 Uku-jima i. Japan
90 D1 Ukwi Botswana
90 D1 Ukwi Pan salt pan Botswana
36 C2 Ulaanbaatar Mongolia
36 B2 Ulaangom Mongolia
50 G2 Ulan Austr.
Ulan Bator see Ulaanbaatar
38 C1 Ulan Buh Shamo des. China
21 H6 Ulan Erge Rus. Fed.
21 H6 Ulan-Khol Rus. Fed.
38 C1 Ulansuhai Nur l. China
38 A1 Ulan Tohoi China
36 C1 Ulan-Ude Rus. Fed.
35 G2 Ulan Ul Hu l. China
28 F2 Ulaş Turkey
49 G2 Ulawa I. i. Solomon Is
31 E4 Ulāy, Kūh-e h. Iran
42 E5 Ulchin S. Korea
7 L7 Ulefoss Norway
7 U7 Ülenurme Estonia
33 A2 Ulhasnagar India
36 B2 Uliastay Mongolia
12 C3 Ulicoten Neth.
6 X2 Ulita r. Rus. Fed.
37 F6 Ulithi i. Micronesia
50 H3 Ulladulla Austr.

10 C3 Ullapool U.K.
6 S5 Ullava Fin.
8 E3 Ullswater l. U.K.
42 F5 Ullŭng-do i. S. Korea
16 D6 Ulm Ger.
12 E4 Ulmen Ger.
7 N8 Ulricehamn Sweden
12 E1 Ulrum Neth.
42 E6 Ulsan S. Korea
6 L5 Ulsberg Norway
11 D3 Ulster Canal canal Rep. of Ireland/U.K.
50 D3 Ultima Austr.
28 B1 Ulubat Gölü l. Turkey
28 C2 Uluborlu Turkey
28 B1 Uludağ mt Turkey
44 B5 Ulu Kali, Gunung mt Malaysia
28 E3 Ulukışla Turkey
91 J4 Ulundi S. Africa
36 A2 Ulungur Hu l. China
44 □ Ulu Pandan Sing.
Uluru h. see Ayers Rock
28 D1 Ulus Turkey
10 B4 Ulva i. U.K.
12 C3 Ulvenhout Neth.
8 D3 Ulverston U.K.
7 O6 Ulvsjön Sweden
31 H1 Ul'yanovo Uzbek.
20 J4 Ul'yanovsk Rus. Fed.
20 H4 Ul'yanovskaya Oblast' div. Rus. Fed.
65 C4 Ulysses U.S.A.
21 D5 Uman' Ukr.
31 G4 Umarao Pak.
34 E5 Umaria India
34 D6 Umarkhed India
35 E6 Umarkot India
34 B4 Umarkot Pak.
62 C2 Umatilla U.S.A.
24 E3 Umba Rus. Fed.
71 H2 Umbagog Lake l. U.S.A.
48 E2 Umboi i. P.N.G.
6 R5 Umeå Sweden
6 Q4 Umeälven r. Sweden
91 J4 Umfolozi r. S. Africa
29 L7 Umgharah Kuwait
91 J4 Umhlanga S. Africa
54 H3 Umingmaktok Can.
58 E2 Umiujaq Can.
91 J5 Umkomaas S. Africa
91 J4 Umlazi S. Africa
29 K6 Umma Iraq
30 D5 Umm al Qaywayn U.A.E.
30 C5 Umm Bāb Qatar
87 E3 Umm Keddada Sudan
29 L6 Umm Qasr Iraq
87 F3 Umm Ruwaba Sudan
87 E1 Umm Sa'ad Libya
30 C5 Umm Sa'id Qatar
62 A3 Umpqua r. U.S.A.
89 B5 Umpulo Angola
34 D5 Umred India
34 C5 Umreth India
91 H5 Umtata S. Africa
91 J5 Umtentweni S. Africa
86 C4 Umuahia Nigeria
82 B3 Umuarama Brazil
91 H5 Umzimkulu S. Africa
91 J5 Umzinto S. Africa
82 E1 Una Brazil
18 G2 Una r. Bos.-Herz./Croatia
28 F6 'Unāb, W. al watercourse Jordan
82 C2 Unaí Brazil
31 H3 Unai Pass Afgh.
54 B3 Unalakleet U.S.A.
10 C2 Unapool U.K.
81 D2 Unare r. Venez.
28 E6 'Unayzah Jordan
32 B4 'Unayzah S. Arabia
29 G5 'Unayzah, Jabal h. Iraq
63 E4 Uncompahgre Plateau plat. U.S.A.
91 H4 Underberg S. Africa
50 C3 Underbool Austr.
62 C2 Underwood U.S.A.
20 E4 Unecha Rus. Fed.
50 F2 Ungarie Austr.
59 G2 Ungava Bay b. Can.
58 F1 Ungava, Péninsule d' pen. Can.
42 F2 Unggi N. Korea
21 C6 Ungheni Moldova
31 E2 Unguz, Solonchakovyye Vpadiny salt flat Turkm.
20 J3 Uni Rus. Fed.
82 B4 União da Vitória Brazil
81 B4 Unilla r. Col.
78 F4 Unini r. Brazil
82 A4 Unión Para.
71 J2 Union ME U.S.A.
67 D5 Union SC U.S.A.
70 C6 Union WV U.S.A.
68 E5 Union City OH U.S.A.
70 D4 Union City PA U.S.A.
67 B4 Union City TN U.S.A.
90 E6 Uniondale S. Africa
73 F4 Union, Mt mt U.S.A.
67 C5 Union Springs U.S.A.
70 D5 Uniontown U.S.A.
69 F4 Unionville U.S.A.
62 E3 Unita Mts. mts U.S.A.
23 E7 United Arab Emirates country Asia
5 C3 United Kingdom country Europe
53 E6 United States of America N. America
57 H4 Unity Can.
71 J2 Unity ME U.S.A.
62 C2 Unity OR U.S.A.
34 C5 Unjha India
13 F3 Unna Ger.
34 E4 Unnão India
42 C4 Ŭnp'a N. Korea
42 C3 Ŭnsan N. Korea
42 D4 Ŭnsan N. Korea
10 □ Unst i. U.K.
13 K3 Unstrut r. Ger.
35 G2 Unuli Horog China
35 F5 Upar Ghat reg. India
81 E2 Upata Venez.
89 C4 Upemba, Lac l. Congo(Zaire)
89 C4 Upemba, Parc National de l' nat. park Congo(Zaire)
43 C5 Upi Phil.
81 B3 Upía r. Col.
90 D4 Upington S. Africa
34 B5 Upleta India
6 W3 Upoloksha Rus. Fed.
49 J3 Upolu i. Samoa
70 B4 Upper Arlington U.S.A.
56 F4 Upper Arrow L. l. Can.
56 F4 Upper Arrow Lake B.C. Can.
51 E4 Upper Hutt N.Z.
68 B4 Upper Iowa r. U.S.A.
71 K1 Upper Kent Can.
62 B3 Upper Klamath L. l. U.S.A.
62 B3 Upper L. l. U.S.A.
72 A2 Upper Lake U.S.A.
56 D2 Upper Liard Can.
11 D3 Upper Lough Erne l. U.K.
70 E5 Upper Marlboro U.S.A.
44 □ Upper Peirce Res. resr Sing.
59 J4 Upper Salmon Reservoir Can.
70 B4 Upper Sandusky U.S.A.
71 F2 Upper Saranac Lake l. U.S.A.
51 D4 Upper Takaka N.Z.
7 P7 Uppsala Sweden
58 B4 Upsala Can.
71 H2 Upton U.S.A.
29 L7 Uqlat al 'Udhaybah well Iraq
29 L6 Ur Iraq
81 A2 Urabá, Golfo de b. Col.
38 C1 Urad Qianqi China
38 C1 Urad Zhonghou Lianheqi China
30 E4 Ūrāf Iran
40 H3 Urakawa Japan
50 F2 Ural h. Austr.
50 H1 Uralla Austr.
4 J2 Ural Mountains mts Rus. Fed.
26 D1 Ural'sk Kazak.
Ural'skiy Khrebet mts see Ural Mountains
88 D4 Urambo Tanz.
50 F3 Urana Austr.
50 F3 Urana, L. l. Austr.
82 D1 Urandi Brazil
57 H3 Uranium City Can.
50 F3 Uranquity Austr.
81 E4 Uraricoera Brazil
81 E4 Uraricoera r. Brazil
81 E4 Uraricuera r. Brazil
81 E3 Uraucaima, Sa mt Brazil
73 H2 Uravan U.S.A.
30 B5 'Urayq ad Duḩūl sand dunes S. Arabia
21 F5 Urazovo Rus. Fed.
65 C5 Urbana IL U.S.A.
70 B4 Urbana OH U.S.A.
18 E3 Urbino Italy
78 D6 Urcos Peru
21 H5 Urda Kazak.
20 J2 Urdoma Rus. Fed.
8 F3 Ure r. U.K.
20 H3 Uren' Rus. Fed.
24 J3 Urengoy Rus. Fed.
49 G3 Uréparapara i. Vanuatu
51 F3 Urewera National Park N.Z.
20 H4 Urga r. Rus. Fed.
26 E2 Urgench Uzbek.
28 E2 Ürgüp Turkey
31 G2 Urgut Uzbek.
6 V2 Urho Kekkosen Kansallispuisto nat. park Fin.
81 B2 Uribia Col.
7 S6 Urjala Fin.
12 D2 Urk Neth.
21 H7 Urkarakh Rus. Fed.
19 M5 Urla Turkey
11 D5 Urlingford Rep. of Ireland
31 H2 Urmetan Tajik.
Urmia see Orūmīyeh
Urmia, Lake salt l. see Orūmīyeh, Daryācheh-ye
39 □ Urmston Road chan. H.K. China
19 J3 Uroševac Yugo.
31 H2 Ŭroteppa Tajik.
35 F3 Urru Co salt l. China
38 A1 Urt Mongolia
82 C1 Uruaçu Brazil
74 D5 Uruapan Mex.
78 D6 Urubamba r. Peru
79 G4 Urucara Brazil
79 K5 Uruçuí Brazil
82 D2 Urucuia r. Brazil
79 K5 Uruçuí Preto r. Brazil
79 G4 Urucurituba Brazil
80 E3 Uruguaiana Brazil
77 E6 Uruguay country S. America
80 E4 Uruguay r. Arg./Uru.
Urukh see Erech
Urumchi see Ürümqi
36 A2 Ürümqi China
21 G6 Urup r. Rus. Fed.
27 H2 Urup, O. i. Rus. Fed.
21 H7 Urus-Martan Rus. Fed.
21 G5 Uryupinsk Rus. Fed.
20 J3 Urzhum Rus. Fed.
19 M2 Urziceni Romania
41 B8 Usa Japan
20 J4 Usa r. Rus. Fed.
28 B2 Uşak Turkey
89 B6 Usakos Namibia
85 B5 Usarp Mts mts Ant.
80 E8 Usborne, Mt h. Falkland Is
24 J1 Ushakova, O. i. Rus. Fed.
30 B5 'Ushayrah S. Arabia
41 B8 Ushibuka Japan
27 F2 Ushtobe Kazak.
80 C8 Ushuaia Arg.
13 G4 Usingen Ger.
24 G3 Usinsk Rus. Fed.
9 E6 Usk U.K.
9 E6 Usk r. U.K.
35 E4 Uska India
20 C4 Uskhodni Belarus
13 H3 Uslar Ger.
21 F4 Usman' Rus. Fed.
7 S8 Usmas Ezers l. Latvia
20 J2 Usogorsk Rus. Fed.
36 C1 Usol'ye-Sibirskoye Rus. Fed.
14 F4 Ussel France
40 D1 Ussuri r. China/Rus. Fed.
36 F2 Ussuriysk Rus. Fed.
20 H3 Usta r. Rus. Fed.
25 M4 Ust'-Barguzin Rus. Fed.
21 G5 Ust'-Buzulukskaya Rus. Fed.
21 G6 Ust'-Donetskiy Rus. Fed.
18 E5 Ustica, Isola di i. Sicily Italy
25 M4 Ust'Ilimsk Rus. Fed.
36 C1 Ust'-Ilimskiy Vdkhr. resr Rus. Fed.
24 G3 Ust'-Ilych Rus. Fed.
16 G5 Ústí nad Labem Czech Rep.
Ustinov see Izhevsk
16 H3 Ustka Pol.
25 S4 Ust'-Kamchatsk Rus. Fed.
27 G2 Ust'-Kamenogorsk Kazak.
36 C1 Ust'-Kut Rus. Fed.
25 P2 Ust'-Kuyga Rus. Fed.
21 F6 Ust'-Labinsk Rus. Fed.
7 V7 Ust'-Luga Rus. Fed.
25 P3 Ust'-Maya Rus. Fed.
24 G3 Ust'-Nem Rus. Fed.
25 Q3 Ust'-Nera Rus. Fed.
20 J2 Ust'-Ocheya Rus. Fed.
25 N2 Ust'-Olenek Rus. Fed.
25 Q3 Ust'omchug Rus. Fed.
36 C1 Ust'-Ordynskiy Rus. Fed.
25 S3 Ust'-Penzhino Rus. Fed.
24 K3 Ust'-Port Rus. Fed.
20 G2 Ust'-Shonosha Rus. Fed.
24 G3 Ust'-Tsil'ma Rus. Fed.
20 H2 Ust'-Ura Rus. Fed.
20 G2 Ust'-Vayen'ga Rus. Fed.
20 H2 Ust'-Vyyskaya Rus. Fed.
20 G2 Ust'ya r. Rus. Fed.
20 F3 Ust'ye Rus. Fed.
20 F3 Ust'ye r. Rus. Fed.
24 G5 Ustyurt Plateau plat. Kazak./Uzbek.
20 F3 Ustyuzhna Rus. Fed.
41 B8 Usuki Japan
20 D4 Usvyaty Rus. Fed.
73 G2 Utah div. U.S.A.
73 G1 Utah Lake l. U.S.A.
6 U4 Utajärvi Fin.
30 C5 Utayyiq S. Arabia
7 T9 Utena Lith.
31 G5 Uthal Pak.
44 A2 U Thong Thai.
44 C2 Uthumphon Phisai Thai.
71 F3 Utica U.S.A.
15 F3 Utiel Spain
56 F3 Utikuma Lake l. Can.
91 F3 Utlwanang S. Africa
35 E4 Utraula India
12 D2 Utrecht Neth.
91 J3 Utrecht S. Africa
15 D4 Utrera Spain
6 U2 Utsjoki Fin.
41 F6 Utsunomiya Japan
21 H6 Utta Rus. Fed.
44 B1 Uttaradit Thai.
34 D4 Uttar Pradesh div. India
9 F5 Uttoxeter U.K.
49 G3 Utupua i. Solomon Is
55 M2 Uummannaq Greenland
55 N2 Uummannaq Fjord in. Greenland
55 O4 Uummannarsuaq c. Greenland
6 T5 Uurainen Fin.
7 R6 Uusikaupunki Fin.
81 C4 Uva r. Col.
65 D6 Uvalde U.S.A.
21 G5 Uvarovo Rus. Fed.
88 D4 Uvinza Tanz.
91 J5 Uvongo S. Africa
36 B1 Uvs Nuur l. Mongolia
41 C8 Uwajima Japan
87 E2 Uweinat, Jebel mt Sudan
9 G6 Uxbridge U.K.
38 C2 Uxin Ju China
38 C2 Uxin Qi China
36 B1 Uyar Rus. Fed.
38 C1 Üydzin Mongolia
25 Q3 Uyega Rus. Fed.
86 C4 Uyo Nigeria
78 E8 Uyuni, Salar de salt flat Bol.
20 H4 Uza r. Rus. Fed.
29 K4 'Uzaym, Nahr al r. Iraq
23 E5 Uzbekistan country Asia
14 G4 Uzès France
21 B5 Uzhhorod Ukr.
19 H3 Užice Yugo.
20 F4 Uzlovaya Rus. Fed.
20 G3 Uzola r. Rus. Fed.
28 C3 Üzümlü Turkey
31 H2 Uzun Uzbek.
29 L3 Üzün Darreh r. Iran
21 C7 Uzunköprü Turkey
21 D5 Uzyn Ukr.

V

7 T5 Vaajakoski Fin.
91 H3 Vaal r. S. Africa
6 U4 Vaala Fin.
90 F4 Vaalbos National Park S. Africa
91 H3 Vaal Dam dam S. Africa
91 H2 Vaalwater S. Africa
6 R5 Vaasa Fin.
31 G1 Vabkent Uzbek.
17 J7 Vác Hungary
80 F3 Vacaria Brazil
82 A3 Vacaria r. Mato Grosso do Sul Brazil
82 D2 Vacaria r. Minas Gerais Brazil
82 A3 Vacaria, Serra h. Brazil
72 B2 Vacaville U.S.A.
20 G4 Vad r. Rus. Fed.
34 C6 Vada India
7 K7 Vadla Norway
34 C5 Vadodara India
6 V1 Vadsø Norway
16 D7 Vaduz Liechtenstein
6 N3 Værøy i. Norway
20 G2 Vaga r. Rus. Fed.
7 L6 Vågåmo Norway
18 F2 Vaganski Vrh mt Croatia
6 □ Vágar i. Faroe Is
6 Q4 Vägsele Sweden
6 □ Vágur Faroe Is
6 S5 Vähäkyrö Fin.
7 T7 Vaida Estonia
33 B4 Vaigai r. India
73 G5 Vail U.S.A.
12 B5 Vailly-sur-Aisne France
49 H2 Vaitupu i. Tuvalu
31 J2 Vakhan Tajik.
31 H2 Vakhsh Tajik.
33 C5 Valachchenai Sri Lanka
69 K2 Val-Barrette Can.
7 P6 Valbo Sweden
83 C4 Valcheta Arg.
18 D2 Valdagno Italy
20 E3 Valday Rus. Fed.
20 E3 Valdayskaya Vozvyshennost' reg. Rus. Fed.
15 D3 Valdecañas, Embalse de resr Spain
7 S8 Valdemārpils Latvia
7 P7 Valdemarsvik Sweden
14 G2 Val-de-Meuse France
15 E3 Valdepeñas Spain
14 E2 Val-de-Reuil France
69 K3 Val-des-Bois Can.
83 D4 Valdés, Península pen. Arg.
54 D3 Valdez U.S.A.
83 B3 Valdivia Chile
69 J1 Val-d'Or Can.
67 D6 Valdosta U.S.A.
7 L6 Valdres v. Norway
29 J1 Vale Georgia
62 C2 Vale U.S.A.
56 F4 Valemount Can.
82 E1 Valença Brazil
14 G4 Valence France
15 F3 Valencia Spain
81 D2 Valencia Venez.
15 F3 Valencia div. Spain
15 C3 Valencia de Alcántara Spain
15 D1 Valencia de Don Juan Spain
15 G3 Valencia, Golfo de g. Spain
11 A6 Valencia Island i. Rep. of Ireland
14 F1 Valenciennes France
40 D3 Valentin Rus. Fed.
73 F4 Valentine AZ U.S.A.
64 C3 Valentine NE U.S.A.
65 B6 Valentine TX U.S.A.
43 B3 Valenzuela Phil.
7 M6 Våler Norway
81 C2 Valera Venez.
19 H2 Valjevo Yugo.
7 U8 Valka Latvia
7 T6 Valkeakoski Fin.
12 D3 Valkenswaard Neth.
21 E5 Valky Ukr.
92 C4 Valkyrjedomen ice feature Ant.
74 G4 Valladolid Mex.
15 D2 Valladolid Spain
15 F3 Vall de Uxó Spain
7 K7 Valle Norway
81 D2 Valle de la Pascua Venez.
81 B2 Valledupar Col.
83 C1 Valle Fértil, Sa de mts Arg.
78 F7 Valle Grande Bol.
65 D7 Valle Hermoso Mex.
72 A2 Vallejo U.S.A.
18 F7 Valletta Malta
9 C4 Valley U.K.
64 D2 Valley City U.S.A.
62 B3 Valley Falls U.S.A.
70 C5 Valley Head U.S.A.
56 F3 Valleyview Can.
15 G2 Valls Spain
57 H5 Val Marie Can.
7 T8 Valmiera Latvia
15 E1 Valnera mt Spain
20 C4 Valozhyn Belarus
58 E4 Val-Paradis Can.
82 B3 Valparaíso Brazil
83 B2 Valparaíso Chile
68 D5 Valparaiso U.S.A.
83 B2 Valparaíso div. Chile
14 G4 Valréas France
34 C5 Valsād India
90 F3 Valspan S. Africa
37 F7 Vals, Tanjung c. Indon.
20 H1 Val'tevo Rus. Fed.
6 V5 Valtimo Fin.
21 G6 Valuyevka Rus. Fed.
21 F5 Valuyki Rus. Fed.
15 C4 Valverde del Camino Spain
44 C3 Vam Co Tay r. Vietnam
7 S6 Vammala Fin.
33 C2 Vamsadhara r. India
29 J2 Van Turkey
29 K1 Vanadzor Armenia
65 E5 Van Buren AR U.S.A.
71 K1 Van Buren ME U.S.A.
44 D2 Vân Canh Vietnam
71 K2 Vanceboro U.S.A.
70 B5 Vanceburg U.S.A.
56 E5 Vancouver Can.
62 B2 Vancouver U.S.A.
56 D5 Vancouver Island i. Can.
56 A2 Vancouver, Mt mt Can./U.S.A.
66 B4 Vandalia IL U.S.A.
70 A5 Vandalia OH U.S.A.
91 G3 Vanderbijlpark S. Africa
68 E3 Vanderbilt U.S.A.
70 D4 Vandergrift U.S.A.
56 E4 Vanderhoof Can.
90 F5 Vanderkloof Dam resr S. Africa
48 D3 Vanderlin I. i. Austr.
73 H4 Vanderwagen U.S.A.
48 D3 Van Diemen Gulf b. Austr.
7 T7 Vändra Estonia
7 N7 Vänern l. Sweden
7 N7 Vänersborg Sweden
70 E3 Van Etten U.S.A.
89 E6 Vangaindrano Madag.
29 J2 Van Gölü salt l. Turkey
65 B6 Van Horn U.S.A.
69 K3 Vanier Can.
49 G3 Vanikoro Is is Solomon Is
48 E2 Vanimo P.N.G.
36 G2 Vanino Rus. Fed.
33 B3 Vanivilasa Sagara resr India
33 B3 Vaniyambadi India
31 H2 Vanj Tajik.
31 H2 Vanj, Qatorkŭhi mts Tajik.
25 V3 Vankarem Rus. Fed.
71 F2 Vankleek Hill Can.
Van, Lake salt l. see Van Gölü
6 R1 Vanna i. Norway
6 Q5 Vännäs Sweden
14 C3 Vannes France
37 F7 Van Rees, Pegunungan mts Indon.
90 C5 Vanrhynsdorp S. Africa
7 O6 Vansbro Sweden
7 T6 Vantaa Fin.
49 G3 Vanua Lava i. Vanuatu
49 H3 Vanua Levu i. Fiji
47 H5 Vanuatu country Pac. Oc.
70 A4 Van Wert U.S.A.
90 D5 Vanwyksvlei S. Africa
90 D5 Vanwyksvlei l. S. Africa
39 B6 Văn Yên Vietnam
90 E3 Van Zylsrus S. Africa
33 A3 Varada r. India
7 U8 Varakļāni Latvia
30 C3 Varāmīn Iran
35 E4 Varanasi India
6 V1 Varangerfjorden chan. Norway
6 V1 Varangerhalvøya pen. Norway
18 G1 Varaždin Croatia
7 N8 Varberg Sweden
33 B2 Vardannapet India
19 K4 Vardar r. Macedonia
7 L9 Varde Denmark
30 B1 Vardenis Armenia
6 W1 Vardø Norway
13 G1 Varel Ger.
83 C2 Varela Arg.
7 T9 Varėna Lith.
18 C2 Varese Italy
40 C2 Varfolomeyevka Rus. Fed.
7 N7 Vårgårda Sweden
82 D3 Varginha Brazil
12 D3 Varik Neth.
6 U5 Varkaus Fin.
19 M3 Varna Bulg.
7 O8 Värnamo Sweden
7 N6 Värnäs Sweden
20 H3 Varnavino Rus. Fed.
28 D4 Varosia Cyprus
6 U5 Varpaisjärvi Fin.
16 J7 Várpalota Hungary
31 H2 Varsaj Afgh.
29 H2 Varto Turkey
35 E4 Varuna r. India
70 D3 Varysburg U.S.A.
30 D3 Varzaneh Iran
82 D2 Várzea da Palma Brazil
20 H2 Vashka r. Rus. Fed.
Vasht see Khāsh
20 H2 Vasilevo Rus. Fed.
7 U7 Vasknarva Estonia
17 N7 Vaslui Romania
69 F4 Vassar U.S.A.
7 P7 Västerås Sweden
7 N6 Västerdalälven r. Sweden
6 P3 Västerfjäll Sweden
7 Q7 Vasterhaninge Sweden
7 P8 Västervik Sweden
18 F3 Vasto Italy
21 D5 Vasyl'kiv Ukr.
14 E3 Vatan France
10 A4 Vatersay i. U.K.
33 A2 Vathar India
19 M6 Vathy Greece
5 E4 Vatican City country Europe
6 E4 Vatnajökull ice cap Iceland
17 M7 Vatra Dornei Romania
7 O7 Vättern l. Sweden
63 F5 Vaughn U.S.A.
12 B4 Vaulx Belgium
81 C4 Vaupés r. Col.
14 G5 Vauvert France
49 J3 Vava'u Group is Tonga
86 B4 Vavoua Côte d'Ivoire
33 C4 Vavuniya Sri Lanka
20 C4 Vawkavysk Belarus
7 O8 Växjö Sweden
33 B3 Vāyalpād India
20 H1 Vazhgort Rus. Fed.
89 E5 Vazobe mt Madag.
44 B2 Veal Vêng Cambodia
13 G2 Vechta Ger.
12 E2 Vechte r. Ger.
13 H3 Veckerhagen (Reinhardshagen) Ger.
33 B4 Vedaranniyam India
7 N8 Veddige Sweden
19 L3 Vedea r. Romania
21 H7 Vedeno Rus. Fed.
29 K2 Vedi Armenia
83 E2 Vedia Arg.
20 E2 Vedlozero Rus. Fed.
68 D5 Veedersburg U.S.A.
12 E1 Veendam Neth.
12 D2 Veenendaal Neth.
65 C5 Vega U.S.A.
6 M4 Vega i. Norway
57 G4 Vegreville Can.
7 U6 Vehkalahti Fin.
34 B3 Vehoa r. Pak.
34 B4 Veirwaro Pak.
13 H5 Veitshöchheim Ger.
15 D4 Vejer de la Frontera Spain
7 L9 Vejle Denmark
81 B1 Vela, Cabo de la pt Col.
33 B4 Velanai I. i. Sri Lanka
12 F3 Velbert Ger.
19 K3 Velbŭzhdki Prokhod pass Macedonia
90 C6 Velddrif S. Africa
18 F2 Velebit mts Croatia
12 E3 Velen Ger.
18 F1 Velenje Slovenia
19 J4 Veles Macedonia
81 B3 Vélez Col.
15 D4 Vélez-Málaga Spain
15 E4 Vélez-Rubio Spain
82 D2 Velhas r. Brazil
21 H6 Velichayevskoye Rus. Fed.
18 G2 Velika Gorica Croatia
19 J2 Velika Plana Yugo.
20 J3 Velikaya Rus. Fed.
25 T3 Velikaya r. Rus. Fed.
20 D3 Velikaya r. Rus. Fed.
20 E2 Velikaya Guba Rus. Fed.
40 E2 Velikaya Kema Rus. Fed.
20 D3 Velikiye Luki Rus. Fed.
20 H2 Velikiy Ustyug Rus. Fed.
33 B3 Velikonda Ra. h. India
17 Q2 Velikooktyabr'skiy Rus. Fed.
19 L3 Veliko Tŭrnovo Bulg.
20 F3 Velikoye Rus. Fed.
20 F3 Velikoye, Oz. l. Rus. Fed.
20 G4 Velikoye, Oz. l. Rus. Fed.
18 F2 Veli Lošinj Croatia
86 A3 Vélingara Senegal
17 P3 Velizh Rus. Fed.
16 H7 Veľký Meder Slovakia
49 F2 Vella Lavella i. Solomon Is
33 B4 Vellar r. India
13 H5 Vellberg Ger.
13 H3 Vellmar Ger.
33 B3 Vellore India
13 J2 Velpke Ger.
20 G2 Vel'sk Rus. Fed.
13 M2 Velten Ger.
12 D2 Veluwe reg. Neth.
12 E2 Veluwezoom, Nationaal Park nat. park Neth.
57 J5 Velva U.S.A.
96 G5 Vema Fracture sea feature Atl. Ocean
93 J4 Vema Trough sea feature Ind. Ocean
33 B4 Vembanād L. l. India
10 D4 Venachar, Loch l. U.K.
83 E2 Venado Tuerto Arg.
18 F4 Venafro Italy
81 E3 Venamo r. Guyana/Venez.
81 E3 Venamo, Co mt Venez.
82 C3 Venceslau Bráz Brazil
14 E3 Vendôme France
20 F4 Venev Rus. Fed.
Venezia see Venice
18 E2 Venezia, Golfo di g. Europe
77 D2 Venezuela country S. America
81 C2 Venezuela, Golfo de g. Venez.
96 E4 Venezuelan Basin sea feature Atl. Ocean
33 A3 Vengurla India
18 E2 Venice Italy
67 D7 Venice U.S.A.
14 G4 Vénissieux France
33 B3 Venkatagiri India
33 C2 Venkatapuram India
12 E3 Venlo Neth.
7 K7 Vennesla Norway
12 D3 Venray Neth.
7 S8 Venta Lith.
7 R8 Venta r. Latvia/Lith.
83 D3 Ventana, Serra de la h. Arg.
91 G4 Ventersburg S. Africa
91 G3 Ventersdorp S. Africa
91 F5 Venterstad S. Africa
9 F7 Ventnor U.K.
14 G4 Ventoux, Mont mt France
7 R8 Ventspils Latvia
81 D3 Ventuari r. Venez.
72 C4 Ventucopa U.S.A.
72 C4 Ventura U.S.A.
50 E5 Venus B. b. Austr.
80 D3 Vera Arg.
15 F4 Vera Spain
74 E5 Veracruz Mex.
34 B5 Veraval India
18 C2 Verbania Italy
18 C2 Vercelli Italy
6 M5 Verdalsøra Norway
83 D4 Verde r. Arg.
82 C2 Verde r. Goiás Brazil
82 B2 Verde r. Goiás Brazil
82 C2 Verde r. Goiás/Minas Gerais Brazil
82 B2 Verde r. Mato Grosso do Sul Brazil
60 E6 Verde r. Mex.
80 E2 Verde r. Para.
73 G4 Verde r. U.S.A.
82 D1 Verde Grande r. Brazil
43 B3 Verde Island Pass. chan. Phil.
13 H2 Verden (Aller) Ger.
83 D3 Verde, Pen. pen. Arg.
65 E4 Verdigris r. U.S.A.
14 H5 Verdon r. France
14 G2 Verdun France
91 G3 Vereeniging S. Africa
69 J2 Vérendrye, Réserve faunique La res. Can.
83 G2 Vergara Uru.
71 G2 Vergennes U.S.A.
15 C2 Verín Spain
21 F6 Verkhnebakanskiy Rus. Fed.
17 Q3 Verkhnedneprovskiy Rus. Fed.
24 K3 Verkhneimbatskoye Rus. Fed.
6 W2 Verkhnetulomskiy Rus. Fed.
25 O3 Verkhnevilyuysk Rus. Fed.

20 D1 Verkhneye Kuyto, Oz. l. Rus. Fed.
21 H5 Verkhniy Baskunchak Rus. Fed.
21 J5 Verkhniy Kushum Rus. Fed.
6 W3 Verkhnyaya Pirenga, Oz. l. Rus. Fed.
20 H2 Verkhnyaya Toyma Rus. Fed.
20 G2 Verkhovazh'ye Rus. Fed.
20 F4 Verkhov'ye Rus. Fed.
21 C5 Verkhovyna Ukr.
25 P3 Verkhoyansk Rus. Fed.
25 O3 Verkhoyanskiy Khrebet mts Rus. Fed.
12 B5 Vermand France
82 B1 Vermelho r. Brazil
57 G4 Vermilion Can.
68 C5 Vermilion r. U.S.A.
73 F3 Vermilion Cliffs cliff U.S.A.
68 A2 Vermilion Lake l. U.S.A.
68 A2 Vermilion Range h. U.S.A.
64 D3 Vermillion U.S.A.
57 L5 Vermillion Bay Can.
71 G3 Vermont div. U.S.A.
92 B2 Vernadsky Ukr. Base Ant.
62 E3 Vernal U.S.A.
69 G2 Verner Can.
90 D5 Verneuk Pan salt pan S. Africa
56 F4 Vernon Can.
73 H4 Vernon AZ U.S.A.
71 G4 Vernon CT U.S.A.
65 D5 Vernon TX U.S.A.
73 F1 Vernon UT U.S.A.
67 D7 Vero Beach U.S.A.
19 K4 Veroia Greece
18 D2 Verona Italy
83 F2 Verónica Arg.
14 F2 Versailles France
13 G2 Versmold Ger.
14 D3 Vertou France
91 J4 Verulam S. Africa
12 D4 Verviers Belgium
14 F2 Vervins France
12 C5 Verzy France
18 C3 Vescovato Corsica France
24 G4 Veselaya, G. mt Rus. Fed.
21 E6 Vesele Ukr.
21 G6 Veselovskoye Vdkhr. resr Rus. Fed.
21 G5 Veshenskaya Rus. Fed.
12 B5 Vesle r. France
14 H3 Vesoul France
40 D3 Vesselyy Yar Rus. Fed.
12 D3 Vessem Neth.
6 O2 Vesterålen is Norway
6 N2 Vesterålsfjorden chan. Norway
92 C3 Vestfjella mts Ant.
7 L7 Vestfjorddalen v. Norway
6 N3 Vestfjorden chan. Norway
6 □ Vestmanna Faroe Is
6 C5 Vestmannaeyjar Iceland
6 C5 Vestmannaeyjar is Iceland
6 K5 Vestnes Norway
6 F4 Vesturhorn hd Iceland
Vesuvio volc. see Vesuvius
18 F4 Vesuvius volc. Italy
20 F3 Ves'yegonsk Rus. Fed.
16 H7 Veszprém Hungary
6 S5 Veteli Fin.
7 O8 Vetlanda Sweden
20 H3 Vetluga Rus. Fed.
20 H3 Vetluga r. Rus. Fed.
18 E3 Vettore, Monte mt Italy
12 A3 Veurne Belgium
16 C7 Vevey Switz.
73 F3 Veyo U.S.A.
30 C4 Veys Iran
14 E4 Vézère r. France
28 E1 Vezirköprü Turkey
7 P5 Vi Sweden
78 C6 Viajas, I. de las i. Peru
79 K4 Viana Brazil
15 B2 Viana do Castelo Port.
12 D3 Vianen Neth.
Viangchan see Vientiane
82 C2 Vianópolis Brazil
18 D3 Viareggio Italy
7 L8 Viborg Denmark
18 G5 Vibo Valentia Italy
15 H2 Vic Spain
92 B2 Vicecomodoro Marambio Arg. Base Ant.
72 C5 Vicente, Pt pt U.S.A.
18 D2 Vicenza Italy
78 D3 Vichada r. Col.
81 C3 Vichada r. Col.
20 G3 Vichuga Rus. Fed.
83 B2 Vichuquén Chile
14 F3 Vichy France
73 F5 Vicksburg AZ U.S.A.
65 F5 Vicksburg MS U.S.A.
82 D3 Viçosa Brazil
68 A5 Victor U.S.A.
50 B3 Victor Harbour Austr.
83 E2 Victoria Arg.
56 E5 Victoria Can.
83 B3 Victoria Chile
Victoria see Labuan
18 F6 Victoria Malta
65 D6 Victoria U.S.A.
50 E4 Victoria div. Austr.
48 D3 Victoria r. Austr.
55 L2 Victoria and Albert Mts mts Can.
75 J4 Victoria de las Tunas Cuba
89 C5 Victoria Falls waterfall Zambia/Zimbabwe
55 O1 Victoria Fjord in. Greenland
39 □ Victoria Harbour chan. H.K. China
67 F7 Victoria Hill Bahamas
54 G2 Victoria Island i. Can.
88 D4 Victoria, Lake l. Africa
50 C2 Victoria, Lake l. N.S.W. Austr.
50 F5 Victoria, Lake l. Vic. Austr.
59 J4 Victoria Lake l. Can.
92 B5 Victoria Land reg. Ant.
35 H5 Victoria, Mt mt Myanmar
48 E2 Victoria, Mt mt P.N.G.
88 D3 Victoria Nile r. Sudan/Uganda
51 D5 Victoria Range mts N.Z.
48 D3 Victoria River Downs Austr.
59 F4 Victoriaville Can.
90 E5 Victoria West S. Africa
83 D3 Victorica Arg.
92 D3 Victor, Mt mt Ant.
72 D4 Victorville U.S.A.
83 D2 Vicuña Mackenna Arg.
73 E4 Vidal Junction U.S.A.
19 L2 Videle Romania
19 K3 Vidin Bulg.
34 D5 Vidisha India
10 □ Vidlin U.K.
20 E2 Vidlitsa Rus. Fed.
17 N3 Vidzy Belarus
20 J2 Vidz'yuyar Rus. Fed.
13 L5 Viechtach Ger.
83 D4 Viedma Arg.
80 B7 Viedma, L. l. Arg.
13 K1 Vielank Ger.
12 D4 Vielsalm Belgium
13 J3 Vienenburg Ger.
16 H6 Vienna Austria
66 B4 Vienna IL U.S.A.
71 F5 Vienna MD U.S.A.
70 C5 Vienna WV U.S.A.
14 G4 Vienne France
14 E3 Vienne r. France
44 B1 Vientiane Laos
83 B3 Viento, Cordillera del mts Arg.
75 L5 Vieques i. Puerto Rico
6 U5 Vieremä Fin.
12 E3 Viersen Ger.
16 D7 Vierwaldstätter See l. Switz.
14 F3 Vierzon France
65 C7 Viesca Mex.
7 T8 Viesīte Latvia
18 G4 Vieste Italy
6 Q3 Vietas Sweden
23 K8 Vietnam country Asia
39 B6 Viêt Tri Vietnam
43 B2 Vigan Phil.
18 C2 Vigevano Italy
12 A4 Vignacourt France
14 D5 Vignemale mt France
18 D2 Vignola Italy
15 B1 Vigo Spain
6 T4 Vihanti Fin.
34 C3 Vihari Pak.
7 T6 Vihti Fin.
6 T5 Viitasaari Fin.
34 C3 Vijainagar India
33 A2 Vijayadurg India
33 C2 Vijayawada India
6 D5 Vík Iceland
6 U3 Vikajärvi Fin.
57 G4 Viking Can.
6 M4 Vikna i. Norway
7 K6 Vikøyri Norway
86 □ Vila da Ribeira Brava Cape Verde
86 □ Vila de Sal Rei Cape Verde
86 □ Vila do Tarrafal Cape Verde
15 B3 Vila Franca de Xira Port.
15 B1 Vilagarcía de Arousa Spain
91 K2 Vila Gomes da Costa Moz.
15 C1 Vilalba Spain
15 B2 Vila Nova de Gaia Port.
15 G2 Vilanova i la Geltrú Spain
86 □ Vila Nova Sintra Cape Verde
15 C2 Vila Real Port.
15 C2 Vilar Formoso Port.
33 B4 Vilavankod India
82 C1 Vila Velha Brazil
78 D6 Vilcabamba, Cordillera mts Peru
6 P4 Vilhelmina Sweden
78 F6 Vilhena Brazil
7 T7 Viljandi Estonia
91 G3 Viljoenskroon S. Africa
7 S9 Vilkaviškis Lith.
7 S9 Vilkija Lith.
25 L2 Vil'kitskogo, Proliv str. Rus. Fed.
78 E6 Villa Bella Bol.
15 C1 Villablino Spain
83 E2 Villa Cañás Arg.
15 E3 Villacañas Spain
16 F7 Villach Austria
18 C5 Villacidro Sardinia Italy
83 E2 Villa Constitución Arg.
60 D6 Villa Constitución Mex.
83 D1 Villa del Rosario Arg.
83 D1 Villa del Totoral Arg.
83 D1 Villa Dolores Arg.
65 F5 Village, Lake U.S.A.
83 F3 Villa Gesell Arg.
83 E1 Villaguay Arg.
74 F5 Villahermosa Mex.
83 D2 Villa Huidobro Arg.
83 D3 Villa Iris Arg.
15 F3 Villajoyosa Spain
65 C7 Villaldama Mex.
83 D3 Villálonga Arg.
83 D2 Villa María Arg.
83 E1 Villa María Grande Arg.
78 F8 Villa Montes Bol.
89 E6 Villandro, Tanjona pt Madag.
91 H1 Villa Nora S. Africa
81 B2 Villanueva Col.
15 D3 Villanueva de la Serena Spain
15 E3 Villanueva de los Infantes Spain
80 E3 Villa Ocampo Arg.
65 B7 Villa O. Pereyra Mex.
18 C5 Villaputzu Sardinia Italy
83 C3 Villa Regina Arg.
83 B3 Villarrica Chile
80 E3 Villarrica Para.
83 B3 Villarrica, L. l. Chile
83 B3 Villarrica, Parque Nacional nat. park Chile
83 B3 Villarrica, Volcán volc. Chile
15 E3 Villarrobledo Spain
18 F5 Villa San Giovanni Italy
83 E2 Villa San José Arg.
83 C1 Villa Santa Rita de Catuna Arg.
80 C3 Villa Unión Arg.
83 D2 Villa Valeria Arg.
81 B3 Villavicencio Col.
78 E8 Villazon Bol.
14 F4 Villefranche-de-Rouergue France
14 G4 Villefranche-sur-Saône France
69 H2 Ville-Marie Can.
15 F3 Villena Spain
14 E4 Villeneuve-sur-Lot France
14 F2 Villeneuve-sur-Yonne France
65 E6 Ville Platte U.S.A.
12 B5 Villers-Cotterêts France
12 D5 Villerupt France
14 G4 Villeurbanne France
91 H3 Villiers S. Africa
16 D6 Villingen Ger.
57 G4 Vilna Can.
7 T9 Vilnius Lith.
21 E6 Vil'nyans'k Ukr.
7 T5 Vilppula Fin.
13 K5 Vils r. Ger.
33 B4 Viluppuram India
12 C4 Vilvoorde Belgium
20 C4 Vilyeyka Belarus
25 O3 Vilyuy r. Rus. Fed.
25 M3 Vilyuyskoye Vdkhr. resr Rus. Fed.
7 O8 Vimmerby Sweden
12 A4 Vimy France
72 A2 Vina U.S.A.
83 B2 Viña del Mar Chile
71 J2 Vinalhaven U.S.A.
15 G2 Vinaròs Spain
66 C4 Vincennes U.S.A.
92 C6 Vincennes Bay b. Ant.
6 Q4 Vindelälven r. Sweden
6 Q4 Vindeln Sweden
34 C5 Vindhya Range h. India
71 F5 Vineland U.S.A.
71 H4 Vineyard Haven U.S.A.
44 C1 Vinh Vietnam
44 C1 Vinh Linh Vietnam
44 C3 Vinh Long Vietnam
44 C3 Vinh Rach Gia b. Vietnam
39 B6 Vinh Yên Vietnam
65 E4 Vinita U.S.A.
18 H2 Vinkovci Croatia
21 D5 Vinnytsya Ukr.
92 B3 Vinson Massif mt Ant.
7 L6 Vinstra Norway
68 A4 Vinton U.S.A.
33 B2 Vinukonda India
18 D1 Vipiteno Italy
13 L1 Vipperow Ger.
43 C3 Virac Phil.
34 C5 Viramgam India
29 G3 Viranşehir Turkey
34 B4 Virawah Pak.
57 J5 Virden Can.
14 D2 Vire France
89 B5 Virei Angola
82 D2 Virgem da Lapa Brazil
69 H1 Virginatown Can.
11 D4 Virginia Rep. of Ireland
91 G4 Virginia S. Africa
68 A2 Virginia U.S.A.
70 D6 Virginia div. U.S.A.
71 E6 Virginia Beach U.S.A.
72 C2 Virginia City U.S.A.
53 K8 Virgin Islands (U.K.) terr. Caribbean Sea
53 K8 Virgin Islands (U.S.A.) terr. Caribbean Sea
73 F3 Virgin Mts mts U.S.A.
7 T6 Virkkala Fin.
44 C2 Virôchey Cambodia
68 B4 Viroqua U.S.A.
18 G2 Virovitica Croatia
7 S5 Virrat Fin.
12 D5 Virton Belgium
7 S7 Virtsu Estonia
33 B4 Virudunagar India
88 C3 Virunga, Parc National des nat. park Congo(Zaire)
18 G3 Vis i. Croatia
7 U9 Visaginas Lith.
72 C3 Visalia U.S.A.
34 B5 Visavadar India
43 B4 Visayan Sea sea Phil.
13 G2 Visbek Ger.
7 Q8 Visby Sweden
54 G2 Viscount Melville Sound str. Can.
12 D4 Visé Belgium
18 H3 Višegrad Bos.-Herz.
24 J2 Vise, O. i. Rus. Fed.
79 J4 Viseu Brazil
15 C2 Viseu Port.
33 C2 Vishakhapatnam India
7 U8 Višķi Latvia
34 C5 Visnagar India
19 H3 Visoko Bos.-Herz.
18 B2 Viso, Monte mt Italy
16 C7 Visp Switz.
13 H2 Visselhövede Ger.
72 D5 Vista U.S.A.
82 A2 Vista Alegre Brazil
19 L4 Vistonida, Limni lag. Greece
81 C3 Vita r. Col.
83 B3 Vitakri Pak.
18 E3 Viterbo Italy
18 G2 Vitez Bos.-Herz.
78 E8 Vitichi Bol.
15 D2 Vitigudino Spain
49 H3 Viti Levu i. Fiji
36 D1 Vitim r. Rus. Fed.
36 D1 Vitimskoye Ploskogor'ye plat. Rus. Fed.
82 E3 Vitória Brazil
Vitoria see Vitoria-Gasteiz
82 E1 Vitória da Conquista Brazil
15 E1 Vitoria-Gasteiz Spain
14 D2 Vitré France
12 A4 Vitry-en-Artois France
14 G2 Vitry-le-François France
20 D4 Vitsyebsk Belarus
6 R3 Vittangi Sweden
18 F6 Vittoria Sicily Italy
18 E2 Vittorio Veneto Italy
94 F3 Vityaz Depth depth Pac. Oc.
15 C1 Viveiro Spain
91 H1 Vivo S. Africa
Vizagapatam see Vishakhapatnam
74 B3 Vizcaino, Sierra mts Mex.
21 C7 Vize Turkey
33 C2 Vizianagaram India
20 J2 Vizinga Rus. Fed.
12 C3 Vlaardingen Neth.
17 L7 Vlădeasa, Vârful mt Romania
21 H7 Vladikavkaz Rus. Fed.
40 D3 Vladimir Primorskiy Kray Rus. Fed.
20 G3 Vladimir Vladimir. Obl. Rus. Fed.
40 C3 Vladimiro-Aleksandrovskoye Rus. Fed.
36 F2 Vladivostok Rus. Fed.
20 G4 Vlaimirskaya Oblast' div. Rus. Fed.
91 H2 Vlakte S. Africa
19 K3 Vlasotince Yugo.
90 D7 Vleesbaai b. S. Africa
12 C1 Vlieland i. Neth.
12 B3 Vlissingen Neth.
19 H4 Vlorë Albania
13 G2 Vlotho Ger.
16 G6 Vltava r. Czech Rep.
16 F6 Vöcklabruck Austria
20 F2 Vodlozero, Ozero l. Rus. Fed.
10 □ Voe U.K.
12 D4 Voerendaal Neth.
13 H4 Vogelsberg h. Ger.
18 C2 Voghera Italy
13 L4 Vogtland reg. Ger.
13 L5 Vohenstrauß Ger.
Vohimena, Cape c. see Vohimena, Tanjona
89 E6 Vohimena, Tanjona c. Madag.
13 G3 Vöhl Ger.
7 T7 Võhma Estonia
88 D4 Voi Kenya
86 B4 Voinjama Liberia
14 G4 Voiron France
7 L9 Vojens Denmark
19 H2 Vojvodina div. Yugo.
20 H3 Vokhma Rus. Fed.
20 D1 Voknavolok Rus. Fed.
62 F2 Volborg U.S.A.
83 B1 Volcán, Co del mt Chile
Volcano Bay b. see Uchiura-wan
Volcano Is is see Kazan-rettō
7 K5 Volda Norway
12 D2 Volendam Neth.
21 H6 Volga r. Rus. Fed.
68 B4 Volga r. U.S.A.
21 G6 Volgodonsk Rus. Fed.
24 F5 Volgograd Rus. Fed.
21 H5 Volgogradskaya Oblast' div. Rus. Fed.
16 G7 Völkermarkt Austria
20 E3 Volkhov Rus. Fed.
20 D3 Volkhov r. Rus. Fed.
12 E5 Völklingen Ger.
91 H3 Volksrust S. Africa
40 B3 Vol'no-Nadezhdinskoye Rus. Fed.
21 F6 Volnovakha Ukr.
25 L2 Volochanka Rus. Fed.
21 C5 Volochys'k Ukr.
21 F6 Volodars'ke Ukr.
21 J6 Volodarskiy Rus. Fed.
26 E1 Volodarskoye Kazak.
17 O5 Volodars'k-Volyns'kyy Ukr.
17 N5 Volodymyrets' Ukr.
21 C5 Volodymyr-Volyns'kyy Ukr.
20 F3 Vologda Rus. Fed.
20 G3 Vologodskaya Oblast' div. Rus. Fed.
21 F5 Volokonovka Rus. Fed.
19 K5 Volos Greece
20 D3 Volosovo Rus. Fed.
17 P2 Volot Rus. Fed.
21 F4 Volovo Rus. Fed.
21 H4 Vol'sk Rus. Fed.
86 B4 Volta, Lake resr Ghana
82 D3 Volta Redonda Brazil
18 F4 Volturno r. Italy
19 K4 Volvi, L. l. Greece
20 J4 Volzhsk Rus. Fed.
21 H5 Volzhskiy Rus. Fed.
89 E6 Vondrozo Madag.
20 G1 Vonga Rus. Fed.
6 F4 Vopnafjörður Iceland
6 F4 Vopnafjörður b. Iceland
20 B2 Vörå Fin.
17 M3 Voranava Belarus
20 J3 Vorchanka Rus. Fed.
20 E2 Vorenzha Rus. Fed.
24 H3 Vorkuta Rus. Fed.
7 S7 Vormsi i. Estonia
21 G5 Vorona r. Rus. Fed.
21 F5 Voronezh Rus. Fed.
21 F5 Voronezh r. Rus. Fed.
21 G5 Voronezhskaya Oblast' div. Rus. Fed.
20 G3 Voron'ye Rus. Fed.
Voroshilovgrad see Luhans'k
17 Q3 Vorot'kovo Rus. Fed.
21 E5 Vorskla r. Rus. Fed.
7 T7 Võrtsjärv l. Estonia
7 U8 Võru Estonia
31 H2 Vorukh Tajik.
90 E5 Vosburg S. Africa
31 H2 Vose Tajik.
14 H2 Vosges mts France
7 K6 Voss Norway
Vostochno-Sibirskoye More sea see East Siberian Sea
36 B1 Vostochnyy Sayan mts Rus. Fed.
40 D1 Vostok Rus. Fed.
92 C5 Vostok Rus. Fed. Base Ant.
46 M5 Vostok Island i. Kiribati
40 D2 Vostretsovo Rus. Fed.
24 G4 Votkinsk Rus. Fed.
82 C3 Votuporanga Brazil
12 C5 Vouziers France
14 E2 Voves France
20 J3 Voya r. Rus. Fed.
66 A1 Voyageurs Nat. Park U.S.A.
6 W4 Voynitsa Rus. Fed.
20 G2 Vozhega Rus. Fed.
20 F2 Vozhe, Ozero l. Rus. Fed.
21 D6 Voznesens'k Ukr.
40 C3 Vrangel' Rus. Fed.
25 T2 Vrangelya, O. i. Rus. Fed.
19 J3 Vranje Yugo.
19 M3 Vratnik pass Bulg.
19 K3 Vratsa Bulg.
19 H2 Vrbas Yugo.
18 G2 Vrbas r. Bos.-Herz.
91 H3 Vrede S. Africa
91 G3 Vredefort S. Africa
90 B6 Vredenburg S. Africa
90 C5 Vredendal S. Africa
12 C5 Vresse Belgium
33 B4 Vriddhachalam India
12 E1 Vries Neth.
7 O8 Vrigstad Sweden
19 J2 Vršac Yugo.
90 F3 Vryburg S. Africa
91 J3 Vryheid S. Africa
20 D2 Vsevolozhsk Rus. Fed.
19 J3 Vučitrn Yugo.
19 H2 Vukovar Croatia
24 G3 Vuktyl' Rus. Fed.
91 H3 Vukuzakhe S. Africa
18 F5 Vulcano, Isola i. Italy
73 F5 Vulture Mts mts U.S.A.
44 C3 Vung Tau Vietnam
7 U6 Vuohijärvi Fin.
6 U4 Vuolijoki Fin.
6 R3 Vuollerim Sweden
6 U3 Vuostimo Fin.
20 H4 Vurnary Rus. Fed.
89 D4 Vwawa Tanz.
34 C5 Vyara India
20 J3 Vyatka Rus. Fed.
20 J3 Vyatka r. Rus. Fed.
20 E4 Vyaz'ma Rus. Fed.
20 G3 Vyazniki Rus. Fed.
21 H5 Vyazovka Rus. Fed.
20 D2 Vyborg Rus. Fed.
20 J2 Vychegda r. Rus. Fed.
20 H2 Vychegodskiy Rus. Fed.
20 C4 Vyerkhnyadzvinsk Belarus
20 D4 Vyetryna Belarus
20 E2 Vygozero, Ozero l. Rus. Fed.
20 G4 Vyksa Rus. Fed.
21 D6 Vylkove Ukr.
17 L6 Vynohradiv Ukr.
20 E3 Vypolzovo Rus. Fed.
20 D3 Vyritsa Rus. Fed.
9 D5 Vyrnwy, Lake l. U.K.
21 F6 Vyselki Rus. Fed.
20 G4 Vysha Rus. Fed.
21 D5 Vyshhorod Ukr.
20 E3 Vyshnevolotskaya Gryada ridge Rus. Fed.
20 E3 Vyshniy-Volochek Rus. Fed.
16 H6 Vyškov Czech Rep.
21 D5 Vystupovychi Ukr.
20 F2 Vytegra Rus. Fed.

W

86 B3 Wa Ghana
12 D3 Waal r. Neth.
12 D3 Waalwijk Neth.
58 B3 Wabakimi L. l. Can.
56 G3 Wabasca Can.
56 G3 Wabasca r. Can.
68 E5 Wabash U.S.A.
68 E5 Wabash r. U.S.A.
68 A3 Wabasha U.S.A.
69 E1 Wabatongushi Lake l. Can.
88 E3 Wabē Gestro r. Eth.
88 E3 Wabē Shebelē Wenz r. Eth.
57 K4 Wabowden Can.
58 C2 Wabuk Pt pt Can.
59 G3 Wabush Can.
59 G3 Wabush L. l. Can.
72 C2 Wabuska U.S.A.
67 D6 Waccasassa Bay b. U.S.A.
13 H4 Wächtersbach Ger.
65 D6 Waco U.S.A.
31 G5 Wad Pak.
50 G4 Wadbilliga Nat. Park Austr.
87 D2 Waddān Libya
12 C1 Waddeneilanden is Neth.
12 C2 Waddenzee chan. Neth.
56 D4 Waddington, Mt mt Can.
12 C2 Waddinxveen Neth.
9 C7 Wadebridge U.K.
57 J4 Wadena Can.
64 E2 Wadena U.S.A.
12 E5 Wadern Ger.
33 A2 Wadgaon India
12 E5 Wadgassen Ger.
87 E3 Wadi el Milk watercourse Sudan
87 F2 Wadi Halfa Sudan
87 E3 Wadi Howar watercourse Sudan
87 F3 Wad Medani Sudan
72 C2 Wadsworth U.S.A.
42 B4 Wafangdian China
29 L7 Wafra Kuwait
13 G2 Wagenfeld Ger.
13 J2 Wagenhoff Ger.
55 K3 Wager Bay b. Can.
50 F3 Wagga Wagga Austr.
34 C2 Wah Pak.
72 □1 Wahiawa U.S.A.
13 H3 Wahlhausen Ger.
64 D3 Wahoo U.S.A.
64 D2 Wahpeton U.S.A.
73 F2 Wah Wah Mts mts U.S.A.
33 A2 Wai India
72 □1 Waialee U.S.A.
72 □1 Waialua U.S.A.
72 □1 Waialua Bay b. U.S.A.
72 □1 Waianae U.S.A.
72 □1 Waianae Ra. mts U.S.A.
51 D5 Waiau r. N.Z.
16 G7 Waidhofen an der Ybbs Austria
37 F7 Waigeo i. Indon.
51 E2 Waiharoa N.Z.
51 E2 Waiheke Island i. N.Z.
51 E2 Waihi N.Z.
51 E2 Waihou r. N.Z.
37 D7 Waikabubak Indon.
51 B6 Waikaia r. N.Z.
72 □1 Waikane U.S.A.
51 D5 Waikari N.Z.
51 E2 Waikato r. N.Z.
51 F2 Waikawa Pt pt N.Z.
50 B3 Waikerie Austr.
72 □1 Waikiki Beach beach U.S.A.
51 C6 Waikouaiti N.Z.
72 □2 Wailuku U.S.A.
51 D5 Waimakariri r. N.Z.
72 □1 Waimanalo U.S.A.
51 C4 Waimangaroa N.Z.
51 F3 Waimarama N.Z.
51 C6 Waimate N.Z.
72 □1 Waimea HI U.S.A.
72 □2 Waimea HI U.S.A.
34 D5 Wainganga r. India
37 E7 Waingapu Indon.
9 C7 Wainhouse Corner U.K.
57 G4 Wainwright Can.
54 C2 Wainwright AK U.S.A.
51 E3 Waiouru N.Z.
51 E3 Waipa r. N.Z.
51 B7 Waipahi N.Z.
72 □1 Waipahu U.S.A.
51 F3 Waipaoa r. N.Z.
51 B7 Waipapa Pt pt N.Z.
51 D5 Waipara N.Z.
51 F3 Waipawa N.Z.
51 F3 Waipukurau N.Z.
51 F3 Wairakei N.Z.
51 E4 Wairarapa, L. l. N.Z.
51 D4 Wairau r. N.Z.
51 F3 Wairoa N.Z.
51 F3 Wairoa r. Hawke's Bay N.Z.
51 E1 Wairoa r. Northland N.Z.
51 F3 Waitahanui N.Z.
51 B6 Waitahuna N.Z.
51 E2 Waitakaruru N.Z.
51 C6 Waitaki r. N.Z.
51 E3 Waitara N.Z.
51 E2 Waitoa N.Z.
51 E2 Waiuku N.Z.
51 B7 Waiwera South N.Z.
39 F5 Waiyang China
41 E6 Wajima Japan
88 E3 Wajir Kenya
41 D7 Wakasa-wan b. Japan
51 B6 Wakatipu, Lake l. N.Z.
57 H4 Wakaw Can.
41 D7 Wakayama Japan
64 D4 Wa Keeney U.S.A.
69 K3 Wakefield Can.
51 D4 Wakefield N.Z.
8 F4 Wakefield U.K.
68 C2 Wakefield MI U.S.A.
71 H4 Wakefield RI U.S.A.
70 E6 Wakefield VA U.S.A.
Wakeham see Kangiqsujuaq
46 H2 Wake Island i. Pac. Oc.
40 G4 Wakinosawa Japan
40 G2 Wakkanai Japan
91 J3 Wakkerstroom S. Africa
50 E3 Wakool Austr.
50 D3 Wakool r. Austr.
59 G2 Wakuach, Lac l. Can.
16 H5 Wałbrzych Pol.
50 H1 Walcha Austr.
16 E7 Walchensee l. Ger.
12 C4 Walcourt Belgium
16 H4 Wałcz Pol.
71 F4 Walden Montgomery U.S.A.
16 F6 Waldkraiburg Ger.
9 C7 Waldon r. U.K.
70 E5 Waldorf U.S.A.
92 C6 Waldron, C. c. Ant.
9 D5 Wales div. U.K.
48 E5 Walgett Austr.
92 A3 Walgreen Coast coastal area Ant.
88 C4 Walikale Congo(Zaire)
68 B4 Walker IA U.S.A.
64 E2 Walker MN U.S.A.
72 C2 Walker r. U.S.A.
90 C7 Walker Bay b. S. Africa
67 E7 Walker Cay i. Bahamas
72 C2 Walker Lake l. U.S.A.
92 A3 Walker Mts mts Ant.
72 C4 Walker Pass U.S.A.
69 G3 Walkerton Can.
64 C2 Wall U.S.A.
62 C2 Wallace U.S.A.
69 F4 Wallaceburg Can.
50 A2 Wallaroo Austr.
9 D4 Wallasey U.K.
50 F3 Walla Walla Austr.
62 C2 Walla Walla U.S.A.
13 H5 Walldürn Ger.
90 B5 Wallekraal S. Africa
50 G3 Wallendbeen Austr.
71 F4 Wallenpaupack, Lake l. U.S.A.
9 F6 Wallingford U.K.
71 G4 Wallingford U.S.A.
47 J5 Wallis and Futuna terr. Pac. Oc.
49 J3 Wallis, Îles is Pac. Oc.
71 F6 Wallops I. i. U.S.A.
62 C2 Wallowa Mts mts U.S.A.
10 □ Walls U.K.
57 H2 Walmsley Lake l. Can.

92 B2 Wilkins Coast coastal area Ant.
92 B2 Wilkins Ice Shelf ice feature Ant.
62 B2 Willamette r. U.S.A.
9 D7 Willand U.K.
50 E2 Willandra Billabong r. Austr.
62 B1 Willapa B. b. U.S.A.
70 B4 Willard U.S.A.
71 F5 Willards U.S.A.
73 H5 Willcox U.S.A.
13 H3 Willebadessen Ger.
12 C3 Willebroek Belgium
75 L6 Willemstad Neth. Ant.
57 H3 William r. Can.
50 D4 William, Mt mt Austr.
73 F4 Williams AZ U.S.A.
72 A2 Williams CA U.S.A.
68 A5 Williamsburg IA U.S.A.
70 A6 Williamsburg KY U.S.A.
68 E3 Williamsburg MI U.S.A.
70 E6 Williamsburg VA U.S.A.
67 F7 Williams I. i. Bahamas
56 E4 Williams Lake Can.
59 H1 William Smith, Cap c. Can.
70 E3 Williamson NY U.S.A.
70 B6 Williamson WV U.S.A.
68 D5 Williamsport IN U.S.A.
70 E4 Williamsport PA U.S.A.
67 E5 Williamston U.S.A.
71 G3 Williamstown MA U.S.A.
71 F3 Williamstown NY U.S.A.
70 C5 Williamstown WV U.S.A.
71 G4 Willimantic U.S.A.
90 D5 Williston S. Africa
67 D6 Williston FL U.S.A.
64 C1 Williston ND U.S.A.
56 E3 Williston Lake l. Can.
9 D6 Williton U.K.
72 A2 Willits U.S.A.
64 E2 Willmar U.S.A.
56 F4 Willmore Wilderness Prov. Park res. Can.
56 D3 Will, Mt mt Can.
50 A1 Willochra r. Austr.
56 E4 Willow r. Can.
57 H5 Willow Bunch Can.
70 E4 Willow Hill U.S.A.
56 F2 Willow Lake l. Can.
90 E6 Willowmore S. Africa
68 C3 Willow Reservoir U.S.A.
72 A2 Willows U.S.A.
65 F4 Willow Springs U.S.A.
50 H1 Willow Tree Austr.
91 H6 Willowvale S. Africa
71 G2 Willsboro U.S.A.
48 C4 Wills, L. salt flat Austr.
50 B3 Willunga Austr.
50 B2 Wilmington Austr.
71 F5 Wilmington DE U.S.A.
67 E5 Wilmington NC U.S.A.
70 B5 Wilmington OH U.S.A.
71 G3 Wilmington VT U.S.A.
9 E4 Wilmslow U.K.
13 G4 Wilnsdorf Ger.
50 B1 Wilpena r. Austr.
13 H1 Wilseder Berg h. Ger.
64 D4 Wilson KS U.S.A.
67 E5 Wilson NC U.S.A.
92 B5 Wilson Hills h. Ant.
73 E3 Wilson, Mt mt CO U.S.A.
73 E2 Wilson, Mt mt NV U.S.A.
64 D4 Wilson Res. resr U.S.A.
71 H2 Wilsons Mills U.S.A.
50 F5 Wilson's Promontory pen. Austr.
50 F5 Wilson's Promontory Nat. Park Austr.
12 E2 Wilsum Ger.
68 B5 Wilton IA U.S.A.
71 H2 Wilton ME U.S.A.
12 D5 Wiltz Lux.
48 C4 Wiluna Austr.
9 J7 Wimereux France
50 D4 Wimmera r. Austr.
68 D5 Winamac U.S.A.
91 G4 Winburg S. Africa
9 E6 Wincanton U.K.
71 G3 Winchendon U.S.A.
58 E4 Winchester Can.
9 F6 Winchester U.K.
68 B6 Winchester IL U.S.A.
68 E5 Winchester IN U.S.A.
70 A6 Winchester KY U.S.A.
71 G3 Winchester NH U.S.A.
67 C5 Winchester TN U.S.A.
70 D5 Winchester VA U.S.A.
54 E3 Wind r. N.W.T. Can.
62 E3 Wind r. U.S.A.
64 C3 Wind Cave Nat. Park U.S.A.
8 E3 Windermere U.K.
8 E3 Windermere l. U.K.
89 B6 Windhoek Namibia
64 E3 Windom U.S.A.
48 E4 Windorah Austr.
73 H4 Window Rock U.S.A.
68 D4 Wind Pt pt U.S.A.
62 E3 Wind River Range mts U.S.A.
9 F6 Windrush r. U.K.
13 J5 Windsbach Ger.
50 H2 Windsor Austr.
59 J4 Windsor Nfld Can.
59 H5 Windsor N.S. Can.
69 F4 Windsor Ont. Can.
59 F4 Windsor Que. Can.
9 G6 Windsor U.K.
71 G4 Windsor CT U.S.A.
67 E5 Windsor NC U.S.A.
71 F3 Windsor NY U.S.A.
70 E6 Windsor VA U.S.A.
71 G3 Windsor VT U.S.A.
71 G4 Windsor Locks U.S.A.
75 M5 Windward Islands is Caribbean Sea
75 K5 Windward Passage chan. Cuba/Haiti
67 C5 Winfield AL U.S.A.
68 B5 Winfield IA U.S.A.
65 D4 Winfield KS U.S.A.
8 F3 Wingate U.K.
50 H1 Wingen Austr.
12 B3 Wingene Belgium
12 F6 Wingen-sur-Moder France
69 G4 Wingham Can.
58 C2 Winisk Can.
58 C2 Winisk r. Can.
58 C3 Winisk L. l. Can.
58 C3 Winisk River Provincial Park res. Can.
44 A2 Winkana Myanmar
57 K5 Winkler Can.
71 J2 Winn U.S.A.
86 B4 Winneba Ghana
68 C3 Winnebago, Lake l. U.S.A.
68 C3 Winneconne U.S.A.
62 C3 Winnemucca U.S.A.
72 C1 Winnemucca Lake l. U.S.A.
64 D3 Winner U.S.A.
65 E6 Winnfield U.S.A.
64 E2 Winnibigoshish L. l. U.S.A.
57 K5 Winnipeg Can.
57 K4 Winnipeg r. Can.
57 K4 Winnipeg, Lake l. Can.
57 J4 Winnipegosis Can.
57 J4 Winnipegosis, Lake l. Can.
71 H3 Winnipesaukee, L. l. U.S.A.
65 F5 Winnsboro U.S.A.
73 G4 Winona AZ U.S.A.
68 C2 Winona MI U.S.A.
68 B3 Winona MN U.S.A.
65 F5 Winona MS U.S.A.
71 G2 Winooski U.S.A.
71 G2 Winooski r. U.S.A.
12 F1 Winschoten Neth.
13 H2 Winsen (Aller) Ger.
13 J1 Winsen (Luhe) Ger.
9 E4 Winsford U.K.
73 G4 Winslow U.S.A.
71 G4 Winsted U.S.A.
67 D4 Winston-Salem U.S.A.
13 G3 Winterberg Ger.
67 D6 Winter Haven U.S.A.
71 J2 Winterport U.S.A.
72 B2 Winters U.S.A.
12 E3 Winterswijk Neth.
16 D7 Winterthur Switz.
91 H4 Winterton S. Africa
71 J1 Winterville U.S.A.
71 J2 Winthrop U.S.A.
48 E4 Winton Austr.
51 B7 Winton N.Z.
9 G5 Winwick U.K.
50 B2 Wirrabara Austr.
9 D4 Wirral pen. U.K.
50 C4 Wirrega Austr.
9 H5 Wisbech U.K.
71 J2 Wiscasset U.S.A.
13 H1 Wischhafen Ger.
68 C3 Wisconsin div. U.S.A.
68 B4 Wisconsin r. U.S.A.
68 C4 Wisconsin Dells U.S.A.
68 C4 Wisconsin, Lake l. U.S.A.
68 C3 Wisconsin Rapids U.S.A.
70 B6 Wise U.S.A.
10 E5 Wishaw U.K.
17 J4 Wisła r. Pol.
16 E4 Wismar Ger.
9 J7 Wissant France
68 B3 Wissota L. l. U.S.A.
56 D4 Wistaria Can.
91 H2 Witbank S. Africa
90 C2 Witbooisvlei Namibia
9 H6 Witham U.K.
9 G4 Witham r. U.K.
71 G2 Witherbee U.S.A.
8 H4 Withernsea U.K.
12 D1 Witmarsum Neth.
9 F6 Witney U.K.
91 J2 Witrivier S. Africa
12 C5 Witry-lès-Reims France
91 G5 Witteberg mts S. Africa
68 C3 Wittenberg U.S.A.
13 K2 Wittenberge Ger.
13 K1 Wittenburg Ger.
14 H3 Wittenheim France
13 J2 Wittingen Ger.
12 E5 Wittlich Ger.
13 F1 Wittmund Ger.
13 L1 Wittstock Ger.
48 E2 Witu Is is P.N.G.
89 B6 Witvlei Namibia
13 H3 Witzenhausen Ger.
42 D3 Wiwon N. Korea
16 J3 Władysławowo Pol.
17 J4 Włocławek Pol.
71 H2 Woburn Can.
50 F4 Wodonga Austr.
13 F6 Wœrth France
12 D5 Woëvre, Plaine de la plain France
13 G4 Wohra r. Ger.
12 E5 Woippy France
37 F7 Wokam i. Indon.
40 B1 Woken r. China
35 H4 Wokha India
9 G6 Woking U.K.
9 G6 Wokingham U.K.
68 D5 Wolcott IN U.S.A.
70 E3 Wolcott NY U.S.A.
13 M1 Woldegk Ger.
12 F1 Woldendorp Neth.
56 C2 Wolf r. Can.
68 C3 Wolf r. U.S.A.
62 D2 Wolf Creek U.S.A.
63 F4 Wolf Creek Pass U.S.A.
71 H3 Wolfeboro U.S.A.
69 J3 Wolfe I. i. Can.
13 L3 Wolfen Ger.
13 J2 Wolfenbüttel Ger.
13 H3 Wolfhagen Ger.
56 C2 Wolf Lake l. Can.
62 F1 Wolf Point U.S.A.
16 G7 Wolfsberg Austria
13 J2 Wolfsburg Ger.
12 F5 Wolfstein Ger.
59 H4 Wolfville Can.
78 □ Wolf, Volcán volc. Galapagos Is Ecuador
16 F3 Wolgast Ger.
16 G4 Wolin Pol.
80 C9 Wollaston, Islas is Chile
57 J3 Wollaston Lake Can.
57 J3 Wollaston Lake l. Can.
54 G3 Wollaston Peninsula Can.
50 H3 Wollongong Austr.
91 F3 Wolmaransstad S. Africa
13 K2 Wolmirstedt Ger.
50 C4 Wolseley Austr.
90 C6 Wolseley S. Africa
8 F3 Wolsingham U.K.
12 E2 Wolvega Neth.
9 E5 Wolverhampton U.K.
68 E3 Wolverine U.S.A.
12 C3 Wommelgem Belgium
12 F5 Womrather Höhe h. Ger.
50 E1 Wongalarroo Lake l. Austr.
50 G2 Wongarbon Austr.
35 G4 Wong Chu r. Bhutan
39 □ Wong Chuk Hang H.K. China
42 D5 Wŏnju S. Korea
50 F4 Wonnangatta Moroka Nat. Park Austr.
42 D4 Wŏnsan N. Korea
50 E5 Wonthaggi Austr.
48 D3 Woodah, Isle i. Austr.
9 J5 Woodbridge U.K.
70 E5 Woodbridge U.S.A.
56 G3 Wood Buffalo National Park Can.
62 B2 Woodburn U.S.A.
68 E4 Woodbury MI U.S.A.
71 F5 Woodbury NJ U.S.A.
70 A6 Wood Creek Lake l. U.S.A.
72 C2 Woodfords U.S.A.
72 C3 Woodlake U.S.A.
72 B2 Woodland U.S.A.
63 F4 Woodland Park U.S.A.
44 □ Woodlands Sing.
49 F2 Woodlark I. i. P.N.G.
48 D4 Woodroffe, Mt mt Austr.
62 E3 Woodruff U.S.A.
70 C5 Woodsfield U.S.A.
50 F5 Woodside Austr.
48 D3 Woods, L. salt flat Austr.
57 L5 Woods, Lake of the l. Can./U.S.A.
50 F4 Woods Pt Austr.
59 G4 Woodstock N.B. Can.
69 G4 Woodstock Ont. Can.
68 C4 Woodstock IL U.S.A.
70 D5 Woodstock VA U.S.A.
71 F5 Woodstown U.S.A.
71 G2 Woodsville U.S.A.
51 E4 Woodville N.Z.
70 E3 Woodville NY U.S.A.
65 E6 Woodville TX U.S.A.
65 D4 Woodward U.S.A.
8 E2 Wooler U.K.
48 D5 Woomera Austr.
71 H4 Woonsocket U.S.A.
70 C4 Wooster U.S.A.
13 J3 Worbis Ger.
90 C6 Worcester S. Africa
9 E5 Worcester U.K.
71 H3 Worcester U.S.A.
16 F7 Wörgl Austria
8 D3 Workington U.K.
9 F4 Worksop U.K.
12 D2 Workum Neth.
62 F2 Worland U.S.A.
13 L3 Wörlitz Ger.
12 C2 Wormerveer Neth.
13 G5 Worms Ger.
9 C6 Worms Head hd U.K.
90 B1 Wortel Namibia
13 G5 Wörth am Rhein Ger.
9 G7 Worthing U.K.
64 E3 Worthington U.S.A.
94 G5 Wotje i. Pac. Oc.
37 E7 Wotu Indon.
12 C3 Woudrichem Neth.
64 C3 Wounded Knee U.S.A.
12 F5 Woustviller France
37 E7 Wowoni i. Indon.
Wrangel Island i. see Vrangelya, O.
56 C3 Wrangell U.S.A.
56 C3 Wrangell I. i. U.S.A.
54 E3 Wrangell Mountains U.S.A.
10 C2 Wrath, Cape c. U.K.
64 C3 Wray U.S.A.
9 F5 Wreake r. U.K.
90 B4 Wreck Point pt S. Africa
13 J2 Wrestedt Ger.
9 E4 Wrexham U.K.
43 C4 Wright Phil.
62 F3 Wright U.S.A.
65 E5 Wright Patman L. l. U.S.A.
73 G6 Wrightson, Mt mt U.S.A.
56 E2 Wrigley Can.
16 H5 Wrocław Pol.
16 H4 Września Pol.
38 E2 Wu'an China
38 D2 Wubu China
42 D1 Wuchang Heilongjiang China
39 E4 Wuchang Hubei China
39 D6 Wuchuan Guangdong China
39 C4 Wuchuan Guizhou China
38 D1 Wuchuan Nei Monggol China
38 C2 Wuda China
38 D3 Wudang Shan mt China
38 C3 Wudang Shan mts China
42 A4 Wudao China
35 H2 Wudaoliang China
38 E2 Wudi China
39 B5 Wuding China
38 D2 Wuding r. China
38 B3 Wudu China
39 D4 Wufeng China
39 D5 Wugang China
38 C3 Wugong China
38 C2 Wuhai China
39 E4 Wuhan China
38 E3 Wuhe China
38 F4 Wuhu China
39 E6 Wuhua China
34 D2 Wüjang China
39 C6 Wujia China
39 C4 Wu Jiang r. China
86 C4 Wukari Nigeria
35 H3 Wulang China
34 C2 Wular L. l. India
42 B5 Wuleidao Wan l. China
38 F3 Wulian China
39 B4 Wulian Feng mts China
36 C4 Wuliang Shan mts China
37 F7 Wuliaru i. Indon.
39 C4 Wuling Shan mts China
39 C4 Wulong China
39 B5 Wumeng Shan mts China
39 C6 Wuming China
13 H1 Wümme r. Ger.
38 A4 Wungda China
39 E4 Wuning China
13 G3 Wünnenberg Ger.
13 L4 Wunsiedel Ger.
13 H2 Wunstorf Ger.
36 B4 Wuntho Myanmar
73 G4 Wupatki National Monument res. U.S.A.
39 E5 Wuping China
12 F3 Wuppertal Ger.
90 C6 Wuppertal S. Africa
38 C2 Wuqi China
38 E2 Wuqiao China
38 E2 Wuqing China
13 H5 Würzburg Ger.
13 L3 Wurzen Ger.
38 B3 Wushan Gansu China
38 C4 Wushan Sichuan China
38 D4 Wu Shan mts China
39 C4 Wusheng China
39 C6 Wushi China
13 H3 Wüstegarten h. Ger.
Wusuli Jiang r. see Ussuri
38 D2 Wutai China
38 D2 Wutai Shan mt China
48 E2 Wuvulu I. i. P.N.G.
38 E4 Wuwei Anhui China
38 B2 Wuwei Gansu China
38 F4 Wuxi Jiangsu China
38 C4 Wuxi Sichuan China
Wuxing see Huzhou
39 C6 Wuxu China
39 C6 Wuxuan China
38 D3 Wuyang China
39 F4 Wuyi China
36 E2 Wuyiling China
39 E5 Wuyi Shan mts China
39 E4 Wuyuan Jiangxi China
38 C1 Wuyuan Nei Monggol China
38 D2 Wuzhai China
38 D4 Wuzhen China
38 C2 Wuzhong China
39 D6 Wuzhou China
68 B5 Wyaconda r. U.S.A.
50 F2 Wyalong Austr.
69 F4 Wyandotte U.S.A.
68 C5 Wyanet U.S.A.
50 G2 Wyangala Reservoir Austr.
50 D4 Wycheproof Austr.
9 E6 Wye r. U.K.
9 F6 Wylye r. U.K.
9 J5 Wymondham U.K.
48 C3 Wyndham Austr.
65 F5 Wynne U.S.A.
54 G2 Wynniatt Bay b. Can.
57 J4 Wynyard Can.
68 C5 Wyoming IL U.S.A.
68 E4 Wyoming MI U.S.A.
62 E3 Wyoming div. U.S.A.
62 E3 Wyoming Peak summit U.S.A.
50 H2 Wyong Austr.
50 D3 Wyperfeld Nat. Park Austr.
8 E4 Wyre r. U.K.
71 E4 Wysox U.S.A.
17 K4 Wyszków Pol.
9 F5 Wythall U.K.
70 C6 Wytheville U.S.A.
71 J2 Wytopitlock U.S.A.

X

88 F2 Xaafuun Somalia
29 M1 Xaçmaz Azer.
90 E1 Xade Botswana
35 H3 Xagquka China
34 D1 Xaidulla China
35 G3 Xainza China
89 D6 Xai Xai Moz.
Xalapa see Jalapa Enríquez
37 C4 Xam Hua Laos
44 B1 Xan r. Laos
89 C6 Xanagas Botswana
38 B1 Xangd China
38 D1 Xangdin Hural China
89 B5 Xangongo Angola
29 L2 Xankändi Azer.
19 L4 Xanthi Greece
44 C2 Xan, Xé r. Vietnam
78 E6 Xapuri Brazil
29 M2 Xaraba Şähär Sayı i. Azer.
29 M2 Xärä Zirä Adası is Azer.
35 F3 Xarba La pass China
38 F1 Xar Burd China
38 E1 Xar Moron r. Nei Monggol China
38 D1 Xar Moron r. Nei Monggol China
15 F3 Xátiva Spain
89 C6 Xau, Lake l. Botswana
79 J6 Xavantes, Serra dos h. Brazil
44 C3 Xa Vo Đat Vietnam
70 B5 Xenia U.S.A.
42 A3 Xi r. China
42 F1 Xiachengzi China
39 D6 Xiachuan Dao i. China
38 B3 Xiahe China
39 E5 Xiajiang China
38 E2 Xiajin China
39 F5 Xiamen China
38 C3 Xi'an China
38 E3 Xiancheng China
38 C2 Xianchengbu China
39 C4 Xianfeng China
38 D3 Xiangcheng China
38 D3 Xiangfan China
38 D1 Xianghuang Qi China
44 B1 Xiangkhoang Laos
34 D3 Xiangquan He r. China
39 F4 Xiangshan China
39 D5 Xiangtan China
39 D5 Xiangxiang China
39 D4 Xiangyin China
39 F4 Xianju China
39 E4 Xianning China
39 E5 Xianxia Ling mts China
38 E2 Xian Xian China
38 C3 Xianyang China
39 F5 Xianyou China
39 C6 Xiaodong China
39 D4 Xiaogan China
36 E1 Xiao Hinggan Ling mts China
38 B4 Xiaojin China
35 H2 Xiaonanchuan China
39 F4 Xiaoshan China
39 E5 Xiaotao China
38 E2 Xiaowutai Shan mt China
38 E3 Xiao Xian China
39 B4 Xiaoxiang Ling mts China
38 D2 Xiaoyi China
39 F5 Xiapu China
42 A2 Xiawa China
38 D3 Xiayukou China
39 B5 Xichang China
38 B4 Xichong China
39 B6 Xichou China
38 D3 Xichuan China
39 B4 Xide China
81 D4 Xié r. Brazil
39 C6 Xieyang Dao i. China
38 E3 Xifei He r. China
39 C5 Xifeng Guizhou China
42 C2 Xifeng Liaoning China
38 C3 Xifengzhen China
27 G4 Xigazê China
38 C3 Xihan Shui r. China
38 B3 Xihe China
38 A1 Xi He watercourse China
38 B3 Xiji China
39 D6 Xi Jiang r. China
35 G2 Xijir China
35 G2 Xijir Ulan Hu salt l. China
38 B2 Xijishui China
38 D1 Xil China
42 B2 Xiliao r. China
39 B5 Xilin China
38 E1 Xilinhot China
38 D1 Xilin Qagan Obo Mongolia
38 A1 Ximiao China
39 F4 Xin'anjiang China
39 F4 Xin'anjiang Sk. resr China
91 K2 Xinavane Moz.
42 C3 Xinbin China
38 E3 Xincai China
39 F4 Xinchang China
38 A2 Xincheng Gansu China
39 C5 Xincheng Guangxi China
38 C2 Xincheng Ningxia China
38 C2 Xinchengbu China
39 D6 Xindu Guangxi China
38 B4 Xindu Sichuan China
39 E5 Xinfeng Guangdong China
39 E5 Xinfeng Jiangxi China
39 E6 Xinfengjiang Sk. resr China
39 D5 Xing'an China
39 E5 Xingan China
42 A4 Xingangzhen China
38 F1 Xingcheng China
39 E5 Xingguo China
27 H3 Xinghai China
38 D1 Xinghe China
38 F3 Xinghua China
39 F5 Xinghua Wan b. China
40 C2 Xingkai China
Xingkai Hu l. see Khanka, Lake
39 E5 Xingning China
39 D4 Xingou China
38 C3 Xingping China
39 B5 Xingren China
38 A3 Xingsagoinba China
38 D4 Xingshan China
38 E2 Xingtai China
79 H4 Xingu r. Brazil
79 H6 Xingu, Parque Indígena do nat. park Brazil
39 B4 Xingwen China
38 D2 Xing Xian China
38 D3 Xingyang China
39 B5 Xingyi China
39 E4 Xingzi China
39 D5 Xinhua China
38 B2 Xinhuacun China
39 C5 Xinhuang China
39 D6 Xinhui China
38 A2 Xining China
39 E4 Xinjian China
38 D3 Xinjiang China
36 A2 Xinjiang Uygur Zizhiqu div. China
38 C2 Xinjie China
38 B4 Xinjin Sichuan China
42 B4 Xinjin China
42 B1 Xinkai r. China
42 B3 Xinmin China
39 D5 Xinning China
39 A5 Xinping China
39 E5 Xinquan China
39 D5 Xinshao China
38 E3 Xintai China
39 D5 Xintian China
38 E4 Xin Xian Henan China
38 D2 Xin Xian Shanxi China
38 D3 Xinxiang China
39 D6 Xinxing China
38 E3 Xinyang Henan China
38 E3 Xinyang Henan China
38 D3 Xinye China
38 F3 Xinye r. China
39 D6 Xinyi Guangdong China
38 F3 Xinyi Jiangsu China
39 C7 Xinying China
39 E5 Xinyu China
38 D2 Xinzhou China
15 C1 Xinzo de Limia Spain
42 B3 Xiongyuecheng China
38 E3 Xiping Henan China
38 D3 Xiping Henan China
38 A3 Xiqing Shan mts China
79 K6 Xique Xique Brazil
39 C4 Xishui Guizhou China
39 E4 Xishui Hubei China
36 D2 Xi Ujimqin Qi China
39 F4 Xiuning China
39 C4 Xiushan China
39 E4 Xiushui China
39 E4 Xiu Shui r. China
39 C5 Xiuwen China
38 D3 Xiuwu China
42 B3 Xiuyan China
39 D6 Xiuying China
35 F3 Xixabangma Feng mt China
38 D3 Xixia China
38 E3 Xi Xian Henan China
38 D2 Xi Xian Shanxi China
38 C3 Xi Xiang China
39 F5 Xiyang Dao i. China
39 B5 Xiyang Jiang r. China
27 G3 Xizang Gaoyuan plat. China
36 B3 Xizang Zizhiqu div. China
42 A4 Xizhong Dao i. China
35 H3 Xoka China
44 C3 Xom An Lôc Vietnam
44 C3 Xom Duc Hanh Vietnam
38 F4 Xuancheng China
39 C4 Xuan'en China
38 C4 Xuanhan China
38 B2 Xuanhepu China
38 E1 Xuanhua China
44 C3 Xuân Lôc Vietnam
39 B5 Xuanwei China
38 D3 Xuchang China
29 M1 Xudat Azer.
88 E3 Xuddur Somalia
39 C5 Xuefeng Shan mts China
35 H2 Xugui China
35 E2 Xungba China
35 F3 Xungru China
38 C3 Xun He r. China
39 D6 Xun Jiang r. China
39 E5 Xunwu China
38 E3 Xun Xian China
38 C3 Xunyang China
38 C3 Xunyi China
39 D5 Xupu China
35 F3 Xuru Co salt l. China
38 E2 Xushui China
39 D6 Xuwen China
38 F3 Xuyi China
39 B4 Xuyong China
38 E3 Xuzhou China

Y

39 B4 Ya'an China
50 D3 Yaapeet Austr.
86 C4 Yabassi Cameroon
88 D3 Yabēlo Eth.
36 C1 Yablonovyy Khrebet mts Rus. Fed.
38 B2 Yabrai Shan mts China
38 B2 Yabrai Yanchang China
28 F5 Yabrūd Syria
42 E1 Yabuli China
81 C2 Yacambu, Parque Nacional nat. park Venez.
39 C7 Yacheng China
39 C5 Yachi He r. China
78 E6 Yacuma r. Bol.
33 B2 Yadgir India
61 K4 Yadkin r. NC U.S.A.
20 H4 Yadrin Rus. Fed.
40 G2 Yagishiri-tō i. Japan
30 D2 Yagman Turkm.
87 D3 Yagoua Cameroon
35 E3 Yagra China
35 H2 Yagradagzê Shan mt China
83 F1 Yaguari r. Uru.
Yaguarón r. see Jaguarão
44 B4 Yaha Thai.
28 D2 Yahşihan Turkey
28 E2 Yahyalı Turkey
31 H4 Yahya Wana Afgh.
41 F6 Yaita Japan
41 F7 Yaizu Japan
39 A4 Yajiang China
28 F3 Yakacık Turkey
31 G4 Yakhehal Afgh.
62 B2 Yakima U.S.A.
62 B2 Yakima r. U.S.A.
30 D3 Yakinish Iran
31 G2 Yakkabag Uzbek.
31 F4 Yakmach Pak.
86 B3 Yako Burkina
56 B3 Yakobi I. i. U.S.A.
40 C2 Yakovlevka Rus. Fed.
40 G3 Yakumo Japan
41 B9 Yaku-shima i. Japan
56 B3 Yakutat U.S.A.
56 B3 Yakutat Bay b. U.S.A.
25 O3 Yakutsk Rus. Fed.
21 E6 Yakymivka Ukr.
44 B4 Yala Thai.
69 F4 Yale U.S.A.
50 F5 Yallourn Austr.
39 A5 Yalong Jiang r. China
28 B1 Yalova Turkey
21 F6 Yalta Donets'k Ukr.
21 E6 Yalta Krym Ukr.
42 C3 Yalu Jiang r. China/N. Korea
42 C4 Yalujiang Kou river mouth N. Korea
28 C2 Yalvaç Turkey
40 G5 Yamada Japan
40 G5 Yamagata Japan
41 B9 Yamagawa Japan
41 B7 Yamaguchi Japan
24 H2 Yamal, Poluostrov pen. Rus. Fed.
57 G2 Yamba Lake l. Can.
81 C4 Yambi, Mesa de h. Col.
87 E4 Yambio Sudan
19 M3 Yambol Bulg.
24 J3 Yamburg Rus. Fed.
38 A2 Yamenzhuang China

Z

ACKNOWLEDGEMENTS

Pages 12-13
Photos : **Pictor International - London**

Pages 24-25
Photos : **Science Photo Library**
Data : **Telegeography Inc, Washington DC**
www.telegeography.com
Petroleum Economist Ltd., London
www.petroleum-economist.com
Network Wizards
www.nw.com